Communism in the United States—A Bibliography

COMMUNISM IN THE
UNITED STATES—
A BIBLIOGRAPHY

COMPILED AND EDITED BY

JOEL SEIDMAN

Graduate School of Business and Division of the
Social Sciences, University of Chicago

Assisted by OLIVE GOLDEN
and YAFFA DRAZNIN

Cornell University Press

ITHACA AND LONDON

PREFACE

In 1955 the Fund for the Republic published its "Bibliography on the Communist Problem in the United States," a listing of some 5,000 books, pamphlets, and magazine articles, with brief annotations. The work of preparing the bibliography was directed by Charles Corker, formerly professor of law at Stanford University. While the bibliography was primarily concerned with the communist movement in the United States, beginning with its inception in 1919, appendices dealt with several related subjects, including native American radicalism, communist ideology and theory, world communist parties, left-wing periodicals, and microfilm records of communist trials. A companion volume, "Digest of the Public Record of Communism in the United States," listed and annotated legislative hearings, committee reports, and other public documents.

The bibliography, in turn, was part of a comprehensive study of communism in this country, "Communism in American Life," sponsored by the Fund for the Republic and directed by Professor Clinton Rossiter of Cornell University. Over the intervening years a series of volumes, fruits of the project, have greatly enlarged our knowledge of communist history, the social origins of American communists, the training of communists, Marxist teachings, and communist influence in literature, education, religion, and government.

Although the series as a whole found a very favorable reception, in the scholarly world as well as in more popular journals, the bibliography was criticized for having omitted a number of works, many of these critical of the communist position. Bibliographers in this field, it should be recognized, work under the handicap that official Party publications are readily available since they appear in official journals or are sponsored by Party-connected publishing houses, whereas material critical of communism may appear in any number of magazines, many of them unlisted in any digest, or in books or pamphlets the titles of which often give no clue as to the contents, sponsored by a wide variety of organizations and publishers. Despite any bibliographer's best intentions and most diligent efforts, gaps may appear in the lists of publications opposed to the communist view.

I undertook revision of the bibliography in the belief that the task would prove the relatively simple one of identifying the gaps and then filling them in. I soon concluded, however, that the bibliography's usefulness would be increased if most of the abstracts were expanded to some extent, and the work organized on a somewhat different basis. I decided also that many of the items originally abstracted could be omitted, to keep the revised work within manageable proportions. The result has been a substantial revision, along with an expansion and updating, of the original work. In this work I have had the advantage of consultation with other authors in the series, each of whom did pioneering work in the area of his particular interests. I wish to express my appreciation of their assistance, along with my debt to the staff members who prepared the original bibliography.

I wish to express my appreciation also to Clinton Rossiter for his cooperation, his wise counsel, and his patience during the long period over which this work extended. For the initial grant that permitted the work to be started I am grateful to the Fund for the Republic; the supplementary funds that allowed the work to be carried to completion were made available by the Graduate School of Business and the Division of the Social Sciences of the University of Chicago and by the Lilly Foundation. While all the librarians and staff employees at the various libraries where work was done were cooperative, those at the Tamiment Institute in New York City were particularly helpful.

Finally, acknowledgment must be made to my associates, Olive Golden and Yaffa Draznin, who carried much of the burden during the earlier period while I was busy with other projects; and to Paul Halpern, Stephen Kaplan, J. B. Ritchie, John Stuckey, Donald Wellington, and Lula White, who served as research assistants at various times during the life of the project.

Joel Seidman

Chicago
January 10, 1967

CONTENTS

Although I have no wish to duplicate information readily available from other sources, and already known to the sophisticated user of this work, it may prove helpful to others who consult this bibliography to provide, in capsule form, a record of the major changes through which the communist movement has passed in its history of half a century.

The Bolshevik seizure of power in Russia in November 1917 was followed by a period of civil war, followed in turn by the consolidation of Soviet rule. Left-wing groups in this country, as elsewhere in the world, most of them belonging to the left wing of the socialist movement, then split off to form the communist movement. In this country two communist organizations appeared simultaneously at the beginning of September 1919—the Communist Labor Party of America and the Communist Party of America. The heads of the Communist Party of the USSR, expecting revolutions to break out soon in the advanced capitalist countries, summoned their supporters to a congress in 1919 at which the Third, or Communist, International was formed.

From that time until its dissolution as a tactical measure during World War II, the Communist International, or Comintern, exercised careful surveillance over its constituent parties, including the American, instructing it in matters of organization and objectives, criticizing its tactics and its press, and changing the leadership when its purposes would be better served by another. Changes of line by the Comintern bound the American party, as it did all other affiliates. Control of the American party was exercised, not merely by directives adopted at congresses or by the executive committee between congresses, but by representatives sent to the Party here—representatives who laid down the line to the nominal heads of the Party and who often wrote the key resolutions at Party conventions. Back of the Comintern, in turn, and dominating it, were the heads of the Communist Party of the Soviet Union. Far from objecting to this control from the USSR through the Comintern, the Party here gloried in it, looking to Lenin and then to Stalin as the generalissimo of the world revolutionary movement which they were proud to serve.

Bitter factional conflict among the American groups led to the formation of the United Communist Party in May 1920, its merger with others into the Communist Party of America in May 1921, and the formation of the Workers Party of America as the legal front for the underground CPA in December 1921. In 1923 the underground organization was liquidated, in 1925 the name of the Party was changed to Workers (Communist) Party, and four years later it was changed again to the Communist Party of the U.S.A.

By 1921 the revolutionary movement outside Russia had ground to a halt, most workers continuing their allegiance to the socialist and trade union movements. Retreating internally, the leaders of the USSR encouraged some forms of private enterprise with their New Economic Policy. Elsewhere the prime political objective of the communists was to break up the socialist parties in their countries, while on the union front they sought to build cells within conservative organizations in order to win control of them. This policy, directed internationally through the newly formed Red International of Labor Unions or Profintern, was carried out in the United States by the Trade Union Educational League under the leadership of William Z. Foster. During this conservative period of the communist movement, when the temporary stabiliza-

tion of world capitalism was accepted, the Party here sought to start farmer-labor parties, and to infiltrate and capture those started by others.

The defeat of Trotsky by Stalin, and the consolidation of the Soviet Union under his rule, marked a leftward turn in the international movement, as Stalin sought to undercut the leftist policies of Trotsky and his followers as well as to eliminate right-wing opposition leaders in the Soviet Union. Any purge started there spread throughout the affiliated parties, as national leaders who were identified with any of the deposed leaders in the USSR were removed in turn. Thus the Trotskyist followers here were expelled in 1928, as was the Lovestone or right-wing group the following year. As part of the ultra-revolutionary "third period," attacks were intensified on the socialist parties, labeled "social-fascist"; the tactic of the "united front from below" developed to divide the socialist leaders from their rank and file; and revolutionary unions formed to fight the conservative labor movement. In line with this policy the Trade Union Educational League transformed itself into a trade union center, the Trade Union Unity League, to challenge the unions of the American Federation of Labor.

The rise of Hitler, with his threat to the USSR, brought about the change in 1935 to the popular front, with its effort to create collective security against aggression through a coalition of the USSR with democratic capitalist states. Since no popular front could be built without the cooperation of the conservative labor movement, the revolutionary unions were liquidated, their members being told to gain admittance to the conservative unions as best they could. By a coincidence, fortunate for the communists, the CIO was just getting under way here at that time, with John L. Lewis eager to find experienced organizers and confident that he could control the communists whom he hired. Taking advantage of their opportunity, they entrenched themselves in many of the newer CIO organizations, not to be displaced until still another turn in the Party line made them vulnerable after World War II.

The Nazi-Soviet pact, signed in August 1939, signaled yet another major communist change. Now the communists centered their criticism on Britain and France as imperialist powers which were equally responsible with Nazi Germany for the war in Europe. Becoming supermilitant on the trade union front, the Party here sabotaged aid to Britain, while proclaiming America's aloofness from the war. Hitler's invasion of the USSR in June 1941, in turn, made the communists eager to have the United States enter the war to take the pressure of the German armies off Russia. Following Pearl Harbor they pressed, for the same reason, for the early opening of a second front on the European mainland, while on the labor front they became as cooperative as they had previously been militant, opposing all interruptions with production and advocating incentive wages to maximize output. Projecting the wartime cooperation of labor and management into the postwar period and envisaging an indefinite period of class peace, Browder liquidated the Communist Party, turning the movement instead into the Communist Political Association.

As the war in Europe neared its end Stalin signaled another change in line, appropriate to the cold war that was soon to follow. His instrument for this purpose was the French communist Jacques Duclos, whose attack on Browder's policies in a French communist journal in April 1945 caused a quick reversal of Party policies here.

Browder was deposed, the CPUSA reconstituted, and the class struggle again enthroned. The communist attack on the Marshall Plan for rebuilding the European democracies placed union leaders loyal to the Party in opposition to CIO policy; this was compounded in 1948 when the Party formed an important part of the Henry Wallace movement, while the CIO as a whole gave its support to Truman. The resulting purge cost the Party much of its influence in the labor movement. Meanwhile the government was moving against the Party, with the Taft-Hartley noncommunist affidavit, prosecutions under the Smith Act, and other anticommunist legislation. State legislatures also joined in the attack.

Then came the 1956 revelations by Khrushchev of the sins of Stalin, followed in a few months by the Red Army's suppression of the Hungarian uprising. The result was chaos and confusion in the ranks of the Party, as disillusioned members fell away by the thousands, as leaders rediscovered the values of democracy, and as factions formed to battle over the remains of a once powerful movement. Meanwhile the world communist movement lost its monolithic character; first the Titoist heresy in Yugoslavia withstood the might of the USSR, then the other national parties regained some measure of independence, and finally the Chinese party challenged the USSR leadership, seeking to form a coalition of leftist communist parties under its leadership. Fragmented and weakened, the CPUSA at the close of the period covered by this bibliography was but a pale shadow of the powerful movement it had once represented.

For information about the communist movement the reader is referred to the various volumes of the series "Communism in American Life," particularly to the historical treatments by Theodore Draper and David A. Shannon. Numerous other works, including Daniel Bell's essay in "Socialism and American Life," the history by Irving Howe and Lewis Coser, and J. Edgar Hoover's "Masters of Deceit," trace the development of the communist movement or characterize its philosophy, organization, and methods of operation. Lewis Lorwin in his "International Labor Movement" has done the same for the Communist International and the Red International of Labor Unions.

The original bibliography, published in 1955, covered the period from the inception of the communist movement here in 1919 until shortly before the volume went to press. The present work provides systematic coverage through 1959, with the inclusion of items of unusual interest published since that time. Some cut-off date had to be established to permit completion of the work; and the diminishing importance of the communist movement in this country after 1959 suggested that little would be lost by the failure to provide more comprehensive coverage after that date.

One-fifth or more of the approximately 5,000 items in the old bibliography have been dropped, as of relatively minor importance. Some 3,000 new items have been added, however, to make a total of almost 7,000 items in the present work. Where the annotation in the former work appeared ample it has been retained, sometimes being rewritten in the style of the present work. In most cases, however, the annotation has been expanded somewhat, to provide the reader with a maximum of information within the available space. In general the annotations have been held to about fifty words for magazine articles or short pamphlets and to one hundred words for books, although longer annotations have been provided for unusually important items. Efforts have been made to identify the author politically when that information would aid in understanding the item.

A preliminary section of the present bibliography contains 138 items dealing with antecedent movements, including the socialist and anarchist movements, leftist union groups such as the Industrial Workers of the World, and labor or third party political efforts. This section consists predominantly of books, supplemented by a few pamphlets or magazine articles of unusual interest or importance. Those who wish to examine the socialist movement more exhaustively will find a careful treatment, with thorough documentation, in the two-volume work, "Socialism and American Life," edited by Donald Drew Egbert and Stow Persons.

All the rest of the material is presented in the main body of the bibliography, organized alphabetically by author. The works by each author are presented chronologically, rather than alphabetically as in the earlier edition, in the belief that this form of organization will permit identification of the phase of the author's career during which a particular item was written. There are numerous cases in which an author, after a period as a Party member, became allied with a dissident communist grouping, before renouncing communism altogether. The titles of the items, together with the periodical or publisher used, may change sharply from one period to another of an author's career. In such cases the mere chronological listing of the works will provide a summary of the author's political history.

In some cases an item could have been put into either the antecedent section or the main bibliography, since it includes material appropriate to both. Duplications have been avoided by classifying the item in the section most appropriate to the bulk of its material, with the annotation covering the item in its entirety. Publications by Party members are placed in the main body of the bibliography, even where the subject is an antecedent organization, since the point of view was felt to be more controlling than the subject matter. It is hoped that the index, which covers the entire bibliography, will guide the reader to all items in which he is interested, whether these are listed in the antecedent section or in the main bibliography. Although the main bibliography properly begins with the formation of communist parties here in 1919, a few items relating to the predecessor left wing of the Socialist Party have been included, dealing with the period in which the left wing had broken ideologically with democratic socialism and was in the process of splitting away to form the communist movement.

It was not an easy matter to delineate the areas that the bibliography should cover. All writings of any consequence by a member of the Party are included, whether these relate specifically to this country or to other portions of the world, and without regard to the particular topic or method of treatment; thus an item may deal with civil liberties, labor organization, war or peace, imperialism, economic conditions, race relations, foreign policy, or Marxist philosophy, as it may also be presented in the form of fiction or poetry. Comment on similar topics by noncommunists is not included, however, unless the author specifically criticized the Party's position or discussed an issue with which the Party was clearly identified, such as the Scottsboro case or self-determination of the Black Belt. The publications of radical groups, such as the Socialist Party, the Socialist Labor Party, and dissident communist groups, were subjected to the same tests as writings of liberals and conservatives, and included only when the Party's views were the subject of discussion. The bibliography is meant to deal with the official Party, not with communism in the broader sense, embracing Trotskyist, Lovestoneite, and other dissident communist tendencies.

The writings of fellow-travelers and the publications of front organizations presented more difficulties. While the Attorney General's list provides an index to front organizations, one has to be careful about the period of Party control where communists captured an organization that they did not start; and there are degrees of influence short of control, as with individuals there are degrees of sympathy, or sympathies limited to particular issues, that fall short of fellow-traveling. To have included all publications of organizations that the Party controlled, or in which it had influence, or all writings of individuals who agreed with the Party's position on key issues, would have helped expand the size of the bibliography to unmanageable proportions. The objective has been, therefore, to include only those items that clearly promoted the Party line, or that addressed themselves specifically to some issue involving the Party, such as the charge of communist domination.

At point after point the lines between inclusion and exclusion have had to be sharply drawn, lest the bibliography expand far beyond its present size. How much material should be included, for example, on the USSR, on the Communist International, on the eastern European satellite countries or communist China or the Cuban revolution? To what extent should Marxist philosophy or Marxist interpretations of conditions in the United States be covered? How far should the bibliography go into race relations, civil liberties, national security, loyalty oaths, the Fifth Amendment, espionage, McCarthyism, or the Progressive Party? How extensive should the coverage be of espionage or loyalty-security cases such as those of Hiss and Chambers, J. Robert Oppenheimer, Owen Lattimore, Judith Coplon, or the Rosenbergs? How much of the proletarian literature of the 1930's or of later works of fiction in which communist characters figured should be included? What about congressional or state investigating committees, federal or state anticommunist legislation, and the resulting prosecutions and judicial decisions? And what about items published abroad, or published here in languages other than English?

The principle that guided our answers to questions such as these was that the items to be listed in the bibliography had to be centrally concerned with the problem of communism in the United States. Thus, out of the enormous literature in English on the USSR, only a few items have been included—because they were written by members of the American Party or by confirmed fellow-travelers, or because they have strongly influenced opinion in this country toward communism. Criticism of the Soviet Union or of other communist countries by non-communists living here has generally been excluded, as beyond the scope of the present work. Publications of the Communist International and its leaders, whether Russians or other nationals, have been included when they specifically addressed themselves to American questions, or in a few cases when they laid down important changes of line that of course bound the CPUSA, along with all other affiliated parties. We have been very selective, similarly, with regard to Marxist philosophy or Marxist criticism, including only a few publications by communists or former communists or works that sought to explain the American communists' point of view or method of approach. Although a few items published abroad have been included, the bibliography excludes material printed in languages other than English, even though published in this country.

Areas such as race relations and civil liberties, in which the communists have had a great interest, have been treated selectively, with items included in the bibliography only when the communist aspect was emphasized. Other subjects, such as national security, loyalty oaths, espionage cases, investigating committees, and federal or state anti-communist legislation, have received somewhat more extensive treatment, when the communist issue was explicitly or implicitly involved. Items that contrasted communism with capitalism or Christianity were included if specific references were made to the United States, or if the author was an American. Writings directed against communism as an external threat were generally excluded, though items seeking to lessen communism's appeal here were included.

The area of creative writing presented special difficulty. During the 1930's a great many writers were sympathetic, to a greater or lesser degree, to the Party, though most of these have turned against communism in more recent years. To have included the novels, short stories, plays, and poems written in the 1930's by persons sympathetic to the Party would have added a large literature to the bibliography; here, indeed, it would have been difficult to know where to stop, since writers friendly to the Party shaded off into those merely critical of existing society. Of this large volume of literature only a small selection has been made, embracing works written by Party members, a few leading examples of the proletarian novels of the 1930's, and occasional more recent works that revolve around a Party theme, or in which a communist character is central to the plot. Those who wish to explore this area further will find guidance in Walter B. Rideout's "The Radical Novel in the United States: 1900-1954" and in Daniel Aaron's "Writers on the Left."

Although the intention was to include magazine articles, along with books and pamphlets, but to exclude newspaper stories, it was not always easy to draw the line between them. Where newspapers have magazine supplements, such as the "New York Times Magazine," articles in them are included in the bibliography. Similarly, a series of articles in a newspaper is sometimes treated as a magazine-type publication. Radical groups without a theoretical organ tend to use their newspapers for more extensive articles of an analytical nature, as well as for more topical stories reporting recent developments; in such cases the former are sometimes included, but not the latter. When a magazine article is also published in pamphlet form, only one annotation is included, usually to the item more readily available, with a note as to the other form of publication. There are doubtless cases, however, in which we were not aware of the other form of publication, or in which a change in title disguised the fact that the item had been published before. Other cases of dual publication include excerpts from a book published in a magazine; in such instances we have not abstracted the magazine article separately, but instead refer to it at the end of the entry on the book.

A special issue of a magazine devoted to a topic pertinent to the bibliography is given an entry in its own right, along with annotations of particular articles, listed under the names of their authors, that are important enough to be included. Often the entry for the issue tells which articles are annotated separately. Sometimes, as in the case of "Party Organizer," no single article was thought significant enough for such treatment, though an issue as a whole deserves to be included. Magazines that contain scattered material pertinent to the bibliography, such as organs of unions under communist domination, have no separate entries, though particular articles are abstracted if they are of sufficient importance.

A volume that contains contributions from various authors is listed under the name of its editor, though a contribution of unusual importance is also listed separately. If the volume as a whole is not pertinent to the bibliography, though one of the contributions is, that contribution only is included, under the name of its author.

A publication with multiple authors is listed only under the name that appears first on the item. If no author is given, the magazine or sponsoring organization is listed as author. Where resolutions adopted by an organization are presented, however, that organization is listed as author, even though an affiliated group may publish the resolutions; thus the Communist International might be listed as author, with the CPUSA as publisher, in publications that reproduce Comintern proceedings or decisions.

All publications of the CPUSA appear in one grouping, whether published by the national organization, its affiliated departments or committees, or state or local units. Since no difference in position was permitted, it seemed simpler to present the material this way, though the sub-unit issuing the material is always identified. However, the Teachers Union of the City of New York, Local 5, is listed under "Teachers" instead of under the American Federation of Teachers, even when it was an affiliate of that organization, since its point of view was independent— indeed, differed sharply—from that of the parent body.

While the bibliography is limited almost entirely to published materials, occasionally an unpublished work of unusual interest, such as a master's thesis or doctoral dissertation, has been included. Similarly, a small number of mimeographed items, or works produced by multilith or offset process, have been included, although the presumption has been against nonprinted materials. Government publications have been excluded as more appropriate to the "Digest of the Public Record of Communism in the United States," although occasional items from nongovernment sources have been included even though they appeared in a government publication, such as privately written articles of a research nature published in the "Monthly Labor Review."

The use of pseudonyms, particularly in the early days of the communist movement here, gives particular trouble. Representatives of the Communist International assigned to the Party here regularly wrote under pseudonyms, sometimes using more than one. Members of the United States Party who attended meetings of the Communist International similarly published their reports under pseudonyms, and for a time, in the early underground period of the movement, it was fashionable for active members to have revolutionary names, sometimes used in publications. In other cases pseudonyms were used to conceal the writer's identity from the government, or to prevent his discharge and blacklisting by private employ-

ers, in the event he was not employed by the Party or an organization controlled by it. In still other cases foreign-sounding names were Anglicized or American-sounding names adopted instead, sometimes for all purposes and sometimes just for publication. In rare cases persons who broke with the Party changed their names before starting life anew.

The bibliographer in this field is therefore presented with problems of identification that are seldom encountered in other areas. Where a pseudonym was used and the identity of the author is known to us, a note to that effect is included, although the item is listed under the name used in the publication. If we do not know the author's real name, we simply note that a pseudonym has been used. When an author has written under his real name and also under a pseudonym, items are listed under both, with appropriate notations. If an author has changed his name for all purposes, no notation of his original name is made unless the earlier name also appears in the bibliography, in which case an appropriate reference is made. Use of a pseudonym is followed by "pseud.," with the real name given if it is known to us, whereas a name changed for all purposes may have the other name simply given in brackets.

The publications of radical groups are difficult to work with, because of their irregularity of appearance and carelessness with regard to dates and identifying issue and volume numbers. Libraries, moreover, are apt to have incomplete sets, when they have any at all. Readers who are interested in learning of the publications of the various radical groups are referred to Walter Goldwater's "Radical Periodicals in America, 1890-1950." The title "Communist" is particularly confusing, because of the tendency of almost every communist group, in the early days of the movement, to give their publication this name. For this reason we have identified the sponsoring organization, whenever the newspaper or magazine bears this title.

Publications of an author appear chronologically, with the books and pamphlets published in any one year arranged alphabetically, followed by magazine articles of that year arranged chronologically.

The three periods always stand for the name of only one author; they are never used to represent several names. When the first entry under a name is of multiple authorship, followed by work of the principal author only, the name is repeated. Each item is numbered, those in the section on antecedents without a letter, and all others with the letter appropriate to the author's last name. This form of numbering will afford those using the index with quick access to items in the bibliography.

Communism in the United States—A Bibliography

A

1 AARON, Daniel. "Men of Good Hope: A Story of American Progressives." New York: Oxford University Press, 1951. 329 pp. Bibliog. Ind.
Five of the nine chapters are devoted to "prophetic agitators": Henry George, the single tax theorist and social reformer; Edward Bellamy, author of the widely read "Looking Backward"; Henry Demarest Lloyd, who wrote the influential "Wealth against Commonwealth"; William Dean Howells, popular writer of fiction, whose works like the utopian novel, "The Traveler from Altruria," expressed a middle class radicalism; and Thorstein Veblen, whose "The Theory of the Leisure Class" and other books helped to satirize business and social leadership and undermine popular faith in business enterprise.

2 ADAMIC, Louis. "Dynamite: The Story of Class Violence in America." Rev. ed. New York: Viking, 1934. 495 pp. Bibliog. Ind.
The evolution of violence in the class struggle in America, presented as a criticism of our capitalist-democratic civilization. The stories of the Molly Maguires, the Great Riots of 1877, the Haymarket tragedy, the Homestead strike, the Pullman strike, violence in the West, the Haywood trial and the IWW, the McNamara affair, the Ludlow massacre, the Mooney-Billings case, the 1919 steel strike, Centralia outrage, Sacco and Vanzetti, labor racketeering, and the Auto-Lite strike of 1934 are dramatically told. The author predicts that American workers will be violent until they organize into unions with revolutionary aims to power.

3 ADAMS, Frederick B., Jr. "Radical Literature in America." Stamford, Conn.: Overbrook Press, 1939. 66 pp. Ind.
An address on pioneer communistic communities in the U.S., some of them religious and others secular in inspiration. Among those discussed are New Harmony, Brook Farm and other phalanxes following Fourier, and the Oneida community. Early anarchist and socialist groups and the IWW are treated briefly. A list of radical publications shown in an exhibition is included.

4 AMERINGER, Oscar. "If You Don't Weaken: The Autobiography of Oscar Ameringer." New York: Holt, 1940. 476 pp. Ind.
The experiences of a German immigrant who spent most of his life as a socialist propagandist and as editor of socialist and labor papers. Influenced more by Bellamy than by Marx, Ameringer was at his best preaching socialism in simple, humorous language to farmers in Oklahoma and miners in Illinois, though he was also successful as socialist organizer and writer in Milwaukee. Though always a right-wing socialist, he opposed World War I and was indicted for his stand, though never brought to trial.

5 AVELING, Edward, and AVELING, Eleanor Marx. "The Working-Class Movement in America." London: Swan Sonnenschein, Lowrey, 1888 (2d ed. 1891). 212 pp.
Reflections upon labor conditions and upon labor and radical organizations in America by leaders of the Social Democratic Federation, the original Marxist group in England, following a 15-week tour of the U.S. in 1886 under the auspices of the Socialist Labor Party. The object of the tour was to present a socialist viewpoint in English, instead of in the German in which it had usually been preached. The book contains comments upon the Knights of Labor, the Socialistic (or Socialist) Labor Party, the United Labor Party of 1886, the anarchists, and Henry George's land reform movement.

B

6 BELL, Daniel. The Background and Development of Marxian Socialism in the United States. Ch. 6 of "Socialism and American Life," ed. by Donald Drew Egbert and Stow Persons. Princeton, N.J.: Princeton University Press, 1952. 1:213-405.
An able, critical analysis of the American socialist movement, dealing with the first Marxist groups in this country, the formation and character of the Socialist Labor Party, and the conflicts of the SLP with anarchists and later with Gompers and his fellow conservative leaders of the AFL. The author, a former editor of the socialist "New Leader," describes the formation of the Socialist Party in 1901 by a merger of an SLP faction led by Hillquit with the Social Democracy of America led by Debs, and discusses the "golden age" of American socialism (1902-12), with emphasis on internal differences and quarrels. The decline and fall of American socialism during the following World War I are treated in some detail.

7 BELLAMY, Edward. "Looking Backward: 2000 - 1887." Boston: Ticknor, 1888. 470 pp.
The most widely read and influential utopian novel by an American writer, describing the organization of society in the year 2,000 as seen by a New Englander, after a sleep of 113 years. He found poverty replaced by plenty, the result of the nationalization of all industry. Selfishness, ignorance, ugliness, war, crime, and the other familiar blights on the social life of earlier ages had all disappeared. The novel enjoyed its greatest influence in the five years following publication, when over 150 clubs and two publications were founded to support its principles.

8 BERKMAN, Alexander. "Now and After: The ABC of Communist Anarchism." New York: Vanguard Press and Jewish Anarchist Federation, 1929. 300 pp. Bibliog.
A restatement in simple terminology of the anarchist philosophy by a leading member of the communist anarchist group, who believed that government could be abolished only by a social revolution and who advocated social ownership and sharing according to need. In addition to attacking capitalism, the author stresses his points of disagreement with socialists, the Bolsheviki, and rival types of anarchist thought. (A life-long associate of Emma Goldman, Berkman played a leading role in the anarchist movement of this country from 1892, when he tried to assassinate Henry Clay Frick during the Homestead strike, until his deportation to Russia in December 1919.)

9   BESTOR, Arthur Eugene, Jr. "Backwoods Utopias: The Sectarian and Owenite Phases of Communitarian Socialism in America: 1663-1829." Philadelphia: University of Pennsylvania Press, 1950. 288 pp. App. Bibliog. essay. Ind.

A study of the early utopian movement in America, before the spread of Fourier's ideas in the 1840's and 1850's. Most of the volume is devoted to Owenism—to Robert Owen's ideas, the enthusiasm with which they were received in the U.S., the experiment at New Harmony, and the influence of Owenism in this country. Brief attention is given to earlier sectarian communities, including those of the Moravians, the Shakers, Ephrata, and the Rappites. The author explores the links between the societies, some of which were religious and some secular, and some of which were German-speaking and others English-speaking. An appendix lists 130 communities founded between 1663 and 1858, with type and location.

10   BIMBA, Anthony. "The History of the American Working Class." 3d ed. New York: International Publishers, 1936. 385 pp. Ind.

A history of American labor told from the communist point of view. The author interprets movements and events from the standpoint of the materialist conception of history; far from claiming to be impartial, he "openly takes side with the working class against the bourgeoisie." Attention is paid to the role of the state in the class struggle. Among the topics dealt with are the era of utopian socialism, the rise and decline of the Knights of Labor, the formation and growth of the AFL, the Haymarket bomb and the Pullman strike, the struggle between the Socialist Labor Party and the AFL, the rise of the Socialist Party, the IWW, the socialist reaction to World War I, and the beginning of the communist movement.

11   BOUDIN, Louis B. "The Theoretical System of Karl Marx in the Light of Recent Criticism." Chicago: Kerr, 1910. 286 pp. App. Ind.

One of the ablest expositions of Marxism by an American writer, the volume served both as an explanation of the Marxist system and a defense against critical views, whether of revisionists within the socialist movement or defenders of capitalism from without. Based on a series of articles that appeared originally in the "International Socialist Review," the volume devotes particular attention to the materialist conception of history, the labor theory of value, the economic contradictions in capitalism, and the role of the proletariat in the social revolution. One of the intellectual leaders of the left wing of the Socialist Party in the period prior to the Bolshevik revolution, Boudin was active in the Communist Labor Party formed in the 1919 split.

12   . . . . "Socialism and War." New York: New Review Publishing Association, 1916. 267 pp.

Six lectures delivered in 1914 by one of the leaders of the left wing of the Socialist Party, presenting the theoretical basis for the left wing's antiwar position. The author advocates a return to the orthodox Marxist interpretation of war. Asserting that intellectual developments are shaped by economic conditions, he analyzes the economic causes of the war. He opposes the bourgeois, nationalistic approach to war, urging the Marxist view that only the class struggle can play a progressive role. Defensive wars may be supported by socialists only if the socialist objective is being pursued, if the class struggle continues, and if the aggressor is viewed merely as a government representing at most the governing class.

13   BRISSENDEN, Paul Frederick. "The I.W.W.: A Study of American Syndicalism." 2d ed. New York: Columbia University Press, 1920. 432 pp. App. Bibliog. Ind.

A study of the IWW from its formation in 1905 until World War I. The launching of the IWW is described, with attention to the various participating groups. The factional groups that comprised the IWW are discussed, as are their bitter disputes over politics and decentralization. The defections and splits that plagued the organization are reviewed. Attention is given to the leading strikes and free speech campaigns in which the IWW engaged, as well as to the developments that made the organization predominantly one composed of unskilled migratory workers of the West.

14   BROOKS, John Graham. "American Syndicalism: The I.W.W." New York: Macmillan, 1913. 264 pp. Bibliog. Ind.

A portrayal of syndicalist philosophy, with emphasis on the IWW, and with attention to European socialist and syndicalist thought as well as to the relations of the IWW with socialists and conservative trade unionists. The general strike is discussed, as are IWW strategy and tactics in strikes of more limited scope. Direction, action, and sabotage are also considered.

15   BUCHANAN, Joseph R. "The Story of a Labor Agitator." New York: Outlook, 1903. 461 pp.

The account of his experiences by one of the leading figures in the turbulent labor struggles of the 1880's. A member of the general executive board of the Knights of Labor in 1884 and 1886, Buchanan helped to lead a number of important strikes during the 1880's, and tried to prevent the breach between the K of L and the trade unions. A life-long socialist, Buchanan occupied leading positions in the People's Party in Colorado and in the International Workmen's (or Workingmen's) Association, and was a member for a time of the Socialist Labor Party. He was friendly with several of the anarchist leaders who were convicted following the Haymarket bombing, and was active in efforts for their release.

16   BUCK, Solon Justus. "The Granger Movement: A Study of Agricultural Organization and Its Political, Economic and Social Manifestations, 1870-1880." Cambridge: Harvard University Press, 1913. 384 pp. Bibliog. Ind.

A study of the formation, growth, achievements, and decline of the Patrons of Husbandry, better known as the Grange. Attention is paid to the grievances of the farmers in the post-Civil War period; to the farm organizations and independent political parties that they formed; to the legislation they sought and accomplished, particularly with regard to the regulation of railroads; and to the establishment of cooperatives in an effort to make the farmers independent of middlemen and manufacturers. The Granger movement is seen as an effort to preserve the political and economic democracy of a simple agricultural community from destruction at the hands of concentrated wealth in the modern industrial state.

17   . . . . "The Agrarian Crusade: A Chronicle of the Farmer in Politics." New Haven: Yale University Press, 1921. 215 pp. Bibliog. note. Ind.

An account of the movement of agrarian protest from the close of the Civil War to the collapse of the People's Party following the campaign of 1896. The book deals with the causes of agricultural unrest, and with the successive economic or political movements of protest— the Grange, the Greenback movement, the Farmers' Alliance, and the People's Party. The Populists, after considerable success in 1890 and 1892, virtually merged into the Democratic party in 1896 by supporting Bryan and free silver.

18 BUSHEE, Frederick A. Communistic Societies in the United States, "Political Science Quarterly," 20 (Dec. 1905), 625-64.

A survey of cooperative communities started in this country, divided into four groups: the Owenite Societies of the 1820's; the Fourierist groups of the 1840's - 1850's; societies organized between 1890 and 1905 under the influence of modern socialistic and cooperative theories; and religious societies, which proved to be the most successful and the longest lived. The author analyzes the reasons for failure of the various societies. A chart is appended of 107 communities, showing in each case the type of community, the years it existed, location, membership, and causes of closing.

C

19 CALMER, Alan. "Labor Agitator: The Story of Albert R. Parsons." New York: International Publishers, 1937. 126 pp.

A dramatic communist interpretation of the life of Albert Parsons, one of the men hanged in connection with the Haymarket bombing of 1886. A detailed account is given of the events in Haymarket Square in Chicago and of the subsequent trial and execution.

20 CALVERTON, V. F. "Where Angels Dared to Tread." Indianapolis and New York: Bobbs-Merrill, 1941. 381 pp. App. Ind.

An account of the principal communitarian groups established in America, including the Lebadists, Kelpius and the Society of the Woman in the Wilderness, Ephrata, the Rappite and Zoarite communities, Bethel and Aurora, the Shakers, Amana, Bishop Hill, the Mormons, the Owenite experiment, Brook Farm, Hopedale, Fruitlands, Oneida, Josiah Warren's Modern Times, Zion City, and Father Divine's heavens. An interpretation of the religious experiments is offered in terms of the Christian heritage.

21 CARROLL, Mollie Ray. "Labor and Politics: The Attitude of the American Federation of Labor toward ·Legislation and Politics." Chicago: University of Chicago Libraries, 1920. 206 pp. Bibliog. Ind.

A carefully documented study of the AFL's attitudes toward legislation, law, and political action. The author notes the Federation's preference for securing gains through collective bargaining, along with its support of legislation to protect special groups of wage-earners, such as children and women, or to deal with problems too broad to be settled by bargaining with particular employers. The Federation's arguments for its nonpartisan political program are reviewed, as is the socialist criticism of that policy. The author urges AFL concern with increasing efficiency in production.

22 CHAPLIN, Ralph. "Wobbly: The Rough-and-Tumble Story of an American Radical." Chicago: University of Chicago Press, 1948. 435 pp. Ind.

The life story of one of the leaders of the IWW. Author of the popular labor song, "Solidarity Forever," and editor of "Solidarity," the IWW paper, Chaplin was a defendant in the wartime prosecution of the Wobblies under the Espionage Act. The book discusses his experiences as IWW activist and editor, IWW reactions to the war, the trials and convictions of the IWW leaders, and their prison experiences. Chaplin welcomed the Bolshevik Revolution in Russia enthusiastically, only to become disillusioned as he saw dissent crushed by dictatorship and police methods. Active in early communist-front organizations, he soon became a bitter opponent of the communists, whose influence he fought in his later years as a labor editor on the West coast.

23 COLEMAN, McAlister. "Eugene V. Debs: A Man Unafraid." New York: Greenberg, 1930. 345 pp. Bibliog. Ind.

A biography of the five-time socialist candidate for president of the U.S. The volume follows his early career as an officer of the Firemen, the first successes of the American Railway Union, and the famous Pullman strike of 1894. Attention is given also to the formation and growth of the Socialist Party and the factional conflicts within it, to the career of the IWW, to the antiwar stand of the socialists, and to the splitting off of the socialist left wing to form an American communist movement.

24 COMMONS, John R., and Associates. "History of Labour in the United States." New York: Macmillan, 1918, reissued 1926. Vol. 1 (to 1860), 623 pp.; vol. 2 (1860-1896), 620 pp. Bibliog. Ind.

The standard history of the American labor movement. The first volume deals, among other topics, with the various utopian efforts in the period prior to 1860. The second volume traces the history of the earliest revolutionary organizations in American labor, including the American sections of the International Workingmen's Association (1864-76); the formation of the Socialist Labor Party (1876, present name adopted in 1877); and the growth of an anarchist movement in the 1880's. Also treated are the formation, growth, and decline of the Knights of Labor, and their struggle with the "pure-and-simple" unionists of the AFL; and the efforts of the SLP under Daniel De Leon to win influence within both the Knights and the AFL, efforts that failed and led to De Leon's ill-starred venture in dual unionism.

D

25 DAVID, Henry. "The History of the Haymarket Affair." New York: Farrar & Rinehart, 1936. 579 pp. Bibliog. Ind.

A scholarly analysis of the Haymarket bombing of May 4, 1886, and its aftermath. Chicago, where the International Working People's Association had its greatest strength, was also the center of the eight-hour movement of May 1, 1886. In the hysteria that followed the hurling of the bomb into police ranks on May 4 a group of anarchists were arrested, tried, and quickly convicted, though no evidence connected them with the throwing of the bomb. Four of the men were hanged, and the survivors were pardoned in 1893 by Governor Altgeld, who was convinced that all of the defendants were innocent. In the author's view the conviction of innocent men was made possible by a biased judge, a prejudiced jury, perjured evidence, an indefensible theory of conspiracy, and the temper of Chicago.

26   DEBS, Eugene V. "Debs: His Life, Writings and Speeches." St. Louis: Wagner, 1908. 515 pp.
A collection of Debs' most important writings and speeches between 1895 and 1908, together with a biography by Stephen Marion Reynolds.

27   . . . . "Speeches of Eugene V. Debs." Introd. by Alexander Trachtenberg. New York: International Publishers, 1928. 95 pp.
A compilation of Debs' speeches, part of the Party's attempt to claim Debs as its own. In a critical introduction, Trachtenberg praises Debs as a revolutionary industrial unionist, a hater of class collaboration, an opponent of the Socialist Party leadership, and a supporter of the Russian Revolution. However, he criticizes Debs for pacifist utterances, lack of clarity with regard to proletarian dictatorship, and failure to join the Community Party.

28   . . . . "Writings and Speeches of Eugene V. Debs." New York: Hermitage Press, 1948. 486 pp. Bibliog.
A collection of Debs' most important writings and speeches, including most of those in the 1908 collection, and a great deal of later material going through his 1920 campaign for president waged from Atlanta prison. There is a brief introduction by Arthur M. Schlesinger, Jr.

29   DESTLER, Chester McArthur. "American Radicalism, 1865-1901: Essays and Documents." New London: Connecticut College, 1946. 276 pp. Ind.
A study of western radicalism in terms of the ideological interchange and conflict between western agrarians and urban radicals. While much of the volume is devoted to currency reform and antimonopoly movements, one chapter is on the anarchists and three deal with the labor-populist political alliance of the 1890's, with attention to the role of the socialists.

30   DIAMOND, Martin. "Socialism and the Decline of the American Socialist Party." Unpublished doctoral dissertation, University of Chicago Library, 1956. 211 pp. Bibliog.
An analysis of the failure of the Socialist Party to acquire a mass following in the U.S. The author points to the absence of a feudal past, our greater social mobility, the middle-class character of America, ethnic and racial heterogeneity, the nature of the American political system, and American hostility to doctrinaire thought. World War I and the triumph of Bolshevism in Russia were serious blows to the Socialist Party here, and the rise of fascism, the development of communist totalitarianism, and the popularity of the New Deal and the welfare state all furthered the socialist decline.

31   DOMBROWSKI, James. "The Early Days of Christian Socialism in America." New York: Columbia University Press, 1936. 208 pp. Bibliog. Ind.
A study of the Christian socialist movement in this country in the last three decades of the nineteenth century. The author traces the growth of social Christianity in that period to the pressures exerted by an expanding labor movement; and to widespread criticism of religion for its conservatism, its teaching of meekness, and its dependence on a wealthy ruling class. Among the leading figures treated are Stephen Colwell, Henry George, Richard T. Ely, Edward Bellamy, W. D. P. Bliss, Henry Demarest Lloyd and George D. Herron. Attention is also given to the Christian Labor Union (1872-78), the Society of Christian Socialists, the radical religious press, and the Christian Commonwealth colony in Georgia.

32   DORFMAN, Joseph. "Thorstein Veblen and His America." New York: Viking, 1934. 556 pp. Bibliog. Ind.
A comprehensive study of the life and thought of Veblen, the most original economic thinker that America has produced. Though not a Marxist, Veblen was sharply critical of the existing economic and social structure of society. He satirized the leisure class, with its patterns of conspicuous consumption, and saw a conflict between those who worked industriously and the predatory interests that preyed upon them. He believed the price system to be a temporary one, incapable of stability. Though Veblen's work was little noticed by economists during his life, his influence grew during the depression years that followed soon after his death.

33   DOWD, Douglas F. (ed.). "Thorstein Veblen: A Critical Reappraisal." Ithaca: Cornell University Press, 1958. 328 pp. Bibliog.
A collection of 17 lectures and essays by as many authors, exploring various aspects of Veblen's thought. Among the topics are the source and impact of Veblen's thought, his critique of the orthodox economic tradition, Veblen's and Keynes' cycle theories, Veblen and Marx, Veblen's theory of economic growth, his view of American capitalism, the ideology of the engineers, and Veblen's view of cultural evolution.

34   DOWELL, Eldridge Foster. "A History of Criminal Syndicalism Legislation in the United States." Baltimore: Johns Hopkins Press, 1939. 176 pp. App. Ind.
A study of criminal syndicalism legislation, designed to outlaw the advocacy of crime, violence, or sabotage as a means of industrial or political reform. Twenty states and two territories enacted legislation of this type, aimed primarily at the IWW, between 1917 and 1920. The author concludes that the statutes, by punishing the advocacy of doctrines even when there was no imminent danger to society, violated the concept of civil liberties guaranteed in the Constitution.

35   DRINNON, Richard. "Rebel in Paradise: A Biography of Emma Goldman." Chicago: University of Chicago Press, 1961. 349 pp. Bibliog. essay. Ind.
A recent biography of the noted anarchist leader, who played an important role in labor struggles and radical controversies in the U.S. and other countries from the 1890's until her death in 1940. She was closely associated with Alexander Berkman, who tried to assassinate Henry Clay Frick of the Carnegie Steel Company in 1892. Deported to her native Russia following the Bolshevik seizure of power, she opposed rationalized terror there as she had fought rationalized conformity here. Always she fought unreservedly for the individual, and for the rights of free speech, press, and assembly.

36   DULLES, Foster Rhea. "Labor in America: A History." 2d ed. New York: Crowell, 1955. 421 pp. Bibliog. Ind.
The book deals, among other topics, with the anarchists and the Haymarket riot of 1886, the Knights of Labor, the American Railway Union (Pullman) strike of 1894, socialist influence in the labor movement, the conservative philosophy of Gompers and the AFL, the philosophy and tactics of the IWW, and the steel strike of 1919 led by William Z. Foster.

introduced by a short discussion, followed by brief comments on the various items.

41   ELY, Richard T. Recent American Socialism, "Johns Hopkins University Studies in Historical and Political Science," 3 (April 1885), 231-304.
An early critique of the aims and techniques of American socialists by a liberal economist, written shortly after he had completed a study of the French and German socialist movements. After dealing briefly with utopian communities and Henry George's land reform program, the author devotes most of his attention to the Socialistic Labor Party and the anarchist International Working People's Association. He concludes that the danger of extremist movements is growing, and calls for a program of reform to meet the just criticism of society made by labor and socialist groups.

42   .... "The Labor Movement in America." Rev. ed. New York: Crowell, 1890. 399 pp. App. Ind.
First published in 1886, this early survey of the labor and radical movement by a noted economist deals with early American communism, with special attention to the Shakers, the Oneida Perfectionists, and the Fourieristic phalanxes; the growth of labor organizations, including national craft unions and the Knights of Labor; the economic and educational value of unions; cooperation; the beginnings of modern socialism in America, especially among German refugees; the International Working People's Association (anarchist) and the propaganda of deed; and the Socialistic Labor Party. Ely advocated moderate reform, Christian morality, education, and equality in the administration of the law to ward off revolutionary excesses.

43   .... "Socialism: An Examination of Its Nature, Its Strength and Its Weakness, with Suggestions for Social Reform." New York: Crowell, 1894. 449 pp. App. Bibliog. Ind.
An influential book in its time, written by a leading economist on the University of Wisconsin faculty. Usually cited as "Socialism and Social Reform," the volume is a balanced and dispassionate treatment of socialist strength and weakness by an author who was conservative but a believer in social reform. He urges the socialization of monopoly, along with land reform and a series of other economic and political changes. Appendices quote socialist programs in Europe and the U.S., and describe the movement and its growth in Germany and France.

E

37   EASTMAN, Max. "Max Eastman's Address to the Jury in the Second Masses Trial." New York: Liberator Publishing Co., n.d. [1918]. 46 pp.
Eastman's summation for the defense in the second conspiracy trial of the editors of the "Masses" for conspiracy to promote mutiny in the army and obstruct recruitment during World War I. Denying the charges, Eastman pleaded for freedom of the press, the socialist faith, and the right of conscience in opposition to conscription. (The other indicted editors were Art Young, John Reed, and Floyd Dell; the jury voted eight to four for acquittal.)

38   .... "Enjoyment of Living." New York and London: Harper, 1948. 603 pp. App. Ind.
An account of the first 33 years (1883-1917) of the life of a leader of the left-wing intelligentsia in the period prior to America's entrance into World War I and the Russian Revolution. Invited to become unpaid editor of the "Masses," Eastman changed its policy from the extreme right to that of left socialism, also making it a vehicle for a creative literature being stifled by commercial journalism. The magazine became a meeting ground for revolutionary labor and the radical intelligentsia. While considering himself a socialist, Eastman opposed the dogmatic aspects of socialism, as he opposed all dogma. The book includes Eastman's recollections of radical leaders such as John Reed and Bill Haywood, with whom he was associated in this pre-CP period.

39   EBERT, Justus. "The I.W.W. in Theory and Practice." Rev. ed. Chicago: Industrial Workers of the World, n.d. [1937?]. 124 pp. App.
The fifth revised edition of a booklet, first published in 1920, dealing with the growth of modern capitalism, the earlier unions formed in America, the formation and history of the IWW, and its principles, forms, and ideals. The type of shop organization advocated by the IWW is explained, along with the work of the shop committee and the job delegate. The industrial union and the general strike are advocated, and both the AFL and the CIO attacked as evasions of real unionism.

40   EGBERT, Donald Drew, and PERSONS, Stow (eds.). "Socialism and American Life." Princeton: Princeton University Press, 1952. Vol. 1. 776 pp.; vol. 2, 575 pp. Bibliog. Ind.
The definitive study of socialist influence on various aspects of American life, with contributions by 14 leading students. Contributions deal with terminology and types of socialism, socialism in Europe, the religious basis of western socialism, Christian communitarianism in America, the secular utopian socialists, Marxian socialism in the U.S. (by Daniel Bell; see separate entry), the socialist philosophy of history, the philosophical basis of Marxian socialism in the U.S., the influence of Marxian economics on American thought and practice, American Marxist political theory, sociological aspects of American socialist theory and practice, the psychology of American socialism, American writers on the left, and socialism and American art. An exhaustive bibliography by Seymour Bassett, arranged topically, comprises volume 2. Each section is

F

44   FINE, Nathan. "Labor and Farmer Parties in the United States: 1828-1928." New York: Rand School of Social Science, 1928. 445 pp. Ind.
The volume traces the history of the socialist movement in the U.S., beginning with German Marxist groups organized in the 1850's, and the formation of the Socialist Labor Party in 1876 (under another name, changed to SLP the following year). Under the leadership of Daniel De Leon in the 1890's, the socialists sought to capture the Knights of Labor and to discredit the Gompers-AFL type of "pure and simple" unionism. The book also outlines the history of the various groups that came together to form the

Socialist Party in 1901. The rising fortunes of the Socialist Party to its peak strength in 1912 are also portrayed, along with the impact of World War I upon the socialist organization and the split of the left-wing elements in 1919 to launch the communist movement.

45   FORBES, Allyn B. The Literary Quest for Utopia, 1880-1900, "Social Forces," 6 (Dec. 1927), 179-89.
An analysis of the wave of utopian novels that swept over America between 1880 and 1900. The period was one of profound social changes, including industrialization and urbanization, tension between capital and labor, and widespread demands for reform. The authors of the novels typically sought economic solutions for the problems of society, emphasizing redistribution of wealth, monetary reforms, and changes in inheritance and landholding. A list of 49 utopian novels published in the period is appended.

46   FORD, Earl C., and FOSTER, William Z. "Syndicalism." Chicago: Wm. Z. Foster, 1912. 47 pp.
An appeal for the abolition of the wage system, not through political action, but through a syndicalist revolutionary union movement. The authors trace the history of syndicalism, show its inevitability, describe the organization of industries under it, and discuss the use of the general strike. They solicit support for the Syndicalist League of North America. (This pamphlet was used against Foster during his leadership of the steel strike of 1919.)

G

47   GEIGER, George Raymond. "The Philosophy of Henry George." New York: Macmillan, 1933. 581 pp. Ind.
A comprehensive account of the life and thought of one of the most original social thinkers that America has produced. Observing the effect of land monopolization in California, George made the place of land central in his analysis and proposed that the community recapture for social purposes, through taxation, its full rental value. The author deals with both the economic and the ethical aspects of George's thinking. A chapter is devoted to the connections between George and the socialist movement in England and America. George's impact on land tax practices in various parts of the world is traced, as is his influence on later thinkers.

48   GEORGE, Henry. "Progress and Poverty." San Francisco: Hinton, 1879. 512 pp.
One of the most widely read and influential works written by an American economic thinker. Living in California in the post-Civil War period, George saw wages fall and unemployment increase as the population grew. The reason, he believed, was the private ownership of land, which permitted its owners, through rising rents, to obtain the full benefit of social development. George argued that the entire value of land, being a social creation, should be taxed by society; this, he held, would enable both employers and workers to enjoy the full fruit of their labor, while providing more than enough revenue to defray all government expenditures. (George was the

labor candidate for mayor of New York City in 1886.)

49   GIDE, Charles. "Communist and Co-operative Colonies." New York: Crowell, n.d. 223 pp. Ind.
A translation of Professor Gide's book, which was published in France in 1928. Two chapters are devoted to American communities: one to Protestant communities, including the Shakers, the Oneida Perfectionists, and the Mormons; and one to those of socialist origin, including Owenite, Fourierist, and Icarian. The author discusses the general characteristics of the communities, and the reasons for their dissolution.

50   GINGER, Ray. "The Bending Cross." New Brunswick: Rutgers University Press, 1949. 459 pp. Ind.
A definitive biography of the socialist leader who has become one of the heroes of the Communist Party. The author, dealing with Debs and the communists, pictures a vacillating leader of the Socialist Party, in serious disagreement with both socialists and communists, but more in accord with the communists than with his own party. He differed from the communists, however, in his sensitivity to the views of American workers and farmers, as he disagreed with the communist emphasis on Marxist theory and Party discipline. He broke sharply with them in 1924 on the issue of La Follette, whom he supported and they opposed.

51   GOLDBERG, Harvey (ed.). "American Radicals: Some Problems and Personalities." New York: Monthly Review Press, 1957. 308 pp.
A collection of essays on radicals of various types in American history. Included are chapters on Vito Marcantonio by Richard Sasuly (pp. 145-59); on Eugene V. Debs by Bert Cochran (pp. 163-77); on William Haywood and syndicalism by Carl E. Hein (pp. 179-97); on Daniel De Leon and the rise of Marxist politics by David Herreshoff (pp. 199-215); and on Thorstein Veblen and capitalist culture by Arthur K. Davis (pp. 279-93).

52   GOLDMAN, Emma. "Living My Life." 2 vols. New York: Knopf, 1931. (1 vol. ed., 1934.) 993 pp. Ind.
The autobiography of a leading figure in the radical movement in America from the early 1890's until the close of World War I. Exposed to Nihilist thinking while still a young girl in Russia, Emma Goldman became an anarchist as a result of the hanging of the Chicago anarchist leaders following the Haymarket bomb explosion of 1886. Thereafter, until her deportation in December 1919, she was in the thick of social struggles, including strikes, free speech campaigns, demonstrations of unemployed, and the Mooney-Billings case. The volume deals with divisions within anarchist ranks, besides detailing their common differences with the socialists of various schools. As a result of her experiences in Russia between January 1920 and December 1921, her initial enthusiasm for the October revolution turned to disillusionment.

53   GOMPERS, Samuel. "Seventy Years of Life and Labour: An Autobiography." 2 vols. New York: Dutton, 1925. 557 and 629 pp. App. Ind. Rev. ed. by Philip Taft and John A. Sessions. New York: Dutton, 1957. 334 pp. Ind.
The autobiography of the life-long leader of the AFL, who more than any other person formulated its philosophy of "voluntarism," craft autonomy, concentration upon immediate objectives, reliance upon economic action, and opposition to state intervention. Sympathetic to socialism of the Marxist variety in his early years, Gompers evolved into a bitter opponent of socialists as a result of their emphasis upon political action, their efforts to undermine

the AFL type of unionism, and their bitter attacks upon him personally.

54   GRONLUND, Lawrence. "The Co-operative Commonwealth: An Exposition of Socialism." Rev. ed. Boston: Lee and Shepard, 1893. 304 pp.
A revision of a work that first appeared in 1884, Gronlund's book was one of the earliest attempts by an American socialist to avoid the charge of utopianism. He urged replacement of a competitive society by one based on cooperation, which could be achieved by a gradual extension of state activity. Gronlund's work influenced Debs and may have led indirectly to Bellamy's "Looking Backward."

H

55   HAYNES, Fred E. "Third Party Movements Since the Civil War with Special Reference to Iowa: A Study in Social Politics." Iowa City, Iowa: State Historical Society of Iowa, 1916. 564 pp. Ind.
The history of five third-party movements, including the Granger Anti-Monopoly and Reform parties of the 1870's, the Greenback movement of the 1870's and 1880's, and the Populists of the 1890's. While developments in Iowa are told in greatest detail, full accounts are given of the national movements of which the Iowa parties formed a part. While labor formed a series of independent local parties of its own in the 1880's, the period of 1870-1900 was one in which farmers, unionists, and reformers usually cooperated in political action, with agrarian groups in the leadership.

56   . . . . "Social Politics in the United States." Boston and New York: Houghton Mifflin, 1924. 414 pp. Bibliog. Ind.
An account of the principal social and economic movements in our political life. Chapters are devoted to utopian socialism in the United States; Marxian socialism, including the anarchist movement; the labor movement, including the Knights of Labor and the AFL; Henry George and the single tax; Edward Bellamy's "Looking Backward" and his "nationalist" movement; third parties, including Grangers, Greenbackers, and Populists; La Follette and the progressive movement; the Socialist Party prior to World War I; the IWW; the impact of the war on the socialist movement and the formation of the earliest communist parties; and the Nonpartisan League.

57   HAYWOOD, William D., and BOHN, Frank. "Industrial Socialism." 6th ed. Chicago: Kerr, 1911. 64 pp.
An argument for industrial unionism and socialism by the leader of the IWW and an associate editor of the "International Socialist Review." Workers are urged to organize in class, not craft, unionism for the purposes of the class struggle, at the same time uniting in the Socialist Party to win control of government. Once this was achieved, production and necessary social institutions would be controlled by democratic industrial government, with political government ceasing to exist. This pamphlet presented the program of the left wing of the Socialist Party.

58   HAYWOOD, William D. "Bill Haywood's Book: The Autobiography of William D. Haywood." New York: International Publishers, 1929. 368 pp. App.
The autobiography of the foremost leader of the IWW, written in Moscow in 1927 shortly before the author's death. The volume traces Haywood's experiences in the metal mines of the West, his rise to a position of leadership in the Western Federation of Miners, and the part played by the Western Federation in the launching of the IWW. Haywood's strike, trial, and prison experiences are given in detail. Haywood, who was recalled from the Socialist Party's national executive committee in 1912, joined the communists soon after that movement developed in this country, though his primary allegiance remained with the IWW. He fled to Russia in 1920, following his conviction in the wartime trials of the IWW. (It was widely believed that this volume, published after Haywood's death, was edited to suit Communist Party purposes.)

59   HELD, Abraham. "The Launching of the Communist Party of the United States." Unpublished M.A. thesis, University of Chicago Library, 1939. 136 pp. App. Bibliog.
The study outlines the radical movement of 1900-1914, with attention to factional divisions within the Socialist Party and the IWW, and to the impact of World War I upon the socialist parties of Europe. The antiwar position of the Socialist Party here is described, as is the formal organization of the left wing early in 1919 and its split into two communist parties late that summer. The study deals with the underground period of the two communist parties, their relations with each other and with other labor and radical groupings, and their merger to form a legal Workers' Party at the end of 1921.

60   HERRON, George D. "The New Redemption: A Call to the Church to Reconstruct Society According to the Gospel of Christ." New York and Boston: Crowell, 1893. 176 pp.
A statement of the Christian socialist position by the leading figure in that movement in the 1890's. A Congregational minister and a member of the faculty of Iowa (now Grinnell) College until his unconventional views on property and marriage ended both connections, Herron reached wide audiences with his arguments that capitalism was in conflict with Christianity; that cooperation rather than competition was the natural law of material as well as moral progress; and that industrial democracy would realize Christianity in social affairs.

61   HICKS, John D. "The Populist Revolt: A History of the Farmers' Alliance and the People's Party." Minneapolis: University of Minnesota Press, 1931. 473 pp. App. Bibliog. Ind.
An account of the populist movement of the 1890's, told against a background of agrarian discontent. Falling prices for agricultural products in the post-Civil War decades sparked a protest movement of the agrarian and debtor West against the financial, railroad, and industrial magnates of the East. The Populists received support from Knights of Labor groups, and supported labor demands along with other measures, among which currency reform was most important. After a promising start as an independent national party in 1892, the People's Party fused with the Democrats four years later following the latter's nomination of Bryan on a free silver platform. A number of political and economic reforms remain as a heritage of the movement.

62   HILLQUIT, Morris. "Socialism in Theory and Practice." New York: Macmillan, 1909. 361 pp. App. Ind.
A comprehensive statement of the industrial, political,

administrative, and social reforms proposed by the Socialist Party on the eve of its greatest membership and electoral success, written by a leading party theoretician. The author deals with the relationship of socialism to individualism, ethics, law, the state, and politics. He analyzes various types of social reforms, asserting that the aim of socialist reform is to strengthen the working class and pave the way for the socialist state. An appendix contains brief historical sketches of the socialist movement in various countries.

63   HILLQUIT, Morris. "History of Socialism in the United States." 5th ed. New York and London: Funk & Wagnalls, 1910. 389 pp. App. Ind.

A comprehensive history of the socialist movement in the U.S., from the utopian experiments in the early and middle portions of the nineteenth century through the formation of the Socialist Party in 1901. The volume traces the ideas and experiments of the four main types of utopian communities—the sectarian or religious communities, the Owenite experiments, the phalanxes inspired by Fourier, and the Icarian communities following Cabet. The beginnings of the "scientific" or Marxist socialist movement in this country are described, and the Socialist Labor Party is treated in some detail. The SLP split into rival factions, one of which combined with the Social Democratic Party led by Debs to form the Socialist Party in 1901. (Hillquit was one of the leaders of the "Rochester" faction of the SLP in the merger negotiations with the Social Democratic Party, and thereafter played a leading role in the Socialist Party.)

64   . . . . "Loose Leaves from a Busy Life." New York: Macmillan, 1934. 339 pp. Ind.

The autobiography of one who played a leading role in the American socialist movement for almost half a century. An early member of the Socialist Labor Party, he led the opposition to De Leon's policies until his faction joined with Debs' Social Democratic Party to form the Socialist Party in 1901. Thereafter Hillquit was one of the most influential members of the party, as a member of its national executive committee, as candidate for mayor of New York and other offices, as delegate to international socialist congresses, and as co-author of the antiwar declaration of 1917. Accounts are given of important cases in which Hillquit served as counsel.

65   HINDS, William Alfred. "American Communities." Rev. ed. Chicago: Kerr, 1902. 433 pp.

A greatly enlarged version of a work that first appeared in 1878, based largely upon personal observations. Among the communities discussed at some length are Ephrata, the Shakers, George Rapp's Harmonists, the Separatists of Zoar, Robert Owen's experiments, the Oneida Perfectionists, Hopedale, Brook Farm and the North American Phalanx, Fruitlands, Skaneateles, Amana, the Bethel-Aurora communities, the Swedish community at Bishop Hill, Cabet and the Icarians, and the Brotherhood of the New Life. Many other communities receive briefer treatment. The author, who was an early member of the Perfectionists, retained an abiding faith in communism as the ultimate basis of human society, though he strongly opposed ill-considered and ill-conducted social experiments.

66   HOLBROOK, Stewart H. "Dreamers of the American Dream." Garden City, N.Y.: Doubleday, 1957. 369 pp. Bibliog. Ind.

The story of various kinds of dreamers and reformers, including brief accounts of the Oneida Perfectionists, the Populists, Henry George, the Homestead strike, the Knights of Labor, Coxey's Army, Debs and the American Railway Union strike, the Haywood-Moyer-Pettibone case, and the IWW.

67   HOLLOWAY, Mark. "Heavens on Earth: Utopian Communities in America, 1680-1880." New York: Library Publishers, 1951. 240 pp. Bibliog. note. Ind.

A sympathetic account of the principal utopian communities established in the U.S., including the Shakers, the Rappites and Zoarites, Owen's New Harmony, the Fourierist phalanxes, the Inspirationists of Amana, the Oneida Perfectionists, and Cabet and the Icarians. There is a summary of the achievements and limitations of the community movement.

68   HOWELLS, William Dean. "A Traveler from Altruria." New York: Harper, 1894. 318 pp.

A utopian novel in the Edward Bellamy tradition, written by the best-known American writer converted to socialism following publication of Bellamy's "Looking Backward." Howells criticized American economic and social structure through the eyes of a citizen of the imaginary Altruria, a newly discovered continent whose economic practices and social structure were based on Christian principles. Howells' work, one of a large number of utopian novels written in imitation of Bellamy, satirized middle-class American standards.

69   HOXIE, Robert F. 'The Rising Tide of Socialism': A Study, "Journal of Political Economy," 19 (Oct. 1911), 609-31.

A discussion of centers of socialist strength at the time of the movement's greatest public acceptance and of reasons for its success, written by a University of Chicago professor. Most of the recent electoral victories, he concluded, were largely fortuitous so far as theoretical socialism was concerned, resulting from peculiar local conditions such as poor municipal government. With responsibility, Hoxie argued, socialists were hard to distinguish from liberal reformers, so that socialist success was a training school for constructive democracy.

70   . . . . "Trade Unionism in the United States." 2d ed. New York: Appleton, 1924. 468 pp. App. Bibliog. Ind.

Chapter 6 on "The Industrial Workers of the World and Revolutionary Unionism" focuses on the failure of the IWW to develop greater strength and stability. Reasons for its weakness are found in its internal conflicts, its lack of sound finances, and its failure to develop stable leadership. Revolutionary unionism of the socialist variety is also discussed briefly.

71   HUGHAN, Jessie Wallace. "American Socialism of the Present Day." New York: John Lane, 1911. 265 pp. Bibliog.

A survey of the socialist movement in the U.S., written when it was near the peak of its numerical strength and influence. The book contains material on socialist theory, socialist history in America, immediate as well as ultimate aims, and party organization and tactics. The author's sympathies were with the right-wing "revisionists" or "constructionists," as she prefers to call them, as against the revolutionists. Other differences within the movement related to Christian socialists as against atheists, and intellectuals as against manual workers. Socialists also differed on the issue of industrial or craft unions, and the desirability of forming a labor party.

72   HUNTER, Robert. "Labor in Politics." Chicago: Socialist Party, 1915. 202 pp.

A review, from a socialist point of view, of the ineffectiveness of the AFL in political and legislative activity, contrasted with labor's political influence and power in many European countries. Asserting the folly of political harmony between capital and labor, the author argues that labor must build its own political party. Now that the Socialist Party is in existence, he suggests that the unions support it, so that there would be two cooperating working-class movements, one in the economic and the other in the political sphere.

J

73   JENSEN, Vernon H. "Heritage of Conflict: Labor Relations in the Nonferrous Metals Industry up to 1930." Ithaca, New York: Cornell University Press, 1950. 495 pp. Bibliog. Ind.

A study of the violent struggles of the metal miners of the West, organized in the class-conscious and militant Western Federation of Miners. Scornful of the conservativism and craft separatism of the AFL, the WFM played a key role in the launching of the IWW in 1905, only to break with that organization three years later. As the WFM shifted to a more conservative type of unionism it affiliated with the AFL in 1911, changing its name in 1916 to the International Union of Mine, Mill and Smelter Workers. (In 1950 this union was one of those expelled from the CIO because of communist domination.)

74   JOHNSON, Oakley C. "The Day is Coming: Life and Work of Charles E. Ruthenberg, 1882-1927." New York: International Publishers, 1957. 192 pp. Bibliog. Ind.

The life of a key figure in the radical movement between 1911 and 1927, who played a leading part in the transformation of the left wing of the Socialist Party into the communist movement. A leader of the Socialist Party in Ohio, Ruthenberg helped draft the antiwar resolution adopted by the national organization in 1917, and played a leading role in the party split two years later. He served as general secretary of the short-lived Communist Party formed in September 1919, and of the Workers Party that succeeded it.

K

75   KARSNER, David. "Debs: His Authorized Life and Letters." New York: Boni and Liveright, 1919. 244 pp. App.

An authorized biography of Debs, written by a sympathetic reporter who covered the story of his trial for violation of the Espionage Act and accompanied him on his trip to the penitentiary following his conviction. Half the book is taken up with his trial, including his speech to the jury, and his prison experiences. The other half, dealing with his earlier life, includes an account of the American Railway Union strike of 1894 and Debs' subsequent conviction for contempt of court; and his activities in four presidential campaigns as socialist standard-bearer. Portions of his Canton, Ohio, speech of June 16,

1918, which led to his indictment and conviction, are reproduced in an appendix.

76   KARSON, Marc. "American Labor Unions and Politics, 1900-1918." Carbondale: Southern Illinois University Press, 1958. 358 pp. Bibliog. Ind.

Concerned primarily with political attitudes of the AFL, Karson also devotes two chapters to the Industrial Workers of the World. The section dealing with the AFL treats in some detail socialist efforts to commit the federation to a labor party, as well as to such legislation as the 8-hour day. The chapters on the IWW deal with the founding of that organization, its philosophy, its internal conflicts, its strikes and free speech campaigns, and the crippling of the organization by arrests and prosecutions for its opposition to World War I. Relations of the Socialist Party and the Socialist Labor Party to the IWW are explored.

77   KENT, Alexander. Cooperative Communities in the United States, "Bulletin of the Department of Labor," 6 (1901), 563-646.

An account of cooperative or communistic communities formed in this country, including such older ones as the Shakers, the Amana Society, the Separatist Society of Zoar, the Rappites, and the Oneida Community, along with the Ruskin Community and others founded in the 1890's. The author observes that most of the communities have been very short lived; democracy, he notes, has thus far proved a source of weakness. The most prosperous and longest-lived communities have been under a rigorous discipline exercised by a central authority.

78   KIPNIS, Ira. "The American Socialist Movement: 1897-1912." New York: Columbia University Press, 1952. 496 pp. Bibliog. Ind.

An account of the socialist movement in the U.S. in the formative period of the Socialist Party and during that party's period of greatest influence. Attention is paid to developments within the Socialist Labor Party before 1901 and to the formation of the Socialist Party that year by merger of the Social Democratic Party of Debs with the "Rochester" faction of the SLP led by Morris Hillquit. The bulk of the book is concerned with factionalism within the SP from its formation until 1912. The author supports the left or revolutionary wing of the party, led by William D. Haywood and Debs, over the right-center coalition led by Hillquit and Victor Berger.

79   KORNBLUH, Joyce L. (ed.). "Rebel Voices: An I.W.W. Anthology." Ann Arbor: University of Michigan Press, 1964. 419 pp. Notes. Bibliog.

A collection of IWW writings, songs, and cartoons, emphasizing the philosophy of industrial unionism; the tactics of direct action; IWW itinerants; free speech campaigns; experiences in the textile, agricultural, lumbering, and mining industries; and war and prison. The industrial unionism and militant tactics of the IWW influenced the CIO, and left an impress on the American labor movement and American society.

80   KUHN, Henry, and JOHNSON, Olive M. "The Socialist Labor Party during Four Decades, 1890-1930." New York: New York Labor News Co., 1931. 126 pp.

Sketches by Socialist Labor Party members of their party history and the party press. The authors focus upon Daniel De Leon's ideas and actions, upon party finance, and upon defections from the party line.

L

81   LAIDLER, Harry W. "Socialism in Thought and Action." New York: Macmillan, 1920. 546 pp. Bibliog. Ind.

A statement of the socialist indictment of capitalism and of socialist theory and objectives by a leading American writer long associated with the Socialist Party. Written shortly after the end of World War I, the book devotes considerable attention to the Russian revolution and to other events since 1914 involving the socialist movement, in other countries as well as in the U.S.

82   LENS, Sidney. "Left, Right & Center: Conflicting Forces in American Labor." Hinsdale, Ill.: Regnery, 1949. 445 pp. Bibliog. Ind.

An attempt to explain the triumph of business unionism over labor radicalism through a survey of labor history. Among the topics treated are socialist influence in the trade unions, the IWW, labor racketeering, craft versus industrial unionism, and the Trade Union Educational League. The author makes a strong plea for the formation of an independent labor party, and urges the creation of a consolidated non-Stalinist left wing within the labor movement.

83   LEVINE, Louis. The Development of Syndicalism in America, "Political Science Quarterly," 28 (Sept. 1913), 451-79.

A brief account of the formation and history of the IWW, the most effective syndicalist organization in America. Attention is paid to the character of the AFL and to the formation of the IWW by groups antagonistic to the Federation. Conflicts within the IWW are described, as are its free speech fights, its chief strikes, and its aggressive methods. There is a comparison of the IWW with French syndicalism.

. . . . See also LORWIN, Lewis.

84   LINDSEY, Almont. "The Pullman Strike: The Story of a Unique Experiment and of a Great Labor Upheaval." Chicago: University of Chicago Press, 1942. 385 pp. Bibliog. Ind.

The leading study of one of the most famous strikes in American labor history. The book traces the development of the Pullman Palace Car Company, the building of the model town of Pullman, and the outbreak of the strike precipitated by wage cuts, while the company as landlord refused to reduce rents. The recently established American Railway Union, led by Eugene V. Debs, supported the strike by boycotting Pullman cars. Injunctions and federal troops broke the strike, while Debs and other leaders of the ARU were given jail terms for violation of an injunction. Emerging from prison a socialist, Debs converted the remnants of the ARU into the Social Democratic Party, a forerunner of the Socialist Party of America.

85   LLOYD, Henry Demarest. "Wealth against Commonwealth." New York: Harper, 1894. 563 pp. App. Ind.

A widely read, influential book that helped arouse America to the evils in our economic and political life for which the newly developed trusts were responsible. The story of the rise of the Standard Oil Company, the volume exposed its ruthless treatment of competitors and its manipulation of government agencies. (Lloyd was interested in socialist colonization plans in the latter years of the century and helped to form the Brotherhood of the Co-operative Commonwealth in 1896.)

86   LONDON, Jack. "The Iron Heel." New York: Macmillan, 1907. 354 pp.

A novel by a socialist author forecasting bloody strife between workers and capitalists in the period between 1912 and 1932, and particularly describing the revolt of the Chicago proletariat and its suppression by the Oligarchy, into which the ruling capitalists were organized. London forecast a series of revolts in the next three centuries before the world movement of labor was to triumph over the united oligarchies of the world. (Only 31 when the novel was written, London was already one of America's most widely read authors.)

M

87   MACY, John. "Socialism in America." Garden City, N.Y.: Doubleday, Page, 1916. 249 pp. Ind.

An informal sketch of the socialist movement, written by a Harvard graduate who was a member both of the Socialist Party and of the IWW. The 1912 Socialist Party program is analyzed in detail. There is also a brief discussion of the contest between anarchists and socialists, and a chapter on the IWW.

88   MADISON, Charles A. "Critics & Crusaders: A Century of American Protest." New York: Holt, 1947. 572 pp. Bibliog. Ind.

An account of six groups of American radicals or reformers—abolitionists, utopians, anarchists, dissident economists, militant liberals, and socialists. The growth and influence of each of these types of thought is described, as is the life and thought of three main figures of the group. Included are the utopians Albert Brisbane and Edward Bellamy; the individualist anarchists Henry David Thoreau and Benjamin R. Tucker, and the rebel Emma Goldman; economic thinkers Henry George and Thorstein Veblen; liberals John Peter Altgeld and Lincoln Steffens; and socialists Daniel De Leon, Eugene Victor Debs, and John Reed.

89   McMURRY, Donald L. "Coxey's Army: A Study of the Industrial Army Movement of 1894." Boston: Little, Brown, 1929. 331 pp. App. Bibliog. Ind.

The leading account of the marches on Washington by unemployed groups in the depression year of 1894. While Coxey, a populist businessman of Massillon, Ohio, organized and led the best publicized contingent, others that were organized independently were larger and traveled greater distances. The announced purpose of Coxey's march was to obtain passage by Congress of his bill to provide work for the unemployed, by building a road system financed by an issue of legal-tender notes. The number participating in the marches was far smaller than anticipated, and Coxey's own efforts reached an anticlimax in Washington when the police prevented him from speaking from the Capitol steps.

90   McVEY, Frank L. The Populist Movement, "Economic Studies," 1 (Aug. 1896), 131-209. App. Bibliog.

A study of the origins and program of the Populists. The movement was made up of two factions, the laborers and the much more numerous farmers, with no real common bond except discontent. The party's most important proposals, such as those relating to money and to government ownership of railroads, are examined, and compared to the program of the socialists. Despite the party's electoral successes in 1892 and 1894, the author predicts that it will be a transient one because of its lack of fundamental principles.

91   MORGAN, H. Wayne. "Eugene V. Debs: Socialist for President." Syracuse: Syracuse University Press, 1962. 257 pp. Notes. Ind.

An account of the five campaigns in which Debs was the socialist candidate for president, with attention to Debs' role and personality and to the factional conflict within the Socialist Party between a left wing that leaned to syndicalism and advocacy of violence and a right wing concerned with social reform and electoral success. Though Debs agreed with the Left in its militancy, revolutionary zeal, and advocacy of industrial unionism, he never lost faith in the democratic process. Despite initial sympathy for the Bolshevik revolution, he opposed the denial of human rights there and the use of terror as an instrument of rule.

N

92   NASH, Howard P., Jr. "Third Parties in American Politics." Washington, D.C.: Public Affairs Press, 1959. 326 pp. Bibliog. Ind.

A review of the various third parties, whatever their social base and objectives, that have appeared in this country's history. The Greenback-Labor and Populist Parties are discussed in some detail, with brief mention of the Socialist Party. Contemporary political cartoons are reproduced.

93   NOMAD, Max [pseud.]. "Apostles of Revolution." Boston: Little, Brown, 1939. 467 pp. Bibliog. Ind.

A chapter is devoted to Johann Most, "terrorist of the word," who came to this country in 1882 after an active career in the radical movement of Europe and became the leading editor and propagandist of the anarchist movement, which then flourished chiefly among German and other immigrant workers. Most preached terrorism as a social weapon, urging his followers to arm themselves and publishing information on the manufacture and use of explosives. His two best-known disciples, both of whom later broke sharply with him, were Emma Goldman and Alexander Berkman.

94   NORDHOFF, Charles. "The Communistic Societies of the United States." New York: Harper, 1875. 439 pp. Bibliog. Ind. Reprinted by Hilary House in 1960.

A description of the principal communitarian groups in existence in America at the time, based upon personal visit and observation. Among the communities discussed are Amana, the Harmonists at Economy, the Separatists of Zoar, the Shakers, the Oneida and Wallingford Perfectionists, the Aurora and Bethel communes, the Icarians, and the Bishop Hill colony. In a concluding chapter the author analyzes and compares the different customs and practices of the communities, and attempts to state the conditions necessary for success and the influences of the colonies, for good and evil, upon members and neighbors.

95   NOYES, John Humphrey. "History of American Socialisms." Philadelphia: Lippincott, 1870. 678 pp. Ind.

A history of the various communities established in the U.S. on socialist principles, whether secular or religious in inspiration. About half the book is devoted to the many phalanxes following Fourierism, and attention is also given to Owenite experiments, particularly the one at New Harmony. Communities with a religious base, notably those of the Shakers and of the Oneida Perfectionists, which Noyes himself founded, are also examined, as are the efforts of the Unitarians at Brook Farm (later a phalanx) and the Universalists at Hopedale. Analyzing the failure of most of the experiments, the author concluded that earnest religion was the factor that distinguished the successful ones.

O

96   OLSON, Frederick I. "The Milwaukee Socialists, 1897-1941." Unpublished doctoral dissertation, Harvard College Library, 1952. 603 pp. Bibliog.

An extensive study of the Milwaukee socialists, their relations with other socialists, and their experiences in local government affairs.

P

97   PARKER, Carleton H. "The Casual Laborer and Other Essays." New York: Harcourt, Brace, and Howe, 1920. 199 pp. App.

Four essays on labor unrest, the casual laborer, the IWW, and motives in economic life by a University of Washington economist who stressed the psychological factors in economic behavior. As investigator for the state of California and the federal government, Parker was particularly concerned with migratory, casual laborers, and with the IWW, which organized them. He viewed the IWW as "a psychological by-product of the neglected childhood of industrial America." An appendix contains his report to the governor of California on the Wheatland hop-fields riot of 1913.

98   PARRINGTON, Vernon Louis, Jr. "American Dreams: A Study of American Utopias." Provi-

dence, R.I.: Brown University, 1947. 234 pp. Bibliog. Ind.

A study of the American utopian novel, with particular stress on late nineteenth century works. Edward Bellamy's work is discussed in detail, and his precursors and followers likewise receive attention. There is a bibliography of utopian novels and related literature published in America between 1659 and 1946.

99   PERLMAN, Selig, and TAFT, Philip. "History of Labor in the United States, 1896-1932." Commons series, vol. 4. New York: Macmillan, 1935. 683 pp. Bibliog. Ind.

The standard history of the American labor movement over the period in which the AFL grew rapidly and became the dominant labor organization in the U.S. The book also tells the story of the militant Western Federation of Miners; the formation, internal conflicts, strikes, and free speech fights of the IWW; and the formation of the Socialist Party and the factional conflicts that followed. Attempts of socialists to influence the AFL are described, as are the Federation's political efforts, the impact of World War I upon the various labor and radical groups, and the efforts of the newly-formed communist movement to "bore from within" the AFL.

100   PETERSEN, Arnold. "Daniel De Leon: Social Architect." New York: New York Labor News Co. Vol. 1 (1941), 313 pp.; vol. 2 (1953), 400 pp. Ind. Add.

A collection of speeches and writings by the national secretary of the Socialist Labor Party on various aspects of De Leon's work. The bulk of the two volumes consists of addresses at the annual De Leon commemorations. Various addresses deal with De Leon as pioneer socialist editor, contributor to Marxian science, educator, social architect, orator, disciplinarian, internationalist, social scientist, and emancipator.

101   POWDERLY, Terence V. "The Path I Trod: The Autobiography of Terence V. Powderly." Ed. by Harry J. Carman, Henry David, and Paul N. Guthrie. New York: Columbia University Press, 1940. 460 pp. App. Ind.

The autobiography of the leading figure of the Knights of Labor, its Grand Master Workman from 1879 to 1893, covering the period of its importance as a labor organization. Written many years later, the book serves to explain and justify his actions or lack of them in the strikes or other controversies in which he and the Knights were involved. His belief in the solidarity of all labor, his dislike of strikes and his efforts to terminate them, his political career from Greenback-Labor to Republican, and his advocacy of producers' cooperation and of land reform are emphasized in the volume. A long chapter deals with the opposition of leading members of the Catholic hierarchy to the Knights, growing out of the early policy of secrecy and the ritual.

102   PRESTON, William, Jr. "Aliens and Dissenters: Federal Suppression of Radicals, 1903-1933." Cambridge, Mass.: Harvard, 1963. 352 pp. Bibliog. note. Notes. Ind.

An account of the federal government's efforts to suppress dissent during three decades of radical change, when fear of radicals and foreigners mounted in intensity. Most of the book deals with the IWW, with the government's efforts to exclude radicals, deport alien IWW's, or deny them citizenship. Attention is given to the military repression of the IWW during World War I, to their prosecution under the Espionage Act, and to deportations following the war. The volume also treats the rise of the communist movement here, the Red raids of 1919-20, and the deportation of alien communists.

Q

103   QUINT, Howard H. "The Forging of American Socialism: Origins of the Modern Movement." Columbia: University of South Carolina Press, 1953. 409 pp. Bibliog. Ind.

An account of the development of American socialism between 1886 and 1901. Attention is paid to the pioneer Marxist groups here in the 1850's and 1860's; to the formation and character of the Socialist Labor Party; to the relations of socialists to the AFL, the single-tax movement, and the Knights of Labor; to the popularization of socialist views with Edward Bellamy's "Looking Backward"; to the formation of a Christian socialist movement; to the sectariansim of the Socialist Labor Party under De Leon; and to the homespun flavor of J. A. Wayland's "The Coming Nation" and "Appeal to Reason." The formation of the Socialist Party in 1901 united most of the socialist groups in this country.

R

104   RAYBACK, Joseph G. "A History of American Labor." New York: Macmillan, 1959. 459 pp. Bibliog. Ind.

A recent labor history, viewing labor events against the background of American economic, political, and social developments. Among the topics treated are the Knights of Labor, the Haymarket affair, the formation and growth of the AFL, the Socialist Labor Party, the Pullman strike, the formation and influence of the Socialist Party, the IWW, the attack on the radicals during and immediately following World War I, and the formation of the communist movement.

105   REED, Louis S. "The Labor Philosophy of Samuel Gompers." New York: Columbia University Press, 1930. 191 pp. Bibliog. Ind.

A doctoral dissertation tracing the development of Gompers' philosophy of "voluntarism" or individualism, as well as his key role in building and leading the AFL. Originally socialist in his thinking, Gompers was repelled by the tactics of the socialists, their obsession with political action, and their indifference to trade unionism. As Gompers evolved into a "pure and simple" trade unionist, his tolerance of socialism turned to bitter hatred as a result of socialist criticism and attempts at the destruction of the AFL. Gompers distrusted the state, though he turned to it occasionally for the solution of some problems. His policies proved congenial to the skilled workers, who could advance their interests by economic action without dependence on legislation.

106   ROCHESTER, Anna. "The Populist Movement in the United States." New York: International Publishers, 1943. 128 pp.

The story of agrarian revolt in the U.S. in the decades following the Civil War, told from a communist point of view. Attention is paid to the Granger movement, the Greenback Party, and the Farmers' Alliances as precursors of the Populists. The formation of the People's Party, its program and first electoral successes, and its fusion with the Democrats in support of Bryan in 1896 are also discussed. The relation of populist thinking to socialism is emphasized. Henry A. Wallace, vice-president when the book was written, is treated as the outstanding current heir of the Populists.

107   ROGOFF, Harry. "An East Side Epic: The Life and Work of Meyer London." New York: Vanguard, 1930. 311 pp.
London's political career—his election to Congress on the Socialist ticket in 1914, 1916, and 1920—is presented against a background of life in the lower East Side of New York City, during the formative period of the Jewish needle trades unions. The right-left split within the Socialist party, giving rise to the communist movement after the Bolshevik revolution in Russia, is portrayed. London was a leading member of the right wing, and as such a frequent target for attacks from the leftist elements. The book throws light upon the radical movement among the immigrant Jews in New York City from the days of the Socialist Labor Party, to which London briefly belonged, to the rise of the communist movement.

S

108   SAVAGE, Marion Dutton. "Industrial Unionism in America." New York: Ronald Press, 1922. 344 pp. Bibliog. Ind.
A study of the most important industrial unions that had appeared in the United States by 1922, whether within the AFL or independent. Among the unions to which chapters are devoted are the Western Federation of Miners, called the International Union of Mine, Mill, and Smelter Workers after 1916; the Industrial Workers of the World; and the One Big Union, formed in Canada in 1919, which spread soon after to the U.S. The other industrial unions covered in the book include those in brewing, coal mining, the garment industries, and textiles. The book concludes with an analysis of the class consciousness of industrial unions, their efforts to develop democracy, and their social idealism.

109   SCHUSTER, Eunice Minette. "Native American Anarchism: A Study of Left-Wing American Individualism." Smith College Studies in History, vol. 17, 1931-32. 202 pp. Bibliog. Ind.
An account of the several varieties of anarchism that have appeared in American history. The volume considers individualism in the Colonial period, with particular attention to the Antinomians and the Quakers; individualism in the "Romantic" period (1812-60), especially Perfectionism and Nonresistance; the period of native anarchism, with emphasis on the doctrines of Josiah Warren, the influence of Proudhon, and the school of "scientific anarchism" led by Benjamin R. Tucker and Lysander Spooner; and the more recent anarchist communists, led first by Johann Most and then by Emma Goldman and Alexander Berkman.

110   SHANNON, David A. "The Socialist Party of America: A History." New York: Macmillan, 1955. 320 pp. Bibliog. essay. Ind.
A history of the Socialist Party from its formation in 1901 until its virtual disintegration in the New Deal period. Approximately half the book is devoted to a history of developments and an analysis of party problems between 1901 and 1919, when the left wing split off to form the communist movement. Attention is given to the regional differences within the party in its early years, to its character as a coalition of the American left broad enough to include various radical tendencies. The leading inner-party squabbles prior to 1917 are related, as are the party's opposition to World War I and the persecution it suffered as a result. The effect of the war on the composition of the party is also analyzed. A number of factors explain the party's failure to grow into a more significant movement.

111   SOCIALIST LABOR PARTY, National Executive Committee. "Daniel De Leon: The Man and His Work: A Symposium." New York: SLP, 1920. Book 1, 136 pp.; book 2, 186 pp. Ind.
Seven sketches of De Leon, his ideas and Socialist Labor Party activities, written by followers. The volume contains material on De Leon's life and political campaigns, as well as on the many factional disputes and quarrels with other labor and radical groups in which he engaged. His activities in the IWW and his relations with the Socialist Party receive attention.

112   SOCIALIST PARTY, National Executive Committee. Report of National Executive Committee: Document on Internal Situation in Socialist Party Read Before National Emergency Convention in Chicago by James Oneal, New York "Call," Sept. 3, 1919, p. 2.
A review of the right-left conflict within the Socialist Party from the St. Louis convention of 1917 until the emergency convention of 1919. The left wing is accused of waging a systematic campaign of lies against the SP, of wrecking the attempt to hold an amnesty convention, of engaging in organized treachery and corrupt practices.

113   SPARGO, John. "Socialism: A Summary and Interpretation of Socialist Principles." Rev. ed. New York: Macmillan, 1909. 349 pp. Ind.
A statement of the socialist position written by one of the leading popularizers of socialist ideas in this country. The book deals with the utopian socialist movement, the "Communist Manifesto" and scientific socialism, the materialist conception of history, the class-struggle theory, socialist economics, and the socialist state. The author advocates a legal, gradual change to socialism.

114   . . . . "Applied Socialism: A Study of the Application of Socialistic Principles to the State." New York: Huebsch, 1912. 333 pp. App.
A suggested outline of the socialist society of the future, by a leading right-wing socialist theoretician. Among the topics dealt with are the socialist state, property and industry under socialism, personal liberty, labor and its remuneration, incentive, the family, intellectual service, and religious freedom. An appendix contains the program of the German Social Democratic Party.

115   . . . . "Syndicalism, Industrial Unionism and Socialism." New York: Huebsch, 1913. 243 pp. App. Bibliog. note.
A discussion of syndicalism, the general strike, and sabotage by a leading right-wing American socialist, who carefully differentiated the Socialist Party's position from that of syndicalists, including those in the IWW. The

author argued that it was as dangerous for the socialist movement to compromise with anarchism in its syndicalist guise as to compromise with capitalist political parties.

116   SPARGO, John. "Americanism and Social Democracy." New York: Harper, 1918. 326 pp. App.
A statement of the position of the prowar minority of the Socialist Party. Spargo, a leading right-wing intellectual associated with the party and a member of its national executive committee, resigned from the party to support World War I. The appendix contains a number of documents dealing with the controversy within socialist ranks created by the war.

117   SPEEK, Peter Alexander. "The Singletax and the Labor Movement." Bulletin of the University of Wisconsin, Economics and Political Science Series, vol. 8, no. 3, 1917. 180 pp. App.
A study of the United Labor Party of New York (1886-88), with attention to the clash between socialists and single taxers for control. The book surveys the single tax philosophy, the growth and problems of the Central Labor Union of New York, the formation of a labor party in 1886, and Henry George's campaign that year as mayoralty candidate of the United Labor Party. The expulsion of members of the Socialist Labor Party from the United Labor Party in 1887 is also dealt with, as is the party's effort to run a national campaign in 1888 and its subsequent collapse.

118   SPRAGUE, Philo W. "Christian Socialism: What and Why." New York: Dutton, 1891. 204 pp. App.
A statement of the Christian socialist point of view. Chapters deal with the nature of socialism, the spirit of the present economic system, why socialists believe in collective ownership and control of land and capital, the relationship of Christianity to socialism, and the transition to socialism by just and orderly methods.

119   STALVEY, James Benjamin. "Daniel De Leon: A Study of Marxian Orthodoxy in the United States." Abstract of an unpublished University of Illinois doctoral dissertation. Urbana, Ill., 1946. 22 pp.
An analysis of De Leon's ideas and of his role in the Socialist Labor Party, together with an estimate of his influence upon other socialists. The more important of his writings, along with discussions of him, are cited.

120   SYMES, Lillian, and CLEMENT, Travers. "Rebel America: The Story of Social Revolt in the United States." New York and London: Harper, 1934. 392 pp. Bibliog. Ind.
An account of movements of social protest in American history, from the utopian socialist experiments of the 1820's to the radical groups of the early 1930's. Attention is paid to the utopian communities of the nineteenth century, to labor and farmer political protest movements, to the Socialist Labor Party under De Leon and the Socialist Party led by Debs, to the anarchist movement of the 1880's, and to the appearance of the IWW early in this century. The effect of World War I upon radical groups is portrayed, as is the split of the Socialist Party and the emergence of the communist movement.

T

121   TAFT, Philip. "Organized Labor in American History." New York, Evanston, and London: Harper & Row, 1964. 818 pp. Notes. Ind.
A comprehensive history of the American labor movement, including treatments of the various working class industrial and political organizations. Anarchist, socialist, and communist activities are described, as are the unions that radicals of these types formed or were active in. Pertinent references include those to the Socialist Labor Party, the anarchists and the Haymarket riot (pp. 127-35), the Industrial Workers of the World (pp. 290-98 and 334-40), the Socialist Party (pp. 323-27, etc.), the Trade Union Educational League (pp. 391-96) and Ch. 47 (pp. 618-30) on "Communist Activity in Organized Labor."

122   THOMPSON, Fred (compiler). "The I.W.W.: Its First Fifty Years (1905-1955)." Chicago: Industrial Workers of the World, 1955. 203 pp. Ind.
A history of the IWW, emphasizing the groups that founded it, the factionalism that developed, and the leading strikes and free speech fights in which the organization engaged. Attention is given to IWW opposition to World War I, to arrests and convictions of its leaders under the Espionage Act, and to the reign of terror against IWW lumber workers in the Centralia, Washington, area. Though the IWW applauded the Russian Revolution, it rejected affiliation with the Third International and the RILU. In this country relations between the IWW and the communists soon shifted from comradely disagreement to open hostility.

123   TUCKER, Benj. R. "Instead of a Book, by a Man Too Busy to Write One." New York: The author, 1893. 512 pp. Ind.
A collection of writings by the leader of the American school of individualistic, philosophical anarchism. Tucker's writings, selected from his journal, "Liberty," deal with state socialism and anarchism; the individual, society, and the state; money and interest; land and rent; socialism and communism; and methods. Arguing that all forms of social organization should be voluntary, Tucker proposed the gradual abolition of the state and the substitution of voluntary cooperation for all necessary or desirable purposes. He opposed all participation in the state or its activities, including voting, the payment of taxes, and military service.

U

124   U.S. COMMISSION ON INDUSTRIAL RELATIONS. "Final Report and Testimony." Washington: Government Printing Office, 1916. 11 volumes.
Volume 2, pp. 1441-1579, consists of public hearings on

the American Federation of Labor, the Socialist Party, and the Industrial Workers of the World. Samuel Gompers was principal spokesman for the AFL, Morris Hillquit and Max S. Hayes spoke for the socialists, and Vincent St. John and Joseph J. Ettor for the IWW. Testimony dealt, among other subjects, with the strength, structure, tactics, and objectives of each organization. Interesting exchanges occurred as Gompers and Hillquit cross-examined each other on the methods and aims of their respective organizations. Hillquit sought to show that the ultimate objectives were similar, since the unions' efforts to increase labor's share would not stop until the working class as a whole received the entire product.

V

125   VEBLEN, Thorstein. "The Theory of the Leisure Class." New York: Macmillan, 1899. 400 pp.
The first and most widely read of Veblen's books, which together constituted a savage indictment of existing society. An economist and philosopher who had read widely in anthropology, Veblen asserted that the leisure class had emerged during the transition from primitive and peaceful savagery to warlike barbarism. In the predatory stage of society, work became unworthy and wealth was sought because it conferred honor. The leisure class became exempt from all useful employment, while developing practices of conspicuous consumption. With the depression Veblen's work gained in influence; he helped to undermine popular respect for the economic and social leaders of the present social order.

126   VORSE, Mary Heaton. "A Footnote to Folly: Reminiscences of Mary Heaton Vorse." New York: Farrar & Rinehart, 1935. 407 pp.
An autobiography, covering the years 1912 to 1922, of a labor writer who covered many of the great strikes of the period. Among these were the Lawrence textile strike of 1912 and the Mesaba Range strike of 1916, both led by the IWW, and the great steel strike of 1919. The book also deals with the wartime persecution of the IWW, the Palmer "Red" raids following the war, and the Sacco-Vanzetti case.

W

127   WACHMAN, Marvin. "History of the Social-Democratic Party of Milwaukee, 1897-1910." Urbana: University of Illinois Press, 1945. 90 pp. App. Bibliog. Ind.
A study of one of the most successful units of the Socialist Party of America, during the years of its formation, growth, and initial electoral victories. Formed as Branch One of the Social Democracy of America in 1897, the Milwaukee socialist organization, led by Victor L. Berger,

retained the Social-Democratic name after the formation of the Socialist Party in 1901. Socialism was a tradition among a substantial segment of the dominant German population of the city; and a strong party organization, capitalizing upon this sentiment along with a practical program of municipal reform, carried socialist candidates into city office.

128   WAGNER, Donald O. (ed.). "Social Reformers: Adam Smith to John Dewey." New York: Macmillan, 1934. 749 pp. Ind.
A collection of passages from the writings of a wide variety of European and American social reformers of the century and a half prior to publication. Among the Americans to whom chapters are devoted are Henry George and Thorstein Veblen; and among those who have had a strong influence on American thought or developments are Robert Owen, Charles Fourier, and Karl Marx and Friedrich Engels. A variety of other Europeans whose writings also had some influence in America are also covered, including anarchists or syndicalists, and various types of socialists, ranging from Christian to guild socialists.

129   WALLING, William English. "Socialism as It Is: A Survey of the World-Wide Revolutionary Movement." New York: Macmillan, 1912. 452 pp. Ind.
A comparative account of the ideas and development of various socialist groups in the U.S. and Europe, written by a leading American socialist of the period before World War I. Part of the book is an attack on right-wing or reformist socialist leaders such as Victor Berger of Milwaukee. The volume shows a friendly attitude toward syndicalism. (The author was one of the large number of socialist leaders who left the party in order to support World War I.)

130   . . . . "The Larger Aspects of Socialism." New York: Macmillan, 1913. 406 pp. App. Ind.
An attempt, by a leading theorist of the pre-World War I socialist movement, to reformulate socialist philosophy in pragmatic rather than in the traditional materialistic terms.

131   . . ., and others. "The Socialism of To-Day: A Source Book." New York: Holt, 1916. 642 pp. App. Ind.
A collection of documents and statistics relating to the socialist movements in the various countries of the world. Four chapters are devoted to the Socialist Party of this country. The socialist position on a wide variety of questions is shown by means of reports and resolutions of socialist congresses, speeches by socialist members of parliaments, and articles in socialist publications.

132   WARE, Norman J. "The Labor Movement in the United States, 1860-1895: A Study in Democracy." New York and London: Appleton, 1929. 409 pp. App. Bibliog. Ind.
A study of the American labor movement over a 35-year period that covers the rise and decline of the Knights of Labor and the emergence of the AFL. The book deals with the Knights' formation and growth, philosophy and tactics, structure and leadership, internal problems, achievements and failures, and periodic conflicts with employers and with the weak but developing national trade unions. The eight-hour movement of 1886, culminating in the Haymarket bomb and the trial of the anarchists, is treated. The author views the Knights as an expression of the ideal of labor solidarity, and the AFL as a strategic retreat by the craft unions, fearful for their own safety in the light of the remarkable growth of the Order in the middle '80's.

133 WARE, Norman J. "Labor in Modern Industrial Society." Boston: Heath, 1935. 561 pp. Ind.
A sympathetic review of American labor history, with emphasis upon the social setting within which unionism originates and functions. Attention is paid to labor and farmer-labor political developments; to the Knights of Labor, the AFL, and the IWW; to socialist and anarchist influences within the labor movement; to leading strikes, such as the Pullman strike of 1894, and to other evidences of class conflict or class collaboration. The author believes that employers face a choice between union recognition and further government control.

134 WEBBER, Everett. "Escape to Utopia: The Communal Movement in America." New York: Hastings House, 1959. 444 pp. Bibliog. Ind.
A review of the communal societies established in the U.S. The societies whose stories are told include the Shakers, the Rappites, Francis Wright's colony at Nashoba, Robert Owen's New Harmony experiment, the Phalanx movement, Fruitlands, Cabet and his Icarians, James Strang's offshoot of Mormonism at Beaver Island, the Community of the True Inspiration at Amana, Thomas Lake Harris' Brotherhood of the New Life, and the Oneida Perfectionists led by John Humphrey Noyes.

135 WOOSTER, Ernest S. "Communities of the Past and Present." Newllano, La.: Llano Colonist, 1924. 155 pp.
Brief accounts of the leading communitarian experiments in the U.S., including the Harmonists or Rappites, the Separatists of Zoar, the Owenite communities, the Fourierist phalanxes, the Icarians, the Nevada Colony, the Shaker communities, Amana, the Perfectionists at Oneida, and Llano Co-operative Colony. The author concludes that the religious colonies were more successful than the secular ones because of strong leadership and because the community was but a means to a more important religious end; secular colonies, on the other hand, tended to fail because attention was focused on material success, with members jealous of their rights and privileges.

Y

136 YELLEN, Samuel. "American Labor Struggles." New York: Russell, 1936. 398 pp. Ind.
An account of ten of the most significant labor struggles in American history, including the railroad uprisings of 1877, the Haymarket tragedy, the Homestead lockout of 1892, the Pullman strike of 1894, the Lawrence textile strike of 1912 led by the IWW, and the steel strike of 1919. In each case the author has sought to tell the story of the strike, its causes, its sequence of events, and its consequences.

137 YOUNG, Arthur Nichols. "The Single Tax Movement in the United States." Princeton, N.J.: Princeton University Press, 1916. 340 pp. App. Bibliog. Ind.
A history of the single-tax movement, covering the background of Henry George's doctrines, the formulation of his ideas and their reception, his efforts in labor politics, and the attempts of his supporters in various parts of the country to enact his tax proposals. Although their legislative achievements in this country were few, his followers achieved greater success in western Canada, Australasia, and elsewhere. Attention is paid to criticism of the single-tax philosophy and proposals, and to the relations between single taxers and socialists.

Z

138 ZIMAND, Savel. "Modern Social Movements: Descriptive Summaries and Bibliographies." New York: Wilson, 1921. 260 pp.
Among the social movements treated in the book are trade unionism, the single tax, socialism, guild socialism, syndicalism, bolshevism, and anarchism. The book is primarily valuable for the extensive bibliographies on each of these movements, although there is also a brief description of each.

A

A1 AARON, Benjamin. Statutory Regulation of Internal Union Affairs: The Control of Communism, "Proceedings of New York University Fifth Annual Conference on Labor." Albany: Bender, 1952. Pp. 389-412.
A discussion of congressional efforts to control communism in unions through the Taft-Hartley Act's noncommunist affidavit. Reviewing experience in its administration, the author asserts that the affidavit has not accomplished its purpose. He doubts that communist-dominated unions threaten national security. We need inquiry and reflection, not new legislation.

A2 AARON, Daniel. "Writers on the Left: Episodes in American Literary Communism." New York: Harcourt, Brace and World, 1961. 460 pp. Notes. Ind.
An account of the influence of the communist movement upon the American literary world. Disillusioned with capitalism in the 1930's by depression and the rise of fascism, large number of writers accepted the political leadership of the CPUSA. The influence of the "Masses," the "Liberator," and the "New Masses" is appraised, as is that of the John Reed Clubs and the League of American Writers. With the signing of the Hitler-Stalin pact writers, as other intellectuals, turned from the communists in disillusionment. Attention is paid to the views of Max Eastman, Floyd Dell, V. F. Calverton, Joseph Freeman, Mike Gold, Malcolm Cowley, Granville Hicks, John Dos Passos, Edmund Wilson, and other leading figures of the literary left.

A3 ABBOTT, Roger S. The Federal Loyalty Program: Background and Problems, "American Political Science Review," 42 (June 1948), 486-99.
A discussion of the employee loyalty program in the federal service under the executive order of March 21, 1947. The author deals with the background of the program, its purpose, and its operation and procedures. The functioning of agency loyalty boards and of the central Loyalty Review Board is described.

A4 ABBOTT, Wilbur C. "The New Barbarians." Boston: Little, Brown, 1925. 25 pp. Ind.
A critical discussion of radical tendencies in the United States in the early and mid-'twenties. The author attacks Marxian socialists, and those who use socialism as a disguise for subversion. Arguing for the individualism on which U.S. society was based, he opposes centralized government, dependence, dictatorship, and reliance on the mass. He finds much of our trouble with the newer immigration, too large a percentage ignorant of our traditions, unskilled, and the cause of social problems.

A5 ABERN, Martin. Notes on Shop Nuclei, "Workers Monthly," 4 (Jan. 1925), 123-24.
Following directives of the Communist International, the Workers Party is to be reorganized with shop nuclei as the basic Party units, eventually replacing territorial branches. This is the best way to bolshevize or Leninize the Party. Distinctions between the shop nucleus, the shop committee, and the TUEL are clarified.

A6 . . . . Work of the Organization Conference of the Workers (Communist) Party, "Workers Monthly," 5 (April 1926), 277-81.
Description of a three-day national organizational conference held in Chicago in February. Major topics discussed were the Party's trade-union work and its progress in reorganization from language sections to street and shop nuclei. Other topics included a campaign for protection of the foreign-born and methods for developing a labor party.

A7 ABERNATHY, Glenn. "The Right of Assembly and Association." Columbia: University of South Carolina Press, 1961. 263 pp. Ref. Ind. of cases. Subject ind.
A review of American constitutional provisions, legislation, and court decisions dealing with the rights of assembly and association. Federal and state legislation and local ordinances dealing with communists, and cases arising under them, are treated on pp. 201-24. Among the issues discussed are the lawfulness of membership in the Communist Party, access of the CP to the electoral process, bars to government employment, access to NLRB services, and naturalization and deportation.

A8 ABRAHAM LINCOLN BATTALION. "The Story of the Abraham Lincoln Battalion: Written in the Trenches of Spain." New York: Friends of the Abraham Lincoln Brigade, n.d. [1937?]. 32 pp.
Series of accounts of the battle experiences of the Battalion, including excerpts from letters and diaries, and emphasizing antifascist unity. (Though many noncommunist Americans fought with the Battalion, it was always dominated by the Party.)

A9 ABRAHAM LINCOLN SCHOOL, Chicago. "Teach Yourself to Write English." Chicago: The School, n.d. [1942 or 1943]. 19 pp.
A reading primer for foreign-born workers issued by a Party school, utilizing material that supports the "antifascist war." Suggested subjects for talks include revolutionary faith, courage to build new worlds, and our democratic allies.

A10 ABT, John. "The People vs. McCarthyism." New York: Civil Rights Congress, 1953. 20 pp.
Address before the People's Conference to Fight the McCarran Law Prosecutions, October 24, 1953, in New York City, with an introduction by William L. Patterson, executive secretary, Civil Rights Congress. Abt analyzes the McCarran Act, calling it an enabling act for American fascism. He calls for unity of labor and liberals to prevent outlawry of the Party and to repeal the McCarran Act.

A11 ADAMIC, Louis. What the Proletariat Reads, "Saturday Review of Literature," 11 (Dec. 1, 1934), 1-2.
"Proletarian literature" is propaganda addressed to workers, emphasizing their plight under capitalism and offering salvation in revolution. But few American workers read serious works, nor do they like exaggerated descriptions of social evils. Working class characters are shown as

too virtuous, while middle-class and capitalistic characters are villains.

A12 ADAMIC, Louis, and ADDES, George F. "Foreign-born Americans and the War." New York: American Committee for Protection of Foreign Born, 1943. 22 pp.
Reprint of two addresses delivered at the Tenth Anniversary National Conference of the American Committee for Protection of Foreign Born, New York City, October 30-31, 1943. Adamic, head of the Committee of South-Slavic Americans, urges the government to make use of antifascist sentiment among immigrant groups in the U.S. Addes, secretary-treasurer of the UAW-CIO, calls for unity against tyranny and reaction.

A13 ADAMS, Grace. Comrades, Lay Off! "Harper's Magazine," 176 (Jan. 1938), 218-20.
An explanation of why the author would never join the Party, despite her liberal views and her dislike of war. She does not like to be told what things to do, nor the manner in which the communists tell her to do them. She objects to their fanaticism and to their resentment of the slightest criticism of the USSR.

A14 "ADVANCE," An Outrageous Performance—Which Every Intelligent Union Member Must Oppose, 9 (May 15, 1925), 7-8.
Condemnation of the picketing and rioting before the general offices of the Amalgamated Clothing Workers by the Workers Party and TUEL adherents. The action, ostensibly to reinstate workers to jobs, constituted a deliberate provocation of both the union officials and the police.

A15 . . ., Wings in Needledom, 12 (Jan. 28, 1927), 6-7.
Editorial comment in the organ of the Amalgamated Clothing Workers on the activities of the TUEL in the clothing unions of New York. Decrying the division into left and right wings, the editorial attacks the TUEL opposition for reckless tactics, dishonesty, and indecency. Methods used by the Amalgamated could bring constructive and stable order to the garment unions.

A16 . . ., The Furred Claws of Factionalism, 12 (June 10, 1927), 6-7.
An editorial in the organ of the Amalgamated Clothing Workers, deploring factionalism in the current New York fur strike, led by the communist faction of the furriers' union. Only the employers can gain from the strike; the left wing (and perhaps even the right) is criticized for preferring to ruin a union if it cannot control it.

A17 ALAN, Robert [pseud.]. Paul Robeson—The Lost Shepherd, "Crisis," 58 (Nov. 1951), 569-73.
Robeson, who overcame discrimination and won world acclaim for his artistry, now spouts communist propaganda and accepts Kremlin dictates without hesitation. A bewildered man, he is more to be pitied than damned. His assertion that American Negroes would not fight in any war with Russia was denounced by Negro leaders once his close associates.

A18 ALBERTSON, William. "The Trucks Act: Michigan's Blueprint for a Fascist State." New York: New Century, 1952. 24 pp.
An attack by the Party's state secretary in Michigan on the Trucks Act, requiring registration with the state police, under penalty of fine and imprisonment, of the Party and all members in the state. The Party is testing the Act before the Supreme Court. The author analyzes other Michigan legislative efforts, denounced as fascist, to control Party activities.

A19 ALEXANDER, Robert J. Splinter Groups in American Radical Politics, "Social Research," 20 (Autumn 1953), 282-310.
A history of splinter groups in the American radical movement from the close of the Civil War to the end of World War II. The growth of rival factions in the communist movement from 1919 to 1940 is traced (pp. 292-306). Reasons are given why Marxian socialism has never become a major force in the U.S.

A20 ALFRED, Helen (ed.). "Toward a Socialist America: A Symposium of Essays." New York: Peace Publications, 1958. 223 pp.
A collection of essays by contemporary writers, along with excerpts from earlier socialist authors, dealing with the need for socialism, the transition to a socially based economy, and an American people's party. Some of the authors represent a democratic socialist approach, whereas others have been associated at one time or another with the communist movement. Among the latter are John Howard Lawson, Herbert Aptheker, Victor Perlo, Scott Nearing, W. E. B. DuBois, and Philip S. Foner.

A21 ALINSKY, Saul. "John L. Lewis: An Unauthorized Biography." New York: Putnam, 1949. 387 pp. Bibliog. Ind.
A biography, favorable to Lewis, which discusses Lewis' use of communists to build the CIO and his fight against them at other times. The author de-emphasizes the close relationship between Lewis and the communists until the Nazi attack on the USSR in June 1941, and offers apologies for their entrance into and their influence in the CIO.

A22 ALLAN, Anne (comp. and ed.). "Sing America." New York: Workers Bookshop, n.d. [1944 or 1945]. 64 pp.
Lyrics, with some music, of workers' songs, patriotic songs, topical songs (in praise of Roosevelt, the war, patriotism), and simple group songs, reflecting the communist wartime position.

A23 ALLEN, Devere. The False Lure of Class War, "World Tomorrow," 16 (March 22, 1933), 276-79; (March 29), 302-3.
An examination and repudiation of the communist emphasis on violence as a technique of social change, written from the pacifist-socialist point of view. A seizure of power in the U.S. in this period would require class war, with wholesale violence and subsequent dictatorship. A parallel is drawn with the peaceful elimination of slavery in many countries.

A24 ALLEN, James S. "The American Negro." New York: International Publishers, 1932. 31 pp.
Advocacy and explanation of the right of self-determination for Negroes in the Black Belt, including the right of separation from the U.S. if desired. The author, a leading Party theoretician on Negro questions, describes the Negro class structure and social and economic conditions. He attacks the leadership of the AFL as anti-Negro, and charges that middle-class Negro leaders (as exemplified by the NAACP) betray the Negro masses.

A25 . . . . "Negro Liberation." New York: International pamphlets, 1932. 35 pp. Rev. ed., 1938. 46 pp.
Communist advocacy of the Negro "nation's" right to self-determination. Whereas the earlier edition uses class-conscious, belligerent language, the later version reflects the shift to the popular front. In 1938 the immediate struggle to defeat all reactionary forces is said to offer the best and most direct path to Negro liberation.

A26   ALLEN, James S. Awakening in the Cotton Belt,
       "New Masses," 8 (Aug. 1932), 11-12.
An account of poverty and exploitation of Negro sharecroppers in the cotton plantation country of the South.
However, a new spirit is spreading, with revolutionary
native white workers replacing Georgia "crackers" and
communists replacing Negro "Uncle Toms."

A27   . . . . "Smash the Scottsboro Lynch Verdict."
       New York: Workers Library, 1933. 16 pp.
A communist view of the Scottsboro case, defending the
accused and the role of the Party-organized International
Labor Defense. The case will be won, not in the courts
alone, but by an ever-growing mass movement. Victory
for the boys will be a blow for Negro liberation, as well
as liberation of the toiling masses from capitalism.

A28   . . . . The Scottsboro Struggle, "Communist," 12
       (May 1933), 437-48.
A discussion of the Scottsboro case in the light of its
sharpening of class and race antagonisms. Early in the
case the struggle was between the revolutionary forces
led by the CP and reformist forces led by the NAACP.
The CP, having won decisively over the NAACP, can now
broaden the struggle into one for the national liberation of
the Negro people.

A29   . . . . Lenin and the American Negro, "Com-
       munist," 13 (Jan. 1934), 53-61.
Whereas Marx and Engels viewed national-revolutionary
movements as forces for the overthrow of feudalism,
Lenin viewed them as forces for the overthrow of imperialism. The struggle for Negro self-determination in
the Black Belt is vital in the struggle against imperialist
aggression. Lenin viewed the struggle of American
Negroes as a revolutionary movement that must be
supported.

A30   . . . . The Black Belt: Area of Negro Majority,
       "Communist," 13 (June 1934), 581-99.
There exists in the South a continuous and well-defined
area, consisting of some 192 counties from southeastern
Virginia to Mississippi, where Negroes are the majority.
The area of the Black Belt has its roots in chattel
slavery. This is not, as some argue, a "mechanical"
application of the theory of national self-determination to
an inappropriate area.

A31   . . . . The Communist Way Out, "Crisis," 42
       (May 1935), 134-35 ff.
The communist program for Negroes, calling for the
right of self-determination for Negroes in the Black Belt
of the South. The workers and peasants there might wish
to remain in the U.S., should we have a Soviet government,
or secede, should the U.S. remain capitalist. In other
parts of the country the Party demands equal rights for
Negroes. (Part of a symposium on "Which Way Out for
the Negro?")

A32   . . . . "The Negro Question in the United States."
       New York: International Publishers, 1936. 224 pp.
       App. Maps. Ref. notes. Ind.
A communist history of the Negro question, emphasizing
the historical and economic forces behind the present
exploitation and repression of Negroes. The author traces
the economic survivals of slavery in sharecropping, and
describes the influence of industrialization upon institutions in the Black Belt. The communist proposal of self-
determination for Negroes in the Black Belt is presented.

A33   . . . . "Reconstruction: The Battle for Democracy
       (1865-1876). New York: International Publishers,
       1937. 256 pp. Ref. notes. App. Bibliog. Ind.

A communist history attempting to correct "distortions"
concerning the reconstruction period perpetuated in U.S.
histories. Condemning the conventional treatment of
Radical Republicans and the Negro people, the author
seeks to show the heroic proportions of both groups. He
points out the class forces at play during Reconstruction,
applauds the attempt to establish democracy in the South,
and attributes the triumph of the counterrevolution to the
regrouping of class forces in the nation. He concludes
that, with the help of the working class and other progressive elements, the Negro people can complete reconstruction, obtaining suffrage, civil rights, and land.
(Chap. 2 appeared under the title, "The Struggle for Land
during the Reconstruction Period," in "Science and
Society," Spring 1937.)

A34   . . . . "Thomas Paine: Selections from his Writ-
       ings." New York: International Publishers, 1937.
       96 pp.
Selections from "Common Sense," "The American Crisis," "Rights of Man," and "The Age of Reason,"
issued during the Party's popular-front period. The
author gathers Paine into the embrace of the Communist
Party, describing him as an active revolutionary and
militant democrat, opposed by the royalists of his day and
disliked by the "economic royalists" of the present.

A35   . . . . America and Neutrality, "National Issues:
       A Survey of Politics and Legislation," 1 (April
       1939), 13-16.
A communist call, prior to the Hitler-Stalin pact, for the
repeal of the Neutrality Law, to be followed by a complete
embargo against Germany, Italy, and Japan. We can
avoid involvement in a world-wide war only by standing
with the USSR and the other democracies against Hitler
and his allies.

A36   . . . . American Imperialism and the War, "Com-
       munist," 18 (Nov. 1939), 1046-53.
A discussion of the designs of American finance capital
to take advantage of world economic realignment due to
the war. In Latin America and the Far East, American
business sees opportunity to replace Germany, Britain,
and Japan. However, world imperialism now has a
strong opponent in world socialism, which will prevent
such exploitation.

A37   . . . . The Farmers and the Struggle against the
       War Program, "Communist," 19 (July 1940),
       628-48.
A report to the Farm Conference at the Party's national
convention, May 31, 1940, stressing the importance and
the means of winning farmers to the communist-led antiwar movement. War cannot reduce farm surpluses and
will not increase purchasing power. Communists must
develop the struggle for farmers' immediate demands,
connecting these with the fight against the war party.

A38   . . . . "The Crisis in India." New York: Workers
       Library, 1942. 31 pp.
A call to Americans to oppose British policy in India and
support Indian independence. The author criticizes
Ghandi's policies as appeasement, and supports Nehru.
The Indian Communist Party line, defended by Allen, is
to create an Indian military force on the basis of Moslem-
Hindu unity, and outside of, but not in open opposition to,
the British government.

A39   . . . . The Far Eastern Front in the War against
       the Axis, "Communist," 21 (March 1942), 143-62.
An analysis of Japanese action in the Pacific as a
tactic to divert U.S. efforts from Europe. Since this
would hurt the Soviet Union, the nations of the Pacific

Islands and Asia must be mobilized to fight that front while the United Nations strike their main blow at Germany.

A40   ALLEN, James S. The Pacific Front in the Global War, "Communist," 21 (Dec. 1942), 1012-20.
A criticism of the "America-first" approach to the Pacific front, with an assertion that Henry R. Luce and others have imperialistic objectives in the Far East. We are closer to victory because we have strengthened the whole Anglo-Soviet-American coalition and taken the offensive in the war.

A41   . . . . Bretton Woods and World Security, "Communist," 23 (Dec. 1944), 1078-86.
The Bretton Woods proposals for an International Monetary Fund and an International Bank will bring international economic cooperation. The U.S. should favor the proposals, which will help speed the European recovery needed to provide foreign markets for American goods.

A42   . . . . "World Cooperation and Postwar Prosperity." New York: New Century, 1945. 63 pp.
Advocating continued economic cooperation among the allies of World War II, the author looks forward to a postwar capitalist society in which barriers to democratic growth and expansion of the economy are reduced as a result of a coalition including labor, progressive middle classes, and antifascist industrialists. (The pamphlet follows the wartime line of the Party before publication of the Duclos letter.)

A43   . . . . World Assembly at San Francisco, "Political Affairs," 24 (April 1945), 291-301.
The San Francisco Conference is the culmination of the many events that have built the United Nations coalition. It will set up a permanent UN, consisting of a General Assembly and a Security Council. U.S. adherence to the world security organization must be assured.

A44   . . . . "The Cartel System." New York: International Publishers, 1946. 32 pp. Ref. notes.
A communist analysis of differences among cartels, trusts, and combines, pointing out that conflicts of interest are continued in cartels, though not in other forms of monopoly. Both domestic and international cartels are discussed. Though the degree of monopoly is limited, cartels represent the general trend toward combination.

A45   . . . . "Who Owns America?" New York: New Century, 1946. 47 pp.
A description of the great corporations of America, said to be controlled by an oligarchy of finance-capitalists who seek to take over the raw materials, markets, and industries of all other countries. After blackmailing the country into doing its bidding during the war, the oligarchy has been milking the "boom" period in anticipation of a crash, one that will precipitate a world crash as well. The USSR has shown what socialist planning can do to avoid such a crash.

A46   . . . . "World Monopoly and Peace." New York: International Publishers, 1946. 288 pp. Ref. notes. Ind.
An extensive treatment of post-World War II economic problems by a communist author, who analyzes postwar monopoly capitalism and relations among the major capitalist countries as well as between them and the USSR. The author deals with monopoly in the U.S. and Britain, with Anglo-American rivalry, and with monopoly in defeated Germany and in Japan. He argues that American capitalism plans world hegemony, based on the expansion of the monopoly giants, and supported by a reactionary turn in foreign policy. He also deals with the economy and foreign policy of the USSR.

A47   . . . . Enlightened American Imperialism in the Philippines, "Political Affairs," 25 (June 1946), 526-40.
Philippine independence, due July 4, will witness creation of a puppet republic that will repress the popular democratic movement and safeguard the American imperialist stake in the Islands. President Manuel A. Roxas is the symbol of collaboration with the Japanese. American capitalists have effective control over the Philippine economy.

A48   . . . . The Policy of Anti-Soviet Encirclement, "Political Affairs," 25 (Oct. 1946), 879-92.
Hostile encirclement of the Soviet Union is the foundation of the Administration's bipartisan foreign policy. The Administration seeks to weaken and isolate the Soviet Union, expand American imperialist interests throughout the world, restore Germany and Japan as anti-Soviet outposts, and support reactionary and fascist forces everywhere.

A49   . . . . The Negro Question (A Discussion Article), "Political Affairs," 25 (Nov. 1946), 1046-56; (Dec.), 1132-50.
A critique of Doxey Wilkerson's article, "The Negro and the American Nation," in "Political Affairs," July 1946, rejecting Wilkerson's view of the Negro people as a national minority rather than as a separate nation. Population and economic trends in the Black Belt of the South are reviewed to show that Wilkerson's views do not accord with the facts.

A50   . . . . The Marshall Plan, "Political Affairs," 26 (July 1947), 563-70.
The Marshall Plan is an offer to Western Europe, not to Europe as a whole; it threatens and bullies the Soviet Union, the countries of Eastern Europe, and the Communist Parties and antifascist movements of Western Europe. It is a bold act of dollar piracy attempting again to divide Europe and the world into hostile blocs, endangering American economic well-being and security as well.

A51   . . . . "Marshall Plan—Recovery or War?" New York: New Century, 1948. 64 pp.
A communist assertion that the Marshall Plan, far from being a scheme for world recovery, is designed for economic and political aggression. It operates as reactionary pressure on Europe, and merges with the Truman Doctrine and U.S. China policy into a single interventionist and expansionist drive that must be backed with force.

A52   . . . . The New War Economy, "Political Affairs," 27 (Dec. 1948), 1055-74.
The U.S. garrison state is assuming concrete form, with few traces of freedom and with 34 per cent of the federal budget allocated for military spending. The military, which is playing an increasing role in the economic, political, and social life of the country, is merging with Big Business as we move toward a cartel economy. War production and profits will be centralized as never before, while the people's living standards will be drastically reduced.

A53   . . . . "Atomic Energy and Society." New York: International Publishers, 1949. 95 pp. Ref. notes.
A communist analysis of the dangers and potentials of "atomics," the new technology for the production and

utilization of nuclear fuel. The U.S., by concentration on armaments, restrictions on exchange of technical information, and military censorship, is said to have fallen far behind the USSR in the development of constructive uses of the new power source. Only by solving the deep conflicts in our own society, by turning to socialism, can we lay the foundation for the positive outcome of atomics.

A54   ALLEN, James S., and WILKERSON, Doxey A. (eds.). Introductory essay by William Z. Foster. "The Economic Crisis and the Cold War." New York: New Century, 1949. 113 pp.
Report of a conference of Communist Party economic experts, held in May, 1949. An introductory essay by Foster gives the conclusions that the conference should (and did) reach: that the crisis of American capitalism was deepening, that Keynesian "managed economy" measures could not solve the problem, that American foreign policy as represented by the Marshall Plan would only intensify the crisis. The mass of people, in turn, would organize to defend themselves against unemployment, destruction of living standards, and the drive toward war.

A55   ALLEN, James S. "Atomic Imperialism: The State, Monopoly, and the Bomb." New York: International Publishers, 1952. 288 pp.
An exposé by a communist spokesman of the atomic munitions industry, which represents a merger of state and monopoly politics. The author describes the scope and content of this new industry, the eminence of the munitions giants of the past, the role of the military, and U.S. atomic diplomacy as represented by the Baruch atomic energy control plan. He supports Soviet Union objectives, urging the people to repudiate U.S. atomic imperialism and embrace the growing antiwar and neutrality movement.

A56   .... Democratic Revival and the Marxists, "Masses & Mainstream," 8 (Oct. 1955), 1–11.
A call by a prominent communist theoretician for a rethinking of the role of Marxists and progressives in the reconstitution of the democratic camp. Though many groups from the center to the left have an anticommunist bias, a reassessment by the Marxists can help overcome this. Marxists should play their part in coalition movements as a clearly defined trend.

A57   .... Problems of Foreign Policy, "Political Affairs," 36 (Dec. 1957), 19–31.
Based on a report given for the Party's foreign affairs committee to the National Executive Committee, October 24, 1957, and approved unanimously. It views American foreign policy as in a crisis, the result of the Soviet successes in outer space and the repudiation of the Eisenhower Doctrine by the Arab countries of the Middle East.

A58   .... The American Road to Socialism, "Political Affairs," 37 (Sept. 1958), 1–7; Program Questions, Pp. 8–27.
A member of the editorial subcommittee of the Draft Program Committee opens public discussion on the Party's program. Questions deal with the socialist goal, the fight for peace, living standards, cultural advance, democracy, the labor movement, Negro freedom, farmers, the urban middle strata, monopoly, political action, the transition to socialism, and the role of the Party.

A59   ALLEN, Jo. "The Big Squeeze: Crisis on the Campus." New York: American Youth for Democracy, 1946. 23 pp.
A discussion of the crisis in education, which is traced to government expenditures for battleships rather than scholarships, to capitalist emphasis on department stores

instead of dormitories. The AYD calls for more federal spending for education, an end to discrimination, and academic freedom for faculty and students. (AYD, a Party-dominated youth organization, functioned between 1943 and 1949.)

A60   ALLEN, Mary L. "Education or Indoctrination." Caldwell, Idaho: Caxton Publishers, 1955. 211 pp.
An account of the controversy in the Pasadena public school system in which Superintendent Willard E. Goslin was removed, following an investigation into subversive influences by California's Dilworth Committee in 1950. Goslin was an exponent of progressive education, of which the author is highly critical. She argues that the philosophy of John Dewey has been reinterpreted by radical thinkers and procommunist sympathizers, who use indoctrination in the schools to achieve extreme changes in the social pattern of the community.

A61   ALLEN, Raymond B. "Communism and Education: An Open Letter to Friends of the University of Washington." Seattle: University of Washington Press, 1948. 11 pp.
The president of the University of Washington asserts that academic freedom has not been abridged by the State's Joint Legislative Fact-finding Committee on Un-American Activities. Pending further legislative action or judicial decision as to the loyalty to the U.S. of members of the Communist Party, the University of Washington will judge communist faculty members according to the University's administrative code.

A62   .... Communists Should Not Teach in American Colleges, "Educational Forum," 13 (May 1949), 433–40.
An assertion by the president of the University of Washington that communists should not be allowed to teach because they are not free men, but slaves to dogma and to a clandestine organization masquerading as a political party. Academic freedom at the University has been strengthened, not violated, by the dismissal of communists. (For a contrary view see George E. Axtelle, "Should Communists Teach in American Universities?" in the same issue.)

A63   ALLEN, William. "Your House on Alger Street— the Gordy Case." Detroit: Michigan Worker, n.d. [1952?]. 24 pp.
The case of a Detroit Negro whose home was invaded and who, in self-defense and to defend his son, killed one policeman and wounded another. The pamphlet sees this attack on Gordy as part of anti-Negro police brutality in Detroit, and calls for the release of Gordy and the end of police brutality.

A64   ALMAZOV, S. "Ten Years of Biro-Bidjan, 1928–1938." New York: ICOR, 1938. 32 pp.
A glowing account of the achievements of the Jews in Biro-Bidjan, a Jewish autonomous territory in the USSR. The experiment is said to be progressing despite the efforts of anti-Soviet Jews to defame it. (ICOR is the American organization to create friends for Biro-Bidjan, to defend the Soviet Union, and to fight against fascism and anti-semitism.)

A65   ALMOND, Gabriel A. "The Appeals of Communism." Princeton, N.J.: Princeton, 1954. 415 pp. App. Ind.
A study of 221 ex-communists, of whom 64 are Americans (the others being British, French, or Italian), to discover how they came to communism, what attracted and what repelled them, and why and how they finally broke with the movement. Susceptibility to communism is found to

be basically either situational (self-oriented, group-oriented, or ideological) or neurotic (as hostility, isolation, or self-rejection). The break, in turn, may be due to career-related dissatisfaction, pressures on personality and personal relations, endangered group loyalties, or conflict of moral standards. Differences among the four countries, and among the respondents according to social class, period of joining, and Party rank achieved, are examined.

A66 ALSOP, Joseph. The Strange Case of Louis Budenz, "Atlantic Monthly," 189 (April 1952), 29-33.
A critical examination of Budenz's conflicting charges and testimony with regard to the membership of Owen Lattimore and John Carter Vincent in the Communist Party. Criticizing Budenz for hearsay accusations of treason, Alsop concludes, on the basis of his own knowledge, that we lost China through grossly bad judgment, not treason.

A67 . . ., and ALSOP, Stewart. Will the CIO Shake the Communists Loose? "Saturday Evening Post," 219 (Feb. 22, 1947), 15-16 ff; (March 1), 26-27 ff.
A report on communist infiltration and tactics in CIO unions, with a strong plea to Philip Murray to take a decisive stand to defeat them. Unions having at least 19 per cent of the CIO's total membership are now communist-dominated. The case of the United Electrical Workers is cited as an example of communist tactics.

A68 . . ., and ALSOP, Stewart. "We Accuse: The Story of the Miscarriage of American Justice in the Case of J. Robert Oppenheimer." New York: Simon & Schuster, 1954. 88 pp.
A defense of Oppenheimer and an indictment of the government's security system. The authors assert that Oppenheimer became an active fellow-traveler in the 30's out of naïveté and misplaced emotionalism, that he saw the folly of his earlier views during and after the war and has since been strongly anti-Soviet, and that many of his critics were out to "get" him for reasons unrelated to his political reliability. (Printed first as an article in "Harper's," October 1954; a rebuttal to this thesis appears in "U.S. News & World Report," December 24, 1954.)

A69 ALSOP, Stewart. Wanted: A Faith to Fight For, "Atlantic Monthly," 167 (May 1941), 594-97.
Marxism, though not necessarily the Communist Party, appealed to youth during the depression because it offered an alternative to bread lines in the cities while wheat rotted on farms, and because in foreign affairs the USSR, alone of the great powers, opposed aggression and injustice. That dream faded with the Russo-German alliance and other USSR misdeeds. With war against fascism impending, American Youth now needs a faith to fight for.

A70 ALSTON, Christopher C. "Henry Ford and the Negro People." National Negro Congress and Michigan Negro Congress, n.d. [1940?]. 22 pp.
Issued by a Party front organization, the pamphlet argues that the Ford Motor Company hires Negroes on a Jim Crow basis and assigns them to the hardest jobs. Attacking Ford's Dearborn "Independent" for its reactionary views and the company for its treatment of Negroes, the pamphlet urges Negro Ford employees to support the UAW-CIO.

A71 AMERICAN ARTISTS' CONGRESS AGAINST WAR AND FASCISM. "Papers and Proceedings of the First Congress." The Congress, 1936. 104 pp.
The record of the first Artists' Congress, held in New York City, February 14-16, 1936. This was a communist-front group of the popular front period, whose avowed purpose was to achieve unity of action among artists of recognized standing, and to fight war, fascism, and reaction. Included are addresses and papers on the anti-fascist theme, on the social responsibility of the artist, and on economic problems of American artists.

A72 AMERICAN ASSOCIATION FOR THE ADVANCE-MENT OF SCIENCE, Board of Directors. Strengthening the Basis of National Security, "Science." 120 (Dec. 10, 1954), 957-59.
Criticism of the internal security program for too much emphasis on screening in order to reduce danger of leaks to a potential enemy. This risks interference with scientific progress and the technological superiority necessary for victory. We should seek to maximize our gains, not minimize our losses.

A73 AMERICAN ASSOCIATION OF UNIVERSITY PRO-FESSORS, Committee Y. "Depression, Recovery and Higher Education." New York: McGraw-Hill, 1937. 543 pp. Ind.
Chapter 14 (pp. 307-23) surveys student political activity during the depression. Student organizations focusing on economic, social, and political questions have increased their activity. On the left, the American Student Union, the Student League for Industrial Democracy, and the National Student League have attracted most attention. There are also middle and right-wing student groups. General economic conditions, not college teaching, are held responsible for whatever movement to the left has occurred.

A74 . . . . Freedom at Harvard, "AAUP Bulletin," 35 (Summer 1949), 313-34. (Reprinted from "Harvard Alumni Bulletin," June 25, 1949.)
Exchange of letters between Frank B. Ober and Harvard University officials concerning extracurricular activities of professors. Asserting that two faculty members gave aid to communism, Ober refused to subscribe to the Harvard Law School Fund. In reply, Grenville Clark, fellow of Harvard College, explained and defended Harvard's refusal to control professors' activities as citizens.

A75 . . . . Academic Freedom and Tenure in the Quest for National Security: Report of a Special Committee of the AAUP, "AAUP Bulletin," 42 (Spring 1956), 49-107.
A restatement of the AAUP position on communism and academic freedom, arguing that Party membership is not prima-facie evidence of unfitness to teach. The report discusses recent college actions against communism, the effect of refusals to testify, the record on academic freedom and tenure, and the University of California oath controversy.

A76 . . . . The University of Kansas City, "AAUP Bulletin," 43 (Spring 1957), 177-95.
Report on an investigation by an AAUP committee of the dismissal of Professor Horace B. Davis by the University of Kansas City following his refusal to answer questions as to Communist Party membership and activities. The committee found both sides at fault—the University for a dismissal without demonstrated adequate reason, and Davis for his refusal to make disclosures.

A77 AMERICAN BAR ASSOCIATION, House of Delegates. Communists in U.S.: Registration Urged by A.B.A. House of Delegates, "American Bar Association Journal," 34 (April 1948), 281-82.
The text of a resolution adopted by the House of Delegates of the American Bar Association on February 24, 1948, favoring compulsory registration of communists and communist organizations, and recommending publicity, pros-

ecution of subversive acts, and education, as safeguards against communism.

A78   AMERICAN BAR ASSOCIATION, Special Committee on Communist Tactics, Strategy and Objectives. "Brief on Communism: Marxism-Leninism—Its Aims, Purposes, Objectives and Practices, with Reports and Recommendations." New York: The Association, 1951. 60 pp.

A brief supporting the Bar Association's resolution to expel and recommend disbarment of all lawyers who belong to the Party or who advocate Marxism-Leninism. Excerpts from communist classics show the Party's conspiratorial aims and the loss of liberty and property under communism. Problems involved in disbarring communists and in determining Party membership are discussed.

A79   . . . , Special Committee on Communist Tactics, Strategy and Objectives. "Report of the Special Committee to Study Communist Tactics, Strategy and Objectives; Recommendations Adopted by the House of Delegates of the American Bar Association." Chicago: The Association, 1951. 16 pp.

The recommendations call for the expulsion from the Association and disbarment of anyone who is a member of the CP or who advocates Marxism-Leninism. The report deals with communist tactics and strategy, objectives of the Party, Marxism-Leninism, and the nature of the Communist Party of the U.S.

A80   . . . . "Brief on Communism." Notre Dame, Indiana: Ave Maria Press, 1952. 64 pp.

A reprint of the "Brief on Communism" prepared by the American Bar Association's Special Committee on Communist Tactics and Objectives. Also included are two statements by J. Edgar Hoover before committees of Congress on the menace of communism, and a bibliography on world communism prepared by the American Legion's National Americanism Commission.

A81   . . . , Special Committee on Communist Tactics, Strategy and Objectives. "Resolutions and Report." Chicago: The Association, 1959. 34 pp. Notes. App.

A review of court decisions relating to communism, with recommendations for legislation for the dismissal of security risks from Federal service, and the denial of passports to persons engaged in subversive activities or activities furthering international communism. Current fallacies about communism are discussed.

A82   . . . , Special Committee on Education in the Contrast Between Liberty Under Law and Communism. "Instruction on Communism and Its Contrast with Liberty Under Law." Chicago: The Association, 1962. 24 pp. App. Bibliog.

The Bar Association's view of the need for instruction in schools and colleges on the subject of communism, especially on its contrast with liberty under law. The present treatment of communism in the high school curriculum is outlined, and ways suggested for the legal profession to assist educational authorities to develop programs of instruction on the subject.

A83   "AMERICAN BAR ASSOCIATION JOURNAL," Communism and Communists; Association Votes Support of Mundt-Nixon Bill, 34 (Oct. 1948), 899-901 ff.

A report on the American Bar Association meeting in Seattle, September 6-9, 1948, which resolved unanimously that any lawyer supporting the world communist movement could not become or remain an ABA member. Any ABA member refusing to answer questions as to whether he is a communist should be expelled. The Mundt-Nixon bill was strongly endorsed.

A84   . . . , Proposed Anti-Communist Oath: Opposition Expressed to Association's Policy, 37 (Feb. 1951), 123-26.

Communications from members of the New York bar, the Committee on Law Reform of the New York City Bar Association, and the Executive Committee of the Massachusetts Bar Association, opposing the endorsement by the ABA annual meeting of the anticommunist oath for lawyers. The oath is opposed as repetitious of the professional oath, unfounded, and of questionable constitutionality.

A85   AMERICAN BUSINESS CONSULTANTS. "Red Channels: The Report of Communist Influence in Radio and Television." New York: Counterattack, 1950. 213 pp.

A listing, by a right-wing group, of about 150 entertainers, writers, singers, and critics, connected with radio or television, who have been affiliated with front groups or procommunist organizations. Ostensibly designed to discourage actors and artists from supporting communist causes in the future, the listing lends itself to a counterattack, presumably economic in nature, urged by the authors. The book contains a list of procommunist organizations, with citations from the public record to support such labeling.

A86   AMERICAN CIVIL LIBERTIES UNION. "Annual Reports."

These reports contain material on the rights of communists, as these are affected by federal, state or local action. Legislative enactments, judicial decisions, and administration regulations are included. Freedom of expression and association, due process under law, and equality before the law are among the areas of concern.

A87   . . . . "The Michigan Communist Trials." New York: ACLU, 1922. 4 pp.

A protest against the arrest and trial of communist leaders, seized at the national convention at Bridgeman, Mich., and charged with violating the Michigan criminal syndicalism law. Asserting that freedom of speech and assembly was violated, ACLU appeals for funds for the defense.

A88   . . . . "The Nation-Wide Spy System Centering in the Department of Justice." New York: ACLU, 1924. 15 pp.

An exposé of the growth of a government secret police system, engaged in espionage, intimidation, propaganda, and provocative acts. Anti-Red activities of the Bureau of Investigation are reviewed.

A89   . . ., Executive Committee. "Free Speech and the Workers Party." New York: ACLU, 1925. 4 pp.

Denunciation of the actions of the Workers (Communist) Party for denying free speech to their opponents, while demanding it for themselves. Despite their attitude, ACLU will continue to defend the right of free speech for communists.

A90   . . . . "The California Red Flag Case." New York: ACLU, 1930. 8 pp.

The facts in the case of five young women who were convicted in California in 1929 for displaying a red flag at a children's camp in violation of an anti-red-flag law, and who were sentenced to prison terms of six months to five years.

A91   AMERICAN CIVIL LIBERTIES UNION. "Police Lawlessness Against Communists in New York." New York: ACLU, 1930. 12 pp.

A review of the unemployment demonstration organized by the communists on March 6, 1930, of the violent police attacks on the demonstrators, and of the criminal prosecutions that followed. The ACLU recommends a complete change in police policy and tactics to avoid future violence.

A92   .... "Still the Fish Committee Nonsense: The Answer of the Press to the Fish Committee Proposals to Outlaw Free Speech for Communists." New York: ACLU, 1932. 8 pp.

A pamphlet reprinting sample editorials from leading papers, all condemning the Fish Committee's recommendations for outlawing the Communist Party. The ACLU urges readers to write to their representatives to oppose such bills.

A93   .... "The Attempted Deportation of John Strachey: Abstract of the Proceedings Before the District Director of Immigration at Chicago." New York: ACLU, 1935. 40 pp.

Abstract of the proceedings before the District Director of Immigration at Chicago in the case of John Strachey, then a communist, who had come from Britain to lecture in the U.S. The Bureau of Immigration argued that a communist necessarily advocated overthrow of government by force, a doctrine prohibited to an alien by law. The case was dropped when Strachey voluntarily returned to England.

A94   .... "Crisis in the Civil Liberties Union." New York: ACLU, 1940. 46 pp. App.

An unofficial minority report protesting the ACLU's 1940 resolution barring advocates of totalitarian governments from office and removing Elizabeth Gurley Flynn from the board of directors. The report charges that the resolution departs from traditional ACLU policy and seriously compromises its work.

A95   .... "A Statement to Members and Friends of the American Civil Liberties Union: Concerning the Resolution Fixing Qualifications for Membership on our Guiding Committees and Staff." New York: ACLU, 1940. 15 pp.

Explanation of the action of the Board of Directors of ACLU on participation of communists in the guidance of ACLU policy. The resolution asserts that it is inappropriate for any person to serve on the organization's governing committees or staff who, by political membership or public declaration, supports totalitarian dictatorship in any country. The events and issues that led to the resolution are reviewed. (See ACLU, "A Crises in the ACLU" for the opposing position.)

A96   .... "It's Not Only Communists' Rights! The ACLU's Stand on Outlawing the Communist Party, Loyalty Tests, House Un-American Activities Committee, Communist Students in the Colleges, Alien Communists, Anti-Communist Oaths by Union Officials." New York: ACLU, 1948. 8 pp.

A compendium of ACLU's stands on these questions, opposing all efforts to penalize opinion or association rather than action. ACLU, therefore, opposes laws to outlaw the Communist Party, loyalty or security checks for government employees, and the noncommunist affidavit provision of the Taft-Hartley Act.

A97   .... "Violence in Peekskill: A Report of the Violations of Civil Liberties at Two Paul Robeson Concerts near Peekskill, N.Y., August 27 and September 4, 1949." New York: ACLU, 1949. 51 pp.

Analysis of the events leading up to and following the riots of August 27 and September 4. Starting as an anti-communist demonstration sparked by scheduled Robeson concerts, the disorders culminated in a violent anti-Negro and anti-Jewish riot. Finding no evidence of communist provocation, the report placed blame upon the local press for inflaming veterans and other residents, and also upon the town and county police for tacitly consenting to the violence.

A98   .... "The Smith Act and the Supreme Court." New York: ACLU, 1952. 39 pp. App.

Opposition to the Smith Act of 1940, making unlawful a conspiracy to advocate the violent overthrow of the government, as an infringement on freedom of speech and as unwise. The decision of the Supreme Court upholding the constitutionality of the Smith Act threatens our fundamental liberties. Portions of the majority, concurring, and dissenting decisions appear in the appendix.

A99   .... "The States and Subversion." New York: ACLU, 1953. 11 pp. Bibliog.

A review of federal and state measures to curb subversion. ACLU concludes that these laws intimidate dissent, instill fear of false accusations as communists or fellow-travelers, and create pressures to conform to majority views.

A100   AMERICAN COMMITTEE FOR DEMOCRACY AND INTELLECTUAL FREEDOM. "The Activities of the Dies Committee: An Analysis." New York: The Committee, 1940. 14 pp.

A front organization urges Congress to cut off all Dies Committee funds because of its witch hunts, particularly in leading universities. The Dies Committee is charged with threatening intellectual freedom, freedom of association and debate, and freedom to read what one likes. Excerpts from Dies Committee hearings document the charges.

A101   AMERICAN COMMITTEE FOR PROTECTION OF FOREIGN BORN. "The Schneiderman Case: United States Supreme Court Opinion." Introduction by Carol King. New York: The Committee, 1943. 46 pp.

A reprint of the majority opinion of the U.S. Supreme Court in the case of William Schneiderman, Party leader whose naturalized citizenship had been revoked. The opinion held that Party membership did not necessarily commit a man to overthrow of the government by violence. Besides the majority opinion, the pamphlet contains concurring opinions and favorable newspaper comments. (See FFR, "Digest of Public Record of Communism in the U.S.," pp. 171 ff.)

A102   .... "The Supreme Court on the Bridges Case." Introduction by Carol King. New York: The Committee, 1945. 15 pp.

A reprint of the Supreme Court ruling which set aside the deportation proceedings against Harry Bridges on the grounds that the meaning given "affiliation" improperly made cooperation with proscribed groups grounds for deportation, and the procedure used in reaching the finding of Party membership denied due process. Justice Murphy, in a concurring opinion reprinted in the pamphlet, weighed the wider constitutional question, concluding that the Bill of Rights protected aliens as well as citizens.

A103   .... "The Walter-McCarran Law." New York: The Committee, n.d. [1953]. 35 pp.

Reprints of 111 excerpts from statements on the Walter-McCarran Law, made at public hearings held by the President's Commission on Immigration and Naturalization in 11 cities during October 1952. All the excerpts oppose the law.

A104 AMERICAN COMMITTEE FOR STRUGGLE AGAINST WAR. "The World Congress Against War." New York: The Committee, n.d. [1932]. 31 pp.
A report on the communist-sponsored World Congress Against War, held in Amsterdam, August 27-29, 1932. The U.S. delegation was dominated by members of communist front groups, notably John Reed Clubs and TUUL unions. (The American Committee for Struggle Against War, formed following the World Congress, was succeeded a year later by the American League Against War and Fascism, the Party's most successful front.)

A105 AMERICAN COMMITTEE FOR THE DEFENSE OF LEON TROTSKY. "World Voices on the Moscow Trials." New York: Pioneer Publishers, 1937. 64 pp.
A compilation from the labor and liberal press of the world dealing with the Moscow purges. Editorials reprinted from the "Manchester Guardian," the "New Statesman and Nation," the "New Republic," and like publications are concerned more with justice than with Trotsky's position.

A106 AMERICAN COUNCIL FOR A DEMOCRATIC GREECE. "American Intervention in Greece." The Council, n.d. [1948]. 22 pp.
An attack by a Party-front organization on the Greek Royalist government for its military offensive against the "Democratic Government of Free Greece," on British intervention from 1944 in Greek affairs, and on U.S. intervention in 1947 under the Truman Doctrine. The pamphlet denounces American economic royalists and the war clique.

A107 AMERICAN FEDERATION OF LABOR, METAL TRADES DEPARTMENT. Communism and the American Labor Movement, "Bulletin," 20 (Nov. 1938), 3 ff.
A report on communists in the American labor movement, asserting that their opportunity to secure a directive part came with the formation of the CIO. The control of CIO members over their unions is now menaced by the communists. Charges of Red-baiting should be ignored by opponents of communism.

A108 A.F. of L. Trade Union Committee for Unemployment Insurance and Relief. "Behind the Scenes of the Fifty-third Annual Convention of the A.F. of L." New York: The Committee, 1934. 48 pp.
A denunciation of the 1933 AFL convention, which praised the NRA, honored government officials, and ejected a delegation sent by the Second A.F. of L. Rank and File Conference. Resolutions introduced by delegate R. Suny opposing service of AFL officials on NRA boards and calling for the elimination of labor racketeering are reproduced, with discussion on them. AFL leaders are accused of class-collaboration policies and growing fascist activities.

A109 . . . . "Labor Fights for Social Security: Why the A.F. of L. Rank and File Supports the Workers Bill (H.R. 2827)." New York: The Committee, 1935. 39 pp.
Reproduction of statements before the subcommittee of the House Committee on Labor by Louis Weinstock and others from various AFL locals endorsing the communist-sponsored workers' bill for unemployment and old age and social insurance, and condemning the Administration-

sponsored Wagner-Lewis bill. The workers' bill is reprinted, with a list of locals endorsing it.

A110 AMERICAN FEDERATION OF TEACHERS. Report of the Council on the Investigation of Local 5, "American Teacher," 25 (Jan. 1941), 4-5.
A report in the form of a resolution by the Council of the American Federation of Teachers, recommending the expulsion of a big New York local found to be dominated by communists.

A111 . . ., Commission on Educational Reconstruction. Teachers and Communism: Resolution Adopted at the Chicago Meeting, Commission on Educational Reconstruction, Sept. 25-26, 1948, "American Teacher," 33 (Dec. 1948), 4.
Membership in the Communist Party is held not compatible with service in educational institutions in the U.S. The government is declared to have a right and obligation to assure itself of the loyalty of those in public service, including education. However, governmental investigations should use procedures which safeguard the rights of individuals.

A112 "AMERICAN FEDERATIONIST," A Message from Chicago, 30 (Oct. 1923), 849-51.
An open letter to AFL affiliates from President John Fitzpatrick and Secretary Edward N. Nockels of the Chicago Federation of Labor, asserting that the Chicago Federation does not disagree with the rest of the AFL on the subject of amalgamation, and that it has no connection with the Trade Union Educational League.

A113 AMERICAN INSTITUTE OF PACIFIC RELATIONS. "Commentary on the McCarran Report on the I.P.R." New York: The Institute, 1953. 94 pp. App. Mimeo.
A defense of the Institute from the charge by the McCarran Subcommittee on Internal Security that communists in the IPR were responsible for the communist victory in China. Denying that communists ever exerted any significant influence on IPR programs or policies, the organization attacks the Subcommittee for presumption of guilt, bias, sensational publicity, illegal seizure of files, reliance on untrustworthy witnesses, distortion of evidence, and disregard of favorable testimony.

A114 AMERICAN JEWISH COMMITTEE. "Now They Admit It: Communist Confession of Crimes Against Jews." New York: The Committee, 1956. 14 pp.
An indictment of the current Soviet anti-Semitic program which previously had been denied by all communist organs concerned with Jewish life. The pamphlet compares the revealed facts and present admissions with past denials to illustrate the cynicism with which communists manipulate truth.

A115 "AMERICAN JEWISH COMMITTEE REPORTER," Communism: Threat to Voluntary Groups, 2 (Sept.-Oct. 1954), 4-5 ff.
An analysis of the united front tactic of the communists, so successful in the 1930's and early 1940's, and revived in the fall of 1952 following increasing isolation during the "cold war" period. Centering their unity line around anti-McCarthyism, the Party has sought to infiltrate non-communist groups.

A116 AMERICAN JEWISH CONGRESS, Commission on Law and Social Action. "The Civil Rights and Civil Liberties Decisions of the United States Supreme Court for the 1957-1958 Term: A Summary and Analysis." New York: The Congress, 1958. 73 pp. Mimeo.

An analysis of cases decided in this session on loyalty oaths, passports, refusals to testify, armed forces, legislative investigations, the Smith Act, deportation, denaturalization, expatriations, and privilege against self-incrimination. Some of the cases are concerned with government procedures for dealing with communists, and others with individuals who are charged with subversive activity or who are testing validity of loyalty oaths, etc.

A117 AMERICAN LEAGUE AGAINST WAR AND FASCISM. "Manifesto and Program: Adopted at the U.S. Congress Against War, New York City, September 29-October 1, 1933." New York: The League, 1933. 4 pp.
German fascism, Japanese militarism, and the struggles in Latin America between British and American imperialism are examples of the dangers of imperialist war. This Congress, which launched the American League Against War and Fascism, pledges a drive to stop munitions expenditures, end militarization, and support the peace policies of the Soviet Union. (Also published in "Communist," Nov. 1933.)

A118 . . ., Youth Section. "Youth Manifesto Against War and Fascism." New York: The League, 1933. 8 pp.
Manifesto adopted at the Youth Conference held at the time of the United States Congress Against War, September 29-October 1, 1933. Participants resolved to fight efforts to militarize youth, to aid the struggle of youth in colonial countries against imperialist domination, to support the peace policies of the Soviet Union, and to organize Youth Committees Against War in key organizations.

A119 . . . . "Youth Against War and Fascism." New York: The League, n.d. [1934]. 11 pp.
Selections from a manifesto adopted by the Second Youth Congress Against War and Fascism, held in Chicago, September 28-30, 1934. The alleged connections of American imperialism, Wall Street, and the New Deal with Nazi Germany are denounced. The Youth Section pledges to fight all efforts to militarize the younger generation.

A120 . . . . "Capone, Karpis, Luciano. . . Convicted! How Much Longer Will This Vilest Racketeer of All Get Away with It?" New York: The League, 1936. 14 pp.
An attack by a Party front organization on William Randolph Hearst, called a warmonger and supporter of Hitler, whose papers never tell the truth. A boycott of the Hearst press is called for.

A121 . . . . "Proceedings, Third U.S. Congress Against War and Fascism." New York: The League, 1936. 60 pp.
Proceedings of the Congress that met in Cleveland, Jan. 3-5, 1936. Reports and speeches, many of them closely paralleling the Party line in the early days of the united front, deal with trade unions, agriculture, religion, education, national and racial minorities, veterans, war and fascism, women, youth, and organization.

A122 AMERICAN LEAGUE FOR PEACE AND DEMOCRACY. "The Dies Committee Inquisition: 20th Century Witch Hunt." New York: The League, 1939. 22 pp.
A call for the abolition of the Dies Committee, which is accused of violating democratic procedures, engaging in character assassination, and making charges of guilt by association. The Committee is said to rely on antilabor witnesses, to ignore the activities of fascists and racists, and to smear liberal and progressive candidates in local elections.

A123 . . . . "7 1/2 Million." New York: The League, n.d. [1939]. 52 pp.
A report of the American Congress for Peace and Democracy held in Washington, D.C., on January 6-8, 1939. The Congress favored collective security and the maintenance of social reforms already gained under the New Deal. Addresses by National Chairman Harry F. Ward and others are reprinted, along with reports by commissions on domestic and foreign affairs.

A124 AMERICAN LEGION, National Americanism Commission. "Isms—A Review of Alien Isms, Revolutionary Communism and Its Active Sympathizers in the United States." Indianapolis: The Legion, 1937. 287 pp.
A compendium on communism and related activities, designed to expose the menace of communism and the workings of its front organizations. Included are a history of the Party and of Soviet spy activities in the U.S., accounts of Party activities among youth and labor, and names of bookshops and presses. There are many quotations from Earl Browder's testimony before the House Committee on Un-American Activities, the report of the Lusk Committee, the "Daily Worker," and communist publications. Affiliated and sympathetic groups are listed.

A125 . . ., National Americanism Commission. "The 'Red' Exposure: A Study of Subversive Influences." Indianapolis: The Legion, 1948. 234 pp. Mimeo.
Addresses at a countersubversion seminar sponsored by the Legion's Americanism Commission, November 17-20, 1947. Among the speakers who dealt with aspects of communism in the U.S. were Ben Gitlow on the history and structure of the CPUSA, Samuel M. Birnbaum on legal aspects, Isaac Don Levine on government, Howard Rushmore on espionage, Ben Stolberg on the cultural field, Suzanne La Follette on women's movements, J. B. Matthews on front organizations, and Edward B. Wilcox on religious bodies.

A126 . . ., National Americanism Commission. "How You Can Fight Communism." Indianapolis: The Commission, n.d. [1950?]. 12 pp.
Suggestions on how to recognize communist-front organizations, with a call for protests to any company or sponsor that hires Party members, sympathizers, or fellow-travelers. A list of organizations and publications cited as communist fronts by official federal, state, or municipal agencies is included.

A127 . . ., All American Conference. "Proceedings, 1950." New York (?): The Legion, 1950. 101 pp.
Addresses given by noted anticommunists at a conference called by the Legion to discuss Party strategy and ways to combat it.

A128 "AMERICAN LEGION MAGAZINE." Watch Out for these Commie Swindles, 52 (May 1952), 14-15 ff.
Warnings by four authorities on the communist conspiracy of attacks against us now in the making. Victor Riesel writes on labor, Louis F. Budenz on world politics, George E. Sokolsky on culture, and Fred Woltman on race and religion.

A129 "AMERICAN MERCURY," The Meaning of Violence: Editorial, 39 (Nov. 1936), 347-50. (Reply by William Henry Chamberlain, 40 [April 1937], 504-5.)
An editorial argument that communists, who advocate violent overthrow of government, should be deprived of freedom of speech and be punished for their conspiracy against the Republic (Chamberlain replies that communists

are funny, not formidable, and that countries which have allowed them the greatest freedom of speech have least to fear from them.)

A130 "AMERICAN MERCURY," Whittaker Chambers Meets the Press, 68 (Feb. 1949), 153-60.
An abbreviated version of a "Meet the Press" radio interview. Chambers, outside the protection of congressional immunity, repeated his charge that Alger Hiss had once been a member of the Communist Party. (The accusations on this radio broadcast brought suit by Hiss against Chambers for slander and libel; this, in turn, led to the other Chambers' disclosures.)

A131 ..., Gerhart Eisler Meets the Press, 69 (July 1949), 5-14.
An abbreviated version of a "Meet the Press" radio interview, held after Eisler was called the real boss of American communists and before he jumped bail and fled the U.S. Repudiating this accusation (which was made both by his sister and by Louis Budenz), Eisler denied having any position of influence in the CPUSA.

A132 ..., Young Communist Meets the Press, 69 (Aug. 1949), 194-201.
An abbreviated reprint of Hans Freistadt's remarks on a radio interview, "Meet the Press." Friestadt was an admitted young communist who was a student at the University of North Carolina and a recipient of an Atomic Energy Commission fellowship. Among the topics discussed was the relative freedom of those holding minority views in the U.S. and Russia.

A133 ..., Judge Kenyon Meets the Press, 70 (June 1950), 700-8.
Reprint of a "Meet the Press" broadcast in which Judge Dorothy Kenyon, replying to accusations by Senator McCarthy, acknowledges membership during the 1930's in organizations later labeled subversive, but denies that she is a communist or a fellow-traveler. Asserting that Alger Hiss was a sacrifice to hysteria, she calls for the defense of civil rights.

A134 ..., Louis Budenz Meets the Press, 71 (July 1950), 90-99.
A reprint, slightly cut, of a "Meet the Press" telecast. Budenz asserts that communists count, not on numbers, but on discipline and the positions their members attain. The test in our loyalty program should not be Party membership, but rather a record indicating that the employee is either gullible or constantly deceived by the communists.

A135 ..., Former O.S.S. Agent Meets the Press, 71 (Aug. 1950), 199-207.
A reprint of a "Meet the Press" telecast in which Frank Bielaski, former Director of Investigation of the Office of Strategic Services, discusses the "Amerasia" case. Telling of the raid on the "Amerasia" offices, in which he was involved, he calls for a more complete investigation.

A136 ..., Box Score on The Supreme Court, 87 (Oct. 1958), 27-28.
Statistics presented by Senator James O. Eastland to the U.S. Senate on July 10, 1958, showing a consistent pattern of procommunism by the Supreme Court. Since Oct. 1953, when Earl Warren became Chief Justice, the Court has heard 39 cases concerning communism, sustaining the communist position in 30 of them.

A137 ..., Senate Internal Security Subcommittee Report on Racketeer and Communist Dominated

Unions, 88 (April 1959), 78-112.
An alliance of the teamsters, the Maritime Union, and the two longshoremen's unions threatens national security because many of the leaders are tainted with corruption and communism. Recommendations for investigation and prosecution are made.

A138 ..., Communists Invade Our Courts, 89 (July 1959), 123-30.
A condensation of a report by the House Un-American Activities Committee on "Communist Legal Subversion," concerned with the increase of communist lawyers in the U.S. and their effect on American government and law. The communist lawyer owes his primary loyalty to an international revolutionary conspiracy.

A139 AMERICAN NEGRO LABOR CONGRESS. "Constitution and Program of the American Negro Labor Congress." Chicago: The Congress, 1925. 40 pp.
The constitution and program adopted at the first convention of the Congress, held in Chicago, October 25-31, 1925. Inviting the participation of all Negro organizations, as well as organizations of Negro and white workers and farmers, the Congress sought to form local councils in all communities with Negro workers. (Originally organized as the League of Struggle for Negro Rights, this Party front changed its name in 1936 to National Negro Congress.)

A140 AMERICAN PEACE MOBILIZATION, National Labor Committee Against War. "Not Labor's War." New York: The Committee, 1941. 4 pp.
An appeal to labor, during the Hitler-Stalin pact period, to help lead the struggle for peace. The war in Europe is called one for profits; our involvement would mean impoverishment of the American people and a new depression.

A141 AMERICAN RANK AND FILE LABOR DELEGATION TO SOVIET RUSSIA. "Report of the First American Rank and File Labor Delegation to Soviet Russia." New York: International Publishers, 1928. 48 pp.
A laudatory report on the state of the Russian workers, signed by about 20 American trade unionists. The delegates visited plants in the coal, steel, oil, and textile industries. They report favorably on Soviet trade unions, cooperatives, the housing campaign, health and safety, workers' education, and international relations. They urge cooperation between the American and Russian labor movements.

A142 "AMERICAN SCHOLAR," Communism and Academic Freedom: American Scholar Forum, 18 (Summer 1949). 323-53.
A resume of the academic freedom cases at the University of Washington, followed by a statement by President Raymond B. Allen of the University and statements by the three dismissed professors. Essays by Arthur O. Lovejoy and T. V. Smith defend the handling of the cases by the University, while articles by Max Lerner and Helen M. Lynd criticize it.

A143 AMERICAN STUDENT UNION. "Keep Democracy Working by Making It Serve Human Needs: Report of Proceedings, Fourth National Convention, American Student Union, December 27-30, 1938." New York: ASU, 1938. 96 pp.
Report on the fourth annual convention of ASU, which discussed (1) aspects of university life such as curriculum, student government, student press, the National Youth Act, and campus cooperatives; (2) domestic affairs, including political action, Negro problems, the professions, civil liberties; (3) foreign policy issues such as Spain, Latin America, the Orient, refugees, neutrality, national defense;

(4) organizational aspects of the ASU, including work in the high schools. The major convention debate was on the ASU's peace program, favoring collective security.

A144 AMERICAN STUDENT UNION. "Students Serve Democracy: An Introduction to the American Student Union." New York: ASU, n.d. [1939?]. 30 pp.
The aims of the ASU, and its educational, citizenship, and peace activities. The Oxford Pledge, an early rallying slogan, is opposed, and international collaboration to maintain peace, in tune with the Stalinist line of the popular front period, is substituted. Sections on ASU organization, publications, growth, constitution, officers, and finances are included.

A145 "AMERICAN TEACHER," Referendum on Expulsion of Locals 5, 192 and 537, 25 (April 1941), entire issue.
Pros and cons on the referendum to expel three locals, charged with being communist led, from the American Federation of Teachers. The Executive Council argued that, because the teaching profession is dependent on the confidence of the general public, an organization of teachers that is led by communists will be discredited and hence unable to organize or service its membership. The accused locals deny communist domination, point to democratic internal practices, and accuse the Executive Council of attempting to expel its opposition.

A146 AMERICAN TRADE UNION DELEGATION TO THE SOVIET UNION. "Russia After Ten Years." New York: International Publishers, 1927. 96 pp.
A favorable report on Russia by an American trade union delegation, consisting of four trade unionists and 12 technical and advisory assistants. The report asserts that, though strikes are legal, few occur because workers see no reason to strike against themselves. It denies that the state controls trade unions and finds improvements in living standards and wages. The report criticizes housing for Russian workers and the lack of civil liberties, particularly the inability of "counterrevolutionaries" to defend themselves, though it denies secret executions of counterrevolutionaries. The report calls for U.S. recognition of Russia.

A147 AMERICAN WORKERS PARTY, Provisional Organizing Committee. "Toward an American Revolutionary Labor Movement: Draft Program of the American Workers Party." 2d and rev. ed. New York: The Party, 1934. 46 pp.
Program adopted following discussions between the Musteite AWP and the Trotskyite Communist League of America. Shortcomings of the CPUSA are analyzed, and its ideas of united front from below, self-determination in the Black Belt, and social fascism are viewed as absurd and vicious. Reliance on Moscow has led the CP to intellectual decay, praise of an infallible leadership, and abandonment of revolutionary morality and decency in dealings with other working-class groups.

A148 . . ., Provisional Organizing Committee. The Communist Party Apes Fascism, "Labor Action," 2 (March 1, 1934), 5.
Denunciation of the CPUSA for breaking up a socialist rally protesting the killing of Austrian workers by fascists. This gangster attack on socialist fellow-workers is the final proof that, far from leading the workers' revolutionary movement, the CP is a stumbling block in its path.

A149 AMERICAN WRITERS CONGRESS. "In Defense of Culture: Official Program of the 4th American Writers and Artists Congress." Held June 6-8, 1941, under the auspices of the League of American Writers, the American Artists Congress, and the United American Artists, CIO. New York: The Congress, 1941. 46 pp.
Program of a Party front organization during the period of the Nazi-Soviet pact. The League asserts that steps being taken toward entry into the European war will bring fascism here and betray the American people. An introduction by Henry Hart gives a brief history of the League, and describes its present stand as traditional Americanism, opposed to economic royalists, wars, and fascism. (The list of speakers consisted largely of well-known communists and fellow-travelers.)

A150 AMERICAN YOUTH CONGRESS, Continuations Committee. "Program of the American Youth Congress: Adopted by Delegates from 79 Organizations with Total Membership of 1,700,000, New York City, August 15-17, 1934." New York: The Congress, 1934. 16 pp.
The program adopted at the First American Youth Congress. Called by the Central Bureau for Young America, under the leadership of Viola Ilma, the Congress rejected the program proposed by the Central Bureau in favor of one opposing war and fascism, and favoring a cooperative world and a social order based on production for use rather than profit. Delegates from communist organizations were elected to the Continuations Committee, along with socialists and others.

A151 . . . . "Proceedings of the Third American Youth Congress, Cleveland, Ohio, July 3-5, 1936." New York: The Congress, 1936. 46 pp.
Proceedings of the Third American Youth Congress, which witnessed a struggle for control between the Young Communist League and the Young People's Socialist League. The struggle centered on an effort to limit the powers of paid functionaries, and an effort to limit the Congress to political activities agreed upon unanimously by its National Council. Both efforts were defeated. A letter from President Roosevelt greeted the Congress. Earl Browder was the CP representative at a symposium on "What My Party Offers American Youth."

A152 . . . . "Congressional Record, Model Congress of Youth, Fourth Session, Milwaukee, July 2-5, 1937." N.publ., 1937. 86 pp.
Proceedings of the Fourth American Youth Congress, organized along the lines of the U.S. Congress, at which the Young Communist League consolidated control, over opposition from the Young People's Socialist League. Controversial issues included a Bill of Rights, which YPSL opposed as "left-liberal" and not radical, and the report on peace, following the Party's collective security line of the popular-front period. Reports on labor, education, democratic liberties, agriculture, recreation, leisure time and cultural opportunities, and housing were adopted without opposition.

A153 . . . . "Youngville U.S.A.: American Youth Tells Its Story." New York: The Congress, n.d. [1937]. 64 pp.
Contains a picture of the social and economic conditions of American youth during the depression, a discussion of the Civilian Conservation Corps and the National Youth Administration, a short history of the American Youth Congress, and the text and a defense of its proposed American Youth Act designed to solve the youth problem.

A154 . . . . "Proceedings of the Congress of Youth, New York City, July 1-5, 1939." New York: The Congress, 1939. 52 pp.
A major issue was adoption of a statement opposing

communist as well as fascist dictatorship. Under pressure from anticommunists, delegates of the Young Communist League supported a statement opposing all forms of dictatorship, on the grounds that no such thing as a communist dictatorship existed. Other activities included panel reports on interfaith and interracial understanding, participation in politics and government, and opportunities in education.

A155 AMERICAN YOUTH CONGRESS. "This Is Youth Speaking: Record of National Youth Citizenship Institute." New York: The Congress, 1940. 30 pp. Mimeo.
Record of the National Citizenship Institute of the American Youth Congress, held in Washington, D.C., February 9-12, 1940, during the Hitler-Stalin pact period. Highlights included a speech by President Roosevelt, who was cooling toward AYC; a question-and-answer session with Eleanor Roosevelt, still friendly to it; and a speech by John L. Lewis. Only sporadic opposition to domination by the Young Communist League developed.

A156 .... "Youth Defends America: Report of the Sixth American Youth Congress, College Camp, Lake Geneva, Wisconsin, July 3-7, 1940." New York: The Congress, n.d. [1940]. 47 pp.
Report of the Sixth American Youth Congress, the second held during the Hitler-Stalin pact period, which adopted an anti-Roosevelt, anti-collective security resolution, despite opposition by a "New Deal" minority. Noncontroversial topics included civil liberties, the proposed American Youth Act, and opposition to poll taxes in the South. The "New Deal" minority was led by Joseph Lash, former leader of the AYC, and by representatives of the National Student Federation, Jewish youth organizations, and the YWCA.

A157 AMERICUS [pseud. for Earl Browder]. "Labor and Socialism in America." The author, 1948. 46 pp. Multilithed.
The former leader of the CPUSA asserts that American communists, after ten years of leadership of unionism in the mass production industries, are again being isolated from the labor movement. He finds the causes in the defects, weaknesses, and mistakes of the Party's left-wing leadership.

A158 .... "Parties, Issues and Candidates in the 1948 Elections." The author, 1948. 18 pp. Multilithed.
Henry A. Wallace is supported for raising the peace issue and reminding the masses of the Roosevelt heritage. However, it is illusory to expect his election, to view his movement as anti-imperialist in the sense of the people's movements of Europe, or to think that his organization can become the future labor party.

A159 .... "Where Do We Go from Here?" The author, 1948. 57 pp. Multilithed.
A review of the 1948 national convention of the CPUSA by its former leader, who examines critically the convention record on the war and its results, the Wallace movement, the Marshall Plan, trade union unity, Marxian theory, and the Party. He concludes that not since 1929 had a Party convention so lost contact with the working class.

A160 AMIDON, Beulah. An Old Fashioned Strike, "Survey," 56 (April 1, 1926), 10-12 ff.
An account of the background and events of the Passaic, N.J., textile strike. The author hopes that the communist philosophy of the strike leader, Albert Weisbord, along with other sensational aspects of the strike, will not divert public attention from the textile industry's economic and social predicament.

A161 AMIS, B. D. "Lynch Justice at Work." New York: Workers Library, n.d. [1930?]. 31 pp.
Denunciation of lynchings as the work of the white ruling class and its agents, the Socialist Party and Negro reform organizations. Only the American Negro Labor Congress supports the struggle of Negroes for full social, economic, and political equality. The right of self-determination for Negroes in the Black Belt is supported.

A162 .... The Negro National Oppression and Social Antagonisms, "Communist," 10 (March 1931), 241-48.
The plantation tenancy system, a remnant of slavery, keeps the Negroes in a state of subjugation, while making huge profits for the white ruling class. Peonage is enforced by convict labor and the chain gang. Only a revolution under communist leadership will free this oppressed potential nation.

A163 .... For a Strict Leninist Analysis on the Negro Question, "Communist," 11 (Oct. 1932), 944-49.
Criticism of J. S. Allen's pamphlet, "The American Negro," for lack of theoretical clarity. Allen views persecution of Negroes as based on race, instead of seeing the question as a national one. The right of self-determination is a major slogan, not part of the general struggle for Negro rights. The Negro majority would rule the while minority as well as themselves.

A164 .... How We Carried Out the Decision of the 1930 C. I. Resolution on the Negro Question in the United States, "Communist International," 12 (May 5, 1935), 498-514.
An analysis of the Party's work among Negroes, pointing to its growing influence but criticizing its lack of understanding on the issue of self-determination of the Black Belt. The Party has not used the united-front-from-below tactic properly in the Scottsboro agitation, nor has it exposed the bourgeois leadership of Negro groups, or the anti-Negro nature of relief and WPA job allotments.

A165 AMTER, Israel. The Black Victims of Imperialism, "Communist International," 3, nos. 26-27, n.d. [1923], 113-19.
An account of the sufferings of the Negro people, victims of imperialism in Africa and the West Indies and of bestial treatment in the U.S. Race prejudice keeps Negroes out of unions and makes them scab against white workers. Only the Communist International can unite Negroes with revolutionary workers and peasants to struggle against exploitation.

A166 .... Political Progress in the United States, "International Press Correspondence," 3 (March 15, 1923), 201-3.
A discussion of political action in the U.S., describing the political consciousness of the American farmer in optimistic terms.

A167 .... Proletarian Forces in the United States, "International Press Correspondence," 3 (March 22, 1923), 221-22.
The American proletariat, despite favorable objective conditions, is not class conscious. This is attributed to the reactionary leaders of the AFL, and the yellow leaders of the Socialist Party. Communists are influencing a strong, progressive left wing, in which sentiment for an independent labor party is growing.

A168 .... Labor Party Movement in the United States, "International Press Correspondence," 3 (April 5, 1923), 245-46.
The Socialist Party is criticized for successfully excluding

communist delegates from the December 1922 Conference for Progressive Political Action, and for the failure of that conference to form a labor party. Sentiment in the unions for a labor party is likely to grow before the next conference on the labor party question.

A169 AMTER, Israel. The Workers Party of America, International Press Correspondence,'' 3 (April 19, 1923), 274-75.
A summary of the drawbacks and achievements of the Workers Party of America, through which the communists seek to proselytize the masses. Despite inexperience, a small and predominantly foreign-language membership, government harrassment, and AFL opposition, the WP has resolved its factional conflict, adopted a more satisfactory communist program, and achieved close relations with the TUEL.

A170 .... The Communist International and the American Movement, "Communist International," new series, no. 1, n.d. [1924?], 185-87.
A tribute, on the fifth anniversary of the Communist International, to the correctness of its decisions on internecine warfare in the American communist movement. The author outlines open Party activities—creation of the Workers Party, united front activities, and creation of the Federated Farmer Labor Party—advocated by the Comintern and proved correct.

A171 .... The American Communists and LaFollette, "International Press Correspondence," 4 (June 12, 1924), 334-35.
Senator La Follette's statement repudiating any party of which communists are a part is viewed as a service to the farmer-labor movement in which the communists are active, since it will drive vacillating elements away. La Follette's statement shows that the farmer-labor movement that includes the communists is the only threat to him and to the capitalist class.

A172 .... The Elections in the United States, "International Press Correspondence," 4 (Oct. 9, 1924), 796-97.
A communist analysis of the 1924 election campaign. Coolidge, a Rockefeller man, and Davis, a Morgan man, are the candidates of the two Wall Street parties. La Follette's movement consists of petty-bourgeois elements under the control of big finance. La Follette's repudiation of any organization supported by communists forced the communists to run candidates in their own name. The communist campaign is summarized.

A173 .... Discussion in the American Party, "International Press Correspondence," 5 (Jan. 22, 1925), 68-69.
The minority view within the Workers Party of America on tactics during the 1924 election. Amter opposes giving up the effort to create a farmer-labor party, as advocated by William Z. Foster, arguing that the conditions making for a farmer-labor party continue to exist, and that the slogan brings communists into political contact with the mass of American workers.

A174 .... The Situation of the Rubber Workers, "Workers Monthly," 5 (Dec. 1926), 640-43.
A description of the wretched conditions in the Akron rubber industry, including declining wages, a vicious speed-up, poor working conditions, and company unionism. There is a weak AFL union.

A175 .... "Is the Socialist Party a Party of the Workers?" New York: Communist Party, USA, District 2, n.d. [1932]. 16 pp.

A "third period" pamphlet, charging the Socialist Party with helping to starve workers, helping to cut wages, working with gangsters, breaking strikes, betraying Negroes, helping lynchings, and supporting the war machine. Led by social fascists who are bitter enemies of the USSR, the Socialist Party is a third party of capitalism.

A176 .... "Industrial Slavery—Roosevelt's 'New Deal.'" New York: Workers Library, 1933. 16 pp.
Issued in July 1933, this pamphlet by a leading communist characterizes the NIRA as the Industrial Slavery (Recovery) Act, under which cartels will grow and minimum wages become maximum wages. Employers' associations submit codes which government amends and approves, with workers allowed only to discuss what employers and government have agreed to in advance.

A177 .... "The March Against Hunger." New York: Workers Library for the National Committee, Unemployed Councils, 1933. 15 pp.
A description of the hunger march on Washington on December 6, 1933, telling how the march was organized, how the marchers were met with government terror, and how they entered Washington and presented their demands for unemployment insurance and winter relief to Congress. This mass action reveals the rising class consciousness of the working masses.

A178 .... The Revolutionary Upsurge and the Struggles of the Unemployed, "Communist," 12 (Feb. 1933), 112-22.
The communists have played an important role in unifying the forces of unrest set in motion by the depression. Though the prestige of the Party, the TUUL, and the Unemployed Councils has risen, organizational gains are limited. The broadest united front of unemployed and employed workers must be built.

A179 .... Unity in the Struggle for Social Insurance, "Communist," 12 (July 1933), 650-58.
A presentation of the Party program of social insurance, to be paid for by the government and the capitalists and to be administered by commissions of workers. The unified struggle of the masses will force the government to provide social insurance.

A180 .... "Why the Workers' Unemployment Insurance Bill? How It Can Be Won." Rev. ed. New York: Workers Library, 1934. 23 pp.
An attack on the New Deal, citing conditions of the depression, and calling for the passage of the workers' unemployment and social insurance bill, introduced by Congressman Lundeen. A copy of the bill and a defense of it are included.

A181 .... Force the Enactment of the Workers' Bill! "Communist," 13 (Sept. 1934), 845-61.
Pointing out the inadequacy of government relief programs, the author urges enactment of the communist-supported workers' bill for unemployment insurance. He calls for local, county, and state conferences and marches, leading up to a mass conference in Washington in January 1935, when Congress assembles.

A182 .... "A Labor Party for New York Workers." New York: New York District, CPUSA, 1935. 15 pp.
Third period pamphlet advocating formation of a labor party in opposition to Democrats, Republicans, and other "betrayers of the working class" such as socialist and AFL leaders. NRA and AAA are attacked as steps toward

fascism and war. Unity of the workers is urged "from below," and a statewide and eventually a national labor party is proposed under CP leadership.

A183 AMTER, Israel. "Social Security in a Soviet America." New York: Workers Library, 1935. 47 pp.
A survey of the terrible conditions under which American workers live, with no security under the capitalist system. The author denounces Roosevelt and the arms program, claiming that only the Soviet Union stands against imperialist war. Only a Soviet America, he concludes, would offer full social security to workers.

A184 .... "Working Class Unity or Fascism?" New York: Communist Party, New York District, 1935. 16 pp.
A call for the united front of all workers and workers' organizations, particularly the Socialist Party, as the only method of providing a program for the American working class. The pamphlet attacks the New Deal. Failure to achieve working-class unity, the author predicts, will result in fascism.

A185 .... "Youth and the Fight for Unemployment and Social Insurance: What Can We Young Workers Expect from the 'New Deal'?" New York: Youth Publishers, n.d. [1935?]. 24 pp.
Criticism of "New Deal" promises to American workers. Roosevelt's inadequate unemployment program is contrasted with the Communist Party's "workers unemployment and social insurance bill." Other effects of the capitalist depression on youth are suggested: the Scottsboro frame-up, crime, prostitution, militarization, hunger. Young workers are urged to fight unemployment by joining a local unemployment council and the Young Communist League.

A186 .... The National Congress for Unemployment and Social Insurance—And After, "Communist," 14 (Jan. 1935), 33-44.
On the occasion of the National Congress, to be held in Washington January 5-7, the author contrasts the comprehensive social insurance plan embodied in the CP-sponsored workers' bill with Roosevelt's inadequate program. The National Congress will intensify pressure for the workers' bill.

A187 ..., and KRUMBEIN, Charles. "Dollars for Democracy." N.p. [New York?]: n.publ. [CPUSA], n.d. [1936?]. 14 pp.
Plea for funds for the New York State Communist Party building fund with an outline of its proposed uses, principally the maintenance of schools and issuance of publications.

A188 .... Organizational Changes in the New York District of the Party, "Communist," 15 (May 1936), 465-73.
A report on efforts of the New York district to adapt its organizational form to the situation in its locality. County committees are necessary to strengthen the farmer-labor party movement. Weaknesses in organizing assembly branches are discussed, and experiences in building industrial units are reviewed.

A189 .... New Party Organizational Forms Prove Their Value, "Communist," 15 (June 1936), 537-41.
In the Party reorganization some branch units have been too large, with resulting insufficient guidance of members and high turnover. The industrial units have had higher attendance and less turnover, but have been concerned with trade-union issues, with little effort to convert noncommunists.

A190 .... The Elections in New York, "Communist," 15 (Dec. 1936), 1141-53.
In the New York elections, the American Labor Party supported Roosevelt, the socialist vote decreased, and the communist vote increased. Although the Party achieved its main task of defeating the Republicans, it failed to increase the circulation of the "Daily Worker" or recruit many new members.

A191 .... Significance of the Coming Municipal Elections in New York, "Communist," 16 (July 1937), 647-60.
A listing of the reactionary versus the progressive forces in the New York City election. Tammany Hall is called the main enemy; the forces enlisted to defeat it include the American Labor Party, the Fusion Party and the Progressive Committee, the Negro people, the Socialist Party, and the Communist Party.

A192 .... Development of the Farmer-Labor Party Movement in the Municipal Election Campaign, "Communist," 16 (Oct. 1937), 925-33.
The farmer-labor party movement is growing rapidly, with many AFL as well as CIO members supporting the various parties. In New York, the American Labor Party's program includes many communist-supported demands. Unlike the Socialist Party, the Communist Party is supporting the ALP and its mayoralty candidate, La Guardia.

A193 .... Work Among National Groups—a Central Communist Task, "Communist," 17 (Aug. 1938), 722-31.
The Party has neglected the national groups, thinking them unimportant with immigration cut off. It forgot that descendants of immigrants are greatly influenced by their national backgrounds. The Party must bring them into the democratic front by stressing the revolutionary traditions in their homelands and by aiding them to solve their particular problems. (Based on a report to the Party's tenth national convention, May 27-31, 1938.)

A194 .... The Democratic Front Moves Ahead in New York, "Communist," 17 (Oct. 1938), 909-18.
A realignment is occurring in New York politics, with progressive Democrats and Republicans supporting the New Deal and reactionaries in both parties opposing it. The American Labor Party supports progressives in either party. The socialists and AFL leaders oppose the ALP. The Communist Party campaigns hard for the ALP, while using the campaign to recruit members and build the circulation of its press.

A195 .... "May Day, 1939." New York: Workers Library, 1939. 15 pp.
A call for the unity of American labor; for the unity of all progressives in the democratic front for social and national security; and for a united stand by the U.S. and the USSR, the only two democracies that stand firmly for resistance to Hitler. (Published several months before negotiation of the Nazi-Soviet pact.)

A196 .... "A Program for Manhattan's Millions." New York: CPUSA, n.d. [1939]. 16 pp.
The program of the Party's candidate for the City Council from the Borough of Manhattan in the 1939 municipal elections. Emphasis is placed on defeating reaction, as well as on more adequate relief, public housing, health, education, a people's taxation program, and a youth program to avoid crime.

A197 .... "The Truth About Finland." New York: Communist Party, New York State Committee, n.d. [1939]. 16 pp.

A defense of the Red Army's invasion of Finland, charging Finnish hostility to the USSR, backed by England, France, and U.S. Finland is said to have been a tool of the imperialists since 1918, to be headed by reactionaries, and to have been forced by native fascist groups to cooperate with Hitler. The U.S. is urged to remain out of the war.

A198 AMTER, Israel. "Americans All." New York: Workers Library, n.d. [1940?]. 15 pp.
A defense of the Party line during the Hitler-Stalin pact period. Addressed to America's foreign born, the pamphlet argues that the drive toward war has resulted in persecution of noncitizens and naturalized foreign born. Soviet conquest of neighboring countries is hailed as liberation of their people. Support of national groups for Browder and Ford, party candidates in 1940, is urged.

A199 . . . . "The Truth About the Communists." New York: Workers Library, n.d. [1940?]. 15 pp.
A statement of communist aims by a veteran Party member, who asserts that the communists stand for economic and political liberty, organization of the unorganized, industrial unionism, unemployment insurance and relief, peace, civil rights, and a people's front to block the economic royalists.

A200 . . . . The Organization of an Election Campaign, "Communist," 19 (April 1940), 344-49.
The conduct of the Party's election campaign in New York's 14th Congressional District is reviewed as a pattern for future campaigns. The most experienced Party workers from all parts of the city were assigned to the District. Attention is paid to campaign literature, agitational activities, election day organization, and finances.

A201 . . . . "May Day, 1941." New York: Workers Library, 1941. 15 pp.
A communist May Day pamphlet, published during the period of the Hitler-Stalin pact. Addressed principally to workers, the pamphlet contains a bitter attack on the European war.

A202 . . . . The National Groups—A Powerful Force in the Struggle Against Fascism, "Communist," 20 (Aug. 1941), 712-23.
A program for work among national groups on a new basis, following the Nazi invasion of the Soviet Union. The national groups are determined to destroy Hitlerism. Independent mass movements should be built within each national group on a local scale, with sectarianism avoided.

A203 . . . . Norman Thomas—A Spearhead of Fascism, "Communist," 21 (June 1942), 450-57.
The socialist leader, Norman Thomas, is opposed to American participation in the war, which he calls an imperialist war. He opposes a second front in Europe, seeks to break up the Allied coalition by calling Russia a dictatorship, and tries to disrupt the war effort by fomenting strikes. In these ways he serves as a fifth columnist for Hitler.

A204 . . . . The War and the New York Election Primaries, "Communist," 21 (Sept. 1942), 732-35.
The Party candidate for governor of New York stresses the importance of the win-the-war issue in the New York primaries and in the coming November elections.

A205 . . . . Twenty-six Years of Struggle and Glory, "Communist," 22 (Nov. 1943), 980-88.
A glowing review of the development of the Soviet Union,

praising the Soviet people for their courageous contribution to the Allied cause.

. . . . See also FORD, J.

A206 ANDELSON, Robert Vernon. You Conform . . . . or Else, "American Legion Monthly," 57 (Aug. 1954), 24-25 ff.
An account by a former student at the University of Chicago of his publication of an article exposing alleged communist influences among students and faculty, and of the subsequent refusal of the theological faculty to admit him to candidacy for the master's degree. Communist student groups were permitted to exist on campus, and there was a softness for communist ideas among faculty and students.

A207 ANDERSON, Franklin J. Union Wreckers at the Switch, "Plain Talk," 1 (April 1947), 19-22.
An exposé of communist influence in the United Electrical, Radio and Machine Workers by an executive board member of UE Local 475 and one of the UE Members for Democratic Action. He traces the struggle with the communists, showing how several hundred Party members in key spots can control the union. A house cleaning is under way.

A208 . . .; JULIANELLE, Joseph A.; and FORD, Matthew [pseud.]. The Red Electric Machine, "Plain Talk," 1 (Sept. 1947), 23-30.
Three short, separate articles by members of the United Electrical, Radio and Machine Workers, exposing Party control of the union. Anderson sketches the procommunist background and affiliations of James J. Matles, the union's organization director. Julianelle tells of the attempt of the union's communist leadership to purge its Bridgeport local. "Ford" describes a strike defeat of a communist-led local in Clifton, N.J.

A209 ANDERSON, Jack, and MAY, Ronald W. "McCarthy: The Man, the Senator, the Ism." Boston: Beacon, 1952. 431 pp. Ind. App.
A critical account of McCarthy's career, covering his childhood, his war record, his first campaign for the Senate, the scandals with which he was connected, and his exploitation of the communist issue. Some of his controversial Senate committee hearings involving the communist issue are analyzed. The authors conclude that, not only did he detect no spies or communist agents in our government, but by his activity he stimulated the growth of communism throughout the world.

A210 ANDERSON, Paul H. "The Attitude of the American Leftist Leaders Toward the Russian Revolution (1917-1923)." Notre Dame, Ind.: University of Notre Dame, 1942. 107 pp. Sources and Ref.
An account of the reaction of American radicals to the Bolshevik revolution. Groups surveyed included socialists, communists, pro-Bolshevik and anti-Bolshevik liberals, and anarchists. The right and center of the Socialist Party opposed Lenin's seizure of power because of his anti-democratic and terrorist methods, while the socialist left became the Communist Party. The anarchists, after initial sympathy, became anti-Bolshevik because of the total disregard of individuals.

A211 ANDERSON, Sherwood. "Beyond Desire." New York: Liveright, 1932. 359 pp.
Written while the author was under the influence of the Party, the novel uses the Gastonia strike as a background for a story of a confused young American who is attracted to communism and who is killed by another confused American, serving in the National Guard.

A212 ANDRASSY, Stella. Communist Voices of America, "American Mercury," 81 (July 1955), 131-36.
An attack on the fellow-traveling foreign language press in the U.S., said to have a combined circulation of 137,000, as compared to less than 10,000 for the "Daily Worker." The circulation figures vastly underestimate the number of people, at home and abroad, who are exposed to the false and misleading information of these publications.

A213 ANDREWS, Bert. "Washington Witch Hunt." New York: Random House, 1948. 218 pp.
A self-styled conservative asserts that a communist "witch hunt" is unnecessary and useless. He fears encroachment on traditional American liberties by actions of the State Department and the House Committee on Un-American Activities. Using answers by William Z. Foster as illustrations, he concludes that communism is refuted merely by listening to evasions and glib generalities of communists.

A214 ..., and ANDREWS, Peter. "A Tragedy of History: A Journalist's Confidential Role in the Hiss-Chambers Case." Washington, D.C.: Luce, 1962. 235 pp. App. Ind.
An analysis of the Hiss-Chambers case, partially written by Bert Andrews, a Washington newspaperman, and after his death in 1953 completed by his son from the father's files and reports. Brought into the case by Richard Nixon, Bert Andrews saw in the Hiss-Chambers clash one of the greatest news stories of the period. Though the case against Hiss was very strong, some mysteries have never been cleared up.

A215 ANDREWS, Lillian. "Youth of the Happy Land." New York: Youth Publishers, n.d. [193-?]. 44 pp.
The "happy land" is the Soviet Union in this communist pamphlet directed toward American youth. Emphasis is placed on Soviet employment, education, sports, agriculture, the Red Army and peace, and the Comsomols.

A216 ANGELL, Ernest. Should Congress Investigate? II: A New Procedure for the Congressional Committee, "Saturday Review of Literature," 38 (Feb. 26, 1955), 9-10 ff.
A reply by the chairman of the board of ACLU to Robert Morris' article in the February 19 issue defending the purposes and procedures of the Senate Internal Security Subcommittee. Criticizing specific practices in which the subcommittee has engaged, Angell asserts that fair rules of procedure will not interfere with congressional investigating power.

A217 ANGOFF, Charles. Wallace's Communist-Front Party, "American Mercury," 67 (Oct. 1948), 413-21.
An assertion that Wallace's third party is foreign in conception, basic ideology, real leadership, and general direction. Among the leaders at the party's convention were a number who have consistently followed the communist line. The Progressive Party is the largest communist front organized in our history.

A218 ANONYMOUS. "Who Are the Hacks in the NMU?" No publication information. 15 pp.
An attack on Joseph Curran and the group he formed within the union in 1943 to fight union control by communists. The pamphlet, which carries the names of 38 members without attributing authorship, attacks Curran for sabotaging the union's 1945 program, for using former communists for Red-baiting, and for making the union powerless.

A219 ANONYMOUS. A Professor Joins the Communist Party, "New Masses," 25 (Oct. 5, 1937), 3-7.
Answering Stuart Browne's complaints against the burdens of Party membership (see "A Professor Quits the Communist Party" in "Harper's Magazine," July 1937), the author asserts that he has made many new friends since joining the Party, that he has made better use of his time, and that his intellectual life is more integrated with real life.

A220 ANONYMOUS. Why I Am Not an Active Communist, "New Masses," 27 (May 17, 1938), 13-14.
A sympathizer who accepts all the fundamental premises of communist ideology has not joined the Party because he is unwilling to spend his evenings at meetings and conferences, because he cannot afford to give up his job, and because he has small children to be cared for.

A221 ANONYMOUS. The Strange Case of Miss X, "Nation," 177 (Dec. 12, 1953), 491-93.
The experience of a federal employee who underwent a loyalty investigation and was ordered dismissed (later reversed) for denying present or past membership in a communist organization. The author had belonged to the League for Peace and Democracy, later placed on the Attorney General's list of communist organizations.

A222 ANONYMOUS. Communists Are Using Our Churches, "American Mercury," 85 (Oct. 1957), 87-89.
In an article excerpted from the "Christian Beacon," an anonymous author asserts that the National Council of Churches has ignored all warnings and proofs of infiltration, and that its leaders have worked closely with communist leaders and collaborators.

A223 ANSTROM, George. "The American Farmer." New York: International Publishers, 1932. 31 pp.
An assertion that the American farm is being crushed by capitalism, as the capitalists hope to climb out of the crises through the misery and hunger of the farm population. However, farmers are waking up, and under the leadership of the United Farmers League (supported by the Communist Party) are agitating for emergency relief for food, and relief from taxes and from foreclosures.

A224 .... "The Government Takes a Hand in the Cotton Patch." New York: Workers Library, 1933. 20 pp.
Condemnation of the perpetrators of the sharecroppers' system, and of Hoover, Roosevelt, and the New Deal for using the A. A. A. to gouge the poor farmer. Negro and white cotton croppers must struggle together, through the Sharecroppers' Union and in Committees of Action, against the capitalists.

A225 ANTI-DEFAMATION LEAGUE OF B'NAI B'RITH. "Hitler's Communism Unmasked." Chicago: The League, 1938. 30 pp.
A pamphlet refuting Hitler's identification of Jews with communism. The League points out that in the U.S. the proportion of Jews in the CP is insignificant, that prominent spokesmen against communism in the U.S. are Jewish, and that Jews have been in the forefront in acts of heroism and loyalty to our country. Jews are also shown to have been a minority of the Bolsheviks in Russia.

A226 .... "Primer on Communism: A Fact-by-Fact Expose." New York: The League, 1955. 87 pp. Bibliog.
The revised edition of a handbook on communism that appeared in 1951. The portion on communism in the free world deals with the communist program, movement, and strategy. Fellow-travelers, front organizations, and the

Party record in labor unions are included. The section on the Soviet world traces zigzags in communist strategy, and covers the Soviet empire, Soviet totalitarianism, and economy and labor in the Soviet world.

A227   APTHEKER, Bettina. "Big Business and the American University." New York: New Outlook, 1966. 40 pp.
A tracing by a youthful communist, a leader of the Free Speech Movement at Berkeley, of the relations between Big Business and the University. The corporate connections of the University of California regents and of the Harvard Corporation and Board of Overseers are shown. A program to democratize the universities is outlined.

A228   APTHEKER, Herbert. "The Negro in the American Revolution." New York: International Publishers, 1940. 47 pp. Bibliog.
An examination of the activities of Negroes before and during the American Revolution. The author, a leading communist historian, finds that the desire for freedom is the central theme in the history of American Negroes, and that failure to free them postponed the final victory of the American forces.

A229   . . . . "American Negro Slave Revolts." New York: Columbia University Press, 1943. 409 pp. Bibliog. Ind.
A well-documented history of the slave revolts and conspiracies prior to the Civil War, showing that Negro's response to bondage was not one of passivity. The study, by a leading communist historian, concludes that discontent and rebelliousness were characteristic of American Negro slaves. The findings support the Party's contention that the Negro people have an inherent revolutionary potential.

A230   . . . . "Essays in the History of the American Negro." New York: International Publishers, 1945. 216 pp. App. Bibliog.
Four essays on the Negro's role in early U.S. history, written by a leading communist spokesman on the Negro question. Included are "Negro Slave Revolts in the United States, 1526-1860"; "The Negro in the American Revolution"; "The Negro in the Abolitionist Movement"; and "The Negro in the Civil War." The history of the Negro in this country is rife with examples of courage, honesty, intelligent organization, and perseverance, though the slavocracy has sought to keep this history and heritage hidden. A chronology of slave revolts is appended.

A231   . . . . "The Negro People in America; a Critique of Gunnar Myrdal's 'An American Dilemma.' " Introd. by Doxey Wilkerson, 1946. New York: International Publishers, 1946. 80 pp. Ref. notes.
A condemnation of "An American Dilemma," contending that its philosophical premises are superficial and dishonest, its historiography distorted and false, its ethics vicious, and its analysis of the Negro question weak, mystical, and dangerous. The author asserts that the Negro question is basically a material one, not a moral one, and that there is no American dilemma for believers in democracy and full rights for all.

A232   . . . . "To Be Free: Studies in American Negro History." New York: International Publishers, 1948. 256 pp. Ref. notes. Ind.
An effort to show that the struggle for Negro liberation is interwoven with the general effort to preserve and extend freedom for all Americans, and to point up the indigenous and deep-rooted nature of revolutionary sentiments. Chapters deal with slave guerilla warfare, buying freedom, militant abolitionism, Negro casualties in the Civil War,

Negroes in the Union navy, organizational activities of southern Negroes in 1865, and Mississippi reconstruction and the Negro leader, Charles Caldwell.

A233   . . . . Communism and Chaos, "Masses & Mainstream," 1 (Sept. 1948), 18-29.
Ridicule of anticommunist explanations as to why communists sometimes promote good legislation and back worthy causes. While communists believe that only a fundamental socio-economic change will eliminate the roots of grievances, leadership of day-to-day struggles of the masses will earn their devotion, so that the Party becomes a vanguard.

A234   . . . . "Why Defend the Rights of Communists?" New York: New Century, 1949. 16 pp.
An assertion that the author was gagged by the judge when he appeared as defense witness in the trial of the Party leaders. He calls upon the American people to defend the communists in order to stop this type of fascism.

A235   . . . . The Schlesinger Fraud, "Masses & Mainstream," 2 (Oct. 1949), 23-35. Reprinted as "The Schlesinger Fraud, a Critique of the Third Force in America." New York: "Masses & Mainstream," 1949. 15 pp.
A review of Schlesinger's "The Vital Center," and other writings, attacking him for misquotations, fabrication, and arrogance in his analysis of communism. Schlesinger's views on American democracy and foreign policy are said to be groomed to the needs of a ruling class seeking war and fascism.

A236   . . . . (ed.). "A Documentary History of the Negro People in the United States." Preface by W. E. B. Du Bois. New York: Citadel, 1951. 942 pp. Ind.
A collection of documents by a leading communist scholar relating to American Negro history from 1661 to 1910. Material is grouped under eight heads: through the revolutionary era, the early national period, the abolitionist era, the Civil War, the reconstruction years, the early post-reconstruction period, the appearance of imperialism, and the twentieth century.

A237   . . . . "America's Racist Laws: Weapon of National Oppression." New York: Masses & Mainstream, 1951. 23 pp.
The author, associate editor of "Masses & Mainstream" and instructor at the Jefferson School of Social Science, reviews city, state, and federal statutes on race, and finds that racist legislation forms an organic part of official U.S. policy and practice. He views the fight against racism as part of the fight against imperialism, fascism, and war.

A238   . . . . Communism and Truth: A Reply to Sidney Hook, "Masses & Mainstream," 6 (Feb. 1953), 31-42.
A reply to Hook, following Hook's refusal to debate publicly on his assertion that present CPUSA members cannot fulfill the obligation of a teacher or scholar to the ethics of scientific inquiry. The reply covers Party control over members' views, the Negro question, science, and the Rosenberg case.

A239   . . . . Behind the Hiss Frameup, "Masses & Mainstream," 6 (Oct. 1953), 1-13.
An argument that an innocent Alger Hiss was framed by the FBI and that the Hiss conviction supports the McCarthy view that the Roosevelt Administration was infiltrated by communists. The result, for many Americans, was an identification of the New Deal with communism, and of communism with espionage and treason. Weaknesses in the case against Hiss are reviewed.

A240   APTHEKER, Herbert. "Laureates of Imperialism: Big Business Re-writes American History." New York: Masses & Mainstream, 1954. 96 pp. Bibliog.
An attack on business historians for defending American capitalism by portraying capitalists as the heroes of American history, whereas in fact they have raped America. Apologies for American imperialism and for current U.S. foreign policies are also criticized, as is the treatment of American populist, working-class, radical and protest movements. Fortunately, there is evidence of a counter-current in American historiography. The last section is devoted to an attack on the "New Conservatism," and on such idols of the movement as Henry Adams and James C. Calhoun.

A241   . . . . "History and Reality." New York: Cameron Associates, 1955. 288 pp.
A collection of essays that have appeared in "Masses & Mainstream," "Political Affairs," and "Science and Society," 1947 to 1955. They are presented as examples of Aptheker's application of Marxist historical materialism to the contemporary scene. The first article, "History and Reality," is a critique of bourgeois philosophies of history and an effort to counterpose the essential features of historical materialism. Eighteen other articles are grouped under four heads: (1) Polemics on the "New Conservatism," (2) Polemics on the Liberal Illusion, (3) Polemics on Policies of Reaction, and (4) Polemics on Class Justice. (Republished in 1962 by Marzani & Munsell as "The Era of McCarthyism.")

A242   . . . . New Light on the Rosenberg-Sobell Case, "Masses & Mainstream," 8 (June 1955), 33-42.
An attack on O. John Rogge, former Progressive Party leader and lawyer for the Greenglasses, as being the master hand behind the Rosenberg frameup. Rogge is accused of having suppressed a document that would have helped establish the innocence of the defendants.

A243   . . . . "Toward Negro Freedom." New York: New Century, 1956. 191 pp.
A collection of essays previously published (except for the last three chapters) in the "Journal of Negro History," "the Daily Worker," the "Communist," "Masses & Mainstream," the "New Masses," "Science and Society," and "Political Affairs." The author's themes are that the Negro people have been in the main stream of revolutionary struggle against oppression in America, and that only the Marxist analysis can explain the persistence of racism in America.

A244   . . . . A Discussion with Critics, "Political Affairs," 35 (Nov. 1956), 15-23.
Widespread discussion of the past, present, and future of the CPUSA is in progress. The Party is defended against both friendly and hostile critics, some of whom call for the liquidation of the Party in the interests of the working class and socialist movements. Though these critics have not proved their case, a re-examination of Party policies is necessary.

A245   . . . . "The Truth About Hungary." New York: Mainstream Publishers, 1957. 256 pp.
A Party analysis of the events in Hungary and an apology for the entry of Soviet troops into that country on November 4, 1956. While the Hungarian people had legitimate complaints stemming from the "mistakes" of former leaders, their discontent was taken advantage of by the reactionary forces of imperialism and by Hungarian counterrevolutionary elements. The intervention of Soviet troops did not occur until this became clear.

A246   . . . . The United States and China: Peace or War? "Political Affairs," 37 (Oct. 1958), 1-20.
An attack on the China policy of the Eisenhower Administration, asserting that there will not be peace and justice until Taiwan is returned to the Chinese government. U.S. national interests, as well as peace, require that the U.S. recognize the Chinese People's Republic and withdraw its forces from Chinese territory, and that the Chinese People's Republic be seated in the UN and on its Security Council.

A247   . . . . "A History of the American People." Vol. 1. "The Colonial Era." New York: International Publishers, 1959, 158 pp. Ref. notes. Bibliog. Ind. Vol. 2. "The American Revolution, 1763-1783." New York: International Publishers, 1960. 304 pp. Ref. notes. Bibliog. Ind.
A multi-volume history of America, of which the first two volumes are listed above. The author, a leading Marxist historian, has long been identified with the Party.

A248   . . . . "On the Nature of Revolution: The Marxist Theory of Social Change." New York: New Century, 1959. 31 pp.
A discussion of revolution and social change by a leading Marxist scholar, who denies that violence is an organic part of the process of revolution or that revolution and democracy are antithetical. The differences between non-socialist and socialist revolutions are explored. (Based on a series of radio broadcasts in February-April, 1959.)

A249   . . . . (ed.). "A Symposium: Disarmament and the American Economy." New York: New Century, 1960. 64 pp.
A collection of papers presented at a Conference on Disarmament and the American Economy, held in New York City on January 30, 1960, with one paper delivered at a symposium on the same subject in Chicago in March. Papers show the economic feasibility of disarmament, the fact that depression need not result, and the constructive uses to which the wealth thus saved might be put. Participants, besides Aptheker, include James S. Allen, Robert W. Dunn, Hyman Lumer, Victor Perlo, George Wheeler, John Eaton, and Jurgen Kuczynski.

A250   . . . . "Dare We Be Free? The Meaning of the Attempt to Outlaw the Communist Party." New York: New Century, 1961. 128 pp. Bibliog.
An assertion that the Smith and McCarran Acts, with their upholding by the Supreme Court, represent heavy blows against democracy in the U.S. Their implementation will be a major step to fascist-like tyranny. Hope is placed in the public sense of injustice to reverse the decisions. Among other topics treated are informers, "Un-American Committees," subversion, Marxism and violence, and the right danger.

A251   . . . . "Mission to Hanoi." Prefaces by Tom Hayden and Staughton Lynd. New York: International Publishers, 1966. 128 pp. Bibliog.
An account of the author's ten-day trip to North Vietnam around Christmas, 1965, in company with Professor Lynd of Yale and Tom Hayden, founding president of Students for a Democratic Society. Aptheker describes his impressions of North Vietnam, including his interview with the Prime Minister. Attacking the "insane" U.S. policy of aggression, he calls on the U.S. to stop bombing North Vietnam and get out of the area. The war, in his view, is now predominantly waged by the U.S., with support of its Saigon puppets, against the people in North and South Vietnam.

A252 ARCHER, Gleason L. "On the Cuff." Boston: Suffolk University Press, 1944. 249 pp.
Criticism of Roosevelt's New Deal for deficit spending, bureaucracy, and radical attacks on individual liberty. Chapter 10, pp. 140-64, deals with "Communistic Activities in America." Pointing to parallels between Party and New Deal objectives, the author implies that the communist program is being steadily advanced by the Administration's vast bureaucracy.

A253 ARENDT, Hannah. The Ex-Communists, "Commonweal," 57 (March 20, 1953), 595-99.
An analysis of the differences between "former" communists and "ex-" communists. The ex-communist dichotomizes the world into faith and counter-faith, whereas the former communist does so into freedom and tyranny, or else points to a plurality of forces. The faith-counter-faith dichotomy leads to an exaltation of the informant, an assertion that the end justifies the means, and advocacy of methods inimical to freedom.

A254 ARMFIELD, Eugene. The Second Writers' Congress, "Saturday Review of Literature," 16 (June 12, 1937), 7 ff.
A review of the Congress that closed June 6, 1937, with D. O. Stewart as president. The only political notion advocated was democratic opposition to fascism and reaction, with emphasis on Spain. The temper of the Congress was lethargic, and the left-wing literary movement seemed ingrown.

A255 ARMSTRONG, Arnold B. [pseud.]. "Parched Earth." New York: Macmillan, 1934. 430 pp.
A propagandistic novel about pioneers in the Tontos Valley of Southern California who are led in a strike by a communist organizer against the opposition of the local bourgeoisie.

A256 ARMSTRONG, O. K. Treason in the Textbooks, "American Legion Magazine," 29 (Sept. 1940), 8-9 ff.
A listing of 71 textbooks found by the Americanism Commission of the American Legion to be subversive. Advocates of progressive education seek to debunk our national heroes and create opinions favorable to collectivism and socialist control. Advocating a Dies Committee investigation, the author urges parents to investigate and bring pressure on school boards where Un-American texts are used.

A257 ARNOLD, John, and HARRIS, Leon. "It's Happening in New York: Anti-Semitism Must Be Stopped." New York: New York State Jewish Buro, Communist Party, n.d. [1938?]. 16 pp.
An account of the rise of organized anti-Semitism in New York City, held to be a tool of the Tory open-shoppers and isolationists. A call for unity of all Jews and support of progressive candidates, most importantly those of the American Labor Party and the Communist Party, as a means of fighting anti-Semitism.

A258 ARNOLD, J. R.; KALVEN, Harry, Jr.; and UREY, Harold. "The Implications of the Oppenheimer Case." (University of Chicago Round Table) Chicago: University of Chicago Press, 1954. 23 pp.
Agreeing that Oppenheimer is loyal, University of Chicago faculty members disapprove of the finding by the Grey Board that Oppenheimer is a security risk; they argue that this decision, rather than insuring our nation's security, will only damage and undermine it. Selections from the hearings and from the report of the security board are included.

A259 ARNOLD, Thurman. The Case Against the Federal Loyalty Program. Pp. 53-74 in "The Strengthening of American Political Institutions," by A. S. Mike Monroney, and others. Ithaca, N.Y.: Cornell University Press, 1949.
A leading Washington attorney, formerly Assistant Attorney General and federal judge, asserts that the loyalty program is destroying American political institutions. He cites the motion picture blacklist and the discharge of Dorothy Bailey from a government position as disloyal, solely on the basis of secret information that she was not permitted to learn about. ("Additional Thoughts on the Federal Loyalty Program," by Arthur E. Sutherland, Jr., appears on pp. 74-78.)

A260 ARTISTS' FRONT TO WIN THE WAR. "Program Held at Carnegie Hall, October 16, 1942." New York: n.publ., 1942. 12 pp.
Program of a meeting held in Carnegie Hall, with Charles Chaplin as honorary chairman and Sam Jaffee as chairman. The program contains a list of hundreds of sponsors from the theatre, the music world, literature, science, and education, plus statements by prominent people calling for opening a second front.

A261 ASCOLI, Max. Our Political D.P.'s, "Reporter," 2 (April 25, 1950), 9-11.
The editor of "Reporter" takes issue with Isaac Deutscher's view, expressed in the same issue, that ex-communists should observe rather than take part in political affairs. The ex-communists, Ascoli asserts, are the ones who understand freedom, since conscience made them revolt.

A262 ASHE, David I. The Expulsion of Communists Upheld, "American Federationist," 57 (July 1950), 21-22.
A discussion, by the attorney for the Brotherhood of Painters, Decorators and Paperhangers, of the New York Supreme Court's decision upholding the union's expulsion of three members solely because of their communist affiliations. This decision opens the way for all unions to rid themselves of this scourge.

A263 ASHEIM, Lester. Layman vs. Librarian, "Library Journal," 80 (Feb. 1, 1955), 253-58.
A report on an exchange of letters between the librarian author and an intelligent layman as to whether procommunist books should be allowed on library shelves. They concluded that libraries should include materials presenting the communist viewpoint, along with all other shades of opinion on controversial issues.

A264 ASSOCIATION OF AMERICAN UNIVERSITIES. Policy of Colleges Toward Communist Teachers, "U.S. News & World Report," 34 (April 10, 1953), 65-67.
A statement, signed by the heads of 37 leading universities, on the nature of a university and the responsibilities of faculties. Membership in the Communist Party makes integrity and independence impossible and extinguishes the right to a university position. Where no law is violated, however, discipline is a university responsibility that should not be assumed by political authority.

A265 ASSOCIATION OF THE BAR OF THE CITY OF NEW YORK, Committee on Federal Legislation. "Report on Internal Security Act of 1950 (McCarran Act)." New York: The Association, 1950. 24 pp. App.
An outline and brief discussion of the McCarran Act, passed by Congress over the President's veto, covering its provisions on control of communist organizations and

members, security, immigration and deportation, naturalization, and emergency detention. The report does not consider the desirability or undesirability of the substantive provisions. The appendix contains an outline of the legislation.

A266 ASSOCIATION OF THE BAR OF THE CITY OF NEW YORK, Committee on Federal Legislation. "Report on Proposed 'Subversive Activities Control Act, 1949' (S.2311, 81st Congress)." New York: The Association, 1950. 15 pp.
While mindful of the meance of communism, the committee unanimously opposes enactment because of the bill's sedition provisions. A majority also disapprove either because the harm to our free society would outweigh the limited effectiveness against communism, or because the measure is undesirable in any form.

A267 .... "Report and Recommendations of the Special Committee on the Matter of Communist Lawyers." New York: The Association, 1955. 18 pp.
The committee recommends approval of the present policy of preventing the admission of communists to the bar, calls for disciplinary action against communist lawyers, favors the disbarment of lawyers engaged in communist activities, and calls for investigation where a lawyer invokes the Fifth Amendment in a proper inquiry as to communist activities. (Some, but not all, of these recommendations were approved by the Association.)

A268 .... "Report of the Special Committee on the Federal Loyalty-Security Program." New York: Dodd, Mead, 1956. 301 pp. App. Ind.
A review of the entire personnel security system, prepared by a special committee of the New York Bar Association. The communist threat is analyzed, and the need for vigilance in international security is emphasized. After describing and analyzing the specific personnel security programs in force, the committee presents its conclusions and recommendations for improving the program. Appendices contain texts of statutes, orders, and regulations relating to the personnel security programs.

A269 .... "Freedom to Travel: Report of the Special Committee to Study Passport Procedures." New York: Dodd, Mead, 1958. 144 pp. App. Ind.
A discussion of U.S. passport policies, whether by administrative regulation or statutory proposal, restricting the freedom of citizens to travel outside the U.S. Passports have been refused to Party members or those under its control, or to those whose travel would knowingly advance the communist movement. These grounds are criticized by the committee, which would restrict travel only where it would constitute a danger to U.S. national security.

A270 ATHEARN, Clarence R. How an Anti-Red Committee Works, "New Republic," 87 (May 13, 1936), 8-10.
A former employee of the U.S. Chamber of Commerce's Committee on Combating Subversive Activities criticizes the committee's methods, particularly attacking its chairman, Felix Marcus McWhirter, an Indianapolis banker, for seeking to connect President G. Bromley Oxnam of De Pauw University with radicalism and communistic activity.

AUERBACH, Sol. See ALLEN, James S.

A271 AUSTIN, John. Reorganizing the Fur Workers, "New Masses," 3 (Dec. 1927), 14-16.
A caustic account of the efforts of the AFL to defeat the progressive leadership of the fur workers in New York City by setting up a dual union and seeking, with the aid of employers and gangsters, to force workers to register with it. As a result, wages are being cut, sweat shops are increasing, and the workers are helpless.

A272 AUSUBEL, Nathan. "Jewish Culture in America: Weapon for Jewish Survival and Progress." New York: New Century, 1948. 32 pp.
A communist analysis of Jewish culture in America. Rejecting bourgeois assimilationism, the author calls for an identification with the progressive struggles of the Jewish people. He urges Jews to infuse Jewish life with new hope and meaning, and to stand with other progressive Americans to preserve world peace.

A273 AVERY, Andrew. "The Communist Fifth Column; What's the Truth About It and What Isn't." Chicago: Chicago Journal of Commerce, 1946. 47 pp.
Reprints of articles that appeared between June 24 and July 11, 1946, in the "Journal of Commerce," exposing communist influence in labor and liberal organizations. Affected unions, Party fronts, and individuals are listed, and a program to combat infiltration is presented.

A274 .... Murray as Peace Maker in CIO, "New Leader," 29 (Oct. 5, 1946), 5.
A report of rumors that Philip Murray may give up the presidency of the CIO. There are conflicting reports that Murray does not believe high CIO officers to be communists, and that he would feel freer to fight them if he were not CIO president. The September 16 issue of "CIO News" was the most procommunist one within memory.

A275 .... "Communist Power in U.S. Industry." Chicago: Chicago Journal of Commerce, 1947. 61 pp.
Reprint of 15 articles on communists in labor unions that appeared in the Chicago "Journal of Commerce," January 13 to 31, 1947. The author gives particular attention to unions in the electrical, farm equipment, packinghouse, and fur industries, among others, as well as to communist power in the national CIO office. Criticizing business for tolerating Reds out of self-interest, he presents a program for combatting them in unions.

A276 AXELROD, Donald. How Red Is the Teachers Union? "Common Sense," 9 (Feb. 1940), 20-22.
An appraisal of communist influence in the American Federation of Teachers, which has been under attack in conservative publications and hurt by the resignation of well-known anticommunists. Though the New York City branch is dominated by communists, the national organization, since the Nazi-Soviet pact and the election of George Counts as president, is not.

A277 AXTELLE, George E. Should Communists Teach in American Universities? "Educational Forum," 13 (May 1949), 425-32.
An assertion that communists should be allowed to teach, provided that they are otherwise competent, in order to have an informed citizenry in a democracy. A free and critical atmosphere is the best protection against error. Freedom of ideas, teaching, and discussion are essential to self-rule. (For a contrary view see Raymond B. Allen, "Communists Should Not Teach in American Colleges," in the same issue.)

A278 .... Communism and Academic Freedom, "Standard," 36 (Dec. 1949), 99-107.
An argument by a professor of education at New York University against excluding members of the Communist Party as such from teaching. Denying that Party discipline automatically makes traitors and liars out of members, Axtelle points to the constant procession in and out of the Party, to the danger that reactionary forces would intimidate liberals, and to the disastrous effects of political control of thought.

B

B1 "H.B." Unemployment—An Old Struggle under New Conditions, "Communist," 17 (May 1938), 419-28.
A survey of the unemployment due to the current recession. The working class now rejects the inevitability of unemployment, placing responsibility on the business interests. The program to alleviate unemployment includes unemployment insurance and public works.

B2 BAARSLAG, Esther. Pity the Poor Witness, "American Mercury," 81 (Nov. 1955), 5-10.
An account of abuse directed by witnesses at congressional hearings against those who question them about communist affiliation. Every chairman of an investigating committee, and especially Senator McCarthy, suffered outrageous insults from Fifth Amendment communists. Their prime target is the person who assists the government with information about the communist conspiracy.

B3 BAARSLAG, Karl. "Communist Trade Union Trickery Exposed: A Handbook of Communist Tactics and Techniques." Washington, D.C.: Argus, 1947, 80 pp.
A former general chairman of the Radio Officers Union, AFL, drawing on his own experience, tells how to identify communists and how to defeat them in unions. He describes such communist techniques as factional organization, character assassination, terror, and parliamentary maneuvering, and outlines ways to combat them. Besides organization, courage, and intelligence, an anticommunist group must have a constructive union program.

B4 . . . . How to Spot a Communist, "American Legion Magazine," 42 (Jan. 1947), 9-11 pp.
A listing of communist tactics to help others identify Party members and sympathizers. Tactics discussed include use of paper organizations to pack meetings, united front activities, denunciation of others as company spies or fascists, and use of smears to discredit enemies of the Party. Readers are warned against crypto-communists, non-Party members who follow its line.

B5 . . . . Slick Tricks of the Commies, "American Legion Magazine," 42 (Feb. 1947), 19-21 ff.
A discussion of communist tactics in unions and other organizations, including disciplined fractions to undermine confidence in noncommunist officers, secret caucuses, seating arrangements to maximize influence or disrupt meetings, filibustering and passing Party-line resolutions after others have left, and use of phony opposition slates to split the anticommunist vote.

B6 . . . . 17 Ways of Spotting the Communist Racket, "Plain Talk," 1 (April 1947), 31-34.
A listing of 17 telltale characteristics by which communists may be identified. Among them are defense of the Soviet Union, use of blackmail, direction of expenditures to Party members, "divide and conquer" tactics, false accusations, kangaroo courts, the innuendo, control of meetings through tedium, phony opposition, and use of the smear.

B7 BACHRACH, Marion. Bail Granted! "Political Affairs," 27 (April 1948), 315-18.
An account of a successful hunger strike for release on bail, staged by five "political prisoners" who were held at Ellis Island on deportation charges. The five included Ferdinand Smith, Irving Potash, Charles Doyle, John Williamson, and Gerhart Eisler, the German communist. Potash and Williamson are members of the Party's National Board.

B8 . . . . "The Federal Jury Is Stacked Against You." New York: Communist Party Defense Committee, 1949. 22 pp.
An assertion that the federal jury system, as evidenced in the trial of the Communist Party leaders under the Smith Act, is unjust. Statistics are cited to show that members of minority groups and manual workers, discriminated against under the system, rarely serve as federal jurors. (The author became a Smith Act defendant, as a second-string Party leader, two years later.)

B9 . . . . "You Are On Trial." New York: New Century, 1949. 18 pp.
A pamphlet urging everyone to take action against the outlawing of the Communist Party. This is declared a prelude to smashing rights of trade unions, hounding of all progressives, and destruction of all civil liberties.

B10 . . . . This Obvious Violence, "Political Affairs," 28 (Jan. 1949), 16-22.
The case of Eugene Dennis, convicted for contempt of Congress, is compared with the Dred Scott decision. Dennis, general secretary of the Party, was convicted following failure to respond to a subpoena of the House Un-American Activities Committee. Dennis' arguments that the committee exceeded its authority are reviewed.

B11 . . . . "Amnesty." New York: New Century, 1952. 23 pp.
Proposal of an amnesty program to release the members of the Communist Party imprisoned under the provisions of the Smith Act.

B12 BACHRACH, Peter. "Problems in Freedom." Harrisburg, Pa.: Stackpole, 1954. 468 pp. Table of cases. Ind.
A collection of court decisions, briefs, statements by public officials and private parties, and other materials, dealing with a series of problems in civil liberties. Topics include the clear and present danger doctrine, the Taft-Hartley oath, the federal loyalty program, the Internal Security Act of 1950, and state loyalty laws and oaths.

B13 BAIRD, William T. The Lightfoot Case, "American Socialist," 2 (April 1955), 16-17.
An account of the conviction of Claude Lightfoot, executive secretary of the Communist Party of Illinois, under the membership section of the Smith Act. No overt acts were charged against him, nor was there proof that he believed in overthrow of the government. The only accusation was

that he was a knowing member of a society advocating overthrow of the government by violence.

B14   BAKER, E. T. Maryland Betrays Its Past, "New Republic," 120 (April 25, 1949), 15-17.
A staff member of the Baltimore "Sun" summarizes the provisions of Maryland's recently enacted anti-subversion and sedition law (the Ober Act), the most comprehensive such measure yet passed in the U.S. He is disturbed by the ease with which it was passed and the lack of vocal opposition to it.

B15   BAKER, Roscoe. "The American Legion and American Foreign Policy." New York: Bookman, 1954. 329 pp. App. Bibliog. Notes. Ind.
Chapter 4, "The Legion Battle Against Communism" (pp. 74-109), describes the Legion's opposition to international communism (it opposes Soviet recognition), and to communism in the U.S. Attention is paid to the Legion's educational campaign against communist techniques, direct action by legionnaires in breaking strikes and interfering with communist meetings, and Legion efforts to outlaw the Party, bar it from the ballot, and control subversion through legislation.

B16   BAKER, Royal A. "The Menace Bolshevism." Detroit: Liberty Bell Publishers, 1919. 46 pp.
An analysis of Russian Bolshevism, warning workers against communist infiltration of American labor unions. Lenin and Trotsky are declared agents of the German war machine who successfully subverted the Kerensky government. Bolshevism is viewed as a more brutal and morally corrupt form of Prussianism, and also as an international movement and a threat to America.

B17   BAKER, Sidney. May the States, by Statute, Bar Subversive Groups from the Ballot? "Notre Dame Lawyer," 25 (Winter 1950), 319-29.
An examination of recent state laws barring the Communist Party from the ballot by name, description, or oath. Court tests indicate a trend toward unconstitutionality. Legislatures should have the right to bar from positions of trust in government those who seek to overthrow government by force and violence.

B18   BAKER, Tom [pseud.] (as told to Mabel Travis Wood). UE - A Red Time Bomb: An Ex-Communist's Story, "Plain Talk," 4 (March 1950), 18-24.
An ex-communist, who was close to the leadership of the United Electrical, Radio and Machine Workers, tells what continued communist control of that union would mean to America's defense. The communist associations of UE leaders are outlined. The UE represents the Party's last real stronghold in trade unionism.

B19   BAKER, Vincent. We Are Not Deceived, "Interracial Review," 16 (Oct. 1943), 152-54.
Negro youth are warned in a Catholic interracial publication against listening to communist claims. The Young Communist League has just decided to change its name and broaden its activity. Christian groups will launch a constructive, democratic youth movement to combat the communists.

B20   . . . . The Communists Try to Capture the Negro, "America," 70 (Nov. 20, 1943), 180-81.
A discussion of the influence of the Young Communist League and the American Youth Congress upon Negro youth from 1939 to 1942. The appeal of the Congress was based on the communist demand for Negro equality. Later the YCL formed itself into the American Youth for Democracy, with membership broadened to include noncommunists.

B21   . . . . Communism and Negro Youth Today, "America," 76 (Jan. 4, 1947), 375-76.
An account of the defeat of the communist bloc in the "Modern Trend" progressive group, a Negro social club in New York City's Harlem. The author cautions anticommunists against two other communist fronts—the American Youth for Democracy and the New York Youth Council.

B22   BALABANOFF, Angelica. John Reed's Last Days, "Modern Monthly," 10 (Jan. 1937), 3-6.
Angelica Balabanoff, who was close to Reed before his death in Moscow, tells of Reed's arguments with Zinoviev, his disgust at Zinoviev's demagogy and intrigue, and his disillusionment with the Communist International. She asserts that this disillusionment contributed to his illness and death.

B23   BALCH, D. E. Denaturalization Based on Disloyalty and Disbelief in Constitutional Principles, "Minnesota Law Review," 29 (June 1945), 405-35.
A discussion of denaturalization as related to the principles of the Constitution. Among the cases discussed is that of Schneiderman v. U.S., in which the Supreme Court in 1943 held that admitted communist activity before naturalization was not unequivocal enough to permit cancellation of naturalization.

B24   BALDINGER, Wilber H. Time to Act, Mr. Murray, "New Leader," 29 (Sept. 14, 1946), 3.
An account of recent anticommunist stirrings within the UE, the United Public Workers, the Furniture Workers, the Shoe Workers, and the National Maritime Union. Philip Murray will be forced to take a more definite stand on communist influence in the CIO.

B25   . . . . Witnesses for Hire, "Progressive," 19 (Feb. 1955), 15-17.
An exposé of the corps of professional former communists who testify as prosecution witnesses before congressional committees and at governmental trials. Though many of them may be experienced and informed, the record shows them to be perjurors and persons of unreliable character, although they have never been prosecuted for their fanciful revelations.

B26   . . . . The Endless Chase, "Progressive," 19 (June 1955), 8-11.
An account of the workings of the Internal Security Act of 1950, designed to force the CP and its fronts to expose themselves by registering with the Attorney General. The case to force the CP to register is still pending, as are cases against the Labor Youth League and other fronts. The Subversive Activities Control Board has been dignified and fair.

B27   BALDWIN, Roger N. "Should Alien Communists Be Deported for their Opinions?" New York: American Civil Liberties Union, 1931. 12 pp.
Speech by Baldwin in a March, 1931, debate with Hamilton Fish, Jr., before the Boston Foreign Policy Association. As head of a congressional committee investigating communist activities, Fish advocated deportation of all alien Party members. Opposing these views, Baldwin argued that freedom of expression was essential to orderly progress in a democracy, that suppression would drive the communist movement underground and provide no answer to the evils on which communism grows. He would deport only those guilty of overt acts of political violence or direct incitement to them.

B28   . . . . Red Scare: 1935, "Common Sense," 4 (March 1935), 8-10.

An assertion that the current anti-Red drive, while aimed primarily at the CP, could be used against strikers and other radical groups, clearing the road to fascism. Among proposed measures are a sedition act aimed at advocacy of overthrow of government by violence, barring all publications of seditious groups from the mails, making deportation easier, and creation of a federal political secret service.

B29   BALDWIN, Roger N. Liberalism and the United Front. Pp. 166-84 in "Whose Revolution?" ed. by Irving DeWitt Talmadge. New York: Howell, Soskin, 1941. 296 pp.
The director of the American Civil Liberties Union supports the united front against fascism and war, despite the Party's attempts to dominate such fronts to its own advantage. The united front is the only practicable means of uniting popular forces with any chance of overcoming reaction. A main weakness of united fronts has been communist control of the administrative machinery.

B30   BALES, James D. "Communism: Its Faith and Fallacies: An Exposition and Criticism." Foreword by Herbert A. Philbrick. Preface by Hollington K. Tong. Grand Rapids, Mich.: Baker Book House, 1962. 214 pp. Ind.
A critique of the philosophy of communism, with emphasis on atheism, dialectical and historical materialism, the dialectic and conduct, the dialectic and reality, the concept of class and class struggle, revolution, the attitude toward religion, the doctrine of morality, and the nature of the Party. Attention is focused on the international communist movement, with only scattered references specifically to this country.

B31   BALLAM, John J. The Cleveland Convention— Building a New Trade Union Center, "Communist," 8 (April 1929), 163-71.
The Trade Union Unity Convention, called by the TUEL for June 1, 1929, will consolidate all existing class-struggle unions, including new unions and revolutionary minorities in old unions. The sharpening class struggle provides the background. The Party must lead the new labor movement in all encounters with capitalism.

B32   . . . . Southern Textile Workers Organize, "Communist," 16 (Nov. 1937), 1023-36.
A review of the activity of the United Textile Workers, AFL, in the South, and a description of the CIO's entrance into the textile industry through the Textile Workers Organizing Committee. The Party will actively support the CIO and the TWOC.

        . . . . See also MOORE, John.

B33   BALLISTER, James [pseud. for Robert Minor]. Legal and Illegal Activities, "Communist," (organ of Communist Party of America), 1 (Feb.-March 1922), 12-18.
A discussion of a legal as opposed to an illegal communist party in the U.S. The Party must defeat the government's effort to confine it to underground channels, in which it is concealed from the masses. However, the Party can give up its underground machinery only after the capitalist state has been overthrown.

B34   . . . . The Blight of Purity, "Communist," (organ of the Communist Party of America), 1 (July 1922), 6-10.
Defense of the compromise theses adopted by the Central Executive Committee of the CPA on its relations to a legal political party. The compromise theses are clear that force is necessary to take over state power, and this

principle is to be made clear to those who join the Party. But one should not invite legal harrassment by using the rhetoric of violence.

B35   BAMBRICK, James J., Jr. Is There a Left-Wing Union Pattern? "Conference Board Management Record," 10 (May 1948), 274-76.
Review of a contract by a left-wing local of the Retail, Wholesale and Department Store Union, CIO, which cannot obtain union security clauses under Taft-Hartley because of failure to file noncommunist affidavits. The contract, which circumvents the law, may set a precedent for other left-wing unions.

B36   . . . . Left-Right Fight in CIO, "Conference Board Management Record," 11 (Dec. 1949), 514-16.
A review of actions of the Cleveland convention of the CIO to rid itself of communist influence. The most hotly debated resolution, passed by a ten-to-one vote, changed the constitution to bar communists from membership on the CIO's executive board. The UE was expelled, and charges filed against the ten remaining left-wing unions.

B37   BARAN, Felix. "Peace—And Price Cuts, Too! The Facts About Price Cuts in the Soviet Union." New York: New Century, 1951. 24 pp.
Living costs in the Soviet Union are said to have fallen due to the USSR peace policy, while rising in the U.S. because of our war policy. The author asserts that the Soviet Union wants peace, while the Truman government wants war.

B38   BARBASH, Jack. "Labor Unions in Action: A Study of the Mainsprings of Unionism." New York: Harper, 1948. 270 pp. Notes and ref. Ind.
A book on American trade unions with a chapter (pp 202-18) on communist unionism. The author argues that communists' views on domestic and international affairs reflect foreign policy needs of the USSR, and that the communist line in unions is a shifting strategy designed to accumulate power and maximize prestige. (This chapter was expanded and updated in the author's later book, "The Practice of Unionism.")

B39   . . . . "The Practice of Unionism." New York: Harper, 1956. 465 pp. Ref. Suggested reading. Ind.
Revision of an earlier book "Labor Unions in Action," with a chapter (pp. 324-66) on communist unionism. The author's thesis is that communists use unions as vehicles to gain power on behalf of a foreign government. He traces the development of communist union strategy, the circumstances under which communists penetrate unions, the techniques they use, and the counter-movements that arise. Sources of communists' strength and weakness in unions are analyzed.

B40   BARD, Phil. "No Jobs Today: A Story of a Young Worker in Pictures." Introduction by Robert Minor. New York: Young Communist League, n.d. [1932?]. 32 pp.
A collection of pictures for use among unemployed young workers about 1932, designed to sell the Party's "class-struggle" line of that period.

B41   . . . . "It Happens Every Day: A Story in Pictures." New York: Youth Publishers, n.d. [1933?]. 32 pp.
A collection of pictures designed to attract young people to the Communist Party during its militant "third period."

B42   BARD, Philip, and others. "Report to the Executive Committee of the American Association for the

Advancement of Science.'' New York: The Association, 1948. 77 pp. Mimeo.
A report of the Special Committee on the Civil Liberties of Scientists, criticizing secrecy as applied to science and objecting to features of the security and loyalty programs. Specific revisions of the loyalty order, conceptual as well as procedural, are recommended, along with relaxation of secrecy regulations as applied to scientists and revision of the personnel security provisions of military and atomic energy establishments. Such provisions, by slowing scientific advance, do more harm than good.

B43   BARDI, Gino. ''Are We Aryans?'' New York: Workers Library, 1939. 39 pp.
Originally published in Italian by the International Workers Order, the pamphlet is designed to counteract anti-Semitism among Italian-Americans. The author argues that the concept of pure races is false, and denies that Italians are ''Aryans.'' He lists Jewish contributions to Italian culture, attacking Italian fascist groups in the U.S. for adopting anti-Semitism.

B44   BARGERON, Carlisle. Our Communists Reconvert, ''Nation's Business,'' 33 (Sept. 1945). 80-88.
An account of the leftist postwar line of the Party, precipitated by the letter written by the French communist leader, Jacques Duclos, criticizing Browder for rewriting Marxism. The peacetime communist line is reviewed. The new declaration shows that the communists are primarily concerned with world affairs.

B45   BARMINE, Alexander. The New Communist Conspiracy, ''Reader's Digest,'' 45 (Oct. 1944). 27-33.
An ex-Soviet high official asserts that the ''dissolution'' of the Communist Party marked the beginning of an even more dangerous conspiracy to penetrate and conquer American political, social, and governmental institutions. He warns against current communist quests for power in the CIO and in liberal and New Deal groups.

B46   BARNES, Joseph. American Dream, ''Atlantic Monthly,'' 159 (Jan. 1937), 111-16.
A discussion of the Communist Party's effort to adopt traditional American issues and slogans in the popular-front period. The American dream was largely one of freedom; in a period in which social and economic problems have replaced geographical frontiers as a primary concern, the Party's appeal is on the promise of abundance, the desire for security, and a revolt against injustice.

B47   .... The Foreign Policy of the American Communist Party, ''Foreign Affairs,'' 26 (April 1948). 421-31.
An analysis of the Communist Party's foreign policy, which is devoted to vituperation rather than to development of a positive program. The Party's foreign-policy objectives are collaboration with the Soviet Union, support of new Eastern European ''democracies,'' reconstruction of coalition governments, aid to colonial peoples, and nonintervention in China.

B48   BARNES, Ralph V. National Unity and the Coming Elections, ''Communist,'' 21 (April 1942). 250-61.
The Party's main tasks in the congressional elections are to promote labor and national unity and further the war effort. The defeatists, unable openly to oppose the war, criticize America's allies and attack the trade unions. Americans must subordinate special interest to the national interest, and vote for any candidate who supports an energetic war effort.

B49   .... Inflation and Economic War Mobilization,

''Communist,'' 21 (Sept. 1942), 736-47.
The obstructionists propose to curb inflation by a wage freeze and heavy taxes on the workers. Such a program would hamper the war effort without stopping inflation. The Party proposes that inflation be curbed by high taxes on profits, price control, and rationing, and that war mobilization be improved by central planning of the economy.

B50   .... Lessons of the Primary Elections, ''Communist,'' 21 (Oct. 1942), 819-25.
Many appeasers and defeatists won in the primaries. Their success was due to the Administration's hesitation to open a second front, which led to widespread apathy. The Communist Party favors a coalition government of all the win-the-war political leaders. It intends to back all win-the-war candidates in the coming election.

B51   BARNETT, J. On the Draft Program of the United Farmers' League, ''Communist,'' 12 (Nov. 1933), 1140-51.
A discussion of the UFL draft program, which bases its work on the class struggle, stands for an alliance with the city proletariat, and is learning to speak in farmers' language. A broad Party program in rural areas is proposed.

B52   .... Leninism and Practical Work Among the Farmers, ''Communist,'' 13 (Jan. 1934), 39-46.
A report on the Party-supported Farmers Second National Conference held in Chicago, and attended by 702 delegates from 36 states. The conference adopted a genuinely revolutionary program, and opposed creation of farmer-labor and liberal third-party movements. However, the middle-class composition of the farmers' movement must be overcome.

B53   BARNETT, James. The Struggle Against Capitalist Rationalization, ''Communist,'' 9 (Sept. 1930), 795-804.
Capitalist rationalization sharpens the fundamental contradictions of capitalism. It beats down the conditions of work and stimulates class consciousness and political understanding. Whereas capitalist rationalization pushes the system of exploitation to destruction, socialist rationalization leads the proletariat to a new society.

B54   .... ''Speeding Up the Workers.'' New York: International Pamphlets, 1932. 31 pp.
A denunciation of the systematic speed-up to which workers have been subjected in the open-shop drive after World War I, as part of capitalist rationalization. The author condemns the enemies within labor's ranks who aid this movement, and calls for its defeat through organization of militant industrial unions.

B55   BARNETT, John. The United Farmers League Convention, ''Communist,'' 13 (Aug. 1934), 810-19.
A discussion of the first national convention of the United Farmers League, pointing out strengths and weaknesses in its platform and organization. The main danger is that the organization is overweighted with middle-class farmers, who believe that New Deal policies, cooperative schemes, and a farmer-labor party will solve farmers' problems.

B56   .... ''The Farmers' Way Out: Life Under a Workers' and Farmers' Government.'' New York: Workers Library, 1935. 31 pp.
An attack on the New Deal's agricultural policies, calling for control of the country by soviets of factory workers, toiling farmers, soldiers and sailors. The author describes the soviet government that could be set up, and

attacks the farmer-labor movement, asserting that his program can be accomplished only by the Communist Party.

B57   BARNETT, John. Unity of the Farming Masses—A Paramount Issue, "Communist," 14 (Feb. 1935), 175-83.
In the past two years the New Deal and progressive movements have been directing farmer discontent into harmless channels. The CP must take leadership into its own hands, fight for the most exploited sharecroppers and farmers, and work to unite the toiling rural masses and the workers against the New Deal.

B58   BARNETTE, Henlee H. "C o m m u n i s m: W h o? What? Why?" Nashville, Tenn.: Broadman Press, 1962, 64 pp. Bibliog.
Questions and answers about communism throughout the world. Chapter 6 on "Communism in the United States" (pp. 42-48) deals with Party organization, its link to Moscow, Party strength, communist fronts, anticommunist legislation, the Party press, activities among the clergy and Negroes, espionage, and the Party's aims.

B59   BARON, Rose. "They Gave Their Freedom!" New York: International Labor Defense, 1935. 30 pp.
An appeal for financial and moral support of the Prisoners' Relief Department of ILD, which helps the families of "victims of class justice." Letters of thanks from widows and orphans are included, along with an analysis of the "frame-up" system and histories of famous political prisoners still in jail.

B60   BARRETT, Edward L. "The Tenney Committee." Ithaca: Cornell University Press, 1951. 400 pp. App. Ind.
One of the Cornell series on civil liberties, this book studies the Committee on Un-American Activities of the California Legislature from 1941 to 1951, evaluating its procedures and results. The author describes the origins of the legislative investigation of subversion in California under Senator Jack Tenney, analyzing the hearings and reports, and describing the various investigations. He concludes that the committee, despite its sincerity, frequently operated with irresponsible zeal. The harmful effects of the Committee's activities are evident, while its achievements in pinpointing communists are negligible.

B61   BARRETT, William. Culture Conference at the Waldorf, "Commentary," 7 (May 1949), 487-93.
A report on the Cultural and Scientific Conference for World Peace held in New York City in March 1947, emphasizing the confusion of many liberals in the face of a communist-dominated affair. The Conference, by hand-picking the participants and avoiding anticommunists, prevented any genuine intellectual exchange. No American organization is adequate to fight Stalinist propaganda on an intellectual level.

B62   BARRON, Samuel. The Communists Fight for the Nation, "Jewish Life," 2 (Oct. 1948), 10-12.
A presentation of the communist view of the class nature of American "democracy," and of the objectives of monopoly capitalism and American imperialism. The two-party system of Big Business is denounced, and support urged for the Progressive Party. The Communist Party must nevertheless continue to exist, because of its advanced Marxist outlook.

B63   BARRY, Dennis P. Communism and Academic Freedom, "American Mercury," 78 (June 1954), 116-21.
A veteran of the Korean War asserts that communists

have no claim by their own beliefs to any rights or freedoms, including academic freedom. A communist teacher is an agent with a mission, who violates the rights of his students.

B64   BARRY, George Francis. The Commissar and the Free Lance Writer, "Catholic World," 164 (Jan. 1947), 328-35.
Denunciation of a plan, proposed by James Cain in the organ of the communist-dominated Screen Writers' Guild, for formation of an American Authors' Authority, to which all American writers would have to submit their work before offering it for publication. Free-lance writers are fighting this plan. Communists have infiltrated American publications, using WPA writing projects for recruitment and training.

B65   BARTH, Alan. "The Loyalty of Free Men." New York: Viking, 1951. 253 pp. Ind.
An analysis of the assault upon freedom of thought and speech in the U.S. today. While understanding the conspiratorial nature of American communism and approving of counterespionage, the author opposes any restraint upon advocacy of communist ideas and criticizes the House Un-American Activities Committee for questioning the right to silence and privacy. He discusses the congressional committees, loyalty programs, and assaults upon academic freedom, by which the nation has lost portions of its freedom, and deplores the easy identification of dissent with disloyalty. Only by working toward, not against, individual freedom, can America command the loyalty of all free men.

B66   . . . . The High Cost of Security, "Reporter," 5 (July 24, 1951), 13-16.
The loyalty program is a doubtful protection of national security and a threat to civil liberties. Suspicion and ungrounded fear may disqualify a person for government employment, and the need for him to prove his innocence diminishes individual rights. A sober, objective assessment of the loyalty program by an impartial commission is needed.

B67   . . . . McCarran's Monopoly, "Reporter," 5 (Aug. 21, 1951), 25-28.
As chairman of the judiciary subcommittee on Internal Security, Senator McCarran has surveillance over the Subversive Activities Control Board and power to thwart the President's attempt to set up an independent Commission on Internal Security and Individual Rights. He is setting up a sort of private Gestapo on loyalty matters.

B68   . . . . "Government by Investigation." New York: Viking, 1955. 231 pp. Ind.
A critical view of the use by Congress of its power to investigate, asserting that this power cannot properly be used to expose individuals and voluntary organizations, to embarrass dissent, or to silence speech. Congress does not need to expose individuals in order to expose the dimensions of the communist problem. The Smith Act of 1940, the McCarran Internal Security Act of 1950, and the Communist Control Act of 1954 all breached the freedom that should properly be accorded voluntary associations in the U.S.

B69   BARTLETT, Frances P. The Atomic Brain Trust and the Young Scientists, "American Mercury," 81 (July 1955), 75-78.
An attack on the scientists, educators, and commentators who have come to Dr. Oppenheimer's defense. The records of such Oppenheimer defenders as Dr. Sidney Weinbaum and Dr. Linus Pauling are revealed. Educators are warned against coddling potential traitors, even though they may be top scientists.

B70   BARTON, Ann. "Mother Bloor." New York: Workers Library, 1935. 25 pp.
A biographical sketch of a woman who had been part of the fibre and legend of the Communist Party since its founding in Chicago in 1919. Nearly 73 years of age, she is pointed to as an inspiring example of one who has been woman, mother, and class fighter. (For a later edition, following adoption of the popular-front line, see the author's "Mother Bloor: The Spirit of 76.")

B71   . . . . "Mother Bloor: The Spirit of 76." New York: Workers Library, 1937. 31 pp.
An account of the life of the famous communist organizer and agitator, somewhat different from the 1935 pamphlet (see the author's "Mother Bloor.") Emphasis is changed with the change in Party line: now Mother Bloor is one with the great patriotic fighters for freedom in the American tradition.

B72   BARY, Arthur. The Denver Elections, "Political Affairs," 26 (Jan. 1947), 47-53.
A report on the role of the Communist Party in the election of John Carroll to Congress. The Party joined other progressive forces in an independent political organization that sponsored Carroll. This organization will now concentrate on insuring that the Democratic Party nominates progressive candidates.

B73   BASS, Cyrus. "Joe McCarthy: Apostle of Communism." Chicago: Atomic Age Publishers, 1954. 46 pp.
An assertion that Senator McCarthy actually fosters communism under the guise of fighting it. The author shows how the communists helped elect him in 1946; how he confused and immobilized the American people, while the communists sought to convert the rest of the world; and how, by his activities in the Fort Monmouth investigation, he has wrecked that vital installation more thoroughly than any Soviet saboteur could have done. The author concludes that McCarthy's record would convict him, before his own investigating committee, of being a communist agent or dupe.

B74   BASSETT, Theodore R. "Why the Negro People Should Vote Communist." New York: Workers Library, n.d. [1940]. 15 pp.
An electioneering pamphlet for Browder and Ford addressed to Negroes. The author terms the Party the only consistent defender of the political, economic, and civil rights of the Negro people. The Party stands for the right of self-determination of the Black Belt, and the repeal of fascist conscription, which would impose a new despotism on the Negro masses. (Written during the "isolationist" period of the Nazi-Soviet pact.)

B75   . . ., and BERRY, A. W. The Negro People and the Struggle for Peace, "Communist," 19 (April 1940), 320-35.
The Democrats and Republicans, who support Jim Crow, are trying to win Negro support for a war in which the Negro would die, but in which only the capitalists would win freedom. The CP, though small, has made unique contributions to Negro rights.

B76   . . . . The Third National Negro Congress, "Communist," 14 [19] (June 1940), 542-53.
A description of the Congress, held in Washington, April 26-28. President A. Philip Randolph is attacked for anti-communist and anti-Soviet slanders, and the top leadership of Negro reformist organizations is criticized for yielding to the war aims of American imperialism. Weaknesses in the work of the Congress are pointed out.

B77   . . . . The Negro People and the Fight for Jobs, "Communist," 20 (Sept. 1941), 805-17.
Description of an intensified drive led by the National Negro Congress and other Negro groups to counter discriminatory hiring policies. The trade unions are urged to assist Negroes to secure jobs.

B78   . . . . The New People's Party and the Negro People, "Political Affairs," 27 (July 1948), 600-8.
A pre-convention article on the draft resolution for the Party's national convention, discussing developments in the Negro liberation movement resulting from the rise of the Wallace party. There is growing Negro mass support for Wallace and the new party, though some Negro leaders favor Truman. Concrete programs which embody their demands and struggles for them can win the vote of the Negro people for Wallace.

B79   BATT, Dennis E. Situation in the Metal Industry, "Labor Herald," 1 (May 1922), 8-9.
Decrying the small number of workers organized in metals by the craft unions, the author finds organization hampered by high initiation fees, separate craft jurisdiction, industry financial power, and the class-collaboration attitude of union leaders. Progressives must fight within the unions for amalgamation and eventual worker-control of the industry.

B80   BEACON PRESS. "Bishop Oxnam and the Un-American Activities Committee." Boston: 1953. 45 pp.
A collection of material dealing with Methodist Bishop G. Bromley Oxnam of Washington and the House Un-American Activities Committee. In an article in the Washington "Post," April 5, 1953, Bishop Oxnam reviewed his file released by the Committee, commenting on each item. A transcript of the American Forum of the Air program of April 26, 1953, in which Bishop Oxnam criticized and Rep. Donald L. Jackson of the Committee defended its methods, is included, along with an address by Bishop Oxnam in Washington, May 25, 1953.

B81   BEAL, Fred E. "Proletarian Journey: New England, Gastonia, Moscow." New York: Hillman-Curl, 1937. 352 pp.
Autobiography of the communist leader of the Gastonia, N.C., textile strike, who fled to the Soviet Union to escape a prison sentence. Disillusioned by what he saw of Russian communism in operation, he returned to the U.S., where he was bitterly attacked by the Party. Pages 109-221 describe the Gastonia strike, and the role that he and the Party played in it. The latter part of the book deals with the Soviet Union.

B82   . . . . I Was a Communist Martyr, "American Mercury," 42 (Sept. 1937), 32-45.
The story of an American communist, leader of the Gastonia, N.C., textile strike of 1929. Sentenced to 17 to 20 years in prison following the killing of a police chief, Beal and six fellow-communist defendants jumped bail and went to the USSR. There Beal and four of the others were quickly disillusioned by the labor slavery they saw.

B83   . . . . "The Red Fraud: An Exposé of Communism." Introd. by Ferdinand Lundberg. Preface by James T. Farrell. New York: Tempo Publishers, 1949. 86 pp.
An account of the career of the author in the labor movement and in the Party, of his leadership of the Gastonia, N.C., textile strike of 1929 and his sentence to 20 years in prison following the killing of the local police chief, of his flight to Russia and his subsequent disillusionment with communism. He returned to the U.S., even though this meant serving his prison term. (Part of the material of

the author's "Proletarian Journey" is included.)

B84 BEALLE, Morris A. "Red Rat Race." Washington, D.C.: Columbia Publishing Co., 1953. 287 pp. Ind.
An anti-Roosevelt, anti-CIO, and anticommunist book, drawing heavily on the various hearings of the House Committee on Un-American Activities. The author asserts that communist agents are in government, labor unions, schools and colleges, publishing and the press, motion pictures and theaters, and even churches; and that Russian spy rings are infiltrating every field of American activity.

B85 BEATY, John Owen. "Iron Curtain over America." Dallas: Wilkinson Publishing Co., 1951. 268 pp. Ind.
An attack on the Democratic administrations of 1933-53, ascribing all the evils of the Democratic Party to the machinations of its East European Jewish members, who are denounced for promoting communist aims in the federal government.

B86 BECK, Carl. "Contempt of Congress: A Study of the Prosecutions Initiated by the Committee on Un-American Activities, 1945-1957." New Orleans: Hauser, 1959. 263 pp. App. Table of cases. Bibliog. Ind.
A critical review by a University of Pittsburgh professor of the procedures and the use of the contempt citation by the House Committee on Un-American Activities. Many of the cases arose from investigations of communist activities.

B87 BECK, Dave. Communism and American Labor Unions, "Vital Speeches of the Day," 17 (Dec. 1, 1950), 107-11.
The Teamsters Union, its president asserts in an address to the Commonwealth Club of San Francisco, refuses membership to communists, and expels anyone who advocates communist philosophy. Communism thrives on hunger and squalor. The problem of communism in American labor can be solved if labor and business work together.

B88 BECKER, William. The Role of Socialists and Communists in the Trade Union Movement, "Call," 13 (July 22, 1946), 3.
Responding to attacks by Philip Murray and George Addes on "outside groups" in the labor movement, a socialist distinguishes between the roles played by Stalinists and by socialists. The CP's "Stalin-first" ideology makes it an unprincipled and a continual menace to the labor movement, whereas socialists believe in union democracy and trade union principles.

B89 BECKNER, Earl R. The Trade Union Educational League and the American Labor Movement, "Journal of Political Economy," 33 (Aug. 1925), 410-31.
An account of the TUEL and its influence in the American labor movement. Though the author favors industrial unionism, he criticizes William Z. Foster for having embraced communism. He opposes dual unionism because he believes that radicals should seek to transform the AFL from within.

B90 BEDACHT, Max. The Economic Anatomy of Five Conventions, "Liberator," 7 (Aug. 1924), 13-15.
Analysis of the 1924 conventions of the Republican Party, the Democratic Party, the Conference for Progressive Political Action, the Socialist Party, and the National Farmer-Labor Party. Having recognized the need for class political action, the last of these is the most politically advanced. But the CPPA has again confused the

masses, and thus the Workers Party must run candidates in its own name.

B91 . . . . What Is Workers' Education? "Workers Monthly," 4 (April 1925), 262-63.
Capitalist education seeks to make the worker a useful tool while paralyzing his intellect. Proletarian education seeks to create proletarian consciousness and anticapitalist conventions. Workers' education cannot be nonpartisan; it must be communist education or it is nonrevolutionary.

B92 . . . . The Fourth Convention of the Workers' (Communist) Party of America, "International Press Correspondence," 5 (Sept. 24, 1925), 1056-58.
A member of the Ruthenberg "political" faction in the Workers (Communist) Party reviews the factional fight prior to and at the Party's fourth national convention. The "trade union" faction led by William Z. Foster is accused of opposing Ruthenberg's labor party policies, not on questions of principle, but in terms of personal struggles for power.

B93 . . . . The A. F. of L. Convenes Again, "Workers Monthly," 4 (Oct. 1925), 543-46.
A prediction that the coming convention of the AFL will ignore the pressing problems of the working class. Built on the basis of skilled workers, the AFL is a caste organization ideologically, not a class one, and therefore sterile and reactionary. A left wing must be crystallized within it, to challenge the procapitalist and antiproletarian leadership.

B94 . . . . Class War or Class Collaboration? "Workers Monthly," 5 (Dec. 1925), 91-93.
A discussion of the current strike of nearly 160,000 anthracite miners. Strikes are welcomed as developing workers' strength and consciousness of strength, as well as smashing the class collaborationist views of conservative trade-union leaders. John L. Lewis is attacked for keeping maintenance men at work, thereby protecting the owners' property, prolonging the strike, and betraying the workers.

B95 . . . . "The Menace of Opportunism." Chicago: Daily Worker Publishing Co., 1926. 46 pp.
An attack upon Ludwig Lore, editor of the New York "Volkzeitung," Workers (Communist) Party German language newspaper, for obstructing bolshevization of the Party. Lore is accused of avoiding the revolutionary class struggle, opposing the highly disciplined organizational form of the Party, and objecting to alliances with farmers and the creation of shop nuclei. Loreism, like all opportunism, looks for every means to avoid revolution, and hence should be eliminated from the Party.

B96 . . . . Do Workers Pay Taxes? "Workers Monthly," 5 (Jan. 1926), 103-7.
A refutation of the view held by some Marxists that workers pay no taxes. Taxes are an indirect means used by capitalists to force wages down, as well as a method of forcing the exploited to pay for the system of exploitation. Those who own the government should pay for the expenses of government.

B97 . . . . What Do the Elections Mean to Us? "Workers Monthly," 5 (Sept. 1926), 486-88.
An explanation of the reasons for communist participation in. election campaigns. Because workers are interested in politics only at this time, communists can then teach them that their miseries result, not from elected officials, but from the system itself. Though labor parties are

reformist, communists urge their support, to hasten the day of working-class revolt.

B98   BEDACHT, Max. After Elections—What Now? "Workers Monthly," 5 (Dec. 1926), 627-30.
A communist analysis of the 1926 election results, which show signs of the disintegration of American capitalism. In the stage of imperialism the big bourgeoisie, itself divided because of antagonistic interests, exploits all other groups in society. The exploited masses are moving toward independent political action.

B99   . . . . American Labor at Cross Roads, "Workers Monthly," 5 [6] (Feb. 1927), 726-29.
Although American workers are intensely exploited, they are ideologically backward because of their comparatively short hours and high wages. Socialists, bosses, and reactionary union leaders are seen in a united front against the class interests of American labor.

B100   . . . . C. E. Ruthenberg, "Communist," 6 (April 1927), 67-71.
Obituary of Charles E. Ruthenberg by the editor of the "Communist," who traces Ruthenberg's efforts to transform the Socialist Party into a truly revolutionary party and outlines his role in the Workers (Communist) Party. Bedacht equates true Marxism with Americanization as well as bolshevization (revolutionary struggle by the proletariat), calling Ruthenberg the leader of this movement.

B101   . . . . The Present Trend in the Labor Movement, "Communist," 6 (June 1927), 207-12.
A review of reactionary trends in the labor movement, emphasizing the need to organize the unorganized, transform craft into industrial unions, end class collaboration, and make the unions instruments of proletarian struggle.

B102   . . . . The Sixth Convention of Our Party, "Communist," 8 (March 1929), 101-7.
The Party is transforming itself from a propaganda society into a mass party of action. Its immediate task is to mobilize the working class against imperialist war. It must oppose social reformism and the right danger, fight against Trotskyism, and end factionalism.

B103   . . . . Ten Years of the Communist Party in the United States, "Communist," 8 (Sept. 1929), 481-87.
The dominant effort in the ten-year history of the Party has been to get rid of the mirage of "American exceptionalism." The history of ideological and factional battles is traced, and the Comintern credited with setting the Party on the road to bolshevization. Each wave of exodus, whether forced or voluntary, and including the latest one, has been a cleansing process.

B104   . . . . A Labor Party—Or? "Communist," 8 (Dec. 1929), 673-81.
The immediate task of communists is to develop political consciousness on the part of American workers, now rapidly drifting leftward. The labor party slogan cannot be used unqualifiedly at this time. The communists must build political united fronts from below, which requires complete bolshevization of the Party.

B105   . . . . The Major Problem Before the Seventh Convention of the C.P.U.S.A., "Communist," 9 (June 1930), 494-99.
The major task facing the Party is to transform itself from an agitational and propaganda sect into a revolutionary, mass party of action, firmly anchored in the factories, shops, and mines. Though this task of bolshevization was slowed down by factionalism, the factional struggle has now been eliminated.

B106   . . . . American Democracy on the Way to Facism, "Communist," 9 (Oct. 1930), 877-83.
The government of the U.S. is rapidly becoming fascist. Among the signs are the criminal syndicalism prosecutions, the Fish Committee and its recommendations, and the general corruption. The Party must mobilize the masses of workers against this transformation.

B107   . . . . "Anti-Soviet Lies and the Five-Year Plan: The 'Holy' Capitalist War Against the Soviet Union." New York: Workers Library, 1931. 128 pp.
An outline of USSR accomplishments, including the five-year plan, industrialization, rising living standards, workers' democracy, and cultural advances. The charge of forced labor is denounced as anti-Soviet poison. In contrast capitalism is declared to be slavery, free labor under capitalism a myth, and democracy a cloak for capitalist dictatorship. Trade with the USSR is advocated as creating jobs in the U.S. The U.S. government is charged with waging economic war against the USSR.

B108   . . .; DON, Sam; and BROWDER, Earl. "Karl Marx: 1883-1933." New York: Workers Library, 1933. 32 pp.
A pamphlet issued on the 50th anniversary of the death of Karl Marx, opposing revisionism and asserting the Party's monopoly of Marxist-Leninist orthodoxy. Bedacht commemorates Marx's life and work. Don attacks socialists, Lovestoneites, and other non-Party radicals as outside the Marxist pale. Browder defends the Party's Workers School against charges of dogmatism.

B109   . . . . Fifteen Years of Our Party, "Communist," 13 (Sept. 1934), 862-74.
A review of main developments in the life of the Party since its formation out of the left wing of the Socialist Party in 1919. Attention is paid to early divisions in the communist movement, the underground period, bolshevization, development of discipline, orientation toward the shops, defeat of the Lovestone leadership, and the laying of the basis for a mass party.

B110   . . . . The I.W.O.—Workers' Fraternalism, "Communist," 17 (June 1938), 541-52.
An account of the membership and finances of the International Workers Order as reported to its fourth national convention, with a discussion of the role of fraternal organizations in the labor movement. Despite its largely proletarian membership, the fraternal movement has been a conservative force in America. The IWO mission is to make the movement a progressive force.

    . . . . See also MARSHALL, James A.

B111   BEECHER, John. The Sharecroppers Union in Alabama, "Social Forces," 13 (Oct. 1934), 124-32.
An analysis of the communists' organization of the Sharecroppers Union, following the Sixth World Congress of the communists in 1928. The mob violence that resulted in Alabama is described. Though white fear and hatred have been intensified, the movement might have been exploited as race war even if it had been conservative in social ideology.

B112   . . . . California: There She Goes, "Nation," 172 (June 30, 1951), 603-5.
A discussion of California's Levering Act, which makes all public employees civil defense workers and requires of them, among other restrictions, a loyalty oath. The author, an instructor in social sciences at San Francisco

State College, refused to sign the oath, viewing it as a weapon for the destruction of free institutions and popular rights. The public mood in California is like that which has always preceded fascism.

B113 BEECHER, Katherine. "Wives or Widows?" New York: Women's Division, New York Council, American Peace Mobilization, n.d. [1941?]. 31 pp.
A pamphlet addressed to women, opposing American entry into World War II. Written shortly before Hitler's invasion of the USSR, the pamphlet emphasizes the loss of sons and husbands, the high cost of living in wartime, and the impact of war preparations on housing and rents. It opposes the conscription of women, and urges the U.S. to keep out of the war.

B114 BEFFEL, John Nicholas. Political Prisoners, 1931, "Nation," 132 (April 29, 1931), 475-76.
An enumeration of political prisoners, their offenses, and the statutes under which they were convicted. Pennsylvania, California, and Oregon are the principal prosecutors of political heresy, with members of the CP their chief victims.

B115 BEGEMAN, Jean. Loyalty Tests for Teachers, "New Republic," 121 (Oct. 10, 1949), 15-16.
A discussion of the spread of state-prescribed teachers' oaths, including both pledges to support the Constitution and oaths that one is not a communist or communist sympathizer. The loyalty oaths have brought fear and confusion to the ranks of teachers.

B116 . . . . The California Loyalty Oath. 'New Republic," 122 (March 27, 1950), 11-12.
An account of the loyalty oath controversy at the University of California, an aftermath of the work of a state legislative committee. The faculty refused to sign oaths that they were not Communist Party members, though they accepted a compromise proposal that they endorse university regulations prohibiting employment of communists.

B117 BEGUN, Isidore, and DIGBY, Robert. The Farmers and National Unity, "Communist," 22 (Oct. 1943), 934-43.
An appeal for increased government aid to farmers both during and after the war. The smallest progress in war adjustment is said to have been in agriculture; the reactionary farm bloc in Congress is blamed for alleged exploitation of farmers.

B118 BEICHMAN, Arnold. Communist Morale Sabotage —And How to Combat It, "New Leader," 33 (Aug. 12, 1950), 9-10.
Communists have denounced socialists and liberals to the press and authorities as "communists" in order to weaken morale, and may do so more frequently in the future. We must protect ourselves from these professional revolutionaries by cooperating with security agencies, while the FBI must show more political sophistication.

B119 BEIER, Norman S., and SAND, Leonard B. The Rosenberg Case: History and Hysteria, "American Bar Association Journal," 40 (Dec. 1954), 1046-50.
A defense of the manner in which the Rosenbergs were tried by Judge Irving Kaufman, written by two of his former law clerks. The Communist Party has tried to convince the public that the two spies were innocent scapegoats of a fear-ridden, prejudiced society. The authors defend Judge Kaufman and the fairness of American justice.

B120 BEIRNE, Joseph A. " 'Communism Is a Criminal Conspiracy': Statement of Joseph A. Beirne, President of Communications Workers of America-CIO, to the Task Force of the Senate Subcommittee on Internal Security." Communications Workers of America, 1954. 15 pp.
The president of the Communications Workers of America opposes the Communist Control Bill of 1954 on the ground that it will not punish communists, but serve to destroy legitimate American unions. American labor has remained relatively free of communist domination because it knows that communism is a criminal conspiracy against our way of life.

B121 BELFRAGE, Cedric. "A Faith to Free the People." New York: Dryden Press, 1944. 317 pp. App.
A sympathetic biography of Claude Williams, Presbyterian minister active in the International Labor Defense, the Workers Alliance, and the Southern Tenant Farmers Union in Arkansas and Tennessee, and for a time Presbyterian industrial chaplain in Detroit. Disillusioned with institutionalized Christianity, Williams organized the People's Institute of Applied Religion to carry on his work for labor organization, interracial cooperation, and reform. (This book, originally published in England in 1939 under the title, "Let My People Go," and in the U.S. in 1940 as "South of God," was brought up to date for the present publication. The author, editor of the "National Guardian," was deported to his native Britain in 1955 as a former member of the Communist Party.)

B122 . . . . "The Frightened Giant: My Unfinished Affair with America." London: Secker & Warburg, 1957. 235 pp. App.
An account of his experiences by an author and newspaper man, long resident in America, who was deported to his native Britain in 1955 as a former member of the Communist Party. A founder and editor of the "National Guardian" newsweekly, Belfrage refused to answer questions as to his political views and associations for the Immigration Service and House and Senate investigating committees. He writes of his jail experiences, his defiance of Senator McCarthy, and his work with the "National Guardian," particularly in publicizing the Rosenberg case.

B123 BELL, Daniel; MacDONALD, Dwight; and WRIGHT, Quincy. "How to Deal with Communist Subversion." Chicago: University of Chicago Press, 1952. 18 pp.
Transcript of a radio discussion on the University of Chicago Round Table, plus a selection from an article by Robert E. Cushman on "American Civil Liberties in Mid-Twentieth Century." The participants disagree on the extent to which communists should be barred from employment, and what to do about known communists in positions of influence not affecting security.

B124 BELL, Daniel. The Origins of American Communism, "New Leader," 35 (May 26, 1952), 15-18.
An account of the early years of the American communist movement, from the formation of rival parties in 1919 until the expulsion of the Trotskyists in 1928 and of Lovestone and his followers in 1929. The various factional rivalries and splits are reviewed, and the control from Moscow is emphasized. After 1929 the CPUSA was Moscow's pliant tool.

B125 . . . . Communism and Intellectuals, "Jewish Labor Committee Outlook," 1 (Autumn 1954), 5-8.
An analysis of the role of the intellectual in Bolshevik theory, and of the appeals of communism to intellectuals.

In the U.S. intellectuals are important to the communist movement because it has not become a mass working class movement. Reactionaries now seek to drive a wedge between intellectuals and the rest of society, thus driving intellectuals into the hands of the communists.

B126 BELL, James. Eight out of 12 Vote Hiss Guilty, "Life," 27 (July 18, 1949), 37 ff.
An account of the June-July 1949 trial of Alger Hiss, charged with perjury. The reporter reviews the evidence and testimony submitted at the trial which led to a hung jury. (The real issue in the case was whether or not Hiss had furnished classified government documents to a Soviet espionage ring in Washington.)

B127 BELL, Laird. Are We Afraid of Freedom? "American Association of University Professors Bulletin," 35 (Summer 1949), 301-12.
A statement by the chairman of the Board of Trustees of the University of Chicago in response to a resolution of the state legislature of Illinois calling for an investigation of communist indoctrination at the University. Denying that any such indoctrination occurs or that any communist professor is employed, Bell defends the University's tradition of freedom. A statement by Vice-President Lynn A. Williams, Jr., of the University is included.

B128 BELL, Tom. "The Movement for World Trade Union Unity." Chicago: Daily Worker Publishing Co., 1925. 48 pp.
An appeal for world trade union unity, following the example of the British workers in the Anglo-Russian Unity Committee and the leadership of the Red International of Labor Unions. The class-collaboration policy of the AFL is attacked, and the Amsterdam International is denounced as dominated by capitalist agents in the labor movement.

B129 . . . . The Fight for World Trade Union Unity, "Workers Monthly," 4 (April 1925), 268-70.
A description of the fight between communists and social democrats for leadership of the European working class. The RILU leads the fight for unity "from the bottom up," while the right-wing leaders of the Amsterdam federation oppose unity. The AFL, the labor wing of American imperialism, will join the Amsterdam federation in order to struggle against unity.

B130 BELL, Thomas. "All Brides Are Beautiful." Boston: Little, Brown, 1936. 360 pp.
A story of the early years of married life of a young working-class couple during the depression. The hero, who accepts communism at the beginning of the novel, at the end is prepared to act upon his beliefs.

B131 BELLAMY, Ralph. Observations on the Communist Problem, "Equity," 38 (Oct. 1953), 5-6 ff.
While protesting against those who see a communist menace everywhere, including in "Equity," the president of Actors Equity agrees with Circuit Court Judge Learned Hand that the CPUSA represents a danger to our free institutions, that it plans to infiltrate his union, and that it constitutes a conspiracy.

B132 BENDINER, Robert. Browder's Mission to Moscow, "Nation," 162 (May 11, 1946), 568-70.
Discussion of the implications of Earl Browder's trip to Russia after his expulsion from the Communist Party. An associate editor of the "Nation" suggests that a major difference of opinion is being decided in the Kremlin, and that the issue is collaboration with the West or continuation of the present distrust.

B133 . . . . C.I.O. Tightrope Act, "Nation," 163 (Nov. 30, 1946), 601-2.

Caucusing at the CIO convention was concerned primarily with the left-right struggle. The anticommunist resolution that resulted was not as strong as anticommunist forces there wanted. Murray, who encouraged left-wing hopes by giving them a greater voice on the board, holds a precarious and ambiguous position.

B134 . . . . Civil Liberties and the Communists: Checking Subversion Without Harm to Democratic Rights, "Commentary," 5 (May 1948), 423-31.
Civil rights under our constitution include the right of communists to maintain their own party openly, and the right of all to advocate peaceful change; but there is no right to a government job nor a right to revolution. Some sort of disclosure plan, requiring information about propaganda groups, would curb extremists without violating democratic traditions.

B135 . . . . Murray's Limited Purge, "Nation," 167 (Dec. 18, 1948), 685-86.
Philip Murray severely censured the communists at the Portland CIO convention, but refused to expel them. His fire was directed against smaller left-wing unions rather than the giant UE, the Fur Workers, or Harry Bridges' Longshoremen. Murray's moderation in practice, if not in language, is called wise and necessary.

B136 . . . . Communists on Trial, "Nation," 168 (Jan. 29, 1949), 118-19.
The associate editor of the "Nation" reports on the early proceedings in the Dennis case, describing the obstructionist tactics of the defense attorneys. The issue on which American communists should be tried is not force or violence, but slavish service to another state.

B137 . . . . Politics and People: From Lenin to Dennis, "Nation," 168 (April 9, 1949), 405-6.
A description of the contradictions in the stand of both sides in the Dennis trial. The prosecution identified defendants with revolutionary doctrines that they had not espoused for years, whereas the defense took a reformist position that Lenin had bitterly attacked. The Party's only consistency has been in serving the immediate interests of the Soviet regime.

B138 . . . . Trial of Alger Hiss, "Nation," 168 (June 11, 1949), 650-51; (June 25), 699-700; 169 (July 16), 52-55.
Reports of the associate editor on the first Hiss trial, written respectively at the start of the trial, at the end of the prosecution's case, and after the jury failed to agree. Chambers' case proved much stronger than Bendiner had anticipated, whereas defense arguments proved evasive, particularly with regard to documentary evidence. The truth behind the drama remains impenetrable.

B139 . . . . Showdown in the C.I.O., "Nation," 169 (Oct. 15, 1949), 361-63.
Speculation as to the expected showdown on the communist issue at the coming CIO convention. Outlining the CIO case against the communists, the author predicts that in less than a month they will be outside the great bodies of organized labor. Behavior of the leftists shows that they expect to be ousted.

B140 . . . . Marx in Foley Square, "Nation," 169 (Oct. 22, 1949), 388-90.
A summary of the trial of 11 leading communists under the Smith Act by the associate editor of the "Nation," who asserts that the Act threatens the guarantees of the First Amendment. The Communist Party, unbeaten by the convictions, can be defeated only by social progress and by being exposed as the lackey of a foreign power.

B141   BENDINER, Robert. Surgery in the C.I.O., "Nation," 169 (Nov. 12, 1949), 458-59.
A report of the CIO convention at which action was finally taken against the communist unions. Prior to the ousting of the UE and the setting of trials for the other communist unions, speaker after speaker told how the communists shifted trade-union strategy to serve the changing purposes of the Communist Party and the Soviet Foreign Office.

B142   . . . . Ordeal of Alger Hiss. I. Second Trial Strategies, "Nation," 170 (Feb. 4, 1950), 100-3; II. Psychiatry, Law and Politics, (Feb. 11), 123-25.
A discussion of significant aspects of the second Hiss trial, showing how both defense and prosecution applied lessons learned at the first trial. While the testimony of psychiatrists and the personality of Whittaker Chambers stirred up controversy, the case was decided on the evidence of the typewriter and the documents.

B143   . . . . Has Anti-Communism Wrecked Our Liberties? "Commentary," 12 (July 1951), 10-16.
A review of the impact of anticommunism upon our freedom. Despite loyalty oaths, communist espionage trials, McCarthyism, and the McCarran Act, the U.S. has not become hysterical. It must be remembered that Soviet spies are at work here, that Russia sees the U.S. as her chief enemy. Liberals must fight the enemies of liberty on both the right and the left.

B144   . . . . The U.S. Communists—Rebellion in a Microcosm, "Reporter," 15 (Dec. 13, 1956), 20-24.
An analysis of the impact on the CPUSA of the Khrushchev revelations and the Polish and Hungarian events. The Party controversy that followed is the first in a quarter century, though there are signs that the bureaucracy is clamping down again. The February convention will lead in one of two directions: either free discussion will split the Party into harmlessly warring sects, or a return to Moscow orthodoxy will occur.

B145   BENEDICT, Agnes E. Youth Enlists for Peace on Earth, "Parents' Magazine," 13 (Dec. 1938), 20-21 ff.
A laudatory account of the communist-controlled second World Youth Congress, held at Poughkeepsie, N.Y., in August 1938, with delegations from 53 countries present. The Vassar Peace Pact of Youth, pledging fraternal collaboration between youth of all nations and condemning wars of aggression, is reproduced.

B146   BEN-HARIN, Meir. Communism and the Faith in Man, "Reconstructionist," 20 (Feb. 26, 1954), 9-16.
Although the author agrees with Whittaker Chambers as to the menace of the communist conspiracy to our democratic institutions, he denies that faith in man, rather than faith in God, is the source of the menace. The choice is rather between a liberal faith and a total faith in either man or God. Democracy requires a rejection of both forms of total faith, not a choice between them.

B147   BENJAMIN, D. The Question of a Labor Party, "Revolutionary Age," 1 (Jan. 1, 1930), 6-7.
Lovestoneite criticism of the abandonment by the CPUSA of the labor party slogan, which is an example of the abandonment of united front tactics. The new Party line is based on a false estimate of the radicalization of the masses, making united-front tactics unnecessary. As a result the Party is isolated and impotent.

B148   BENJAMIN, George. A Communication, "Nation," 183 (July 28, 1956), inside front cover, ff.

A letter to the editor, criticizing the communists for depriving the American public of radical leadership, overestimating their role in history, lack of originality, vindictiveness, and anti-intellectualism. The CPUSA, having outlived its time, should dissolve, to make way for a new radical movement in which every shade of progressive or radical opinion could find some common meeting ground.

B149   BENJAMIN, Herbert. "How to Organize and Conduct United Action for the Right to Live." New York: Workers Library for the National Committee, Unemployed Councils, 1933. 23 pp.
A call by the national organizer of the Unemployed Councils for militant and sustained mass struggles to force the ruling class to secure the rights of the unemployed. He lists issues and grievances, calls for the formation of Committees of Action in each block or neighborhood and their election of delegates to an Unemployed Council, and discusses direct relief, propaganda activities, and finances.

B150   . . . . "Shall It Be Hunger Doles or Unemployment Insurance?" New York: National Committee, Unemployed Councils, 1933 (rev. ed., 1934), 24 pp.
A denunciation of the proposed Wagner-Lewis social security bill, with a plea for the support of the workers' unemployment and social insurance bill, sponsored by this communist-directed organization. Workers can win real social insurance, as in the Soviet Union, only by fighting against labor misleaders and supporting the workers' bill.

B151   . . . . The Unemployment Movement in the U.S.A. from March Sixth, 1930, Through the Second New Deal Year, "Communist," 14 (June 1935), 528-47.
An analysis of the organization of the unemployed argues that relief programs, inadequate as they are, were won through struggle, and were not a result of the "humanity" of capitalist governments. Now more systematic organization is needed, with more attention to political education. New Deal proposals for social security are demagogic maneuvers to avoid responsibility. The need for a single organization of the unemployed is more imperative than ever.

B152   . . . . "A Handbook for Project Workers." New York: National Unemployment Council, 1936, 39 pp.
A handbook for WPA workers by the national secretary of the National Unemployment Council, attacking WPA regulations and urging jobs at useful work, adequate cash relief for the jobless, and genuine social insurance. Advice is given on organization of project workers, fees and dues, democratic control, and cooperation with trade unions.

B153   . . . . "Relief and Work Standards." New York: National Joint Action Committee for Genuine Social Insurance, 1936. 30 pp.
A plea for the passage of H.R. 11186, the Marcantonio relief and work projects standards bill, drafted on the initiative of the party-controlled National Unemployment Councils and related groups, and based on the principle that relief is a federal responsibility. The bill is reproduced in the pamphlet.

B154   . . . . Unity in the Unemployment Field, "Communist," 15 (April 1936), 327-36.
The alliance of the communist-sponsored National Unemployment Council and the socialist-sponsored Workers' Alliance is a great gain for working class unity in the fight against the inadequate relief program of the Roosevelt Administration. Unity of the unemployed is an important step in solidifying the united front of the entire working class.

B155 BENJAMIN, Herbert. Unification of the Unemployed Organizations in the USA, "International Press Correspondence, 16 (May 16, 1936), 628-29.
A report on the merger of communist and socialist organizations of unemployed in April, 1936, to form the Workers Alliance of America. Old-guard socialists opposed the merger, and Trotskyist attempts at disruption were unsuccessful. The program is substantially that of the former communist group, the Unemployed Councils.

B156 .... Six Months of Unity of the Unemployed, "Communist," 15 (Nov. 1936), 1056-70.
Despite the election, reactionary politicians in both parties continued their drive to cut unemployment relief. Unification of the unemployed in the Workers Alliance, achieved in April, provides the unemployed with a better instrument of struggle. Where Trotskyites had influence in organizations of unemployed they sabotaged the unity program. The unemployed must have the support of working-class political parties.

B157 .... Extending the Unity of the Unemployed Movement, "Communist," 16 (Aug. 1937), 761-70.
A protest against the liquidation of the federal relief work program and a discussion of the Third Annual Convention of the Workers Alliance. The convention consolidated its unity, in line with the people's front policy, and prepared for great struggles ahead. Its activities will culminate in a mass march on Washington for jobs.

B158 .... Meeting Reaction's Assault on the Unemployed, "Communist," 18 (Aug. 1939), 689-700.
In six months four major battles have been fought in Congress over appropriations for unemployment relief through a federal works program. The reactionaries, who support the sit-down strike of Big Business, seek to discredit the Administration and its supporters as treasury-raiders, and demoralize WPA workers, the unemployed, and the Workers' Alliance.

B159 .... After a Decade of Mass Unemployment, "Communist," 19 (March 1940), 259-77.
The former general secretary of the Workers Alliance surveys attempts from 1930 to 1940 to solve the unemployment problem, appraising the WPA and the work of the Party-led Workers Alliance. The Alliance proposes a public works program to replace the WPA and a guaranteed minimum wage. Attacks on labor are viewed as part of the drive towards war.

B160 .... Civilian Defense and Morale—A Vital Factor in the Struggle against Hitlerism, "Communist," 20 (Dec. 1941), 1072-78.
It is important to build civilian defense, both for its own sake and as a morale booster. So far, little has been done to implement the federal government's civilian defense program. Trade unions should become more active in this work.

B161 BENNETT, A. J. The Struggle on Two Fronts: The Coming Convention of the Workers' Party of America, "Communist International," 6 (Jan. 15, 1929), 114-18.
A new Trotskyist faction, led by Cannon, has appeared in the U.S. The American Party must struggle on two fronts, against the right opportunist errors and against the left deviations which are its shadows. A declaration by the Central Executive Committee of the American Party on right-wing dangers and on Trotskyism is criticized for lack of clarity.

B162 BENNETT, John Coleman. "Christianity and Communism." New York: Association Press, 1948. 128 pp.
Written for students and young people, the book analyzes the differences between Christianity and communism, the nature of communism, alternatives to it, and the proper approach of Christians. Believing that communism is a compound of half-truth and positive error, the author sees it as a threat to freedom, yet argues that its errors result from the failure of Christians to be true to their own faith. The extension of communism can be prevented, not by negative propaganda, but only by offering a sounder faith and a better program to meet human needs and unsolved problems. (Revised edition, 1960, under the title, "Christianity and Communism Today.")

B163 .... Turn Communists to Christianity, "Christian Century," 68 (April 18, 1951), 494-96.
A professor of theology at Union Theological Seminary asserts that many who have been concerned enough about social injustice to become communists may be open to the Christian message if disillusionment sets in. Despite the church's poor record of dealing with social issues, the teachings of Christianity offer a path for the concerned.

B164 .... Can We Ever Support Communism? "Christian Century," 69 (June 11, 1952), 696-98.
A warning of the dangers of half-hearted opposition to communism because its teachings contain some truth. The good elements in it are the entering wedge for the evil. No help should be given to communism to gain power; if independent political action is impossible, faithful waiting is the best choice.

B165 .... "Communism and the West . . . the Basic Conflicts." New York: Church Peace Union, 1953. 30 pp.
An analysis of tensions between communism and the Western world by a leading Protestant theologian, who discusses four conflicts: the international conflict, the conflict between communism and capitalism as economic systems, the conflict between communist totalitarianism and an open and pluralistic society, and the conflict between communism as a faith and Christianity.

B166 .... The Church between East and West. Pp. 75-91 in John A. Hutchison (ed.), "Christian Faith and Social Action." New York: Scribner, 1953.
The author sees the conflicts as between capitalism and communism as economic systems; as between totalitarian imperialism and an open and pluralistic society; as between communism and Christianity as faiths; and, on the international scene, as one of extensions of power of communism and the West. He outlines the world churches' rejection of communism in each of these areas, pointing out that the churches must propose affirmative as well as negative action.

B167 .... The Protestant Clergy and Communism, "Christianity and Crisis," 13 (Aug. 3, 1953), 107-10.
A reply to the charges by J. B. Matthews ("Reds and Our Churches," in the "American Mercury," July 1953) on communist sympathizers among the Protestant clergy. The group of Protestant ministers who identify with the communist cause have never been so isolated as today. Others have participated in organizations because of the cause and despite the communists, or left after the communists gained control.

B168 BENSON, Ezra Taft. "The Red Carpet." Salt Lake City: Bookcraft, 1962. 325 pp. Ind.
A former Secretary of Agriculture sees the communist threat in America as a very real one, and views creeping socialism as the road to communism.

B169 BENSON, H. W. The CP at the Crossroads: Toward Democratic Socialism or Back to Stalinism, "New International," 22 (Fall 1956), 139-78. Reprinted in pamphlet form by New International Publishing Co., 1957. 40 pp.
A contribution to the discussion in the CPUSA following the Khrushchev revelations and the Hungarian uprising of 1956, addressed particularly to the Gates faction. If the CPUSA is to move sincerely toward democratic socialism it must adopt a principled stand on democracy everywhere, including the Soviet Union, and reject Stalinism as unequivocally as capitalism.

B170 BENTLEY, Elizabeth. "Out of Bondage: The Story of Elizabeth Bentley." New York: Devin-Adair, 1951. 311 pp.
The story of a Columbia University student who was attracted to the Communist Party in the depression 1930's through the American League Against War and Fascism, and who was later recruited into underground work in the service of the Russian secret police. Married to Jacob Golos, member of the powerful Central Control Commission of the American Party and an agent of the Russian secret police, she served principally as a contact for an espionage ring in government service in Washington from 1941 until early 1945, collecting material which she turned over to the Russians. Becoming disillusioned both with the leadership of the American Party and the Russian agents under whom she worked, she renounced communism and told her story to the FBI in 1945. (A condensed version appeared serially in "McCall's Magazine" before publication in book form.)

B171 BENTLEY, Eric. Broadway's Missing Communist: Theater Without Candor, "Commentary," 22 (Sept. 1956), 244-48.
A drama critic reports on the lack of candor in the theatrical world with regard to communism, the only political force with any staying power over the past quarter century. Most of the communists on Broadway profess to be progressives or antifascists. A character is missing from American plays that touch on communism —the communist hero.

B172 BERDIAEFF, Nicholas. Christianity and Communism, "Commonweal," 18 (Sept. 8, 1933), 440-42.
A member of the Russian Orthodox church expelled from the Soviet Union asserts that communism, above all, is a spiritual and religious problem. He finds the roots of its godlessness in the bourgeois capitalist philosophy of the 18th century. To compete with communism Christianity must become free and vital, not irrevocably a defender of the existing social order.

B173 BERENBERG, David P. The Bankruptcy of American Communism, "American Socialist Quarterly," 3 (Dec. 1934), 38-50.
A socialist analysis of the failure of the Communist Party to gain influence among American workers and in American life. The primary reason is found in its domination by the Communist International. Communist policy in the trade unions, in "innocent" clubs, and with the Negroes is reviewed. "Self-criticism," as practiced by the communists, never becomes free discussion.

B174 BERG, Louis. How End the Panic in Radio-TV? The Demagogic Half-Truth vs. the Liberal Half-Lie, "Commentary," 14 (Oct. 1952), 315-25.
Censure, both of "Red Channels" and of Merle Miller's rejoinder, "The Judges and the Judged," for slanting evidence to support their respective positions. We must acknowledge the facts of communist influence in TV and radio, judge fellow-travelers on present and future conduct, and have a board of inquiry deal with hard core Party-liners.

B175 BERGER, Hans [pseud. for Gerhart Eisler]. On the Third Anniversary of the Soviet-German Non-Aggression Pact, "Communist," 21 (Aug. 1942), 610-19.
The Western democracies are now collaborating with Russia. If Britain and France had followed the same policy, the war would never have occurred. Instead they tried to maneuver Hitler into attacking Russia. Once they were defeated, Hitler attacked Russia as the one big barrier to his design of world conquest. (Gerhart Eisler was a Comintern representative assigned to the U.S.)

B176 .... Our Nation Discovers the Soviet Union, "Communist," 21 (Nov. 1942), 886-93.
The war is bringing Americans a true understanding of Russia. They are ceasing to believe the lies that Russia is a technologically backward tyranny, and are beginning to see that Russia is an industrially advanced nation inhabited by a free people who are fighting to preserve their national existence and democratic rights.

B177 .... The Nazi Peace Offensive, "Communist," 22 (March 1943), 266-73.
The Nazis, having suffered military defeats, seek to break up the United Nations alliance. They are trying to destroy popular American support of the alliance by having their dupes here assert falsely that Russia intends to subjugate Eastern Europe.

B178 .... Remarks on the Discussion concerning the Dissolution of the Communist International, "Communist," 22 (Nov. 1943), 1018-29.
The Communist International has been dissolved to facilitate antifascist unity. The American press falsely asserts that the dissolution was a Russian move to gain American aid in return for giving up control of communist parties in other countries. But neither the Russian government nor the Communist International has ever dominated other communist parties.

B179 .... Notes on the Dumbarton Oaks Conference, "Communist," 23 (Oct. 1944), 911-18.
The Dumbarton Oaks Conference, slanderously attacked by the Republicans, is working to build an international organization based on close cooperation of big and small powers. Such an organization would have saved the world from Nazi attack because it would have confronted Hitler with overwhelming power.

B180 .... From Teheran to Fulton, "New Masses," 59 (April 16, 1946), 3-6.
An effort to show, on the occasion of Churchill's Fulton, Missouri, speech, that Truman has abandoned FDR's foreign policy, under the influence of American imperialism, in favor of hostility toward the USSR. One indication is that Truman, knowing what Churchill would say at Fulton, chose to be present.

B181 BERGMAN, Walter G. State Dept. McCarthyism: The Passport Division in Action, "Socialist Call," 22 (Jan. 1954), 19-22.
An account by a socialist of the lifting of his passport while he was abroad on charges of his having belonged to two organizations on the subversive list, having followed the communist line in a trade union years earlier, and having attended an antifascist meeting linked by some informants to the CP. The arbitrary actions of State Department officials are criticized.

B182 BERKELEY, Martin. Reds in Your Living Room, "American Mercury," 77 (Aug. 1953), 55-62.
An account of the infiltration of radio and television unions by the communists, emphasizing the "red" Radio Writers Guild and the communist-instigated Television Writers of America. The author deplores the television industries' fear of the anticommunist as a controversial figure, feeling that they thus abet communist control.

B183 BERMAN, Arnold. On Method in Political Economy: A Discussion Article, "Political Affairs," 35 (June 1956), 44-57.
An application of communist "self-criticism" following the Twentieth Congress of the CPSU. The Party's economic writing is criticized for seeing a major depression at every sign of downturn in the American economy. This is a departure from Marxist method in economic analysis.

B184 BERN, Gregory. "Behind the Red Mask." Los Angeles: Bern Publications, 1947. 324 pp.
An attack upon communism and the New Deal from the extreme right. While attacking Soviet crimes around the world and the existence of slave-labor camps within Russia, the author finds a parallel between the New Deal and the Nazi regime in Germany and criticizes war acts of the Roosevelt Administration prior to Pearl Harbor. He describes the origin of the Communist Party in this country and the organization of front groups, and charges that Soviet collaborators in the U.S. State Department encouraged Soviet espionage here.

B185 BERNS, Walter. "Freedom, Virtue & the First Amendment." Baton Rouge: Louisiana State University Press, 1957. 264 pp. Table of cases. Ind.
A study of Supreme Court decisions in First Amendment cases. Chapter 9, pp. 198-227, on "Freedom and Loyalty," discusses the Smith Act and the Dennis case, concluding that the Smith Act at best was a crude device based on the conception of law as punishment and loyalty as patriotism.

B186 BERNSTEIN, George. The People's Fight for Progressive Taxation, "Political Affairs," 24 (Dec. 1945), 1097-1108.
A description of and argument for an eight-point reconversion tax program sponsored by 16 national organizations. The tax program of these labor and progressive organizations seeks to sustain mass purchasing power, tax according to ability to pay, and raise adequate revenues to finance human and industrial demobilization.

B187 BERNSTEIN, Walter. Furriers' Gold, "New Masses," 63 (May 6, 1947), 11-14.
An account of the career and achievements of Ben Gold, president of the International Fur and Leather Workers, and a member of the CIO executive board and of the national committee of the Communist Party. Emphasis is placed on struggles against gangsters, factionalism, and employers.

B188 BERRY, A. W., and others. "The Road to Liberation for the Negro People." New York: Workers Library, 1937. 15 pp.
Sixteen Negro communist leaders tell of the Party's role in leading the struggle for Negroes. Mention is made of economic struggles led by the communists, the Scottsboro case, the Herndon case, and fights for political equality, democratic rights, and trade-union equality.

B189 BERRY, Abner W. The Future of Negro Music, "Masses & Mainstream," 6 (Feb. 1953), 15-20.
Negro music is being diverted from its true path as a folk music by subjectivism and dead-end formalism. From its functional beginnings as social music, Negro music and

musicians were driven into honky-tonks, finally arriving at be-bop. This is a misfortune for Negro liberation music and for all democracy.

B190 . . . . Ira Aldridge: A Negro Actor's Triumph, "Masses & Mainstream," 7 (Feb. 1954), 2-6.
A biographical sketch of the New York-born Negro, said to be the world's most celebrated interpreter of Shakespeare from 1833 to 1867. Aldridge is compared to Paul Robeson, "our greatest living Othello," who today is barred from all commercial outlets because of his courageous fight for peace.

B191 BERRY, Lewis. A Dead Horse . . . and Its Galloping Ghost, "Workmen's Circle Call," 19 (Jan. 1951), 2-4.
An assertion that it is the duty of the liberal anticommunist to educate others to the dimensions of the communist threat. This requires that he overcome his repugnance against speaking out against our communist enemies.

B192 BERT, Erik. Notes on the Strength of American Capitalism, "Communist," 9 (April 1930), 321-35.
A review of the recent development of American finance capital, showing the inherent contradictions of capitalism. The credit system has had unprecedented parasitic growths, goods have been disposed of through stock market "prosperity" and installment selling, and American imperialism increasingly has been forced to find markets abroad.

B193 BESSIE, Alvah. What Is Freedom for Writers? "New Masses," 48 (March 12, 1946), 8-10.
An attack on Albert Maltz for his views in "What Shall We Ask of Writers?" ("New Masses," February 12, 1946). Maltz is charged with holding the bourgeois concept that art is unconnected with beliefs. None of the reactionary writers praised by Maltz was a major talent to start with. We need more, not fewer, Party artists to understand and act upon working class theory.

B194 . . . . (ed.). "The Heart of Spain." New York: Veterans of the Abraham Lincoln Brigade, 1952. 494 pp. Bibliog.
An anthology of fiction, nonfiction, and poetry, containing Spanish, other European, and American contributions, all written in 1936-39. Central themes are the struggles of the Loyalists and the justness of the fight against Franco. A large percentage of the items are by communists or sympathizers.

B195 . . . . "The Un-Americans." New York: Cameron Associates, 1957. 383 pp.
A novel about American communists who fought for the Loyalists in Spain and who were later subjected to unwarranted persecution by fascist-minded forces in the U.S. in control of a congressional investigating committee and other positions of power. The communists are presented as the true patriots, the opponents of fascism during the war and the defenders of democracy and progress during the peace. (Bessie, who fought for the Spanish Loyalists, was one of the "Hollywood Ten," indicted in 1947 for refusing to tell his political beliefs to the House Un-American Activities Committee; convicted, he served a year in prison.)

B196 . . . . "Inquisition in Eden." New York: Macmillan, 1965. 278 pp. Ind.
An account of Bessie's experiences during and after the House Un-American Activities Committee's investigation of communist infiltration of the motion picture industry. Refusing to answer questions as to his present or past

membership in the Communist Party, Bessie was one of the "Hollywood Ten" convicted for contempt of Congress. The book, written in the form of a scenario, describes the blacklist from which he suffered, his efforts to earn a living, and his experiences in prison while serving his year's sentence.

B197　BIANCA, Michael. How to Fight McCarthyism, "Political Affairs," 30 (Oct. 1951), 23-30.
Fascism is not here, though the tempo of fascization has accelerated at the hands of an Administration that hypocritically proclaims devotion to democracy. Truman demagogically seeks to make the struggle against McCarthyism a main issue in 1952. We must appeal to Truman supporters against McCarthyism, showing them that united action for restoration of the Bill of Rights is in their own interest.

B198　BICKEL, Alexander M. The Communist Cases, "New Republic," 144 (June 19, 1961), 15-16.
Comment on decisions by the U.S. Supreme Court requiring the CPUSA to register as a communist-action organization under the Subversive Activities Control (McCarran) Act of 1950, and affirming the conviction of Junius Irving Scales under the Smith Act for active membership in the Party. The Court need not have decided the cases on constitutional grounds.

B199　BIDDLE, Francis. Security and Liberty, "New Republic," 123 (Aug. 14, 1950), 11-14.
A former Attorney General of the U.S. evaluates the Truman loyalty program. Despite its general fairness, it will discourage government employees from association with any liberal movement and will lead to comparable state legislation. Loyalty probes are essentially un-American.

B200　. . . . Sickness of Fear, "Bulletin of the Atomic Scientists," 7 (Nov. 1951), 323-26.
The former Attorney General discusses the larger meaning of loyalty investigations and their impact on traditional free thought. In our fear of communism, in his view, we have perverted the need for internal security into a movement to control thought. He considers loyalty tests and oaths, and the registration of communists, to be futile.

B201　. . . . "The Fear of Freedom." Garden City, N.Y.: Doubleday, 1952. 263 pp.
An analysis of civil liberties by a former U.S. Attorney General, focusing discussion on the current obsession with anxiety and fear, its historical background and present expression, and its effect on national security and American institutions. Chapters deal with the House Un-American Activities Committee, the federal loyalty program, state investigations of un-American activities, and loyalty oaths for teachers. The book is less a discussion of communism than a protest against the steps taken to protect against subversion. Though not denying that risks exist, the author warns against futile and harmful measures that would endanger our traditional freedoms.

B202　. . . . Ethics in Government and the Use of FBI Files, "Reporter," 10 (Jan. 5, 1954), 13-16.
Criticism of Attorney General Herbert Brownell for using FBI files for political purposes, and an attack on ex-President Truman for appointing Harry Dexter White to office. Brownell's assertion that White was known at the time of appointment to be a Russian spy was based on his interpretation of unevaluated material in secret FBI files.

B203　. . . . Subversives in Government, "Annals of the American Academy of Political and Social Science," 300 (July 1955), 51-61.

A former U.S. Attorney General examines the meaning of subversion, the various phases of the loyalty-security program, and the present program, making suggestions for its improvement. Although internal dangers from communists are largely in the past, fear and hysteria have increased as the threat has subsided.

B204　. . . . "In Brief Authority." Garden City, N.Y.: Doubleday, 1962. 494 pp. Ind.
An account of the public life of the prominent attorney who served, among other public offices, as chairman of the National Labor Relations Board, Solicitor General, Attorney General, and American member of the International Military Tribunal at the Nuremberg trial. Chapter 19, pp. 296-307, deals with Biddle's unsuccessful effort while Attorney General to deport Harry Bridges as a member of the Communist Party.

B205　BIGMAN, S. K. The New Internationalism Under Attack, "Public Opinion Quarterly," 14 (Summer 1950), 235-61. Correction in 15 (Winter 1950-51), 767.
An analysis of the opposition by both the extreme left and the extreme right to proposals for a world federation. The communists cry "American imperialism"; the arch-conservatives cry "A communist plot." A study of the latter group's use of the word "communist" follows.

B206　BINGHAM, Robert K., and ASCOLI, Max. Case of Alger Hiss, "Reporter," 1 (Aug. 30, 1949), 4-7.
An account of the first Hiss trial, satirizing the exploitation of emotion and drama by both sides. There are two cases: the trial of Hiss for perjury, and the "Case of Alger Hiss" which, with its espionage overtones, appears to many as an indictment of the liberalism of the 1930's and the New Deal.

B207　BI-PARTISAN LEAGUE OF OHIO. "Secret Communist Party Manual on Organization." Columbus, Ohio: The League, n.d. 41 pp.
A reprint of "The Communist Party: A Manual on Organization," by J. Peters.

B208　BIRDSEYE, Clarence F. "American Democracy versus Prussian Marxism." New York and Chicago: Revell, 1920. 371 pp. Ind.
A contrast of American Democracy with Marxism, which the author finds sterile and rooted in Prussian autocracy and ruthlessness. He exposes the inherent weaknesses of Marx's political theories and the falseness and baseness of his political philosophy, which are reflected in Lenin's conduct in the USSR. Describing and defending "purposive" democratic government in the U.S., the author asserts that we must choose between it and Prussian Marxism.

B209　BISHOP, Hillman M. "The American League Against War and Fascism." The author, 1936. (rev. ed., 1937). 46 pp. App. Mimeo.
A critical account of the League, giving its history and program, and showing how the Communist Party controls it mechanically and undemocratically for Party purposes. The League is not primarily a peace organization; its foremost purpose is to aid the Soviet Union in the way determined by the Party. Most organizations active in the League are under Party orders and discipline.

B210　. . ., and HENDEL, Samuel. "Basic Issues of American Democracy." 3d ed. New York: Appleton-Century-Crofts, 1956. 484 pp.
A book of readings that first appeared in 1948. Section III, "What Limits on Free Speech?" (pp. 72-154), deals, among other topics, with the advocacy of revolution and the problem of loyalty and security. Topic 24, "Reply to the Communist Challenge," appears on pp. 351-70.

B211 BITTELMAN, Alexander. A Memorandum on the Present Situation in the Communist Movement in America, Adopted by the Communist Unity Committee for Submission to the Executive Committee of the Third Communist International, "Communist Unity," 1 (Feb. 1, 1921), 3-4.
A discussion of the formation of the communist organization here and the struggle for control between the English-speaking elements and the foreign-language federations.

B212 .... "Parties and Issues in the Election Campaign." Chicago: Literature Department, Workers Party of America, n.d. [1924]. 23 pp.
A study of the main parties and political groupings in the U.S.: the Republican, the Democratic, the Socialist-La Follette-Gompers alliance, and the Workers (Communist) Party. Attitudes are presented on a series of issues, ranging from imperialism and war to the Dawes plan, a labor party, trade union organization, the Negro, unemployment, the League of Nations, the Communist International, recognition of Russia, and the Ku Klux Klan.

B213 .... In Retrospect: A Critical Review of Our Past Labor Party Policy in the Light of the Present Situation, "Workers Monthly," 4 (Dec. 1924), 85-90.
A detailed analysis of the largely unsuccessful efforts of the Workers Party to apply united front tactics to the political scene since December 1922. Positions of the Ruthenberg group and of the opposing Foster-Cannon faction, to which Bittelman belonged, are clarified; Bittelman blames the Ruthenberg caucus for the WP's failures. After the 1924 election the Foster-Cannon proposal to drop the farmer-labor party idea, as a slogan as well as an organizational force, was adopted.

B214 .... A Conference of Progressive Reactionaries, "Workers Monthly," 4 (Feb. 1925), 166-67.
A communist view of the Conference for Progressive Political Action, to be held in Chicago, February 25, 1925, as the tail-end of the LaFollette movement, seeking to establish a third, bourgeois party. The CPPA and the LaFollette movement represent rich farmers, small and medium capitalists, and labor bureaucrats. Workers are urged to join the communists instead in a real struggle for real demands.

B215 .... On the Road to a Bolshevik Party in America, "Workers Monthly," 4 (Sept. 1925), 483-85.
A report on the national convention of the Workers (Communist) Party held in Chicago, August 21-30, 1925. The decisions of the convention on imperialism, a labor party, trade union work, reorganization, and deviationism are reviewed. The Party will support united labor tickets in municipal elections as a step toward a labor party, and will reorganize on the basis of shop nuclei. Opportunist elements such as "Loreism" must be rooted out.

B216 .... American Capitalism Prepares for Class War, "Workers Monthly," 5 (Nov. 1926), 605-6.
Denunciation of industrial mobilization plans and of Mayor James Walker's appointment of a Committee on Industrial Organization and Defense of New York City. Such committees will strive to develop into fascist organizations for the class struggle.

B217 .... History of the Communist Movement in America, in "Investigation of Communist Propaganda: Hearings." U.S. Congress, House of Representatives, Special Committee on Communist Activities in Government. Washington, D.C.: Government Printing Office, 1930. Part V, 4:435-48.
A sketch, in outline form, of the history of the American communist parties, ending with the unification of the

splintered parties in September 1922. Contains an inside account of the splits in the pre-communist left wing of the Socialist Party, as well as in the communist parties. Unity was achieved, Bittelman states, only as a result of Comintern pressure.

B218 .... "Revolutionary Struggle against War vs. Pacifism." New York: Workers Library, n.d. [1931]. 48 pp.
An argument by a leading Party theoretician that imperialist war grows out of rivalry for markets, spheres of influence, and colonies, and that, when it breaks out, the masses should transform it into civil war and destroy capitalism. He attacks the "dangerous illusion" of humanitarian pacifists that imperialist war is separate from capitalism, that it is possible to abolish war without ending capitalism.

B219 .... The Party Anniversary in the Light of Our Present Tasks, "Communist," 10 (Dec. 1931), 975-84.
The twelfth anniversary of the Party finds it free from factionalism, united on the line of the Communist International, and extending its influence among the masses. The Party has had three periods: (1) separation from social reformism, (2) development into a propagandist organization, and (3) conversion into a mass political party of the working class.

B220 .... "The Communist Party in Action." New York: Workers Library, 1932. 48 pp.
Instructions to new members about Party aims during the "third period." Emphasis is on the vanguard role of the Party, its monopoly as a source of Marxist-Leninist wisdom, and the need for reducing turnover in Party membership. Chapters deal with the revolutionary nature of the Party, the capitalist parties and their social-fascist agents, activity and discipline, Leninism, the world-wide Party, its strategic aim, the main lines of the struggle, and the fight against deviations.

B221 .... From Left Socialism to Communism, "Communist," 12 (Sept. 1933), 846-63.
An account of the development of the left wing of the Socialist Party of 1918-19 into the Communist Party. The central issue was not socialism versus anarchism, but the dictatorship of the proletariat, or revolutionary Marxism, versus reformism or bourgeois democracy. Other issues were revolutionary struggle against imperialist war versus social chauvinism, and the Communist International versus the Second International. (Also published in pamphlet form.)

B222 .... (ed.). "A Documentary Account of the Advance of the United Front." New York: CPUSA, Central Committee, 1934. 70 pp.
Documents dealing with a proposed united front with the socialists, 1933-34, from the communist point of view. The Socialist Party leadership is blamed for the failure of the socialists to accept the communist united-front offer. In effect the socialist rank and file is appealed to over the heads of its leaders. The pamphlet includes various communist statements on the necessity for the united front, and correspondence between the top leaderships of the two parties. Bittelman contributes an introduction.

B223 .... "Fifteen Years of the Communist Party." New York: Workers Library, 1934. 52 pp.
Reprints of three articles by Bittelman that appeared in the "Communist," in December 1931, September 1933 (also published as a pamphlet), and March 1934. The articles are offered as an introduction to the study of

Party history. The Party was able to give effective leadership to the San Francisco general strike of 1934, the author asserts, because of the correct line established at its 1933 and 1934 conventions.

B224 BITTELMAN, Alexander. The New Deal and the Old Deal, "Communist," 13 (Jan. 1934), 81-98; (Feb.), 182-92.
A detailed comparison of Hoover and Roosevelt policies to show that the New Deal represents neither a revolution nor a continuation of the old order, but a turn to war and fascism in the search for a capitalist solution of the depression crisis. The function of the AFL bureaucracy in the NRA is to make the trade unions an organ of fascist oppression.

B225 . . . . Milestones of Comintern Leadership, "Communist," 13 (March 1934), 235-48.
A listing, with brief discussion, of the outstanding events in the history of the American Party, marked by advice from the Comintern. Among those listed are consolidation of all revolutionary workers into one party, breaking through illegality, building a left wing in the reformist unions, the labor party move, the program for Negro liberation, emphasis on unemployment insurance, and liquidation of factionalism.

B226 . . . . For a Bolshevik Anti-War Struggle, "Communist," 13 (Aug. 1934), 755-72.
American imperialism, with the rest of the capitalist world, is preparing feverishly for war, whereas the Soviet Union follows a consistent peace policy. War is the capitalist way out of the crisis. August 1 must be a day of mass actions against hunger, fascistization, and war. The antiwar struggle must be brought into the basic factories and the united front against war and fascism strengthened.

B227 . . ., and JEROME, V. J. Leninism Is the Only Marxism of the Imperialist Era, "Communist," 13 (Oct. 1934), 1033-56; (Nov.), 1125-56. Reprinted in pamphlet form as "Leninism, the Only Marxism Today."
A review article of Lewis Corey's "The Decline of American Capitalism." Although Corey declares socialism to be inevitable, he has a wrong conception of imperialism, of the revolutionary process, of the role of the proletarian party. He does not reject social democracy and bourgeois constitutionalism, he makes no reference to the united front, and he leaves out of his program the objective—Soviet power. (As Louis Fraina, Corey had been a leader of the left wing of the socialist party in the early formative period of the communist movement.)

B228 . . . . Developments in the United Front, "Communist," 13 (Dec. 1934), 1195-1213.
A review of efforts to achieve a united front between communists and socialists since Hitler's rise to power in May 1933. Socialists have been for the united front only because of pressure from their ranks, organized principally by the communists. The main CP efforts must still be on the united front from below.

B229 . . . . "How Can We Share the Wealth? The Communist Way versus Huey Long." New York: Workers Library, 1935. 32 pp.
Communist critique and attack on the "Share the Wealth" scheme of Huey Long of Louisiana, counterposing the revolutionary position of the Communist Party to the "fascist" proposals of Long.

B230 . . . . For Leninism—For a Soviet America! "Communist," 14 (Jan. 1935), 6-22.

An appeal, on the 11th anniversary of Lenin's death, to workers not to accept the reformist philosophy of the New Deal, AFL, or Socialist Party. Their programs further entrench the bourgeois dictatorship and are obstacles to the establishment of the united front. The overthrow of capitalism will come only through violence.

B231 . . . . The Socialist Revolution in the United States, "Communist," 14 (Feb. 1935), 127-47.
A chapter from a forthcoming book views the proletarian revolution as a world-wide force trying to break an imperialist capitalist chain. The link formed by American capitalism will inevitably break, as monopoly imperialism turns international and the Negro intensifies his fight for self-determination.

B232 . . . . Report to the National Agitation and Propaganda Conference, January 18, 1935, "Communist," 14 (March 1935), 240-61.
Communists must demonstrate that Roosevelt leftists like Sinclair and the socialists and conservative Republicans all seek through alternative ways to preserve capitalism. Communists should use strikes to make workers more hostile to capitalism. In trade unions, the labor party, and united fronts, communists should seek to convert the masses to the communist cause.

B233 . . . . Approaching the Seventh World Congress of the Communist International, "Communist," 14 (June 1935), 518-27.
A discussion outline for Party units, prepared for the Agit-Prop Commission of the Party's Central Committee. The thesis is that the Communist International's prognosis has been confirmed by history, while the hopes and prophecies of the Socialist Parties and trade-union reformists have been shattered.

B234 . . . . The Supreme Court, the New Deal and the Class Struggle, "Communist," 14 (July 1935), 579-603.
Criticism of the Supreme Court's decision holding the NRA unconstitutional, as a fresh capitalist offensive against the rights of the masses. The whole New Deal is a capitalist tool, and the NRA merely an attempt to placate the workers. The solution is to strengthen the united front with a union base, which will lead to an independent labor party.

B235 . . . . The United Front Against Imperialist War, "Communist," 14 (Aug. 1935), 675-85.
An interpretation of the switch to collective security, written shortly before the Seventh World Congress of the Comintern. The main job of the working class is to fight war and fascism through united fronts of communists and socialists. Yet Bittelman defends, as in the interests of peace, Stalin's approval of the national defense policies of France.

B236 . . . . Problems of the Struggle for Peace, "Communist," 14 (Nov. 1935), 1034-43.
An introduction to discussions on the Seventh World Congress of the Comintern, delivered to the National Bureau of the Young Communist League, September 30, 1935. The main emphasis is the struggle against the war danger. Communists must concentrate their struggle against German and Italian fascism, the chief instigators of war.

B237 . . . . Winning the Masses to Fight for Peace, "Communist," 14 (Dec. 1935), 1171-81.
A speech at the November meeting of the Party's Central Committee, pointing out the obstacles to wide acceptance of the united front, antifascist movement. Chief among these are bourgeois isolationists and left socialists.

B238 BITTELMAN, Alexander. "Going Left: The Left Wing Formulates a 'Draft Program for the Socialist Party of the United States.' " New York: Workers Library, 1936. 46 pp.
An analysis of the draft program of the left wing of the Socialist Party, in an attempt to intervene in the factional struggle in that party. The author seeks to channel the socialist leftward movement toward the Communist Party rather than toward the Trotskyists, while preparing the left socialists for the popular-front line.

B239 .... "How to Win Social Justice: Can Coughlin and Lemke Do It?" New York: Workers Library, 1936. 47 pp.
Communist critique and attack on the "Social Justice" scheme of Father Coughlin and the candidacy of the proto-fascist Lemke for the presidency. (The communists attacked depression movements which, while anticapitalist in ideology, were thought fascist in nature.)

B240 .... "The Townsend Plan: What It Is and What It Isn't." New York: Workers Library, 1936. 46 pp.
A critical evaluation of the Townsend Plan by a prominent communist. The pamphlet is one of a series criticizing quasi-radical movements of the depression, and differentiating them from the Party's program. The author urges political action toward more fundamental economic and social reform based on Marxist theory.

B241 .... "Break the Economic and Political Sabotage of the Monopolists." [New York?]: no publ. [CPUSA], n.d. [1937]. 10 pp.
Reprint of a speech assessing the causes of the mid-depression economic downturn and presenting the Party's political and legislative program to cope with it. The Party's Political Bureau calls for higher wages, shorter hours, unionization, peace through collective security, nationalization, and a people's front government.

B242 .... "Milestones in the History of the Communist Party." New York: Workers Library, 1937. 92 pp.
A reprint, with additional material, of Bittelman's "Fifteen Years of the Communist Party," which appeared in 1934. A brief survey, on the occasion of the 18th anniversary of the Party, is added; entitled "The Vanguard Role of the Communist Party," it appeared in the "Communist," August and September 1937.

B243 .... "Problems of Party Building." New York: Workers Library, 1937. 30 pp.
A speech delivered to Party functionaries in 1937, emphasizing the vanguard role of the Party, the need to recruit membership and to increase "Daily Worker" circulation, the failure of many Party organizations to engage in sufficient independent activity, and the favorable opportunity for the mass propaganda of Marxism, working class power, and socialism. Despite the policy of the united and people's front, however, the Party must engage in more independent activities to build itself into a mass Bolshevik party.

B244 .... "Trotsky the Traitor." New York: Workers Library, 1937. 30 pp.
A recitation of the case against Trotsky as it emerged at the Moscow trials, involving territorial concessions to fascist states for help in coming to power, and the restoration of capitalism. Bittelman seeks to show that Trotsky's record was one of struggle against Lenin and Bolshevism, of treachery throughout. The confessions, he argues, should all be believed.

B245 .... The Party and the People's Front, "Communist," 16 (Aug. 1937), 709-15.

Political alignments in the U.S. are shifting. In order to split the Democratic Party and destroy the New Deal, the reactionaries are trying to draw the conservative Democrats to their side. The communists are trying to build a mass progressive party, while increasing their own party membership. (Excerpts from a speech to a plenary meeting of the Party's Central Committee, June 17-20, 1937.)

B246 .... The Vanguard Role of the Communist Party: On the Occasion of the Eighteenth Anniversary of the C.P.U.S.A., "Communist," 16 (Sept. 1937), 808-23.
The role of the Party as the vanguard of the working class is discussed in terms of the new people's front. The Party must both lead the working class, and labor within it, to attract workers with new demands, organize them into mass movements, educate the masses in Marxism, and show them the superiority of communist to reformist solutions of current problems.

B247 .... Some Problems Before the Tenth Convention of the Communist Party, "Communist," 17 (July 1938), 624-29.
A speech to the convention, asserting that a democratic front, in which the working class would play an important but not leading role, is the appropriate mass progressive organization for the U.S. Its failure might result in acceptance of the capitalist program for recovery. Marxist thought must be brought to American workers.

B248 .... A Historic View of the Struggle for Democracy, "Communist," 17 (Aug. 1938), 711-21.
At various times in American history the masses have united to extend democratic rights. The first struggle with monopoly capitalists came with Populism, which, however, was influenced by bourgeois illusions. Later social democratic leaders betrayed the masses by collaborating with capitalism. With the depression, monopoly capitalism turned to fascism. Now the democratic front against fascism is the appropriate organization.

B249 .... The Reaction to European Events, "World News and Views," 19 (April 19, 1939), 395-96.
Hitler's march into Czechoslovakia has discredited Chamberlain's appeasement policy and forced American isolationism into retreat. Efforts on the part of the capitalist press to interpret Stalin's recent speech as evidence that an alliance between Stalin and Hitler is afoot are branded as fantastic lies.

B250 .... For a Democratic Progressive Front at the Presidential Elections, "World News and Views," 19 (May 20, 1939), 619-20.
A summary of decisions of the national committee of the CPUSA in May, 1939, to broaden the popular front into a democratic-front coalition of workers, farmers, and middle classes in support of Roosevelt.

B251 .... "Jewish Unity for Victory." New York: Workers Library, 1943. 63 pp.
A plea for Jewish unity and a criticism of the recent American Jewish Conference for not making winning the war and Jewish contribution to victory its central theme. Blaming this omission on both the Labor Zionists and the Jewish Labor Committee, the author advances a program for American Jews which includes winning the war, uprooting anti-Semitism and the fifth column, establishing close friendship with USSR Jews, and denunciation of Jewish Red-baiters.

B252 .... Government Intervention in the National Economy, "Communist," 23 (Oct. 1944), 893-910.
A defense of government planning, with a brief account of

the Soviet economy, in answer to Republican critics of New Deal "bureaucracy" or "socialism." The U.S. government must play an important role in our economic affairs in the transition to peace. It is already preparing for a wide expansion of our foreign trade.

B253 BITTELMAN, Alexander. "The Jewish People Face the Post-War World." New York: Morning Freiheit Association, 1945. 31 pp.
A communist view of problems facing American Jews at the end of World War II. The danger of fascism in America, with its accompanying anti-Semitism, is emphasized. Noncommunist Jewish organizations are denounced as lackeys of American imperialism. A cooperative struggle of Arabs and Jews against British imperialism in Palestine is urged.

B254 . . . . Cartels and the Economic Disarmament of Germany, "Political Affairs," 24 (March 1945), 229-45.
Proposals for revision of international economic relations to destroy German cartels, which are called the economic base of German imperialism. Problems of the United Nations in economic collaboration are considered.

B255 . . . . What Is the Outlook for the Jewish People? "Political Affairs," 24 (Oct. 1945), 918-34.
A reappraisal of the Party's domestic and international Jewish policy, correcting errors caused by Browder's revisionism. The Party did not sufficiently emphasize a leading role for Jewish workers in Jewish antifascist unity, safeguard their ideological independence, expose reactionary tendencies in Zionism, or insist on a free and democratic Palestine.

B256 . . . . "Palestine: What Is the Solution?" New York: Morning Freiheit Association, 1946. 15 pp.
A warning against partition of Palestine as a reactionary and imperialist proposal, with a call for a free and independent Palestine of Jews and Arabs. A democratic Jewish-Arab solution will promote peace and democracy, and open the road to socialism. (Reprinted from "Jewish Life," November 1946.)

B257 . . . . How Shall We Fight for Full Employment? "Political Affairs," 25 (Jan. 1946), 50-66.
With present-day unemployment over five million, the result of reconversion and demobilization, it is vital that we reach the objective of sixty million jobs, as outlined in Henry Wallace's book. Yet Wallace holds the illusions that we can maintain full employment without a planned, socialist economy, and that we can persuade the monopolies that this is a desirable and profitable national objective.

B258 . . . . Wages and Profits under Monopoly Capitalism, "Political Affairs," 25 (May 1946), 423-37.
A review of arguments of the auto and steel industries that wage increases must be followed by price increases to keep their rate of profit the same. A Marxist interpretation of labor as the source of all value shows that profit is unpaid labor. Labor's fight is a political one in the interests of the entire population.

B259 . . . . The Anglo-American Bloc, "Political Affairs," 25 (July 1946), 588-96.
U.S. and British imperialism are acting as a bloc against the Soviet Union and all other democratic and peace forces of the world. Present American foreign policy serves only international reaction, whose main driving force is the American monopolies. The American and British governments support each other's imperialist claims in order to maintain their dominating positions.

B260 . . . . The Twenty-Seventh Party Anniversary, "Political Affairs," 25 (Oct. 1946), 867-78.
A review of Party history emphasizing left and right deviation movements and especially the revisionism of Browder, who overestimated the strength of American monopoly capitalism and suggested that the Party abdicate its vanguard role.

B261 . . . . Economic Trends and Perspectives, "Political Affairs," 25 (Nov. 1946), 1001-10.
Cites declining trends and sharp breaks on the stock exchange as signals of economic crisis, and lists issues upon which the masses must make their stand against the economic sabotage of the monopolists.

B262 . . . . Exchange of Letters with Editor, "Congress Weekly," 13 (Dec. 13, 1946), 13-15.
An exchange of letters concerning an editorial by the editors of "Congress Weekly" on the Communist Party resolution on the Jewish problem. Bittelman denies that communists are hostile to Jewish immigration to Palestine or to the progressive developments of Jewish culture in Palestine. The editors point up the disingenuousness of Bittelman's arguments and reassert their opposition to the communist view.

B263 . . . . "Study Guide on the Jewish Question." New York: National Jewish Commission of the Communist Party, n.d. [1946 or 1947]. 14 pp. Mimeo.
A study outline for a communist class on the Jewish question, reflecting the Party's position about 1946. The outline opposes both bourgeois assimilationism and bourgeois chauvinism, and calls for Arab-Jewish unity against British imperialism in Palestine.

B264 . . . . "Program for Survival: The Communist Position on the Jewish Question." New York: New Century, 1947. 63 pp.
Report to a special Party conference in 1946 on the Jewish question. The author denounces the main obstacles to antifascist unity of the Jewish democratic forces: the reactionary Jewish nationalists, assimilationists, and Social Democrats. Resolutions call for efforts to achieve united action and labor unity, present the position of the Party on Palestine and on Jewish immigration, and urge a progressive Jewish culture in America.

B265 . . . . The Role of Jewish Communists, "Jewish Life," 1 (Jan. 1947), 6-8.
A letter to "Congress Weekly," organ of the American Jewish Congress, criticizing its view of the Party position on Jewish work. Bittelman denies that the Party opposes Jewish immigration to Palestine or progressive developments in Jewish culture there. He calls for an independent Palestine of Jews and Arabs guaranteeing equal national rights to both peoples.

B266 . . . . A Communist Wage Policy, "Political Affairs," 26 (March 1947), 221-38.
A call for labor to use both its economic and political power to raise the level of wages. The Nathan Report, "A National Wage Policy for 1947," is generally approved, despite some theoretical defects and weak points of policy. Both the right opportunism of AFL reactionary leadership and the left opportunism of renegade communists are denounced.

B267 . . . . A Democratic Solution for Palestine, "Political Affairs," 26 (July 1947), 576-85.
Support for the "just and democratic" principles for the solution of the Palestine crisis proposed by the USSR at the UN General Assembly. The Soviet proposal calls for abolition of the British mandate, building Arab-Jewish

understanding, and setting up an Arab-Jewish independent and democratic state.

B268 BITTELMAN, Alexander. The Struggle against the Approaching Economic Crisis, "Political Affairs," 26 (Sept. 1947), 836-54.
All signs point to a maturing economic crisis in the U.S. that may break in 1948. Temporary props have sustained the postwar boom; the crisis could be postponed if mass purchasing power were raised in sufficient volume and quickly enough. A program to fight the economic crisis is outlined.

B269 .... "To Secure Jewish Rights: The Communist Position." New York: New Century, 1948. 39 pp.
The "cold-war" communist line, identifying the interests of the Jewish people with opposition to the Truman Doctrine, the Marshall Plan, and Wall Street's offensive for world domination. The first duty of the Jewish people is to promote the Wallace-for-President movement. The author supports the UN partition plan for Israel, denounces Zionism, and warns against Anglo-American imperialists.

B270 .... New Tasks and Realignments in the Struggle for the Jewish State in Palestine, "Political Affairs," 27 (Feb. 1948), 146-55.
The UN decision to establish two independent states in Palestine, one Jewish and one Arab, is hailed as a triumph of justice and truth, though there is danger that Anglo-American imperialism may seek to violate the UN decision. The new Jewish state must ally itself firmly with anti-imperialist world forces. (From a report to the Party's National Jewish Commission, December 12, 1947.)

B271 .... The New State of Israel, "Political Affairs," 27 (Aug. 1948), 720-30.
An appraisal of the role of communists in the emergence of the Jewish state in Israel and of the effect of the new nation on American Jews. Democratic unity of the Jewish people in the U.S. must be built as part of the general American peace coalition, while a similar coalition is built in Israel to fight the supporters of imperialism among the Jewish people.

B272 .... The Beginning of the Economic Crisis in the United States, "Political Affairs," 28 (July 1949), 22-32; (Aug.) 22-34.
An analysis of the crisis in the American economy, covering farm prices, unemployment, retail sales, and exports. Capitalist efforts to avert the crisis through the Marshall Plan, rearmament, and attacks on living standards of workers will prove ineffective. Bittelman supports the official Stalinist position on the question of whether Western capitalism will experience a postwar economic convulsion, and attacks Browder for revisionist economic theories.

B273 .... Our Party's Thirtieth Anniversary. "Political Affairs," 28 (Sept. 1949), 1-13.
The two main principles of the Party are close ties with the masses and adherence to Marxist theory. These principles are fulfilled in the Party's policy of a united front led by a strong Party organization. The united front is an antimonopoly coalition of many mass organizations, each also fighting for specific issues. The Foster tradition has been to carry out this policy.

B274 .... Credo of a Communist, "Jewish Life," 3 (Oct. 1949), 15-21.
Excerpts from notes, in the form of questions and answers, prepared by Bittelman for his appearance before a commissioner of the U.S. Immigration Service, which was seeking his deportation. Subjects covered include labor conditions, American anti-Semitism, the Russian revolution,

Jewish equality, and monopolies. Bittelman denies that he or the Party ever advocated violent overthrow of the American government.

B275 .... Wall Street Optimism and the Developing Crisis, "Political Affairs," 28 (Oct. 1949), 26-32.
An analysis of steel production, unemployment, and farm receipts in the U.S. during the first eight months of 1949 and of currency devaluations in Europe in the same period, to show the imminence of an economic crisis. Murray and Reuther have taken responsibility for Wall Street's plans to drive down American labor's living standards.

B276 .... Reverse Wall Street's Verdict and Prevent the Outlawing of a Working-Class Political Party! "Political Affairs," 28 (Nov. 1949), 1-9.
An editorial article discussing the implications for the American people and particularly for the working class of the conviction of 11 leading communists in New York under the Smith Act. It calls for the reversal of the verdict and for the defense of the Party's right to an open and legal existence.

B277 .... Jerusalem, National Independence and Peace, "Political Affairs," 29 (Jan. 1950), 66-77.
An accusation that Britain and the U.S. deliberately undermined the 1947 UN decisions on the partition of Palestine in order to get control of the oil resources of the Near East. The Israel government is capitulating to Wall Street, which would turn Israel into a semi-colony.

B278 .... The Course of the Developing Economic Crisis, "Political Affairs," 29 (March 1950), 46-57.
An analysis of unemployment, industrial production, and exports during 1948 and 1949, showing the development of an economic crisis in the U.S. While the general crisis of capitalism deepens, the Soviet Union and the People's Democracies are making amazing economic progress. Truman's "welfare state" masks preparations for a new world war.

B279 .... We Are the Vanguard Party of Peace, "Political Affairs," 29 (Sept. 1950), 1-14.
The Party, now celebrating its 31st anniversary, is the vanguard party of peace because it is the party of Marxian-Leninism and therefore of anti-imperialism. It condemns Wall Street's imperialist intervention in Korea. The Circuit Court of Appeals has confirmed the conviction of the 11 communist leaders because the Party threatens the war preparations of American imperialism.

B280 .... Wall Street's War Preparations and the People's Living Standards, "Political Affairs," 29 (Oct. 1950), 58-74.
Wall Street's acts of aggression and preparations for world war are worsening the economic conditions and living standards of the masses of the American people. The fight against the warmakers requires the workers' united front and the people's front against war and fascism.

B281 .... Where Is the "Monthly Review" Going? "Political Affairs," 30 (May 1951), 34-53.
Criticism of "Monthly Review," the "independent socialist" magazine, for lack of confidence in the working class and in the vanguard role of the Party. It reflects imperialist and white chauvinist ideology, tends to political passivity, and opens the door to Titoism and Trotskyism. It is negative and even dangerous from the standpoint of the camp of peace, democracy, and socialism. (For the reaction of the editors of the "Monthly Review," see that publication's issue of November 1951.)

B282 BITTELMAN, Alexander. Who Are the Conspirators? "Political Affairs," 30 (July 1951), 9-21.
An attack on the Supreme Court decision upholding the Smith Act and the conviction of the 11 communist leaders. A process of fascistization of bourgeois rule is now going on in the U.S. The real conspirators are those seeking to drag America into a new world war. Communists will continue to fight for peace, democracy, and socialism.

B283 .... Mass Tasks Facing the Party Today, "Political Affairs," 30 (Sept. 1951), 15-28.
An examination of the Party's tasks on the 32nd anniversary of its founding. Emphasis is placed on the current profascist offensive, the deteriorating economic position of the masses, the pending economic crash, the contradictions of the war economy, and the fight for labor unity and political independence in the 1952 national elections.

B284 .... Lenin's Teachings and the Liberation of Humanity, "Political Affairs," 31 (Jan. 1952), 1-11.
Marxist-Leninist theory has been influential because it is objectively true. It is not a dogma, but a living science that is a guide to action. Mastering Marxism-Leninism means absorbing its substance and spirit, and learning to use it to solve practical problems of the class struggle.

B285 .... Corruption, Warmongering, and the Pro-Fascist Reaction, "Political Affairs," 31 (March 1952), 1-14.
Corruption in the federal government is blamed on monopoly ruling circles, which dominate the government and set the moral tone in national politics. Corruption in government and politics is inseparable from war profiteering, warmongering, racism, and profascist reaction.

B286 .... New Economic Dangers and How to Meet Them, "Political Affairs," 32 (May 1953), 30-47.
The accelerating economic crisis is the result of the war policies and the war economy of the U.S. monopolists. Crisis looms in agriculture and in foreign trade, while the market for most industries is saturated. The first answer of the monopolies is wage cuts and speed-up. The economic and political power of the monopolies must be curbed.

B287 .... Key Problems of Party Program, "Political Affairs," 37 (Feb. 1958), 36-44.
An answer to criticism by William Z. Foster of Bittelman's views on the Party crisis (see Foster's "The Party Crisis and the Way Out," in "Political Affairs," December 1957, and January 1958). Asserting that Foster's article shows no awareness of the need for new methods in mass work, Bittelman analyzes capitalist development in the U.S. and concludes that only the welfare state will permit a peaceful transition to socialism.

.... See also RAPHAEL, A.

B288 BIXLER, Paul. Let's Make up Our Minds, "Antioch Review," 7 (March 1947), 151-55.
Writing for the editorial board of the "Review," Bixler poses the dilemma liberals face when communists call on them for cooperation. The board holds that communists may be excluded from liberal organizations, since they enter them in order to control. The CIO, the American Veterans Committee, and the popular-front youth groups are cited as examples.

B289 .... Anti-intellectualism in California, "Antioch Review," 10 (Dec. 1950), 537-42.
A discussion of implications of the loyalty oath at the University of California, emphasizing two issues: the Board of Regents should understand their relation to the faculty and the general public, not merely reflect the sentiment of business leaders; faculty members too frequently reject America uncritically, thus creating a link in the public eye between themselves and communists.

B290 BLACK, Archie. Millionaire Communist: A Case Study of Frederick Vanderbilt Field, "Plain Talk," 3 (May 1949), 25-30.
An account of Field's affiliation with the Party and with various of its front organizations from the mid-1930's to 1949, emphasizing his leadership of front groups such as the American Peace Mobilization, his services to the Party as an "authority" on the Far East, and his financial contributions to Party causes.

B291 BLACK, Henry. Religion and Communism—A Parallel, "Christian Century," 51 (June 27, 1934), 861-62.
A sketch of "religious types," including the missionary, the theologian, the doubter, and the lay worker, found among the students in a labor school dominated by communists. Some knowledge of religious psychology will be necessary for an understanding of American communism.

B292 .... "Radical Periodicals: Their Place in the Library." Mena, Ark.: Commonwealth College, 1937. 11 pp. Mimeo.
A short essay on why libraries should include important radical publications, with an annotated list of radical periodicals published in 1937. The author, later librarian for the Jefferson School of Social Science in New York, rates Party-oriented periodicals as important, but dismisses socialist and Trotskyist publications as of doubtful value.

B293 .... War Invades the Libraries, "Masses & Mainstream," 5 (Nov. 1952), 52-57.
An assertion that libraries are yielding to reactionaries and Washington's war program, despite some opposition within the American Library Association. Until recently the low quality of book selection reflected commercial book reviewing and lack of information, but since World War II overt censorship has been growing.

B294 BLACKWOOD, George D. The Battle for Local 600, "New Leader," 36 (Aug. 10, 1953), 10-11.
A discussion of reasons for strong communist influence within UAW Local 600 at Ford's River Rouge plant. Local president Carl Stellato, formerly anticommunist, is now allied with them against Reuther. Hostility toward the international union officers, resentment against the company, attention by the communists to workers' grievances, and frequent elections help to explain the communists' success.

B295 "BLACK WORKER" (Brotherhood of Sleeping Car Porters), Communists and the Labor Movement, 6 (Aug. 1940), 4.
An editorial warning union members that communists are a menace to the trade-union movement and a danger to its democracy.

B296 ..., Communists—A Menace to Black America, 11 (Nov. 1945), 1 ff.
An editorial attack on the Party for having betrayed the colored people during World War II. During the Nazi-Soviet pact period the communists deserted the cause of the Negro, and during the war they opposed the fight for jobs for Negroes on the ground it would hold up war production.

B297 ..., The Problem of Communists, 13 (May 1947), 3 ff.

While opposing communism, the editor asserts that reaction threatens all progressive ideas under the guise of suppressing communism. Instead of outlawing the Party, Americans should learn how to find and expose communists; the labor movement must combat communism with democratic ideals and deeds.

B298 BLAIR, Fred B. Some Remarks on Rural Politics, "Communist," 18 (April 1939), 364-70.
The Party chairman in Wisconsin urges development of broad united movements in the townships and counties in order to elect progressive-minded town chairmen and county officials. Control of local administration is a prerequisite to victory in the state. Relief and WPA should be centralized to lighten taxes on small and middle farmers.

B299 .... "The Ashes of Six Million Jews." Milwaukee: People's Book Shop, 1946. 23 pp.
A poem to the memory of the Jews killed by Hitler's Germany, written by the chairman of the Communist Party of Wisconsin. The author points to the USSR as a state that has abolished race hatred and offers the goal of a socialist society that will destroy the roots of famine, greed, prejudice, and war.

B300 BLAKE, Ben. "The Awakening of the American Theatre." Introduction by John Howard Lawson. New York: Tomorrow Publishers for the New Theatre League, 1935. 64 pp.
An account of new tendencies in the theatre of the depression years, written by a participant in the proletarian theatre. The history of such groups as the Theatre Guild, the Workers Drama League, New Playwrights Theatre, the agitprop theatre, Rebel Players, the Theatre Union, the Theatre of Action, and the New Theatre League is given. Representative proletarian plays are discussed.

B301 .... (ed.). "Twelve Plays for Boys and Girls." New York: Federation of Children's Organizations and Junior Section of International Workers Order, 1935. 79 pp.
A collection of working-class plays, to be staged as well as read. Organizations staging them are urged to bring out the social background of the play and the relations of the characters to real life, and to do this in a manner interesting to children.

B302 BLAKE, George. The Party in Harlem, New York, "Party Organizer," 11 (June 1938), 14-20.
A report on recruiting, membership fluctuation, and membership education in the Party's Harlem Division. Though growth has been rapid, membership has fluctuated heavily, especially among the Negroes; in part this is due to insecurity and discrimination suffered by Negroes, and in part to the Party's failures. (From a report to a convention of the Harlem Division, May 6-8, 1938.)

B303 .... "Who Pays for the Cold War? How the Marshall Plan Affects Your Living Standards." New York: New Century, 1949. 23 pp.
An attack on the Marshall Plan by the chairman of the New York County Committee of the Party, who asserts that the Plan has deepened both the European and the American economic crises. He connects expenditures for imperialist purposes with American inflation and unemployment, and views the Plan as part of Wall Street's drive toward World War III.

B304 ..., and TERESTMAN, Al. The People Win with Marcantonio, "Political Affairs," 28 (Jan. 1949), 85-94.
The reelection of Marcantonio to Congress from New York was the outstanding progressive victory in the 1948 elections. With the Roosevelt coalition breaking up, the reactionaries tried to destroy the ALP and Marcantonio. The Republicans attacked the ALP directly, while the Democrats tried to seduce progressives with liberal pledges.

B305 .... The Marcantonio Election Campaign, "Political Affairs," 30 (Jan. 1951), 80-90.
An analysis of the defeat of Vito Marcantonio in the 18th Congressional District, at the hands of a reactionary coalition organized by social democracy. Contributing factors included the uprising in Puerto Rico, an element of defeatism in the conduct of the campaign, and weaknesses in the candidate's position on the Negro question. The dangers of reaction, fascism, and war are growing.

B306 .... The Trade Union Movement and the McGee Case, "Political Affairs," 30 (Aug. 1951), 23-32.
The lynching of Willie McGee symbolizes the savage oppression directed against the Negro people by the forces of reaction. However, Negro workers and the general working-class movement responded well, although there were weaknesses and sectarian errors, as in not broadening the struggle sufficiently against the Truman Administration.

B307 .... The Supreme Court Will Not Have the Last Word! "Political Affairs," 31 (March 1952), 15-21.
The Supreme Court accelerates monopoly's drive toward fascist rule and war by decisions sustaining New York's Feinberg Law, upholding the contempt sentences of the lawyers for the 11 leading communists, and supporting the Attorney General's right to hold without bail individuals facing deportation.

B308 BLANKFORT, Michael. "A Time to Live." New York: Harcourt, Brace, 1943. 343 pp.
An autobiographical novel exposing the hold that Marxism as a doctrine and communism as an organization had upon so many Americans in the 1930's. The impact of the Moscow trials and the Nazi-Soviet pact upon a fellow-traveler is shown.

B309 BLANSHARD, Paul. Communism in Southern Cotton Mills, "Nation," 128 (April 24, 1929), 500-1.
A report on the strike of the communist-led National Textile Workers Union in Gastonia, N.C. The strike, charged with fear and bitterness, resembles civil war. Behind the excitement over communism lie the grievances of the mill workers. The strike is hanging in the balance today.

B310 .... "Communism, Democracy, and Catholic Power." Boston: Beacon, 1951. 340 pp. App. Bibliog. Notes. Ind.
A comparison of communism and Catholicism, emphasizing their similarity as patterns of power. Each has a dictator, a method of deification, thought control, a disciplined elite, deceptive propaganda, and a strategy of penetration. Americans are urged to oppose the political power and authoritarian spirit of both the Vatican and the Kremlin, as totalitarian agencies whose aims and methods are incompatible with democratic ideals.

B311 BLAUFARB, Douglas. WPA Terror: CP Demands Tribute in Exchange for Relief Jobs, "New Leader," 21 (July 9, 1938), 1 ff.
First of a series of articles on communist control of the WPA Artists', Writers', and Theatre Projects. CPUSA members in supervisory positions engage in such practices as giving preferential treatment to Party members or

sympathizers, forcing writers to pay "Daily Worker" assessments, and spending their time on Party work. (Later articles in this series by Blaufarb are: "Jobless Anti-Stalinites Persecuted by CP-Controlled Workers Alliance," July 16, 1 ff; "CP Members Ordered to Drive Trotskyites Off WPA," July 23, 1 ff; and "C.P. Plans Reprisals for Exposure of WPA Terror," July 30, 1 ff.)

B312 BLEDSOE, Thomas. Hierarchy over Washington, "Protestant," 8 (Jan. 1949), 11-16; (Feb.), 8-10; (March), 5-10.
A comparison of President Truman's loyalty order and federal legislative moves against communists with the Holy Inquisition of the Catholic Church. The procedure of the New Inquisition is examined in Loyalty Board hearings.

B313 BLEDSOE, William. Revolution Came to Hollywood, "American Mercury," 49 (Feb. 1940), 152-61.
An analysis by the editor of "Screen Guild Magazine" of communist activities in Hollywood during the popular-front period. He describes meetings of the Party and its front groups, money-raising functions, and infiltration of studio labor organizations. Names of active Stalinists are listed. Disillusionment set in, however, with the signing of the Nazi-Soviet pact.

B314 BLIVEN, Bruce, Jr. The Fifth American Youth Congress, "New Republic," 99 (July 19, 1939), 302-3.
A Coughlinite-sponsored move to bar communists from membership in the American Youth Congress was defeated at its Fifth Annual Convention, and a resolution condemning all dictatorships, fascist or communist, was adopted. Young Communist League delegates voted for this resolution. The author denies that the AYC is communist-dominated.

B315 . . . . Two Worlds at Foley Square, "New Republic," 120 (May 9, 1949), 12-14.
An account of the famous communist trial, now in progress for 14 weeks, emphasizing the tactics of the defense attorneys and the conduct of the trial by Judge Harold R. Medina. The editorial director of the "New Republic" seeks to capture the atmosphere of the trial and the undercurrents present.

B316 BLOOR, Ella Reeve. "Women in the Soviet Union." New York: Workers Library, 1938. 15 pp.
The text of a radio address broadcast from Moscow to England and the U.S., November 2, 1937, discussing the position and achievements of women in the Soviet Union. Attention is paid to the number of women in the professions, their prominence in political life, their equal rights and equal responsibilities with men.

B317 . . . . "We Are Many: An Autobiography." Introd. by Elizabeth Gurley Flynn. New York: International Publishers, 1940. 319 pp. Ind.
The autobiography of "Mother" Bloor, one of the founding members of the communist movement in the U.S. The book tells of her early life and formative years, her activities in the Socialist Party before the Bolshevik Revolution, and her later participation successively in the Communist Labor Party, the Workers Party, and the Communist Party. Chapters deal with her work with the Party's trade union and civil rights organizations and her trips to the USSR.

B318 . . ., and FLYNN, Elizabeth Gurley. Women in the National Front Against Hitler, "Communist," 20 (Oct. 1941), 897-909.
While fascism is the greatest world menace, it is woman's greatest enemy in a special way. By subjecting women to the will of the state in determining the labor they perform and their role in sex and childbearing, fascism destroys the very dignity of women. American women must organize a strong front to push the war effort.

B319 BLUM, Emanuel, and FIGUEIREDO, Joseph C. "What's Ahead for Textile Workers." Boston: Communist Party of New England, 1948. 47 pp.
An attack on employers as parasites who live on the labor of textile workers, and who seek war and destruction through the Marshall Plan. The authors condemn Emil Rieve and the Textile Workers Union as agents of the bosses, and urge support for the Progressive Party and the communists.

B320 BLUM, Emanuel. The Steel Settlement and a Look Ahead, "Political Affairs," 34 (Sept. 1955), 48-59.
The 15-cent wage increase in steel, a victory for all labor, followed a 20-cent auto wage settlement. Steel labor could have won more had it been fully mobilized. Demands of the union's social democratic leadership for extension of the guaranteed annual wage should not be permitted to divert the workers from the main lines of struggle.

B321 BLUMBERG, A. E. The 78th Congress, "Communist," 22 (Aug. 1943), 711-19.
The reactionaries of the 78th Congress have defeated much of the Administration's domestic policy and hence have disrupted the war effort. The trade unions are being mobilized to put popular pressure on the members of Congress to support the Administration.

B322 . . . . Notes on the Electoral Outlook for '52, "Political Affairs," 30 (April 1951), 53-63.
A review and analysis of recent political developments, based on a report to the Party's national committee, March 5, 1951. Evidence of growing labor support for a labor or farmer-labor party is cited. The Progressive Party, despite its important role, is not an adequate base for a third party. The outlook for an independent peace ticket in 1952 is improving.

B323 . . . . The November Elections and the Party Program, "Political Affairs," 33 (Dec. 1954), 3-13.
The November congressional elections constituted a rebuff to Eisenhower, a defeat for the GOP, and a sharp setback for the McCarthyites. An analysis of the returns shows that labor was the main driving force in the GOP defeat. A positive program for peace must be placed in the center of the anti-Administration movement.

B324 . . . . Labor, Congress, and the '56 Elections, "Political Affairs," 34 (Jan. 1955), 33-43.
Setbacks for McCarthy and for the allied "War Now" conspirators led by Knowland open opportunities for a labor-based movement for peaceful co-existence. In order to oust the Eisenhower Administration in 1956, labor must become a distinct force within the framework of the two-party system. A fight for labor and the people must be made in the new Congress.

B325 . . ., and MAGIL, A. B. Peace and the 1956 Elections, "Political Affairs," 34 (May 1955), 9-19.
The decisive issue in the 1956 elections will be peace. A new tactical rift is developing within the bourgeoisie. The Democratic Party opposes, not the bipartisan war program as a whole, but only its most bellicose features. Labor, the key to the 1956 elections, must develop an independent, active policy for peace.

B326 . . ., and HALL, Rob. Congress and '56, "Political Affairs," 34 (Dec. 1955), 1-13.

60

Though the first session of the 84th Congress contributed to peace, it retained the cold-war approach to legislation and the budget. Its failures, especially in civil rights, were glaring. The second session should advance peace, while restoring the Bill of Rights and enacting a domestic program blocked by a decade of cold war.

B327 BLUMBERG, A. E. The '56 Elections, "Political Affairs," 35 (Jan. 1956), 19-35.
A report to the Party's national conference, December 3-5, 1955, emphasizing the opportunity of the '56 elections to win victories for labor and the people, strengthen labor independent political action, and increase the role of the left in the people's democratic coalition. The Party must help end the cold war, restore the Bill of Rights for all, and assure its legal existence.

B328 BLUME, Peter. American Artists Today, "New Masses," 19 (May 12, 1936), 20-21.
A historical analysis of the role of artists in class society. Since the great depression, their illusions have been shattered. Now they are fighting war and fascism, and helping to create a better social order.

B329 BLYNE, Murray (comp.). "Guide to Readings on Communism." New York: New York Workers Book Shop, n.d. [1935?]. 22 pp.
An annotated list of Marxist-Leninist writings, compiled for those "who are finding their way to Communism." Selections are grouped under 11 heads: Introduction to communism, the rise and decline of capitalism, the labor and trade union movement, the dictatorship of the proletariat, the fight against war and fascism, working class unity, the Soviet Union, the Negro question, dialectical materialism, problems of communism, and literature.

B330 BOAS, George, and WHEELER, Harvey (eds.). "Lattimore the Scholar." Baltimore: Lattimore Defense Fund, 1953. 61 pp.
A collection of letters attesting to the scholarly standing of Owen Lattimore in the field of Sinology (study of China). Written when Lattimore faced perjury charges for denial of communist sympathies, and when his scholarly status had been challenged, these 37 opinions regard him as one of the leading Sinologists in this country. While no judgment is made of his political or social views, there is an implied assumption that these do not prejudice his scholarly work.

B331 BODENHEIM, Maxwell. "Run, Sheep, Run." New York: Liveright, 1932. 234 pp.
The story of a proletarian who, after being sidetracked in bohemianism, is brought back to the ranks of the workers after he becomes involved in a communist demonstration. He and his working class sweetheart work together for the revolution.

B332 .... "Slow Vision." New York: Macaulay, 1934. 247 pp.
The protagonist, at the start in the grip of petty-bourgeois illusions, within a year is ready to join a red union and to strike.

B333 BOHN, William E. Who Created Matusow? "New Leader," 38 (March 21, 1955), 6-7.
"False Witness," the book by the turncoat informer, tells much about why people become communists, how they feel, and why they leave. An active member of the Communist Party, Matusow turned against them, helping send a number to jail, then returned to the Party fold and denounced his former testimony as false. Political degeneration permits degenerates to play a part.

B334 .... U.S. Communists on the Spot, "New Leader," 39 (April 9, 1956), 6.
A review of "Daily Worker" reactions to the de-Stalinization campaign. After long remaining paralyzed and speechless, the Party leaders here acknowledge that they should have showed more independence. But they still do not ask the important questions, such as what sort of people head the Soviet government.

B335 BOLLER, Paul F., Jr. Academic Freedom and Communist Professors, "Christian Scholar," 42 (March 1959), 16-29.
In some fields, as fine arts and sciences, a communist may be outstanding; the problem is more complicated in the social sciences and the humanities. Nevertheless a communist teacher who possesses the professional qualifications for university work, who makes his position candidly known, and who is willing to meet colleagues in discussion and debate can be a valuable asset on a university faculty.

B336 BOLSOVER, Philip. "America over Britain." New York: International Publishers, 1953. 128 pp.
A communist effort to analyze American foriegn policy. The book, written primarily for a British audience, explains American foreign policy as an effort of American imperialism to supplant the British. The Marshall Plan and the Truman Doctrine were designed to create subservient governments in Europe as a military base for war against the "socialist camp." The International Confederation of Free Trade Unions is seen as an effort by American imperialism to split the World Federation of Trade Unions. In contrast, the policies of the "socialist camp" are for peace and progress.

B337 BONOSKY, Philip. "Brother Bill McKie: Building the Union at Ford." New York: International Publishers, 1953. 192 pp.
A communist interpretation of the unionization of the Ford Motor Company, emphasizing the key role of the Party in the organization of the auto industry. A portrait is given of Bill McKie, an important leader in the struggle, who finally joined the Party. The author praises the working class spirit which organized the Ford empire whole holding off the Reuthers, the supporters of "creeping fascism."

B338 .... "Burning Valley." New York: Masses & Mainstream, 1953. 288 pp.
A first novel by a Party functionary, revolving around the conflict between Catholicism and Marxism in the mind and heart of a boy in a coal-mining town. The young adolescent eventually lines up with his father and his father's communist friends.

B339 .... Salute to Mike Gold, "Masses & Mainstream," 7 (April 1954), 43-49.
A tribute to a leading Marxist writer who chose truth over comfort, who stayed close to the people, who scorned the chase after dollars. Of all the writers coming up from formerly unrepresented classes, from workers, Negroes, and the children of foreign-born, Gold best represented what was truly proletarian.

B340 BONTECOU, Eleanor. Does the Loyalty Program Threaten Civil Rights? "Annals of the American Academy of Political and Social Science," 275 (May 1951), 117-23.
A review of the federal loyalty program, concluding that, despite many corrections of unfair procedures, it violates accepted principles of due process of law. The compilations of dossiers on a large scale by the FBI involves obvious dangers, despite FBI policy not to evaluate the information it gathers. The investigation of disloyalty,

involving thought as well as action, is being left to amateurs.

B341 BONTECOU, Eleanor. "The Federal Loyalty-Security Program." Ithaca: Cornell University Press, 1953. 377 pp. App. Ind.
An examination of civil liberties issues arising from Acts to eliminate subversives from government service. The volume describes the origins, legal basis, and operation of the loyalty program through 1952, discussing the mechanics of adjudication, the problems of the investigated, the impact of loyalty and security cases, the Attorney General's list of subversive organizations, and the relationship of the loyalty-security program to legal tradition. While approving in general of the administration of the program, the author finds that unnecessary violations of due process and other faults result from the terms of the Loyalty Order, unwise administration, and the "curse of bigness." She warns that maintenance of basic freedoms is necessary to national security.

B342 . . . . Due Process in Security Dismissals, "Annals of the American Academy of Political and Social Science," 300 (July 1955), 102-9.
A critical examination of the procedure used by the federal government in dismissals of civilian employees on security grounds. The accused is not informed fully as to the information against him or given the right to face his accusers. Particular problems are presented by paid informers and professional anticommunist witnesses. Well-defined standards that apply in all cases should be developed.

B343 BORKENAU, F. "World Communism: A History of the Communist International." Introd. by Raymond Aron. Ann Arbor: University of Michigan Press, 1962. 442 pp. Bibliog. notes. Ind.
A recent edition of a work that was first published in this country in 1939, the year after it appeared in Britain as "The Communist International." The author, who had been a communist in his youth, traces the three periods of the Comintern: first as an instrument for revolution, then as a factor in Russian factional struggles, and finally as a tool of Soviet foreign policy. He shows how the Bolsheviks split the socialist movement in other countries, weakened the leftist parties, and made inevitable their defeats in Hungary, Germany, and elsewhere. There are scattered references to the communist movement in the U.S.

B344 BORNET, Vaughn D. Historical Scholarship, Communism and the Negro, "Journal of Negro History," 37 (July 1952), 304-24.
Critical comments on Wilson Record's "The Negro and The Communist Party," and on William A. Nolan's "Communism Versus the Negro." Record is criticized for not covering available resources, whereas Nolan commits methodological errors because he is a scholar turned propagandist. Further areas for scholarship are suggested.

B345 . . . . The Communist Party in the Presidential Election of 1928, "Western Political Quarterly," 11 (Sept. 1958), 514-38.
A description of the behavior of the Party and its leaders in the 1928 campaign, emphasizing their antagonistic attitude toward democratic institutions and their belief that only struggle would bring them to power. Their objectives in the campaign were to mobilize the working class, increase class consciousness, and overthrow existing society. Viewing the election as a "sham" one, they participated for publicity reasons.

B346 BOSSE, A. G. The Economic Situation in the United States During 1926, "Communist," 6 (March 1927), 17-24.
A survey of economic conditions in the U.S., concluding that prospects for continued prosperity are unfavorable, although there are some compensating features.

B347 . . . . The American Coal-Mining Situation, "Communist International," 4 (May 1, 1927), 123-25.
A report on the election battle in the United Mine Workers between the reactionary John L. Lewis and the progressive elements, led by John Brophy and supported by the Party. The Lewis machine, following its use of illegal methods, proclaimed a victory. The union faces disaster.

B348 . . . . American Militarism, "Communist," 6 (Sept.-Oct. 1927), 347-57.
A review, on the occasion of the naval disarmament conference in Geneva, of military preparations and militarism in the U.S. The U.S. will play a leading part in any new war; the era of its passive role as vendor of supplies and moneylender is over.

B349 . . . . The National Hunger March to Washington, "International Press Correspondence," 11 (Dec. 24, 1931), 1165-66.
A description and analysis of the Hunger March to Washington, organized by the Unemployed Councils and supported by the CPUSA, the Trade Union Unity League, and the Workers International Relief. When the four columns from various parts of the country converged on Washington, there were demonstrations, a conference, and demands on Congress to pass the workers unemployment insurance bill.

B350 . . . . The Plenum of the CC of the CPUSA, "International Press Correspondence," 12 (May 19, 1932), 443-44.
A resumé of the work of the Fourteenth Plenum of the Central Committee, CPUSA, held April 16-19, 1932. The foremost task outlined was the struggle against the imperialist war now being organized against the Soviet Union. Other topics included a turn to mass work, methods of mobilizing the membership in this direction, and work in the 1932 presidential elections.

B351 . . . . The Results of the American Elections, "International Press Correspondence," 12 (Dec. 8, 1932), 1179-81.
A review of the 1932 election campaign. The Democratic landslide means that the masses of workers and petty-bourgeois cleaned house as effectively as their class consciousness permitted. Since Roosevelt will carry out the same basic policies, and since there is no end in sight, mass discontent will deepen. The result will be greater influence for the Communist Party.

B352 . . . . Eighth Convention of the CPUSA, "International Press Correspondence," 14 (June 1, 1934), 861-62.
A brief review of the convention, summarizing Browder's report on membership and on criticism of Party work, particularly in the shop nuclei and in the TUUL unions. The Party's task in the coming period is to win the workers and allied groups for the struggle against war and fascism and for the revolutionary way out of the crisis.

B353 . . . . The United Front in the USA, "International Press Correspondence," 14 (Oct. 5, 1934), 1372-74.
A review of united-front activities, including the Party's effort to build a united front with the socialists, who are charged with delaying tactics. The CP does not use the

united front as a maneuver to discredit the socialist leaders. The YCL and the YPSL are making joint efforts to win control of the American Youth Congress.

B354 BOSSE, A. G. The Result of the USA Elections, "International Press Correspondence," 14 (Dec. 1, 1934), 1600-1.
The 1934 landslide victory of the New Deal was a vote by the American working class for the lesser of two evils. Communists improved their votes in comparison with the Socialist Party, which declined. The CP must lead the masses in struggles against the New Deal trend toward fascism and toward lower living standards, and also counteract SP efforts to form a third party.

B355 .... The CPUSA and the Question of a Labor Party, "International Press Correspondence," 15 (April 6, 1935), 416-17.
Summary of two resolutions passed by the Central Committee of the CPUSA in January 1935, taking a more favorable view of a labor party. The first has to do with the labor party line in general, while the second deals specifically with the Minnesota Farmer-Labor Party. The effort is to reconcile the new line with the united front from below, not yet abandoned by the CP.

B356 BOUDIN, Leonard B. The Constitutional Privilege in Operation, "Lawyers Guild Review," 12 (Summer 1952), 128-49.
An examination of recent cases involving the privilege against self-incrimination, with criticism of its treatment in certain courts. Congressional committees continue to compel witnesses to incriminate themselves, with those who resist facing contempt citations. The attack upon the privilege occurs in a pattern of social repression.

B357 BOUDIN, Louis B. From Foster to La Follette: The United Front and the Third Party Movement, "American Labor Monthly," 2 (July 1924), 32-37.
A critical analysis by a former intellectual leader of the left wing in the Socialist Party of the effort of the Workers Party to join the La Follette movement. Like the reformists in the pre-war Socialist Party, the Workers Party now seeks an alliance with small capital against big capital. It wants to establish a coalition with La Follette and William Jennings Bryan.

B358 .... Seditious Doctrines and the Clear and Present Danger Rule, "Virginia Law Review," 38 (Feb. 1952), 143-86; (April), 315-56.
A discussion of the clear and present danger doctrine as it relates to the Communist Party, with emphasis on its demise in the Dennis case. The theory of the prosecution was that Marxism-Leninism is a doctrine of force and violence, in violation of the clear and present danger rule. Defendants were not indicted for actual conspiracy, but for teaching a doctrine that might have that effect.

B359 BOULWARE, L. R. "What to Do about Communism in Unions." General Electric Company, Employee and Plant Community Relations Service Division, 1952. 22 pp.
Reprint of a letter from a high management official to a Senate subcommittee, urging Congress to eliminate communists from positions of power and influence in unions, and set up an independent government agency to designate such persons. Government, not employers, should determine who are communist leaders. The labor movement has done little to solve this problem.

B360 BOUSCAREN, Anthony T. "America Faces World Communism." Introd. by George Creel. New York: Vantage Press, 1953. 196 pp. App. Bibliog. Ind.
The author, a political scientist at the University of San Francisco, sees our foreign policy as a sequence of appeasements and betrayals, including actual treason. He discusses the Korean War, the evolution of our foreign policy, the new Soviet leadership following Stalin, the situation in the Middle East and in Europe, the Soviet fifth column in America, and the Institute of Pacific Relations as a case history of communist influence on American Far Eastern policy. He urges the U.S. to lead the entire non-Soviet world in an offensive to eliminate the Soviet cancer.

B361 .... "Imperial Communism." Washington, D.C.: Public Affairs Press, 1953. 256 pp. Bibliog. Ind.
An analysis, by a conservative political scientist, of the imperialistic aims of the Soviet Union. Though most of the book is concerned with other countries, one chapter (pp. 221-42) is devoted to the communist offensive in the U.S. Asserting that American communists operate solely as tools of Soviet policy, the author discusses violations of security and evidence of espionage in the cases of "Amerasia," the Institute of Pacific Relations, the Rosenbergs, and Alger Hiss.

B362 .... Khrushchev and the Twentieth Party Congress, "Catholic World," 183 (August 1956), 363-67.
The Twentieth Congress seeks to appease discontent within the Soviet sphere, extend neutralism abroad, and weaken anticommunists in the U.S. Despite Khrushchev's denunciation of Stalin, there is no basic change in communist doctrine. The U.S. should increase its anticommunist activities at home and abroad.

B363 .... Nature of Communist Fronts, "National Republic," 44 (Dec. 1956), 21-22.
A description of the way in which communists operate through front organizations. A list of front organizations is given, and ways to identify them are listed.

B364 .... The Anatomy of American Communism, "Catholic World," 184 (Feb. 1957), 334-39.
A review of Party strength and organization in the U.S., with attention to the types of persons who are attracted to it. Among these are mission-minded intellectuals, psychologically maladjusted individuals, adventurous spirits, and embittered professionals. The Party is now reverting to its popular-front line to gain respectability and reach the masses.

B365 .... "A Guide to Anti-Communist Action." Chicago: Regnery, 1958. 244 pp. Notes. App. Bibliog.
A discussion of the communist threat, both external and internal, and how to combat it. Part II, pp. 103-213, deals with the internal communist threat. Among the topics considered are communist penetration into the U.S., why people become communists, identification of communists and communist fronts, and the fight against communism, with particular attention to education. The Christopher movement to encourage positive action against communism is described. Herbert R. O'Conor contributes a chapter on the impact of the 1957 Supreme Court decisions on communism.

B366 .... "You Can Stop Communism." Foreword by Herbert A. Philbrick. New Rochelle, N.Y.: America's Future, 1961. 19 pp.
A discussion of the danger of communism to the U.S. and the entire free world, with suggestions of anticommunist actions in which individuals and groups may engage. Ways of identifying communists and communist fronts are outlined, and typical communist arguments, with refutations, are presented.

B367 BOUSCAREN, Anthony T. "A Textbook on Communism." Milwaukee: Bruce, 1965. 216 pp. App. Bibliog. Ind.
A textbook presenting the essentials of communist theory, the internal structure and foreign policy of the USSR, the rise of other communist states, and the international communist movement. Chapters 17-18, pp. 152-71, deal with communism in the U.S., including Party history, front organizations, congressional investigations, anticommunist legislation, subversive activities, and current strength. Chapter 19, pp. 172-78, tells how to identify communists and communist fronts, and chapter 21, pp. 185-93, outlines a strategy for America.

B368 BOW, Frank T. Ohio Fights Communism, "National Republic," 41 (May 1953), 1-2.
An Ohio Congressman describes the investigation by the Ohio Un-American Activities Commission of the communist movement in that state. The principal work of the Party is carried on through front groups, which are listed.

B369 BOXLY, George T. The Twelve: A Lawyer Looks at the Case, "Masses & Mainstream," 1 (Dec. 1948), 26-34.
An assertion that the current trial of the 12 national committeemen of the Party will vindicate or destroy the constitutional foundation of American freedom for years to come. The legal basis of the indictments is examined against the background of American constitutional history. The issue is thought control versus the Bill of Rights.

B370 BOYD, Ernest. Challenge to Communists, "Atlantic Monthly," 156 (Dec. 1935), 727-33.
An analysis of the new popular front line of the CPUSA, emphasizing past errors in the Party's estimate of America. If communism is to win adherents here, it must drop Russian Marxism for a theory corresponding to American needs and circumstances.

B371 .... Marxian Literary Critics, "Scribner's Magazine," 98 (Dec. 1935), 342-46.
A satirical survey of Marxist literary criticism and its class-conscious interpretation of literature. Among those ridiculed are "Robert Forsythe," Michael Gold, Granville Hicks, and Joshua Kunitz, who seek to foster a literature of interest only to Union Square. We should support those who would preserve the cultural heritage of Western civilization.

B372 .... The Literary Comrade: A Portrait, "American Mercury," 40 (Jan. 1937), 78-82.
A caustic caricature of communist literary figures who seek economic security while following the Party line and glorifying the class conscious worker.

B373 .... The United Affront, "American Mercury," 42 (Nov. 1937), 275-83.
Criticism of all totalitarians, communist as well as fascist, and of intellectuals who accept the communist-inspired united front. The idea that the whole structure of Western civilization must be torn down to solve the economic problem for the benefit of one class, the proletariat, constitutes the United Affront.

B374 BOYD, Julian P. Subversive of What? "Atlantic Monthly," 182 (Aug. 1948), 19-23.
A comparison of Jefferson's opposition to the Alien and Sedition Acts with the passage of the Subversive Activities Control Act. Promise of human improvement depends on the freedoms which Jefferson advocated. Cases involving teachers, scientists, and the banning of textbooks show the mounting demand for conformity. (Also published in "Bulletin of the American Association of University Professors," Autumn 1948, pp. 527-38.)

B375 BOYD, Thomas. "In Time of Peace." New York: Minton, Balch, 1935. 309 pp.
The story of an unsophisticated white-collar worker who loses his naiveté and his job, and ends up by joining a communist demonstration. He then realizes that one must prepare for class war, to fight against injustice and oppression.

B376 BOYER, Richard O. Challenge to Youth, "New Masses," 61 (Oct. 22, 1946), 6-9.
An appeal to youth to join the communists, to the end that the people, not monopoly, will own the American earth. The communists are said to be the inheritors of the best in the American tradition. Their internationalism recognizes that one cannot love his country until he loves mankind.

B377 .... "The Dark Ship." Boston: Little, Brown, 1947. 306 pp.
A procommunist account of the National Maritime Union. Part I describes the voyage of an NMU-manned ship to Liverpool during World War II, picturing the typical day-by-day work of the union during this period. Part II tells the story of shipping before the NMU, and the subsequent history of the NMU. The author describes Joseph Curran, union president, as a new type of labor leader, and condemns President Truman's antilabor stand in the 1946 waterfront strike.

B378 .... They're Jailing Anti-Fascists, "New Masses," 44 (July 29, 1947), 3-4.
A protest against the sentencing to prison terms of 11 leaders of the Joint Anti-Fascist Refugee Committee for refusing to furnish names to the House Un-American Activities Committee. This is part of the drive against civil liberties in this country. Freedom of the victims can be won by the growth of a new party that rejects Red-baiting.

B379 .... "If This Be Treason." New York: New Century, 1948. 31 pp.
Protesting the indictment of the 12 Communist Party leaders under the Smith Act, the author argues that communists are as American as were the Jeffersonians, always fighting for the welfare of the majority. He traces his own commitment to the Party, relating it to his view of Americanism. Charging that monopoly capitalism seeks fascism here, he calls for support of the Progressive Party and Henry Wallace.

B380 .... "Hold High the Torch!" New York: New Century, 1951. 15 pp.
A protest by an editor of "Masses & Mainstream" against the outlawing of the Communist Party, because, he charges, reaction disliked its peace platform. The author protests against the sentencing of the officers of the Civil Rights Congress. He asserts that this nation became great by the efforts of men who were often called traitors and sometimes jailed.

B381 .... Gestapo, U.S.A., "Masses & Mainstream," 4 (Jan. 1951), 15-22.
A favorable review article of "The Federal Bureau of Investigation," by Max Lowenthal. In support of the status quo, J. Edgar Hoover is creating a police state, getting Americans to spy on their neighbors and nearly destroying the Constitution. His special province is thought control and the spoken word, both protected by the First Amendment. His special targets are organized labor, Negroes, and communists.

B382 .... Hear the Accents Our Fathers Spoke, "New World Review," 19 (Sept. 1951), 4-10.
Denunciation of the Supreme Court's approval of the Smith

Act, under which communists are being convicted. This is part of a war on civil rights and supporters of peace. The fight of the communists to preserve the Bill of Rights and prevent war is compared to the fight of our forefathers against the Alien and Sedition Acts.

B383 BOYER, Richard O. Pettis Perry: The Story of a Working-Class Leader, "Masses & Mainstream," 4 (Dec. 1951), 15-32.
A eulogy of Perry, currently under indictment for violation of the Smith Act. Perry's life is traced, from boyhood on a tenant farm in Alabama, through life as a migratory worker, to his career as a Party leader. Aroused by the Scottsboro case, he joined the ILD and then the Party in 1932, rising to become a member of its national committee and a leader in its Negro and farm work. (Also published in pamphlet form.)

B384 .... "The Cold-War Murder: The Frame-up against Ethel and Julius Rosenberg." Introd. by William L. Patterson. New York: Civil Rights Congress, 1952. 47 pp.
An account of the lives of Ethel and Julius Rosenberg and a brief analysis of their alleged "frame-up." An analysis of the trial by D. N. Pritt, an English communist, concludes that the convictions violate all Anglo-Saxon standards of justice. The international campaign for clemency for the Rosenbergs is described and supported.

B385 .... Elizabeth Gurley Flynn: An Epic of American Labor, "Masses & Mainstream," 5 (May 1952), 5-20.
A biographical tribute to Elizabeth Gurley Flynn, written at the time of her trial in New York City under the Smith Act. Because she is a threat to Wall Street's plans for war, she is threatened with prison. But she still stands as a pioneer of industrial unionism and a leader of some of the most important strikes in the annals of American labor.

B386 ..., and MORAIS, Herbert M. "Labor's Untold Story." New York: Cameron Associates, 1955. 402 pp. Ind.
A communist history of the American labor movement from the Civil War to the present day. It tells little of specific unions, instead drawing a picture of opposed forces: trade unions, farmers, small businessmen, the Negro people, America as pitted against Wall Street, reaction, the "iron heel," monopoly, and sell-out labor leaders. The authors end with a condemnation of the hot- and cold-war, and call for a new coalition of the American people under labor leadership.

B387 BRADEN, Anne. "House Un-American Activities Committee: Bulwark of Segregation." Los Angeles: National Committee to Abolish the House Un-American Activities Committee, n.d. [1964]. 49 pp. Ref. notes.
An assertion that advocates of civil rights are persistently called communists and the integration movement labeled as subversive, the result of false charges made by the House Un-American Activities Committee, the Senate Internal Security Subcommittee, or one of several state committees modeled after these. The history and activities of these federal and state committees are outlined.

B388 BRADLEY, Hugh. "Next Steps in the Struggle for Negro Freedom." New York: New Century, 1953. 48 pp.
A report to the national conference of the Party. Emphasis is placed on the struggle against war and fascism, the fight for jobs for Negroes, the amnesty movement for Negro victims of the Smith Act, and the fight against Jim Crow. The NAACP top leadership is attacked for capitulation to the Eisenhower Administration and for Red-baiting. The National Negro Labor Council is praised for achievements, but warned to follow a firm united front policy. Current tasks include developing the Negro youth movement and building the Party in key Negro centers.

B389 .... The N.A.A.C.P. Convention, "Political Affairs," 32 (Nov. 1953), 54-60.
An extract from the report on Negro work at the Party's recent national conference, praising the NAACP convention for a progressive program, a good resolution on labor, and an improved foreign policy statement, but criticizing Walter White for Red-baiting and support of Eisenhower, and attacking the passage of an anticommunist resolution.

B390 BRAHMS [BRAHNS], George. Monopolies, Prices and Profits, "Communist," 17 (June 1938), 553-61.
An assertion, in view of demands for a congressional investigation of monopolistic practices, that only a tiny fraction of profits is reinvested. The bulk of profits goes into stock market gambling, financing fascist gangs, supporting private luxury, or is simply idle.

B391 BRAHNS, George. Has the Crisis Run Its Course? "Communist," 17 (Aug. 1938), 743-48.
Roosevelt's recovery program cannot reverse the downward economic trend. The crisis may surpass the deepest one of 1932; the present-day monopolistic economy cannot lift itself automatically from the deepest point. The recovery program of the democratic front is the only way out of the crisis for the American people.

B392 .... Idle Money—Doom or Boon? "Communist," 18 (July 1939), 648-56.
An analysis of the detrimental effect of surplus capital on small business, workers, and the economy. Monopoly control of capital, with the large surplus which is generated, will never provide for sufficient investment to meet the needs of the workers. Therefore government must limit monopolies, invest the surplus, and nationalize the banks.

B393 .... The Impact of the War on the Structure of Capitalism, "Communist," 19 (May 1940), 451-62.
The contradiction between steadily increasing productive capacity and lagging markets is the cause of capitalist crises and, ultimately, of war. Capitalism, weakened in the second imperialist war, will be unable to switch back to a peace economy, with resulting general economic chaos in the capitalist world. The capitalist war economy is based on class collaboration.

B394 BRAMELD, Theodore. Karl Marx and the American Teacher, "Social Frontier," 2 (Nov. 1935), 53-56.
Teachers who advocate the Marxist goal of a socialist society must consider the means Marx proposed. They must use, not merely persuasion, but revolutionary opposition to the present system. As members of the working class, they must organize trade unions and foster class consciousness.

B395 .... American Education and the Social Struggle, "Science and Society," I (Fall 1936), 1-17.
A discussion of the relationship between Marxism and our educational system. The notion of class struggle is a scientific hypothesis which is key to the understanding of modern society. Teachers who accept the hypothesis have a legitimate right to indoctrinate their students, so long as they present, scrupulously and completely, evidence on both sides of the issue.

B396 .... "Ends and Means in Education: A Mid-

Century Appraisal.'' New York: Harper, 1950. 244 pp. Ind.

In chapter 12, ''Communism and the American Teacher'' (pp. 107-17), the author asserts that the primary task of education should be to reconstruct a culture which, left alone, would collapse of its own conflicts. The author in part sympathizes with and in part opposes the Marxist approach to education. Teachers are urged to reject antidemocratic solutions, whether from right or left.

BRANSTEN, Richard. See MINTON, Bruce.

B397   BRANT, Irving. Sentence First, Verdict Afterwards, ''New Republic,'' 131 (Dec. 20, 1954), 10-13.

An assertion that the Gwinn Amendment to the National Housing Act, denying occupancy of the housing to persons belonging to organizations held subversive by the Attorney General, is a bill of attainder and unconstitutional. Test cases are on their way to the Supreme Court.

B398   BRENNER, Anita, and WINTHROP, S. S. ''Tampa's Reign of Terror.'' New York: International Labor Defense, n.d. [1934]. 16 pp.

A protest against flagrant violations of civil liberties in Tampa, Fla. Because of injuries to two policemen, 15 men and women are serving sentences on chain gangs and county farms, under such brutality that three have gone insane. Many others have been jailed, deported, or beaten by vigilantes. Unemployed cigar workers are victims of the terror, especially directed against radicals, Negroes, and Spanish-Americans. (Part of this appeared under the same title in the ''Nation,'' December 7, 1932.)

B399   BREWER, Daniel Chauncey. ''The Peril of the Republic: Are We Facing Revolution in the United States?'' New York: Putnam, 1922. 354 pp.

The danger of revolution is traced to the decadence of American democracy, combined with large-scale immigration. Both public school graduates and their teachers are held ignorant of American democracy, and the trend of education is deplored as socialistic. Revolutionary literature from IWW, socialist, and communist sources is quoted. The author proposes to block revolution by reducing the size of government, having the schools teach democracy instead of sociology, regulating the alien population, and censoring the non-English press.

B400   BREWER, James L. Smith Act Decision Plagues American Conscience, ''Protestant,'' 8 (July-Aug.-Sept. 1951), 3-10.

A review, by a member of the New York Bar and the National Lawyers' Guild, of the reaction to the Supreme Court's decision upholding the Smith Sedition Act as constitutional and the conviction under it of the 11 Party leaders, in effect outlawing the Party. Opinions viewing the decision as a defeat for democracy and urging a rehearing are quoted.

B401   BREWSTER, Frank, and COLTON, Peter. On the Question of Sectarianism in Our Peace Activity, ''Political Affairs,'' 31 (Sept. 1952), 21-32.

Though conditions are favorable in the U.S. for a major advance in peace organization, communists have often limited their peace activity to the advanced peace centers, and have sometimes operated so as to exclude all elements but the left from the centers. These forms of sectarianism must be overcome, in order to enlist all mass organizations in a united front for peace.

B402   BREWSTER, Frank, and LOGAN, Mark. Automation: Abundance for Whom? ''Political Affairs,'' 34 (Oct. 1955), 44-53; (Nov.), 31-42.

Automation can either improve the material conditions of the masses or reduce them to dire poverty. It does not ease the intensity of labor or the rate of exploitation. With the gains going to the few, it is clear that automation plus intensified exploitation leads to depression. A program for coping with automation is presented.

B403   BRICKMAN, William W. Communism and American Education, ''School and Society,'' 71 (March 25, 1950), 180-88. Bibliog.

The question of communists in the schools is one of the most significant issues in contemporary education in the U.S. The doctrine of academic freedom should not be used to defend communists, who cannot teach objectively. No one has the privilege of teaching in a democracy who is committed to the destruction of democracy.

B404   BRIDGES-ROBERTSON-SCHMIDT DEFENSE COMMITTEE. ''The Law and Harry Bridges.'' San Francisco: The Committee, 1952. 26 pp.

Issued on the eve of hearing before the 9th Circuit Court of Appeals of the case of Harry Bridges, I. R. Robertson, and Henry Schmidt on charges of conspiracy and perjury. Government efforts to deport Bridges are reviewed. The pamphlet argues that there is no substantial evidence to prove that Bridges was a member of the Communist Party, and quotes Supreme Court justices to the effect that he is being persecuted and that the judicial process is being subverted.

B405   BRIEHL, Fred. National Unity and the Farmers, ''Communist,'' 23 (March 1944), 275-81.

A denial of alleged assertions by the congressional farm bloc that the Administration favors labor while exploiting farmers. A joint stand of workers and farmers on political, economic, and social issues is urged.

B406   BRIGGS, Cyril. The Negro Question in the Southern Textile Strikes, ''Communist,'' 8 (June 1929), 324-28.

Trade-union organizers sent by the Party into the South must overcome antagonism between white and Negro workers, and carry on a determined campaign against white chauvinism. The organizers have retreated shamefully before white chauvinism, in one case permitting a wire to separate Negro from white strikers.

B407   .... The Negro Press as a Class Weapon, ''Communist,'' 8 (Aug. 1929), 453-60.

A survey of the Negro press and the possibilities of its use to spread communist propaganda. The revolutionary past of the Negro press still largely motivates its present. If the Party leads the struggles of the Negro masses against terrorism, segregation, and discrimination, its activities will be reported in most Negro periodicals.

B408   .... Our Negro Work, ''Communist,'' 8 (Sept. 1929), 494-501.

Prior to the Sixth World Congress white chauvinism in both factions of the Party prevented progress among Negroes. Although much progress has since been made, white chauvinism still exists within the Party.

B409   BRIGGS, H. E. '' 'New Deal' for the Vets.'' New York: Workers Library, 1933. 16 pp.

An attack on the government's treatment of veterans and on right-wing veterans' leaders. Veteran support is urged for the bonus, veterans' benefits without cuts, and relief for the unemployed and farmers.

B410   .... ''The Veterans Fight for Unity.'' New York: American League of Ex-Servicemen, 1935. 47 pp.

The history and program of this communist front group,

formerly the Workers Ex-Servicemen's League, which struggles against the reactionary, officer-controlled organizations of veterans. Emphasis is placed on the class-conscious nature of the group, and the reactionary opposition it faces.

B411   BRINSER, Ayers. Radicals in the Labor Movement: I.W.W., T.U.U.L., C.P.L.A. or A.F. of L.? "Common Sense," 3 (Jan. 1934), 16-20.
A review of the efforts of radicals and progressives to organize labor in America. The IWW and the Trade Union Unity League are discussed at length. The author, sympathetic to the IWW, criticizes the postwar left wing, under communist influence, for its confusion. He calls for an "American" approach, such as A. J. Muste's group exemplifies.

B412   BRINTON, Job W. "Communist Primer: The Primary Facts About Criminal Communism, with a Review of William Z. Foster's 'Toward A Soviet America.'" Hollywood: Job W. Brinton Foundation, 1950. 96 pp.
An attempt to demonstrate the criminality of communism, based on the writings of Marx, Lenin, Stalin, and Foster; on the activities of the IWW; and confirmed by the 1949 conviction of 11 top leaders of the Party, led by Dennis, for criminal conspiracy.

B413   BRODSKY, Merle. On the Role of the Party, "Political Affairs," 36 (Jan. 1957), 46-54.
The role and organizational forms of the American left should be determined by class and political developments in the U.S. A mass socialist movement must emerge from the working class. The Party must become part of the labor and people's movement, letting the question of "vanguard" be resolved by unfolding events.

B414   BRODY, Alter; BAYER, Theodore M.; SCHNEIDER, Isidor; and SMITH, Jessica (eds.). "War and Peace in Finland: A Documented Survey." New York: Soviet Russia Today, 1940. 128 pp.
Defense of the Russian invasion and annexation of Finnish territory, on the grounds that these acts ended the anti-Soviet war base being prepared in Finland, reinforced Soviet neutrality, and protected the east Baltic from war dangers. The Allies, it is charged, planned to use Finland as a northern front in the war against Germany and a base for attacking the USSR. The Russians, who were not imperialistic, demanded only such territorial cessions as were necessary to Soviet defense.

B415   BRODY, Alter. "Behind the Polish-Soviet Break." Introd. by Corliss Lamont. New York: Soviet Russia Today, n.d. [1943?]. 24 pp.
A defense of the Soviet break with the World War II "Polish Government-in-Exile" and the Soviet demand for a boundary adjustment with Poland. The Polish charge that the Russians murdered 10,000 Polish officers is declared false. Eastern Poland is said to be populated by White Russians and Ukranians, not by Poles. Lamont stresses the need for American support of the Russian position as essential to the war effort.

B416   BROMFIELD, Louis. Back of the Brannan Plan, "Freeman," 1 (April 9, 1951), 425-28.
Charges of communist infiltration in American agriculture, through the Farmers Union and the Department of Agriculture, a haven of Party members and fellow-travelers. The Farmers Union formulated the Brannan plan on the Soviet model in an effort to bring small farmers and organized labor together, as the basis of a socialist labor government.

B417   BROOKS, Alexander D. "A Bibliography of Civil Rights and Civil Liberties." New York: Civil Liberties Educational Foundation, 1962. 151 pp.
A bibliography, with brief abstracts, on civil liberties, civil rights and intergroup relations, immigration and naturalization, the rights of women, international rights, pertinent works of fiction and biography, and audio-visual materials. Among the subjects included are loyalty and security programs, legislative investigating committees, espionage and perjury cases, freedom of the mass media, and academic freedom.

B418   BROOKS, Walter. Setting the Stage for Moscow, "American Legion Magazine," 55 (Sept. 1953), 14-15 ff.
Criticism of the Federal Theatre Project for hiring non-actors and for presenting red propaganda plays of the Living Newspaper type. Red infiltration of Hollywood, radio, television, and the Broadway theatre is traced to the policies and personnel of the project.

B419   BROUN, Heywood. It Seems to Heywood Broun, "Nation," 130 (Jan. 15, 1930), 63; (Feb. 5), 145; (March 26), 353; (April 23), 483.
A series of articles on communism during the "third period," accusing the communists of hysterical tactics, American Legion-type attacks on socialists, and unrealistic propaganda about the predatory nature of American capitalism. Broun questions the seriousness with which communists seek to make a social revolution.

B420   . . . . All Quiet Along the Rubicon, "Common Sense," 2 (July 1933), 4-5.
The well-known newspaper writer announces that he has left the Socialist Party because it is not radical enough, but cannot join the Communist Party because it is not "American" enough, and lacks proper regard for native peculiarities. A new radical American party is needed.

B421   . . . . Apology for Not Being a Communist, "Nation," 141 (Sept. 4, 1935), 274.
A noncommunist left-winger states his reasons for giving democracy a last try. Though logically Broun should be a communist, he sees no immediate prospects for a revolution in America; the bulk of the middle class, in his view, would fight against communism.

B422   . . . . We Want a United Front, "Nation," 141 (Dec. 11, 1935), 673.
A discussion of the recent debate between Norman Thomas and Earl Browder. Broun finds Browder the stronger participant and criticizes Thomas for his rejection of a united front with communists. Broun urges a united front of socialists and communists now because of the rapid growth of fascism here.

B423   . . . . Shoot the Works, "New Republic," 93 (Jan. 12, 1938), 280-81.
Criticism of Dr. John Dewey by a leading columnist for asserting that the CIO accepts members and even organizers who are communists, and that the communists are attempting to divide labor. Broun argues that barring radicals from existing unions would make dual unionism imperative. The Party, he asserts, now opposes divided unionism.

B424   BROWDER, Earl R. Gompers Attacks the League, "Labor Herald," 1 (May 1922), 16-17 ff.
Passage by the Chicago Federation of Labor of a resolution calling for amalgamation of unions alarmed the AFL conservatives. At a meeting in Chicago of local officials, Gompers denounced the TUEL, Foster, and the position of the Chicago Federation. Progressives should view this opposition to the League as the greatest compliment.

B425 BROWDER, Earl R. Progress of the Amalgamation Movement, "Labor Herald," 1 (Oct. 1922), 3-6.

A progress report on the TUEL's drive for union amalgamation. Labor bodies, including state federations and central labor councils, which support amalgamation are listed. Particular strength exists in the metal, needle, and printing trades.

B426 . . . . The League's Labor Party Referendum, "Labor Herald," 2 (June 1923), 12-13.

A referendum in the Trade Union Educational League shows overwhelming support for a labor party, despite opposition from AFL officials. The next step in the formation of such a party will be the July 3 convention in Chicago, to which all local unions are urged to send delegates.

B427 . . . . Reactionaries Smashing Ladies Garment Workers, "Labor Herald," 2 (Nov. 1923), 13-16.

An account of the struggle in the ILGWU. The reactionary leaders are charged with a campaign of expulsions and dictatorship which threatens the life of the union. When the fight is carried back into the shops, the union wreckers will be swept into oblivion by the outraged rank and file.

B428 . . . . Fascism in the United States, "International Press Correspondence," 3 (Dec. 29, 1923), 848-49.

While fascism as a well-defined institution has not yet appeared in the U.S., its roots (the Ku Klux Klan, American Legion, and Minute Men of the Constitution) are here. The Anti-Fascist Alliance, created largely by the communists, has so far neutralized the fascist movement. The AFL bureaucracy, by supporting the American Legion, helps American fascism to develop.

B429 . . . . "Class Struggle vs. Class Collaboration." Chicago: Daily Worker Publishing Co. for Workers Party of America, n.d. [1924?]. 31 pp.

One of the "Little Red Library" series, attacking labor banks, the B. & O. plan for union-management cooperation, and union insurance plans as substitutes for labor unions and the class struggle. The AFL is attacked as the headquarters of reaction, whose officials are swinging to the right as the workers are swinging to the left.

B430 . . . . "Unemployment: Why It Occurs and How to Fight It." Chicago: Workers Party of America, 1924. 14 pp.

An assertion that unemployment is a normal phase of capitalist society, and that the present crisis is the beginning of capitalism's breakdown. Condemning reformist methods and class collaboration, the author advocates, as the only solution for unemployment, the revolutionary program of the Workers Party.

B431 . . . . The Changing Political Situation in the United States, "International Press Correspondence," 4 (March 20, 1924), 182-83.

An evaluation of prospects for independent political action in the 1924 elections. An emerging third party movement may endanger the communist-supported farmer-labor movement. Scandals in both Democratic and Republican parties have led many progressives to call a conference on July 4, after the major party conventions. July 4 will witness another betrayal of the farmers and workers.

B432 . . . . Our Timid Progressives, "Labor Herald," 3 (April 1924), 50-51.

A rejoinder to an article by Benjamin Stolberg in "Hearst's International" about the left-wing movement in the trade unions. Denying Stolberg's assertion that the left wing has caused irreparable damage to the American labor movement, Browder asserts instead that it has cleared away misunderstanding by taking away a rotten support.

B433 . . . . The American Labour Movement and the Presidential Elections, "International Press Correspondence," 4 (July 31, 1924), 553-54.

A communist interpretation of the 1924 political alignment. Coolidge and Davis represent the bipartisan forces of Wall Street; La Follette heads the middle class and the labor bureaucracy; and Foster, running on the Workers Party ticket and endorsed by the farmer-labor national committee, leads all forces that stand against capitalism.

B434 . . . . Chicago, St. Paul, Cleveland, "Labor Herald," 3 (Aug. 1924), 166-68.

An analysis of the failure of the movement for a farmer-labor party in 1924, blaming misleaders of labor who followed the Gompers policy of nonpartisan political action. The communists were willing to endorse La Follette only if he ran as a farmer-labor candidate on a farmer-labor program. The Workers Party felt that only in its own name could it campaign for independent working class political action in 1924, and therefore it nominated William Z. Foster for president.

B435 . . . . Industrial Depression or Prosperity? "Workers Monthly," 4 (March 1925), 218-20.

A recent revival of U.S. industry is traced to temporary factors such as agricultural prosperity, increased exports, and a continued building boom. While capitalists receive tremendous profits, workers are subjected to more intense exploitation. Organization of workers into labor unions, and the vanguard into the Workers (Communist) Party, is advocated.

B436 . . . . Communism on the Streets of America, "Workers Monthly," 4 (May 1925), 299-301.

Demonstrations protesting the arrival of Abramovich, "agent of counterrevolution," in the U.S. are cited as examples of a united and vital revolutionary movement. The breaking up by communists of meetings for Abramovich sponsored by various socialist and liberal groups is defended, and protests by the ACLU are brushed aside.

B437 . . . . What Is Collaboration of Classes? "Workers Monthly," 4 (June 1925), 366-68.

A denunciation of class collaborationism, on the occasion of a debate between Scott Nearing and J. B. S. Hardman (Salutsky) in "Advance," journal of the Amalgamated Clothing Workers. Nearing is called confused, though he is moving toward the communist position. Hardman, a former communist, opposes class collaboration in the abstract, while approving it in practice.

B438 . . . . Left-Wing Advances in the Needle Trades, "Workers Monthly," 4 (July 1925), 403-6.

A review of left-wing successes, under TUEL leadership, in the needle trades. The left wing has won control of the New York Joint Board of the Furriers, and now controls the three great locals of the ILGWU in New York City. It is growing in the Capmakers, and resisting expulsions and removal of elected officers in Local 5 of the Amalgamated Clothing Workers.

B439 . . . . Opportunism Within the Trade-Union Left Wing, "Workers Monthly," 4 (Aug. 1925), 468-69.

A criticism of opportunism and sectarianism within the left wing of the trade unions, errors related in a political sense to "Loreism," which the Comintern has denounced. Illustrations are drawn from the UMW, where the left wing has resisted centralized leadership and failed to register its strength, and from the ILGWU, where the leading militants object to suggestions and directions from the Party leadership.

B440 BROWDER, Earl R. Fourth National Convention of the Workers (Communist) Party of America, "International Press Correspondence," 5 (Oct. 8, 1925), 1089-90.
A member of the Foster "trade union" faction presents its views on the factional struggle with the Ruthenberg "political" faction at the fourth national convention of the Workers (Communist) Party. The two factions were given equal representation on the Central Executive Committee, with the Comintern representative serving as chairman. The Comintern representative has voted with the Ruthenberg faction, giving it control of the Party.

B441 . . . . The Congress of the American Federation of Labour, "International Press Correspondence," 6 (Nov. 18, 1926), 1307-9.
The October 1926, AFL convention was an orgy of reaction, characterized by increased class collaboration and a renewed war of extermination against the Trade Union Educational League. The reactionary John L. Lewis raised the issue of Moscow against the Brophy opposition, showing his intention to split the union rather than give up power.

B442 . . . . The Five Day Week, "Workers Monthly," 6 [5] (Jan. 1927), 695-97.
The spread of the five-day week, now accepted by both Henry Ford and the AFL, was made possible by the successful strike of the Fur Workers in New York City under communist leadership. The economic base is the increase in productivity. The five-day, 40-hour week issue has stirred the masses and will become a storm center in the American labor movement.

B443 . . . . China and American Imperialist Policy, "Communist," 6 (Sept.-Oct. 1927), 388-93.
America's seemingly wavering policy in China can be understood only against the background of a complicated struggle against Japan and Britain. American policy, aiming at complete control of China, is more dangerous than the British, because it is more powerful and fights with subtler weapons.

B444 . . . . The Bankruptcy of American Trade Unionism: The Forty-Seventh Convention of the American Federation of Labour, "Labour Monthly" (London), 9 (Dec. 1927), 754-64.
The Los Angeles convention of the AFL is called the most reactionary on record. Browder attacks AFL officials for class-collaboration practices, cooperation with the police, ignoring the struggle of the miners, perpetuation of the myth of prosperity, and glorification of the unifying slogan of "Down with Communism."

B445 . . . . The T.U.E.L. Must Be Reorganized: A Criticism and New Proposals for the American R.I.L.U. Section, "Labor Unity," 3 (Feb. 1929), 6-8.
A call for drastic reorganization of the TUEL, whose campaign to organize the unorganized has failed. The word "educational" is too limited; Trade Union Unity League is better. The TUUL must become the left-wing trade union center, with a central body in each city, and give special attention to organizing the Negro masses and internationalizing the left wing.

B446 . . . . Reinforcements for a Discredited Bureaucracy: The New Progressives in the American Federation of Labor, "Labor Unity," 3 (March 1929), 22-25.

An attack upon the new "progressivism," as presented in a manifesto in the February "Labor Age." Though framed in near-left terms, the manifesto is said to be in reality an attack against the left wing and the Trade Union Educational League. The same "progressives" who destroyed the 1922-23 left-wing campaign play a treacherous role as bearers of social reformism in left-wing ranks.

B447 . . . . The October Plenum of the Central Committee, C.P.U.S.A., "Communist," 8 (Nov. 1929), 575-83.
The October plenum of the Central Committee was one of the Party's most constructive meetings. It wholeheartedly endorsed the struggle against the Right danger and the expulsion of the Lovestone group. It reviewed the Party's trade union and Negro work, and registered the liquidation of factionalism and the basic unification of the Party.

B448 . . . . The Wall Street Crash and the Class Struggle, "Communist," 8 (Dec. 1929), 643-50.
The Wall Street crash, caused by the production of surplus values, has brought crises to the entire capitalist system. Both the crash and the sharpening class struggle originated in the conflict between productive forces and market limitations. The crash reveals that war is imminent and makes it more so.

B449 . . . . "Out of a Job." New York: Workers Library, n.d. [1930]. 32 pp.
Claiming the inevitability of unemployment in a capitalist society, the author denounces Hoover, the socialists, the AFL, and their proposed fake cures for unemployment. The final solution for unemployment, he asserts, has been found in the Soviet Union through the dictatorship of the proletariat.

B450 . . . . Some Experiences in Organizing the Negro Workers, "Communist," 9 (Jan. 1930), 35-41.
The experiences of J. W. Johnstone in organizing the Stock Yards Labor Council in Chicago in 1919, and the story of the combined assault upon and betrayal of it by the packers, their Negro agents, the government, and reactionary AFL officials.

B451 . . . . Preparing for the Seventh Party Convention, "Communist," 9 (May 1930), 439-44.
A review of a plenum of the Party's Central Committee, held March 31 to April 4, 1930, prior to the Party convention. The economic crisis has ended such "exceptionalist" theories of American capitalism as those of Jay Lovestone. The AFL is plainly a fascist organization, in contrast to the Socialist Party, which is social fascist. The plenum also clarified its views on the imminence of the war danger.

B452 . . . . The Bolshevization of the Communist Party, "Communist," 9 (Aug. 1930), 684-93.
A review of Party efforts to integrate itself with the Communist International, eliminate deviationists, liquidate factionalism, and turn toward mass work. The task of the seventh convention was to overcome the gap between our influence over the masses, and our narrow organizational strength. There are still tendencies to deviate to both left and right.

B453 . . . . Next Tasks of the Communist Party of the USA, "Communist," 9 (Nov.-Dec. 1930), 972-78.
The old method of linking immediate demands with the ultimate aim of Soviet power, which made them seem equally distant, must be done away with. We must link them up in the Bolshevik way, showing how the revolutionary struggle led by communists is the most practical producer of immediate relief.

B454 BROWDER, Earl R. "Secret Hoover-Laval War Pacts." New York: Workers Library, 1931. 15 pp.
A charge that a new constellation of imperialist forces has emerged, with France, Japan, and the U.S. in leading positions and Germany and Italy in subordinate roles, to lead the bourgeois front against the rising tide of world revolution. The imperialists are organizing war on the USSR, the socialist fatherland.

B455 .... "War Against Workers' Russia." New York: Communist Party of the U.S.A., 1931. 30 pp.
Speech delivered before the Executive Committee of the Communist International in Moscow in 1931, accusing the U.S. and other capitalist countries of preparing an aggressive war against the Soviet Union.

B456 .... Report of the Political Committee to the Twelfth Central Committee Plenum, CPUSA, November 22, 1930, "Communist," 10 (Jan. 1931), 7-31.
Report of the Political Committee to the Twelfth Central Committee Plenum, CPUSA, November 22, 1930, calling for concretization of the line laid down at the Sixth World Congress of the Communist International. Opportunities are outlined for doing this in the Red unions, in strike struggles, in shop committees, and in work among the unemployed, the foreign-born, youth, and Negroes.

B457 .... Masses Fight Against Hunger in America, "International Press Correspondence," 11 (Feb. 15, 1931), 96-97.
An analysis of the depression's effect on the radicalization of the working class, concluding that the forces of revolution are maturing in the heart of world capitalism. Credit is given the Party for organization of the unemployed councils, and for hunger marches and other mass demonstrations.

B458 .... One Year of Struggle of the Unemployed in the USA, "International Press Correspondence," 11 (March 19, 1931), 291-92.
An analysis of the unemployed movement on its first anniversary. The drop in turnout on "Unemployment Day" (February 25) from 1,250,000 in 1930 to 400,000 in 1931 is but a superficial indication that the movement is declining. Those still supporting the movement show improved quality and fighting power, and the movement's program has improved in quality.

B459 .... Faith in the Masses—Organization of the Masses! "Communist," 10 (July 1931), 600-14.
The Party is completing its turn toward the masses. Its next step in preparing the workers' struggle against capitalism is to weld the Party to the masses through organization. The Party is still weak in its trade-union and antiwar work. All Party units must carry forward their practical work under a planned system, periodically revised.

B460 .... Putting the XI Plenum Decisions Into Life, "Communist," 10 (Aug. 1931), 685-92.
The chief task of communist parties as outlined by the ECCI at its Eleventh Plenum is to transform revolutionary trade union oppositions and independent unions into mass organizations to lead workers' economic battles and serve as transmission belts into the Party. Browder evaluates such progress in the National Miners Union of the TUUL and in the UMW.

B461 .... To the Masses—To the Shops! Organize the Masses! Extracts from the Report of the Political Bureau to the Central Committee, 13th Plenum,

C.P.U.S.A., August 21, "Communist," 10 (Oct. 1931), 797-817.
A discussion of specific application of the Communist International line in building Party organization. "Phrase mongering" is criticized; words must be transformed into concrete action. Party organization and mass activity have improved, but insufficiently in view of objective possibilities.

B462 .... Some Problems of Mass Work, "Communist," 10 (Nov. 1931), 875-81.
A review of the program for mass work set forth at the Thirteenth Plenum of the Central Committee, CPUSA. Browder warns against bureaucratic procedures that are cutting the Party off from sympathetic contact with the masses; he also warns against interpreting the drive against bureaucracy as a breakdown in internal Party discipline.

B463 .... "The Fight for Bread." New York: Workers Library, 1932. 16 pp.
Keynote speech at the Party's 1932 national convention. The Party's major slogan will be: "Class against class!" Only the fight of the masses can win social insurance, stop wage cuts, bring relief to farmers, secure self-determination for the Black Belt, end capitalist terror, prevent imperialist war, and defend the Chinese people and the USSR.

B464 .... For National Liberation of the Negroes! War Against White Chauvinism! "Communist," 11 (April 1932), 295-309.
Extracts from a report to American students at a communist school on behalf of the Central Committee, CPUSA, on relations between white and Negro students at the school. The Central Committee insists that quarreling between white and Negro Party members end immediately. This can only be done by raising the questions bothering each group to a political level, and applying Bolshevik theory.

B465 .... Place the Party on a War Footing: Extracts from Report for the Central Committee, at District Convention, District No. 2, June 11-12, 1932, "Communist," 11 (July 1932), 590-605.
The imminent danger of war affects all phases of Party work. We must close the gap between words and deeds, and strengthen the bolshevization of the Party. Neighborhood and shop units, not the office, are the Party's supreme expression. We are weak in work among Negroes, as a result of white chauvinism, and also among Latin-Americans.

B466 .... "Is Planning Possible Under Capitalism?" New York: Workers Library, 1933. 16 pp.
A speech by Browder in a debate with George Soule, asserting that there can be no planned economy so long as capitalists own the means of production. The planning that takes place within an industry under capitalism intensifies the anarchy of capitalist production as a whole.

B467 .... "The Meaning of Social-Fascism: Its Historical and Theoretical Background." New York: Workers Library, 1933. 48 pp. App.
A "third period" pamphlet, calling socialist parties social-fascist because, while pretending opposition to fascism, they help it come to power. Illustrations from England and Germany are given, and socialist leaders here are attacked for allegedly justifying fascism, supporting World War I, and criticizing the USSR. The Party must win the workers from social-fascist leadership.

B468 .... "What Every Worker Should Know About the

N.R.A.' New York: Workers Library, 1933. 24 pp.
Denunciation of the National Recovery Act, during the Party's ultra-leftist "third period," as a scheme permitting strike-breaking and greater trustification, and constituting a step toward war. Workers are urged to expose this plan of capitalist oppression, and fight to overthrow capitalism.

B469 BROWDER, Earl R. "What is the New Deal?" New York: Workers Library, 1933. 23 pp.
A picture of the New Deal and the National Industrial Recovery Act, during the Party's leftist "third period," as forerunners of American fascism. The task of the Party, its general secretary asserts, is to break down the illusions of the masses about the New Deal, by presenting demands when codes are being written that expose the real nature of this "slavery" act.

B470 .... The Revisionism of Sidney Hook, "Communist," 12 (Feb. 1933), 133-46; (March), 285-300.
Continuation of the discussion of Hook's Marxism started by V. J. Jerome ("Unmasking an American Revisionist of Marxism," in "Communist," January 1933). Hook submitted a reply, charging that Jerome had distorted his meaning. Reproducing portions of Hook's reply, Browder answers it point by point, asserting that Hook is critical toward Marx, Engels, and Lenin, and that Hook uses John Dewey's theories as the basis for a revised Marxism.

B471 .... The End of Relative Capitalist Stabilization and the Tasks of Our Party, "Communist," 12 (March 1933), 222-48; (April), 352-70.
Excerpts from Browder's report to the Sixteenth Plenum, Central Committee, CPUSA, January 28, 1933. Browder outlines the tasks of the Party as laid down by the Twelfth Plenum, Executive Committee of the Communist International, and appraises progress to date. Emphasis is placed on the fight against social fascism, application of the united front policy, mistakes in trade union work, the struggle against white chauvinism, and theoretical understanding.

B472 .... Why an Open Letter to Our Party Membership, "Communist," 12 (Aug. 1933), 707-69.
Report for the Political Buro to the Extraordinary Party Conference, New York City, July 7, 1933. It appraises the economic situation and outlines the Party's program. An Extraordinary Party Conference and an Open Letter are necessary because the CPUSA has not yet become a revolutionary mass Party, in spite of a mass revolutionary upsurge.

B473 .... The Open Letter and the Struggle Against the N.R.A., "Communist," 12 (Oct. 1933), 963-72.
An evaluation of Party efforts to translate into action the dictates of the Open Letter issued in July 1933. Browder attributes Party successes to the improvement in its political line and methods of work and its correct analysis of the NRA and New Deal, and to the struggles and radicalization of the workers. Much of the article responds to criticisms of the Open Letter by a "Comrade Bell."

B474 .... "The Communist Party and the Emancipation of the Negro People." New York: Harlem Section of the Communist Party, n.d. [1934?]. 16 pp.
Report to the eighth convention of the Communist Party, April 2-8, 1934. A restatement of the CP position on the Negro question, characterizing Negroes in America as an oppressed nation. Browder emphasizes the communist struggle in the Scottsboro case and analyzes the ideology of the Negro bourgeoisie, which works to stem the struggle

of the Negro masses through utopian schemes. He calls for support of the League of Struggle for Negro Rights.

B475 .... "Report of the Central Committee to the Eighth Convention of the Communist Party." New York: Workers Library, 1934. 128 pp.
An analysis of the economic crisis of capitalism, emphasizing the dangers of fascism and imperialist war. Browder discusses the work of the Party, elaborates the theory of social-fascism, and asserts that the New Deal, in political essence, is the same as fascism. He analyzes the work of the Trade Union Unity League, and communist work among farmers, students, Negroes, youth, and in the American League Against War and Fascism. The Party line of united front from below is elaborated. Browder asserts that the bolshevization of the Party is moving too slowly, and that self-criticism must be developed.

B476 .... Situation in the United States of America, "Communist International," 11 (Jan. 15, 1934), 75-80.
Browder's speech at the Thirteenth Plenum of the ECCI, reviewing developments in the U.S., with emphasis on the fascist direction of Roosevelt's policies, the AFL and the TUUL, the strike movement and the Red unions, the antiwar and antifascist movement, and the Party's inner situation.

B477 .... Forward in Struggle against Hunger, Fascism, and War! "Communist," 13 (Feb. 1934), 145-77.
Report to the 18th plenary meeting of the Central Committee, CPUSA, January 16, 1934. Following the views of the Thirteenth Plenum of the Executive Committee of the Communist International, Browder asserts that the period of capitalist stabilization has ended, and that the international proletariat must turn the capitalist crisis into the victory of the proletarian revolution.

B478 .... Communism and its Renegades, "Modern Thinker," 4 (March 1934), 281-89.
The text of an interview in which Browder attacks Trotskyites, Lovestoneites, the New Deal, and the leadership of the Socialist Party. Rank-and-file socialist movements toward the Communist Party are supported. The Party has grown in numbers and influence in the last four years because it foresaw the crisis and advocated a revolutionary solution.

B479 .... The Role of the Socialist Party Leaders in the Struggle Against War and Fascism, "Communist," 13 (April 1934), 323-35.
A review of Socialist Party defections from united front activities in the year since the communists issued their United Front Manifesto. The latest episode is the withdrawal of the SP leaders from the national committee of the American League Against War and Fascism. Browder charges that the SP leaders from the beginning sought to prevent communist participation and, failing, withdrew.

B480 .... Approaching the Seventh World Congress and the Fifteenth Anniversary of the Founding of the C.P.U.S.A., "Communist," 13 (Sept. 1934), 835-44.
A review of 15 years of Party history in the light of three periods of world-wide capitalist development: 1918-23, a period of revolutionary upsurge following the Russian revolution; 1923-28, a period of partial stabilization of capitalism; 1928 to the present, the "third period" of world economic crisis and renewed revolutionary upsurge.

B481 .... The Struggle for the United Front, "Communist," 13 (Oct. 1934), 931-67.
Report to a meeting of the CPUSA Central Committee,

September 5-6, 1934, reviewing Party activities since its eighth convention in April, 1934. The New Deal has not brought a capitalist recovery, and resulting radicalization reached a new level in the 1934 strike wave. The bulk of the report discusses communist activities in the West Coast strikes and united-front activities with socialists.

B482 BROWDER, Earl R. "Communism in the United States." Introd. by Alex Bittelman. New York: International Publishers, 1935. 352 pp. Ind.
A collection of writings, speeches, and reports by the general secretary of the Party between 1932 and April, 1935, covering the latter part of the ultra-left "third period" and the transition to the more moderate tone of the people's front. Among the topics dealt with are strikes, NRA planning under capitalism, unemployment insurance, formation of a labor party, Negroes, farmers, the exploited middle classes, USSR successes, the growth of reaction in the U.S., relations with the Communist International, the united front against war and fascism, and religion.

B483 . . ., and STACHEL, Jack. "How Do We Raise the Question of a Labor Party?" New York: Workers Library, 1935. 24 pp.
Excerpts from reports to the Party's central committee meeting in January, 1935, and the resolution on a labor party adopted there. The documents rationalize the Party's opposition to a labor party from 1928 to 1935. Still opposing farmer-labor parties of the populist type and labor parties dominated by union bureaucrats or socialists, the Party will support only a labor party on a trade union base, led by communists.

B484 . . . . "Unemployment Insurance: The Burning Issue of the Day." New York: Workers Library, 1935. 23 pp.
In the three speeches contained in this pamphlet, the author denounces the Wagner-Lewis bill, endorses instead H.R. 2827 (the workers' unemployment and social insurance bill) as the only one which gives workers real social insurance, and predicts that failure to pass the latter will pave the way for a new government representing socialism.

B485 . . . . Education—An Ally in the Workers' Struggle, "Social Frontier," 1 (Jan. 1935), 22-24.
Before the school system can become an effective instrument of social change, revolutionary or otherwise, it must itself be revolutionized. The progressive educator must link issues in the educational world with the political and economic interests of the masses. Though education is secondary to the class struggle, it can be an ally if educators realize the importance of fighting fascism.

B486 . . . . For the Workers' Bill, "Communist," 14 (Feb. 1935), 148-57.
A speech before the National Congress for Social and Unemployment Insurance, Washington, January 6, 1935, presenting the case for the communist-initiated workers' bill to "tax the rich and feed the poor."

B487 . . . . New Developments and New Tasks in the U.S.A., "Communist," 14 (Feb. 1935), 99-116.
A review of developments which have led to the new Party policies of supporting a labor party and working within AFL unions. United-front successes have been achieved, particularly in the fight against war and fascism. The Party must assume leadership of the daily mass struggles of the workers.

B488 . . . . Report to the Central Committee Meeting of the C.P.U.S.A., January 15-18, 1935, "Communist," 14 (March 1935), 195-216.

An appeal for Party support of the new line, with explanation for policy changes. Emphasis is placed on the transition from independent unions to working within the AFL, on increased effort to establish a broad united front, on the necessity of establishing a labor party, and on the shift to working within the mass Negro organizations.

B489 . . . . Religion and Communism, "Communist," 14 (April 1935), 350-65.
A discussion of the relationship of religion and communism with students of Union Theological Seminary, February 15, 1935. Browder upholds the Party's negative stand on religion; religious persons may join the CP, but must expect systematic criticism of their beliefs. Religious radicals may cooperate with communists on such issues as opposition to war.

B490 . . . . What Is Communism? "New Masses," 15 (May 7, 1935), 9-10; (May 14), 13-15; (May 21), 18-19; (May 28), 16-17; (June 4), 18-20; (June 11), 18-20; (June 18), 11-13; (June 25), 13-14; 16 (July 2), 9-10; (July 9), 9-10.
Among the topics discussed, toward the end of the revolutionary third period and in the early period of the people's front, are the New Deal, differences between socialism and communism, leadership in the revolution, wages, middle-class gains from the revolution, religion, how the Party works, Americanism, a labor party, and a glimpse of a Soviet America. While socialism, as the Soviet Union has shown, is superior to capitalism in material production, its greatest achievement is the production of superior types of human beings. (Some of the material in this series later appeared in Browder's book of the same name.)

B491 . . . . Recent Political Developments and Some Problems of the United Front, "Communist," 14 (July 1935), 604-24.
A report to a meeting of the Party's Central Committee, May 25-27, 1935, attesting to the growing political influence of the Party. Browder opposes sectarian views within the Party, advocates a broad national united front with the socialists as in France, and outlines next steps in the struggle for a labor party.

B492 . . . . For Working Class Unity! For a Workers' and Farmers' Labor Party! "Communist," 14 (Sept. 1935), 787-99.
A speech to the Seventh World Congress of the Communist International on the formation of a united working-class front and a broad people's antifascist front in the U.S. Though a labor party cannot achieve socialism, the communists will support it because it will fight fascism, attract middle class as well as worker support, and show the masses the need for a revolutionary party.

B493 . . . . New Steps in the United Front: Report on the Seventh World Congress, "Communist," 14 (Nov. 1935), 990-1014.
A report on the Seventh World Congress to an open Party membership meeting, October 3, 1935. While the rise of fascism was a defeat for the working class, it gave a powerful impetus to united action by communists and socialists. The whole work of the Congress was on speeding up the united front. In the U.S. the concept of a labor party must be broadened to include farmers and the middle class. (Also published in pamphlet form.)

B494 . . . . The United Front—The Key to Our New Tactical Orientation, "Communist," 14 (Dec. 1935), 1075-1129.
A report to the November plenum of the Party's Central Committee, applying the new line of the Seventh World Congress of the Comintern to the U.S. In order to fight

fascism and defend the Soviet Union from imperialistic capitalism, communists must establish united fronts and create a farmer-labor party, whose existence would force the capitalist parties to make concessions to the workers.

B495 BROWDER, Earl R. "Build the United People's Front: Report to the November Plenum of the Central Committee of the Communist Party of the U.S.A." New York: Workers Library, 1936. 70 pp.
Discussion of the application to the American scene of the popular front line adopted at the Seventh Congress of the Communist International. New conditions require united fronts of communists, socialists, and other fighters for peace, in the youth field, among the unemployed, etc. The policy of self-determination of Negroes in the Black Belt is soft-pedaled. Roosevelt is seen as having abandoned his profascist tendencies of 1933-34.

B496 .... "The Communist Position in 1936: Radio Speech Broadcast March 5, 1936." New York: Workers Library, 1936. 16 pp.
Election campaign speech calling for formation of a farmer-labor party, and containing a sharper attack on Roosevelt than in other Party documents of this period. Appended is a Party statement calling for impeachment of judges who usurp the democratic rights of the people, and amendment of the Constitution to prohibit the Supreme Court from declaring laws unconstitutional.

B497 .... "Earl Browder Reports to the 9th Convention of the Communist Party." New York: Workers Library, 1936. 47 pp.
The communist program in the early days of the people's front, stressing the meance of fascism in the U.S. and calling the issue one of democracy or fascism, not socialism. Browder attacks the Landon-Knox ticket as the chief enemy, yet refuses to support Roosevelt. Hope is placed in the growing farmer-labor party, though it is unable to run a presidential ticket in this campaign. (Also published under the title, "Democracy or Fascism.")

B498 .... "Hearst's 'Secret' Documents in Full." New York: Workers Library, 1936. 22 pp.
Text of a speech by Browder which was used by the pro-Landon Hearst press to show a close linkage between Roosevelt and the communists. The bulk of the speech dealt with the Chicago conference called by the Minnesota Farmer Labor Party, in the hope of forming a national party. The CPUSA opposed formation of this party because Labor's Nonpartisan League viewed it as inopportune. Attacking the Hearst press, Browder insists that the communists oppose Roosevelt.

B499 .... "Lincoln and the Communists." New York: Workers Library, 1936. 14 pp.
Lincoln's birthday speech, delivered at Springfield, Ill., discussed by the general secretary of the Party. In 1936, as in 1860, there is a crisis of parties and of the Constitution. Browder calls for raising the number of judges on the Supreme Court and for the appointment of progressive judges; and he urges formation of a broad, all-inclusive farmer-labor party that would carry forward Lincoln's tradition. He quotes Lincoln on the people's revolutionary right to overthrow a government of which they have grown weary.

B500 .... "The People's Front in America." New York: Workers Library for State Campaign Committee, Communist Party, 1936. 16 pp.
Reprint of a speech in Brooklyn, N.Y., August 27, 1936, calling for a people's front against fascism and war. Attacking the false and sectarian policies of the Socialist Party, Browder calls for a genuine united front with Socialist Party members. Criticizing Roosevelt gently, he attacks Landon severely.

B501 .... "The Results of the Elections and the People's Front." New York: Workers Library, 1936. 87 pp.
A report to the plenum of the Central Committee of the Party during the period of the Spanish Civil War. Browder saw Spain as the first stage of a general world war prepared by fascism against democracy everywhere, and the USSR as rallying all antifascist and peace-loving nations, and progressive circles everywhere, to the defense of democracy, progress, and peace. He saw in the reelection of Roosevelt in 1936 a great chance for the people's front to move forward, along with improved prospects for a national farmer-labor party.

B502 .... "What Is Communism?" New York: Vanguard, 1936. 254 pp. App. Ind.
An account by the secretary of the Party of its program in the early days of the people's front. Browder stresses the development of native American fascism, the need for a united front of all workers to prevent fascism and war, and the desirability of a farmer-labor party. The ruling class, as capitalism disintegrates, will destroy democracy; the working class, if it cannot prevent war, will turn imperialist into civil war. Other topics dealt with include trade unions, the Negro people, religion, the family, and the methods of operation of the Party. (An excerpt was published by the Workers Library in 1936 in pamphlet form as "Who Are the Americans?" Some of the material in the book appeared earlier in the "New Masses," May 7 to July 9, 1935.)

B503 .... "Zionism." New York: Yidburo Publishers, 1936. 24 pp.
Text of a speech in New York City, June 8, 1936, in which blame for Palestine's unrest is attributed to Zionist nationalism and subservience to British imperialism. Browder proposes unity of Arab and Jewish workers, which will come about once the Zionist policy of conquest is abandoned.

B504 .... The Party of Lenin and the People's Front, "Communist," 15 (Feb. 1936), 120-29.
An attempt to justify the current slogan for a united front party in terms of Lenin's philosophy. Formation of a farmer-labor party is supported by Lenin's emphasis on the vast difference in interests between capitalists and workers.

B505 .... The Farmer-Labor Party—The People's Front in the U.S.A., "Communist International," 13 (Sept. 1936), 1118-26.
The task of building a people's front against reaction, fascism, and war is being carried on in the U.S. through formation of a farmer-labor party. Hundreds of such local parties, and several state parties, have been or are being formed. A unified farmer-labor party in the U.S. necessarily involves inclusion of the communists.

B506 .... The Presidential Elections in the United States, "Communist International," 13 (Dec. 1936), 1582-91.
Roosevelt's 1936 election victory, in the face of overwhelming newspaper opposition, is seen as a sharpening of class lines in the U.S. The vote represented sentiment for a people's front against fascism and war, though the Administration is not a people's front. Further movement to the left will be achieved by strengthening progressive people's organizations and unions.

B507 BROWDER, Earl R. "China and the U. S. A."
New York: Workers Library, 1937. 16 pp.
Opening the communist municipal election campaign,
Browder declares the solidarity of the American Communist Party with the Chinese Communist Party and
Chinese people in their struggle against imperialism and
the Japanese. He calls on the American government to
sever economic relations with Japan, in cooperation with
all Pacific nations which want peace.

B508 . . . . "The Communists in the People's Front."
New York: Workers Library, 1937. 126 pp.
A report by the general secretary of the Party to the
plenary meeting of the Central Committee of the Party
held June, 1937. The report selects four points of concentration for the Party: (1) building the people's front
in the U.S., (2) the struggle for progressive industrial
unionism as exemplified by the CIO, and the need for
AFL-CIO unity, (3) organizing the mass movement for an
effective peace policy, and (4) building the Party and the
"Daily Worker." The report looked toward the emergence
of a national farmer-labor party as a people's front in the
U.S.

B509 . . ., and ARNOLD, John. "The Meaning of the
Palestine Partition." New York: New York State
Jewish Buro, Communist Party, 1937. 32 pp.
Reprints of two articles from "Jewish Life." Browder's
article called on Jewish workers who had been antagonistic
to the Party because of its attacks on Zionism to rethink
their position in the light of the British proposal for the
partition of Palestine. Arnold's article called for Jewish-
Arab unity in Palestine in a struggle against British imperialism. Also included is a statement of the Communist
Party of Great Britain opposing the partition and calling
for an independent Arab state with full rights of citizenship for Jews.

B510 . . . . "Talks to America." New York: Workers
Library, 1937. 48 pp.
Reprints of eight radio speeches during the 1936 campaign
by the Party's candidate for president. The talks deal
with democracy or fascism, foreign policy and peace,
unemployment, youth, Spain, and other issues. Major
emphasis is on the defeat of Landon, the need for a farmer-
labor party, and support of a New Deal type of program
while opposing Roosevelt. The socialists are attacked for
arguing that the issue is socialism versus capitalism; the
issue, rather, is democracy versus fascism.

B511 . . . . "Trotskyism Against World Peace." New
York: Workers Library, 1937. 15 pp.
The text of a speech by the general secretary of the Party,
pointing to the Moscow trials as proof that Trotsky and
his associates had plotted with fascism for world war.
Since they could come to power only through foreign armed
power, Trotsky's group agreed with Germany and Japan
to partition Soviet territory and grant economic privileges
to those imperialist states.

B512 . . . . The Results of the Elections and the People's
Front, "Communist," 16 (Jan. 1937), 14-49.
With Roosevelt's victory, the Party achieved its first
objective of defeating fascism. It laid the basis for realizing its second objective, formation of a mass people's
front. Its main shortcoming was failure to propagandize
communist doctrines and recruit widely. Now its main
task is to ally itself with noncommunist progressives to
create a people's front against fascism. (A report to the
plenum of the Party's Central Committee, December 4-6,
1936.)

B513 . . . . Lenin and Spain, "Communist," 16 (Feb.

1937), 112-19.
The American government's policy of neutrality and
refusal to aid the Spanish Loyalists is contrary to the
American tradition of helping other democracies against
tyranny. Communist policy is to create a people's front
to agitate for the Loyalists and send them money and men.

B514 . . . . The Struggle for the People's Front in the
United States, "Communist International," 14 (June
1937), 391-96.
A review of the 1936 election campaign, emphasizing the
success of the "Communism is Twentieth-Century Americanism" line, while denying that the Party has given up
its emphasis on the farmer-labor party movement as the
main American form of the popular front. The CPUSA
seeks to link sentiment for peace with a policy of collective security, while associating itself with American
revolutionary traditions.

B515 . . . . The Communists in the People's Front,
"Communist," 16 (July 1937), 594-627.
A report to a plenary meeting of the Party's Central Committee, June 17-20, 1937. The four main tasks of the
Party are to build a mass people's front, aid the CIO
organizing drive, organize a mass peace movement to
support economic sanctions on aggressors, and recruit
many more new members. Turnover in membership must
be reduced.

B516 . . . . Revolutionary Background of the United
States Constitution, "Communist," 16 (Sept. 1937),
793-807.
The Communist Party is in line with the American tradition of revolutionary struggle for freedom that began with
the fight to include the Bill of Rights in the Constitution.
In each struggle the contestants were the monied interests
and the democratic masses. The slogan, "Communism is
Twentieth-Century Americanism," is advanced.

B517 . . . . For a Common Front Against the War-
Makers, "Communist," 16 (Nov. 1937), 1041-44.
The text of an address to the convention of the Communist
Party of Canada, asserting that only Russia has opposed
the aggressions of Germany, Italy, and Japan. However,
communists can begin supporting Roosevelt, now that his
foreign policy has become more hostile to the fascist
nations. (Also published in pamphlet form.)

B518 . . . . Twenty Years of Soviet Power, "Communist," 16 (Nov. 1937), 986-95.
Twenty years ago Russia was economically prostrate
while the U.S. was the foremost economic power. Now
the U.S. is in economic collapse while Russia is undergoing rapid economic growth. Democracy has been precariously kept alive in America by the formation of trade
unions to balance the trusts, but the latter are now turning
to fascism.

B519 . . . . Issues, Parties and Men in the Last Elections, "International Press Correspondence," 17
(Nov. 13, 1937), 1202-03.
A report on the Communist Party's support of the American Labor Party, its increased prestige on the American
scene, and the leftward evolution of the Roosevelt Administration. This evolution has gone far enough for the
Communist Party to find in it its place as a co-worker.

B520 . . . . The People's Front Moves Forward, "Communist," 16 (Dec. 1937), 1082-1102.
A report to the Party's Political Bureau, applauding
Roosevelt's decision to abandon neutrality in favor of
concerted action with the other democracies, and also his
decision to take vigorous action against the recession.

Browder denies Roosevelt's claim that communists seek violent revolution, and reviews the recent election successes of the communist-backed people's fronts.

B521 BROWDER, Earl R. "Concerted Action or Isolation: Which Is the Road to Peace?" New York: International Publishers, 1938. 64 pp.
A collection of seven articles by the then general secretary of the Party, one from the "New Republic" and the others from the "New Masses," advancing the collective security policy of the Party in the period between the rise of fascism and the signing of the Hitler-Stalin pact. Arguing that Germany, Italy, and Japan were destroying peace, Browder called for an embargo upon all economic transactions with those countries to be applied jointly by the U.S., France, Britain, and the Soviet Union to force the warmakers to change their policies.

B522 .... "The Democratic Front for Jobs, Security, Democracy and Peace: Report to the Tenth National Convention of the Communist Party of the U.S.A." New York: Workers Library, 1938. 95 pp.
The Party line in 1938 seeks to broaden the popular front, enunciated in 1936, into the democratic front. Only the unity of the camp of democracy and progress in support of the New Deal can stop the reactionaries. The democratic front must be based upon workers, farmers, middle classes, and professionals through independent, but pro-New Deal, political organizations. Problems involved in building a broad Communist Party, and in working in noncommunist mass organizations, are discussed, and the communist program is linked to the Jeffersonian tradition, to show that communism is twentieth-century Americanism.

B523 .... "A Message to Catholics." New York: Workers Library, 1938. 15 pp.
An appeal to Catholics, in which Browder maintains that membership in the Catholic Church is no bar to joining the communist movement, for communists respect all religious beliefs. Moreover, there is no foundation for practical differences on questions of ethical standards, or family and social morality. He invites the great mass of democratic Catholics to unite with communists for their common salvation.

B524 .... "The Nazi Pogrom: An Outcome of the Munich Betrayal." New York: New York State Committee, Communist Party, 1938. 12 pp.
In a speech delivered before the Nazi-Soviet pact, Browder asserts that only the Soviet Union opposed Munich and stood firm against Germany.

B525 ..., and LAWRENCE, Bill. "Next Steps to Win the War in Spain." New York: Workers Library, 1938. 23 pp.
An address by Browder, December 9, 1937, launching the campaign for 50,000 members of the Friends of the Abraham Lincoln Battalion. He advocates an end to defeatist propaganda, suppression of the Trotskyist POUM, and more material help for Republican Spain. Lawrence, until recently a political commissar at a Spanish military base, calls for unity of all antifascist forces in Spain, and help from the international working class and democratic countries.

B526 .... "The People's Front." New York: International Publishers, 1938. 354 pp. Ind.
A collection of reports, speeches, and articles written in 1936 and 1937 by the Party's general secretary. The material is organized under three heads: "Parties and Issues," "The American Tradition," and "The United

States and World Affairs." While many domestic topics, such as unions, Wall Street, social insurance, freedom of the press, and the 1936 elections are dealt with, along with Trotskyism, Spain and the achievements of the USSR, the main emphasis is on building a people's front against fascist aggression.

B527 .... "Social and National Security." New York: Workers Library, 1938. 46 pp.
Report to the national committee of the Party on policies and strategy in the light of Munich and the 1938 U.S. elections. Browder calls for achievement of working-class unity, national and international, and for recreating the New Deal coalition to extend democracy, curb monopoly capital, and defend liberty and independence. He urges collaboration with the USSR to halt fascist world conquest.

B528 .... "Traitors in American History: Lessons of the Moscow Trials." New York: Workers Library, 1938. 32 pp.
A defense of the Moscow trials on the ground that similar plots by American leaders against the American government have occurred—those of Benedict Arnold, Aaron Burr, the southern Confederacy, and others. The USSR's one-party system is likened to that during the first 20 years of U.S. history. Soviet collectivization of agriculture and the suppression of the kulaks is compared to our Civil War, said to have been caused by agrarian reform. Stalin is hated, it is said, by the same people who hate Roosevelt.

B529 .... Toward the American Commonwealth: The Present Communist Position, "Social Frontier," 4 (Feb. 1938), 161-64.
An assertion that democracy has been almost completely deprived of its original economic foundation, and that socialism is the only final guarantee of democracy. A people's front is necessary today to prevent fascism, reaction, and war.

B530 .... The Trade Unions and Peace, "New Masses," 26 (March 22, 1938), 5-6.
The trade-union movement increasingly favors concerted action to restrain the warmakers. Evidence is found in affiliations with the American League for Peace and Democracy, and in statements by William Green, the National Maritime Union, the United Mine Workers, and the Ohio CIO convention.

B531 .... Mastering Bolshevik Methods of Work, "Communist," 17 (June 1938), 500-8.
An address to the Party's National Training School, April 28, 1938. Emphasis is placed on collective work and individual initiative, alertness to our mistakes, learning from the masses in order to lead them, and mastery of materialist dialectics.

B532 .... The Tenth National Convention of the CPUSA, "International Press Correspondence," 18 (June 25, 1938), 769-70.
A summary of the actions of the Party's tenth national convention, held May, 1938. The Party's chief task is to form a democratic front, to prevent election of a reactionary majority to Congress. The convention extended the democratic front to include religious organizations, consolidated the influence of the Party, and adopted a new constitution.

B533 .... Summation Speech at the Tenth National Convention, "Communist," 17 (July 1938), 594-99.
An assertion that the Party has now reached maturity. The convention was a demonstration that the Party is the most completely democratic organization in America.

The Party is now prepared to make its voice heard in determining the fate of the U.S. and the world.

B534 BROWDER, Earl R. Three Years' Application of the Program of the Seventh World Congress, "Communist," 17 (Aug. 1938), 699-703.
Three years ago the American press mistakenly interpreted Dimitroff's united-front report, which became the program of the Seventh World Congress, as urging communists to infiltrate democratic institutions to destroy them. Instead the report calls on communists to exploit divisions in fascist ranks in order to safeguard democracy.

B535 .... The United States and the New International Situation, "World News and Views," 18 (Oct. 29, 1938), 1179-80.
The capitulation of Britain and France to fascism at Munich poses a direct threat to the U.S. Friendly relations between the U.S. and the Soviet Union are vital. The CPUSA should facilitate these friendly relations, combat isolationism, and help unify all democratic and progressive forces within the U.S. and internationally around an action peace policy.

B536 .... Concerning American Revolutionary Traditions, "Communist," 17 (Dec. 1938), 1079-85.
The Party's slogan, "Communism is Twentieth-Century Americanism," recognizes the Party as the modern expression of America's revolutionary tradition. It represents the national interest by leading the fight against reactionary attempts to exploit the masses. The form of socialist society that the Party seeks to establish in any country is determined by its national characteristics.

B537 .... The Democratic Front in the 1940 Elections, "World News and Views," 18 (Dec. 31, 1938), 1391-92.
A prediction that the Republicans will not pick a reactionary candidate in 1940. A combination of forces to guarantee victory over the reactionaries, whether or not Roosevelt runs again, must be achieved. This requires further progress along New Deal lines.

B538 .... "America and the Second Imperialist War." New York: New York State Committee, Communist Party, 1939. 15 pp.
A speech delivered just after the Nazi-Soviet pact was signed. Responsibility for the war is placed on the fascist dictatorships of Germany, Italy, and Japan. While the USSR alone pressed for a solid peace front, it refused to be tricked into a war for aims that Chamberlain alone would decide. Support is declared for Poland's national independence.

B539 .... "The Economics of Communism: The Soviet Economy in its World Relation." New York: Workers Library, 1939. 23 pp.
An examination of the Soviet Union's continuous economic advance, showing that it rose rapidly between 1929 and 1933 while U.S. and world production declined sharply, and that its rate of advance since then has far outpaced the moderate recovery elsewhere. This has been true both of production and consumption goods. Browder urges friendship between the U.S. and the USSR.

B540 .... "Fighting for Peace." New York: International Publishers, 1939. 256 pp. Ind.
A collection of Browder's articles, speeches, and reports between February 2, 1938, and February 27, 1939. Published before the Nazi-Soviet pact, the volume emphasizes American foreign policy and the need for concerted action against fascism. Among the topics dealt with are collective security, the isolationist united front, the trade unions and peace, lessons of the Moscow trials, unity for peace, the Munich betrayal, social and national security, Lenin and America, and the Soviet economy.

B541 .... "Finding the Road to Peace." New York: New York State Committee of the Communist Party, 1939. 4 pp.
A radio address delivered August 29, 1939, following the signing of the Hitler-Stalin pact, praising the peace policy of the USSR and its nonaggression pact with Germany. In obtaining a guarantee that Germany would not attack it, the USSR won a victory for the peace of the whole world.

B542 .... "The 1940 Elections: How the People Can Win." New York: Workers Library, 1939. 47 pp.
A report to the national committee in May, 1939, in the popular-front period just prior to the Hitler-Stalin pact. Browder stressed the need to build an antifascist front of the peace forces of the world, including of course, the USSR, as essential to U.S. national security; he also urged a third term for Roosevelt in 1940 to prevent profascist reaction from winning the government. Along with emphasis on the united front, Party fractions in unions and other mass organizations were reported dissolved, and shop newspapers were also to be abolished.

B543 .... "Religion and Communism." New York: Workers Library, 1939. 15 pp.
In a speech at Community Church, Boston, Browder asserts that the Party stands for freedom of religious belief and worship, and pleads for common action to combat fascism. He urges friendship with the USSR as a bulwark against fascism.

B544 .... "Socialism, War and America." New York: Workers Library, 1939. 15 pp.
Speech delivered by the Party's general secretary in November 1939, calling for an end to the "imperialistic" war. Delivered two months after the signing of the Hitler-Stalin pact, the speech is highly critical of the policies of the Roosevelt Administration.

B545 .... "Stop the War." New York: Workers Library, 1939. 15 pp.
Speech delivered by the general secretary of the Party shortly after the signing of the Nazi-Soviet nonaggression pact. Denouncing the war in Europe as an imperialist one, he demands that it be ended, though American capitalists want it to continue indefinitely for their profits. Browder finds the U.S. in an economic mess, going backwards, while the USSR forges ahead.

B546 .... "Theory as a Guide to Action." New York: Workers Library, 1939. 16 pp.
Address at the fifteenth anniversary of the Party's Workers School, calling for an overhauling of the Party's educational system. Marxist-Leninist theory must not be restricted to small circles within the Party. Old courses tending toward sectarianism must be overhauled. The role of the Workers School is to advance the Party, master the theory of Marxism-Leninism, and transmit it to the broadest masses.

B547 .... "Unity for Peace and Democracy." New York: Workers Library, 1939. 95 pp.
The text of the report by the general secretary of the Party to an enlarged meeting of its national committee, September 1-3, 1939, the week after the announcement of the Nazi-Soviet pact. Browder called for moral and economic help to the Polish people, under attack from Hitler, and for an embargo on Japan and Germany. He urged support of the peace policy of the USSR, unity of the American people around the New Deal, and a people's democratic front to defeat reaction in 1940.

B548 BROWDER, Earl R. "Whose War Is It?" New York: Workers Library, 1939. 16 pp.
Denunciation of the war as an imperialist one, for which both sides are equally guilty. The Soviet Union's march into Poland is seen as defensive, redeeming the Poles from Nazi rule. The war must be stopped before the U.S. is dragged into it. American democracy and the progressive measures of the New Deal are endangered by reaction, which seeks first to outlaw the Communist Party.

B549 .... Mastery of Theory and Methods of Work, "Communist," 18 (Jan. 1939), 17-24.
The concluding speech at the plenary session of the Party's national committee, December 5, 1938, urging communists to come closer to the Catholics, and combat the Dies Committee's charge that communism is seditious and un-American. The Party must support the Spanish Loyalists, urge an embargo on aggressors, and fight for both social and national security.

B550 .... America and the Communist International, "Communist," 18 (March 1939), 209-15.
American communists do not take orders from Moscow. They act according to their convictions, taking the advice of outstanding leaders like Lenin, Stalin, and Dimitroff, who are well-qualified Marxists with a good grasp of American problems. Today Americanism means interventionism, American collaboration with other democracies against fascism.

B551 .... Perspectives of the 1940 Presidential Election, "Communist," 18 (June 1939), 497-510.
The electorate is divided into three approximately equal groups, Democrats, Republicans, and progressives. The Democratic Party has been successful only when its candidate appealed to the progressives. Regardless of the third-term tradition, it should nominate Roosevelt. To bring economic recovery, the New Deal must expand its public works program.

B552 .... America and the Non-Aggression Pact, "National Issues: A Survey of Politics and Legislation," 1 (Sept. 1939), 11-14.
The text of Browder's radio speech, August 29, 1939, together with his radio interview over the NBC network on August 26. Defending Stalin's pact with Hitler, Browder asserts that the USSR won a victory for the peace of the whole world. Chamberlain is charged with seeking to inveigle the Soviet Union into a war with Germany, while opposing a system of collective security.

B553 .... Some Remarks on the Twentieth Anniversary of the Communist Party of the United States of America, "Communist," 18 (Sept. 1939), 788-803.
The Communist Party was the first American party with a consistent Marxist theory. Weak during its first decade because of the Palmer raids and the struggle against Trotskyite and Lovestoneite factions, the Party gained great influence during its second decade. It supports the New Deal as the best barrier to fascism, though earlier it suspected that the New Deal was a camouflage for reaction.

B554 .... On the Twenty-Second Anniversary of the Socialist Revolution, "Communist," 18 (Nov. 1939), 1016-27.
Britain and France rejected cooperation with Russia in the hope of turning German aggression against Russia. Instead Germany, fearing Russian strength, signed the non-aggression pact. In the U.S. many New Dealers seek to repeal the Neutrality Act and send aid to the Allies. The Party, while supporting the Neutrality Act, does not associate itself with reactionary isolationists who also back American neutrality.

B555 .... "An American Foreign Policy for Peace." New York: Workers Library, 1940. 13 pp.
Speech by Browder in the 1940 presidential campaign, during the period of the Hitler-Stalin pact. The CPUSA, during this period, advocated American neutrality with respect to events in Europe.

B556 .... "Earl Browder Takes His Case to the People." New York: Workers Library, 1940. 31 pp.
Two speeches delivered the day Browder was sentenced for passport violation: his presentation of the case at a Party rally; his summation before the jury. In the first speech, Browder insists that his excessive sentence proves that the New Deal has gone reactionary and is starting a campaign to curb the labor movement. In his summation to the jury, he argues that the so-called "fraud" was just a misunderstanding, and that he should be found not guilty.

B557 .... "Earl Browder Talks to the Senators on the Real Meaning of the Voorhis 'Blacklist' Bill." New York: Workers Library, 1940. 29 pp.
The author's testimony against a bill to require registration of foreign-controlled organizations. Asserting that communists do not oppose establishment of controls over foreign agents in the U.S., he argues that the present bill is capable of much more damage than service. Legitimate trade unions, he declares, would be injured by the measure.

B558 .... "Internationalism: Results of the 1940 Election." New York: Workers Library, 1940. 31 pp.
Report to the Party's emergency national convention, held during the period of the Hitler-Stalin pact. Browder opposes the policies of Roosevelt and raises the slogan of "proletarian internationalism"—solidarity with, and defense of, the Soviet Union.

B559 .... "The Jewish People and the War." New York: Workers Library, 1940. 23 pp.
The Nazi-Soviet pact "line" as directed to the Jews. The author states that the present war is an imperialist war and that the Jewish people, like the toiling masses as a whole, have nothing to gain from an Allied victory. He calls on Jews in the U.S. to help keep America out of war.

B560 .... "The Most Peculiar Election: The Campaign Speeches of Earl Browder." New York: Workers Library, 1940. 94 pp.
The 1940 campaign speeches of the Party's candidate for president, during the period of the Nazi-Soviet pact. Browder declares that the Yanks are not coming, demands an end to the sale of war materials, and denounces Roosevelt for dictatorship and for leading Wall Street's imperialist march. The election is called the most peculiar because a federal judge has forbidden Browder's travel across the country.

B561 .... "The People Against the War Makers." New York: Workers Library, 1940. 31 pp.
A report to the national committee of the Party in February 1940, during the period of the "phony war" in Europe. Browder interpreted the war as an effort by British-French imperialism to break the Hitler-Stalin pact and force the Nazis to carry out the original program of war against the Soviet Union. Roosevelt was now charged with having assumed leadership of the camp of reaction in the U.S., to scrap the New Deal and drag America into the war. Far from favoring a third term for Roosevelt, Browder now urged formation of a third party.

B562 .... "A People's Platform for Peace; Keep

America Out of the Imperialist War." New York: National Election Campaign Committee, CPUSA, 1940. 4 pp.

Acceptance speeches of Earl Browder and James W. Ford, communist candidates for president and vice-president, June 2, 1940. Conducted during the Hitler-Stalin pact period, the Party campaign criticized the Roosevelt Administration, urging it to follow a neutralist policy.

B563 BROWDER, Earl R. "The People's Road to Peace." New York: Workers Library, 1940. 63 pp.

A report from the national committee to the eleventh national convention of the Party, held May 30-June 2, 1940. Browder viewed the war as an imperialist conflict for the redivision of the world. Condemning both the Nazis and the Western democracies, he attacked Roosevelt for taking the U.S. step by step into the war. He urged a people's program for peace and prosperity and an end to the shipment of munitions to the Allies.

B564 .... "The Second Imperialist War." New York: International Publishers, 1940. 309 pp. Ind.

A collection of speeches, articles, and reports by the general secretary of the Party between March 1939, and May 1940, just prior to and during the period of the Nazi-Soviet pact. Whereas prior to the pact Browder urged U.S. cooperation with the USSR and other countries to block fascist aggression, after its signing and the beginning of Nazi attacks on neighboring states he denounced the war as an imperialist one and opposed American involvement. The material is grouped under three heads: "Fateful Days," "The Second Imperialist War," and "The People Against the War-Makers."

B565 .... To the People Will Belong the Victory, "Communist," 19 (Feb. 1940), 116-21.

The text of an address to the Lenin Memorial Meeting, New York, January 22, 1940. Browder asserts that the Roosevelt Administration has capitulated to reaction and warmongering, and has started to curb the labor movement by persecuting communists. Workers should support the Communist Party in 1940 as the only party desiring peace.

B566 .... The Domestic Reactionary Counterpart of the War Policy of the Bourgeoisie, "Communist," 19 (July 1940), 597-609.

Selections from the general secretary's report for the national committee to the Party's national convention, May 30-June 2, 1940. Now that Roosevelt has cast the progressives aside in favor of the reactionaries, there is little difference between the Democratic and Republican parties. Both seek imperialist objectives, differing only in tactics. Only the Communist Party stands for peace.

B567 .... Election Platform of the Communist Party of the U.S.A., 1940: Basic Political Outline for the Platform; Text of the Platform, "Communist," 19 (Sept. 1940), 791-804.

Excerpts from Browder's report to the Party's national convention, May 30 to June 2, 1940, asserting that the Democratic and Republican parties are trying to drag the U.S. into war although most Americans want peace. Only the Communist Party seeks peace. The Party platform calls for opposition to warmongers, protection of civil liberties, and improvement of living standards.

B568 .... The Most Peculiar Election Campaign in the History of the Republic, "Communist," 19 (Oct. 1940), 884-89.

Browder, convicted of a passport violation, was prohibited by Federal Judge Knox from leaving the state of New York.

He accuses Roosevelt of giving the directive to silence the only rival candidate who opposes his designs of assuming dictatorial power and bringing the U.S. into the war on Britain's side.

B569 .... The 1940 Elections and the Next Tasks, "Communist," 19 (Dec. 1940), 1075-85.

A report to the Party's national committee, November 16-17, 1940, asserting that, although the Democratic and Republican parties are both controlled by Wall Street, they were forced by mass pressure to favor peace in the recent election campaign. During the campaign communists agitated for peace and a labor party, and fought to put the Communist Party on the ballot.

B570 .... "Communism and Culture." New York: Workers Library, 1941. 47 pp. Bibliog.

Writings and speeches of the author between 1935 and 1941 on the role of the intellectual in the struggle against reaction and exploitation. Asserting a community of interest between writers and the Communist Party, he explains the value of Marxist-Leninist theory as a guide to action. Interpreting the Party's stand on religion, he hails the growing friendly contacts between communists and religious communicants.

B571 .... "The Communist Party of the U.S.A.: Its History, Role and Organization." New York: Workers Library, 1941. 47 pp.

Excerpts from the writings and speeches of Earl Browder, then general secretary of the Party, between 1935 and March, 1941, dealing with the history, role, and organizational principles of the Party. Other topics treated include Party unity and discipline, qualities of communist leadership, the work of the Party branch, the need for vigilance against spies and provocateurs, and the tasks of the Young Communist League.

B572 .... "Earl Browder Says—." New York: Workers Library, 1941. 23 pp.

Compiled from the writings and speeches of the general secretary of the Party, then in federal prison for irregularities on a passport application. Published shortly before the Nazi invasion of the Soviet Union, the pamphlet includes quotations on war and peace, the struggle for democracy and civil rights, the role of the working class, the Soviet Union, and socialism as the way out of capitalist exploitation and imperialist war.

B573 ...; MINOR, Robert; FORD, James W.; and FOSTER, William Z. "The Path of Browder and Foster." New York: Workers Library, 1941. 22 pp.

Texts of a speech written by Browder, and speeches of Minor, Ford, and Foster, delivered at Madison Square Garden, New York City, March, 1941, at a meeting ostensibly to celebrate Foster's 60th birthday. The speeches dealt in most part with the "unjust" imprisonment of Browder (convicted of passport fraud), urging that he be released for the good of the war effort.

B574 .... "The Road to Victory." New York: Workers Library, 1941. 46 pp.

A compilation from writings and speeches of the general secretary of the Party between November 1, 1938, and May 30, 1940, asserting that the western democracies had planned to use Nazi Germany to destroy the Soviet Union, but that the Hitler-Stalin pact prevented this. The pamphlet, published after Hitler's invasion of the USSR, has a foreword by Gil Green calling for an all-out American effort to defeat German fascism.

B575 .... "The Way Out." New York: International

Publishers, 1941. 255 pp. Ind.

A compilation of speeches, articles, and reports between May 1940 and February 1941, expressing the Party's position during the period of the Hitler-Stalin pact. Emphasis is placed on the imperialist nature of the war and the need for the U.S. to refrain from aiding either side and to avoid an armaments program. The items are grouped under three headings: "The Road to Peace," "The Most Peculiar Election," and "The Way Out of the Imperialist War." The second section is so-named because Browder, though Party candidate for president, was forbidden by a federal judge to leave the jurisdiction of his court.

B576   BROWDER, Earl R. "The Way Out of the Imperialist War." New York: Workers Library, 1941. 14 pp.

An argument by the general secretary of the Party, written during the Hitler-Stalin pact period, that America can avoid involvement in the "imperialist" war if the American laboring masses cease to support the Roosevelt war program.

B577   .... On Some Aspects of Foreign Policy, "Communist," 20 (Jan. 1941), 35-37.

Browder clarifies his formulation of a "Washington-Moscow-Chungking Axis" proposed in a Boston speech, October 6, 1940. He denies press implications that he advocated alliance of the U.S. and Russia in an "imperialist war." The peace-loving American masses must put pressure on their government to collaborate with Russia in working for peace.

B578   .... Education and the War, "Communist," 20 (Feb. 1941), 132-37.

The reactionaries are trying to destroy the teachers' union, remove progressive and communist teachers, and limit academic freedom in order to mislead people into supporting their war program. The Communist Party has no conspiratorial attitude towards the schools; it merely wishes to publicize Marxist thought, confident that people will see its truth.

B579   .... We Represent the Future, "Communist," 20 (March 1941), 197-201.

An address in New York City, February 24, 1941, shortly before Browder's imprisonment, denouncing U.S. defense measures and asserting that the government is unjustly persecuting him in convicting him for a passport violation. Roosevelt is guilty of the crime of betraying the peace and prosperity of the American people.

B580   .... "Earl Browder on the Soviet Union." New York: Workers Library, 1942. 47 pp.

Pamphlet compiled from writings and speeches of Browder dealing with the Soviet Union and the need for an American foreign policy based on friendship and collaboration with the USSR. The material is reproduced from books published between 1935 and 1941.

B581   .... "Production for Victory." New York: Workers Library, 1942. 48 pp.

Report to the Communist Party on expediting war production, emphasizing the role of labor unions and advocating stricter economic controls. Browder calls for wage stabilization, price fixing, and payment of wage incentives. He opposes strikes, urges strengthening of labor-management committees, and calls for greater agricultural productivity. All else must be subordinated to unity and winning the war.

B582   ..., and others. "Speed the Second Front." New York: Workers Library, 1942. 15 pp.

Speeches by Earl Browder, William Z. Foster, Israel Amter, and Max Weiss at a "second-front rally" in New York City, September 24, 1942. Defeatist influences are said to delay the second front, which is necessary for U.S. victory and survival.

B583   .... "Victory—and After." New York: International Publishers, 1942. 256 pp.

A wartime book by the Party's leader addressed to the general public, dealing with the war, national unity, the United Nations (the world coalition of governments fighting the Axis), economics of war, and the postwar world. Browder appeals for national unity, arguing that Tories, communists, and all others can cooperate. He calls for equality of sacrifice, and a centralized war economy with labor's active participation. The central postwar problem is whether the coalition of nations set up to prosecute the war can deal with world economic and political reconstruction.

B584   .... "Victory Must Be Won." New York: Workers Library, 1942. 15 pp. Reprinted from "Communist," Aug. 1942.

A speech delivered July 2, 1942, at a meeting welcoming Browder after 14 months' imprisonment for irregularities in a passport application. Asserting that only the USSR was pulling its full weight in the war, Browder called for national unity and the opening of a second front in Europe now. He ascribed his jailing to efforts by world reaction to prevent realization of the U.S.-USSR alliance.

B585   .... Should the United States Government Join in Concerted Action against the Fascist States? "Communist," 21 (Jan. 1942), 22-37.

Reprint of a speech delivered in 1938, asserting that an isolationist policy encourages further fascist aggression. Isolationists excuse fascist aggressors as have-not countries, though their victims are even less wealthy. Marxists and Americans have always distinguished between good and bad governments and should urge the U.S. to embargo aggressors.

B586   .... On the Anniversary of the Patriotic War of the Soviet Union, "Communist," 21 (July 1942), 485-90.

The American people realize that the German attack on Russia transformed an imperialist into a people's war and that the U.S. had to join in the war. Fifth columnists in the U.S. slander Russia; after first predicting its defeat, they now say it will become too strong. They also oppose a second front and urge persecution of communists.

B587   .... The Communist Party and National Unity, "Communist," 21 (Sept. 1942), 679-91.

The demand that the Party be liquidated in the interests of national unity is inspired by Hitler and peddled by his U.S. agents. The Party has always striven for democratic objectives and American national interests. It backs close collaboration with Russia as necessary to defeat Germany.

B588   .... The Economics of All-Out War, "Communist," 21 (Oct. 1942), 791-808.

A speech to the Party's New York State convention, August 29, 1942, advocating centralized control of the nation's economy. High war production would be assured by high real wages, without strikes. To solve the problem of limited supply and unlimited demand, the free market should be replaced by a planned economy, with participation of labor leaders in central planning.

B589   .... One Year Since Pearl Harbor, "Communist," 21 (Dec. 1942), 976-84.

Address delivered in Detroit, November 12, 1942, acclaiming the Anglo-Soviet-American coalition and urging immediate opening of a second front in Europe. The American war effort is handicapped by prewar attitudes—underestimation of Russia's strength, unwillingness to accept centralized planning of the economy, and suspicion of communists.

B590   BROWDER, Earl R., and SOKOLSKY, George E. Is Communism a Menace? (A debate.) New York: "New Masses," 1943. 47 pp.
Sokolsky, columnist for the New York "Sun," asserts that communism is a menace because the Party is part of an international political instrument controlled by the USSR for its purposes, and because it seeks to destroy the spiritual and intellectual basis of American civilization. Denying that communism is a menace, Browder declares that everywhere in Europe we must choose between the democratic mass movement, including communists, and seedy aristocrats and profiteers. Communism cannot come to the U.S., he states, unless the American people choose it democratically.

B591   BROWDER, Earl R. "Make 1943 the Decisive Year." New York: Workers Library, 1943. 15 pp.
A plea for an invasion of Europe to win the war in 1943, and a condemnation of Churchill because the USSR must fight alone. Conservative and reactionary groups in the U.S. are said to support Churchill's strategy of delay. Browder calls for a genuine Anglo-Soviet-American alliance. (Also published under the title, "The Speech the Papers Lied About.)

B592   . . . . "Policy for Victory." New York: Workers Library, 1943. 96 pp.
Articles and speeches between July 1942 and April 1943, urging a second front, a Chinese coalition, and people's resistance movements in eastern Europe. Browder charges that a defeatist clique with the NAM is engaged in a conspiracy against the war. He attacks the fear in this country of sharing victory with the Soviet Union, and denounces the alleged Ehrlich-Alter conspiracy in the U.S. to overthrow the USSR.

B593   . . . . "A Talk About the Communist Party." Introd. by Robert Minor. New York: Workers Library, 1943. 23 pp.
Two speeches by Earl Browder, one in 1942 and one in 1943, to small gatherings of Party leaders. Browder calls for a party of thought and action, one close to the people, and one properly organized. He predicts a much more powerful Party in the near future.

B594   . . . . "Wage Policy in War Production." New York: Workers Library, 1943. 23 pp.
An abridged version of Browder's address to production workers and trade union officials in New York City, February 23, 1943, supporting incentive pay, which the entire noncommunist labor movement in the U.S. opposed. Distinguishing the new methods of computing incentive rates from the arbitrary bonus system, he urges acceptance as a patriotic duty.

B595   . . . . Production for Victory, "Communist," 22 (Jan. 1943), 10-29.
The abridged text of a report to the Party's National Conference held in New York City, November 29-December 1, 1942, analyzing war production and the problems involved. Attention is paid to production schedules, utilization of labor, and the role of organized labor in production.

B596   . . . . Hitler's Secret Weapon—the Bogey of Com-

munism, "Communist," 22 (March 1943), 198-204.
At a time when Germany is suffering military defeats, Hitler won a victory when Congress again declared its confidence in Martin Dies, who continually slanders Russia and the communists. Some cabinet members oppose close collaboration with Russia, a policy backed by most Americans. (An address in Baltimore, February 12, 1943.)

B597   . . . . The Carrot and the Club, or the Copperhead Cabal, "Communist," 22 (April 1943), 297-300.
Russian victories are causing contemporary American copperheads to oppose the opening of a second front on the grounds that a quick victory over Germany would cause power to pass from the U.S. to Russia, since the U.S. would be left fighting Japan. This proposal would be a double cross of a trustworthy ally, Russia.

B598   . . . . The Anti-Soviet Conspiracy in the United States, "Communist," 22 (May 1943), 399-402.
A speech suggesting that Ehrlich and Alter, executed for conspiracy to overthrow the Russian government, were sponsored in their attempt by Russo-Americans, N. Chanin, David Dubinsky, and Abe Cahan, who now denounce the Russian government for its action. Their activities are part of a conspiracy to break up the United Nations alliance.

B599   . . . . The Strike Wave Conspiracy, "Communist," 22 (June 1943), 483-94.
Bitter criticism of efforts on the part of some trade union leaders, including Walter and Victor Reuther and John L. Lewis. They hope to create a crisis in the U.S. that will prevent the opening of the second front in Europe to crack Hitler in 1943. The no-strike policy is labor's policy in labor's war.

B600   . . . . Hold the Home Front! "Communist," 22 (July 1943), 579-98.
A report to a plenary meeting of the Party's national committee, June 11-13, stressing communist objectives to strengthen the Soviet-American alliance, defeat John L. Lewis' strike policy, stimulate war production by incentive wages, reelect Roosevelt, and centralize the economy. The Communist International has been dissolved to help achieve national unity in the U.S. and in other United Nations countries.

B601   . . . . The Future of the Anglo-Soviet-American Coalition, "Communist," 22 (Oct. 1943), 867-73.
A speech delivered in New York City, September 2, 1943, reviewing the consequences of the failure to open a second front in Europe in 1943. Serious coalition warfare can be carried on only if a second front is opened in Europe to engage a considerable fraction of Hitler's forces. (Also published in pamphlet form.)

B602   . . . . The Three-Power Conference at Moscow, "Communist," 22 (Dec. 1943), 1059-64.
A favorable review of the decisions of the Moscow Conference of the foreign ministers of Britain, Russia, and the U.S. Agreement was reached to open a second front, continue collaboration after the war, punish German war criminals, and facilitate the return of democratic government to Italy and Austria.

B603   . . . . "Communists and National Unity: An Interview of 'PM' with Earl Browder." New York: Workers Library, 1944. 23 pp.
The text of Browder's interview with Harold Lavine of the New York newspaper "PM," March 15, 1944. While stressing national unity and points of similarity of the communists with other progressive groups, Browder

asserts that the existence of the communists bolsters up these groups. The communists, because of their mastery of the art of organization, can contribute to the general progressive cause.

B604 BROWDER, Earl R. "Economic Problems of War and Peace." New York: Workers Library, 1944. 15 pp.
Explanation and approval of the Dumbarton Oaks and Bretton Woods conferences and criticism of their opponents. Expanded world trade is urged as the only way to ensure full employment after reconversion.

B605 . . . . "Moscow, Cairo, Teheran." New York: Workers Library, 1944. 23 pp.
An article by Browder on "The Three-Power Conference in Moscow," combined with a "Daily Worker" editorial on "The Historic Teheran Meeting" and several communiques issued by the allied governments on war policies and peace objectives. Applauding the success of the Moscow conference, Browder attacks Trotskyite and other critics of the agreements reached.

B606 . . . . "The Road Ahead to Victory and Lasting Peace." New York: Workers Library, 1944. 40 pp.
Browder's speeches at the convention, May 20-22, 1944, which dissolved the Communist Party and established the Communist Political Association. He urges cooperation on the policies agreed upon at Teheran to win the war, and proposes postwar national unity for full employment, higher wages, and international economic collaboration. He calls for the reelection of Roosevelt in the interests of national unity and victory.

B607 . . . . "Teheran and America: Perspectives and Tasks." New York: Workers Library, 1944. 48 pp.
The main report and concluding remarks of the Party's general secretary at the meeting of its national committee on January 7-9, 1944. Browder hails the determination of the U.S., Britain, and the USSR to cooperate in the peace as well as in the war. He calls for national unity both during the war and in the postwar world, and supports the transformation of the Party into a political association.

B608 . . . . "Teheran: Our Path in War and Peace." New York: International Publishers, 1944. 128 pp.
Browder calls for the indefinite extension of national wartime unity into the postwar period, full postwar operation of the national economy, and an end to colonialism. He advocates reelection of Roosevelt to prevent reaction at home. (A chapter, "What Marxism Contributes to America," appeared in "Communist," September 1944.)

B609 . . . . On the Negroes and the Right of Self-Determination, "Communist," 23 (Jan. 1944), 83-85.
Official announcement of, and rationalization for, the wartime abandonment by the Party of its line of self-determination in the Black Belt. The WPA in the South, the organizing drives of the CIO, and the struggle to abolish the poll tax have shaken the old semifeudalism and opened up opportunity for Negro equality within the context of American capitalism. The decision to integrate is an exercise of the right of self-determination.

B610 . . . . "Teheran—History's Greatest Turning Point," "Communist," 23 (Jan. 1944), 3-8.
The Teheran Conference declaration that the Allies plan close collaboration in the postwar world means that the Soviet Union has been accepted as a permanent partner. Since each partner accepts the other's regime, American communists must cooperate with anyone who supports the Allied coalition.

B611 . . . . Marxism Arms Communists to Meet and Solve Issues Today, "Communist," 23 (Feb. 1944), 102-6.
Concluding remarks to the meeting of the Party's national committee, January 9, 1944, attesting to the flexibility of Marxism in solving problems arising from new situations. In its efforts to support the Teheran decisions, the Party will remain independent, joining neither the Democratic nor the Republican Party.

B612 . . . . Partisanship—A Luxury America Cannot Afford, "Communist," 23 (March 1944), 195-200.
Criticism of the American press for repeating the Nazi lie that conflict instead of cooperation will develop between Russia and the U.S. in the postwar world. Americans should press Roosevelt to accept the Democratic nomination because he is the one leader who can maintain national unity and uphold the policies of Teheran.

B613 . . . . Unity for Victory, for the Elections and for Post-War Security, "Communist," 23 (June 1944), 485-500.
Report to the national convention of the Communist Political Association, May 20, 1944, pledging communist support of the Teheran decisions. In order to promote the necessary national unity the Association takes a non-partisan stand. It accepts capitalism in America in order to help secure postwar markets, the end of racial discrimination, and the reelection of Roosevelt.

B614 . . . . America's Election and the Teheran Concord, "Communist," 23 (Dec. 1944), 1059-66.
The reactionaries' strategy in 1944 was to capture both major parties and break up the progressive coalition by sowing labor disunity and stirring up racial discrimination. Although they gained control of the Republican Party, they failed to prevent Roosevelt's re-election, and America is now firmly committed to the Teheran concord.

B615 . . . . "America's Decisive Battle," New York: New Century, 1945. 31 pp.
A report to the national committee of the Communist Political Association, March 10, 1945, approving the decisions at the Yalta Conference, and outlining strategy for the coming local elections. Those who reject the Yalta decisions are attacked as taking Hitler's side, and John L. Lewis is denounced for his strike threat. The success of the Communist Political Association since its formation the year before is attributed to its understanding of Marxist science.

B616 . . . . "Why America Is Interested in the Chinese Communists." New York: New Century, 1945. 16 pp.
An indictment of the Kuomintang's conduct during the war and a contrast of its regime with that of the Chinese communists. The Kuomintang is corrupt and has paralyzed the economy, whereas the communist regime has expanded production, worked military miracles against the Japanese, and given rise to democracy.

B617 . . . . The Study of Lenin's Teachings (On the Twenty-First Anniversary of Lenin's Death), "Political Affairs," 24 (Jan. 1945), 3-10.
The present communist policy of cooperation with capitalism is only apparently contradictory to Lenin's denunciation of class collaboration, for circumstances in the U.S. are not the same as in the Russia of 1917. America is now allied with the Soviet Union, and many of its capitalists have become more progressive.

B618 . . . . A Political Program of Native American Fascism, "Political Affairs," 24 (Feb. 1945), 99-107.

An examination of the speeches of Thomas E. Dewey and Dr. Virgil Jordan, president of the National Industrial Conference Board, shows that reactionaries are forced to hide behind specious programs. This confirms the communist argument that many American capitalists are no longer reactionary and imperialist.

B619 BROWDER, Earl R. The Big Three in the Crimea, "Political Affairs," 24 (March 1945), 203-9.
Approval of the decisions of the Crimean (Yalta) Conference as the logical continuation of those reached at Teheran. The agreement, providing for broad democratic unity and for self-determination for Poland and Yugoslavia, furnishes the pattern for all liberated Europe.

B620 .... Roosevelt's Heritage and the Task Ahead, "Political Affairs," 24 (May 1945), 389-91.
Commemorating Roosevelt's death, Browder urges the nation to carry on Roosevelt's policies of cooperation with Britain and Russia, support of the prospective world organization, raising of American living standards, and furtherance of national unity.

B621 .... After V-E Day—What Next? "Political Affairs," 24 (June 1945), 483-86.
Churchill's belief that the Big Three coalition should not continue into peacetime, the seating of Argentina in the UN, and the refusal to seat Poland are manifestations of an Anglo-American alliance against the Soviet Union. The conflict is viewed as one of mood and opinion, not interest.

B622 .... On the Question of Revisionism, "Daily Worker," July 24, 1945. Section 2, pp. 1-2 ff.
A defense of Browder's position against the attacks on it by Jacques Duclos and Foster. Accusing Foster of being the revisionist, Browder deals with criticisms of his position with regard to the power of U.S. monopoly capital, collaboration of capitalism and socialism, a socialist revolution in Europe, postwar national unity, the labor-management charter, revisionism and foreign markets, the expansion of the domestic market, economic crisis, and liquidation of the Party. (For Foster's reply see his "Browder on Revisionism" in the "Daily Worker," July 25, 1945.)

B623 .... "The Writings and Speeches of Earl Browder from May 23, 1945 to July 26, 1945." New York: The author, n.d. [1946]. 67 pp. App.
Browder's defense against the attack on him by the French communist leader, Jacques Duclos, that culminated in his expulsion from the Party. Included are speeches at Party meetings and articles in which Browder stated his point of view and pleaded for genuine discussion. Printed as an appendix is Browder's appeal to Party members following his expulsion. (Duclos' article signaled the shift from wartime cooperation with the USSR to the "cold war," and the Party's return to militancy.)

B624 .... Report on Russia, "New Republic," 115 (Aug. 5, 1946), 126-30; (Aug. 12), 163-65; (Aug. 19), 194-96; (Aug. 26), 222-25; (Sept. 2), 255-58; (Sept. 9), 289-91.
A report on the USSR by the former head of the CPUSA, expelled from the Party earlier that year, following his fifteenth trip to the Soviet Union. He reports on the issue of a durable peace or a new war, problems of reconversion, the Soviet Union and its neighbors, an American loan to the USSR, everyday life in Russia, and the question as to whether America wants cooperation. He offers a program for lasting peace based on equality and cooperation.

B625 .... "War or Peace with Russia?" New York: Wyn, 1947. 190 pp.

The former leader of the Party attributes deterioration of Soviet-American relations after 1945 to American denial of equality to the Soviets. Following Roosevelt's death, he asserts, the U.S. abandoned his policy of cooperation with the USSR, instead making anti-Sovietism a decisive factor in American policy; the USSR, in contrast, seeks to apply Roosevelt's policies. Arguing that peace and cooperation between the U.S. and the USSR are possible without abandonment by either country of its economic system, he urges collaboration on an equal basis as the only hope for world peace.

B626 .... "Answer to Vronsky." New York: n.publ., n.d. [1948?] 11 pp. Multilithed.
Browder's answer to an attack on his book "World Communism and U.S. Foreign Policy," by the editor of the Cominform journal, "For a Lasting Peace, for a People's Democracy." Browder charges Vronsky with misstating his position and slandering his attitudes toward the Soviet Union and toward the opening of the second front during World War II.

B627 .... "The Decline of the Left Wing of American Labor." New York: The author, 1948. 38 pp. Mimeo.
Sharp criticism of communist trade union leadership, three years after Browder's expulsion from the Party. Criticizing the disintegration of the left wing at the 1948 CIO convention, Browder asserts that it lacked a coherent or consistent policy, and that there was no difference in principle between left and right CIO unions on wage policy.

B628 .... "The 'Miracle' of Nov. 2d: Some Aspects of the American Elections." New York: The author, 1948. 40 pp. Mimeo.
Truman's reelection, due to a regathering of the Roosevelt coalition, is seen as a mandate for peace and progress. Nevertheless the Truman Administration is seen as unstable and opportunist. The collapse of the Wallace campaign is laid to the faulty judgments and clumsy direction of the Foster leadership of the Party. The left wing is now in a blind alley, without authoritative leadership.

B629 .... "World Communism and U.S. Foreign Policy: A Comparison of Marxist Strategy and Tactics After World War I and World War II." New York: The author, 1948. 55 pp.
An assertion that reaction has controlled the government since Roosevelt's death, making anti-Sovietism the keynote of U.S. foreign policy. The Truman Doctrine, openly directed against the USSR, and the Marshall Plan, organizing Europe as an anti-Soviet fortress, logically end in a new war. The progressive coalition that supported Roosevelt has lost by default, from confusion and lack of leadership. Browder urges unity of the progressive majority to restrain the war-makers and restore Roosevelt's foreign policy of peace and world progress.

B630 .... "Chinese Lessons for American Marxists." New York: The author, 1949. 48 pp. Mimeo. Ref. notes.
An analysis of the success of Marxism in China contrasted with its failure in the U.S., made three years after Browder's expulsion from the Party. He finds the basic reasons in the Chinese party's rejection of dogmas, its refusal to copy unthinkingly from any other country. In the U.S., however, the dogmatists in control have driven away their allies in the trade unions and wrecked the movement by arrogance and stupidity.

B631 .... "The Coming Economic Crisis in America." New York: The author, 1949. 47 pp. Mimeo.

A prediction by the former leader of the Party that a major economic crisis is developing, intensified by growing monopoly domination. The U.S. must choose between progressive economic relations with the world, on the basis of agreement with the USSR, or seek to conquer world markets by military power. The peaceful path, which is possible for America, should be the goal of all progressive effort.

B632 BROWDER, Earl R. "How to Halt Crisis and War: An Economic Program for Progressives." New York: The author, 1949. 40 pp. Mimeo.
A plea for a "progressive" export policy, denying that exports serve exclusively as an instrument of imperialism, and asserting that the domestic market cannot replace the foreign one. The cold war must be stopped before foreign trade can be increased. The alternative to a progressive export policy is a blundering descent toward disaster.

B633 .... "In Defense of Communism: Against W. Z. Foster's 'New Route to Socialism.'" Yonkers, N.Y.: The author, 1949. 70 pp.
A criticism of the defense in the 1949 conspiracy trial of the communist leaders, and of Foster's pamphlet, "In Defense of the Communist Party and the Indicted Leaders." Browder charges Foster with revisionist views on the subjects of violence, the route to socialism, the theory of correspondence between capitalism and socialism, the theory of spontaneity, and state power. Foster's views must be repudiated to restore a Marxist party here.

B634 .... "More About the Economic Crisis: Discussion on 'The Coming Economic Crisis.'" [New York?]: The author, 1949. 16 pp.
Criticism of the Communist Party's "left-deviationism." The author, general secretary of the Party before his expulsion, argues that true Leninists should support state capitalism in the U.S. as a transition to ultimate socialism, so as to soften the inevitable economic crises.

B635 .... "U.S.A. & U.S.S.R.: Their Relative Strength." New York[?]: n.publ., 1949. 48 pp. Mimeo.
Refuting the conclusions reached by a "New Republic" symposium, Browder asserts that the USSR is stronger economically and politically than the U.S. liberals admit. The "New Republic" findings are said to overestimate U.S. strength while underestimating that of the USSR, to be based on distortions of facts and unsound methodology, and to ignore American weakness in the form of surplus of commodities and role of classes.

B636 .... "War, Peace and Socialism." New York: The author, 1949. 38 pp. Mimeo.
Browder argues, three years after his expulsion from the Party, that capitalism and socialism, though inevitably in conflict in the long run, in the short run must find a way to co-exist. The American left must develop a peace program through unity with nonsocialists. Communists must also deal with the question of foreign markets for American goods, the key problem of the Marshall Plan.

B637 .... "Earl Browder Before U.S. Senate: The Record and Some Conclusions." Yonkers, N.Y.: The author, 1950. 64 unnumbered pp.
Reproduction of newspaper and Congressional Record statements on Senator McCarthy's attack on Owen Lattimore and the U.S. policy in China, together with Browder's testimony on the matter before the Senate committee. The author criticizes the conduct of both the McCarthy group and the Communist Party with regard to Browder's testimony: the former exhibits the rage and frustrations

of the war party; the "Daily Worker" attacks on Browder show that present Party leadership cares only for its narrow factional interests.

B638 .... "Is Russia a Socialist Community?" Yonkers, N.Y.: The author, 1950. 24 pp.
Affirming Russia's socialism on evidence of the USSR's economic accomplishments and peaceful motives, Browder argues for peaceful coexistence between the U.S. and Russia and predicts the ultimate success of Marxism in America.

B639 .... "Keynes, Foster and Marx." Yonkers, N.Y.: The author, 1950. In two parts, 56 pp. and 93 pp. Mimeo.
An attack on Foster's thinking, especially as revealed in the recent volume, "The Economic Crisis and the Cold War." Foster is attacked for not understanding Marxism, for groping blindly for a policy since becoming Party leader in 1945. Among other topics, Browder discusses capitalism, world markets, socialism, progress under capitalism and its limits, labor's role, bourgeois progressives, and Marxists as fighters for progress. He attacks Foster for nihilism, and for seeking to defeat such progressive candidates as Senator Douglas and Senator Humphrey. Browder advocates a progressive program of labor organization, rising living standards, and domestic reforms on which nonsocialists and socialists can unite.

B640 .... "Modern Resurrections & Miracles." Yonkers, N.Y.: The author, 1950. 55 pp.
A reply to an attack on Browderism by Gilbert Green (see "The Browderite Conception of History," in "Political Affairs," October 1949). Browder calls the Fosterite conception of history, like its policies, anti-Marxist. He attacks Foster's "coup d'etat" in the Party in 1945, explaining why he refused to organize resistance. He denies that the government's prosecution of the Party leadership proves that Foster has restored Marxism-Leninism or followed sound policy.

B641 .... "Toward an American Peace Policy." Yonkers, N.Y.: The author, 1950. 24 pp.
A plea for peace with the USSR, based on Stalin's peaceful overtures. Although rejecting the role of "professional anticommunist," Browder attacks the leadership of the CPUSA for failing to support this peace policy.

B642 .... "Contempt of Congress: The Trial of Earl Browder." Introd. by Louis B. Boudin. Yonkers, N.Y.: The author, 1951. 192 pp.
A collection of testimony, Senate resolutions, articles, court opinions, and personal commentary bearing on the author's citation for contempt of Congress for refusing to answer certain questions put to him by the Senate Foreign Relations Subcommittee (Tydings Committee), looking into alleged disloyalty of State Department personnel. (The contempt citation led to acquittal in a Federal District Court.) At the time of the hearing Browder, although expelled from the Party, insisted that he remained a communist, at least that he held the same ideas he had held for most of his adult life.

B643 .... "The Meaning of MacArthur: Letter to a Friend. Yonkers, N.Y.: The author, 1951. 13 pp. Multilithed.
The MacArthur-Truman split expresses a split in the decisive circles of the American bourgeoisie. Though both sides are bourgeois and imperialist, the Truman Administration recognizes that the USSR and its allies cannot be defeated by military means, while its critics led by MacArthur, ignore or deny this.

B644 BROWDER, EARL R. "Four Letters Concerning Peaceful Co-existence of Capitalism and Socialism." Yonkers, N.Y.: The author, 1952. 68 pp.
Four letters stimulated by an article by the Italian communist leader, Palmiro Togliatti. Asserting that peaceful co-existence is both desirable and possible, Browder denies that the only alternatives are fascism and war, or socialism and peace. He declares that Marxist theory will have to be applied in terms of U.S. history and experience, not repeated mechanically from Europe.

B645 . . . . "Marx and America: A Study of the Doctrine of Impoverishment." Introd. by Broadus Mitchell. New York: Duell, Sloan and Pearce, 1958. 146 pp. Ind.
A volume based on lectures delivered at Rutgers University in 1957, and expanded at the New School for Social Research in 1958. The former leader of the CPUSA emphasized Marx's imperfect understanding of America, which he never visited; the higher standard of living of workers here, Marx thought, would not continue inevitably, to exempt the proletariat from the intolerable misery that he saw around him in industrialized Europe.

B646 . . . . How Stalin Ruined the American Communist Party, "Harper's Magazine," 220 (March 1960), 45-51.
A discussion of the reasons and consequences of his purge by the former head of the Party in the U.S. The Duclos article, which Stalin initiated, signaled Browder's purge, and marked the beginning of the cold war. As a result the Party, placed under the leadership of the sectarian William Z. Foster, was wrecked. Now Khrushchev has adopted the co-existence heresy for which Browder was expelled.

B647 BROWDER, Irene. For a Correct Approach to the Problems of the National Groups, "Communist," 17 (Sept. 1938), 797-804.
A report delivered May 27, 1938, to the Commission on National Groups at the Party's tenth convention, listing the major national groups for Party work and the approach to be followed with each. The influence of fascism and of its Trotskyite and Lovestoneite agents must be counteracted.

B648 . . . . Problems of the National Groups in the United States, "Communist," 18 (May 1939), 456-66.
The importance of winning national groups to the support of progressive and democratic forces is emphasized. The national groups played an important part in the early socialist movement and provided the main base for the CP on its formation. More recently reactionary influences have been growing among them. This process can and must be reversed.

B649 . . . . The National Groups in the Fight for Democracy: On the Occasion of the Twentieth Anniversary of the Communist Party of the United States, "Communist," 18 (Sept. 1939), 857-66.
A historical account of national groups in American life, emphasizing their roles in the American Revolution, in the rise of Jeffersonian democracy, in the Civil War and the battle for Negro rights, in the rise of the labor movement, and in the development of the Communist Party.

B650 BROWDER, Robert P. The United States, the Soviet Union, and the Comintern, 1933-1935, "Russian Review," 12 (Jan. 1953), 25-39.
An account of the negotiation of, and experience with, the pledge of noninterference through propaganda and subversive activity made by the Soviet Union to the U.S. as the price of diplomatic recognition. The two governments disagreed as to whether the pledge applied to the Communist

International and its American section, the CPUSA. The American view is regarded as naïve.

B651 BROWN, F. The Tasks Among the Foreign-Born Workers, "Communist," 12 (Aug. 1933), 810-17.
Proposals for increased activity of the Party's language organizations. The International Workers Order, the Party's fraternal-benefit society, can carry the campaign for unemployment and social insurance to foreign-born workers. Activities of the language groups should be better coordinated with those of factory and shop committees and nuclei.

B652 . . . . Through Concentration to a Mass Proletarian Party, "Communist," 12 (Sept. 1933), 864-74.
A discussion of the importance of concentrating Party activities in specific areas, particularly industrial centers, in order to create a mass Communist Party, one that will be overwhelmingly proletarian.

B653 . . . . For Improving the Work of the Party Among the Foreign-Born Workers, "Communist," 13 (July 1934), 700-10.
A speech delivered at the eighth convention of the Communist Party, reviewing Party success in consolidating the language organizations in the period between the seventh and eighth conventions. New tasks are outlined.

B654 . . . . The Organizational Tasks Arising from the Plenum Decisions, "Communist," 14 (March 1935), 262-73.
An analysis of changes in Party work needed following the January 1935 decisions of the CPUSA Central Committee, which altered the line on trade-union work, the united front, and the labor party. Despite Party improvements in united-front and trade-union work, it has not sufficiently increased membership or circulation of the "Daily Worker."

B655 . . . . Toward the Study of Fascization in the United States, "Communist," 14 (June 1935), 558-68.
A discussion article analyzing the rising tide of fascism in the U.S. and the communist role in counteracting it. Differences in American, Italian, and German capitalism are outlined. The orientation of the American bourgeoisie toward fascism is expressed primarily through the Roosevelt Administration.

B656 . . . . "Who Are the Communists and What Do They Stand For?" New York: Workers Library, 1936. 13 pp.
Popularly written pamphlet of the people's front period, stating that communists stand for full employment, educational opportunities, Negro rights, and peace.

B657 . . . . Building the Party During the Election Campaign, "Communist," 15 (Oct. 1936), 966-74.
An appeal at the ninth convention of the Party to use the national election as a means of increasing the membership from 50,000 to 100,000. The Party recruited 12,000 new members in its latest drive, though the proportion of industrial workers, native-born Americans, Negroes, and women was not as high as desired.

B658 BROWN, Fred [pseud. for F. Marini]. The Importance of the Present Recruiting Drive for the Future of Our Party, "Communist," 16 (Oct. 1937), 915-24.
A discussion of preparations for a two-month recruiting drive which will avoid weaknesses of past drives. The time is ripe, since workers in newly organized unions have seen the good work of communists. Party members must be well trained in theory and able to answer the

questions of potential or new recruits. (Fred Brown was a pseudonym for F. Marini, also known as Mario Alphi, a Comintern representative in the United States.)

B659 BROWN, Fred. For Concerted Action—Against Isolation and War! "Communist," 17 (March 1938), 251-65.
A report to a plenary session of the Party's Central Committee and National Party Builders Congress, February 18-21, 1938, condemning a neutrality philosophy and advocating active international peace fronts. The American League for Peace and Democracy must be strengthened, democratic Spain and China supported, and actions of the bourgeois-democratic countries consolidated with that of the Soviet Union against all aggressors.

B660 BROWN, George. Railroad Workers Raise Struggle Against Consolidation, "Communist," 15 (Aug. 1936), 698-706.
A discussion of demands for consolidation of railroad facilities, and of the role of unions in defeating merger efforts. The gravest danger to the railroad unions is the threat of mass layoffs through consolidations. The move to amalgamate the railroad unions is growing.

B661 BROWN, Jay G. The Farmer-Labor Party Side, "American Labor Monthly," 1 (Sept. 1923), 33-37.
Criticism of the Workers Party by the secretary of the National Farmer-Labor Party for capturing the July 1923, conference at which the Federated Farmer-Labor Party was formed. Inspired by Moscow, the program will be unacceptable to the bulk of workers, and the chance to increase sentiment for independent political action has been lost.

B662 BROWN, John. The Causes and Effects of McCarthyism, "Political Quarterly," 26 (April-June 1955), 178-85.
An Englishman who has lived in the U.S. traces McCarthyism to conditions in America which make it possible for demagogues to prey on the fears of ordinary people. He reviews the cases of Lattimore and others accused of communist sympathy, asserting that they served as scapegoats for the failure of American policy in China. Career diplomats have been dismissed for giving unpalatable advice.

B663 BROWN, John M. Can They Ever Learn? "Workers Monthly," 5 (Nov. 1926), 592-93.
The IWW is criticized for its avoidance of political action. The workers' economic organization is met with the political as well as the economic power of the capitalists. Therefore the workers must conquer the state, using political action under the leadership of a revolutionary political party.

B664 BROWN, John Mason. "Through These Men: Some Aspects of Our Passing History." New York: Harper, 1952. 302 pp. Ind.
A book of essays by a leading literary and theatrical critic on personalities in recent political developments. Chapter 10, pp. 228-91, is devoted to the case of J. Robert Oppenheimer and the question of his security clearance. The various investigations of Oppenheimer on loyalty grounds are reviewed.

B665 BROWN, Joseph M. Labor Out of the Red, "Plain Talk," 2 (Feb. 1948), 10-12.
An account of the setbacks suffered by communists in unions during 1947. The communists were defeated in the American Newspaper Guild, the New Jersey State Industrial Union Council, the National Maritime Union, and the United Automobile Workers. Though communists still lead several important unions, the CIO promises to become a truly American federation.

B666 BROWN, Lloyd. "Young Workers in Action: A Story of the South River Strike." Introd. by National Executive Committee, Young Communist League. New York: Youth Publishers, n.d.[193-]. 15 pp.
An account of the strike of 1,700 needle trades workers, most of them young girls, in South River, N. J., helped by the Young Communist League and led by the Needle Trades Workers Industrial Union. The Republican mayor, the police, the Democratic governor, and the U.S. Department of Labor all aided the employers.

B667 BROWN, Lloyd L. Iron City. New York: Masses & Mainstream, 1951. 255 pp.
A story by a Party functionary, dealing with the efforts of three Negro communists, imprisoned as "politicals" just before Pearl Harbor, to organize a protest strike outside the prison for another Negro awaiting execution for a crime he did not commit.

B668 .... Which Way for the Negro Writer? "Masses & Mainstream," 4 (March 1951), 53-63; (April), 50-59.
An expression of disagreement with writers who feel that Negroes should not be preoccupied with the Negro problem, but should write on more universal themes. The dominant force behind such sentiment is the chauvinistic ideology of American imperialism. The real trouble with Negro literature is that it has not been Negro enough.

B669 .... "Stand Up for Freedom! The Negro People vs. the Smith Act." New York: New Century, 1952. 15 pp.
An appeal to American Negroes to defend the Negro communists indicted under the Smith Act. The author, a Negro communist, states that the author of the Smith Act is one of the most vicious and powerful enemies of the Negro people. The Smith Act, he asserts, would be used against Negroes who fight for antilynching legislation, fair employment, and civil rights, and who seek to repeal Jim Crow laws.

B670 BROWN, Louise Fargo. The Great Teacher That Teaches Nothing. "Survey Graphic," 37 (Aug. 1948), 366-67.
A plea by a historian that we avoid a witch hunt against communism, that we not abandon our tradition of freedom out of fear. She criticizes the guilt-by-association features and the punishment of opinion in the Taft-Hartley and Smith Acts and the Mundt-Nixon bill.

B671 BROWN, Ralph S., Jr. 6,000,000 Second-Class Citizens, "Nation," 174 (June 28, 1952), 644-47.
Examination by a Yale University law professor of the problems that the loyalty program has created for government employees, whose liberties have been diminished by procedural shortcomings, reduced ability to find other employment, and reduced freedom of political and social thought and action.

B672 ..., and FASSETT, John D. Loyalty Tests for Admission to the Bar, "University of Chicago Law Review," 20 (Spring 1953), 480-508.
An examination of loyalty requirements for admission to the bar throughout the U.S. The authors recommend that there be a lessening of loyalty tests, though inquiries about criminally subversive activities are not improper. Applicants should not be barred for "disloyalty," because of the elusiveness of the concept.

B673 ..., and FASSETT, John D. Security Test for Maritime Workers: Due Process under the Port Security Program, "Yale Law Journal," 62 (July 1953), 1163-1208.

An analysis of the Coast Guard port security program, noting that denial of clearance to a seaman bars him from practicing his calling. The authors review the incidence of communism in the shipping industry, assert that Congress probably had the right to authorize a screening program, list inadequacies in the review and appeal arrangements, and discuss the constitutional requirement of due process.

B674 BROWN, Ralph S., Jr. Lawyers and the Fifth Amendment: A Dissent, "American Bar Association Journal," 40 (May 1954), 404-7.
A Yale Law School professor opposes the position of the House of Delegates of the American Bar Association that a lawyer who claims the privilege against self-incrimination should not be permitted to practice. For various reasons one who was never a member of the Communist Party might invoke the protection of the Fifth Amendment.

B675 .... The Operation of Personnel Security Programs, "Annals of the American Academy of Political and Social Science," 300 (July 1955), 94-101.
A discussion of the federal security program for civilian employees under Executive Order 10450, with special attention to the role of the security officer. The process of investigation is described, as are the evaluation of FBI reports by security officers, the standards employed, the nature of the charges made, the hearing, the review, and the powers of security officers.

B676 .... "Loyalty and Security: Employment Tests in the United States." New Haven, Conn: Yale University Press, 1958. 524 pp. Ind.
A study of the loyalty and security aspects of employment tests developed in private industry and government during the cold-war decade. The author describes the standards, procedures, and effects of these tests, examines their justification, considers the alternatives in a security context, and offers recommendations for improvement.

B677 BROWN, Sam. The Proposals of the Communist Party for United Front with the S. P. in the U.S.A., "Communist International," 11 (Nov. 5, 1934), 740-42.
The CPUSA has proposed united front action to the new "left" leadership of the Socialist Party which, in view of rank-and-file sentiment, does not dare reject it openly. It now favors effective local united-front action, though in the past the SP leadership has prohibited such action without national approval. (Written by an English member of the Anglo-American Commission of the Communist International.)

B678 BROWN, William Montgomery. "Communism and Christianism Analyzed and Contrasted from the Marxian and Darwinian Points of View." Galion, O.: Bradford-Brown Educational Co., n.d. [1925]. 223 pp.
An attempt by a former Episcopalian bishop, who was convicted of heresy by his church, to show that Christianity and organized religion are an abomination, and that Marxism embodies all of both religion and politics that are good for the world.

B679 .... "Communism: The New Faith for a New World." Galion, O.: Bradford-Brown Educational Co., 1933. 42 pp.
An address by an unfrocked bishop, who regarded the Marxian communism of the Soviet Union as the final religion and politics, to the World Fellowship of Faiths at the Chicago World's Fair of 1933. He describes existing economic problems, praises the Soviet revolution, and asserts that communism can usher in the brotherhood of nations.

B680 BROWNE, Stuart [pseud.]. A Professor Quits the Communist Party, "Harper's Magazine," 175 (July 1937), 133-42. Reprinted in "New Leader," 20 (July 3, 10, 17, 1937).
The experiences of a professor and his wife in the Communist Party. The author, who spent 30 months in one CP unit, records his activities for one week, and describes his withdrawal, ending his useless activity. He finally saw that his activities were furthering a dictatorship in the name of democracy.

B681 BROWNELL, Herbert, Jr. Immunity from Prosecution vs. Privilege against Self-Incrimination, "Federal Bar Journal," 14 (April-June 1954), 91-112.
The attorney general of the U.S. discusses the history of the privilege against self-incrimination, the way in which congressional investigations have been thwarted by resort to the privilege, and the pending proposal before Congress to exchange immunity from prosecution for testimony.

B682 .... Attorney General Says: Reds Are Trying to Wreck Informant System of FBI, "U.S. News & World Report," 38 (April 1, 1955), 68-71.
The text of an address by Attorney General Herbert Brownell on March 21, 1955, asserting that the latest communist tactic is to smear government witnesses. Describing the case of Harvey Matusow, Brownell urges us to keep up our defenses against this sort of attack.

B683 BRUHN, Alfred W. "Stop Communism Now." Chicago: Midwest Publishers, 1952. 144 pp.
A statement from the extreme right, contrasting New Dealers with "good Americans," and reciting characteristics in which New Dealers are communistic—as in tax and spending policies, deception, confusion of issues, suppression of the press, control of education, protection of communists, and use of controls. The author proposes the outlawry of communism, the requirement of anticommunist oaths of all public officials, the establishment of an anticommunist court with Senator McCarthy as chief prosecutor, and the formation of anticommunist cells in schools and places of employment.

B684 BRUHNS, Fred C. The Appeal of Communism, "Pacific Spectator," 6 (Autumn 1952), 413-27.
An assertion that the appeal of communism is not in its political doctrine, but in its function as a moral faith and a religion. The communist faith, based on the class struggle, grew out of the European class structure, and is unsuited to U.S. conditions. Democracy must overhaul its public and educational approach to the problem of communism.

B685 BRUNINI, John G. A Catholic Paper vs. Communism, "Commonweal," 19 (Nov. 24, 1933), 96-98.
A report on the "Catholic Worker," a new labor paper to educate Catholic workers in the labor teachings of the Church and to oppose communism by fighting for social justice for workers. The paper was started in May 1933, by Dorothy Day, formerly associated with communist publications, and Peter Maurin, a French Catholic workingman and apostle to the radicals.

B686 BRYSON, Lyman. "Which Way America? Communism—Fascism—Democracy." New York: Macmillan, 1939. 113 pp.
A popularly written analysis of the forms of government and economic organization in Russia, Italy, Germany, and the United States by a staunch defender of the democratic

process, who is willing to accept economic and political changes to which people are persuaded by honest argument and facts. Both communism and fascism, he asserts, seek to disguise themselves in American form to get support.

B687 BUCHWALD, Nathaniel. The Off-Broadway Theatre, "Masses & Mainstream," 8 (June 1955), 13-18.
An evaluation of the current off-Broadway theatre, with a review of the history of the little theatre and of the social theatre of the '20's and '30's. Though the present off-Broadway movement does not have the same social mission, any resistance to conformity is welcome, despite confusion and lack of clear social orientation.

B688 BUCKLEY, Wm. F., Jr., and BOZELL, L. Brent. "McCarthy and His Enemies: The Record and Its Meaning." Prologue by William Schlamm. Chicago: Regnery, 1954. 413 pp. App. Notes. Ind.
A vigorous defense of McCarthy's efforts to purge the government service of procommunists. The authors describe communist infiltration of the federal government, especially the State Department, dealing particularly with the cases of Dorothy Kenyon, Haldore Hanson, Philip Jessup, Esther Brunauer, Frederick Schuman and Harlow Shapley, Gustavo Duran, John Stewart Service, and Owen Lattimore. McCarthy's methods and record are defended. McCarthy serves as a prosecutor, not concerned with establishing "guilt," but with creating security standards stringent enough to protect the country against camouflaged communists.

B689 ..., and the editors of "National Review." "The Committee and Its Critics: A Calm Review of the House Committee on Un-American Activities," New York: Putnam, 1962. 352 pp. Notes. Ind.
In the opening chapter, "The Committee and Its Critics" (pp. 13-33), Buckley raises the question whether the open society can tolerate communists, and calls for a standing House Committee on Communist Activities. In chapter 3, "Subversion in the Twentieth Century" (pp. 66-89), Willmoore Kendall discusses communist efforts at subversion in the U.S. Chapter 6, pp. 143-75, by Ralph de Toledano, deals with the Hiss case. The remaining chapters review other aspects of the work of the Committee.

B690 BUDENZ, Louis F. A.F. of L. Unity Is Threatened by the Executive Council, "Communist," 15 (Sept. 1936), 845-56.
A protest against the suspension of CIO unions by the AFL's Executive Council, in violation of the AFL constitution. Reactionary union heads who support the suspension have no right to speak for their membership, since they have not called conventions of their unions for years. A flood of union resolutions for reinstatement is urged.

B691 .... "May Day, 1937: What It Means to You." New York: Workers Library, 1937. 16 pp.
Applauding the rise of unionism in the steel and automobile industries, and on the ships and docks, Budenz calls for the organization of those workers still unorganized, and for a fight in Congress and state legislatures for democracy and the welfare of the common people. He hails the peace policies of the Soviet Union, the bulwark of peace and democracy.

B692 .... "Red Baiting: Enemy of Labor." New York: Workers Library, 1937. 23 pp.
Vitriolic communist attack on William Green, the Liberty League, Homer Martin (then president of the United Automobile Workers), and others who draw sinister inferences

from communist backing of labor unions. Though communists help build CIO industrial unions as a step to socialism, those who equate the CIO with communism are using Red-baiting to wreck the unions. Included is a letter from Earl Browder to Martin, protesting statements against communists and attacking the Lovestone group.

B693 .... "May Day 1940." New York: Workers Library, n.d. [1940]. 16 pp.
A call, during the Hitler-Stalin pact period, for opposition to the imperialist war and for a militant struggle for better economic conditions and democracy. Only socialism can achieve peace and security. The unity of Soviet workers is pledged in the battle for peace, security, and a socialist world.

B694 .... "Save Your Union! The Meaning of the 'Anti-Trust' Persecution of Labor." New York: Workers Library, 1940. 30 pp.
A plea by the managing editor of the "Daily Worker" to all labor to denounce the Department of Justice drive to use the antitrust laws against certain union activities. The prosecutions, he asserts, seek to destroy unions and to bind labor to the war machine.

B695 .... The Reactionary Political Role of the Vatican, "Communist," 19 (May 1940), 431-50.
A denunciation of the papacy in protest against the appointment of Myron C. Taylor as personal envoy of the President to the Pope. The CP has unified Catholic and non-Catholic workers in struggles against poverty and war, whereas the Catholic hierarchy has always played a reactionary role in the U.S., helping capitalists against the workers and supporting fascism here and in Spain.

B696 .... The President's Message to Congress, "Communist," 22 (Feb. 1943), 157-64.
The defeatists were rebuffed when Roosevelt, in his speech to Congress, called for offensives on all fronts. Renewed defeatists' efforts to obstruct the war effort must be routed. New taxes will be needed for the war, and trade unions must exert pressure to make the taxes progressive and achieve central economic planning.

B697 .... May Day for Victory and the Teheran Goal, "Communist," 23 (May 1944), 387-96.
Objectives for labor include victory over the Nazis; closer cooperation among the American, British, and Soviet trade unions; and the program of Teheran, with its promise of lasting peace. The AFL Executive Council, under defeatist influence, will not participate in the World Labor Congress opening in London next month.

B698 .... Notes on the Democratic Convention, "Communist," 23 (Sept. 1944), 813-18.
The Democratic convention is commended for its nomination of Roosevelt and for advocating quick victory in the war, United Nations collaboration, the Good Neighbor policy towards Latin America, independence for Puerto Rico, and prolabor legislation.

B699 .... Fuehrer Lewis Runs a Convention, "Communist," 23 (Nov. 1944), 1043-55.
A scathing review of the United Mine Workers convention held in Cincinnati, September 1944. Lewis is denounced for dictatorial procedures; progressives are urged to rally the miners behind Roosevelt in spite of the opposing stand of the UMW.

B700 .... "This Is My Story." New York: McGraw-Hill, 1947. 379 pp. Ind.
A member of the Party from 1935 to 1945, Budenz was

managing editor of the "Daily Worker" when he broke with communism. He had joined the Party when the popular front line seemed to promise a democratic, although still revolutionary, communist movement. Disillusioned with the Party's intellectual dishonesty and strait-jacket discipline, and convinced that it was the agent of a foreign power, Budenz left it to rejoin the Catholic Church. His autobiography offers valuable insight into the workings of the Party and the perspectives of a prominent anticommunist.

B701   BUDENZ, Louis F. How the Reds Snatched Henry Wallace, "Collier's," 122 (Sept. 18, 1948), 14-15 ff.
An assertion that Wallace was a prisoner of the communists. Instructed by the USSR to support Wallace, the communists here chose him as the candidate, loading the ranks of his advisers. If he should win, communists would be entrenched in government, and we would be on our way to overthrow of democracy as in Czechoslovakia.

B702   . . . . The Red Web in U.S. Labor, "Collier's," 122 (Oct. 23, 1948), 13-14 ff.
A former communist editor analyzes the methods used by communists to get control of American unions. Masters of the smear, they use fraud, trickery, falsehood, and treachery. They also lure good union men with sweet talk. Examples are given from the fight in the United Electrical Workers and from other unions with communist activity.

B703   . . . . The Red Plan for S-Day, "Collier's," 122 (Nov. 20, 1948), 16-17 ff.
On the day the Soviets declare war on the U.S., American communists will spring into action with disruptive tactics in preparation for 25 years. A former leading communist outlines the master plan prepared for S-Day (Soviet Day), and discusses the tools, organizations, and methods that will be used.

B704   . . . . Capture of the Innocents, "Collier's," 122 (Nov. 27, 1948), 92-95.
A former high-ranking communist reveals uses to which the Party puts the endorsements of front groups by gullible intellectuals. Describing some of the front groups which he helped establish, he argues that similar technique is used for such postwar front groups as the Civil Rights Congress.

B705   . . . . "Men without Faces: The Communist Conspiracy in the U.S.A." New York: Harper, 1950. 305 pp. Ind.
An exposure of the Party, its activities and methods of operation, by a former managing editor of the "Daily Worker" who had been a Party member from 1935 to 1945. Budenz outlines the organizational structure of the CP, showing that it is not a political party in the American sense. He describes the communist web in organized labor, the Party's manipulation of front groups, and its espionage operations for the Soviet Union. A fifth column for the USSR, the Party is laced with deceit, conspiracy, and double-dealing; it constitutes a "clear and present" danger to the U.S.

B706   . . . . How the Reds Invaded Radio, "American Legion Magazine," 49 (Dec. 1950), 14-15 ff.
The former managing editor of the "Daily Worker" tells of the communist campaign in late 1943, in which he played a leading part, to infiltrate radio and television. Taking advantage of sympathetic radio artists and government officials, the Party was able to get friendly script writers and commentators on the air.

B707   . . . . I. W. O.—Red Bulwark, "American Legion Magazine," 50 (March 1951), 14-15 ff.
An assertion by a former high-ranking communist that the medical and insurance functions of the International Workers Order serve as cover-up for red subversion. An IWO lodge cannot be distinguished in its political tone from a Party branch. Attached to IWO are a number of foreign language societies, in each of which an espionage apparatus operates.

B708   . . . . Do Colleges Have to Hire Red Professors? "American Legion Magazine," 51 (Nov. 1951), 11-13 ff.
An assertion that an aggressive and growing minority of college professors are committed to the communist cause and serve repeatedly on front organizations. The activities of a number of such faculty members are traced. Loyalty oaths for educators and thorough investigations of colleges and universities are advocated.

B709   . . . . "The Cry Is Peace." Chicago: Regnery, 1952. 242 pp. Ind.
An account of communist penetration into American life, written during the Korean War by a former leading communist. He traces communist influence in the State Department, in communications, in higher education, and in social service institutions. The communist "peace" crusade has bewildered us, preventing a firm stand against a foe bent on world domination. A call for firmness against Stalin abroad and his agents at home.

B710   . . . . "The Techniques of Communism." Chicago: Regnery, 1954. 342 pp. Ind.
Analysis of the objectives of international communism and of its organizational techniques, using the CPUSA for illustration. The author discusses changes in the Party line, relating them to the needs of Soviet foreign policy. Detailed accounts of communist infiltration into labor organizations, education, the sciences, minority groups, and government agencies are presented. The gravest threat to national security stems, not from espionage, but from infiltration which influences policy.

B711   . . . . The Plight of the Liberals, "American Mercury," 80 (April 1955), 27-32.
An assertion that liberals, in the name of democracy and freedom, advance the communist line—the greatest present danger to our freedom. The author condemns such liberals as Theodore H. White, Henry Steele Commager, Jerome Davis, and others who, because they have only negative viewpoints, take a "moral" stand for the most immoral of all forces, communism.

B712   . . . . The Reds and Labor Have Nothing in Common, "American Mercury," 81 (Aug. 1955), 87-93.
A former leading Party member reviews communist activity in labor unions to show that Soviet Russia is interested in unions solely to turn them into puppets. The expulsion of communist-led unions by the CIO is reviewed, along with the efforts of the expelled groups to enter the AFL through mergers. Communism should never be confused with the labor movement.

B713   . . . . McCarthyism Vindicated, "American Mercury," 81 (Oct. 1955), 19-24.
The author finds McCarthyism vindicated by the refusal of the Wisconsin Republican convention to support the censure of McCarthy. Since McCarthyism was halted on the national scene, moreover, communist objectives have won out in the U.S. in the acceptance once more of the "Yalta atmosphere."

B714   BUDISH, J. M. In collaboration with Labor Research Association. "People's Capitalism: Stock Ownership and Production." New York: International Publishers, 1958. 64 pp. Ref. notes.

An assertion that common stocks are narrowly owned and controlled, that employee and consumer stock-ownership plans are designed to make people believe that monopolies are owned by the people. The process of monopolization in industry continues. The Soviet economic system, in contrast, mobilizes the nation's resources and energies for socially useful ends.

B715 BUDISH, J. M. In Collaboration with Labor Research Association. "The Changing Structure of the Working Class." New York: International Publishers, 1962. 64 pp.
A communist view of the size and composition of the working class, asserting that it is growing both absolutely and relatively, absorbing ruined elements of the middle strata, while undergoing shifts in distribution between employed and unemployed, commodity and service-producing occupations, and production and nonproduction workers. Problems of union organization and job security are considered.

B716 .... "Is Communism the Next Stage? A Reply to Kremlinologists." New York: International Publishers, 1965. 128 pp. Bibliog.
A discussion of the aims of communist society and the problems of the USSR economy, by a labor publicist and economist who had served on the staff of the Soviet's Amtorg Trading Corporation here, and also as an editor of the communist Yiddish paper, "Morning Freiheit." The author discusses the meaning of socialism and communism and the difference between them, and considers conventional "cold-war" preconceptions concerning the USSR.

B717 "BULLETIN OF THE ATOMIC SCIENTISTS," American Visa Policy and Foreign Scientists, 8 (Oct. 1952).
A special issue, under the editorship of Edward A. Shils, devoted to the problems raised for scientists by American visa policy. Leading American scientists criticize the policy, and British, French, and other foreign scientists describe their difficulties in obtaining visas. An editorial by Shils condemns the two McCarran Acts—the Internal Security Act of 1950 and the Immigration and Nationality Act of 1952—and their excessively rigid administration by the State Department as harmful to scientific advance, democratic reputation, and national security.

B718 ..., The Oppenheimer Case, 10 (May 1954), 173 ff.
Documents in the Oppenheimer case, including the charges against Oppenheimer and the suspension of his security clearance by the Atomic Energy Commission, Oppenheimer's reply, the AEC statement on procedures in the case, and statements by scientists affirming faith in Oppenheimer.

B719 ..., Special Section: The Oppenheimer Case, 10 (June 1954), 241-56.
Included are an editorial, "What is a Security Risk?"; "A Slippery Slope," by Edward Shils; the Report of the Special Personnel Security Board; the minority report by Dr. Ward V. Evans; the request of Dr. Oppenheimer's attorney for a review by the Personnel Security Review Board; and an open letter to President Eisenhower from the Federation of American Scientists on security policy.

B720 ..., The Fort Monmouth Investigations, 10 (June 1954), 225-26.
A summary of the findings of the Committee on Loyalty and Security of the Federation of American Scientists on the Fort Monmouth security investigations. The committee concludes that there was no evidence of espionage, that those responsible for security were of doubtful competence, that the laboratories' work was greatly damaged, and that many employees suffered severe hardship.

B721 ..., In the Matter of J. Robert Oppenheimer, 10 (Sept. 1954), 270-82.
Documentary material on the Oppenheimer case, including a letter from Oppenheimer's lawyer, Lloyd K. Garrison, to General Nichols; the findings and recommendations of General Nichols; and the majority, concurring, and dissenting opinions of the Atomic Energy Commission. (Statements from leading scientists expressing confidence in Oppenheimer, and reports by two Washington correspondents, follow.)

B722 ..., Secrecy, Security, and Loyalty, 11 (April 1955).
A special issue, edited by Edward Shils, reviewing and criticizing American policy in the areas of loyalty and security. Included are discussions of security policy by Shils, Raymond Aron, Ralph S. Brown, Jr., and Harold Green; reviews of the Atomic Energy Act and the AEC security program; criticism of State Department policy by Hans J. Morgenthau; a discussion of the task of the security officer and reviews of some individual cases; a British view of American policy; and suggestions for a positive security program.

B723 "BULLETIN OF THE METAL TRADES DEPT.," Communism and the Committee for Industrial Organization, 18 (Dec. 1936), 3 ff.
A portion of the officers' report to the 28th convention of the Metal Trades Department of the AFL, asserting that the communists, unable to "bore from within" the AFL, changed their line in order to infiltrate the CIO. The officers suggest that trade unions exclude communists from membership.

B724 ..., C.I.O. Is under Communist Domination, 20 (Sept. 1938), 2-3 ff.
A description of communist activities within the CIO, based on the testimony of John P. Frey (president of the Metal Trades Department) to the House Un-American Activities Committee.

B725 BULLOCK, Edward T. The Real Strength of American Communism, "Current History," 18 (June 1923), 419-22.
A survey, suggested by the raid on the Bridgman, Mich., communist convention in 1922, and by Foster's trial under the Michigan criminal syndicalism law. The author assesses the program and strength of communism here and its relation to the USSR. Though few in number, the communists are influential, particularly in times of industrial strife.

B726 BUNDY, Edgar C. "Christianity or Communism?" Wheaton, Ill.: The author, 1951. 22 pp.
An address delivered at the Pan-American Evangelical Conference, San Paulo, Brazil, July 20, 1951, attempting to link theological modernism and liberalism with communism. Dr. G. Bromley Oxnam, one of the presidents of the World Council of Churches, is a particular object of attack.

B727 .... "Collectivism in the Churches: A Documented Account of the Political Activities of the Federal, National, and World Councils of Churches." Wheaton, Ill.: Church League of America, 1958. 354 pp. App. Bibliog. Ind.
A work from the extreme right wing of the Protestant Church. The author opposes the social gospel as preached and practiced in the churches, and sees in this "collectivist" sentiment an alliance with socialists, procommunists, communists, and "one-worlders," to the grave detriment of the true message of the Protestant Church.

B728 BUNTING, David E. "Liberty and Learning: The Activities of the American Civil Liberties Union in Behalf of Freedom of Education." Introd. by George S. Counts. Washington, D.C.: Public Affairs Press, 1942. 197 pp. App. Bibliog. Ind.
A Ph.D. thesis on the history of American Civil Liberties Union activities in the field of educational freedom. Chapter 8, "The Future of Freedom," discusses academic freedom for teachers, chiefly communists, who belong to groups seeking antidemocratic ends. ACLU opposes dismissal because of organizational affiliation or expression of opinions, but upholds dismissals of teachers who have not lived up to responsibilities of academic freedom, who have used assumed names, are guilty of perjury, have resorted to deliberate deception, and the like.

B729 BURCHAM, Brantley. "Red Challenge to America: A Guide for Intelligent Action." New York: Exposition Press, 1955. 222 pp. Bibliog. Ind.
An account of the spread of communism and of U.S. relations with the communist world. Chapter 17, pp. 158-86, "Dark Cloud Over America," deals with the communist movement in the U.S., with attention to espionage, influence in the labor movement, infiltration of government, and security legislation.

B730 BURCHETT, Bessie R. "Education for Destruction." Foreword by P. M. Allen. Philadelphia: The author, 1941. 170 pp. Ind.
A plea for schools free of communist teachers and communist-influenced curriculum by a Philadelphia teacher, a follower of Elizabeth Dilling, who believes that the public schools have been organized into a political machine operated by the Communist Party.

B731 BURCK, Jacob. "Hunger and Revolt: Cartoons by Burck." New York: Daily Worker, 1935. 248 pp.
A collection of cartoons of social protest published in the "Daily Worker" during the previous four years.

B732 BURKE, Kenneth. My Approach to Communism, "New Masses," 10 (March 20, 1934), 16-20.
An outline of four approaches to communism: rational, ethical, historical, and aesthetic. The first shows why capitalism must break down, the second demonstrates its moral adequacy to replace capitalism, the third presents it in historical sequence, and the fourth considers it as the base for a new equilibrium in society and art.

B733 BURLINGAME, Roger. "The Sixth Column." Philadelphia and New York: Lippincott, 1962. 258 pp. Bibliog. Ind.
An account of the "sixth column," composed of anticommunists who under the guise of patriotism spread fear and suspicion in the U.S., promote police-state methods, and attempt to suppress free speech and free assembly. In reality they are communism's strongest allies, weakening us by their instigation of panic. Among the targets of the volume are the red raids of 1919-20, the investigations of the Dies Committee and the House Un-American Activities Committee, the antiradical activities of the American Legion, the government loyalty purges, and the John Birch Society.

B734 BURNHAM, Grace M. "Work or Wages." New York: International Pamphlets, 1930. 39 pp. 2d ed. entitled "Unemployment: Work or Wages, the Challenge of Unemployment." 1932. 40 pp.
A communist view of unemployment problems during the great depression. AFL out-of-work benefits and insurance-fund schemes are denounced as class collaboration. Only organization under TUUL leadership can bring some relief. Millions of unemployed are meeting the inter-national crisis of capitalism with new protest and organized struggle.

B735 .... "Dangerous Jobs." New York: International Publishers, 1932. 23 pp.
An examination of industrial injuries and of the inadequacy of existing remedies. Workers must get over the illusion that compensation laws were made and are carried out in their interest. The Party's solution is health and safety codes, enforced by workers, with costs paid by employers and government.

B736 .... "Social Insurance." New York: International Pamphlets, 1932. 31 pp.
A contrast of the inadequacy of unemployment and health insurance programs in the U.S. with the generosity of USSR provisions in this area. The author presents the Communist Party's proposal for unemployment insurance, to be paid for by employers and administered by the workers.

B737 BURNHAM, James. "The People's Front: The New Betrayal." New York: Pioneer Publishers, 1937. 64 pp.
A Trotskyite pamphlet condemning the people's front as a means of preparing the masses for national unity in support of the coming war, to be fought for their own imperialism under the slogan of democracy against fascism. The revolutionary Marxists also prepare for the war by urging revolutionary defeatism, the turning of imperialist war into class war. The struggle against Stalinism, according to the author, is a necessary condition for the defense of the Soviet Union.

B738 .... His Excellency's Loyal Opposition, "Socialist Appeal," 3 (Jan. 1937), 2-6.
Earl Browder's report to the Party in December 1936 is viewed merely as an open expression of old policies. The Party is no longer to disguise its opportunism with revolutionary language, but is now to become the Roosevelt Administration's "loyal opposition," criticizing it gently.

B739 .... "How to Fight War." New York: Socialist Workers Party, 1938. 15 pp.
Trotskyite plea for workers to stay out of the coming "imperialist" war, with an attack on Earl Browder and the communists for siding with the imperialists in the people's front.

B740 .... The Sixth Turn of the Communist Screw, "Partisan Review," 11 (Summer 1944), 364-66.
A discussion of the history of the communist movement, divided into six periods, during which the pendulum has swung from left to right and back again. The current period, that of Teheran, is farthest to the right.

B741 .... "The Struggle for the World." New York: John Day, 1947. 248 pp.
An argument that total war with the USSR is inevitable, and a call to the U.S. to play a positive role in the world struggle. The ultimate goal of communism is conquest of the world. World domination will be organized in this period of history, and only two power groupings can attempt this: communism, with its Soviet base, or a noncommunist coalition under U.S. leadership.

B742 .... "The Coming Defeat of Communism." New York: John Day, 1949. 278 pp.
A proposal for an offensive to defeat world communism, with specific proposals for countermeasures against communism in the U.S. The Third World War is already taking place, in the form of subversive, ideological, and guerilla warfare. The communists are committed to a

struggle for world domination. In all nations they seek control of the labor movement, though their labor influence in the U.S. has been weakened since 1947. American businessmen are criticized for ignorance, greed, reactionary views, and cowardice in relation to the struggle against communism. The defeat of communism is inevitable.

B743 BURNHAM, James. How the IPR Helped Stalin Seize China, "Freeman," 2 (June 30, 1952), 643-54.
An account of the infiltration of the Institute of Pacific Relations by the communists and of its functioning as an instrument of Soviet policy, based on a study of the McCarran Committee record. The IPR influenced persons in the State Department to view the Chinese communists as agrarian reformers.

B744 .... "The Web of Subversion: Underground Networks in the U.S. Government." New York: John Day, 1954. 247 pp. Ind.
An examination of the complex network of communist underground activity that operated in Washington in the 1930's and 1940's, made up of knowing and unknowing agents of the communist and Soviet conspiracy. The author explores the personnel and activities of the three exposed communist cells among high government officials, following their record of penetration into New Deal, war, and postwar agencies. Concluding that the activities of the web were among the deciding factors in world-wide defeats by communism, he gives advice on improving or supplementing methods now used to combat communism in government.

B745 BURNHAM, Louis E. "Smash the Chains." New York: American Youth for Democracy, n.d. [1946]. 24 pp.
Recruiting pamphlet by the executive secretary of the Southern Negro Youth Congress, asserting that no young American can be truly free until white supremacy has been destroyed and the oppression of 13,000,000 Negroes ended. (American Youth for Democracy was the post-World War II communist youth organization.)

B746 .... "Behind the Lynching of Emmet Louis Till." New York: Freedom Associates, 1955. 16 pp.
The murder of a Negro youth in the South is related to the basic communist analysis of the Negro question in that area. The author calls for a federal program to break up the plantation system, with other benefits for share-croppers and tenant farmers. Negro freedom will come because we live in an epoch of liberation of the colonial peoples.

B747 BURNHAM, Philip. The Hollywood Affliction, "Commonweal," 47 (Nov. 7, 1947), 84-85.
The executive editor of "Commonweal" discusses communism in the movie industry and the current investigation of Hollywood by Representative Thomas' Un-American Activities Committee. The danger is not Soviet propaganda in the movies, but financial aid from movie figures for the Party and Party-sponsored purposes.

B748 BURNS, Emile. Science, Art and Superstructure, "Masses & Mainstream," 6 (Sept. 1953), 46-53.
A Marxist analysis of science and art in relation to modes of production in society. Bourgeois science has expanded, restricted, or falsified, depending on the stage of the society's development and the needs of the dominant class. An analogous situation exists in art; what is of permanent value in art must be understood in light of the stage of development of bourgeois society.

B749 .... "What Is Marxism?" New York: International Publishers, 1957. 91 pp.

An exposition of basic Marxist principles in simple language. Chapters deal with the laws of social development, capitalist society, the imperialist stage of capitalism, class struggles and the state, socialist society, the Marxist view of nature, and the fight for socialism.

B750 BURNSHAW, Stanley. Notes on Revolutionary Poetry, "New Masses," 10 (Feb. 20, 1934), 20-22.
Much of the revolutionary poetry of recent years shows a cleavage between subject matter and expression, or fails to constitute a powerful mass literature. Revolutionary poets should avoid modes of expression of despair and decay, avoid obscure writing, make greater use of satire, and create a vital literature.

B751 .... Middle-Ground Writers, "New Masses," 15 (April 30, 1935), 19-21.
Criticizing Marxists for their attacks on the "middle-ground" writer, this article prepares for the Party's more permissive popular-front line in the cultural sphere. The liberal writer, a potential ally of the working class, must realize that middle ground is illusory, and that he must choose between communism and fascism.

B752 BUROKER, L. Peres. Left Wingers in the Church, "National Republic," 26 (March 1939), 1-2 ff; (April), 21-22 ff.
An assertion by a minister that the Church League for Industrial Democracy, directed by Rev. William B. Spofford, is a front for communist activities. Through the CLID communist theories have made inroads into the thinking of the Episcopal Church and the nation. CLID activities, including cooperation in the American League for Peace and Democracy, are reviewed.

B753 BURT, Eric. "Eyes on Washington! A Program for People's Legislation: What Labor and the People Can Do to Influence Congress in 1956." New York: New Century, 1955. 16 pp.
An attack on the "Cadillac-Cabinet," the Republican Party, and the Dixiecrat wing of the Democratic Party. The author calls for an end to the "cold war," tax cuts on low and middle incomes, a $1.25 minimum wage, a 35-hour week, 90 per cent parity for farm prices, federal aid to education and to low- and middle-cost housing, enforcement of the desegregation decision, and abolition of federal agencies that investigate or regulate subversive activities.

B754 BURTON, Bernard. "A New Depression?" New York: New Century, 1949. 24 pp.
A "Daily Worker" staff member examines signs of a growing economic crisis which is being produced by the basic contradictions in capitalism. He proposes domestic economic measures to raise wages, lower hours, and eliminate unemployment, and foreign-trade policies such as restoring trade with the Soviet Union, and ending the Marshall Plan and military pacts. This program, opposed by Republicans and Democrats, is supported by the Progressive Party.

B755 .... "The Big Lie of War 'Prosperity.'" New York: New Century, 1952. 24 pp.
An assertion during the Korean War that Americans must choose between "guns and butter," that war production cannot solve capitalist contradictions because war curtails living standards. A program based on the demand for peace includes reduction of arms appropriations, promotion of world trade, internal economic reform, and repeal of legislation aimed at advocates of peace.

B756 .... "We Can Have Peace and Jobs!" New York: New Century, 1953. 16 pp.
A call for the end of all restrictions on foreign trade with

the Soviet Union, China, and Eastern Europe, arguing that this would solve the problem of three and a half million unemployed and prevent further increase in unemployment.

B757 BURTON, Bernard. "How to Keep Your Job: Must We Have Depression?" New York: New Century, 1955. 16 pp.
Communist analysis of the economic downswing of 1954-55. Though the economy was stimulated in 1949 by increase of war production, easing of credit, and expansion of productive facilities through "rapid amortization" tax policies, these measures will be self-defeating in the long run. A program of sweeping domestic social and economic legislation is advocated to prevent a sharp slump.

B758 BUSCH, Bonnie, and MAXWELL, Lucia Ramsey. "The Red Fog." Washington: National Patriotic League, 1929. 105 pp.
The authors see communism-socialism pitted against women, children, God, and the Bible. The Christian Church is urged to dispel the Red Fog, which brings confusion, madness, and death.

B759 BUSCH, Francis X. "Guilty or Not Guilty?" Indianapolis and New York: Bobbs-Merrill, 1952. 287 pp.
Four unusual criminal cases, including that of Alger Hiss (pp. 197-287). Placing the case in the context of communist espionage revelations in America following World War II, the author traces the entire case, from the House Un-American Activities testimony of Elizabeth Bentley and Whittaker Chambers to the jailing of Alger Hiss after the second trial. He presents Hiss' background, details of his appearance before the House committee, and highlights of testimony by Hiss and Chambers at the two trials. The implication is that Hiss was justly convicted, although the author allows the testimony and the arguments of counsel to speak for themselves.

B760 . . . . "Enemies of the State." Indianapolis and New York: Bobbs-Merrill, 1954. 299 pp.
A discussion of the Rosenberg case (pp. 235-99), along with three other American trials. The author outlines the background of the case, starting with the conviction of Dr. Allen Nunn May and following the cases of Fuchs, Gold, and Greenglass; he describes the trial of the Rosenbergs and Sobell, the appeals that followed, and the execution of the Rosenbergs on June 19, 1953. He lists disturbing questions that still remain, that will make the case a "cause célèbre" in American criminal annals.

B761 BUSH, Vannevar. To Make Our Security System Secure, "New York Times Magazine," March 20, 1955. 9 ff.
An appeal by a noted scientist, wartime head of the Office of Scientific Research, for an entirely new system of loyalty clearance. We need a program that is alive to subversion and equally alive to the rights of citizens. Problems that arise under the present system are discussed.

B762 "BUTCHER WORKMAN," Communist Conspiracy in Packingtown, 38 (Oct. 1952), 4-6.
Report in the organ of the Amalgamated Meat Cutters and Butcher Workmen of the AFL of an ex-communist's testimony before the House Committee on Un-American Activities about the Armour local of the United Packinghouse Workers, CIO. The 6,000-member local is said to be dominated by communists.

B763 BUTLER, Nicholas Murray. Our Bolshevik Menace, "Forum" 63 (Jan. 1920), 49-56.
The president of Columbia University suggests the Americanization of aliens and a vigorous counterpropaganda program as means of easing the unrest created by Bolshevik agitators. A wrong idea cannot be reached by force, but only by a right idea. A class struggle would destroy civilization.

B764 BYRNS, Ruth Katherine. Communism and Complacency, "Catholic World," 137 (June 1933), 257-61.
An assertion that, if communism grows, the fault will lie with those guilty of shortsighted complacency. The author calls on Catholics to counter Godless communism by suggesting solutions to our current problems based on Christian ethics, moral philosophy, and Catholic principles.

B765 BYSE, Clark. A Report on the Pennsylvania Loyalty Act, "University of Pennsylvania Law Review," 101 (Jan. 1953), 480-508.
A critical examination of the Pennsylvania Act of December 22, 1951, requiring loyalty oaths of all employees of the state or its political subdivisions, and providing machinery to weed out subversives. The author concludes that there has been no demonstration of need for the law, which contributes little or nothing to security, harms innocent persons, and spreads fear and mistrust.

B766 . . . . Teachers and the Fifth Amendment, "University of Pennsylvania Law Review," 102 (May 1954), 871-83.
A University of Pennsylvania professor of law discusses whether teachers who invoke the privilege against self-incrimination when asked about communist affiliations, should automatically be barred from teaching. He concludes that automatic dismissal violates academic freedom and tenure rights vital to free inquiry. Dismissal should not be imposed without ascertaining all relevant facts.

C

C1   CABLE, George W. "A Southerner Looks at Negro Discrimination: Selected Writings of George W. Cable." Ed. by Isabel Cable Manes. Introd. by Alva W. Taylor. New York: International Publishers, 1946. 48 pp.
George W. Cable, a Southerner who fought with the Confederate Army, wrote about the shame of discriminating against the Negro; while loving the South, he viewed the caste system as un-Christian, undemocratic, and unfair. His daughter, who praises the communists for seeking full economic, political, and social equality for Negroes, has compiled some of Cable's writings, as part of the communist effort to pose as inheritors of all antidiscrimination sentiment in America.

C2   CACCHIONE, Peter V. "Italian-Americans and the War." New York: Workers Library for National Election Campaign Committee, Communist Party of the United States, 1940. 11 pp.
A pamphlet designed to win political support for the author among Italian-Americans. It attacks the anti-alien legislation being passed in the U.S., and opposes American entry into the "imperialist" war.

C3   . . . . "5¢ Fare or 10¢ Fare—Which Is Fair?" Brooklyn: The author, n.d. [1942?]. 23 pp.
An argument by a communist member of the New York City Council in favor of keeping the five-cent fare on the New York subways. (This battle helped to break Michael Quill, head of the Transport Workers Union, and his organization away from the Party line, since the union supported the increase in order to win its wage demands.)

C4   . . . . "How to Save the 5¢ Fare." Brooklyn, N.Y.: The author, 1942. 14 pp.
A communist member of the New York City Council argues against raising the five-cent subway fare to ten cents, urging instead that the fare be frozen for the duration of the war and that the law be changed to permit transit deficits to be made up from general taxation.

C5   . . . . "Public Speaking: A Speaker's Guide Book." New York: Workers Library, 1942. 30 pp.
Illuminating tips for communist public speakers by a successful communist candidate for the City Council in New York City.

C6   . . . . "Is Drew Guilty?" Brooklyn, N.Y.: The author, n.d. [1944]. 23 pp.
The case of a member of the police force, James LeRoy Drew, charged with having belonged to subversive fascist organizations. A communist member of the City Council in New York City calls for his removal from the police force.

C7   . . . . "The Truth about Luigi Antonini." Brooklyn, N.Y.: Peter V. Cacchione Association, n.d. [1944?]. 24 pp.
An attack by a communist member of the New York City Council on a vice-president of the ILGWU and the head of its Local 89 of Italian dressmakers. Antonini is attacked for criticizing the communists in radio addresses, for opposing the Soviet Union, and for allegedly spreading disunity in the American Labor Party.

C8   . . . . "Wall Street on the Warpath." New York: New Century, 1947. 23 pp.
A denunciation of Wall Street bankers and monopolists who have moved into Washington, where they have been responsible for reactionary Red-baiting, for the Marshall and Truman plans, and for the Taft-Hartley Act, all designed to advance the interests of the big-money people.

C9   CADDEN, Joseph. "Spain 1936: Findings of an International Youth Commission." New York: The Commission, n.d. [1936]. 22 pp.
One of the leaders of the American Youth Congress reports the findings of an International Youth Commission on the Spanish Civil War. U.S. members of the Commission included representatives of the YCL and communist-front groups, along with others. The pamphlet defends the Spanish Republicans and discusses the united front of all antifascist forces in Spain. Cadden urges antifascist groups in the U.S. to unite, as in Spain.

C10   CADE, Dozier C. Witch Hunting, 1952: The Role of the Press, "Journalism Quarterly," 29 (Fall 1952), 396-407.
A member of the journalism faculty at Northwestern asserts that American newspapers play a vital role in the current "witch hunt" by featuring unsubstantiated charges, and by failing to interpret adequately news reports which give only one side of the story. He offers suggestions for counteracting this tendency without suppressing news.

C11   CAHAN, Abraham (ed.). "Hear the Other Side: A Symposium of Democratic Socialist Opinion." New York: n.publ., 1934. 71 pp.
Seven articles of vigorous protest against "socialism" as practiced in the USSR, written by leading spokesmen for right-wing socialists in the U.S. The tactics of the communists here are exposed, particularly the hypocrisy of their call for a united front with socialists.

C12   CAHN, Bill. "Mill Town." New York: Cameron & Kahn, 1954. 286 pp. Bibliog.
The story of Lawrence, Mass., in pictures and prose by a procommunist author, who dramatizes the fight to unionize an industrial town. The struggle, he asserts, was first against violence and frame-ups, then against company unions, and is now against runaway shops. He writes of two kinds of people, those who work the machines and those who own them.

C13   CAIN, Harry P. Security of the Republic, "New Republic," 132 (Jan. 31, 1955), 6-10.
Reprint of a speech by a member of the Subversive Activities Control Board. In our concern with internal security we have not been vigilant enough against abuses. Though our security system has worked well, there have been too many injustices, three of which are cited. Suggestions are offered to improve the security system.

C14   "CALL," The ALP Fight, 9 (Aug. 20, 1943), 8.
A socialist editorial attack on both the communists and the right wing in the struggle for control of New York's American Labor Party. The Stalinists seek to use the ALP to obtain a new political lease on life. The Amalgamated Clothing Workers, following Sidney Hillman, promote the interests of Franklin Roosevelt. The ILGWU, with the same objective, at least battles the Stalinists.

C15   CALLER, Fay. "Shall It Be Girls in Uniform?"
       New York: New Age, 1941. 16 pp.
Designed to appeal to young women, this pamphlet opposes American entry into the "imperialist" war, attacks plans allegedly made to conscript women, and advances the program of the Young Communist League.

C16   . . . . "In Freedom's Cause." New York: New
       Age, 1943. 32 pp.
A leader of the Young Communist League of the U.S. outlines the heroic fight of Soviet youth against fascism, and discusses the benefits for young people in the Soviet Union.

C17   CLAMER, Alan. Depression Fictioneers, "New
       Masses," 9 (Sept. 1933), 20-21.
Trashy, commercial fiction, using the depression as a background, constitutes the literature of the American masses, parroting the psychology and propaganda of the bourgeoisie. Fiction dealing with the unemployed usually depicts them as idlers and racketeers; Negroes are shiftless and stupid; industrial workers, if shown at all, are minor characters.

C18   . . . . The Proletarian Short Story, "New Masses,"
       16 (July 2, 1935), 17-19.
Criticism of proletarian short story writers for lack of concern with literary tradition and experiment, and for naïve notions of what revolutionary literature should be. Hackneyed endings are a symptom of the vulgar approach to proletarian literature. Writers should create literary works of emotion and feeling, not sociological tracts masquerading as literature.

C19   . . . . Portrait of the Artist as a Proletarian,
       "Saturday Review of Literature," 16 (July 31,
       1937), 3-4 ff.
A collective portrait of the young proletarian writer coming of literary age in the John Reed Clubs. Although told to use literature as a weapon, he knew that a political line could not be substituted for personal experience, and moved away from the communist brand of literature. With a change in the leftist line, a united front of intellectuals welcomed him back.

C20   CALOMIRIS, Angela. "Red Masquerade: Under-
       cover for the F.B.I." New York: Lippincott, 1950.
       284 pp. App.
An account of the experiences of a New York City photographer who joined the Communist Party at the request of the FBI. She rose to be co-organizer of her Party section, and was financial secretary of her branch when she testified for the government in the 1949 Smith Act conspiracy trial of the top 11 Party leaders. The book gives an inside picture of the workings of the Party, as seen by an active member. A sampling of communist literature, emphasizing the revolutionary aim of the movement, appears in an appendix.

C21   CALVERTON, V. F. "The Newer Spirit: A Socio-
       logical Criticism of Literature." Introd. by Ernest
       Boyd. New York: Boni & Liveright, 1925. 284 pp.
An early attempt by the Marxist editor of the "Modern Quarterly" to formulate a theory of literary criticism,

under which literary works are viewed in the light of existing class relationships, themselves the product of the stage of economic development of the society. Walt Whitman is viewed as a product of changes which gave economic and political significance to the proletariat. Revolutions in esthetics result from revolutions in ideas, which in turn result from revolutions in the social structure produced by prevailing material conditions.

C22   . . . . Social Forces in Late American Literature,
       "Workers Monthly," 4 (Sept. 1925), 509-12.
A review of the impact of economic and social forces upon American literature from the 1850's to the 1920's. The influence of economic growth, imperialism, and optimism upon creative literature is traced. William D. Howells and Harold Bell Wright, among others, reflect these influences, whereas realism and social protest are exemplified by Walt Whitman, Edward Bellamy, Frank Norris, and Upton Sinclair.

C23   . . . . The International and Marxian Literature,
       "Modern Quarterly," 4 (June-Sept. 1927), 162-65.
A brief survey of Marxian classics and literature issued by International Publishers. Though others, including Kerr, the Dial Press, and the Rand School, have published radical classics here, International Publishers has attained unique distinction for Marxist publications in the U.S.

C24   . . . . Literature and Economics, "Communist,"
       6 (June 1927), 225-31; (July-Aug.), 313-18; 7
       (March 1928), 181-89; (April), 247-51; (June),
       378-81.
An attack on the concept that art and literature reflect individual expression detached from reality; one must look at literature in terms of social environment. In the feudal period the dominant aristocratic class determined the nature of literature. The rise of the bourgeoisie in the commercial revolution was reflected in literature which exalted the virtues of the merchant. The industrial revolution gave rise to a proletarian trend in literature.

C25   . . . . Revolt among American Intellectuals, "New
       Masses," 4 (April 1929), 3-5.
The American milieu has discouraged the development of a profound intelligentsia. Our only significant philosophers have been pragmatists. There is now a revolt among the intellectuals, but not against anything fundamental. Not until radicals change American conditions can we expect greater thinkers and finer artists.

C26   . . . . Humanism: Literary Fascism, "New
       Masses," 5 (April 1930), 9-10.
A critique of the philosophy of humanism as expressed by Norman Foerster. Humanism exalts philosophic individualism and attacks the authority of science; it is anti-collectivist, escapist, and reactionary, interested in self-reform rather than social reform.

C27   . . . . A Challenge to American Intellectuals: A
       Controversy: The Revolutionary Approach, "Mod-
       ern Quarterly," 5 (Winter 1930-31), 411-21.
Disagreeing with Lewis Mumford (see "The Evolutionary Approach," pp. 407-10), Calverton calls for a revolutionary approach to the new society and a revolutionary, communist logic. Soviet Russia alone is successful today because the Russians have overthrown the old order of control and instituted a new one.

C28   . . . . Left-Wing Literature in America, "English
       Journal," 20 (Dec. 1931), 789-98.
A view that a tradition of radical literature is developing in the United States. No distinction is made between writers interested in social revolt, and those who look to the Soviet Union as the pattern of the new society. John

Dos Passos, Mike Gold, and Charles Yale Harrison are among the novelists in this tradition.

C29   CALVERTON, V. F. "For Revolution." New York: John Day, 1932. 24 pp.
An argument by a prominent literary and social critic, who was friendly to the Party in the 1920's but who soon afterward became anti-Stalinist, that only a revolution could solve our social problems. An attempt to avert or delay the revolution would only result in worse chaos when it came.

C30   .... "The Liberation of American Literature." New York: Scribner's, 1932. 500 pp. Ind.
A Marxist analysis of American literature in terms of the American cultural pattern, shaped as it has been by conflicting class interests. The proletarian-literature movement, as expressed in the "Masses," the "Liberator," and the "New Masses," is described on pp. 450-67. Proletarian writers, who are not necessarily proletarians, are those who express in their work the revolutionary point of view of the proletarian ideology. The work of current leading proletarian writers in America is described.

C31   .... Leftward Ho! "Modern Quarterly," 6 (Summer 1932), 26-32.
An assertion that intellectuals are turning left, because economic individualism is bankrupt and because middle-class idealism has collapsed. The promise of the country's potentialities has disappeared, and the intellectuals are protesting against the entire structure of our civilization. Whereas once the dominant note in American literature was optimistic, today leading literary intellectuals are swinging left.

C32   .... Can We Have a Proletarian Literature? "Modern Quarterly," 6 (Autumn 1932), 39-50.
Tracing the history of literature as an expression of the ideology of a particular social class, the author asserts that we do not yet have a true proletarian literature in America. The best we can do is to encourage a proletarian literature in the future by bringing literature back to the masses.

C33   .... Literature Goes Left, "Current History," 41 (Dec. 1934), 316-20.
Proletarian literature expresses the morality of a working class striving toward a collective society; the worker naturally becomes the hero, while the capitalist and his allies are the villains. Proletarian literature in the U.S., beginning with Upton Sinclair and Jack London, is now in the mainstream of American letters. Leading writers such as Edmund Wilson and John Dos Passos have joined the movement.

C34   .... Literature as a Revolutionary Force, "Canadian Forum," 15 (March 1935), 221-27.
An analysis of the historical antecedents and promise of American proletarian literature of the 1930's. The author views this literature, a working class literature inspired by revolutionary purpose, as the culmination of a century-long rise in American realism. While its promise is evident, American proletarian literature is in a state of becoming rather than fulfillment.

C35   .... Proletarianitis, "Saturday Review of Literature," 15 (Jan. 9, 1937), 3-4 ff.
Proletarian literature based on the Soviet pattern under Stalin has superimposed a type of literary terrorism in America which has accelerated a shift of intellectuals from the Stalinist to the socialist camp. We need writers who will resist dictation from abroad and dictation by politicians, administered by converts to the cult of proletarianitis.

C36   .... Land of Literary Plenty, "Saturday Review of Literature," 22 (May 11, 1940), 3-4 ff.
In the 1920's our literature was characterized by nihilism. The proletarian literature movement of the 1930's, inspired from Russia, was contrived and artificial, and now is happily dead. Genuine proletarian literature is acquiring form and significance in the work of Steinbeck and Wright.

C37   CAMERON, Angus and others. "Publisher on Trial: A Symposium: The Case of Alexander Trachtenberg." New York: Committee to Defend Alexander Trachtenberg, 1952. 47 pp.
Speeches delivered at a public meeting in defense of the head of International Publishers, June 12, 1952, together with extracts from articles and editorials on the case. Trachtenberg's trial is denounced as an effort to suppress freedom of the press, deprive the reading public of the Marxist classics, and institute thought control.

C38   CAMERON, Donald A. "Chemical Warfare: Poison Gas in the Coming War." New York: International Pamphlets, 1930. 31 pp.
An argument that chemicals will be used in the next war by the capitalists against civilians and workers as well as at the front. The author urges understanding between the free chemical workers of the USSR and the exploited workers of the U.S., and organization of all U.S. chemical workers in the Trade Union Unity League to fight war. (This pamphlet appeared in successive editions, revised with shifts in the Party line. A third edition, under the title "Poison Gas in the Coming War," was published in 1934.)

C39   CAMPION, Bruce. Security and Common Sense, "American Legion Magazine," 62 (April 1957), 27 ff.
Our security program, concerned with the form rather than the substance of security, sometimes concentrates on the wrong people. While we need protection from Soviet espionage and the placement of communists and sympathizers in key government posts, we should not endanger the rights of government employees and defense workers. Those who are loyal but are nevertheless security risks should not be trusted with vital information.

C40   CAMPION, Martha. "Who Are the Young Pioneers?" Illustrated by Mary Morrow. New York: New Pioneer Publishing Company, 1934. 32 pp.
Recruiting pamphlet for the children's organization of the Communist Party, containing stories about the work of the Young Pioneers in various sections of the country, in schools, as workers, in Germany under Hitler, and in the Soviet Union. There are questions and answers about what the Young Pioneers stand for, why children should not join the Boy Scouts, and what the magazine "Young Pioneer" offers to members.

C41   .... (ed.). "New Pioneer Story Book." Introd. by Max Bedacht. New York: New Pioneer Publishing Company, 1935. 110 pp.
Stories that "tell you the truth about the conditions of the workers and their children and what they must do in order to better these conditions." Addressed to the children of workers and farmers, the stories are intended, from a communist point of view, to help them understand the life around them, and to become masters, not pawns, of destiny.

C42   CANNON, James P. "The Fifth Year of the Russian Revolution." New York: Workers Party, n.d. [1923]. 21 pp.

95

A lecture given by the national chairman of the Workers Party and delegate to the Executive Committee of the Communist International, following his visit to the USSR in the summer of 1922. He reports on economic reconstruction, trade unionism, the workers and the Red Army, and the workers and internationalism.

C43   CANNON, James P. The St. Louis Conference of the C.P.P.A., "Labor Herald," 3 (March 1924), 25-26.
The gesture toward formation of a labor party at the St. Louis convention of the Conference for Progressive Political Action, in February 1923, was a device for buying time. The CPPA will meet again on July 4, after the convention of the two major parties. Those who want a Farmer-Labor Party must therefore support the May 30 conference of farmer-labor forces in St. Paul.

C44   . . . . The Bolshevization of the Party, "Workers Monthly," 4 (Nov. 1924), 34-37.
A speech before the New York Workers' School, October 5, 1924, stressing the importance of revolutionary theory in the work of communists. The Workers' School must be a weapon in Bolshevization, a fighting instrument against all deviations. The American party is not yet a Leninist monolithic party; Bolshevization requires elimination of factionalism.

C45   . . . . Trade-Union Questions, "Communist," 7 (July 1928), 406-12.
Accepting much of the criticism leveled by the Red International of Labor Unions and by Losovsky, its head, at the Workers Party trade union policy, Cannon calls for organizing the unorganized into new unions, without abandoning work in the old unions. (His views differ in emphasis and tone rather than in fundamentals from the position of the Central Executive Committee [defended by Foster in the same issue of the "Communist"].)

C46   . . .; ABERN, Martin; and SHACHTMAN, Max. For the Russian Opposition! Against Opportunism and Bureaucracy in the Workers (Communist) Party of America! "Militant," 1 (Nov. 15, 1928), 1-2.
Statement by the Trotskyists following their expulsion from the Workers (Communist) Party on October 27, 1928. The article outlines the points of disagreement between the Cannon group and the Lovestone leadership of the Party on the one hand, and with the Foster-Bittelman opposition, with whom the Cannonites had previously been allied, on the other. The main danger to the Workers (Communist) Party is from the Lovestoneite right; the same danger exists in the Communist International.

C47   . . ., and others. The Right Danger in the American Party, "Militant," 1 (Nov. 15, 1928), 7; (Dec. 1), 7; (Dec. 15), 7; 2 (Jan. 1, 1929), 7; (Jan. 15), 7.
A document submitted by the delegation of the Opposition in the Workers (Communist) Party to the Sixth World Congress of the Communist International, July 1928, prior to the expulsion of the Cannon group as Trotskyists. The document, signed by Cannon, William Z. Foster, William F. Dunne, Alex Bittelman, J. W. Johnstone, Manuel Gomez, and George Siskin, identifies the Lovestone leadership as the Right danger in the American Party, and accuses it of opportunism.

C48   . . . . Our Appeal to the Party Members, "Militant," 2 (Jan. 1929), 1-2.
Cannon's speech to the Central Executive Committee of the Workers (Communist) Party, December 17, 1928, calling for the reinstatement of the Trotskyists. Both the Pepper-Lovestone leadership and the Foster opposition are charged with gangster attacks on Trotskyists. The

Cannon group will work for Party unity, provided free discussion and democracy are restored.

C49   . . ., and others. Platform of the Communist Opposition: Addressed to the Sixth National Convention of the Workers (Communist) Party, "Militant," 2 (Feb. 15, 1929), 1-8; (March 1), 7.
Platform of the Trotskyite opposition to the Workers (Communist) Party. The Stalinist "third period" line is analyzed, and errors in the CPUSA's trade-union policy, as well as bureaucratization and Stalinization of the Party, are criticized. The Party membership is urged to demand the reinstatement of the Cannon opposition.

C50   . . . . Conference of the Opposition Communists: Formation of the Communist League of America (Opposition), "Militant," 2 (June 1, 1929), 1 ff.
Summary of the national conference of supporters of Trotsky held in Chicago, May 17-19, 1929, at which the Communist League of America (Opposition) was created. The conference adopted a constitution, elected a national committee, and undertook to organize communists, inside and outside the Party, on the platform of the Opposition.

C51   . . . . The Crisis in the Communist Party, "Militant," 2 (Aug. 1, 1929), 3.
Analysis of the crisis in the CPUSA following the expulsion of the Lovestoneite leadership. Lovestone, who was supported by 90 per cent of the delegates to the Party convention, is now expelled as an opportunist and renegade. No help in rebuilding the Party can be expected from the leadership, which is dependent on Moscow, the source of all disruption.

C52   . . . . The New Unions and the Communists, "Militant," 2 (Nov. 30, 1929), 5.
The leader of the Trotskyist opposition group attacks the Party for importing into the new TUUL unions the arts of the labor fakers, as shown at a district convention of the National Miners Union where Party leaders exercised mechanical control. Cannon urges a struggle to make the new unions democratic, and proposes a united front of the Party with progressives.

C53   . . . . "The History of American Trotskyism: Report of a Participant." Introd. by Joseph Hansen. New York: Pioneer Publishers, 1944. 268 pp. Ind.
An informal history of the Trotskyist movement in the U.S., first delivered as a series of lectures. Cannon, the founder of American Trotskyism, describes the beginning of the communist movement here, the factional struggles that developed, the beginning of the Left Opposition within the Party in this country, and the crystallization of Trotsky's following into new parties and a new international. The strike activities of the Trotskyists are described, as are the fusion with the Muste group in 1934 to form the Workers Party of the U.S., the entry into the Socialist Party in June 1936, and the formation of the Socialist Workers Party a year and a half later. (Chapters appeared in the "Fourth International" in February, March, and May 1944.)

C54   . . . . "American Stalinism and Anti-Stalinism." New York: Pioneer Publishers, 1947. 48 pp.
An attack by a leading American Trotskyite on Stalinism in the U.S. and abroad. Stalinism, which originated in the disbelief of Soviet bureaucrats in the capacity of workers to overthrow capitalism, has relied on slander and mass murder, while American Stalinists have sold out the workers and become the most blatant jingoes in the American war camp.

C55 CANNON, James P. "The Road to Peace According to Stalin and According to Lenin." New York: Pioneer Publishers, 1951. 48 pp.
A Trotskyite attack on the peace campaign of the Stalinists, who urge peaceful coexistence between the capitalist and socialist states. This means abandonment of the revolutionary struggle for socialism in capitalist countries, and for independence in colonial areas. A return to Lenin's teaching of class struggle and revolution is advocated.

C56 . . . . "Notebook of an Agitator." New York: Pioneer Publishers, 1958. 362 pp.
A collection of articles and speeches over a period of three decades by one of the founders and early leaders of American communism, and then of American Trotskyism. Included are writings on the Sacco-Vanzetti case, on the 1934 strike of the Minneapolis Teamsters, and on the San Francisco maritime strike of 1936-37; and articles on a wide variety of topics written for the Trotskyist paper, "The Militant," in the 1940's and early 1950's.

C57 . . . . "The First Ten Years of American Communism: Report of a Participant." New York: Stuart, 1962. 343 pp. Ind.
Notes on important issues, developments, and personalities in the history of American communism, from its emergence out of the left wing of the socialist movement until the expulsion of the Trotskyists in 1928. Cannon, a left-wing factional communist leader before he founded the Trotskyist movement here, prepared the material to answer questions raised by Theodore Draper, the historian of American communism. Though the letters are episodic rather than systematic, and depend primarily upon memory, they shed light upon the inner workings of the communist movement, in the USSR as well as in the United States. (First published in "Fourth International," later in the "International Socialist Review," Summer 1954 to Spring 1957.)

C58 CANTWELL, Robert. "The Land of Plenty." New York: Farrar & Rinehart, 1934. 369 pp.
A strike novel, one of the best products of the proletarian literature movement of the 1930's, in which workers in a veneer factory strike against economic injustice and undeserved discharges. Though the strike is lost to strikebreakers and police violence, the workers grow in solidarity and knowledge of the class struggle.

C59 . . . . The Communists and the CIO, "New Republic," 94 (Feb. 23, 1938), 63-66.
Criticism of Benjamin Stolberg's "Inside the CIO" for its inaccuracies and for its treatment of the communist issue. Stolberg's main point was that the communists were in control of many CIO unions and were disrupting others. With emphasis on the United Automobile Workers, Cantwell charges Stolberg with superficiality and bias, with exaggeration and distortion of the communist role. (For Stolberg's response and Cantwell's further comment see the March 16 "New Republic," pp. 168-69.)

C60 CAPELL, Frank A. "Treason is the Reason (847 Reasons for Investigating the State Department)." Zarephath, N.J.: Herald of Freedom, 1965. 168 pp.
An assertion that communists, sympathizers, fellow-travelers, and assorted security risks have infiltrated the U.S. government, beginning with our recognition of the USSR. Names of alleged subversives or security risks in government service, currently or in the past, are given. No action was taken on a list of 847 security risks prepared by the late Scott McLeod when he headed the State Department's security section. (Along with Party members or sympathizers, the author lists as security risks such persons as Adlai Stevenson, Dean Rusk, Arthur J. Goldberg, and Arthur M. Schlesinger, Jr.)

C61 CAREY, James B. The CIO Role in the WFTU, "New Leader," 31 (July 24, 1948), 5 ff.
A reply to an article by Matthew Woll in the July 3, 1948, "New Leader," asserting that, in order to fight the communists, one must get into organizations with them, not harangue them from the outside. The CIO will continue the struggle on behalf of the free trade-unionists in Europe, through organizations like the World Federation of Trade Unions.

C62 . . . . We've Got the Reds on the Run, "American Magazine," 146 (Sept. 1948), 30-31 ff.
A review of successful efforts by democratic trade unionists in the CIO to drive communists out of the United Automobile Workers, the National Maritime Union, the Transport Workers Union, city and state industrial-union councils, and the national CIO office. An effective democratic movement, with rank-and-file involvement and a progressive program, is required to defeat the communists.

C63 . . ., (as told to Sidney Shallet). Why the CIO Bowed Out, "Saturday Evening Post," 221 (June 11, 1949), 28-29 ff.
The secretary-treasurer of the CIO describes its effort to cooperate with Russia in the World Federation of Trade Unions, 1945-49. Carey traces WFTU origins, and experiences of CIO delegates at various WFTU conferences. A series of betrayals, including the Soviet attempt to use the WFTU to propagandize against the Marshall Plan, finally forced the CIO and the British Trades Union Congress to withdraw.

C64 CARLISLE, Harry (ed.). "On the Drumhead: A Selection from the Writings of Mike Quin." San Francisco: Pacific Publishing Foundation, 1948. 244 pp.
A memorial volume to a communist writer, Paul William Ryan, who wrote under the name of Mike Quin, and who died in 1947. The volume includes columns and articles from "The Daily People's World," some poems, and a few radio broadcasts. A biographical sketch by the editor is included.

C65 CARLSON, Frank. "Let's Get off the Dime." San Francisco, Calif.: Communist Party of California, n.d. [1946?]. 24 pp.
A Party member who also belongs to Local 6 of the International Longshoremen's and Warehousemen's Union attacks capitalism as causing depression and layoffs and appeals to workers to join the Party.

C66 CARLSON, John Roy [pseud. for Arthur Derounian]. "The Plotters." New York: Dutton, 1946. 408 pp. Ind.
An exposé of antidemocratic elements of both the Left and the Right, assessing their impact on veterans' organizations. Posing as a disgruntled World War II veteran, the author sought entrance into many veterans' groups. In chapter 9 he describes the National Veterans Committee of the CP, and the Party's attempt to infiltrate the American Legion. Chapter 10 deals with AFL and CIO activities in veterans' affairs, with attention to communist influence in the CIO.

C67 CARLSON, Oliver. The Communist Record in Hollywood, "American Mercury," 66 (Feb. 1948), 135-43.
An exposé of the communist record in Hollywood since 1935, listing the names of active front organizations,

members, and fellow-travelers. The author also discusses the unions which have either capitulated to or withstood the communist assault. The era of good will that the communists enjoyed in Hollywood is now over.

C68   CARLSON, Oliver. Hollywood's Red Fadeout? "Plain Talk," 3 (Aug. 1949), 17-23.
An account of communist influence in Hollywood since the "unfriendly ten" writers and directors refused to tell the House Committee on Un-American Activities whether they were Party members. Anticommunists from Hollywood who appeared before the Committee lost employment or were subjected to smear campaigns. The influence of the ten has steadily diminished, however.

C69   CARNEY, William P. "No Democratic Government in Spain; Russia's Part in Spain's Civil War; Murder and Anti-Religion in Spain." New York: America Press, n.d. [1937]. 20 pp.
Publication by the Catholic journal "America" of three short articles attacking the Spanish Republicans as anti-democratic, dominated by communists, and enemies of the Church. The author, a Catholic writer recently returned from Spain, is not openly pro-Franco, but indicates that many Spaniards want neither fascist nor communist rule.

C70   "CARPENTER," Clever, these Communists, 58 (April 1938), 10-12.
An editorial attack by a leading AFL craft-union organ on John L. Lewis, whose leadership of the CIO permits the communists to wreck legitimate American unions wherever they can drive a wedge. The communists use attractive slogans like "unity" and "people's front" to mislead the gullible.

C71   CARPENTER, David. The Communist Party— Leader of the Struggle of the Unemployed, "Political Affairs," 28 (Sept. 1949), 82-96.
A summary of Party work among the unemployed from 1929 to 1949. The author discusses the Trade Union Unity League, the Unemployed Councils, unemployment insurance, and a program to protect the interests of the unemployed presented by the national committee of the Party in its 1949 Labor Day Manifesto.

C72   CARPENTER, G. D. America's War Economy and the Unemployed, "Communist," 20 (Feb. 1941), 138-50.
Chronic mass unemployment in the U.S. cannot be alleviated by a war economy. Protection of the unemployed is a vital task of the trade unions, while the Workers Alliance can play an important role. A program for improvements in social security legislation is outlined.

C73   CARPENTER, Willard. Supreme Court Colloquy: Conversation on the Smith Act, "Nation," 183 (Dec. 8, 1956), 500-1.
An account by an official of the American Civil Liberties Union in California of oral argument before the U.S. Supreme Court on the membership clause of the Smith Act. Earlier cases before the court dealt with the conspiracy section of the Act. Convictions of Junius Scales and Claude Lightfoot, who admitted membership in the Communist Party but who denied that it advocated violence, are involved.

C74   CARR, James [pseud. for Ludwig E. Katterfeld]. Some Facts about the Communist Party of America, "International Press Correspondence," 2 (March 8, 1922), 134-36.
The first article in "International Press Correspondence" describing American communism, while it was still underground. The article discusses the Party's organizational

apparatus, its membership composition, its factional problems, and the role of the Communist International in uniting the two communist parties in the spring of 1921.

C75   CARR, Robert K. (ed.). Civil Rights in America, "Annals of the American Academy of Political and Social Science," 275 (May 1951).
Robert E. Cushman discusses "American Civil Liberties in Mid-Twentieth Century"; a section on "Protection of Civil Rights Against Government" includes "Does the Loyalty Program Threaten Civil Rights?" by Eleanor Bontecou; "Do State Antisubversive Efforts Threaten Civil Rights?" by William B. Prendergast; and "Do Anti-subversive Efforts Threaten Academic Freedom?" by Edward C. Kirkland. (All these articles are abstracted separately.)

C76   . . . . "The House Committee on Un-American Activities, 1945-1950." Ithaca: Cornell University Press, 1952. 489 pp. App. Ind.
Part of the Cornell series on the impact on civil liberties of the government security programs and investigations. The author, professor of law and political science at Dartmouth, discusses Committee hearings on communism: the Gerhart Eisler hearings, labor unions, Hollywood, espionage, Hawaii, security legislation, the Remington hearings, the Lee Pressman hearings, and others. He appraises the Committee's personnel and staff, the conduct of its investigations, and its publications. The good things the Committee has done, he concludes, are outweighed by the bad. (Portions of the book appeared in the "Louisiana Law Review," March 1951, and the "University of Chicago Law Review," Spring 1951.)

C77   . . . . National Security and Individual Freedom, "Yale Review," 42 (June 1953), 496-512.
Though we have acted vigorously to meet the international communist threat, we are not clear as to the nature of the less substantial domestic threat. We seek safeguards against internal communist subversion through criminal statutes, Congressional investigations, and loyalty oaths. The use of these safeguards endangers freedom, it is pointed out.

C78   . . . . Academic Freedom, the American Association of University Professors, and the United States Supreme Court, "AAUP Bulletin," 45 (Spring 1959), 5-24.
An examination of recent Supreme Court decisions bearing on authority and liberty, on the threats posed by the national security program to academic freedom, tenure, and due process. Among the cases are those of teachers dismissed or found guilty of contempt for refusing to answer questions of investigating committees about communist membership or associations. The Court has found a satisfactory balance between authority and freedom.

C79   CARRINGTON, Walter. Laws to Suppress Anarchy and Sedition, "Virginia Law Quarterly," 5 (Dec. 1919), 606-9.
The author states his approval of a Missouri Bar Association resolution advocating punishment or deportation of individuals who advocate forcible overthrow of the government.

C80   CARROLL, Gordon. Revolution in Michigan, "American Mercury," 40 (April 1937), 385-99.
The managing editor of the "American Mercury" characterizes the Michigan automobile strikes as a serious economic upheaval staged by a handful of left-wing racketeers—communists, socialists, anarchists, and miscellaneous agitators—whose radical connections he lists.

C81 CARROLL, Raymond G. Aliens in Subversive Activities, "Saturday Evening Post," 208 (Feb. 22, 1936), 10-11 ff.
An assertion that there is inadequate U.S. supervision of aliens and immigrants, who come largely from countries represented in the Comintern, and are easy prey for the CPUSA. The nature and extent of communist activities in the U.S., both among noncitizens and citizens, are described.

C82 CARSEL, Wilfred. "A History of the Chicago Garment Workers Union." Chicago: Normandie House, 1940. 323 pp. Bibliog. Ind.
In chapter 16, "Lefts and Rights" (pp. 178-92), the author describes the bitter factional struggle in the Chicago ILGWU between the Trade Union Educational League "lefts" and right-wing union elements, 1923-27. The struggle, during which the TUEL under communist leadership for a time controlled the Chicago Joint Board of the ILGWU, duplicated the fight in New York.

C83 CARSON, Saul. On the Air: Trial by Sponsor, "New Republic," 123 (Sept. 11, 1950), 22-23.
A denunciation of Jean Muir's dismissal from her job as Mother Aldrich by the National Broadcasting Company because of alleged communist affiliations, based on listings in "Red Channels." The author attacks the blacklisting effect of "Red Channels," and the cowardice of the networks and advertisers.

C84 CARTER, Jack. Communist Rule in White Collar Union Drives Out Anti-Stalinites, "New Leader," 21 (Nov. 12, 1938), 2.
A description of "democracy" as practiced in a union under communist control. Local 16 of the United Office and Professional Workers in New York City suspended a member for expressing opinions critical of the union administration. The local, having issued instructions to its delegates to the national convention, had prohibited members from publishing contrary views.

C85 CARTER, Joseph. Stalinism and the War, "New International," 7 (May 1941), 68-73.
Writing during the period of the Hitler-Stalin pact, a Trotskyist traces the changes in CPUSA attitudes toward the Roosevelt Administration, showing that these coincided with Stalin's foreign policy aims. Stalin will seek to maintain his alliance with Hitler if Hitler permits; if Russian foreign policy so requires, the American communists will join the prowar chorus.

C86 CASEY, James. "What Is Fusion?" New York: Communist Party Election Campaign Committee, n.d. [1934]. 15 pp.
An attack on the Fusion movement in New York City as under the control of Wall Street, and on Fiorello La Guardia, its candidate for mayor, as an enemy of the workers. The Communist Party alone offers a comprehensive program, presented in detail, for the working population.

C87 .... "Hearst: Labor's Enemy No. 1." New York: Workers Library, 1935. 23 pp.
A picture of William Randolph Hearst as the chief mouthpiece of fascist forces, an imperialist warmonger, and the arch enemy of labor. The author urges a boycott of the Hearst press.

C88 .... "The Crisis in the Communist Party." New York: Three Arrows Press, n.d. [1937]. 24 pp.
Written for the Socialist Party by a former managing editor of the Communist Party's "Daily Worker." The pamphlet attacks the CP for its abandonment of Marxism and Leninism in the popular-front line, its lack of internal democracy, membership demoralization, and the like, and appeals to the Party rank and file to fight its leadership. The socialists welcome a united front with the CP on specific issues, such as the defense of the Soviet Union and the prevention of imperialist wars.

C89 CASEY, William J. Communism and Your Labor Relations, "Forbes," 58 (Aug. 1, 1946), 14-15 ff.
Advice to employers on combatting communist strategy in the plant, and ways to spot a communist. Noncommunist union leaders seek stable relations with management in order to get the greatest possible economic benefits for their unions, but communist tactics may disrupt stable relations.

C90 CASHMAN, Joseph T. "America Asleep: The Menace of Radicalism." New York: National Security League, 1923. 15 pp.
A speech delivered in Scranton, Pa., by a member of the National Security League's "Flying Squadron" on the danger of radicalism in the U.S., with emphasis on the communist movement and the Trade Union Educational League. A number of quotations from a report of the United Mine Workers issued September 10, 1923, appear as footnotes.

C91 CATER, Douglass. A Senate Afternoon: The Red Hunt, "Reporter," 3 (Oct. 10, 1950), 27-30.
An account of the Senate debate on the McCarran-Mundt-Ferguson bill to control subversives. The attack on the bill's registration provision as "ineffectual" by Senator Douglas and Senator Humphrey upsets traditional civil-liberty alignments. The bill passed, although the President and many leading newspapers have denounced it as a threat to our civil liberties.

C92 .... The Great Attack on Fort Monmouth, "Reporter," 10 (Jan. 5, 1954), 19-23.
A comparison of methods used by reporters of the Washington "Times-Herald" and the Washington "Post" in reporting the Fort Monmouth "espionage" case. The former played McCarthy's game, printing McCarthy's accusations and assertions of espionage as though they were facts; the latter traced the true story, finding no proof of communist espionage at Fort Monmouth.

C93 "CATHOLIC DIGEST," Red Fadeout in Radio (condensed from "The Sign"), 14 (Nov. 1949), 41-49.
A description of an alleged communist blacklist in the radio-TV field which kept numerous anticommunists from work before the campaign was started to remove the Reds from the air waves.

C94 CATHOLIC INFORMATION SOCIETY. Booklets on Communism.
A series of 26 popularly written pamphlets on various aspects of communism, including its place in fields such as religion, education, philosophy, and the like.

C95 "CATHOLIC WORLD," Communism: Who's to Blame, 166 (Jan. 1948), 291-95.
An assertion that the Catholic Church is responsible for the rejection of Catholicism and the embracing of communism by so many working people. Communism could not have made a start if Catholics had been doing their job. The Catholic Church must go again to the working-men and the poor, not give greater favor to the rich; it must get back to fundamentals.

C96 CAUDWELL, Christopher. "Illusion and Reality: A Study of the Sources of Poetry." 2d ed. New York: International Publishers, 1955. 342 pp.

A communist literary and philosophic classic, originally published in 1937, by an English writer who died fighting with the International Brigade in Spain. Tracing the development of poetry through each stage in mankind's development, from primitive communism through bourgeois culture to the communism of the Soviet Union, the author shows how the form of poetry was determined by the society in which it existed. At the highest stage of bourgeois development poetry was most cut off from life and reality, but with the coming of communism it was anchored in reality once again.

C97   CAUGHEY, John. A University in Jeopardy, "Harper's Magazine," 201 (Nov. 1950), 68-75.
A former professor at the University of California, dismissed because of refusal to sign the institution's loyalty oath, describes the dispute between the faculty and the regents. Though the oath has not exposed a traitor, it has put academic freedom in jeopardy, taken away faculty rights and guarantees, undermined faculty self-government, and shattered faculty morale.

C98   .... "In Clear and Present Danger: The Crucial State of Our Freedoms." Chicago: University of Chicago Press, 1958. 208 pp. Bibliog. Ind.
An assertion that America's traditional freedoms are in danger of being critically narrowed in the name of national security. McCarthyism and the House Un-American Activities Committee are discussed at some length. Communism in the U.S. is considered, with emphasis upon it as an academic freedom issue. Extra-legal actions against communists, and state and federal enactments against communism and subversion are discussed, as is the federal government's security program. The death of McCarthy has not ended McCarthyism.

C99   CAYTON, Horace R., and MITCHELL, George S. "Black Workers and the New Unions." Chapel Hill, N.C.: University of North Carolina Press, 1939. 473 pp. App. Bibliog. Ind.
A study of Negro workers in iron and steel, meat-packing, and railroad-car shops, and of the impact on them of the CIO organizing drives. In the discussion of the steel industry, chapter 6, "The Communists Take the Field," deals with the Steel and Metal Workers Industrial Union of the Trade Union Unity League. Pages 337-41 refer to communist activity in Birmingham, where many of the packinghouse workers were Negroes.

C100   CAZDEN, Norman. How Pure Is Music? "Masses & Mainstream," 2 (April 1949), 20-30.
An assertion that the concept of "pure" musical form is an illusion, that musical form depends completely on the historical, human substance which is its reason for being. The same is true of esthetic thought.

C101   CECIL, John. "Shall We Repeal Russian Recognition?" New York: American Women Against Communism, 1941. 15 pp.
An assertion that the USSR, under the cloak of recognition, is promoting communist subversion in the U.S. The Communist Party here is a totally un-American revolutionary movement, under the control of the Soviet government. Hundreds of communist organizations reach into almost every field of American society.

C102   "CENSORED!" Behind the Hoax in Foley Square, 1 (Sept. 1950), 10-15.
An account of the Smith Act trial of the communist leaders in a publication of the Civil Rights Congress. The hoax is the view that communism is a menace to America. Judge Medina is criticized for his biased conduct of the trial, as well as for showing prejudice even before the trial began.

The prosecution is attacked for using paid liars and stool-pigeons as witnesses.

C103   CESTARE, Frank. "Meet the Young Communist League." New York: YCL, 1943. 26 pp.
An account of YCL efforts in the fight against fascism, and the fight for such wartime policies as a planned economy, widespread use of incentives, welfare of servicemen, war-bond drives, salvage collection, immediate opening of a second front, abolition of poll taxes, and friendship with the USSR. The organizational structure of the YCL is described.

C104   CHAFEE, Zechariah, Jr. A Contemporary State Trial—The United States vs. Jacob Abrams et al, "Harvard Law Review," 33 (April 1920), 747-74. Corrections and further statements by the author, 35 (Nov. 1921), 9-14.
A description from the record of the trial of Russian aliens charged with violating the Espionage Act of 1918 by distributing pro-Bolshevik leaflets protesting the anti-Bolshevik foreign policy of the U.S. The author criticizes the convictions as violations of the free speech guarantee of the Constitution.

C105   .... "Free Speech in the United States." Cambridge: Harvard University Press, 1941. 634 pp. Bibliog. note. App. Ind.
A study of free speech in the U.S., with attention to prosecutions during World War I, along with sedition laws, deportation cases, and criminal syndicalism cases that followed the war. The alien registration law of 1940 is also examined, as is the exclusion of communists from the ballot. Appendices list federal and state statutes affecting freedom of speech.

C106   .... Freedom and Fear, "American Association of University Professors Bulletin," 35 (Autumn 1949), 397-433.
An analysis of the Mundt-Johnston bill for registration and public disclosure by communist or communist-front groups. The author dissents from the bill's assumption that the world communist movement presents a clear and present danger to free American institutions. Except for a fanatical inner circle, most communists love this country, but resent real or fancied injustices. The Mundt-Johnston bill will intensify rather than solve the problem.

C107   .... "The Free and the Brave: A Letter to the House Un-American Activities Committee on the Mundt-Nixon Bill." Foreword by Patrick Murphy Malin. New York: American Civil Liberties Union, 1950. 41 pp.
Opposition to the bill by a professor of law at Harvard, on the ground that it would water freedom down by borrowing hateful totalitarian practices. Doubting that the communists present a clear and present danger to free American institutions, he argues that present legislation is sufficient to cope with them. Provisions of the proposed measure are analyzed.

C108   .... The Registration of Communist-Front Organizations in the Mundt-Nixon Bill, "Harvard Law Review," 63 (June 1950), 1382-90.
Condemnation of the subversive activities control section of the Mundt-Nixon bill, particularly as it relates to communist-front organizations. These provisions interfere with freedom of discussion through organization. The vague characterization of communist-front organizations may be used to suppress many desirable organizations.

C109   .... Investigations of Radicalism and Laws against Subversion, pp. 46-84 in "Civil Liberties

under Attack," by Henry Steele Commager, etc., Philadelphia: University of Pennsylvania Press, 1951. 155 pp.
A discussion of congressional investigating committees in relationship to domestic communists, and of the Internal Security Act of 1950. Since investigating committees act like courts, their procedures should be reshaped to give a citizen rights like those in a criminal trial. The Internal Security Act (the McCarran Act) creates new kinds of criminal activity, and penalizes men for fear they might in the future engage in bad acts.

C110 CHAFEE, Zechariah, Jr. Civil Liberties in the United States and the Communist Threat, "Ammunition" (United Automobile Workers—CIO), 10 (May 1952), 40-46.
An address to the union's fifth annual educational conference, warning that the communist danger must not become a pretext for suppression of civil liberties. Several recent cases are discussed.

C111 .... The Freedom to Think, "Atlantic Monthly," 195 (Jan. 1955), 27-33.
An assertion that loyalty oaths and considerations of national security, while seeking to protect us against communist subversion, have undermined free thought and discussion. The danger in our colleges is not radical teachers, but uninspiring ones; we will get the latter at a university engaged in a campaign of suppression.

C112 .... "The Blessings of Liberty." Philadelphia and New York: Lippincott, 1956. 350 pp. Notes.
Compilation, in book form, of articles and addresses on freedom and civil liberties by a professor at the Harvard Law School. He is primarily concerned with the encroachment by government (and private groups) upon the Bill of Rights and the freedoms guaranteed the individual under our form of government. Among the topics dealt with are the Subversive Activities Control Act (the McCarran Act) of 1950 (chapter 5, pp. 116-56), and the proposal of the American Bar Association for noncommunist oaths for lawyers (chapter 6, pp. 157-78).

C113 CHAILLAUX, H. L. What Next, Tovarich? "American Legion Magazine," 28 (May 1940), 18-19 ff.
The director of the National Americanism Commission of the Legion traces the history of the recently disbanded American League for Peace and Democracy, and its predecessor, the American League Against War and Fascism, showing the communist inspiration, support, and control of both organizations. Prominent Party members and fellow-travelers who were active in the two groups are identified.

C114 CHALMERS, Allan K. "They Shall Be Free." Garden City, N.Y.: Doubleday, 1951. 255 pp. Ind.
The inside story of the Scottsboro case, told by the Congregational minister who became head of the Scottsboro Defense Committee in December 1935. The case lasted 19 years, from the arrest of nine Negro youths in Scottsboro, Alabama, in 1931 for a crime of rape that had not been committed, until the release of the last defendant in 1950. The part played by the communists and their International Labor Defense is told; the communists are criticized for their financial practices, and their willingness to lose the case in order to dramatize weaknesses in American legal practice. The defendants were more valuable to the communists in jail than out, for fund-raising and propaganda purposes.

C115 CHAMBER OF COMMERCE OF THE UNITED STATES. "Combating Subversive Activities in the United States." Washington, D.C.: The Chamber, 1934. 29 pp.

A report to the Chamber's Board of Directors, with recommendations for the forthcoming annual meeting. The report deals with the communist creed, Soviet domination, the Party here and its doctrines, its size and alien composition, auxiliary organizations, strike activity, and activity in the Army and Navy. Proposals for legislation are offered.

C116 .... "Safeguards against Subversive Activities." Washington, D.C.: The Chamber, Committee on Subversive Activities. 1935-39. Mimeo.
A periodical with summaries of published material, organizational actions, legislation, and other measures to combat subversive activities.

C117 .... "Communist Propaganda among American Youth." Washington, D.C.: The Chamber, 1936. 39 pp.
A reproduction of "Young Communists in Action: Handbook for Young Communists," issued by the Young Communist League (District 13), Educational Department. The handbook describes the basic aims, organization, and work of the YCL, with attention to shop and street units, unit officers, the section committee and organizer, and fractions in mass organizations. A supplement tells the origin of the Young Communist International and the YCL.

C118 ..., Committee on Socialism and Communism. "Communist Infiltration in the United States: Its Nature and How to Combat It." Washington, D.C.: The Chamber, 1946. 38 pp. Bibliog.
A pamphlet for popular distribution, dealing with the communist creed, communism in practice, the Comintern, why people become communists, communist fronts, what communism means to America, communists in the labor movement, communist penetration of government, and communist techniques to influence public opinion. Ways to combat communism are suggested.

C119 ..., Committee on Socialism and Communism. "Communists within the Government: The Facts and a Program." Washington, D. C. and New York: The Chamber, 1947. 57 pp. App.
A survey of communist infiltration into the federal government and a review of the methods used, with condemnation of the government's lax policies. A program for action in this area is outlined. One of the appendices analyzes the dangerous role of the United Public Workers, a communist-controlled union with access to government files and information.

C120 .... "Communists within the Labor Movement: A Handbook on the Facts and Countermeasures." Washington, D.C.: The Chamber, 1947. 60 pp. Bibliog.
A management view of ways in which communist domination of unions may be fought. The publication shows why and where communist influence is felt in unions, points out the difference between a procommunist and simply a militant labor leader, and advises employers how best to deal with the former without prejudicing normal labor relations. While the workers must resolve the issue, the employer can help.

C121 .... "A Program for Community Anti-Communist Action." Washington, D.C.: 1948. 56 pp. Bibliog.
A proposal that community leaders undertake an informed anticommunist campaign. Leaders are urged to be informed about communism, locally as well as nationally and internationally; to form a community organization on communism; to inform the public on communism; to protect the community against communist propaganda; to see

that legislators are informed on communism; and to give assistance to private anticommunist national research groups. Suggestions on how to get such a program under way are presented.

C122 CHAMBER OF COMMERCE OF THE UNITED STATES, Committee on Communism. "Communism: Where Do We Stand Today?" Washington, D.C.: The Chamber, 1952. 55 pp. App.
The international communist and imperialist movement controlled by Moscow is called the only major threat to world peace and freedom in 1952. The Communist Party here, while weakened, is still active, especially in the civil rights field. Communist influence in government and labor unions and among minority groups is described. Communists should be barred as entertainers and teachers, as well as government employees.

C123 .... "A Citizen's Course in Freedom vs. Communism: The Economics of Survival." Washington, D.C.: The Chamber, 1961. Set of eight pamphlets.
The economic systems of the U.S. and the USSR are contrasted with attention to the role of consumers, profit motive or master plan, distribution of income, the role of government, output and income, meeting the economic challenge, and what the citizen can do. The final pamphlet in the series, "What You Can Do About Communism," contains on pp. 6-16 a discussion of communism in the U.S.

C124 CHAMBERLAIN, John. The Literary Left Grows Up, "Saturday Review of Literature," 12 (May 11, 1935), 3-4 ff.
A largely favorable review of the First American Writers' Congress, held in New York in 1935. The author suggests that the menace of fascism has made Marxists more amenable to compromise, though he still hopes for a less dogmatic Party line. Personalities at the conference and recent proletarian literary efforts are discussed.

C125 .... Was It a Congress of American Writers? "Common Sense," 6 (Aug. 1937), 14-16.
Criticism of the National Congress of American Writers, which met in New York on June 4, for assuming that the U.S. could not stay out of a world war, for being intolerant of differences of opinion on the left, and for emphasizing the war in Spain while saying little about democracy in the U.S. Issues that dealt with the conduct of Soviet foreign policy were not discussed.

C126 .... School for Treason, "Plain Talk," 4 (April 1950), 13-16.
A sketch of New York City opinion-making in the 1930's to explain how a man of Alger Hiss' background and education could become a communist.

C127 CHAMBERLAIN, Lawrence H. "Loyalty and Legislative Action: A Survey of Activity by the New York State Legislature, 1919-1949." Ithaca: Cornell University Press, 1951. 254 pp. Ind.
A survey by the dean of Columbia College of legislative investigations of subversive activities in New York State, particularly in the school system: the Lusk investigation of 1919, the loyalty laws and investigations between 1934 and 1939, the Rapp-Coudert investigation of 1940-41, and New York City Board of Education activities resulting from the Rapp-Coudert investigation of 1941 and the Feinberg law of 1949. He finds them all guilty, in greater or lesser degree, of violating civil liberties. He doubts whether such investigations achieve their avowed purpose, and whether democracy is not better served by tolerating the few communists in the public school system.

C128 CHAMBERLIN, William H. Red Queen of California, "American Mercury," 52 (June 1941), 711-19.
A humorous portrait of Mrs. Kate Crane-Gartz, a "muddled millionairess" with a weakness for procommunist letter writing, subsequently published in book form. She is a bored lady of wealth gone red, engaging in comfortable make-believe revolution.

C129 .... "America's Second Crusade." Chicago: Regnery, 1950. 372 pp. Bibliog. Ind.
A sweeping condemnation of World War II as unnecessary, poorly conducted, and Soviet-inspired. Roosevelt is said to have sought the war, which was a military success but a failure in terms of our professed war aims—the Atlantic Charter and the Four Freedoms. The author attacks major blunders in the West's diplomacy during the war, and the one-sided appeasement followed at Teheran and Yalta. Sympathy for communism among American intellectuals, and communist influence in the State Department and other U.S. government agencies, are held partly responsible.

C130 .... Fallacies about Communism, "Freeman," 1 (July 2, 1951), 628-30.
A discussion of common misconceptions regarding communism. Its threat lies in its power as a disintegrating idea, as a blueprint for espionage and sabotage, and as a snowballing empire. It must be counteracted by a campaign of truth about Soviet conditions, by vigorous police action, and by balance-of-power politics against imperialist expansion.

C131 CHAMBERS, Whittaker. Can You Make Out Their Voices, "New Masses," 6 (March 1931), 7-16.
A short story, written when Chambers was a communist, about a group of armed farmers, led by a communist, who stormed a town to take food from the Red Cross and local stores for their starving families. The story was based on actual events in a town in Arkansas. Chambers' story was hailed as one of the best examples of proletarian literature in the 1930's. (Also published by International Pamphlets in 1932 as "Can You Hear Their Voices?" and made into a play by Hallie Flanagan and Margaret Ellen Clifford under the title, "Can You Hear Their Voices? A Play of Our Time.")

C132 .... "Witness." New York: Random House, 1952. 808 pp. Ind.
An account of the life of one of the most articulate, as well as the most famous, of the ex-communists. A member of the Party from 1925 to 1938, Chambers was on the editorial staff of the "Daily Worker" and the "New Masses" before serving as an underground agent. In his underground activities he was in contact with a communist cell in Washington, D.C., following which, after his break with the Party, he became the chief protagonist in the Alger Hiss affair. The book explains Chambers' motivations for entering and leaving the party, and sheds light on Party operations. (The book ran serially in the "Saturday Evening Post" from February 9 to April 12, 1952, under the title, "I Was the Witness.")

C133 .... Is Academic Freedom in Danger? "Life," 34 (June 22, 1953), 90-91 ff.
An account of investigations of communism in colleges made by the Senate Committee on the Judiciary and the House Committee on Un-American Activities. Chambers contends that liberals overdo the "reign of terror" view of the investigations; unless communism is curbed, freedom itself will be academic.

C134 .... What Is a Communist? "Look," 17 (July 28, 1953), 27-31.

Answers to questions on the nature of communism. The widespread confusion about communism is the result, not of stupidity, malice, or lack of facts, but of communism's different moral standard. Communists have made the morality of war their permanent standard.

C135 CHAMBERS, Whittaker. "Cold Friday." Ed. and introd. by Duncan Norton-Taylor. New York: Random House, 1964. 327 pp.
A collection of papers by the author of "Witness," published three years after his death. A number of the papers contain references to the author's experiences as a communist, developments in the international communist movement, or his reasons for breaking with communism.

C136 CHANCEY, Martin. The Doctrine of Criminal Conspiracy and the American Labor Movement, "Political Affairs," 33 (Dec. 1954), 32-46.
The doctrine of criminal conspiracy is the main legal foundation for the Smith Act and the Communist Control Act. The use of the doctrine in American labor history is traced. For the McCarthyites it is an unexcelled propaganda device; it convicts people without proof of criminal acts, and it covers whole groups of unionists and class-conscious workers.

C137 CHAPLIN, Ralph. "American Labor's Case against Communism: How the Operations of Stalin's Red Quislings Look from inside the Labor Movement." Seattle: Educator Publishing Company, 1947. 111 pp.
A polemic against communism and the communist conspiracy in the American labor movement by a former IWW leader, author of "Solidarity Forever." The author equates the Political Action Committee of the CIO with communism, without qualification. He names a number of alleged communists, gives their affiliations, and lists "front" organizations. (The author's anti-CIO bias makes his work of little informative value.)

C138 CHAPMAN, Abraham. "Nazi Penetration in America." New York: American League for Peace and Democracy, 1939. 32 pp.
Tracing the rise of anti-Semitism in the U.S. to Nazi influence, the author relates anti-Semitism and Nazism to the needs of the economic royalists, and calls for support of the American League for Peace and Democracy.

C139 .... "The North Atlantic Pact: For Peace or War?" New York: New Century, 1949. 16 pp.
The editor of "Fraternal Outlook," organ of the International Workers Order, attacks the North Atlantic Pact as part of the imperialistic drive of American capitalism. He calls for peaceful co-existence between the U.S. and the Soviet Union, based on a pact of peace and friendship.

C140 .... Subversion in New York's Schools, "Jewish Life," 3 (March 1949), 5-7.
An attack on the Board of Education of New York City for its crusade against progressive teachers and progressive ideas, and its denial of the use of school rooms after class hours to labor and progressive organizations. The Board has barred the International Workers Order from holding classes and lectures in the city schools.

C141 CHAPPELL, Winifred L. When the Docile Stir, "Christian Century," 51 (March 7, 1934), 317-18.
A report on the communist-led National Convention Against Unemployment held in Washington, and on a victory won by the unemployed members of the Marine Industrial Union in Baltimore. The workers unemployment and social insurance bill is described, as is the militant mood of the unemployed.

C142 CHAPPLE, John B. "La Follette Road to Communism: Must We Go Further along That Road?" Ashland, Wisconsin: The author, 1936. 170 pp. Ind.
A denunciation of Governor Philip La Follette of Wisconsin for leading the state into communism, which is held responsible for the decline of religion, morality, and economy in the state.

C143 CHARNEY, George Blake. Lessons of the Congressional By-Election in N.Y., "Political Affairs," 25 (April 1946), 362-70.
A report on a special election held February 19, 1946, in the 19th Congressional District of New York in which an American Labor Party candidate, run in opposition to the Democratic candidate, came close to victory. This confirms the tactic to be used by the Communist Party in the 1946 congressional elections—to support progressive labor candidates outside the Democratic Party.

C144 ..., and LEVIN, Harry A. An Analysis of the New York Elections, "Political Affairs," 33 (Jan. 1954), 33-50.
The election results in New York City represented a defeat to Big Business, reflecting growing opposition of labor and other broad strata of the population to Eisenhower's foreign and domestic policies. The outline of a broad people's program has emerged, that can unite labor and its allies in a program for democracy and peace and against McCarthyism. Our Party's main struggle in the elections had to be directed against left sectarianism and isolation.

C145 .... New Features in the Struggle against McCarthyism, "Political Affairs," 33 (May 1954), 43-55.
The anti-McCarthy movement, now embracing a majority of the people, cuts across party and class lines. There is a growing awareness that McCarthyism is fascism. While the main fire in the 1954 elections must be directed at the Republicans, the fight against McCarthyism and McCarranism must be conducted in both parties.

C146 CHARTENER, William H. Reds in Trade Unions, "Editorial Research Reports," 2 (July 22, 1949), 463-82.
An analysis of communist activities in the U.S. labor movement, from the "boring from within" period of the 1920's to the rise of communist-dominated unions and the recent decline of communist influence. The author discusses Marxist doctrine on union functions, communist methods to control unions, and government and union efforts to curb left-wing elements in the unions.

C147 CHASE, Harold W. "Security and Liberty: The Problem of Native Communists, 1947-55." Garden City, N.Y.: Doubleday, 1955. 88 pp.
An analysis of the security-liberty syndrome. The author analyzes the problem of subversion in America; explores the legal doctrines under which subversive control is weighed against individual liberty; evaluates the general control measures that were adopted; and explores the various programs of loyalty-security in government employment, among aliens, and within organized labor. He concludes that only a clear and present danger warrants measures which forestall espionage and sabotage; in all other cases, civil liberties must be preserved.

C148 CHASE, Ray P. "Are They Communists or Catspaws? A Red Baiting Article." Anoka, Minn.: The author, 1938. 60 pp.
An assertion, by an active Republican, that communism in Minnesota was masked as the Farmer-Labor Party and

promoted by the state administration. Cited as evidence are the activities of Governor Elmer A. Benson in various peace fronts and the Communist Party's support of him.

C149 CHASE, Stuart. Mr. Dies Is a Communist, Too, "New Republic," 102 (Jan. 29, 1940), 137-39.
By using the logic employed by the "professional" anticommunists—a system which incriminates by association—the author demonstrates that he can prove anyone, including Dies and Pegler, to be a communist.

C150 .... The Twilight of Communism in the U.S.A., "Reader's Digest," 39 (Sept. 1941), 25-28. Condensed from "Forbes."
An assertion that scientific progress has made Marx's revolutionary theories obsolete. The change from the machine age to the power age has done away with the army of proletarians, changing large numbers from overalls to white collars. Though skilled workers may strike for higher wages, they will not accept Marx's view of class struggle.

C151 .... Jumpin' Joe McCarthy—His Motives and Methods, "Progressive," 14 (June 1950), 11-13.
A summary of McCarthy's motives, his methods, and the results of his campaign against the State Department. While he has not yet located a single card-carrying communist, he has damaged the reputations of innocent persons, made government service dangerous, and seriously discredited democracy.

C152 .... Nineteen Propositions about Communism, "Saturday Review," 35 (April 5, 1952), 20-21.
Though the U.S. was in mild danger of communism at the bottom of the great depression, no such danger exists today. Communist danger here is exaggerated because the official faith in Russia is communist. By using "communist" loosely, demagogues are splintering the nation when unity is needed.

C153 CHERNE, Leo. How to Spot a Communist, "Look," 11 (March 4, 1947), 21-25.
The executive secretary of the Research Institute of America gives classifications to help identify persons or organizations that follow the communists' lead. Communist tactics in trying to seize control of an organization are presented, and characteristics of the communist mind are outlined.

C154 CHEW, Geoffrey. Academic Freedom on Trial at the University of California, "Bulletin of the Atomic Scientists," 6 (Oct. 1950), 333-36.
An account of the loyalty oath controversy at the University of California by a former faculty member, who discusses faculty objections to the oath, and the division within the Board of Regents.

C155 CHILDS, John L. Democracy, Education, and the Class Struggle, "Social Frontier," 2 (June 1936), 274-78.
Disagreement with John Dewey's argument ("Social Frontier," May 1936) that teachers should view reorganization as a social, not a class, idea. The choice is between rival social ideas; one is a democratic, planned reorganization to meet community needs, whereas the other serves only the interests of owners. The educator should work in alliance with the working class, playing a leadership role in both classroom and community.

C156 ..., and COUNTS, George S. "America, Russia and the Communist Party in the Postwar World." New York: John Day, 1943. 92 pp.
An attempt to outline the conditions for American-Soviet

cooperation after the war, viewing the CPUSA as a major obstacle to American-Soviet friendship and suggesting that the correction of social injustice will lead to the Party's dissolution. (A publication of the Commission on Education and the Postwar World of the American Federation of Teachers.)

C157 .... Liberty in America: Communists and the Right to Teach, "Nation," 168 (Feb. 26, 1949), 230-33.
A professor of the philosophy of education at Teachers College, Columbia University, supports the decision of the Board of Regents of the University of Washington that members of the Communist Party should not be permitted to teach. The Party requires them to use their position to advance communist purposes. (For an opposing view see Carey McWilliams, "Liberty in America: The Test of a Teacher," in the "Nation," March 5, 1949.)

C158 CHILDS, Marquis. The Hiss Case and the American Intellectual, "Reporter," 3 (Sept. 26, 1950), 24-27.
An effort to explain the phenomenon of Alger Hiss. The American intellectual was alienated from political life until the New Deal, when he came in to "do good" in government, without real public support. Hiss' willingness to pass State Department documents to communists stemmed from a belief that extraordinary steps were necessary to save Western freedom.

C159 CHILDS, M. H. The American Social Fascists, "Communist," 11 (Aug. 1932), 708-15.
An attack on the Socialist Party program as a capitalist way out of the crisis, and on Norman Thomas for advocating purchase of industries at reasonable valuations. The revolutionary way out of the crisis, as in Russia, is the only way. The communist program is to wrest political power from the capitalist class and confiscate industry and landed estates.

C160 CHILDS, M. [Morris]. Permanent Counter Revolution: The Role of the Trotskyites in the Minneapolis Strikes, "Communist," 13 (Oct. 1934), 1015-32.
The second Minneapolis truck drivers' strike exposed the Trotskyite leadership as strikebreakers, as the vanguard of the counterrevolutionary bourgeoisie. They cooperated with the Farmer-Labor Party and the labor bureaucrats, supported martial law, covered up the strikebreaking role of the state, and helped organize anti-Red hysteria. (Expanded and reprinted in pamphlet form under joint authorship with William F. Dunne.)

C161 .... Our Tasks in the Light of Changed Conditions, "Communist," 14 (April 1935), 299-311.
A defense and elaboration of the new Party line calling for work within the AFL and endorsing a labor party. Emphasis is on experiences in Wisconsin. The Party's new line recognizes changing conditions, which Trotskyite and Lovestoneite critics fail to do.

C162 .... Forging Unity against Reaction in Illinois, "Communist," 15 (Aug. 1936), 769-83.
A report to the Party's ninth convention from the Chicago district, one of the Party's major areas of concentration, describing efforts toward a united front in Chicago industry and politics. The movement toward independent political action by labor is described.

C163 ..., and MEYER, Frank. Philosophic Nihilism Serves Reaction, "Communist," 17 (May 1938), 468-80.
Pragmatism is condemned for denying the significance of

theory, without which man cannot gain understanding. He could only perceive separate, disjointed things, not recognizing the validity of general concepts like fascism, unemployment, and class struggle. Pragmatism serves the reactionaries by making workers feel that they have no common cause against the exploiters.

C164 CHILDS, Morris. Building the Democratic Front in Illinois, "Communist," 17 (Sept. 1938), 811-17.
A speech to the Party's tenth national convention, May 29, 1938, by the Party's secretary in Illinois, discussing activities in the Illinois elections and the growth of the Party in the district.

C165 . . . . Strengthening National Unity in the Elections, "Communist," 21 (June 1942), 440-49.
A communist analysis of the first elections since Pearl Harbor, the Illinois primaries held April 14. Anti-Hitlerism is viewed as the year's chief election issue; Democratic victories will further national unity.

C166 . . . . "Unity behind Roosevelt Will Defeat the Modern Copperheads in Illinois." Chicago: Illinois Communist Political Association, n.d. [1944]. 16 pp.
The modern Copperheads in Illinois, led by the Chicago "Tribune" and using Hitler's weapons, can be defeated by unity behind Roosevelt. National unity to win the war is needed. Labor, including communists, should cooperate with existing organizations, mobilizing the broadest section of the population.

C167 . . . . The Daily Worker—Problems and Prospects, "Political Affairs," 25 (Sept. 1946), 827-36.
A report delivered July 18, 1946, at the plenary meeting of the Party's national committee, criticizing the semi-independent status of the "Daily Worker" in the Browder period and suggesting measures to restore the paper's role as a militant voice of Party policy. The aim of the "Worker" is not to compete with the capitalist dailies, but to stage a militant fight against capitalism.

C168 "CHRISTIAN CENTURY," Dissent Is Not Treason, 70 (Nov. 18, 1953), 1317-19.
The November 2 statement by the General Council of the Presbyterian Church, U.S.A., on communism and American politics is highly praised. The statement denounced the use of the "big lie" in American politics, insisted that truth be preserved at all times, and asserted that police measures alone could not stay the forces of disintegration. The document demonstrates calmness, wisdom, and faith.

C169 "CHRISTIAN REGISTER," Can a Real Unitarian Be a Real Communist? A Symposium, 126 (Oct. 1947), 391-95 ff.
Earl Browder, former national chairman of the CPUSA, asserts that there is nothing incompatible with Unitarian or other religious beliefs in the political program of communism. In the view of Rev. Donald Harrington, a Party member will join a Unitarian church only if he is stupid, schizoid, or a scoundrel. Rev. Howard G. Matson and Rev. Curtis W. Reese object to driving any men of good will away, or limiting tolerance to familiar ideas. Alfred Stiernotte calls for critical independence from all socialist and communist groups.

C170 . . . . Man, God, and the Soviets: 52 Religious Liberals Speak Up. Boston: Christian Register, 1952. 74 pp.
Selections from the publication of the American Unitarian Association, between 1947 and 1952, on various aspects of the struggle with communism. The authors, many of them prominent in American life and most of them Unitarians,

discuss such topics as communism, America's job in the world today, the USSR and the "people's democracies," the United Nations, the Wallace party, loyalty, and academic freedom

C171 CHRISTIE, Robert A. "Empire in Wood: A History of the Carpenters' Union." Ithaca: Cornell University Press, 1956. 356 pp. App. Bibliog. Ind.
Pages 253-66 of this history of the United Brotherhood of Carpenters and Joiners deal with the communist challenge to the conservative administration of William Hutcheson during the 1920's. Organized into the Trade Union Educational League, the communists offered a small but lively opposition until their expulsion from the union in 1928.

C172 CIMA, Anthony P. "Counterfeit Humanitarians." New York: Bookcraft, 1935. 448 pp.
A bitterly antilabor book, attacking the A F L as parasitical, tyrannical, and arrogant. The author argues that organizing workers into professionally-led unions is dangerous because these unions will eventually be dominated by communists, racketeers, and demagogues. Communism in the U.S., he asserts, is multiplying rapidly, encouraged by government officials and well financed from mysterious sources.

C173 CITIZENS COMMITTEE FOR HARRY BRIDGES. "In the Matter of Harry R. Bridges," 1939 and 1941. Washington, D.C.: National Federation for Constitutional Liberties, 1941. 30 pp.
A digest of briefs recently submitted in the pending deportation proceedings against Bridges. The theory of the prosecutors is called a threat to the entire trade union movement, since under it an alien could be subject to deportation for accepting aid from an organization labeled subversive.

C174 CITIZENS' COMMITTEE TO FREE EARL BROWDER. "America Speaks for Earl Browder." New York: The Committee, 1941. 31 pp.
An account of the September 24, 1941, meeting in Madison Square Garden, New York City, held to promote a pardon for Earl Browder, then imprisoned on a passport charge. Comments of a number of trade union leaders on the Browder case are included.

C175 . . . . "The Browder Case: A Summary of Facts." New York: The Committee, 1941. 22 pp.
Listing Browder's contributions to the cause of freedom, the Committee urges his release from the federal penitentiary. It argues that his sentence was excessive, that he falsified his passport application for unselfish ends, and that his only offense was to deny that he had ever had a passport before.

C176 . . . . "Mr. President—Free Earl Browder." New York: The Committee, 1942. 47 pp.
A report, prepared by Sasha Small, of the proceedings of the National Free Browder Congress, held March 28-29 in New York City. Browder had then been imprisoned for a year for passport fraud. Highlights of the Congress include excerpts from speeches, reports of panels, and the text of a resolution to President Roosevelt urging Browder's release.

C177 CITIZENS COMMITTEE TO PRESERVE AMERICAN FREEDOMS. "Courage Is Contagious: The Bill of Rights versus the Un-American Activities Committee." Los Angeles: The Committee, 1953. 32 pp.
An attack on the House Un-American Activities Committee by a communist-front group in Southern California that seeks to abolish HUAC and discredit the FBI. The pamphlet

criticizes HUAC activities in Los Angeles, particularly its investigation and alleged blacklisting of people in the motion picture industry, along with lawyers and other professionals.

C178 CITRON, Alice. Teachers in Battle, "Masses & Mainstream," 3 (July 1950), 64-69.
A defense of their fitness to teach by one of the eight members of the New York Teachers Union, suspended in May 1950, for refusing to answer questions as to association with the Party. This is an attempt to eliminate the union, not to remove teachers for unfitness to teach or for indoctrination of pupils.

C179 CIVIL RIGHTS CONGRESS. "America's 'Thought Police': Record of the Un-American Activities Committee." Foreword by Henry A. Wallace. New York: The Congress, 1947. 46 pp.
An account of the "illegal" and "unconstitutional" actions of the House Un-American Activities Committee. The Congress links the Committee and its supporters to reactionary and anti-Semitic groups, and claims that, under the guise of anticommunism, the Committee threatens all progressive movements and the liberties of the American people. In his foreword Wallace denounces as bigots the men first known as the Dies Committee, then the Rankin Committee, and now the Thomas Committee.

C180 .... "It's You They're After!" Los Angeles: The Congress, n.d. [1949?]. 32 pp.
A defense of those who were brought before the Grand Jury in Los Angeles in 1948 and 1949, asked about communist activities, and convicted of contempt and jailed because they refused to answer. Comparing the convictions with events in Nazi Germany, the Congress calls for mass demonstrations to free the prisoners and defend civil liberties.

C181 .... "Deadly Parallel." New York: The Congress, n.d. [1949 or 1950?]. 32 pp.
An illustrated pamphlet comparing U.S. policies which the Civil Rights Congress opposes with those of Nazi Germany. Opponents of communism are identified with racists in the South as well as with Nazi stormtroopers.

C182 .... "Voices for Freedom." New York: The Congress, 1951. 39 pp.
A collection of opinions criticizing the recent Supreme Court decision upholding the Smith Act and the conviction of the 11 communist leaders. The dissents of Justice Black and Justice Douglas are included, as are newspaper and magazine editorials, and the statements of individuals and labor groups.

C183 .... "Voices for Freedom No. 2: An Additional Collection of Opinions on the Supreme Court Decision Upholding the Smith Act, an Act for the Persecution of All Political Non-Conformists." New York: The Congress, 1951. 39 pp.
Reprints of newspaper editorials and statements by trade union leaders and others opposing the Supreme Court's decision upholding the conviction of the top 11 communist leaders under the Smith Act.

C184 .... "We Charge Genocide: The Historic Petition to the United Nations for Relief from a Crime of the United States Government against the Negro People." New York: The Congress, 1951. 238 pp.
A brief submitted to the United Nations listing hundreds of incidents of murder and attempted murder of Negroes, which the petitioners contend is part of a conspiracy to destroy the Negro people. The brief was presented to the U.N. under the terms of the Convention on the Prevention

and Punishment of the Crime of Genocide. A cold-war weapon to embarrass the U.S. Government, the brief was a major activity of the Congress.

C185 .... "The Heat Is On!" The Congress, n.d. [1952?]. 14 unnumbered pp.
An assertion by the Party's front organization in the civil rights field that the Supreme Court is under reactionary pressure to support attacks on civil liberties and in particular to uphold the Smith Act convictions. The Congress calls for a program of mass pressure on the Supreme Court to defeat the attacks on civil liberties.

C186 .... "Lawyers under Fire." New York: The Congress, 1952. 24 pp.
The story of the five lawyers jailed for contempt of court for their fearless and able defense of the eleven CPUSA leaders in the Smith Act trial. Two have also been disbarred, with disbarment proceedings pending against the others. Three Supreme Court justices, reviewing the contempt convictions, refused to join in the frameup.

C187 .... "The Bill of Rights: How Safe Are You?" New York: The Congress, n.d. [1954?]. 16 pp.
An assertion that under the "Communist Control Act of 1954" not only communists, but all progressives and liberals, are in danger of losing their civil liberties. A call for the repeal of the law.

C188 CLAIBORNE, Robert. Twilight on the Left, "Nation," 184 (May 11, 1957), 414-18.
An assertion that the Party is on its way out as an organization. It succeeded to the degree that it did in the past because it looked at America rather than its ideology. From a membership of 90,000 it is now down to fewer than 10,000, with more leaving every day.

C189 CLARK, Evans. "Facts and Fabrications about Soviet Russia." New York: Rand School of Social Sciences, 1920. 96 pp. Bibliog.
A defense of the USSR by the former director of the Department of Information, Bureau of the Representative in the United States of the Russian Socialist Federal Soviet Republic. He claims that stories of Soviet atrocities are false. The volume includes a bibliography of articles and books said to describe the events in Soviet Russia accurately.

C190 CLARK, James C. The Economic Situation of the Youth, "Communist," 16 (Feb. 1937), 153-60.
A description of the problems of American youth in the depression. The government has provided little vocational training. Its work agencies, the WPA and the CCC, employ only a fraction of the unemployed youths, and pay them low wages. The communists support the American Youth Act, which will provide vocational training, more work projects, and high wages.

C191 CLARK, Joe C. "Life with a Purpose: Why You Should Join the Young Communist League." New York: National Committee, YCL, n.d. [193-?]. 15 pp.
Recruiting literature, emphasizing unemployment and low wages, and the dangers of war and fascism. Advocating passage of the American Youth Act and formation of a farmer-labor party, the author calls for a new social order to abolish the profit system and end the menace of war and fascism.

C192 CLARK, Joseph. "We the People." New York: New Age, 1937. 31 pp.
A pamphlet of the popular-front period commemorating the adoption of the U.S. constitution, at a time when the

Party's slogan, "Communism is Twentieth Century Americanism," sought to show that its aims were in line with American traditions. The pamphlet urges a firm stand against the "Tories" of the twentieth century.

C193 CLARK, Joseph. "Who Are the Young Communists?" New York: New Age, 1941. 15 pp.
A recruiting pamphlet for the Young Communist League during the period of the Hitler-Stalin pact. Urging that the U.S. stay out of the war, the author attacks imperialism, both German and British, as responsible. He denies that the communists advocate force, or that they are agents of a foreign power.

C194 .... "Men of Liberty." New York: New Age, 1942. 15 pp.
An appeal for a Presidential pardon for the release from prison of Earl Browder, whose struggle for freedom and national unity is compared with those of George Washington, Abraham Lincoln, and Frederick Douglass.

C195 .... Planners of Atomic Imperialism, "Political Affairs," 25 (June 1946), 555-60.
An attack on the policies outlined in the "Report on the International Control of Atomic Energy" prepared by a board of consultants for the Secretary of State's Committee on Atomic Energy. These policies are based on imperialist power politics.

C196 .... Atomic Energy—For War or Peace, "Political Affairs," 25 (Aug. 1946), 713-23.
A discussion of atomic energy control, centering upon the dispute between the U.S. and the Soviet Union over the use of the veto in atomic matters. The Baruch plan, which calls for the elimination of the veto in atomic matters, would give the U.S. complete control because the U.S. controls the majority of votes in the UN.

C197 .... The Disarmament Question, "Political Affairs," 26 (Feb. 1947), 122-31.
A discussion of the UN resolution adopted December 14, 1946, calling for world-wide reduction of arms and troops, and control of the atomic bomb. The author welcomes the resolution on arms reduction, criticizes the West for failing to agree with the Russian plan for troop reduction, and opposes the Baruch plan for atomic control.

C198 .... "What's Behind the Berlin Crisis." New York: New Century, 1948. 24 pp.
An argument that the creation of an independent West German republic by the U.S., in violation of the Potsdam agreement, provoked the Berlin "air-lift" crisis. The author calls for American-Russian negotiations to solve the German question, maintaining that the Soviet Union wants peaceful co-existence with the U.S. and all other nations.

C199 .... American Labor and the German Working Class, "Political Affairs," 27 (April 1948), 337-43.
Forces making for a progressive German trade-union movement, united in all four zones, are maturing. It is being opposed by American Military Government, in league with reactionary forces in Germany. U.S. policy is to turn Germany into an anti-Soviet military base.

C200 ..., and WEINSTONE, William. "The Atom Bomb and You." New York: New Century, 1950. 15 pp.
An appeal to sign the world peace petition to outlaw the atom bomb, sponsored by the World Peace Congress. The atom bomb is called a weapon of aggression and of mass slaughter, not an instrument of war. The U.S. proposal on atomic energy, the Baruch plan, is termed a fake. Wall Street is said to be alarmed by the peace petition, already signed by 273,000,000 people.

C201 .... "Hell-Bomb or Peace?" New York: New Century, 1950. 15 pp.
Criticism of President Truman for orders to make the hydrogen bomb and of Secretary of State Acheson for refusing to search for peace with Russia. Opposition from scientists, clergymen, and others to preparation of H-bombs is cited, and an end urged to the cold war with the USSR.

C202 .... "Must There Be War?" New York: New Century, 1951. 24 pp.
A plea for peaceful co-existence and the outlawing of atomic warfare. Tracing the history of the Soviet fight for peace, the author argues that American capitalism and Wall Street block the road to peace because of American capitalism's imperialist plans and the economy's needs for war production.

C203 .... "The Real Russia: A Former Moscow Correspondent—Who Saw Harrison Salisbury See Russia—Tells Why the New York Times Correspondent Forgot His Own Eye-Witness Reports from the U.S.S.R." New York: New Century, 1954. 32 pp.
An attempt at a point-by-point refutation of articles which appeared in the "New York Times" in 1954, written by Harrison Salisbury after his return from the Soviet Union. "Daily Worker" foreign correspondent Clark compares these articles with ones Salisbury wrote in Moscow, pointing out contradictions—contradictions that censorship could not explain.

C204 .... "Geneva: Road to Peace." New York: New Century, 1955. 16 pp.
The Geneva summit conference of 1955 is termed a major step to peaceful co-existence. The American position on Germany is criticized as calling for a united Germany tied to the North Atlantic Treaty Organization; the author urges, instead, a neutral Germany allied neither with NATO nor the Warsaw Pact. The Geneva conference took steps toward disarmament and inspection, but its greatest benefit was contact between East and West.

C205 CLAY, Robert. Farm Problems and Legislation, "Communist," 16 (May 1937), 446-55.
A review of congressional policy with regard to AAA, soil conservation, floods, rural electrification, and the like. Slashing of farm relief is criticized, as is legislation favoring larger and more prosperous farmers. A vigorous drive for progressive farm legislation is advocated.

C206 CLEMENT, Travers. Red-Baiters' Holiday in Sacramento: The Criminal-Syndicalism Trial, "Nation," 140 (March 13, 1935), 306-8.
The trial of 14 members of the Communist Party and one of the Workers' Party under the California criminal-syndicalism law. The trial seeks to punish efforts to organize migratory workers in California's large-scale agriculture. The result may decide the future of labor in California.

C207 "Cleveland Federation of Labor Quarterly," You Can't Compromise with Communism, 19 (Spring 1950), 15-55.
Many quotations from Lenin, Stalin, and J. Peters' "Manual on Organization" are used to demonstrate the inflexibility of communist thinking.

C208 CLEVELAND, Harlan. Short Cuts to Disaster: Communism and McCarthyism, "Progressive," 18 (June 1954), 10-13.
Both communists and McCarthyites seek to sow distrust among the American people. McCarthy and his tactics help the communists, who strive to present McCarthyism or communism as the alternatives. We who wish to protect

our freedoms by remaining part of the tolerant center must guard against extreme actions.

C209 CLIFFORD, Arthur. "The Truth about the American Youth Congress." Detroit: Committee of 76, AYC, 1935. 32 pp.
An official history of the AYC, issued on the eve of the Second American Youth Congress in Detroit. Emphasis is placed on the First American Youth Congress the previous year, the position of the AYC (then hostile to the New Deal), and procedures to be followed at the Detroit meeting.

C210 COAN, Blair. "The Red Web." Chicago: Northwest Publishing Company, 1925. 301 pp. App.
An examination of radical tendencies in the U.S. between 1918 and 1925, by a former newspaperman. Viewing Bolshevism as a mental disorder, and holding that the differences between the socialist and the communist movements are minor, the author argues that red radicalism is less of a menace than pink radicalism. A defender of the actions taken by Attorney General A. Mitchell Palmer and Attorney General Harry M. Daugherty against radical groups, Coan thinks the La Follette-Wheeler ticket of 1924 was an agency for the mobilization of leftist groups.

C211 COBLENTZ, L. A. "Russia Up to Date As Seen by a Minnesota Farmer, Together with an Account of World's Most Horrible Atrocities." Red Lake Falls, Minnesota: The author, n.d. [1937?]. 63 pp.
Following his return from a trip to Russia, the author refutes "atrocity stories" about the Soviet Union. The real atrocities, he says, are those committed by fascism, war, and capitalism.

C212 COCHRAN, Bert. The Split in the Socialist Party, "American Socialist," 2 (Feb. 1955), 12-17.
An account of the development of the communist movement in 1919 out of the left wing of the Socialist Party. The effect of World War I and the Bolshevik Revolution of 1917 on the various socialist factions is reviewed, as are the expulsions of left-wing groups by the SP National Executive Committee, the left-wing national conference preceding the SP convention in 1919, the SP convention itself, and the immediate formation of two communist parties, the Communist Party and the Communist Labor Party.

C213 .... The Communist Convention, "American Socialist," 4 (March 1957), 5-7.
A report on the factionalism at the CPUSA's 16th national convention. John Gates and his followers, who sought independence from Moscow, failed to fight for their program. They allied themselves with the Dennis wing in order to block Foster's and the Russians' attack.

C214 .... The Birth of American Communism, "American Socialist," 4 (June 1957), 8-13.
An account of the early years of American communism, as it tried to get its bearings in the U.S. while its admiration for Soviet achievements made it subservient to the USSR.

C215 .... Two Radical Decades in American History, "American Socialist," 5 (June 1958), 13-20.
A discussion of the two peaks of socialist radicalism in the U.S., the Debs period and the communist heyday of 1935-45. Communism in the Browder period bore some similarity to the earlier Hillquit-Berger socialism. The CPUSA gained strength through militant campaigns for the unemployed, striking workers, Negro rights, and civil liberties.

C216 CODE, Joseph B. "The Spanish War and Lying Propaganda." New York: Paulist Press, 1938. 48 pp.
A pro-Franco pamphlet by a member of the History Department of Catholic University, attacking the Protestants, Jews, socialists, and communists for spreading lying propaganda about the Spanish war.

C217 COE, Charles J. "Farmers in 1944." New York: Farm Research, 1944. 55 pp.
A call to farmers to support agreements reached at Teheran, which call for postwar peace through full farm production. Attacking the 78th Congress for sabotaging this program, the author urges readers to vote for Roosevelt in 1944 to assure peace and abundance, as planned at Teheran.

C218 .... "Food Now or Coffins Later: The Meaning of the World Food Crisis." New York: Farm Research, 1946. 32 pp.
A communist attack on American "scuttling" of the UNRRA program to provide food for the peoples of the world. The author calls for continuation of UNRRA, supervision of food distribution by the World Federation of Trade Unions, encouragement of land-reform programs, and long-term loans to help countries industrialize. He urges formation of a new, progressive, People's Party in the U.S.

C219 .... "Eisenhower's Farm Crisis." New York: Farm Research, 1953. 33 pp.
A communist critique of the Eisenhower farm program. It proposes reduced farm taxes, full-parity price supports, social security for farmers and agricultural workers, low-cost credit, restored East-West commerce, aid for small farmers, and a permanent farm debt moratorium law.

C220 COGLEY, John. The Failure of Anti-Communism, "Commonweal," 52 (July 21, 1950), 357-58.
An assertion that the long crusade of American Catholics against communism has failed, because Catholics have given too little time to Christianity itself. Almost anyone, from the Christian Fronters of 1940 to Senator McCarthy of 1950, could get sizable Catholic support by peddling anticommunism. A minority has stressed Catholic social thought and positive action.

C221 .... "Report on Blacklisting." Fund for the Republic, 1956. 1: "Movies." 312 pp. 2: "Radio-Television." 287 pp. App. Ind.
A report by the executive editor of "Commonweal" on the use of the blacklist to bar alleged communists or communist sympathizers from employment in Hollywood or in the radio-television industry. The Hollywood blacklist followed the 1947 movie hearings of the House Un-American Activities Committee, whereas in radio and television it began with the publication of "Red Channels," listing persons who were linked to communist causes. Reports by Harold W. Horowitz on legal aspects and by Dorothy B. Jones on film content are included in the volume on movies, as is a study by Marie Jahoda on employment policies in the volume on radio and television.

C222 COHEN, Elliot E. "The Yellow Dog Contract." New York: International Publishers, 1932. 15 pp.
Communist pamphlet describing the history and use of yellow dog contracts (anti-union employment contracts). Workers can prevent their use, not by joining AFL "phony" unions, but only by militant organization under Trade Union Unity League leadership.

C223 COHEN, Maximilian. The Executive Committee's Statement, "New York Communist," 1 (May 24, 1919), 6-7.

A letter to the New York "Call" which was refused publication, giving the left-wing version of the developing split in the Socialist Party. The right-wingers are accused of illegal "reorganization" of Local New York when faced with the threat of losing their majority in the Central Committee. Members are urged to oppose the state referendum on expulsion of the left wing.

C224   COHEN, Morris R. Why I Am Not a Communist, "Modern Monthly," 8 (April 1934), 138-42.
Cohen rejects communism because its program of civil war and dictatorship would bring more miseries than the communists seek to remove. The gains to mankind from free inquiry, free discussion, and accommodation should not be belittled. The forces of intolerance should not be strengthened. (Part of a symposium on communism, reprinted as "The Meaning of Marx: A Symposium.")

C225   COHEN, Murray, and FUCHS, Robert F. Communism's Challenge and the Constitution, "Cornell Law Quarterly," 34 (Winter 1948), 182-219; (Spring 1949), 352-75.
An analysis of the conspiratorial nature of the Communist Party and of the defeated Mundt-Nixon bill as the pattern for future antisubversive legislation. Constitutional validity would have to rest on proof of clear and present danger. Yet a great deal may be accomplished by publicity.

C226   COHEN, Simon. I Accuse the Communist Party, "American Federationist," 46 (Dec. 1939), 1330-35. Also published in "Painter and Decorator," Sept. 1939.
An indictment of the communists who transformed Russia into a prison state, sabotaged the republic in Germany, undermined the people's front in France, and in the U.S. destroyed the Farmer-Labor Party in 1923 and split the Socialist Party twice. Though they now pretend to love America, they have not changed their character.

C227   COHN, Roy M. A Struggle to the Death with the Communists: Stop Investigating the Investigators, "Vital Speeches of the Day," 21 (Oct. 15, 1954), 789-93.
A view of the work and methods of congressional investigating committees as indispensable and justified. Much of the propaganda against congressional committees which have been fighting communism stems from communist sources; this has diverted the public's attention from its real enemies, the communists.

C228   COLE, Albert M. The Red Trail in New Deal Washington, "National Republic," 38 (Oct. 1950), 3-4 ff.
An account by a Congressman from Kansas of the communist penetration of the federal government, beginning with the formation of a Party cell in the Agricultural Adjustment Administration in 1934. Efforts of the House Committee on Un-American Activities to expose communist influence in government are reviewed. The "Amerasia" case is reported in some detail.

C229   COLEGROVE, Kenneth, and BARTLETT, Hall. "The Menace of Communism." Princeton, N.J.: Van Nostrand, 1962. 294 pp. App. Bibliog. Ind.
An analysis of communism for high school use, almost all of it reprinted from Colegrove's "Democracy versus Communism." Most of the volume deals with the USSR and other countries under communist control. Chapter 12, pp. 253-74, on the Party program in the U.S., deals with the origin and growth of the Party here, its methods of operation, and federal controls of communist activities.

C230   COLEMAN, Jerry. Farm Legislation and the

People's Front, "Communist," 16 (Oct. 1937), 946-53.
The Party must make progressive farm legislation an integral part of the people's front program. The author proposes amendments to the AAA, endorses the Boileau farm tenancy bill, and discusses proposals for farm mortgaging and refinancing.

C231   .... "A Square Deal for the Farmer." New York: Workers Library, 1938. 15 pp.
A communist defense of the Agricultural Adjustment Administration during the popular front period. Asserting that the New Deal is working in the interests of the small farmers, the author urges support of Roosevelt's progressive farm program.

C232   .... Farmers Advance in the Movement for the People's Front, "Communist," 17 (Feb. 1938), 169-76.
The pact between the Farmers' Union and Labor's Non-partisan League is hailed as an indication of growing accord in the demands of farmers and workers. The formation of farmer-labor legislative conferences throughout the country is urged in preparation for the 1938 congressional elections.

C233   COLEMAN, McAlister. Who Are the Communists? "World Tomorrow," 15 (Oct. 5, 1932), 323-25.
One of a series of articles on the personnel of the various political parties. The author analyzes the backgrounds of communist leaders, including Foster, Browder, Engdahl, Weinstone, Minor, Dunn, and Amter. Some of the best communist intelligences in this country, such as Lovestone, Cannon, and Weisbord, are outside the official Party.

C234   .... Communism Strikes, "Today," 1 (May 26, 1934), 3-4.
Communists often provoke rioting in strikes and before relief agencies to get publicity and to teach their young people the technique of street fighting. They seek to infiltrate strikes, to get a foothold in the labor movement. They have "spheres of influence" through the International Labor Defense, the National Student League, and other Party-controlled organizations. (For a communist response see William Francis Dunne, "Raymond Moley: Provocateur-in-Chief for the New Deal," in "New Masses," June 26 and July 3, 1934.)

C235   COLLINS, Karl. The Rise and Decline of a Crusader, "New Leader," 29 (May 11, 1946), 8 ff.
An account of the news and editorial policies of the newspaper "PM" under Ralph Ingersoll, who hired mostly Party-liners and supported Party policies. Ingersoll had expected to publish a popular-front paper, but the line had changed by the time "PM" appeared. His efforts to discharge anticommunists created a problem for the Party-dominated Newspaper Guild in New York.

C236   COLLINS, Mary. "Democracy in Danger." New York: Workers Library for the National Campaign Committee of the Communist Party, 1938. 15 pp.
Political campaign pamphlet of the popular front period calls for the election of a progressive, New Deal Congress, the defeat of all reactionaries, and a collective security foreign policy.

C237   .... "The Fight for Recovery: Stop the Sit-Down Strike of Big Business." New York: Workers Library for the National Campaign Committee of the Communist Party, 1938. 24 pp.
Popular front period political campaign pamphlet stating that reactionaries and big business withhold production,

causing massive unemployment. Creation of a genuine democratic front behind the New Deal, despite its inadequacies, will stop reaction and keep the New Deal and Roosevelt from vacillating from a progressive program.

C238 COLLINS, Richard. Confessions of a Red Screenwriter, "New Leader," 35 (Oct. 6, 1952), 7-10.
The writer of the idyllic film, "Song of Russia," a member of the CP from 1937 to 1947, tells why he joined the Party and later broke with it. Communists have a sense of personal security, with an answer for every question; they view the world in terms of black and white. It was impossible for the author to be a communist and the kind of writer he wanted to be.

C239 COLMAN, Louis. "Night Riders in Gallup." New York: International Labor Defense, 1935. 14 pp.
An account of the "frame-up" murder prosecution of union leaders of the Gallup-American Coal Company as a means of smashing the United Mine Workers and the Unemployed Councils. An appeal is made for protests to the governor and to the secretary of labor, as well as for contributions.

C240 .... "'Equal Justice': Year Book of the Fight for Democratic Rights, 1936-1937." Introd. by Anna Damon. New York: International Labor Defense, 1937. 104 pp. Bibliog.
A record of the year's activities of the ILD, including cases arising under criminal syndicalist laws and growing out of strikes and vigilante actions. The work of other defense organizations is summarized.

C241 COLONY, David C. The Church Made Communism, "Forum," 92 (Aug. 1934), 67-72.
An assertion that communism has become the force it is today because organized religion has ignored social evils. The author recommends that all religious groups unite on a program of social reform. Only in this way can communism be combatted.

C242 .... Which Churches Are American? "Forum," 99 (June 1938), 338-40.
An assertion that organized Christianity will be to blame if either fascism or communism comes to the U.S. Both the Protestant and Catholic hierarchies are indicted for willingness to embrace a totalitarian philosophy (communism in the former's case, fascism in the latter's) in order to combat the totalitarian tendencies of the other.

C243 COLTON, Peter. The Eisenhower Congress and the 1954 Elections, "Political Affairs," 32 (Nov. 1953), 36-53.
The 1954 congressional elections will test the reactionary, prowar policies of the Eisenhower-Big Business Administration. Big Business has had its way in the Eisenhower 83rd Congress, with "give-aways," the ending of price controls, and tax policy. Eisenhower has not opposed McCarthyism-McCarranism. Issues on which broad legislative struggles can be developed are outlined.

C244 COLUM, Mary M. Marxism and Literature, "Forum," 91 (March 1934), 145-49.
An assertion that Marxian precepts are not a guide to literature, but rules for trade writing. Recent proletarian writing reveals a total ignorance of literature. Though one who wants to write a pamphlet about the class struggle can use any of these proletarian novels as models, one who wants to write literature must look elsewhere for inspiration.

C245 .... Literature and the Social Left, "Saturday Review of Literature," 13 (Nov. 2, 1935), 3-4 ff.
A discussion of proletarian writers, most of whom are leftist only in a social sense, based on selections from "Proletarian Literature in the United States," edited by Granville Hicks, and "The American Writers Congress," edited by Henry Hart. These writers who aim at propaganda produce neither literature nor good trade writing, nor good propaganda.

C246 "COLUMBIA LAW REVIEW," Federal Sedition Bills: Speech Restriction in Theory and Practice, 35 (June 1935), 917-27.
A history of efforts to enact sedition legislation since the days of World War I. Such legislation has been used to combat demands of labor groups, rather than to meet imminent danger of violent overthrow of the government.

C247 ..., Constitutionality of the Taft-Hartley Non-Communist Affidavit Provision, 48 (March 1948), 253-64.
A discussion of legal questions arising from the noncommunist affidavit provision of the Taft-Hartley Act, including equal protection of the laws, freedom of association, freedom of speech, and guilt by association. The provision is opposed as unwise and of doubtful constitutionality.

C248 ..., Designation of Organization as Subversive by Attorney General: A Cause of Action, 48 (Nov. 1948), 1050-67.
An organization listed by the Attorney General as subversive has standing to challenge the constitutionality of the action, since it is damaged in property and reputation. Constitutional questions are to be found in possible lack of due process in the Attorney General's investigation and determination.

C249 ..., Self-Incrimination and Federal Anti-Communist Measures, 51 (Feb. 1951), 206-19.
An analysis of the Supreme Court interpretation of the Smith Act in the Dennis case, emphasizing the need to ascertain which individuals or groups are communist, and the effect on this of the Fifth Amendment guarantee against self-incrimination. Attention is paid to federal employment, legislative hearings, the Taft-Hartley affidavit, and the McCarran Internal Security Act.

C250 ..., The Internal Security Act of 1950, 51 (May 1951), 606-60.
A detailed examination of the Internal Security Act of 1950, with attention to Congressional findings, the requirement of registration for communist action and communist-front groups, sedition, control of communist aliens, and emergency detention provisions. Problems of constitutionality, effectiveness, and reconciliation of national security with civil liberties are considered.

C251 ..., The Rosenberg Case: Some Reflections on Federal Criminal Law, 44 (Feb. 1954), 219-60.
A discussion of six legal issues raised by the Rosenberg case: the admission of evidence of Party affiliation, the definition of a conspiracy for procedural purposes, the necessity for corroboration of accomplice testimony, the constitutionality of the death penalty here, the Supreme Court's power to vacate a stay of execution, and the Atomic Energy Act's implied repeal of the Espionage Act. The article concludes that, whether or not the Rosenbergs were guilty, their rights were not fully protected in the last stage of the litigation.

C252 COMBS, Richard E. How Communists Make Stooges out of Movie Stars, "American Legion Magazine," 46 (May 1949), 14-15 ff.
An account of communist infiltration of the motion picture industry, written by the chief counsel of the California

State Senate Fact-Finding Committee on Un-American Activities. The Party has sought to lure screen celebrities into front organizations, to raise funds in Hollywood, and to win control of studio unions. A list of leading Party fronts is attached, with the names of Hollywood figures who have joined each.

C253 COMERFORD, Frank. "The New World." New York: Appleton, 1920. 364 pp.
A critical account of Bolshevik objectives and practices in Russia and of the Third International. Chapter 19, pp. 224-49, deals with "Bolshevism in the United States." It describes the program of the left wing of the Socialist Party and the development out of it of two rival communist parties, the Communist Labor Party and the Communist Party of America. The IWW is viewed as a third Bolshevik group.

C254 COMMAGER, Henry Steele. Washington Witch-Hunt, "Nation," 164 (April 5, 1947), 385-88.
A detailed criticism of President Truman's executive order on loyalty by a professor of history at Columbia University, who calls it an invitation to witch-hunting. The provisions, which are loosely drawn, are said to invoke the doctrine of guilt by association.

C255 .... Should We Outlaw the Communist Party? "New York Times Magazine," Aug. 22, 1948. 7 ff.
An argument against outlawing the Communist Party, based on careful consideration of effectiveness, constitutionality, and policy. Outlawing the Party would only drive communists further underground, and could easily lead to suppression of free speech and thought.

C256 .... Red-Baiting in the Colleges, "New Republic," 121 (July 25, 1949), 10-13.
A discussion of the University of Washington's dismissal of three faculty members because of Communist Party membership, which was considered conclusive evidence of incompetence and professional unfitness. A faculty committee had recommended that the cases turn on proof of incompetence. Though abuse is possible, complete freedom of inquiry is essential in our universities.

C257 ..., and others. "Civil Liberties under Attack." Foreword by Clair Wilcox. Philadelphia: University of Pennsylvania Press, 1951. 155 pp.
A series of lectures appraising the current state of civil liberties, under attack as a result of the current fear of communism. Lectures include "The Pragmatic Necessity for Freedom," by Henry Steele Commager; "Progress in Civil Rights," by Robert K. Carr; "Investigations of Radicalism and Laws Against Subversion," by Zechariah Chafee, Jr.; "Security, Secrecy, and the Advancement of Science," by Walter Gellhorn; "Censorship and the Arts," by Curtis Bok; and "Freedom in Education," by James P. Baxter, III. (The Chafee lecture is abstracted separately.)

C258 .... Guilt—and Innocence—by Association, "New York Times Magazine," Nov. 8, 1953, 13 ff.
A professor of history at Columbia denounces the doctrine of guilt by association as wrong logically, legally, practically, historically, and morally. Defended as a way of detecting subversives, it subverts democratic principles, destroys constitutional guarantees, and corrupts faith in ourselves and our countrymen.

C259 .... "Freedom, Loyalty, Dissent." New York: Oxford University Press, 1954. 155 pp.
A collection of essays that appeared over a six-year period. The argument in all is that we must preserve freedom of inquiry and dissent; that freedom, far from being a luxury for periods of security, prosperity, and enlightenment, is antecedent to these and necessary for their attainment. Essay titles include "The Necessity of Freedom," "The Necessity of Experimentation," "Free Enterprise in Ideas," "Guilt by Association?" and "Who is Loyal to America?"

C260 COMMITTEE FOR A DEMOCRATIC FAR EASTERN POLICY. "Facts and Documents Concerning the Far East for the Delegates to the National Conference on American Policy in China and the Far East, New York City, January 24-25, 1948." New York: The Committee, n.d. [1948]. 71 pp. Mimeo.
Material compiled by a communist front organization for a conference called by it. The section on China asserts that the United Nations Relief and Rehabilitation Administration was used by the U.S. to aid Chiang Kai-Shek and fight the communists. Material favorable to the Chinese communists is included. The sections on Japan, Korea, the Philippines, Indonesia, Viet Nam, and India criticize American policy in these areas.

C261 .... "Facts on the Korean Crisis." New York: The Committee, n.d. [1950]. 12 pp.
A communist front organization opposes American participation in the Korean War, suggesting that the South Koreans were really the aggressors. U.S. policy in Formosa is also opposed.

C262 .... "Far East Spotlight: The Korean Crisis: An Analysis of American Policy." New York: The Committee, n.d. [1950]. 22 pp. Mimeo.
Opposition to U.S. participation in the Korean war, and support for North Korea, by a communist front group. It calls for withdrawal of all foreign troops from Korea, UN peace negotiations including North Korea and communist China, U.S. recognition of communist China, and its admission to the UN.

C263 .... "Far East Spotlight: U.S. Dilemma in Japan an American Disaster in the Making." New York: The Committee, n.d. [1950 or 1951?]. 16 pp.
An assertion that American Far Eastern policy is based on a rebuilt and remilitarized Japan, and an attack on utilization of Japanese naval bases by the American fleet. However, the Japanese increasingly resist American military, political, and economic repression, and American policy is alienating the people of Asia, who rightfully fear the revival of Japanese imperialism, from the U.S.

C264 COMMITTEE FOR DEFENSE OF CIVIL RIGHTS OF COMMUNISTS. "The Conspiracy against Free Elections." Pittsburgh: The Committee, n.d. [1940]. 24 pp.
A presentation of the case of 30 defendants in Pittsburgh, tried on various charges in connection with nominating petitions for Communist Party candidates. The indictments, the pamphlet charges, are part of a move against the Communist Party by the Roosevelt Administration, to silence the only real opponents of the war program.

C265 COMMITTEE IN DEFENSE OF CARL MARZANI. "The Case of Carl Marzani." New York: The Committee, n.d. [1947]. 16 pp.
A defense of Carl Marzani, convicted of perjury for denying that he was a Party member when working for the OSS during World War II. Included are a statement by his lawyer, Arthur Garfield Hays; an article by I. F. Stone; and statements by such people as Henry A. Wallace, Eleanor Roosevelt, and Congressman Adolph J. Sabath.

C266 COMMITTEE OF EXPELLED AND SUSPENDED CITY COLLEGE STUDENTS. "City College and

War: Why Were Twenty-One Students Expelled?"
New York: The Committee, 1933. 19 pp.
A defense of students, expelled from or suspended by City College following a riot on May 29, 1933, caused by rival parades, one organized by the college's Military Science Department and the other by communist and socialist student groups. Mass struggle is urged to reinstate the City College "fighters for peace," and organized mass action is called for to stop the war makers.

C267 COMMITTEE TO COMBAT COMMUNISM. "Souvenir Booklet of Anti-Communist Mass Meeting, January 9, 1931." New York: The Committee, 1931. 32 pp.
Speeches at a meeting of patriotic societies, protesting communist activity and urging the outlawing of the Communist Party, the vigorous use of existing laws to keep it under surveillance and control, the boycott of USSR goods, and the continued nonrecognition of the USSR. Speakers included Martin Littleton, Matthew Woll, Rev. Edmund Walsh, and Hamilton Fish.

C268 COMMITTEE TO DEFEND ALEXANDER TRACHTENBERG. "Books on Trial: The Case of Alexander Trachtenberg." New York: International Publishers, 1952. 23 pp.
A defense of the director of the communist publishing house, International Publishers, charging that Trachtenberg's indictment under the Smith Act was aimed at freedom of the press. A biography of Trachtenberg is included.

C269 COMMITTEE TO DEFEND THE PITTSBURGH FIVE. "The Frame-up of Benjamin Lowell Careathers." Pittsburgh: The Committee, 1953. 24 pp.
The opening statement to the Court by Careathers, defendent in the Smith Act trial in Pittsburgh. He defends the Party, denies that it advocates overthrow of the American government by force, and attacks the entire Smith Act proceedings.

C270 COMMITTEE TO SUPPORT THE CHINA DAILY NEWS. "The Facts behind the China Daily News Case." New York: The Committee, n.d. [1952?]. 16 pp.
An attack on the indictment of the "China Daily News," Chinese-language paper published in New York, and its editor, Eugene Moy, under the "Trading with the Enemy Act." Details of the harrassment of the paper by pro-Chiang Kai-Shek elements in the Chinese-American community are given.

C271 "COMMON SENSE," Radical Parties (II): The Communist Party of America, 3 (Nov. 1934), 12-14.
A survey of the membership (26,000 with 500,000 sympathizers), fronts, and publications of the Party, with a short history of it, written by the editors. Attention is paid to splits in the movement and to obstacles to its growth; among the latter are the belief that the end justifies the means, the attitude toward democracy and civil liberties, the view of the New Deal, and the terminology used.

C272 . . ., The Red Menace Again, 7 (March 1938), 3-5.
Editorial regret that a "red scare" is in progress in the U.S. The communists have shown energy and courage in organizing unions and the unemployed, and have had success with intellectuals and liberals. But their strategy is determined by the Comintern, which is dominated by Soviet foreign-policy needs.

C273 "COMMONWEAL," Despotisms and Democracy, 25 (Dec. 4, 1936), 141-43.
An assertion that the Methodist Federation for Social

Service has permitted itself to become an instrument for communist propaganda by publishing the attack against the Vatican by Dr. Harry F. Ward, one of the secretaries of the Federation, and also chairman of the American Committee Against War and Fascism. Ward's statement is attacked as deceptive.

C274 . . ., The Communist Threat, 71 (Oct. 30, 1959), 131-34.
Four previous editorials on communism, asserting that, as long as communism is a political and military force as well as an ideology, we will have to emphasize guns in addition to giving the world bread; that, while anticommunist oratory is on the upswing, military budgets are being cut; that conflict between the U.S. and the Soviet Union will persist as long as communism remains what it is; and that the foreign aid program is a valuable asset in fighting communism.

C275 "COMMUNIST" (organ of the Communist Party of America), The Communist Party and the Communist Labor Party, 1 (Sept. 27, 1919), 10-12.
Comment on events which culminated in the creation of two communist parties in Chicago in 1919. The Communist Labor Party's membership, composition, and program are criticized. Documents exchanged between the two parties are reproduced.

C276 . . ., The Workers' Struggle Calls You Comrades: Proclamation to the Party Membership, 1 (Nov. 29, 1919), 6-7.
Recommendations to the Party membership on activity in the face of raids and arrests. Without specifically saying so, the leadership advocates going underground. Party shop branches are advocated, to distribute leaflets and facilitate agitation. Problems of membership growth are discussed.

C277 . . ., The Party Crisis, 2 (May 1, 1920), 2 ff.
Denunciation of the pro-Ruthenberg "secessionist" faction in the Communist Party of America, from the viewpoint of the foreign language federation majority of the Central Executive Committee. The CEC accuses Ruthenberg of equivocation on the question of force and violence and other matters of principle, in an effort to "run after the masses."

C278 . . ., Statement to the Membership, 2 (May 1, 1920), 3 ff.
An account of the controversy of the Central Executive Committee majority (in control of the foreign language federations) with the pro-Ruthenberg, "secessionist" faction. Negotiations between the two factions having reached an impasse, the Ruthenberg faction withdrew from the CPA. The membership is called upon to support the CEC, and is reminded that only the CEC can call a convention.

C279 . . ., At Last the Centrists Unite! 2 (July 1, 1920), 3 ff.
An attack on the United Communist Party, recently formed by merger of the Ruthenberg faction, formerly in the CPA, with the Communist Labor Party. Ruthenberg is held responsible for various mistakes and omissions in the UCP program. The UCP position on violence, parliamentarianism, industrial unionism, and party organization indicates that it has renounced Bolshevism.

C280 . . ., Constitution of the Communist Party of America, Adopted at Its Second Convention, 2 (Aug. 1, 1920), 3 ff.
The constitution adopted at the second convention of the CPA. Also included is a resolution on boycotting the

coming elections. (The second convention of the CPA followed the departure of the Ruthenberg faction, which merged with the Communist Labor Party to form the United Communist Party.)

C281 "COMMUNIST" (organ of the Communist Party of America), A Criticism of the Program and Constitution of the United Communist Party, 2 (Aug. 1, 1920), 4-5 ff.
The newly formed UCP is characterized as Menshevik and centrist. Its constitution, by breaking up the language federations, guarantees control to the centrists. The UCP merely amalgamated two small organizations of adventurers and charlatans. (The UCP united the Ruthenberg faction, formerly in the CPA, with the Communist Labor Party.)

C282 . . ., The Program of the Communist Party of America: Adopted at Its Second Convention, 2 (Aug. 1, 1920), 1 ff.
The program reaffirms the CPA's belief in the revolutionary nature of the class struggle, aimed at conquest of political power. Parliamentarianism must be restricted to use of a forum for revolutionary agitation. (The second convention of the CPA followed the departure of the Ruthenberg faction, which merged with the Communist Labor Party to form the United Communist Party.)

C283 . . ., The Second Convention of the Communist Party of America," 2 (Aug. 1, 1920), 6 ff.
A description of actions taken at the CPA's second convention, held following the departure of the Ruthenberg faction (which merged with the Communist Labor Party to form the United Communist Party). The CPA admits having lost 65 per cent of its membership, though it denies Ruthenberg's claim that a majority joined the UCP. Major issues at the convention were questions of parliamentarianism and the degree of centralization.

C284 . . ., Answer of the Central Executive Council, Communist Party of America to Communist International Appeal for Unity, 2 (Sept. 15, 1920), 3-6.
The CPA reviews the history of unity negotiations, discusses how it differs in program from the United Communist Party, questions whether any party can become a "mass organization" as required by the Comintern, and describes the CPA's policy toward unionism. A change in the UCP's program and leadership, plus an opportunity for the CPA to present its views to the Comintern, must precede unification.

C285 . . ., Resolution adopted by the Executive Committee of the Communist International in the Fraina Case, 2 (Nov. 15, [1920]), 1. Also appears in "Communist" (organ of the United Communist Party), no. 11 n.d. [Nov. 1920?], 8.
Official decision by the Executive Committee of the Communist International in the case of Louis C. Fraina, charged by Santeri Nuorteva, Secretary of the New York Soviet Bureau, with having been a Department of Justice agent. The ECCI decided unanimously that Fraina was innocent; after hearing new evidence from Nuorteva, it sustained its decision. Nuorteva was warned to discontinue his charges against Fraina and to make a public apology.

C286 . . ., The Unity Proceedings between the Communist Party and the United Communist Party of America, 2 (Nov. 15, 1920), 4 ff.
Reports from representatives to the Second Congress of the Communist International, correspondence, and commentary on the unity proceedings between the CPA and the UCP. The major issue was the basis of representation in a unified group. (Despite Comintern pressure, unification did not take place until May 1921. Additional

correspondence appears in "Communist" [organ of the Communist Party of America], 2 [Dec. 15, 1920], 8, and 2 [Jan. 5, 1921], 5 ff.)

C287 . . ., Constitution of the Communist Party of America: Adopted by the Third Convention, February, 1921, 2 (March 1, 1921), 6-7.
The constitution adopted at the third convention of the CPA. Section 9 on discipline defines, more precisely than before, offenses in violation of Party discipline.

C288 . . ., Program of the Communist Party of America: Adopted at the Third Convention, February, 1921, 2 (March 1, 1921), 3-5.
The program adopted at the CPA's third convention, which followed the second congress of the Communist International. The major dispute occurred over the section on armed insurrection, which was modified to conform to the theses of the Communist International. Other topics included types of political action, the trade union question, factory committees, communist nuclei, imperialism and the colonial question, and problems of agricultural labor.

C289 . . ., Report of the Third Convention, 2 (March 1, 1921), 1-2.
An account of the third convention of the Communist Party of America, held secretly in February 1921, and attended by 50 delegates representing 6,819 members. The convention unanimously adopted the 21 points of the Communist International. The secretary's report is summarized. Debates occurred over the wording on armed insurrection, and over unity negotiations with the United Communist Party.

C290 . . ., The United Communist Party and the Communist Party of America United: An Account of the Joint Unity Convention, 1 (July 1921), 1-3.
Report on the unity convention, held on the insistence of the Comintern with a Comintern representative present. The convention, which had to overcome numerous deadlocks, lasted two weeks. The program was largely that of the old CPA, with additions dealing with labor organizations.

C291 . . ., Our Attitude toward the Workers Party, 1 (Jan. 1922), 1-6.
Report of the establishment of the Workers Party of America, the "legal arm" of the underground CPA. The group was created primarily by two organizations—the American Labor Alliance, made up of auxiliary communist organizations, and the Workers Council, composed of recently-expelled socialists who endorsed the Third International. The Workers Council group was opposed to continuation of an underground party. (A Left Opposition, opposing the formation of the Workers Party, split for a time from the Communist Party.)

C292 . . ., Decisions of the Second Annual Convention, 1 (Aug.-Sept. 1922), 3-5.
A report of decisions made at the secret second convention of the CPA, held in Bridgman, Mich., in August 1922. Decisions dealt with trade union policy, relations with a legal political party, the program of the legal party, return of a leftist faction, the function of Party discussion, forbidding of caucuses, formation of a Party council, and composition of the executive committee. (The convention ended prematurely with a raid by federal and local authorities.)

C293 . . ., A View of Our Party Condition: Extract from Report of the Representative of the C.I. to the Presidium of the C.I., 1 (Aug.-Sept. 1922), 10-14.
The report of the Comintern representative on the second

convention of the Communist Party of America, held at Bridgman, Mich., in August 1922. The Comintern representative forced the factions to maintain unity, personally drafting many of the resolutions. The main issues were whether to engage in open, legal activity, and whether to liquidate the underground Party.

C294 "COMMUNIST" (organ of the 1922 Left Opposition to the Communist Party of America), Constitution of the Communist Party of America: Adopted at the Emergency Convention, January, 1922, 1 (Feb. 1922), 3-7.
Constitution adopted by the 1922 Left Opposition to the Communist Party of America at an emergency convention in January 1922. (This new splinter group also adopted the name "Communist Party of America.")

C295 . . ., Emergency Convention, 1 (Feb. 1922), 1-3.
A report of the convention of the Left Opposition to the Communist Party of America, which opposed endorsement by the CPA of its legal arm, the Workers Party of America. The convention favored, for the future, creation of another legal political party, but under direct control of the Communist Party, to co-exist with an illegal party.

C296 . . ., Documents Received from Executive Committee of the Communist International, 1 (June 1922), 5.
Resolution adopted by the Executive Committee of the Comintern, March 11, 1922, ordering the Communist Party of America and its Left Opposition to reunite. The split had occurred in January 1922, because the Left Opposition opposed creation of the Workers Party of America, a legal political party.

C297 "COMMUNIST" (organ of the Ruthenberg faction formerly in the Communist Party of America), Agreement for a Unity Conference: Between the Communist Party and Communist Labor Party, 2 (May 22, 1920), 3.
This document, agreed to by the Communist Labor Party and the Ruthenberg faction in the Communist Party of America, contains seven "fundamental principles" in harmony with the position of the Third International, upon which all parties who agree shall unite.

C298 "COMMUNIST" (organ of the CPUSA), The Significance of the Comintern Address, 8 (June 1929), 291-302.
An account of the Comintern's decisions on the American Party, following the Sixth World Congress. The Comintern Address, prepared by its commission on the American question, was accepted by the representatives of the American Minority, but not by Gitlow, Lovestone, and some other members of the Majority. A struggle must now be carried on against a concealed opposition in the American Party, with which Lovestone is now aligned. (In late June 1929, Lovestone and his followers were expelled from the Party.)

C299 . . ., The Internal Situation in the C.P. of U.S.A.: Resolution Adopted by American-Canadian Students in the Lenin School, Moscow, 9 (Jan. 1930), 86-92.
Criticism of the CPUSA for having failed to concretize and put into practice the line of the Communist International. Remnants of Lovestoneism are to be found, particularly in the draft program submitted to the Cleveland Trade Union Conference (where the Trade Union Unity League was formed).

C300 . . ., U.S. Agriculture and Tasks of the Communist Party, U.S.A., 9 (Feb. 1930), 104-20; (March), 280-85; (April), 359-75.
Draft program proposed by the Central Executive Committee of the Party for general discussion. The farm crisis can be resolved only by collectivization. The Party must broaden the base and improve the program of the United Farmers Educational League, and recruit agrarians into the CP and into the agricultural workers union of the Trade Union Unity League.

C301 . . ., Draft Program for Negro Farmers in the Southern States, 9 (March 1930), 246-56.
Almost all Negro farmers in America are part of the agrarian proletariat of agricultural laborers, small farmers, tenants, or sharecroppers. Only by an alliance with the working class for the overthrow of capitalism and the establishment of a proletarian dictatorship can they save themselves from ruin.

C302 . . ., Resolution on the Negro Question in the United States, 10 (Feb. 1931), 153-67.
The final text of the resolution, confirmed by the Executive Committee of the Communist International, setting forth the CPUSA line of self-determination in the Black Belt. If the proletariat has come into power in the U.S., communists will oppose separation of the Negro republic, though the Negro population of the Black Belt will have freedom of choice.

C303 . . ., The Fight against the Capitalist Offensive and the Unity of the Employed and the Unemployed, 11 (Sept. 1932), 771-85.
Prosperity is not just around the corner, despite the capitalist press. U.S. imperialists, aided by the AFL, seek to divide the employed and the unemployed. The Communist Party is for united struggle of employed and unemployed. The Red unions should fight for unemployment insurance, and for development of unemployed councils on the broadest united-front basis.

C304 . . ., Forward in the Line of the Twelfth Plenum of the E.C.C.I., 12 (Jan. 1933), 3-17.
The growth of the Soviet Union and the crisis of world capitalism have created a revolutionary upsurge. The CPUSA reaffirms the line of the Twelfth Plenum of the Communist International that a majority of the working class will be won by directing the main blows against the social democracy; the major tactic is the united front from below.

C305 . . ., For United Action against Fascism, 12 (April 1933), 323-36.
An editorial following Hitler's rise to power in Germany, noting that the Communist International is willing to engage in united action with the Second International against fascism. The Communist International has always been willing, but the Second International has refused. The CPUSA has issued a similar call to the AFL, the Socialist Party, and the Conference for Progressive Labor Action.

C306 . . ., The Roosevelt Program—An Attack upon the Toiling Masses, 12 (May 1933), 419-25.
An editorial attack upon the Roosevelt program as a desperate effort to save finance capitalism that will further lower the living standard of the masses. Among the specific measures discussed are those dealing with banking, public works, and agriculture.

C307 . . ., The Eighth Convention of Our Party, 13 (May 1934), 427-29.
Many of the convention delegates were industrial workers, native Americans and Negroes, showing that the Party has taken advantage of the depression to recruit widely. To combat a high turnover in membership, recent recruits must be better indoctrinated.

C308 . . ., The Lessons of May Day, 13 (June 1934), 515-23.

Many more people participated in the May Day parades organized by the Communist Party and its United Front than in those organized by the socialists. Not enough effort was made to recruit new members and to distribute communist propaganda, as distinct from that of the United Front.

C309 "COMMUNIST" (organ of the CPUSA), The Darrow Report, 13 (July 1934), 611-15.
The report demonstrated that NRA, like any planning within capitalism, has led to the growth of monopolies, injuring small business. The communists can profit if they can convince small business that trust-busting is a poor remedy, compared to aiding the workers to overthrow capitalism.

C310 . . ., In the Midst of Great Historic Battles, 13 (Aug. 1934), 739-50.
An editorial view of current strikes, especially the San Francisco general strike, as representing higher forms of class action. The strikes show a growing political character, as American capitalism becomes more fascist. AFL leaders, supported by the Socialist Party, again played a strikebreaking role. The Communist Party provided revolutionary leadership.

C311 . . ., Results and Lessons of the Elections, 13 (Dec. 1934), 1187-94.
The election success of New Deal candidates was due to Roosevelt's "Left" demagogy. The vote for CP candidates, though larger than in the past, was not large enough. This reflects a failure to politicalize economic struggles, and to expose the demagogy of Roosevelt and his trade-union reformist supporters.

C312 . . ., Roy Howard's Interview with Joseph Stalin, 15 (April 1936), 337-45.
The text of the talk between Stalin and Roy Howard of the Scripps-Howard publications. Stalin said that Germany and Japan are the countries most menacing to Russia, that the American Communist Party was created by and is controlled by Americans, and that Russians have the most personal freedom because they are freed from exploitation and want.

C313 . . ., Special Party Convention Supplement, 15 (Aug. 1936), 747-93.
Reports from the four concentration districts to the Party's Ninth Convention, June 24-28, 1936. William Weinstone reports on Detroit, B. K. Gebert on Pittsburgh, Morris Childs on Chicago, and John Williamson on Cleveland. The reports outline Party activities in union organizing drives, in forming shop nuclei, and in stimulating farmer-labor political organization.

C314 . . ., Election Campaign Outline for 1936, 15 (Sept. 1936), 819-28.
The communist platform for 1936, including adequate relief, higher wages, a 30-hour week, taxation of the rich, nationalization of banks and monopolies, cooperation with Russia, and collective security for peace. The Republicans oppose these demands, the Democrats are ineffective in achieving them, the Union Party ignores them, and the socialists favor only some of them.

C315 . . ., Twenty Years of the Communist Party of the U.S.A., 1919-1939, 18 (Sept. 1939).
A special issue reviewing the entire 20-year period of the communist movement in the U.S. Included are Earl Browder, "Some Remarks on the Twentieth Anniversary of the Communist Party of the USA"; William Z. Foster, "Twenty Years of Communist Trade Union Policy"; James W. Ford, "The Struggle for the Building of the Modern Liberation Movement of the Negro People"; Ella Reeve Bloor, "The American Woman"; V. J. Jerome, "Forerunners"; Irene Browder, "The National Groups in the Fight for Democracy"; Alexander Trachtenberg, "The Soviet Union and the American People"; and Robert Minor, "Data on the Development of American Agriculture in the Twentieth Century." (The articles by Earl Browder, Foster, Ford, Irene Browder, and Minor are abstracted separately.)

C316 . . ., Convention Number: Resolutions and Reports, 19 (July 1940).
Reports and resolutions of the Party's eleventh national convention, May 30-June 2, 1940. Included are Earl Browder's report, "The Domestic Reactionary Counterpart of the War Policy of the Bourgeoisie"; William Z. Foster's speech, "The Three Basic Tasks of the Communist Peace Policy"; the resolutions adopted by the convention; and James S. Allen's report to the Farm Conference of the convention, "The Farmers and the Struggle against the War Program." (Each item is abstracted separately.)

C317 . . ., Browder 50th Birthday Number, 20 (June 1941).
An entire issue dedicated to Earl Browder, with many tributes from Party leaders and attempts to further the campaign to free him from prison. Articles emphasize his contribution to the fight for peace, his analysis of the imperialist war, his defense of the oppressed peoples of the Americas, his leadership in the Party, his friendship for the youth, and his contributions to the solution of Party problems in the South and on the West Coast.

C318 . . ., The Working Class and the National Front against Hitlerism: An Editorial Article, 20 (Sept. 1941), 763-75.
The working class must be united in a national front that will work to defeat Hitlerism. Although the CIO has gone far in this direction, many workers are still misled by John L. Lewis and other appeasers. Workers' rights and living standards must be maintained, profiteering prevented, and workers' representatives given a voice in the direction of industry.

C319 . . ., The Battle of Production, 20 (Oct. 1941), 851-67.
A plea to workers to recognize that an efficient production system is of the highest priority. Strikes and other interruptive activities are not appropriate, because the Hitler threat can be met only by full employment of all resources to supply materials for the Eastern front and prepare to open a Western front.

C320 . . ., Labor Unity—The Demand of the Hour, 20 (Oct. 1941), 868-75.
Labor unity is of increased importance because national unity is needed to defeat Nazi Germany. The working class must be the backbone of the national front against Hitlerism. The Party recommends to the coming AFL and CIO conventions that no steps be allowed to sharpen the conflict between them, while a joint committee explores possibilities of merger.

C321 . . ., Toward Labor Unity, 21 (March 1942), 99-113.
An editorial acclaiming establishment of the Labor Victory Board as the right step toward joint labor action in the war emergency. The Board, which will provide for labor participation in government policies, represents progress toward organic labor unity.

C322 . . ., Labor Must Act to Open a Western Front Now: An Editorial Article, 21 (June 1942), 387-401.

A plea to the working class and trade unions to demand immediate opening of a Western front against Germany. Washington hesitates to act decisively, relying on an air offensive and on supplying Russia with material. The Nazi armies, weakened by the Red Army and by guerilla warfare in occupied areas, can be smashed with the present resources of the United Nations.

C323 "COMMUNIST" (organ of the CPUSA), No Delay in Opening the Western Front! An Editorial, 21 (Aug. 1942), 579-91.
The recent signing of the U.S.-Soviet-British pacts must be translated into action through opening a new military front. The AFL is criticized for rejecting cooperative action with the Anglo-Soviet Trade Union Committee. Support for all "win-the-war" candidates is urged in the coming congressional elections.

C324 . . ., The Stalin-Churchill Meeting and After, 21 (Oct. 1942), 809-15.
Although the Stalin-Churchill meeting points to a closer collaboration between the Allies, it is not certain that Britain and the U.S. will soon launch a second front. Communists must maintain popular pressure for the opening of a second front.

C325 . . ., To the Offensive! An Editorial Article, 21 (Oct. 1942), 771-90.
The failure to open a second front against Hitler results, not from the complacency of the people, but from the efforts of a small group who encourage appeasement, hope for a negotiated peace, and advocate an overcautious approach to the war. Results of elections around the country and the strong win-the-war programs of the unions show that the people demand action.

C326 . . ., National Committee Plenary Meeting Issue, 22 (July 1943).
Reports and speeches at the plenary meeting of the Party's National Committee, held in New York, June 11-13, including reports by Earl Browder on "Hold the Home Front!," by Eugene Dennis on "Victory and the 1944 Elections," by Roy Hudson on "Crucial Problems Before Labor Today," and by John Williamson on "Gearing Organizational Forms and Methods to the War Effort." (All of the above are abstracted separately.) Speeches by Gilbert Green, James W. Ford, William Schneiderman, and Arnold Johnson are also included, together with plenum resolutions and statements.

C327 "COMMUNIST" (organ of the United Communist Party), At Last! 1 (June 12, 1920), 1.
A report on the convention at which the former Communist Labor Party and the majority of the Communist Party of America, led by C. E. Ruthenberg, merged to form the United Communist Party. This is an illegal party, urging the necessity of civil war as the final form of struggle with capitalism.

C328 . . ., Constitution of the United Communist Party, 1 (June 12, 1920), 6-7.
The constitution of the United Communist Party, formed by merger of the Communist Labor Party with the faction of the Communist Party of America led by Ruthenberg. The constitution was adopted by the new illegal party at a secret convention.

C329 . . ., Program of the United Communist Party, 1 (June 12, 1920), 8-16.
The program of the United Communist Party, formed by merger of the Communist Labor Party and the faction of the Communist Party of America led by Ruthenberg. The program contains sections on the collapse of capitalism, immediate tasks, and the communist reconstruction of society. The UCP favors workers' mass action, which it will seek to organize for the final struggle.

C330 . . ., The Communist International to the American Movement, [1] (Aug. 15, 1920), 5 ff. Appears also in "Communist" (organ of the Communist Party of America), 2 (Oct. 15, 1920), 9, and in "Revolutionary Radicalism," 2 (1908-9).
Full text of the statement by the Executive Committee of the Communist International to the Executive Committees of the Communist Party of America and the Communist Labor Party, requiring the two groups to merge. The major differences between the two groups, concerning how to split from the Socialist Party in 1919, do not justify a division.

C331 . . ., From the U.C.P. to the International, [1] (Aug. 15, 1920), 7. Reprinted as The Answer of the U.C.P. to the C.E.C. of the Communist International, "Communist" (organ of the Communist Party of America), 2 (Sept. 15, 1920), 2.
A reply to a directive from the Executive Committee of the Communist International, calling for unity between the Communist Party of America and the Communist Labor Party. While declaring its substantial agreement with the ECCI, the UCP points out that working with the IWW is impossible. (The Ruthenberg faction of the CPA had already merged with the CLP to form the UCP.)

C332 . . ., Program of the United Communist Party, 1, no. 13 [1920], 2-7.
The program adopted by the second convention of the United Communist Party, dealing with parliamentary democracy, "socialist" reform parties, mass action, penetration of military units, imperialism and war, colonial problems, unemployment, Negroes, agriculture, and labor unions and shop committees.

C333 . . ., The Second United Communist Party Convention, 1, no. 13, n.d. [1920], 1.
A report on the second convention of the United Communist Party. This "underground" convention ratified the theses adopted at the Second Congress of the Communist International, and discussed the question of unity with the Communist Party of America. A major issue protracting the negotiations was a dispute over the basis of representation at a unity convention.

C334 . . ., United Communist Party of America Constitution, 1, no. 13, n.d. [1920], 8.
The constitution of the United Communist Party adopted at its second convention. The constitution makes no provision for organization of separate language federations. Instead, provision is made in Article 5 for education and propaganda activity in the various foreign languages, with control in the hands of the district organizations.

C335 . . ., Communist Unity, 1, no. 15, n.d. [March 1921], 5.
The United Communist Party blames the Communist Party of America for the breakdown in unity negotiations between the two organizations, particularly criticizing the CPA for having rejected the proposal of the Unity Committee appointed by the Executive Committee of the Communist International.

C336 . . ., "New Stage in the Unity Proceedings," 1, no. 15, n.d. [March 1921], 3.
Correspondence revealing efforts of the Communist International to break the deadlock in unity negotiations between the Communist Party of America and the United Communist Party. The proposal of a Unity Committee representing both parties and the CI was rejected by the CPA, and accepted with qualifications by the UCP.

C337 "COMMUNIST" (organ of the United Communist Party), "The Third International Has Acted!" 1, no. 16, n.d. [April 1921], 3.
A letter from the American Agency of the Communist International to the Communist Party of America and the United Communist Party, informing them that the Executive Committee of the Comintern has empowered it to unite the parties by June 1, 1921. The basis on which unification is to take place is outlined, and Comintern policy on points of controversy between the two groups is stated.

C338 "COMMUNIST" (organ of the Workers Party), Special Plenum Number, 7 (July 1928).
Material relating to the May 1928 plenum of the Central Executive Committee of the Workers Party appears on pp. 387-433. It includes the plenum's "Resolution on Trade Union Work," William Z. Foster's "Old Unions and New Unions," James P. Cannon's "Trade-Union Questions," the plenum's "Resolution on the Report of the Political Committee," and Jay Lovestone's remarks on "Some Immediate Party Problems." (All these items are listed separately.)

C339 COMMUNIST INTERNATIONAL, Central Executive Committee. "An Appeal by the Central Executive Committee of the Communist International to the I.W.W." Central Executive Committee of the Communist Party of America, n.d. [1920]. 12 pp.
An appeal to the IWW to unite all unions of a class-conscious, revolutionary character for revolutionary mass action, and to cooperate with the Communist Party for the abolition of capitalism through the dictatorship of the proletariat. In an introduction the Communist Party of America attacks the IWW for having renounced direct action and become a peaceful instead of a revolutionary organization. IWW members are urged to oust their opportunist leaders, so that cooperation will be possible.

C340 . . ., Executive Committee. The Communist International to the American Comrades, "Communist International," nos. 11-12 (June-July 1920), 2495-500.
Pointing to the harm done by the rupture of the American communist movement into two parties, with no serious difference in principle between them, the Executive Committee insists on immediate reunion. A congress to achieve unity is to be called at once. The communists must work closely with the radical labor groups, while engaging in both legal and illegal work.

C341 . . ., Executive Committee. "From the Fourth to the Fifth World Congress: Report of the ECCI." Great Britain: Published for the Communist International by the Communist Party of Great Britain, 1924. 122 pp.
A summary of the activity of the ECCI and of its various national "sections." The Workers Party of America is dealt with on pp. 76-80, with major attention to its policy, tactics, and factional disputes with respect to the Farmer-Labor Party. This dispute is to be submitted to the Fifth World Congress for decision.

C342 . . . . Reorganization of the Workers Party: Resolution of the Communist International, "Liberator," 7 (Oct. 1924), 26-27.
A resolution adopted by the Fifth Congress of the Communist International, confirming decisions of its Executive Committee that the world's communist parties must be reorganized on the basis of factory nuclei. The reorganization will distinguish the revolutionary parties from the reformist social-democratic parties based on electoral districts, and insure majority membership of industrial proletarians.

C343 . . ., Organization Department. Resolution on the Results of the Reorganization of the Workers (Communist) Party of America, "Party Organizer," 1 (April 1927), 5-9.
Organizational promise for a real Communist Party has been created by reorganization on the basis of factory and street nuclei. Despite language difficulties, progress has been made in welding the separate federations into a united, centralized party. Shortcomings of the reorganization are considered, and immediate organizational tasks outlined.

C344 . . . . The International Situation and the Tasks of the Communist International, "International Press Correspondence," 8 (Nov. 23, 1928), 1567-77.
Theses of the Sixth World Congress, which called for militancy appropriate to the "third period" of capitalist crisis and imperialist wars. Thesis no. 52 (p. 1576), while recognizing some successes of the Workers (Communist) Party of America, criticizes its shortcomings with regard to relations with the socialists, the unorganized, Negroes, and American imperialism in Latin America. The Party's most important task is to end factional strife.

C345 . . . . Theses on the Revolutionary Movement in the Colonies and Semi-Colonies, "International Press Correspondence," 8 (Dec. 12, 1928), 1659-76.
Thesis no. 39 (pp. 1674-75) of the Sixth World Congress deals with the Negro question in the U.S. and elsewhere. Communists in the U.S. are to struggle for complete equality for Negroes, eliminate white chauvinism, resist lynchings, organize Negroes into the Party and unions, organize Southern peasants and agricultural workers, struggle against petty bourgeois tendencies among Negroes, and advocate the right of self-determination for Negroes in the southern Black Belt.

C346 . . . . "Problems of Strike Strategy." Decisions of the International Conference on Strike Strategy Held in Strasburg, Germany, Jan. 1929. Foreword by A. Lozovsky. Preface to the American edition by Bill Dunne. New York: Workers Library for the TUUL, 1929. 49 pp.
A report on the conference which laid down stike strategy for the Red International of Labor Unions in the "third period," foreshadowing the transformation of the Trade Union Educational League into the Trade Union Unity League. The strategy calls for barring reformist union officials from strike committees, creating the united front from below, converting every strike into a political struggle, and doing everything possible to liquidate reformist unions.

C347 . . . . "Program of the Communist International." New York: Workers Library, 1929. 96 pp.
The program, constitution, and rules of the Communist International, as adopted at the Sixth World Congress, September 1, 1928. Sections deal with the world system of capitalism, its general crisis, the ultimate aim of world communism, the period of transition, the dictatorship of the proletariat, and the strategy and tactics of the Communist International.

C348 . . . . C. I. Resolution on Negro Question in U.S.A., "Daily Worker," 5 (Feb. 12, 1929), 3.
The Negro working class can play a part in the class struggle against American imperialism and lead the oppressed Negro masses in a national revolutionary movement, influencing the revolutionary struggle of Negroes oppressed by imperialism all over the world. The Party in America must fight for emancipation of Negroes and their right to national self-determination in the South.

C349 COMMUNIST INTERNATIONAL, Executive Committee. Open Letter of the E.C.C.I. to the Convention of the Workers (Communist) Party of America, "International Press Correspondence," 9 (March 1, 1929), 208-12.

An open letter from the Executive Committee of the Communist International to the Sixth Convention of the Workers (Communist) Party, criticizing both the Lovestoneite majority and the Foster-Bittelman opposition for continuing the factional fight, to the detriment of the important tasks confronting the Party. Expulsions are threatened if the struggle is not ended at the convention.

C350 ..., Executive Committee. To All Members of the Communist Party of the United States: An Address by the Executive Committee of the Communist International, "International Press Correspondence," 9 (June 7, 1929), 598-600.

Decision of the Executive Committee of the Communist International settling the factional fight between the Lovestoneites and the Foster-Bittelman opposition. While both groups are criticized, Lovestone is held primarily responsible for the errors of the Party. The ECCI insists on the dissolution of all factions, and removes Lovestone and Bittelman, the leading factionalists, from work in the CPUSA.

C351 ..., Executive Committee. Decision of the Tenth Plenum of the ECCI on the Appeal of J. Lovestone, Member of the ECCI, against His Expulsion from the C.P. of the United States, "International Press Correspondence," 9 (Aug. 9, 1929), 818.

Lovestone's appeal from the decision of the CPUSA is viewed as merely a maneuver; his flouting of Comintern discipline and his efforts to split the CPUSA show he has no intention of remaining in the Party. Nevertheless, the International Control Commission is instructed to deal with his appeal at the earliest possible date.

C352 ..., International Control Commission. Decision of the International Control Commission of the C.I. in the Matter of John Pepper, "International Press Correspondence," 9 (Sept. 13, 1929), 1067.

The International Control Commission decision, dated August 19, 1929, to expel John Pepper (Josef Pogany), former Comintern Representative in the U.S., from the Communist International. Pepper's improper actions included his refusal to follow Comintern discipline, and his continued participation in factional activities, in association with Jay Lovestone of the CPUSA, even after the Comintern repudiated the line of that group.

C353 .... C. I. Resolution on Negro Question in U.S., "Communist," 9 (Jan. 1930), 48-55.

The text of a resolution of the Communist International, calling for the right of Negroes to self-determination in the South. A strong Negro revolutionary movement in the U.S. will influence Negroes oppressed by imperialism elsewhere. Areas and organizations in which the Party should concentrate its work are pointed out. (The final text of the resolution appeared in "Communist International," Jan. 15, 1931.)

C354 .... To the Central Committee CPUSA: Organization Letter from Comintern, "Party Organizer," 3 (June-July, 1930), 2-5.

Emphasis on the need to strengthen the Party organization, in order to consolidate the Party's ideological influence. The chief problem is the numerical weakness and the unsatisfactory composition of the leading cadres. Party members must be activized, special shock brigades formed for concrete tasks, and the factory nuclei converted into the Party's fundamental organizations.

C355 .... Conditions of Admission to the Communist International, "Party Organizer," 4 (Feb. 1931), 27-32.

The 21 conditions for admission of parties to the Third or Communist International, as drawn up by the Second World Congress, held in Moscow, August 1920. Parties were required to renounce social-patriotism and reformism, support the Red International of Trade Unions, organize on the principle of democratic centralization, and accept as binding all resolutions of the Communist International and its Executive Committee. (The 21 conditions were reprinted in a number of places, including "Communist" (Communist Party of America), Oct. 1, 1920, and in a 1921 pamphlet of the Communist Party of America, "The Theses and Statutes of the Communist International.")

C356 ..., Executive Committee. Comintern Documents, "Communist," 10 (May 1931), 402-8.

Directives from the Executive Committee of the Communist International to the CPUSA, endorsing the line of the CPUSA and ordering its translation into concrete activity. The Party is to concentrate in the areas of unemployed, trade union, and agrarian work. The Party is also to direct the struggle for Negro rights.

C357 ..., Executive Committee. "The Next Step in Britain, America and Ireland." New York: Workers Library, n.d. [1932]. 88 pp.

Speeches and reports to the twelfth Plenum of the ECCI. The main report by S. Gusev, "The End of Capitalist Stabilization and the Basic Tasks of the British and American Sections of the C.I." (pp. 2-35), calls for attacks on social-democracy, winning over the proletariat and poor farmers, organizing a disciplined Party, and strengthening its general staff. "Jack Pringle" reports on "The Situation in U.S.A." (pp. 67-79), covering wage cuts, farmers' and veterans' movements, and Party growth. (Reprinted from "Communist International," nos. 19 and 17-18.)

C358 .... Lessons of the Strike Struggles in the U.S.A.: Resolution of the E.C.C.I., "Communist," 11 (May 1932), 402-13.

An analysis of shortcomings in the conduct of strikes of miners and textile workers. Leadership of the miners' strike is criticized for weak preparatory work, failing to strengthen the Party, failures in activating the masses and mobilizing outside support, and the way the strike ended. The textile strikes showed sectarian tendencies and improper use of the united front from below tactic. (Also published in the pamphlet, "Toward Revolutionary Mass Work." Workers Library, 1932.)

C359 .... Executive Committee. The Tasks of the Communist Sections Regarding Municipal Policy, "Communist," 13 (Sept. 1934), 913-20.

Resolution on municipal policy adopted by the Enlarged Presidium of the Executive Committee of the Communist International, February 1930, reprinted as a guide for communists in local elections.

C360 .... Comintern Documents on the United Front, "Communist," 14 (May 1935), 470-73.

The resolution of the Fourth Congress of the Comintern calls upon communist parties, without giving up freedom to agitate on their own, to try to attract noncommunist workers into united fronts. The Comintern's 1933 manifesto directs communist parties to join with social democratic parties in organizations and demonstrations against fascism.

C361 .... The Communist International—From the

Sixth to the Seventh Congress—1928-1935, "Communist," 14 (Oct. 1935), 921-23.
Resolution of the Seventh Congress enjoining all Communist Parties to come out of isolation and induce social democratic leaders and workers to join them in a common fight against fascism.

C362   COMMUNIST INTERNATIONAL, Seventh Congress. The Offensive of Fascism and the Tasks of the Communist International in the Fight for the Unity of the Working Class against Fascism, "Communist," 14 (Oct. 1935), 924-39.
Resolution on the report of Georgi Dimitroff adopted by the Seventh Congress of the Comintern, August 20, 1935. The victory of socialism in the Soviet Union, the crisis in world capitalism, the offensive of fascism, and the bankruptcy of European social democracy make necessary a united front of the working class. Communists must establish the closest cooperation with the left social democrats.

C363   . . . . "Blueprint for World Conquest." Introd. by William Henry Chamberlin. Washington and Chicago: Human Events, 1946. 264 pp. Ind.
Chamberlin's introduction emphasizes the conspiratorial nature of international communism, as well as the frankness with which this conspiracy is blueprinted in Comintern documents. Since the communist program for organized subversion has not been repudiated, U.S. leadership must acquaint itself with the enemy it faces. Documents reproduced include the theses and statutes of the Communist International, its program, and its constitution and rules.

C364   "COMMUNIST INTERNATIONAL," Editorial Comment on the Negro Question, n.s., no. 8, n.d. [1924 or 1925]. 53-54.
Emphasis on the necessity to expose the class basis behind the antagonism between white and Negro workers. Unless the Party fights for full equality regardless of race, the Negro liberation movement in America will be led by nationalist petty bourgeoisie under a "Back to Africa" slogan. (The Party line before the "self-determination" formulation for U.S. Negroes.)

C365   . . ., Future of the La Follette Movement, n.s., no. 9, n.d. [1925]. 27-37.
A discussion of the La Follette movement and its relationship to the Workers (Communist) Party. Though not a working class party, the La Follette movement separates workers, farmers, and petty bourgeois from the capitalists. Antagonisms among the groups constituting the La Follette movement will likely lead to its disintegration, which the Workers (Communist) Party, temporarily isolated, must help achieve.

C366   . . ., Unemployment in the U.S.A., 8 (Jan. 15, 1931), 58-64.
Analysis of the extent of unemployment in the U.S., the condition of the unemployed, sources of relief, and remedial measures proposed by various political groups. The Party must quickly devise methods of agitation and struggle if it is to take advantage of the sharpening crisis.

C367   . . ., Review of the "Daily Worker," U.S.A.: In the Order of Checking Up and Carrying Out the Tasks Put before the Communist Party of the USA by the E.C.C.I., 10 (Nov. 1, 1933), 726-39.
A detailed criticism of the "Daily Worker" during June and July 1933. The paper has failed to popularize such policies as the Open Letter to the membership, it has failed to supply good agitational and organizational material, and it has had weak relations with local Party and other organizations. Proposals to remedy these weaknesses are presented.

C368   "COMMUNIST LABOR" (organ of Communist Labor Party), Progress in C.L.P. and C.P. Unity, 1 (May 15, 1920), 5-7.
Exchanges of correspondence between the Communist Labor Party and the Communist Party of America on their proposed unification, accompanied by the CLP interpretation of the state of negotiations. The negotiations were complicated by a factional struggle within the CPA between the Ruthenberg group and the leadership of the foreign-language federations.

C369   COMMUNIST LEAGUE OF AMERICA (OPPOSITION), National Committee. Back to Lenin! Manifesto to the Rank and File and Seventh National Convention of the C.P.U.S.A., "Militant," 3 (June 14, 1930), 1 ff.
The Stalinist leadership of the Communist Party is following disastrous policies foisted on it by the Communist International. The so-called "third period" is an effort to explain away the crimes and blunders of the Stalin-Bucharin bloc in the International. Both the Lovestoneites and the Fosterites in the Party are denounced.

C370   . . ., National Committee. Thesis for the Pre-Convention Discussion, "Militant," 4 (July 25, 1931), 3-5.
The main draft thesis of the Trotskyist Communist League of America (Opposition) for its Second National Conference, September 1931. The thesis rejects the CPUSA view of working class radicalization, disagrees with its "social fascism" line, and discusses the reasons for the stagnation and bureaucratization of the Party.

C371   . . ., National Committee. For a New Party and a New International! "Militant," 6 (Sept. 30, 1933), 1.
Announcement that the Communist League of America (Opposition) no longer regards itself as a faction of the official Stalinist Party. The statement of the American Trotskyists calls for formation of a new Communist Party. In view of the collapse of both the Social Democracy and the Communist International in Germany, a new revolutionary organization of the proletariat must be created.

C372   COMMUNIST LEAGUE OF STRUGGLE. "The Struggle for Communism: The Position of the Internationalist-Communists of the U.S." New York: The League, 1935. 54 pp.
An appraisal of world depression, together with the League's solution as opposed to those of the CPUSA or the Lovestone or Cannon groups. Critical of Stalin, the League nevertheless regards the USSR as a true workers' state and urges a united front of communists to return to true Leninism. (The League was led by Albert Weisbord, former Party union leader, who went into the Trotskyist movement with Cannon before forming this splinter group.)

C373   COMMUNIST PARTY (MAJORITY GROUP). "The Crisis in the Communist Party, U.S.A.: Statement of Principles of the Communist Party (Majority Group)." New York: Revolutionary Age, 1930. 77 pp.
Lovestoneite analysis of the current crisis in the Comintern and in the Communist Party, USA. The Stalin clique within the Comintern is attacked, as is the Foster faction presently leading the Party here. The current opportunist and sectarian Party line is said to have resulted in internal organizational chaos, and is discrediting the name of communism. Creation of a new party is rejected; the effort is rather to win the CPUSA back to true Leninism.

C374 COMMUNIST PARTY (MAJORITY GROUP). The Present Situation and Our Tasks, "Revolutionary Age," 1 (June 15, 1930), 10-15.
Draft thesis for the National Conference of the Lovestoneite "Communist Party (Majority Group)," to be held July 4, 1930, one year after their expulsion from the CPUSA. The 51 "theses" making up the document deal with world capitalism, contradictions of American capitalism, economic crisis and reaction in the U.S., the labor movement, the CPUSA, and the situation and tasks of the Lovestone group.

C375 .... Recent New Union Developments, "Revolutionary Age," 2 (Aug. 22, 1931), 4.
A statement by the Lovestone opposition group asserting that increased activity by the dual unions of the Trade Union Unity League resulted from the objective conditions of the depression; attacking the splitting and sectarian tactics of the Party in trade-union work; and calling for trade-union unity.

C376 COMMUNIST PARTY OF AMERICA, National Organization Committee. Call for a National Convention, for the Purpose of Organizing the Communist Party of America, "Communist," (organ of the Communist Party of America, National Organization Committee), 1 (July 19, 1919), 1-2.
Call to a convention to organize a Communist Party of America, to meet in Chicago on September 1, 1919. The group issuing this call opposed attempting to take over the Socialist Party as a step to forming the Communist Party. It was composed of foreign language federations expelled from the Socialist Party and led by Alexander Stoklitsky, and the Socialist Party of Michigan.

C377 .... Manifesto, Program and Constitution, "Communist," (organ of the Communist Party of America), 1 (Sept. 27, 1919), 6-9 ff. Reprinted as a pamphlet, "Manifesto and Program." Chicago: Communist Party of America, 1919. Also reprinted in New York State Legislature, Joint Legislative Committee Investigating Seditious Activities, "Revolutionary Radicalism," 1:776-98. Excerpts appear in "American Labor Yearbook," 1919-1920, pp. 414-19.
The CPA opposes both the Socialist Party and a labor party, instead supporting mass strikes as having revolutionary potential. The aim is not to capture the bourgeois parliamentary state, but to conquer state power in order to overthrow it and replace it with the dictatorship of the proletariat. Participation in parliamentary activity is permitted only for the purpose of revolutionary propaganda.

C378 ..., Central Executive Committee. "Proletarian Revolution or Wage Slavery." [New York?]: CPA Central Executive Committee, n.d. [192-?]. 6 pp.
An openly and uncompromisingly revolutionary demand for mass action to achieve a soviet government, using parliamentarianism and trade unions for propaganda purposes. Manifesto issued in the early 1920's by one of the predecessors of the CPUSA.

C379 .... "Stenographic Report of the 'Trial' of Louis C. Fraina." [Chicago?]: Central Executive Committee of the CPA, 1920. 48 pp.
Fraina, intellectual leader of the left wing and one of the founders of the communist movement here, was charged with being a Department of Justice agent in the Communist Party of America, one of the forerunners of the CPUSA. The charge was made by Santeri Nuorteva, secretary of the Russian Soviet Bureau in the U.S., while Fraina was serving as international secretary of the CPA. This is an account of hearings before the Central Executive Committee, which exonerated Fraina. (Later, as Lewis Corey, Fraina became a leading anticommunist and an author of noted economic studies.)

C380 ..., Central Executive Committee. "Program and Constitution (Adopted at Joint Unity Convention of the United Communist and Communist Parties, May, 1921)." New York: The Committee, 1921. 63 pp.
The background and objectives of the Communist Party of America and its constitution, with provisions for membership, organization, finances, Party press, and discipline. (Also published in "Communist," [organ of Communist Party of America], July 1921.)

C381 ..., Central Committee. "The Theses and Statutes of the Communist International as Adopted by the Second World Congress, July 17-August 7, 1920." New York: Contemporary Publishing Association, 1921.
Though existing trade unions are part of the military apparatus of the bourgeoisie, they are becoming agencies of struggle for the proletariat, against the opposition of the old bureaucracy. Communists must not leave the old trade unions voluntarily to form separate unions, lest they isolate themselves from the masses; where splits have occurred, however, they support the more revolutionary union. The unions must be subordinated to the Party, the advanced guard of the revolution. The 21 conditions for admission of parties to the Third or Communist International are included. (Also reprinted in "Blueprint for World Conquest, as Outlined by the Communist International.")

C382 ..., Central Executive Committee. Theses on the Relations of the Communist Party to a Legal Political Party, "Communist," (organ of the Communist Party of America), 1 (July 1922), 1 ff.
The winning formula in the factional fight on the underground versus the legal political party that erupted following organization of the Workers Party of America, a legal political party. The Communist Party cannot function openly unless it can advocate armed insurrection. Even then, the "open" party must co-exist with an underground until the Soviet Republic has been established. (This formula was essentially the position of the "goose caucus" rather than that of the "liquidators.")

C383 COMMUNIST PARTY OF PUERTO RICO, Central Committee. "The Case of Puerto Rico: Memorandum to the United Nations." New York: New Century, 1953. 16 pp.
An assertion that Puerto Rico, despite U.S. statements to the contrary, remains an American colony in which American imperialism works to subjugate the people. The United Nations is called upon to demand that the U.S. recognize the right of the Puerto Rican people to a free and independent republic.

C384 COMMUNIST PARTY OF THE USA (OPPOSITION), National Committee. Unite and Strengthen Our Party, "Workers Age," 2 (Oct. 15, 1932), 1-2.
Despite growing working class unrest resulting from the economic crisis, labor leadership, including the communists, is bankrupt. The Opposition will continue its fight to return the CPUSA to the line of Lenin. CPUSA members are urged to join the Opposition.

C385 .... "For Unity of the World Communist Movement." New York: CPUSA (Opposition), 1934. 14 pp.
A letter to the Independent Labor Party of Great Britain from the Communist Party, USA (Opposition), stating the Lovestoneite indictment of the Communist International's ultra-left sectarian tactics.

C386 COMMUNIST PARTY OF THE USA (OPPOSITION). "Why a Labor Party." New York: Communist Party (Opposition), 1934. 16 pp.
Draft resolution of the Lovestoneite group approved by the plenum of its national committee. Since workers, despite rising discontent, are not yet ready to accept a revolutionary party or communist leadership, a labor party is urged to advance working class consciousness, and to draw the more advanced workers into the communist movement. (This resolution signified abandonment by the Lovestoneites of efforts to re-establish their leadership within the CPUSA or to be reinstated by the Communist International.)

C387 . . . . On the New Line of the Comintern: Letter to the Central Committee and Members of the CPUSA, "Workers Age," 3 (Oct. 1, 1934), 3 ff.
Lovestoneite letter to the CPUSA, citing changes in the Comintern line as evidenced by the united front in Germany and France with socialists, dropping of the theory of social fascism, and liquidation of the red unions. But the changes in the U.S. are half-hearted. Unity is urged, since differences are being eliminated.

C388 COMMUNIST PARTY, USA. "On the Road to Bolshevization." New York: Workers Library, 1929. 46 pp.
Materials dealing with the Comintern's "third period" line and the expulsion of Trotskyists and Lovestoneites from the Party. Included are excerpts from theses of the Sixth World Congress, open letter from the Comintern to the Sixth Convention of the CPUSA ("Daily Worker," March 4, 1929), address of the Comintern to the membership of the CPUSA ("Daily Worker," May 20, 1929), and the decision of the Central Committee of the CPUSA on the Comintern's address ("Daily Worker," May 20, 1929).

C389 . . . . "Why Every Worker Should Join the Communist Party." New York: Workers Library, n.d. [1929?]. 30 pp.
A description of economic crises and the class struggle, and an attack on capitalistic parties, including the Socialist Party. The program and organization of the Communist Party are presented, with an explanation of the need to expel Trotskyists and Lovestoneites. Workers of all countries must protect USSR achievements by preventing imperialist war.

C390 . . . . "Working Class against Capitalist Class: Main Election Issue of the Communist Party." New York: CPUSA, n.d. [1929]. 30 pp.
Assertions that capitalist dictatorship oppresses the workers, that the capitalist parties deceive them, and that a new war is in the making, for colonies and markets. Workers are urged to support the USSR, to demand unemployment relief and social insurance, and to join revolutionary unions. The persecution of Negroes and the exploitation of poor farmers must be ended.

C391 . . ., New York State Committee. "How to Build It!" New York: The Committee, n.d. [193-]. 15 pp.
Ways to increase the circulation of the "Daily Worker" in shops, neighborhoods, and unions. The paper serves as a means of organizing, and as an agency of communication—downward, through its news columns, and upward, through workers' correspondence and political contacts between distributors and readers.

C392 . . ., Central Committee. "American Working Women and the Class Struggle." New York: Workers Library, n.d. [1930?]. 40 pp.

Working women are urged to recognize their class interests and to join the Trade Union Unity League and the CPUSA. The AFL and women's organizations such as the YWCA and the Women's Trade Union League are attacked. Working women are urged to join with the entire working class to fight against imperialist war, for defense of the Soviet Union, and for a workers' government.

C393 . . . . "Another War Coming and the Workers Pay Its Price." New York: CPUSA, 1930. 31 pp.
The Party's antiwar line during its "third period." Wars are fought for profits, power, and territories, not moral principles. Capitalists want to wipe out the example of the Soviet Union; this explains their war preparations. American workers must fight against war preparations, and prepare to turn the imperialist war into a civil war.

C394 . . . . "Death Penalty Demanded: The Case of Georgia against the Communist Party." New York: CPUSA, 1930. 31 pp.
Denunciation of the "capitalist justice" which has imprisoned and tried two communist organizers on the charge of violating a Georgia statute dating from the slavery era, under which the prosecutor is demanding the death penalty. The pamphlet denounces the masters of the South and their exploitation, and proudly pleads guilty to the crime of organizing and leading the working class.

C395 . . . . "Struggles Ahead! Thesis on the Economic and Political Situation and the Tasks of the Communist Party: Adopted by the Seventh National Convention, June 20-25, 1930." New York: CPUSA, 1930. 32 pp.
The Party line in the "third period," calling for activation and Bolshevization of the Party, transformation of the Party base from street to shop nuclei, and building of mass industrial unions. Sections deal with war dangers, unemployment, American fascism and imperialism, opposition to a labor party, the united front from below, the TUUL, Negro self-determination, and the "right" danger of Lovestoneism.

C396 . . ., Central Committee. "Thesis and Resolutions for the Seventh National Convention of the Communist Party of the USA, by the Central Committee Plenum, March 31-April 4, 1930." New York: The Committee, 1930. 95 pp.
Documents containing the proposals of the Party leadership to the Seventh Convention, laying down the line for the "third period." The proposals, following the line of the Communist International, signify the liquidation of Lovestoneite opportunism. The documents include a thesis on the economic and political situation, and resolutions on the Trade Union Unity League, District Eight (Chicago), tasks of the Party in the South, organization of factory nuclei, Party fractions, language work, and keeping new members.

C397 . . ., Waterfront Section. "United We Stand." New York: The Section, n.d. [1930]. 12 pp.
An appeal to longshoremen to oppose racist discrimination against Negroes in the industry and to support the New Deal and the Communist Party. The Party believes that socialism will end unemployment, poverty, and racial discrimination, as in the Soviet Union.

C398 . . . . "Communist Call to the Toiling Farmers." New York: Workers Library, 1931. 16 pp.
An appeal to farmers to join the Party and unite with revolutionary city workers to struggle against capitalism. Despite the richness of our country, farmers suffer untold misery; and when they revolt against their misery, the full force of government is thrown against them.

C399 COMMUNIST PARTY, USA, New York District. "Communist Election Program against Hunger, Wage Cuts, Speed-Up and War; New York Elections, 1931: Vote as You Strike—Communist." New York: The District, 1931. 25 pp.

Party platform for the 1931 New York City municipal election, featuring a proposal for full unemployment insurance. Other demands include unemployment relief, civil liberties, release of all political and class war prisoners, repeal of the criminal anarchy law, and federal recognition of the USSR.

C400 . . . . "Race Hatred on Trial." [New York]: CPUSA, n.d. [1931?]. 47 pp.

Abridged proceedings of a "trial" held by the New York District of the Party of a member accused of white chauvinism for stating that he did not want Negroes to use the Finnish bath house. The defendant, Yokinin, had pleaded guilty before the trial, which was held before an audience of 1,500 white and Negro workers in Harlem. The jury's decision, expelling Yokinin for a specified time but giving him a number of tasks for which he could earn readmission, was adopted unanimously by the meeting.

C401 . . ., Central Committee. "Shop Paper Manual: A Handbook for Comrades Active in Shop Paper Work." New York: The Committee, n.d. [1931?]. 42 pp.

Instructions on preparation of shop papers, termed the communist's sharpest weapon in mass agitation. The paper must express the Party's political interpretations, and at the same time champion the worker in his day-to-day struggles in the shop. The tone must be vigorous, not patronizing. Advice is given on financing and on technical details.

C402 . . ., District Eight (Chicago). "Smash the Bosses' Program of Hunger and War! Vote Communist!: Chicago Election Platform of the Communist Party." Chicago: The District, n.d. [1931]. 14 pp.

"Third period" mayoralty election platform of the Communist Party in Chicago. The main slogan of this election is WORKING CLASS AGAINST THE BOSS CLASS! The Democrats, Republicans, and Socialists are the parties of capitalism, whereas the CP leads the workers in their struggle for lower prices, unemployment relief, and against wage cuts and police terror.

C403 . . ., Central Committee. "Unemployment Relief and Social Insurance: The Capitalist Program of Starvation." New York: Workers Library, 1931. 31 pp.

A "third period" publication denouncing the capitalist system for precipitating America into the worst economic crisis in the history of the brutal system. The reformist programs of the AFL and the Socialist Party are denounced, and the government attacked for preparing for war against the USSR. A workers' struggle for adequate relief, under Party leadership, will be the first step toward overthrowing capitalist slavery and starvation.

C404 . . ., Central Committee, 13th Plenum. Resolution on Work among the Unemployed, "Communist," 10 (Oct. 1931), 838-50.

The main gains have been made in the organization of demonstrations and hunger marches, though these have yet to be crystallized into organizational gains. Slogans to be emphasized, and organizational forms (such as Councils of the Unemployed) to be utilized, are discussed in detail.

C405 . . ., Central Committee, 13th Plenum. Tasks in the Struggle against Hunger, Repression and War: Resolution of the 13th Plenum, Central Committee, C.P.U.S.A., on the Main Tasks in the Organization of Mass Struggles against the Offensive of the Capitalists, "Communist," 10 (Oct. 1931), 818-37 ff.

A call on the Party to close the gap between the spontaneous revolutionary activity of the masses and its organizational consolidation under Party influence. An analysis is made of failures and proposals for improvements in all spheres of Party activity: unemployed struggles, union organizations, antiwar work, and work among Negroes, youth, and the foreign born.

C406 . . ., National Campaign Committee. "Communist Election Platform: Against Imperialist War—For Jobs and Bread." New York: Workers Library, 1932. 16 pp.

Election platform for the 1932 presidential campaign. Immediate demands include unemployment and social insurance at the expense of the state and employers, opposition to Hoover's wage-cutting policy, emergency relief for impoverished farmers, equal rights for Negroes and self-determination for the Black Belt, opposition to capitalist terror and imperialist war, and defense of the Chinese people and the Soviet Union.

C407 . . ., National Election Campaign Committee. "The Democratic Twin of the Hoover Hunger Movement." New York: Workers Library, n.d. [1932]. 16 pp.

Election campaign pamphlet declaring that the Democratic majority in Congress has supported Hoover's "hunger government" and similarly attacked the working class. Roosevelt's record as governor of New York is condemned, as is the Democratic platform. John N. Garner, Democratic candidate for vice-president, is called "the lynch-law candidate." Only the Communist Party stands for the revolutionary way out of the present crisis.

C408 . . . . "The Farmers' Way Out." New York: Workers Library, 1932. 16 pp.

An appeal to farmers to support the Party's platform and vote for its candidates in the 1932 election. The Party's program is presented—emergency relief for impoverished farmers; their exemption from taxes; no forced collection of rents, debts, or mortgages; and opposition to imperialist war and race discrimination.

C409 . . . . "Fundamentals of Communism." New York: Workers Library, n.d. [1932?]. 45 pp.

A short outline of communist theory, covering capitalism and communism; imperialism, war, and the Soviet Union; the class struggle, reformism, and revolutionary Marxism; and the nature and organization of the Party, and the tasks of its members.

C410 . . ., National Election Campaign Committee. "Hoover: The Great Engineer after Four Years." New York: Workers Library, 1932. 16 pp.

A charge that Hoover lied in 1928 when he said that unemployment was disappearing, and an attack upon his public works program, his reduction of federal salaries, his refusal to hire Negroes at the Hoover dam, and his arms preparations. Promises of capitalist parties are empty, and their solutions aid the rich. Even the Socialist Party serves the capitalists. Only the Communist Party is a party of the workers.

C411 . . ., Central Committee. "Toward Revolutionary Mass Work." New York: Workers Library, 1932. 64 pp.

Resolutions adopted by the Central Committee of the Party, a resolution on strike struggles in the U.S. adopted by the

Executive Committee of the Communist International, and directives on how these resolutions are to be put into practice. A decisive turn toward mass work, so far attempted only in a mechanical way, is required. The key task is to improve the revolutionary unions of the Trade Union Unity League. A reduction in the central Party apparatus and the activization of more comrades are also necessary. The masses must be organized around the issues of opposition to imperialist war and defense of the Soviet Union.

C412 COMMUNIST PARTY, USA, National Election Campaign Committee. "Will Beer Bring Back Prosperity?" New York: Workers Library, 1932. 16 pp.
Election campaign pamphlet asserting that the main issue is not beer, but bread, and that the argument that beer will bring back prosperity is nonsense. Only the communist program of unemployment and social insurance at the expense of the state and the employers will relieve unemployment, and only the overthrow of the capitalist system will abolish it.

C413 . . ., Central Committee. The Tasks of the Communist Party U.S.A.: Resolution for the Central Committee Plenum, "Communist," 11 (April 1932), 310-24.
The CPUSA has not yet overcome its isolation from the masses of the American proletariat. The struggle against social fascism must be sharpened, and sectarianism overcome. Directives for work in specific spheres of activity, such as in trade unions, and among the unemployed and Negroes, are presented, as are details on participation in the election campaign.

C414 . . ., Central Committee. Lessons of the Bonus March, "Communist," 11 (Sept. 1932), 792-804.
Analysis of the march of veterans on Washington in July 1932, claiming a major role for the communist-supported Workers Ex-Servicemen's League, although leadership of the march was lost to petty bourgeois elements. The role of petty bourgeois and social-fascist elements in the veterans' movement should be exposed, and the movement linked to the class struggles of revolutionary workers.

C415 . . ., Central Committee. The Sharpening Capitalist Offensive, the Rising Tide of Mass Struggles and the Next Tasks of the Party: Resolution of the Fifteenth Plenum of the Central Committee, C.P.U.S.A., "Communist," 11 (Oct. 1932), 902-17.
The Fifteenth Plenum finds the Communist Party not yet a mass party, still competing with the social fascists for leadership of the working class. The Party must be strengthened, and mass campaigns conducted to aid the unemployed, employed workers, veterans, and farmers. The struggle against imperialist war must be intensified.

C416 . . . . "The Communist Position on the Farmers' Movement." New York: Workers Library, 1933. 48 pp.
Resolution adopted at a Party conference in July 1933 criticizing the bourgeois leadership of a recent farm conference which made no effort to stress the need for mass struggle. The Party supports a revolutionary alliance of the proletariat with poor and small farmers, while struggling against the big farmers who are allied to finance capital. Included are speeches by H. Puro, outlining the task of the Party in work among farmers, and by a "Comrade M" on the Sharecroppers Union.

C417 . . . . "The Communist Position on the Negro Question: Self-Determination for the Black Belt." New York: Workers Library, n.d. [1933?]. 64 pp.

A collection of articles, speeches, and resolutions on the Negro question during the "third period." Included are two articles by Earl Browder, C. A. Hathaway's nominating speech for James W. Ford as vice-presidential candidate in 1932, an article by Harry Haywood, and two resolutions by the Communist International.

C418 . . ., New York District. "Election Platform, Communist Party, New York Municipal Elections, 1933." New York: The District, 1933. 23 pp.
Party municipal platform during the "third period," calling for higher wages, unemployment relief, the right to organize labor unions, equality for Negroes, self-determination in the Black Belt, and militant struggle against imperialist war.

C419 . . . . "For United Action against Fascism." New York: CPUSA, 1933. 16 pp. (Reprint of editorial from April 1933 issue of "Communist," especially for Madison Square meeting against fascism, April 5, 1933.)
An analysis of German fascism, predicting that Hitler and the Nazi movement will be defeated by a German proletarian revolutionary upsurge. Although the German Social Democratic Party is "the moderate wing of fascism," the Communist International calls for a united front from below with Social Democratic workers. American workers are urged to defend their living standard, oppose imperialist war, and support the fight of German workers against fascism.

C420 . . ., Central Committee. "An Open Letter to All Members of the Communist Party: Adopted by the Extraordinary National Conference of the Communist Party of the USA, Held in New York City, July 7-10, 1933." New York: The Committee, 1933. 24 pp.
An expression of concern with attempts to turn the Party to mass work during a period of economic crisis, war preparations, and renewed attacks on the workers. The Party's policy is declared to be correct, but execution of it is faulty. The united front, under Party initiative, is to be the organizing tactic. Party factionalism is declared the greatest crime; sectarian opposition to the line is to be rooted out, and isolation of the bureaucracy from the Party masses ended.

C421 . . ., District Five, (Pittsburgh). "Plan of Work: Main Tasks and Perspectives, Jan. 15—May 1st, 1933." Pittsburgh: The District, 1933. 11 pp.
An attempt to apply the "third period" line of the Party in one district. Main tasks are to mobilize the unemployed and part-time workers into united front committees of action, to conduct hunger marches, and to fight against wage cuts, and for relief and unemployment insurance. Social fascism must be defeated through the united front from below. The struggle against imperialist war must be connected with local struggles.

C422 . . ., District Eight (Chicago). "Resolution and Plan of Concentration for the Communist Party, District 8." Chicago: The District, 1933. 23 pp.
A practical, daily guide for Party members, aimed at expanding their operations in the heavy industries around Chicago, including steel, coal, railroads, and packing. An effort to translate into action the open letter adopted at the Party's national conference in 1933, calling for intensified "mass work."

C423 . . ., Chicago District. "Smash the Bosses' Program of Hunger and War! Vote for Workers Candidates Endorsed by the Communist Party: Chicago Election Platform of the Communist Party, Alder-

manic Elections, Feb. 28, 1933.'' Chicago: The District, 1933. 16 pp.
Election program for the Chicago aldermanic elections in 1933, in which the Party endorsed 26 candidates. Chicago Federation of Labor officials are charged with supporting the police terror of Chicago's "red squad." Platform demands range from emergency relief appropriations to defense of the Soviet Union.

C424 COMMUNIST PARTY, USA, Election Campaign Committee. "Socialist Party: Words and Deeds." New York: The Committee, n.d. [1933?]. 15 pp.
A contrast of Socialist Party platform pledges with the actions of socialists elected to office in Milwaukee and Bridgeport, in the areas of relief, evictions, corruption, and taxation. Leaders of the Socialist Party, the third party of capitalism, pave the way to fascism, slander the USSR, prepare to support imperialist war, and destroy worker solidarity by rejecting united-front actions with the communists.

C425 . . ., Election Campaign Committee. "Unemployment and the Election Campaign: New York Municipal Elections." New York: The Committee, 1933. 15 pp.
Municipal election platform calling for unemployment relief, social insurance, higher wages, right to form unions and strike without injunctions or police interference, equality for Negroes, self-determination in the Black Belt, a struggle against imperialism, and defense of the Soviet Union and the Chinese people.

C426 . . ., New York District Committee, District Two. "An Urgent Letter to Every Communist in New York." New York: The Committee, 1933. 16 pp.
Letter to all New York Party members on the critical state of work among the unemployed. The Party is isolated from the masses, it negotiates with social fascist leaders of reformist unemployed movements instead of utilizing the united front from below, and the revolutionary unions neglect work with the unemployed. The Party must mobilize for the second united front conference of unemployed scheduled for August 19, 1933.

C427 . . ., Political Bureau. The Scottsboro Struggle and the Next Steps: Resolution of the Political Bureau, "Communist," 12 (June 1933), 570-82.
A resolution adopted following the death verdict against Heywood Patterson in the Scottsboro case. The case, which is interrelated with the Negro struggle generally, is beginning to be led by Negro proletarians and the Party. Recent mass demonstrations on the case have been successful to the degree that the CP and the ILD have pursued the tactic of the united front from below, and discredited the petty bourgeois and reformist deceivers of the Negro masses.

C428 . . ., Central Committee, Resolution of the 17th Central Committee Meeting of the Communist Party, U.S.A., "Communist," 12 (Nov. 1933), 1088-95.
A reaffirmation of the Open Letter, with a plea for greater Party mobilization. The New Deal, as a capitalist solution of the crisis, is bankrupt. The bourgeoisie is using more fascist methods against workers' struggles. We must penetrate the AFL, and organize the broadest united front in the workers' struggle for economic and political demands. (Also published in "International Press Correspondence," Nov. 3 and 10, 1933.)

C429 . . ., Central Committee. "The Advance of the United Front." New York: The Committee, 1934. 70 pp.

A collection of documents exchanged between the Communist and Socialist Parties of this country between March 1933 and October 1934, relating to united front activities, together with an introduction by Alexander Bittelman. (In this period of "united front from below," communists appealed to socialists and their local branches for immediate united-front struggles on specific issues, regardless of the status of negotiations between the national leaderships.)

C430 . . ., Illinois. "Congressional Platform of the Communist Party, 1934." Chicago: Communist Party State Election Headquarters in Illinois, 1934. 16 pp.
A "third period" campaign document, attacking the Socialist Party for "misleadership" and AFL officials for strikebreaking. Workers are urged to break with the Farmer-Labor and Socialist Parties as well as with the Democrats and Republicans. The CP is said to represent the immediate needs of workers, poor farmers, the Negro people, and the impoverished middle class, besides leading the struggle toward a Soviet America.

C431 . . . . "Draft Resolution of the Eighth Convention of the C.P.U.S.A." New York: Workers Library, 1934. 47 pp.
Stress is placed on the depression and the New Deal's failure to ameliorate it, except by a program of fascism and war. Theses and decisions of the Thirteenth Plenum of the Executive Committee of the Communist International are included.

C432 . . . . "Guide for Party Functionaries." CPUSA, n.d. [1934?]. 8 pp.
Directives of an unidentified Party District Committee on the work of membership committees and the handling of new members. Fluctuating membership is viewed as a serious problem. Instructions deal with procedure in accepting new members, training and follow-up, improving quality of recruiting, handling of transfers, and keeping individual attendance records.

C433 . . ., District Six, Ohio. "Into Mass Work: Ohio District Resolution and Four Month Control Plan, Adopted at Conference, August 24-26, 1934." Cleveland: The District, n.d. [1934]. 23 pp.
The chief task of Party members in Ohio is preparation to lead the expected strike wave in basic industry. All eligible Party members are to join unions, concentrating in steel, automobile, and rubber plants. Opposition groups within AFL unions are to be formed, while affiliates of the Trade Union Unity League are to be built. Work is also to be carried on among unemployed, Negroes, and youth.

C434 . . ., Chicago District. "A Manifesto to the Workers of Chicago from the Ninth Convention of the Communist Party Chicago District, April 1, 1934." Chicago: CPUSA, Chicago District, 1934. 10 pp.
Application of the Party line of the "third period" to the Chicago scene, with attacks on the "Roosevelt-Horner, Kelly Administration," on leading Chicago capitalists, and on the Chicago Socialist Party and its leaders. United action of socialists and communists is called for, within the formula of the "united front from below."

C435 . . ., New York State Election Campaign Committee. "Platform of Struggle for Urgent Needs of Toilers: Election Platform of the Communist Party, New York State, 1934." New York: CPUSA, New York State Election Campaign Committee, 1934. 23 pp.
A "third period" campaign document, stressing unemploy-

ment, falling wages, and the ineffectiveness of the New Deal in coping with the depression. Roosevelt is accused of taking fascist measures. The basic orientation of the Party is unity of the working class against the capitalist class.

C436 COMMUNIST PARTY, USA. "The Program of Struggle of the Negro People for Defense of Ethiopia, for Bread and Work, for Equal Rights." New York: Workers Library, n.d. [1934?]. 24 pp.
An attack on the treatment of Negroes, including discussions of police violence, unemployment, segregation, and slums and firetraps. The pamphlet proposes organization of Negro domestics, plus a program for veterans and youth. It urges defense of Ethiopia against fascist attack, and unity of all workers against capitalism, fascism, war, and racism.

C437 .... "Report of the Central Committee to the 8th Convention of the Communist Party, U.S.A., Cleveland, Ohio, 1934." New York: Workers Library, 1934. 128 pp.
The official line in 1934, before the popular-front era, when Roosevelt's New Deal was reviled almost as much as were the leaders of the AFL and the Socialist Party. Objectives and strategies are outlined, with special attention to labor, Negroes, and youth.

C438 ..., Ohio District. "Resolution and Control Tasks: April 1st-August 1st, 1934." Cleveland: CPUSA, Ohio District, 1934. 24 pp.
A resolution adopted at the Ohio District convention, March 31-April 1, 1934, reviewing the problems of the depression and Party gains and shortcomings in Ohio since the last convention. Tasks to be accomplished in the months ahead are outlined.

C439 ..., Election Campaign Committee. "Teachers! Where Do You Stand Today, 1934?" New York: The Committee, 1934. 14 pp.
A plea for teachers to vote communist in the 1934 state elections in New York, to protest overcrowded classes and reduced educational budgets. Communist candidates are pledged to release funds for education, repeal the teachers' loyalty oath, and adopt unemployment insurance legislation.

C440 .... "Theses and Decisions, 13th Plenum of the E.C.C.I.; Draft Resolutions of the Eighth Convention of the C.P.U.S.A." New York: Workers Library, 1934. 47 pp.
The Comintern's picture of world conditions, with its program for a united front from below. The Party's draft resolutions adapt this view to U.S. conditions, emphasizing separate unions and mass strikes, condemning Roosevelt and his "liberal" supporters as fascists, and also attacking A. J. Muste's American Workers Party.

C441 .... "The Way Out: A Program for American Labor." New York: Workers Library, 1934. 99 pp.
Manifesto and principal resolutions adopted by the eighth convention of the Party, April 2-8, 1934. The NRA is seen as a strikebreaking agency, and such pending measures as the Wagner and the 30-hour bills are evidence of fascization. The workers are rapidly becoming radicalized, as a wave of militant strikes indicates, despite actions of AFL misleaders. The Party must form opposition groups within the AFL while building the unions of the TUUL.

C442 ..., New York District Committee. "Why You Should Vote Communist." New York: CPUSA, New York District Committee, 1934. 24 pp.

A "third period" election appeal, blaming the capitalists, their politicians, and the Socialist Party for the current crisis. Only the CP fights for the interests of all toilers. Workers are urged to vote for CP candidates to help prepare for a Soviet America, since the only way out for the American working class is the Soviet way.

C443 ..., Central Committee. Tasks of Our Party for Winning the Majority of the Working Class, "Communist," 13 (Feb. 1934), 178-81.
Resolution of the Central Committee, CPUSA, January 16, 1934, endorsing the thesis of the Thirteenth Plenum of the ECCI. This plenum, following Hitler's rise to power, called for a revolutionary upsurge of the German proletariat led by the German CP. In the U.S. the New Deal is seen as a movement toward fascism and war preparations.

C444 ..., National Organizational Department. Facts and Material on Organizational Status, Problems, and Organizational Tasks of the Party (Prepared for 8th National Convention, April 2-8, 1934), "Party Organizer," 7 (May-June 1934), 5-18.
A statistical report on membership growth, dues payments, new shop nuclei, and penetration of new territories and basic industries in the four-year period between the seventh and eighth national conventions.

C445 ..., Eighth National Convention. Lessons of Economic Struggles, Tasks of the Communists in the Trade Unions, "Communist," 13 (May 1934), 456-76.
Trade union resolution of the eighth national convention of the Party, Cleveland, April 2-8, 1934. The American working class is growing more militant, and it may be possible to form a new trade-union center independent of the AFL. However, CP leadership in trade union work has been weak. The Party must increase its work in AFL and in independent unions, without weakening the TUUL.

C446 ..., Eighth National Convention. The Present Situation and the Tasks of the Communist Party of the U.S.A., "Communist," 13 (May 1934), 430-55.
Main resolution of the eighth national convention of the Party, Cleveland, April 2-8, 1934. Capitalism is in a state of deepening crisis, with the only alternative a revolutionary communist one. The New Deal, supported by such social fascists as the AFL leadership and the Socialist Party, leads to fascism and war.

C447 ..., Eighth National Convention. The Winning of the Working Class Youth Is the Task of the Entire Party, "Communist," 13 (May 1934), 477-90.
Resolution of the eighth convention of the CPUSA, Cleveland, April 2-8, 1934. The Roosevelt Administration is worsening the conditions of and militarizing youth. A united front from below should be formed with the Young People's Socialist League, while exposing its leadership as social-fascist. The National Student League should be transformed into a mass revolutionary student organization.

C448 ..., Central Committee. Unify the Forces of All Steel Workers for Aggressive Unionism, "Communist," 13 (July 1934), 655-63.
"False friends" of the steel workers, including AFL President William Green, Mike Tighe of the Amalgamated Association, and the Committee of Ten are condemned, as well as NRA conciliation, for getting the AA to call off the steel strike. Steel workers are urged to organize under the leadership of the Steel and Metal Workers Industrial Union, and to join the Party.

C449 ..., Central Committee. Lessons of Recent Strike

Struggles in the U.S.A., "Communist," 13 (Oct. 1934), 968-84.
Resolution adopted September 5-6, 1934, reviewing recent strike history. Isolated strikes on economic issues have developed into general strikes, as in San Francisco, reflecting opposition to the New Deal and government strikebreaking, and growing class consciousness. Recent strike struggles confirm the correctness of Party trade union policies.

C450 COMMUNIST PARTY, USA, New York District. "Day of Solidarity and Unity in Struggle: May 1." New York: The District, n.d. [1935]. 22 pp.
A call to the annual May Day demonstration, with denunciation of Mayor La Guardia as a strikebreaker and workers' enemy and of the NRA as a program of fascization. Roosevelt is attacked for readying the country for war. A Soviet America would triple workers' living standards.

C451 . . ., New York Election Committee. "The Fight for Labor's Rights." New York: CPUSA, 1935. 23 pp.
Municipal election program, calling for expanded social welfare measures, a 30-hour week, the right to organize and strike, a housing program, and abolition of sales taxes. The pamphlet attacks the Socialist Party, and calls for a Labor Party and for a people's front against war and fascism.

C452 . . ., "A Guide to the Study of Comrade Dimitroff's Speech Delivered at the 7th World Congress of the C.I." New York: CPUSA, n.d. [1935?]. 6 pp.
A communist catechism on the contents of the major address announcing the turn to the popular front at the Seventh World Congress of the Communist International. Questions are divided into sections, dealing with the major headings of Dimitroff's address.

C453 . . ., Ohio State Committee. "Hope in Ohio for Jobs, Security, Democracy, Peace." Cleveland: The Committee, n.d. [1935?]. 15 pp.
An attack on Big Business for slashing relief and fighting labor organizations, and on the profit system for producing unemployment, bankruptcies, and monopoly. The unity of the people against reaction is urged.

C454 . . ., District Six. "Key Tasks: Tactics in the Trade Union, United Front & Labor Party Questions." Cleveland: CPUSA, District Six, 1935. 15 pp.
A resolution of the Ohio District Committee of the Party, adopted January 26-27, 1935, asserting that new strike struggles are maturing and outlining the central tasks of the Party with regard to trade-union work, united-front struggles, the fight for a labor party, and work among the Negro masses.

C455 . . ., New York District. "May First: Day of Solidarity and Unity in Struggle; Capitalism and Its Twins: War and Fascism." New York: The District, n.d. [1935]. 24 pp.
A call for workers to march on May Day, under the leadership of the Communist Party, for the right to organize unions of their own choosing, the 30-hour week and higher wages, against injunctions, and for the Workers Unemployment and Social Insurance Bill. Typical "third period" attacks are made on AFL leaders, the Roosevelt Administration, and La Guardia's program. A Soviet America is called for.

C456 . . ., Central Committee, Agit-Prop Committee. "Outline for Discussion on Trade Union Work." New York: CPUSA, 1935. 16 pp.

An outline of the Party's new trade union objectives and tactics, indicating the shift from support of the Trade Union Unity League to re-entry into the AFL. While the previous tactics were correct, new conditions require that the TUUL be disbanded. Communists must not push sectarian aims, but convince the membership that they are a constructive force.

C457 . . . "The Program of the Unemployed for Jobs, Union Wages, Cash Relief, Social Insurance: 1935 Election Platform of the Communist Party." New York: CPUSA, 1935. 23 pp.
The Party's program in the 1935 New York municipal election, attacking the Democratic, the Fusion-Republican, and particularly the Socialist Party. Sections deal with high rents, clothing, youth, Negro discrimination, the sales tax, and unemployment insurance.

C458 . . ., District Six. "A Year in Review and Our Next Tasks: Draft Resolution for the District Convention, June 22-23, 1935." Cleveland: The District, 1935. 31 pp.
A review of economic conditions and strike struggles in the past year, with attention to the role of the Party in developing militancy and overcoming NRA illusions. The struggle for the united front must be the basis of the Party's mass policy. Tasks confronting the Party in the coming months are outlined.

C459 . . ., Central Committee. On the Main Immediate Tasks of the C.P.U.S.A., "Communist," 14 (Feb. 1935), 117-26.
Resolution adopted by the Central Committee plenum, January 15-18, 1935, on the Party's revised labor policy: to work toward abolishing independent red unions, concentrate Party work within the AFL, seek trade union unity, and support proposals for a labor party. United front efforts with the socialists are to be intensified, and sectarian tendencies within the CP combatted.

C460 . . ., Central Committee. Forge a Mighty United Front for May Day! "Communist," 14 (April 1935), 291-98.
A May Day manifesto urging the masses to form a united front in opposition to fascist business, press, and government, and especially criticizing the NRA for compelling workers to join company unions. The only solution to the six-year bankruptcy of capitalism is the Communist Party.

C461 . . . . The Eighteenth Anniversary of the October Revolution, "Communist," 14 (Nov. 1935), 979-84.
A contrast of the great progress of communism in the Soviet Union with the decay and failure of the capitalist-imperialist world. The CP offers the only solution for curbing the fascist trend in the U.S. as evidenced by Negro lynching, increased production of armaments, slave wages on government relief projects, militarization of American youth, and continued unemployment.

C462 . . ., Central Committee. The Farmer-Labor Party and the Struggle against Reaction, "Communist," 14 (Dec. 1935), 1186-96.
A resolution adopted at the November plenum of the Central Committee, concentrating new united front efforts on the development of a farmer-labor party. Discontent with the Roosevelt regime, resulting from its failure to reduce unemployment, creates the basis for a successful farmer-labor party. In drumming up support for it, communists should emphasize immediate demands.

C463 . . ., Central Committee. The Seventh World Congress of the Communist International and the

Tasks of Our Party, "Communist," 14 (Dec. 1935), 1182-85.

Resolution adopted at the November plenum of the Central Committee, reorienting the Party to the line of the Seventh Congress of the Communist International. Emphasis is to be placed on building the united people's front, on opposing fascism and war, and on thwarting imperialist attacks on the USSR. Sectarianism within the Party must be eradicated.

C464   COMMUNIST PARTY, USA, National Campaign Committee. "Acceptance Speeches: Communist Candidates in the Presidential Elections." New York: Workers Library, 1936. 16 pp.

Nominating and acceptance speeches of Earl Browder as presidential candidate and James W. Ford as vice-presidential candidate. Browder minimized his attack on Roosevelt and the New Deal, asserting that the main goal was to defeat Republican reaction. Ford accepted the nomination as a tribute to the entire Negro people, and appealed to white workers to join the Negroes in their struggle.

C465   . . . . "Appeal to Socialists." New York: CPUSA, n.d. [1936?]. 15 pp.

Communist Party leaders warn the Socialist Party against Trotskyite influence, and invite socialists to collaborate in a people's front.

C466   . . . . "The Communist Election Platform." New York: Workers Library, 1936. 16 pp.

The central issue is declared to be democracy or fascism, progress or reaction. Formation of a great farmer-labor party is urged. The Party's platform includes jobs and living wages, social insurance, opportunity for youth, aid to indebted farmers, taxation of the rich, civil liberties, Negro rights, and prevention of war.

C467   . . ., New York State Housing Commission. "Manual on Housing." New York: CPUSA, n.d. [1936?]. 32 pp.

A view of the housing problem as an opportunity for the Party to penetrate neighborhoods and build influence and membership. All tenants can be united in a struggle for safe, decent, and economical housing, and small landlords won over to their side. Tenant organization can stimulate building of a people's front. Tips on organization of a tenants' union are given.

C468   . . . . "Resolutions of the Ninth Convention of the Communist Party." New York: Workers Library, 1936. 64 pp.

The Party position early in the popular front period. Three key resolutions are reproduced in full: on the struggle against reaction, fascism, and war; on the struggle for peace; and on building a mass party. The issue is declared to be, not capitalism versus socialism, but progress versus reaction. Independent political goals are temporarily sacrificed to a collective struggle for peace.

C469   . . ., Central Committee. For a Powerful United A.F. of L., "Communist," 15 (March 1936), 281-88.

The struggle for industrial unionism in the AFL is in reality the struggle to organize the unorganized. The AFL Executive Council's demand that the CIO be liquidated is a splitting tactic. Unity of the AFL is to be desired, but on the basis of industrial unionism. (Also published in pamphlet form.)

C470   . . ., Central Committee. For a United Front May Day, "Communist," 15 (May 1936), 405-10.

An assertion that the time is ripe for a socialist America. The road to victory is the fight for a six-hour day and a five-day week, a strong AFL, equality for Negroes, jobs for the youth, a farmer-labor party, and support of the Soviet Union.

C471   . . ., Jewish Bureau, Central Committee. On the Communist Approach to Zionism, "Communist," 15 (July 1936), 666-70.

The Zionists are Jewish capitalists in league with British imperialism. Whereas the Zionists want to expel the Arabs from Palestine and restrict immigration to pro-Zionists, the communists advocate free immigration and unity of Arab and Jewish workers against Zionist capitalists.

C472   . . ., Central Committee. The Communist Party on the Results of the Elections, "Communist," 15 (Dec. 1936), 1104-11.

Roosevelt's victory was a decisive defeat of fascism as represented by Coughlin, Hearst, and the Republicans. To achieve their demands, people should now put pressure on the Roosevelt Administration through trade unions and the Farmer-Labor Party, which should be established throughout the country.

C473   . . ., New York County Election Campaign Committee. "The Communist Election Platform." New York: The Committee, n.d. [1937]. 16 pp.

A call for the election of four communist candidates to the New York City Council, and for support of the American Labor Party as a progressive, antifascist party opposed to the Wall Street Tammany Tories. The program of the communist candidates includes passage of relief, social insurance, and civil rights measures, as well as public ownership and control of utilities.

C474   . . ., Bronx County, New York, Committee. "The Communist Election Platform: Vote Labor and Communist." New York: CPUSA, 1937. 15 pp.

Political campaign material during the popular-front period, defending the CIO and the progressive wing of the AFL, and urging the voters to elect American Labor Party candidates. The communists, as part of their popular-front orientation, advocate socialist objectives to be gained by democratic methods.

C475   . . ., Massachusetts Central Committee. "A Confession of Faith: We State Our Case to the Legislative Committee." [Boston?]: The Committee, n.d. [1937]. 31 pp.

Letter to a state legislative committee set up to investigate communist, fascist, and Nazi activities, asserting that the Communist Party is loyal and American, the inheritor of our revolutionary traditions. The real objects of the attack, the letter states, are the progressive and labor movements. The legislators are urged to investigate fascist and semi-fascist groups, a list of which is attached.

C476   . . ., Massachusetts. "Declaration of Principles and Constitution of the Communist Party of Massachusetts." Introd. by Otis Archer Hood and Phil Frankfeld. Boston: Communist Party of Massachusetts, 1937. 24 pp.

The principles and constitution of the Massachusetts unit of the Party during the popular front period, when collective security against fascist aggression was the major objective. In their introduction the state chairman and state secretary call for a powerful people's front for great social change.

C477   . . . . "First Convention of the Waterfront Section, New York Port, June 26, 27, 1937." New York: CPUSA, 1937. 58 pp. Mimeo.

A view of communist tactics among seamen, whose Party program calls for uniting into a National Maritime Union, affiliating with the CIO, supporting the American Labor Party, and building the Communist Party. Speeches by Foster, Hudson, and Amter relate the work of the marine section to the general 1937 CP line. A list of resolutions is included.

C478 COMMUNIST PARTY, USA, New York State Committee Education Department. "A Manual for Unit Educational Directors." New York: The Committee Education Department, 1937. 16 pp.

The educational director's task is to guide all educational work within the Party unit, and also to develop communist education in the territory or mass organization in which the unit operates. Sources of aid and of speakers, such as Party units and front organizations, are recommended. The "Daily Worker" is to be the center of educational work, and unit discussions the chief form of Party education.

C479 . . ., Illinois State Committee. "Socialism Triumphant in the USSR: 20th Anniversary, USSR, 1917-1937." Chicago: The Committee, 1937. 78 pp.

A pamphlet commemorating the twentieth anniversary of the Bolshevik revolution. Among the contents are a description of life and labor in the USSR; a tribute to Lenin by Stalin; an article, "The USSR a Beacon Light," by Morris Childs, Illinois State Secretary of the Party; quotations from Gorki; and two articles by Earl Browder, "Life in a Soviet America," and "Communism 20th Century Americanism."

C480 . . . . "Tell It to Millions!" New York: CPUSA, Publicity Department, n.d. [1937?]. 32 pp.

A guide for Party members in preparing press releases and gaining other publicity through radio and press.

C481 . . ., Central Committee. Building the Party in the Struggle for Proletarian Unity and the People's Front, "Communist," 16 (Aug. 1937), 735-48.

The resolution on Browder's report adopted at the plenary session of the Party's Central Committee, June 17-20, 1937, calling on the Party to build a people's front that will include progressives in the Democratic Party. The people's front will fight for the immediate demands of the masses, economic sanctions on aggressors, and trade union unity that recognizes industrial unionism. While also fighting for these goals, the Party will continue its independent role.

C482 . . ., Central Committee. Rally the People against Vigilantism and Reaction, "Communist," 16 (Aug. 1937), 749-53.

A statement of the Central Committee, rallying the Party against opponents of Roosevelt's proposed Supreme Court reorganization and against anti-CIO reactionaries. The reactionaries are trying to force Roosevelt to break with the CIO, while trying to force the CIO to expel its left-wing members. Roosevelt should ally himself more firmly with the workers; the CIO should organize more workers, seek unity with progressives in the AFL, and ally itself with the middle class.

C483 . . . . "Communist Election Platform, 1938: For Jobs, Security, Democracy and Peace." New York: Workers Library, n.d. [1938]. 16 pp.

A popular-front period election platform, asserting that the issue is democracy or fascism, not socialism or capitalism. The Party calls for a united front of all the people to fight monopoly and reaction and to support the New Deal. Roosevelt's collective-security foreign policy is supported, and an extension urged of the New Deal's work relief, social security, and farm program. Also demanded are an end to Jim Crow, curbing of monopolists' power, and extension of civil liberties.

C484 . . . . "Constitution and By-Laws of the CPUSA. Adopted by the Tenth National Convention, 1938." New York: Workers Library, 1938. 31 pp.

The constitution of the Communist Party, USA, during the popular front period. The preamble pledges the Party's defense of the U.S. Constitution and of the immediate interests of workers, and states the Party's objective to be the preparation of the working class for socialism as the logical extension of democracy.

C485 . . ., New Jersey State Committee. "Hague over Jersey." The Committee, n.d. [1938?]. 19 pp.

An attack on Mayor Frank Hague of Jersey City for corruption and crushing of democracy, for building a dictatorship on violence and robbery, and for using the "red" cry to deny civil liberties and keep out unions. Nevertheless the CIO unions are growing in New Jersey, as is Labor's Non-Partisan League.

C486 . . ., Negro Commission of the National Committee. "Is Japan the Champion of the Colored Races?" New York: Workers Library, 1938. 17 pp.

An appeal to Negroes during the popular front period to ignore Axis portrayals of Japan as champion of the colored races against white imperialism. Support of Japan is called support of Mussolini, the symbol of fascist colonial oppression. Negroes are urged to join the progressive whites and colored persons, and, with the USSR, to oppose fascism everywhere.

C487 . . ., Central Committee. "The La Follette Third Party: Will It Unite or Split the Progressive Forces?" New York: Workers Library, 1938. 32 pp.

An argument, in the popular front period, that progressive Americans need, not further division, but greater unity; not new minority political parties, but a majority coalition into a single democratic front to beat back the reactionary monopolies and solve the grave economic problems. Only reactionaries and fascists, who seek to split the progressive forces, welcome the La Follette move. Also, the La Follette program is reactionary, not progressive.

C488 . . ., New York State Committee. "A People's Constitution for New York." New York: The Committee, n.d. [1938]. 32 pp.

Party proposals for a New York State constitutional convention, calling for strengthening of civil liberties, changes in the power of courts, a unicameral legislature elected by proportional representation, the initiative and referendum, liberalization of voting requirements, broadening public ownership, and use of taxation powers for social welfare purposes.

C489 . . ., New York State Committee. "Proceedings, 10th Convention, Communist Party, New York State." New York: The Committee, 1938. 330 pp.

The discussion, reports, and decisions of the tenth convention of the Communist Party of New York State, held May 20-23, 1938. The proceedings cover a wide range of subjects, including problems of building the Party, the democratic front and the elections, work in trade unions and among the unemployed, and organizational efforts among women, Negroes, and national groups.

C490 . . . . "Resolutions of the 10th Convention of the Communist Party, U.S.A." New York: Workers Library, 1938. 22 pp.

Resolutions adopted by the Party's tenth national convention, May 27-31, 1938, on the offensive of reaction and the building of the democratic front, the 1938 elections, and Party building. Emphasis is placed on unification of democratic forces behind a single progressive candidate to defeat the candidates of reaction and fascism.

C491 COMMUNIST PARTY, USA, New York State, Women's Commission. "Women Voters, Save Your Home and Family! Vote Labor and Progressive." New York: The Commission, n.d. [1938]. 4 pp.

An appeal to women to vote for American Labor Party and progressive candidates. Issues expected to appeal to women, such as equal pay for equal work, lower living costs, and peace, are emphasized.

C492 . . ., National Committee, Educational Department. Political Forces and Issues, "Communist," 17 (Oct. 1938), 891-908.

A comparison of communist, progressive, and reactionary planks for the 1938 congressional elections, on such issues as economic recovery, social security, health and education, agriculture, youth, Negroes, monopolies, democracy, and peace. Included in the progressive column are the New Deal Democrats, Labor's Non-Partisan League, the Farmer-Labor Party of Minnesota, the American Labor Party of New York, the Washington Commonwealth Federation, and the Progressive bloc in Congress. In the reactionary listing are the reactionary Democrats, the Republican Party and the National Progressives.

C493 . . ., National Committee Organizational-Educational Commission. "How to Organize Mass Meetings." New York: Workers Library, 1939. 48 pp.

Instructions to Party units on the preparations for and organization of large meetings. Topics include date of meeting, location of hall, admission fee, publicity, entertainment, conducting the meeting, selling literature, open-air meetings, and use of radio and films.

C494 . . ., Waterfront section. "Sure—I'm a Red! The Story of an American Longshoreman." New York: The Section, 1939. 8 pp.

A recruiting pamphlet addressed to longshoremen, purporting to show how one longshoreman came to join the Party.

C495 . . ., Waterfront Section. "United We Stand." New York: The Section, n.d. [1939]. 12 pp.

An appeal to longshoremen to oppose racist discrimination in the industry and to support the New Deal and the Communist Party. The Party, following the principles of socialism, will end unemployment, poverty, and racial discrimination, as the workers have done in the Soviet Union.

C496 . . ., New York State Committee. "What about the Dies Committee?" New York: The Committee, n.d. [1939?]. 4 pp.

A call for withholding further appropriations from the Dies Committee, which engages in a Red hunt but does nothing to stop the spread of fascism in the U.S.

C497 . . ., National Committee. Keep America Out of the Imperialist War! "Communist," 18 (Oct. 1939), 899-904.

Britain and France rejected the Russian offer of collaboration in a peace front, instead abetting a German attack on Russia. The Soviet government forestalled Allied treachery by signing the Soviet-German nonaggression pact. Now an imperialist war has broken out between the Allies and Germany. America must keep out, giving no help to either side.

C498 . . ., Political Committee. America and the International Situation: Resolution Unanimously Adopted October 13, 1939, by the Political Committee of the Communist Party of the United States of America, "Communist," 18 (Nov. 1939), 995-1001.

The present imperialist war has altered international relations and changed class and political alignments within each capitalist nation. The nonfascist Allied powers are no longer on the side of peace. In order to keep the U.S. out of the war, Americans must not aid either side. Many New Dealers are now enemies of the working class, for they want the U.S. to aid Britain and France.

C499 . . . . "Campaign Book: Presidential Elections, 1940." New York: Workers Library, 1940. 128 pp. Suggested readings. Ind.

Included are biographies of the Party's candidates, the 1940 election platform, attacks on the other parties, and brief discussions of peace, jobs, social security, civil rights, monopoly, farmers, Negroes, youth, women, the Soviet Union, and socialism.

C500 . . ., Eastern Pennsylvania, Negro Commission. "Democracy Means Jobs for Negroes." Philadelphia: The Commission, n.d. [1940?]. 14 pp.

A presidential election pamphlet addressed to Negroes, asserting that the Party alone champions their full social, economic, and political equality. Defense industries are attacked for refusing to hire Negroes while talking of democracy.

C501 . . . . "Election Platform of the Communist Party, 1940." New York: Workers Library, 1940. 15 pp.

The Party's national election platform during the period of the Hitler-Stalin pact. Wall Street is said to want to enter the war unleashed by the imperialist ruling classes of both sides, whereas the American people want peace, jobs, education, and equal rights. A national farmer-labor party is urged as an anti-imperialist third party of the people.

C502 . . ., New York State Committee. "No Career in No Man's Land." New York: CPUSA, n.d. [1940]. 30 pp.

A denunciation, during the period of the Nazi-Soviet pact and the USSR attack on Finland, of the head of Labor Stage and his associates, who are soliciting aid for the Finns. Such efforts are labeled part of the drive to embroil the U.S. in imperialist war. Supporting the USSR's "consistent peace policy," the Party urges that we keep America out of war, reduce unemployment, and maintain civil liberties.

C503 . . ., National Committee. Resolutions Adopted by the National Committee of the Communist Party, U.S.A., in Plenary Session, February 17-18, 1940, "Communist," 19 (March 1940), 211-31.

Resolutions deal with the political situation and the role of the working class and the Party, the presidential campaign, defense of the Party, the anti-lynching bill, farmers and the war, and solidarity with the Irish people. Emphasis is placed, during the Hitler-Stalin pact period, on attacking the Roosevelt Administration for curtailing social welfare in the interests of its imperialist, pro-Allied, war policy.

C504 . . . . Resolutions Adopted by the Eleventh National Convention of the Communist Party, U.S.A., "Communist," 19 (July 1940), 615-27.

The resolutions include an acceptance of Browder's analysis of the war as an imperialist conflict. Other resolutions back democratic rights in the South, support Latin America against any attempted subjugation by the U.S., acclaim communist success in building Russia, and oppose U.S. persecution of foreign born.

C505 COMMUNIST PARTY, USA. Constitution of the Communist Party, U.S.A., "Communist," 19 (Dec. 1940), 1086-92.
The Party's constitution adopted in May 1938, as amended in November 1940. Provisions relate to membership, dues, International Solidarity Fund, rights and duties of members, structure of the Party, national organization, and disciplinary procedure.

C506 . . ., National Committee. Defeat Roosevelt's War-Powers Bill! Get Out and Stay Out of the War! "Communist," 20 (Feb. 1941), 115-19.
The communists protest against the war-powers bill which will enable Roosevelt to lend war material to Britain. The bill is a means by which American capitalism hopes to drag the U.S. into the war and make Britain a junior partner in its effort to gain world domination.

C507 . . . . Support the U.S.S.R. in Its Fight against Nazi War! "Communist," 20 (July 1941), 579-80.
The Party's statement following the Nazi attack on Russia, urging Americans to defeat any attempt at a new "Munich conspiracy" against the Soviet Union, and to give full support to the USSR in its struggle against Hitlerism.

C508 . . ., National Committee. The People's Program of Struggle for the Defeat of Hitler and Hitlerism, "Communist," 20 (Aug. 1941), 678-82.
A review of Soviet policy with respect to the Second World War, which has changed character as a result of Hitler's attack on the Soviet Union. The Party calls on all Americans to go to the aid of Russia, whose destruction would endanger the independence of all nations and the freedom of all peoples.

C509 . . ., National Committee. Everything for Victory over World-Wide Fascist Slavery! "Communist," 20 (Dec. 1941), 1043-44.
A statement following the Japanese attack on Pearl Harbor, pledging full support in the fight against the Berlin-Rome-Tokyo axis and calling on all America, especially labor, to join in that pledge.

C510 . . ., Montana. "Arvo Fredrickson — Hard-Rock Miner and Organizer: Selections from his Speeches and Writings." Butte, Montana: Communist Party of Montana, 1942. 32 pp.
A memorial pamphlet for the Montana Party chairman, who died while in the Army preparing to go overseas. Included are statements by leading communists and by the Butte local of the Mine, Mill and Smelter Workers, as well as speeches and articles by Fredrickson himself.

C511 . . ., National Committee. Attack Hitler Now! Open a Western Front in Europe! "Communist," 21 (May 1942), 291-96.
A May Day Manifesto calling for the United Nations to force Hitler to face wars on two fronts. A Western front would thwart Nazi victory plans and offer great help to the gallant Red Army. American workingmen are praised for not striking and urged to give their all for the Victory Production Program. (Also published in pamphlet form.)

C512 . . ., National Committee. Enforce the Fourteenth Amendment! Strengthen the War Effort by Abolishing the Poll Tax, "Communist," 21 (May 1942), 380-84.

A letter sent on March 23 by the national committee of the Party to the subcommittee of the Senate Judiciary Committee which was holding hearings on legislation to outlaw the poll tax. The poll tax, which violates the U.S. Constitution, should be abolished to permit the survival of democracy.

C513 . . ., National Committee, Organization Department. "Party Building: A Handbook for Branch Officers." New York: CPUSA, n.d. [1943]. 15 pp.
Guidance to branch officers in the Party building campaign, emphasizing the key position of the Party branch. Sections deal with recruiting, conditions of Party membership, typical arguments to be answered, welcoming and activizing new members, initiation of members, and the agenda of branch meetings.

C514 . . . . "Stages in the History of the Communist Party: A Political Review." New York: CPUSA, 1943. 39 pp.
A booklet for new members of the Party, taken from the brief submitted by the Party in the deportation proceedings against Harry Bridges. Tracing its formation and history, the Party denies that it advocates the forcible overthrow of the U.S. government. This is termed a distortion of Marxism by the Attorney General. The Party bases its principles on the scientific law of social development.

C515 . . ., National Committee. May Day Manifesto of the Communist Party, "Communist," 22 (May 1943), 387-93.
An appeal to carry the war to the Western front and achieve increased unity with the Soviet Union. The key to victory is a unified world labor movement fighting for a common cause.

C516 . . ., National Committee, Organization Department. "Manual for Community Club Leaders: A Handbook for the Use of Officers and Committees of Communist Community Clubs." New York: The Committee, 1944. 64 pp.
Ideas and suggestions for officers and committees of communist community clubs, prepared after the decision was made to drop the word "Party," but before the transformation to the Communist Political Association was made. The Community Club unites all members living in a specific geographic area. Responsibilities of each of the officers are outlined.

C517 . . . . "Shall the Communist Party Change Its Name?" New York: CPUSA, National Committee, 1944. 23 pp.
Excerpts of speeches by Earl Browder, Eugene Dennis, Roy Hudson, and John Williamson at the January 1944 meeting of the national committee of the Communist Party. Asserting that the concept of "party," not of "communist," prevents cooperation with other democratic groups, Browder calls for transforming the CPUSA into the Communist Political Association. The others support the change in terms of political activity and work in the labor movement.

C518 . . ., National Committee. Decisions of the National Committee of the Communist Party, Unanimously Adopted on January 9, 1944, at the Final Session of its Plenary Meeting, "Communist," 23 (Feb. 1944), 107-8.
The national committee endorses Browder's report evaluating the Teheran Conference and decides to convene a national convention in May, 1944, at which it will propose that the Communist Party be reorganized under the name of the Communist Political Association.

C519 COMMUNIST PARTY, USA, National Committee. Statement to the Press, "Communist," 23 (Feb. 1944), 99-101.
A statement pledging the Party's cooperation, within the framework of the existing system of free enterprise, in carrying out the allied powers' wartime and postwar objectives. The proposal to change the Party's name to Communist Political Association at a national convention to be held in May is set forth.

C520 . . ., New York State. "Constitution of the Communist Party of the United States of America, together with By-Laws of the Communist Party of the State of New York." New York: Communist Party of the State of New York, 1945. 32 pp.
The constitution of the Communist Party adopted July 28, 1945, when the Communist Political Association reconverted itself back into the Communist Party. It is similar to the constitution of 1938. (Also published in "Daily Worker," August 12, 1945.)

C521 . . ., Labor Committee. Labor and the Problems of Reconversion, "Political Affairs," 24 (Sept. 1945), 771-81.
A call for government action to provide jobs, increase unemployment insurance, raise the minimum wage, increase wages by 20 per cent, ensure full employment, stimulate foreign trade, and provide health insurance. The labor movement should achieve labor unity, organize the unorganized, and reassert the right to strike.

C522 . . . . Present Situation and the Next Tasks, "Political Affairs," 24 (Sept. 1945), 816-32.
The resolution adopted by the national convention, July 28, 1945, that liquidated the Communist Political Association and reconstituted the CPUSA. The resolution repudiates Browder's revisionism, condemns Party bureaucracy, and acknowledges errors on the Negro question. Cooperation with all democratic and antifascist forces is pledged. (Also published in pamphlet form; an earlier draft of the resolution appeared in "Political Affairs," July 1945.)

C523 . . ., National Board. The People's Fight for Wages, Jobs and Security, "Political Affairs," 24 (Nov. 1945), 997-1002.
Labor's program is in the interests of the nation because it will raise purchasing power and thus increase production and employment. Big Business wants to continue its profiteering at the expenses of labor and the people. The Truman Administration will not fight for its program, which is being cut to pieces by Congress. Only through unity can labor lead the people's fight in Congress.

C524 . . ., National Education Department. "Browder's Revisionism and His Struggle against the Party." New York: CPUSA, 1946. 14 pp.
A chronological summary of events leading up to Browder's expulsion in 1946.

C525 . . ., National Veterans Committee. "On the Struggle against Revisionism." New York: The Committee, 1946. 112 pp.
Booklet for returning communist servicemen to acquaint them with the struggle inside the Communist Party against Browderism. Besides the article by Jacques Duclos, the French communist leader, which announced the Comintern's condemnation of Browderism, the booklet includes articles and letters by William Z. Foster, Eugene Dennis, and John Williamson, the preamble to the Party's constitution, and the resolution adopted by the Party's national convention on July 28, 1945, on "The Present Situation and the Next Tasks."

C526 . . . . On the Expulsion of Earl Browder from the Communist Party, "Political Affairs," 25 (March 1946), 215-18.
The February 5, 1946, statement of the Party's national board unanimously recommending Browder's expulsion, together with the February 13 resolution of the national committee unanimously approving the recommendation. The expulsion was based on gross violation of Party discipline and decisions, active opposition to the Party line and leadership, factional activity, and desertion to the class enemy.

C527 . . ., National Secretariat. Defeat the Anglo-U.S. Imperialist War Drive! Restore Big 3 Unity to Preserve World Peace! "Political Affairs," 25 (April 1946), 291-93.
A statement by the Party's national secretariat on March 5, 1946, attacking Churchill's Fulton, Mo., speech as a defection from the wartime coalition and a proposal for an Anglo-American campaign to attack Russia and gain world domination.

C528 . . ., National Groups Commission. Communist Work among the American Jewish Masses: Resolution of the National Groups Commission of the C.P.U.S.A., October, 1946, "Political Affairs," 25 (Nov. 1946), 1025-45.
The major task in achieving antifascist Jewish unity in the U.S. is to isolate and defeat the reactionary Jewish social-democrats. United Jewish-Arab struggle against reactionary and imperialist schemes of fake independence for Palestine is called for. Jewish bourgeois nationalism and assimilationism in the U.S. are opposed, and Jewish participation in the progressive movement of the American people is advocated.

C529 . . ., National Board. Statement by the National Board of the Communist Party on the Recent Expulsions of Vern Smith, Ruth McKenney, Bruce Minton, and William F. Dunne, "Political Affairs," 25 (Nov. 1946), 1011-15.
The expelled group is charged with opposition to the Party line since the emergency convention of July 1945 that repudiated Browder revisionism. Their line of struggle against the Party is semi-Trotskyist and unprincipled leftist adventurism. Posing as the only true opponents of Browderism, they falsely charged that the Party is still revisionist in policy and practice.

C530 . . ., National Groups Commission. Jewish Nationality Group Problems, "Jewish Life," 1 (Dec. 1946), 19-21.
A resolution of the Party's National Groups Commission calling for a progressive mass culture as part of the struggle against bourgeois nationalism and assimilationism in the American Jewish nationality group. While participating in the antifascist activities of the Jewish people of all countries, progressive Jews must be part of the labor-democratic coalition in America.

C531 . . ., National Committee. "The Communist Position on the Negro Question." New York: New Century, 1947. 61 pp.
Excerpts from major speeches on the Negro question by William Z. Foster and others at the plenary meeting of the national committee, January 3-4, 1946. (A pamphlet by Benjamin Davis, "The Path of Negro Liberation," contains the report on which the discussion was based.) The resolution adopted, while supporting in principle the right of self-determination for the Negro people, does not propose this as a slogan of action, instead advocating equality and integration.

C532 COMMUNIST PARTY, USA. "What Do Communists Really Want?" New York: CPUSA, 1947. 12 pp.

A call for united action of progressives to achieve higher wages; a progressive tax policy; social programs for labor, veterans, and farmers; projects such as the Missouri Valley Authority; advancement of Negro rights; government ownership of certain basic industries; and a peace policy that includes total disarmament, relief for needy countries, and restoration of "Big Three" unity.

C533 .... "What You Should Know about The Communists—Who They Are—What They Believe In—What They Fight For." New York: CPUSA, 1947. 16 pp.

A prediction that in the next six months 30,000 people who believe in peace, progress, equality, and socialism will join the Party, and an argument that we have poverty, Jim Crow, anti-Semitism, and the cold war because a handful of people organized into huge trusts control our economic life. The Party disavows violence, declaring that leading capitalists are the ones who practice it.

C534 ..., Veterans Commission. "Who Ruptured Our Duck?" New York: New Century, n.d. [1947]. 15 pp.

A pamphlet, addressed to veterans, denouncing high prices and the lack of jobs and housing. The immediate program of communist war veterans is presented, along with the Party's long-range plan to introduce socialism as in the USSR.

C535 ..., National Committee. Special Plenum Issue, "Political Affairs," 26 (Jan. 1947).

An issue devoted almost entirely to reports to and remarks at the plenary meeting of the Party's national committee, held December 3-5, 1946. (A number of the reports are abstracted separately.)

C536 ..., National Committee. Resolution on the Question of Negro Rights and Self-Determination, "Political Affairs," 26 (Feb. 1947), 155-58.

Adopted by the national committee at its December 3-5 meeting, the resolution supports the right of the Negro people to realize self-government in the Negro majority area in the South, without raising self-determination as an immediate slogan of action. The importance of Negro-white working class unity and of Negro alliances with other minority groups is stressed.

C537 ..., National Board. United Labor Action Can Halt Reaction, "Political Affairs," 26 (May 1947), 387-90.

The May Day appeal of the Party to workers and all liberty-loving Americans, calling for unity of labor and the people to defeat reaction and fascism. Emphasis is placed on defending the trade unions, protecting civil liberties, preventing imperialist expansion, and halting the drive to reaction.

C538 ..., National Board. Statement on the Question of Affiliation to the Information Bureau of the Nine Communist Parties, "Political Affairs," 26 (Dec. 1947), 1141-42.

A statement issued November 2, 1947, hailing the establishment of the Information Bureau as a contribution to peace and to the struggle against Marshall Plan imperialism, but declining to affiliate in order not to provide a pretext for further repression in this country.

C539 .... "An Open Letter to All Members of the Communist Party." New York: CPUSA, n.d. [1948]. 12 pp.

An appeal, under the signatures of Eugene Dennis, William Z. Foster, and Henry Winston, on behalf of the Party's national committee, to increase the circulation of the "Daily Worker" and the "Worker," as a major task of the Party's membership.

C540 ..., National Educational Department. "Theory and Practice of the Communist Party: First Course." New York: New Century, 1948. 48 pp.

A post-Browder pamphlet summarizing the Party line of 1948, and outlining the structure of the Party. Subjects covered include capitalism and the class struggle, imperialism, war and fascism, the Negro question, socialism, and the Communist Party. Criticism of Browder's "revisionism" appears throughout. A reading list and study-guide questions are included.

C541 .... Communist Position on the Marshall Plan, "Political Affairs," 27 (April 1948), 304-14.

A statement to the Foreign Affairs Committee of the House of Representatives, opposing the proposed European Recovery Program as part of the cold war against the USSR. It is designed to rebuild Western Germany's war potential, prop up capitalism, undermine the sovereignty of the participating countries, and forge a reactionary Western bloc under Wall Street's domination.

C542 .... A Call to the American People, "Political Affairs," 27 (May 1948), 387-88.

A statement released to the press April 30, 1948, calling for the defeat of Senator Mundt's proposed Subversive Activities Control Act to outlaw the Party and "front" organizations on the Attorney General's list. Passage would constitute a long step toward fascism and World War III.

C543 ..., National Committee. Draft Resolution for the National Convention, C.P.U.S.A. "Political Affairs," 27 (June 1948), 483-513.

A draft resolution for the convention to be held August 3-6, 1948, emphasizing Wall Street's drive for world rule, the growing danger of war, the reactionary offensive and the growth of fascism at home, Wall Street's attacks upon the people's economic standards, the resistance of the American people, and the need to build a mass vanguard Communist Party.

C544 .... 1948 Election Platform of the Communist Party, "Political Affairs," 27 (Sept. 1948), 937-44.

The Party's election platform emphasizes opposition to war and fascism, defense of labor's living standards against inflation caused by the trusts, defense of civil rights and Negro rights, and support of the Progressive Party. (Also published in pamphlet form.)

C545 ..., 14th National Convention. Approaching the 30th Anniversary of the Communist Party, U.S.A. "Political Affairs," 27 (Nov. 1948), 1006-12.

A statement adopted by the convention, August 6, 1948, summarizing the history of the Party as the champion of labor and the people. The Party has fought against imperialism, supported unions, struggled for relief and jobs, and opposed fascism and war, while avoiding right opportunism and left sectarianism.

C546 ..., New York State Committee. The Election Results in New York, "Political Affairs," 27 (Dec. 1948), 1082-87.

A report on the American Labor Party vote and the victory of Vito Marcantonio in New York City. The state-wide Democratic victories are attributed to the "lesser evil" voting of most citizens, whose first thought was to defeat Republican candidates. Communists must renew their efforts to combat Truman's warlike and fascist policies.

C547 COMMUNIST PARTY, USA, Waterfront Section. "Maritime Workers at the Crossroads." [New York]: CPUSA, n.d. [1949?]. 23 pp.
A pamphlet addressed to maritime workers, calling for labor unity in the current contract negotiations. The communists denounce Red-baiting, and call for higher wages, the 40-hour week, saving the hiring hall, ending discrimination against Negroes, the four-watch system, and unemployment compensation. They also call for world peace and trade based on Soviet-American friendship.

C548 .... "Not 12 Men on Trial, but Everybody! New York: CPUSA, 1949. 13 pp.
An agitational pamphlet, with pictures and striking format, protesting the indictment of 12 Party leaders under the Smith Act. Freedom for the 12 is demanded as necessary to save democracy for 145,000,000 people.

C549 . . ., National Education Department. "The Struggle against White Chauvinism: Outline for Discussion and Study Guide for Schools, Classes, Study Groups." New York: CPUSA, 1949. 19 pp.
A publication for internal Party use, explaining white chauvinism as the ideology used to perpetuate the Wall Street national oppression of the Negro people and to support the drive of American imperialism to world domination. The Party calls for the eradication of white chauvinism, together with its opposite, petty-bourgeois nationalism.

C550 . . ., National Committee. Labor Must Take the Offensive to Win Substantial Wage Increases! "Political Affairs," 28 (Feb. 1949), 1-4.
A statement issued by the national committee, CPUSA, on January 5, 1949, demanding higher wages for all workers to offset the decrease in the dollar's purchasing power. The Party calls for equal rights for Negro workers; Negro-white unity in the struggle against the trusts; and economic security, democracy, and peace.

C551 .... The Mexican-Americans—Their Plight and Struggles, "Political Affairs," 28 (May 1949), 71-80; (July), 75-84.
Two resolutions adopted at the fourteenth national convention, CPUSA, August 3, 1948, outlining the tasks facing the Party among the Mexican-American migratory workers of the American Southwest. A discussion of the traditions of the Mexican-Americans and of their current economic, social, and political status follows.

C552 . . ., National Committee. A Momentous Youth Gathering, "Political Affairs," 28 (July 1949), 85-87.
The formation of the National Organizing Conference for a Labor Youth League is applauded. Objectives are to stimulate study of Marxism, promote unity of American youth, oppose the warmongering of the capitalists, strive for friendship between Russia and the U.S., support trade unions, and defend civil rights. (A draft of principles for the Labor Youth League appears on pp. 87-89.)

C553 . . ., National Committee. Resolution on the Question of Negro Rights and Self-Determination, "Political Affairs," 28 (Sept. 1949), 49-53.
A resolution adopted by the special plenum of the national committee, CPUSA, December 1946, which reaffirmed the national character of the Negro people's struggle. It is republished as part of the celebration of the Party's 30th anniversary.

C554 . . ., National Education Department. "Prevent World War III." New York: The Department, 1950. 8 pp.

Information on various aspects of Party work in New York County, linked to the New York State goal of 1,500,000 signatures on peace petitions. Topics include opposition to the Korean War, Party recruiting, the role of the Negro people in the fight for peace and freedom, the Smith Act trial of the 11 communist leaders, and the 1950 election campaign.

C555 . . ., National Committee. The Cold-War Rulings of the Supreme Court, "Political Affairs," 29 (June 1950), 3-6.
A statement issued by the national committee of the Party, May 10, 1950, attacking the Supreme Court for its decisions of May 8 upholding the Taft-Hartley Law, supporting a state ban on picketing against Jim Crow employment practices, and restoring the contempt citations of congressional witch-hunters.

C556 . . ., National Secretariat. Halt Wall Street Aggression in Asia! "Political Affairs," 29 (Aug. 1950), 1-3.
American intervention in Korea has been instigated by Wall Street to defeat the people's revolt against their fascist rulers. The Party demands the cessation of American intervention in Korea, the outlawing of the atom bomb, and the seating of the Chinese government in the Security Council of the UN.

C557 . . ., National Committee. The Sovereignty of the American People Cannot Be Revoked by any Act of Congress, "Political Affairs," 29 (Oct. 1950), 30-31.
A statement issued September 23, 1950, following passage of the Internal Security Act (McCarran Act). It is characterized as a legislative blueprint for fascism, destructive of the Bill of Rights.

C558 .... "The McCarran Conspiracy against the Bill of Rights: The Communist Party's Answer to the Charges of the Attorney-General under the McCarran Act." New York: CPUSA, 1951. 23 pp.
Denunciation of the petition filed by the Attorney General with the Subversive Activities Control Board (set up under the McCarran Act) requesting that the Communist Party be ordered to register under the Act. The McCarran Act, the Party asserts, is unconstitutional, its function being to deny freedom of association and create the new crime of political heresy. The Party denies that it is a conspiracy or that it is subject to foreign domination.

C559 .... Working-Class and People's Unity for Peace! (Main Resolution of the 15th National Convention, C.P.U.S.A.), "Political Affairs," 30 (Jan. 1951), 1-37.
Sections of the resolution deal with the growing war danger and the fight for peace, the menace of fascism and the struggle for democracy, the need for a fighting and united working class, the Negro liberation movement, the need for independent political action, working farmers as the main ally of the working class, and problems faced by the Party.

C560 . . ., National Committee. America's Hour of Peril—Unite! Save Democracy and Peace! "Political Affairs," 30 (July 1951), 1-8.
A statement issued following the U.S. Supreme Court decision upholding the conviction of the 11 communist leaders and their lawyers. The Bill of Rights is said to be nullified, with thought control instead of free speech. Only united action and popular resistance can save us from full-fledged fascism and a third world war.

C561 . . ., National Election Campaign Committee.

"1952 Election Platform of the Communist Party."
New York: The Committee, n.d. [1952]. 16 pp.
The issue is said to be peace or war, democracy or fascism. The platform includes an immediate cease fire in Korea, outlawing the atom bomb, reducing armaments, elimination of the North Atlantic Pact, repeal of the Smith, McCarran, and Taft-Hartley Acts, abolition of the House Committee on Un-American Activities, and the end of segregation. Vincent Hallinan and Charlotta Bass, Progressive Party candidates in 1952, are supported.

C562 COMMUNIST PARTY, USA. "Steel Labor's Road to Economic Security, Peace and Democracy: A Communist Viewpoint." New York: CPUSA, 1953. 96 pp.
Analysis of problems in the steel industry. The corporations are charged with establishment of a vicious, feudal-type system to add every possible penny to already fabulous profits. The union is the key in the fight for economic security as well as in political and legislative action. A program of militant local union action is outlined.

C563 . . ., National Committee. On Conviction of the Thirteen Communist Leaders, "Political Affairs," 32 (Jan. 1953), 1-4.
A statement issued on the conclusion of the second Foley Square trial at which 13 "second-string" CP leaders were convicted. The verdict is denounced as a thought-control conviction, a product of the present war hysteria, and a typical example of a frame-up in a hostile capitalist court.

C564 . . ., National Committee. Resolution on the Situation Growing out of the Presidential Elections (Final Text), "Political Affairs," 32 (July 1953), 5-16.
Eisenhower's election is viewed as a victory for reaction; it gave control to the party of monopoly and increased the dangers of fascism and of spreading the war. It showed that communists must build a united front, because the working class is not ready to create a mass third party. Our Party must help build a political coalition embracing labor, Negroes, and the democratic forces. (An earlier version of this resolution appeared in "Political Affairs," Dec. 1952.)

C565 . . ., National Committee. The Rosenbergs: Heroes of Democracy, "Political Affairs," 32 (July 1953), 1-4.
Ethel and Julius Rosenberg were murdered by the ruling class to intimidate the fight for peace and democracy. The Rosenbergs died innocent, heroes of democracy, refusing to "finger" the progressive and Marxist movement as an espionage conspiracy.

C566 . . ., National Committee. Restore Democratic Rights! "Political Affairs," 32 (Oct. 1953), 1-4.
A denunciation of the recent arrests of two communist leaders, fugitives from a Smith Act conviction, and of four others for allegedly harboring them, as another blow against democratic liberties. The secret police should be abolished and the Bill of Rights saved.

C567 . . ., Illinois. "Illinois Faces the '54 Elections." Chicago: Communist Party of Illinois, n.d. [1954]. 12 pp.
A call for political independence of labor as it works within the Democratic Party, and for the ultimate establishment of a party of the people, with labor as the main base. Objectives in the coming election should be to open the door to peace, elect anti-McCarthy candidates, and increase Negro representation in elected office.

C568 . . ., New York State. "Patriotism against McCarthyism." New York: CPUSA, New York State, n.d. [1954]. 16 pp.
The full text of a speech by New York Party Chairman Robert Thompson, made when sentenced to an additional four-year term for contempt for failure to surrender in the original Smith Act case. Part of the speech was undelivered, having been stopped by the judge when Thompson attempted to describe McCarthyism as the real danger to America.

C569 . . ., National Committee. Answer the Attack on the Communist Party and the Labor Movement, "Political Affairs," 33 (Sept. 1954), 2-6.
The Communist Control Act of 1954, a major triumph of McCarthyism, is the most extreme step in our country's history against political and democratic liberties. It is based on the Big Lie that the Communist Party advocates violent overthrow of the U.S. government. Under pretext of communist domination, it establishes a system of government licensing of trade unions.

C570 . . . . The American Way to Jobs, Peace, Democracy: Program of the Communist Party, "Political Affairs," 33 (Oct. 1954), 1-20.
The Party's post-Stalinist program, emphasizing the dangers of depression and war and the menace of McCarthyism. The communist program calls for raising the people's purchasing power, spending for human welfare, ending the cold war, strengthening democracy, and winning equal rights for Negroes. The present issue is not communism, but peace, security, and democracy versus monopoly, fascism, and war. (Also published in pamphlet form. A preliminary draft of this program appeared in "Political Affairs," April 1954.)

C571 . . . . "The Farm Crisis." New York: New Century, 1955. 23 pp.
An attack upon the federal government's handling of agricultural problems, and especially upon Secretary of Agriculture Benson for denying that a farm crisis exists. The Party's program includes raising the purchasing power of the people, curbing the trusts, spending for human welfare instead of warfare, strengthening democracy, winning equal rights for Negroes, ending the cold war, and promoting friendship and trade with communist countries.

C572 . . . . "Call to the 16th National Convention, Communist Party, USA, February 9-12th, 1957, New York City." New York: CPUSA, n.d. [1956]. 4 pp.
Call for a Party convention with a declaration on the state of the American people and the Party. As a result of these developments, plus revelations of serious weaknesses and injustices in the Soviet world, Party members are debating all possible issues. Provisions for apportionment and election of delegates are included.

C573 . . . . "Draft Resolution for the 16th National Convention of the Communist Party, U.S.A., Adopted Sept. 13, 1956." New York: New Century, 1956. 62 pp.
The draft resolution for the February 1957 Party convention, following the Khrushchev revelations of Stalin's excesses and the Hungarian and Polish events. The resolution favored Negro integration in American life, a political realignment, and unity of all socialist-minded elements. It criticized the Party's left sectarian errors, and called for Party democracy and the independence and equality of Marxist parties.

C574 . . ., Labor Committee. "Greetings to the American Working People on the Occasion of the First Anniversary of the Great Labor Merger, AFL-CIO! New York: The Committee, n.d. [1956]. 8 pp.

Praise and support for the merger, although need exists for more political action, organization drives, solving jurisdictional disputes, etc. The AFL-CIO is criticized for lacking a full program for peace, and some of its leaders are attacked for their hostility toward the recent Soviet intervention in Hungary.

C575 COMMUNIST PARTY, USA, National Committee. Statement of the National Committee, C.P.U.S.A., "Political Affairs," 35 (July 1956), 34-36.
Khrushchev's speech on the evils of Stalinism calls for an analysis by the leadership of the CPSU of how such perversions could continue for 20 years. We justified many Soviet policies now shown to be wrong. Relations between Marxists of various countries must be based on serving the interests of each people and all progressive humanity, equality of parties, and the right and duty of friendly criticism of the Marxists of any country.

C576 . . ., National Committee. On the Events in Hungary, "Political Affairs," 35 (Dec. 1956), 1-5.
The text of an open letter to the Party membership, November 19, 1956, on the Hungarian situation. Members of the Committee hold a common view on events in Hungary preceding November 4, when the USSR intervened, but differ with regard to subsequent events. While presenting the Soviet assertion that intervention was necessary to forestall fascism, the Committee refuses either to justify or to condemn the intervention.

C577 . . . . "Constitution of the Communist Party of the United States of America." New York: New Century, 1957. 24 pp.
The text of the Party constitution adopted by the sixteenth national convention, February 9-12, 1957. The preamble advocates a "peaceful, democratic road to socialism through the political and economic struggles of the American people within the developing constitutional process." Article 7 provides for the expulsion of any member who advocates force, violence, or terrorism, or who conspires or acts to weaken or overthrow institutions of American democracy.

C578 . . . . "Main Political Resolution Adopted by the 16th National Convention of the Communist Party, U.S.A., February 9-12, 1957." New York: New Century, 1957. 81 pp.
The resolution calls for the formation of an antimonopoly coalition composed of labor, farmers, the Negro people, small business people, and professionals, and advocates a peaceful and constitutional road to socialism in the U.S. Errors in the Party's fight for peace and against the fascist danger are reviewed, with warnings against both left-sectarian and right-opportunist dangers. Social Democratic organizations are to be dealt with fraternally, not as enemies.

C579 . . . . "Proceedings (Abridged) of the 16th National Convention, Feb. 9-12, 1957." New York: CPUSA, 1957. 351 pp.
Proceedings of the Party convention following that of the Twentieth Party Congress of the Communist Party of the Soviet Union and the Hungarian and Polish revolutions of 1956. The convention was marked by a three-way struggle between the supporters of William Z. Foster, an anti-Foster group centered around "Daily Worker" editor John Gates, and a middle group led by Party secretary Eugene Dennis. Issues over which major controversy took place were the name and form of the Party, the American (i.e., peaceful) road to socialism, the nature of the errors of the Party in the postwar period, and the procedures for election of the incoming national committee. The main political resolution adopted by the convention appears on pp. 253-328.

C580 . . ., State Board and National Convention Delegation. Communist Activity Today: A Program for Minnesota, "Political Affairs," 36 (May 1957), 7-23.
A program prepared prior to the April state convention, which adopted it unanimously. The program stresses the need for Marxist study of Minnesota and the Upper Midwest. A program for Minnesota should be developed, covering the state's economy and monopoly growth, the economic outlook, the tax program, peace, and discrimination.

C581 ., National Executive Committee. Statement on the Declaration of 12 Communist Parties, "Political Affairs," 37 (Jan. 1958), 1-4.
A statement concerning the declaration adopted in Moscow in November 1957, approved by the National Executive Committee of the CPUSA on December 22, 1957, by a vote of 11 to 7, with two abstaining and two absent. The statement asserted that only the CPUSA could chart the American road to socialism. Though the 12 parties viewed right opportunism as the main danger at present, the CPUSA looks upon left sectarianism as the major obstacle. (For the minority view see Robert Thompson, On the 12-Party Declaration, "Political Affairs," Feb. 1958.)

C582 . . ., National Committee. On the Resignation of John Gates, "Political Affairs," 37 (March 1958), 7-9.
A resolution submitted by Jack Stachel and approved at the February meeting of the national committee by a vote of 36 to 12, with seven abstentions. The resolution attacks Gates for liberal-reformist political views, for opposition to a Marxist-Leninist party, and for abandonment of the concept of proletarian internationalism. Departure of such persons will strengthen the Party.

C583 . . ., National Committee. On Uniting and Strengthening the Party and Its Mass Base, "Political Affairs," 37 (March 1958), 1-6.
A resolution submitted by Eugene Dennis to the national committee meeting of February 14-16 and approved by a vote of 32 to 20, with three abstentions. Emphasis is on the growth of a dangerous right-opportunist, revisionist viewpoint, exemplified by Gates; and on the assertion that the Party is not a temporary organization, but is here to stay.

C584 . . ., National Executive Committee. On the Peace Manifesto and the 12-Party Declaration, "Political Affairs," 37 (June 1958), 22-26.
A statement hailing the Soviet Union's announcement of unilateral suspension of nuclear weapons tests, the Manifesto for Peace issued by representatives of 64 communist parties in Moscow, and the Declaration of the Twelve Communist and Workers' Parties (the parties which govern socialist states).

C585 . . ., National Committee. A Policy for American Labor, "Political Affairs," 37 (Aug. 1958), 1-17.
A statement adopted June 29, 1958, asserting that the U.S. once again is in an economic crisis, and calling for wage increases, a fight for peace, a shorter work week, organization of the South, a Negro-labor alliance, independent political action, strengthening of united labor action, an end of racketeering and business unionism, and rebuilding the influence of the left.

C586 . . ., National Committee. Draft Political Resolution, "Political Affairs," 38 (Sept. 1959), 24-44.
The draft of a resolution approved by the national committee for Party discussion prior to the national convention on December 10-13, 1959. The resolution deals with

the U.S. need for a peace policy, the domestic economic and political situation, the importance of an antimonopoly people's coalition, the 1960 presidential election, and the role of the Party. (For criticism see William Z. Foster, On the Draft Resolution, "Political Affairs," Dec. 1959.)

C587 COMMUNIST PARTY, USA, 17th National Convention. "The Negro Question in the U.S.A." New York: New Century, 1960. 23 pp.
The resolution on the Negro question adopted by the convention, asserting that Negroes, though a specially oppressed part of the American nation, are not constituted as a separate nation. The proposal for self-determination, formerly advanced by the Party, is discarded as deficient. The report of Claude Lightfoot to the convention on "The Negro Question Today" is included. (Earlier drafts of the resolution appeared in "Political Affairs" in January and September, 1959.)

C588 . . ., New York State. "Subways Are for Sitting." New York: Communist Party of New York State, n.d. [1962]. 20 pp. Ref. Multilithed.
A program to meet New York's transit crisis, pointing out that many other countries are far ahead of us in the quality of transit service. Suggestions are made for expanding the subway network, improving equipment and service, financing the program, and improving transit labor conditions.

C589 . . . . "New Program of the Communist Party, U.S.A. (A draft)." Foreword by Gus Hall. New York: Political Affairs Publishers, 1966. 128 pp.
Finding our society in crisis, the result of monopoly, the cold war, and imperialist aggression against colonial revolutions, the program calls for the creation of a new people's party comprising the working class, the Negro people, farmers, intellectuals, professionals, small business, and youth. The new party would challenge monopoly, expand democracy, improve the well-being of the people, increase working class strength, secure peace, and halt the arms race. Within the larger coalition the communists will seek a political majority for a socialist reconstruction of society. Unity of the left is urged.

C590 COMMUNIST POLITICAL ASSOCIATION, New York State. "Constitution of the Communist Political Association together with By-Laws of the C.P.A. of New York State." New York: CPA of New York State, n.d. [1944]. 32 pp.
The constitution of the Communist Political Association, formed as a successor to the CPUSA under Browder's leadership. The Association is declared to be a nonparty organization based on the working class, and carrying forward the traditions of Washington, Jefferson, Paine, Jackson, and Lincoln, under the changed conditions of modern industrial society.

C591 COMMUNIST POLITICAL ASSOCIATION. "The Path to Peace, Progress and Prosperity: Proceedings of Constitutional Convention of the Communist Political Association, New York, May 20-22, 1944." New York: Communist Political Association, 1944. 140 pp. App.
Record of the convention which unanimously dissolved the Communist Party, USA, and formed the Communist Political Association. The abolition of "partisan purpose" but not the abandonment of Marxian principles was declared the future Party policy. The new turn of the communist movement was an effort to achieve national unity, to avoid postwar class struggles, and to realize postwar Anglo-Soviet-American cooperation within the spirit of Teheran. Quick victory and a lasting peace were held to depend on a broad coalition of democratic forces in each country.

C592 . . . . "Serve and Learn." [New York]: CPA, n.d. [1944].
A brochure designed to integrate the membership of the Communist Political Association into its activities. It emphasizes a broad approach and a loose conception of membership, appealing for national unity for a speedy victory and enduring peace.

C593 . . . . National Unity for Victory, Security and a Durable Peace (Resolution adopted by the National Convention of the Communist Political Association on the Report of Earl Browder), "Communist," 23 (June 1944), 501-5.
The Communist Political Association pledges to subordinate all other aims to the strengthening of national unity necessary to hasten victory and realize the objectives of Teheran. To achieve national unity, it seeks the re-election of Roosevelt, larger domestic markets through increased purchasing power, broader foreign markets, and an end to discrimination against minorities.

C594 . . . . Resolutions Adopted by the National Convention, "Communist," 23 (July 1944), 663-72.
The resolutions include demands for government aid for reconversion, higher wages for steel workers, the vote for all servicemen, government aid in finding jobs for them, abolition of the poll tax, and American encouragement of unity between the Kuomintang and the Chinese communists.

C595 . . . . Resolutions Adopted by the National Convention, "Communist," 23 (Aug. 1944), 761-68.
The resolutions call for adequate financial aid to wives and children of soldiers killed or disabled in battle, aid to farmers through price supports, legislative action against racial discrimination in the South, and American participation in international trade union unity.

C596 . . . . The Twenty-Fifth Anniversary of the Founding of the American Communist Organization (Resolution adopted by the National Convention of the Communist Political Association held May 20-23, 1944, at New York), "Communist," 23 (Sept. 1944), 778-81.
Resolution of the Communist Party to relinquish its status as an electoral party and, in the form of the Communist Political Association, to continue Marxist activities as a working class political-educational association.

C597 . . ., National Board. The 1945 Municipal Elections: Memorandum Submitted by the National Board to the Meeting of the National Committee, C.P.A., March 10-12, 1945, "Political Affairs," 24 (April 1945), 339-41.
Guides for the conduct of city elections to assure consolidation of the democratic coalition which elected Roosevelt. They call for unity of all progressives behind one popular, progressive candidate, and emphasis on the vital issues.

C598 . . . . The Present Situation and the Next Tasks, "Political Affairs," 24 (July 1945), 579-90.
Resolution adopted by the Party's national convention, July 28, 1945, marking the turn from wartime collaboration of the U.S. with the USSR to the cold war. Revisionist errors of the Party under Earl Browder are criticized, and the idea that sections of monopoly capital can play a progressive role is rejected. The dissolution of the Communist Party and formation of the Communist Political Association are also criticized. (Also published in pamphlet form, with introduction by William Z. Foster.)

C599 COMRADE X. I Was a Communist in the U.S.A.,

"Liberty," 16 (July 15, 1939), 10-11; (July 22), 51-54; (July 29), 30-34; (Aug. 5), 47-51.
A Party member for four years, who claims to have risen to its innermost councils, asserts that the Party can paralyze U.S. transportation and communications, destroy every American fort and battleship, and deliver this country to Russia. He discusses the role of sex in luring college boys into red ranks, the power of the Party in American labor unions, and the use that Stalin makes of the New Deal. The Party, he says, fears only the American Legion and the Catholic Church. He calls on the president to use the FBI to stamp out treason.

C600 COMRADE X. Why Earl Browder Sued Liberty, "Liberty," 17 (Feb. 24, 1940), 7-8.
An assertion that Browder sued "Liberty" for libel, as a result of Comrade X's earlier articles (see "I Was a Communist in the U.S.A.," in the July 15 to August 5, 1939, issues) in an effort to learn his identity. Exposures of communist activities by known writers have never resulted in libel suits. Comrade X's credentials are reproduced without identifying names and numbers.

C601 CONANT, James B. "Law vs. Communists in Schools and Colleges." New York: American Civil Liberties Union, 1949. 6 pp.
Statement by the president of Harvard University before a committee of the Massachusetts legislature, February 9, 1948, opposing a bill to prohibit employment of communists as teachers.

C602 CONFERENCE FOR PROGRESSIVE LABOR ACTION. "CPLA: Program—Policies." New York: CPLA, National Executive Committee, n.d. [1933?]. 16 pp.
Policies and program of group led by A. J. Muste, declaring its adherence to the class struggle and to a genuine united front with all other working class groups, including communists. CPLA asserts that influence of the CPUSA is declining due to its sectarianism, its disruptive tactics in unions, its dual unionist adventures, and its mechanical domination of mass organizations. The American section of a world-wide class struggle movement must be rooted in the American working class, not dominated by an outside agency such as the Russian Party.

C603 CONGRESS OF INDUSTRIAL ORGANIZATIONS. "Report of the CIO Delegation to the Soviet Union." Washington, D.C.: CIO, n.d. [1946]. 28 pp.
The report by a CIO delegation of an eight-day visit to the USSR in October 1945. The delegation, which included, along with others, a number who were very close to the Communist Party, submitted a glowing, uncritical report. Among the topics covered were wage rates, purchasing power, production, social security, and trade union structure.

C604 . . . . "Official Reports on the Expulsion of Communist Dominated Organizations from the C.I.O." Washington, D.C.: CIO, 1954. 125 pp.
Contains resolutions of the 1949 CIO convention on the expulsion of the United Electrical, Radio and Machine Workers and the Farm Equipment Workers, and the reports of the committees which investigated charges of communist domination against nine other CIO unions. Each committee reviewed the charges, analyzed the evidence, considered the defense of the accused unions, and concluded that the unions have consistently pursued Communist Party rather than CIO objectives and policies. Revocation of the certificates of affiliation of these unions is recommended. (These reports, but not the resolutions, are reprinted in a Report of the Subcommittee on Labor and Labor-Management Relations of the Committee on Labor and Public Welfare, "Communist Domination of Certain Unions." U.S. Senate, 82nd Congress, 1st Session, 1951, Document No. 89.)

C605 "CIO NEWS," Murray Blasts Progress in Three Fields: Probe of Organizational Failures Authorized, 11 (Nov. 29, 1948), 2 ff.
A report of Philip Murray's speech to the CIO convention, with discussion of a resolution calling on the executive board to investigate CIO affiliates which have failed to make progress in organizing. The resolution was aimed at communist-dominated affiliates in the white collar, government, and retail fields.

C606 . . ., Leftists Warned: Follow C.I.O Policy or Quit Board, 12 (May 23, 1949), 3 ff.
The CIO Executive Board has ordered all unions and other CIO bodies to support its national policies. Resolutions rebuke the Mine, Mill and Smelter Workers for attacking Philip Murray, and again order the Farm Equipment Workers to merge with the Automobile Workers.

C607 "CONGRESS WEEKLY," The Jewish Line of American Communism, 13 (Nov. 22, 1946), 3-6.
An editorial analyzing and criticizing the recent CPUSA resolution on communist work among the Jewish masses. The communist resolution ignores the common desire of Jews to survive as a people. The communists' advocacy of unity between Jews and Arabs shows indifference to Palestine realities, as their proposal to leave the refugees in the hands of a UN commission indicates callousness.

C608 "CONGRESSIONAL DIGEST," Congress and Un-American Activities, 18 (Nov. 1939), 259-88.
An issue devoted to a review of the activities of the Dies Committee to investigate un-American activities and the question of its continuation. Its history and record are reviewed, and speeches by congressmen for and against its continuation are reprinted. A glossary of terms, an excerpt from the committee's report, and a statement by the American League for Peace and Democracy are included.

C609 "CONGRESSIONAL QUARTERLY WEEKLY REPORT," Un-American Activities Committee, 11 (March 13, 1953), 321-23.
An examination of the House Un-American Activities Committee, its goals, its predecessor, its main reports. Despite criticism, the Committee has enjoyed widespread support. Roll calls since 1945 indicate diminishing congressional opposition.

C610 . . ., Loyal Workers for Uncle Sam, 11 (June 5, 1953), 721-23.
An analysis of the Eisenhower loyalty-security program, comparing it with previous programs for federal employees. Basic innovations made by the Eisenhower program are emphasized.

C611 CONN, Harry. Communist-Led Unions and U.S. Security, "New Republic," 126 (Feb. 18, 1952), 16-17.
An appraisal of the hearings before a Senate subcommittee on the problem of communist-dominated unions, some of them in vital defense industries. Testimony of union officers, including Murray, Green, and Hayes, is reported, as are various proposals for legislation.

C612 CONNER, Stuart W. Communism and Religion: Our Survival Demands We Understand Communism, "Vital Speeches," 20 (April 15, 1954), 408-11.
A speech on the nature of communism by a special

assistant to the attorney general of New Hampshire, who discusses communist theory, Marxist opposition to religion and to the Judaic-Christian concept of morality, communist plans to take over the U.S., and espionage and subversive activities of communist sympathizers in our government.

C613   CONRAD, Earl. "Harriet Tubman: Negro Soldier and Abolitionist." New York: International Publishers, 1942. 47 pp. Bibliog.
A biographical sketch of a slave who fled to the North and became a leader in the underground railroad and the antislavery movement. (A part of the communist literature glorifying Negroes who fought against slavery, in an effort to show that the Negro revolutionary tradition ends in the Party.)

C614   . . . . "Harriet Tubman." Washington, D.C.: Associated Publishers, 1943. 248 pp. Ind.
A full-scale, documented biography of a Negro slave who became a leader in the underground railroad, expanded from a pamphlet published by International Publishers the year before. (Among those to whom the author offers acknowledgements are Party leaders Angelo Herndon, Cyril Briggs, Herbert Aptheker, and Ella Reeve Bloor. The book is part of the Party's literature showing the Negro as a bearer of a revolutionary tradition that culminated in the Communist Party.)

C615   . . ., and GORDON, Eugene. "Equal Justice under Law." New York: Committee for Equal Justice for Mrs. Recy Taylor, n.d. [1944 or 1945]. 16 pp.
A plea for justice for Mrs. Recy Taylor, an Alabama Negress who charged that she was raped by a group of white youths whom the jury refused to prosecute. Her case is compared with the cases of Negroes accused of rape who, on the flimsiest of evidence, were convicted and severely punished, even lynched. (The pamphlet concludes with a list of the committee's officers and sponsors, including, among others, leading Party members and sympathizers.)

C616   CONROY, Jack. "The Disinherited." New York: Covici, Friede, 1933. 310 pp.
One of the few proletarian novels actually written by a working-class author. The hero, a drifter who shifts from one job to another, is patterned after the author himself. The hero eventually embraces communism.

C617   . . . . "A World to Win." New York: Covici, Friede, 1935. 348 pp.
A story of two half-brothers who grew up, separated, traveled widely divergent routes, and finally came together again as communists.

C618   CONSTITUTIONAL EDUCATIONAL LEAGUE. "Communism's Iron Grip on the CIO." New Haven, Conn.: The League, n.d. [1937]. 60 pp.
Its text taken from a speech by Representative Clare E. Hoffman of Michigan in the House of Representatives on June 1, 1937, the pamphlet charges that the CIO is a communist body, that John L. Lewis employs communist organizers, and that Lewis and the communists around him are fomenting widespread disorders as part of a communist plot to establish proletarian dictatorship here.

C619   . . . . "Department of Justice Memo Re: American Youth Congress." New Haven, Conn.: The League, n.d. [1942]. 8 unnumbered pages.
A confidential FBI document sent to federal department heads in connection with an investigation into subversives on the government payroll. Since its inception the AYC is said to have been controlled by communists and manipulated by them to influence American youth.

C620   COOK, Fred J. Hiss: New Perspectives on the Strangest Case of Our Time, "Nation," 185 (Sept. 21, 1957), 142-80.
A detailed defense of Alger Hiss in a reevaluation of the Hiss-Chambers controversy by a leading crime reporter. The author reviews the life histories of the two men, along with the conflicting testimony about their personal associations, the car, the rug, the name by which Hiss knew Chambers, relations to the Party, and the typewriter. Resolving most doubts and conflicts in Hiss' favor, Cook concludes that an innocent man was convicted.

C621   . . . . The Remington Tragedy: A Study of Injustice, "Nation," 185 (Dec. 28, 1957), 486-500.
An account of the William Remington case, telling of his personal life, the testimony of Elizabeth Bentley and his ex-wife naming him as an espionage contact, his loyalty board hearing, his conviction for perjury for denying membership in the Communist Party, and the reversal of the conviction on appeal. He was then convicted for perjury in his first trial, on the ground that he had passed secret documents to Miss Bentley. His murder in prison is described.

C622   . . . . "The Unfinished Story of Alger Hiss." New York: Morrow, 1958. 184 pp. Ind.
A review of the Hiss-Chambers case, the central issues of which were the duel of credibility between Hiss and Chambers, the documents, and the typewriters. The author believes that Hiss won the duel of credibility, though Chambers won the final battle. While Hiss may have been guilty, the prosecution's case contained so many flaws, in the author's view, that they force the conclusion that an innocent man was convicted. The vital question is whether Chambers had official collaborators in the perfection of his story and the completion of his deed.

C623   . . . . "The FBI Nobody Knows." New York: Macmillan, 1964. 436 pp. Ind.
A critical account of the FBI and of the dictatorial rule and right-wing views of its director, J. Edgar Hoover. Among the topics treated are the Red raids of 1919-20, the "Amerasia" case, and the cases of Alger Hiss, William Remington, Julius and Ethel Rosenberg, Harry Dexter White, and Judith Coplon. The author criticizes the FBI's release of material from its files for the congressional witch-hunts of 1948, and the close relations between Hoover and Senator McCarthy.

C624   COOK, Thomas I. Democracy, Leisure and Communism, "Journal of Politics," 12 (Aug. 1950), 530-46.
Because of the communists' unrelaxing efforts to capture our institutions, the convinced democrat faces a dilemma. Either he becomes vigilant in public affairs, sacrificing leisure, or he must allow his institutions to be taken over by the communists. That is why he tolerates repressive measures.

C625   . . . . "Democratic Rights vs. Communist Activity." Garden City, N.Y.: Doubleday, 1954. 56 pp.
A professor of political science at Johns Hopkins argues for the suppression of some types of speech. Our traditional civil liberties, he asserts, should not protect a conspiracy to overthrow government by force. He proposes outlawing of the Communist Party, and citizen participation at the group level to thwart communist tactics and control.

C626   COOKE, Alistair. "A Generation on Trial: U.S.A. v. Alger Hiss." New York: Knopf, 1950. 342 pp. Ind.

An account of the Hiss case by a British correspondent, who analyzes the two trials against the background of the 1930's which strongly influenced Hiss. The chronology prior to the opening of the legal cases is given, and the cases are reported at length. Attention is drawn to the radically different political contexts in which Hiss allegedly committed his crime and was tried. Hiss is regarded as a tragic figure of great stature.

C627 COOLIDGE, David. The Foster-Browder Debate and the New Turn in the CPA, "Labor Action," 9 (June 18, 1945), 1 ff; (July 2), 4; (July 9), 3; (July 16), 4: (July 23), 4.
A series of articles on the "debate" between Foster and Browder currently in progress within the Communist Political Association. Foster appears as leader of the "opposition," while Browder is the sole defender of the wartime line of American Stalinists. Foster argues that Browder defended capitalism in a reactionary instead of a progressive way. Foster's line today is a return to the spurious radicalism of the period of the Hitler-Stalin pact, in order to protect the interests of the Kremlin.

C628 COOPER, Leo. "Universal Military Training: Program for Peace or Weapon for War?" New York: New Century, 1948. 24 pp.
A call for an end to militarization of American life, with an attack on universal military training as part of a reactionary, prowar program linked with the reactionary and imperialist nature of American foreign policy.

C629 COREY, Lewis. "The Decline of American Capitalism." New York: Covici, Friede, 1934. 622 pp. Notes. Sources. Ind.
An effort by an unaffiliated Marxist (formerly a communist leader under the name of Louis Fraina) to show that the depression of the 1930's is more fundamental and more permanent than previous capitalist crises. State capitalism, intervening through the NIRA, seeks to protect profit, not wages. Arguing that the forces of production are more highly developed than the forces of consumption, and that monopoly and imperialism have contributed to the depression, Corey predicts the coming of a proletarian revolution. (For criticism by leading CPUSA members see Alex Bittelman and V. J. Jerome, "Leninism Is the Only Marxism of the Imperialist Era," in "Communist," Oct. 1934.)

C630 . . . . "The Crisis of the Middle Class." New York: Covici, Friede, 1935. 379 pp. Notes.
A Marxist analysis of the development of the middle class and of its role in the overthrow of feudalism and the development of democratic ideals. Formerly a class of small businessmen and farmers, it has become a class of propertyless professionals and supervisors. The middle class must now choose between fascism, the last resort of capitalism, and socialism. (The author, under the name of Louis Fraina, was an early leader of the communist movement here.)

C631 . . . . Marxism Reconsidered, "Nation," 150 (Feb. 17, 1940), 245-48; (Feb. 24), 272-75; (March 2), 305-7.
An examination of the fatal shortcomings of all variants of Marxism by one of the founders of the communist movement here, who asserts that the Russian fulfillment of Marxism is a totalitarian nightmare. He discusses ways of achieving and maintaining a more democratic economic order without sacrificing political democracy. The economic crisis can be solved only by progressive transformation of capitalism toward democratic socialism.

C632 . . . . What Is Henry Wallace? 1. The Betrayal of

Peace; 2. Imperialism and War-Mongering; 3. The Betrayal of Democracy, "New Leader," 31 (Oct. 2, 1948), 8-9 ff; (Oct. 9), 4 ff; (Oct. 16), 7.
Criticism of Wallace on the grounds that his foreign policy is 100 per cent pro-Soviet, and that the Progressive Party was promoted by and is controlled by communists. Wallace fails to criticize communist destruction of democracy in Eastern European nations. He betrays democracy in allowing himself to be used by the communists.

. . . . See also FRAINA, Louis C.

C633 CORK, Jim. Eighth Communist Party Convention, "Workers Age," 3 (May 1, 1934), 5.
A Lovestoneite report on the eighth convention of the CPUSA. Despite the tragic working-class defeat in Germany, contributing errors are not corrected. The social fascism theory is reaffirmed, and the TUUL is to be continued under a different name.

C634 CORNFORTH, Maurice. "Historical Materialism." New York: International Publishers, 1954. 206 pp. Bibliog. Ind.
A theoretical work on historical materialism, dealing with its general principles, the way in which society develops according to its tenets, and the reasons why socialism and communism are inevitable in the future. The author asserts that the scientific socialist theory of Marxism-Leninism has been proved in practice in the Soviet Union; and that the working class, by embracing socialism under the leadership of the Communist Party, will achieve truly human conditions of existence for mankind.

C635 CORSI, Edward. "In the Shadow of Liberty: The Chronicle of Ellis Island." New York: Macmillan, 1935. 321 pp. Ind.
The former U.S. Commissioner of Immigration and Naturalization, New York Division, tells of his experiences on Ellis Island. Pages 177-200 deal with the exclusion and deportation of radicals, particularly communists and anarchists.

C636 CORT, John C. Labor's Chances Look Bad, "Commonweal," 37 (Feb. 12, 1943), 417-20.
A discussion of obstacles to labor unity, including jurisdictional disputes, jobs, prestige, and the presence of communists in the CIO. However, the right wing of the CIO peace committee is in favor of labor unity if it can be obtained with honor and without sacrifice of principle.

C637 . . . . Hillman, C.P.A. and P.A.C.—What's It All About? "Commonweal," 41 (Oct. 20, 1944), 6-9.
Sidney Hillman and the Political Action Committee are defended against Republican charges of communism. Hillman has made only one bad error, his alliance with the Stalinists in New York. Only one member of the National PAC board of 76 is CP-controlled, though there are dangers in the national legal setup and in certain local PAC's.

C638 . . . . Comrades Have a Crisis, "Commonweal," 42 (Aug. 10, 1945), 406-8.
The associate editor discusses Browder's sudden dismissal as head of the Communist Party. The ensuing discussions in the "Daily Worker" by communist leaders give insight into the machinations of the Party.

C639 . . . . The Labor Movement: The CIO Convention, "Commonweal," 45 (Dec. 13, 1946), 231-32.
An appraisal of the 1946 CIO convention's successes and failures in limiting its powerful communist minority. Unfortunately, Philip Murray wanted an anticommunist resolution that the communists would accept. The com-

munists won some minor victories, as on the foreign policy resolution.

C640 CORT, John C. Labor Cleans House. "Progressive," 11 (May 19, 1947), 5 ff.
A review of the infiltration of communists into the labor movement and of AFL and CIO actions against them. Communist-controlled and anticommunist unions in the CIO are listed. Though Murray is indecisive, the tide is running against the communists.

C641 .... The Mundt-Nixon Bill, "Commonweal," 48 (July 2, 1948), 285-86.
The associate editor joins the AFL and CIO in their opposition to the "guilt by association" features of the bill, the excessive power given the Attorney General, and the loosely worded definitions. The Association of Catholic Trade Unionists also opposes the bill.

C642 .... The C.I.O. Expels Its Communist Unions, "Commonweal," 51 (Nov. 25, 1949), 211-12.
Praise for the CIO's expulsion of communist unions, including the strong UE, at its recent convention. The decision to hold hearings to determine if ten other unions are Stalinist-controlled shows that the CIO has not simply yielded to anticommunist hysteria. A full-fledged communist labor federation within three months is predicted.

C643 .... The Hearn's Strike, "Commonweal," 58 (July 17, 1953), 367-69.
An assertion that the Distributive, Processing and Office Workers Union, formed by three formerly communist-controlled unions, has broken with the CP and has again been chartered by the CIO. In the DPOW strike against Hearn Department Stores in New York, the employer has falsely raised the communist issue. Arthur Osman and his DPOW colleagues are suffering from the sins of their Stalinist period.

C644 CORWIN, Edward S. Bowing Out Clear and Present Danger, "Notre Dame Lawyer," 27 (Spring 1952), 325-59.
The history of the clear and present danger doctrine from its origin in an opinion by Justice Holmes in 1919. The doctrine found its way into a majority opinion of the Supreme Court nearly 20 years later. Its use in various espionage and criminal syndicalist cases is reviewed, as is its restricted application in the Dennis case of 1951.

C645 COSER, Lewis. The Age of the Informer, "Dissent," 1 (Summer 1954), 249-54.
An objection to the tendency of "liberal" anticommunists to extol the informer, and to elevate informing from expediency to duty. While informants are justified in cases of espionage, this does not justify identifying Stalinists of the 1930's who now see their mistakes.

C646 COSTELLO, William. The Facts about Nixon: The Hiss Case, "New Republic," 141 (Dec. 7, 1959), 10-16.
A description of Richard Nixon's career in Congress, dealing principally with his role in the Alger Hiss case and the Mundt-Nixon bill. It was Nixon who transformed the House Un-American Activities Committee into a functioning legislative organism.

C647 COULTON, Thomas Evans. "A City College in Action: Struggle and Achievement at Brooklyn College, 1930-1955." Foreword by Harry D. Gideonse. New York: Harper, 1955. 233 pp. Ind.
An account of the history of Brooklyn College by its Dean of Freshmen. Chapter 4 deals with the college's struggle against Stalinism. The college inherited some Stalinist

influence when it was founded in 1930 as a unification of the Brooklyn branches of Hunter and City Colleges. Swift administrative actions to deal with the problem were on the basis of illegal actions by groups and individuals, not on the basis of the beliefs they held. The author discusses the hearings by the New York State Joint Committee on the State Education System (Rapp-Coudert Committee), and those by the Senate Internal Security Subcommittee.

C648 COUNTRYMAN, Vern. "Un-American Activities in the State of Washington: The Work of the Canwell Committee." Ithaca: Cornell University Press, 1951. 405 pp. Ind.
One of the Cornell University studies on civil liberties and security, by a member of the Yale Law School faculty. It is a study of the Canwell Committee in the state of Washington, 1947-49, which investigated communism and the influence of the Party. The author appraises the record of the Committee, the techniques it used, its function and procedures, the objectivity of press coverage, and the validity of its conclusions. He concludes that the activities of the Canwell Committee and its allies are more subversive of established legal processes than any activities disclosed by its investigation.

C649 .... The Bigots and the Professionals, "Nation," 174 (June 28, 1952), 641-43.
A Yale University law professor reviews the record of attacks by the House Committee on Un-American Activities on the loyalty of lawyers, ministers, doctors, and newspapermen. Organizations such as the National Lawyers Guild and the Methodist Federation for Social Action have been particular targets.

C650 .... Loyalty Tests for Lawyers, "Lawyers Guild Review," 13 (Winter 1953 [1954]), 149-57.
Arguments by a member of the Yale Law School faculty against loyalty tests for members of the bar. The objective of current oaths and investigations is to exclude those who are attached to the CP or its policies. Exclusion from the legal profession should never be based on political beliefs.

C651 COUNTS, George S. Whose Twilight? "Social Frontier," 5 (Feb. 1939), 135-40.
An account of conflicts within Teachers College at Columbia University, answering criticism in the "Nation." Communists are condemned for using undemocratic means at the school, for making malicious and irresponsible attacks, and for injuring the cause of democracy in education. They are acting as midwives to the fascism they profess to oppose.

C652 .... Is Our Union Controlled by Communists? "American Teacher," 24 (Dec. 1939), 5-6.
A denial by the new president of the American Federation of Teachers that the union is run by communists, with a call for teachers to resist communist influence in the union. Communists are termed foreign agents.

C653 .... The Fight for the American Labor Party, "New Leader," 27 (Feb. 5, 1944), 7.
The New York State chairman of the American Labor Party describes the fight being waged to save the ALP from a bloc of communists allied with followers of Sidney Hillman, president of the Amalgamated Clothing Workers and chairman of the CIO Political Action Committee. Victory for the communists would discredit the ALP.

C654 .... Kulturfest at the Waldorf: Soapbox for Red Propaganda, "New Leader," 32 (March 19, 1949), 1 ff.

A prediction that the forthcoming Cultural and Scientific Conference for World Peace, to be held at the Waldorf-Astoria Hotel in New York City, will be a communist-inspired gathering, attacking the U.S. and glorifying the USSR. The conference is sponsored by the National Committee for the Arts, Sciences and Professions, which has long followed the Party line.

C655 COWAN, William Wallace. "The Red Hand in the Professor's Glove." Manchester, N.H.: The author, 1933. 31 pp.
An exposé of socialist and communist sympathizers in U.S. colleges and universities by an author who groups the two movements together in contrast to Americanism. Though most of the pamphlet deals with socialists, there are scattered references to communist activities. (A reprint of articles that first appeared in "Industry and Labor," published by the author.)

C656 COWL, Margaret. "The Soviet Union—Your Questions Answered." New York: Workers Library, 1933. 48 pp. Bibliog.
Questions and answers on the Soviet Union relating to sources of capital, unemployment, wages and prices, social insurance, trade unions, factory committees, forced labor, population, housing, education, the press, churches, the position of women, the building of socialism, the Red Army, and relations with capitalist states.

C657 .... "Women and Equality." New York: Workers Library, 1935. 15 pp.
A denunciation of the capitalist system, which discriminates against women through lower wages and the speed-up; only in the Soviet Union have women won complete equality with men in practice. The Party urges immediate demands, not only to better conditions now, but as part of the fight for freedom and happiness that only a socialist society can give.

C658 .... "The High Cost of Living: How to Bring It Down." New York: Workers Library, 1937. 16 pp.
A pamphlet in dialogue form addressed primarily to women, asserting that the way to reduce the high cost of living is to build the people's antimonopoly coalition, and, beyond that, to do away with the profit system. It tells what a Soviet America would look like and invites those who agree to join the Party.

C659 .... We Must Win the Women, "Communist," 16 (June 1937), 545-54.
A review of struggles for women's rights in the U.S. and other countries, and of communist insistence upon the economic independence of women as the basis for social and political equality. Progress of women in the USSR is reviewed. Attention must be given by the trade unions and the Party to the special problems of women.

C660 .... Woman's Place in the People's Front, "Communist," 17 (Jan. 1938), 46-53.
An assertion that the Equal Rights Amendment, supported by reactionary elements, jeopardizes protective laws for women. Instead the Women's Charter movement, which has trade union support, is endorsed and viewed as part of the people's front. This recognizes that the demand for equality is inseparable from the demand for higher living standards for women.

C661 .... The Struggle for Equal Rights for Women, "Communist," 19 (Sept. 1940), 856-64.
An argument that discrimination against and exploitation of women is inherent in capitalism. The inferior status of jobs held by women, their substandard pay, and indifference to the economic burden of motherhood will not be tolerated by women's movements now gaining momentum. The CP represents women's only hope for equality.

C662 COWLEY, Malcolm. Ivory Towers to Let, "New Republic," 78 (April 18, 1934), 260-63.
By the early 1930's writers had become politically minded. Though the Marxists find the cause in the depression, the author feels that it resulted from the rebellious escapism of the 1920's. Finding no escape, writers began to recognize realities, leave their ivory towers, and choose sides in the class struggle.

C663 .... A Note on Marxian Criticism, "New Republic," 81 (Jan. 30, 1935), 337.
One of the magazine's editors appraises Marxian criticism, finding it limited in that it is sociological rather than psychological. While it can explain the social effects of a novel or drama, it is inadequate with regard to the personal reason for writing. No social elements may be connected with a whole group of human emotions based on biological sorrows and satisfactions.

C664 .... Stalin or Satan? "New Republic," 89 (Jan. 20, 1937), 348-50.
A reply to Edmund Wilson's "Complaint: I. The Literary Left" in the same issue. Though Wilson's thesis is noble, Cowley objects to his ambiguous and condemnatory use of the term "Stalinist." Wilson wants to attack certain evils in American left-wing writing, but has adopted a method likely to make them worse instead of better.

C665 .... Notes on a Writers Congress, "New Republic," 99 (June 21, 1939), 192-93.
A view of the recent American Writers Congress as by far the best of the three held by the League of American Writers. More writers were there, and more attention was paid to strictly literary matters. The excellent results may encourage writers to think of one another as partners rather than as rivals.

C666 .... In Memoriam, "New Republic," 103 (Aug. 12, 1940), 219-20.
An assertion that the report of the Third Writers Congress, just published, has the air of a memorial to something that has died, since it belongs to the popular-front period now repudiated by the League. The League now follows the Party line that this war is another imperialist conflict. Quoting from his letter of resignation, Cowley makes clear his opposition to the League's present policy.

C667 .... Some Dangers to American Writing, "New Republic," 131 (Nov. 22, 1954), 114-17.
The current loyalty crusade is accompanied by anti-intellectualism and an economic crisis in publishing and book selling. The result is a greater political and economic threat to American writing than at any other time in the century.

C668 COX, Oliver C. The New Crisis in Leadership among Negroes, "Journal of Negro Education," 19 (Fall 1950), 459-65.
In the past, Negro leadership has faced two major crises, the conflict between protest and collaboration, and the conflict between protest and nationalism. Today it faces the conflict between protest and revolution. W. E. B. Du Bois and Paul Robeson have identified other protest leaders with the ruling class and subjected them to severe attack.

C669 COYNE, June. My Communist Friends, "Commonweal," 26 (Aug. 27, 1937), 415-16.
A description of intellectual friends who are communists or socialists, atheists, and believers in the infallibility of

psychology. The author deplores the lack of Catholic secular literature that would appeal to such groups.

C670 CRAIG, George N. Labor Sets an Example, "American Legion Magazine," 48 (April 1950), 14-15 ff.
The national commander of the Legion tells of the successful efforts of American labor unions to free themselves of communist control. Among the cases cited are the recent expulsions of the United Electrical Workers and the Farm Equipment Workers by the CIO, the earlier struggles in the needle trades, and the upheaval in the National Maritime Union. The conflict in the World Federation of Trade Unions is also summarized.

C671 .... Terror by Law, "American Legion Magazine," 49 (July 1950), 14-15 ff.
An assertion by the national commander of the Legion that the communists have organized a nationwide legal machine to intimidate anticommunists by lawsuits, to help communist spies and conspirators escape punishment, to discredit the courts, and to plant communist lawyers in high government posts for espionage purposes. A series of legal fronts serve these ends.

C672 CRAMTON, Roger C. Supercession and Subversion: Limitations on State Power to Deal with Issues of Subversion and Loyalty, "University of Chicago Law School Record, Special Supplement," 8 (Autumn 1958), 24-53.
A discussion of the precedence of federal over state power in dealing with subversion. Attention is centered on the Supreme Court's 1956 decision in Pennsylvania v. Nelson, which held that the states could not punish for sedition directed against the U.S. government; on limitations on state legislative investigations, as laid down in Sweezy v. New Hampshire in 1957; and on limitations on state power to impose civil disqualifications.

C673 CRARY, Ryland W., and STEIBEL, Gerald L. "How You Can Teach about Communism." New York [?]: Anti-Defamation League of B'nai B'rith, 1951. 48 pp.
A handbook for teachers, dealing with the roots of communism in Russia and in Marxism, and with the communist line on class struggle, social justice, peace, human rights, and free institutions. Answers to each communist assertion are presented, and democratic principles and achievements are stressed. Questions for communists are included, along with suggested readings.

C674 CRAWFORD, John D. Federal Legislation: Free Speech and the Internal Security Act of 1950, "Georgetown Law Journal," 39 (March 1951), 440-65.
An analysis of the Internal Security Act, with attention to points of doubtful constitutionality. Among the provisions discussed are those relating to conspiracy, identification of communist organizations, membership, deportation, denaturalization, and employment in defense facilities. Questionable provisions of the measure should be amended or deleted.

C675 CRAWFORD, Kenneth G. Open Season on Reds, "Nation," 148 (May 6, 1939), 519-20.
Representative Howard W. Smith, member of the House Rules Committee, is cited as a symbol of congressional red hunts. Smith's omnibus bill to curb communists and aliens is a spiritual twin of the infamous Alien and Sedition Acts of 1798.

C676 CRAWFORD, Ruth Elizabeth. I Have a Thing to Tell You, "Nation," 176 (Jan. 24, 1953), 76-78.

A former member of the United Nations staff, dismissed on grounds of previous membership in the Communist Party, admits past membership and defends her right to her political opinion. She tells of her background, her reasons for joining, and her ordeal since her dismissal.

C677 CRENSHAW, Files, Jr., and MILLER, Kenneth A. "Scottsboro: The Firebrand of Communism." Montgomery, Ala.: Brown Printing Co., 1936. 336 pp. App.
A view that the Scottsboro defendants were guilty as charged, and that all sympathy for them was inspired by the communists, who seized upon the case to gain a propaganda weapon and to stir up racial antagonism in the Black Belt of the South. A verbatim copy of all testimony in the case is included.

CRICHTON, Kyle. See FORSYTHE, Robert.

C678 "CRISIS," Negro Editors on Communism: A symposium of the American Negro Press, 41 [39] (April 1932), 117-19; (May), 154-56 ff.
The views of 14 leading Negro editors on the subject of communism. The replies attest to the appeal of communism to Negroes, primarily because the communists practice and fight for racial equality. Some of the editors endorse communism for this reason. Others, however, disagree with the communists' means, distrust their goals, or fear that Negroes will suffer because of the association.

C679 ..., The NAACP and the Communists, 56 (March 1949), 72.
An editorial calling attention to the communist campaign of misrepresentation of the NAACP, in the hope of discrediting its leadership and taking control of the organization. The communist line on Negroes and Negro organizations is reviewed, to show its subordination to Soviet needs. Members are warned against communist infiltration and disruption.

C680 CRIST, Judith. A Blow for Freedom, "Nation," 169 (Dec. 10, 1949), 566-67.
A newspaper writer specializing in education applauds the decision of Justice Schirick of the New York Supreme Court that the Feinberg law, disqualifying members of a subversive organization from employment in the school system, is unconstitutional. The fumbling and inability to cooperate of individuals and groups opposed to this law is deplored.

C681 CROCKETT, George W., Jr. "Freedom Is Everybody's Job! The Crime of the Government against the Negro People." New York: National Non-Partisan Committee to Defend the Rights of the 12 Communist Leaders, 1949. 16 pp.
The summation before the jury by one of the lawyers for the communist leaders in the first Smith Act trial. Asserting that he differs with the communists on many issues, he supports their struggle for Negro rights, particularly the idea of self-determination. He charges that the communists are being framed because the Party throughout its history has acted as the conscience of America on the Negro issue. (The pamphlet also contains Crockett's statement when being sentenced for contempt of court.)

C682 CROCKETT, Sam. "Frankfurter's Red Record." Union, N.J.: Christian Educational Association, 1961. 66 pp. Ind.
Anti-Semitic literature attacking Felix Frankfurter's alleged communist record before and during his membership on the Supreme Court, and proposing his impeachment.

C683 CRONIN, John F. "Communism: A World Menace." Washington, D.C.: National Catholic Welfare Conference, 1947. 31 pp.
A discussion of the theory and practice of world communism and of the strength and tactics of the American Communist Party by the assistant director of the Department of Social Action of the National Catholic Welfare Conference. The author discusses the organization of front groups, boring from within other organizations, disloyalty in government, and communists in the labor movement. He outlines a program of action for anticommunists.

C684 .... Labor's Great Divide, "Plain Talk," 1 (March 1947), 30-33.
A discussion of the importance of labor in the plans of communism in the U.S. Control of unions enables the Party to enroll recruits, control industry, divert funds, and employ Party functionaries. The CIO has both pro-communist and anticommunist unions. Communists must be defeated in local unions, with the aid of socialists, Jewish labor groups in New York, and Catholics throughout the country.

C685 .... "Communism: Threat to Freedom." Washington, D.C.: National Catholic Welfare Conference, 1962. 80 pp.
A critical view of communist theory and practice, and of communist tactics and strength, both home and abroad, by the assistant director of the Department of Social Action of the National Catholic Welfare Conference. The author discusses our world-wide struggle against communism, the danger of internal subversion, and communist opposition to religion. Reading lists and study questions are included.

C686 CROOK, Wilfrid H. "Communism and the General Strike." Hamden, Conn.: Shoe String Press, 1960. 483 pp. Notes. Bibliog. Ind.
An updating of the author's "The General Strike: A Study of Labor's Tragic Weapon in Theory and Practice" (University of North Carolina Press, 1931), to show, among other objectives, how the Communist Party has seized upon the general strike, often abusing and misusing it. Economic and political general strikes throughout the world are described. Chapters 8 and 9, pp. 107-48, are devoted to the San Francisco general strike of 1934, with emphasis on the part played by the communists in organizing and leading the strike.

C687 CROSBY, Percy. "Three Cheers for the Red, Red and Red." McLean, Va.: Freedom Press, 1936. 507 pp. App.
A rambling attack on Roosevelt and the New Deal, and also on literature, magazines, the daily Hearst press, and professors for advancing communist doctrine in America. Roosevelt is charged with suppressing criticism and with terrorizing Congress and the military, and Professor Rex Tugwell's thought is compared with that of Marx.

C688 .... "Would Communism Work Out in America?" McLean, Va.: Freedom Press, 1938. 316 pp. App.
Most of the book is an attack on the Roosevelt Administration. The two final chapters point out the hollowness of communist ideals and their incompatibility with the American way of life.

C689 CROSSMAN, Richard (ed.). "The God That Failed." New York: Harper, 1949. 273 pp.
A collection of six autobiographical essays by writers and intellectuals, including Arthur Koestler, Richard Wright, Louis Fischer, Ignazio Silone, Andre Gide, and Stephen Spender on how and why they were attracted and committed to communism, and how and why they finally turned away from it. The hold that communism has upon the intellectual is revealed in many different ways, and the act of de-commitment is registered in candor and intimacy. The compulsion to repudiate ideas that had become a part of their personalities, but whose debasement they could no longer avoid recognizing, is the theme. Richard Wright and Louis Fischer are the two Americans in the group.

C690 CROSSWAITH, Frank R. The Communists and the Negro, "Interracial Review," 16 (Nov. 1943), 166-68.
A Negro labor leader denounces communists for creating disorder and suspicion wherever they go. Their disruptive activities in the labor movement and among Negroes are related. The communists have done nothing to further Negro progress; rather, they have hampered progressive forces by their tactics.

C691 CROUCH, Paul. Southern Conference for Human Welfare: The Anatomy of a Front, "Plain Talk," 3 (March 1949), 7-13.
A former Party official who helped to form the Southern Conference for Human Welfare tells how the communists controlled that organization, at a time when the Party's slogans and immediate aims were like those of progressive Southerners in general. The Southern Conference weakened when the Hitler-Stalin pact cost the communists most of their mass following.

C692 .... Soviet Underground, U. S. A., "Freeman," 1 (Feb. 26, 1951), 336-39.
A former communist reports on the extent and methods of the communist underground network in the U.S. Ex-communists, if called upon, can render invaluable service to our country and to the cause of freedom.

C693 .... Communism in the South, "National Republic," 42 (June 1954), 13-14 ff.
An account by a former Party leader in the South of communist activities in that area. The Southern Conference Educational Fund, successor to the Southern Conference for Human Welfare, is said to be one of the major organizations through which the Reds carry on subversive activities there. Leading Party members in the South are named.

C694 CRUDEN, Robert L. "The End of the Ford Myth." New York: International Publishers, 1932. 15 pp.
A communist account of Ford's "tyranny" toward employees in the early depression. This tyranny can be combatted only by a working class organization leading to the overthrow of capitalism.

C695 ..., and DUNN, Robert W. How the Crisis Hit the Auto Workers, "Communist," 11 (March 1932), 230-38.
The results of a field study of Detroit auto workers by the Labor Research Association, which analyzed wage rates, working time, deductions from wages, accidents, and speed-up. The study also covered debts, food costs, and unemployment relief. Conditions, now bad, will become increasingly serious as the year advances.

.... See also STEELE, James.

C696 CUNARD, Nancy (ed.). "Negro Anthology, 1931-1933." London: Wishart, 1934. 854 pp.
An anthology reflecting Negro life in America and elsewhere in the world, including selections from Theodore Dreiser, Michael Gold, Langston Hughes, W. E. B. Du Bois, and many others. Sections in this anthology deal with Negro history, race relations, literature, Marxism,

the Scottsboro case, poetry, and other aspects of life, in the West Indies, South America, Europe, and Africa, as well as in the U.S. The author advocates the communist world-order as the solution of the race problem for the Negro.

C697 CURRAN, Dale. "A House on a Street." New York: Covici, Friede, 1934. 285 pp.
The story of a man, out of a job in 1929, who finds employment as an apartment house manager in Greenwich Village, where he learns the realities of life and is converted to communism.

C698 . . . . Only One Subject, "New Masses," 15 (April 9, 1935), 21-22.
An assertion that only those who live in the proletarian strata of civilization can write about it authentically. From his own experiences, the author tells how the proletarian writer develops class consciousness. Literature produced today, if it is to be honest, must reflect the new world in birth.

C699 CURRAN, Edward Lodge. "Facts about Communism." Brooklyn: International Catholic Truth Society, 1937. 208 pp. Bibliog.
A Catholic analysis of communism, in question and answer form. The author traces the origin and development of communism up through the "democratic" Soviet constitution of 1936, emphasizing its totalitarian aspects. He discusses the philosophy of communism, showing its destructive errors vis-à-vis religion, morals, and economics. He shows how the communists operate in the U.S., how they malign everyone opposed to them as "fascist," how they falsely claim to favor peace, how they propagate their ideas, and how we can and must oppose them. The encyclical letter by Pope Pius XI on "Atheistic Communism" is reproduced.

C700 . . . . "The Hand of Pilate: A Reply to Earl Browder's Message to Catholics." Brooklyn: International Catholic Truth Society, n.d. [1938]. 24 pp.
Warning Catholics against communist efforts to recruit them, the president of the Society denounces communist deceit, atheism, responsibility for war, persecution of religious believers, destruction of parental authority and the family, immorality, terrorism, intolerance, and hypocrisy.

C701 CURRAN, Joseph E. "The N.M.U. Forges Ahead: A Report on the Status of the National Maritime Union of America." New York: NMU, 1940. 31 pp.
A report delivered to the NMU national council while Curran and the union were still following the Party line. A bitter attack is made on a group of NMU officers, led by Jerry King, who sought to expose the union's procommunist leadership. The current war "hysteria" is denounced, and the slogan, "The Yanks are Not Coming," is endorsed. Attacks are made on AFL elements said to be plotting to prevent maritime unity.

C702 "CURRENT HISTORY," Meet Earl Browder, 45 (Oct. 1936), 93-97.
A biographical sketch of Earl Browder, general secretary of the Party since 1931. An early convert to socialism, Browder was jailed during World War I for resisting the draft. An active communist since 1919, he participated in left-wing activities here and in China before becoming head of the Party.

C703 . . ., 29 (Oct. 1955), 197-260.
An issue devoted to problems of security in a free society. Included are Henry Steele Commager on "The Right of

Dissent," Sidney Warren on "The Threat of Internal Communism," Hans J. Morgenthau on "Government Administration and Security," M. Stanley Livingston on "The Scientist and Security," Donald W. Mitchell on "Military Security," John P. Roche on "Security and the Press," W. Howard Mann on "Security and the Constitution," and David Denker on "American Security Viewed from Abroad." (The Warren, Morgenthau, and Mann articles are abstracted separately.)

C704 CURTIS, Charles P. "The Oppenheimer Case: The Trial of a Security System." New York: Simon and Schuster, 1955. 281 pp. Ind.
A popular treatment of the J. Robert Oppenheimer case, very favorable to Oppenheimer. Excerpts from testimony at the hearing are presented at some length. Criticizing the decision against Oppenheimer, the author concludes that the entire security system is at fault, that it stultifies our judgment where doubt can be presumed.

C705 CUSHING, Richard Cardinal. "Questions and Answers on Communism." 3d rev. ed. Boston: Daughters of St. Paul, 1961. 236 pp.
A booklet by a leading Roman Catholic prelate, consisting of the questions most frequently asked in classrooms and lecture halls, with answers taken mainly from communist writings, and with quotations from papal encyclicals, reports of congressional committees, and other sources. Topics include the nature of communism, class war, reforms, the Catholic church, religion, morality, the state, the workers, communism in the U.S., communist history, the current line, the economics of Marxism-Leninism, and the defeat of communism.

C706 . . . . "Conferences on Communism." Boston: Daughters of St. Paul, 1962. 76 pp.
A pamphlet by a leading Catholic prelate, mostly concerned with the world-wide communist threat, but with some treatment of Party activities specifically in the U.S., notably with respect to the "peace" campaign to prevent our winning the war in Korea.

C707 CUSHMAN, Robert E. The Purge of Federal Employees Accused of Disloyalty, "Public Administration Review," 3 (Autumn 1943), 297-316.
An examination of the policy, procedure, and constitutionality of congressional and executive branch programs dealing with the loyalty of federal employees. The test of loyalty should be clarified and carefully defined, with adequate procedural safeguards.

C708 . . . . The President's Loyalty Purge, "Survey Graphic," 36 (May 1947), 283-87 ff.
An examination of President Truman's executive order of March 21, 1947, providing for loyalty investigations of federal civilian employees and their dismissal if reasonable grounds exist for belief that they are disloyal. The effect on the morale of the federal service, and the dangers to individuals and to organizations, are considered, and suggestions for improvements are made.

C709 . . . . The Repercussions of Foreign Affairs on the American Tradition of Civil Liberty, "American Philosophical Society Proceedings," 92 (Oct. 1948), 257-63.
A professor of government examines our paradoxical position as a world leader in civil liberties, while fear of Russia and communist infiltration lead us to legislation which endangers these very liberties.

C710 . . . . American Civil Liberties in Mid-Twentieth Century, "Annals of the American Academy of Political and Social Science," 275 (May 1951), 1-8.

A review of recent gains and losses in the area of national civil liberties. Despite impressive gains in some areas, there are dangers resulting from the cold war and our almost pathological fear of communism. Grave threats to civil liberty arising from legislative investigative committees, loyalty oaths, and such legislation as the McCarran Act are pointed out.

C711 CUSHMAN, Robert E. "Civil Liberties in the United States: A Guide to Current Problems and Experiences." Ithaca: Cornell University Press, 1956. 248 pp. Ind.

A summary, by a professor of government at Cornell University, of the state of our civil liberties since the close of World War II. He discusses each civil liberty, summarizes developments of the past decade respecting it, and lists current or unsolved problems. In chapter 7, "Civil Liberties and National Security" (pp. 166-205), he discusses the statutes, executive orders, court decisions, and practices constituting our arsenal against communism and subversion. Included in his treatment are laws to prevent espionage or alien subversion, loyalty and security programs, registration and communist control acts, and legislative investigations. He concludes that, in our campaign against communism and subversion, we have deviated from long-established traditions of civil liberty.

C712 CUTLER, S., and OLEY, S. J. The Clear and Present Danger Test—Schenck to Dennis, "Georgetown Law Journal," 40 (Jan. 1952), 304-20.

Defense of the holding of the courts in the Dennis case as a realistic application of the clear and present danger rule, correcting its overly lenient application between 1936 and 1950. The authors trace the history of the rule from the Schenck case in 1919 to the present, showing the first modification in the Douds case. The Dennis case revealed the inherent weaknesses in the rule.

C713 CVETIC, Matthew (as told to Pete Martin). I Posed as a Communist for the F.B.I., "Saturday Evening Post," 223 (July 15, 1950), 17-19 ff; (July 22), 34-35 ff; (July 29), 30 ff.

The experiences of an FBI informant in the Communist Party in western Pennsylvania. Cvetic tells of the effect on his own life of posing as a communist. He also tells of Party activities and membership, naming people with whom he dealt as communists, and gives a detailed account of how the Party took over the American Slav Congress.

C714 . . . . "The Big Decision: Based on the Experiences of Matt Cvetic, Former FBI Counterspy." Hollywood, Calif.: n.pub., 1959. 216 pp.

The experiences of a Pittsburgh resident who joined the Communist Party in 1943 as an undercover man for the FBI. Assigned first to the Party's professional branch, he worked his way up in the Party, participating in work with nationality groups, training Red agents, raising funds for the Party, building front organizations, serving on a disciplinary commission, and attending the Party's 1945 national convention. His Party work broke up his home and cost him his Civil Service job. He ended nine years of double life with testimony against the communists before the House Un-American Activities Committee.

D

D1　J. D. [Carl Ross]. On Chauvinism against the Mexican-American People, "Political Affairs," 31 (Feb. 1952), 51-56.
A discussion of the tasks facing Party members in overcoming the widespread feeling of superiority which many Americans, including communists, have toward the Mexican-American minority.

D2　DABNEY, Virginius. Reds in Dixie, "Sewanee Review," 42 (Oct.-Dec., 1934), 415-22.
A Richmond, Va., newspaperman suggests that a liberal policy of letting the Reds talk is a more effective means of withstanding them than suppression or imprisonment. An example is given of official violence against the Unemployed Councils in Richmond, Va., which only helped to swell the ranks of the communists.

D3　DAHL, Leif. "The Way Out for Milk Producers." Philadelphia: Farmers National Committee for Action, n.d. [1934]. 24 pp.
A militant dairy program, including higher prices to farmers, lower prices to consumers, cancellation of debts of impoverished farmers, and passage of the workers unemployment insurance bill. The New Deal is attacked as an instrument for the exploiters to further pauperize small farmers and city workers.

D4　DAHLBERG, Edward. "Bottom Dogs." New York: Simon & Schuster, 1930. 269 pp.
A novel about a drifter, a down-and-outer in the lower layers of society. Then in his proletarian writer phase and close to the Party and its front organizations in the literary-intellectual field, Dahlberg shocked the reader by his description of life in the depths of society.

D5　. . . . "Those Who Perish." New York: John Day, 1934. 242 pp.
An examination, in fictional form, of the effect in America of the Nazi pogroms and the menace of fascism. Although the heroine comes to believe that communism is the hope of the future, she poisons herself because she belongs to the decaying old world.

D6　DAILY WORKER PUBLISHING COMPANY. "Red Cartoons from the Daily Worker, The Workers' Monthly and the Liberator." Chicago: 1926. 64 pp.
One of a series of cartoon collections from communist publications. (Others were published in 1927, 1928, and 1929.)

D7　. . . . "How to Sell the Daily Worker." New York: n.d. [193-]. 30 pp.
Advice to Party members on where and how to sell the official Party paper. Distribution of the paper is an important recruiting activity of the Party.

D8　. . . ."How the Auto Workers Won." New York: 1937. 14 pp.
Articles and editorials from the "Daily Worker," hailing the victory of the United Automobile Workers of the CIO over General Motors. The union victory is held the result of the progressive trade union policies and tactics employed.

D9　" 'DAILY WORKER.' Fighting Words: Selections from Twenty-Five Years of 'The Daily Worker.' " New York: New Century, 1949. 239 pp.
Excerpts from columns of the official paper of the Communist Party, covering the period from 1924 to 1949. Commentary on news events, on the people in the news, and special signed articles are all reproduced here. The collection is a valuable source of Party material on a wide variety of subjects.

D10　DALE, Thelma. Reconversion and the Negro People, "Political Affairs," 24 (Oct. 1945), 894-901.
A description of discriminatory treatment of Negroes in industry and in the armed forces. The Party will combat these conditions through Commissions on Negro Work to be set up in major cities throughout the country.

D11　DALLIN, David J. American Labor's Anti-Cominform, "American Mercury," 73 (Oct. 1951), 14-23.
A review of anticommunist efforts by American labor in the area of international affairs. The author praises the AFL for its stand against the WFTU, its help in forming the ICFTU, and its advice and assistance in fighting the communists through its labor representatives abroad. Though the CIO has been far less active, labor's efforts are impressive.

D12　. . . . "Soviet Espionage." New Haven: Yale, 1955. 556 pp. Notes. Ind.
An account of Soviet espionage activities in Europe and North America. Chapter 9 (pp. 389-492) is devoted to the U.S., covering the period from the late 1920's to 1950. The activities of Soviet spies George Mink, Jacob Golos, J. Peters, Juliet Stuart Poyntz, and Whittaker Chambers in the 1930's are described, as are the industrial, political, and atomic espionage carried on by the USSR here during World War II. The case of Judith Coplon is discussed at length (pp. 479-90).

D13　DALY, John Jay. Red Blight in Union Gardens, "Nation's Business," 34 (Sept. 1946), 57-59 ff.
A popularly written article on communist influence in the American labor movement. The Communist Party, whose object is to sovietize the U.S., has come into the open. Its members are at work on all fronts, particularly the labor front. Active communists in the labor movement are identified, and their methods of work outlined.

D14　DAMON [pseud. for C. E. Ruthenberg]. Make the Party a Party of Action, "Communist," (pro-Ruthenberg), 2 (April 25, 1920), 4.
An account of factional conflict within the Communist Party of America, between the majority of the Central Executive Committee and the group led by Ruthenberg, the executive secretary. Disagreeing with the Committee majority, who primarily represented the language federations, Ruthenberg wanted to build a strong Party organization and make the Party one of action. (Shortly afterward the Ruthenberg

group merged with the Communist Labor Party to form the United Communist Party.)

D15   DAMON, and MARSHALL [pseud. for Max Bedacht]. Problems of Communist Organization in the U.S., "Communist," (organ of the Communist Party of America), 1 (July 1922), 23-24.
An argument for liquidation of the underground Communist Party in the 1922 factional fight with the "goose caucus." The weak underground Party is in no condition to participate effectively in workers' struggles. Establishment of a legal political party is a first step toward creation of an open Communist Party. (This position was rejected for that advocated by the "goose caucus.")

D16   DAMON, Anna (ed.). "Victory: Decision of the United States Supreme Court in the Case of Angelo Herndon." Chicago: International Labor Defense, 1937. 30 pp.
The text of the majority decision of the U.S. Supreme Court in which Angelo Herndon, sentenced for an attempt to incite insurrection in Georgia, was ordered discharged. (See "Digest of the Public Record of Communism in the United States," p. 251.) The ILD had charged that Herndon was convicted, not on substantive grounds, but because he was a Party organizer. Anna Damon asserts that the Supreme Court's decision was prompted by the President's court reform proposal, made three days earlier.

D17   DAMON, Anna. The Struggle against Criminal Syndicalist Laws, "Communist," 16 (March 1937), 279-86.
The reversal by the Supreme Court of the conviction of communist Dirk De Jonge under an Oregon criminal syndicalist law is hailed as a victory, although the reversal was based on incorrect application of the law rather than unconstitutionality. The history of such repressive legislation is recited, along with the struggle against it of forces such as the ILD.

D18   DAMON, David [pseud. for C. E. Ruthenberg]. What Kind of Party? An Answer to the Majority Group of the C.E.C., "Communist," (organ of the Communist Party of America, pro-Ruthenberg), 2 (May 8, 1920), 3-4 ff.
A statement of the differences between the Ruthenberg-led minority and the language federations majority on the Central Executive Committee of the CPA. Differences concerned relations to the Third International, interpretation of "mass action," the language federations, which was the legal CEC, and responsibility for factionalism. (Shortly afterward the Ruthenberg group merged with the Communist Labor Party to form the United Communist Party.)

D19   DANIEL, Hawthorne. "Judge Medina: A Biography." New York: Wilfred Funk, 1952. 373 pp. App. Ind.
The story of the life of the judge who presided at the long and often disorderly trial of the 11 leaders of the Communist Party charged in 1949 under the Smith Act with advocating the overthrow of the government by violence. A long chapter describes the trial, the abusive tactics of the communists and their attorneys, the delays and confusion for which they were responsible, and the manner in which the judge conducted the proceedings. The statement made by the judge when he sentenced the defending attorneys for contempt of court is given in full, as is his charge to the jury.

D20   DANIELS, Robert V. "The Nature of Communism." New York: Random House, 1962. 398 pp. Bibliog. note. Ind.
A discussion of various aspects of communism, including Marxist theory, revolution, the Party, its strategy of struggle, Russia, the Eastern world, and the industrial revolution. Chapters on communism as totalitarianism and as a faith, and a view of the future of communism, complete the study. Though there are only scattered explicit references to the U.S., the description of communist objectives and behavior applies here as to all other countries in which the communists have not attained power.

D21   DANISH, Max D. "The World of David Dubinsky." Cleveland and New York: World Publishing Co., 1957. 347 pp. Ind.
A biography of the president of the ILGWU by the editor of its publication. Chapter 4 describes the communist drive for power in the needle trades unions, and chapter 20 deals with Dubinsky's efforts throughout his career to expose the Party's threat to organized labor. Dubinsky's experiences during the war with the communists, his activities in the American Labor Party and the Liberal Party, and his role in the formation and split of the World Federation of Trade Unions are included.

D22   DARCY, Sam. "The Challenge of Youth: Why Every Young Worker Should Join the Young Communist League." Chicago: Young Workers (Communist) League of America, 1926. 52 pp.
An appeal to young workers to join the communists and fight capitalism, child labor, and war profiteering. "Warmongering" organizations such as the Girl Scouts are condemned.

D23   . . . . The Big Stick in Latin America—Its Size and Cost, "Workers Monthly," 5 (March 1926), 215-18.
An attack on American military ventures in Cuba, Haiti, Santo Domingo, and Panama, and financial penetration and manipulation elsewhere. The American military, fostered by this imperialism, is said to be four times as large as the armed forces of the Soviet Union, which has more to defend and has the bourgeois governments of the whole world plotting against it.

D24   . . . . Join the Army—, "Workers Monthly," 5 (May 1926), 315-18.
A description of alleged atrocities against U.S. Army enlisted men, including the court-martial convictions of Paul Crouch and Walter Trumbull for communist activities in Hawaii. Military graft and war profits are also discussed. The communists must win over the soldiers, who come from the working class, whereas the officers come from the bourgeoisie.

D25   . . . . The Great West Coast Maritime Strike, "Communist," 13 (July 1934), 664-86.
A report written during the course of the San Francisco maritime strike, detailing plans, strategies, and problems of the strike. Despite efforts by the AFL and Socialist Party reformists to sell the workers out, the Marine Workers Industrial Union is represented in the Joint Strike Committee and the strike shows signs of developing into a general one.

D26   . . . . The San Francisco Bay Area General Strike, "Communist," 13 (Oct. 1934), 985-1004.
An analysis of the San Francisco general strike, which grew out of a strike by longshoremen and marine workers. It was not the intention of the general strike to seize power, though it stopped all production in the Bay area and raised the level of class consciousness. It was "sold out" by labor fakers and AFL bureaucrats, who seized the leadership.

D27   DARCY, Sam. "An Eye-Witness at the Wreckers' Trial." New York: Workers Library, 1937. 63 pp.
An account, by an American communist, of the trial in Moscow in January 1937 of a group of Trotskyites headed by Piatakov and Radek. The defendants were convicted of sabotage, murder, robbery, espionage for fascism, and treason. Darcy testifies to the fairness of the trial and the guilt of the defendants.

D28   . . . . "What's Happening in the USSR?" New York: Workers Library, 1937. 16 pp.
A defense of the Moscow trials for the American public. The author charges that fascist spies and wreckers had been sent into Russia, where they cooperated with Trotsky, Bucharin, and others; and that wrecking and treason were committed, in an effort to return capitalism to the USSR. Norman Thomas is attacked for supporting the Trotskyites, who are labeled agents of fascism.

D29   . . . . "The Battle for Production." New York: Workers Library, 1942. 47 pp.
A call to Americans to increase production to fight the Axis. Industry is urged to complete its conversion to war production and monopolies are asked to stop raising prices. Labor should be given full representation on government boards, the labor movement must heal its split, and a second front should be opened now.

D30   . . . . The Elections in Philadelphia, "Communist," 22 (Dec. 1943), 1121-32.
A review of political line-ups in the Philadelphia elections and the work of communists in support of win-the-war candidates. The defeat of William C. Bullitt, Republican candidate for mayor, is acclaimed a victory.

D31   DARROW, Clarence. "Argument in the Case of the Communist Labor Party in the Criminal Court." Chicago: Kerr, 1920. 116 pp.
Summation for the defense in the trial of the Communist Labor Party leaders who were indicted and convicted in 1919 of violation of the Illinois criminal syndicalism statute. Darrow based the defense on the defendants' rights to express their opinions and to be free of illegal search and entry. He stressed the political idealism of his clients, the prejudices and propaganda of the prosecution, and the need to protect the freedoms guaranteed by our Constitution.

D32   DASCH, Al. Confusion Reigns in Ranks as C.P. Veers to Labor Party, "New Militant," 1 (April 13, 1935), 3.
A Trotskyist analysis of Earl Browder's announcement, at the Washington Conference for Unemployment Insurance, that the CP favors a labor party. The announcement caused surprise, since for five years such a policy has been viewed as social fascism. But the monolithic Party structure gave the new policy unanimous acceptance.

D33   DAVENPORT, Walter. Trouble in Paradise, "Collier's," 118 (Aug. 10, 1946), 14-15 ff.
The editor of "Collier's" speculates on possible changes in Party policy and leadership on Browder's return from Moscow, where he was received as a distinguished guest. He had been replaced with Foster, and his policies reversed, following an attack on him by a French communist leader, Jacques Duclos. Past policy changes are reviewed, and an account given of current membership drives.

D34   DAVID, Rex. "Schools and the Crisis." New York: International Pamphlets, 1934. 46 pp.
An assertion that the crisis in American education is catastrophic, that high schools and colleges are for the well-to-do, and that teachers' salaries, already low, are declining. The schools are attacked for Jim Crow education and for propagandizing for war. Education in the USSR is contrasted with the poor condition here. The author calls for mass action by teachers and students.

D35   DAVIDSON, Bill. The People Who Stole It from Us, "Look," 21 (Oct. 29, 1957), 87-88 ff.
An account of the activities of Julius and Ethel Rosenberg and those involved with them. Though many believe them innocent, a special report by the Attorney General's office shows this not to be true.

D36   DAVIES, A. Powell. Loyalty Needs Better Friends, "New Republic," 126 (Feb. 4, 1952), 11-13.
A protest by a leading Unitarian minister against the oppressive and unjust procedures used in the testing of loyalty of government employees. The morale of loyal government workers is being undermined by intimidation. Cases of unjust dismissals, based on earlier membership in or association with the Party, are reviewed.

D37   . . . . "The Urge to Persecute." Boston: Beacon, 1953. 219 pp.
A Unitarian minister discusses the effects of loyalty investigations on our basic freedoms and the principles of democracy. Communism as an ideology is of minor importance in America, except as it permits exploitation of fear and destruction of traditional American liberalism. He sees in our "urge to persecute" a release from our frustrations, not only about communism but about the responsibilities of freedom. (A chapter appeared in "Progressive," Jan. 1954, under the title, "What Makes a Communist?")

D38   . . . . The Bewitchment of Rebecca West, "New Republic," 128 (June 8, 1953), 14-15.
Criticism by a leading Unitarian minister of articles by Rebecca West seeking to quiet British fears about McCarthy, and dispel the myth of our anticommunist hysteria. Miss West is charged with trickery, apologizing for McCarthy, and ignoring the treacherous enemies, other than communism, that we face.

D39   . . . . Congress Moves in on the Churches, "New Republic," 129 (Aug. 3, 1953), 7-8.
Condemnation by a Washington, D.C., Unitarian minister of the congressional committee that questioned G. Bromley Oxnam. Oxnam's inquisitors are trying to substitute conformity for judgment, anticommunism for the Judeo-Christian ethic, and authoritarianism for the American founding principles.

D40   DAVIES, Joseph E. Is Communism a Menace to Us? "New York Times Magazine," April 12, 1942. 3 ff.
A former U.S. ambassador to Russia asserts that Russian communism has nothing to offer the American people. He traces the decline of the Party's vote here from 1932 to 1940, cites the turnover in Party membership, and lists the privileges of Americans under democracy. He concludes that there is no menace of communism here.

D41   DAVIS, Arthur K. Behind the Civil Rights Crisis, "Monthly Review," 3 (Sept. 1951), 138-47.
An associate professor of sociology at Union College asserts that the mounting civil rights crisis is that thought control, penalties, and coercion are being applied to nonconformists. The equation, "Change = Communism = Russia," is a distortion of reality. He calls for the rejection of this false equation, support for socialism, and participation in battles for civil rights. (Reprinted in pamphlet form with article by Florence Luscomb under the title, "Red Baiting and Civil Liberties.")

D42   DAVIS, Arthur K. Anti-Communism and Fascism, "Monthly Review," 5 (June 1953), 69-75.
An examination of the spread of communism abroad, especially in the relatively backward countries, and of the rise of American interventionism, with its intensification of anticommunism at home. So long as anticommunism remains the core of American policy, we are headed for fascism.

D43   DAVIS, Benjamin J., Jr. "James W. Ford: What He Is and What He Stands For." New York: Workers Library, 1936. 30 pp.
A glowing biography of James W. Ford, Party candidate for vice-president of the U.S. The author asserts that communism is twentieth-century abolitionism, and that the Party candidates are the only ones for the Negro people.

D44   .... The Negro People in the Elections, "Communist," 15 (Oct. 1936), 975-87.
The Republicans have forsaken Lincoln in favor of Wall Street, Hearst, and the Liberty League. The Democrats are corrupted by its Southern faction, which forms a coalition with the Ku Klux Klan. Only the CP, with a Negro vice-presidential candidate, James Ford, offers a program of equality.

D45   .... The Communists, the Negro People and the War, "Communist," 21 (Aug. 1942), 633-39.
In a letter to the editor of the New York "Age," a Harlem weekly, Davis denies assertions in that paper's June 27 editorial that the Communist Party had given up its struggle for Negro rights when this country entered the war.

D46   .... "The Negro People and the Communist Party." New York: Workers Library, 1943. 15 pp.
An appeal to Negroes to follow Davis' example and join the Communist Party to help win the war and fight Jim Crow. Telling how he became a communist, Davis emphasizes the Negro's stake in victory, the achievements of the Soviet Union, and the role of the Party in the fight for Negro rights.

D47   .... Reply to a Libel, "New Masses," 50 (Feb. 15, 1944), 8-9.
A reply to attacks on the Party's civil rights line made by the New York "World Telegram" and the "Herald Tribune." Davis asserts that the Party, far from inciting the Negro people to violence, is a stabilizing force, as shown by its role in curbing rioting in Harlem in August 1943. Nevertheless it insists that all racial discrimination must go.

D48   .... "The Path of Negro Liberation." New York: New Century, 1947. 22 pp.
The 1946-47 reinterpretation of the earlier "self-determination of the Black Belt" slogan, as presented to the Party's national committee in December 1946. Davis asserts that Negroes want full equality and first-class citizenship in America, without Red-baiting; as they develop a national consciousness, they will desire self-determination. The statehood envisioned now is binational, like the Canadian.

D49   .... "Why I Am a Communist," New York: New Century, 1947. 23 pp. Reprinted from the June 1947, issue of "Phylon," an Atlanta University quarterly.
The author, communist leader and New York City councilman, asserts that he joined the Party because he sought freedom and equal rights, although the immediate cause was the Herndon trial, in which he participated as defense attorney. The issue today is said to be democracy vs. fascism, with the Party and the Negro on one side and American imperialism on the other. Organized labor and Negroes, natural allies, will soon be working together in a national third party against the policies of Wall Street.

D50   .... Summary Remarks on the Discussion of the Resolution on Negro Rights, "Political Affairs," 26 (Jan. 1947), 59-63.
A summary of the discussion of Negro problems at the plenary meeting of the Party's national committee, December 3-5, 1946. The position on self-determination taken in the resolution eliminates Browder's revisionism while avoiding our sectarianism of the past.

D51   .... Build the United Negro People's Movement, "Political Affairs," 26 (Nov. 1947), 996-1006.
Since V-J Day the status of the Negro people has rapidly grown worse. Reaction seeks to divide them and to disrupt the unity between them and organized labor and white progressives. The broadest unity among the Negro people is urged. (Based on a report to a Party national conference on the problems of the Negro people, Sept. 19-20, 1947.)

D52   .... The Negro People's Liberation Movement, "Political Affairs," 27 (Sept. 1948), 880-98.
American imperialism is intensifying the national oppression of the Negro people, who are fighting for full citizenship. The Progressive Party stands for Negro rights as against the twin parties of reaction. Weaknesses in the Communist Party's work among Negroes are analyzed, and suggestions offered for improvement. (Based on Davis' report to, and the discussion in, the Negro-South panel of the Party's fourteenth national convention.)

D53   .... "In Defense of Negro Rights." New York: New York State Committee, Communist Party, 1950. 64 pp.
Excerpts from Davis' testimony at his trial for violation of the Smith Act. Davis denounces both the judge and American justice, and asserts that, because of the verdict and his sentence, the American people are being reduced to the second-class citizenship of the Negroes.

D54   .... The Negro People in the Fight for Peace and Freedom, "Political Affairs," 29 (May 1950), 101-14.
A report to the plenum of the national committee, CPUSA, March 23-25, 1950, warning of an intensified profascist offensive against the Negro people. The struggle for Negro liberation is linked to the fight for peace. Right-wing Negro reformists, social democrats, and bourgeois nationalists are serving as agents of imperialism.

D55   .... On the Use of Negro Troops in Wall Street's Aggression against the Korean People, "Political Affairs," 29 (Oct. 1950), 47-57.
By using Negro troops in Korea, American imperialism conceals the racist character of its aggression. Negro soldiers are brutally mistreated, especially in Korea, while the armed services continue their Jim Crow policy.

D56   .... On the Colonial Liberation Movements, "Political Affairs," 29 (Dec. 1950), 37-49.
Throughout the world colonial peoples, often under communist leadership, are freeing themselves from imperialistic rule. The Korean War has exposed the U.S. as an imperialist power seeking to subjugate darker peoples. The American working people must make common cause with the colonial peoples in the fight against Wall Street.

D57   .... "The Negro People in the Struggle for Peace." New York: New Century, 1951. 23 pp.

A report to the CPUSA national convention, December 28-31, 1950, in which the Party's support of the Negro liberation movement is made an integral part of the offensive against participation in the Korean war. Winning the Negro masses is called the first step toward advancing the struggle against fascism and war.

D58   DAVIS, Benjamin J., Jr. The Struggle for Peace and the Negro Liberation Movement, "Political Affairs," 31 (June 1952), 51-57.
The Negro liberation movement is seen as a strong deterrent to the drive to fascism and another world war. It is objectively a movement for peace, for mobilizing a people whose right to self-determination and nationhood in the Black Belt is denied by imperialism. (Excerpts from a report to the fifteenth national convention, CPUSA, Dec. 1950.)

D59   .... "The Negro People on the March." New York: New Century, 1956. 48 pp.
Text of a report to the Party's national committee, June 23-24, 1956, representing a sharp change in the Party's position on the Negro question. The "self-determination" plank is repudiated, and a united front program with other Negro leaders and organizations is supported. Asserting that the number of Negroes in leading Party positions has declined, Davis demands that the Party ends its lag behind many other organizations in this respect.

D60   .... The Challenge of the New Era, "Political Affairs," 35 (Dec. 1956), 14-27.
Though he voted for and still supports the Draft Resolution, Davis presents his reservations. These deal with the resolution's equivocation on Marxism-Leninism, its inadequate treatment of the Negro question, its weak stand on American imperialism, and its underplaying of the role of the Party.

D61   .... The Pilgrimage to Washington, "Political Affairs," 36 (July 1957), 14-20.
The May 17 prayer pilgrimage to Washington, in which 30,000 participated, was the most massive demonstration of the Negro people for first-class citizenship since the Civil War. Along with the great significance of the pilgrimage there were some shortcomings—the scant presence of white workers and the appearance of Red-baiting.

D62   DAVIS, Elmer. The Red Peril, "Saturday Review of Literature," 8 (April 16, 1932), 661-62.
Though communism is unlikely to come to America, American literature will some have its Red peril, since intellectuals are most susceptible to communism. The Red infiltration into literature imports alien and irrelevant values. Communists will be good artists only to the extent that they are bad communists.

D63   .... Makers of Martyrs, "Harper's Magazine," 167 (Aug. 1933), 341-51.
An assertion that over-zealous persons and communists alike make martyrs by fighting for vindication of a principle, no matter what the cost may be to innocent defendants. The Scottsboro case is used as an illustration of the methods of the communists, who are interested in martyrs and propaganda, not in the acquittal of defendants.

D64   ..., and HICKS, Granville. A Debate: Lattimore and the Liberals, "New Leader," 33 (May 27, 1950), 16-18.
Davis criticizes Hicks for his repudiation of Lattimore in a "New Leader" article on May 6, and for his implied injunction to keep quiet about defending accused men, lest they be proved guilty. Hicks replies that just because McCarthy says a man is guilty, this does not make him innocent; and he may be a communist even though he is well-informed and appears honest and forthright.

D65   .... History in Doublethink, "Saturday Review of Literature," 35 (June 28, 1952), 8-9 ff.
An attack on the arrogance of excommunists, many of whom shift from the extreme left to the extreme right and may be as wrong in their present views as when they were communists. Some become experts in "doublethink," misreading history and remembering what they wish to remember. Whittaker Chambers and John Dos Passos are cases in point.

D66   .... "But We Were Born Free." Indianapolis and New York: Bobbs Merrill, 1954. 229 pp.
A collection of essays with a common theme, the need for Americans to defend their freedoms, under attack by professional anti- and excommunists. The former head of the Office of War Information decries the excesses of McCarthy and other hunters of subversives, arguing that the communist threat to our country is the external, not the internal, one. He asserts that American democracy is endangered more by the McCarthyites than by the activities of communists and fellow-travelers.

D67   DAVIS, Horace B. "Labor and Steel." New York: International Publishers, 1933. 304 pp. Ref. notes. App. Ind.
A description of the life and grievances of steel workers and the structure of the industry, with an outline of its history of unionism. A chapter on the steel strike of 1919 stresses the heroic role of William Z. Foster. Subsequent attempts to organize are reviewed, with emphasis on the progressive role of the Metal Workers Industrial League (later the Steel and Metal Workers Industrial Union) and the Trade Union Unity League.

D68   .... "Shoes: The Workers and the Industry." New York: International Publishers, 1940. 257 pp. Ind.
One of the studies of industrial conditions by the procommunist Labor Research Association. The author describes the depressed conditions of the shoe industry, the personnel policies followed by the shoe companies, and their use of violence and spies to defeat unionism. He deplores the defeatist attitude of the AFL union in the industry, the lack of good leadership on the part of the independent unions, and the failure of the workers to develop class consciousness.

D69   DAVIS, Jerome. "Contemporary Social Movements." New York & London: Century, 1930. 901 pp. Bibliog. App. Ind.
A textbook of readings, with some original analysis, on contemporary social movements. Though most of book 4 (pp. 219-421), dealing with communism, is devoted to the USSR, the last portion (pp. 366-421), deals with its significance for the U.S. Among the authors in this section are E. A. Ross, Lenin, Davis, Frank R. Kellogg, Edwin R. A. Seligman, Lyford P. Edwards, and Harold J. Laski.

D70   .... Capitalism and Communism, "Annals of the American Academy of Political and Social Science," 156 (July 1931), 62-75.
Opposition by a Yale professor to the proposal of the Fish committee to outlaw the Communist Party. Davis argues that, despite evidence of dictatorship and lack of freedom for opponents, economic progress is being made in Russia, as contrasted with the condition of American capitalism in the depression. He urges recognition of Russia.

D71   .... "Behind Soviet Power: Stalin and the Russians." Introd. by Joseph E. Davies. New York: Readers Press, 1946. 120 pp.

An attempt by a professor of sociology and social ethics at the Yale Divinity School to explain Russia to Americans, giving a sympathetic analysis of its system of government, economic controls, and democratic leanings. The author contends that Russia champions the oppressed masses the world over, and that the charge that foreign observers see only what the Russians want them to see is untrue.

D72   DAVIS, Jerome. "Character Assassination." New York: Philosophical Library, 1950. 259 pp. App. Ind.

Criticism of all types of "prejudice," which is viewed as any opposition, founded or unfounded, on religious, social, or political grounds. Charges of communist sympathy in trade unions, churches, and schools are deplored as prejudice and character blackening in a period of hysteria, without discrimination between legitimate and illegitimate accusations. Pages 175-220 deal with the House Committee on Un-American Activities and the federal loyalty program, whose procedures are declared conducive to suspicion, hatred, fear, and intolerance.

D73   DAVIS, John P. "Let Us Build a National Negro Congress." Washington: National Sponsoring Committee, National Negro Congress, 1935. 31 pp.

The secretary of the national sponsoring committee of a Party front organization recites the evidence of the Negro's second-class citizenship in the U.S.—denial of constitutional rights, joblessness, Jim Crow unionism, the plight of farmers on Southern plantations, discrimination in relief, legal lynching, and the like—and calls for the formation of a national Negro congress to right these wrongs.

D74   DAVIS, Saville R. "Toward Freedom and Security." Foreword by Wesley F. Rennie. New York: Association Press, 1955. 48 pp.

A discussion, in a YMCA publication, of the menace of communism and the decline in the spirit of freedom. The author, an editor of the "Christian Science Monitor," asserts that both liberty and security are vital to the American system, and that nonconformity occupies a vital place in our democratic existence. Even in time of crisis we cannot limit the freedom we seek to make secure.

D75   DAWIDOWICZ, Lucy S. Liberals and the CP Line on McCarthyism. "New Leader," 35 (April 21, 1952), 16-18.

The Communist Party's policy toward McCarthy is based on confusing legitimate anticommunism with "McCarthyism." This is part of the new united-front policy of the communists, which is directed toward specific issues. The Party believes that the U.S. is in the incipient stage of fascism, the result of Truman's warlike policy, and that this policy feeds the rabid McCarthy forces.

D76   .... Anti-Semitism and the Rosenberg Case: The Latest Communist Propaganda Trap, "Commentary," 14 (July 1952), 41-45.

The communists seek to exploit minority fears and sympathies by presenting the conviction of Julius and Ethel Rosenberg for atomic espionage as an anti-Semitic plot by the American government. Jews are cautioned to be on guard, since similar campaigns have strengthened anti-Semitic forces elsewhere.

D77   .... Trojan Horse Returns, "New Leader," 36 (March 9, 1953), 12-14.

The new communist line, following Eisenhower's victory, calls for dropping the Progressive Party, an attempt to cooperate with the CIO's Political Action Committee and the AFL's Labor's League for Political Education, and efforts by individual communists to infiltrate the NAACP, the ADA, the Liberal Party, and the Democratic Party.

D78   .... False Friends and Dangerous Defenders, "Reconstructionist," 19 (May 1, 1953), 9-15.

An analysis of the communist line on anti-Semitism in America. Communists insist that American anti-Semitism is promoted deliberately by the American government. In fact, the communists encourage, provoke, and fan anti-Semitism by spreading the anti-Semitic stereotype of the Jew as communist.

D79   DAWSON, Christopher. The Significance of Bolshevism, "American Review," 1 (April 1933), 36-49.

A discussion of the reasons for the triumph of the Bolsheviks in Russia and of aspects of Bolshevik ideology that repel citizens of Western countries or are attractive to them. Communists are disciplined members of a party and priests of an idea, not representatives of the people. Western civilization is more than bourgeois culture; it is socially and spiritually complex.

D80   DAWSON, Henry. Reaction Bids for Farm Support, "Communist," 15 (Oct. 1936), 956-65.

A survey of the farm crisis, contrasting the farmer-labor movement's farm program with those of the Democratic and Republican parties. The Republicans would restrict the uses to which payments could be put. The Democratic plan, while providing more relief, could drive smaller farmers out of commercial production. The farmer-labor program would guarantee farmers their cost of production without harming consumers.

D81   DAY, Dorothy. "From Union Square to Rome." Silver Spring, Md.: Preservation of the Faith Press, 1938. 173 pp.

An account of the author's life until she joined the Catholic Church in 1927 at the age of 29. A staff member at various times of the socialist New York "Call," the "Masses," and its successor "The Liberator," she had been active in various radical groups and in the pacifist movement during the first world war. For brief periods a member of the Socialist Party and the IWW, she had been active in various communist front organizations and sympathetic to the Communist Party, though with reservations, before rejecting communism for Catholicism.

D82   .... "The Long Loneliness: The Autobiography of Dorothy Day." New York: Harper, 1952. 288 pp. Ind.

The autobiography of one of the founders of the Catholic Worker Movement. There is a brief account of the author's earlier activities in the radical movement, when she worked as a reporter for the socialist New York "Call," and wavered among socialism, syndicalism (the IWW), and anarchism. Later she was a member of the editorial staff of the "Masses," followed by a period with its successor, "Liberator." Much of the latter portion of the book is devoted to the Catholic Worker Movement, which she founded with Peter Maurin; and to its publication, the "Catholic Worker," its "houses of hospitality," and its picket line activities, in which Catholics and communists often cooperated.

D83   DAYKIN, Walter L. The Operation of the Taft-Hartley Act's Non-Communist Provisions, "Iowa Law Review," 36 (Summer 1951), 607-28.

An analysis of the operation of Section 9 (h) of the Taft-Hartley Act, describing its provisions, explaining the NLRB's jurisdiction over noncomplying unions, outlining the area of bargaining between an employer and a noncomplying union, and exploring the problem of compliance of the local and its parent organization.

D84 DAYKIN, Walter L. The Communist Employee: What Grounds for Discharge? "Personnel," 36 (Jan.-Feb., 1959), 64-68.
A review of arbitrators' decisions on the discharge of employees for Party membership or refusal to answer questions under the Fifth Amendment. Party membership alone is not generally held a valid ground for discharge. A federal ruling is usually required to justify discharge as a security risk.

D85 DEAN, Elwood M. "The Story of the Trenton Six." New York: New Century, 1949. 23 pp.
An exposé of the case of six New Jersey Negroes said to be unjustly convicted of a murder charge, written by the education director of the Party in New Jersey.

D86 DEAN, John. The Socialist Administration in Reading and Our United Front Tasks, "Communist," 15 (Jan. 1936), 84-88.
In the recent municipal elections in Reading, the communists supported the successful socialists. The socialists will not meet the workers' demands, as for adequate relief, and the workers may become disillusioned. As they are more likely to turn to the capitalist parties than to the weak CP, we should put mass pressure on the socialists to meet their demands.

D87 DeBOER, John J. Communism and Fascism in the Schools, "School and Society," 70 (Oct. 29, 1949), 273-75.
Our schools are failing to teach students the meaning of democracy through the realities of everyday living. If our schools would convert the symbols of freedom into these realities, we would not need to fear communism. Youth must compare the communist effort to suppress free inquiry, not with the Dies Committee, etc., but with the teachings of Jefferson, Lincoln, and Roosevelt.

D88 DECTER, Moshe (ed.). "The Profile of Communism: A Fact-by-Fact Primer." New York: Collier Books, 1961. 160 pp. Bibliog.
A primer on communism in question-and-answer form. Part one, on "World Communism: Strategy and Tactics," includes sections on the program, movement, tactics, and techniques of communism. Part two, on "Communist Rule," covers the Soviet empire, the totalitarian nature of the Soviet world, economy and labor in the Soviet world, and communist China. Though only a small portion of the illustrative material deals explicitly with the U.S., the description of communist strategy and tactics applies to this as to all other countries not under communist rule. (Revision of the "Profile of Communism," by Joseph L. Lichten and Oscar Cohen, which was based on a 1951 pamphlet, "Primer on Communism," by Frank N. Trager and Joseph L. Lichten.)

D89 DEGRAS, Jane (ed.). "The Communist International: Documents, Vol. I (1919-1922)." London, New York, Toronto: Oxford University Press, 1956. 463 pp. Ind.
Two documents in this compilation deal specifically with American communism: (1) A letter from the Communist International to the Industrial Workers of the World; (2) The thesis of the Fourth Congress of the Communist International on the Negro question.

D90 DELANEY, Martin. "Journal of a Young Man." New York: Vanguard, 1936. 300 pp.
A story of young Bohemians, living poverty-stricken and hopeless lives in the Greenwich Village of the 1930's. An anticlerical novel, it focuses on the hopeless love affair between a Marxist and a girl who dislikes his radical activities.

D91 DELANEY, Robert Finley. "The Literature of Communism in America: A Selected Reference Guide." Washington, D.C.: Catholic University, 1962. 433 pp. App. Ind.
A fairly comprehensive listing of pertinent writings, with brief abstracts, organized under the heads of reference works, general works, philosophy and theory of communism, the communist state in reality, world communist literature, biographies, American communism and civil rights, history of American Marxism, American communist literature, procommunist literature, anticommunist literature, and official anticommunist publications. Most of the above sections are in turn subdivided. An appendix lists titles that appeared while the manuscript was being prepared for publication.

D92 DELL, Floyd. "Intellectual Vagabondage: An Apology for the Intelligentsia." New York: Doran, 1926. 261 pp.
Reproduction, with additional material, of a series of articles on "Literature and the Machine Age" that appeared in "Liberator." The machine civilization of our time, its associate editor asserts, has produced a generation of intellectual vagabonds unable to find a place in society. He hopes that younger intellectuals, recognizing the promise of the Russian Revolution, will live more joyously and more responsibly.

D93 .... A Literary Self-Analysis, "Modern Quarterly," 4 (June-Sept., 1927), 148-52.
An attempt by Dell to explain why, though he had been associated with the socialist movement and now regards himself as a communist, his fictional works contain so little political, social, or economic realism. His fictional work, he says, represents an attempt to work out unsolved psychological conflicts.

D94 .... "Homecoming: An Autobiography." New York: Farrar and Rinehart, 1933. 368 pp.
The autobiography of a leading radical literary figure of the period of World War I and later. An associate editor of the "Masses" and its successor, "Liberator," Dell was first a left-wing socialist and then a supporter of communism, although he never joined the Party. (Later, after his break with communism, he was attacked by the Party.) Political issues and events receive only minor attention in this volume.

D95 DEMBITZ, Nanette. Swearing to One's Loyalty, "Antioch Review," 12 (June 1952), 195-202.
The author, for several years an attorney in the Department of Justice, weighs the demerits of loyalty oaths against their dubious advantages and effectiveness. The benefits of free expression, she holds, are as much lost when it is sacrificed through fear as when it is suppressed.

D96 DENNIS, Eugene. The Wisconsin Elections and the Farmer-Labor Victory, "Communist," 15 (Dec. 1936), 1125-40.
A communist leader acclaims the victory of the Farmer-Labor Progressive Federation in Wisconsin. The communists, over the opposition of the Federation's leadership, worked directly among the Federation's adherents in support of its campaign. As a result some known communists were elected to office, and communist propaganda influenced many people.

D97 .... The Socialist Party Convention, "Communist," 16 (May 1937), 401-20.
The socialists continued their sectarian view that the key conflict is between capitalism and socialism. Failing to see that fascism is a much more serious threat than bourgeois democracy, they did not favor a people's front

to fight fascism. The socialist resolutions reflect the power of the Trotskyites in the leadership.

D98 DENNIS, Eugene. Problems of the People's Front in the United States, "Communist International," 14 (Nov. 1937), 795-803.
Justification for a shift in Party emphasis away from the farmer-labor movement as the specific American form of the people's front. Efforts should be made to encourage union and progressive groups to organized action within the Democratic Party, while eradicating the influence of those, such as Trotskyites, who oppose the people's front.

D99 . . ., and GREEN, Gilbert. Notes on the Defense of American Democracy, "Communist," 17 (May 1938), 410-18.
The Party fought against bourgeois democracy, as in postwar Germany, when it was the principal obstacle to socialism. Now the Party defends a capitalist democracy under fascist threat because fascism would lessen the workers' and Party's freedom of action and make the realization of socialism more difficult.

D100 . . . . Some Questions Concerning the Democratic Front, "Communist," 17 (June 1938), 534-40.
The concept of the democratic front as expounded by Hathaway (see "Building the Democratic Front," in "Communist," May 1938) needs clarification. It is wrong to view the democratic front as having a less clear program than a people's front or as working only within the major parties. It is merely an attempt to combine a wider range of progressives in the fight against fascism than would come into a people's front.

D101 . . . . Preparing for the Opening of Congress: Next Steps of the Democratic Front, "Communist," 17 (Nov. 1938), 993-99.
In the 1938 election campaign, labor must seek closer collaboration with New Deal Democrats in pushing and extending New Deal policies. People must be shown that the legislative record of Republicans belies their liberal proclamations.

D102 . . . . The President's Message—an Editorial, "National Issues: A Survey of Politics and Legislation," 1 (Feb. 1939), 3-5.
Enthusiastic endorsement of the President's message to Congress on January 4, which recognized that social reform, economic recovery, and resistance to fascism are inseparable planks of the progressive program. Progressives in both parties must act jointly to offset the reactionaries.

D103 . . . . Recovery Demands a Bold Progressive Program, "Communist," 18 (June 1939), 523-34.
By curtailing loans and agitating for an end to public works, the capitalists caused the 1937 recession. They hope to prolong it so that the people will turn against the New Deal and its social legislation. To prevent this, the government must expand public works, and nationalize the banks to make cheap credit available to small businesses.

D104 . . . . Roosevelt, the War, and the New Deal, "Communist," 19 (Jan. 1940), 21-40.
Roosevelt has embarked on an imperialist war policy of aiding Britain and France, subjugating South America and the Far East, and abetting Finnish opposition to Russia. A huge arms program at the expense of social welfare implements this policy. Labor should lead a people's front opposed to both the Democrats and the Republicans.

D105 . . . . The Bolshevization of the Communist Party of the United States in the Struggle against the Imperialist War, "Communist," 19 (May 1940), 403-17.
A critique of the current status of the Party and a program for improvement. The Party is criticized for failing to recognize the imperialist nature of the war and the need for proletarian opposition to U.S. involvement. The Party must lead the labor-farmer-Negro-intellectual coalition in opposition to Roosevelt and the capitalists.

D106 . . . . Labor and the Elections, "Communist," 19 (Sept. 1940), 820-41.
Although workers oppose Wall Street's imperialist policy, they vote Democratic because their class consciousness has been dimmed by the slogan of national unity and the fear of war, because social democrats and labor leaders have labeled the Democrats a lesser evil, and because progressives have failed to form a people's front party. The communists favor formation of such a party.

D107 . . . . America and the United Nations, "Communist," 21 (March 1942), 114-24.
The basic task is to build an American, British, and Russian alliance with an integrated strategy that concentrates on defeating Germany. To accomplish this, Britain and the U.S. must supply Russia with munitions. Emphasis on the defeat of Germany does not imply slackening of the war effort against Italy and Japan.

D108 . . . . For a Second Front in Europe! To the Offensive against Hitler! "Communist," 21 (April 1942), 199-213.
Britain and the U.S. should open a second front, catch Germany between two fronts, and engineer its immediate defeat. Communists reject as treacherous the go-slow advice of the old isolationists; nor do they accept the view that an early peace would leave Russia too strong. There is nothing to fear from Russian strength, since Russia wants only a just peace.

D109 . . . . The Second Front and the Winter of 1942-43, "Communist," 21 (Nov. 1942), 894-902.
In failing to open a second front, Britain and the U.S. are missing an opportunity to defeat Germany now, and are running the risk that Germany may defeat Russia and emerge even stronger. Therefore the Party asserts that a second front should be opened immediately.

D110 . . . . The New Stage of the War in Europe, "Communist," 22 (Feb. 1943), 99-113.
The tide of war is turning against Germany, as many Allied offensives are being launched. The British and Americans have landed in Africa and many resistance movements are tying down German troops. The biggest offensive is the Russian. Now that Germany has begun to retreat, the time is opportune for the opening of a second front on the European continent.

D111 . . . . Victory and the 1944 Elections, "Communist," 22 (July 1943), 599-612.
An abridgment of a report to a plenary meeting of the Party's national committee, June 11-13. Dennis describes political alignments in the U.S. for the coming elections and stresses mobilization of all "win-the-war" forces, particularly labor groups, to bring about a Democratic victory and promote collaboration between the Willkie forces and the Roosevelt Administration.

D112 . . . . The Moscow Conference, National Unity, and the Elections, "Communist," 22 (Dec. 1943), 1083-1102.
The abridged text of a report to a Midwest conference of Party leaders, November 10, approving the Moscow Conference's decisions as providing a basis for postwar allied

cooperation. Labor and other win-the-war forces should help the Roosevelt Administration to implement those decisions.

D113 DENNIS, Eugene. "The Elections and the Outlook for National Unity." New York: Workers Library, 1944. 46 pp.
The abridged text of a report to the national board of the Communist Political Association, November 17, 1944. Dennis hails Roosevelt's reelection over Dewey as a victory for the nation, and urges consolidation of the victorious coalition to win the war, build a durable peace, and achieve abundance and maximum employment. He identifies anticommunism with profascist reaction.

D114 .... The Outlook for a Durable Peace, "Communist," 23 (Feb. 1944), 109-21.
Marxist theory says only that capitalist society can give no guarantee against the outbreak of war. Hence it is possible for communists to back the Teheran Conference declaration of Allied collaboration in seeking lasting peace.

D115 .... For Victory in the War and the Elections, "Communist," 23 (July 1944), 598-607.
Abridged text of the report by the chairman of the resolutions committee of the national convention of the Communist Political Association, presenting the main political resolution calling for national unity behind Roosevelt. The realization of this resolution involves scuttling all third parties, protecting property rights, and allowing private enterprise to function.

D116 .... A Resolute Non-Partisan Policy to Strengthen National Unity, "Communist," 23 (Sept. 1944), 806-12.
The importance of achieving unity of "win-the-war" forces behind Roosevelt in the 1944 elections. Common action among divergent groups on points of common interest is urged in order to build strong nonpartisan backing for the fourth term.

D117 .... "America at the Crossroads: Postwar Problems and Communist Policy." Foreword by William Z. Foster. New York: New Century, 1945. 48 pp.
A report to the Party's national committee, November 16-18, 1945, shortly after the Party had been reconstituted. The report deals with American imperialism's drive for world domination, the domestic struggle for jobs and security, the need to organize a national antifascist and antimonopoly party, and the necessity to continue the struggle within the Party against revisionism and sectarian tendencies.

D118 .... Yalta and America's National Unity, "Political Affairs," 24 (April 1945), 302-10.
New conditions exist for strengthening U.S. national unity. Progressive Republicans are shaking off isolationist leadership. Continued cooperation with Russia requires nonpartisan support of the Dumbarton Oaks and Bretton Woods proposals. The trade unions must support this foreign policy, recognizing that long-term collaboration between capitalism and communism is possible. (Remarks at the meeting of the CPA national committee, March 10, 1945.)

D119 .... Postwar Labor-Capital Cooperation, "Political Affairs," 24 (May 1945), 415-22.
A highly favorable report on the "New Charter for Labor and Management" signed by Eric Johnston, Philip Murray, and William Green. Dennis urges labor's support because, unlike Gomper's old collaboration with reactionary capital, the charter unites progressive capitalists with the labor movement.

D120 .... America Needs the Communist Party, "Political Affairs," 24 (Oct. 1945), 867-75.
A speech by Dennis, September 18, 1945, on the twenty-sixth anniversary of the CPUSA, describing the role of the Communist Party in combating fascist influences in the U.S. Dennis denounces the House Committee on Un-American Activities and its proposed investigation of the change in the Party line. (Republished in pamphlet form with a speech by William Z. Foster on the same occasion entitled "The Menace of American Imperialism.")

D121 .... The London Conference, "Political Affairs," 24 (Nov. 1945), 963-73.
The London meeting of the Council of Foreign Ministers ended without agreement because the U.S. and Britain are sabotaging de-Nazification of Germany and excluding Russia from policy determination on Japan. Russia is an obstacle to U.S.-British imperialist plans. They charge that Russia dominates Eastern European countries, whereas Russia merely enjoys great prestige and respects national sovereignty.

D122 .... "Peace or War: The People against the Warmakers!" New York: New Century, 1946. 16 pp.
Speech delivered at a May Day rally of the Party in Cleveland, condemning Anglo-American foreign policy. Dennis attacks unilateral American action, the maintaining of strategic military posts that encircle the Soviet Union, and intervention in the internal affairs of China, the Philippines, Puerto Rico, and other countries. Effective opposition to American foreign policy requires a broad, anti-imperialist peace front—among AFL and CIO workers, veterans, farmers, Negroes and whites, communists and noncommunists.

D123 .... "The People against the Trusts: Build a Democratic Front to Defeat Reaction Now and Win a People's Victory in 1948." New York: New Century, 1946. 64 pp.
Political report to a plenary meeting of the national committee of the CPUSA. The general secretary of the Party analyses the outcome of the 1946 congressional elections, minimizing Republican gains and prophesying a new impetus to independent political action. He urges a democratic coalition for a progressive presidential ticket in 1948.

D124 .... "The Red-Baiters Menace America." New York: New Century, 1946. 11 pp.
Address to the Party's twenty-seventh anniversary meeting. The author attacks Red-baiting, seeing its chief target as not just the Party, but the CIO and the whole labor movement, American democracy, and world peace.

D125 .... "The Un-Americanism of Hearst's John Sentinel." Milwaukee: Communist Party of Wisconsin, n.d. [1946]. 16 pp.
Speech delivered in Milwaukee during the Allis-Chalmers strike, in answer to articles in the Milwaukee Hearst paper under the name of John Sentinel. Sentinel, Dennis charges, is out to break the strike, destroy Local 248 of the UAW, and defeat the pro-Roosevelt slate in November's elections. Dennis denies that the communists controlled the Allis-Chalmers local and were using the strike to advance Russian ends.

D126 .... "What America Faces." New York: New Century, 1946. 62 pp.
The text of the report by a member of the Party's National Secretariat to the plenary meeting of the national committee held in February 1946. Written in the early stages of the cold war, the report attacked the Truman Administration for its imperialist course in foreign affairs, and

called for the friendship of the U.S. and Britain with the USSR and an end to U.S. imperialist interference abroad. Dennis also urged education leading to a third party, and defended the expulsion of Browder for refusing to accept the Party line.

D127 DENNIS, Eugene. Defeat the Imperialist Drive toward Fascism and War, "Political Affairs," 25 (Sept. 1946), 778-809.
The text of the report for the national board, delivered on July 16 to the plenary meeting of the Party's national committee. It accuses American monopoly capital of an aggressive imperialist policy in international affairs and a reactionary domestic offensive against the American people. Promotion by the communists of a new people's party, led by labor, is advocated.

D128 .... "I Challenge the Un-Americans." New York: CPUSA, 1947. 16 pp.
A denunciation of the House Un-American Activities Committee, which refused to hear the author's testimony against the anticommunist bills. Dennis' reply to Chairman J. Parnell Thomas, challenging the legality of the Committee, is included.

D129 .... "Is Communism Un-American?" New York: New Century, 1947. 15 pp.
Contains the full text of the statements by the then general secretary of the Party on nine questions posed by New York "Times" reporter A. H. Raskin. Dennis asserts that the first and only loyalty of the Party is to our working class, people, and country, and denies that it receives instructions and financial support from Russia or that it seeks a violent overthrow of the American system. The Party maintains, he states, a maximum degree of inner-party democracy, until decisions are reached that are mandatory on all members.

D130 .... "Let the People Know: The Truth about the Communists Which the Un-American Committee Tried to Suppress." New York: New Century, 1947. 32 pp.
Statement by the general secretary of the Party which he was not allowed to present at the House Un-American Activities Committee's hearings on the Rankin and Sheppard bills. Opposing both bills as unconstitutional, the author quotes from the Communist Party constitution, as well as from Jefferson, Lincoln, and Roosevelt, to show the democratic and progressive nature of the Party.

D131 .... Concluding Remarks on the Plenum Discussion, "Political Affairs," 26 (Jan. 1947), 8-19.
Closing remarks at the plenum of the Party's national committee, December 3-5, 1946, stating the Party's policy of self-determination for the Negroes and its support of the UMW in its judicial struggle with the U.S. government. The speech criticizes the "Daily Worker" for attacking Wallace, and forecasts an economic recession for the U.S.

D132 .... The Progressives Can and Must Unite, "Political Affairs," 26 (March 1947), 195-203.
The abridged text of a speech to a mass meeting in Chicago, February 4, 1947, calling on all progressives to unite against the monopolists and defeat profascist reaction. The present disunity of the progressives is the cause of the recent successes of the reactionaries.

D133 .... American Democracy Must Not Commit Suicide, "Political Affairs," 26 (April 1947), 291-92.
A statement to the press by the Party's general secretary, March 11, 1947, in response to the proposal of Secretary of Labor Lewis B. Schwellenbach that the Communist

Party be outlawed. Defending the Party's record, Dennis attacks the proposal as profascist.

D134 .... The Truth about the Communists: A Statement to America, "New Masses," 63 (April 8, 1947), 10-18.
The full text of the statement which Eugene Dennis, CP general secretary, could not make on March 26 before the House Committee on Un-American Activities. Dennis denies that the CP is an agent of a foreign power, that it advocates use of force and violence, or that it is a conspiracy. He calls for checking the profascist conspiracy evident in pending measures.

D135 .... Challenge to the Legality of the Thomas-Rankin Committee, "Political Affairs," 26 (May 1947), 395-402.
The text of the letter in which Dennis refused to appear before the House Committee on Un-American Activities on the grounds that the committee was not a lawful one of Congress, its authority was not properly defined, it usurped police authority, its objectives lay outside congressional functions, and John E. Rankin of Mississippi was not lawfully elected. (Dennis' conviction for contempt was affirmed by the U.S. Supreme Court in 1950.)

D136 .... The Foreign Agent Lie, "Political Affairs," 26 (May 1947), 391-94.
A letter from the Party's general secretary to the U.S. Attorney-General, responding to one to him from the House Committee on Un-American Activities, requesting prosecution of communist officials for failure to comply with the McCormack and Voorhis Acts. Dennis asserts that the CP is an American political party; though its foreign policy has often coincided with that of the USSR, it accorded with the interests of the U.S.

D137 .... Concluding Remarks on the Plenum Discussion, "Political Affairs," 26 (Aug. 1947), 688-700.
Dennis' concluding remarks at the June 27-30 plenary meeting of the Party's national committee, emphasizing labor militancy, united labor action, and the need for a broad political coalition. A Democratic coalition candidate, backed by third-party forces, is the only hope to defeat the Republican candidate in 1948; if the third-party movement cannot influence the Democratic Party's choice, it will run an independent ticket.

D138 .... "Dangerous Thoughts: The Case of the Indicted Twelve. New York: New Century, 1948. 15 pp.
An address by the general secretary of the Party on September 23, 1948, denouncing the trial of the top communist leaders as an example of ripening American fascism, and calling for mass demonstrations against the trials.

D139 .... "Eugene Dennis Indicts the Wall Street Conspirators." New York: National Office, CPUSA, 1948. 15 pp.
The text of an address by the general secretary of the Party to a mass meeting in connection with the Party's fourteenth national convention, August 2, 1948. His speech answers the arrest on July 20 of the twelve members of the Party's national board, indicted for advocacy of violence and conspiracy to overthrow the U.S. government by force.

D140 .... "The Third Party and the 1948 Elections." New York: New Century, 1948. 61 pp.
The text of the general secretary's political report to the Party's national committee in February 1948. Citing the

increased dangers of fascism and war to the U.S. and the growing resistance of the people, Dennis hails Wallace's presidential candidacy and calls for a progressive political alignment that will lead to an antimonopoly and anti-imperialist government. Communists, while building their own Marxist party, will support the third-party movement.

D141 DENNIS, Eugene. The Role of the Communist Party in the Present Situation, "Political Affairs," 27 (March 1948), 207-23.
Part of the report on the political situation to a meeting of the Party's national committee, February 3-5, 1948. The report stresses communist support of the developing third-party movement, the need to strengthen the Communist Party as a vanguard party, and the struggle for Marxist-Leninist theory within the Party.

D142 .... The Fascist Danger and How to Combat It, "Political Affairs," 27 (Sept. 1948), 778-819.
The main political report to the Party's fourteenth national convention, August 3, 1948. The development of fascism in the U.S. is now a serious menace. Wall Street's drive toward war and fascism can be defeated if a new people's coalition is led by the working class and its most class-conscious sector. The new Progressive Party is crusading for peace, American-Soviet friendship, civil liberties, and Negro rights. (Reprinted in pamphlet form.)

D143 .... The Main Lessons of the 1948 Elections, "Political Affairs," 27 (Dec. 1948), 1047-54.
A communist view of the 1948 election results, arguing that the masses rejected the party of Big Business and showed that they wanted peace and progress, not reaction and war. The Progressive Party emerged as an influential force in U.S. political life with a bright political future. Reasons for the low Wallace vote are explored.

D144 .... "The Case for the Communist Party: Opening Statement to the Jury." Introd. by Elizabeth Gurley Flynn. New York: New Century, 1949. 32 pp.
Dennis' opening statement to the jury on behalf of himself and 11 other Party leaders in their trial for conspiracy under the Smith Act. Dennis points out that no overt acts are charged, that the defendants are accused only of political organization and advocacy of Marxism-Leninism, and that the history of the CP since 1919 shows that it does not advocate force and violence.

D145 .... "In Defense of Your Freedom." New York: New Century, 1949. 64 pp.
Summation to the jury by one of the defendants in the 1949 Smith Act trial of communist leaders, in which he seeks to refute charges that the Party's aims are based on force and violence. Some portions summarized in the court presentation are presented here in full. (This summation is included in the book by Dennis, "Ideas They Cannot Jail.")

D146 .... "Ideas They Cannot Jail." Introd. by William Z. Foster. New York: International Publishers, 1950. 192 pp.
Speeches, reports, and articles by the general secretary of the Party between January 1946 and May 1950. Included are his statements before Judge Pine during his trial for contempt of Congress, his statement that the House Committee on Un-American Activities refused to allow, and his summation to the jury in the Foley Square trial in October 1949. Other items are speeches, including one on the eve of his imprisonment; articles in the communist press, here and abroad; and his closing remarks at a meeting of the Party's national committee in March 1950.

D147 .... "Twenty-One Questions about War and Peace." New York: New Century, 1950. 48 pp.
Questions and answers originally published by "Challenge," Communist Labor Youth League publication. Topics include prevention of war, outlawing of atomic warfare, peace aspirations of the USSR, peaceful co-existence, Soviet pressure on Yugoslavia, the Marshall Plan, trade with eastern Europe and China, relationship of foreign to domestic policy, and whether the Party is subversive.

D148 .... Lenin, Stalin, and the Mid-Century, "Political Affairs," 29 (March 1950), 1-6.
A contrast of the "path of decline and decay" taken by world capitalism from 1900 to 1950 with the advances achieved in the same period by world socialism. Dennis is confident that the second half of the twentieth century will find American workers marching on the path of socialism.

D149 .... For Communist Clarity and Resoluteness to Forge Working-Class and People's Unity, "Political Affairs," 29 (May 1950), 41-58.
A report by the general secretary of the CPUSA to the plenum of its national committee, March 23-25, 1950, dealing with problems in forming a united front, the fight against the Mundt bill, Party objectives in the 1950 congressional elections, and the trial of Dennis and ten other communists in New York under the Smith Act.

D150 .... Let Us March Forward with Supreme Confidence, "Political Affairs," 29 (July 1950), 9-20.
Dennis' farewell address, on May 2, 1950, shortly before his imprisonment under the Smith Act. He praises Marxism-Leninism, summarizes the Party's struggle against Wall Street, expresses confidence in those who will take over Party leadership, and gives instructions on fighting for peace and building the Party.

D151 .... The Un-Americans, "Masses & Mainstream," 3 (July 1950), 46-51.
Part of the letter written by Dennis, general secretary of the Party, to J. Parnell Thomas, then chairman of the House Committee on Un-American Activities, explaining his refusal to appear before the Committee and challenging its constitutionality. (As a result Dennis was sentenced to a year's imprisonment for contempt.)

D152 .... "The MacArthur Ouster: A Letter to Members of the Communist Party." New York: CPUSA, 1951. 16 pp.
Though MacArthur may have precipitated his ouster by Truman to advance his own political ends, Dennis asserts that the major reason for dropping him was the U.S. military failure in Korea, along with sharpening differences faced by the Anglo-American imperialists. The ouster does not indicate any change in foreign policy. (Reprinted from "Political Affairs," May 1951.)

D153 .... Peace—the Supreme and Over-Riding Issue, "Political Affairs," 30 (April 1951), 1-9.
The text of Dennis' March 21 speech, following his release from prison, hailing the upsurge of peace sentiment in the midst of Wall Street's drive toward fascism and a third world war. He calls for an end to the Korean War, prevention of West German rearmament, and friendship with the USSR.

D154 .... The Fascist Danger, "Political Affairs," 31 (April 1952), 14-25.
The opening section of Dennis' report to the Party's fourteenth convention, held in 1948. Dennis asserts that American capitalism is turning to fascism because it

needs wars and huge arms expenditures to make up for lost markets in countries that have gone communist. Evidence of the movement toward fascism here are cited.

D155 DENNIS, Eugene. "The Communists Take a New Look." New York: New Century, 1956. 48 pp.
A report, on behalf of the Party's national board, to a meeting of the national committee held April 28 - May 1, 1956. Asserting that most of the Party's mistakes since 1945 had been left sectarian, Dennis called for a major political realignment, the organization of a mass party of socialism, and an end to dogmatism. The communists advocate a peaceful and democratic road to socialism in the U.S. (Part of the report appeared in "Political Affairs" in June 1956.)

D156 .... "Letters from Prison." New York: International Publishers, 1956. 157 pp.
Prison letters from a leading communist to his wife and son between 1951 and 1955, with commentaries on local and world issues. The letters, selected and edited by Mrs. Dennis, give the communist point of view on some of the major events of this period. (Dennis was imprisoned first for contempt of Congress, and then for violation of the Smith Act.)

D157 ..., and GATES, John. "What America Needs: A Communist View." New York: New Century, 1956. 24 pp.
Party and the editor of the "Daily Worker" since their imprisonment for violation of the Smith Act. Expressing faith in the necessity of the Party, Dennis asserted that cooperation of communists and noncommunists can thwart the men of corporate wealth who threaten the world with rule or ruin. Gates charged that the reactionaries do not want democracy in the South because it would threaten the GOP-Dixiecrat coalition in Congress.

D158 .... After Five Years, "Political Affairs," 35 (Feb. 1956), 1-11.
A speech delivered January 20, 1956, after Dennis' release from prison, hailing the Geneva peace conference, the AFL-CIO merger, and the progress of Negro liberation, and asserting that the Party is indestructible. While working to defeat the warmongers, open shoppers, and white supremacists in 1956, the Party will promote united and independent political action of workers and progressives.

D159 .... Questions and Answers on the XXth Congress, CPSU, "Political Affairs," 35 (April 1956), 21-26.
The general secretary of the Party answers questions concerning the Khrushchev revelations about Stalin, as well as about the new line that war is not inevitable and there are many roads to socialism. He admits that the CPUSA, in defending the Soviet Union against capitalist slanders, glossed over CPSU shortcomings. The chief lesson is the need for self-criticism and collective leadership.

D160 .... Towards the Party Convention, "Political Affairs," 35 (Oct. 1956), 46-55.
A speech at the Party's national election campaign conference, supporting the draft resolution proposed by the national committee. Dennis defends the draft resolution from criticism that it is a compromise that decides nothing, that it departs from Marxism-Leninism, and that it does not change Party form and structure enough.

D161 .... What Kind of a Change? "Political Affairs," 36 (Jan. 1957), 27-42.
Asserting that the chief internal problem confronting the Party in this period of crisis is left-sectarianism and

dogmatism, Dennis nevertheless disagrees with the views of John Gates (see "Time for a Change," in "Political Affairs," Nov. 1956). Dennis calls for a fighting Marxist-Leninist vanguard, a party to lead the struggle against monopoly and crusade militantly for Negro rights and labor organization.

D162 .... H-Bomb Testing and Our National Interest, "Political Affairs," 36 (Sept. 1957), 1-13.
A report by the secretary for national affairs to the July meeting of the Party's national committee, and accepted by it, emphasizing the development of the anti-H-bomb movement and the need to center mass activity on the banning of all nuclear tests. The peace camp is compelling the imperialist war bloc to accept the conditions of peaceful coexistence.

D163 .... The Struggle for Peace, "Political Affairs," 37 (Aug. 1958), 18-36.
A report to the Party's national committee, June 28, 1958, reviewing developments in France, Yugoslavia, and Hungary, and discussing preparations for top-level East-West negotiations. Emphasis is placed on the continuing advance of socialism, and suggestions are offered for advancing the American people's struggles for peace.

D164 .... "Toward the 1960 Elections." New York: New Century, 1959. 16 pp.
A report to the Party's national committee, December 6, 1958, evaluating the 1958 congressional elections, which showed a majority protest against the Administration's recession, farm, and brinkmanship policies. Our country needs a people's democratic coalition, under working-class leadership, to curb monopolies and defeat the atom-maniacs, racists, and open shoppers.

D165 .... Post-Election Perspectives, "Political Affairs," 39 [38] (Jan. 1959), 1-15.
An appraisal of the 1958 elections, asserting that the people won some important victories and that they are moving in the direction of a democratic-front type of coalition. They disapprove of the Administration's recession and farm programs at home and its brinkmanship abroad. The Eighty-sixth Congress includes the largest number of liberal and prolabor congressmen since the New Deal.

D166 DENNIS, Lawrence. The Real Communist Menace, "American Mercury," 44 (June 1938), 146-55.
An assertion by an American fascist that the Communist Party's idealism, revolutionary ideology, and revolutionary strategy constitute the real communist menace. Afraid only of fascism, the communists are instigating a holy war between liberalism and fascism in order to come into power themselves.

D167 DENNISON, Tom. "How Fare Youth?" New York: American Youth for Democracy, 1947. 31 pp.
Youth fought during World War II, but returns to civilian life to face a housing shortage, an impending depression, no adequate GI Bill of Rights, overcrowded high schools, and unemployment. American Youth for Democracy, successor to the Young Communist League, calls for an American Youth Act to provide youth with education, jobs, health, recreation, and equal treatment regardless of race, religion, or political conviction.

DEROUNIAN, Arthur. See CARLSON, John Roy.

D168 DERRY, George Hermann. "How the Reds Get That Way (Some Big Words to Discuss)." New Haven, Conn.: Knights of Columbus, Supreme Council, Division of Social Education, 1948. 20 pp. Bibliog.

A statement and refutation of the basic tenets of communism, with a guide for study. The causes of communism and social unrest are found in the abuses of unrestricted capitalism, and the remedy suggested is the organization of industry councils of owners, workers, and the public, to plan production for the general welfare.

D169   DE SANTILLANA, Giorgio. Galileo and J. Robert Oppenheimer, "Reporter," 17 (Dec. 26, 1957), 10-18.
A comparison of the Galileo trial before the tribunal of the Inquisition in Rome with the hearing of J. Robert Oppenheimer before the Atomic Energy Commission's Personnel Security Board. Parallels in specific instances are drawn, and the highlights of Oppenheimer's case are repeated.

D170   DE TOLEDANO, Nora. The Harvey Matusow Story, "American Mercury," 80 (June 1955), 141-60.
The case of Harvey Matusow, progovernment witness in two criminal cases against communists, and witness before numerous congressional committees, who repudiated his former testimony and asserted that Roy Cohn, McCarthy Committee counsel, induced him to make false statements. A careful check of documents and the story in his book shows that his past testimony was true.

D171   DE TOLEDANO, Ralph. Stalin's Hand in the Panama Canal, "Plain Talk," 1 (Nov. 1946), 31-39.
An analysis of the procommunist background of the leaders of the United Public Workers, which is seeking to organize workers in this key defense area. With this organization has come an upsurge of communist activity in the Canal Zone. The author calls for congressional investigation and action against subversion.

D172   ..., and LASKY, Victor. "Seeds of Treason: The True Story of the Hiss-Chambers Tragedy." New York: Funk & Wagnalls, 1950. 270 pp.
An account of the Chambers-Hiss controversy, based on fresh material obtained from Chambers as well as the trial record. The book deals with Chambers' background, the espionage ring in Washington of which he was a part, Hiss' background and motivations, the relations between the two, the hearings, and the two Hiss trials. The authors conclude that the proof that Hiss engaged in espionage was incontrovertible. Their book is also an indictment of the New Deal. (The book was summarized in "Reader's Digest" in May 1950.)

D173   .... Grave-diggers of America: I. The Book Reviewers Sell Out China; II. How Stalin's Disciples Review Books, "American Mercury," 73 (July 1951), 72-78; (Aug.), 14-20.
In Part I the author shows that procommunist book reviewers perpetuated their ideas about China by "assassinating" anticommunist books. Part II is a more general discussion of the influence of literary fellow-travelers. The author asserts that the book review columns of the "Saturday Review of Literature," the "New York Herald Tribune" and the "New York Times" show hostility to literary conservatism.

D174   .... Operation Storm! "Collier's," 128 (Oct. 6, 1951), 16-17.
Biographical sketches of Gus Hall, Robert Thompson, Gilbert Green, and Henry Winston, four convicted defendants in the communist conspiracy case who jumped bail. The author, a staff member of "Newsweek," asserts that these four were the general staff of "Operation Storm," a campaign of treason and sabotage culminating in revolution and Soviet invasion.

D175   .... "Spies, Dupes, and Diplomats." New York: Duell, Sloan and Pearce, 1952. 244 pp. App. Ind.
Drawing upon confessions, court records, communist documents, and Internal Security Committee hearings, the author shows how our Far Eastern policy was distorted by Soviet agents and fellow-travelers. He points to the influence of Owen Lattimore, Lauchlin Currie, Harry Dexter White, the Institute of Pacific Relations, "Amerasia," and others on American policy. Though not all were spies, the indictment must run against dupes and diplomats as well.

D176   .... The Alger Hiss Story, "American Mercury," 76 (June 1953), 13-20.
A review of the events in Hiss' life which led to his conviction, written shortly before his release from his five-year jail term for perjury. The author concludes that part of a generation sinned, and still sins, with Hiss.

D177   .... The Road to Anti-Communism, "American Mercury," 78 (April 1954), 29-36.
An account of how the author reached his position of conservative and militant anticommunism. Somewhat sympathetic during his student days, he was shaken by the Moscow trials and accounts of GPU mass executions of Loyalist soldiers during the Spanish Civil War. The Hitler-Stalin pact, the murder of Carlo Tresca, and finally the Hiss case completed the transformation.

D178   .... Whose Civil Liberties? "American Legion Magazine," 56 (May 1954), 20-21 ff.
A critical interpretation of the record of the American Civil Liberties Union, asserting that, while not a communist front, it serves communist purposes through its propaganda and has a double standard in evaluating civil liberties issues, one for the left and another for the right. Though impartial in litigation, it has issued crudely partisan press releases and reports.

D179   .... The Noel Field Story, "American Mercury," 80 (April 1955), 5-8.
A review of the strange case of Noel Field, the procommunist who worked in government posts primarily in Europe, and whose family and friends have disappeared behind the Iron Curtain. The author suggests that their recent appearance at a U.S. consulate and subsequent disappearance was a hoax and that the Fields may have been murdered.

D180   .... It's Still the Soviet Party, "National Review," 3 (Jan. 5, 1957), 11-12.
The CPUSA is far from dead; when the Soviet Politburo has resolved its differences, the CPUSA will fall back into line, its present disunity evaporated. Though membership has fallen, the Party's infiltration tactics are as successful as ever.

D181   ..., and DE TOLEDANO, Nora. Love that Book! "American Legion Magazine," 63 (Aug. 1957), 14-15 ff.
An attack on individuals like Morris Ernst and Max Lerner, and on papers like the New York "Times" and the Washington "Post," for their attention to Alger Hiss' book, "In the Court of Public Opinion."

D182   .... This We Face: Subversion by the Communist Underground Remains the Strongest Weapon against U.S.A., "American Mercury," 88 (April 1959), 38-46.
Communism's strongest weapon against the U.S. is subversion. Communists, seeking to break our will to resist, have succeeded to an impressive degree. The communist method of subversion is outlined and its successes are listed.

D183 DEUTSCHER, Isaac. What Can Ex-Communists Do? "Reporter," 2 (April 25, 1950), 4-9.
An analysis of the several contributions to "The God that Failed," with Deutscher's reasons for advising excommunists to observe rather than take part in political affairs. Their confusion of intellect and emotion makes them poorly suited for political activity. They may try to suppress a sense of guilt and uncertainty, or may be concerned only with self-justification. (For a contrary view, see Max Ascoli, "Our Political D.P.'s," in the same issue.)

D184 DEVERALL, Richard L-G. Commonwealth College, "Commonweal," 30 (April 28, 1939), 9-11.
A description of the routine, work, and study at a labor college in the Ozarks, said to be run by communists. Catholic workers should emulate the practices of this school as a realistic way of fighting communism.

D185 DeVOTO, Bernard. The Ex-Communists, "Atlantic Monthly," 187 (Feb. 1951), 61-65.
While views of excommunists are of value, the presumption should be in favor of minds that were never deceived. The conversion of intellectuals to communism was a phenomenon of the depression 1930's. Those who resisted communism had faith in political reform, as evidenced in the New Deal, and saw that the enemy was absolutism, not fascism. The excommunist has discovered what the noncommunist knew all along.

D186 DEWEY, John. Why I Am Not a Communist, "Modern Monthly," 8 (April 1934), 135-37.
Dewey rejects communism because it is not founded on American background and traditions, because its philosophy of history is unacceptable, because class war may not result in social advance, because communism's emotional tone is repugnant to him, and because a violent revolution in a modernized society would result in chaos. (Part of a symposium on communism, reprinted as "The Meaning of Marx: A Symposium.")

D187 .... Class Struggle and the Democratic Way, "Social Frontier," 2 (May 1936), 241-42.
For educators to put faith in the class struggle and violent revolution as the only method of social reconstruction is to negate faith in the role of education. Recognition of social injustice does not of itself determine educational policies and methods. Educators should be alert to the need of a social rather than a class reorganization of American society.

D188 ..., and others. "Not Guilty: Report of the Commission of Inquiry into the Charges Made against Leon Trotsky in the Moscow Trials." New York: Harper, 1938. 422 pp. App. Ind.
A study of the Moscow trials of August 1936 and January 1937 at which Leon Trotsky and his son, Leon Sedov, were charged with crimes against the Soviet government and its leaders. The Commission, under the chairmanship of John Dewey, suspecting political persecution in judicial form, investigated the trials and concluded that they were frameups.

D189 DICKINSON, Edwin D. Political Subversives: An Appraisal of Recent Experience and Forecast of Things to Come, "Record of the Association of the Bar of the City of New York," 2 (Dec. 1947), 350-61.
A description of communist tactics and front operations, along with activities of other subversives, by a University of California law school dean, who opposes employment of Party members or fellow-travelers in the public service or their induction into the armed services. However, he would abolish "un-American" legislative committees and he opposes plans to outlaw the Party.

D190 DIES, Martin. The Real Issue Is Plain, "Vital Speeches of the Day," 4 (Sept. 15, 1938), 731-34.
Reprint of a radio speech by the Texas congressman who headed the Committee on Un-American Activities and Propaganda, listing communist front organizations and exposing communist influence in labor and other groups. Some of those who assert that the evidence given the Committee is false have attacked the investigators instead of answering the charges.

D191 .... "The Trojan Horse in America." New York: Dodd, Mead, 1940. 366 pp. Ind.
A description of the communist conspiracy and communist tactics by the first chairman of the House Special Committee on Un-American Activities, who views the united front tactic as the "Trojan Horse" technique. Chapters on particular aspects of communist activity, including their work with labor unions, the unemployed, Negroes, and youth, illustrate their techniques of infiltration and propaganda, using all the resources of the Party and imposing the will of the Party upon front groups and captured organizations.

D192 .... More Snakes Than I Can Kill: Behind the Scenes in the Probe of Un-Americanism, "Liberty," 17 (Jan. 13, 1940), 6-10; (Jan. 20), 16-19; (Jan. 27), 17-22; (Feb. 3), 37-42; (Feb. 10), 42-46.
An account by an early congressional investigator of communist activities in the U.S., of efforts by the Roosevelt Administration to sabotage the work of his committee. He was refused assistance by the heads of executive departments, and told that it would be a mistake to investigate the CIO simply because some communists were in it. Defending the CIO to Dies, Roosevelt had suggested that fascism should be investigated instead. Government agents investigated Dies' financial affairs and his record in law practice in an effort to discredit him.

D193 .... The Reds in Hollywood, "Liberty," 17 (Feb. 17, 1940), 47-50.
An assertion by the chairman of the House Committee on Un-American Activities that many prominent film actors and writers and a few producers were Party members or followed the Party line, and that Hollywood was becoming the powerhouse of communist propaganda. The producers, many of them Jewish, were more fearful of fascism.

D194 .... Is Communism Invading the Movies? "Liberty," 17 (Feb. 24, 1940), 57-60.
An account of the growth of communist membership and influence in the film industry in Hollywood, where Party policy is to prevent production of anticommunist pictures while stressing the weak points in the American system. Substantial sums have been raised in Hollywood for the Party and its front organizations.

D195 .... "Martin Dies' Story." New York: Bookmailer, 1963. 283 pp. Notes. App. Exhibits. Ind.
An account of the work of the Dies Committee, the Special Committee on Un-American Activities of the House of Representatives, which Dies headed for seven years, beginning in 1938. The Committee's investigations of communist activities, in the Party, in Party fronts, and in trade union, student, and other groups is described. The author believes that we are losing the cold war, and that the Executive Department, in cooperation with left-wing commentators and columnists, seeks to smear and discredit investigations of communists.

D196 DIGBY, Robert. For Farmer-Labor Unity in the Elections and in the Food-for-Victory Campaign, "Communist," 21 (Aug. 1942), 620-32.
Farmer-labor unity is essential to national unity, which is essential to victory. Farmer-labor collaboration will win the farm vote from the defeatist farm bloc in Congress. Increased farm production is needed, as is joint farmer-labor action to break bottlenecks and bring agriculture into the war program.

D197 .... Three Wartime Farm Conventions, "Political Affairs," 24 (Feb. 1945), 182-92.
A review of recent conventions of the three national farm organizations: the Farmers Union, the National Grange, and the Farm Bureau. Farmers are abandoning their former isolationism for international cooperation. This year's farm conventions suggest that large sections of the farmers can be won to the national unity camp.

D198 ..., and HARRIS, Lem. Danger Signs in Postwar Farm Perspectives, "Political Affairs," 25 (Feb. 1946), 156-73.
A review of postwar developments in agriculture. The Administration has failed to find adequate outlets at home or abroad for farm products. Labor is urged to stand by the farmers in resisting the scarcity plans of the monopolists. A program for agriculture is outlined.

D199 .... The Second Chronic Crisis in Agriculture, "Political Affairs," 26 (Jan. 1947), 89-96; (Feb.), 182-92.
A discussion of the causes of the disparity between farm markets and farm output. Included in the discussion are farm mechanization, marketing problems, proletarianization in agriculture, the effect of the war, monopoly's program for agriculture, and imperialism and restrictionism. United political action of workers and farmers is advocated.

D200 DILLING, Elizabeth. "The Red Network: A Who's Who and Handbook of Radicalism for Patriots." Kenilworth, Ill.: The author, 1934. 352 pp.
A listing of organizations and persons by an author of the extreme right, who lumps socialism, anarchism, pacifism, and the New Deal with communism as forces that are undermining America. She lists 460 organizations and 1,300 individuals under the communist label, applying this term indiscriminately to all types of social reform as well as to radical groups.

D201 .... "The Roosevelt Red Record and Its Background." Kenilworth and Chicago, Ill.: The author, 1936. 439 pp. Ind.
An attack on Roosevelt as one engaged in a plan to change the U.S. form of government to a red dictatorship. Roosevelt's program is compared with that set forth in the "Communist Manifesto," and attention is directed to his radical support, his radical appointees, and radical influences within the CIO and the Federal Council of Churches. Mrs. Roosevelt is charged with having pet red organizations.

.... See also JOHNSON, Frank Woodruff.

D202 DIMITROFF, Georgi. "Working Class Unity—Bulwark against Fascism." New York: Workers Library, 1935. 71 pp.
Dimitroff's report to the Seventh World Congress of the Communist International, held in Moscow, July 25 to August 20, 1935. Dimitroff's call for a united front against fascism signaled a change in the communist line, which bound the CPUSA as all other affiliates of the Communist International.

D203 .... The Threat of Fascism in the United States, "Communist," 14 (Oct. 1935), 903-10.
Excerpts from Dimitroff's remarks at the Seventh Congress of the Communist International in which he attributes the rise of fascism in the U.S., not to Roosevelt (the former communist line), but to the most reactionary circles of American finance capital which oppose him.

D204 .... "The United Struggle for Peace." New York: Workers Library, 1936. 22 pp.
A statement of the united-front policy by the general secretary of the Communist International, who finds fascism the instigator of the impending war. He calls for a united front of peace, including the Soviet Union, the international working class and peasantry, the oppressed nations, and the peoples whose independence is threatened by the warmongers.

D205 .... Communists and the United Front, "Communist," 16 (June 1937), 508-16.
A restatement of united front objectives set forth at the Seventh World Congress of the Communist International. To combat fascism, the main enemy of the working class, the workers must form a people's front with other classes. Russia, the only socialist state, is the inner bastion of the working class. The main job of communists, even while promoting democratic goals in the people's front, is to work for a communist revolution.

D206 .... "The United Front: The Struggle against Fascism and War." New York: International Publishers, 1938. 287 pp. Ind.
Reports, speeches, and articles by the general secretary of the Communist International, beginning with his report to the Seventh World Congress of the Communist International held in Moscow, August 1935. This collection shows the development of the united-front policy from 1935 to the end of 1937. While Dimitroff is primarily concerned with the rise of fascism in Germany, Italy, and Spain, there are scattered references to the U.S. (An abridged version of Dimitroff's speeches at the Congress was published by the Workers Library as "The United Front against Fascism and War.")

D207 DINAMOV, Sergei. Sinclair Lewis' Communists, "International Literature," 4 (April 1937), 96-103.
The author chides Lewis' portrayal of communists in "It Can't Happen Here" as narrow dogmatists, ineffectual people with little understanding of political realities. While showing the menace of fascism to America, Lewis does not understand that the communists, through the united people's front, have become the bulwark of democracy.

D208 DISKIN, Lou. The Courageous Action of the New York High School Students, "Political Affairs," 29 (July 1950), 71-78.
Enthusiastic endorsement of a strike of New York City high school students, April 25-28, 1950, in support of reinstatement of extracurricular activities and higher salaries for teachers. The Party is rebuked for its lack of activity during the strike, which provided opportunity for blows against the forces of war and fascism.

D209 DLUGIN, Sam. "Blood on the Sugar (The Terror in Cuba)." New York: New York District, International Labor Defense, n.d. [1935]. 14 pp.
An account of terrorism by the Mendieta-Batista government in Cuba against students, strike leaders, and workers, and of low wages and starvation. American imperialists, who control the sugar industry, are responsible for this savage warfare against the Cuban people.

D210 DODD, Bella V. "School of Darkness." New York: P. J. Kenedy & Sons, 1954. 264 pp. Ind.

An account of her life by a leader of the New York City teachers who was drawn to the communist movement by its antifascist activity and its support for the Teachers Union. For eight years the legislative representative of Teachers Union Local 5, she accepted Party discipline long before she joined openly. Later the legislative representative of the New York district of the Party, a member of both the national and state committees of the Communist Political Association, and then of the national committee of the reconstituted Party, she was alienated by the dictatorial control, duplicity, and cynicism that she found there. Expelled in 1949 after she had lost all sympathy for communism, she finally rejoined the Catholic Church of her youth.

D211 DOERFLER, Ernest. Socialism and the Negro Problem, "American Socialist Quarterly," 2 (Summer 1933), 23-28.

A discussion of the Negro problem by a socialist, who ridicules the communist proposal of self-determination of the Black Belt. Exposing the fallacies behind the proposal, in which he sees the hand of the Comintern, he contrasts it with the sanity and realism of the socialist solution.

D212 DOHERTY, John. Red Spain Tactics on Fourteenth Street, "America," 60 (Jan. 7, 1939), 318-19.

A description of anti-Catholic demonstrations staged by Spanish Loyalist communists in New York City during the fall of 1938, culminating in the defacement of a Catholic church. The demonstrations are denounced as the first glimpse here behind the cause of Spanish "democracy."

D213 DOLSON, Hildegarde. Proletariat with Duncan Phyfe Legs, "New Yorker," 27 (Oct. 13, 1951), 126-32.

A humorous account of the author's experience with a proselytizing communist while both were writing advertising for home furnishings for a New Jersey department store.

D214 DON, Sam. Fear of Communism and War Preparations in the Election Campaign, "Communist," 9 (Oct. 1930), 900-13.

The deepening economic crisis and the success of the Soviet five-year plan make the American ruling class more vicious and more active in preparations for war against the Soviet Union. Bourgeoisie strategy is to prepare for a social-fascist labor party. Our Party must link up immediate issues with the campaign against war and with the defense of the USSR.

D215 . . . . The Emergence of an American Revolutionary Proletariat: Toward the Study of the Application of Marxism-Leninism to the American Class Struggle, "Communist," 12 (March 1933), 267-75.

In America, free land meant there was no feudal period and hence little class consciousness. With rapid industrialization the stage was set for a revolutionary worker movement that has not yet become strong because it was misdirected by socialist and IWW leaders. (The remainder of the article failed to appear.)

D216 . . . . The Study of Marxism-Leninism and the Role of the Party in Promoting National Unity, "Communist," 21 (Dec. 1942), 1021-38.

There is unity of theory and action in Marxism-Leninism. More than mere analysis, it is a guide to action that has enabled communists to formulate correct policies on fighting fascism, industrializing Russia and mobilizing its people, distinguishing when wars are imperialist or

national, and uniting the workers. (Also published in pamphlet form.)

D217 . . . . Our Nation's Democratic Historical Path, "Communist," 22 (Sept. 1943), 824-35.

A contrast of the development of capitalism in Germany and in the U.S., emphasizing the significance of American revolutionary ideology. Founded in the Revolution, this ideology has been followed by progressives from 1776 to the present.

D218 . . . . Leninism and Foreign Policy, "Communist," 23 (Jan. 1944), 13-24.

A presentation of Lenin's views on imperialism, war, and the role of the working class in shaping foreign policy. We should make the most of his teachings to achieve speedy victory and an enduring peace.

D219 DONAHUE, George R. "The World Federation of Trade Unions: Facts about a Communist Front." Introd. by James B. Carey. Washington, D.C.: International Union of Electrical, Radio & Machine Workers, AFL-CIO, n.d. [1958?]. 81 pp. App.

An account of the formation, structure, and activities of the World Federation of Trade Unions, formed in 1945 by the labor movements of a number of countries, including the CIO. Communists, in control, used the organization to criticize the U.S. and other western democracies, oppose the Marshall Plan, and attack the CIO and other democratic labor groups as agents of American imperialism. The CIO, with the British, Dutch, and other non-communist unions, left the WFTU in 1949.

D220 DONDERO, George A. Communism in Our Schools, "National Republic," 34 (Aug. 1946), 1-2.

A member of Congress from Michigan asserts that this country is being systematically communized through its educational institutions. A congressional investigation of subversion in our school systems is essential. Investigations by state legislatures have proved that the menace is real but have been ineffective in checking it.

D221 DONNER, Frank J. Smith Act, Baltimore Version, "Nation," 175 (Nov. 8, 1952), 426-28.

The editor of the "Civil Liberties Reporter" questions the decision of the U.S. Court of Appeals in the Baltimore case affirming the convictions of six persons on a charge of conspiracy to violate the Smith Act. This decision extends the Smith Act to punish membership in an organization and circulation of literature. This is clearly unconstitutional.

D222 . . . . "The Un-Americans." New York: Ballantine, 1961. 312 pp.

A critical account of the House Un-American Activities Committee, emphasizing its abuse of power. The author tells how HUAC began, who supports it in Congress, why it needs headlines for existence, and how it works with the FBI and private patriotic groups. Though it has spent the most money and called the most witnesses, it is responsible for the least legislation of any congressional committee. HUAC, forever yelping that the Reds are at our throats, depends for its existence on a falsehood—that the U.S. is threatened by subversion with which the regular agencies of government cannot deal.

D223 DONOVAN, William J., and JONES, Mary Gardiner. Program for a Democratic Counter Attack to Communist Penetration of Government Service. "Yale Law Journal," 58 (July 1949), 1211-41.

Communism is viewed as a menace to national security which justifies such efforts as the President's loyalty program. The authors examine the program and the

Loyalty Review Board, answer criticism of the program, and recommend some changes in recruitment. (The senior author was wartime head of the Office of Strategic Services.)

D224 DOOB, Leonard W. "Propaganda: Its Psychology and Technique." New York: Holt, 1935. 424 pp. App. Ind.
An examination of the psychology of people and of the nature, sweep, and vehicles of propaganda. Chapter 15 (pp. 236-68) is devoted to the Communist Party, with particular attention to communist tactics and the Scottsboro case. The Party concentrates upon mass appeals; it operates, however, in an environment hostile to communism.

D225 DORAN, Dave. "The Highway of Hunger: Story of America's Homeless Youth." New York: Youth Publishers, 1933. 14 pp.
A discussion of the plight of unemployed, homeless youth, denied adequate relief and wanted only for cannon-fodder. The Young Communist League leads the fight for food, shelter, and relief, not military camps. The Unemployed Councils are organizing the homeless youth.

D226 .... Youth in Industry, "Communist," 16 (May 1937), 471-80.
The Young Communist League must not be a small sect of convinced communists, but a mass youth organization attracting the youth, especially young workers, with a sports and social program, and instruction in job skills and trade union work. After recruiting members the YCL will try to convert them to communism.

D227 DORCHESTER, Daniel, Jr. "Bolshevism and Social Revolt." New York: Abingdon Press, 1919. 124 pp. Ind.
An attack on Bolshevism in Russia as a universal menace, with an estimate of its strength in this country, centered in New York City. Not limited to the proletarian and criminal classes, it is attracting some people of property, along with left-wing socialists and union members. Bolshevism is viewed as an epidemic due to diseased social conditions; the remedy is God's righteousness in the minds and hearts of mankind.

D228 DORSEY, John. Progressive International Committee of the United Mine Workers of America, "Labor Herald," 2 (March 1923), 10-11.
A report of the February 10 meeting at which UMW militants organized and adopted a program calling for socialization of the coal mines, opposition to dual unionism, a labor party, amalgamation, and similar measures. The meeting attacked the mismanagement and treason of the UMW officials.

D229 DOSCH-FLEUROT, Arno. "How Much Bolshevism Is There in America?" New York: Press Publishing Co. (New York "World"), 1921. 21 pp.
A series of articles by a European staff correspondent of the "World," who had lived under the Bolsheviks in Russia and who toured the U.S. studying social unrest. Contrasting the industrial situation here with the war-impoverished countries of Europe, he portrays the industrial unrest he found, in which Bolshevism plays a very small part. (The articles appeared in the "World," Jan. 16-20, 1921; bound with them is a series by Hector Boon, a businessman recently returned from the USSR, entitled "Russia from the Inside.")

D230 DOS PASSOS, John. Back to Red Hysteria! "New Republic," 63 (July 2, 1930), 168-69.
A discussion of the recent arrests of communists or alleged communists in Newark, Chester, Atlanta, and the Imperial Valley, cases being fought by the International Labor Defense with help from the American Civil Liberties Union. An important issue is the attitude of middle-class liberals.

D231 ..., and EVANS, Robert. A Discussion: Intellectuals in America, "New Masses," 6 (Aug. 1930), 8-9.
Dos Passos pleads with intellectuals to protest against the bestiality of class war as evident in murders, lynchings, etc. Evans replies that appeals to the white collar class are a waste of time. Only the workers, the class with the least stake in the game, can be called upon to preserve civilization.

D232 .... The Communist Party and the War Spirit, "Common Sense," 6 (Dec. 1937), 11-14.
A leading novelist, once close to the communists, criticizes their advocacy of war between fascism on one side and communism and the capitalist democracies on the other. Our involvement in war may make us a totalitarian state. Fascism, a disease of sick capitalism, must be fought at home.

D233 .... "Adventures of a Young Man." New York: Harcourt, Brace, 1939. 322 pp.
A leading novelist, at one time under Party influence, writes a novel dealing with communist infiltration of the American labor movement in the 1930's and later of the Loyalist forces in Spain. The leading figure, who started as a communist organizer in this country, meets his death as a Trotskyist in the Spanish Civil War.

D234 .... "Most Likely to Succeed." New York: Prentice-Hall, 1954. 310 pp.
An anticommunist novel dealing with the activities of a left-wing drama group and the subsequent careers of several members in Hollywood as communists or fellow-travelers.

D235 DOTY, Margaret. Our Misunderstood Communists, "Forum," 90 (Oct. 1933), 242-46.
An account of the objectives and techniques of the communist movement in the U.S., with brief sketches of the most important deviationist sects. The communists expect to seize power during a general strike caused by worsening conditions; the communists, as a disciplined group, will organize the strikers under their leadership, and be in power within 48 hours.

D236 DOUGLAS, Jack. "Veterans on the March." Foreword by John Dos Passos. New York: Workers Library for Veterans Publication Society, 1934. 376 pp. Ind.
An account of the veterans' bonus march on Washington in 1932, told from the point of view of the Party-led Workers Ex-Servicemen's League. The heads of organizations such as the American Legion and the VFW are ridiculed as lackeys of the Administration, and Roosevelt is attacked for seeking, through forestry camps, to develop the veterans into fascist storm troops.

D237 DOUGLAS, Paul H. The Threat of the McCarran Law, "New Leader," 33 (Sept. 30, 1950), 16-18; (Oct. 7), 12-14.
In articles adapted from a Senate speech, Senator Douglas argues that the real danger from American communists lies in spying and sabotage. The McCarran bill, which fails to deal with these activities, would facilitate smearing noncommunist and anticommunist organizations.

D238 DOUGLAS, William O. Dialectical Materialism, A

Challenge to our Political Competence, "Vital Speeches of the Day," 15 (April 1, 1949), 359-63.
An assertion that communism and democracy are in irreconcilable disagreement. Douglas advocates an understanding of communist purposes and methods, an end to the identification of communism with liberal reform, increasing our political consciousness, and developing effective democratic government.

D239 DOUGLAS, William O. Communists Here and Abroad, "U.S. News & World Report," 35 (Dec. 4, 1953), 110-12.
The text of an address by a justice of the U.S. Supreme Court, condemning the current witch-hunt that threatens everyone from the communist to the one who protests against the witch-hunt. The decline in our respect for the Bill of Rights has serious effects, both at home and abroad.

D240 DOUGLASS, Paul F. "Six upon the World: Toward an American Culture for An Industrial Age." Boston: Little, Brown, 1954. 443 pp. Bibliog.
Biographies of six men, each of whom was influential in some one institutional pattern. Chapter 2 (pp. 57-123) is devoted to William Z. Foster, whose field is given as revolutionary socialism. A favorable view is presented of Foster's career, with attention both to his experiences in the labor and radical movements before he became a communist and to his factional fights with Browder after he joined the Party. Quotations from Foster illustrate the Party line in various periods.

D241 DOWNING, Francis. Loyalty Affidavits, "Commonweal," 50 (Aug. 26, 1949), 483-85.
Philip Murray of the CIO finally agreed to sign the Taft-Hartley noncommunist affidavit because his refusal to sign gave communists a claim to respectability, and because of the need for the Steelworkers to get on the ballot in organizing drives. Communist-dominated unions, often resorting to subterfuges, have also been compelled to sign.

D242 . . . . Stockholm and Detroit, "Commonweal," 52 (Aug. 18, 1950), 458-60.
Support for the policy of Ford Local 600 of the UAW in Detroit, requiring officers to pledge that they are not members of the Communist Party, do not support Soviet policies, and will not distribute petitions favoring such policies (the Stockholm "peace" petition). A voluntary organization has the right to bar from its administration those who oppose its policies.

D243 . . . . Bankrupt's Oath, "Commonweal," 52 (Sept. 15, 1950), 555-57.
An unflattering portrait of Lee Pressman, whose reasons for leaving the Party, as revealed in his August 10, 1950, "confession," are said to be as hollow and insincere as his motives for joining. No penitence is evident, little frankness or truth, and no pity or shame.

D244 . . . . Communist Arrests, "Commonweal," 54 (July 13, 1951), 332-33.
An analysis of the Supreme Court's affirmation of the constitutionality of the Smith Act in the Dennis case. While questioning the wisdom of the Smith Act, the author believes that Justice Holmes would never have applied the "clear and present danger" test in this case.

D245 . . . . Substitute for Debate, "Commonweal," 54 (July 27, 1951), 378-79.
Condemnation of the Grand Central Airport Co. of Tucson, Arizona, for distributing literature to its employees during a UAW-CIO organizing drive charging the UAW and the CIO with communism. Along with such literature by a fascist writer and others, it distributed unidentified reprints from communist sources attacking Reuther and the UAW. The NLRB should set the election aside.

D246 DOYLE, C. A., and others. "Five Men on a Hunger Strike." New York: Civil Rights Congress and American Committee for Protection of Foreign Born, 1948. 16 pp.
A description of the arrests of Charles Doyle, Gerhart Eisler, Irving Potash, Ferdinand C. Smith, and John Williamson in deportation proceedings and their detention without bail on Ellis Island, telling how they won their freedom through a five-day hunger strike and the protests of hundreds of thousands of Americans.

D247 DRAKE, Lawrence. Our Communists' New Line, "Nation's Business," 32 (July 1944), 35-38.
Comment on the transformation of the CPUSA into the Communist Political Association, which repudiates class conflict and endorses free enterprise. The new line is a maneuver, double-talk to disarm the business man while the Reds go underground. The communists want to undermine capitalism by liquidating small business.

D248 DRAPER, Harold E. (ed.). "Out of Their Own Mouths: A Documentary Study of the New Line of the Comintern on War." New York: Young People's Socialist League, Greater New York Federation, n.d. [1936?]. 39 pp.
An assertion that the Communist Party now defends certain types of imperialist wars, in contrast to the traditional socialist opposition to all imperialist wars. The "new factor" justifying the change is the presence of the Soviet Union. The Comintern itself opposed all imperialist wars until a month before the signing of the Franco-Soviet pact, which brought about the shift in the line.

D249 DRAPER, Theodore. America's Youth Rejects Fascism, "New Masses," 12 (Aug. 28, 1934), 11-13.
An account of the First American Youth Congress held in New York in August 1934. Viola Ilma, its organizer, is described as an admirer of the Hitler Youth program, the New Deal, and President Roosevelt. Liberal, socialist, and communist youth organizations created a united-front caucus, which won a majority of delegates and took over the Congress from the Ilma group.

D250 . . . . City College's Rebel Generation, "New Masses," 13 (Nov. 27, 1934), 13-15.
The development of the National Student League at CCNY is traced. Antiwar feelings, an impoverished student body, and the leadership of the Social Problems Club made NSL possible. Events leading to expulsions, first on an individual and later on a mass basis, are described.

D251 . . . . "The Roots of American Communism." New York: Viking, 1957. 498 pp. Notes. Ind.
An account of the early years of American communism, which emerged from two major sources, native American radicalism and the imported radicalism of immigrant groups. Early factional struggles within the communist movement are reviewed, with emphasis on the relationship of American communism to the Communist International. The early Communist Parties turned to the Comintern as the final arbiter of their organizational and ideological controversies, becoming transformed into the American appendage of a Russian revolutionary power. The classic twists in the CP line, from sectarian orthodoxy to "opportunistic" efforts at mass influence, have always begun and ended on Russian initiative. (Part of the series on "Communism and American Life" edited by Clinton Rossiter.)

D252 . . . . "American Communism and Soviet Russia: The Formative Period." New York: Viking, 1960. 558 pp. Notes. Ind.

The story of the American communist movement from its beginning until the expulsion of Lovestone and his followers in 1929. The earliest years of the movement, explored in Draper's earlier "The Roots of American Communism," are summarized, following which the author deals with the political and trade union ventures of the Party, the effort at bolshevization, Party life, the death of Ruthenberg and the rise of Lovestone, communist policy on the Negro question, the 1928 expulsion of Cannon and his Trotskyite group, and the 1929 expulsion of Lovestone and his followers. Emphasis throughout is placed on factional developments in the Party here and on their relationship to the alignment of forces within the USSR.

D253 DREHER, Carl. The Intellectuals and the Left, "Monthly Review," 5 (Feb. 1954), 490-99.
Criticism of Harold C. Urey for having broken off association with the left, despite his later support of the Rosenbergs. Urey is seen as the prototype of the American intellectual whose confidence the left must win if it is to survive. A potential leader of those who may hold the balance of power between capitalist democracy and fascism, Urey needs the support and counsel of the left.

D254 DREISER, Theodore. "Dreiser Looks at Russia." New York: Liveright, 1928. 264 pp.
A report of the author's 11-week trip to the USSR in the fall of 1927 at the invitation of the Soviet government. Dreiser tells of many aspects of life in the Soviet Union—the economic plan, the theory and practice of communism, the tyranny of communism, the life of peasants and workers, the position of women, religion, and art, literature, and music. On the whole his report is a favorable one, although he disapproves of the atmosphere of espionage and the pervading social regulations.

D255 .... "Tragic America." New York: Liveright, 1931. 435 pp. Ind.
An indictment of conditions in the U.S., written during the great depression by a leading novelist. Dreiser describes living conditions, the role of business as government, the Supreme Court and the Constitution, the position of labor, the church, and crime. Arguing that the U.S. is ruled by a Wall Street oligarchy, he proposes an executive power not unlike the communist Central Committee in Moscow, which would confiscate all basic industries as well as needed institutions, pool all wealth, and distribute the fruits equitably. (Dreiser joined the Communist Party in 1945, shortly before his death.)

D256 ..., and others. "Harlan Miners Speak: Report on Terrorism in the Kentucky Coal Fields." New York: Harcourt, Brace, 1932. 348 pp.
The report of a committee organized by Dreiser, then chairman of the National Committee for the Defense of Political Prisoners, a Party front, to investigate crimes and abuses inflicted on striking members of the National Miners Union, a TUUL affiliate, in Harlan County, Kentucky. Most of the volume reproduces testimony taken from miners and their wives in Pineville and Harlan, along with testimony of the sheriff and prosecuting attorney. Early chapters, by members of the delegation, deal with class war in the Kentucky coal fields, organizing the union, ownership of the mines, the lawlessness of the law, treatment of reporters, and living conditions.

D257 .... "America Is Worth Saving." New York: Modern Age, 1941. 292 pp.
An argument, written during the Nazi-Soviet pact period, that the U.S. should not become involved in the war in Europe. Critical of American business and labor conditions, Dreiser is even more critical of England's imperialism, colonial tyranny, and undercover fascism. (Four years later Dreiser joined the Communist Party.)

D258 .... The Logic of My Life...., "Mainstream," 1 (Spring 1947), 225-27.
A letter written by Dreiser shortly before his death (on June 20, 1945) to William Z. Foster, expressing his desire to become a member of the American communist organization, as the final step in his belief in the greatness and dignity of man.

DRIDZO, S. A. See LOSOVSKY, A.

D259 DRINAN, Robert F. Deporting Our Subversive Aliens, "America," 91 (Aug. 21, 1954), 495-97.
Though the government has the right to revoke citizenship and deport alien subversives, its laws and administrative machinery may work undue hardship upon possibly innocent people. The author analyzes laws and administrative rulings resulting in injustice, and suggests that Congress reappraise substantive and procedural law dealing with aliens charged with disloyalty.

D260 .... The Right to Silence, "America," 95 (April 28, 1956), 106-8.
An analysis of the meaning of the statute granting immunity from criminal prosecution for those who would otherwise refuse to testify about subversive activity by reason of the Fifth Amendment. The author feels that this immunity statute will inflict great injustice upon repentent excommunists.

D261 DRIVER, Martha M. Constitutional Limitations on the Power of Congress to Punish Contempts of Its Investigating Committees, "Virginia Law Review," 38 (Nov. 1952), 887-911; (Dec.), 1011-33.
An exploration of the restrictions placed by the Constitution on congressional probes, through the First, Fourth, and Fifth Amendments. The courts have been too lenient in enforcing these substantive restrictions, and have not enforced procedural limitations on the investigatory powers of the Congress.

D262 DRUMMOND, Roscoe. Are Communists Traitors to America? "American Mercury," 67 (Oct. 1948), 389-96.
The chief of the Washington Bureau of the "Christian Science Monitor" compares the American Constitution with the rules of the Communist International. As a section of the Communist International, the CPUSA is not a genuine political group, its members having surrendered their civil rights to a foreign power.

D263 DUBINSKY, David. The Struggle for the Revival of Our Union, "American Federationist," 36 (Dec. 1929), 1437-42.
An analysis by the acting president of the ILGWU of the fight in the union, 1924-29, with the communists. He describes the long and disastrous 1926 strike in New York City, led by the communists. Now the union has been rebuilt under noncommunist leadership.

D264 .... A Warning against Communists in Unions, "New York Times Magazine," May 11, 1947, 7 ff.
An assertion by the president of the ILGWU that communism's aim and spirit are hostile to trade unionism. Though the Party has been defeated in the ILGWU and some other unions, it maintains a stranglehold on others, some in strategic industries. Real progressives are their foremost targets; they will support a reactionary who favors a pro-Soviet line. Rules for defeating communist tactics are given.

D265 .... How I Handled the Reds in My Union, "Saturday Evening Post," 225 (May 9, 1953), 31 ff.
The president of the ILGWU tells how members of his

union were converted from communism and how excommunists were used to defeat Party workers. Excommunists who are sincere, who want to fight the communists and not merely quit them, can be helpful. Persons who want to break away from the Party, a difficult thing to do, can thus be helped.

D266 DUBINSKY, David. Instead of the McCarthy Method, "New York Times Magazine," July 26, 1953, 9 ff.
Citing communist history in the U.S., particularly with regard to the ILGWU, Dubinsky criticizes the McCarthy method for failure to convert communists to democracy, for confusing the issue, for interfering with the work of security agencies, for inducing cynicism, and for weakening our international prestige. He outlines a plan to fight communism while avoiding these pitfalls.

D267 DuBOIS, W. E. B. The Negro and Communism, "Crisis," 38 (Sept. 1931), 313-20.
The editor of "Crisis," NAACP organ, replies to communist critics of NAACP's role in the Scottsboro case. Communist tactics of threatening judges and calling for mass action by southern white workers will cause the Scottsboro boys to be murdered. Accusations that the NAACP is guilty of misuse of funds and lack of interest in the case are stupid and malicious.

D268 . . . . "Color and Democracy: Colonies and Peace." New York: Harcourt, Brace, 1945. 143 pp.
A leading Negro fellow-traveler and author questions whether the world, in the postwar period, will admit the colored races of the world into full equality with the European powers; if not, the possibility of lasting peace is remote. He denounces the imperialism of the U.S. and Britain, and praises the Soviet Union's lack of race discrimination and its practice of democracy.

D269 . . . . "Behold the Land." Birmingham, Ala.: Southern Negro Youth Congress, 1946. 15 pp.
An address by a prominent Negro fellow-traveler to a front organization, bidding Southern Negro youth to regard the South as the battleground of a great crusade, and to publicize the infamies of whites against Negroes in the South, so as to rescue the land by sacrifice.

D270 . . . . The 13th, 14th and 15th Amendments, "Lawyers Guild Review," 9 (Spring 1949), 92-95.
An assertion that these amendments were never meant to serve the cause of freedom. The Thirteenth was passed to avoid war, and the Fourteenth to protect property. The Fifteenth was dead before it was born, because democracy in America was subordinated to industry rather than to human freedom.

D271 . . ., and WHITE, Walter. Paul Robeson, Right or Wrong, "Negro Digest," 8 (March 1950), 8-18.
DuBois defends Robeson's pro-Soviet politics, pointing to the USSR's opposition to prejudice and colonialism and its love of peace. Criticizing Robeson's views, White denies the Russian democratic claim, asserting that its one-party regime is rigid in discipline and destructive of freedom.

D272 . . . . "I Take My Stand for Peace." New York: Masses & Mainstream, 1951. 15 pp.
A pamphlet written while DuBois, with four others, was under indictment for activities in the Peace Information Center, a front group, during the Korean War. The author asserts that the U.S. alone wants war, forces other nations to fight, and asks its citizens to prepare for a world war wanted only by rich Americans who profit from it.

D273 . . . . "In Battle For Peace: The Story of My 83rd Birthday." New York: Masses and Mainstream, 1952. 192 pp. App.
Autobiographical account by a leading Negro fellow-traveler, who finally joined the Party nine years later. He tells of his activities with various front groups, including the Council on African Affairs, the Peace Congresses, and the Peace Information Center; of his candidacy for U.S. senator on the Progressive ticket in 1950; and of his indictment for not having registered as a foreign agent as director of the Peace Information Center and his acquittal. He concludes that his advocacy of peace threatens the imperialists of the world, but that to silence him, through courts and national hysteria, would mean the death of democracy.

D274 . . . . Negroes and the Crisis of Capitalism in the U.S., "Monthly Review," 4 (April 1953), 478-85.
The U.S. is seen in a crisis in which American industry is making unparalleled efforts to usurp government. White North America, by its continued efforts to enslave Asia and Africa, is driving Negroes toward socialism. Negroes, divided into the masses and the capitalist upper class, are repelled by the custom of calling agitation for Negro rights "communism."

D275 DUCLOS, Jacques. On the Dissolution of the Communist Party of the United States, "Political Affairs," 24 (July 1945), 656-72. (Reprinted from the April issue of "Cahiers du Communisme," theoretical organ of the Communist Party of France.)
An assertion by a French communist leader that, while national unity was to be desired, Browder erred in seeking national unity by liquidating the CPUSA as an independent party. Browder's line was also revisionist in its belief in the possibility of long-term class peace. (This article, accepted in the American communist movement as the views of Moscow, precipitated the liquidation of the Communist Political Association, the reconstitution of the CPUSA, and the turn to the "hard" postwar Party line appropriate to the cold war.)

D276 DUFFY, Frank. Disturbers in Our Midst, "Catholic World," 135 (June 1932), 307-13.
Asserting that socialism and Bolshevism are the same, an AFL vice-president denounces both, together with their subsidiaries, as disrupters in the ranks of labor. Neither will ever be recognized by the AFL.

D277 DUFFY, John F., Jr. Communism Rejected by American Workers, "Christianity and Crisis," 9 (May 30, 1949), 67-70.
A review of communist attempts to gain influence in the American labor movement, and of the successful efforts to defeat them. The communists "bored from within" under the Trade Union Educational League, set up dual unions with the Trade Union Unity League, and entrenched themselves in a number of CIO unions. In many of these their domination is now being ended.

D278 DUGAN, James. Meet Four Communists, "New Masses," 33 (Oct. 31, 1939), 7-9.
Sketches of Israel Amter, Isidore Begun, Peter V. Cacchione, and Paul Crosbie, Communist Party councilmanic candidates in New York City who were ruled off the ballot by the Board of Elections. Their program for jobs, civil rights, housing, and peace is given, and write-in votes appealed for.

D279 DUNCAN, Leonard. Organizational Development among Clerical Workers, "Communist," 17 (April 1938), 359-68.

Mechanization of clerical work, concentration of clerical workers into large offices like factories, and the disappearance of personal relationships with their employers have shaken illusions of superiority held by clerical workers and led to growing accord with demands of manual labor. CIO efforts to organize clerical workers are described.

D280 DUNHAM, Barrows. How We Know, "Mainstream," 10 (Aug. 1957), 21-43.
A discussion of the theory of knowledge developed by Marx and Engels, and how its "truth" is determined. A philosophical discussion of how we "know" and how Marxism heightens knowledge.

D281 DUNN, Robert W. "American Company Unions: A Study of Employee Representation Plans, 'Works Councils' and Other Substitutes for Labor Unions." Conclusions by William Z. Foster. Chicago: Trade Union Educational League, n.d. [1926]. 66 pp. Ind.
A study of company unions, covering definition, extent of their use, reasons for their installation, specific cases, their tactics, and organized labor's case against them. Foster's conclusions contain a program for the fight against company unionism.

D282 .... "The Americanization of Labor: The Employers' Offensive against the Trade Unions." Introd. by Scott Nearing. New York: International Publishers, 1927. 272 pp. Ind.
A discussion, by a long-term fellow-traveler active in Party-oriented research and trade union affairs, of efforts by U.S. business to keep workers from unionizing during the 1920's. He describes such techniques as employee stock ownership, piece work with bonuses, personnel work, welfare activities, the company union, the blacklist, and the spy system, and urges the trade union movement to combat them with state welfare and minimum wage protection, amalgamation of craft unions, aggressive industrial unions, and a labor party.

D283 .... "Company Unions: Employers' Industrial Democracy." Introd. by Louis Budenz. New York: Vanguard, 1927. 206 pp.
A description of a number of company unions, with analysis of common characteristics, written by the executive secretary of the Party-affiliated Labor Research Association. Company unions are not unions at all, but a form of labor regulation to serve employers' needs. Unions can fight them by boring from within, attacking from without, amalgamating craft unions into industrial unions, and organizing the unorganized into industrial unions. Company unions will remain part of the employers' machinery of exploitation until militant labor, seeking full fruits of workers' toil, destroys them. (An elaboration of the author's pamphlet published by the TUEL in 1926.)

D284 .... "Labor and Automobiles." New York: International Publishers, 1929. 224 pp. Ind.
One of a series of industrial studies sponsored by the Labor Research Association, a Party front which Dunn long served as executive secretary. He stresses the deplorable conditions of workers in automobile plants, contrasting their low wages with high industry profits. Asserting that the AFL will not be able to organize the industry, he proposes industrial unionism built on a shop-committee basis.

D285 .. , and HARDY, Jack [pseud. for Dale Zysman]. "Labor and Textiles: A Study of Cotton and Wool Manufacturing." New York: International Publishers, 1931. 256 pp. Ref. notes. App. Ind.
One of a series of labor and industry studies sponsored

by the Party-oriented Labor Research Association. The book gives a comprehensive account, from the communist point of view, of organizational problems confronting workers in wool and cotton manufacturing. It contains a history of labor organization in the textile industry and a description of the deplorable conditions giving rise to worker discontent. (Dunn, a veteran fellow-traveler, long served as executive secretary of the Association. Jack Hardy is the Party name of Dale Zysman, a New York public school teacher active in teacher-union affairs.)

D286 .... "Spying on Workers." New York: International Publishers, 1932. 31 pp.
An account of the types and activities of spies in the ranks of labor, including company spies, government spies, and labor union officials' stool pigeons who inform on militants and progressives. The spy system will continue, the author asserts, as long as there are classes in society and class struggles.

D287 .... "What War Means to the Workers." New York: Workers Library, 1933. 23 pp.
A denial, addressed to workers, that war will bring back prosperity. Instead workers are the victims of war, as casualties in the armed forces and as certain losers because the cost of living mounts faster than wages, while capitalists receive profits from mass murder. The New Deal is called a part of war preparations.

D288 .... American Imperialism Prepares for War, "Communist," 12 (July 1933), 625-35.
The U.S. government is preparing for war to protect the interests of Wall Street throughout the world and to extend its foreign markets and investments. The importance of the Navy in war preparations shows this. The AFL is cooperating in procurement planning for war.

D289 .... How the Cards Are Stacked in the New Deal, "Labor Unity," 8 (Aug. 1933), 11-14.
A bitter attack on the National Industrial Recovery Act as a plan under which workers will share poverty while profits rise, and wages will be kept around the minimum despite soaring profits. Company unions are to be fostered, while employers and the police help the AFL against the left-wing unions. The entire plan is seen as part of the preparations for the approaching imperialist war.

D290 .... "Company Unions Today." New York: International Publishers, 1935. 31 pp.
An assertion that company unions have spread widely under the New Deal, encouraged by government and indirectly by AFL officials through their support of NRA. In all the plans the employer has the controlling voice, aided by coercion and terror. Purposes are to control the workers, keep them out of real unions, increase exploitation, and increase profits.

D291 .... "The Bill of Rights in Danger." New York: International Labor Defense, 1940. 31 pp.
An assertion that the Bill of Rights is endangered by the "inquisition" of the Dies Committee, as well as by reactionary legislation against labor and noncitizens and by the "antisubversive" drive against labor and progressives opposed to war and fascism. U.S. ruling circles are held responsible for the danger to our rights.

D292 ..., and others. "Crisis in the Civil Liberties Union." [New York]: The authors, 1940. 46 pp. App.
A pamphlet issued by Dunn, Nathan Greene, A. J. Isserman, Corliss Lamont, William B. Spofford, and Mary van Kleeck, giving the position of the minority on the ACLU

board of directors on its resolution of February 5, 1940, which barred from its governing committees and staff anyone who supports totalitarian dictatorship in any country. Harry F. Ward resigned from the board of directors in protest, and Elizabeth Gurley Flynn, a Party member, was removed. Their statements, along with others protesting the resolution, are included as appendices.

D293   DUNN, Robert W. (ed.) "The Palmer Raids." New York: International Publishers, 1948. 80 pp.
A detailed account of the round-up of communists and anarchists in January 1920 under the leadership of Attorney General A. Mitchell Palmer. Those raids, the author asserts, show how a government agency can be corrupted to the purposes of big corporations and used to undermine constitutional rights. He draws a parallel between those raids and the anticommunist "hysteria" of post-World War II.

D294   DUNNE, William F. "Wm. F. Dunne's Speech at the A.F. of L. Convention, Portland, 1923." Chicago: Trade Union Educational League, 1923. 15 pp.
The author, an elected delegate to the convention, denounces the efforts of the AFL officialdom to unseat him because of his membership in the Workers (Communist) Party and his criticism of AFL officers and policies. Defending his record in the trade union movement, he charges convention delegates with being closer to the bosses than they ever were to the workers.

D295   .... The Cleveland Con Conference, "Labor Herald," 1 (Jan. 1923), 24-25.
Criticism of the Second Conference for Progressive Political Action, Cleveland, Ohio, December 11-12, 1922. Workers Party delegates were excluded because they had the clearest understanding of the necessity for a labor party. Farmer-labor delegates, led by John Fitzpatrick of the Chicago Federation of Labor, sought to form a labor party, but were defeated by 12 votes.

D296   .... Labor's Chamber of Commerce, "Labor Herald," 2 (Nov. 1923), 3-5.
A bitter report on the AFL convention in Portland at which the author was unseated. He presents his view of the episode, describing the efforts of professional labor leaders to outdo Chambers of Commerce in denunciation of anything that could be viewed as un-American. At Portland the offensive against the left wing reached its height.

D297   .... Organization of the Metal Mining Industry, "Labor Herald," 2 (Feb. 1924), 11-15.
The metal mining industry is characterized by monopoly control and, since the wrecking of Butte Miners' Local No. 1 of the Western Federation of Miners, by lack of effective worker organization. The story of its destruction is told. The new Butte local is part of the Mine, Mill and Smelter Workers. The miners must now be organized around their job interests.

D298   .... Workers and Farmers on the March, "Labor Herald," 3 (April 1924), 38-40.
The series of conferences in Minnesota during March constituted a victory for those who want to form a labor party on a working-class basis. The next step in the formation of a powerful working-class political organization will be the June 17 farmer-labor party conference, to be held in St. Paul.

D299   .... Revolutionary Strike Strategy, "Labor Herald," 3 (Sept. 1924), 201-4.

The text of a speech to the Third Congress of the Red International of Labor Unions, July 16, 1924. In America a weak trade union movement confronts the strongest capitalism in the world. Since the trade union bureaucracy is capitalist, communists must initiate strikes among the unorganized, so that the masses see there is no hope without destruction of capitalism.

D300   .... Shop Committees—a Revolutionary Weapon, "Workers Monthly," 4 (Nov. 1924), 29-31.
Elaboration of the thesis of the Red International of Labor Unions that the shop committee is the natural center around which organized and unorganized workers should be grouped. Such committees, under communist leadership, will revolutionize the unions and organize the masses for the overthrow of capitalism.

D301   ..., and FOSTER, William Z. The A.F. of L. and Trade Union Unity, "Workers Monthly," 4 (Jan. 1925), 130-34.
An assertion that the AFL plans to affiliate with the Amsterdam International in order to block the drive of the RILU for world trade-union unity. The AFL bureaucrats, who act as policemen for American imperialism, will establish themselves in Europe as the auxiliary of the Dawes Plan, and in continuation of their policy of war on the left wing.

D302   .... Negroes in American Industry, "Workers Monthly," 4 (March 1925), 206-8; (April), 257-60.
A view of race hatred as an artificial development based on falsehood, and encouraged by unscrupulous capitalists. Solidarity of whites and blacks is found only among the communists and the most intelligent and militant workers outside Party ranks. Capitalism exploits race prejudice to beat down living standards.

D303   .... The Negroes as an Oppressed People, "Workers Monthly," 4 (July 1925), 395-98.
A description of capitalism's world-wide oppression of Negroes, who are oppressed as a race, not as individuals. The horrors of European imperialism in Africa are reviewed. American Negroes have two allies—the U.S. white working class and African Negroes. They should unite their race internationally, joining it with the world working-class struggle.

D304   .... The A.F. of L. and World Trade Union Unity, "Workers Monthly," 5 (Dec. 1925), 64-67.
An attack upon the recent AFL convention for its treatment of Purcell, fraternal delegate from the British Trades Union Congress, who advocated world-trade unity, opposed recognition of the USSR. The AFL, instead, collaborates with capitalism and wars on the left wing at home, and unites with the traitors to labor wherever American imperialism operates abroad.

D305   .... "Worker Correspondents." Chicago: Daily Worker Publishing Company, n.d. [1926?]. 35 pp.
Instructions to the Daily Worker's "worker correspondents" on the gathering and writing of news. The worker correspondent is declared essential to a communist press that must both reflect and mould the struggles of workers. Instructions on news stories and interpretive articles are given, and the importance of factory and job news is emphasized.

D306   ..., and WEINSTONE, William. The Left Wing at Two Conventions, "Workers Monthly," 5 (Feb. 1926), 171-78.
A description by Dunne of the 1925 convention of the ILGWU held in Philadelphia, and by Weinstone of the Fur Workers' convention held in Boston the same year. Activities of the left-wing delegates of both unions, among

whom there were many communists, are discussed, and their successes and failures pointed out. The left-wing groups must be broadened and consolidated.

D307 DUNNE, William F. American Imperialism's Black Mass, "Workers Monthly," 5 (Aug. 1926), 445-46.
An attack on the Eucharistic Congress of the Catholic Church in Chicago, and a view of its favorable reception in the capitalist press as evidence of an alliance of the archreactionaries in the Vatican with Protestant American capitalism and American imperialism.

D308 .... The N.A.A.C.P. Takes a Step Backward, "Workers Monthly," 5 (Aug. 1926), 459-61.
Criticism of the June 1926 conference of the National Association for the Advancement of Colored People, which failed to take a militant stand on such issues as antidiscrimination in trade unions, and which rejected the program proposed by the American Negro Labor Congress delegate, James Ford. The reason is found in the middle-class composition of the conference.

D309 .... "The Threat to the Labor Movement: The Conspiracy against the Trade Unions." n.pub., n.d. [1927?]. 40 pp.
An argument that the current attack by AFL reactionaries against labor progressives is part of a combination of union officials, the capitalist press, employers, and government against the threat posed by progressive forces to their imperialist designs. Socialists and union officials are labeled labor agents of imperialism.

D310 .... The Thirtieth Convention of the United Mine Workers of America, "Communist," 6 (March 1927), 32-40.
A review of the recent convention in which the Lewis machine defeated John Brophy's "Save the Union" faction and wiped out the union's militant, class conscious tradition. The Party must strengthen its fractions in the UMW and aid the left wing, which is under noncommunist leadership.

D311 .... Surrender Raised to a System: The Work of the Last A.F. of L. Convention, "Communist," 6 (Nov. 1927), 413-22.
The AFL convention was dominated by conscious reaction. It did not deal with the injunction meance, political organization of labor, organization of the unorganized, or the danger of imperialist war. Dodging unpleasant reality, it reported a more friendly employer attitude toward unions. No rank-and-file expression was permitted.

D312 .... The Crisis in the American Labor Movement: How to Meet It, "Labor Unity," 2 (Feb. 1928), 1-2 ff.
The labor movement is in a crisis, due to corrupt union officials who expel militant workers, spread class-peace poison, and support the political parties of capitalism. Purposes are to smash the labor movement at home and assist imperialism and war abroad. The TUEL fights against this program.

D313 .... The Crisis in the United Mine Workers, "Communist," 7 (Feb. 1928), 105-9.
The United Mine Workers are crippled by John L. Lewis' policy of peace with the coal barons at the expense of the miners. Strikes in Pennsylvania, Ohio, and West Virginia are developing unfavorably because of his leadership. Communists are urged to save the union on the basis of a militant program.

D314 .... "Gastonia, Citadel of the Class Struggle in

the New South." New York: Workers Library, 1929. 58 pp.
A description, by a veteran Party editor and labor leader, of the strife in Gastonia, N.C., growing out of a strike led by the Party-controlled National Textile Workers Union. The killing of the local chief of police resulted in the arrest of 13 union members on murder charges; besides defending them, the pamphlet describes the "reign of terror" by the company and the police that led to the strike.

D315 .... Gastonia—The Center of the Class Struggle in The New South, "Communist," 8 (July 1929), 375-83.
The National Textile Workers Union strike in Gastonia, N.C., shows the rapid development of class conflict in the South. A police attack on union headquarters and on a tent colony of evicted strikers was met with bullets. Now 15 organizers and strikers are charged with murder.

D316 .... The Struggle against Unemployment and the Communist Way Out of the Crisis, "Communist," 11 (Jan. 1932), 17-26.
With permanent unemployment and mass misery in the U.S., the immediate task of communists is to prepare for the revolutionary struggle, for the communist way out of the crisis. It is not enough to fight for unemployment insurance. Greater use of Marxist-Leninist classics will destroy the illusions of American workers.

D317 .... Three Months of the New Deal, "New Masses," 8 (June 1933), 14-17.
A characterization of Roosevelt's New Deal as an extension of the program of Wall Street imperialism. Roosevelt has established forced labor camps, cut relief for the unemployed, used troops against workers and farmers, persecuted the foreign born, formed a united front with Japanese imperialism, and raised the cost of living.

D318 .... NIRA—Strikebreaker, "New Masses," 8 (Aug. 1933), 16-18.
An attack on the NIRA for breaking the strike of Western Pennyslvania coal miners, and on the leaders of the United Mine Workers for class collaboration and corruption. The recovery act is a slave pact, used by AFL officials to protect capitalism from the wrath of the working class.

D319 .... The Seal of the N.R.A. on the A.F. of L. Convention, "Communist," 12 (Nov. 1933), 1078-87.
Cooperation between the AFL and the NRA is traced, as is the active part of AFL leaders in framing industrial codes. The NRA program is one of strikebreaking and suppression, while strengthening monopoly capitalism. The working class can organize for struggle against NRA and its fascist trend by forming a mass opposition movement within the AFL.

D320 .... "The Great San Francisco General Strike." New York: Workers Library, 1934. 80 pp.
An analysis by a veteran communist of the 1934 general strike in the San Francisco Bay area. He denounces the reactionaries in the Central Labor Council and the "fascist terror" of the police, and praises the influence of the Party in the waterfront unions. He asserts that the general strike was betrayed from within, not defeated.

D321 ..., and CHILDS, Morris. "Permanent Counter-Revolution: The Role of the Trotskyites in the Minneapolis Strikes." New York: Workers Library, 1934. 56 pp.
An attack by two prominent Party members on the Trotskyite leadership of the Minneapolis teamsters' union (in

which three brothers of Dunne played leading roles). Governor Olson, Farmer-Labor Party office-holder, is also attacked. The authors conclude that an opposition faction must be organized among the drivers to expose the traitorous Trotskyite leadership. (Expanded from an article by Childs in "Communist," Oct. 1934.)

D322 DUNNE, William F. One Year of the New Deal, "New Masses," 10 (March 6, 1934), 11-14.
Though the admitted purpose of the New Deal is to save capitalism, it has set wages at the level of the beginning of the century. The communists seek to organize the working class against the NRA, which smells of fascism.

D323 . . . . Raymond Moley: Provocateur-in-Chief for the New Deal, "New Masses," 11 (June 26, 1934), 9-13; 12 (July 3, 1934), 13-15.
An attack on Raymond Moley, former head of Roosevelt's "brain trust" and now editor of "Today," for publishing an article critical of the communists (see McAlister Coleman, "Communism Strikes," in "Today," May 26, 1934). The real crime of the Communist Party is exposing the monopoly capitalist character of NRA. Unlike the tabloids, Moley tries to hide his incitement to fascist methods with hypocritical phrases.

D324 . . . . Fascism in the Pacific Coast Strike, "New Masses," 12 (July 31, 1934), 9-11.
An account of fascist terrorism in the San Francisco general strike. An American Legion Anti-Red Committee became virtually part of the police department, engaged in antilabor espionage, and later amalgamated with Citizens' Committees. Fascist storm squads have raided workers' homes, slugged strikers, destroyed workers' halls. The Roosevelt Administration is encouraging the use of fascist bands against communists.

D325 . . . . San Francisco General Strike: Its Significance, Betrayal and Great Lessons, "Labor Unity," 9 (Aug. 1934), 5-7 ff.
An analysis of two general strikes, one by longshoremen and maritime workers of the entire Pacific Coast and the other by shore trade unions in the San Francisco area, by a member of the national executive board of the Trade Union Unity League. The strikes showed growing labor solidarity, despite the treachery of the labor bureaucracy. They were fought by armed force, the intervention of the federal government, a fascist reign of terror against communists, and the threat of martial law.

D326 . . . . "The Supreme Court's Challenge to Labor." New York: Workers Library, 1935. 23 pp.
Although opposed to the National Industrial Recovery Act on principle, this communist pamphlet assails the U.S. Supreme Court's declaration of its unconstitutionality as the opening gun in the new offensive against the working class by the trusts and monopolies.

D327 . . . . "Why Hearst Lies about Communism." New York: Workers Library, 1935. 48 pp.
Three open letters to William Randolph Hearst by a veteran communist, denouncing misrepresentation by the Hearst newspapers, and asserting that Hearst, in his drive against wages, unions, and communism, is driving for fascism in the U.S., with the knowledge and approval of the Roosevelt Administration.

D328 . . . . "The Struggle against Opportunism in the Labor Movement—for a Socialist United States." New York: New York Communications Committee, n.d. [1947]. 87 pp.
A call for the unity of Marxist forces in the U.S. to establish a socialist society and end mass unemployment, poverty, and war. The author attacks revisionism of Marxism-Leninism, opportunism and defeatism, and surrender to suppression of the democratic rights of workers. (A charter member of the communist movement here, Dunne had opposed Browder's liquidation of the Party during World War II. Following reconstitution of the Party, he preferred charges against leading comrades for forging quotations and was himself expelled.)

D329 DURR, Clifford J. How to Measure Loyalty, "Nation," 168 (April 23, 1949), 470-73.
A case study of the dismissal, under President Truman's loyalty order, of a government employee on charges of having been a leader of the American Peace Mobilization, of having followed the Party line, and of having sympathized with policies advocated by the "Daily Worker." Despite his denial of the charges and the lack of evidence supporting them, the employee was dismissed.

D330 D'USSEAU, Arnaud. The Theater as a Weapon, "New Masses," 59 (June 25, 1946), 15-18.
A playwright calls for a theater dealing with social issues that will challenge audiences and change the world. Art should be a weapon, though we must also respect theory and learn technique. The author seeks an experimental theater, a living-newspaper theater, a repertory theater, and, above all, a labor theater.

D331 DYCHE, John A. "Bolshevism in American Labor Unions: A Plea for Constructive Unionism." New York: Boni & Liveright, 1926. 224 pp.
A critical view of the ILGWU by a former leading officer of the union who for the past ten years had been an employer in the industry. Himself Jewish, he emphasizes the radical characteristics of the "Yiddish" immigrant workers in the garment industry. He uses the term "Bolshevism" to denote radicalism rather than the Third International.

E

E1 EASTMAN, Max. The Chicago Conventions, "Liberator," 2 (Oct. 1919), 5-19.
A report on the 1919 convention of the Socialist Party and the founding conventions of the Communist Labor Party and the Communist Party of America. The factional fight in the national left-wing organization that led to creation of two communist parties is reviewed. The CPA is controlled by the Slavic language leaders, whereas the CLP consists of English-speaking leftists and centrists. The two communist groups do not differ on principle.

E2 . . . . An Opinion on Tactics, "Liberator," 4 (Oct. 1921), 5-6.
An appeal for the recently amalgamated, but still underground Communist Party to give up its infantile leftism. In the two years since two half-parties were formed, nothing of value to the cause of communism has been done. Though they blame their underground status on the ruthlessness of capitalism, it is their romanticism that accounts for their isolation. Eastman calls for a legal party and press, to save workers from laborism and yellow socialism.

E3 . . . . A Christmas Party, "Liberator," 5 (Feb. 1922), 5-7.
The author hails formation of the Workers Party of America on Christmas Day, 1921, combining all leftward elements from the Socialist Party, an IWW group, and AFL workers devoted to "boring from within." It comprises all genuinely revolutionary elements in the U.S. except antipolitical dogmatists, romantics of the "infantile left," and Eugene Debs.

E4 . . . . "Since Lenin Died." New York: Boni and Liveright, 1925. 158 pp. App.
One of the earliest accounts of the factional differences developing between Trotsky and the Stalin group within the Communist Party of the Soviet Union. Highly critical of the CPSU, this book became a center of controversy within the American communist movement. (The leading intellectual supporter of American communism in its early years, Eastman subsequently became the first Trotskyist sympathizer in the U.S., then a leading intellectual of the anti-Stalinist left, and finally a political conservative.)

E5 . . . . Karl Marx Anticipated Freud, "New Masses," 3 (July 1927), 11-12.
An assertion that Marx's theory of history and his attitude to human thought and culture anticipated Freudian psychology, applied, however, to the ills of society rather than to those of the individual.

E6 . . . . Lenin Was an Engineer, "New Masses," 3 (Nov. 1927), 14-16.
An effort to appraise Lenin's contribution to Marxist thinking. Lenin was a practical thinker, an engineer of revolution, though other Marxist thinkers charged him with heresy. Lenin's concept of the professional revolutionist is explored. (For criticism of Eastman's views see Bertram D. Wolfe, "Eastman Revises Marx—and Corrects Lenin," in "Communist," Nov. 1927.)

E7 . . . . Artists in Uniform, "Modern Monthly," 7 (Aug. 1933), 397-404.
A critical account of the Soviet organization of artists and writers and of its American branch. In the USSR artists and writers are viewed as soldiers whose methods and objects are dictated by the Party. Communist authors and writers here similarly accept unquestioningly the tasks assigned by the Stalinist hierarchy, before which they abase themselves.

E8 . . . . "Artists in Uniform: A Study of Literature and Bureaucratism." New York: Knopf, 1934. 261 pp. Notes. Ind.
An account of bigotry and bureaucratism in the sphere of arts and letters in the USSR in the early period of the Stalinist regime, written by a leading American intellectual and radical who at the time still supported the Soviets, though he opposed Stalin. He describes the program of the 1930 Kharkov congress of artists and authors which, viewing art as a class weapon, called for the abandonment of individualism and the collectivization of artistic creation under the discipline of the Party. Subsequently Russian writers had to conform, confessing their errors, or keep silent.

E9 . . . . John Reed and the Old Masses, "Modern Monthly," 10 (Oct. 1936), 19-22 ff.
Sharp disagreement with the portrait painted of John Reed in Granville Hicks' biography, "The Making of a Revolutionary." The portrait suffers because of Hicks' Stalinist politics and associations. Eastman tells of Reed's association with him on the "Masses," an association ignored by Hicks. (This article, with additional material, later appeared as a chapter in Eastman's "Heroes I Have Known.")

E10 . . . . John Reed and the Russian Revolution, "Modern Monthly," 10 (Dec. 1936), 14-21.
Eastman's version (in a critique of Granville Hicks' biography of Reed, "The Making of a Revolutionary") of Reed's last days in Russia. Eastman's view, based on information from Louise Bryant and Angelica Balabanoff, is that Reed lost faith in communism before he died.

E11 . . . . "Marxism: Is It Science?" New York: Norton, 1940. 394 pp. App. Notes. Ind.
An assertion by a leading American radical intellectual, who turned first against Stalinism and then against any form of socialism, that dialectical materialism is animistic and metaphysical, and as such cannot be scientific. Though Marxists profess to reject religion for science, they believe that the universe must evolve in the direction in which they want it to go. Marx substituted materialism for Hegel's idealism, without making his effort any more scientific. Marxism is contrasted with true scientific thought. The contributions of anarchists, syndicalists, and Bolsheviks to a revolutionary understanding of society are outlined, and Lenin's scientific revolutionary attitude is contrasted with Marx's metaphysical socialism. (Much of the volume appeared earlier in other publications.)

E12 EASTMAN, Max. Stalin's American Power, "American Mercury," 53 (Dec. 1941), 671-80.
An examination of three leading communist-front organizations—the American Youth Congress, the League of American Writers, and the American People's Mobilization (successor to the American League Against War and Fascism and the American League for Peace and Democracy)—to show how they fool the innocent and follow the Party line. Rules to follow before joining any organization today are given.

E13 . . . . "Heroes I Have Known: Twelve Who Lived Great Lives." New York: Simon and Schuster, 1942. 326 pp.
Chapter 9 (pp. 201-37) deals with John Reed and the Russian Revolution. Based upon Eastman's associations with Reed and with others who were close to him, it portrays Reed as a sincere revolutionist who was repelled by many actions of the early Soviet leaders. Eastman criticizes severely the picture of Reed presented by Granville Hicks in "John Reed, the Making of a Revolutionary." Chapter 3 (pp. 45-68) deals with the trial of Eugene Debs.

E14 . . . . Proletarian Novelists, Old and New, "American Mercury," 54 (April 1942), 496-500.
An analysis of three books by Upton Sinclair, who is called a great writer of socialist novels and a great socialist pamphleteer, but who is said to lack the courage to face up to Soviet totalitarianism. Eastman also reviews Ward Moore's "Breathe the Air Again," a proletarian novel with passion for the proletariat that is nevertheless strongly anti-Stalinist.

E15 . . . . Why We Must Outlaw the Communist Party! "Reader's Digest," 57 (Sept. 1950), 42-44.
An assertion that the Communist Party is a conspiracy posing as a legitimate political party. Its outlawry, far from violating our tradition of democratic freedom, will preserve freedom of opinion. A government that fails to suppress a conspiracy to overthrow it is weak, not democratic.

E16 . . . . Can Truman Be Educated? "American Mercury," 71 (Dec. 1950), 726-32.
An assertion that the Truman-Marshall-Acheson school of diplomacy is ignorant of communism, when such ignorance, in makers of our foreign policy, is more dangerous than treason. Roosevelt had stated in 1940 that the USSR was a dictatorship, but during the war, as a result of self-deception, he spoke of it as a democracy and a peace-loving nation.

E17 . . . . "Reflections on the Failure of Socialism." New York: Devin-Adair, 1955. 127 pp.
A series of essays by the former editor of the "Masses" and the "Liberator," who played a leading role in the literary-intellectual life of the socialist and then the communist movement in the U.S. from 1912 on. A biographical introduction traces his early socialist beliefs, his support for communism following the Bolshevik triumph in Russia, his disillusionment with Stalinism and his connections with Trotsky, and his final rejection of democratic socialism as well as revolutionary communism. The essays deal with some of these themes, besides presenting his current beliefs that political freedom and the free market are interdependent and that a wider distribution of private property within the structure of the capitalist system should be one of our goals.

E18 . . . . "Love and Revolution: My Journey through an Epoch." New York: Random House, 1964. 665 pp. Ind.

The second part of the autobiography of one of the leading literary figures associated with the communist movement in this country, covering the period from 1917 to 1941. (His earlier years had been described in "Enjoyment of Living.") Eastman tells about his associations with the "Masses," his adherence to the Communist Labor Party when the left wing split from the Socialist Party in 1919, his pilgrimage to Russia and support of Trotsky in his fight with Stalin, and his final loss of faith in both communism and socialism.

E19 EBENSTEIN, William. "Today's Isms." 2d ed. Englewood Cliffs, N.J.: Prentice-Hall, 1958. 243 pp. Ind.
A discussion of the struggle between totalitarianism and the free way of life, with chapters on totalitarian communism, totalitarian fascism, democratic capitalism, and democratic socialism. A section on "Individual Freedom and National Security" (pp. 144-56) treats of anticommunist legislation, administrative regulations, and investigating committees in the U.S., with cases that have arisen under them.

E20 EBON, Martin. "World Communism Today." New York: Whittlesey House, 1948. 536 pp. App. Bibliog. Ind.
A study of world communism in the light of the strategies successively adopted in the 30-year period from 1918 to 1948. Sections of the volume are devoted to communism's world-wide pattern, eastern Europe, western Europe, the western hemisphere, the Orient and Africa, and the challenge of communism. Chapter 23 (pp. 275-96) deals with the U.S., which is called the main target of communist agitation throughout the globe. The emergence of the Party here is described and its development outlined, with emphasis on the roles of Foster and Browder. Attention is given to Soviet spying here.

E21 EDELMAN, Irwin. "The Myth of the Iron Curtain." Los Angeles: The author, n.d. [1948?]. 32 pp.
A former Party member, expelled in 1947, appeals for the coexistence of capitalism (the U.S.) and socialism (the Soviet Union). He argues that the curtain separating the peoples of the world is woven of such materials of imperialistic American foreign policy as the Truman Doctrine and the Marshall Plan.

E22 . . . . "Freedom's Electrocution." Los Angeles: The author, n.d. [1952]. 22 pp.
A view of the Rosenberg case as the American Dreyfus case, as a frame-up linked to fascist elements, with the victims both Jews and radicals. The government's claim that an atom-bomb secret existed was fraudulent. The conduct of the judge, and also of the defense, is criticized.

E23 EDUCATIONAL POLICIES COMMISSION OF THE NATIONAL EDUCATION ASSOCIATION OF THE U.S. AND THE AMERICAN ASSOCIATION OF SCHOOL ADMINISTRATORS. "American Education and International Tensions." Washington, D.C.: National Education Association, 1949. 54 pp.
A statement by a group of distinguished educators, chaired by Professor John K. Norton of Teachers College, Columbia University, on current international tensions and ways in which the schools may respond. The statement recommends (pp. 37-40) that young citizens learn about the principles and practices of communism, that advocacy not be permitted in American schools, and that members of the CPUSA not be employed as teachers.

E24 "EDUCATIONAL RECORD," It Did Happen at Rutgers: Basic Documents Concerning the Case of Two Professors Who Refused to Answer Questions Asked by the Internal Security Subcommittee of the U.S. Senate, 34 (April 1953), 154-78.

Documents in the case of two professors dismissed by Rutgers University for pleading the Fifth Amendment in testimony before the Senate Internal Security Subcommittee. Although pleading the Fifth Amendment was lawful, and although a special Faculty Committee of Review opposed dismissal, the Board of Trustees dismissed the professors.

E25 "EDUCATIONAL RECORD," It Also Happened at Harvard, 34 (Oct. 1953), 359-70.
Documents in the cases of Wendell H. Furry, Leon J. Kamin, and Helene Deane Markham, Harvard University professors who refused to answer questions before congressional investigating committees. Harvard found that Furry had engaged in "grave misconduct," though he was not dismissed; no action was taken against Kamin; Markham was retained until the end of her term, but was not to be reappointed.

E26 ..., "Are There Alternatives to Congressional Investigations? A Symposium," 35 (April 1954), 94-107.
Papers presented at the October 8-9, 1953, meeting of the American Council on Education. Harold M. Keele deals with the history of legislative inquiry and the legal right of congressional committees to investigate subversive activities. J. Walter Yeagley describes and supports the work of the Department of Justice under the Internal Security Act of 1950. Erskine R. Myer shows how the University of Colorado, by acting promptly, dealt effectively with problems of subversion. Hollis F. Price fears that congressional investigations of communism in education may produce excessive conformism. Harry D. Gideonse asserts that Senator Jenner's committee, avoiding McCarthy's abuses, has made valuable information available to the schools.

E27 EDWARDS, E. For an Intensive Struggle against Right Opportunism, "Communist," 12 (Nov. 1933), 1096-1107.
Right opportunism is the erroneous belief that communists must conceal Party affiliation for fear that workers will not fight under communist leadership. Although communists provide fine leadership in workers' organizations, by concealing their identity as communists, they help keep workers suspicious of the Party.

E28 EDWARDS, George. The Birth of a Student Union, "Socialist Call," 1 (Jan. 11, 1936), 10.
The national chairman of the American Student Union writes on the founding convention, held in Columbus, Ohio, December 1936. Delegations from socialist and communist youth groups, as well as unaffiliated delegates, attended. The most controversial plank in the program was the Oxford Pledge opposing all wars.

E29 EDWARDS, H. [pseud. for Irving Potash]. The New York Painters Strike and Its Betrayers, "Workers Age," 2 (Oct. 15, 1932), 5; (Nov. 15), 5; (Dec. 1), 5 ff; (Jan. 15, 1933), 6.
An account of the strike of the New York painters, called July 13, 1932, and of its betrayal by the AFL leadership, socialist bureaucrats, and a wing of the TUUL. The left wing, which alone could offer a program of action and lead the workers in a genuine struggle, failed to unite all progressive and left-wing groups.

E30 EDWARDS, Willard. The Reformation of Harry Cain, "American Mercury," 81 (Oct. 1955), 39-44.
An account of the turnabout of this former arch-conservative who, as a member of the Subversive Activities Control Board, has attacked the whole federal security

system. The author, who strongly disagrees with Cain's new line, suggests political ambition as well as a type of religious conversion as possible reasons.

E31 EGBERT, Donald Drew. Socialism and American Art. Ch. 14 of "Socialism and American Life," ed. by Donald Drew Egbert and Stow Persons. Princeton, N.J.: Princeton University Press, 1952. 1:621-751.
An analysis of utopian socialist and Marxist influence on American art. Included in the discussion are the various Party cultural organizations of the 1920's and 1930's, the "art as a weapon" line of the Party, the Party line on art after 1945, Party influence on liberal American artists, Mexican communist artists and American art, and communist influence through motion pictures. The modern art movement, the federal art projects under the New Deal, and the postwar appeal of peace are also treated. The author concludes that revolutionary art and revolutionary politics are frequently dissociated, and that the artist's problem is to relate both to his special talent and to his fellow men.

E32 ..., and PERSONS, Stow. (eds.). "Socialism and American Life." 2 vols. Princeton: Princeton University Press, 1952. 776 and 575 pp. Ind.
A valuable reference book for the student of the communist movement in America. Volume 1 contains an introduction, followed by fourteen essays, of which the first six deal with the history of European and American socialism, the remainder discussing socialism in relation to American ideals, economics, politics, psychology, literature, and art. (For further comment see entries under names of Daniel Bell, Willard Thorp, and Donald Drew Egbert.) Volume 2 is a selective and critical bibliography by T. D. Seymour Bassett, each section of which deals with a particular aspect of American socialism.

E33 EGGLESTON, Arthur. Labor and Civil Liberties, "Nation," 174 (June 28, 1952), 647-50.
A former newspaper labor reporter opposes legislation being considered by a U.S. Senate subcommittee to curb communists in unions. Employers are blamed for the witch-hunt attack on the labor movement, which is a threat to all the learned professions as well. While some unionists appearing before the subcommittee invited government intervention, others warned strongly against it.

E34 EHLERS, Henry (ed.). "Crucial Issues in Education: An Anthology." New York: Holt, 1955, 277 pp. Ind.
A source book containing readings and bibliography reflecting opposing viewpoints on such issues as loyalty, censorship, racial segregation, progressive education, teaching of communism, and the rights of communist teachers. Among the authors dealing with the latter subjects are William F. Russell, Lawrence H. Chamberlain, and Howard Mumford Jones. Supreme Court decisions and statements by the Association of American Universities and the American Association of University Professors are included.

E35 EHRMANN, Henry W. The Zeitgeist and the Supreme Court, "Antioch Review," 11 (Dec. 1951), 424-36.
A discussion of the issues in the Dennis case by a political science professor at the University of Colorado. The Communist Party is a threat, not because it is revolutionary, for it is not, but because it is a conspiratorial arm of a foreign government. Civil liberties must be extended even to communists for the sake of the American community at large.

E36   EIBERGER, Carl F., Jr. Judicial Notice and the
        Communist Party, "Notre Dame Lawyer," 29
        (Fall 1953), 97-115.
An analysis of decisions concerning whether a court
should take judicial notice that the Communist Party
advocates violent overthrow of the government. The issue
is much too disputed to be properly a subject of judicial
notice.

E37   EISENSCHER, Sigmund G. Witch-Hunt in the Jew-
        ish War Veterans, "Jewish Life," 2 (Feb. 1948),
        17-21.
A letter to the commander of the Milwaukee post of the
Jewish War Veterans of the United States, protesting a
request for his resignation under a constitutional amendment barring avowed communists. Eisenscher asserts
that the amendment conflicts with the JWV stand on civil
liberties, that obligations of membership in the JWV and
the CP are not inconsistent, and that the amendment
imperils the JWV program to defend the Jewish people.

E38   EISLER, Gerhart. Budenz Is a Liar, "New
        Masses," 61 (Dec. 17, 1946), 13-16.
Abridged text of a speech by Eisler, replying to charges
made against him by Louis Budenz, the House Committee
on Un-American Activities, and the Hearst press. Denying that he is a spy or a "boss" to the CPUSA, Eisler
asserts that he is simply a German antifascist refugee.

E39   . . . . "Eisler Hits Back: A Reply to the Rankin
        Men." New York: German-American, n.d.
        [1947?]. 14 pp.
An address given by Eisler at a meeting organized by
"German-American" (a newspaper for which he wrote),
in which he asserts that he is not an international agent
or boss of the Reds in the U.S., as charged by Louis
Budenz before the House Un-American Activities Committee, but a German antifascist who wants to return home
to fight against a resurgence of Nazis there. (Eisler, a
Comintern representative in the U.S., fled this country in
1949 after conviction for contempt of Congress and passport fraud.)

E40   . . . . "My Side of the Story." New York: Civil
        Rights Congress, 1947. 22 pp.
The statement that Eisler was prevented from reading
prior to being sworn in before the House Un-American
Activities Committee. In it, he repudiates Louis Budenz'
assertion that he is the Comintern's commissar in the
U.S., asserting that he is simply a German communist who
came here as an antifascist refugee. The Communist
Party, he says, is not a conspiracy, nor does it hide its
adherence to an international organization of the workers.
(Part of this statement was published in the "New
Masses," Feb. 18, 1947.)

       . . . . See also BERGER, Hans.

E41   EISMAN, Harry. "An American Boy in the Soviet
        Union." New York: Youth Publishers, 1934. 63 pp.
An enthusiastic report on the USSR by a young communist,
who describes his travels and observations in the Soviet
Union, his work and education in the factory school, his
reprimand for not behaving properly as a Comsomol, and
the process of socialist competition.

E42   ELIEL, Paul. "The Waterfront and General
        Strikes, San Francisco, 1934." San Francisco:
        Hooper Printing Co., 1934. 256 pp. Exhibits.
        Chronology. Ind.
A documented account, based largely on newspaper
sources, of the 1934 San Francisco strikes by an official
of the Industrial Association of San Francisco, covering

events from May 9 to about July 31. Exhibits include
union-management agreements, decisions of government
boards, statements and advertisements by the parties,
letters and telegrams, and proclamations by public officials. The extent of communist influence in the strikes
is touched on at various points.

E43   ELIOT, George Fielding. How the States Are Deal-
        ing with Communism, "American Legion Maga-
        zine," 47 (Oct. 1949), 22 ff.
An account of state legislative efforts to deal with internal
security, including sedition laws, criminal anarchy and
criminal syndicalism laws, exclusion of subversive
groups from the ballot, exclusion of members of subversive
groups from state office or employment, loyalty oaths, and
required registration of subversive organizations. Though
all but three states now have legislation along one or more
of these lines, the job is declared less than half done.

E44   ELISTRATOVA, A. New Masses, "International
        Literature," 1 (1932), 107-14.
An appraisal of the "New Masses" in the central organ of
the International Union of Revolutionary Writers. The
magazine's mistakes and shortcomings are traced to its
insufficient politization, its lack of a sufficiently militant
party line in its cultural political work. In some cases
the "New Masses" empiricism is a repudiation of the
revolutionary class struggle.

E45   ELL, Jay [pseud. for Jay Lovestone]. The Work-
        ers Party of America and the United Front,
        "International Press Correspondence," 2 (June
        20, 1922), 376-77.
While the Workers Party is wholeheartedly committed to
united-front tactics, such tactics will not overthrow
capitalism because of the level of class consciousness of
the American worker. On the trade union front, the WP
emphasizes amalgamation, and on the political front it
favors a national, federated, labor party.

E46   ELLINGTON, Duke. No Red Songs for Me, "New
        Leader," 33 (Sept. 30, 1950), 2-4.
An assertion by Ellington that an engagement in Stockholm
was used by the communists to fake his name to the
Stockholm peace petition. Denying that he signed the
petition or had any inclination to do so, he attacks the role
of the CP in the falsification.

E47   ELLIS, Fred, and others. The Charkov Conference
        of Revolutionary Writers, "New Masses," 6 (Feb.
        1931), 6-8.
A report by the American delegation—Fred Ellis, Michael
Gold, William Gropper, Joshua Kunitz, A. B. Magil, and
Harry Alan Potamkin—on the Second World Plenum (Conference) of the International Bureau of Revolutionary
Literature, November 6-15, 1930. The Conference supported the defense of the Soviet Union and the struggle
against social fascism, heard a definitive discussion of
the creative method in proletarian literature, and laid out
a program to guide work in the U.S.

E48   ELLISON, Ralph. "Invisible Man." New York:
        Random House, 1952. 439 pp.
An anticommunist novel in which the protagonist is drawn
into a "Brotherhood" (a euphemism for the Communist
Party) and rises to become its Harlem spokesman. A riot
started by the Brotherhood shows him that the organization, following a change in its line, will sacrifice its members.

E49   ELMHURST, Ernest F. "The World Hoax." In-
        trod. by William Dudley Pelley. Asheville, N.C.:
        Pelley Publishers, 1939. 243 pp. Ind.

Anti-Semitic literature, based on the premise that communism is world Jewry in action, seeking to smash all gentile governments in order to make Jews supreme. Chapter 6, pp. 165-96, tells what communism would mean to the U.S., and Chapter 7, pp. 197-210, asserts that the CIO is the opening wedge.

E50   EMBREE, Edwin R. "13 against the Odds." New York: Viking, 1944. 261 pp.
The stories of 13 distinguished American Negroes, whose achievements place them at the top in their respective fields. Among them are four who at various times were members of or close to the Communist Party: Richard Wright, Langston Hughes, W. E. B. Du Bois, and Paul Robeson. Their political views and affiliations receive little attention in these sketches, though Wright's sympathies with communism are mentioned, as is the great impression that racial equality in the USSR made on Robeson.

E51   EMERSON, Thomas I., and HELFELD, David M. Loyalty among Government Employees, "Yale Law Journal," 58 (Dec. 1948), 1-143.
A comprehensive analysis of the demand for loyalty among government workers, tracing the development of the current program and analyzing its impact. The problem of communists in federal employment was not of serious proportions when the loyalty order was issued. The injurious effect of the order on government service far overshadows the danger of harboring disloyal personnel. The program should apply only to employees in key jobs or performing secret work.

E52   EMERSON, Thomas I. Answer to Report of the House Committee on Un-American Activities on the National Lawyers Guild, "Lawyers Guild Review," 10 (Summer 1950), 45-46.
An answer by the Guild president to the report in which the House Committee requested the Attorney General to cite the Guild as subversive. Denying that the Guild is controlled by the Party, Emerson asserts that its views are those of independent liberal lawyers, and that some of its positions conflict with those of the Party.

E53   . . . . An Essay on Freedom of Political Expression Today, "Lawyers Guild Review," 11 (Winter 1951), 1-17.
A review of freedom of expression by the president of the National Lawyers Guild. The nation loses more than it gains from repressive measures such as the Smith Act. The prosecution of the communist leaders in 1948 has weakened the "clear and present danger" rule. The McCarran Act establishes the legal foundation for a police state.

E54   . . ., and HABER, David. "Political and Civil Rights in the United States." Foreword by Robert M. Hutchins. Buffalo: Dennis, 1952. 1209 pp. Ind. (2d ed., 1958. 1536 pp.)
A collection of cases, statutes, and other legal materials relating to civil rights, compiled by two members of the faculty of the Yale Law School. This book is intended primarily as a case book for law school use. Issues dealt with include the Smith Act, the Internal Security Act of 1950, the Communist Control Act of 1954, the Taft-Hartley noncommunist affidavit, passport restrictions and freedom of movement, loyalty qualifications for employment, legislative investigating commissions, and academic freedom.

E55   EMERY, Lawrence. Days with Eugene Dennis, "New Masses," 63 (June 17, 1947), 6-10.
An early associate of Eugene Dennis, general secretary of the Party and one of the defendants on trial for contempt of Congress, tells of Dennis' activities in the Party and in the Trade Union Unity League in southern California in the late 1920's and early 1930's.

E56   EMERY, Robert C. "Thirty Years from Now." St. Paul: The author, 1934. 62 pp.
Anti-Olson campaign literature, presenting a picture of life in the Soviet State of Minnesota as seen by a traveler returning in 1964, 30 years after Floyd Olson's election as governor.

E57   EMMET, Christopher. Communist Agents and Freedom of the Press, "New Leader," 28 (June 16, 1945), 8-9.
An assertion that the arrest of four pro-Soviet journalists and three State Department officials in the "Amerasia" case shows that some information was "leaking" to the communists. National security, not freedom of the press, as the communists wish us to believe, is the issue in this case.

E58   . . . . The Mundt-Nixon Bill, "Commonweal," 48 (June 25, 1948), 253-56.
An outline of the Mundt-Nixon bill to combat communism. While not hampering legitimate political activity, the bill will keep a foreign power from using our political machinery, mails, and radio for its own ends. Arguing that the bill is constitutional, the author deplores the campaign against it by reputable liberals as well as by procommunists.

E59   . . . . The McCarthy Muddle, "Commonweal," 51 (April 7, 1950), 673-75.
A call for a middle way between McCarthy's reckless smearing of honest liberals and the Tydings method of ignoring the dangers of communist infiltration. McCarthy's irresponsible labeling has confused the issue about CP-front groups. In the present struggle, liberals cannot merely be noncommunist; they must give priority to the cause of liberation.

E60   . . . . McCarran's Blunderbuss, "Commonweal," 53 (Nov. 3, 1950), 89-91.
An outline of the provisions of the McCarran anti-subversive law, an example of the defects of hasty legislation. The measure calls for the registration of communists and communist-front groups, provides for the internment of communists after a national emergency is declared, and bans aliens who were ever affiliated with a totalitarian party.

E61   ENGDAHL, J. Louis. Sam Gompers Is Not Dead, "Workers Monthly," 5 (Nov. 1925), 10-14.
A critical account of the AFL convention where President William Green sought to incite mob spirit against progress and the TUEL. The labor aristocrats of the convention are attacked for class collaborationism and reactionary views. Progressive resolutions were rejected or sidestepped, while socialists and former militants lined up with the official machine. The left wing was very small and almost inarticulate.

E62   . . . . Wall Street's Congress Convenes, "Workers Monthly," 5 (Dec. 1925), 60-64.
The Congress that assembles this month shows the bankruptcy of capitalist parliamentarism here. Congress is no longer vital to capitalism, which relies instead on the executive branch under Coolidge and the judicial branch under William Howard Taft. No fight will be made for workers and poor farmers in this Congress; they can expect no quarter from the capitalist dictatorship.

E63   . . . . Build for the Third Year, "Workers Monthly," 5 (Jan. 1926), 134-37.

The "Daily Worker," on the eve of its second anniversary, is being molded into an invincible weapon of the Bolshevik revolution, patterned on the daily press in the Soviet Union; it not only reports events for workers to read, but makes the workers feel as though they are a part of such events.

E64 ENGDAHL, J. Louis. The Capitalist Offensive against the Foreign-Born Workers, "Workers Monthly," 5 (April 1926), 259-63 ff.
An attack on immigration legislation, proposed alien registration laws, and publicity campaigns against the foreign-born as an effort of Big Business to weed out prospective agitators in the ranks of labor. While the AFL is criminally inactive, resistance to new restrictive legislation is being organized by the Councils for the Protection of the Foreign-Born.

E65 . . . . It Still Moves—, "Workers Monthly," 5 (June 1926), 370-73.
An analysis of the recent national convention of the Socialist Party. Engdahl criticizes all three leaders—Debs, Berger, and Hillquit. The Debs leadership does not actively function, while the position of the others offers no basis for socialist growth. The socialists, who have no strength in basic industries, rejected a united front with the communists.

E66 . . . . After Gompers—What? Answered, "Workers Monthly," 5 (Dec. 1926), 631-35.
A communist view of the 1926 AFL convention. Though Gompers is remembered only faintly, reaction is still in control. No communist or left-wing delegate was present. The convention opposed recognition of Soviet Russia, disapproved of the British general strike, and viewed Mexican labor imperialistically and hypocritically.

E67 . . . . "The Tenth Year: The Story of the Rise and Achievements of the Union of Socialist Soviet Republics." New York: Workers Library, 1927. 36 pp.
This pamphlet, first in a series to be called the "Workers Library," describes the achievements of the USSR during its first decade, and urges American workers to demand diplomatic recognition. Denying that the Soviet Union has destroyed the trade unions, the author argues that their function in a state ruled by the working class is to be an instrument of government.

E68 . . . . Peasantry or Power, "Workers Monthly," 6 [5] (Jan. 1927), 691-94.
An analysis of American agriculture, concluding that American farmers are being driven toward peasantry and that they must combine with city labor, opposed to the capitalist class, to win power. The breaking away of farmers from the two capitalist parties is shown in the developing farmer-labor movement.

E69 . . . . American Communist Party Develops Defeatist Campaign against U.S. Imperialism, "International Press Correspondence," 8 (Feb. 16, 1928), 174-75.
A contrast of demonstrations by communists against the presence of U.S. marines in Nicaragua with past campaigns. Whereas in past campaigns the Party has merely called for withdrawal of troops, this campaign urges defeat of Wall Street imperialism, using the slogan, "Civil War against Imperialist War!" The campaign is viewed as a rehearsal for future antiwar struggles.

E70 . . . . The Victors in the American Elections, "International Press Correspondence," 8 (Nov. 16, 1928), 1499-1500.

While the communists did not elect any candidates in 1928, the Party has made tremendous progress since 1924. It was on the ballot in 34 states, as contrasted with 14 in 1924; it appeared on a national scale; and it carried, for the first time, a parliamentary campaign to the workers in the shops.

E71 . . . . "Sedition! To Protest and Organize against War, Hunger and Unemployment." New York: International Labor Defense, n.d. [1930]. 31 pp.
An attack by a veteran Party member who served as general secretary of the ILD on the sedition or criminal syndicalism laws on the statute books of 35 states. He reviews leading cases under the statutes since the formation of the communist movement, and appeals for support of the ILD, the Party, and the USSR.

E72 . . . . The Presidential Elections in the U.S., "International Press Correspondence," 12 (Oct. 13, 1932), 949-51.
A pre-election review of major and minor party candidates and issues in the 1932 election. Only the CPUSA fights for the workers' way out of the crisis. While a larger vote than that received in 1928 is expected, the Party's strength is among the disfranchised masses. Because of the American electoral system, even a million votes would probably not give the Party a single seat in Congress.

E73 ENGEL, Leonard. Fear in Our Laboratories, "Nation," 166 (Jan. 17, 1948), 63-65.
A review of eight cases in which guilt by association has resulted in dismissal of scientists from private industry and government. The cases show hostility to trade unions (in three cases) and represent illegal probing by private industry into thoughts and lives of employees. Valuable scientific research has been disrupted.

E74 ENGLESTEIN, David, and HIRSCH, Carl. "A Tale of Two Workers." New York: New Century, 1949. 23 pp.
A tale by two Party functionaries in Illinois of American and Russian workers who compare the two systems under which they live. The conclusion is that the Russians have built a superior economic system from which American workers can learn.

E75 ENGLISH, Richard. What Makes a Hollywood Communist? "Saturday Evening Post," 223 (May 19, 1951), 30-31 ff.
A biographical sketch of Edward Dmytryk, movie director and one of the "Hollywood Ten," who joined the Communist Party in 1941, and was cited for contempt by the House Committee on Un-American Activities in 1947 for refusing to answer questions as to Party membership. He served four months in prison in 1950. His reasons for finally rejecting communism are outlined.

E76 . . . . We Almost Lost Hawaii to the Reds. "Saturday Evening Post," 224 (Feb. 2, 1952), 17-19 ff.
Communist activities in the Hawaiian labor movement as described to a "Post" reporter by Jack Kawano, Hawaiian labor leader and for 13 years a leading communist. Repressive labor practices provided the ILWU with a fertile field of discontent. The ILWU and the communists have successfully infiltrated the Democratic Party.

E77 EPSTEIN, Albert, and GOLDFINGER, Nathan. Communist Tactics in American Unions, "Labor and Nation," 6 (Fall 1950), 36-43.
A review of the Party's trade union policy and a description of recent communist tactics in American unions. The Party, not the union, determines union policy, while communist union leadership parrots the Party line. Party

policy, in turn, is governed by the Communist International in the light of Soviet objectives.

E78   EPSTEIN, M. "May Day, 1934." New York: CPUSA, New York District, 1934. 18 pp.
A May Day pamphlet by a staff member of "Freiheit," Yiddish Party paper in New York, during the "third period." It attacks the Roosevelt Administration, the National Recovery Act, AFL and socialist leaders, and La Guardia, asserting that only the Party fights for the vital needs of workers and Negroes, and that unity must come from below.

E79   EPSTEIN, Melech. Jewish Labor in the U.S.A.: An Industrial, Political and Cultural History of the Jewish Labor Movement. Vol. 1: 1882-1914. New York: Trade Union Sponsoring Committee, 1950, 456 pp. Vol. 2: 1914-1952. New York: The Committee, 1953, 466 pp. Index.
Portions of volume 2 contain information on communist activity in the Jewish labor movement. Chapter 8 (pp. 98-123) analyzes communism in the U.S., with attention to personalities, splits, and factions. Chapter 9 (pp. 124-56) describes the civil war in the ILGWU in the 1920's between communists and anticommunists. Chapter 12 (pp. 220-39) tells of communist activities in the CIO, the role of Jewish labor leaders vis-a-vis the communists, the communist capture of the American Labor Party, and the break of the Jewish unions from the ALP to form the Liberal Party.

E80   .... "The Jew and Communism, 1919-1941." New York: Trade Union Sponsoring Committee, 1959. 438 pp. Notes. Ref. Ind.
An attempt to evaluate communist influence among Jews in the U.S. in the period between the two world wars, written by one who was a communist until the fall of 1939. Communism found its early converts among middle-class intellectuals and skilled workers, not the unorganized and unskilled. A unique environment favored the spread of communism among Jews, in America as in Europe, and here it entrenched itself behind a number of important institutions. The communists betrayed both democracy and world Jewry in 1939-41.

E81   ERNEST, Gifford. "William Z. Foster—Fool or Faker?" Chicago: The author, 1923. 16 pp.
An attack on Foster as a sinister influence in the labor movement, as a trickster interested only in his own career. Formerly an advocate of decentralization, he now believes in centralized dictatorship; his views on political action, similarly, are now the opposite of his earlier ones. His actions with regard to the farmer-labor party and industrial unionism are attacked for insincerity and destructiveness.

E82   ERNST, Morris, and BALDWIN, Roger. Liberals and the Communist Trial, "New Republic," 120 (Jan. 31, 1949), 7-8.
Ernst argues that the U.S. government has the legal and moral right to try the 12 communists indicted under the Smith Act in New York. Criticizing the indictment, Baldwin asserts that there was no allegation of overt acts and that no "clear and present danger" exists.

E83   ERNST, Morris L. "Some Affirmative Suggestions for a Loyalty Program, "American Scholar," 19 (Autumn 1950), 452-60.
A lawyer who believes that a loyalty program is necessary outlines the virtues and defects of the present program.

He proposes that the loyalty program be limited to sensitive jobs. Calling for disclosure rather than suppression, he would allow the fullest latitude to the review boards.

E84   ..., and LOTH, David. "Report on the American Communist." New York: Holt, 1952. 240 pp.
A first step toward exploring the psychological basis of Party membership, based on interviews with nearly 300 excommunists. The typical recruit is found to be white, native-born, and well educated, and to have joined for idealistic reasons; yet personal insecurity and psychological maladjustments have much to do with the Party's attraction. Similarly, motives for leaving may be complicated, though a twist in the Party line is sometimes the occasion. The loneliness and fear of discrimination that follow departure have been accompanied by an improved standard of living. The authors, who estimate that 700,000 Americans have left the Party in the past thirty years, present a program to defeat the communist movement.

E85   ..., and LASKY, Victor (Gunnar Back, moderator). What Shall We Do with the American Communists? "Town Meeting," 18 (April 14, 1953). 15 pp.
Lasky advocates outlawing the Party, which is already underground, praises the work of congressional committees such as the House Committee on Un-American Activities, and denounces the hatred of excommunists. Opposing outlawry, because ideas can't be outlawed, Ernst favors provision of jobs for those who have left the movement.

E86   EULAU, Heinz. World Labor and the A.F. of L., "New Republic," 112 (Feb. 26, 1945), 286-87.
Criticism of the AFL for its refusal to attend the World Trade Union Conference in London, February 1945, because of anticipated communist domination. The AFL attitude, allegedly due in part to opposition to the CIO, is said to betray political immaturity.

E87   .... Communism and the Abuse of Free Speech, "Antioch Review," 12 (Sept. 1953), 316-28.
Advocacy of a federal disclosure law applying to all political propagandists which, without suppressing speech, would enable the public to identify the sources. Communist Party propaganda undermines the free trade in ideas that is essential to democratic government, because it is highly organized and because it parades its ideas under false organizational colors.

E88   EVANS, Louis H. The Present Responsibility of Our Churches: Combatting the Rising Tide of Communism, "Vital Speeches of the Day," 20 (July 15, 1954), 602-8.
A Presbyterian minister presents the church's program in its fight against communism. The church seeks individual freedom, Christian democracy, and the sovereignty of God in the hearts and lives of men. Christians should fight for their ideals—peace, love of the common people, and racial equality—with as much zeal as the communists.

E89   EVANS, Robert [pseud. for Joseph Freeman]. Pilgrims of Confusion, "New Masses," 7 (Feb. 1932), 8-10.
An attack on literati who flounder between an old world which they distrust and a new one which they do not understand. They do not realize that the answer to the crisis lies, not with the captains of industry, but with the revolutionary class. Under pressure of the economic crisis, some intellectuals have begun to see the correct way out.

F

F1   "FACTORY MANAGEMENT AND MAINTE- NANCE," You Can't Laugh Off the Reds, 104 (June 1946), 82-86.
A discussion of the extent to which communists have wormed their way into industry and of what management can do about it. Communists are dangerous because they have the direct backing of the Soviet, because their ideology gains followers, because their target today is labor, because their leaders' influence is felt far beyond their own unions, because they operate under cover, and because every industrial setback aids them.

F2   ..., The Red Menace in Labor and How to Fight It, 106 (Sept. 1948), 106-12.
An account of the impact of leftist leadership on unions and the companies involved, showing how communists make use of management's mistakes to gain power in unions and how honest labor leaders lose control to communists. Management can help, as by cooperating in every lawful way with anticommunist elements and by settling gripes and grievances.

F3   FAGAN, Myron C. "Moscow over Hollywood." Los Angeles: R. C. Cary, 1948. 108 pp.
An account of communist influence in Hollywood and of the author's efforts to combat it. He asserts that Hollywood is as red-controlled as Moscow, that the communists wrecked his production of an anticommunist play, that Hollywood finances communist propaganda and hires European Reds as writers and actors. Over a hundred communists and supporters in Hollywood are named.

F4   .... "Communism by Any Other Name...!" Hollywood: Cinema Educational Guild, 1949. 26 pp.
"Further documentation" is given of Fagan's charges that the United World Federalists is a communist organization; also included are a plea for support of a bill to deport Charles Chaplin, and a brief history of the Cinema Educational Guild.

F5   .... "Hollywood Reds are 'On the Run' !" Cinema Educational Guild, 1949. 24 pp.
A report of the activities of the Cinema Educational Guild, which the author credits with putting film-industry communists on the run, and with having led to the indictment for contempt of Congress of ten Hollywood screen writers. The author's list of loyal Hollywood stars is included.

F6   .... "Moscow Marches On in Hollywood." Hollywood: Cinema Educational Guild, 1949. 30 pp.
Praising the Cinema Educational Guild, the author calls for picketing theatres showing films which are procommunist or have procommunist actors in them. He attacks communist efforts to infiltrate women's groups, the One World and United World Federalists movements, and the film, "We Were Strangers," as procommunist.

F7   .... "Red Treason in Hollywood." Hollywood: Cinema Educational Guild, 1949. 120 pp.
A popularly written exposé of communist activities in Hollywood. The author charges that threats of bodily harm were used to keep actors from appearing in an anticommunist play that he wrote. He asserts that Hollywood, controlled by Stalin, is a propaganda machine for communism, the result of a Moscow plot to break down America's defenses by first capturing films and radio. The Screen Writers' Guild was the first stronghold of the communists, who later formed the Actors' Lab and infiltrated the Actors' Guild.

F8   .... "Reds behind World Federalism." Hollywood: Cinema Educational Guild, 1949. 36 pp.
An accusation, from the extreme right, that the United World Federalists is a treasonable organization, directed by a group of "red-fronters."

F9   .... "Unmasking the Reds in Hollywood." Hollywood: Cinema Educational Guild, 1949. 25 pp.
Charging that communism is widespread in the film industry, the author particularly labels Charles Chaplin and Eddie Cantor as communists or supporters of Party-front organizations and activities.

F10   .... "'Crusade for Freedom' is a Whodunit." Hollywood: Cinema Educational Guild, 1950. 23 pp.
Another attack on the Eisenhower-supported Crusade for Freedom, which Fagan claims is also a communist-infiltrated organization.

F11   .... "Documentation of the Red Stars in Hollywood." Hollywood: Cinema Educational Guild, 1950. 92 pp.
This booklet, in support of "Red Treason in Hollywood" by the same author, gives lists of Hollywood personages and the communist fronts or causes which they supported. This is in further documentation of his thesis that the film industry has long been Moscow's most effective fifth column in America.

F12   .... "Documentation of the Reds behind World Federalism." Hollywood: Cinema Educational Guild, 1950. 26 pp.
An assertion that the "One Worlders," such as the American Association for the United Nations and the United World Federalists, are part of the communist transmission belt of front organizations.

F13   .... "Reds in 'Crusade for Freedom.'" Hollywood: Cinema Educational Guild, 1950. 24 pp.
A charge that the idea of world government is directed by Moscow, and that the Crusade for Freedom organization is a blind behind which the fellow-travelers and the "red-fronters" in Hollywood hide.

F14   .... "Reds in the Anti-Defamation League." Hollywood: Cinema Educational Guild, 1950. 42 pp.
A charge that the League is run by communists and World Federalists, whose main weapon is to brand all anticommunists as anti-Semites.

F15 FAGAN, Myron C. "Hollywood Backs U.N. Conspiracy." Hollywood: Cinema Educational Guild, 1951. 20 pp.
A right-wing attack on the United Nations, which, it alleges, was created by Stalin, and on Columbia Pictures for producing a pro-UN film. The author supports the Bricker amendment to the Constitution.

F16 .... "Red Treason on Broadway." Hollywood, Calif.: Cinema Educational Guild, 1954. 95 pp.
An assertion that the communist conspiracy has gained absolute control of the entertainment world, including stage, screen, radio, and television, and also the magazine and book publishing and newspaper fields. This was accomplished partly through individuals, and partly through control of the various trade unions. Methods used by the communists are revealed. A list of 300 top red stars, writers, directors, and producers in television, stage and radio is included.

F17 FAGEN, Melvin M. Congress Finds a Scapegoat, "New Republic," 82 (March 20, 1935), 152-54.
Condemnation of the various proposals in Congress to outlaw the Communist Party and other organizations advocating radical social change. Responsibility is placed on the Chamber of Commerce, the Hearst press, and the American Legion.

F18 FAHAN, R. What Makes Henry Run?: Wallace's Social and Political Role, "New International," 14 (Feb. 1948), 54-57.
A Trotskyist analysis of Henry Wallace's candidacy in 1948 and of the role of the Stalinists in his campaign. Stalinist support of Wallace is to be understood only in terms of Stalin's foreign policy. Wallace's opposition to the Marshall Plan plays a key role. The Wallace movement may appeal to desires for peace and full employment, but it is little more than a Stalinist-inspired hot-house plant.

F19 FAIRFIELD, William S. How the Reds Came to Haugen, Wisconsin, "Reporter," 10 (Jan. 5, 1954), 24-26.
An account of the formation of a local chapter of the communist-front Civil Rights Congress in a small northern Wisconsin community, which had been settled by Bohemian freethinkers, and of the opposition led by the local Catholic priest and American Legion post.

F20 FALK, Julius. American Student Movement: A Survey, "New International," 15 (March 1949), 84-91.
A history of the student movement since the 1920's, emphasizing the dominant role since the 1930's of Stalinist-controlled youth groups. Stalinists initially mobilized antiwar sentiment, but changes in line, prowar hysteria, and economic recovery dissipated the movement. In the postwar period a political vacuum exists.

F21 ..., and HASKELL, Gordon. Civil Liberties and the Philosopher of the Cold War, "New International," 19 (July-Aug. 1953), 184-227.
A review and critique of "Heresy Yes, Conspiracy No," by Sidney Hook. The authors question the usefulness of distinguishing heresy from conspiracy as a basis for government measures against political organizations. Hook overemphasizes the organizational threat of the CP and underemphasizes its ideological threat, underestimates the extent and impact of the witch hunt, and misunderstands the threat to academic freedom.

F22 .... The Origins of the Communist Movement in the United States, "New International," 21 (Fall 1955), 151-73; (Winter 1955-56), 239-68; 22 (Spring 1956), 49-58.
Discussion of the origin of the American communist movement in the left wing of the Socialist Party. The first article deals with some left wing pre-history; the second discusses aspects of the left wing's "sectarian malady"; the third deals with formation of a split American communist movement, and summarizes factors responsible for the decline of American radicalism in the post-World War I period.

F23 FARBER, Maurice L. The Communist Trial: College Student Opinion and Democratic Institutions, "Public Opinion Quarterly," 14 (Spring 1950), 89-92.
A report on student opinion at an Eastern university regarding the sentences given 11 communist leaders convicted under the Smith Act. Fifty-two per cent of the students favored penalties more severe than the law allows; there were considerable differences according to sex, income, and religion.

F24 FARR, Finis. To the Aid of the Party, "National Review," 5 (May 31, 1958), 517-19 ff.
The case of R. Lawrence Siegel, New York attorney active in civil liberties cases, who was disbarred for perjury and obstructing justice in connection with the legal troubles of Harvey M. Matusow, government witness in communist cases who recanted. Though Siegal's motive was not clear, the benefit has gone to the Party.

F25 FARRAGUT, Clinton. The Clergy in the Red Vineyard, "National Republic," 41 (July 1953), 3-4 ff.
An account of communist sympathizers among the Protestant clergy in the U.S., with attention to G. Bromley Oxnam, William Montgomery Brown, A. J. Muste, Claude Williams, Harry F. Ward, and William Howard Melish. Exposure of their activities does not violate religious freedom.

F26 FARRAR, Larston D. Consumers Union: A Red Front, "Freeman," 2 (July 28, 1952), 726-28.
An assertion, based on the alleged procommunist record of officers and employees, that Consumers Union is a communist front. Its propaganda attacks American business, disparages the private enterprise system, and praises government controls.

F27 FARRELL, James T. "A Note on Literary Criticism." New York: Vanguard, 1936. 221 pp.
In this extended discussion of Marxist aesthetics from a Marxist point of view, a leading novelist attacks both the "revolutionary sentimentalism" of Mike Gold and "mechanical Marxism" represented by Granville Hicks. Both these leftist tendencies have ignored the aesthetic aspect and weakened Marxist criticism. By treating both the novel and the strike bulletin as weapons in the class struggle without differentiation, Farrell asserts, Marxist critics have led revolutionary literature into confusion and sterility. (Farrell's views were criticized by Isidor Schneider in "New Masses," June 23, 1936; defended by Hicks in "New Masses," July 14, 1936; and gave rise to other opinions in "New Masses," July 10, 1936, pp. 21-23. This essay was written during Farrell's procommunist phase, which ended soon afterward.)

F28 .... The Last Writers' Congress: An Interim Report on Its Results, "Saturday Review of Literature," 16 (June 5, 1937), 10 ff.
A look at the literary output of the promising proletarian writers so brightly hailed at the First Writers' Congress in 1935. Finding the output meagre, Farrell asks, on the eve of another writers' congress, what they have been doing.

F29 FARRELL, James T. Dos Passos and the Critics, "American Mercury," 47 (Aug. 1939), 489-94.
A review of Dos Passos' "The Adventures of a Young Man," criticizing its reception by other reviewers. These other reviews constitute a warning to writers not to stray off the reservation of the Stalinist-controlled League of American Writers, to which a number of the critics belong.

F30 .... The End of a Literary Decade, "American Mercury," 48 (Dec. 1939), 408-14.
An analysis of political aspects of literature in the 1930's. In the early years of the decade, major controversies centered on Marxism and the nature of proletarian literature. During the later popular front period emphasis was on defense of culture and democracy, while American writers of liberal or radical persuasion who opposed the Stalinist line were subjected to a pernicious witch hunt.

F31 .... "The League of Frightened Philistines and Other Papers." New York: Vanguard, 1945. 210 pp.
A collection of essays, including "Literature and Ideology" (pp. 90-105) and "The Short Story" (pp. 136-48). The former is a defense of the political freedom of the artist, whether attacked by the advocates of proletarian literature, as in the 1930's, or by supporters of the current war effort. "The Short Story," a paper read at the First American Writers Congress in 1935, is an appraisal of the revolutionary short story.

F32 .... Stalinist Literary Discussion: An Answer to Maltz and the "New Masses," "New International," 12 (April 1946), 112-15.
Comment on the controversy raging in the "New Masses" over the article by Albert Maltz, What Shall We Ask of Writers? in the February 12 issue. The Stalinist movement, which has always used literature as a Party instrument, viciously attacked Maltz's confused attempt to separate artistic ability from political conviction.

F33 .... "Literature and Morality." New York: Vanguard, 1947. 304 pp.
A collection of essays of literary criticism and interpretation of the American literary scene. In the chapter on "The Literary Popular Front" (pp. 150-67), written in 1937, Farrell analyzes the proletarian literature movement of the early and middle 1930's, and criticizes "third period" sectarianism. Even in the people's front period dogmatism and disfavor greeted writers who maintained independence of judgment.

F34 .... The Literary Left in the Middle '30's: From Proletarian to People's Front Literature, "New International," 13 (July 1947), 150-55.
The Communist International's formula for novels in the early 1930's required correct social motives and an explicit political orientation, views that were sidetracked in the popular front period. Any skeptic of the Moscow trials, however, remained "an enemy of the people." Literary criticism by the official left has nothing to do with literature.

F35 .... "The Road Between." New York: Vanguard, 1949. 463 pp.
A novel about a writer in the 1930's who struggles to survive and preserve his integrity against commercial and political (Communist Party) pressures.

F36 .... "Yet Other Waters." New York: Vanguard, 1952. 414 pp.
An anticommunist novel, of a semi-autobiographical nature, centering around the relationship of the writer to the communist movement in the 1930's. Though the protagonist, a novelist, was never a member of the Party, he is torn between attraction to its stated aims and repulsion at its rigid control of thought and art. When he finally breaks with his Party friends, he is vilified in the left-wing papers and reviews.

F37 .... "Reflections at Fifty and Other Essays." New York: Vanguard, 1954. 223 pp.
A collection of essays, including "Literature—Free or in Bondage" (pp. 22-34) on the relationship between literature and politics, in the USSR and in the U.S. This essay includes comments on Albert Maltz's plea in the "New Masses" of February 12, 1946, for more freedom for the writer, the bitter attacks on him in the Party press, and his subsequent "confessions."

F38 FAST, Howard "The American: A Middle Western Legend." New York: Duell, Sloan and Pearce, 1946. 337 pp.
A novel, Marxist in spirit, about the life and times of John Peter Atlgeld, featuring the Haymarket Affair and Altgeld's pardoning of the surviving convicted anarchists.

F39 .... Art and Politics, "New Masses," 48 (Feb. 26, 1946), 6-8.
Albert Maltz is charged (see "What Shall We Ask of Writers?" in "New Masses," Feb. 12, 1946) with seeking to liquidate Marxist and all progressive creative writing, and with advocating the artist's retreat from politics on the ground that art and politics do not mix. This would mean exiling himself from civilization and therefore abandoning art.

F40 .... Toward People's Standards in Art, "New Masses," 49 (May 7, 1946), 16-18.
Reprint of a paper read at a symposium on "Art is a Weapon," held in New York City, April 18, 1946. Standards in art are determined most basically by the economic system and the class structure. Great artists express the highest objective reality of their time in masterly fashion. We can use art as a weapon only by understanding the standards of the people.

F41 .... Dreiser's Short Stories, "New Masses," 60 (Sept. 3, 1946), 11-12.
An evaluation of Dreiser's work by a communist writer and literary critic, who asserts that Dreiser has no peer in the American short story and is a unique genius in American letters. The key to Dreiser the artist is compassion, which led him to become a champion of Russia and to join the Communist Party of the U.S.

F42 .... "Clarkton: A Novel." New York: Duell, Sloan & Pearce, 1947. 239 pp.
The story of a postwar strike in a one-industry town in Massachusetts, presenting a group of communists as human beings with quite human virtues and shortcomings.

F43 .... "May Day 1947." New York: United May Day Committee, 1947. 13 pp.
Recalling the glorious history of May Day, the author urges readers to protest, this May Day, the fall in workers' wages, the emergence of antilabor legislation, Red-baiting, and the effort to outlaw the Communist Party.

F44 .... "Departure, and Other Stories." Boston: Little, Brown, 1949. 238 pp.
A collection of short stories by a leading communist writer, who presents communists as good and heroic human beings. The book is dedicated to the men of the Abraham Lincoln Brigade.

F45   FAST, Howard. "Intellectuals and the Fight for Peace." New York: Masses & Mainstream, 1949. 32 pp.
A polemic against American intellectuals who have retreated in the battle against injustice and who today, because of fear, are either mute or have climbed on the anticommunist bandwagon. Intellectuals must realize that the attack on the Communist Party is part of the attack upon themselves.

F46   .... Cultural Forces Rally against the Warmakers, "Political Affairs," 28 (May 1949), 29-38.
A report on the Cultural and Scientific Conference for World Peace held in New York City, March 1949, which was a success despite the disruptive efforts of the State Department, Trotskyites, and renegades. The resolution adopted by the conference provides a coalition platform for the peace movement.

F47   .... "Literature and Reality." New York: International Publishers, 1950. 128 pp. Ref. notes.
Marxist aesthetic criticism, defending the concept of socialist realism in literature. Realism is a matter of content, not just form. Bourgeois realism is simply formalism, a superficial realistic method that is a retreat from the struggles of humanity. Socialist realism, on the other hand, is a result of the struggle for truth. In order for the writer today to write literature, he must face up to the reality of communism, and love mankind and freedom.

F48   .... We Have Kept Faith, "Masses & Mainstream," 3 (July 1950), 23-28.
One of the board of directors of the Joint Anti-Fascist Refugee Committee, sentenced to prison for refusal to produce its records to the House Committee on Un-American Activities, reviews the case and defends their action. He asserts that they and others are being jailed to clear the ground for a new world war, that this is the last moment before fascism.

F49   .... "May Day, 1951," New York: United Labor and People's Committee for May Day, 1951. 14 pp.
Publicizing the 1951 May Day march, the author, a leading Party literary figure, declares that the march will be for peace, freedom, equality, and the Constitution.

F50   .... "Peekskill, U.S.A.: A Personal Experience." New York: Civil Rights Congress, 1951. 127 pp.
A procommunist version of the riots at Peekskill, N.Y., where Paul Robeson appeared twice for outdoor concerts, both times being attacked, together with his audience, by local anticommunist groups. Such actions are denounced as portents of the imminent peril of fascism.

F51   .... "Spain and Peace." New York: Joint Anti-Fascist Refugee Committee, n.d. [1951?]. 17 pp.
A pamphlet recalling the gallant battle of the Spanish Loyalists against the Hitler-Mussolini-Franco Axis and hailing the March 1951 general strike in Barcelona. Describing terror and poverty in Spain, the author condemns the actions by the Truman government to cement a military and economic alliance between the U.S. and Franco.

F52   ..., and others. "Steve Nelson: A Tribute by 14 Famous Authors." New York: Provisional Committee To Free Steve Nelson, n.d. [1952]. 32 pp.
A tribute to the Pittsburgh communist currently being tried under the Smith Act. There are poems about his heroism, essays of reminiscences of his work in Spain,

condemnation of his persecution, and appeals to him to remain steadfast in his hour of trial. Among the contributors are Howard Fast, I. F. Stone, Luis Aragon, John Howard Lawson, Alvah Bessie, Albert Kahn, William Patterson, and Albert Maltz.

F53   .... "Silas Timberman." New York: Blue Heron Press, 1954. 311 pp.
A novel about a liberal college professor who signed a petition against the atom bomb circulated by communists during the Korean War period, and who spoke at a protest meeting when another faculty member was suspended. Following his appearance before a Senate subcommittee headed by a chairman modeled on McCarthy, he was wrongly indicted for perjury and sentenced to jail. (A Party member when he wrote this novel, Fast left the Party in the fall of 1956 after Khrushchev's revelations on Stalin.)

F54   .... A Letter from Howard Fast, "New Leader," 39 (July 30, 1956), 16-18.
Replying to an open letter from Eugene Lyons ("New Leader," July 9, 1956), Fast defends the role of American communism despite the Party's shortcomings, and lists evils in American society. (In a rejoinder, pp. 18-20, Lyons asserts that Fast is shouting down his doubts and feelings of guilt.)

F55   .... "The Naked God: The Writer and the Communist Party." New York: Praeger, 1957. 197 pp.
The account by a writer, long a member of the Party, of his reasons for joining, his experiences while a member, his resistance to the dissolution of his beliefs, and his final break occasioned by the Khrushchev report on the bestialities of Stalin, including the anti-Semitism of the Stalinist regime. He writes at length about his ordeal as a creative writer while under Party discipline. Despite his disillusionment with the communist movement, he retains his beliefs in socialism, justice, and brotherhood. (Excerpts were published in the "Saturday Review," November 16, 1957.)

F56   .... My Decision, "Mainstream," 10 (March 1957), 29-38.
The author's explanation of his break with the Party. He was shocked by the horror of Khrushchev's report on the Stalin era; nine months later, this "socialism by slaughter and terror" is still going on. The communist movement here is a party to this guilt, its very organization leading to a brutalized practice of power. (Comment by the editors appears on pp. 39-47.)

F57   .... The Only Honorable Thing a Communist Can Do, "Progressive," 22 (March 1958), 35-38.
The transcript of Fast's television interview with Martin Agronsky, shortly after the novelist broke with the Party. Fast asserts that during his fellow-traveling period, before he joined the Party in 1943, he was fearful of the communist threat to freedom. Fascism, however, was an even bigger threat during that period. The Khrushchev revelations destroyed his faith in the communist movement.

F58   FAULK, John Henry. "Fear on Trial." New York: Simon and Schuster, 1964. 398 pp.
An account of the experiences of a radio performer, active in the American Federation of Television and Radio Artists, who was falsely accused of procommunist sympathy by AWARE, Inc., an organization that combatted communists in the entertainment and communications industries. The leaders and supporters of AWARE, defeated in an AFTRA election, retaliated by charging Faulk and his as-

sociates with communist sympathies, bringing pressure on companies to cease sponsoring Faulk's show. The book describes the lawsuit that Faulk filed and won, in a fight that lasted over an eight-year period.

F59   FAULKNER, Stanley. Security Program in the Armed Forces, "Lawyers Guild Review," 15 (Winter 1955-56), 145-52.
Criticism of the operation of the security program in the armed forces since Senator McCarthy's attack on the Army for its favorable treatment of Major Irving Peress. Steps in the security program in the armed forces are traced, and the effects of a less-than-honorable discharge are outlined. Legal issues presented to the courts are listed, and the cases reviewed.

F60   FEDERATION OF AMERICAN SCIENTISTS, Committee on Loyalty and Security. "The Fort Monmouth Security Investigations, Aug. 1953-April 1954." The Federation, 1954. 49 pp. Reprinted by the Atomic Scientists of Chicago as "The Scientists Examine the Investigation."
A detailed report of the Fort Monmouth investigations by a group of scientists, most of them connected with Yale University. They present a chronology of events, describe the engineering laboratories and the Fort, and analyze the security threat as charged first by McCarthy and then by the Army. They conclude that the damage to our security through loss of key personnel and the disruptive effort on research was tremendous, pointing out that no charges of espionage were made and that most accusations were irresponsible.

F61   FEELY, Raymond T. "Just What Is Communism?" New York: Paulist Press, n.d. [1935]. 32 pp.
A presentation of the Catholic case against communism, emphasizing its atheism, its materialist philosophy of life, and its destruction of personal rights. Communism in the USSR is viewed as a Godless religion.

F62   .... "Communism and Union Labor: Where Do You Stand?" New York: Paulist Press, 1937. 48 pp.
The author, a Jesuit at the University of San Francisco, urges union members to get rid of the communist "phonies" who run their unions, who use workers for their own selfish purposes. He depicts the bitter life of labor in the Soviet Union, and refers his readers to books which describe the tactics of the communists in detail. He asks Congress to expose the communists, so that workers can cleanse their labor unions of these traitors.

F63   .... "Fascism—Communism—the U.S.A." New York: Paulist Press, n.d. [1937] 32 pp. Bibliog.
A Catholic view of the contrasts and parallels of fascism and communism, emphasizing the essential elements of each. The author argues that Americans can achieve economic security while retaining natural liberties.

F64   .... "Communism Today or Red Fascism." New York: Paulist Press, 1945. 47 pp. Bibliog.
A Catholic pamphlet on the theme that communism is a red form of fascism that crushes civil liberties and political opposition, and that is essentially atheistic, though religious persecution in Russia was lessened as a war measure. Despite the alleged dissolution of the Third International, world communism is portrayed as more insidious than ever, and a grave threat to our victory in Europe.

F65   FEINSTEIN, Isidor. How to Make a Riot, "New Republic," 79 (June 27, 1934), 178-80.
Censure of the police for attacking a demonstration of the unemployed in front of relief headquarters in New York

City, and of the newspapers for inaccurate and slanted news coverage. The United Action Committee, which led the demonstration, is partly communist in leadership and membership.

F66   FELHABER, Elmer. "The Coal Miners and You." New York: New Century, 1950. 15 pp.
A defense of the striking coal miners by the editor of the Ohio edition of "The Worker," who views the attacks on the strike as part of a conspiracy against the entire labor movement, peace, and the Bill of Rights. Emphasis is placed on aid given the strikers by the Communist Party and front organizations.

F67   FENDEL, J. Lenin and the American Labor Movement, "Workers Monthly," 5 (April 1926), 256-58; (May), 319-22.
Lenin viewed the U.S. as a highly developed capitalist country, whose bourgeois democracy was in reality a bourgeois dictatorship. The battle in the U.S. must be led by a revolutionary vanguard of a proletariat that is internally divided and politically and organizationally backward.

F68   FERGUSON, Homer, and KILGORE, Harley M. (Theodore Granik, moderator). Controlling Red Activities, "American Forum of the Air," 13 (April 8, 1950), 1-11.
Senator Ferguson asserts that his bill, co-sponsored by Senators Mundt and Nixon, would reach only those who enter into the communist conspiracy, not those who merely think or speak. Senator Kilgore, opposing the measure, fears that it would drive communists underground and make martyrs of them; and that the loose definition of "communist" would permit application to others in a period of hysteria.

F69   ..., and BIRKHEAD, Leon M. (Orville Hitchcock, moderator). How Should We Deal with American Communists and Front Organizations? "Town Meeting," 16 (Sept. 5, 1950). 16 pp.
Ferguson defends current legislative proposals as necessary to force the Party into the open and prevent its conspiratorial activities. While granting congressional duty to legislate on conspiracy, espionage, and sabotage, Birkhead asserts that current proposals would restrict advocacy of ideas.

F70   ..., and MUNDT, Karl. The Internal Security Act: Joint Statement Upholding Bill, "Vital Speeches of the Day," 17 (Oct. 15, 1950), 6-9.
A rebuttal of the President's veto message by two senators, who answer each of his seven points against the legislation. They also analyze the bill, contending that, far from weakening our liberties, it will strengthen democracy in its battle against totalitarian communism.

F71   FERGUSON, I. E. The Communist Party Convention, "Communist" (organ of the Communist Party of America), 1 (Sept. 27, 1919), 4-5 ff.
An account of the founding convention of the Communist Party of America, at which three groups were represented: the foreign language federations, the Michigan organization earlier expelled from the Socialist Party, and the former National Left Wing Council of the SP. Factional issues among the three groups are described, as are the constitution and leadership of the CPA.

F72   FETTER, Frank W. Witch Hunt in the Lincoln Country, "South Atlantic Quarterly," 53 (July 1954), 349-57.
An analysis of sources of support for and opposition to the Broyles bills against subversion in Illinois, 1947-1953. The bills' author, Paul Broyles, was spokesman for a sec-

tor of white, Protestant, Anglo-Saxon, small-town and rural America. Opposition came largely from minorities—teachers, clergymen, and those with a background of wealth and education. Broyles is visionless and sincere, whereas McCarthy is shrewd and scheming.

F73   FEY, Harold E. Catholicism Fights Communism, "Christian Century," 62 (Jan. 1945), 13-15.
An appraisal of efforts of the Catholic Church to stem the growth of communism in labor unions through the National Catholic Welfare Conference, the Association of Catholic Trade Unionists, the Catholic Labor Alliance, and the Catholic Worker group. (One of a series, "Can Catholicism Win America?")

F74   .... Bishop Oxnam's Challenge, "Christian Century," 70 (Aug. 5, 1953), 885-87.
The executive editor of the "Christian Century" describes and analyzes the confrontation of the House Committee on Un-American Activities by a most courageous churchman, G. Bromley Oxnam. He denounces the Committee for not apologizing for its unsubstantiated accusations.

F75   FIEDLER, Leslie A. Hiss, Chambers and the Age of Innocence: Who Was Guilty—and of What? "Commentary," 12 (Aug. 1951), 109-19.
A review of the Hiss-Chambers case in the light of the self-images of the two leading figures. Hiss lied, instead of presenting his higher allegiance to the Soviet Union as his defense, because his was the popular-front mind at bay, incapable of honesty. Unless we understand this, we will not be able to move from a liberalism of innocence to a liberalism of responsibility.

F76   .... A Postscript to the Rosenberg Case, "Encounter," 1 (Oct. 1953), 12-21.
An analysis of world reaction to the Rosenberg case, appearing in a magazine published in England. To their supporters the Rosenbergs were symbols, not people. The Rosenbergs also thought of themselves as cases rather than people. They committed their kind of treason because they were incapable of telling treason from devotion.

F77   .... "An End to Innocence: Essays on Culture and Politics." Boston: Beacon, 1955. 214 pp. Ind.
Part one, "An Age of Innocents," consists of three chapters—one on Hiss and Chambers (pp. 3-24), one on the Rosenbergs (pp. 25-45), and one on "McCarthy and the Intellectuals" (pp. 46-87). Hiss is viewed as the embodiment of the popular-front era. The discussion of the Rosenbergs, assuming their guilt, discusses the legendary case later presented by the communists to world opinion.

F78   FIELD, B. J., and HERBERG, Will. The Crisis in Communism, "Modern Monthly," 7 (June 1933), 279-88.
Two criticisms of the official communist movement, one by a Trotskyist and the other by a Lovestoneite. Communists, according to the former, must either adopt the Trotskyist view or give up active support of the world revolution. The Lovestoneite view is that sectarianism has demoralized and made impotent the official communist parties outside the USSR.

F79   FIELD, Ben. The Black Belt, "New Masses," 8 (July 1933), 8-11.
A first-hand report on conditions in the Black Belt of the South, with impressions of working and living conditions among Texas cotton-share tenants, cotton pickers in Georgia, sugar-cane workers in Louisiana, and sap dippers, sorghum grinders, and tobacco and rice workers. Everywhere anger is slowly gathering among white and Negro farmers, sharecroppers, and laborers.

F80   FIELD, Frederick V. "The People Are Sovereign." New York: American Peace Mobilization, 1941. 14 pp.
Call to an "American People's Meeting" in the fight against war, to be held in New York City, April 5-6, 1941. The basic demands of this meeting are to oppose World War II, defend democracy, work for the rights of labor, and promote a people's peace in support of the peace policy of the Soviet Union. (The American Peace Mobilization was the Party's peace front during the period of the Hitler-Stalin pact, 1939-41.)

F81   .... "China's Greatest Crisis." New York: New Century, 1945. 32 pp.
An account of the political and military crisis in China, told from the point of view of the Chinese communists, who are said to lead the national struggle for democratic, anti-Japanese unity. Roosevelt is applauded for trying to bring about a government of all elements in China willing to fight the Japanese.

F82   .... Mexico City—On the Road from Yalta to San Francisco, "Political Affairs," 24 (April 1945), 318-28.
At the Mexico City conference the U.S. no longer looked on Latin-American countries as in its sphere of influence. It is now concerned with their part in eradicating fascism. However, the conference did not take stern enough action against Latin-American fascists, especially in Argentina. The conference recognized that Latin-American countries need American aid to develop beyond semi-feudalism.

F83   .... San Francisco Balance Sheet, "Political Affairs," 24 (Aug. 1945), 675-87.
A discussion of the United Nations Charter, drafted at the San Francisco Conference. The basis of the Charter is Big Five collaboration, which is guaranteed by the veto in the Security Council. The reactionaries succeeded in seating Argentina in the UN, protecting colonialism, and excluding the World Federation of Trade Unions.

F84   .... The Record of American Imperialism in China, "Political Affairs," 25 (Jan. 1946), 31-41.
American intervention against Chinese democracy is part of a general pattern of American imperialism's foreign policy. American policy in China is traced, from the "old imperialism" of the nineteenth century through the period when American monopoly came of age. With its main competitors drastically weakened by the war, American imperialism today seeks to monopolize the China field.

F85   .... American Imperialist Policy in the Far East, "Political Affairs," 25 (Nov. 1946), 988-1000.
American imperialist policy has been carried furthest in the Far East, where the U.S. position is virtually unchallenged by its imperialist rivals. The vista opened here to American imperialists ends with world domination. American imperialism in the Far East must be destroyed on the picket lines at home, as well as by the fight of the heroic Chinese people.

F86   .... The New China Program of the American Interventionists, "Political Affairs," 27 (Jan. 1948), 51-64.
U.S. imperialists are hysterical because the military and political initiative has passed to the democratic forces in China. William C. Bullitt's report, an imperialist classic, would make China a U.S. colony. The U.S. should withdraw all military forces from China and stop all aid to the reactionary Nanking government.

F87   .... Wall Street's Aggression in Korea and the

Struggle for Peace, "Political Affairs," 29 (Sept. 1950), 15-29.

American imperialism's assault upon the Korean people is part of Wall Street's program of military aggression against the whole of Eastern Asia. Syngman Rhee's police state in South Korea was well prepared for its aggression on behalf of American imperialism. The USSR has presented Korean peace proposals to the UN Security Council. American workers should be the foundation of a vast U.S. peace movement.

F88   FIELD, Frederick V. China, Korea and the Struggle for Peace, "Political Affairs," 29 (Dec. 1950), 16-24.

The invasion of Korea by American imperialists has brought the whole world to the edge of disaster. U.S. forces have violated the Chinese border, following Japan in attacking China from Korea. The AFL and CIO labor bosses have sold themselves to imperialism. Peace-loving Americans must be organized into a broad and powerful movement.

F89   FIELD, Noel. Hitching Our Wagon to a Star, "Mainstream," 14 (Jan. 1961), 3-17.

The thoughts and experiences of the former State Department official who was imprisoned in Hungary from 1949 to 1954 on charges, which he calls false, of espionage. Field reveals that he and his wife had become communists in thought and action by the time World War II began. After their release from prison they decided to remain in Hungary, their views unchanged.

F90   FIELDING, Bernard. Communism across the Counter, "Plain Talk," 1 (Jan. 1947), 19-23.

An exposé of the five department-store locals of the United Retail, Wholesale, and Department Store Employees that are controlled by communists, and that work with four other communist-dominated locals in New York City against the leadership of the national union. The author tells how the communist leadership persecutes opponents and retains control.

F91   FILLER, Louis. Political Literature: A Post Mortem, "Southwest Review," 39 (Summer 1954), 185-93.

An assertion that the writers of the 1930's wrote poorly because they were more interested in a "correct line" than in literature. Art, consciously or unconsciously, became a class weapon. Our present-day free, if largely aimless, writers are preferred for their individualism, wit, and willingness to write about dignity and love.

F92   FILLEY, Jane. "An American Holiday: May Day 1939." New York: United May Day Provisional Committee, 1939. 14 pp.

Tracing the history of May Day from the fight for the eight-hour day in 1886 until the present, the author appeals for the unity of all workers, AFL and CIO, on this May Day.

F93   FINCH, Roy. An Observer Reports on the Communist Convention, "Liberation," 2 (March 1957), 4-6.

One of the noncommunist observers at the recent Party national convention records his impressions. The Khrushchev revelations about Stalin and the Russian action in Hungary have greatly weakened the Party. The demand for democracy within the Party was overwhelming.

F94   FINE, Fred. Against Opportunism in Practice, "Political Affairs," 27 (Aug. 1948), 743-49.

A discussion of organizational and ideological weaknesses of the Party which must be remedied at the national con-

vention, to be held August 3-6, 1948. Formalism and opportunism are attacked, and emphasis on the department and the shop is advocated. Specific changes in Party organization and activities are proposed.

F95   .... Tasks before the Peace Camp, "Political Affairs," 28 (Oct. 1949), 1-18.

A report to a meeting of the Party's national committee, September 16-18, 1949, asserting that a peace movement is growing here as the U.S. arms its allies in preparation for war against the Soviet Union. A people's democratic front, uniting all honest partisans for peace, must be built. The principal task now is to defeat Truman's military-aid bill, designed to rearm Western Europe.

F96   .... Notes on the 1950 Elections, "Political Affairs," 29 (May 1950), 131-37.

In the 1950 congressional elections, the Democrats will pursue Wall Street objectives while proclaiming a liberal platform. The Progressive Party must not retreat from its peace platform. The Communist Party will work for the Progressive Party wherever the latter runs candidates. Elsewhere it will support candidates who oppose war, the Taft-Hartley Act, Negro discrimination, and anticommunist legislation.

F97   .... The Anti-Labor Drive and Business Unionism, "Political Affairs," 36 (June 1957), 1-15.

The struggle against the open-shop drive of the corporations and the movement for clean, democratic, and more militant unions must go hand in hand. Big Business hopes to split the labor movement into warring factions, break up the merger, and turn the country's antimonopoly sentiment away from itself and against labor.

F98   FINE, Nathan. Left and Right in the Needle Trades Unions, "Nation," 118 (June 4, 1924), 639-40.

A discussion of the bitter and persistent left-right struggle at the conventions of the ILGWU, the Amalgamated Clothing Workers, and the Fur Workers. The heads of the three unions oppose the vicious tactics of the left against the leadership, and will not tolerate the dictation of outside organizations. The ILGWU convention unseated sixteen communist delegates.

F99   FINEBERG, S. Andhil. "The Role of Religion in Combating Communism." New York: American Jewish Committee, 1951. 12 pp.

An address by the Director of Community Services of the American Jewish Committee to an anticommunist conference in March 1951. Communism is attacked as a totalitarian creed, antithetical to all religious precepts; and communist fraud, deceit, and immorality are declared opposed to all religious teachings. Religion must expose the communists and preserve American democracy.

F100   .... "The Rosenberg Case: Fact and Fiction." New York: Oceana Publications, 1953. 159 pp. App. Ind.

A detailed account of the Rosenberg case, affirming the guilt of the Rosenbergs, and condemning the communist attempt outside the court room to prove them innocent. The author reviews the testimony and the verdict of guilty, commending the quality of justice displayed. He describes at length the post-trial efforts of the Party to convince the public of the Rosenbergs' innocence, analyzing the activities of the National Committee to Secure Justice in the Rosenberg Case.

F101   .... They Screamed for Justice, "American Legion Magazine," 55 (July 1953), 22-23 ff.

An account of the activities and conviction of Julius and Ethel Rosenberg, central figures in a World War II spy ring now under sentence of death. The drive to save them, started by the Kremlin, is managed by the National Committee to Secure Justice in the Rosenberg Case, the largest and most successful communist front in the U.S. The communists ignored the case until it was evident that the Rosenbergs would not turn informers.

F102 FINEMAN, Hayim. Jew-Baiting and the "New Masses," "Jewish Frontier," 2 (Jan. 1935), 7-9.
Criticism of the articles on anti-Semitism by John Spivak as superficial, and as ignoring anti-Semitism among workers and Negroes and in the liberal professions. The communists use the issue of anti-Semitism merely to exploit Jewish agony for Party expansion.

F103 FINKELSTEIN, Sidney. "Art and Society." New York: International Publishers, 1947. 288 pp. Bibliog. notes. Ind.
A Marxist analysis of art and society, condemning romanticism, classicism, and abstraction, along with "art for art's sake," and praising socialist realism, which reveals the process of conflict and resolution that makes up the movement of history. Folk art and nationalism in art are healthy when directly connected with political movements for national freedom. American art is stifled by industrialization and monopolization of art production, whereas the USSR has made great cultural achievements.

F104 .... "Jazz: A People's Music." New York: Citadel Press, 1948. 278 pp. Ind.
An interpretation of jazz by the music critic of the "New Masses," discussing the sound of jazz, the blues and the folk song, improvisation and composition, the pop tune, styles in bands, experimental music, and the new jazz. The author condemns the popular-tune market for restricting the talent and scope of jazz artists, and sees in jazz almost limitless possibilities for use in larger forms of composition.

F105 .... The New Criticism, "Masses & Mainstream," 3 (Dec. 1950), 76-86.
A new body of writing has sprung up since World War II to fit the needs of monopoly capital and destroy the humanist achievements of the past. It is a reactionary creed, embraced by French Catholic intellectuals, British reactionaries, and Southern writers of aristocratic pretensions.

F106 .... Psychoanalysis and the Arts, "Masses & Mainstream," 4 (Aug. 1951), 69-79.
Criticism of all three phases of the psychoanalytic theory of history and the arts: the original Freudian view of the artist as a neurotic; Jung's theory of the collective unconscious, which laid a theoretical base for Nazi propaganda; and the "social-democratic" belief that each cultural stage embodies its own neurosis in its art.

F107 .... Dreiser: The Hollywood Twist Again, "Masses & Mainstream," 4 (Oct. 1951), 11-14.
Hollywood, in filming Dreiser's "An American Tragedy" as "A Place in the Sun," completely distorted the meaning of this powerful novel by a man who proudly announced in 1945 that he was a communist.

F108 .... "How Music Expresses Ideas." London: Lawrence & Wishart, 1952. 128 pp. Gloss. Ref. notes.
The art and music critic of the "Daily Worker" writes on the development of music, applying the standards of socialist realism to contemporary music. Chapter 10 on "Music in the United States" (pp. 106-18) states that the greatest, almost only, genuinely American music is that of the Negro people. The author regrets that in America the composer and musician are isolated, with low income,

and that concert halls and opera houses are for the rich. A basic problem is the barrier between popular and art music, said to be higher in the U.S. than in any other country.

F109 .... Abstract Art Today: Doodles, Dollars and Death, "Masses & Mainstream," 5 (Sept. 1952), 22-31.
An attack on abstract art as decadent. The author criticizes museums exhibiting such art, the artists themselves, the art critics who cannot see that abstract art is bankrupt. The hope of art in America lies in artists who are mastering realism, making their art a force in the struggle for peace and democracy.

F110 .... The Negro Composer, "Masses & Mainstream," 6 (Oct. 1953), 52-58.
Exploitation of the Negro is true of the concert as well as the jazz field; classical, like popular, music, must speak a language that the average listener can understand. The music industry, which tried to choke off the best in Negro jazz and classical music, is challenged by modern jazz and bebop. The commercial musical world must be fought.

F111 .... "Realism in Art." New York: International Publishers, 1954. 190 pp. Ref. notes. Ind.
A Marxist esthetic critique in which the author, art critic of the "Daily Worker," defends the concept of socialist realism in art. Tracing the development of art from primitive society to the present time, he sees art as a force aiding mankind's adjustment to the reality of life. He attacks the corruptive influence of abstract art in America, and concludes that realism in art, by showing the humanity of people the world over as against obscurantism, is helping to bring peace and the unlimited development of people. (This thesis of Finkelstein is opposed, in an article in "Mainstream," by a group of "progressive" California artists who protest replacement of esthetic by political judgment. See "Painters on the Left," in "Mainstream," Aug. 1957.)

F112 .... How Art Began, "Masses & Mainstream," 7 (June 1954), 15-26.
A Marxist view of primitive art as arising in primitive communal life, connected with objects of physical utility or with rituals based on magical beliefs. The function of art is to make society conscious of its world, its real being, its potentialities. With the rise of antagonistic classes, art became subject to classes and class struggle.

F113 .... The World of Science Fiction, "Masses & Mainstream," 8 (April 1955), 48-57.
A review of the increasing popularity of science fiction, whose contents suggest the fears in people's minds in the age of the atom bomb. It is a gadget science, haunted by the myth of a robot or Frankenstein which gets out of hand; this is similar to the real fear of the people in a country that is dominated by a handful of multi-million dollar corporations.

F114 .... John Sloan: American Painter, "Masses & Mainstream," 8 (July 1955), 17-27.
A eulogy to the painter who died in 1951 at the age of 80. Art editor of the "Masses," he contributed more than 50 drawings and covers to it. His importance in the art world is appraised, as is his political point of view.

F115 .... The Artist and His World, "Mainstream," 10 (Sept. 1957), 37-46.
A reply to the group of California painters who criticized his book, "Realism in Art." Seeking to clarify the meaning of realism, Finkelstein calls it the duty of a social-minded critic to point to the work of artists whose work

expresses the brotherhood of peoples, though those who express only subjectivity and anguish also deserve respect.

F116 FINKELSTEIN, Sidney. "Composer and Nation: The Folk Heritage of Music." New York: International Publishers, 1960. 333 pp. Ref. notes. Ind.
A view of music as national expression, based on its folk heritage, and reflecting class structure and antagonism. Problems of a people's music in the USSR are examined, as is American jazz as folk and art music.

F117 FINNEGAN, Les. The Last Days of the UE, "New Leader," 33 (April 1, 1950), 5 ff.
An assertion that the United Electrical Workers, which the communists have staffed almost completely, is evaporating after ouster from the CIO. It has lost over 200,000 members in five months, with bargaining rights in many plants being won by the newly-formed IUE. Communism's greatest field day in an American union is ending.

F118 FISCHER, Ernst. "Is This a War for Freedom?" New York: Workers Library, 1940. 39 pp.
The communist view of the European war during the Nazi-Soviet pact period as unjust and imperialistic, to be opposed by the workers. The antifascism of the British imperialists is said to be really anticommunism. Only the Soviet Union works untiringly for peace. The working class should struggle against the bourgeoisie to end capitalism and the imperialist war.

F119 .... The People's Front of Yesterday—The National Freedom Front of Today and Tomorrow, "Communist," 21 (Oct. 1942), 841-48.
When formation of People's Fronts in a number of countries defeated efforts of reactionaries to sow disunity by Red-baiting, the reactionaries tried to subjugate the masses in a fascist dictatorship. The Party proposes that the present war-inspired unity of the masses be continued after the war in a National Freedom Front.

F120 FISCHER, Stephen. Notes on the CIO Convention, "Monthly Review," 1 (Dec. 1949), 245-47.
The CIO convention, engaging in a five-day orgy of attacks on the left, expelled the UE, its third largest affiliate, and authorized the executive board to expel other unions on the grounds of communism. These powers are dangerous to any future minority group. The convention was dominated by adherents of Americans for Democratic Action and the Catholic Church.

F121 FISH, Hamilton. The Menace of Communism, "Annals of the American Academy of Political and Social Science," 156 (July 1931), 54-61.
The New York Congressman, chairman of a congressional investigating committee, outlines the principles and objectives of communism, gives a brief historical sketch, explains conditions of labor in Russia and methods of communists, and shows communism's incompatibility with the American way of life. He defends the Fish Committee's proposal that the CPUSA be outlawed. (These proposals are criticized by Jerome Davis in the same issue of the "Annals.")

F122 .... "The Challenge of World Communism." Milwaukee: Bruce Publishing Co., 1946. 224 pp. App.
A former chairman of the House Special Committee to Investigate Communist Activities seeks to awaken the people to the dangers of communism. While most of the book deals with communism in other parts of the world, chapter 6 (pp. 136-78) is on "Communism in America."

Fish defends his opposition in 1940 to World War II because it sacrificed American lives for communism, and condemns the past foreign policy of "communism's friend," Franklin D. Roosevelt. He explains the nature of the Party, points to its influence in the CIO, and asserts that it will use any camouflage to carry out its aim to sovietize America. In an appendix he urges formation of a national anticommunist organization, for which he solicits suggestions and contributions.

F123 .... "The Red Plotters." New York: Domestic and Foreign Affairs Publishers, 1947. 103 pp.
An expose, by a former chairman of the House Special Committee to Investigate Communist Activities, of the communist conspiracy directed from Moscow. In chapter 2, "Communism in America" (pp. 17-35), he charges that a conspiracy of radicals and communists, all now in the Democratic Party, seeks to sovietize America and end private enterprise and property. He urges Christians to form a united front against communism as anti-Christ. He proposes that communists be cleaned out of all government positions, and that labor unions, colleges, and schools do the same. He offers help in forming a militant, nationwide, anticommunist organization.

F124 FISHER, Hilda. Labor and the Communists, "Current History," 12 (March 1947), 199-204.
A survey of labor's attitude to recognition of Soviet Russia, 1917-33. The AFL's opposition to recognition was based on its general foreign policy view, as well as on its reaction to communist "boring from within." Among the more influential unions, the Amalgamated Clothing Workers led the pro-recognition movement.

F125 FISKE, Mel. "McCarthyism in the Courts: The Story of the Steve Nelson Frame-Up." New York: Provisional Committee to Free Steve Nelson, 1953. 30 pp.
Denunciation of the trial and 20-year sentence of Steve Nelson, Pittsburgh communist leader, as an example of ruthless exploitation of the communist scare by politicians. An indictment, not only of Judge Michael Musmanno, but also of the Mellons and Morgans who control the 28 largest Pittsburgh industries, and who are said to be aiming, through the anticommunist front, to reestablish the old-fashioned, antilabor spy system.

F126 FITCH, John A. The CIO and Its Communists, "Survey," 85 (Dec. 1949), 642-47.
An account of the crackdown by the CIO national convention on the unions that consistently followed the communist line. Events leading up to the convention action, and the specific charges against communist-led unions, are reviewed. Much depends on whether the members of the expelled unions are brought back into newly chartered CIO organizations.

F127 FITCH, Robert E. Heresy Trial in California, "Christianity and Crisis," 10 (June 12, 1950), 77-79.
A review of the loyalty oath issue at the University of California, criticizing some of the regents for hysteria and arrogance, and some of the faculty for unrealism and irresponsibility. While a theoretical Marxist may meet academic standards, a member of the Party is disqualified by the Party's contempt for liberty and truth.

F128 FLANAGAN, Hallie. "Arena." New York: Duell, Sloan and Pearce, 1940. 475 pp. Bibliog.
The story of the Federal Theatre Project written by its former director, following its abolition on charges of communist infiltration. Viewing the Project as a pioneering effort to establish a people's theatre, she describes

its inception, activities, and achievements. She denies communist sympathy on her part or any infiltration by communist sympathizers or members.

F129 FLANAGAN, Hallie "What Was Federal Theatre?" Washington, D.C.: American Council on Public Affairs, 1940. 23 pp.

An appraisal of the Federal Theatre Project by its former director, stressing its human and economic achievements and its socially valuable service to the public. She gives a chronology of the events which led to investigation by a congressional committee and subsequent denial of appropriations.

F130 FLEISCHER, Louis. The International Economic Conference, "Political Affairs," 31 (May 1952), 1-10.

A report on the conference, held in Moscow, April 3-12, 1952, at which Russia offered to aid backward countries and increase trade with the U.S. and Western Europe. The trade offer was very welcome to European countries suffering from a dollar shortage. The U.S. government tried to keep Americans from attending, even though the purpose, by developing close relationships, was to help prevent war.

F131 FLEISCHMAN, Harry; KORNBLUH, Joyce Lewis; and SEGAL, Benjamin D. "Security, Civil Liberties and Unions." Foreword by William F. Schnitzler. New York: National Labor Service, 1956. 52 pp.

An analysis of the five official security programs in effect at this time, their influence upon the civil rights of Americans in general and union members in particular, and the part unions play in their administration. The authors are concerned over abuses in the administration of the security programs. Viewing the Fifth Amendment as a great privilege of a free people, they condemn the assumption that its use is a confession of guilt.

F132 FLEISHER, Henry. Frey's Red Scare Tales about CIO Filled with Errors, Distortions, "CIO News," 1 (Aug. 20, 1938), 3-5.

Criticism of John P. Frey of the AFL for his testimony before the House Committee on Un-American Activities, especially for making public a list of alleged communists in the CIO containing many errors.

F133 .... New C.I.O. Electrical Workers Union Launched, "CIO News," 12 (Dec. 5, 1949), 1 ff.

A report on the founding convention of the new electrical workers' union of the CIO, and on its plans for a campaign to oust the communist-controlled union from the industry. Enthusiastic comments are made on the spirit of the convention, and on the policies, goals, and potential strength of the union.

F134 .... 4 CP-Dominated Unions Expelled; Mine, Mill Now, 3 Others March 1st, "CIO News," 13 (Feb. 20, 1950), 6-7.

The four expelled unions are the Mine, Mill and Smelter Workers, the United Office and Professional Workers, the Food, Tobacco and Agricultural Workers, and the United Public Workers. A summary of CIO action with regard to communists since November is presented, along with an analysis of the hearings of these unions before the special trial committees.

F135 FLEMING, D. F. Are We Moving Toward Fascism? "Journal of Politics," 16 (Feb. 1954), 39-75.

A research professor at Vanderbilt University asserts that the current concern over Reds in America is manufactured by right-wing elements who are anxious to repress all nonconservative thought; and that obsessive anticommunism and enforced orthodoxy and loyalty are leading us toward fascism.

F136 FLETCHER, Charles, and VANCE, John. Unemployment and the Works Program in 1939, "Communist," 18 (Feb. 1939), 147-55.

An analysis of the country's economic situation and the relief program to show the need for increased relief expenditures. In addition, America needs a long-range program of public works and low-cost housing construction, along with improved social insurance, all financed with the wealth of monopoly capitalists.

F137 FLEXNER, Eleanor. "American Playwrights: 1918-1938: The Theatre Retreats from Reality." Pref. by John Gassner. New York: Simon and Schuster, 1938. 331 pp. Ind.

A study of two decades of the American theatre by an editor of "New Theatre" magazine. Chapter 7, "The New Realism" (pp. 283-309), deals with the social protest and militant labor plays of the depression 1930's. Among the playwrights discussed are John Howard Lawson, Clifford Odets, Albert Maltz, George Sklar, Elmer Rice, Irwin Shaw, and Marc Blitzstein.

F138 FLYNN, Elizabeth Gurley. "Debs, Haywood, Ruthenberg." New York: Workers Library, 1939. 48 pp.

Biographies by a prominent Party member and veteran radical of three U.S. radical leaders: Eugene V. Debs, perennial presidential candidate of the Socialist Party; William D. Haywood, leader of the Industrial Workers of the World; and Charles E. Ruthenberg, founder of the CPUSA.

F139 .... "I Didn't Raise My Boy to Be a Soldier—for Wall Street." New York: Workers Library, 1940. 15 pp.

A pamphlet addressed to women during the Hitler-Stalin pact period, calling the European war an unjust one and urging women to help form "The Yanks Are Not Coming Committees." The author proposes that the war be starved while America is fed, and that bankers and their sons fight to protect Wall Street's dollars.

F140 .... "Earl Browder, the Man from Kansas." New York: Workers Library, 1941. 30 pp.

Brief biography of Browder, presenting him as a home-grown radical, and written to combat the idea that all communists are foreigners. The author asks that Browder be freed from federal prison, where he is serving a sentence for a passport violation.

F141 .... "Coal Miners and the War." New York: Workers Library, 1942. 15 pp.

An assertion that, though miners all over the world seek to win the war and open a second western front, coal production here is hampered by John L. Lewis' evasive position on the war. A veteran Party leader appeals to U.S. coal miners to produce for victory in 1942.

F142 .... "Daughters of America: Ella Reeve Bloor and Anita Whitney." New York: Workers Library, 1942. 15 pp.

Written for a July fourth commemorative celebration for Anita Whitney and Ella Reeve (Mother) Bloor, this pamphlet gives an account of their lives, showing how they have struggled for political equality, economic security, and happiness in freedom for all people.

F143 .... "Women in the War." New York: Workers Library, 1942. 31 pp.

The communist position toward women during World War II, seeing their tasks as on the home front, as registering for war work, and as working side by side with men in the factories. Deploring past prejudice against women workers, the author calls for child-care centers, good housing, union organization, and equal pay for equal work.

F144   FLYNN, Elizabeth Gurley.   The New Role of Women in Industry, "Communist," 22 (April 1943), 348-57.
Citing the increasing employment of women in war industries, a veteran communist leader urges their participation in the trade union movement.

F145   . . . . "Women Have a Date with Destiny." New York: Workers Library, 1944.   31 pp.
A plea to women to register and vote for Roosevelt, as well as to support total victory, planning for reconversion, and the Teheran agreement. An example of the "win-the-war" line of the Party during World War II, before the onset of the cold war

F146   . . . . "Meet the Communists."   New York: CPUSA, 1946.   23 pp.
A recruiting pamphlet by a veteran American communist, who asserts that communists lead struggles everywhere for the rights of the people. Declaring that the U.S. has a ruthless and reactionary capitalist class and that poverty exists here in the midst of plenty, she appeals especially to veterans, Negroes, women, and youth to join the Party.

F147   . . . . "Woman's Place—In the Fight for a Better World." New York: New Century, 1947.   16 pp.
A leading woman Party leader calls on American women to insist on a lasting peace, and to end the "get tough" policy of the U.S. toward the Soviet Union. The author expresses confidence in the devotion of American women to the cause of peace.

F148   . . . . International Women's Day, 1947, "Political Affairs," 26 (March 1947), 216-20.
The history of International Women's Day, the program for the 1947 celebrations, and the communist position on women's rights.

F149   . . . . "The Twelve and You." New York: New Century, 1948.   23 pp.
The author denounces the Smith Act indictment of the leading communists, of whom she is one, asserting that it is not the communist leaders who are guilty of force and violence, but the oppressive capitalist system and the profiteers who swindle and starve the American family. She appeals for contributions for a defense fund.

F150   . . . . 1948—A Year of Inspiring Anniversaries for Women, "Political Affairs," 27 (March 1948), 259-65.
A review of American women's fight for equality on the 100th anniversary of the first Women's Equal Rights Convention and the publication of the "Communist Manifesto," and the fortieth anniversary of International Women's Day.

F151   . . . . They Must Go Free! "Political Affairs, 27 (Dec. 1948), 1075-81.
The indictment of the twelve Party leaders under the Smith Act is called an attack on the entire labor movement. The Truman Administration is responsible for this trial for advocacy of ideas. Mass protest must be mounted to compel dismissal of the indictments.

F152   . . . . "Labor's Own William Z. Foster: A Communist's Fifty Years of Working-Class Leadership and Struggle." New York: New Century, 1949. 48 pp.

A eulogistic biography of Foster which also gives highlights of Party history, particularly in the 1920's. Foster's efforts to unionize the steel industry after World War I are described, as is his leadership of the Trade Union Educational League and the Trade Union Unity League. He is praised as a great American as well as a communist trade union leader.

F153   . . . . "Stool-pigeon." New York: New Century, 1949.   23 pp.
An attack on the use of spies and stool-pigeons to give false testimony at the Smith Act trials of the communist leaders. The author charges that the spies and informers used in the case also spy on trade unions, and asserts that a fair hearing is impossible in this circus atmosphere.

F154   . . . . "Debs and Dennis: Fighters for Peace." New York: New Century, 1950.   24 pp.
A comparison of the conviction of Eugene Dennis for contempt of the Un-American Activities Committee with that of Debs thirty years earlier. Both men, the author says, opposed a bosses' war, and both had a federal jury stacked against them. She calls for amnesty for Dennis.

F155   . . . . "The Plot to Gag America." New York: New Century, 1950.   15 pp.
An analysis of Red-baiting hysteria in the U.S., starting with the 1940 Smith Act and ending with the Mundt-Nixon bill. The author urges repeal of the Smith Act, rejection of the Mundt bill as the blueprint of a police state, and stopping thought control before fascism is upon us.

F156   . . . . Mass Action Can Free the Eleven, "Political Affairs," 29 (May 1950), 150-54.
Release of the 11 Party leaders on bail was the result of a mass campaign. Their fight against the Smith Act can be won if the Party develops a powerful movement of struggle to back the courtroom defense. The campaign to repeal the Smith Act should be coordinated with the fight against the Mundt bill.

F157   . . . . "Elizabeth Gurley Flynn Speaks to the Court." New York: New Century, 1952.   30 pp.
Elizabeth Gurley Flynn's opening statement to the court and jury in the case of 16 Smith Act defendants. Acting as her own attorney, she tells her life story; argues that it is not the communists who flaunt the Constitution and Bill of Rights, but always the employing class; and asserts that the Party is fighting for its democratic rights, not advocating violence.

F158   . . . . Freedom for the Communist Leaders! "Political Affairs," 31 (July 1952), 1-6 ff.
A leading communist calls for a mass movement for the release of communists imprisoned under the Smith Act and a state sedition law The Bill of Rights was violated and literature and history distorted in a trial of books, in which the real issue was the struggle against war and fascism.

F159   . . . . "The Communists and the People: Summation Speech to the Jury in the Second Foley Square Smith Act Trial of Thirteen Communist Leaders." New York: New Century, 1953.   48 pp.
An assertion that the defendants are being persecuted for opposing the "status quo," and that there is no evidence of conspiracy to overthrow the U.S. government by violence. Declaring that the communists are a legally constituted political party, a veteran Party leader charges that they are on trial for opposing policies leading to an atomic world war.

F160   . . ., and others.   "Thirteen Communists Speak to the Court." New York: New Century, 1953. 95 pp.

Statements to the court by 13 leading communists, found guilty in 1953 of violating the Smith Act, just before they were sentenced. The statements all denounce the judge, the rigged jury, and the framed testimony by stool-pigeons and professional informers. All end with appeals to the idealism of Washington, Jefferson, Douglass, and the Communist Party.

F161 FLYNN, Elizabeth Gurley. "I Speak My Own Piece." New York: Masses& Mainstream, 1955. 326 pp.
The autobiography of a woman who had been active in the radical and labor movements of this country for the past half century. A socialist at the age of sixteen, she joined the IWW soon after its formation and participated in many of its struggles. Her book, which carries her story down to 1927, deals with many of the strikes, free speech fights, and civil liberties cases of the preceding twenty years, and sketches many of the personalities in the radical movement. (The author joined the Communist Party in 1937; along with other communist leaders she was imprisoned under the provisions of the Smith Act.)

F162 .... "The Alderson Story: My Life as a Political Prisoner." New York: International Publishers, 1963. 223 pp. App.
The prison experiences of a leading member of the CPUSA, the only woman member of its national board, who was convicted in 1952 under the Smith Act, and who was confined in the Federal Reformatory for Women in West Virginia from January 1955 until April 1957.

F163 FLYNN, Fabian. "Catholicism, Americanism and Communism." New York: Paulist Press, 1937. 38 pp.
A popular exposition of the evils of communism, written in question-and-answer form. Asserting that communism is contrary to American democratic ideals, the author discusses the extent to which it contemplates revolution, the size of its organization here, and the fate of the Catholic Church should it obtain power. He summarizes the communist attitude toward religion, and shows how this force of immorality and class hatred can be fought.

F164 FLYNN, John T. "The Road Ahead: America's Creeping Revolution." New York: Devin-Adair, 1949. 160 pp.
A right-wing treatise directed, not against the communists (whom the author despises but feels are not significant), but against socialists and "social planners" who, while bitterly opposing communists, would bring the same kind of social control to America. In chapter 10, "The Kingdom of God" (pp. 106-19), the author asserts that the Federal Council of Churches of Christ in America is directed by men who are using its machinery to promote a socialist revolution in America.

F165 .... "While You Slept: Our Tragedy in Asia and Who Made It." New York: Devin-Adair, 1951. 192 pp. Ref.
An argument that Roosevelt had made commitments, later carried out by Truman under the guidance of Dean Acheson and General George Marshall, to deliver most of Europe and Asia into the hands of Russian communism. This policy had been promoted by communist sympathizers in the State Department who constantly sought to undermine Chiang Kai-shek and promote the Chinese communists. The American people, the author argues, did not protest because they had been drugged by propaganda—from books, literary critics, magazines, motion pictures, and radio—controlled by communists and their sympathizers. In this network of propaganda supporting the communist cause in Asia, the Institute of Pacific Relations played an important part.

F166 .... "The Lattimore Story." New York: Devin-Adair, 1953. 118 pp. Ind.
An account of the Owen Lattimore case, based on Senate committee hearings. Lattimore is called a pro-Soviet agent who promoted Stalin's policies in the U.S. and against the U.S. throughout the world. The loss of China to the communists is attributed to the State Department's softness toward communism and to activities of men like Lattimore.

F167 .... Twenty-four Steps to Communism, "American Mercury," 77 (Dec. 1953), 3-6.
An outline of the communist over-all plan for wrecking the American system without revealing openly its communist label. Starting with a change from a federal republic into a powerful central state, the plan proceeds through excessive controls on business and infiltration of schools and labor unions to weakening of our economic system and infiltration of government.

F168 .... "McCarthy: His War on American Reds and the Story of Those Who Oppose Him." New York: America's Future, 1954. 15 pp.
A right-wing defense of the Senator and his actions, based on a radio broadcast of May 2, 1954. Favorably reviewing McCarthy's activities against communists in government, the author asserts that, while Party smears against McCarthy are vicious but understandable, attacks on him by liberals are inexcusable.

F169 FOLEY, Ellery, and BRANDON, Arthur. Communist Influence Killed Growing Washington Federation, "New Leader," 25 (Feb. 21, 1942), 4.
A charge that the Washington Commonwealth Federation, under the leadership of Hugh De Lacy, follows the Communist Party line. Howard Costigan, executive secretary from 1934 to 1940, was quickly dropped for supporting Roosevelt in 1940.

F170 FOLLETT, Wilson. Letter to a Communist Friend, "Atlantic Monthly," 162 (Oct. 1938), 460-69.
An analysis of the incompatibility of communist theory with contemporary American society. The author argues that Americans do not find any sense in the abstraction of the class struggle, that the communist urge for justice is false, and that the justification of dictatorship for some theoretical good must be rejected.

F171 FONER, Philip S. (ed.). "Abraham Lincoln: Selections from His Writings." New York: International Publishers, 1944. 93 pp.
An example of communist efforts to attach themselves to American traditions, written during the Party's "win-the-war" phase. Lincoln is pictured here as the forerunner of the Communist Party, in sentiment if not in actual pronouncement.

F172 .... "Morale Education in the American Army." New York: International Publishers, 1944. 64 pp.
A communist historian, during the Party's "win-the-war" phase, praises the efforts of the American and British armies to inform their soldiers of the issues in the war. He tells the story of similar efforts during three previous people's wars in our history, the War for Independence, the War of 1812, and the Civil War. The resulting boost in morale among the armed forces, then as now, was crucial to victory.

F173 .... (ed.). "Frederick Douglass: Selections from His Writings." New York: International Publishers, 1945. 95 pp. Ref. notes.
Another in the American history cycle of communist "win-the-war" interpretations of history. Frederick Douglass is claimed as the progenitor of all communist

pronouncements on race equality and freedom. In the introduction, the editor sees him as inspirer of anti-fascists everywhere today, who now seek victory, enduring peace, security, and freedom because of him.

F174 FONER, Philip S. "The Jews in American History, 1654-1865." New York: International Publishers, 1945. 96 pp. Bibliog.
A communist interpretation of history, asserting that Jewish heroism and fighting spirit in the Revolutionary War, the War of 1812, and the Civil War were of the same order as in the present conflict against fascist barbarism.

F175 .... "History of the Labor Movement in the United States." Vol. 1. "From Colonial Times to the Founding of the American Federation of Labor." New York: International Publishers, 1947. 576 pp. Ref. notes. Biographical sketches. Ind. Vol. 2. "From the Founding of the American Federation of Labor to the Emergence of American Imperialism." New York: International Publishers, 1955. 480 pp. Ref. notes. Ind. Vol. 3. "The Policies and Practices of the American Federation of Labor, 1900-1909." New York: International Publishers, 1964. 477 pp. Ref. notes. Ind. Vol. 4. "The Industrial Workers of the World, 1905-1917." New York: International Publishers, 1965. 608 pp. Ref. notes. Ind.
The definitive communist study of U.S. labor history, viewing all previous histories as apologies for Gomperism and craft unionism. Emphasis is placed on the role of the working class in democratic and social struggles, on strike militancy, and on efforts at independent political action. The author attacks the AFL for narrow craft interests, for failure to organize Negroes and the unskilled, and for class collaborationist policies.

F176 .... (ed.). "Jack London, American Rebel." New York: Citadel Press, 1947. 533 pp. Bibliog.
A collection of London's social writings, preceded by a long biographical essay. London is said to be one of America's most significant writers, the first to portray his class sympathetically, and one of the few to use literature to build the foundations of a future society.

F177 .... Labor's Story: Myth and Reality, "New Masses," 64 (Aug. 26, 1947), 3-6.
The author presents the "true" or Marxist interpretation of American labor history, so long distorted, in his view, by the Commons school. A summary of the point of view developed in full by the author in his volumes on American labor history.

F178 .... "The Fur and Leather Workers' Union: A Story of Dramatic Struggles and Achievements." Newark, N. J.: Nordan Press, 1950. 708 pp. Ind.
The history of the only openly communist-controlled labor union in the country, by a high-ranking procommunist historian. The author, after describing sweatshop conditions in the industry, tells of the formation of the Furriers' Union, the factional battles during the 1920's for its control, the break with the AFL and the entry into the CIO, the amalgamation with the Leather Workers, and the union's battles within the CIO through the 1949 convention. Ben Gold, communist president of the union, receives the highest praise.

F179 .... (ed.). "The Life and Writings of Frederick Douglass." 4 vols. New York: International Publishers, 1950-55. Bibliog. Ref. Inds.
An extensive collection of Douglass' writings, speeches, letters, and editorials by a communist historian, who interprets Douglass' life and times. (Douglass has been chosen by the Party as the one who gave the clearest articulation of Negro protest, militance, and hope.)

F180 .... "The Case of Joe Hill." New York: International Publishers, 1965. 127 pp. Ref. notes.
A communist view of the case of Joe Hill (Joseph Hillstrom), IWW activist and songwriter, who was executed in Utah in 1915 on a charge of murdering a grocer and his son. The author is convinced that Hill, under suspicion because of an unexplained wound, was framed because of his IWW activities and because the Mormon Church and powerful corporations in the state were bitter foes of trade unionism.

F181 FONTAINE, A. B. "Subterfuge." Green Bay, Wis.: The author, 1934. 175 pp.
An attack on Roosevelt's New Deal as a controlled, regimented economy leading inevitably to communism. Leading members of the New Deal agencies are portrayed as radicals, many as communists, seeking to realize the principles of the Communist Manifesto. New Deal leaders are asserted to desire a third party to put communism into effect, using the La Follette movement in Wisconsin toward this objective.

F182 FORD, J. [pseud. for Israel Amter], and DUBNER, J. [pseud. for Abraham Jakira]. Theses on the Relations of No. 1 and No. 2, "Communist" (organ of the Communist Party of America), 1 (July 1922), 2-13.
The position of the "goose caucus" in the 1922 factional fight in the Communist Party of America on the question of liquidating the underground Communist Party. While there is a need for a legal political party, its control must be in the hands of the illegal, underground Communist Party. (The final compromise between the "goose caucus" and the "liquidators" more closely paralleled the position of the "goose caucus.")

F183 FORD, James W. "Economic Struggle of Negro Workers: A Trade Union Program of Action." New York: Provisional International Trade Union Committee of Negro Workers, 1930. 20 pp.
An early statement of communist concern for Negroes throughout the world, together with an economic program for Negro workers which includes equal pay for equal work, no forced labor, proper labor legislation, protection of women and youth, freedom of trade unions, better housing and social conditions, free universal education, unlimited civil rights, self determination, and defense of the Soviet Union.

F184 .... "The Negro's Struggle against Imperialism." New York: Provisional International Trade Union Committee of Negro Workers, 1930. 32 pp.
A report to the Second World Congress of the League Against Imperialism, Frankfort, Germany, July 1929. The author traces the development of capitalism, with special reference to the enslavement of the Negro peoples. He denounces the oppression of imperialism today in Africa, the U.S., and the West Indies, and calls for Negro workers to organize along class lines and fight against imperialist war.

F185 .... "Imperialism Destroys the People of Africa." New York: CPUSA, Harlem Section, n.d. [1931?]. 15 pp.
A speech in Switzerland at a conference on African children, by the foremost Negro communist of the time in the U.S. Only by ceaseless struggle against imperialism along the lines of the Comintern program, Ford asserts, can African workers achieve freedom.

F186   FORD, James W. "The Right to Revolution for the Negro People." New York: Harlem Section of the Communist Party, n.d. [1932?]. 21 pp.

A leading Negro communist, Party candidate for vice-president in 1932, explains the Party's slogans of equal rights for Negroes and self-determination for Negroes in the Black Belt. This platform, he says, embodies the revolutionary aims and methods needed to wrest the nation's wealth from the capitalists. Inspired by the Soviet Union and led by the communists, Negroes will change their condition of servitude.

F187   . . . . "World Problems of the Negro People (A Refutation of George Padmore)." New York: Harlem Section, Communist Party, n.d. [1934?]. 24 pp.

The report of the chief organizer of the International Trade Union Committee of Negro Workers to the First International Conference of Negro Workers in Hamburg, Germany, in 1934. George Padmore, former secretary of the ITUCNW, was expelled for petty bourgeois nationalist and antiworking-class activities.

F188   . . . . "Hunger and Terror in Harlem." New York: CPUSA, Harlem Section, 1935. 39 pp.

Occasioned by an outbreak of violence in Harlem on March 19, 1935, the pamphlet indicts Mayor La Guardia, along with bankers and merchants. Police brutality in Harlem shows that the police are an instrument of ruling-class oppression. The author asserts that conditions in Harlem can be remedied only by ceaseless struggle of the masses against the capitalists and their agencies of oppression.

F189   . . . . "The Negro People and the Farmer-Labor Party." New York: CPUSA, Harlem Division, 1935. 12 pp.

A plea for a farmer-labor party by the leading Negro communist of the time. Only under such a party, seeking as its fundamental purpose to develop an antifascist movement, can the problems of the Negro people be dealt with correctly.

F190   . . ., and ALLEN, James S. "The Negroes in a Soviet America." New York: Workers Library, 1935. 47 pp.

The communist program for the Negro in the mid-1930's. The depressed status of the Negro on the farm and in the city is contrasted with the communist ideal of self-determination of Negroes in the Black Belt and a proletarian revolution in the rest of the country. The pamphlet tells how a Soviet U.S. and a Soviet Negro republic will complement each other.

F191   . . ., and GANNES, Harry. "War in Africa: Italian Fascism Prepares to Enslave Ethiopia." New York: Workers Library, 1935. 31 pp.

A Party pamphlet directed to U.S. Negroes, chronicling the attempts of the fascists in Italy to subjugate Ethiopia up to the present time. Negroes are urged to mobilize the widest possible working-class and anti-imperialist allies in support of the Ethiopian people.

F192   . . . . The United Front in the Field of Negro Work, "Communist," 14 (Feb. 1935), 158-74.

Growing disillusionment among Negroes and working people with Negro reformist leaders and their white AFL supporters creates an opportunity for wide united action. Church groups, local unions, and youth groups reject reformists' efforts to discredit the ILD's handling of the Scottsboro case. United fronts with these groups can be developed.

F193   . . ., and SASS, Louis. Development of Work in the Harlem Section, "Communist," 14 (April 1935), 312-25.

A report of Party activities in New York's Harlem, noting that practically every Negro reformist group has at one time or another offered to join it in united action. The Harlem section, in developing a cadre of Negro leaders, gives leadership to the Negro struggle across the nation.

F194   . . . . The Negro Liberation Movement and the Farmer-Labor Party, "Communist," 14 (Dec. 1935), 1130-41.

A speech to the November plenum of the Party's Central Committee, arguing that Negroes, disillusioned with the New Deal, can be won to a farmer-labor or people's party, but that united-front efforts in Negro communities need to be consolidated with the campaign for such a party. This can be accomplished through the trade unions.

F195   . . . . "The Communists and the Struggle for Negro Liberation." New York: Harlem Division of the Communist Party, n.d. [1936?]. 67 pp.

A collection of speeches and reports at international conferences by a leading Negro communist, together with some of his writings of the "third period" and of the transitional period leading to the popular front. They present the Party's position on problems of imperialism, Africa, the West Indies, war, Ethiopian independence, and the struggle for peace. Attention is paid to relations between the Universal Negro Improvement Association (the Garvey movement) and the communists, and to the need for unity in the struggle for Negro rights.

F196   . . ., and BERRY, A. W. The Coming National Negro Congress: A New Phase in the Liberation Struggles of the Negro People, "Communist," 15 (Feb. 1936), 139-42.

The aims of the National Negro Congress, scheduled to convene in February, are far more radical than those in any previous attempt to form a broad Negro organization. The Party fully supports its demands for social, economic, and judicial equality, along with its opposition to war and fascism.

F197   . . . . The National Negro Congress, "Communist," 15 (April 1936), 316-26; Political Highlights of the National Negro Congress (May), 457-64; Build the National Negro Congress Movement (June), 552-61.

An account of the National Negro Congress, held in Chicago in February 1936, with an appeal for Party support for its program. Emphasis is placed on Negro opposition to fascism and war, and specifically to Italy's aggression in Ethiopia. The Congress should be developed into a political, economic, and social activist organization. Though the Congress does not support the entire CP program, Party members should participate, especially in view of the coming election threat of the Republican-Liberty League-Hearst clique.

F198   . . . . The Negro People and the Elections, "Communist," 16 (Jan. 1937), 63-73.

Strong Negro support of Roosevelt in the 1936 election represented a departure from traditional Negro Republicanism. The programs of the major parties are criticized, and the CP united-front fight for Negro equality is viewed as the only one to really benefit the Negroes.

F199   . . . . The Negro Masses in the United States, "Communist International," 14 (June 1937), 403-7.

A picture of the geographic, occupational, economic, and political distribution of Negroes in the U.S. Despite obstacles, Negroes are supporting the progressive wing of the Democratic Party, and are helping in the struggle for a broad Negro people's front in the U.S.

F200   FORD, James W. Uniting the Negro People in the People's Front, "Communist," 16 (Aug. 1937), 725-34.
An enumeration of problems retarding the economic and social life of the Negro people, with an analysis of experiences in building the National Negro Congress. In order to build the Party among Negroes and extend the Negro people's front, our struggle for immediate Negro needs must be renewed. (Based on a speech to a plenary meeting of the Party's Central Committee, June 17-20, 1937.)

F201   . . ., and DAMON, Anna. Scottsboro in the Light of Building the Negro People's Front, "Communist," 16 (Sept. 1937), 838-47.
A discussion of the Scottsboro case as a symbol of Negro oppression. The series of trials, appeals, and retrials supported by the Party and the International Labor Defense gave world-wide publicity to the injustices suffered by Negroes. The popular front which grew up in response to this case provides the basis for further racial and Party action.

F202   . . . . "The Negro and the Democratic Front." Introd. by A. W. Berry. New York: International Publishers, 1938. 222 pp. Ind.
Articles and addresses by James W. Ford, Negro communist leader, illustrating the communist program for Negroes during the popular-front period. Topics covered include a softened version of self-determination, new alignments for Negroes in the people's front for democracy, the National Negro Congress, and the Negro revolutionary past. Ford's solution for the problem facing American workers, progressives, and Negroes is a democratic front against fascism; and its extension to true democracy, which is socialism.

F203   . . ., and BLAKE, George E. Building the People's Front in Harlem, "Communist," 17 (Feb. 1938), 158-68.
An analysis of the election results in Harlem, New York City, in 1937. The Lower Harlem Section of the Party played a decisive role in the election of Oscar Garcia Rivera to the Assembly. Weaknesses in the campaign are reviewed, and tasks for the future are outlined.

F204   . . . . Rally the Negro Masses for the Democratic Front! Communist," 17 (March 1938), 266-71.
A report to a plenary session of the Party's Central Committee and National Party Builders Congress, February 18-21, 1938, advocating support of the National Negro Congress, pressure for the antilynching bill, and formation of a united-front Negro peace movement following the pattern of the Harlem Legislative Conference.

F205   . . . . Forging the Negro People's Sector of the Democratic Front, "Communist," 17 (July 1938), 615-23.
A speech to the Party's tenth convention, May 29, 1938, aligning current Negro activities in the democratic front with the traditions of Negro culture. The Harlem Legislative Conference plans to send an outstanding progressive Negro to Congress. Negroes are being given systematic training in Party schools.

F206   . . . . "Anti-Semitism and the Struggle for Democracy." New York: National Council of Jewish Communists, n.d. [1939]. 19 pp.
Asserting that anti-Semitism is a fascist weapon directed against all progressive Americans, a leading Negro communist calls for unification of Jewish progressives and their alliance with all within the camp of progress, particularly the Negro people.

F207   . . . . "Win Progress for Harlem." New York: Harlem Division, Communist Party, 1939. 31 pp.
The text of a report to the Health-Housing Conference of the Party's Harlem Division, June 23, 1939, outlining the economic crisis in Harlem and the bad health and housing conditions there. Gains made under the New Deal and La Guardia's city administration are reviewed, and the program of I. Amter, communist candidate for the City Council, is presented.

F208   . . . . The Struggle for the Building of the Modern Liberation Movement of the Negro People, "Communist," 18 (Sept. 1939), 817-28.
The CP has been the only political party to recognize that real freedom for the working class is impossible without liberation of the Negroes. The role of labor unions is central in this fight, and the CIO has made an excellent beginning.

F209   . . . . Earl Browder—Leader of the Oppressed, "Communist," 20 (June 1941), 529-35.
A tribute to Earl Browder as the outstanding Marxist-Leninist in the Western Hemisphere and the symbol of fraternity and unity among the toiling peoples of the Americas.

F210   . . . . The Negro People and the New World Situation, "Communist," 20 (Aug. 1941), 696-704.
A reappraisal of Party work among Negroes in light of the changed character of the war, following Hitler's attack upon the Soviet Union. A Nazi victory, with its doctrine of Aryan superiority, would doom Negroes to eternal slavery. (Based on a report to a plenary meeting of the Party's national committee, June 28-29, 1941; reprinted in pamphlet form.)

F211   . . . . Some Problems of the Negro People in the National Front to Destroy Hitler and Hitlerism, "Communist," 20 (Oct. 1941), 888-96.
The statement of a new line on Negro liberation. Following Hitler's invasion of the Soviet Union, the Negroes must now regard defeat of Germany as the first step in their liberation. In order for Negroes to make the maximum contribution to the war effort, all discrimination in industry and the military must be eliminated.

F212   . . . . "The War and the Negro People: The Japanese 'Darker Race' Demagogy Exposed." New York: Workers Library, 1942. 15 pp.
A pamphlet during the Party's "patriotic" phase calling for all-out Negro support of the war effort. The author attacks the Axis nations, stating that the Japanese government is the ally of the worst enemy of colored peoples the world has ever seen. He asks his readers to forget the Party's previous isolationist stand.

F213   . . . . Mobilize Negro Manpower for Victory, "Communist," 22 (Jan. 1943), 38-46.
The labor movement and the Manpower Commission must break down barriers of discrimination and fully mobilize Negro manpower for the war effort. Bottlenecks of discrimination that prevent full integration of Negroes in war industries are reviewed, and a program to prevent discrimination in employment, in training, and in the armed services is presented.

F214   . . . . The Negro People Unite for Victory, "Communist," 22 (July 1943), 642-47.
A speech to a plenary meeting of the Party's national

committee, June 11, 1943, hailing the Negro Freedom Rally as indicative of the increasing national unity behind the war effort. The rally, held in New York on June 7, was organized by the Negro Victory Labor Committee.

F215 FORD, James W. Teheran and the Negro People, "Communist," 23 (March 1944), 260-66.
The objectives of Negroes coverge with the progressive aims of the labor movement and the ideals of the Teheran conference. The participation of the Negro people in American economic, political, and cultural life has steadily increased. The objective of Teheran calls for national unity behind Roosevelt and national integration of the Negro people.

F216 . . ., and others. "Communists in the Struggle for Negro Rights." New York: New Century, 1945. 23 pp.
Contributions of three leading Negro communists to a symposium organized by the "Negro Digest" on the question, "Have the Communists Quit the Fight for Negro Rights?" and published in its December 1944 issue. James W. Ford, Benjamin J. Davis, Jr., and William L. Patterson all deny that the communists have soft-pedaled the fight for Negro rights in the interests of wartime unity, asserting that winning Negro rights and winning the war are linked. Excerpts from a talk by Earl Browder, "On the Negroes and the Right of Self-Determination," are included.

F217 . . . . The 1948 Elections in Bedford-Stuyvesant, "Political Affairs," 28 (Feb. 1949), 70-81.
A description of the role of the Communist Party in the progressive coalition that helped elect a Brooklyn Negro, Bertram L. Baker, to the New York State Assembly, and in the congressional campaign of Mrs. Ada B. Jackson, American Labor Party candidate from Brooklyn.

F218 . . . . The Communist Party: Champion Fighter for Negro Rights, "Political Affairs," 28 (June 1949), 38-50.
White chauvinism is an integral part of monopoly capital's oppression of the Negro people. Among its other achievements, the CPUSA has directed the national liberation struggles of the Negro people. The campaign for Negro rights is part of the struggle against war and fascism.

F219 . . . . Foster and Negro-Labor Unity, "Masses & Mainstream," 4 (March 1951), 21-29.
A eulogy of Foster, in connection with his seventieth birthday, citing his devotion to the rights of Negroes in the labor movement. The author, the Party's Negro candidate for U.S. vice-president in 1932, recalls his own activity in the TUEL, telling how Foster constantly stressed the need to organize Negroes and to support their struggle for civil and economic rights.

F220 FORD, Sherman. "The McCarthy Menace: An Evaluation of the Facts and an Interpretation of the Evidence." New York: William-Frederick Press, 1954. 94 pp. Ind.
A view of Senator McCarthy's type of anticommunism as a greater threat to the U.S. than Hitlerism was to Germany. Analyzing McCarthy's charges against the State Department, the author asserts that by this standard Lincoln could be a communist. He urges McCarthy's recall or his expulsion from the Senate.

F221 FORDHAM UNIVERSITY, Institute of Contemporary Russian Studies. "Four Good Men and True." New York: The Institute, 1953. 11 pp.
A reprint of an article from "Newsweek" by J. Edgar Hoover on the value of the excommunist. Sketches of four excommunists—Louis Budenz, Benjamin Gitlow, Manning Johnson, and Howard Rushmore—and an account of their anticommunist contributions follow.

F222 FORSTER, Arnold, and EPSTEIN, Benjamin. "The Trouble Makers: An Anti-Defamation League Report." Garden City, N.Y.: Doubleday, 1952. 317 pp. Ind.
A report on those who cause trouble in America by means of racial and religious prejudice. While most of the book is concerned with the extreme right, Chapter 6, "Confusion from the Left" (pp. 217-32), deals with the communists, showing how, in the name of antidiscrimination and antiracism, they spread their own propaganda and cause dissention. The cases of Willie McGee, the Rosenbergs, the Trenton Six, the Scottsboro boys, and others are cited as examples.

F223 FORSYTHE, Robert [pseud. for Kyle Crichton]. "Redder Than the Rose." New York: Covici, Friede, 1935. 241 pp.
A collection of Forsythe's humorous and satirical articles, on a wide variety of subjects, that appeared in the "New Masses." One of the rare efforts at humor in communist literature.

F224 . . . . "The World Gone Mad." New York: New Masses, 1936. 12 pp.
An assertion by a "New Masses" critic that war is inevitable under capitalism, whether totalitarian as in Germany or "democratic" as in England. Though only a Soviet world would be a peaceful world, peace can be fought for through a united-front organization such as the American League Against War and Fascism.

F225 . . . . "Reading from Left to Right." Illus. by William Gropper. New York: Covici, Friede, 1938. 255 pp.
A collection of satirical articles, most of them on political topics, that first appeared in the "New Masses." Some comment on the British Tories, whom the author believes to be fascist at heart. Other topics are the USSR, Trotsky and Trotskyists, American politicians and business leaders, and writers.

F226 "FORTUNE," The Communist Party, 10 (Sept. 1934), 69-74 ff.
A survey of the CPUSA describing its history, aims, techniques, and leadership. Though the Party has only 26,000 enrolled members, these are disciplined leaders of a body of 300,000 to 500,000 sympathizers. Leading communist front organizations are described. The communist movement, which fights for the underdog, has been on the upgrade for the past year. (An appendix, pp. 160-62, describes the various communist sects.)

F227 . . ., The Maritime Unions, 16 (Sept. 1937), 123-28.
An analysis of the maritime unions and their leaders, including Bridges of the International Longshoremen's and Warehousemen's Union and Curran of the National Maritime Union. The many communists in leadership positions in the maritime unions do not constitute a danger, since their purpose is only to build strong, class-conscious unions.

F228 . . ., Youth, 21 (May 1940), 88-92 ff.
An article written following the February 1939 National Citizenship Institute of the American Youth Congress, discussing the history of the American Youth Congress, the struggle within it of communists and noncommunists, and the degree to which it reflects accurately the needs of American youth.

F229 "FORTUNE," The C.P. Column, 22 (Nov. 1940), 89 ff.
Stalin's fifth column in the U.S., despite its low prestige and limited success, still has 100,000 adherents seeking to overthrow our capitalist democracy. Its greatest successes have been in penetrating the industrial unions and attracting intellectuals, though in both these areas it has recently lost ground. Its chief weakness has been the zigzagging Party line.

F230 . . ., Hammer and Tongs: The New C.P. Line, 33 (June 1946), 105-7.
A description of the switch in the Party line from its wartime program of class peace to its peacetime program of class war. Five major turns have been required of the CPUSA in the past seven years to keep it abreast of Soviet foreign policy. Changes signaled by the Duclos statement are outlined.

F231 . . ., Alternating Currents in U.E.—C.P.'s Last Base, 39 (March 1949), 175-77.
Communists control the United Electrical Workers by means of patronage and a public-relations program. An opposition group, the UE Members for Democratic Action, is fighting against great odds to arouse the union members against the communist leaders.

F232 . . ., C.I.O. Split Widens, 40 (July 1949), 151-53.
An assertion, in anticipation of the October CIO convention, that the cleavage between the minority communist-line unions and the remainder of the CIO is so deep that expulsions are a foregone conclusion. The effects on the CIO in membership and in wage negotiations are analyzed.

F233 . . ., Civil War in C.I.O. 40 (Nov. 1949), 204-6.
The major problem at the forthcoming CIO national convention in Cleveland will be how to sweep out the communist minority without wrecking the CIO. The effect of this factional warfare on the collective bargaining policies of CIO unions is reviewed.

F234 . . ., The C.P.'s New Labor Line, 43 (March 1951), 38-41.
Due to the CIO's expulsion of communist-led unions, the Party has a new line to break through its isolation. Its labor lieutenants must now cooperate with the right, especially in unions in basic industries. Communists in right-led unions must steer a path between left sectarianism and right opportunism.

F235 . . ., Box Score on Communist Influence in U.S. Labor, 45 (June 1952), 71-76.
A list of present and past Party-line unions, giving membership, leaders, and contracts of each. Communist influence today is an important force in only four unions, with less than two per cent of organized labor's membership, and this summer the dwindling communist influence will be further reduced.

F236 . . ., Curtains for the C.P., 206 (March 1956), 206-8.
Party-dominated unions, once powerful, have been greatly weakened by the Communist Control Act of 1954, following the noncommunist affidavits required by Taft-Hartley and the expulsions from the CIO. A tally of history and present status, 1948 membership and present membership, and major contracts appears on p. 206.

FORT-WHITEMAN, Lovett. See JACKSON, James (1924-25).

F237 FOSTER, William Z. The Great Steel Strike and Its Lessons." New York: Huebsch, 1920. 265 pp.
A detailed account of the 1919 steel strike by its leader, who later joined the communist movement and eventually became its leading figure. Though Foster bitterly criticizes the behavior of the steel company heads and the public officials subservient to them, he asserts that the strike could have been won had the labor movement fully thrown its resources into the fight. Strongly opposing dual unionism, he argues that trade unions, despite their appearance of conservatism, are inherently anticapitalist and should be supported by progressives and radicals.

F238 . . . . "The Revolutionary Crisis of 1918-1921 in Germany, England, Italy and France." Chicago: Trade Union Educational League, 1921. 64 pp.
An outline of the postwar revolutionary movements in these four European countries, with an assertion that they failed because of reformist policies and leadership. The leaders, schooled in the prewar evolutionary advance of labor, were psychologically incapable of leading a revolutionary struggle.

F239 . . . . "The Russian Revolution." Chicago: Trade Union Educational League, n.d. [1921]. 155 pp.
A report of Foster's 14-week stay in Russia during the spring and summer of 1921. He views the Russian Revolution as our own labor movement carried to its logical conclusion. Foster gives the history of the revolution, and describes the Soviet government, the Red Army, the Party, the dictatorship, and the trade unions. Other topics covered include labor laws and working conditions, cooperatives, wages and prices, the organization of industry, and the new economic program.

F240 . . . . "The Bankruptcy of the American Labor Movement." Chicago: Trade Union Educational League, 1922. 62 pp.
An indictment of the American labor movement for refusal to engage in political activity, for tolerating reactionary and incompetent leadership, and for general "bankruptcy." The cause of the backwardness of American workers is found in dual unionism. Now radicals and progressives are organizing in the TUEL to oppose capitalism and craft unionism.

F241 . . . . "The Railroaders' Next Step—Amalgamation." Chicago: Trade Union Educational League, 1922. 48 pp.
A plea for amalgamation of all railroad unions by the leading Party trade-union expert, himself a former railroad worker. Only by united resistance, he says, can the workers resist the greed of the companies. Despite the weaknesses of the railroad craft unions, he counsels against going outside of them to start a new organization.

F242 . . . . Amalgamation or Annihilation, "Labor Herald," 1 (April 1922), 6-8 ff.
A plea for the amalgamation of the 16 principal rail unions at present in retreat before the attacks of the employers. The only objections should come from the well-paid officials of the various organizations. The rank and file must bring about amalgamation, so that united action can be taken against the employers.

F243 . . . . The Railway Employees' Department Convention, "Labor Herald," 1 (June 1922), 16-19 ff.
A description of the latest convention of the railway employees' department as an almost total failure. The conservatives won every floor fight, and the amalgamation question fizzled. Progressives must continue to work among the rank and file so that delegates to the next convention will come instructed to merge the many weak railroad unions.

F244   FOSTER, William Z. The Left Wing in the American Labour Movement, "Labour Monthly," (London), 3 (Sept. 1922), 156-62.
Whereas until a year ago the left-wing program was to replace conservative trade unions with revolutionary organizations, now it is to organize revolutionary nuclei within the old unions under the leadership of the TUEL. Objectives include industrial unionism, a militant working-class political party, affiliation with the RILU, and establishment of a workers' republic.

F245   .... The Chicago Federation of Labor, "Labor Herald," 1 (Dec. 1922), 8-10.
The progressive Chicago Federation of Labor, under the leadership of John Fitzpatrick and Edward Nockels, is one of the bright spots in American labor. Its support of union organizing drives and strikes, its activity in labor defense cases, and its interest in a farmer-labor party and union amalgamation are commended.

F246   .... Five Vital Conferences, "Labor Herald," 1 (Jan. 1923), 11-15.
An account of conferences held during November, which set up national industrial sections (or educational committees) of the TUEL in textiles, the needle trades, the printing industry, the food industry, and the shoe or leather industry. Other sections are being organized.

F247   .... The National Railroad Amalgamation Conference, "Labor Herald," 1 (Jan. 1923), 3-5 ff.
A report on the successful December 9-10 conference in New York City, held to promote union amalgamation in the railroad industry. The conference's program tells the procedure to be followed in the campaign that will be undertaken.

F248   .... The Progressive Miners' Conference, "Labor Herald," 2 (July 1923), 3-6.
A report on the activities of the militants within the United Mine Workers, and of the conference that launched the left-wing movement. Speeches at the conference are reported, along with resolutions opposing dual unionism and the Lewis administration, and calling for recognition of Soviet Russia.

F249   .... The Federated Farmer-Labor Party, "Labor Herald," 2 (Aug. 1923), 3-7.
A report on the July 1923 conference in Chicago at which the Federated Farmer-Labor Party was formed. The author denounces John Fitzpatrick's Farmer Labor Party for weakness in the face of a rank-and-file movement for a federated labor party. Foster denies the charge that the Workers Party "captured" the convention, arguing that its strength was not in numbers but in program.

F250   .... The AF of L Convention, "Liberator," [6] (Nov. 1923), 7-9.
A report on the Portland convention of the AFL at which left-wing proposals for amalgamation of craft unions, a labor party, and recognition of Russia were overwhelmingly defeated, and William Dunne, TUEL member representing the Butte, Montana, central labor council, was unseated. The bureaucratic delegates did not represent the rank and file.

F251   .... "Russia in 1924." Chicago: Trade Union Educational League, 1924. 31 pp.
A speech delivered after Foster's return from sessions of the Communist International in April-May 1924 defending USSR efforts to solve such problems as worker discontent, lack of productivity, unemployment, and industrialization. Hard as this road has been, the world's working class must travel it, since capitalism cannot be patched up.

F252   .... An Open Letter to John Fitzpatrick, "Labor Herald," 2 (Jan. 1924), 6-8 ff.
A reply to statements by Fitzpatrick, head of the Chicago Federation of Labor, that held the Workers Party responsible for the split at the Farmer-Labor Party convention on July 3. Attacking Fitzpatrick bitterly, Foster accuses him of retreating from his former progressive position back to Gompers, injuring the labor movement, and betraying the workers who followed him.

F253   .... The Coming Struggle, "Labor Herald," 2 (Feb. 1924), 3-5.
An assertion that the economic crisis is growing, and the struggle between reactionary and revolutionary forces in the labor movement is becoming sharper. Militant revolutionaries must see that the workers' struggle against their masters is based on the class struggle. The left wing, organized in the TUEL, must take the most active part possible in this fight.

F254   .... The Miners' Convention, "Labor Herald," 3 (March 1924), 3-5 ff.
An analysis of the UMW convention recently held in Indianapolis, characterized by the bitter struggle between the reactionary Lewis administration and progressive forces among the rank-and-file. Despotic methods used against the progressives are described. By the next convention, revolutionary militants must organize and direct the revolt in order to defeat the Lewis machine.

F255   .... Petty Bourgeois Leadership vs. Proletarian Rank and File, "Labor Herald," 3 (May 1924), 75-77.
A denunciation of union officials as petty bourgeoisie interested primarily in their property right in the union. The officials, with their high salaries and job security, fight to maintain the status quo. A new and militant leadership must be developed, inspired by the revolutionary class struggle.

F256   .... The Convention of the Conference for Progressive Political Action, "Liberator," 7 (Aug. 1924), 7-9.
A critique of the Conference for Progressive Political Action and a defense of the Workers Party's withdrawal of support from candidates of the National Farmer-Labor Party. Despite strong working-class support, the CPPA was reduced to another petty-bourgeois mess. The National Farmer-Labor Party remained little more than a skeleton. The Workers Party therefore decided to participate in the elections under its own name.

F257   .... The Next Task of the Left Wing, "Labor Herald," 3 (Sept. 1924), 198-200.
An assertion that the Trade Union Educational League has made great progress in bringing its demands to the attention of the AFL. Now it must register the will of the aroused rank and file and break the resistance of the bureaucrats, who cheat in elections and expel revolutionary members.

F258   .... La Follette, Gompers and Debs, "Labor Herald," 3 (Oct. 1924), 230-32.
The third party movement of 1924 is a united front of the middle class, trade unions, and socialists. La Follette is a militant defender of small capitalists, Gompers is a labor faker, and Debs is a sentimentalist who should have joined the communists. Revolutionists must expose the follies of La Follettism and stem the tide of reformism.

F259   .... The Workers Party to the Fore, "Workers Monthly," 4 (Nov. 1924), 9-11.
The leader of the "trade union" faction within the Workers

Party urges the Party to abandon its labor-party slogan, concentrating instead on workers' immediate struggles in shops and factories. (This position was opposed by the Ruthenberg or "political" wing of the Party.) The Workers Party in the 1924 election must seek to assist the masses to cast off the La Follette illusion, and to unite the more advanced workers into the Workers Party and the TUEL.

F260 FOSTER, William Z. The Significance of the Elections: Three Stages of Our Labor Party Policy, "Workers Monthly," 4 (Dec. 1924), 51-54.
Asserting that the Workers Party was justified in entering the labor party movement in 1922 and in withdrawing from the National Farmer-Labor Party in the summer of 1924 when it became a mere shell, Foster argues that the WP should now drop the farmer-labor party slogan. This slogan, absorbed by the La Follette movement, has become useless in the class struggle. (This view was opposed by C. E. Ruthenberg, leader of the opposing faction.)

F261 . . . . The Elections in the United States, "International Press Correspondence," 4 (Dec. 11, 1924), 943-44.
A review of the 1924 presidential election results. The La Follette vote was a defeat for that movement, while the small Workers Party vote was not indicative of its true strength. A factional struggle is going on inside the Workers Party over the question of forming a farmer-labor party in which the WP will participate.

F262 . . . . "Organize the Unorganized." Chicago: Trade Union Educational League, 1925. 25 pp.
The union strategy to be followed by the left wing, outlined by the Party's leading union expert when the Party supported a policy of "boring from within" the conservative unions. Where there are no AFL unions, Foster states, new unions must be formed and brought into affiliation with the broad labor movement; where old unions exist, left-wing workers must enter them. The dual-union tendency must be combatted.

F263 . . .; CANNON, J. P.; and BROWDER, Earl R. "Trade Unions in America." Chicago: Daily Worker Publishing Co. for the Trade Union Educational League, n.d. [1925]. 36 pp.
An analysis of the membership and structure of the American labor movement, emphasizing corruption and betrayal in the conservative unions and the rise of the TUEL. The TUEL campaign for amalgamation of unions and formation of a labor party is described, and the expulsion of leftists by the conservative union leaders is denounced. TUEL strength in the recent UMW election is pointed to as illustrative of the membership revolt against class collaboration.

F264 . . . . The American Federation of Labor Convention, "Workers Monthly," 4 (Jan. 1925), 103-7.
A review of the AFL convention held November 17-25 at El Paso, which is called the most reactionary in history. The left-wing was practically unrepresented, since only the highest trade-union bureaucrats attend. Resolutions by TUEL militants dealing with a general labor congress, Soviet recognition, union amalgamation, American imperialism, etc., were ignored or defeated overwhelmingly.

F265 . . . . The Left Wing in Trade Union Elections, "Workers Monthly," 4 (Feb. 1925), 147-50 ff.
A description of fights waged by the TUEL within the United Mine Workers, the Carpenters, the Iron, Steel, and Tin Workers, the Machinists, the Fur Workers, the ILGWU,

the Amalgamated Clothing Workers, and the Minneapolis Trades and Labor Assembly. TUEL candidates for office are fought with expulsions, violence, and fraudulent elections.

F266 . . . . Amalgamation from Below, "Workers Monthly," 4 (April 1925), 253-54 ff.
Amalgamation of trade unions is everywhere forced on union bureaucrats by pressure from the bottom. The rank-and-file demand for amalgamation in the U.S., led by the TUEL, is being fought to the death by our stupid and venal bureaucrats. The struggle for amalgamation must be extended and carried on at three distinct but closely related levels—national, local, and shop.

F267 . . . . Party Industrial Methods and Structure, "Workers Monthly," 4 (June 1925), 351-52 ff.
An admission that the TUEL is suffering a decline of influence, its members becoming isolated. The reasons are found in union reverses in industry and a growth of the class collaboration movement. Shop nuclei are needed to strengthen the Party's work in the factories, and a progressive bloc should be organized in the trade unions of ideologically backward masses who are discontented with their reactionary leaders.

F268 . . . . Party Trade Union Fractions, "Workers Monthly," 4 (July 1925), 414-16.
A call for greater effort to build communist fractions in labor unions. The fractions must not be confused with shop nuclei, the basic Party structure for collecting dues and determining and executing Party policies. Communist fractions within the TUEL are usually identical with Party fractions in the trade unions. The TUEL should be a mass organization, not restricted to Party members.

F269 . . . . The Ladies Garment Workers Awaken, "Workers Monthly," 4 (Aug. 1925), 440-42.
A description of the "degeneration" of the leadership of the needle trades unions, including the ILGWU, the Fur Workers, and the Amalgamated Clothing Workers. President Sigman of the ILGWU, engaged in a war against the left wing, has swept out of office 77 members of the executive boards of three local unions on flimsy charges. The healthy movement of revolt runs the danger of dual unionism.

F270 . . . . Company Unions, "Workers Monthly," 4 (Sept. 1925), 497-99.
A description of the growth of company unions, particularly in the steel and railroad industries. They are based on class collaboration, the subjugation of workers' interests to those of employers. Nevertheless they can be fought and even captured. The shop nuclei must discredit or destroy company unions, or capture and transform them into genuine shop committees and trade unions.

F271 . . . . The Left Wing Labor Conference, "Workers Monthly," 4 (Oct. 1925), 538-39.
A report on the second international conference of the International Committee for Amalgamation in the Railroad Industry, which is said to have lost much ground since its 1922 conference. Its failure is attributed to poor union leadership, wholesale wage cuts, class collaboration, and the like.

F272 . . . . The Left Wing in the Needle Trades, "Workers Monthly," 5 (Nov. 1925), 25-28.
A discussion of the fight of the left wing in the ILGWU against the administration of President Sigman, and of the third national conference of the needle trades section of the TUEL. Within the ILGWU the communists avoided dual unionism despite the expulsions, and won a sub-

stantial victory in the settlement. The TUEL conference, attended by 90 delegates, stressed amalgamation and the policies needed to win the union from the reactionaries.

F273 FOSTER, William Z. "Russian Workers and Workshops in 1926." Chicago: Trade Union Educational League, n.d. [1926?]. 60 pp.
A report of a trip through Soviet industry, with stops at steel, railroad, coal, chemical, agricultural machinery, electrical, rubber, textile, and shipbuilding enterprises. Foster presents figures on employment, earnings, and production, and describes workers' clubs, rest houses, and technical schools. Hailing the revolution as an unqualified success, he calls it the inspiration and leader of the world's working class.

F274 . . . . "Strike Strategy." Chicago: Trade Union Educational League, 1926. 88 pp.
An important pamphlet by the Party's leading union expert, classifying strikes into types determined by the state of capitalist development, and specifying the correct strike strategy for each. He lists three strike prerequisites: the development of worker solidarity, the building of a well-organized and militant group leadership, and a Marxian analysis of the problem. He discusses a number of strike issues, including the organization of peripheral activities, principles to hold to in a strike settlement, and post-strike follow-up action.

F275 . . . . Company Unionism and Trade Unionism, "Workers Monthly," 5 (Jan. 1926), 131-33.
Whereas traditionally employers have sought to eradicate trade unions, now they are developing company unions instead, while union bureaucrats' schemes of class collaboration, like the B & O plan, are causing the trade unions to degenerate until they approximate company unions. The left wing must destroy or penetrate company unions, while organizing a progressive bloc within trade unions.

F276 . . . . Trade Union Insurance, "Workers Monthly," 5 (July 1926), 413-15 ff.
The recent development of trade union life insurance is denounced as an insidious aspect of class collaboration. Insurance is an important phase of trade union capitalism, which includes labor banking, ownership of office buildings, etc. The TUEL must war against trade union capitalism.

F277 . . . . The Railroad Employees' Department Convention, "Workers Monthly," 5 (Aug. 1926), 449-51 ff.
A characterization of the convention of the AFL Railway Employees' Department, held in Chicago, June 28 to July 2, as one of surrender to the employers and intensified class collaboration. The left-wing proposes general wage demands, organization of the unorganized, militant struggle instead of class collaboration, amalgamation of unions, and a labor party.

F278 . . . . A Dangerous Situation, "Workers Monthly," 5 (Sept. 1926), 493-95.
An assertion that the United Mine Workers are falling to pieces because of the misleadership of John L. Lewis and the crisis caused by overproduction of bituminous coal. Lewis' program calls for a wage cut in the bituminous fields, class collaboration, and terrorism against the left wing. Disaster can be avoided by supporting John Brophy as a candidate for president against Lewis.

F279 . . . . "Misleaders of Labor." Chicago: Trade Union Educational League, 1927. 336 pp.
A denunciation of the class collaboration policies of the reactionary AFL leadership, and an exposure of graft in the building trades unions, the plundering of union treasuries, the autocratic control of unions, the use of "tainted" labor journalism, and the development of trade-union capitalism to swindle the workers. The author concludes with a TUEL program calling for mass struggle against American imperialism, a united front with all constructive elements among the workers, unionization of semi-skilled and unskilled workers, union democracy, and a fight against class collaboration.

F280 . . . . "The Watson-Parker Law: The Latest Scheme to Hamstring Railroad Unionism." Chicago: Trade Union Educational League, 1927. 48 pp.
Denunciation of a law which is said to continue the disastrous retreat of the railroad unions since 1920-21. Terming the Railway Labor Act of 1926 a fraud and betrayal, Foster calls for a general wage increase, union organization and amalgamation, an end to the B & O Plan and trade-union capitalism, and nationalization and a labor party.

F281 . . . . "Wrecking the Labor Banks." Chicago: Trade Union Educational League, 1927. 60 pp.
A description of the financial collapse of the banks and investment companies of the Brotherhood of Locomotive Engineers to emphasize the destructive effects of trade union capitalism upon the labor movement. Instead of pursuing trade union capitalism, which develops class collaboration, the unions must be redeveloped as fighting organizations.

F282 . . . . The Struggle in the Needle Trades, "Workers Monthly," 6 [5] (Jan. 1927), 688-90.
An assertion that the needle trades constitute the sharpest point in the class struggle in the U.S. now, with the masses under left-wing leadership fighting the bosses and the right-wing socialist union officials. The needle trades unions, becoming company-unionized, support speed-up and class collaboration. The right-wing leaders spread defeatism in strikes led by the left-wing.

F283 . . . , and GITLOW, Benjamin. "Acceptance Speeches." New York: Workers Library for the National Election Campaign Committee of the Workers (Communist) Party, 1928. 47 pp.
The acceptance speeches in the 1928 campaign of Foster, communist candidate for president, and Gitlow, candidate for vice-president, together with the report of the Committee on Nominations and Jay Lovestone's closing remarks at the nominating convention. The candidates emphasize the Party's revolutionary nature and its anti-imperialist, pro-Soviet line, and attack the Socialist Party as the "hangman of the revolution."

F284 . . . . The Crisis in the Labor Movement, "Communist," 7 (Jan. 1928), 10-20.
The labor movement is in a crisis as a result of the breaking up of the United Mine Workers, following victories of the coal operators in strikes in Pennsylvania and Ohio. The employers are trying to undermine all existing unions. Foster urges the Workers Party to organize discontented workers in the TUEL and support labor-party developments.

F285 . . . . Capitalist Efficiency "Socialism," "Communist," 7 (Feb. 1928), 90-104; (March), 169-74.
The current trend toward industrial reform is capitalism's means of assuring rising productivity and liquidating the workers' revolutionary movement. Foster denounces conservative trade unionists and right-wing socialists for accepting the general principles and practices of capitalist efficiency "socialism."

F286 FOSTER, William Z. A Show-down in the Mining Industry, "Labor Unity," 2 (April 1928), 1-4, 22-23.
The economic crisis in the coal industry, combined with the corruption and inertia of the Lewis administration, have brought the union, Foster asserts, to its greatest crisis, with real danger of its destruction. Since no democracy remains in the union, the Save-the-Union Committee must clash openly with Lewis for leadership of the miners.

F287 .... Tasks and Lessons of the Miners' Struggle, "Communist," 7 (April 1928), 195-200.
Description of a united front of rank-and-file union members, formed to oppose the Lewis machine in the United Mine Workers. Plans for organizing the unorganized miners throughout the country are outlined. There has never been a better chance to build the Party in the coal fields.

F288 .... Two Mine Strike Strategies, "Communist," 7 (May 1928), 279-83.
A contrast of the retreat policy of John L. Lewis in the mining strike with that of the "Save-the-Union Movement," which is attempting to broaden and intensify the strike. One is a policy of class surrender, the other of class struggle.

F289 .... Old Unions and New Unions, "Communist," 7 (July 1928), 399-405.
The Party's emphasis in trade union work is to be changed, following criticism by Losovsky of the Red International of Labor Unions, to place main emphasis on the organization of the unorganized into new unions. At the same time the Party will develop a TUEL opposition in old unions of a mass character. (This represented a sharp change in Foster's traditional opposition to dual unionism.)

F290 .... New Tasks of the T.U.E.L., "Labor Unity," 2 (Oct. 1928), 1, 18-20.
The national secretary of the Trade Union Educational League, applying the new line of the Red International of Labor Unions, calls for the TUEL to organize the masses of nonunion, industrial workers into new unions, while intensifying work within the old unions.

F291 .... The Workers (Communist) Party in the South, "Communist," 7 (Nov. 1928), 676-81.
The Party has made a beginning at active work in the South. Rapid industrialization is developing a rich field for the Party, as the leader of the working class and the organizer and defender of the Negro race. There must be no compromise with Jim Crowism or with white chauvinism.

F292 .... The Decline of the American Federation of Labor, "Communist," 8 (Jan.-Feb., 1929), 47-58.
The AFL convention in November 1928 was the most reactionary in its history. It supported American imperialism, capitalist rationalization, a high tariff, and the formation of capitalist trusts. Its decline in membership continues, while it wars against the left. The TUEL must organize the unorganized into new unions, while keeping up its work in the old unions.

F293 .... The Cleveland Unity Convention, "Labor Unity," 3 (April 20, 1929), 3; (April 27), 5; (May 4), 5; (May 11), 5.
A series of articles, in preparation for the June 1 convention, on the need to set up the Trade Union Unity League. The four articles deal respectively with "A New Trade Union Center," "The Organization of the Unorganized," "Fight the Reformist Labor Leaders," and "Organize the Negro Workers, Fight Inequality."

F294 .... Right Tendencies at the Trade Union Unity Congress, "Communist," 8 (July 1929), 369-74.
A warning against right tendencies at the coming Trade Union Unity Convention in Cleveland, August 31. The Muste "Labor Age" group, Cannon-Trotsky elements, and Jay Lovestone's exceptionalism must be guarded against.

F295 .... The Party Trade Union Work during Ten Years, "Communist," 8 (Sept. 1929), 488-93; (Nov.), 609-18.
A review of the Party's achievements and mistakes in trade union work during its first ten years, covering the postwar capitalist offensive of 1920-23, the era of "prosperity" from 1923 to mid-1928, and the present period of sharp class struggles. The outlook for the future is excellent.

F296 .... The T.U.U.L. Convention, "Communist," 8 (Sept. 1929), 528-33.
The Trade Union Unity League convention demonstrated the growing radicalization of the American working class. It endorsed the entire program of the Profintern and the TUEL, responded enthusiastically to slogans against imperialist war and for the defense of the Soviet Union, and crushed the Lovestone group.

F297 .... "Fight against Hunger." New York: Workers Library, 1930. 32 pp.
A statement to the Fish Committee, which was investigating communist activities in the U.S. The author criticizes starvation and unemployment, the brutality of the bosses and police, and the strikebreaking activities of the AFL and the Socialist Party. The Fish Committee is investigating communists, he says, in order to bolster the waning power of the AFL, an instrument of the capitalist class.

F298 .... "Victorious Socialist Construction in the Soviet Union." New York: Trade Union Unity League, n.d. [1930]. 46 pp.
A contrast of the deepening crisis of world capitalism with the astounding growth in the Soviet Union under socialism. Describing the Soviet's five-year plan, Foster attributes USSR successes to the superior organization of socialism, vast financial economies, socialist mass incentive, and the constructive role of the trade unions. Only the TUUL, he concludes, fights with the workers of the world against war, for the defense of the USSR, and for the overthrow of world imperialism.

F299 .... The Trade Union Line of Lovestone and Cannon—Muste Auxiliaries, "Communist," 9 (Oct. 1930), 884-99.
From 1921 until 1928 the communist policy was to work within conservative unions. When capitalism entered into its "third period" of decay and general crisis, the communists formed new revolutionary unions under the TUUL. The Lovestone-Cannon-Musteites, however, would liquidate the revolutionary movement inside as well as outside the conservative unions.

F300 .... "Little Brothers of the Big Labor Fakers." New York: Trade Union Unity League, 1931. 32 pp.
An attack on A. J. Muste and the Conference for Progressive Labor Action. Foster denounces the CPLA as an AFL "left maneuver," and its founder as an advocate of capitalist planned economy, supporter of the AFL betrayal in the South, and a false friend of the USSR. He urges class conscious workers to renounce the CPLA and support the TUUL instead.

F301 .... Calverton's Fascism, "Communist," 10 (Feb. 1931), 107-11.

A reply to Calverton's "Democracy vs. Dictatorship" in the current "Modern Quarterly." Calverton's article is a medley of fascist, social-fascist, and communist conceptions. As a whole it is an essay in fascism, in flat contradiction to Marxian principles. The social-fascist and liberal elements who debate Marxism in the "Modern Quarterly" are defenders of revisionism and capitalism; they are enemies of the revolution.

F302 FOSTER, William Z. On the Question of Trade Union Democracy, "Communist," 10 (March 1931), 199-203.
A call for democracy in the revolutionary unions of the Trade Union Unity League. The Party does not possess all the wisdom; avoiding bureaucracy, it must learn from the masses as well as teach them.

F303 .... Musteism—"Left" Demagogy a la Mode, "Communist," 10 (June 1931), 483-87.
As the crisis deepens, the employers use the most blatant "left" demagogy, such as that of the Conference for Progressive Labor Action, the Muste group, to hold the masses in check. Its radical talk is designed to confuse the workers and draw them into the control of the AFL and SP reactionaries. The Party and the TUUL must struggle militantly against Musteism.

F304 .... The Coal Strike, "Communist," 10 (July 1931), 595-99.
The rapid spread of the coal strike under the leadership of the National Miners Union justifies the Comintern and RILU line, shows the growing radicalization of the workers, supports the program of building the new unions, and demonstrates the growing fascization of the AFL bureaucracy. The strike has been handicapped by the weakness of the Party nuclei in the mine field.

F305 .... "Toward Soviet America." New York: Coward-McCann, 1932. 343 pp.
A full-length statement of Party policy during the "third period." Pointing to depression unemployment and impoverishment, Foster contrasts the injustices and failures of American capitalism with the economic and cultural achievements of the USSR. Defending the dictatorship of the proletariat in Russia as the democracy of the toiling masses directed against the former exploiters, he advocates a similar dictatorship here, which will confiscate large-scale industry and end capitalist robbery and waste. Other results, he says, will be liberation of Negroes, emancipation of women, unshackling of youth, and the ushering in of a profound cultural revolution. The Socialist Party and AFL are declared far advanced toward fascization.

F306 .... "The Words and Deeds of Franklin Roosevelt." New York: Workers Library, 1932. 16 pp.
A speech by the communist presidential candidate in 1932, denouncing Roosevelt, and accusing him of motives as capitalistic as those of his Republican opponents.

F307 .... Our Work in the Reformist Unions, "Labor Unity," 7 (March 1932), 3-6.
Disagreeing with Joseph Zack's views on the tactic of the united front (in "Labor Unity," Jan.-Feb.), the secretary of the Trade Union Unity League doubts that the reformist unions are about to break up. Pointing to the current wave of radicalization, he proposes that the TUUL intensify activities in the reformist unions, starting in the shops and also building minority organizations inside the local unions, but in addition emphasizing a united front with reformist unions wherever they have the masses.

F308 .... Some Elementary Phases of the Work in the

Reformist Trade Unions, "Communist," 11 (June 1932), 509-18.
General agitation in the old unions must give way to struggle over immediate economic demands. During AFL strikes the revolutionary unions must build up united-front contacts with the strikers. Comrades must not, by splitting an old union, transform a powerful opposition into an isolated independent union. We must discredit the labor fakers by every means.

F309 ..., and BROWDER, Earl. "Technocracy and Marxism." New York: Workers Library, 1933. 32 pp.
A Marxist refutation of the Technocrats' economic theory and proposed solution of the world's current economic crisis. The two leading American communists view Technocracy as a degenerate form of Veblenism, representing the dreams of baffled technicians who hope to reestablish themselves and capitalism.

F310 .... Fascist Tendencies in the United States, "Communist," 14 (Oct. 1935), 883-902.
Though a fascist movement is growing in the U.S., its main stream is not (as had previously been argued by the CP) in the New Deal, but in such groups and individuals as the American Liberty League, the American Legion, the "shirt" groups, Hearst, Father Coughlin, Huey Long, etc. A broad, antifascist, farmer-labor party, including sections of the bourgeoisie, must be formed in the U.S.

F311 .... Syndicalism in the United States, "Communist," 14 (Nov. 1935), 1044-57.
An analysis of syndicalism, its development in the U.S., its errors, and its demise with the organization of the Communist Party. The syndicalist movement, formerly strong in America, was destroyed by the Russian communist revolution, which showed the need for a political party of trained revolutionaries.

F312 .... "The Crisis in the Socialist Party." New York: Workers Library, 1936. 70 pp.
A communist assertion that the Socialist Party has failed historically because of opportunism, reformism, and class collaborationism, the result of its petty bourgeois leadership. Avoiding a Marxian class-struggle line, it has never become a mass revolutionary party. The Socialist Party, now being pushed in a revolutionary direction by the radicalization of the masses and the growth of the popular-front movement, is held back by reformism and Trotskyism. (Based on a series of articles that appeared in "Communist" between Oct. 1936 and Jan. 1937.)

F313 ..., and HONIG, N. "Industrial Unionism." New York: Workers Library, 1936. 48 pp.
The position of the Communist Party in the early days of the CIO, before the Party gave the CIO unequivocal support. The authors praise the industrial form of labor organization, telling of their own struggle for it in past years. Nevertheless they criticize the Lewis bloc at the AFL convention for not repudiating craft unionism entirely and for not adopting a class-struggle policy.

F314 .... "Organizing Methods in the Steel Industry." New York: Workers Library, 1936. 24 pp.
The leader of the 1919 steel strike outlines organizing methods to be followed in the steel industry. He deals with union structure and functions, mass agitation and mass organization, special group work, company unions, and special organization work outside the union itself.

F315 .... "Unionizing Steel." New York: Workers Library, 1936. 46 pp.

Reprints of "Daily Worker" articles by Foster on the prospects of steel unionism. Foster shows why the 1936 campaign of the CIO will succeed where the 1919 campaign failed. He predicts that, if the CIO will learn from the lessons of 1919, it can organize, not only the 500,000 steel workers, but also millions of workers in other industries.

F316 FOSTER, William Z. The Industrial Union Bloc in the American Federation of Labor, "Communist International," 13 (May 1936), 624-35.
An analysis of the progressive opposition movement, the CIO, now taking shape within the AFL. Although Lewis and Hillman have not been friends of the communists, the Party will support the CIO's organization campaign, which should start with steel workers.

F317 .... "From Bryan to Stalin." New York: International Publishers, 1937. 352 pp. Ind.
An account of Foster's experiences in union organization and left-wing politics. Early a member of the Socialist Party, Foster was also active in the IWW and headed two small syndicalist organizations before leading the AFL organizing drive in meat packing in 1917-18 and the great steel strike of 1919. In 1920 he formed the Trade Union Educational League to bore from within the mass unions, and in the following year he became a communist. Foster criticizes his early failures to achieve communist orthodoxy, and describes the activities of the TUEL (1920-29) and its successor, the Trade Union Unity League (1929-35).

F318 ..., and others. "How the Auto Workers Won." New York: Daily Worker, 1937. 14 pp.
Articles reproduced from the "Daily Worker" in praise of the victory of the UAW-CIO in Detroit over General Motors, due to the new and progressive trade union tactics used by the workers.

F319 .... "A Manual of Industrial Unionism: Organizational Structure and Policies." New York: Workers Library, 1937. 63 pp.
The nature, structure, and practices of industrial unionism, as represented by the newly formed CIO, with an explanation of its superiority over AFL craft unionism. This superiority is attributed to its recognition of the class struggle and its organization of workers in a single industry as a class. The pamphlet tells how industrial unionism should be organized and operated. Rank-and-file members of AFL craft unions are urged to repudiate their reactionary leaders and unite with the CIO, the railroad brotherhoods, and independent unions.

F320 ...; BITTELMAN, Alex; FORD, James W.; and KRUMBEIN, Charles. "Party Building and Political Leadership." New York: Workers Library, 1937. 127 pp.
Reports to the plenary meeting of the Party's Central Committee, June 17-20, 1937. Foster's report is on "Party Building and Political Leadership," Bittelman's is on "The Party and the People's Front," Ford's is on "Developing Negro Communist Leaders," and Krumbein's is on "Problems of Developing Leading Forces." The first two are published in full, with excerpts from the other two.

F321 .... "Questions and Answers on the Piatakov-Radek Trial." New York: Workers Library, 1937. 79 pp.
A defense of the trial of 17 Trotskyites in Moscow in January 1937 in which they confessed a conspiracy, directed by Trotsky, to overthrow the Soviet government with armed assistance from Germany and Japan. Far from being fantastic, their plot is termed the logical climax of treason, espionage, and sabotage. Foster denies that the Moscow trials were frame-ups, opposes an international trial as demanded by Trotsky, and denounces Trotskyism as a diseased growth of strikebreakers and counterrevolutionaries.

F322 .... "Railroad Workers, Forward!" New York: Workers Library, 1937. 61 pp.
A plea to railroad workers to develop a more militant trade union policy, to prevent exploitation by the owners as in the past. Amalgamation and democratization of the railroad unions are urged, along with formation of a farmer-labor party, a broad people's front.

F323 .... "What Means a Strike in Steel." New York: Workers Library, 1937. 64 pp.
The leader of the 1919 steel strike forecasts another steel strike soon, asserting that proper knowledge of strike preparation, organization, and execution will insure victory. The CIO, in his view, should then organize the unorganized, reunite with the AFL, and help form a national farmer-labor party, the beginning of a broad people's front in the U.S.

F324 .... The Convention of the A.F. of L., "Communist International," 14 (Jan. 1937), 45-50.
A report on the November 1936 convention of the AFL, which confirmed the suspension of the CIO unions. The Party has supported the CIO, which has rosy prospects, with some criticism of CIO policies. The Party proposes trade-union unity and industrial unionism. Foster foresees mass struggles under CIO leadership.

F325 .... The Significance of the Sit-Down Strike, "Communist," 16 (April 1937), 334-41.
A discussion of the circumstances leading to the use of the sit-down strike, and of its revolutionary role in the organization of workers against the capitalists and their allies. The Party should help develop this powerful weapon for maximum possibilities in organization campaigns.

F326 .... The Renaissance of the American Trade Union Movement, "Communist International," 14 (June 1937), 397-402.
A communist view of the rise of the CIO as representing the radicalization of the working masses and the organization of American workers as a class, both economically and politically. A great American People's Front should crystallize from the mass forces grouped around the CIO. The CPUSA seeks to develop the CIO in this direction, while leading mass struggles and championing trade union unity.

F327 .... Political Leadership and Party Building, "Communist," 16 (July 1937), 628-46.
Communist recruitment has lagged despite favorable conditions. In order to recruit, the Party must maintain its leadership role, formulating more advanced goals and slogans. Communists in leadership positions in mass organizations should not conceal their Party affiliation, or the Party will not get credit for their work. While communists should lead front groups, they should not monopolize the offices.

F328 .... For a National Health Program, "Communist," 16 (Aug. 1937), 754-60.
To solve the problem of widespread illness among Americans, a national health program must be set up, based on high wages, good working conditions, stringent food inspection, adequate housing, lengthy vacations, adequate insurance, and a vast system of hospitals and clinics. A mass united front must be organized to push this program.

F329 FOSTER, William Z. American Origins of the People's Front, "Communist," 16 (Dec. 1937), 1103-7.
The accusation that the people's front is an importation from Moscow is false. There has been a long tradition in the U.S. of unity of poorer farmers, petty bourgeoisie, and workers against the capitalists. Unlike the present people's front, these earlier movements were poorly organized, presented a confused program, and were dominated by farmers rather than by workers.

F330 . . . . The Struggle for Trade Union Unity in the U.S.A., "Communist International," 14 (Dec. 1937), 1096-1101.
An analysis of the split in labor's ranks and the formation of the CIO, in whose success the Communist Party plays an important role. The CIO has become the main American trade union center. Foster calls for unity of AFL and CIO on the basis of industrial unionism.

F331 . . . . "Halt the Railroad Wage Cut." New York: Workers Library, 1938. 14 pp.
An attack on the railroads' proposal for a 15 per cent wage cut. This must be defeated and steps taken toward government control of the entire industry. In addition, railroad workers must democratize their unions, become active politically, and establish socialism.

F332 . . . . "Stop Wage-Cuts and Layoffs on the Railroads." New York: Workers Library, 1938. 23 pp.
Written as a reply to an attack on Foster and his views by President T. C. Cashen of the Switchmen's Union, the pamphlet attacks Cashen for lies, strikebreaking, and Red-baiting. Foster urges the six-hour day, amalgamation of related crafts, admission of Negroes, government ownership of the railroads, trade union democracy, trade union unity, and united political action.

F333 . . . . World Fascism and War, "Communist," 17 (April 1938), 322-33.
The fascist powers are planning to attack Russia, the obstacle to their designs for world conquest. They are held back by the growing strength of Russia, disunity in their own ranks, and the increasing resistance of the capitalist democracies. The task of the communists is to strengthen the obstacles to fascist attack.

F334 . . . . The Socialist Party Convention, "Communist," 17 (June 1938), 509-12.
As a result of its left sectarianism, advocating the immediate realization of socialism, the Socialist Party has lost most of its members and trade union influence. Nevertheless its twenty-first convention decided to continue to oppose the democratic front, collective security, the Communist Party, and Russia.

F335 . . . . Win the Western Hemisphere for Democracy and Peace! "Communist," 17 (July 1938), 600-14.
An assertion, in a speech to the Party's tenth convention, that German, Italian, and Japanese fascists are trying to foist fascism on American countries. Cooperation among governments, democratic fronts, trade unions, and communist parties of the Western Hemisphere can prevent this. To fight fascism, the American nations must cooperate with democracies outside the Western Hemisphere.

F336 . . . . The American Federation of Labor and Trade Union Progress, "Communist," 17 (Aug. 1938), 689-98.
The AFL's leftward movement is evidenced by its more militant strike policy, its increased politicalization, and its support of progressive legislation. The formation of the CIO by a great progressive section of the AFL is described. Trade union unity is needed to consolidate industrial and political progress and permit further advance.

F337 . . . . The Communist Party and the Professionals, "Communist," 17 (Sept. 1938), 805-10.
The Party must use the potential strength of professionals, who have been radicalized by depression, fascism, and war. Their value is crucial in the areas of theoretical work, Party education, and the advancement of communism in and through their professions. The Party must develop their revolutionary possibilities, while avoiding the danger of reformist individuals and tendencies among them.

F338 . . . . Panacea Mass Movements: A Problem in Building the Democratic Front, "Communist," 17 (Nov. 1938), 984-92; (Dec.), 1086-93.
The Technocracy, Epic, Utopian Society, Townsend, Social Justice, and Share-the-Wealth movements all arose to meet the grievances of the masses in a depression. Most of these movements were led by reactionaries, and some were organized to split the progressive vote. Although they have mostly died out since Roosevelt's victory, they could again become dangerous. The most effective answer to this danger is a democratic front that will meet the pressing demands of the masses.

F339 . . . . Anent the American Medical Association, "Communist," 17 (Dec. 1938), 1137-40.
The reactionary AMA opposes Roosevelt's health program. Pharmaceutical firms and rich doctors who want to make money out of illness are opposed to any program that will prevent illness. In opposing the government's health program, the AMA blocks the medical advances that would result.

F340 . . . . "Pages from a Worker's Life." New York: International Publishers, 1939. 314 pp.
The autobiography of one of America's leading communists, emphasizing experiences that throw light on the exploitation and struggles of American workers and that contributed to his political development. Included are descriptions of his activities in the IWW, the steel strike of 1919, the Trade Union Educational League, the 1931-32 hunger march, and the CIO campaigns.

F341 . . . . "Your Questions Answered." New York: Workers Library, 1939. 127 pp.
Answers to 115 questions, showing the party line in the period of the popular-front. Chapters deal with the democratic front, the struggle for peace, economic crises, trade unionism, the Negro and Jewish peoples, the Soviet Union, and the Party. Foster argues that only a broad democratic front can defeat the danger of fascism in the U.S., and calls for a policy of collective security, an alliance of the leading nonaggression states, to restrain the fascist war-making states and assist their victims. Though capitalism cannot solve the general crisis of its world system, it will survive somehow until the masses, led by the Communist Party, establish socialism.

F342 . . . . Isolationist Defeatism! "Communist," 18 (Jan. 1939), 40-47.
The isolationists claim that opposition to the fascist nations will bring a war that the democracies will lose; and that, even if they are victorious, war will cause loss of liberty. Foster answers that the democracies are potentially stronger; that their failure to oppose the fascist nations encourages aggression; and that, unlike World War I, only one camp is now the aggressor.

F343 FOSTER, William Z. New Methods of Political Mass Organization, "Communist," 18 (Feb. 1939), 136-46.
Techniques must be improved to win large numbers of people to the "democratic" cause in the face of increasing reactionary opposition. Intensified drives are suggested to increase labor's political role, ally farmers and workers, enact progressive legislation, and coordinate democratic front political forces.

F344 .... The Human Element in Mass Agitation, "Communist," 18 (April 1939), 346-52.
Modern progressives are too unemotional, objective, and statistical. They should be like the old progressives, who eloquently portrayed the hardships and poverty of the masses. Despite a lessening of the brutalities of capitalist exploitation, enough misery exists under modern capitalism to warrant a more eloquent and emotional approach.

F345 .... The Technique of the Mass Campaign, "Communist," 18 (May 1939), 445-55.
A description of the people's technique of mass agitation, organization, and struggle. The elements of a mass political campaign include utilization of the burning issue, developing a plan of action, mobilizing forces, and good execution. Questions of organization must receive far closer attention.

F346 .... Main Organizational Tasks of the Democratic Front, "Communist," 18 (June 1939), 535-41.
An outline of the chief areas of organizational work of the democratic front, with suggestions of ways in which it can be strengthened. Tasks include organizing the mass offensive, consolidating the toilers' ranks, recruiting the people's forces, and administering mass organizations.

F347 .... Building the Western-Hemisphere Democratic Front, "Communist," 18 (July 1939), 606-21.
The Germans and Italians seek to help local fascists seize power in Latin America. Their efforts are balked by the Latin American people's fronts, which seek land reform; the Pan American Peace Front, promising mutual aid against aggression; U.S. reciprocal trade agreements and government loans; and cooperation of Latin American youth and trade union organizations.

F348 .... Secondary Aspects of Mass Organization, "Communist," 18 (Aug. 1939), 701-11.
The democratic front should adapt to secondary influences such as religion, patriotism, ritualism, fraternal insurance, and social activities in order to attract and retain adherents. The front should combat influences such as capitalist illusions, racism, and discrimination against Negroes, women, and youths, because these are inconsistent with the front's primary purposes.

F349 .... Twenty Years of Communist Trade Union Policy, "Communist," 18 (Sept. 1939), 804-16.
A detailed review of changing communist tactics in the American labor movement by the Party's leading trade union expert. He reviews the work of the Trade Union Educational League, the later Trade Union Unity League, and labor progress in the Roosevelt New Deal period. The present central task is to achieve labor unity so as to assure victory in the 1940 elections.

F350 .... Specific Organizational Features of the Democratic Front in the United States, "Communist," 18 (Oct. 1939), 939-50.
Three peculiarly American features must be considered

in organizing a democratic front here: the responsiveness of Americans to the mass agitator, the absence of a working class political party, and the militancy of American workers.

F351 .... "Capitalism, Socialism and the War." New York: Workers Library, 1940. 22 pp.
A leader of the Party urges the strengthening of anticapitalist forces to prevent the imperialists from launching a joint attack upon the USSR. The fact that capitalism is declining in the face of socialist gains makes such aggression imminent.

F352 .... "Roosevelt Heads for War." New York: Workers Library, 1940. 15 pp.
Foster holds the Roosevelt Administration partly responsible for the European war because of its failure to cooperate with the USSR in a peace front against fascist aggressors, and because of its betrayal of Spanish democracy. He attacks Roosevelt's "hunger and war" budget, his war loan to "fascist" Finland, and his assault on the democratic rights of unions and communists. (A pamphlet of the Hitler-Stalin pact period.)

F353 .... "The United States and the Soviet Union." New York: Workers Library, 1940. 15 pp.
Text of a speech by the Party's national chairman to the John Reed Club, Harvard University, during the Hitler-Stalin pact period, urging the U.S. to stay out of World War II. The war is viewed as an imperialist one between rival capitalist states. The U.S. is urged to cooperate with the USSR for a just and lasting peace and for world democracy and prosperity.

F354 .... "The War Crisis: Questions and Answers." New York: Workers Library, 1940. 64 pp.
Questions and answers relating to the war, organized under three heads: the imperialist war, the U.S. and the war, and the Soviet Union. Finding the cause of the war in rival imperialist antagonism, Foster holds both sides responsible. He advocates a policy of neutrality for the U.S. with no aid to either side, and supports the Hitler-Stalin pact as a victory of Soviet diplomacy over world imperialism. He defends the invasion of Finland as necessary to Soviet security.

F355 .... "What's What about the War: Questions and Answers." New York: Workers Library, 1940. 47 pp.
A communist view of the war, during the period of the Hitler-Stalin pact, given in question-and-answer form. Foster holds all the great capitalist states, along with the treachery of the social democrats, responsible for the war. The USSR is blameless, however, since it sought to prevent the war and, only when that proved impossible, became neutral. U.S. entry into the war would not give it a democratic character. This is an unjust war in which the democratic masses have no interest.

F356 .... Seven Years of Roosevelt, "Communist," 19 (March 1940), 232-58.
A critical review of Roosevelt's entire period in office, charging that his early years were spent in buttressing a broken-down capitalist system, and that his concessions to the masses were the result of pressure led by the CP. This aroused the ire of Wall Street, to which Roosevelt yielded. With the outbreak of war in Europe, Roosevelt surrendered to Wall Street, becoming the spokesman of its warmongering.

F357 .... The War Aims of American Imperialism, "Communist," 19 (April 1940), 308-19.
A communist analysis of the war in Europe during the

period of the Nazi-Soviet pact, viewing it as an advanced stage in the general crisis of world capitalism. The program of American imperialism includes war profits, subjugating Latin America and the Far East, supporting the Allies, and injuring Russia. It seeks U.S. entry into the war, asserting that the Allies are fighting for democracy and that war is inevitable.

F358 FOSTER, William Z. World Socialism and the War, "Communist," 14 [19] (June 1940), 500-15.
A communist view of the war in Europe during the period of the Nazi-Soviet pact. Because of betrayal by its socialist leaders, the working class did not exploit the revolutionary opportunity following World War I. Chances are far better for a revolution under communist leadership after the present imperialist war. American capitalism, hostile to Russia, follows a pro-Allied foreign policy for profits and markets.

F359 .... The Three Basic Tasks of the Communist Peace Policy, "Communist," 19 (July 1940), 610-14.
An address to the Party's nominating convention, June 2, 1940. The tasks of the Party in 1940 are to oppose Roosevelt's foreign policy of aiding the Allies and seeking to dominate Latin America and the Far East; to achieve a just and lasting peace by organizing a worldwide movement supporting Russia's peace policy; and to replace capitalism with socialism.

F360 .... The Pan-American Conference in Havana, "Communist," 19 (Sept. 1940), 805-19.
The Pan-American conference gave permission to the U.S. to take over a European-held colony and drive other countries out of Pan-American markets through an economic cartel. Independence of Latin American countries is menaced by agreement for intervention by the American countries to suppress communist subversion. The communists oppose all imperialism, including that of the U.S.

F361 .... The Trade Unions and the War, "Communist," 19 (Oct. 1940), 890-906.
An examination, during the period of the Nazi-Soviet pact, of the stand of the trade unions on the war, with a statement of their task to prevent American involvement. Formation of a third party is necessary to defend labor's standard of living and civil rights, and to struggle against the war-makers.

F362 .... For a People's Policy in U.S.-Soviet Relations! "Communist," 19 (Nov. 1940), 978-89.
Before there can be close collaboration between the U.S. and Russia in a peace bloc the U.S. must pursue a peace policy like Russia's, remain neutral in the imperialist war between the Allies and Germany, and provide its people with security like that afforded the Russians under communism.

F363 .... "Communism versus Fascism: A Reply to Those Who Lump Together the Social Systems of the Soviet Union and Nazi Germany." New York: Workers Library, 1941. 31 pp.
A reply by a leading American communist to charges that the Soviet Union and Nazi Germany are identical in their totalitarianism. He asserts that the social systems of the two countries are at opposite poles in their economic structure, forms of political government, class composition, foreign policies, culture, and outlook on life. The Soviet Union represents peace and democracy, whereas fascism stands for dictatorship and war.

F364 .... "Defend America by Smashing Hitlerism." New York: Workers Library, 1941. 15 pp.

The text of a speech by the Party's national chairman on August 20, 1941, following the Nazi invasion of the USSR. Asserting that a Hitler victory would jeopardize American national interests and independence, Foster calls for full U.S. cooperation with the USSR and Britain, including creation of a great western front. He attacks both isolationism and the "all measures short of war" illusion.

F365 ..., and MINOR, Robert. "The Fight against Hitlerism." New York: Workers Library, 1941. 32 pp.
Abridged texts of two reports to the Party's national committee on June 28, 1941, following the Nazi invasion of the USSR, one by Foster, the Party chairman, and the other by Minor, its acting secretary. Emphasizing the change in the character of the war as a result of Soviet involvement, they call for all possible aid to the USSR and Britain, and for throwing American might against Hitler. They ask for the release of Browder and formation of a united people's movement against Nazism.

F366 .... "The Railroad Workers and the War." New York: Workers Library, 1941. 15 pp.
A warning to railroad workers, in the Party's isolationist phase during the Nazi-Soviet pact, that the great employers and their own union officials are plunging the American people into an imperialist war. The railroad unions should fight instead for better working conditions and peace, and against Red-baiting. However, the only real remedy is socialism as in the USSR.

F367 .... "Socialism: The Road to Peace, Prosperity and Freedom." New York: Workers Library, 1941. 47 pp.
A pamphlet of the Hitler-Stalin pact period, dismissing the war in Europe as an imperialist one, and centering attention on poverty in the midst of plenty in the U.S. and on the spreading fascist danger here. The root cause of mass misery, destruction, and tyranny is found in capitalism. Under socialism, Foster asserts, poverty will disappear, and we will enjoy democracy, peace, and freedom. Proof that socialism solves many economic and political problems is found in USSR experience.

F368 .... "The Soviet Union: Key Bastion of World Freedom, Friend and Ally of the American People." New York: Workers Library, 1941. 31 pp.
A communist view of the war in the period between Hitler's invasion of the USSR and the Pearl Harbor assault. Foster asserts that Soviet entry has transformed the war from an unjust to a just one. Hitler plans first to crush the USSR, then conquer England, and finally attack the U.S. The U.S. is urged to enter the war now, and with Britain open a big western front.

F369 .... Organized Labor's Two Conventions, "Communist," 20 (Jan. 1941), 38-50.
A contrast of the recent AFL and CIO conventions with respect to foreign and domestic policies. Writing during the Hitler-Stalin pact period, Foster assails the support pledged by the AFL to the "war policies of the Wall Street government." While its antiwar position is praised, the CIO is criticized for failure to break with the two-party system and lack of emphasis on friendly collaboration of the U.S. and USSR.

F370 .... World Capitalism and World Socialism, "Communist," 20 (March 1941), 220-37.
A contrast of the capitalist and socialist worlds, written during the Nazi-Soviet pact period. While capitalism is being weakened by internecine wars, anticapitalist forces grow stronger. The two imperialist camps try to beat

down resistance by use of terror and by demagogic appeals for national unity. The Communist International remains true to its peace policy. (Reprinted in pamphlet form.)

F371 FOSTER, William Z. American Fascism Speaks Out, "Communist," 20 (April 1941), 333-49.
Critical commentary on Lawrence Dennis' book, "The Dynamics of War and Revolution," intended as a guide to American fascist development. Dennis' main theme fits the outline of German fascism, combined with elements of Roosevelt's scarcity policy and agreement with many social-democratic concepts.

F372 .... Earl Browder and the Fight for Peace, "Communist," 20 (June 1941), 497-504.
A review of the path of the imperialist powers into war and of the militant efforts of the communists, led by Browder, to prevent American involvement.

F373 .... Yankee Imperialism Grabs for the Western Hemisphere, "Communist," 20 (July 1941), 581-98.
American imperialism seeks conquest of the Western Hemisphere, from which it hopes to exclude British and German imperialism. Its strategy consists of securing military bases, dominating markets and industry, controlling governments, and obtaining popular support through a deceitful Good Neighbor policy.

F374 .... For the Military Destruction of Hitlerism! "Communist," 20 (Sept. 1941), 793-800.
With Hitler engaged in a war against Russia, the one big barrier to his dream of world conquest, his agents in the U.S. are working to prevent American aid to Russia. Acceptance of their illusions about isolationism, coming to terms with Hitler, and letting Russia do all the fighting would free Hitler to concentrate on defeating Russia.

F375 .... The Soviet Union and the Course of the War, "Communist," 20 (Nov. 1941), 961-71.
Since the war became a people's war the German army has suffered great losses, the German war machine is running out of raw materials, and morale is weakening in the Axis countries. Nevertheless the war is far from won, and the U.S. must therefore enter. Labor should cement an alliance among Russia, Britain, and the U.S.

F376 .... The Tasks of the Communist Party in the War, "Communist," 20 (Dec. 1941), 1051-54.
Concluding remarks by the Party's national chairman to the meeting of its national committee, December 7, 1941, asserting that American entry into the war has not changed the Party's tasks. It demands increased efforts for Allied collaboration, national unity, labor unity, and increased war production.

F377 .... "American Democracy and the War." Workers Library, 1942. 14 pp.
Arguing that this is a people's war, needing the fullest support of the masses, Foster urges a number of steps to increase democracy at home. These include more representation of labor in government, more voice in the conduct of industry, an equitable distribution of the economic burdens of the war, and the maintenance of traditional civil liberties.

F378 .... "From Defense to Attack: The United Nations Seize the Initiative." New York: Workers Library, 1942. 15 pp.
A summary of the progress of World War II to date, with support urged for a new offensive drive. Asserting that the entry of the USSR changed the character of the war, Foster calls for overcoming the business-as-usual attitude of the employers, giving full representation to workers,

achieving labor unity, and maintaining the Bill of Rights. He warns that Germany, not Japan, is the main enemy.

F379 .... "Labor and the War." New York: Workers Library, 1942. 23 pp.
A call for national unity in an all-out, antifascist war effort. Labor is asked to ensure production by avoiding strikes. "Fifth columnists" include American reactionaries, Trotskyites, and social-democrats such as Norman Thomas. In return for the no-strike pledge labor must be given a strong voice in war production, and the cost of living must be checked.

F380 .... "Smash Hitler's Spring Offensive—Now! New York: Workers Library, 1942. 15 pp.
A wartime pamphlet calling for vastly increased munitions aid to the USSR and Britain and for getting a big American armed force into the European war zone quickly. Foster declares it imperative for the U.S. and Britain to open a new European front. The U.S. is urged to free Browder, and to permit labor's fullest possible participation in the war effort.

F381 .... "Steel Workers and the War." New York: Workers Library, 1942. 15 pp.
A speech at a win-the-war rally in July 1942 asserting that the biggest task now is to establish the second front. On the home front we must win the battle for production, without strikes. Foster concludes with the Party's usual antifascist slogans of the war period.

F382 .... "The Trade Unions and the War." New York: Workers Library, 1942. 47 pp.
The win-the-war program of the Party, based on a series of articles in the "Daily Worker," April 30 through May 26, 1942. Because this is a people's war, Foster calls upon workers to accept every sacrifice necessary. He lays out a 12-point program for trade unions, including establishing a Western front this spring and cultivation of the closest possible fighting relations between the U.S. and the Soviet Union.

F383 .... "The U.S.A. and the U.S.S.R.: War Allies and Friends." New York: Workers Library, 1942. 15 pp.
An assertion that the USSR is fighting Hitler virtually alone, thus saving the world from Nazi conquest, and a call for the opening of a second front immediately. The opposition to this is said to be political in character, stemming from defeatists and Munichmen who fear the consequences of Hitler's defeat. Hailing the growing friendship and cooperation between the U.S. and the USSR, Foster calls for its continuation into the peace in an effort to abolish war, poverty, and fascism.

F384 .... Trade Unions in the War Emergency, "Communist," 21 (Jan. 1942), 57-70.
Excerpts from the main report of the political committee to the Party's national committee, December 6-7, 1941, analyzing the crucial role of labor in wartime mobilization. While most unions support the war effort, the AFL, CIO, and railroad brotherhoods must be united for maximum efficiency in operating a wartime economy and distributing war burdens equitably.

F385 .... The Rio de Janeiro Conference, "Communist," 21 (March 1942), 131-42.
A report on the Third Conference of the Foreign Ministers of the 21 American Republics, January 15-18, 1942. Its resolution recommending the breaking off of diplomatic relations with the Axis powers is viewed as a step in the right direction. It also arranged for common defense, restricted trade with the fascist nations, and stimulated inter-American trade.

F386 FOSTER, William Z. John L. Lewis and the War, "Communist," 21 (July 1942), 497-506.
Lewis' opposition to the Roosevelt Administration and his autocratic control of the United Mine Workers sabotage the nation's war effort. Cracking Lewis' control of the UMW and eliminating his influence in the labor movement are major tasks in winning the war and protecting American democracy.

F387 . . . . The War and Labor Unity, "Communist," 21 (Sept. 1942), 708-20.
A review of labor's progress in achieving wartime unity of action, essential to support the war program and elect win-the-war congressional candidates. Unity, needed in international as well as the national labor field, is blocked by a defeatist opposition led by Hutcheson of the Carpenters and Lewis of the Miners. The central task today is to open and support a second front in Europe.

F388 . . . . The Miners' Convention, "Communist," 21 (Nov. 1942), 911-21.
A review of the recent convention of the United Mine Workers, at which Lewis disaffiliated his union from the CIO. The way in which Lewis controlled the convention is discussed. Communists and all progressives must defeat his policies.

F389 . . . . "For Speedy Victory—The Second Front Now." New York: Workers Library, 1943. 31 pp.
Calling for a full-scale invasion of France, Foster asserts that this would doom Hitler, whereas delaying the second front would prolong the war. He denounces defeatists who fear casualties, who want us to stand aside while the Russians do the hard fighting. He asserts that the State Department is loaded with antidemocratic, anti-Soviet elements.

F390 . . . . "The People and the Congress." New York: Workers Library, 1943. 15 pp.
An assertion that Congress is blocking an all-out war effort, and that the reactionary wings of the Democratic and Republican parties are defeatist. Urging that the President's war policies be backed, Foster calls for full labor participation, the greatest possible national unity, a centralized war economy, a fight against the fifth column, and a more unified coalition military strategy.

F391 . . . . "Soviet Democracy and the War." New York: Workers Library, 1943. 23 pp.
The military achievements of the USSR against Hitler's armies are declared to be in line with prewar Soviet successes. The basic explanation is found in the democratic system of socialism—in the solidarity of the people, the complete mobilization of economic resources, the fighting morale bred of democracy, and the character of the Communist Party.

F392 . . . . "Soviet Trade Unions and Allied Labor Unity." New York: Workers Library, 1943. 47 pp.
An attack on the AFL's refusal to cooperate with the trade unions of the USSR, because they were not "real" unions. Foster asserts that the Soviet trade unions are far more democratic than those of the U.S. or Britain, and that they are independent of both the Soviet government and the Communist Party. He urges American labor to link itself with the trade unions of the USSR and the rest of the UN.

F393 . . . . The Reactionary Offensive and the War, "Communist," 22 (April 1943), 301-15.
Russian military successes have stimulated U.S. defeatists, who seek to weaken the presidency, persecute trade unions and the communists, and prevent economic centralization. They have hampered war mobilization and post-

poned opening a second front. Win-the-war forces, particularly the AFL and CIO, must unite to prevent further gains by defeatists.

F394 . . . . The Strike of the Coal Miners, "Communist," 22 (June 1943), 527-38.
Although sympathetic to the miners' grievances, Foster supports Roosevelt's seizure of the mines in the 1943 strike called by John L. Lewis. The government's action is necessary to the war effort.

F395 . . . .Labor's General Staffs Meet, "Communist," 22 (Oct. 1943), 894-902.
An account of recent pre-convention meetings of the CIO National Board and the AFL Executive Council, reviewing their policies on trade union unity, the no-strike pledge, wages and cost of living, postwar problems, etc.

F396 . . . . The C.I.O. National Convention, "Communist," 22 (Dec. 1943), 1147-55.
A review of the CIO convention, praising its endorsement of labor's no-strike pledge and its condemnation of John L. Lewis. Foster urges a united political action movement led by the CIO, looking toward eventual trade union unity.

F397 . . . . The Hoover-Dewey-McCormick Election Threat to Teheran, "Communist," 23 (July 1944), 614-19.
A Roosevelt victory in the 1944 elections is necessary to win the war, assure postwar collaboration among allied powers, effect economic reconstruction, and extend democracy. None of these goals could be realized if Dewey, who is backed by defeatists and reactionaries, is elected.

F398 . . . . Dewey and Teheran, "Communist," 23 (Nov. 1944), 1001-14.
A Dewey victory in the 1944 elections would lead to an abandonment of a strong United Nations organization in favor of a weak organization like the League of Nations. A Republican Administration would embark on an imperialist policy of subjugating the world to American domination.

F399 . . . . "The Coal Miners: Their Problems in War and Peace." New York: New Century, 1945. 24 pp.
John L. Lewis is condemned during the Party's "patriotic" phase, for his attempts to smear Roosevelt and for his close friendship with isolationists and reactionaries. The miners are urged to take a more active part in the control of the union, and to support Roosevelt in both the war and postwar periods.

F400 . . . . "The Menace of American Imperialism." DENNIS, Eugene. "America Needs the Communist Party." New York: New Century, 1945. 30 pp.
The text of the speeches by Foster and Dennis, September 18, 1945, on the twenty-sixth anniversary of the CPUSA. Attacking monopolies and American imperialism in world politics, Foster calls for a small peacetime army and the defeat of reactionary Big Business on the home front. (Dennis' speech, published in "Political Affairs," Oct. 1945, is separately abstracted.)

F401 . . . . "Organized Labor Faces the New World." New York: New Century, 1945. 23 pp.
The Party line during the war, when Foster was a vice-president of the Communist Political Association. Trade union tasks are to maintain production at the highest possible levels, honor the no-strike pledge, and fight the reactionary forces that oppose the Roosevelt Administration. Foster looks forward to victory, peace, democracy, and prosperity.

F402 FOSTER, William Z. "The Rankin Witch Hunt." New York: New Century, 1945. 15 pp.
A charge that the House Committee on Un-American Activities, led by John Rankin, is planning national anti-red hysteria to enable the reactionaries to proceed with exploitation at home and imperialist aggression abroad. The communists fight to strengthen democracy, not to destroy it, he asserts, warning against allowing Red-baiting to split the ranks of labor and progressives.

F403 .... "The Strike Situation and Organized Labor's Wage and Job Strategy." New York: New Century, 1945. 23 pp.
The Party's cold war line, presented by its national chairman. Foster attacks the Little Steel formula and declares labor's no-strike pledge no longer in force now that fighting is over. Asserting that economic and political struggles are inseparable, he urges labor to fight against the Truman Administration's tendency to surrender to reaction. The capitalist system is called the cause of all our society's ills.

F404 .... The World Trade Union Conference, "Political Affairs," 24 (March 1945), 220-28.
A report on the World Trade Union Conference, written while the conference was in session in London. The agenda included discussion of the war effort, reconstruction, postwar trade union demands, and formation of a world trade union organization. This new body will help the UN destroy fascism and build a peaceful and prosperous world.

F405 .... A New World Trade Union Federation Is Born, "Political Affairs," 24 (April 1945), 329-38.
The London conference laid the basis for a new world federation of labor, despite AFL refusal to participate. The program adopted dovetails with UN general policies, with special emphasis on workers' needs. Socialist, communist, progressive, and "Christian" union leaders worked together harmoniously. The CIO delegation played a constructive role, and the AFL must join.

F406 .... The Danger of American Imperialism in the Postwar Period, "Political Affairs," 24 (June 1945), 493-500.
A warning against fascist trends in the capitalist countries, and an assertion that drastic changes are needed to prevent resurgence of imperialism. Most reactionary danger is in the U.S., where the more militantly imperialist sections of the capitalists hope to acquire international domination.

F407 .... Foster's Letter to the National Committee, Submitted January 20, 1944, "Political Affairs," 24 (July 1945), 640-55.
A letter to the national committee of the CPUSA when the Party's reorganization as the Communist Political Association was impending, criticizing Browder for seeking national unity at the price of accepting the leadership of a monopoly capitalism that helped fascism and opposed peace. Browder also failed to emphasize the socialist goal of the Party. Foster's letter was rejected by the Political Bureau.

F408 .... "Browder on Revisionism, "Daily Worker," July 25, 1945, Sect. 2, pp. 1-2.
Replying, point by point, to Browder's defense of his position (see "On the Question of Revisionism," in the "Daily Worker," July 24, 1945), Foster accuses Browder of misrepresentation of the positions of Foster and the national committee, of evading issues, of contradictions and double-talk. Browder is charged with seeing only the synthetic danger of syndicalism, not the real dangers of American imperialism abroad or reaction at home.

F409 .... The Struggle against Revisionism, "Political Affairs," 24 (Sept. 1945), 782-99.
Report to the Special Convention of the Communist Political Association, July 26-28, 1945, which reconstituted the Communist Party. The Browder line was revisionist in that it abandoned Marxist theories, gave up the Party's vanguard role, and became subservient to capital. The Communist Party should be reestablished and democratic centralism reconstituted.

F410 ...; DUCLOS, Jacques; DENNIS, Eugene; and WILLIAMSON, John. "Marxism-Leninism vs. Revisionism. Foreword by Max Weiss. New York: New Century, 1946. 111 pp.
Contents include Foster's letter to the Party's national committee, January 20, 1944; Duclos' article, "On the Dissolution of the Communist Party of the U.S.A.," reprinted from the April 1945 issue of "Cahiers Du Communisme"; Foster's report to the national committee, June 18-20, 1945, "On the Question of Revisionism"; Dennis' report, "Some Aspects of Our Policies and Tasks"; Williamson's report, "For the Re-Establishment of Our Marxist Vanguard"; Foster's report to the convention, "The Struggle against Revisionism"; Williamson's report, "The Reconstitution of the Communist Party"; the resolution of the Party's national convention, "The Present Situation and the Next Tasks"; and Foster's summary remarks to the national committee, "For a Fighting Communist Party!"

F411 .... "The Menace of a New World War." New York: New Century, 1946. 15 pp.
Speech delivered at a communist meeting in New York in 1946, protesting Churchill's Fulton, Mo., "iron curtain" address and the new U.S. "get-tough-with-Russia" policy. Denouncing American monopolists' aim for world domination and our government's reactionary, aggressive, and expansionist policies, he warns that war against the USSR would be suicidal.

F412 .... "The Need for Unity among the Maritime Workers." New York: CPUSA, Waterfront Section, n.d. [1946?]. 8 pp.
A call for bringing together all unions in the maritime field. The author praises the actions of the CIO Committee for Maritime Unity, led by Joseph Curran and Harry Bridges, and the new AFL Maritime Trades Department. He lists the bad effects of maritime labor disunity, which causes needless strikes and creates anti-union sentiment.

F413 .... "Our Country Needs a Strong Communist Party." New York: New Century, 1946. 23 pp.
The report of the chairman of the Party to a plenary meeting of the national committee in 1946. Building the Party is seen as the imperative political task in order to curb fascism, prevent union smashing, and block the alleged imperialist aims of the country's leaders. Foster cites areas in which the Party can be strengthened.

F414 .... "Palestine: Problem and Solution." New York: New York State Communist Party, 1946. 5 pp.
Abridged version of a speech by Foster in June 1946 in which he attacks Zionist leadership as reactionary. He calls for an end to colonial oppression in Palestine, and establishment of an independent Palestine with equal national rights for Arabs and Jews.

F415 .... "Problems of Organized Labor Today." New York: New Century, 1946. 48 pp.
A cold war document in which Foster urges the unions to block the drive of American monopolists, fight against

class collaboration, and lead in the building of a mass people's party. Red-baiting must be combatted, unity achieved with the World Federation of Trade Unions, and capitalism eliminated as in the USSR.

F416 FOSTER, William Z. "Reaction Beats Its War Drums." New York: New Century, 1946. 15 pp.
A cold war period attack on the "warmongering" of U.S. trusts and monopolies, and their Social-Democratic and Trotskyist hangers-on. The Truman Administration, departing from Roosevelt's cooperative attitude, bases its policies on reckless and false charges that war is inevitable with the USSR because of the latter's imperialism and attempts at world domination.

F417 .... Leninism and Some Practical Problems of the Postwar Period, "Political Affairs," 25 (Feb. 1946), 99-109.
Leninist teaching strips away the illusion that the U.S. is not imperialist because it has no colonies. The role of the Party is to reveal to Americans the truth of Lenin's teaching, and to lead the workers and other progressive groups against monopoly capitalism.

F418 .... The Wage and Strike Movement, "Political Affairs," 25 (Feb. 1946), 121-29.
Approval of the 1946 union demands for substantial wage increases to maintain wartime take-home pay. Employer resistance may convert this mass wage movement into a militant mass strike movement. The unions must rally all their strength in the present struggle, using propaganda in the mass media and political action to defeat the reactionaries in Congress.

F419 .... On the Expulsion of Browder, "Political Affairs," 25 (April 1946), 339-48.
A review of the struggle against Browder leading up to his expulsion. He held to his opportunist line, refused assignments of Party work, betrayed the Party before the House Committee on Un-American Activities, openly attacked the Party, and boosted American imperialism. The Party must be cleansed of Browderism.

F420 .... Elements of a People's Cultural Policy, "New Masses," 49 (April 23, 1946), 6-9.
The Party line on the "art is a weapon" issue. The ruling classes have always tried to subjugate artists, and to use art to help maintain themselves in power. It is absurd to contend that art is above the battle of the classes. A new people's culture is developing among the masses; communists much enrich culture with Marxist understanding and carry it to the people.

F421 .... On Self-Determination for the Negro People, "Political Affairs," 25 (June 1946), 549-54.
Excerpts from a speech to the Party's national board, March 28, 1946, defending the slogan of self-determination for the Negro people in the Black Belt. The Negro failure to respond favorably to the slogan is ascribed to their lack of national consciousness. Our manner of presenting the slogan must be improved.

F422 .... American Imperialism, Leader of World Reaction, "Political Affairs," 25 (Aug. 1946), 686-95.
World reaction, led by American imperialism, is leading the world in the direction of economic smash-up, fascism, and a new world war. However, the democratic, antifascist, antiwar masses are potentially much stronger than the imperialist forces. Big Three unity must be reestablished and the power of finance capital broken.

F423 .... One Year of Struggle against Browderism, "Political Affairs," 25 (Sept. 1946), 771-77.

Opening remarks at a plenary meeting of the Party's national committee, July 16-18, 1946, reviewing changes in the Party since the expulsion of Browder. The Party, sick as a result of his opportunist regime, has been reorganized and rebuilt, its vanguard role reestablished, and its ideological work strengthened.

F424 .... "American Trade Unionism." New York: International Publishers, 1947. 386 pp. Ind.
Selections from Foster's writings on trade unionism over a 35-year period, drawing most heavily upon his autobiography, "From Bryan to Stalin." The book is divided into four chronological sections: the turn of the century to 1923, 1923 to 1929, the New Deal, and World War II. In each period the author shows the violence of the class struggle in the U.S., contrasting the inadequacy of business unionism and its leaders with the courage of the militant workers. He calls for a united front between communists and progressive forces in labor, defense of industrial unions against the trusts and the AFL reactionaries, a struggle against class collaboration, a fight against corruption, national trade union unity, international labor unity through the WFTU, independent working-class political action, a struggle against Red-baiting, and a fight for a socialist ideology.

F425 ..., and others. "The Communist Position on the Negro Question." New York: New Century, 1947. 61 pp.
The resolution on Negro rights and self-determination adopted at the plenary meeting of the Party's national committee, December 3-5, 1946, with the remarks of Foster, the summary remarks of Benjamin J. Davis, Jr., excerpts from the concluding remarks of Eugene Dennis, and excerpts from the discussion by nine others. The resolution calls for full equality for Negroes and asserts their right to nationhood in the Black Belt.

F426 .... "The Meaning of the 9-Party Communist Conference." New York: New Century, 1947. 23 pp.
A communist interpretation of the purposes of the conference of the nine big communist parties of Europe recently held in Poland, and of the Information Bureau that it set up. The conference, Foster states, called upon the European peoples to defend national independence against Wall Street's attempts to enslave them, and warned of the economic dangers and fascist implications in such recovery programs as the Marshall Plan.

F427 .... "The New Europe." New York: International Publishers, 1947. 128 pp.
An analysis of postwar trends in Europe by a leading American communist, based on a trip through Europe in the winter and early spring of 1947. Foster praises Yugoslavia, Poland, Czechoslovakia, and Bulgaria as advanced democracies, approving of their nationalization of financial institutions and key industries, the division of the landed estates, the mass communist parties, and the new trade unions. Denouncing U.S. policy toward Europe as one of cynical imperialism, which if unchecked will lead to war, he calls for an end to atom-bomb diplomacy and of aid to reactionary minorities with funds and war materials.

F428 .... "Organized Labor and the Fascist Danger." New York: New Century, 1947. 15 pp.
The Taft-Hartley Act is viewed as a step toward state control of trade unions and enslavement of the working class, so that U.S. trusts and monopolies can conquer the world under the guise of the Marshall Plan. The reactionary Truman is helping to put over Wall Street's program. By its fighting policies, united labor can defeat the fascist danger.

F429 FOSTER, William Z. "Quarantine the Warmongers." New York: New Century, 1947. 15 pp.
A warning against a third world war by a leading communist, who protests the warmongering campaign against the Soviet Union currently in progress in the U.S. Labeling the Marshall Plan an instrument of Wall Street imperialism, he asserts that our loans and food reserves are being used to build a military bloc against the USSR.

F430 .... "Workers, Defend Your Unions!" New York: New Century, 1947. 8 pp.
The legislative attack on trade unions is seen as a conspiracy of Wall Street corporations, oppressors of the Negro people, and instigators of reaction. Workers are urged to achieve labor unity, form a great people's party, and force the government to adopt a foreign policy of peaceful collaboration with the Big Five powers.

F431 .... On the Question of Negro Self-Determination, "Political Affairs," 26 (Jan. 1947), 54-58.
Remarks at the plenum of the Party's national committee, December 3-5, 1946, summarizing the discussion on self-determination. The discussion has shown that the Negro people in the Black Belt are a nation, though a young and developing one. While fighting for full participation in American life, they are unifying ranks and developing national consciousness.

F432 .... For a Stronger, More Active Communist Party! "Political Affairs," 26 (Feb. 1947), 152-54.
Excerpts from a speech to the plenum of the Party's national committee, December 3-5, 1946, stressing the necessity, in a period of growing reaction, of ridding the Party of opportunism which flourished under Browder's revisionist leadership.

F433 .... On Building a People's Party, "Political Affairs," 26 (Feb. 1947), 109-21.
Prospects for an independent, antimonopoly, antifascist party are much brighter than in 1924. Problems in building the third party are considered. Building such a new party is the major task of the Communist Party.

F434 .... American Imperialism and the War Danger, "Political Affairs," 26 (Aug. 1947), 675-87.
The text of a report to the June 27-30 meeting of the Party's national committee, asserting that American imperialism's drive for world control creates widespread fears of another world war. Wall Street's imperialist drive has not succeeded because world monopoly capital has been weakened in the war, while world democratic forces have been strengthened. The Truman Doctrine and Marshall Plan are reactionary schemes to fight democracy.

F435 .... Marxism and American "Exceptionalism," "Political Affairs," 26 (Sept. 1947), 794-812.
Though American capitalism appears exempt from the disintegrating forces that have undermined capitalism in other countries, the economic collapse of 1929 showed that it was subject to all the basic economic laws of capitalism. Browder became the most extreme advocate of American "exceptionalism." American capitalism is traveling the same path to decay as capitalism elsewhere.

F436 .... "Beware of the War Danger: Stop, Look, and Listen!" New York: New Century, 1948. 23 pp.
Reactionaries in many countries, led by those in the U.S., are organizing for war against the USSR, although the USSR wants peace. The war that Wall Street wants would be a war of devastation, a lost war, a reactionary war, and a needless war. The warmongers must be smashed.

F437 .... "The Crime of El Fanguito: An Open Letter to President Truman on Puerto Rico." New York: New Century, 1948. 16 pp.
A description of conditions in El Fanguito (The Mudhole), a huge slum in San Juan, Puerto Rico. The President, with his control over legislation and funds for Puerto Rico, is held responsible for the continuance of such slums.

F438 .... "Danger Ahead for Organized Labor." New York: New Century, 1948. 15 pp.
A criticism of organized labor for supporting the bipartisan, imperialist foreign policy of Big Business (the Marshall Plan and the Truman Doctrine). The author sees the rank and file resisting, as shown in growing militancy and support for Wallace's new party. (Reprinted from "Masses & Mainstream," July 1948.)

F439 .... "Labor and the Marshall Plan." New York: New Century, 1948. 23 pp.
Labor is urged to stop supporting the Marshall Plan, which is an attempt by the big corporations to control Europe as part of their scheme to dominate the world. Labor leaders who support the Plan are betraying the workers and the American people to Wall Street. The best answer to Wall Street would be defeat of the Marshall Plan and development of the Progressive Party.

F440 .... "The New York Herald Tribune's 23 Questions about the Communist Party Answered by William Z. Foster." New York: New Century, 1948. 31 pp.
A reprint of questions to Foster and his answers, published in the "Herald Tribune" on January 11, 1948. Foster asserted that the Party was loyal to the Constitution of the United States, that it favored majority rule in any country to determine that country's system of government and economics, that the danger of violence comes from reactionary elements who refuse to accept majority will, and that American communists formulate their own policies without consultation with the Soviet government or international communism.

F441 .... The Political Significance of Keynesism, "Political Affairs," 27 (Jan. 1948), 27-43.
Keynesism, a product of the world-wide capitalist crisis of the 1930's, attempts to save capitalism by mitigating mass unemployment. But it does not remove its fundamental cause, the contradiction between the social character of production and the private character of appropriation. Communists must expose the economic and political fallacies of Keynesism.

F442 .... Organized Labor and the Marshall Plan, "Political Affairs," 27 (Feb. 1948), 99-109.
Top union leaders who support the Marshall Plan are backing Wall Street's program for world domination. These union leaders have taken their labor imperialism into the national election by supporting Truman. Henry Wallace's third party campaign represents the profoundest peace sentiments of the American people.

F443 .... World Democracy's Struggle against American Imperialism, "Political Affairs," 27 (March 1948), 195-206.
A report on the international situation to the meeting of the Party's national committee, February 3-5, 1948. The world has divided into two hostile camps: that of democracy and peace, led by the USSR; and that of imperialism, fascism, and war, led by the U.S. Although capitalist desperation creates the danger of war, the people of the U.S. can halt the warmongers.

F444 .... On the Theoretical Work of the Party, "Political Affairs," 27 (April 1948), 319-26.

The Party is weak in its understanding of Marxist-Leninist theory. There is great need for Marxist-Leninist analysis of the U.S. position in the world economy, Keynesian economics, Dewey's pragmatism, and American history and conditions. Marxist-Leninist theory, stifled under the Browder regime, must be cultivated and developed.

F445   FOSTER, William Z. Specific Features of American Imperialist Expansion, "Political Affairs," 27 (Aug. 1948), 675-89.
An analysis of the characteristics of American capitalist expansion and of the factors facilitating or impeding it. Though American imperialist policy has passed through several stages, including atom-bomb diplomacy, the Truman doctrine, the Marshall Plan, and active preparation for war, its objective has always been to break USSR resistance.

F446   .... Concluding Remarks at the Convention, "Political Affairs," 27 (Sept. 1948), 820-33.
The national chairman's summation of the Party's fourteenth national convention, held August 2-6, 1948. He considers the Party line of supporting the Progressive Party the best means of combatting imperialism, and urges members to work harder to carry out the Party line.

F447   .... The 1948 Elections and the Struggle for Peace, "Political Affairs," 27 (Sept. 1948), 773-77.
The keynote address to the Party's fourteenth national convention, August 2-6, 1948, urging support of the Progressive Party in the coming elections as the best means of avoiding imperialist war. Nevertheless, points of difference exist with many Progressive Party leaders, who hope to save world capitalism.

F448   .... On Improving the Party's Work among Women, "Political Affairs," 27 (Nov. 1948), 984-90.
A report to the Party Commission on Theoretical Aspects of Work among Women, August 9, 1948, stressing the necessity of overcoming theories of male superiority. The Party must exert more influence among the mass of women, whose votes now count so much in the elections.

F449   .... "In Defense of the Communist Party and the Indicted Leaders." New York: New Century, 1949. 96 pp.
The position of the Party on all issues in the case of the 12 leaders on trial under the Smith Act. The U.S. Party, the author states, is an independent political organization, with no organic connections with Communist Parties of other countries. Its great task today is to elect a coalition, antifascist, anti-imperialist government, which would defend the people's interests and protect itself from the capitalists' violent counterrevolution. In the process it would develop into a People's Democracy, which would move inevitably toward socialism.

F450   .... "The Twilight of World Capitalism." New York: International Publishers, 1949. 168 pp.
A leading American communist discusses the decline of world capitalism and the rise of world socialism, along with the growth of American reaction, the progress of American labor, the degeneration of social democracy, and the decline of religion. He discusses the expanding communist movement, the communist fight for peace and freedom, and the advent of socialist man. Socialism has met the test of life in the USSR and the communist countries of Eastern Europe. Socialism brings political and intellectual freedom, sex equality, freedom for youth, national freedom, and a new and free ethics.

F451   ..., and DENNIS, Eugene. Is the Advocacy of

Peace Treason? "Political Affairs," 28 (April 1949), 1-4.
Two declarations of the Party's opposition to war, issued jointly by its chairman (Foster) and its general secretary (Dennis); one was a statement to the press on March 2, 1949, and the other an open letter to President Truman on March 6. The statements assert that peace is threatened by American capitalists' schemes of world domination, the first steps being the building of an aggressive alliance against Russia. Communist opposition to these efforts have been called treasonous.

F452   ..., Cannon, Lovestone, and Browder, "Political Affairs," 28 (Sept. 1949), 14-24.
America has been so prosperous, due to richly endowed land and safety from foreign aggression, that a heresy of American exceptionalism to capitalist contradictions has appeared among communists. The heresy has taken two forms, the right opportunism of Lovestone and Browder, and the left sectarianism of Cannon.

F453   .... Keynote Message of Greetings to the Plenum, "Political Affairs," 29 (May 1950), 9-13.
A letter to the meeting of the Party's national committee, March 23-25, 1950, asserting that the tasks of the Party are to aid the trade unions to maintain wage levels, agitate for social insurance for the unemployed, fight discrimination against Negroes, defend the Party against unfair legislation, and mobilize the masses in a peace movement.

F454   .... People's Front and People's Democracy, "Political Affairs," 29 (June 1950), 14-31.
Clarification of points raised during the Foley Square trial of Party leaders and dealt with in Foster's pamphlet, "In Defense of the Communist Party and the Indicted Leaders." Among the topics are the significance of fascism, the antifascist and antiwar movement, the people's front, a people's front government, the nature and role of a people's democracy, socialist encirclement, and force and violence.

F455   .... The Domination of the Capitalist World by the United States, "Political Affairs," 29 (Dec. 1950), 1-15.
A Marxist-Leninist analysis of American capitalist world hegemony and of its reckless drive for war. American imperialism aims at full world dominion. The Party, with its united-front allies, must fight for peace and democratic rights, protect workers' living standards, and crush the rising wave of fascism.

F456   .... "Outline Political History of the Americas." New York: International Publishers, 1951. 668 pp. Gloss. Maps. Ref. notes. Ind.
A popular political history of the western hemisphere, from colonial times to the present, in the light of Marxist-Leninist social science. Foster emphasizes the attempt by U.S. imperialism to dominate the hemisphere, and the struggle of the American peoples against enslavement by fascist-minded Wall Street. Book 3, "From Capitalism to Socialism" (pp. 355-611), covers the period from World War I to 1951. In this section Foster deals with the Russian revolution and the formation of communist parties, the great depression and the rise of fascism, the New Deal, World War II and its consequences, the drive of U.S. imperialism, and trade unions in the U.S.

F457   .... American Capitalist Hegemony, the National Emergency, and "Isolationism," "Political Affairs," 30 (Feb. 1951), 3-11.
A message to the Party's fifteenth national convention, asserting that American hegemony over the capitalist

world is a product of the general crisis of capitalism, that the state of national emergency definitely increases the danger of war, and that the new "isolationism" does not imply abandonment by American imperialism of its policy of aggression. The Wall Street capitalists seek to make the U.S. fascist and militarist, and to rush the capitalist countries into an anti-Soviet war.

F458 FOSTER, William Z. "History of the Communist Party of the United States." New York: Inter-National Publishers, 1952. 600 pp. App. Ind. Bibliog.
A history of the communist movement in this country, written by its leading figure. More than a fourth of the volume is devoted to predecessor movements, particularly to the Socialist Labor Party and the Socialist Party. The book also deals with the 1919 split in the Socialist Party and the maneuvers of the various leftist factions that culminated in the formation of the Workers Party in 1921. Throughout the volume the point of view is that of the official communist movement, with positions of other groups labeled as "correct" or "incorrect," and with Marxism-Leninism accepted as the authoritative philosophic view. (Chapters on "The Communists and the La Follette Movement of 1924" and "The Formation of the Communist Party [1919-21]" appeared in "Political Affairs," Feb. and Sept. 1952.)

F459 .... "A Letter to Congress: Defeat the Anti-Labor Smith Bill." New York: New Century, 1952. 15 pp.
A letter to the House Committee on the Armed Services, expressing the Party's condemnation of the Smith bill. Calling the bill the most dangerous antilabor measure ever submitted to Congress, Foster denounces it as part of a trend to fascism and as furthering the war aims of Wall Street imperialism.

F460 .... "The Steel Workers and the Fight for Labor's Rights." New York: New Century, 1952. 31 pp.
A call for strike action to settle the steel wage negotiations now in progress, since government seizure is a strikebreaking technique by Truman to prevent the workers from winning a real victory. Contending that the U.S. is following the road to presidential dictatorship, Foster calls for labor and liberal independent political action.

F461 ... (ed.). "The Case of Puerto Rico: Memorandum to the United Nations." New York: New Century, 1953. 16 pp.
A charge that the limited reforms introduced in Puerto Rico by the U.S. do not fundamentally alter the colonial status of the island, with a demand that the U.S. be required to present a report to the United Nations on the status of the colony. The Party calls for a free and independent Republic of Puerto Rico.

F462 .... "Danger Signals for Organized Labor." New York: New Century, 1953. 31 pp.
Declaring that the Eisenhower Administration represents reaction worse than Truman's, the author criticizes the trade union movement for indifference to military preparations of the U.S. and Wall Street (the real cause of the cold war) and McCarthyism. Only the labor movement, he says, can reverse these trends.

F463 .... Fighting War with Peace and Democracy, "Political Affairs," 32 (June 1953), 1-8.
The Soviet and Chinese peoples are fighting the war drive of American imperialism by strengthening their own drive for peace. American imperialism, striving for world domination, seeks a major anti-Soviet war. The USSR fights the war drive with democracy as well as peace.

F464 .... Left Sectarianism in the Fight for Negro Rights and against White Chauvinism, "Political Affairs," 32 (July 1953), 17-31.
The Party must fight against both the main danger of white chauvinism and the lesser dangers of left sectarianism and Negro nationalism. Sectarianism shows up in neglect of work among the Negro masses, the definition of white chauvinism, and attitudes toward Negro national sensitivity and white supremacist terminology.

F465 .... The 34th Anniversary of the Communist Party, "Political Affairs," 32 (Sept. 1953), 1-8.
A brief review of the achievements of the Party in the light of problems of the cold war period, emphasizing the crisis of American labor leadership and the dangers of war and fascism. The main objective today is to shift the labor movement's acceptance of an inevitable world war against the USSR to an acceptance of peaceful coexistence. The basic policy for the mass fight to achieve this is the united front from below.

F466 .... Marxism and the American Working Class, "Political Affairs," 32 (Nov. 1953), 1-19.
Marxist conceptions played and still play an important role in the developing American labor movement. Class collaboration, which has poisoned the ideology of the American working class, is being undermined by domestic and world events. An attack on workers' living standards will shatter bourgeois illusions. We must fight against the warmakers and fascists, against Keynesism and bourgeois illusions.

F467 .... "The Negro People in American History." New York: International Publishers, 1954. 608 pp. Ind.
The chairman of the Communist Party interprets Negro history and presents the Party line on the Negro question. He traces the history of the Negro from his home in Africa to his slave home in America, and on through the Colonial days, the 1776 Revolution, the Civil War, post-Civil War reconstruction, the first World War, the Garvey movement, World War II, and the cold war. Subsequent chapters trace the history of the Communist Party as "the Party of the Negro people," view the Negro people here as an oppressed nation, and tell how the Party reconciles Negro national cohesion with demands for full integration. This solution, according to Foster, will come with the achievement of socialism.

F468 .... Problems of Organized Labour in the U.S., "Labour Monthly" (London), 36 (May 1954), 209-15.
American labor must combat the war drive of Wall Street, the developing economic crisis, and McCarthyite fascism. It must seek unification of all labor, a broad labor-farmer party, and strengthening of class conscious ideology and leadership. There are signs of political awakening and struggle.

F469 .... The War Danger in the Present World Situation, "Political Affairs," 33 (May 1954), 9-17.
An assertion that U.S. aggressive imperialism seeks to master the world through fighting another world war against the USSR and the people's democracies. The Party's fight against the war danger must be continuous, resolute, and energetic, and not carried out mechanically. The people won a great victory in forcing through the Korean truce.

F470 .... The Question of the Peaceful Co-Existence of the U.S.A. and the U.S.S.R., "Political Affairs," 33 (Aug. 1954), 1-15.
Peaceful co-existence between the countries of socialism and capitalism, and especially between the USSR and the

U.S., is the most urgent political question in the world today. The opposition of the American democratic masses has been a vital factor in the defeat of aggressive American imperialism.

F471 FOSTER, William Z. Is the United States in the Early Stages of Fascism? "Political Affairs," 33 (Nov. 1954), 4-21.
Strong fascist trends in the U.S. are evidenced by a mass of reactionary legislation such as the Smith Act, the Taft-Hartley Act, the McCarran Acts, and the infamous Communist Control Act passed in August. Though the danger of fascism in the U.S. is increasing, fascism is not inevitable here. There is imperative need for a broad antifascist, pro-peace political movement.

F472 .... "History of the Three Internationals." New York: International Publishers, 1955. 580 pp. App. Ref. Ind.
A history of the world socialist and communist movements from 1848 to 1955. While most attention is focused on Europe, there are scattered references to developments in the U.S. The Second International is denounced for its opportunism and for its betrayal of the revolutionary cause during World War I. The bulk of the volume is devoted to the Communist International, with a treatment of trade union as well as political developments.

F473 .... The Perspectives for a Labor-Farmer Party in the U.S., "Political Affairs," 34 (Feb. 1955), 3-19.
Although the U.S. is the only major industrial country without a broad labor-farmer party, the time is not yet ripe for launching one. The Party must educate the masses to create a strong movement of workers and their allies, breaking the bourgeois political leadership of the workers and eventually heading towards creation of a labor-farmer party.

F474 .... Notes on the Struggle for Negro Rights, "Political Affairs," 34 (May 1955), 20-42.
A discussion of some of the newer problems in the Party's Negro work. Large numbers of Negroes have migrated from the Black Belt and from the South, becoming urbanized. The Negro class composition is changing and its bourgeoisie developing, with the influence of bourgeois and social-reformist leaders increasing. The working class plays a leading role, which we must strengthen.

F475 .... "Outline History of the World Trade Union Movement." New York: International Publishers, 1956. 592 pp. Ref. Ind.
A history of world trade unionism from a communist point of view, emphasizing the evolution of membership and leadership toward a Marxist basis. Among the topics dealt with are the formation and activities of the Red International of Labor Unions, the World Federation of Trade Unions, and the ICFTU. Attention is paid to the AFL, the CIO, and the CIO's expulsion of communist-dominated unions. (A chapter, "The General Law of Trade Union Progress," appeared in "Political Affairs," July 1955.)

F476 .... Has World Capitalism Become Stabilized? "Political Affairs," 35 (March 1956), 5-16.
Though most of the important capitalist countries are experiencing an industrial boom, their economic situation is basically unhealthy and their political situation is unstable. Meanwhile the socialist countries are making swift advances. The maintenance of peace is a basic condition for the rapid growth of socialism, so that peaceful coexistence of all nations is the key strategy of the workers.

F477 .... The Road to Socialism, "Political Affairs," 35 (April 1956), 4-20; (May), 1-18.
A discussion of the road to socialism in various countries, covering the views of Marx and Lenin, struggles for a parliamentary majority, the use of force and violence, and people's front movements. In the U.S. a democratic election is quite possible, though American monopoly capital would use every means to beat back a militant movement of the masses. The Party does not consider fascism inevitable in the U.S.

F478 .... The "Managed Economy" of the U.S., "Political Affairs," 35 (July 1956), 20-32; (Aug.), 24-31.
The so-called "managed economy" in the major capitalist states is an expression of state monopoly capitalism, not to be confused with the planned economy of the socialist states. Efforts at a managed economy in the U.S. are traced from World War I through the 1929 economic crisis and the New Deal, World War II, and the cold war. The "managed economy" cannot grow into true planned production.

F479 .... Marxism-Leninism in a Changing World, "Political Affairs," 35 (Sept. 1956), 50-58; (Dec.), 54-63.
An attempt to show how Marxism-Leninism must be developed and applied in a rapidly changing world, in the U.S. as well as in the other capitalist countries. In the U.S. much closer attention must be paid to specific American national characteristics, though "American exceptionalism" must be combatted. The U.S., the richest and strongest capitalist country, aims to dominate the world.

F480 .... On the Party Situation, "Political Affairs," 35 (Oct. 1956), 15-45.
Announcement of a decision to vote against the draft resolution now before the Party for discussion because it seriously weakens the Party's stand on Marxism-Leninism. Dennis' proposal to merge the Party with other left groupings will prove a liquidating force. Strong right tendencies have reappeared in the Party for the first time in a decade. The resolution should be changed to take a correct stand on Marxism-Leninism.

F481 .... Marxism-Leninism and "American Prosperity," "Political Affairs," 36 (Feb. 1957), 39-48.
Foster attacks the right tendency within the Party that views Marxism-Leninism as left-sectarian and seeks to replace the Party with a political action organization. Opposing these tendencies as similar to those led earlier by Lovestone and then by Browder, Foster calls for retaining and strengthening the Party.

F482 .... The Party Crisis and the Way Out, "Political Affairs," 36 (Dec. 1957), 47-61; 37 (Jan. 1958), 49-65.
Disagreement with the views expressed by Alexander Bittelman in a series of articles in the "Daily Worker" in October. Foster charges Bittelman with tending in the direction of the Party's right, which views the Party's basic theories and methods as completely out of date. Instead Foster urges the rebuilding of the Party, based on the principles of Marxism-Leninism, and applied with a rising class struggle perspective. (For Bittelman's response see his "Key Problems of Party Program," in "Political Affairs," Feb. 1958.)

F483 .... The Superiority of World Socialism over World Capitalism, "Political Affairs," 47 [37] (May 1958), 19-28.
A review of examples of socialist superiority over capitalism on the occasion of the launching of the Soviet satellite.

American scientists who confessed U.S. inadequacy in many fields were careful not to impugn the capitalist system. A number of reasons for socialist superiority to capitalism are developed.

F484 FOSTER, William Z. The Struggle for a Mass Labor Party in the U.S., "Political Affairs," 38 (May 1959), 1-16.
A discussion of the two-party system in the U.S., through which monopoly capital rules the country, and of the growing efforts of the workers to break away from it. The creation of a strong labor party will be of major importance to the labor movement of the world, not just to the American working class.

F485 .... The Cold War and the People's Welfare, "Political Affairs," 38 (July 1959), 13-22.
The time is over-ripe for ending the cold war, which has increased militarization, reduced social services, injured the industrial potential of the socialist countries, and reduced labor freedom here. Organizations of the people, while preventing war, must carry on union struggles, advance national liberation movements, and build socialism.

F486 .... On the Draft Resolution, "Political Affairs," 38 (Dec. 1959), 49-54.
The current draft resolution (see Communist Party, USA, National Committee, "Draft Political Resolution," in "Political Affairs," Sept. 1959) must be strengthened on a number of subjects. Criticism of the trade union bureaucracy is too mild, more emphasis on the labor party is needed, a youth movement must be organized without delay, the primacy of the right danger must be recognized, and factionalism must be abolished.

F487 .... "The Historic Advance of World Socialism." New York: International Publishers, 1960. 48 pp.
A brief review of the development of world capitalism, pointing out its failures and inadequacies, and of the subsequent rise of communism and fascism. Soviet advance is contrasted with American imperialism. The progressive, socialist movement seeks a path to socialism through peaceful coexistence. The intrinsic superiority of socialism over capitalism is emphasized.

F488 FOUNTAIN, Clayton W. "Union Guy." New York: Viking, 1949. 242 pp. Ind.
The autobiography of an automobile worker, formerly a communist, and then an activist in the battle against the communists in the UAW-CIO. Drawing on his personal experiences, he tells of the struggles between communists and anticommunists in the union's first ten years. Included are accounts of the fight over Homer Martin in 1937, communist sabotage of the defense effort during the Nazi-Soviet pact period, communist super-patriotism during the war, the battle at the 1946 convention, and the triumph of Walter Reuther and the entire anticommunist slate at the 1947 convention.

F489 "FOURTH INTERNATIONAL," The Case of the Eighteen and the Red-Baiting Stalinist Campaign, 5 (June 1944), 163-65.
A review of Stalinist support of the government's prosecution of the Trotskyist "Minneapolis eighteen" under the Smith Act. Stalinism is renewing its attack on Trotskyists because workers are beginning to understand the enormity of Stalinist degeneration, crimes, and betrayals, and because the Trotskyists' struggle for Marxism and Leninism stands out in sharp contrast.

F490 .... American Stalinists to Execute a New Shift in Line, 6 (June 1945), 163-66.

A Trotskyist analysis of the shift in the Stalinist line, as reflected in the Duclos letter to the American Communist Party. Browder's dissolution of the CPUSA in 1944 paralleled the dissolution of the Communist International in 1943, and his postwar perspective flows from Stalin's wartime policy of co-existence. The present change of line, like past changes, reflects the Soviet Union's international position.

F491 .... What the "Daily Worker" "Discussion" Seeks to Cover Up: Leninism vs. Stalinism, 6 (July 1945), 195-97.
The discussion in the "Daily Worker" of Browder's revisionism creates the illusion that the controversy is between opportunism and Marxist-Leninist orthodoxy. But Stalinism is itself a revision of Marxism-Leninism, insofar as it holds that socialism can be built in one country. All subsequent turns in the Stalinist line flow from this basic revisionist policy.

F492 .... American Stalinism—Our Attitude toward It, 14 (May-June, 1953), 70-74.
A resolution adopted by the national committee or tne Socialist Workers Party in May 1953. While the government's witch-hunt has affected the CPUSA, the major reason for its decline is its own moral rottenness. The Trotskyists will continue to compete with the CPUSA in the struggle for the leadership of the working class.

F493 FOWLER, Dan. Case History of a Failure: What the Loyalty Oath Did to the University of California, "Look," 16 (Jan. 29, 1952), 69-71.
An account of the loyalty oath controversy at the University of California. The Board of Regents instituted the oath, and faculty members were told to sign or leave. After the Regents' oath was held unconstitutional, non-signers were reinstated. Two possible communists were discovered, reputations were wrecked, and the university's morale and intellectual power were lowered.

F494 FOX, Jay. "Amalgamation." Chicago: Trade Union Educational League, n.d. [1923?]. 45 pp.
An early TUEL pamphlet, urging amalgamation of craft unions in the U.S. into ten industrial unions, to make their policies and structure conform to current economic conditions. The amalgamation movement is described, as are the advantages of industrial unionism. The TUEL program is outlined.

F495 .... Let's Have a Labor Party, "Labor Herald," 2 (June 1923), 26-27.
The two prime needs of the American proletariat are industrial organization and a labor party. The Gompers leadership in the AFL opposes both. It is therefore up to the workers, in their local unions, to achieve their own political independence through formation of a broad, united front labor party.

F496 .... From Anarchism to Communism, "Workers Monthly," 4 (Feb. 1925), 179-81.
A former anarchist tells of his conversion to communism following the Bolshevik victory in Russia, which showed that no revolution could live without a powerful organization of defense. Emma Goldman is called a traitor for attacking the Soviet Union.

F497 FRAENKEL, Osmond K. "Our Civil Liberties." New York: Viking, 1944. 277 pp. Authorities. Ind.
A survey of the state of civil liberties in the U.S., including a section on sedition (pp. 78-87) in which the Harry Bridges deportation proceedings and the Schneiderman denaturalization cases, among others, are discussed.

There are other scattered references to issues involving communists.

F498 FRAENKEL, Osmond K. Is the Smith Act Constitutional? "Lawyers Guild Review," 10 (Winter 1950), 181-84.
An assertion that the Smith Act is unconstitutional, as interference with freedom of expression. Such interference might be justified if there were imminent danger of attempted violent overthrow of government, but this finding would have to be made by a jury, not, as in the Dennis trial, by a judge.

F499 .... Law and Loyalty, "Iowa Law Review," 37 (Winter 1952), 153-74.
A review of legal restraints on subversion, including loyalty oaths, loyalty investigations, and the registration provisions of the Internal Security Act of 1950. Viewing all such measures as efforts to curb free thought, the author looks forward to court tests of their constitutionality.

F500 .... "The Supreme Court and Civil Liberties." 2d rev. ed. New York: American Civil Liberties Union, 1955. 105 pp. App. Ind.
A work, written in 1937 and first revised in 1952, appraising the Court's protection of civil liberties. The author, who believes that a good society would guarantee civil liberties to communists as to all others, reviews the constitutional issues that have arisen in this area. An appendix lists the leading decisions, indicating which were favorable to civil liberties and which were not. (A further revised and enlarged edition was published in 1960.)

F501 .... The Smith Act Reconsidered, "Lawyers Guild Review," 16 (Winter 1956), 149-54.
A discussion of the new Smith Act cases before the Supreme Court in the spring of 1956. They are the Scales and Lightfoot membership cases, and the Yates and Nelson conspiracy cases. The forthcoming decisions are unlikely to set the constitutional limits of the Smith Act, since the Court avoids constitutional issues whenever possible.

F502 FRAINA, Louis C. "Revolutionary Socialism: A Study in Socialist Reconstruction." New York: Communist Press, 1918. 246 pp.
An argument for revolutionary as against reformist socialism and for the dictatorship of the proletariat as a temporary but necessary instrument, written shortly after the Bolshevik Revolution by a youthful leader of the American socialist left wing, who analyzes the development of imperialism and attacks the reformist Second International for having abandoned the class struggle. The only true revolutionary class is the unskilled proletariat, whose weapon of struggle is mass action. (This book serv... s a theoretical basis for the development of the left wing of the Socialist Party, from which the American communist movement emerged. After helping to lead the Communist Party formed in this country in 1919, Fraina left the movement, later to author economic works under the name of Lewis Corey.)

F503 .... The Swing to Revolutionary Socialism, "Revolutionary Age," 2 (April 12, 1919), 4.
Capitalism is on the verge of collapse as a result of the World War. Even in the American Socialist Party, which was against the war and which favors Russia, it is necessary to organize a revolutionary left wing. This is because the SP leadership rejects revolutionary ideas, emphasizes parliamentary action, and refuses to endorse industrial unionism.

F504 .... Report of Louis C. Fraina, International Secretary of the Communist Party of America to the Executive Committee of the Communist International, "Communist," (organ of the Communist Party of America), 1 (Oct. 11, 1919), 3-4 ff; (Oct. 18), 4-5.
A review of the history of the revolutionary wing of American socialism from the organization of the Socialist Labor Party to the split of the left wing from the Socialist Party. The report accompanies application for admission to the Third International. The program and tactics of both the IWW and the Communist Labor Party are criticized.

F505 .... The International and Unionism, "Communist," (organ of the Communist Party of America), 3 (April 1921), 5-8.
Reprints of speeches made by Fraina, and the minority thesis on unionism advocated by him at the Second Congress of the Communist International. Fraina called for mobilizing the AFL rank and file against the bureaucracy, for creation of shop committees, and for greater attention to mobilizing the unorganized.

.... See also COREY, Lewis.

F506 FRANCE, Royal W. "My Native Grounds." New York: Cameron, 1957. 255 pp.
The autobiography of a liberal attorney who was the friend of many communists and fellow-travelers, though he was critical of some of their beliefs and practices. He describes some of the cases in which he represented them, and criticizes the Smith Act, the McCarran Act (the Internal Security Act of 1950), and the Communist Control Act of 1954 as thought control acts in violation of the Bill of Rights.

F507 FRANCIS, Jean. A War-Time Tax Program for Victory, "Communist," 21 (April 1942), 225-38.
An appraisal of the government wartime tax program, with proposals to strengthen it by making income taxes more progressive, taxing undistributed corporation profits, limiting profits on government contracts, increasing taxes on capital gains, levying fewer excise taxes on consumer goods, and raising personal income tax exemptions to protect the living standards of the poor.

F508 .... The Battle for a Democratic Win-the-War Tax Program, "Communist," 22 (March 1943), 248-57.
A review and appraisal of various tax programs. The communists support the program proposed by the CIO, and urge the use of taxation as a supplement to a planned, centralized war economy.

F509 .... A Tax Program to Speed the Offensive, "Communist," 22 (Nov. 1943), 1030-40.
A favorable analysis of a tax program sponsored by a coalition of the CIO, the National Farmers Union, the Brotherhood of Railroad Trainmen, the League of Women Shoppers, and other groups. It is a more progressive tax program than that proposed by the Treasury.

F510 FRANCIS, John. "It Is Happening Here." Huntington, Ind.: Our Sunday Visitor, n.d. [1937]. 128 pp.
A Catholic report on communist activities in the U.S., communist strength, supporting organizations, and Party influence in labor unions. The communist appeal to the cultured and to the rich is examined. Excerpts from Pope Pius' encyclical of March 1937 and a catechism on communism are included.

F511 FRANK, B. The Struggle against the "New Deal" in the Coal Fields, "Communist," 12 (Oct. 1933), 973-81.

An account of the "isolation" of the communist-led National Miners Union in face of the powerful, NRA-supported United Mine Workers of America.

F512 FRANK, B. "Miners Unite! One Class Struggle Union." New York: Workers Library, 1934. 47 pp.
A call to miners to join the National Miners Union, a new union with a militant class-struggle program, full rank-and-file democracy, and the only program of action that can benefit the miners. The author denounces the United Mine Workers and the Lewis machine. (The NMU was an affiliate of the Party-controlled Trade Union Unity League.)

F513 FRANK, M. Z. R. Our Fifth Column, "Congress Bulletin," 8 (Jan. 10, 1941), 5-6.
A warning against communists who have fanned panic among Jews in connection with anti-Semitism, emphasized the inadequacy of our democratic institutions to deal with the menace, and attacked the American Jewish Committee.

F514 FRANK, Richard. Negro Revolutionary Music, "New Masses," 11 (May 15, 1934), 29-30.
An assertion that the communist movement today is beginning to be expressed in typically American forms, as in native Negro music in the South. New revolutionary songs are being created, and revolutionary words are being added to the music of old spirituals and work songs.

F515 .... The Schools and the People's Front, "Communist," 16 (May 1937), 432-45.
An outline of a program for communist activity in the schools: to direct the rebelliousness of school children, organize teachers in the American Federation of Teachers, advance the people's front movement through Parent-Teacher associations, and counteract bourgeois propaganda with Marxist-Leninist teaching.

F516 FRANK, Waldo. "The Death and Birth of David Markand: An American Story." New York: Scribner, 1934. 542 pp.
A novel by a communist supporter about a man who is dissatisfied, despite a good job and a family, and who wanders through America for four years "in search of life." Surviving many tribulations, he at last records conversion at the graves of two working class comrades, and finds a new life and a new faith.

F517 .... The Writer's Part in Communism, "Partisan Review and Anvil," 3 (Feb. 1936), 14-17.
An address to the International Congress of Writers for the Defense of Culture, held in Paris, in June 1935. Pledging his complete political support to the Communist Party, Frank shows how literature through history has portrayed the organic unity of mankind, which is today embodied in the Marxian dialectic.

F518 .... "In the American Jungle." New York: Farrar & Rinehart, 1937. 302 pp.
A collection of Frank's papers from 1925 to 1936, many of which were previously published in various periodicals. They show his progressively stauncher support of Marxism, the Soviet Union, and the Communist Party. (He subsequently turned away from his procommunist stand.) Among the speeches printed here are one to the U.S. Congress Against War in 1933, one given on the anniversary of the October Revolution in 1935, one at the first session of the American Writers Congress in 1935, and one at the International Congress of Writers for the Defense of Culture in 1935.

F519 .... "The Bridegroom Cometh." New York: Doubleday, Doran, 1939. 628 pp.
A novel set between 1914 and 1924, recording the experiences of a woman who works her way through college, marries into a wealthy Jewish family, is divorced, and finally identifies with the working class and the Communist Party. (A sequel to "The Death and Birth of David Markand.)

F520 .... Anti-Communist Peril: Rediscovering Our Roots, "Nation," 178 (June 19, 1954), 515-21.
While there is a communist peril, at home as well as abroad, the greater peril is in the trend, in our values and institutions, toward man's dehumanization. Professional communist-haters such as Max Eastman and Sidney Hook, in rejecting communism, have come to accept communism's opponent, the American capitalist system.

F521 .... An American Tragedy: The Oppenheimer Case, "Nation," 179 (Sept. 25, 1954), 245-49.
An analysis of the hearings in the J. Robert Oppenheimer case, probing psychological and emotional factors, and interpreting the scientist's feelings, motives, and compulsions. Oppenheimer's failure to speak out for his convictions, his misgivings about the H-bomb, are symbolic of America's tragedy.

F522 FRANKFELD, Phil. The Crisis and the Strike Curve for 1930, "Communist," 10 (May 1931), 444-51.
A communist explanation for the decline of strikes in 1930. While workers are more cautious in periods of unemployment, the strike decline of 1930 was also due to the treachery of the AFL, and to the weakness of the Party and the Trade Union Unity League. The strike of 10,000 workers in Lawrence, Mass., is a turning point in the strike curve.

F523 .... A United Democratic Front Defeated the Ober Law, "Political Affairs," 28 (Oct. 1949), 85-94.
After the Ober Law, which declared it illegal for one to be a member of any subversive group, had been railroaded through the Maryland legislature, a Citizens' Committee was set up to organize a mass campaign against it. Workers, Negroes, and communists participated in the campaign. The law was later held unconstitutional.

F524 FRANKLIN, Francis. For a Free, Happy and Prosperous South, "Communist," 17 (Jan. 1938), 62-74.
A proposal of a popular-front program for the South, to be enacted through progressive forces in the Democratic Party, a strong labor movement of both races, and a farmer-labor coalition. Southern wage differentials can be erased, Negro liberation forwarded, and Northern domination of the Southern economy ended. (Some aspects of this article are criticized by Theodore Bassett in "The 'White' South and the People's Front," in the "Communist" for April 1938.)

F525 .... Problems of the Democratic Front in the South, "Communist," 17 (Sept. 1938), 818-28.
The crisis in the Cotton Belt is evident in the near bankruptcy of plantations, soil deterioration, and the increase in tenancy. Support is urged for Roosevelt's program of sales of land to tenants at low interest rates, with technical assistance to new farm-owners. The political difficulties of the Southern ruling class are increasing.

F526 .... The Cultural Heritage of the Negro People, "Communist," 18 (June 1939), 563-71.
A discussion of early Negro culture in Africa, the development of Negro culture in America, and recent achievements in Negro culture. The work of the Party in developing the new culture of national liberation among Negroes

is emphasized. Negro cultural progress will be made as the basic demands for land and democracy are realized.

F527 FRANKLIN, Francis. The Status of the Negro People in the Black Belt and How to Fight for the Right of Self-Determination (A Discussion Article), "Political Affairs," 25 (May 1946), 438-56.
While repudiating Browder's revisionism and affirming the correctness of the Party's 1930 stand on the Negro nation's right of self-determination, the author asserts that the Negro people in the Black Belt are also an oppressed part of the American nation as a whole. The Negro people want, not separation, but amalgamation with the American nation on the basis of equality. The Party should support this specific form of self-determination. (For a sharp disagreement with Franklin's views see Max Weiss, "Toward Clarity on the Negro Question [A Discussion Article]," in the same issue of "Political Affairs.")

F528 FRANKLIN, John. "National Defense." New York: American League Against War and Fascism, 1936. 19 pp.
An attack on our "enormous" war budgets by a leading front organization, which asserts that we have no enemies beyond our shores. Any war we fight, the author asserts, will be for foreign aggression—for markets and investments, for economic control of new colonial areas—or against our own people. The U.S. army, which is opposed to democracy, poses the threat of military dictatorship.

F529 FRANKLIN, Julian H. Why I Broke with the Communists. "Harper's Magazine," 194 (May 1947), 412-18.
A liberal, active in the American Veterans Committee, tells why he cooperated with communists who controlled his chapter, and how he finally became disillusioned with them. Their dogmatism prevented adjustment to political realities; they violated democratic procedure, caused universal distrust, and isolated themselves from the local community.

F530 FRANTZ, Laurent B., and REDLICH, Norman. Does Silence Mean Guilt? "Nation," 176 (June 6, 1953), 471-77.
A law librarian and a practicing attorney protest the widespread inference that those who plead the Fifth Amendment are guilty. Witnesses may decline to answer as to past Communist Party membership to avoid informing on others or to escape a perjury charge. This use of the Fifth Amendment can seldom block the investigative function of Congress, which is incidental to its duty to legislate.

F531 FRANTZ, Laurent B. H-Bomb for Unions: The Butler Bill, "Nation," 177 (Nov. 28, 1953), 442-45.
Denunciation of Senator Butler's bill providing for the loss of bargaining rights by any union held by the Subversive Activities Control Board to be substantially controlled by communists. Since the tests for communist domination are weak, all unions would be at the mercy of the Board. Accused unions would lose bargaining rights when a complaint is issued, not when final judgment is reached.

F532 .... Tooling Up for Mass Repression, "Nation," 177 (Dec. 12, 1953), 494-99.
A critical evaluation of the Subversive Activities Control Board, covering the statute under which it was established, the composition of the Board, and its methods and functions. The cases of five organizations which the Board will consider are examined, with emphasis on ambiguities and false accusations. The liberty of everyone is threatened by this power over voluntary organizations.

F533 FRAZIER, Gilbert. The NAACP Convention, "Political Affairs," 35 (Sept. 1956), 7-21.
A generally favorable account of the June 26-July 1 convention of the NAACP, hailing its militant posture and the addresses of Martin Luther King and A. Philip Randolph. The convention is criticized, however, for following the government's anticommunist foreign policy line, and for barring cooperation with communist organizations.

F534 FREEDMAN, Blanch L. The Loyalty-Security Program—Its Effect in Immigration and Deportation, "Lawyers Guild Review," 15 (Winter 1955-56), 135-38.
Although the status of the foreign-born has always been uncertain, the impact of the loyalty-security program on them has been devastating. Among the topics considered are investigations, alien registration, deportation, detention, bail, and supervision. The loyalty-security drive has made the noncitizen's position a debased one.

F535 FREEDOM HOUSE. "What's 'Right' and 'Left'? A Guide for Responsible Anti-Communists." New York: Freedom House, n.d. [1962]. 4 pp.
An assertion by an organization dedicated to democratic principles that communism and fascism are basically alike in their attack on democratic institutions and their use of conspiratorial tactics. Irresponsibles on both left and right help to confuse and paralyze American thought and action. Communist views during the Soviet-Nazi pact period and the present cold war period are reviewed and compared with those of the extreme right.

F536 FREEMAN, Donald. "Tax Relief for Whom—the Needy or the Greedy?" New York: New Century, 1947. 15 pp.
An effort to arouse indignation against the tax bill of 1947, as one giving special privilege to favored groups instead of allowing tax relief to those who need it. The author outlines the Party's tax program, which, he urges, should be enacted at once.

F537 .... Toward a People's Tax Program, "Political Affairs," 26 (April 1947), 346-58; (May), 465-70.
A report on federal income taxes from 1939 to 1947, corporation taxes, gift and estate taxes, excise taxes, social security taxes, real estate taxes, sales taxes, etc. Lower income groups bear the brunt of the tax burden. Charges are proposed to stem the drive of monopoly capital toward fascism.

F538 FREEMAN, Joseph. Notes on American Literature, "Communist," 7 (Aug. 1928), 513-20; (Sept.), 570-78.
Analysis of the role of literature in American life, with a brief appraisal of left-wing writers and their works. The author asserts that the literature of Wilsonian middle-class liberalism has reached a dead end, that a bourgeois literature with fascist tendencies is developing, and that a left-wing literature is emerging.

F539 ...; KUNITZ, Joshua; and LOZOWICK, Louis. "Voices of October: Art and Literature in Soviet Russia." New York: Vanguard, 1930. 317 pp. Bibliog.
A study of art and literature in the USSR by American intellectuals who were leading members of the "New Masses" group in the 1930's. Freeman discusses the background of Soviet literature, the new literary groupings, and the methods used by the government to bring art and literature into the lives of all. Kunitz writes on the men and women in Soviet literature. Other chapters deal with the theatre, cinema, painting, architecture, and music.

F540   FREEMAN, Joseph. Social Trends in American Literature, "Communist," 9 (July 1930), 641-51.
An analysis of various trends in literature before the 1929 crash, with special attention to the humanist movement, which has a reactionary and fascist philosophy. Opposing it is a new left-wing school of literary criticism, extending from H. L. Mencken of the "American Mercury" to Henry Hazlitt of the "Nation."

F541   . . . . Ivory Towers—White and Red, "New Masses," 12 (Sept. 11, 1934), 20-24.
Disagreement with an attack on Marxian critics written by Albert Harper for the "Daily Worker." Acknowledging that very little fundamental writing has been produced by the Marxists, Freeman asserts that those dedicated to guiding on the cultural front have been too busy to write. The situation should now improve, since more intellectuals have moved left.

F542   . . . . "An American Testament: A Narrative of Rebels and Romantics." New York: Farrar & Rinehart, 1936. 678 pp. Ind.
The autobiography of a Russian-born writer who became a communist in the early days of the Party here, and whose work on the "Masses," its successor, the "Liberator," and later the "New Masses" brought him into contact with many of the Party's intellectual and political leaders. Freeman discusses the artist's conflict between art and poetry on the one hand and communist political activity on the other. He tells of his experiences in western Europe and in the Soviet Union. The book is valuable for its description of early Party life and leaders, and for its insights into the attitudes of the young poets and radicals who joined the Party in the 1920's. (Freeman's loyalty to the Party and the USSR was shaken by the Moscow trials of the 1930's. The admiration for Trotsky expressed in this book, despite the author's fundamental disagreement with him, led to his denunciation by the Party; thereafter he abandoned politics.)

F543   . . . . The Battle for Art, "New Masses," 18 (Feb. 25, 1936), 8-10.
A report on the meetings of the American Artists Congress which established a permanent League of American Artists. The artists are now united with the millions who struggle for the advancement of culture and against war and fascism.

F544   . . . . Old Fervor and New Discipline, "New Masses," 21 (Dec. 15, 1936), 5-8.
A eulogy of the "New Masses" on its twenty-fifth anniversary. Aware of the dangers of fascism, it continues the fight against capitalism and for socialism, Spain, and the Soviet Union. Through it artists, organized in a people's front, are combatting the forces of evil and darkness.

    . . . . See also EVANS, Robert.

F545   FRIEDMAN, Robert. U.E.: Ten Years Strong, "New Masses," 60 (Sept. 17, 1946), 3-5.
An account of the formation, growth, and achievements of the United Electrical, Radio and Machine Workers of America, CIO. Attention is paid to strike gains, the UE's part in the struggle for peace, and the Red-baiting to which the union has been subjected. The UE leadership is praised.

F546   . . . . "How's Your Health? The Fight for a National Health Program." New York: New Century, 1947. 32 pp.
An assertion that America is in a health crisis, with an appeal for support for the Wagner-Murray-Dingell proposal for a National Health Act. Health problems are intensified among low-income workers, among Negroes and slum-dwellers. Big Business, aided by the American Medical Association, leads the fight against the National Health Act. The achievements of the USSR in the field of health are lauded.

F547   FRIENDLY, Alfred. The Noble Crusade of Senator McCarthy, "Harper's Magazine," 201 (Aug. 1950), 34-42.
A reporter for the Washington "Post," who has covered the McCarthy story since January 1950, points out inconsistencies in the senator's statements about the number of communists in the State Department. McCarthy's charges, particularly about CP influence in our Far East policy, are inaccurate and irresponsible.

F548   . . . . Case History of a Smear, "Progressive," 15 (May 1951), 5-9.
A Washington, D.C., newspaperman's account of the effort to smear Mrs. Anna M. Rosenberg as a communist sympathizer, following her nomination as Assistant Secretary of Defense. The chief accusation, that she had been a member of the John Reed Clubs, was found to be deliberately false, not an honest confusion with another Anna Rosenberg who had belonged. Other charges were equally groundless.

F549   FRIENDS OF THE SOVIET UNION. "Why Soviet Russia Should Be Recognized: Demand Unconditional Diplomatic and Trade Relations Now!" New York: Friends of the Soviet Union, n.d. [1933]. 23 pp.
An effort to mobilize support for diplomatic recognition of the Soviet Union. Anti-Soviet propaganda is called a smokescreen behind which capitalists seek to prevent the American working class from expressing solidarity with Soviet workers and peasants. Even segments of the bourgeoisie now recognize the advantages of diplomatic and commercial recognition. Foreign Commissar Litvinov is quoted to prove that the Soviet Union wants peace.

F550   FRIES, Amos A. "Communism Unmasked." Washington, D.C.: The author, 1937. 204 pp.
A presentation of the basic tenets of communism from the extreme right. Among the topics considered are the nature of communism, communism and religion, the condition of women under communism, its fundamental characteristics, Soviet power and who wields it, the united-front tactic, laws against teaching communism in the D.C. schools, immigration, labor, and national defense.

F551   FRIESSEN, Gordon. "Oklahoma Witch Hunt." Oklahoma City: Oklahoma Committee to Defend Political Prisoners, 1941. 23 pp.
The cases of several Oklahoma citizens who were convicted of criminal syndicalism on grounds of possession and sale of communist books and membership in the Communist Party. The pamphlet urges support of the fight of the International Labor Defense and the National Federation for Constitutional Liberties (both communist-controlled organizations) to reverse the sentences.

F552   FROHOCK, W. M. Another Sort of Communist, "Commonweal," 27 (Dec. 17, 1937), 205-6.
The author sees in the "sincere" communist a man of faith, capable of great renunciation, a general love of humanity, and seriousness combined with the strength of orthodoxy; these are virtues which would produce a good Catholic. To oppose him properly, these traits must be recognized.

F553   FROST, Stanley. "Labor and Revolt." New York: Dutton, 1920. 405 pp.

An account of radical activities following World War I, with a discussion of their relationship to labor's legitimate ends. The chance of revolution is so slight that those who urge revolt are guilty of suicidal folly. The cure is work, reform, and more civilization.

F554 FUCHS, Ralph F., and HUNTER, Robert M. Communists in the Colleges: Two Views, "Antioch Review," 9 (June 1949), 199-209.
Fuchs defends the position of the American Association of University Professors, which opposes using Communist Party membership as prima-facie evidence of unfitness as a college teacher. Hunter defends the prima-facie evidence argument, because of the loyalty implications of Party membership and because intellectual integrity is incompatible with it.

F555 FUERNBERG, F. "Where to Begin? How to Build a Mass Young Communist League." New York: Distributed in the U.S. by the Young Communist League for Youth International Publishers, n.d. [1929?]. 24 pp.
A "self-critical" pamphlet analyzing the reasons why the Young Communist League has not been more successful. Young communists have neglected organizational tasks, it is argued; in emphasizing these, young communists must guard against merely being "practical," as well as

against right-opportunist errors. The YCL must also push shop work in order to make shop nuclei the basis of the organization.

F556 FULLER, Helen. Remington and Lee: New Loyalty Purge, "New Republic," 122 (June 19, 1950), 13-15.
Brief summaries of the records of Michael Lee and William Remington, two U.S. Department of Commerce employees dismissed as security risks. The author asserts that important evidence was overlooked, and that proper dismissal procedures were disregarded.

F557 "FUR AND LEATHER WORKER," The Attack on Ben Gold, 16 (Feb. 1954), 7-14.
A review of the career of Ben Gold and the International Fur and Leather Workers Union, of which he is president; and an impassioned defense of Gold, on trial for perjury in connection with his signing of a noncommunist affidavit under the Taft-Hartley Act.

F558 . . ., Challenge to Labor, 16 (April 1954), 9-20.
A call to organized labor to come to the aid of Ben Gold, president of the union, convicted of perjury after signing a noncommunist affidavit under the Taft-Hartley Act. The editors call the conviction a frame-up.

G

G1 GABRIEL, Gilbert W. Behind the Asbestos Curtain, "Nation," 174 (June 28, 1952), 625-28.
The drama critic for "Cue" discusses the impact of the red hunt on the legitimate theater. The theater is peculiarly subject to picketing and boycotting, since few plays can survive two or three successive empty houses. The threat to freedom in the theater has begun.

G2 GAER, Joseph. "The First Round: The Story of the CIO Political Action Committee." New York: Duell, Sloan and Pearce, 1944. 478 pp.
A popular manual on CIO-PAC, with reproductions of many of its publications, written by a pro-CP author at a time when communists and fellow-travelers were very active in CIO-PAC and in the National Citizens PAC, and when the Party line supported both organizations. The book illustrates the Party line during World War II.

G3 GALENSON, Walter. "The CIO Challenge to the AFL: A History of the American Labor Movement, 1935-1941." Cambridge: Harvard University Press, 1960. 732 pp. Notes. Ind.
A scholarly account of the split in the American labor movement and of the development of unionism in 17 leading industries in the years immediately preceding World War II. Communists were active in a number of these unions, including those in automobiles, electrical and radio manufacturing, women's garments, meat packing, and lumber. Scattered references to communist activity occur in various of the other industries as well.

G4 GALLACHER, William, and BROWDER, Earl. "Anti-Semitism: What It Means and How to Combat It." New York: Workers Library, 1943. 35 pp.
In the first article, "The Meaning of Anti-Semitism," an English communist leader refutes anti-Semitic stereotypes, and asserts that anti-Semitism is the weapon of reaction and fascism to split the working class, confuse the people, and aid the Nazi war effort. In "How to Combat Anti-Semitism," Browder links it with anticommunism, accusing anticommunist Jews of anti-Semitism.

G5 GAMBS, John S. "The Decline of the I.W.W." New York: Columbia University Press, 1932. 268 pp. App. Bibliog. Ind.
A study of the IWW from 1917 to 1931, supplementing the earlier work by Brissenden. Chapter 3 on "Communism and Internationalism" (pp. 75-98) deals with the appeal of the Third International for IWW affiliation, and the IWW rejection of this, because of its refusal to ally itself with politics. In 1922 it also refused to join the RILU. Communist sympathizers within the IWW continued to press for affiliation with Moscow until the split of 1924.

G6 GANLEY, Nat. On the Coming 15th Convention of the United Auto Workers, "Political Affairs," 34 (March 1955), 41-51.
The left auto workers, working with non-left forces, will influence the convention. The UAW's 1955 contract demands will include the guaranteed employment plan, which the left has always supported. Most top officers remain

wedded to the Wall Street cold war program. ACTU pressure may lead the convention to bar communists from UAW membership.

G7 .... The UAW Convention and Coming Struggles, "Political Affairs," 34 (June 1955), 3-12.
The UAW convention was a demonstration of unity and militancy, adopting shorter hours without wage reductions as the next major bargaining goal. While the convention supported the cold war, it proposed an end to it. Left and progressive forces fought for Negro representation in top UAW leadership, but were defeated by Reuther's commitment to a lily-white ticket.

G8 GANNES, Harry, and OSWALD, George. "Youth under Americanism." Chicago: Young Workers League, n.d. [1923?]. 64 pp.
A communist view of class divisions under capitalism, control of the educational system by the capitalist class, and misleading of the young by YMCA, YWCA, and Boy Scouts. Young workers are urged to help in the task of abolishing capitalism.

G9 GANNES, Harry. The Raisins in the Filipino Cake, "Workers Monthly," 5 (March 1926), 213-14.
A denunciation of American imperialism in the Philippines. Despite assertions that America has only the good of the Filipinos at heart, American imperialism, in reality, seeks to retain the Islands for strategic and exploitative reasons.

G10 .... "Yankee Colonies: Imperialist Rule in the Philippines, Porto Rico, Hawaii and Other Possessions." New York: International Pamphlets, 1930. 31 pp.
A description of the economic resources of the islands, of capitalist investments there, of military bases constructed, and of the exploitation by American imperialists and native bourgeois of the workers and peasants. The author calls on American workers to support the campaign of the colonial people for independence.

G11 .... 13 Years of the Soviet Union and the Economic Crisis in the U.S.A., "Communist," 9 (Nov.-Dec. 1930), 979-97.
The achievements of the Soviet five-year plan are contrasted with the depression crisis in the U.S. The five-year plan should be a topic of discussion in every American shop.

G12 .... "Graft and Gangsters." New York: Workers Library, n.d. [1932]. 61 pp.
A Party view of political graft and gangsters as inextricably entwined. Graft and murder are seen as integral parts of capitalist government, whereas the capitalist system, based on profit and exploitation of workers, is the breeding ground of racketeers and gangsters. Only the daily struggles of the Party and the TUUL, and the dictatorship of the proletariat, can end the connection between gangsterism and capitalism.

G13   GANNES, Harry. "Kentucky Miners Fight." New York: Workers International Relief, 1932. 31 pp.
An account of the struggle of the coal miners in Harlan and Bell counties in eastern Kentucky. The story of the strike there, the activity of the National Miners Union, and the violence against strikers and against the Workers' International Relief food kitchens are told in this appeal for help.

G14   . . . . The National Industrial Recovery Act—Spearhead of the Roosevelt Program, "Communist,' 12 (Aug. 1933), 770-83.
A communist analysis of the NIRA, viewing the Act as an attempt to create a super-imperialism, while eliminating the antagonism between exploiters and exploited. NIRA seeks to trustify all industry, prepare it for war, prevent workers' struggles for improved conditions, and use the reformist leaders as strikebreakers.

G15   . . . . Wall Street Faces the Far East, "Communist," 15 (Jan. 1936), 35-46.
An analysis of U.S. and British imperialist designs as related to Japan's aggression in China and Manchuria. The demand for British forces in the Mediterranean, resulting from Mussolini's attack on Ethiopia and Japan's action in China, is bringing about a U.S.-British alliance to protect imperialist interests and make the Soviet Union vulnerable to attack from Japan.

G16   . . . . The United States Supreme Court and the Specter of Fascism, "Communist," 15 (March 1936), 230-44.
The Supreme Court is a capitalist tool whose decisions encourage fascist trends. Because of the Court's record against social legislation, culminating in decisions holding the NRA and AAA unconstitutional, the Party favors restricting the Court's power to nullify legislation.

G17   . . . . "The Munich Betrayal." New York: Workers Library, 1938. 15 pp.
Criticism of the perpetrators of the Munich agreement for handing Hitler one of his greatest triumphs, despite the superiority of the peace forces. Only the USSR has consistently stood for collective security. The Munich settlement has increased Hitler's threat to America.

G18   GANNETT, Betty. Disposal of Government-Owned Plants, "Political Affairs," 24 (June 1945), 527-38.
A survey of government-owned facilities, with proposals for their speedy and orderly postwar conversion to civilian production. Labor should help develop community-wide plans for effective use of the plants.

G19   . . . . "The Communist Party and You." New York: CPUSA, 1946. 48 pp.
A recruiting pamphlet by the Party's assistant organization secretary, emphasizing its role as a vanguard party of fighting action. Its struggles for union organization, democratic rights, a free South, Negro rights, and the unemployed are described, as are Party democracy and unity of action and the meaning of communist discipline.

G20   . . . . Win the Youth for Peace, Democracy and Socialism! "Political Affairs," 27 (Sept. 1948), 916-34.
A call for the formation of a non-Party youth organization, avoiding errors made by the Young Communist League and the American Youth for Democracy. Particular attention is urged to repeal of the draft and to work among young workers and Negro youth. (A report to the youth panel at the Party convention, Aug. 1948.)

G21   . . . . Organization for Struggle, "Political Affairs," 28 (Oct. 1949), 47-58.

A report to the Party's national committee, September 16-18, 1949, discussing recruitment, industrial concentration, and Party organization in a period of legal and extra-legal terror. Party members have shown a good fighting spirit in the face of the latest attacks, participating in many mass campaigns to protect civil rights. Recruiting has been insufficiently planned, however, and too few members have been recruited.

G22   . . . . Wall Street's War against the Korean People, "Political Affairs," 29 (Aug. 1950), 6-18.
An editorial article charging American imperialism with a reckless adventurist war of annihilation against the Korean people, who seek national unification, independence, and a free and democratic life. The million signatures in the U.S. for the World Peace Appeal show the desire of the common people for peace.

G23   . . . . "The Communist Program and the Struggle for Jobs, Peace, Equal Rights, and Democracy." New York: New Century, 1954. 40 pp.
An appeal to all who desire peace to unite for the settlement of disputes through negotiations, to halt the threat of war and fascism. Whereas Browder put his faith in enlightened monopoly capitalists, we avoid his revisionism by placing the organized labor movement in the leading role of a broad popular movement. We advocate socialism, but not force and violence in the change from capitalism to socialism.

G24   GANNETT, Lewis S. Skipping Bail, "Nation," 131 (Oct. 22, 1930), 437-38.
Censure of Fred Beal and four other Gastonia communists, convicted on a conspiracy charge, for skipping bail to flee to Russia. Their flight, which reflects on the labor movement, will affect subsequent political prisoners.

G25   GARDNER, George K. Bailey v. Richardson and the Constitution of the United States, "Boston University Law Review," 33 (April 1953), 176-203.
Criticism by a Harvard Law School professor of the result in the Dorothy Bailey loyalty case, in which a Supreme Court tie vote upheld a lower court decision approving her dismissal from the federal service. Grave injustice was done by preferring the word of absent informants to her supporters.

G26   GARDNER, Virginia. Notes on Un-Americana, "New Masses," 63 (April 8, 1947), 18-20.
A report by the Washington editor of the "New Masses" on hearings before the House Committee on Un-American Activities on the Rankin and Sheppard bills, which would punish by fine and imprisonment Party members or those who express sympathy with it.

G27   . . . . The Case of the Sixteen, "New Masses," 64 (July 15, 1947), 15-17.
A discussion of the appeal of the 16 members of the board of the Joint Anti-Fascist Refugee Committee from their conviction for contempt for failure to turn over Committee records to the House Un-American Activities Committee. The unconstitutionality of HUAC will be a major issue in the appeal.

G28   . . . . Trial by Perjury, "New Masses," 64 (Aug. 5, 1947), 14-16.
An assertion that the government's case against Gerhart Eisler is a frame-up, dependent upon testimony by employers' spies, stool pigeons, and psychopaths that Eisler had been a representative of the Communist International in the U.S. Weaknesses in the testimony against Eisler are reviewed.

G29   GARDNER, Virginia. A Mistake, Mr. Meyer? "New Masses," 64 (Aug. 19, 1947), 14-16.
An unflattering account of the hearing and testimony of Ira P. Meyer, divisional assistant in the State Department's visa division, at the trial of Gerhart Eisler, whose testimony is also reviewed. Admitting former membership in both the Austrian and German communist parties, Eisler denied that he had ever been a Communist International representative.

G30   . . . . Guilty of Anti-Fascism, "New Masses," 44 (Aug. 26, 1947), 13-16.
An account of the final portion of the trial of Gerhart Eisler, who was found guilty by the jury and whose conviction will be appealed. (Although the jury was asked to determine whether Eisler had been affiliated with the CPUSA, had used an alias, or resided here prior to 1941, the real issue was whether he had earlier been a Communist International representative in this country.)

G31   . . . . "The Rosenberg Story." New York: Masses & Mainstream, 1954. 126 pp.
A resumé of the lives of the communist "martyrs," Julius and Ethel Rosenberg, written by a member of the "Daily Worker" staff. Her account, based on interviews with friends, relatives, and associates, originally appeared in that publication. Emphasis is placed on the nobility of the heroic couple, for whose execution President Eisenhower, Attorney General Brownell, and J. Edgar Hoover are held indirectly responsible.

G32   GARLIN, Sender. Upton Sinclair: Reactionary Utopian, "New Masses," 11 (May 22, 1934), 10-12.
A communist critique of the socialist author currently seeking nomination for governor of California on the Democratic ticket. His program, denounced as reactionary utopianism, attracts weary liberals, frustrated clubwomen, and the bankrupt middle class.

G33   . . . . "The Real Huey P. Long." New York: Workers Library, 1935. 47 pp.
An attack on Senator Long for establishing a dictatorship in Louisiana and for ruthlessly attacking the living standards of the masses. Long, who personifies the fascist menace in the U.S., hopes to defeat Roosevelt in 1936 by means of empty promises. His career shows him to be an enemy of strikers and a foe of the Negro people.

G34   . . . . "The Real Rickenbacker." New York: Workers Library, 1943. 23 pp.
An attack on Edward V. Rickenbacker, acclaimed as a national hero after spending three weeks on a rubber raft in the Pacific. Rickenbacker, America First Committee member and labor baiter, was an admirer of the Nazi system in 1940 and has been associated with firms with antilabor records.

G35   . . . . "The Truth About Reader's Digest." New York: Forum Publishers, 1943. 29 pp.
An attack on "Reader's Digest" as dishonest, profascist, and anti-Soviet. It is accused of catering to anti-Semitic, anti-Negro, and antilabor sentiments. The author demands that this defeatist magazine be forced to cease publication.

G36   . . . . "Is Dewey the Man?" New York: Workers Library, 1944. 32 pp.
A communist view of Governor Thomas E. Dewey, Republican candidate for President. Dewey's record as governor of New York and his support of reactionary principles prove him unworthy to lead the country in war and peace. His views on foreign affairs are similar to those of native fascists.

G37   . . . . "Enemies of the Peace: Profile of the 'Hate-Russia' Gang." New York: New Century, 1945. 48 pp.
Attacks on anti-Soviet writers, including William C. Bullitt, Clare Luce, William Henry Chamberlin, Eugene Lyons, Westbrook Pegler, George E. Sokolsky, Max Eastman, Louis Fischer, William L. White, Isaac Don Levine, David Dallin, and Alexander Barmine. The McCormick, Hearst, Scripps-Howard, and Patterson papers are also attacked, along with social democrats and Trotskyists. The author concludes that high circles oppose a democratic, antifascist Europe in which people may choose their forms of government and social systems.

G38   . . . . "Red Tape and Barbed Wire: Close-up of the McCarran Law in Action." New York: Civil Rights Congress, 1952. 48 pp.
Denunciation of and demand for repeal of the McCarran Act, with an analysis of hearings before the Subversive Activities Control Board regarding Soviet domination of the CPUSA. The Act, the author predicts, will be used to persecute unions or civil rights or community groups fighting for progressive measures. He particularly criticizes provisions for the jailing of subversives during national emergencies.

G39   GARRETT, Garet. Federal Theater for the Masses, "Saturday Evening Post," 208 (June 20, 1936), 8-9 ff.
An assertion that the Federal Theater Project, though supported by the U.S. government, uses its funds to denounce and ridicule that government's officials and policies. The author describes the New York City production of a play, "Triple A Plowed Under," whose theme coincides with the objectives of the CPUSA.

G40   GARRISON, Lloyd K. Some Observations on the Loyalty-Security Program, "University of Chicago Law Review," 23 (Autumn 1955), 1-11.
A speech by a former dean of the University of Wisconsin Law School, criticizing the federal government's loyalty-security program. While an effective security program is essential today, the present one works needless injustice on innocent people. Suggestions for reforms are made that will promote, not weaken, our security.

G41   GATELY, Lawrence. Almost a Red, "American Magazine," 120 (Nov. 1935), 61 ff.
The story of a young American who, repelled by the corruption and self-seeking of American political machines, was attracted to the communists because of their idealism, courage, and willingness to sacrifice for their beliefs. He discovered, however, that there was no freedom of discussion within the Party, that its appeal to youth was based on feeling, not thinking.

G42   GATES, Albert. "Incentive Pay: The Speed-up, New Style." New York: Workers Party, n.d., [1943?]. 30 pp.
An anti-Stalinist (as well as anti-Big Business) indictment of incentive pay as another plan to intensify exploitation of workers. Stalinists and the unions they control, interested only in the second front and in supporting Stalin's foreign policy, are declared willing to sell out American workers. Labor must regain the right to strike and win higher wages.

G43   . . . . Slap at Browder Signal for CP Change of Line, "Labor Action," 9 (June 4, 1945), 1 ff.
A Trotskyist analysis of the attack on the Communist Political Association and Earl Browder by Jacques Duclos, French communist leader. So long as Germany was dangerous, Russian policy was to strengthen the Big Three

coalition, though the American communists, going further than in other Western countries, gave up status as a party. Now Stalin wants to make life difficult for the governments of Britain and the U.S.

G44   GATES, Albert. Labor! Beware the Latest Communist "Turn," "Labor Action," 9 (June 11, 1945), 1 ff.
A Trotskyist comment on the change in the line of the Communist Political Association following the criticism by Duclos. The new line can be applied in a peaceful manner, depending on good relations between Russia and the U.S. and Britain, or it can become a militant, class struggle policy if relations deteriorate. The new line, like the old, serves the interests of Russian foreign policy.

G45   . . . . The UE Convention Fight: Is the CIO Heading toward a Split? "New International," 15 (Sept. 1949), 196-98.
A Trotskyist view of the UE fight with the CIO and a report on the opposition within the UE to the Emspak-Matles leadership. The author reports on the UE convention, which concluded with an ultimatum to the national CIO to end hostilities or lose the UE's per capita tax.

G46   GATES, John. The Army and the People, "Communist," 20 (Nov. 1941), 997-1010.
Communist criticism, in the period between Hitler's invasion of Russia and Pearl Harbor, of U.S. reluctance to enter the war as a belligerent. The American army must be made an army of national unity and a decisive military force to annihilate Hitlerism. Pacifism, which is not a working-class ideology, is in the service of Hitler.

G47   . . . . The American Veterans Committee Convention, "Political Affairs," 25 (Aug. 1946), 734-41.
The AVC convention is criticized for not taking a more militant stand on benefits for veterans. The charge that a bonus would cause inflation is ridiculed, and sly Red-baiting behind the scenes is regretted. United action with the labor movement and with other veterans' organizations is advocated.

G48   . . . . Whither the American Legion? "Political Affairs," 25 (Dec. 1946), 1084-91.
A report on the twenty-eighth national convention of the American Legion. Weak participation of World War II veterans is attributed to the Legion's failure to fight vigorously for their demands. Progressive veterans are urged to defeat the convention's reactionary program.

G49   . . . . The 80th Congress and Perspectives for 1948, "Political Affairs," 26 (Aug. 1947), 716-29.
The text of a report to the June 27-30 meeting of the Party's national committee, asserting that the reactionary 80th Congress is moving to impoverish the American people and destroy our democratic liberties. Progressives must help develop the movement for Wallace for President and build a new people's party led by labor.

G50   . . . . The South—The Nation's Problem, "Political Affairs," 27 (Sept. 1948), 899-909.
A report to the Negro-South panel of the Party's fourteenth national convention, August 2-6, 1948, attributing the economic backwardness of the South to the national oppression of the Negro people. The Party's program for achieving national liberation of Southern Negroes and obtaining land for Negro farmers is presented.

G51   . . . . "On Guard against Browderism, Titoism, Trotskyism." New York: New Century, 1951. 15 pp.

A speech by the editor of the "Daily Worker" in December 1950 at a Party convention, attacking Browder for his criticism of the USSR, his treatment of the Negro question, and his aid to the stool pigeon, Budenz. The Titoist clique in Yugoslavia is attacked as fascist, merging with Trotskyism.

G52   . . . . Time for a Change, "Political Affairs," 35 (Nov. 1956), 43-56.
The editor of the "Daily Worker" asserts that the Party is in a deep crisis, having lost members and influence and become isolated. Reviewing the Party's errors, he calls for changes in the approach to Marxist-Leninist theory and to the USSR, and for full democracy within the Party. He attacks the concept of Soviet infallibility and the one-sided relationship between the CPSU and other communist parties.

G53   . . . . "Evolution of an American Communist: Why I Quit after 27 Years, Where I Stand Now." Brooklyn: The author, 1958. 23 pp.
The former editor of the "Daily Worker," who had joined the Party at seventeen and fought both in Spain and in World War II, viewed Soviet military intervention in Hungary in 1956 as a crime. He describes differences with the Foster leadership of the Party in the early and mid-1950's, and the disintegration following Khrushchev's revelations about Stalin. A socialist society demands a high level of political democracy.

G54   . . . . "The Story of an American Communist." New York: Thomas Nelson & Sons, 1958. 221 pp. Ind.
An account of his experiences, by a man who was a leader of the Communist Party of the U.S. until his resignation in January 1958 following the Khrushchev disclosures about Stalin and the Soviet actions in Poland and Hungary. Gates was on the national committee from 1946 and editor-in-chief of the "Daily Worker" from 1947 until he left the Party, after leading the internal struggle against the Foster group to democratize the Party and establish its independence of the communist movement abroad. He calls for democratic socialism, an end to sectarianism, democracy in the USSR, and a new political alignment and a mass popular party in the U.S.

G55   . . . . The Failure of Communism in America, "Progressive," 22 (March 1958), 34 ff.
A former leading communist, editor of the "Daily Worker" and member of the Party's national committee for over a decade, asserts that he recently left the Party because it could not realize democracy, peace, and socialism without a radical transformation; among its defects are its relationship to the Soviet Union, its attitudes toward other radical groups, and the absence of internal democracy.

G56   GATES, Lillian. The People Fight Back for Rent and Housing, "Political Affairs," 26 (April 1947), 316-27.
A call for a broad democratic coalition for the fight to keep rent control, against the financial interest and their tools in Congress. A grass-roots tenants' movement is now being formed. The housing crisis will continue as long as we have capitalism, since the industry cannot and will not build housing at a price most Americans can afford.

G57   GAULD, Charles A. "Dies Committee & Tory Attacks on Federal Government Employees." Washington, D.C.: The author, 1942. 78 pp. Mimeo.
A defense by a government employee charged by the Dies

Committee with affiliation with communist front organizations. One of five employees so charged, the author comments on the various organizations named, showing that well-known, respected persons were connected with them.

G58 GAUSMANN, William C., and FLEISCHMAN, Harry. Wallace Follows Line, Hints at Formation of a Third Party, "Call," 14 (June 25, 1947), 1 ff.
A socialist analysis of the developing Wallace third party movement, charging that it is a hoax through which communist-fronters hope to see a Republican—preferably an isolationist one—elected in 1948, leaving Europe at the mercy of Stalin, and making emergence of a genuine farmer-labor party more difficult. Wallace is criticized for refusing to recognize that the Soviet Union is a totalitarian state.

G59 GEBERT, Bill. The St. Louis Strike and the Chicago Needle Trades Strike, "Communist," 12 (Aug. 1933), 800-9.
An account of strikes of Negro women, under Party leadership, in the nut industry of St. Louis and dress shops in Chicago. The Party must penetrate the big factories, making them fortresses of our movement.

G60 . . . . The Significance of the Party Anniversary for the Polish Workers in the U.S.A., "Communist," 12 (Sept. 1933), 955-60.
A review of the development of communist sentiment among Polish-American workers, with a call to the Party to revitalize its Polish section. The Party must pay more attention to winning the Polish workers, while struggling against Polish fascism and social fascism.

G61 . . . . Mass Struggles in the Chicago District and the Tasks of the Party, "Communist," 12 (Dec. 1933), 1189-1200.
A report on Party successes and failures in the Chicago district, dealing particularly with the labor movement. While the TUUL unions have led a series of successful strikes, these have not taken place in such areas of Party concentration as steel, packing, and railroads.

G62 . . . . Check-Up on Control Tasks in the Chicago District, "Communist," 13 (July 1934), 711-17.
An examination of Party work in the Chicago district, one of the major points of concentration, to determine reasons for its weaknesses. Among the reasons are insufficient guidance to factory nuclei, neglect of work in reformist trade unions, and preoccupation with particular mass organizations.

G63 . . . . The General Strike in Terre Haute, "Communist," 14 (Sept. 1935), 800-10.
A review of the general strike, declared without sanction of the AFL or the Central Labor Union, to protest the importation of gunmen as strikebreakers. The weakness of the AFL leadership and the need for a strong communist movement are emphasized.

G64 . . . . Our Tasks in Developing Activity within the Company Unions, "Communist," 15 (Jan. 1936), 47-57.
In heavy industries such as steel, company unions have a larger membership than genuine unions. Their development has been aided by the failure of reactionary AFL officials to adopt industrial unionism and organize the unorganized. The Party must work within the company unions to transform them into genuine trade unions.

G65 . . . . The United Mine Workers' Union Convention, "Communist," 15 (March 1936), 211-19.

A communist commends the United Mine Workers of America for its stand on industrial unionism, but criticizes John L. Lewis for the anticommunist clause in the UMW constitution, and for his support of Roosevelt in the 1936 elections.

G66 . . . . The Steel Workers Give Their Mandate for Organization, "Communist," 15 (June 1936), 498-507.
A review of the convention of the Amalgamated Association of Iron, Steel and Tin Workers, with attention to conditions in the steel industry and the weakness of union organization. The CIO has offered assistance to the steel union. Communists support the organization drive despite their exclusion from the union.

G67 . . . . Smashing through Barriers to the Organization of the Steel Workers, "Communist," 15 (Aug. 1936), 759-68.
Report to the ninth convention, CPUSA, regarding attempts to break the steel trusts and organize the steel workers. The CP supports the Steel Workers Organizing Committee and hopes for cooperation between AFL and CIO in order to unite all workers in a common front. Communist efforts to unionize steel workers in the Pittsburgh district are described.

G68 . . . . Steel Workers on the March, "Communist," 16 (May 1937), 456-64.
The agreement between the Steel Workers Organizing Committee of the CIO and the Carnegie-Illinois Steel Corporation is hailed as a major advance in the unionization of steel. The organizational drive in other steel areas is reviewed.

G69 . . . . The Convention of 400,000, "Communist," 16 (Oct. 1937), 891-905.
The Milwaukee convention of the United Automobile Workers is acclaimed as a victory for the CIO and the communists. The article comments on the convention's background, problems, resolutions, and officers.

G70 . . . . The Steel Workers in Convention, "Communist," 17 (Feb. 1938), 122-33.
A report on the convention of the Steel Workers Organizing Committee, CIO, held in Pittsburgh in December, stressing the essential unity of the convention while attacking Muste-Trotskyite "wreckers." Unfortunately the resolution against war was passed under isolationist influence.

G71 . . . . The Auto Workers Forge Unity at the Cleveland Convention, "Communist," 18 (May 1939), 435-44.
A review of CIO activities in the automobile industry, and an analysis of the 1939 convention of the United Automobile Workers. The convention represented a victory of the progressive forces, and demonstrated the unity of the auto workers on problems confronting their union and the country as a whole.

G72 GEHMAN, Richard B. Oak Ridge Witch Hunt, "New Republic," 119 (July 5, 1948), 12-14.
The former editor of the Oak Ridge "Journal," official weekly of the atomic-bomb project, discusses the Atomic Energy Commission's loyalty investigations of research scientists and laborers at Oak Ridge, Tenn. He asserts that scientists are being intimidated and harassed in the name of security.

G73 GELLERMANN, William. "The American Legion as Educator." New York: Teachers College, Columbia University, 1938. 280 pp. App. Bibliog.

A study of the American Legion's educational activities, which are found to be an expression of its "Americanism" program; this, in turn, is essentially a war against subversive elements. Chapter 5, pp. 87-134, deals with the "War Against 'Subversive Elements,'" among which communism occupies a leading place. The Legion has opposed foreign influences in America, and sought to suppress subversive and radical groups and to crush disloyalty in the schools. The Legion condemns opponents as "subversive" and "radical," with little attention to the meaning of such words.

G74   GELLERMANN, William. "Martin Dies." New York: John Day, 1944. 310 pp. Notes.
A denunciation of Martin Dies, chairman of the House Committee on Un-American Activities, for fighting the battle of American reaction. The author sketches Dies' background and his life in Congress prior to the formation of the Un-American Activities Committee. He describes the inception of the committee, its hearings, the witnesses who testified before it on the influence of communism in our national life, and the committee's reports. He concludes by comparing Dies to Adolph Hitler.

G75   GELLERT, Hugo. "Karl Marx's 'Capital' in Lithographs." New York: Ray Long and Richard R. Smith, 1934. 120 pp.
A communist effort to present extracts from Marx's major work, dealing with such topics as primary accumulation, commodities, surplus value, the working day, machinery and large-scale industry, and the transformation of surplus value into ground rent, in 60 pages of text, each with an interpretive illustration. In a foreword the author, a Party artist long associated with the "New Masses," attacks Roosevelt for making slaves of all workers under the NRA, while police clubs here as in other "democratic" countries force jobless millions to submit to starvation. Marx's "Das Capital" is our guide, while the USSR builds the future of mankind.

G76   . . . . "Comrade Gulliver: An Illustrated Account of Travel into that Strange Country the United States of America." New York: Putnam, 1935. 44 pp.
A communist view, with text and illustrations, of the U.S. during the depression, emphasizing want in the midst of plenty, race prejudice, police violence against workers, militarism, and other evils attributed to capitalism, as seen by a visitor from the USSR. The author, long a Party member, served as art editor of the "New Masses."

G77   . . . . "Aesop Said So." New York: C o v i c i, Friede, 1936. 41 unnumbered pp.
A series of fables, each with a title and full page drawing by a leading Party artist, to make its application to current America clear. Among the topics treated are the distribution of wealth, the Liberty League, the Supreme Court, the professional patriot, the Negro, fascism, the liberal, Father Coughlin, Hearst, and the Farmer-Labor Party.

G78   GELLHORN, Walter. Report on a Report of the House Committee on Un-American Activities. "Harvard Law Review," 60 (Oct. 1947), 1193-1234.
An analysis of the House Committee on Un-American Activities' report asserting that the Southern Conference for Human Welfare is a communist front. Tracing the history of the Conference, the author finds no evidence to support the accusation. "Guilt by association" is used by the Committee to prove its case.

G79   . . . . In Defense of American Activities, "American Scholar," 17 (Spring 1948), 139-49.
A law professor, active on civil liberties issues, disagrees

with the methods and conclusion of the House Un-American Activities Committee. Its propensity for "guilt by association" endangers America's intellectual life. The House is urged to require fair procedure in legislative investigations.

G80   . . . . "Security, Loyalty and Science." Ithaca: Cornell University Press, 1950. 300 pp. App. Ind.
One of the Cornell University studies in civil liberty. The author cites the growing ties between scientific knowledge and military security, and describes the policies and procedures devised to assure the loyalty of scientists and the security of information vital to national defense. He questions such measures with regard both to their effectiveness in achieving the goal of security and their restriction of the scientific mind and process.

G81   . . . (ed.). "The States and Subversion." Ithaca: Cornell University Press, 1952. 453 pp. App. Ind.
A collection, by a professor of law at Columbia University, of reports on state and local activity in the field of subversion control. Edward L. Barrett, Jr., has condensed his book on "The Tenney Committee" into a chapter on California (pp. 1-53); Lawrence H. Chamberlain has condensed his "Loyalty and Legislative Action" into a chapter on New York (pp. 231-81); and Vern Countryman has made a digest of his book, "Un-American Activities in the State of Washington" (pp. 282-357). E. Houston Harsha writes on the Broyles Commission of Illinois (pp. 54-139), William B. Prendergast on the Ober Anti-Communist Law in Maryland (pp. 140-83), and Robert J. Mowitz writes on the state of Michigan (pp. 184-230). All are critical of the states in one way or another. The editor concludes that at least some of the antisubversion or anticommunist laws are not justified as societal safeguards, and that state committees' hearings are held to publicize conclusions rather than to inquire into the facts. Such state actions may hurt rather than help democracy.

G82   . . . . "American Rights: The Constitution in Action." New York: Macmillan, 1963. 232 pp. Notes. Ind.
Chapter 4, pp. 70-95, on "Free Speech and the Communist Conspiracy," deals with the Smith Act, the Internal Security Act of 1950 (the McCarran Act), and the Communist Control Act of 1954. Criticizing these measures, the author asserts that a free society can better stand the risks of talk than the risks of silence, and urges us to perfect democratic institutions rather than toy with totalitarian-style weapons.

G83   GENDEL, Martin. Criminal Syndicalism, Red Flag Law, "California Law Review," 19 (Nov. 1930), 64-69.
A critical discussion of the effect of the California criminal syndicalism statute and the history of its enforcement. The so-called Red Flag Act is another control measure recently used in California to combat communist activity. Prosecutions invite further growth and stifle free discussion.

G84   GENERAL ELECTRIC COMPANY. "What to do about Communism in Unions." (Statement before a Senate Subcommittee by L. R. Boulware, G. H. Pfeif, and W. J. Barron.) [New York:] General Electric Company, n.d. [1952]. 62 pp.
A statement to a Senate Subcommittee on Labor and Labor-Management Affairs in July 1950 answering charges by James Carey of the IUE that the company and other electrical manufacturers assisted the communist-controlled United Electrical Workers. GE officials offer specific proposals on eradicating communists from positions of power and influence in unions.

G85 GENERAL JEWISH COUNCIL. "Father Coughlin: His 'Facts' and Arguments." New York: The Council, 1939. 59 pp.
A refutation by the American Jewish Committee, B'nai B'rith, the American Jewish Congress, and the Jewish Labor Committee of Father Coughlin's charges that communism is of Jewish origin, that it was introduced into Russia by Jews, and that Nazism arose in Germany to stop the spread of communism by an international Jewish conspiracy. Coughlin's assertions, the pamphlet shows, are malicious lies, identical with those made by Goebbels.

G86 GEORGE, Harrison. "The Red Dawn: The Bolsheviki and the I.W.W." Chicago: IWW Publishing Bureau, n.d. [1918]. 26 pp.
An imprisoned IWW leader, sympathetic to the Bolsheviks, outlines their rise to power. Although conditions are different here, American workers are urged to pattern their methods after those of the Bolsheviks. The Bolsheviks show the road to power that the IWW could take to industrial freedom.

G87 .... "Socialist" Union Wreckers, "Labor Herald," 3 (July 1924), 143-44.
A denunciation of the ILGWU, during the "boring from within" TUEL period, as a perfect picture of despotism. Despite the provocative expulsion policy of the entrenched officials, communist and left-wing elements must fight against the impulse to leave, and continue to fight for the workers' demands.

G88 .... Twenty Years After, "Workers Monthly," 4 (Aug. 1925), 447-48 ff.
An analysis of the mistakes of the Industrial Workers of the World, with suggestions for restoring its vitality. The IWW has tried to be both a political party and a labor union, not having understood that the struggle for power cannot be waged by the same organization as the struggle for bread. If the IWW is to rejoin the revolutionary struggle, it needs a left wing to propound communist ideas within it.

G89 .... "A Noon-Hour Talk on the Communist Party." New York: Central Committee, CPUSA, n.d. [1932?]. 31 pp.
A popularly written "third period" recruiting pamphlet, in the form of a conversation among three workers, one of them a communist. AFL leaders are attacked as sellout thieves, and support is urged for the industrial unions of the Trade Union Unity League. Socialists are denounced as social fascists, and Musteites as artists at selling out with radical talk.

G90 .... The War Threat and the World Peace Conference, "Communist," 15 (Aug. 1936), 692-97.
Neutrality will not keep America out of war because of the pressure of capitalists to protect their investments. War can be prevented only by collective security and a strengthened League of Nations. The American League Against War and Fascism and the National Peace Conference have been formed to agitate for peace.

G91 .... On the Inter-American Peace Conference, "Communist," 15 (Sept. 1936), 865-72.
Americans should exert pressure on the Roosevelt Administration to adopt a real peace policy at the Buenos Aires conference. This would include abolition of the Monroe Doctrine, an end to unequal commercial treaties, and an insistence that the American countries support the League of Nations.

G92 .... "This 4th of July." New York: Workers Library, 1937. 15 pp.

The communists, who express the Americanism of 1937, are compared to the revolutionists of 1776. As patriotic defenders of the U.S., the communists join with all who oppose reaction, fascism, and war.

G93 .... Class Forces in California Agriculture, "Communist," 18 (Feb. 1939), 156-62; (March), 269-73.
A discussion of the structure of California agriculture, its capitalist nature, class differences in the farming population, and farm financing and marketing. The "Pro-Rate Law" in California restricts agricultural production by making free marketing by farmers a misdemeanor. Fascist influence is growing among the rural population, but sentiment for farmer-labor collaboration is also growing.

G94 .... "The Crisis in the C.P.U.S.A." Los Angeles: The author, 1947. 136 pp. App. Ind.
A view of the crisis in the Party by one who had been a member since 1919, only to be expelled in October 1947 on charges of factionalism, after being attacked as a leftist by a member of the State Board. The manuscript, originally written for preconvention discussion, expresses opposition to factionalism as well as to both right opportunism and leftism. George charges in a letter to the State Review Commission, reproduced in the appendix, that Commission functions have been subverted by a right opportunist faction.

G95 GERSH, Harry, and MILTON, Paul R. Radio Writers off the Beam, "New Leader," 35 (Dec. 8, 1952), 12-14.
The authors, members of the anticommunist caucus of the Radio Writers Guild, explain why their group has suffered persistent defeat. Reasons include indifferent anticommunist caucus membership, indignation of members over McCarthyism rather than communism, fear of exposure of passive fellow-traveling in the past, and hardening of battle lines against the Guild by employers.

G96 GERSON, Simon W. The New "Left" Social-Fascism, "Communist," 9 (July 1930), 622-31.
An indictment of an emerging left wing within the Socialist Party. The efforts of this group to reintroduce into the SP a line of class struggle is viewed as a mere juggling with words, demagogically aimed at keeping the workers from following the Communist Party.

G97 .... "It is Happening Here." New York: New York State Committee, Communist Party, 1941. 16 pp.
A Party leader draws a parallel between 1920 and 1941, between the expulsion of five socialist aldermen from the New York legislature in 1920 and the bills currently pending in New York to make communists ineligible for public office, to keep the Party off the ballot, and to outlaw the advocacy of syndicalism. The author asserts that these bills, if enacted, will open the floodgates of reaction, with dire effects on labor and popular liberties.

G98 .... "Pete Cacchione—His Record." New York: Workers Library, 1943. 15 pp.
A campaign pamphlet, urging the reelection of Peter V. Cacchione to the New York City Council. Cacchione, a communist, was elected to the Council in 1941. His record is reviewed, with emphasis on his efforts to keep down living costs, combat race prejudice, and aid civil service employees.

G99 .... Thomas E. Dewey: His Record, "Communist," 22 (May 1943), 461-68.
Thomas E. Dewey, governor of New York and presidential aspirant, has a Hooverite record of opposing the New Deal

and government intervention in the economy. Although not as outspoken as Hoover against the war effort, he does not emphasize its importance. Like Hoover, he is suspicious of Russia.

G100 GERSON, Simon W. Electoral Coalition Problems in New York, "Political Affairs," 26 (Oct. 1947), 894-901.
A call for a progressive, pro-Roosevelt coalition to defeat the Republicans in the 1948 presidential contest for New York's 47 electoral votes. The path to unity is made more difficult by the social-democratic-controlled unions and Liberal Party. Labor and progressive forces must build the American Labor Party and prepare for the Wallace-for-President primary fights in the spring of 1948.

G101 .... "Either the Constitution or the Mundt Bill: America Can't Have Both!" New York: New Century, 1950. 15 pp.
Testimony against the Mundt-Nixon bill, before the House Un-American Activities Committee, by a member of the Party's Public Affairs Committee, who was also legislative chairman of the Party in New York State. Gerson attacks the bill as the domestic expression of "the bipartisan cold war atmosphere," asserting that its aim is not merely to outlaw the Communist Party, but to stifle expression of the American people's will for peace.

G102 .... The Jury System and Democratic Rights, "Political Affairs," 31 (July 1952), 35-44.
An assertion that the juries in the Dennis and Flynn cases were stacked against the defendants, making a fair trial impossible. The jury system is systematically undermined as part of the war camp's drive to destroy the basic rights of the people. Vicious techniques are used to exclude workers and Negroes from federal juries.

G103 .... "The Rights You Save May Be Your Own." New York: New York State Communist Party, 1954. 16 pp.
The legislative chairman of the Party in New York State opposes, before a subcommittee of the House Judiciary Committee, ten bills to outlaw the Party. Attacking the bills as unconstitutional and libelous, he asserts that they would strangle the rights of all Americans and take us on the road to fascism.

G104 .... A Communist at Cornell, "Masses & Mainstream," 8 (July 1955), 28-35.
Impressions by the legislative chairman of the N.Y. Communist Party of his meeting at Cornell University, the first visit of a Marxist to that institution in years. Some of the students' questions following Gerson's debate with a faculty member on "How to Achieve Co-Existence" showed inquiring minds, while others showed the impact of the cold war on the questioners.

G105 GESSNER, Robert. A Task for the Writers' Congress, "New Masses," 15 (April 2, 1935), 39-41.
A report on the All-Union Writers' Congress held recently in Moscow, with emphasis on what the American Writers' Congress, shortly to be held in New York, could learn from the Soviet gathering. Socialist realism, which does not merely photograph life but is based on dialectical materialism, is advocated as an artistic method.

G106 GHENT, William J. "The Reds Bring Reaction." Princeton, N.J.: Princeton University Press, 1923. 113 pp. App.
A former socialist argues that the infatuation of both revolutionaries and "parlor radicals" with Bolshevism has brought such a reaction in the U.S. that even reformist socialism becomes impossible. He discusses the impact

of the Bolshevik Revolution on the American left, the struggle between radical and reformist elements inside the Socialist Party, the rise and decline of the IWW, and the intricacies of communist politics. He concludes that capitalism, with all its evils, is preferable to Bolshevik tyranny.

G107 GIBBONS, Robert D. Recent Legislative Attempts to Curb Subversive Activities in the United States, "George Washington Law Review,' 10 (Nov. 1941), 104-26.
A review of existing and proposed federal antisubversion legislation on the eve of World War II. Outlining the half-hearted anticommunist administrative and legislative efforts and the spottiness of existing legislation, the author suggests a comprehensive statute outlawing all advocacy of overthrow of government by force.

G108 GIBBS, Willa. "The Tender Men." New York: Farrar, Straus, 1948. 246 pp.
The story of a Dakota farm boy who becomes a newspaperman and who, when starving, is recruited by a communist organizer. Schooled in Marxism, he becomes a valuable asset to the Party, but under severe stress he fails to follow directions and is sentenced to death. An exposé of communist methods and strategy, showing how completely individual members are subjected to the Party.

G109 GIDEONSE, Harry D. The Reds Are After Your Child, "American Magazine," 146 (July 1948), 19 ff.
An account of communist efforts to indoctrinate youth and infiltrate campus youth groups. Students are attracted by the ingenious tactics used, plus youthful rebellion. The efforts of the Rapp-Coudert Committee of the New York State Legislature to discover the facts should serve as a model for other investigating agencies.

G110 .... Changing Issues in Academic Freedom in the United States Today, "Proceedings of the American Philosophical Society," 94 (April 1950), 91-104.
A discussion by the president of Brooklyn College of the problem of teachers who accept political discipline, and of the impact of federal security regulations on scholarly activities. Asserting that members of the Communist Party accept discipline in intellectual as well as political matters, Gideonse charges that they use academic freedom and civil liberties to subvert the ideals of liberty and truth.

G111 GILBERT, Brian [pseud.]. New Light on the Lattimore Case, "New Republic," 131 (Dec. 27, 1954), 7-12.
A well-known Washington commentator on political affairs reviews the history of the Owen Lattimore case, analyzing the hearings before the Internal Security Committee. Acting as prosecutor instead of investigator, the committee pressured the Justice Department to stretch the perjury statutes in the hope of finding Lattimore guilty.

G112 .... The Irony of the Peters Case, "New Republic," 132 (June 13, 1955), 11-12.
The case of John P. Peters, professor of medicine at Yale, who was dismissed as a consultant to the U.S. Public Health Service as a security risk. The case came before the Supreme Court on a procedural issue, though the justices learned of the substantive charges through the files of the House Un-American Activities Committee. The author feels, after seeing the list of Dr. Peter's affiliations, that the Loyalty Review Board acted reasonably.

G113 GILBERT, Brian [pseud.]. Judge Youngdahl Wins His Fight, "New Republic," 133 (July 11, 1955), 5-6.
A review of the Lattimore case, asserting that its dropping by the Attorney General is a victory for liberty against political persecution. Congress should not investigate ideas and thinkers, and the Department of Justice should not seek a perjury indictment phrased in general ideological terms.

G114 GILBERT, Dan W. Sovietizing Our Children, "National Republic," 24 (Aug. 1936), 16-17.
An analysis of textbooks written by Professor Harold Rugg and Professor Carl Becker, which allegedly belittle Americanism and exalt communism. Such textbooks are one method of carrying forward the program of sovietizing American school children.

G115 .... "Our Chameleon Comrades: The Reds Turn Yellow!" San Diego, Calif.: Danielle Publishers, 1938. 176 pp.
A vigorous attack on the CPUSA, focusing on Browder's leadership for cowardly plotting against the government behind a front of political respectability. Ridiculing the Party's current effort to claim Lincoln and Jefferson as heroes, in an effort to ally itself to American traditions, the author asserts that he had more respect, even though he disagreed with them, for the older generation of genuine revolutionaries.

G116 .... Un-Americanism in Textbooks, "National Republic," 29 (Oct. 1941), 17-18 ff; (Nov.), 5-6 ff; (Dec.), 3-4 ff; (Jan. 1942), 7-8 ff; (Feb.), 7-8 ff; (March), 7-8 ff.
An assertion that many textbooks used in tax-supported high schools contain pro-Soviet propaganda, giving a wholly false picture of life under the Bolsheviks. Among the textbook authors attacked are Harold Rugg, Leo Huberman, Samuel Grove Dow, and Seba Eldridge and Carroll D. Clark. (Also published in pamphlet form.)

G117 .... Moscow over Hollywood, "National Republic," 34 (Feb. 1947), 3-4 ff; (March), 5-6 ff; (April), 15-16 ff; 35 (May), 17-18 ff; (June), 19-20 ff; (July), 17-18 ff; (Aug.), 19-20 ff; (Sept.), 19-20 ff; (Oct.), 19-20 ff.
An account of an alleged effort to sovietize the film industry and, through it, the thought and life of the movie-attending public. Installments deal with the influence in Hollywood of Russian-born families, the privileges enjoyed by Hollywood Reds, the deception of the common people by the Reds, the glorification of Stalin, Hollywood hypocrisy, racial strife stirred by Hollywood Reds, and the regimentation of screen writers.

G118 .... "What Is Happening in Hollywood." Los Angeles: Jewish Hope Publishing House, n.d. [1950?]. 36 pp.
Attacks are made on communist infiltration in Hollywood, the influence of foreign-born movie heads on American entertainment, the softness of these capitalists toward communism in the industry, and the degenerate sex mores in Hollywood under the atheistic Marxist way of life.

G119 GILES, Barbara. The South of William Faulkner, "Masses & Mainstream," 3 (Feb. 1950), 26-40.
Faulkner's novels seem to portray the degradation and break-up of the South and the Southern myth; in reality they portray the nightmare of believers in white supremacy who see their beloved South debased by industrialization, and by the rise of a new, nonaristocratic-type of Southerner.

G120 .... Brand-Name Culture: The Battle for the Bucks, "Masses & Mainstream," 5 (Dec. 1952), 43-50.
A denunciation of advertising as a destructive cultural force. The "eye appeal" in the big magazines is to money and snobbery. Working-class men and women are rarely presented in fiction or in ads, and Negroes appear only in servile roles. The "typical American" who is portrayed is an Anglo-Saxon.

G121 .... The Noble Money-Makers, "Mainstream," 10 (Sept. 1957), 1-13.
A critical review of recent books which glorify Big Business executives. Among the works discussed are "Executive Suite," "Cash McCall," "The Man in the Gray Flannel Suit," and "Sincerely, Willis Wayde."

G122 GILFILLAN, Lauren [Harriet Woodbridge Gilfillan]. "I Went to Pit College." New York: Viking, 1934. 288 pp.
The experiences of a young Smith College graduate in the western Pennsylvania coal fields in 1931, during a strike conducted by the National Miners Union of the Trade Union Unity League. She reports the misery and degradation that she saw, the rivalry between the striking NMU and the strikebreaking United Mine Workers, the behavior of the state police and the courts, and the activities of the communists who led the strike. Finally the communists forced her to leave, charging her with being a stool pigeon.

G123 GILLARD, John T. The Negro Challenges Communism, "Commonweal," 16 (May 25, 1932), 96-98.
Communism, which rejects religion while apparently embracing humanitarianism, has great appeal to intelligent Negroes, who nevertheless know that communism cannot do what it so readily promises. Yet they may turn to communism unless Catholics act soon to redress their wrongs.

G124 .... "Christ, Color and Communism." Baltimore: Josephite Press, 1937. 138 pp. Ref. notes. Ind.
A discussion of efforts of communists to capitalize on oppression of Negroes in the South. The author describes the techniques the Party used, and evaluates its success to date. He points out that communism uses Negroes and their problems to further its own ends and urges Negroes to accept the solution offered by the Catholic Church.

G125 GILLIS, James M. How Communists Get That Way, "Catholic World," 164 (Feb. 1947), 385-91.
Editorial comment drawing on Andrew Avery's pamphlet, "The Communist Fifth Column," for illustrations of red or pink actors, writers, artists, musicians, educators, and clergy. Various motivations for communist sympathy are listed; the unsolved problem is what has brought them together in the compact, well-organized world communist movement.

G126 .... Communism: Who's to Blame, "Catholic World," 166 (Jan. 1948), 291-95.
The author blames the Catholic clergy for the fact that working people have embraced communism and rejected Catholicism. Communism cannot be destroyed by violence because it is a theology and an ethical system. Thus it must be demolished by the clergy, not by politicians or soldiers; the clergy must cease favoring the rich because of their larger gifts.

G127 GILLMOR, Daniel S. Guilt by Gossip, "New Republic," 118 (May 31, 1948), 15-27.
A critical review of the current governmental campaign

against domestic communists, led by Attorney General Tom C. Clark, J. Edgar Hoover of the FBI, and Chairman J. Parnell Thomas of the House Un-American Activities Committee. They rely on gossip, hold biased hearings, and institute deportation proceedings against alien left-wingers. The culmination of their campaign is the subversive activities control bill now before Congress.

G128   GILLMOR, Daniel S. "Fear, the Accuser," New York: Abelard-Schuman, 1954. 308 pp. Notes. Ind.
A condemnation of the activities, methods, and leadership of congressional subversion investigating committees, which are said to have exhibited a fear of the future, besides violating our traditional civil liberties. Senators McCarthy and Jenner, Rep. Harold H. Velde, and committee counsel Roy Cohn come in for particular criticism. Testimony by former communists Benjamin Gitlow, Manning Johnson, and Elizabeth Bentley is reviewed, and attention paid to the interrogation of Bishop G. Bromley Oxnam, Rev. Jack R. McMichael, Wendell L. Furry, and others.

G129   GINDER, Richard. "The Reds in Our Labor Unions." New York: Catholic Information Society, n.d. [1947?]. 16 pp.
Questions and answers on how Catholics specifically, and all labor union members in general, should deal with communists in labor unions. The author explains how Philip Murray, a devout Catholic, became saddled with so many communists, and what must be done to get rid of them.

G130   GINZBURG, Benjamin. Loyalty, Suspicion and the Tightening Chain, "Reporter," 11 (July 6, 1954), 10-14.
A critical analysis of governmental concern with employee loyalty. President Truman's loyalty program sought to steal the thunder of the "professional investigators"; instead, he should have dealt with the security problem through better counterespionage. The program has added nothing to American security.

G131   . . . . "Rededication to Freedom." Introd. by Reinhold Niebuhr. New York: Simon and Schuster, 1959. 177 pp. Notes. Ind.
A former research director for the Senate Subcommittee on Constitutional Rights asserts that freedom is indivisible, that we cannot abridge the rights of communists without undermining the liberties of all. The freedom guaranteed by the Bill of Rights, in his view, has been imperiled by the hysteria generated by the House Un-American Activities Committee. He attacks the conduct of the Hiss and Rosenberg trials, and argues that the security system is unnecessary, even in so-called sensitive areas.

G132   GITLOW, A. L. The Communist Threat to Labor, "Southern Economic Journal," 16 (April 1950), 458-70.
An analysis of the conflict between communists and "business unionists" in American trade unions. Past differences have centered on union structure and political action, whereas current issues include the WFTU or the ICFTU and the Progressive Party. Basic to all differences are attitudes to our existing economic system and to the USSR.

G133   GITLOW, Benjamin. "The 'Red Ruby' Address to the Jury." New York: Workers' Defense Conference, n.d. [1921]. 15 pp.
Gitlow's address to the jury before he was found guilty of criminal anarchy for publishing the "Left Wing Manifesto" and sentenced to from five to ten years in prison. Defending the Manifesto, which he published in "Revolutionary

Age," Gitlow, a leader of the Communist Labor Party, tried to show that its principles of revolutionary socialism were correct. Excerpts from defense attorney Clarence Darrow's address to the jury, Judge Weeks' thanks to the jury for its verdict of guilty, and comment by Arturo Giovanitti are included. (Gitlow's address got its title from the statement by District Attorney Rorke that "He would make America a Red Ruby in the Red Treasure Chest of the Red Terror.")

G134   . . . . Victimizing Labor Militants, "Labor Herald," 2 (Sept. 1923), 17-18.
An attack on the "Jewish Daily Forward" and the rightwing machine in the needle trades, who are warring against the militants in order to maintain control. The TUEL will not permit itself to be exterminated.

G135   . . . . Why the Anthracite Strike? "Workers Monthly," 5 (Nov. 1925), 15-18.
An attack upon the current strike of anthracite miners as the outcome of John L. Lewis' policies of class collaboration. The operators will benefit, by the opportunity to unload the large supplies above ground. Though the miners will get no material gains, Lewis' reward will be the check-off. Meanwhile meetings of progressive miners are being broken up and their leaders jailed.

G136   . . . . The Passaic Textile Workers Strike, "Workers Monthly," 5 (June 1926), 347-51.
A description of issues and developments in the Passaic textile strike, in progress since January 25. Communists have succeeded in drawing all branches of the labor movement and bourgeois supporters of the strike into a united front. The mayor, the governor, judges, police, and sheriffs are being used by the capitalists in their fight against the workers.

G137   . . . . The Furriers Strike—A Victory for the 40-Hour Week, "Workers Monthly," 5 (July 1926), 406-9.
The New York Fur Workers' Union, with 13,000 members, is the first union of importance in the U.S. to come under communist leadership. Its 17-week strike has ended in victory. Future struggles will be for control of the International Fur Workers Union, unification of left-wing forces in the needle trades, and amalgamation of all needle-trades unions.

G138   . . . . The Crusade of the A.F. of L. against the Reds, "Communist," 6 (June 1927), 213-24.
A review of the fight of the AFL bureaucracy, led by Matthew Woll, against the left-wing forces in the needle trades. The reactionaries are alarmed by communist leadership of strikes of Passaic textile workers, New York furriers, and New York cloakmakers. Their success will smash the unions or transform them into company unions.

G139   . . . . Big Business Can't Lose in 1928. "Communist," 7 (Aug. 1928), 467-72.
Both major parties are said to be spokesmen for Wall Street and American imperialism in 1928. Big Business is now directly taking over the leadership of both parties. Whichever party wins, the result will be further centralization of government, the use of government power against workers, militarization, and imperialism.

G140   . . . . Hoover and Smith—Mouthpieces of Big Business—Accept the Nomination, "Communist," 7 (Sept. 1928), 531-37.
An attack on both major party candidates as tools of Wall Street. Their acceptance speeches are analyzed to show that both favor capitalism, Big Business, and U.S. imperialism. The workers are offered nothing.

G141 GITLOW, Benjamin. What Was the Cleveland TUUL Convention? "Revolutionary Age," 1 (Nov. 1, 1929), 9 ff.; (Nov. 15), 7; (Dec. 1), 13-14.
Charges in the Lovestoneite press that a new revolutionary trade union center was established, not to organize workers, but to fight Lovestone. The result is a communist-dominated organization with incorrect policies, that will isolate itself from the labor movement.

G142 .... The United Front, "Revolutionary Age," 1 (Feb. 1, 1930), 8-9.
Current Party tactics are in effect an abandonment of the united front, according to this Lovestoneite criticism. Many workers, though ready to fight capitalism on some issues, are not ready to overthrow it. The "social fascism" slogan is a Party effort to establish leadership over the masses by name-calling.

G143 .... Foster Tries to Forget the Past: The New Turn of the Party on Trade Union Policy, "Revolutionary Age," 2 (Dec. 6, 1930), 4.
An attack on the Party's trade union line, as outlined by William Z. Foster in the October 1930 issue of "Communist." The author, a leader of the Communist Party (Majority Group), attacks Foster for repudiating his own past policies by abandoning work within conservative unions in order to follow De Leon's errors by seeking to build revolutionary unions.

G144 .... The Road to Isolation: Two Years of the New Trade Union Line, "Revolutionary Age," 2 (May 30, 1931), 4.
Arguing that the Party's current dual union line is sectarian, adventurous, and a failure, a leader of the Communist Party (Majority Group) calls for unity of progressive forces within the mass unions to struggle against the reactionary trade union bureaucracy and capitalism. Observing that the Red International of Labor Unions recognized the failure of the Party's union line, the author asserts that the International proposed no fundamental change.

G145 .... Some Plain Words about Communist Unity! "Workers Age," 1 (May 14, 1932), 1-2; (May 21), 4; (May 28), 4.
A discussion of recent efforts to achieve unity in the communist movement, with reproduction of letters sent by the Lovestone group to the political committee of the Party. Objections to these letters by the Party are answered. The author criticizes the leadership of the Communist International and of the CPUSA for their refusal to discuss the issues, as well as for their growing sectarianism. The Lovestone group, he asserts, will rejoin if guaranteed Party democracy. (Also published in pamphlet form in 1932 under the title, "Some Plain Words on Communist Unity.")

G146 .... "America for the People! Why We Need a Farmer Labor Party." New York: Labor Party Association, n.d. [1933?]. 15 pp.
Calling the Republican and Democratic parties the "Gold Dust Twins of big business," a former leader of the Communist Party calls for a new party to represent organized labor and Negroes and to fight against war. Roosevelt's New Deal is said to favor big business and to have a military bias. A national party on the model of the Farmer Labor Party of Minnesota is called for.

G147 .... U.S. Communists' Lines Show Puppetry to Kremlin, "New Leader," 22 (Sept. 9, 1939), 5-6.
A former communist leader asserts that the Party here has no independent viewpoint, that it is dominated by the Kremlin, and that its very formation was directed by Russian Bolshevik leaders. The Bolsheviks, as shown by the Nazi-Soviet pact, have never abandoned dictatorship.

G148 .... "I Confess: The Truth about American Communism." New York: Dutton, 1940. 611 pp. Ind.
An account of the first ten years of the communist movement in the U.S. by a former leading figure in the Party, who was expelled with Jay Lovestone in 1929 for right opportunism, following a struggle for control of the Party. He describes in detail the development of the American communist movement, its methods of operation, its incessant factional conflicts, and his own expulsion. He emphasizes Moscow's control over the Party here, and the primary concern of American communists to help maintain in power the leaders of the Soviet state. Communist penetration of the American labor movement is described, as is the communist hope, through the CIO, to establish a people's front in the U.S.

G149 .... Communist Party Now Functioning in Underground Apparatus Set Up in '40, "New Leader," 24 (Jan. 4, 1941), 3 ff.
A former communist leader asserts that the Party reorganized its structure at a secret convention in 1940. All ties with the Comintern are to be broken; no cards are to be issued; the members are to submerge themselves in noncommunist organizations, and deny Party membership.

G150 .... U.S. Communist Party Supplied Agents to GPU on Order, "New Leader," 24 (Jan. 11, 1941), 5 ff.
A former top leader of the Party describes its recruitment of spies for the Soviet OGPU. The key figure was Nicholas Dozenberg, alias Dallant, an American communist of Lettish origin, who became head of the OGPU here and in charge of military intelligence for the Red Army. (Subsequent articles in the series appeared in "New Leader" issues of Jan. 18, pp. 5 ff; Jan. 25, p. 4; Feb. 1, pp. 5 ff; and Feb. 8, p. 4.)

G151 .... "The Whole of Their Lives: Communism in America—a Personal History and Intimate Portrayal of Its Leaders." Foreword by Max Eastman. New York: Scribner's, 1948. 387 pp. Ind.
An account of the first three decades of the American communist movement by one of its founders, who was expelled with Lovestone in 1929 and who remained a member of a splinter group before renouncing communism altogether. Gitlow describes the impact of the Bolshevik seizure of power on American radicals, the formative years of the movement here, the factional squabbling over points of doctrine and positions of power, and the final unity in subservience to the USSR and Stalin. The volume, a sequel to the autobiographical "I Confess," throws considerable light on the personalities of the communist movement, and on Party developments here and in the USSR.

G152 .... "How to Think about Communism." Whitestone, N.Y.: Graphics Group, 1949. 30 pp.
Drawing on his book, "The Whole of Their Lives," Gitlow outlines Party strategy in the U.S. with special attention to labor policies. He shows how communists took over many unions, using ignorant rank-and-file members to further an alien cause.

G153 .... William Foster and the Revolution, "American Mercury," 68 (April 1949), 408-17.
A former high-ranking American communist explains Foster's devotion to the Party despite his many disappointments. Foster feared he would be passed by when the

Revolution came to America unless he headed the American communist movement. Events in the relations between Moscow and the CPUSA are detailed, to show Foster's subservience to the Comintern.

G154 GITLOW, Benjamin. What Makes Them Commies? "American Legion Magazine," 46 (June 1949), 11-13 ff.
A former leader of the Party identifies the types attracted to the communist movement. Among them are noncommunist radicals seeking to overcome disappointments in the labor movement, people with inferiority complexes, middle class elements hard hit by depression, frustrated females, and individuals who crave excitement. Though most join for idealistic reasons, they are transformed into cynical, power-hungry communists.

G155 GLADSTEIN, Richard. "Argument to the Jury in the New York Communist Trial." San Francisco: Civil Rights Congress, n.d. [1949 or 1950]. 18 pp.
The text, somewhat abridged, of Gladstein's final argument to the jury in the trial of the communist leaders in 1949. He deals with the history of the right to advocate ideas, its connection with the Bill of Rights, and the consequences of restricting it. He holds that prosecution for political views is not American, and that defendants should not be held responsible for distortions of their beliefs by others.

G156 GLAZER, Nathan. Civil Liberties and the American People: Tolerance and Anti-Communism, "Commentary," 20 (Aug. 1955), 169-76.
An evaluation of Samuel A. Stouffer's "Communism, Conformity, and Civil Liberties," criticizing it for treating communism, not directly but as part of the larger problem of "conformism." Stouffer fails to distinguish between those who are intolerant of communism, as of other views with which they disagree, and those who are concerned about communism and think strong measures are necessary to deal with it.

G157 .... A New Look at the Rosenberg-Sobell Case, "New Leader," 39 (July 2, 1956), sect. 2, 20 pp.
A report by a sociologist on a study of the evidence in the Rosenberg-Sobell case. The author concludes that the jury decided correctly, though he does not believe that the crime deserved death, particularly in the case of Ethel Rosenberg. He charges John Wexley, author of "The Ordeal of Julius and Ethel Rosenberg," with suppressing some evidence and doctoring the rest. (Reprinted as pamphlet by Tamiment Institute, 1956.)

G158 .... "The Social Basis of American Communism." New York: Harcourt, Brace & World, 1961. 244 pp. Notes. Ind.
An examination of the selective appeal of communism in the U.S. to various social groups. From its beginning and through the 1920's the movement was a foreign-speaking one, though the top leadership was generally native-born. The great depression brought large numbers of English-speaking recruits, most of them unemployed, few of whom stayed very long. In some cases, unions were important bases of communist strength. Jews proved more susceptible than most other groups to communist appeals, while Negroes responded less, and with a high degree of fluctuation. American democracy and American wealth are fundamentally responsible for communist failure here.

G159 GLEY, R. L. Freudism—A Psychology of a Dying Class, "Communist," 18 (Nov. 1939), 1066-79.
A Marxist appraisal of the teachings of Sigmund Freud, outlining his main doctrines as well as his social views. Freud, with most of his followers, used his theories to support reactionary conclusions. The Marxist approach to psychological problems is reviewed. (For other articles by Gley on developments in Psychology see "Communist," June and July 1939.)

G160 GLICKSBERG, Charles I. Waldo Frank: Critic of America, "South Atlantic Quarterly," 35 (Jan. 1936), 13-26.
A critical analysis of the career of Waldo Frank, a passionate mystic who swung to the left with the depression. After analyzing his life and work, Glicksberg concludes that Frank will not be bound for long within a utilitarian economic doctrine.

G161 .... Granville Hicks and Marxist Criticism, "Sewanee Review," 45 (April-June 1937), 129-40.
A rebuke to Marxist critics in general and to Hicks in particular for trying to transform a political and economic doctrine into a system of aesthetics. In "The Great Tradition," Hicks views all major nineteenth-century writers as feeble or frustrated because they failed to understand industrialism and class conflict. Literature must be analyzed according to its own laws and processes.

G162 .... Proletarian Fiction in the United States, "Dalhousie Review," 17 (April 1937), 22-32.
A discussion, in a Canadian magazine, of the development of proletarian fiction in the U.S. Left-wing critics have extravagantly praised the novels that presented solutions in line with Marxist doctrines. Proletarian writers must obey Party discipline, at the expense of originality and freedom of thought. Proletarian fiction will progress only if it breaks away from Marxist taboos.

G163 .... V. F. Calverton: Marxism without Dogma, "Sewanee Review," 46 (July-Sept. 1938), 338-51.
A review of the writings of V. F. Calverton, a rare example of a Marxist who is not dogmatic and does not pretend to be infallible. Because he would not conform to Communist Party dictates, his integrity and ability were impugned.

G164 .... Calverton and Marxist Literary Criticism, "Modern Quarterly," 11, no. 7 [1941], 57-60. (V. F. Calverton Memorial Issue.)
An analysis of Calverton's role in the development of Marxist literary criticism in this country. From his early view in "The Newer Spirit" that class concepts determine esthetic concepts, Calverton came to believe that ideas condition people, and that economic systems alone do not explain history and literature.

G165 .... The Decline of Literary Marxism, "Antioch Review," 1 (Dec. 1941), 452-62.
An analysis of the birth and decline of proletarian literature in the U.S. and England from 1930 to 1940, commenting on the dilemma of the literary fellow-traveler, the control of the movement by the Marxist theoreticians, and the defections from the ranks.

G166 .... Communist Students in the Classroom, "School and Society," 71 (March 25, 1950), 177-80.
A professor at Brooklyn College discusses the problems of dealing with communist students, of keeping a determined and disciplined minority from practically taking over a class. The teacher must not allow discussion to degenerate into propagandizing, and must maintain his position as intellectual leader of the group.

G167 .... Anti-Communism in Fiction, "South Atlantic Quarterly," 53 (Oct. 1954), 485-96.
For the most part European novelists such as Koestler, Silone, Orwell, and Sperber have done the best work in

exposing the horrors of communism. In American writing, Lionel Trilling's "The Middle of the Journey" and John Dos Passos' "Adventures of a Young Man" stand out.

G168 GLICKSBERG, Charles I. Anti-Communism in Jewish Fiction, "Congress Weekly," 22 (Feb. 14, 1955), 11-13.
An assertion that Jewish novelists of our time, having lost faith that communism can save mankind, are now exposing in novels the ideological evils of communism, as well as its suppression of the freedom of the spirit. Among the examples cited are Ludwig Lewisohn, Meyer Levin, Irwin Shaw, and Arthur Koestler.

G169 GLOSTER, Hugh M. "Negro Voices in American Fiction." Chapel Hill: University of North Carolina Press, 1948. 295 pp. Notes. Bibliog. Ind.
A review of fiction written by American Negroes, including the proletarian fiction of the depression period. Attention is given (pp. 219-34) to two Negro writers, Langston Hughes and Richard Wright, both of whom moved for a time in the Party's orbit and took leading roles in front organizations. Other writers who were at one time close to the Party are mentioned briefly.

G170 GLYNN, Robert B. L'Affaire Rosenberg in France, "Political Science Quarterly," 70 (Dec. 1955), 498-521.
The Rosenberg case resulted in one of the most successful anti-American propaganda campaigns ever launched in Europe. The French communists, ably capitalizing on the French impulse to protest against apparent injustice anywhere, united France as on no other issue since the war.

G171 GODDEN, G. M. New Communist Attack on Youth, "Catholic World," 143 (May 1936), 148-52.
An analysis of the united front tactic adopted by the Seventh World Congress of the Communist International, as applied in the youth field. The "facade" of communist youth work has changed, but the underlying commitment—destruction of religion under the discipline and leadership of Moscow—has not changed. Communist participation in the American Youth Congress is described.

G172 GOFF, Kenneth. "Why I Left the Communist Party." Wichita, Kansas: Defenders, 1947. 21 pp.
An excommunist explains how his New Deal background prepared him for an introduction to Marxism and ultimately for Party membership. He describes Communist Party educational practices, methods of organization, and techniques of infiltrating and controlling other groups. (Originally published in "Defender," April, May, and June 1947.)

G173 .... "Red Betrayal of Youth." Englewood, Colorado: Pilgrim Torch, 1948. 32 pp.
An account of communist activities among youth by a former member of the Party, who asserts that the Party trains youngsters to hate God and that young communists practice free love. The organization of Party fronts for young people is described, as is red propaganda in schools and communist influence in Hollywood.

G174 .... "This Is My Story." No publication information [1948]. 96 pp.
The story of a Wisconsin newspaperman who was a member of the Party from 1936 until he became a willing witness before the House Un-American Activities Committee in 1939. Much of his testimony before the Committee is reproduced. He reports that Jews controlled the Party, that they alone could hold secret caucuses. The CPUSA is not a Party, but a revolutionary army masked as a political organization.

G175 GOLD, Ben. "Who Are the Murderers?" New York: General Executive Board, Needle Trades Workers Industrial Union, n.d. [1933?]. 21 pp.
A leader of the left-wing garment trades union, an affiliate of the Party-led Trade Union Unity League, accuses the bosses and the conservative garment union officials of an unholy alliance with the underworld to murder insurgents who revolt against their leadership. (National president of the Fur Workers from 1937 until its merger with the Meat Cutters in 1955, Gold was one of the few highly placed union officials who freely admitted Party membership.)

G176 GOLD, Michael. Two Critics in a Bar Room, "Liberator," 4 (Sept. 1921), 28-31.
A report of a conversation, true or imaginary, on the American literary scene between the author and Edgar Holgar Cahill, literary critic for the "Freeman." Gold proclaims himself for the Revolution, whereas Cahill simply thinks of art for its own sake.

G177 .... John Reed and the Real Thing, "New Masses," 3 (Nov. 1927), 7-8.
A tribute to John Reed, an intellectual who identified himself with the working class and the revolution, and helped form the Communist Party in this country. He participated in strikes here and in the revolution in Russia, experiencing famine, war, and chaos.

G178 .... 3 Schools of U.S. Writing, "New Masses," 4 (Sept. 1928), 13-14.
A division of American writing into three schools: (1) that which is oriented toward the outmoded Wilsonian—socialist idea of democracy; (2) that which, like "Transition Magazine," has a furious anarchistic spirit with few roots in reality; (3) the communist school, which prefers struggle to suicide.

G179 .... "120 Million." New York: International Publishers, 1929. 192 pp.
Proletarian sketches and chants by a communist writer who played an important part in the proletarian writers' movement of the 1930's. The bitterness of the American worker's life is emphasized.

G180 .... Floyd Dell Resigns, "New Masses," 5 (July 1929), 10-11.
Comment on Dell's resignation as a contributing editor of the "New Masses," on the ground that the magazine represented a neurotic literary estheticism, not a rebellious literary tendency. Denying that Dell was ever a real revolutionist, Gold calls him an artistic and moral failure, who writes about silly and worthless people.

G181 .... "Jews without Money." New York: Liveright, 1930. 309 pp.
A book of personal reminiscences in novel form by a communist who wrote a column for many years in the "Daily Worker." It describes the teeming life of New York's East Side where the author spent his childhood and youth. The dominant motif is the disfigurement of human character by poverty and fear, by the sweat shop and the hunt for jobs.

G182 .... Wilder: Prophet of the Genteel Christ, "New Republic," 64 (Oct. 22, 1930), 266-67.
A denunciation of the works of Thornton Wilder by a communist literary critic, who views him as the poet of the American genteel bourgeoisie, seeking to escape the real problems of his own time and country. Wilder's silliness and superficiality would be revealed if he tried to write about modern America. (This review precipitated a literary controversy in 1930-31.)

G183 GOLD, Michael. Toward an American Revolutionary Culture, "New Masses," 7 (July 1931), 12-13.
The main purpose of capitalist culture is to dope the
masses, filling their minds with nonsense to keep them
from thinking. The cultural movements spawned by the
Socialist Party and the IWW are worse than nothing, but
the Soviet Union shows that culture can be a weapon of
communist construction.

G184 .... A Bourgeois Hamlet of Our Time, "New
Masses," 11 (April 10, 1934), 28-29.
Criticism of John Howard Lawson, still lost, like Hamlet,
in inner conflict, for failure to realize his early promise
as a playwright. Lawson is said to have no real base of
emotion or philosophy; when he takes what might be a
revolutionary theme, he "botches" it completely. (For
Lawson's response, see "Inner Conflict and Proletarian
Art," in the "New Masses," April 17, 1934.)

G185 .... "Change the World!" Foreword by Robert
Forsythe. New York: International Publishers,
1936. 272 pp.
America in the depression as seen by a communist essay-
ist whose solution to all problems—artistic, moral, economic—is militant mass action to establish a Soviet
America. Most of the selections were first published as
columns in the "Daily Worker," whereas others were
reprinted from the "New Masses" or "Anvil."

G186 .... Migratory Intellectuals, "New Masses," 21
(Dec. 15, 1936), 27-29.
An attack on "super-Leftists" such as Sidney Hook and
James Farrell who, having become disillusioned, slander
the communist program in liberal journals. If one believes
in communism, as these people say they do, one must
accept the Communist Party as the only instrument that
can bring it.

G187 .... Notes on the Cultural Front, "New Masses
Literary Supplement," 25 (Dec. 7, 1937), 1-5.
An attack on Trotskyists, who are used by the bourgeois
press as witnesses to the alleged decay of proletarian
culture. They assert that proletarian literature is dead in
America, murdered by the Communist Party. The fact is
that the political situation has altered, and that new types
of literature are called for.

G188 .... "The Hollow Men." New York: International Publishers, 1941. 128 pp.
A survey of the literature of twentieth century America,
written during the period of the Nazi-Soviet pact by a leading Party writer and literary critic. The author, long the
directing spirit of the "New Masses," was also a "Daily
Worker" columnist. He attacks the skepticism of the
1920's; praises the proletarian literature of the 1930's;
and denounces the bourgeois writers, disguised as Marxists in the 1930's, who reverted to their class interest
during the current "imperialist" war. Real intellectuals,
he says, will continue to fight against the dark force of
Wall Street.

G189 .... William L. Patterson: Militant Leader,
"Masses & Mainstream," 4 (Feb. 1951), 34-43.
A sketch of the career of William L. Patterson, secretary
of the Civil Rights Congress, who was cited for contempt
for refusing to name contributors to his organization for
a congressional committee. A successful lawyer, Patterson resigned from his firm following the Sacco-Vanzetti
case to devote his life to the Party and the International
Labor Defense, predecessor of the Civil Rights Congress.

G190 ..., and NORTH, Joseph. The Masses Tradition,
"Masses & Mainstream," 4 (Aug. 1951), 45-55;
(Sept. 1951), 34-41.

A tribute to the magazine on its fortieth anniversary. In
the first article, covering the period of 1911-1934, Gold
writes of the old "Masses," telling how it started, who
wrote and drew for it, and how its fortunes fluctuated. In
the second article North continues the story from 1934 to
1948, telling of the birth of the new magazine, its financial
difficulties, the opposition it faced, and the support it
received.

G191 .... Thoughts on American Writers, "Masses &
Mainstream," 6 (March 1953), 38-43.
Comments on the blighted and diverted careers of various
writers in America, who started out with proletarian
fervor but who succumbed to corruption. Examples include Ernest Hemingway, Erskine Caldwell, Carl Sandburg, Upton Sinclair, John Steinbeck, Eugene O'Neill, and
Claude McKay. Only a few, as himself, Herb Tank, and
Lloyd Brown, have continued to contribute to the people's
front.

G192 .... "The Mike Gold Reader." Introd. by Samuel
Sillen. New York: International Publishers, 1954.
188 pp.
A collection of writings by an author who devoted his
entire adult life to the communist cause. This publication, covering the period from 1921 to 1953, appeared on
Gold's sixtieth birthday. Included are poetry, stories,
sketches, columns, reportage, and literary criticism which
previously appeared in communist publications, principally
the "New Masses" and the "Daily Worker." Covering a
wide range of subjects, the writings follow every turn and
twist of the Party line.

G193 .... Salute to Hugo Gellert, "Masses & Mainstream," 8 (Jan. 1955), 27-31.
An account of the life and achievements of the Hungarian-
born, procommunist artist who has spent 40 years in
cheerful battle as artist and organizer. Scorning commercial success, he painted labor murals and organized
artists against fascism.

.... See also GRANICH, Irwin.

G194 GOLDBERG, Arthur J. "AFL-CIO: Labor U-
nited." New York: McGraw-Hill, 1956. 315 pp.
Ind. App.
An account of the AFL-CIO merger by one of its architects,
who deals in chapter 10, "Communism and Corruption"
(pp. 170-94), with the entry of communists into the labor
movement; their history within it, especially in the CIO;
and the elimination of their influence from the CIO by the
encouragement of anticommunist groups within some
unions and the expulsion of other unions. The author tells
how the merged federation's constitution was drafted to
deal with this problem in the future.

GOLDBERGER, Alexander. See PETERS, J.

G195 GOLDBLOOM, Maurice J. American Communism:
Party of the Right, "Common Sense," 13 (Sept.
1944), 305-9.
A review of the development of Browder's wartime policies
which culminated in the Party's reorganization as the
Communist Political Association. Surveying the changing
communist line to show its adherence to Russia's political
position, the author questions the stability of the present
right swing in the CPUSA.

G196 .... Stalin Builds a Trojan Horse against America: Warning—Another "Popular Front" in the
Making, "Commentary," 14 (Nov. 1952), 403-12.
An assertion that the communists around the world, following Stalin's statements at the October 1952 congress of the

Communist Party of the Soviet Union, will seek to build new popular fronts, playing on the fears of reborn fascism and war. The situation in 1952 is contrasted with that of the 1930's.

G197 GOLDBLOOM, Maurice J. "American Security and Freedom." Boston: Beacon, 1954. 84 pp.
An exploration, sponsored by the American Jewish Committee, of means of reconciling American security and American freedom. The author analyzes our traditional constitutional guarantees, explores the nature of the communist danger to our security, and evaluates the loyalty and security programs in government and private employment. He calls for procedural safeguards, fairness in legislative investigations, and proper division of responsibility among federal, state, and local authorities.

G198 .... Cost of the Security Programs, "Commentary," 20 (Dec. 1955), 541-47.
A review article of Adam Yarmolinsky's "Case Studies in Personnel Security," and Roland Watts' "The Draftee and Internal Security." These two studies support the author's view that the true threat to internal security stems from espionage, sabotage, and conspiracy, which are not best fought by restricting open propaganda or by confounding prevention with punishment.

G199 .... New Moderation in Security, "Commentary," 22 (Nov. 1956), 408-15.
An analysis of the changed climate in the administration of internal security. Despite recent improvements, there is still a misunderstanding of the real nature of the problem; it is not communist opinion, but certain communist acts, such as espionage and systematic infiltration, that we must guard against.

G200 .... The American Communists Today: Parting of the Ways? "Commentary," 23 (Feb. 1957), 123-34.
An evaluation of the struggle inside the CPUSA following the Khrushchev revelations. This struggle is unlike those of the past, in that there is a faction that is critical of Moscow, of the CPUSA's internal government, and even of Marxism-Leninism. The divisions seem too deep for the coming convention (February 1957) to resolve.

G201 GOLDMAN, Albert. "Charge: Rioting; Verdict: Not Guilty!" Chicago: International Labor Defense, n.d. [1932?]. 47 pp.
In March 1932 a communist-led demonstration in front of the Japanese Consulate in Chicago resulted in bloodshed between police and demonstrators. Thirteen demonstrators were tried for rioting and were acquitted. This pamphlet is the summation to the jury by the attorney for the defense.

G202 .... "From Communism to Socialism." Introd. by Arthur G. McDowell. [Chicago, Ill.?]: n.publ., 1934. 14 pp.
A discussion of left-wing factional issues by a former communist who became a Trotskyist and then joined the Socialist Party. The pamphlet deals with factional quarrels within the Trotskyist group and between them and the socialists, and also with the author's disagreements with the CPUSA and the Communist International. He calls himself a revolutionary socialist who joined the SP because Hitler's victory in Germany brought leftward movements within socialist parties formerly under reformist control.

G203 .... Communists Play "Follow The Leader," "Socialist Appeal," 2 (Aug. 1936), 6-8.
A critique of the recent convention of the CPUSA, which

implicitly endorsed Roosevelt as the lesser evil. This can be justified only on the ground that the working class must now choose between bourgeois democracy and fascism. But fascism arises from capitalist democracy, and the alternative to fascism is therefore socialism.

G204 .... "Why We Defend the Soviet Union." New York: Pioneer Publishers, 1940. 31 pp.
Reprint of six articles from the "Socialist Appeal," explaining that the Socialist Workers Party, a Trotskyist group, defends the Soviet Union (with reference to the Stalin-Hitler pact) as representative of the struggle by socialism against capitalism. Though the SWP does not condone the Stalinist bureaucracy, so long as nationalized property exists the Soviet Union is a workers' state.

G205 GOLDSMITH, Len. "Ideas behind Bars? The Story of the Frame-up of 140,000,000 Americans." New York: Civil Rights Congress, n.d. [1948]. 31 pp. App.
The national director of the Civil Rights Congress protests against the indictment of the 12 national leaders of the CPUSA under the Smith Act for conspiracy to reconstitute the Communist Party and teach Marxism. They are not charged with any overt act against the U.S. government. The trial will determine whether the American people have the right to hear this social philosophy.

G206 GOLDSTEIN, David, and AVERY, Martha Moore. "Bolshevism: Its Cure." Boston: Boston School of Political Economy, 1919. 414 pp.
A critical view of Bolshevism by Catholic authors who view it as only another name for socialism and who look to the Catholic Church as the one power that can resist its advance. Socialist-Bolshevik views of marriage, divorce, and patriotism are outlined, and leftist propaganda within the armed forces and the schools is attacked. Russian developments and Bolshevik views relating to the class struggle, the classless society, the state, dictatorship of the proletariat, democracy, freedom of speech and press, marriage and divorce, world revolution, and violence are presented.

G207 GOLDWATER, Walter. "Radical Periodicals in America, 1890-1950." New Haven: Yale University Press, 1964. 51 pp.
A listing of 321 radical (anarchist, communist, or socialist) periodicals published in the U.S. in English between 1890 and 1950. The political orientation of each publication is given, along with its editor and dates of appearance. Information where pertinent is given about the organization sponsoring the publication, and its relationship to earlier or later publications. A genealogy of radical parties is included.

G208 GOLDWAY, David. "The Communist Political Association." New York: CPA, n.d. [1944]. 30 unnumbered pp.
A popularly written account of the Communist Political Association, picturing communists as leading fighters against fascism, in the armed forces, in production, and in the community. Unity to win the war and achieve postwar prosperity is advocated. The communists, Marxists who believe in scientific socialism, do not raise the issue of socialism now in the interests of national unity.

G209 GOMEZ, Manuel. Labor and Empire "Workers Monthly," 4 (July 1925), 420-24 ff.
An effort to relate anti-imperialism directly to the class struggle and to the needs of the workers. Denouncing traditional labor organizations for abdicating the antiimperialist struggle, the author argues that the Communist International is the only group capable of leading the

struggle, both in the oppressed nations and in the imperialist ones.

G210 GOMEZ, Manuel. La Follettism without La Follette, "Workers Monthly," 4 (Aug. 1925), 435-37.
An assessment of the La Follette movement on the occasion of La Follett's death. Since the movement embodies the class interests of the petty bourgeoisie, communists must take advantage of its temporary demoralization to hasten the separation of the labor party forces. A labor party, however, must be rooted in the trade unions.

G211 .... The Crisis in Philippine Independence, "Workers Monthly," 5 (Oct. 1926), 539-42.
An attack on American imperialism in the Philippines, which has moved speedily since it was discovered that rubber could be grown there profitably. Filipino independence will make progress only when its leaders learn to see through American "generosity." American workers should be in the forefront of the struggle for Filipino liberty.

G212 ... (ed.). "Poems for Workers." Chicago: Daily Worker Publishing Co., 1927. 55 pp.
An anthology of poems from labor periodicals, published for the Workers Party of America. The collection, the editor states, is limited to poems which belong directly to the class struggle, and are written by authors who have been active in the revolutionary proletarian movement.

G213 GOMPERS, Samuel. The Truth about Soviet Russia and Bolshevism, "American Federationist," 27 (Feb. 1920), 159-67; (March), 253-56.
Reciting the use of mass terror tactics by the Bolshevik rulers of Russia, Gompers censures publications such as the "New Republic" and the "Nation" for creating sentiment favorable to the USSR. The support by French socialists of the Third International, while French trade unionists reject it, shows that, while theorists may advocate Bolshevism, the workers see it as a freak and a scourge.

G214 .... The Soviet Camouflage, "American Federationist," 29 (April 1922), 276-78.
The president of the AFL comments on newspaper reports of Third International and Soviet government instructions on boring from within the American labor movement to capture it for revolutionary activity and strikes. Bolsheviks are not to appear in labor unions as such, but as "liberals" or "radicals."

G215 .... Another Attempt at Soviet Dictatorship Unmasked, "American Federationist," 29 (May 1922), 337-45.
An editorial attack on the newly-established Trade Union Educational League as Moscow's new scheme for destroying the AFL. The proposal of the TUEL, which is sponsored and controlled by one man, William Z. Foster, is to amalgamate all unions into ten industrial organizations, replacing all present union officials with Reds subservient to Moscow.

G216 .... American Labor Unshaken, "American Federationist," 29 (Aug. 1922), 573-80.
A report on the debate at the AFL convention in June on recognition of the Soviet Union. After delegates pointed to Russian communist propaganda seeking to destroy the AFL, the convention reaffirmed the AFL stand against Soviet recognition. The committee's report is printed in full.

G217 .... Results of "Bad Company," "American Federationist," 30 (Aug. 1923), 659-61.
An analysis of the capture of the Federated Farmer-Labor Party by the communists in July 1923. The party now has no purpose, since the present time is most inopportune for a third party, and it is also rankless and fileless. No good American trade unionist can give this party the slightest support.

G218 .... Why Labor Opposes Soviet Recognition, "American Federationist," 30 (Oct. 1923), 807-12.
A speech by Gompers at the Cigarmakers' convention in August 1923 on a resolution to send relief to Soviet Russia. Discussing the dictatorship in the USSR, Gompers opposes any action that will open the way for establishment of a communist government in the U.S.

G219 GONZALEZ, Isabel. "Step-Children of a Nation: The Status of Mexican-Americans." New York: American Committee for Protection of Foreign Born, 1947. 14 pp.
A protest, by a Party-front organization, against the status and treatment of Mexican-Americans in the U.S. The author asserts that they are placed in an inferior position, kept in poor health, housed badly, exploited economically, and subjected to the threat of deportation. Demands to ease their plight are listed.

G220 GOODMAN, Walter. Who Promoted Matusow? "New Republic," 132 (March 7, 1955), 12-14.
A resumé of the career of Harvey Matusow and an account of his appearance before the Senate Internal Security Subcommittee after he repudiated testimony on communists and communist activities that he had given to various government agencies and in court. A former communist and later a professional informer, he is now an admitted liar.

G221 GORDON, Charles. The Immigration Process and National Security, "Temple Law Quarterly," 24 (Jan. 1951), 302-19.
A review of federal statutory and administrative provisions dealing with national security and directed against aliens, and of some of the more important cases interpreting them. The exclusion provisions in legislation of 1917-18 and in the Internal Security Act of 1950, and procedures instituted to carry them out, are discussed.

G222 GORDON, Eugene. Negro Novelists and the Negro Masses, "New Masses," 8 (July 1933), 16-20.
Slavery gave rise to an unhealthy Negro culture which emphasized wealth and upper-class virtues. These ideals were reflected in Negro novelists, as in the rising Negro bourgeoisie. Up to 1920, American Negroes had not produced a writer of fiction with a proletarian-revolutionary approach. More recently Langston Hughes pictures the Negro worker as seeing the way out through the class struggle.

G223 ..., and BRIGGS, Cyril. "The Position of Negro Women." New York: Workers Library, 1935. 16 pp.
A condemnation of the "double exploitation" of the Negro woman, and the heavy burden put upon her by capitalism. Only by unity with white workers, under the leadership of the Party, can Negro women fight against their enemy, the white capitalists. (One of the authors, Cyril Briggs, Negro intellectual and editor, was one of the first of his race to join the Party.)

G224 GORDON, Evelyn B. "Weaving the Future." New York: Workers Library, 1937. 23 pp.
Communists are pictured as "master weavers" of an ideal world in this recruiting pamphlet aimed at textile workers. The Party's program, including jobs, housing, peace,

and formation of a farmer-labor party, is presented. A letter from Elizabeth Gurley Flynn to textile workers, inviting them to join the Party, is included.

G225 GORDON, Evelyn B. The Textile Drive, "Communist," 16 (June 1937), 517-25.
A description of communist support of the Textile Workers Organizing Committee of the CIO. The National Textile Act is endorsed.

G226 GORDON, Louis. "White Collar Workers Organize." New York: United Office and Professional Workers, n.d. [1938?]. 23 pp.
A recruiting pamphlet, telling of the successes of the UOPWA (a communist-controlled union) in organizing white collar workers; the union's efforts were inspired by the example of the CIO in the basic industries.

G227 GORDON, Max. The President's Message to Congress, "Communist," 23 (March 1944), 241-51.
A favorable review of Roosevelt's State of the Union Message to Congress, outlining a program of high taxes on profits, continued price controls, cooperation in a peaceful world on the basis of the Teheran decisions, and economic security for Americans. Roosevelt must be reelected to implement this program.

G228 .... What Is Behind the Attack on the C.I.O. Political Action Committee? "Communist," 23 (July 1944), 657-62.
An exposé of the anti-Roosevelt conspiracy that is behind the defeatist attacks on the CIO-PAC. The Republicans have joined the Southern reactionaries in the attacks. The PAC program is a platform for the entire nation for winning the war and the peace.

G229 .... Albany Battleground, "Political Affairs," 24 (Feb. 1945), 169-81.
A review of Governor Dewey's 1945 message to the New York legislature to show its sham liberalism. The problem inside the legislature is to win united action between Democrats and progressive Republicans.

G230 .... The Bretton Woods Hearings, "Political Affairs," 24 (May 1945), 430-40.
A midway report on the hearing on the Bretton Woods credit and currency agreements before the Banking and Currency Committee of the House of Representatives. Gordon criticizes groups such as the American Bankers Association which seek to scuttle the agreements.

G231 .... Issues and Candidates in the New York Elections, "Political Affairs," 24 (Oct. 1945), 882-93.
The reactionary Dewey machine has put forward a stooge, Goldstein, as Republican-Liberal-Fusion candidate for mayor. The Democratic Party is split, with some reactionary Democrats allied with the Liberal Party in opposing O'Dwyer. Progressives are urged to reelect Benjamin Davis and Peter Cacchione, communist members of the City Council.

G232 .... Labor Moves Forward in the New York Elections, "Political Affairs," 24 (Dec. 1945), 1079-87.
The New York City election resulted in a victory for progressives. O'Dwyer's dependence on the ALP in order to win the mayoralty election means that he will not be dominated by reactionary Democrats. Communist councilmen received a record vote, while the Liberal Party's vote fell markedly.

G233 .... New York Is Not Mississippi, "New Masses," 61 (Oct. 22, 1946), 21-23.

Democratic politicians are accused of using mass intimidation to have their communist competitors removed from the ballot in New York State. Signers of communist nominating petitions are terrorized into repudiation of their signatures. New York City Councilman Benjamin J. Davis reminded the judge that he was in New York, not Mississippi.

G234 .... Mr. Truman's Glove and the Mailed Fist, "Political Affairs," 27 (Feb. 1948), 119-24.
An attack on President Truman's 1948 "State of the Union Message" for its sham liberalism, designed to take votes away from Henry Wallace. Truman is concerned with the war-like policies of the reactionaries, not with liberal policies such as civil rights.

G235 .... The Sham Revolt against Truman, "Political Affairs," 27 (May 1948), 440-47.
A discussion of dissatisfaction within the Democratic Party with the Truman Administration. Whether Truman or another candidate runs on the Democratic ticket in 1948, the Democratic Party's war policy will continue. Progressives have chosen a new anti-imperialist, anti-monopoly people's party in 1948.

G236 The "Grand" Old Party, "Political Affairs," 27 (Aug. 1948), 711-19.
A report on the Republican national convention in Philadelphia, which showed that the Republican leaders have imperialist ambitions, differing only in approach. Some, like Dewey, are internationalists, seeking to subject Europe to Wall Street control. Others, like Taft, are nationalists who emphasize American domination of Latin America. The internationalists won at the convention.

G237 .... Popular Mandate vs. Monopoly Policy in the New Congress, "Political Affairs," 28 (Jan. 1949), 75-84.
An analysis of the composition of the 81st Congress, with speculation as to how it will act on foreign policy and on various domestic issues, including civil rights. Illusions that Truman will live up to his election promises must be dispelled, and progressive forces and all workers united in a militant program of mass activity.

G238 GORDON, Rosalie M. "Nine Men against America: The Supreme Court and its Attack on American Liberties." New York: Devin-Adair, 1958. 166 pp. Ind.
An attack on the U.S. Supreme Court for striking down practically every bulwark raised against the communist conspiracy in America, leaving the states helpless in the face of subversion. Among the cases cited are those dealing with state antisedition acts, communist teachers in tax-supported schools, the government's security program, the admission of communists to the bar, efforts to deport communist aliens, the freedom of inquiry of congressional investigating committees, and advocacy of overthrow of government by force and violence.

G239 GORFINKEL, John A., and MACK, Julian W., II. Dennis v. United States and the Clear and Present Danger Rule, "California Law Review," 39 (Dec. 1951), 475-501.
Criticism of the opinions of the Court of Appeals and the U.S. Supreme Court which affirmed the convictions of the 11 communist leaders for conspiring to advocate violent overthrow of the government. The authors trace legal precedents on freedom of speech, discuss the clear and present danger rule, and conclude that the Dennis case failed to reach a proper balance between freedom and security.

G240 GORKY, Maxim. "To American Intellectuals."
      New York: International Publishers, 1932. 31 pp.
In a letter addressed to American intellectuals, a leading
Russian literary figure attacks the intellectual sterility of
bourgeois society in the U.S. He condemns the Christian
Church and contrasts the decadence of culture in bourgeois
countries with cultural progress in the Soviet Union

G241 . . . . An Answer to Some Americans, "New
      Masses," 7 (June 1932), 15-17.
A reply by Maxim Gorky to two American intellectuals
concerned about their role in society. He attacks the
misleadership of the bourgeoisie as well as the role of
the press, the scientist, the artist, and the church in
capitalist society. The working class, in taking political
power, will open the widest possibility for cultural development.

G242 GOSNELL, Harold. "Negro Politicians: The Rise
      of Negro Politics in Chicago." Chicago: Univer-
      sity of Chicago Press, 1935. 404 pp. Ind.
In chapter 15, "Negroes and Communism" (pp. 319-56), a
University of Chicago sociologist analyzes the inroads
made by the communists in the Negro community in
general and in the Chicago Black Belt in particular. He
compares the relative attraction of communist and traditional bourgeois symbols, and gives case histories of
some typical Negro communists. He concludes that,
although the early success of the communists left an
imprint on Negroes, communism did not take deep root in
the Chicago Black Belt.

G243 GOULD, Kenneth. Legislating Loyalty, "American
      Scholar," 4 (May 1935), 345-55.
An exploration of one phase of antisubversive campaigns,
the enactment by states of loyalty oath requirements for
teachers or students. Outlining the provisions of the Ives
Law of New York State, the author concludes that such
oaths violate the right of academic freedom and set a
dangerous precedent.

G244 GOULD, Leslie A. "American Youth Today."
      Foreword by Eleanor Roosevelt. New York: Ran-
      dom House, 1940. 307 pp.
A sympathetic history of the American Youth Congress,
written during the Hitler-Stalin pact period, in which the
author is highly critical of President Roosevelt's "prowar" foreign policy. The author denounces all charges
that the AYC is communist-controlled as "red herrings."
Chapters deal with the 1940 Youth Citizenship Institute,
the origins of the AYC, its structure, testimony of its
leaders before the Dies Committee in 1939, and the problems facing youth, such as jobs and peace, as viewed by
the AYC. An appendix contains the creed of the AYC, its
constitution, the American Youth Act, and a list of organizations cooperating with the AYC.

G245 GRAFTON, Samuel. The Red Scare: A Case His-
      tory, "Nation," 140 (April 24, 1935), 476-78.
An account of the continuing persecutions and charges of
radicalism against the Affiliated Schools for Workers and
one of its constituents, the New York City School for
Workers. Newspapers and patriotic societies hunt for
communist influence, and there is pressure on government
to withdraw relief teachers and have Congress investigate.

G246 GRAHAM, Margaret [pseud. for Grace Lois McDon-
      ald]. "Swing Shift." New York: Citadel Press,
      1951. 494 pp.
An attempt to portray the communist man, the worker-
radical, in a biographical novel. The author writes a left-
wing history of the American labor movement, from the
closing years of the last century to the opening of World

War II, through the activities of a tough and devoted railroad man.

G247 GRAHAM, Shirley. "Paul Robeson, Citizen of the
      World." Foreword by Carl Van Doren. New York:
      Messner, 1946. 264 pp. Bibliog. Ind.
A glowing account of Robeson's life and career, including
his boyhood experiences, his athletic triumphs, his successes as singer and actor, and his interest in social
problems. His favorable impressions of the Soviet Union
are noted.

G248 GRANGER, Lester B. The Negro Congress—Its
      Future, "Opportunity," 18 (June 1940), 164-66.
An assertion by a Negro leader that the National Negro
Congress is no longer representative of the Negro community. Apart from A. Philip Randolph's refusal to stand
for reelection because of communist control, so large an
organization is always in danger of capture by a political
party.

G249 GRANICH, Irwin [Michael Gold]. Towards Prole-
      tarian Art, "Liberator," 4 (Feb. 1921), 20-24.
Whereas the older generation of artists, isolated by the
art ideals of the capitalist world, had no roots in the
people, the masses of Americans are said by a leading
communist literary critic to have awakened, through the
revolutionary movement, to their souls. Following the
example of the proletarian culture now flowering in Russia,
great art must grow from the fields, factories, and workshops of America.

G250 GRANIK, Theodore. Should the Communist Party
      Be Outlawed? "American Mercury," 79 (Aug.
      1954), 59-64.
An outline, in the "American Forum" section of the
"Mercury," of past congressional efforts to outlaw the
Party and of the principal arguments on both sides, as
presented in congressional hearings, House and Senate
debates, and public discussion.

G251 GRANT, David. "A Worker Looks at Jesus."
      Hollywood: Christian Front for Peace and Against
      Fascism, 1938. 48 pp.
An appeal is made, on grounds of religion, for readers to
join the united front against fascism in this country and
abroad.

G252 . . . . "Attack Now! Knock Out Hitler in '42."
      New York: New Age, 1942. 15 pp.
Young Communist League pamphlet seeking to rally
American youth behind World War II. The author argues
that the opening of a western front in Europe by America
and Britain, combined with a Russian offensive, will bring
victory in 1942. He urges a Presidential pardon to Earl
Browder, to strengthen national unity.

G253 GRATTAN, C. Hartley. Red Opinion in the U.S.,
      "Scribner's Magazine," 96 (Nov. 1934), 299-305.
A study of the communist press, to see whether we can
afford the expression of abhorred opinions. The entire
spectrum of left-wing periodicals is reviewed—socialist,
Musteite, Lovestoneite, CPUSA, Trotskyite, and Socialist
Labor Party. The author concludes that the communist
press poses no threat at all.

G254 GRECHT, Rebecca. Paterson—Field of Battle,
      "Workers Monthly," 4 (Nov. 1924), 12-14 ff.
A review of labor conditions and struggles in the Paterson,
N.J., silk industry since 1913, with an account of the
current strike led by the Associated Silk Workers. Wage
cuts, longer hours of work, and the three- and four-loom
systems brought on the walkout. TUEL militants are

agitating for amalgamation and awakening class consciousness.

G255   GREEN [pseud. for Sergei Gusev?]. Some Questions of the Work of the CPUSA, "Communist International," 10 (Sept. 1, 1933), 570-74.
The Party's failure to carry out Comintern instructions stems from a mistaken belief that the main danger is left sectarianism. The CPUSA suffers from the right danger, of following rather than leading the masses. Its chief source of support must come from the employed, though other groups must not be ignored. (The author, not identified, may be a former Comintern representative to the Party here who used this pseudonym.)

G256   GREEN, Abner. "United Nations in America." New York: American Committee for Protection of Foreign Born, 1943. 18 pp.
A report given at the committee's tenth national conference, showing how the foreign born have demonstrated their love and loyalty for the U.S., their hatred of fascism, and their support of the war effort. Though other wartime problems confront us, the author asserts that the only one of importance is winning the war as speedily as possible.

G257   .... "The Fight for the Rights of Foreign-Born Americans: A Report to the Chicago Conference for Protection of Foreign Born." New York: American Committee for Protection of Foreign Born, n.d. [1947]. 15 pp.
The text of a report to the Chicago Conference for Protection of Foreign Born, May 25, 1947, discussing deportations for political opinions, and naturalization cases. Public opinion must be mobilized to aid noncitizens with naturalization and immigration problems.

G258   .... "The Deportation Terror: A Weapon to Gag America." New York: New Century, 1950. 23 pp.
A protest against deportations by the executive secretary of the American Committee for Protection of Foreign Born. The Justice Department is charged with employing guilt-by-association methods, creating a concentration camp, and using deportation to weaken and destroy trade unions.

G259   .... "The Deportation Drive vs. the Bill of Rights." New York: American Committee for Protection of Foreign Born, 1951. 23 pp.
A report by the executive secretary of the American Committee for Protection of Foreign Born to the National Conference to Defend the Bill of Rights held in New York, in December 1950. He depicts a reign of terror by the Justice Department against noncitizens and naturalized citizens, in an attempt to denaturalize and deport them under the Walter-McCarran Act.

G260   .... "The Walter-McCarran Law: Police-State Terror against Foreign-Born Americans." New York: New Century, 1953. 48 pp.
A call for the repeal of the Walter-McCarran Law, which subjects the foreign-born to police-state restrictions. The background and provisions of the law are described, with emphasis on the powers of the Attorney General, the status of noncitizens, preliminary investigations, the right to bail, deportation hearings, deportation, supervisory parole, naturalization, and immigration.

G261   .... "In the Shadow of Liberty: The Inhumanity of the Walter-McCarran Law." New York: New York Committee for Protection of Foreign Born, 1954. 46 pp.
The author uses "human interest" biographies of the noncitizens or naturalized citizens against whom the Walter-McCarran Law is being used (the "little man in the street," Charlie Chaplin, Cedric Belfrage, John Steuben, and Claudia Jones) to show how these people are being persecuted by the Justice Department. He urges the repeal of the Walter-McCarran Law.

G262   GREEN, Charles H. "The Headwear Workers: A Century of Trade Unionism." New York: United Hat, Cap, and Millinery Workers International Union, 1944. 269 pp. Ind.
Chapter 17 gives an account of the battle in the Hat and Cap Workers Union between the lefts and rights. The author analyzes communist tactics in labor unions and tells of the events that led to a temporary ascendency of the left-wingers in this union. The battle for control in Local 43 (Trimmers) and Local 24 (Blockers), the physical battles and the ferment in the millinery district, and the eventual elimination of communists at the 1929 convention are told in detail.

G263   GREEN, Elizabeth Zeleny. I Face an Oklahoma Prison, "Protestant Digest," 4 (Aug.-Sept. 1941), 26-33.
An account of police raids in Oklahoma on the Party headquarters, its bookstore, and the home of the state secretary, followed by charges against 12 persons, including the author, of criminal syndicalism on the basis of Party membership. Some have already been convicted, and sentenced to ten years in prison, although the political views of communists are legal under the U.S. Constitution.

G264   GREEN, Gilbert. The Young Communist League Turns to Struggle, "Communist," 10 (Aug. 1931), 714-19.
A report on the sixth national convention of the Young Communist League. Weaknesses of the League, notably failures to lead white and Negro youth, are cited. This weakness is based on a "right-opportunist underestimation of radicalization." Emphasis of the article is on building YCL trade-union work.

G265   .... "Youth Confronts the Blue Eagle." New York: Youth Publishers, 1933. 29 pp.
The leader of the Young Communist League asserts that the National Recovery Act will lead to deeper crises, more unemployment, greater misery, a new imperialist war, and fascism. He urges youth to work for the creation of a Soviet America.

G266   .... The Open Letter and Tasks of the Y.C.L., "Communist," 12 (Aug. 1933), 818-23.
An analysis of the failure of the Young Communist League to increase its membership, particularly among the working class. The YCL should not relax its demands for activity and discipline among its members. Instead of relying on a few leaders, it should demand that every member exert the utmost effort to recruit new members.

G267   .... "United We Stand for Peace and Socialism." New York: Workers Library, 1935. 64 pp.
The report of the national secretary of the Young Communist League of the U.S.A. on the Sixth World Congress of the Young Communist International, held in Moscow in September 1935. Following the Comintern response to the threat of Hitlerism against the USSR, Green emphasizes the need for a united front of nonfascist youth in defense of democracy, peace, and freedom.

G268   .... "Young Communists and Unity of the Youth." New York: Youth Publishers, 1935. 15 pp.
Speech delivered at the Seventh World Congress of the Communist International, outlining accomplishments and objectives of the Young Communist League in America.

Green emphasizes the threat of fascism, the need to achieve unity between proletarian and middle class youth, the success thus far achieved in the united-front movement, and the necessity to avoid sectarian errors.

G269 GREEN, Gilbert. Roosevelt's "Happy Days" for the Young Generation. "Communist," 14 (July 1935), 661-72.
The youth in the CCC are discontented over low pay, poor food, inadequate housing, poor working conditions, and strict discipline under Army officers. The Party plans to send specially trained youth into selected camps to form strong factions and lead the fight against the CCC authorities.

G270 . . . . Toward Youth Unity. "Communist," 15 (Sept. 1936), 855-64.
The January conference of the Young Communist League adopted a united front policy that would enroll socialists and other noncommunists in the ranks of the YCL. Yet organic unity between the YCL and the Young People's Socialist League is no closer today; united front activity, as in the American Youth Congress and the American Student Union, has been more successful.

G271 . . . . "Facing the 8th Convention of the Young Communist League: Report to the National Conference of the Young Communist League Delivered January 1, 1937." New York: YCL, 1937. 24 pp.
A report written during the Party's collective security period, asserting that the major issue facing the American people is that of democracy versus fascism. Sections of the report deal with the new problems faced by youth in industry, the growing movement towards youth unity and the YCL tasks, and problems connected with building the YCL and the perspective for a united farmer-labor youth organization. The YPSL leadership is criticized for using left phrases to hinder development of the broad youth movement.

G272 . . . . "Make Your Dreams Come True." New York: Workers Library, 1937. 47 pp.
Report to the eighth national convention of the Young Communist League, during the popular front period. Emphasis is placed on fascist aggression abroad, the dangers of the American brand of fascism, and the need for unity in the fight for economic security, peace, and democracy. Support is pledged to the CIO, the American Student Union, and the American Youth Congress. The YCL is to be transformed into an organization broader than the Party, adapted to the desires of youth.

G273 . . . . The Coming Convention of the Y.C.L., "Communist," 16 (Feb. 1937), 120-41.
A report to the National Conference of the Young Communist League, discussing youth problems and the growing youth unity movement. The tasks of the YCL are to help bring industrial youths into trade unions and YCL clubs, to form a united front with other youth organizations, to build youth organizations associated with the Farmer-Labor Party, and to support progressive youth legislation.

G274 . . . . Some Problems of the Youth Movement in the U.S.A., "Communist International," 14 (Nov. 1937), 857-60.
Though the progressive youth movement, exemplified by the American Youth Congress, has greatly expanded in the U.S., there has not been a corresponding increase in the "class conscious" youth movement, the Young Communist League. The eighth national convention of the YCL therefore undertook to transform the YCL into a mass anti-fascist youth organization.

G275 . . . . "The Truth about Soviet Russia." New York: New Age, 1938. 47 pp.
A defense of the USSR by the president of the Young Communist League of America. Asserting that speech and elections in the Soviet Union are free, he justifies the one-party system on the ground that the economic basis for classes has disappeared. He defends the purges and trials as necessary to root out disloyal remnants of the old landlord and capitalist classes, along with the spies and agents of foreign governments.

G276 . . . . The Young Generation and the Imperialist War, "Communist," 18 (Nov. 1939), 1037-45.
The youth, victims of the depression, cannot be helped by the war boom because if America is drawn into the war the youth will have to fight. The task of the YCL is to teach young people that the war is an imperialist war in which neither side has a just cause. It must mobilize the youth in opposition to American aid to the Allies.

G277 . . . . Imperialist War and "Democratic" Demagogy, "Communist," 14 [19] (June 1940), 521-30.
An assertion, during the Soviet-Nazi pact period, that an Allied victory will not save democracy, since both belligerents are imperialists seeking markets. So long as the allies remain capitalistic, they will go to war for markets. Peace and democracy will be advanced by an imperialist defeat, which will hasten proletarian revolution.

G278 . . . . Some Effects of War Economy in the U.S.A., "Communist," 20 (Jan. 1941), 83-96.
Communist criticism of U.S. military appropriations during the Hitler-Stalin pact period. Capitalists approve Roosevelt's war budget because it will give them huge profits, whereas workers will pay for war expenditures through higher prices, higher taxes, and curtailed social welfare benefits. The war policy is impoverishing the nation through the waste of resources on munitions.

G279 . . . . Our Tasks in the Struggle to Defeat Hitlerism, "Communist," 21 (Aug. 1941), 705-11.
Americans must aid Russia because a Russian defeat would leave Germany overwhelmingly powerful. In order to mobilize Americans behind Russia, the Party must emphasize the common loathing of Hitlerism. It will support Roosevelt's defense measures, while criticizing any defects. (Based on a report to a plenary meeting of the Party's national committee, June 28-29, 1941.)

G280 . . . . "New York's Wartime Election." New York: New York State Committee, Communist Party, 1942. 24 pp.
Text of an address by the executive secretary of the New York State Communist Party to the state convention, August 29-30, 1942. Urging the election to Congress and the New York State legislature of win-the-war candidates over defeatists, Roosevelt haters, and labor-baiters, he calls for increased production, stable living costs, labor and national unity, an end to racial discrimination, and an immediate opening of a second front on the European continent.

G281 . . . . The Course of the War and the Present Tasks, "Communist," 21 (April 1942), 214-24.
America must go on the offensive, launching a second front in Europe. It must speed up its production effort. In return for labor's giving up of the strike weapon, price control and rationing must be instituted. Communists hope to use their participation in the war effort to recruit many new members.

G282 . . . . Some Problems of Economic Stabilization, "Communist," 22 (March 1943), 229-39.

An examination of wage and price problems resulting from the war economy, and the possibility of their solution by centralized economic planning, strict price control, and democratic rationing. Creeping inflation is blamed on defeatists whose opposition to cost-of-living adjustments alienates workers and seeks to provoke strikes that would sabotage the war effort. (For a critical commentary see William and Pauline Young, "On Wage Stabilization," in "Communist," May 1943.)

G283   GREEN, Gilbert. The Dubinsky Social-Democrats, "Communist," 22 (July 1943), 633-41.
A report to a plenary meeting of the Party's national committee, June 11, 1943, describing the Dubinsky, "New Leader," "Forward" wing of social democracy and proposing strengthening of the communist position in key industries to defeat its influence.

G284   . . . . The New York City Elections, "Communist," 22 (Dec. 1943), 1103-10.
A speech to Party workers in New York, reviewing the New York City elections in which the win-the-war camp won. The success was not greater because of disunity in the ALP and apathy in the Democratic Party. Two communists, Benjamin J. Davis, Jr., and Peter V. Cacchione, were elected to the City Council.

G285   . . . . "Marxism and the World of Today." New York: New York State Committee, Communist Party, 1944. 23 pp.
Speech to a meeting of New York City communist club leaders, January 20, 1944, supporting Browder's proposals that the wartime national unity line be projected into the postwar period, and that the word "party" be dropped by the communist organization. Postwar production levels must be raised to permit national unity, while world stability can be based on the Anglo-Soviet-American coalition.

G286   . . . . American Capitalism and Teheran, "Communist," 23 (Feb. 1944), 148-52.
The Teheran decisions mean the replacement of old imperialist domination with world stability based on the independence of colonial peoples, the strength of the Soviet Union, and the collaboration of the wartime allies. This stability will help American capitalism by encouraging foreign investments and the growth of foreign markets for American goods.

G287   . . . . Post-War Economic Perspectives, "Communist," 23 (April 1944), 296-309.
A leading postwar objective is to provide sufficient demand for American goods to ensure a full employment economy. Peaceful international relations and industrialization of backward countries will expand export markets, while proper fiscal policy and adequate social security will provide enough purchasing power at home.

G288   . . . . New York in the 1944 Election Lineup, "Communist," 23 (July 1944), 620-31.
New York, the largest state in the union, must be rallied behind Roosevelt in the 1944 elections. Because of apathy in the Democratic Party, the American Labor Party must mobilize support behind Roosevelt. One big task will be to register voters.

G289   . . . . The Outlook for the Municipal Elections, "Political Affairs," 24 (April 1945), 342-47.
In the coming city elections, the proper technique is to promote nonpartisan support of whichever party has a progressive candidate with a good chance of winning. The major objective is to strengthen the coalition around Roosevelt. (Remarks to a meeting of the CPA national committee, March 11, 1945.)

G290   . . . . The Chicago Elections, "Political Affairs," 26 (Dec. 1947), 1112-19.
A report on the Progressive Party's first campaign in Chicago, in which it won more than 16 per cent of the vote. The building of the third-party movement calls for bringing together all who can unite around a common progressive program. People will leave the old parties for the sake of clear-cut issues about which they feel deeply.

G291   . . . . A Few Thoughts on Our Perspectives, "Political Affairs," 27 (Aug. 1948), 731-38.
A preconvention discussion article, seeking to counter the defeatism apparent among some Party members. Green asserts that American imperialist efforts are due to the narrowing of markets in the face of expanding productive facilities. A recession will inevitably come and turn the masses against the ruling class.

G292   . . . . The Browderite Conception of History, "Political Affairs," 28 (Oct. 1949), 65-84; Browder's "Coalition" with Monopoly Capital. (Nov.), 48-57; Capitalism's Crisis—and Mr. Browder's, 29 (March 1950), 68-81.
Browder has criticized the Party for not continuing its wartime coalition with the capitalists in the U.S. and Europe, arguing that American capitalists would be progressive if Roosevelt had lived and if Truman's efforts to collaborate had not been rebuffed by the Party. But capitalism always seeks to destroy the Party. A wartime coalition was possible with the capitalist democracies because both were threatened by the fascists. With fascism overthrown, American and European capitalism engages in imperialist aggression against the USSR. Instead of Browder's unity with monopoly capital, Green calls for a broad antimonopoly, antiwar coalition, based on working-class unity.

G293   . . . . For Communist Vigilance, "Political Affairs," 29 (May 1950), 115-30.
Recommendations for strict controls to combat the infiltration of FBI and Central Intelligence Agency spies into the Party, and to prevent recurrence of the "stoolpigeoning" which took place at the trial of the 11 leading communists in New York.

G294   . . . . "The Enemy Forgotten." New York: International Publishers, 1956. 320 pp.
A book published just as the author, a member of the national committee of the Party, began to serve a jail sentence for violation of the Smith Act. Chapters contrast the progressive 1930's with the reactionary 1950's, and discuss such issues as the Soviet "threat" to America, monopoly, unsolved economic problems, military expenditures, political realignment, labor in politics, the Negro, and the future of socialism in America. The author believes that the enemy of the people is special privilege, and that only by struggle against predatory special interests can peace, democracy, and abundance be achieved.

. . . . See also SWIFT, John.

G295   GREEN, Jack. Labor's Stake in the South, "Political Affairs," 35 (Aug. 1956), 1-12.
The American labor movement faces a tremendous problem in the millions of unorganized Southern workers. The Negro people's struggle for equal rights represents an opportunity, not an embarrassment, to organizing efforts. The crucial test is the projected organizing campaign in the textile industry.

G296   GREEN, John. We Bar Communists as Union Officers, "Labor and Nation," 2 (Nov. 1946), 33-35.

Defense by the president of the Marine and Shipbuilding Workers (CIO) of the union's constitutional clause barring fascists, nazis, and communists from union office. Supporters of these philosophies have their roots abroad and are not primarily concerned with the welfare of American workers.

G297 GREEN, Joseph, and SHAPIRO, Nat. People's Guards at Peekskill, "Jewish Life," 3 (Oct. 1949), 5-8.
An account by two of the guards of their experiences at Paul Robeson's concert near Peekskill on September 4, following disorders the previous week. Despite provocations by police, American Legionnaires, and others, the concert went off successfully. (Many in the audience were attacked after the concert, on the ride home.)

G298 GREEN, P. [pseud. for Sergei Gusev]. Internal Situation of the Workers Party of America, "International Press Correspondence," 5 (Oct. 22, 1925), 1121-22.
The representative of the Communist International reviews the factional struggle in the Workers (Communist) Party of America between the Foster and Ruthenberg factions. The split between the two groups has been sharpened by a contest for Party control. The former issue between them, the labor party question, has been replaced by issues such as Party "bolshevization" and reorganization, and the relationship of the Party to the Communist International.

G299 .... Eight Years of Proletarian Dictatorship, "Workers Monthly," 5 (Nov. 1925), 3-4.
An assertion by the Comintern representative to the American Party that the USSR has made a tremendous step forward in the past eight years, while the rest of Europe has rotted in continuous crisis. Enormous progress has been made in the rehabilitation of industry, in educational and cultural institutions, and in the well-being of the peasants. The greatest danger is war against the USSR, which workers of all countries must prevent.

G300 GREEN, William. "More about Brookwood College: Labor's Answer to Its Critics, Brookwood Defenders." Washington, D.C.: American Federation of Labor, 1929. 6 pp.
The president of the AFL answers criticism of its executive council for having advised affiliates not to support Brookwood. He asserts that Brookwood employs one or more communists as instructors and assists dual organizations formed to destroy AFL affiliates.

G301 .... "Report on Communist Propaganda in America." Washington, D.C.: American Federation of Labor, 1934. 86 pp. Ind.
Report submitted by the president of the AFL to the U.S. State Department when the U.S. was considering recognition of the USSR, offering evidence of subversive activity on the part of communists in the U.S. and of the direction of such activity from Moscow. Sections deal with American affiliates of various Moscow "internationals," the Party program of violence and terror, communism and the Comintern as a world revolutionary organization, the Trade Union Unity League and other united fronts, the work of the OGPU in American factories, Party training and propaganda work, financing of the American Party by Moscow, and examples of the Party line in a variety of fields.

G302 .... Our Immediate Obligation, "American Federationist," 48 (July 1941), 20-21.
An editorial by the AFL president, pointing to recent defense strikes under communist leaders as evidence of the political and social revolutionary objective behind the communist invasion of the labor movement. He supports a ban against all communists' participation in AFL unions.

G303 .... Against Outlawing the Communist Party, "New Leader," 30 (May 31, 1947), 4.
The AFL president argues that outlawing the Communist Party would create more difficulties than it would solve. Our most effective weapons against communism are exposure, public disclosure of sources of funds, and a progressive public policy. Stringent legal devices are inconsistent with our Constitution and likely to defeat their purpose.

G304 GREENAWAY, Emerson. Books—Democratic Defense, "Library Journal," 79 (Sept. 1, 1954), 1437-41.
Remarks to the All-American Conference to Combat Communism, held May 22, 1954, in New York City. A universal collection of books, with diversification, is held essential. Books explaining communism must be included; contrary to assertions often made, most public libraries emphasize books exposing communism.

G305 GREENBERG, Hayim. Are the Communists Repenting? "Jewish Frontier," 5 (June 1938), 16-17.
Comment in a labor Zionist publication on the new constitution of the CPUSA, which endorses democracy and makes religious belief no bar to membership. By giving up their advocacy of revolution by a minority and establishment of a dictatorship, the communists in effect become social democrats, but they owe explanations for their past behavior and beliefs before their honesty can be trusted.

G306 .... Why the Reds Went to Jail, "New Leader," 34 (July 16, 1951), 7-9.
A discussion of legal and philosophical grounds for conviction in the Dennis case. Discussion of freedom of speech is irrelevant, since the Communist Party is primarily a conspiratorial organization, whose goal is to act under orders from abroad. The Party is quite big enough for sabotage and fifth column activity, and its propaganda represents a clear and present danger to our nation.

G307 GREENFIELD, E. C. The Housing Question, "Communist," 15 (Sept. 1936), 873-84.
An analysis of the housing shortage in U.S. industrial cities in terms of Engels' argument that this is another way to exploit the workers. When workers are faced with foreclosures they are more willing to accept low wages in order to save their homes. A governmental program of low rent and cheap loans is advocated.

G308 GREER, Thomas H. "American Social Reform Movements: Their Pattern Since 1865." New York: Prentice-Hall, 1949. 313 pp. Bibliog. Ind.
Chapter 6, "Radical Efforts Since World War I," includes discussions of the formation and development of the Communist Party here (pp. 187-93), its policies during World War II (pp. 196-200), and its present and future (pp. 201-6). Quotations from Browder and excerpts from a resolution adopted at the 1945 convention of the CPUSA appear on pp. 208-12.

G309 GREFTHEN, Emil A. "Communism and Christianity: Their Differences and Their Relation to Socialism." Washington, D.C.: Public Affairs Press, 1952. 16 pp.
A distinction by a Lutheran pastor between ethical socialism, which may have something in common with Biblical Christianity, and Marxian socialism or communism, which is an enemy of Christianity with which no compromise can be considered.

G310 GREGORY, Horace. One Writer's Position, "New Masses," 14 (Feb. 12, 1935), 20-21.
Though his political interests have centered in the Party since 1924, Gregory remains out of organizations in order to remain objective. While admitting that works of art change in meaning over time, he disagrees with the view of left cultural groups that esthetic standards undergo daily revision. (See replies by Edwin Seaver in the "New Masses," Feb. 19, and by Meridel Le Sueur on Feb. 26.)

G311 GRESSMAN, Eugene. So You're Having a Loyalty Hearing! "New Republic," 126 (April 14, 1952), 10-13.
Criticism by a Washington attorney of the application of the "reasonable doubt" standard in loyalty probes. The assault on freedom has lowered the morale of the government service, while the concept of loyalty has itself been forgotten in the drive against intellectualism and liberalism.

G312 .... I Decline to Answer. . . "New Republic," 126 (June 9, 1952), 9-11.
A discussion by a Washington, D.C., attorney of the privilege against self-incrimination, in relation to the hearings conducted by the House Committee on Un-American Activities. Witnesses claim the privilege because of the right of privacy, because of the attitude and record of the Committee, and because they wish to protect others from the Committee's inquiries.

G313 GREY, V. The Case of Owen Lattimore, "Fourth International," 14 (Jan.-Feb., 1953), 18-24.
A Trotskyist analysis of the Lattimore case views him as an honest servant of the bourgeoisie, part of the State Department bourgeois left. In his forthcoming perjury trial a whole generation of liberals will be on trial. Lattimore's pragmatic approach to the Chinese revolution included advocacy of a coalition government between Chiang and Mao. Lattimore still hopes to ally Mao's government with Wall Street against the Soviet Union.

G314 GRISWOLD, Erwin N. The Fifth Amendment: An Old and Good Friend, "American Bar Association Journal," 40 (June 1954), 502-5 ff.
Reprint of an address by the dean of the Harvard Law School, who traces the historical background of the privilege against self-incrimination. He argues that the claim of the privilege by a witness in an investigation of communism is not necessarily inconsistent with the witness' loyalty.

G315 .... The Fifth Amendment Today, "Marquette Law Review," 39 (Winter 1955-56), 191-204.
An assertion by the dean of the Harvard University Law School that the Fifth Amendment has helped to maintain the balance of individual liberties against the pressure for national security. Explaining the legal intracacies involved in invoking the privilege, Dean Griswold expresses dissatisfaction with the Supreme Court's rule on waiver of the privilege by witnesses who answer some questions.

G316 GRODZINS, Morton. "The Loyal and the Disloyal: Social Boundaries of Patriotism and Treason." Chicago: University of Chicago Press, 1956. 320 pp. Notes. Ind.
A study of national loyalty, which is found to depend, in a democratic society, on loyalties to family and other primary groups. The state is advised to promote social diversity, and make harmony among loyalties easy, rather than to destroy lesser allegiances, following the model of the totalitarian nations. Among the topics discussed are the attractions of totalitarianism, the pathology of dis-loyalty, the problem of alienation, and the reverse consequences of national loyalty investigations.

G317 ..., and RABINOWITCH, Eugene (eds.). "The Atomic Age: Scientists in National and World Affairs." New York and London: Basic Books, 1963. 616 pp. Ind.
A selection of articles from the "Bulletin of the Atomic Scientists" between 1945 and 1962. Part 3, "Fear" (pp. 349-493), is concerned with Soviet espionage and secrecy in science, and with loyalty and security. Selections deal, among other topics, with Soviet atomic espionage, atomic spy trials, national loyalty, and the cases of J. Robert Oppenheimer and Linus Pauling.

G318 GRONER, Samuel B. State Control of Subversive Activities in the United States, "Federal Bar Journal," 9 (Oct. 1947), 61-94.
A summary of state legislative efforts to control subversive activities. Some statutes bar subversive groups from political activities, whereas others declare specific subversive acts by individuals to be crimes. The statutes are reviewed in the light of Supreme Court decisions.

G319 GROSSMAN, Aubrey. Lawyers on Trial, "Masses & Mainstream," 4 (Aug. 1951), 25-31.
Condemnation of the political character of the contempt conviction of the defense attorneys in the Foley Square trial of the 11 communist leaders. Disbarment of the lawyers, who conscientiously upheld their clients' constitutional rights, is meant to deny legal representation to political, labor, and Negro victims.

G320 GROVE, George [pseud.?]. The Political and Economic Situation in the United States, "International Press Correspondence," 2 (Nov. 13, 1922), 779-83.
A report to the Fourth World Congress of the Communist International, reviewing recent industrial conflicts in the U.S., the movement toward trade union amalgamation, TUEL success in creating left wings within AFL unions, sentiment for a labor party, the growing influence of the Workers' Party, and the foreign and domestic policy of American capitalism. The working class is moving slowly but surely to the left.

G321 GURSTEIN, A. Artist and Class, "New Masses," 8 (Dec. 1932), 8-9.
Marxism holds that the artist is part of the reality that he portrays. However, every perceiving man is a class subject, and every class apprehends reality in its own way. Moreover, there are different degrees of consciousness of reality among various classes at various epochs. The proletariat now possesses the greatest consciousness of reality.

G322 GUSEV, S. The End of Capitalist Stabilization and the Basic Tasks of the British and American Sections of the C.I., "Communist International," 9 (Oct. 15, 1932), 672-82.
A speech at the Twelfth Plenum of the ECCI by a former Comintern representative to the U.S. (under the name of P. Green), who asserts that the basic tasks of the Party in the U.S. and Britain are to isolate social democracy, win over the majority of the proletariat and poor farmers, develop inner-party democracy based on iron discipline, and strengthen the Party's general staff. (Also published in "Communist," Jan. 1933, pp. 33-49.)

G323 ..., and BROWDER, Earl. "Organize Mass Struggle for Social Insurance." New York: Workers Library, 1933. 32 pp.
The major item, an article by Gusev, criticizes Party failures in the struggle for social insurance, holding sectarian tendencies within the Party responsible. He

discusses tactics to give the campaign a militant, mass character. A speech by Browder, also reproduced, distinguishes the Party's social insurance proposal from the "fake" schemes of employers, reformers, and social fascists. (Gusev, also known as P. Green, was a Comintern representative to the American Party. His article also appeared in "Communist International," May 1, 1933, pp. 260-66.)

. . . . See also GREEN and GREEN, P.

G324 GUTHRIE, R. The U.S.A. Prepares for War. "World News & Views" (London), 20 (June 29, 1940), 362-63; (July 6), 378-79; (July 13), 388.
A denunciation of American domestic and foreign policy during the Hitler-Stalin pact period, for preparing to intervene in the "imperialist" war. Attacks on living standards will occur as New Deal measures are curtailed in favor of defense expenditures. Attacks on civil rights are also predicted.

G325 GUTTMANN, Allen, and ZIEGLER, Benjamin Munn (eds.). "Communism, the Courts and the Constitution." Boston: Heath, 1964. 132 pp. Bibliog.
A collection of materials relating to constitutional issues raised by the communist movement in the U.S. and government efforts to suppress it. Included are authoritative statements of the communist position by the Party or by such leading spokesmen at various periods as Charles E. Ruthenberg, Earl Browder, and Gus Hall; excerpts from U.S. Supreme Court decisions applying the Smith and the McCarran Acts; and writings of Irving Kristol, Alan F. Westin, Sidney Hook, Zechariah Chafee, Jr., and Walter Gellhorn on constitutional aspects of issues involving communists.

G326 GWINN, Ralph W. Sweeping Communists from the U.S. Payroll. "National Republic," 42 (May 1954), 1-2.
A Congressman from New York reports approvingly on the housecleaning in the federal service following Eisenhower's directive to weed out every communist and fellow-traveler security risk. Truman, who had not regarded communism in Washington as a threat, had discharged communists only when they were caught in illegal acts.

H

H1   HAALAND, Jasper. "Farmers and the War." New York: Workers Library, n.d. [1940]. 23 pp.
An antiwar appeal to farmers during the period of the Nazi-Soviet pact. Farmers are said to face conscription of their sons for a useless slaughter, to be followed by loss of democratic rights. Farmers are urged to vote for communist candidates in 1940 in protest against Roosevelt-Wall Street war plans.

H2   HACKETT, Francis. Stuffed Shirts and Red Shirts, "Saturday Review of Literature," 13 (April 4, 1936), 3-4 ff.
The communist intellectual is viewed, not as an advocate of an economic system, but as a rebel against the commercial terms of urban life and the business life that has perverted American values. The intellectual really wants to be recognized on his own merits.

H3   HADLEY, Edwin Marshall. "T.N.T." Chicago: Tower Press, 1931. 105 pp. Bibliog.
An alarmist view of the spread of communism in America from the extreme right. The author asserts that schools, colleges, churches, and liberal organizations have all been heavily infiltrated, and that America is seriously threatened by an unholy alliance of parlor pinks, gutter Reds, and anarchists.

H4   HAERLE, Paul R. Constitutional Law—Federal Anti-Subversive Legislation—The Communist Control Act of 1954, "Michigan Law Review," 53 (June 1955), 1153-65.
A discussion of the Communist Control Act of 1954, emphasizing the hectic legislative activity behind this most unusual measure, and some of the legal problems it raises. It suffers from lack of careful and mature legislative consideration and meaningful draftsmanship. It may be allowed to die on the statute books.

H5   HAESSLER, Gertrude. How Not to Apply the Open Letter, "Communist," 13 (March 1934), 261-71.
Criticism of the views of J. A. Zack (in "How to Apply the Open Letter," in "Communist," Feb. 1934), for speaking first as a union organizer and second as a Party member, and for subordinating Party shop papers to trade union newspapers.

H6   HALDEN, Joseph M. On the 1952 Steel Strike, "Political Affairs," 31 (Nov. 1952), 36-45.
The steel workers' gains in the 1952 strike included a 21-cent package raise and six paid holidays. All their demands were not met because right-wing and reformist labor leaders support the war-making policies of the ruling class.

H7   HALE, William Harlan. Radicals in Straight-Jackets, "Saturday Review of Literature," 10 (June 9, 1934), 737-39.
Using Max Eastman's book, "Artists in Uniform," as a supporting text, the author sees in communism an attempt to deny intellect and art their independent existence. Intellectuals embrace this faith to escape from doubts, artistic skepticism, and personal difficulties. The new totalitarian doctrine curbs the independence and integrity of intellectuals.

H8   HALL, Gus. Improve the Marxist-Leninist Content and Methods in Party Activity, "Political Affairs," 28 (April 1949), 35-47.
The reactionaries are trying to destroy the Party by encouraging the growth of Party factions, by jailing communists, and by calling the Party a foreign agent. The Party has repelled these attacks because it has remained true to Marxist-Leninist theory, even though some members have succumbed to the right-opportunist error of being satisfied with capitalist reforms.

H9   . . . . Thirty Years of Struggle for a Steelworkers' Union and a Working-Class Ideology, "Political Affairs," 28 (Sept. 1949), 54-70.
A description of the Party's role in the unionization of the steel industry from the great steel strike of 1919, through the depression years, to the organization of the CIO's United Steelworkers of America in 1936-37. The present tasks of the Party in the industry are outlined, in view of the reactionary policies adopted by the union from 1937 on.

H10   . . . . United Front Is the Key to Victory over Reaction, "Political Affairs," 28 (Dec. 1949), 18-34.
A letter written in prison, from the chairman of the Party in Ohio to leading Party members of that state. Calling for a bolder and broader united front policy, Hall examines the reasons for weaknesses in applying the united front. He urges a united front of the working class from below and unity of the Negro people. The Party must be flexible on details, not tailor-make a program or hog the leadership.

H11   . . . . "Which Way for Young Americans?" New York: Challenge (Organ of the National Organizing Conference for a Labor Youth League), 1950. 30 pp.
A national leader of the Party compliments the Labor Youth League, the youth organization of the Party, for initiating active mass resistance to war and fascism, despite its small numbers. Resistance to the Korean War is urged, and also to the "big lie" that the Soviet Union is an imperialist aggressor.

H12   . . . . The Coal Miners Lead the Way, "Political Affairs," 29 (March 1950), 18-31.
A survey of the chronically sick coal industry from 1933 to 1950, including working conditions, wages, unionization, and strikes, with particular attention to the mining strike of 1949-50. This long struggle has developed a political character, exposed the role of the state as an employers' instrument, and become the vehicle of a broad rank-and-file movement.

H13   . . . . Through United-Front Struggle to the Victory of Peace! "Political Affairs," 29 (May 1950), 14-40.

A report to the plenum of the national committee, CPUSA, March 23-25, 1950, calling the issue of peace the main concern of the people. The imperialist drive of Wall Street to conquer the world must be defeated. Jingoistic warmongering has become common in American life, and has been accompanied by steps toward fascism at home. The peace movement needs a united, working class core.

H14   HALL, Gus. Raise the Struggle for Peace to New Heights, "Political Affairs," 29 (July 1950), 21-31.
A report to the national committee, CPUSA, May 17, 1950, asserting that the struggle for peace is central in all Party activities. Despite the new tempo of the war drive, peace can be won through all-out mobilization of the peace forces of all strata of the population. The campaign must be mobilized around the world-peace appeal initiated at Stockholm by the World Peace Congress.

H15   . . . . For Marxist-Leninist Leadership in the National Groups Field, "Political Affairs," 29 (Sept. 1950), 30-36.
Summary remarks at a Party conference of leaders in national group work, July 15-16, 1950. Hall calls for more qualified leadership in national group cadres, and warns against viewing national groups as a passing phenomenon rather than as an integral part of the American working class.

H16   . . . . The Present Situation and the Tasks of Our Party, "Political Affairs," 29 (Oct. 1950), 1-29.
A report to the plenary session of the national committee, CPUSA, September 19-20, 1950, asserting that World War III can still be halted and fascism stopped. The war economy, which cannot overcome the cyclical economic crisis, will lower the living standards of the working class and of farmers and other sections of the middle class. The Party's main issues are peace, democratic rights, Negro rights, and economic demands.

H17   . . . . "Marxism and Negro Liberation." New York: New Century, 1951. 24 pp.
Text of a speech by the national secretary of the Party in February 1951 in celebration of Negro History Week. Paying tribute to the Negro people's militancy and skill in the struggle against great odds, he points out that they still suffer hardships resulting from national oppression, and asserts that Negroes and the working class must oppose their common oppressor, capitalism.

H18   . . . . "Peace Can be Won! Report to the 15th Convention, Communist Party, U.S.A." New York: New Century, 1951. 79 pp.
The text of the political report by the Party's national secretary to the national convention held in New York, December 28-31, 1950. Sections deal with the drive toward fascism and war, world realities today, independent political action, correct tactics, the work of the Party, and political perspectives. Special attention is given the working class, the Negro people, poor farmers, youth, and women, and emphasis is placed on the fight for peace.

H19   . . . . On Independent Political Action, "Political Affairs," 30 (Dec. 1951), 33-41.
A section of Hall's political report to the Party's fifteenth national convention in December 1950, published while he was in prison for contempt of court. Viewing electoral activities as an expression of the united front, of the coalition struggle for peace, democratic rights, and workers' living standards, Hall forecasts the appearance of an independent peace ticket in 1952.

H20   . . . . The Importance of Communist Cadres, "Political Affairs," 31 (Jan. 1952), 38-48.

A speech delivered at a meeting of Party activists in Cleveland, June 13, 1951, analyzing the organizational weaknesses of Party cadres and the inadequacies of Party work in the basic industries. The national secretary of the Party protests the terror against communist workers in shops and unions, and calls for Party leadership in economic struggles.

H21   . . . . "The Eleventh Hour—Defeat the New Fascist Threat!" New York: New Currents, 1964. 22 pp.
A report to a national conference of Party leaders following Goldwater's nomination for the Presidency by the Republicans. The aim of the people's democratic forces must be a smashing defeat for this ultra-right reaction. Nevertheless, because of Johnson's aggression in Asia and Cuba and his inadequate program against poverty, the communists do not endorse him.

H22   HALL, Rob Fowler. The Southern Conference for Human Welfare, "Communist," 18 (Jan. 1939), 57-65.
The Party secretary in Alabama reviews the inter-racial Conference, which seeks to replace the reactionary philosophy of the South with progressive movements aimed at complete equality for Negroes and greater prosperity for the South. The Party encourages action based on the Conference objectives.

H23   . . . . New Forces for Peace and Democracy in the South, "Communist," 19 (Aug. 1940), 690-706.
The Southern ruling class was twice threatened by uprisings of united whites and Negroes, following the Civil War and in the populist period. Both times the ruling class regained power because the leaders of the masses were too vacillating. Now, when the masses of whites and Negroes are again becoming active, they must be mobilized behind communist leadership.

H24   . . . . Stop American Intervention in China! "Political Affairs," 24 (Dec. 1945), 1059-68.
An attack on continued American military aid to the dictator, Chiang Kai-shek. The aid is being used for an attack on the popular, democratic forces of China. It is part of the reactionary drive of American imperialism to defeat the Chinese communists, achieve world domination, and support an anti-Soviet bulwark in China.

H25   . . . . Labor in the 1946 Primaries, "Political Affairs," 25 (Aug. 1946), 704-12.
The main objective for labor in the 1946 primaries is to lay the basis for a third party by supporting independent progressive candidates whenever possible. No alliance should be made with Truman, who has turned away from Roosevelt's policies. The Republican strategy of pretending to be liberal must be counteracted.

H26   . . . . "The Record of Truman's 81st Congress." New York: New Century, 1949. 23 pp.
A review of the betrayals and broken promises of Truman's 81st Congress by the Washington correspondent of the "Daily Worker," emphasizing the failure to repeal the Taft-Hartley Act, and the defeat of civil rights and rent control legislation. Failures in the domestic program are contrasted with the passage of cold war measures.

H27   . . . . "FEPC: How It Was Betrayed, How It Can Be Saved." New York: New Century, 1950. 15 pp.
The Washington correspondent of the "Daily Worker" reviews the maneuvers and betrayals in Washington to prevent FEPC from becoming law because it is useful as a campaign issue and because it interferes with the Truman-Wall Street war plans. Both major parties, including Truman, are responsible.

H28 HALLGREN, Mauritz A. "Seeds of Revolt." New York: Knopf, 1933. 369 pp. Ind.
In this study of American life during the depression, the author touches on the subject of communists and communism among the miners, in steel, in auto, and among the unemployed. He finds no group in the country actively preparing for revolution, and analyzes (pp. 334-40) why the communists do not command more support.

H29 HALONEN, George. The Cooperative Movement in America, "Workers Monthly," 5 (Jan. 1926), 129-30.
Communists should help build the cooperative movement, not by defending the interests of "consumers," but by defending the working class and fighting with it to abolish classes. Through practical and responsible work communists can gain the confidence of the masses, drawing the workers into a struggle against capitalism.

H30 .... "Why Cooperation: Consumers' Cooperative Movements in U.S.A." New York: Workers Library, 1928. 31 pp.
An argument that the cooperative movement can teach workers to seek relief from the evils of capitalism through united working class action, provided that cooperatives are an integral part of the labor movement and not neutral on issues other than purely cooperative ones, as urged by some of its middle class theorists.

H31 HALPENNY, Marie. Books on Trial in Texas, "Library Journal," 78 (July 1953), 1179-84.
A review of the successful battle to resist the removal of books by procommunist authors from San Antonio libraries, or the stamping of these books. A group opposed to censorship pointed out that democracy depends on expression of diverse opinions, whereas no totalitarian government allows it.

H32 HALPER, Albert. "Union Square." New York: Viking, 1933. 378 pp.
Glimpses of life around Union Square, written as an impressionistic novel. The author's characters—a radical poet, a warehouse worker, a business man and his mistress, a communist artist—are drawn together in the story of a communist riot on the Square and a tenement fire.

H33 HAMBURG, Carl. Communism, Competence, and the College, "Ethics," 64 (Jan. 1954), 126-31.
Party members, whose political commitments are primary to teaching responsibilities, are security risks who should not be given teaching posts. Those who are loyal to our political institutions, even though they differ from the majority, are competent to teach noncontroversial subject matter. The Marxist position should be represented in higher institutions in balanced departments.

H34 HAMILTON, Iris. Shoot to Kill! on the Coast, "New Masses," 12 (July 17, 1934), 10-12.
An account of the marine transport strike in San Francisco and of orders to the militia to shoot at strikers to kill. The employers are using every classic device to break the strike, including the red scare. Their best weapon is the effort of AFL leaders to split the coastwise marine and longshore rank-and-file unity.

H35 .... General Strike, "New Masses," 12 (July 24, 1934), 9-11.
An account of the developing general strike movement in San Francisco, growing out of the West Coast marine transport strike. The employers have thrown everything into the battle, while government mediators seek only to break the strike. Labor's worst enemy, and the employers'

most powerful ally, is the reactionary AFL leadership. Every charge, including that of being Reds, is made against leaders who stick by the men.

H36 HAMILTON, John W. "I Was Branded with the Number 666." St. Louis: Christian Nationalist Crusade, 1948. 31 pp.
An account of communism in Boston, where the author claims he was encouraged by teachers and professors to join the Young Communist League, which he found to be dominated by Jews.

H37 HANES, John W., Jr. Passports to Trouble, "American Legion Magazine," 67 (Sept. 1959), 14-15 ff.
The administrator of the Bureau of Security and Consular Affairs of the State Department criticizes present law under which passports are granted to communists, aiding their travel to foreign countries where they participate in and aid Soviet ventures. We need legislation denying passports to hard-core supporters of the communist movement.

H38 HANIGHEN, Frank C. Foreign Political Movements in the U.S., "Foreign Affairs," 16 (Oct. 1937), 1-20.
A section on the Communist Party (pp. 1-5) deals with the American Party's formal connection with Moscow through the Third International and describes its consistent adherence to Russian policy.

H39 HANNA, Paul W. The Failure of the Martens Inquiry, "Nation," 110 (March 27, 1920), 396-98.
Criticism of the Senate committee investigating Russian propaganda in America for its indecisive proceedings with regard to Ludwig C. A. K. Martens, a Moscow emissary and propagandist.

H40 HANSON, Ole. "Americanism versus Bolshevism." Garden City, N.Y.: Doubleday, Page, 1920. 299 pp.
The author, mayor of Seattle during that city's general strike in February 1919, describes the strike as an attempted revolution by IWW "Bolshevists." He sketches the history of syndicalism in France, Germany, England, Russia, and the U.S., identifying Bolshevism with syndicalism and with the IWW, and viewing the syndicalist, whether of the Bolshevik or the IWW variety, as a revolutionary criminal. He calls syndicalism the class government of the unfit, the scum, and the failures. His program includes restriction of immigration, teaching of Americanism in all schools, improvement of working conditions, and blacklisting of Reds.

H41 HARAP, Louis. Sartre and Existentialism, "New Masses," 62 (Dec. 31, 1946), 8-11; (Jan. 7, 1947), 21-22.
An account of the development of existentialism, a reactionary philosophy. By interpreting the world in subjective terms, it denies class society and the possibility of social change. Sartre completely misunderstands Marxism. The true revolutionary locates struggles in objective society, with Marxism his most important tool.

H42 .... X-Ray on "Commentary," "Jewish Life," 1 (July 1947), 19-24.
An attack on "Commentary," monthly publication of the American Jewish Committee, as a haven for Trotskyists, social democrats, and other anticommunist "leftists" and a venture in open Red-baiting. The AJC financial supporters are economic royalists more influenced by their class and economic interests than by their care for the Jewish people.

H43   HARAP, Louis. American Jewish Committee as Red-Baiter, "Jewish Life," 2 (June 1948), 23-26.
An attack on the American Jewish Committee for its anti-labor position, for its campaign against communists and progressives in American Jewish life, and for its employment of a staff of Red-baiters obsessed with hatred for progressivism and the USSR. The Jewish community is urged to reject the AJC, the agency among the Jews of the big bourgeoisie, as an appeaser of fascism.

H44   .... "Social Roots of the Arts." New York: International Publishers, 1949. 192 pp. Ref. notes. Ind.
A communist interpretation of arts and society by the editor of the Party magazine, "Jewish Life." The author emphasizes the superiority of socialist realism in art and music. He asserts that all art has a class orientation, that the creation of art is a social act, and that the Marxist artist intends that his influence on society shall be exerted in full consciousness. The author explains how folk art and mass art fall into this frame of reference, and concludes that under socialism "art for art's sake" is replaced by art for the people's sake, as in the Soviet Union today.

H45   .... Program on the Left, "Jewish Life," 4 (March 1950), 23-26.
The final article in a series on the preparedness of American Jewry to meet the threat of fascism in the U.S. Much of the liberal and trade union leadership in the Jewish community, including Americans for Democratic Action, the American Jewish Congress, the New York "Post," and the "Forward"-Jewish Labor Committee group is attacked for its Red-baiting and its role in putting over the cold war hysteria.

H46   .... Comniphobia and the AJ Committee, "Jewish Life," 5 (Dec. 1950), 6-9.
An attack on the American Jewish Committee for deciding that the critical task of the Jewish community is to fight communism, not a threatening fascism. By its plunge into anticommunist hysteria, AJC is leading the Jews down the suicidal path taken by German Jewry.

H47   .... "The Truth about the Prague Trial." New York: Jewish Life, 1953. 31 pp.
A review of the trial of the Rudolf Slansky group in Czechoslovakia in November 1952, written by the managing editor of "Jewish Life," communist Jewish publication here. Denying that anti-Semitism was a factor, he points to confessions that the defendants were involved with U.S. intelligence in a conspiracy against the Czechoslovak people's democracy. (First published in "Jewish Life," in Jan. 1953.)

H48   .... Election Outlook, "Jewish Life," 10 (Oct. 1956), 3-6 ff.
An assertion that the Democratic nominees, Stevenson and Kefauver, can win in November, despite the weak civil rights and the muddy cold war planks in their party's platform. In the absence of a significant third party this year, most Jews will vote Democratic. Progressive congressional and local candidates should be supported regardless of party label.

H49   HARBISON, William. Masterpiece in Double-Talk, "America," 81 (July 16, 1949), 440-41.
An analysis of a 30,000 word defense statement at the Smith Act trial, attributed to William Z. Foster, which defense counsel tried to introduce as evidence. The statement is a masterpiece in double-talk, in which the author expresses illegal sentiments in legal, "Aesopian" language.

H50   HARD, William. Eyes Left! "Nation," 116 (May 16, 1923), 568-69.
An assertion that William Z. Foster, though he believes in the dictatorship of the proletariat, does not really believe in violence and does not belong to the Communist Party, the Workers' Party, or any other political party seeking a proletarian dictatorship. He plans a lot of plain union organizing for years ahead.

H51   .. ., and BLACHLY, Frederick J. O. Communists Invited Out, "Reader's Digest," 49 (Nov. 1946), 17-21.
A description of increasing rebellion against communist influence in various CIO unions. Communist influence is declining in the maritime, shipbuilding, auto, and newspaper writers' unions. Rank-and-file revolts against communists are occurring within Mine, Mill and UE. Philip Murray is nearing the end of his patience with them.

H52   HARDMAN, J. B. S. (ed.). "American Labor Dynamics in the Light of Post-War Developments." New York: Harcourt, Brace, 1928. 432 pp. App. Ind.
A study of the American labor scene in the decade following World War I. Chapter 1, "Postscripts to Ten Years of Labor Movement" (pp. 5-36), touches on the role of the communists in the issues of labor-party and craft-union amalgamation, and analyzes the activity of the left-wing Trade Union Educational League, with particular attention to the communist opposition in the needle trades unions.

H53   HARDMAN, J. B. S. Communism in America, "New Republic," 64 (Aug. 27, 1930), 34-37; (Sept. 3), 63-67; (Sept. 10), 94-97; (Sept. 17), 120-22.
Discussion of the size and strength of the Party, communist influence in the labor movement, the Party's relationship to the Communist International, and factions and personalities in the CPUSA. The Party's influence is found to be declining, largely because of its indifference to American realities. After initial successes in the trade union field, the TUEL was turned into a subcommittee of the Party; the communist dual unions have been complete failures. The Party takes orders from Moscow in blind obedience. In theory indivisible, in practice the movement is torn by violent factionalism.

.... See also SALUTSKY, J. B.

H54   HARDY, Jack [pseud. for Dale Zysman]. "The Clothing Workers: A Study of the Conditions and Struggles in the Needle Trades." New York: International Publishers, 1935. 256 pp.
A procommunist account of unionization in the needle trades. The author traces the history of organization in the clothing industry, giving the left-wing version of the right-left struggle within the ILGWU during the 1920's. He traces the development of the Amalgamated Clothing Workers, and praises the left-wing leadership of the Furriers. All socialist, Lovestoneite, and AFL unions are criticized for their reactionary policies, while the Needle Trades Workers Industrial Union of the Trade Union Unity League is pictured as the only true workers' organization.

H55   .... "The First American Revolution." New York: International Publishers, 1937. 160 pp. Ref. notes. App. Bibliog. Ind.
A communist interpretation of the American Revolution, emphasizing its inevitability and the importance of the masses in bringing it about and carrying it to a successful conclusion. The underprivileged masses, caught in the oppressions of class society, sought to open opportunities through revolt. They created a revolutionary tradition for the working class of today, when the productive forces created by capitalism in turn choke further progress.

H56 HARDY, Jack. Reds Bore into Communications, "National Republic," 34 (Jan. 1947), 3-4 ff.
An account of 20 years of Muscovite infiltration in American communications. Communists won control of the American Radio Telegraphists Association in the mid-1930's, using it and controlled locals of the Commercial Telegraphers Union to form the American Communications Association. Though its membership is small, the ACA and other communist-controlled unions can apply pressure on communications.

H57 .... Smoking Out the Reds in Washington State, "National Republic," 35 (March 1948), 15-17 ff.
An account of hearings by the State Legislature of Washington on subversive activities in the Northwest. Ten members of the legislature were alleged to have constituted a CP fraction within that body. Party activities at the University, in unions, and among old-age pensioners are described.

H58 HARGIS, Billy James. The History of American Communist Fronts, "American Mercury," 87 (Dec. 1958), 26-33.
Communist fronts are as essential to the communist conspiracy as are their schools, cells, and press. Far from being failures, Party fronts have had notable successes, as in calling strikes during the Korean War, aiding the communist takeover of China, and opposing McCarthyism. A partial list of front groups is included.

H59 .... "Communist America: Must It Be?" Tulsa, Okla.: Christian Crusade, 1960. 185 pp.
An account of communist influence in the U.S. by a right-wing Protestant minister, founder of Christian Crusade, who believes that the current U.S. government is heavily procommunist. Chapters deal with communist influence in the press, schools, and labor unions, and communist exploitation of the race issue. The officers of the National Council of Churches are attacked for communist front activities.

H60 .... "The Facts about Communism and Our Churches." Tulsa, Okla.: Christian Crusade, 1962. 252 pp. Notes. Ind.
A Protestant fundamentalist view of the National and World Councils of Churches, and American churches affiliated with the National Council of Churches, as infiltrated by communists. The record of participation by clergymen in communist peace front organizations is reviewed, as is the effort to discredit the House Committee on Un-American Activities and other government committees investigating communism. There are signs of awakening in the churches, which should be in the forefront of the fight against communism.

H61 .... "The Real Extremists—The Far Left." Tulsa, Okla.: Christian Crusade, 1964. 288 pp.
A report on the communist movement in the U.S. by a right-wing fundamentalist, who believes that the entire left-wing movement is of the devil, and that communism internally was responsible for the assassination of President John F. Kennedy. Chapters deal with the history of the Communist Party in the U.S., communist fronts here, fascist allies of the communists, the "far left" press (in which the author includes "Harper's Magazine" and the Washington "Post"), Walter Reuther as the star of the far left, men and movements of the far left, and manipulations of public opinion by it.

H62 HARKNESS, Richard and Gladys. How about Those Security Cases? "Reader's Digest," 67 (Sept. 1955), 202-14; (Nov.), 136-42. Reprinted in part in "U.S. News & World Report," 39 (Nov. 25, 1955), 77-84.
An examination of cases under the Eisenhower security program, showing the use the communists can make of sexual perversions and other weaknesses of government employees. Laxity in the Truman Administration's loyalty program is the cause of current security probes. A uniform and fair code of rights for government employees should be developed.

H63 HARMON, James. Flood Control, "Communist," 16 (June 1937), 569-76.
Criticism of the present flood control and relief programs, with a plea for action by the federal government to control floods and conserve soil. Though TVA thus far has merely created rural refugees, it can do much good if it overcomes the opposition of the power trust and brings cheap power to the Tennessee Valley.

H64 HARPER, Fowler V. "How is Your Americanism?" New York: National Council of the Arts, Sciences and Professions, 1951. 9 pp.
An address at a "Restore Free Speech" rally sponsored by the National Council by a professor of law at Yale, who asserts that the freedoms guaranteed by our founding fathers were unrestricted. Today we are abandoning our tradition of freedom, replacing it with a false and vile "Americanism." We must protest against such abandonment of our political faith.

H65 .... Loyalty and Lawyers, "Lawyers Guild Review," 11 (Fall 1951), 205-9.
A Yale law professor sees the decision in the Dennis case as the worst blow to democracy since the Dred Scott decision. This is true also of the Sachar contempt case, also a conviction for conspiracy, which intimidates lawyers from representing alleged communists, denying them, in effect, their right to a fair trial.

H66 .... The Crusade against Bridges, "Nation," 174 (April 5, 1952), 323-26.
A sympathetic biographical sketch of Harry Bridges by a Yale University professor of law, who reviews the government's six attempts to deport Bridges. Since he led the 1934 longshoremen's strike Bridges has been one of the most effective labor leaders in the U.S. Repeated investigations have failed to show that he was ever a member of or affiliated with the Party.

H67 HARPER, Lawrence A. Shall the Professors Sign? "Pacific Spectator," 4 (Winter 1950), 21-29.
A University of California professor tells the history of the University's loyalty oath controversy and outlines the issues. Some members of the faculty believe that the oath threatens academic freedom, is unconstitutional and un-American, and would not eliminate subversive elements.

H68 .... Legislative Investigation of Un-American Activities; Exhibit A: The Tenney Committee, "California Law Review," 39 (Dec. 1951), 502-24.
Approval of Edward Barrett's book, "The Tenney Committee," by a professor of American history at the University of California. After reviewing the book, the author concludes that the legislative investigating committee is not the most effective way to deal with subversives. Procedural reforms are needed to prevent abuse of power by such committees.

H69 HARPMAN, Bill. Communists Plan Tie-Up of U.S. War Industries through Control of National Labor Board, "New Leader," 23 (Sept. 28, 1940), 1 ff.
An assertion that the communists, organized around National Labor Relations Board member Edwin S. Smith and NLRB secretary Nathan Witt, are pushing for control

of the Board, the key to control of America's war industries. The issue is crucial in view of a vacancy in the Board chairmanship, and communist plans to sabotage our defense.

H70　HARRINGTON, Donald. Wallace and Liberalism, "New Leader," 31 (May 8, 1948), 3 ff.
An assertion that, while Henry A. Wallace has wide support among liberals, his organization is controlled by communists and their fellow-travelers. His platform of peace is really appeasement, while prosperity is wishful thinking. The communists behind Wallace are aiming at 1952.

H71　HARRINGTON, Michael. Rights of the Guilty, "Commonweal," 58 (Aug. 7, 1953), 435-37.
Condemnation of the legal broadening of notions of conspiracy, as exemplified in the Smith Act, and also of the broadening of the view of the conspirator by government agencies and the public. These extensions of the conspiracy doctrine undermine the rights of the innocent as well as of the guilty.

H72　.... The Committee for Cultural Freedom, "Dissent," 2 (Spring 1955), 113-22.
Criticism of the American Committee for Cultural Freedom for its failure to defend the civil liberties of Stalinists. This makes the defense of the civil liberties of anti-Stalinist radicals and liberals more difficult.

H73　.... New Communist Line, "Commonweal," 64 (July 13, 1956), 363-65.
While the CPUSA has not changed in any fundamental way since the Twentieth Party Congress of the Soviet Union, changes which have occurred in Stalinist institutions will make a return to the popular front line all the more seductive. Since communists will not be easily distinguished as such, liberals must put forward a democratic program of opposition to Stalinism.

H74　.... Communism after Hungary: In the United States, "Commonweal," 65 (Feb. 1, 1957), 455-57.
The Soviet Twentieth Party Congress, the Polish uprising, and the Hungarian revolution have split the CPUSA, with one wing under Foster loyal to Moscow and another led by John Gates favoring independence. A genuine democratic political program as an alternative can bring dissident communists of the Gates leaning to the support of democracy. (See further comment by Harrington in "Commonweal," March 8, 1957.)

H75　HARRIS, Herbert. Politics and the C.I.O., "Nation," 149 (Nov. 18, 1939), 543-46.
A discussion of changes made by John L. Lewis to reduce communist influence in the CIO, such as the demotion of Harry Bridges from his post as West Coast director. Other Party-line followers are being removed, while promotions go to staunch anti-Stalinists. Meanwhile the number of Party supporters is being reduced by the Hitler-Stalin pact.

H76　.... "Labor's Civil War." New York: Knopf, 1940. 298 pp. Ind.
An analysis of the AFL-CIO split, including the problem of communists in the CIO. Communist influence there is traced to Lewis' desire in 1936 to obtain organizing help from any quarter. The special Stalinist menace is not that they want to overthrow the government, but that they are part of the foreign apparatus of the Russian government, subordinating CIO interest to that of the Soviet Union.

H77　HARRIS, Lem. "Meat—A National Scandal." New York: New Century, 1946. 23 pp.

An indictment of the meat trust for attempting to blackmail the American people by artifically created meat shortages. The packinghouse workers, through strikes, are combatting the meat monopoly. The question, the answer to which will determine our destiny, is whether the packing monopoly or the people will control the meat industry.

H78　.... A Program for Agriculture, "Political Affairs," 26 (Oct. 1947), 910-22.
A program submitted to the Committee on Agriculture, House of Representatives, on behalf of the Party's Farm Commission. Asserting that every farm home faces the threat of renewed economic crisis and prolonged depression, the program calls for a world food policy, a floor under agricultural income, legal protection for farm workers, a floor under consumption, and financing by reduction of arms expenditures.

H79　...., and DIGBY, Robert. Farm Cooperatives and the Trusts, "Political Affairs," 27 (Jan. 1948), 65-75.
A discussion of the attack by the trusts, led by the National Association of Manufacturers, on independent farm cooperatives. Suggestions on ways to combat this attack are offered. Major cooperatives and their national associations have long served as agents of the NAM, examples of Big Business in overalls. Farmers must be active in coops, shaping their policies.

H80　.... Toward a Democratic Land Program for the South, "Political Affairs," 28 (March 1949), 87-96.
A series of proposals to break up the plantation system of land ownership in the South and redistribute the land among the Negroes and whites who work it. A progressive coalition, led by labor and including the Communist Party, can achieve the economic program that the South needs.

H81　HARRIS, Robert J. The Impact of the Cold War upon Civil Liberties, "Journal of Politics," 18 (Feb. 1956), 3-16.
An assertion that basic civil liberties are endangered as a result of the cold war, to which the executive branch of government has responded with loyalty and security programs and other measures. The Supreme Court has interposed few constitutional obstacles to antisubversive legislation, loyalty and security programs, and legislative investigations.

H82　HARRISON, Charles Yale. An Open Letter to Waldo Frank, "Modern Monthly," 10 (Jan. 1937), 6-8.
Criticism of Waldo Frank, chairman of the First American Writers' Congress and acknowledged leader of Stalinist literary forces in the U.S., for continuing to support the communist movement, despite the evils of Stalin's regime, climaxed by the framed Moscow trials.

H83　.... Crawl, Comrades, Crawl Till the Line Changeth Again, "New Leader," 21 (Oct. 29, 1938), 4 ff.
Comment on repudiation by the American Labor Party of the Communist Party's offer of electoral support. Ridiculing the communists' current efforts at respectability, the author asserts that memories of the Party's manipulation of working-class organizations during its more "revolutionary" periods will not be obliterated.

H84　.... Red Maritime Union Plans Sabotage of U.S. Defense, "New Leader," 23 (July 27, 1940), 1 ff.
An assertion that the U.S. merchant marine, through control of its personnel by the National Maritime Union, has become part of the Comintern's espionage and sabotage

apparatus here. The head of the NMU has boasted of his power to sabotage the movement of American war equipment. The communist background of NMU leaders is listed.

H85   HARRISON, Charles Yale. Maritime Union Works with Gestapo, "New Leader," 23 (Aug. 3, 1940), 1 ff.
An assertion that German-born, pro-Nazi members of the National Maritime Union work in loyal cooperation with the communist leaders of the union. Communists and Nazis within the NMU have collaborated since the signing of the Hitler-Stalin pact. Government agents are investigating a possible espionage link between NMU officials and Gestapo headquarters in Berlin.

H86   .... Stalin's American Merchant Marine, "American Mercury," 51 (Oct. 1940), 135-44.
An account of the Party campaign over the past 15 years to control the waterfront and the merchant marine, with a denunciation of the communist domination of three waterfront or merchant marine unions. While the Nazi-Soviet pact is in force, this domination could make the U.S. powerless before the dictatorships. The communists seek a stranglehold on American industry and defense.

H87   HARRY BRIDGES DEFENSE COMMITTEE. "The Bridges Exile Bill: A Blow at Labor." San Francisco: The Committee, n.d. [1940]. 8 pp.
A denunciation of the bill to deport Bridges, passed by the House of Representatives on June 13, 1940. Bridges, who has not been proved to be a member of the Party, is not a citizen because of the error of an immigration clerk. Employers are trying, by this underhanded blow at Bridges, to damage the longshoremen's union that he leads.

H88   HARRY BRIDGES VICTORY COMMITTEE. "Biddle's Private War against Harry Bridges." San Francisco: The Committee, n.d. [1945]. 14 unnumbered pp.
A popularly written pamphlet attacking Attorney General Biddle for ordering Bridges' deportation at a time when the Bridges plan for maximum production in maritime transport was helping to win the war. Bridges is now classed as a dangerous Red because of his leadership of waterfront labor struggles.

H89   .... "The Harry Bridges' Case." Introd. by Philip Murray. San Francisco: The Committee, 1945. 16 pp.
The dissenting opinion of two judges of the Circuit Court of Appeals for the Ninth Circuit in the Bridges deportation case, in which the majority of the court upheld the Attorney General's order deporting Bridges. In his introduction, Murray tells of the long efforts to deport Bridges, condemning the court's verdict as resting upon hatred and prejudice.

H90   HART, Fred. Stalinism and Negro Intellectuals, "Fourth International," 11 (May-June 1950), 70-74.
An assertion that Negroes are attracted to the Stalinist version of Marxism because it is the only Marxism they know. Negro intellectuals, however, are at fault for allowing Stalinists to claim falsely that they lead the Negro struggle. (Part of a special issue of this Trotskyist journal on "Marxism and the Negro.")

H91   HART, Harold. "The Cry for Peace." New York: Workers Library, 1936. 31 pp.
A pamphlet of the popular-front period, calling for the unity of workers and all friends of peace to prevent war. The danger of war is in German fascism; following his

war against the German people, Hitler, besides endangering all neighboring countries, is preparing a war against the Soviet Union. The USSR, which under socialism has achieved freedom and human dignity, is hailed as the greatest power for peace in the world.

H92   HART, Henry (ed.). "Proceedings of the First American Writers Congress, Held April 26-28, 1935." New York: International Publishers, 1935. 192 pp.
The major papers at the Congress that created the League of American Writers, with a summary of the discussion and proceedings. Held while the Party followed a militant line, the Congress emphasized proletarian literature and revolutionary literary efforts. Among the contributors were Harry F. Ward, Moissaye J. Olgin, Joseph Freeman, Malcolm Cowley, Earl Browder, Waldo Frank, Jack Conroy, Granville Hicks, Edwin Seaver, James T. Farrell, and Langston Hughes.

H93   .... "The Writer in a Changing World." New York: Equinox Cooperative Press for the American Writers Congress, 1937. 256 pp.
Proceedings of the Second American Writers Congress, whose popular-front orientation of opposition to fascism contrasts sharply with the revolutionary fervor of the first Congress. Included are 16 papers by writers such as Joseph Freeman, Newton Arvin, Malcolm Cowley, Earl Browder, Archibald MacLeish, Ernest Hemingway, Donald Ogden Stewart, Albert Rhys Williams, and Granville Hicks. The proceedings of the Congress, with a paraphrase of the extemporaneous speeches, are reproduced. (No mention is made of the furor created by a group of anti-Stalinists who protested against Party control of the Congress.)

H94   HART, Henry. The Tragedy of Literary Waste, "New Masses," 24 (June 29, 1937), 19-20.
The irrational process of publishing under capitalism exposes writer, publisher, and bookseller alike to the evils of economics of scarcity. Writers must join in an organization like the League of American Writers to combat the odds against publication of the truth.

H95   HART, Hornell. "McCarthy versus the State Department." 2d rev. ed., Durham, N.C.: The author, 1952. 34 pp. Notes.
A review of McCarthy's charges of communist influence in the State Department by a professor of sociology at Duke University, who concludes that almost all of McCarthy's charges have been proved false. McCarthy's activities have contributed little or nothing to discovering or weeding out communists in government.

H96   .... McCarthyism versus Democracy, "New Republic," 126 (Feb. 25, 1952), 10-13.
An analysis by a professor of sociology at Duke University of the political career and methods of Senator McCarthy, who responds to factual accusations by invectives, threats, and other improper actions. Though we have had cause for concern in communist infiltration of the State Department in 1937-38, the cleansing process was completed, except for one doubtful case, before McCarthy started his campaign.

H97   HARTFORD, Jerry. U.A.W., Key Union in C.I.O., Swings away from Reds, "Labor Leader" (Association of Catholic Trade Unionists), 10 (Nov. 17, 1947), 1-3.
An account of the 1947 convention of the United Automobile Workers, at which Walter Reuther and a group of anticommunists won complete control of the union.

H98   HARTMAN, Fanny. Problems of Labor in Massachusetts, "Communist," 22 (Nov. 1943), 1051-56.
A discussion of the belated change to a war economy in Massachusetts, and of the political work to be undertaken by the labor movement there in behalf of the war effort.

H99   HARTMAN, Hershl. The Trial on Columbus Avenue, "Jewish Life," 4 (Sept. 1950), 16-19.
An account of the proceedings conducted by the Immigration and Naturalization Service of the Justice Department to deport Andrew Dmytryshyn, vice-president of the Ukranian American Fraternal Union, an affiliate of the International Workers Order, on the ground that the IWO is affiliated with the CPUSA. The proceedings against Dmytryshyn, who openly asserts that he is a communist, affect all American Jews.

H100   . . . . Political Trial of the IWO, "Jewish Life," 5 (April 1951), 25-27.
An account, by a reporter of the "Morning Freiheit," of the efforts of the Insurance Department of New York State to liquidate the International Workers Order, on the basis of testimony by "bought and paid-for" witnesses. This is called the first instance of a proceeding against an insurance company or fraternal benefit organization on political grounds.

H101   HARTMANN, George W. The Behavior of Communists in Unions, "Ethics," 50 (April 1940), 329-35.
A discussion of the ethical aspect of communist behavior in trade unions. Communists, who place Party loyalty above union loyalty, make systematic use of deception and justify the means by the end. By use of caucuses, etc., they are disproportionately represented in union officer ranks, and they attack as Red-baiting any effort to expose their aims and procedures. (A letter of rebuttal by Earl Browder also appears.)

H102   HARTNETT, Robert C. U.S. Communists in the U.N., "America," 88 (Jan. 17, 1953), 421-23.
Federal agencies are increasingly aware of the employment of American communists by the United Nations, whose secretary general is having trouble dismissing suspected employees. Secretary of State Dean Acheson fails to see the harmful effect on the UN of his department's lack of vigilance.

H103   . . . . Commies and Academic Freedom, "America," 89 (April 18, 1953), 77-78; (May 16), 187-90.
Criticism of American higher education for operating in a philosophical vacuum, making it hard to strike a balance between freedom and security on the campus. The ACLU is criticized for its view that communist teachers should be tolerated, provided they do not violate state law. The recent statement of the Association of American Universities, which opposed keeping communists on faculties, evidenced the philosophical vacuum.

H104   HARTNETT, Vincent. New York's Great Red Way, "American Mercury," 76 (June 1953), 66-72.
An assertion that Broadway is the last stronghold of show-business Marxists and their supporters. About half of the legitimate plays on Broadway in the 1952-53 season are said to have contained Party members or friends in their retinues.

H105   "HARVARD LAW REVIEW," Conduct Proscribed as Promoting Violent Overthrow of the Government, 61 (July 1948), 1215-24.
A survey of state and federal statutes and proceedings thereunder which prohibit conduct aimed at the forcible overthrow of the government. Criminal syndicalist laws of 1917-20, sedition acts beginning at that time, and more recent federal and state legislation are discussed. The constitutional limits of antisubversive measures are considered.

H106   . . . , State Control of Subversion: A Problem in Federalism, 66 (Dec. 1952), 327-34.
A survey of state antisubversive legislation, emphasizing the extent of state power in this area and the possibility that some state enactments may conflict with federal law. State statutes proscribing membership in the Communist Party or requiring registration of communists are reviewed.

H107   . . . , Denial of Federally Aided Housing to Members of Organizations on the Attorney General's List, 69 (Jan. 1956), 551-59.
An analysis of constitutional questions raised by the Gwinn Amendment to the Housing Act, which denies federally aided housing to members of organizations on the Attorney General's list. The questions of due process of law and freedom of speech and assembly are discussed.

H108   HARVEY, John. The Young Workers (Communist) League of America and the Struggle against the Right Danger, "International Press Correspondence," 9 (March 15, 1929), 277-78.
The Young Workers (Communist) League has the same right (Lovestoneite) deviations that existed in the Party; the Comintern and the Young Communist International are seeking to eliminate them. The League, because of its greater homogeneity, can help the Party overcome its isolation.

H109   HARVEY, Rowland Hill. "Samuel Gompers: Champion of the Toiling Masses." Palo Alto: Stanford University Press, 1935. 376 pp.
A biography of the founder and leader of the AFL. The role of the communists in the U.S. during Gompers' life is discussed (pp. 301-7), and a summary is given of the activities of the Trade Union Educational League. Gompers emerges as a belligerent and conservative anticommunist, whose anticommunism was the result of his opposition to state intervention in economic affairs, his horror of class conflict, and his distrust of theoretical utopias.

H110   HASKEL, Harry. "A Leader of the Garment Workers: The Biography of Isidore Nagler." Introd. by David Dubinsky. New York: Amalgamated Ladies' Garment Cutters' Union, Local 10, ILGWU, 1950. 351 pp. Bibliog. Ind.
An account of the life and trade-union activities of Isidore Nagler, for the past ten years manager of Cutters' Union, Local 10 of the ILGWU, and for 20 years an ILGWU vice-president. Chapters 8-10, pp. 77-110, deal with the struggle between the communists and anticommunists in the union in the mid-1920's, in which Nagler played a leading role as a leader of the anticommunist forces.

H111   HASS, Eric. "The Socialist Labor Party and the Internationals." New York: New York Labor News, 1949. 187 pp. App. Ind.
The story of De Leon's Socialist Labor Party, its role in the collapse of the Second International, and its disdain for the Third International as a corruption of Marxism. The SLP considered affiliation with the Third International, until it realized that its program of industrial unionism and stateless industrial administration was not taken seriously by Moscow. Appendices contain the SLP declaration on dissolution of the Communist International in 1943, the report of SLP observers at the Congress of the Communist International in 1921, and the 21 conditions for membership in the Communist International laid down in 1920.

H112 HASTINGS, Frederick C. Basing the Party in the Shops, "Political Affairs," 32 (May 1953), 16-29.
In order to win the majority of workers for peace, democracy, and economic security, the Party must be stronger in the trustified industries. Petty bourgeois pressures keep the Party from fully carrying out its concentration policy. The Draft Resolution properly emphasizes the importance of Party shop organizations in the basic industries.

H113 . . . . Unite the Negro People against McCarthyism, "Political Affairs," 33 (Oct. 1954), 36-44.
McCarthyism endangers further advance in the Negro people's struggle for economic, political, and social equality. Negro unity must develop in the context of the struggle of all Americans for democratic liberties. While Walter White of the NAACP is anti-McCarthy, he accepts the McCarthy "Big Lie" that the U.S. faces an internal and external communist danger.

H114 . . ., and MANN, Charles P. For a Mass Policy in Negro Freedom's Cause, "Political Affairs," 34 (March 1955), 7-29.
Condemnation of sectarian tendencies which isolate the Party from mass Negro organizations. The Party should work through these organizations, not to exclude reformists, but to win as many as possible for progress and unity. The Negro people's movement can be allied with labor for peace, economic security, equality, and democracy.

H115 HATHAWAY, Clarence A. The Development of Independent Working Class Political Action in Minnesota, "Labor Herald," 2 (Dec. 1923), 3-6.
A history of the movement for independent working-class political action in Minnesota. It was a struggle between two groups, one advocating nonpartisan political action, and the more radical group demanding an independent working-class political party. The latter group was victorious when, in September 1923, the Farmer-Labor Federation was created.

H116 . . . . The Communists Take the Lead in Minnesota, "Workers Monthly," 4 (March 1925), 214-15 ff.
An account of communist activity and influence in the labor movement of St. Paul and Minneapolis and in the Minnesota Farmer-Labor Party, and of the efforts of the AFL bureaucrats to destroy their influence. Communists have been barred from the Minneapolis Trade and Labor Assembly in violation of the AFL constitution.

H117 . . . . The Fight for Unity in Minnesota, "Workers Monthly," 4 (May 1925), 308-9.
A history of the Farmer-Labor Party of Minnesota, with an assertion that control has now passed to middle class office-seekers. A communist program to benefit poor farmers is presented. Communists will seek to win the rank and file to a program of class struggle, and to build a party of exploited farmers and industrial workers.

H118 . . . . An Examination of Our Failure to Organize the Unemployed, "Communist," 9 (Sept. 1930), 786-94.
Examination of Party failures to capitalize organizationally on the mass demonstrations of the unemployed in recent months. Party comrades have underestimated the seriousness of the crisis and failed to develop concrete slogans by which the class struggle could be linked to the immediate needs of the unemployed.

H119 . . . . On the Use of Transmission Belts in Our Struggle for the Masses, "Communist," 10 (May 1931), 409-23.

The Party's unemployment work has failed to develop an organized mass movement of the unemployed. The Party is still a propaganda party, not a Bolshevik mass party. A series of mass organizations must function as transmission belts to the masses of non-Party workers.

H120 . . . . "Who Are the Friends of the Negro People?" New York: Communist Party National Campaign Committee, Workers Library, 1932. 16 pp.
A speech nominating James W. Ford as Party candidate for vice-president of the U.S. By nominating a Negro, Hathaway asserts, the Party shows in action, not merely words, that it is in the forefront of the struggle for real equality of the Negro people now.

H121 . . . . For a Complete Mobilization of the Party for Real Mass Work in the Election Campaign, "Communist," 11 (May 1932), 418-32.
Extracts from Hathaway's report to the Fourteenth Plenum of the Central Committee, CPUSA, on the election campaign. Emphasis is placed on overcoming sectarian tendencies, popularizing demands, and avoiding opportunist errors. The Party must revolutionize the masses of workers, expose its enemies, answer bourgeois demagogy, and build a broad united-front campaign.

H122 . . . . The Increasing Radicalization of the Masses and the Election Issues, "Communist," 11 (Oct. 1932), 874-88.
The election campaign suffers from a failure to draw in larger numbers of non-Party workers. Greater efforts must be made to expose the bankruptcy of the capitalist parties, combat activities of the social fascists, develop legal election campaign struggles, and broaden united front activities.

H123 . . . . Maneuvers to Sabotage a United Front of Struggle, "Communist," 12 (May 1933), 426-36.
A review of developments in the month since the Central Committee of the CP asked the AFL, the Conference for Progressive Labor Action, and the Socialist Party for joint efforts against fascism and war. These groups seek to avoid fighting unity with the CP. Internal struggles between right and left in these groups are outlined.

H124 . . . . A Warning against Opportunist Distortions of the United Front Tactic, "Communist," 12 (June 1933), 525-37.
Recent events (i.e., the rise of Hitler to power in Germany) have increased sentiment for united front actions between communists and socialists. Because of this, the Socialist Party and the AFL are maneuvering to block broad united action. The author cautions against sectarian views toward the united front in communist ranks.

H125 . . . . "Communists in the Textile Strike: An Answer to Gorman, Green and Co." Foreword by Alex Bittelman. New York: Central Committee, CPUSA, 1934. 24 pp.
Reprints of five "Daily Worker" editorials urging textile workers to continue their current strike, and denouncing the reformist leadership of the United Textile Workers and the AFL for attacking the communists and for supporting arbitration before a National Recovery Administration board. Branding any arbitration board a strike-breaking board, Hathaway insists on full acceptance of the strikers' demands.

H126 . . ., and DON, Sam. "Why a Workers' Daily Press?" New York: Daily Worker, n.d. [1934?]. 20 pp.
Hathaway, editor of the "Daily Worker," describes the paper's achievements and shows how the capitalist press

serves as a weapon of reaction. Don, an associate editor, summarizes Lenin's thoughts on what a revolutionary paper should be.

H127 HATHAWAY, Clarence A. The Struggle for the United Front, "Communist," 14 (June 1935), 510-17.
A discussion article preceding the Seventh World Congress of the Comintern. Efforts of the Communist International, since Hitler's rise to power, to achieve a united front with socialists are reviewed. Though different tactics are used, sometimes a united front from below and at other times from above and below, the objective is always to unite workers on the basis of class struggle, defeat class collaboration, and isolate leaders who block united action.

H128 .... Let Us Penetrate Deeper into the Rural Areas, "Communist," 14 (July 1935), 641-60.
A report to a meeting of the Party's Central Committee, May 25-27, 1935, presenting a program for work among farmers. The author denounces the New Deal for aiding large farmers at the expense of poor and middle farmers. He accuses comrades in the United Farmers League of sectarianism and of failure to penetrate mass farmer organizations, and calls for a united front, particularly on the farmers emergency relief bill.

H129 .... Problems in Our Farmer-Labor Party Activities, "Communist," 15 (May 1936), 427-33.
Two common faults among Party members are sectarianism and right opportunism. Sectarianism is the unwillingness to go out among the masses and arouse support for communist causes like the Farmer-Labor Party. Right opportunism occurs when communists cooperate so closely with noncommunists that they cease to advance Party interests.

H130 .... Fighting for Democracy in Spain, "Communist," 15 (Sept. 1936), 829-44.
A speech delivered in New York City, August 18, 1936, supporting the Spanish government and the people's front movement in Spain, and calling for the defeat of the fascists in the civil war there. The neutrality policy of the U.S. government is attacked, and a mass protest movement, with material support for the Spanish workers, is urged.

H131 .... Trotskyism in the United States, "Communist," 16 (March 1937), 271-78.
The Russian Trotskyites joined the fascists in an effort to sabotage the building of a socialist society. Trotskyites are also dangerous in the U.S., where they infiltrated the Socialist Party and carry on a continued battle to prevent formation of a people's front.

H132 .... The People vs. the Supreme Court, "Communist," 16 (April 1937), 306-12.
The reactionaries oppose Roosevelt's court packing plan, hoping to preserve the Supreme Court's power to block social legislation. The communists favor Roosevelt's plan, while proposing to end the Court's right to declare legislation unconstitutional. The Democratic Party may split, its progressive wing developing into a farmer-labor party. (Also published in pamphlet form.)

H133 .... The Problems of a Worker-Farmer Alliance, "Communist," 16 (Aug. 1937), 716-24.
The incitement of farmers against striking chocolate workers at Hershey, Pa., is a danger signal to militant labor and progressive farmers. Communists must overcome fascist-inspired prejudice among farmers against the CIO.

H134 .... "Collective Security." New York: Workers Library, 1938. 15 pp.

A radio speech by the editor of the "Daily Worker" and a reprint of an article from that paper, both on the collective security theme. In the radio speech, a plea to abandon isolationism and neutrality. Hathaway asserts that radicals and pacifists who oppose collective security thereby strengthen fascism. The article opposes the Ludlow Amendment, which would make any declaration of war subject to referendum; the problem is to prevent war, which can best be done through collective security.

H135 .... The 1938 Elections and Our Tasks, "Communist," 17 (March 1938), 208-19.
A report to a plenary session of the Party's Central Committee and National Party Builders Congress, February 18-21, 1938. In the coming congressional elections, the reactionaries hope to capitalize on the split in the Democratic Party over Roosevelt's Supreme Court reform. A united labor movement must ally itself politically with the farmers and middle class.

H136 .... Building the Democratic Front, "Communist," 17 (May 1938), 404-9.
The Party now seeks to form a democratic front that differs from a people's front in being a looser coalition that will not necessarily try to establish a new party. A democratic front is a first step toward a people's front. It will try to get progressive candidates nominated in the Democratic and Republican primaries. (See a criticism by Eugene Dennis, "Some Questions Concerning the Democratic Front," in "Communist," June 1938.)

H137 HAUSHALTER, Walter M. Our Leftist Clergy: 1. The Enigma; 2. The Remedy, "Freeman," 2 (June 2, 1952), 573-75; (June 16), 618-20.
A clergyman, asking why so many of the American clergy are procommunist, finds that their liberal idealism blinds them to Soviet reality. An economic order cannot bring man to perfection; regeneration must begin with the individual, followed by economic change for the good. The remedy is rededication to historic Christian ideals under the banner of a united church.

H138 HAVIGHURST, R. J., and PECK, R. F. Communism and American Education, "School Review," 57 (Nov. 1949), 453-58.
The year 1949 was the year of the red scare in American education. Public education leaders opposed communists as teachers in American schools, an issue on which leaders in higher education were divided. Teachers participated less in questionable or suspect organizations, though educational leaders protected their civil liberties. Educational leaders proposed the critical study of communism and the Soviet Union in American Schools.

H139 HAWES, Elizabeth. "Hurry Up Please, It's Time." New York: Reynal & Hitchcock, 1946. 245 pp.
A book about the UAW by a fashion designer who became a UAW international representative during World War II. She attacks Walter Reuther and the anticommunists around him for opportunism and Red-baiting, telling of her experiences and those of "Eve," a shop worker who holds similar views. Her sympathies are with the union leaders who are communist-oriented. The author praises the USSR, and reports Eve's views that no party, with the possible exception of the CP, is worth belonging to; should Eve go communist, it would be because of the rottenness of the American capitalist system.

H140 HAWKINS, Carroll. "Communism: Challenge to Americans." East Lansing, Mich.: Michigan State College, Governmental Research Bureau, 1953. 76 pp.
An outline of the development of communism and of

communist activities in the U.S., with emphasis on methods of infiltration, espionage, and formation of front groups. The strength of world communism is analyzed, showing its influence on various groups and classes. The author tells how America can meet this foe by taking advantage of its weaknesses in structure and organization, by keeping ready our military arm, and by waging political, economic, and ideological warfare in support of democratic ideas at home and abroad.

H141 HAYNES, George E. Communists Are Bidding for Negro Loyalty, "Southern Workman" (Hampton Institute), 62 (April 1933), 151-60.
An expression of alarm over communist gains among Southern Negroes since the inception of the Scottsboro case. In contrast, the influence of the Negro press, clergy, and intellectuals seems to be declining. The communist effort, starting as far back as 1925, has made a strong appeal to Negro workers and sharecroppers.

H142 HAYS, Arthur Garfield. "Trial by Prejudice." New York: Covici, Friede, 1933. 369 pp. Ind.
An account by a lawyer active in civil liberties cases of the impact of prejudice in trials. Among the cases discussed are those of Gastonia, Angelo Herndon, Sacco and Vanzetti, and the miners in Harlan and Bell Counties, Kentucky.

H143 .... The Rosenberg Case, "Nation," 175 (Nov. 8, 1952), 422-23.
The general counsel for the American Civil Liberties Union discusses the Rosenberg sentence, questioning the death penalty for giving information to an ally and expressing approval of the lighter sentences for similar offenses in Canada and England.

H144 HAYS, Paul R. Academic Freedom and Communist Teachers, "Commentary," 21 (June 1956), 549-54.
Critical comment, by a professor of law at Columbia University, on a report by the American Association of University Professors defending the right of communists to be college teachers. The AAUP ignores the fact that communism is a conspiracy seeking the destruction of the U.S., and that Party members must use their role as teachers to further that conspiracy.

H145 HAYWOOD, Harry. Against Bourgeois-Liberal Distortions of Leninism on the Negro Question in the United States, "Communist," 9 (Aug. 1930), 694-712.
Criticism of the opportunist view that the American Negro question is one of race, a view that supports chauvinism and opposes the Communist International line. The Negroes in the Black Belt are struggling for bourgeois democracy, for self-determination, while Negro toilers have become potential allies of the proletariat. (Also published in pamphlet form.)

H146 .... The Crisis of the Jim-Crow Nationalism of the Negro Bourgeoisie, "Communist," 10 (April 1931), 330-38.
The crisis is intensifying imperialist oppression of Negro toilers in the U.S. The main Negro reformist organizations, the NAACP and the National Urban League, include white liberals and even imperialist elements. The Negro bourgeoisie supports Jim Crow nationalism, a segregated economy among the Negro masses in the cities.

H147 .... The Theoretical Defenders of White Chauvinism in the Labor Movement, "Communist," 10 (June 1931), 497-508.
An answer to Lovestoneite attacks on the "self-determina-tion" plank of the CP program. The author challenges Will Herberg's contention that Negroes are not a nation and that the CP supports reactionary-separatist tendencies among the Negro masses. Herberg's reactionary stand places the Lovestoneites in a united front of chauvinism against the Party's revolutionary program.

H148 ..., and HOWARD, Milton. "Lynching: A Weapon of National Oppression." New York: International Publishers, 1932. 15 pp.
An assertion that the white ruling class enforces its national oppression of the Negro people through lynching and terrorism. The police, the courts, the well-to-do, the NAACP, and the AFL are responsible, along with the mobs. The Party, however, strikes at the basis of the oppression with its demand for self-determination in the Black Belt.

H149 .... The Scottsboro Decision: Victory of Revolutionary Struggle over Reformist Betrayal, "Communist," 11 (Dec. 1932), 1065-75.
The recent reversal by the U.S. Supreme Court of the lower court decision in the Scottsboro case is a victory of revolutionary struggle over reformist betrayal and a vindication of the Party's policy, although the Court hoped to revive confidence in bourgeois-democratic institutions. The next steps must be to expose the reformist betrayals and broaden the struggles.

H150 .... The Struggle for the Leninist Position on the Negro Question in the U.S.A., "Communist," 12 (Sept. 1933), 888-901.
Negroes in the U.S., as seen by the Sixth Congress of the Communist International in 1928, form an oppressed nation with all requisites for a national revolutionary movement against American imperialism. This is a concrete application of Marxist-Leninist conceptions. Negro struggles against Jim Crowism are part of the struggle of the working class against capitalism.

H151 .... "The Road to Negro Liberation: Report to the 8th Convention of the C.P.U.S.A., Cleveland, April 2-8, 1934." New York: Workers Library, 1934. 63 pp.
The Negro program in the Party's militant "third period," with a condemnation of Negro reform groups such as the NAACP and the Urban League as agents of U.S. imperialism, seeking to halt the growing revolutionary drift of the Negro masses. Only the communists, the report asserts, really fight for Negro freedom. Party members must expose Negro reformist and nationalist "misleaders" through the tactic of the united front from below, and build the League of Struggle for Negro Rights into an independent mass organization around the Party's program for struggles for Negro liberation.

H152 .... Toward a Program of Agrarian Reforms for the Black Belt, "Political Affairs," 25 (Sept. 1946), 855-64; (Oct.), 922-39.
Fundamental agrarian reform, the prime need of the South, is essential if the Negro is to be free. The large plantations must be broken up, and the land distributed among the poor cultivators, Negro and white, who till it. Self-government for the Black Belt is essential. Key issues for immediate struggle are outlined.

H153 .... "Negro Liberation." New York: International Publishers, 1948. 245 pp. Notes. App. Ind.
A postwar statement by a leading Negro Party member of the communist program for American Negroes, consisting of land redivision and self-determination by the Negroes in the South. The Negro problem is seen in the context of the semi-feudal plantation system and the

corrupt rule of monopoly capitalism. Full economic, social, and political equality for Negroes can be achieved only through democratic rule by the Negro people and their allies among disfranchised whites. The Negro liberation movement can lead the Negro people only if it accepts Party leadership on this issue.

H154 HAYWOOD, William D. Revolutionary Problems in America, "Communist International," 3 nos. 16-17 [1921], 77-80.
A review of the concentration of wealth in the U.S., and of the conservative policies of the AFL and its craft unions, by the former leader of the IWW who sought refuge in the USSR. He praises the industrial unionism of the IWW and the militancy of its members in the class struggle.

H155 HAZLETON, Barbara Ann. Communism on the Campus? "Freedom and Union," 3 (Sept. 1948), 6-8.
A University of Michigan graduate minimizes the danger of communism on the campus. Opposing the banning of "subversive" student organizations, she argues that exposure is more effective than denunciation. Only by instilling critical ability in students will educational institutions curb communist influence on campus.

H156 HEALEY, Dorothy R. On the Status of the Party, "Political Affairs," 37 (March 1958), 40-48.
A member of the Party's national committee regrets the fragmentation of the Party, the name-calling and abstract definitions (dogmatism vs. revisionism) that have become substitutes for debate, the over-simplified definitions of right and left dangers. She calls for a Party able to contain divergent points of view. (See James E. Jackson, "A Reply to Comrade Healey," in "Political Affairs," April 1958.)

H157 .... "A Communist Speaks at a Teach-In on Viet Nam." Los Angeles: Southern California Communist Party, 1966. 15 pp.
A call for ending the war now, with an assertion that we are in Vietnam because of the key strategic raw materials and investments in the area. Efforts to find a "legal" base for our presence there are reviewed and ridiculed. Meanwhile, under the guise of anticommunism, democratic rights are being challenged at home. (Based on a speech delivered at UCLA, March 25, 1966.)

H158 HEALY, Paul F. Stalin's American Snoops, "Saturday Evening Post," 223 (Jan. 20, 1951), 22-23 ff.
An exposé of Tass, the official Soviet "news" agency, and of the Americans who serve as its correspondents here. The Tass connections and communist activities of staff members are disclosed.

H159 HEDLEY, George. A Christian View of Communism: Out-perform, Out-think and Out-speak Communists, "Vital Speeches of the Day," 17 (May 15, 1951), 476-80.
A call for Christians to debate the economic theory, repudiate the tyranny, and condemn the dishonesty of the USSR. We can deal with communism by understanding how it works, allowing it to operate, debating it, and combatting its tactics. We must remove the soil in which communism has been able to grow.

H160 HEFFERNAN, Robert E. Communism, Constitutionalism and the Principle of Contradiction, "Georgetown Law Journal," 32 (May 1944), 405-24.
Criticism of the U.S. Supreme Court decision in the Schneiderman denaturalization case as unfortunate and poorly conceived. The Court's ruling that the beliefs of

the Party cannot be imputed to the man seems untenable. Communism and Americanism are incompatible.

H161 HEFFRON, Edward J. McCarthy: The Case for Him, "Commonweal," 57 (Oct. 31, 1952), 87-90.
An assertion that the New Deal's negligent treatment of communism made a thorough investigation necessary. The Democratic Administration's frantic attempts to cover up the facts behind McCarthy's claim that communists were employed in the State Department implies that the charges were warranted.

H162 ..., and SULLIVAN, Daniel J. Pro, Con, McCarthyism, "Catholic World," 179 (Aug. 1954), 326-35.
Heffron, defending McCarthy, asserts that this "man of justice" has single-handedly stood up against the Republican Administration, the Democratic party, the mass media, and the intelligentsia. Sullivan, attacking McCarthy's methods, shows how he labels as communist those who oppose him. He does not support measures, such as the Marshall Plan and the Point Four program, that would stave off communism.

H163 HEIDENHEIMER, Arnold J. The Communists' Last Stand, "New Republic," 124 (May 14, 1951), 15-16.
A report on hearings by the Subversive Activities Control Board to determine whether the CPUSA is a "communist-action organization," under the McCarran Act. While it appears certain that the Party will be curbed, the means employed are essential. Standards to judge abstract concepts like Marxism-Leninism must be set up.

H164 .... Five Long Years of Loyalty, "New Republic," 126 (Feb. 4, 1952), 13-15.
A sympathetic biographical sketch of the public service of Seth Richardson, chairman of the Loyalty Review Board from 1947 to 1952. The author discusses the personnel activities and deliberations of the Loyalty Review Board and the pressures under which it operated.

H165 HELLER, A. A. "Who Wants War?" New York: Friends of the Soviet Union, n.d. [1934?]. 31 pp.
An assertion that Japan and Nazi Germany are making plans to attack the Soviet Union, while the U.S. is preparing for war. Whereas war is part of the capitalist system, the Soviet Union seeks peace. The fight against war is growing, in the U.S. as well as in Europe and Japan.

H166 .... "American Scientist No. 996: The Story of Morton Sobell." New York: The author, n.d. [1955]. 24 pp.
An account of the Sobell case by one who believes him innocent, a scapegoat, along with Julius and Ethel Rosenberg, of the national hysteria of the cold war-McCarthy period. The trial, in the author's view, was a put-up job, a structure of fraudulent testimony and base invention.

H167 HENDERSON, Donald. Reds Bait Midwest Farmers, "National Republic," 21 (April 1934), 17-18.
A report in a right-wing periodical of a meeting in a Nebraska farming community organized by the Young Communist League, at which a young agitator preached revolution for a Soviet America. Only farmers who never prospered and never will under any form of government will listen to such agitation.

H168 HENDERSON, Donald. The Rural Masses and the Work of Our Party, "Communist," 14 (Sept. 1935), 866-80.
May 25-27, 1935, asserting that the Party has failed to win the poor farmers because it has recruited in rural districts from large industrial cities rather than from

agricultural towns and villages. These small towns contain a semi-industrial proletariat, who have good opportunities for organizational contacts in the countryside.

H169 HENDERSON, Samuel T. White Chauvinsim and Negro Bourgeois Nationalism, "Political Affairs," 31 (Dec. 1952), 28-40; 32 (Jan. 1953), 52-63.
White chauvinsim exists within Party ranks because it has increased in the country generally and because we have failed to understand fully the national character of the Negro question. Negro bourgeois nationalism, an anti-working-class ideology, is also influential in Party ranks and among the Negro masses. It is alien to proletarian internationalism and Marxism. White chauvinism and Negro nationalism are two sides of the same phenomenon.

H170 HENDLEY, Charles J. Unionism in the Educational Field, "Social Frontier," 5 (May 1939), 237-40.
A reply to charges of communist control of New York City Local 5 of the American Federation of Teachers (see Henry R. Linville, "How Communists Injure Teachers' Unions," in "Social Frontier," March 1939). Admitting that there are communists in the local, one of its top officers denies that they dominate it or exploit it for ulterior purposes. He describes the local as democracy in action.

H171 HERBERG, Will. Employee Education in Economics, "Workers Monthly," 5 (Sept. 1926), 505-10.
A discussion of the aims and methods of employee education in economics among modern corporations. Though the employers have technical superiority, communists are on the side of the forces of history. Meanwhile communists should use educational and propaganda techniques developed by employers.

H172 .... Are the U.S. Negroes a Nation? A False Orientation to Negro Work, "Revolutionary Age," 2 (Feb. 14, 1931), 3.
A Lovestoneite attack on the CPUSA view of Negroes in the U.S. as an "oppressed nation," with the right of "self-determination in the Black Belt." American Negroes do not satisfy Stalin's criteria of a nation. The new segregationist line makes effective work among Negroes impossible.

H173 .... The Crisis in Communism: The Viewpoint of the International Communist Opposition, "Modern Monthly," 7 (June 1933), 283-88.
Criticism by a leading member of the Lovestone group of the policies of the Communist International and the CPUSA. Charging the official Party with sectarianism, he calls for revolutionary class action, an end to dual unionism, a genuine united front with socialist workers, unification of the communist movement, and democratic centralism with freedom of discussion.

H174 .... The Labor Party Muddle, "Workers Age," 4 (Feb. 2, 1935), 3.
A Lovestoneite analysis of the contradictions in the labor party policy of the Communist Party. The CPUSA first adopted a labor party policy in 1922, repudiated it in 1929, and now denies the repudiation. The current CP policy is phony, since the CP will support a labor party only if it dominates it.

H175 .... The Rise and Fall of Dual Unionism: What Has Happened to the Sectarian Course of the Comintern? "Workers Age," 4 (Sept. 21, 1935), 3-4.
A review of the Party's trade-union line by a leader of the Lovestone group. From establishing revolutionary dual unions and attempting to split or destroy conservative unions, Party policy has changed first to forming left groups within old unions, next to forming united fronts with the old unions, still later to forming an independent federation, and finally to dissolving the federation. Each step was initiated by the Communist International.

H176 .... American CP Writes Its Own Epitaph, "Workers Age," 7 (May 28, 1938), 1 ff.
The proposed amendments to the constitution of the CPUSA show its complete degeneration into an organization to defend bourgeois capitalist democracy against the interests of the working class. It promises to defend American institutions, and threatens expulsion of anyone advocating terrorism or violence.

H177 .... On the Political Nature of the Stalinist Party, "Workers Age," 8 (July 29, 1939), 3; (Aug. 5), 3.
Lovestoneite analysis of reasons why the Young Communist League could introduce resolutions opposing both fascist and communist dictatorships at a recent American Youth Congress. Present-day, non-Russian communist parties have no principles; they seek control to manipulate front groups as the Party line requires.

H178 .... What Is the New Stalinist Party Line Going to Be? "Workers Age,' 8 (Sept. 30, 1939), 1-2.
Lovestoneite critique of the new line announced by the national committee of the Communist Party. Whereas in the popular front period antiwar advocates were "paid agents of Hitler," now the CP sees the war as imperialist and predatory on both sides.

H179 .... From Marxism to Judaism: Jewish Belief as a Dynamic of Social Action, "Commentary," 3 (Jan. 1947), 25-32.
The author, during the 1920's a communist and in the 1930's a Lovestoneite, tells of his disillusionment with Marxism and of his belief that religion, in particular Judaism, provides a more secure groundwork for a mature and effective social radicalism.

H180 .... Jewish Labor Movement in the United States: World War I to the Present, "Industrial and Labor Relations Review," 6 (Oct. 1952), 44-66.
A section of this article, "Inner Disruption and Economic Depression," (pp. 45-52), reviews the drive of the communists for control of the ILGWU, the Fur Workers, and the Amalgamated Clothing Workers through the Trade Union Educational League, and the formation of the Needle Trades Workers Industrial Union of the Trade Union Unity League.

H181 .... Communism, Democracy and the Churches, "Commentary," 19 (April 1955), 386-93.
An account of a conference held in Washington, D.C., to form a religious front against the communist danger. The author, sympathetic to the conference, discusses issues raised there, including the concept of communism as religion and the relationship between religion and democracy.

H182 HERBERT, E. S., and others. Opinion of the Commission of Jurists with Respect to Staff Members of the United Nations Secretariat of United States Nationality, "American Journal of International Law," 47 (July 1953), 87-114.
The report of the committee appointed by the Secretary-General to rule on the rights and immunities of an American member of the UN staff who is alleged to be disloyal or who pleads the protection of the Fifth Amendment. The report concludes that an official may justly be dismissed by the Secretary-General if the latter believes that he is engaged in subversive activities against the host country, or if he claims protection of the Fifth Amendment without justification.

H183 HERBST, Josephine. "Rope of Gold." New York: Harcourt, Brace, 1939. 429 pp.
The story of a family from 1930 to 1937, one of whose members, a communist, plays a heroic role in the sit-down strikes. (The third volume of a trilogy that traces the disintegration of a family, contrasting with it the revolutionary development of some of its members.)

H184 HERMAN, B. Again—A Sharp Change of Line, "Revolutionary Age," 2 (Oct. 24, 1931), 4; (Oct. 31), 3; (Nov. 7), 3.
Comment in a Lovestoneite journal on articles by Ralph Simons in the "Daily Worker," calling for a turn in the Party's trade union policy. The author finds no real turn, only continuation of the splitting role of the Party's Trade Union Unity League. To increase left-wing activity in reactionary unions while building dual unions means disruption of reactionary unions, expulsions of militants, and loss of Party influence with the masses.

H185 . . . . Again the Party Trade Union Course! The Party Doctors Disagree! "W o r k e r s A g e," 1 (March 19, 1932), 3; (March 26), 3.
Pointing to the disagreement over trade-union policy between two Party leaders, William Z. Foster and Joseph Zack, in recent issues of "Labor Unity," the author expresses the disagreement of the Lovestone group with both. Lagging behind a change in the Party line, Zack had attacked the AFL as the bosses' labor agency and called for the organization of workers outside it. For this he was rebuked by Foster, who urged renewed activity in the reformist unions by committees established by each revolutionary union. Zack's view is dismissed by the author as grotesque, and Foster's as a policy of splitting and disruption.

H186 HERMAN, Louis Jay. The "Compass" That Points East, "New Leader," 34 (July 2, 1951), 6-8.
An analysis of the origins and ideology of the New York "Compass," whose needles point due east toward Moscow. Editor Thackrey's procommunist viewpoint is criticized; the Korean War is only one of the issues on which Thackrey followed the CP line.

H187 . . . . The "Nation": The Ideology of Surrender, "New Leader," 37 (Oct. 25, 1954), 15-18.
Critical commentary on the "Nation," its editor, and major writers, for serving as apologists for the Soviet Union. Reviewing its pronouncements from the Korean War to the present, the author concludes that the magazine has lost the right to speak for American liberals or free men anywhere.

H188 . . . . Turmoil in U.S. Communism, "N e w Leader," 40 (Jan. 21, 1957), 7-10.
A detailed analysis of the factional struggle inside the CPUSA following the publication of Khrushchev's anti-Stalin speech. While the Gates faction, favoring greater democracy, seems in control of the Party, only the convention will tell whether the struggle will lead to a walk-out by the Fosterites.

H189 HERNDON, Angelo. "Let Me Live." New York: Random House, 1937. 409 pp. App.
The autobiography of a youthful Negro communist who had been sentenced to 18 to 20 years at hard labor under a Georgia insurrection statute of 1861. Attracted to the Party by its interest in Negroes, Herndon had seen in the movement a way to fight Jim Crow and lynchings. He had also been active in the Unemployed Councils organized by the Party, in the TUUL, and in the Scottsboro defense. The autobiography was written while Herndon awaited a U.S. Supreme Court decision which resulted in his release.

The Herndon case was widely publicized by the communists in the 1930's to dramatize the treatment of Negroes in the South.

H190 . . . . "The Scottsboro Boys: Four Freed! Five to Go." New York: Workers Library, 1937. 15 pp.
A Negro communist congratulates the International Labor Defense, the Party, the Young Communist League, and all the front groups for their efforts which resulted in partial victory. He gives the communists full credit for the freeing of four of the accused, asserting that there shall be no compromise in the fight to free the five remaining boys.

H191 . . . . "You Cannot Kill the Working Class." New York: International Labor Defense and League of Struggle for Negro Rights, n.d. [1937]. 30 pp.
The central figure in one of the Party's celebrated cases writes his autobiography and explains his case, which is pending in the Supreme Court. After pleading his cause, he appeals to workers and Negroes to support the ILD and the LSNR, and join in the struggle to free him and the Scottsboro boys.

H192 HERNDON DEFENSE COMMITTEE. "W i s d o m, Justice and Moderation: The Case of Angelo Herndon." New York: Joint Committee to Aid the Herndon Defense, 1935. 15 pp.
Written after the Supreme Court refused a second review of the Herndon case, the authors review the history of the case, emphasizing the civil liberties aspects of Herndon's conviction order under the antiquated Georgia "insurrection" law. The Committee asks help in circulating a petition to the Governor to free Herndon and repeal the law, and also appeals for contributions.

H193 HERRICK, Robert. Writers in the Jungle, "New Republic," 80 (Oct. 17, 1934), 259-61.
A critical analysis of the proletarian novels of the period. Despite promising experimentation in technique, there is a failure to write in human terms and a failure in objectivity. The writers must learn to overcome their own prejudices.

H194 HEWITT, Nelson E. "How Red is the University of Chicago?" Chicago: Advisory Associates, 1935. 102 pp.
An assertion, based partly on Elizabeth Dilling's "The Red Network," that the University of Chicago is very "Red." Among the evidence are activities of faculty and students in opposition to fascism, support of the Civil Liberties Union, and appearance of such speakers as Felix Frankfurter and Max Eastman.

H195 HICKS, Granville. The Crisis in American Criticism, "New Masses," 8 (Feb. 1933), 3-5.
Criticism, like American literature in general, was emancipated from Victorian morality by 1925. It is now in the stage of the rise of Marxism. However, vulgar Marxism, such as that of V. F. Calverton, must be avoided. Marxian criticism may demand that the theme of a novel be related to the class struggle, that it be approached with intensity, and that the author adopt the communist viewpoint.

H196 . . . . The Social Interpretation of Literature, "Progressive Education," 11 (Jan.-Feb., 1934), 49-54.
An assertion that the conventional methods of teaching English, which give the student cultural polish without challenging his convictions, are well adapted to the demands of capitalist education. Hicks proposes Marxist

analysis of literature as a social phenomenon, though to do so within a capitalist education system is a halfway measure.

H197 HICKS, Granville. Revolution and the N o v e l, "New Masses," 11 (April 3, 1934), 29-31; (April 10), 23-25; (April 17), 24-25; (April 24), 23-25; (May 8), 22-24; (May 15), 23-25; (May 22), 23-25.
Among the topics discussed are the past and future as themes, complex and collective novels, drama and biography as models, character and classes, selection and emphasis, the problem of documentation, and the future of proletarian literature. The revolutionary novel that falls short of the author's intentions is more important than a bourgeois novel that reaches its goal.

H198 . . . . "The Great Tradition: An Interpretation of American Literature since the Civil War." New York: Macmillan. Rev. ed., 1935. 341 pp. Bibliog. Ind.
A Marxist view of post-Civil War American literature, discussing each writer in terms of his comprehension of the contemporary socio-economic scene as well as his artistic achievement. A chapter on the proletarian literature of the 1930's praises the group of revolutionary writers, crediting the Marxian analysis of capitalism with sharpening their perception. Their work is not mere criticism, but is prophetic of the destruction of capitalism. (Revision of a work first published in 1933.)

H199 . . ., and others (eds.). "Proletarian Literature in the United States: An Anthology." Introd. by Joseph Freeman. New York: International Publishers, 1935. 384 pp.
An anthology of fiction, poetry, drama, and literary criticism, representing a cross-section of proletarian literature. The introduction presents the case for the use of art as an instrument in the class struggle. Included also is a concise history of American letters from 1912 to the time of writing, relating art to the contemporary environment.

H200 . . . . Revolutionary Literature of 1934, "New Masses," 14 (Jan. 1, 1935), 36-38.
An assertion that 1934 has been a year of enormous gains in revolutionary literature, with sympathizers drawing closer to the movement and revolutionary writers surpassing themselves. Important revolutionary plays, poems, short stories, and novels have appeared.

H201 . . . . Literature and Revolution, "English Journal" (College ed.), 24 (March 1935), 219-39.
A Marxist interpretation of literature, asserting that intellectual movements of a period cannot be understood without understanding its class alignments. The question about a work of literature is whether it contributes to a world-attitude compatible with the aims of the proletariat. A writer must confront the central issues of his age. (An address to the College Conference on English in the Central Atlantic States, Dec. 1, 1934.)

H202 . . . . Fired for Being a C o m m u n i s t, "New Masses," 15 (June 4, 1935), 9-10.
Hicks charges that he was fired by Rensselaer Polytechnic Institute in May 1935 because he was a communist, not because financial retrenchment, which could have taken place in other ways, was necessary. RPI, under capitalist pressure like most other colleges, refused to face the issue squarely.

H203 . . . . The Timid Profession, "New Masses," 15 (June 18, 1935), 14-15.
Capitalism's grip on our colleges is tragic, not only because it dismisses radicals, but because of the timidity of teachers. The insecurity of the instructor, and the emphasis on "playing the game" to achieve advancement, lead to conformity. The alternative is for teachers to organize.

H204 . . . . "John Reed: The Making of a Revolutionary." New York: Macmillan, 1936. 445 pp.
A sympathetic biography of the American chronicler of the Russian Revolution and one of the founders of the Communist Labor Party, which eventually became part of the Workers (Communist) Party. Among the subjects dealt with are Reed's adventures in Mexico with Villa's men, his life and work as a war correspondent, his participation in and reports of the Russian Revolution, his relations with the Socialist Party, his part in founding the Communist Labor Party, and his final days in Soviet Russia. (Portions of this material appeared in the "New Masses," Dec. 31, 1935, and Jan. 14, 1936.)

H205 . . . . Communism and Academic F r e e d o m, "Christian Register," 115 (Jan. 30, 1936), 71-72.
An assertion that academic freedom in the true sense is virtually nonexistent, and that economics cannot be discussed freely because of business control of boards of trustees. Communists believe that teachers can have as much freedom as they are able to win, and that the true democracy for which communists work will include real academic freedom.

H206 . . . . The Legend of John Reed, "New Masses," 25 (Oct. 19, 1937), 9-11.
Reed has become a legend because his life was genuinely symbolic. Reviewing the known details of Reed's life, Hicks criticizes the picture of him in "Movers and Shakers," by Mabel Dodge Luhan, and also in Max Eastman's writings.

H207 . . . . A "Nation" Divided, "New Masses Literary Supplement," 25 (Dec. 7, 1937), 8-11.
An analysis of the policies of the "Nation," praising its articles and editorials as fair, but criticizing its book review section, under the editorship first of Joseph Wood Krutch, and more recently of Margaret Marshall, for antagonism to the USSR and the communist movement. She is making the book section an organ of Trotskyites.

H208 . . . . "I Like America." New York: Modern Age, 1938. 216 pp.
A leading Party literary critic of the 1930's explains that he embraced communism because he likes America. Addressing himself to the middle class reader who does not suffer economic privation, Hicks presents the case for communism by contrasting present conditions with Party objectives. (The book was written during the popular front period, after Hicks had lost his post at Rensselaer Polytechnic Institute because of his communist affiliation; he left the Party following the Nazi-Soviet pact.)

H209 . . . . What Shall I Read? A Program for Study, "New Masses," 29 (Oct. 4, 1938), 17-18.
Suggested readings for those who agree with the view that poverty and insecurity can and should be abolished. All the works recommended are communist classics or contemporary works. Recommended authors include Marx and Engels, Lenin, Dimitrov, John Strachey, A. B. Magil and Henry Stevens, William Z. Foster, and Earl Browder.

H210 . . . . On Leaving the Communist Party, "New Republic," 100 (Oct. 4, 1939), 244-45.
The author is leaving the Party, not because of the Soviet-Nazi pact, but because the Party has made it clear that he must resign if he could not defend the pact in the Party's terms. There is no justification for altering the domestic

popular front policy to conform to Soviet foreign policy needs.

H211 HICKS, Granville. New Directions on the Left. "New Republic," 102 (June 17, 1940), 815-18.
A discussion of the predicament faced by the former fellow-traveler after the Hitler-Stalin pact. Hicks sees a considerable section of the left supporting a democratic, humanitarian socialism, to be achieved if possible through gradual reform.

H212 .... The Fighting Decade, "Saturday Review of Literature," 22 (July 6, 1940), 3-5 ff.
A review of the literature of the 1930's, asserting that most left-wing writers wrote as they did because their perceptions and emotions found a political as well as a literary expression. Despite the collapse of a political dogma consequent to the Nazi-Soviet pact, the strength in this literature is not invalidated.

H213 .... The Failure of Left Criticism, "New Republic," 103 (Sept. 9, 1940), 345-47.
An analysis of the failure of Marxian literary criticism in the 1930's. Its real weakness lay in the way the critics thought of their function, which was that literary criticism could be a major weapon in changing the world. This naive concept made such criticism less effective than it might otherwise have been.

H214 .... The Blind Alley of Marxism, "Nation," 151 (Sept. 28, 1940), 264-67.
A former communist attributes the faults of the Russian regime and of communist parties in other countries to the failure in Marxist thought to provide checks for the misuse of power. Whereas Marx and Engels relied upon the unrest of the victims of capitalism for the coming of socialism, Lenin built a disciplined party which seized power, resulting in the dictatorship of a handful of politicians.

H215 .... Communism and the American Intellectuals. Pp. 78-115 in "Whose Revolution?" ed. by Irving DeWitt Talmadge. New York: Howell, Soskin, 1941. 296 pp.
An explanation by a former Party member of the attraction of communism in the 1930's, using his experience as an example. A fellow-traveler for four years and then a Party member for four years more, Hicks tells how the Party looks when one is moving toward it, when one is in it, and when one is going away from it. The appeal of communism in the 1930's could be understood only against the background of general paralysis and helplessness.

H216 .... "Only One Storm." New York: Macmillan, 1942. 427 pp.
The story of a New Englander who returns to his home town in 1937 to operate a printing press. A novel of ideas, the book represents the author's effort to reconcile his leanings toward communism with the course of history in the late 1930's.

H217 .... The Spectre That Haunts the World, "Harper's Magazine," 192 (June 1946), 536-42.
An assertion that communist internationalism has developed under the control of Russian nationalism, though persons outside the USSR are drawn to communism by economic and social evils and the energy of communists in attacking them. (Though the article has only a few explicit references to the U.S., the analysis applies to the communist movement here as to all other countries outside the USSR.)

H218 .... The Politics of John Dos Passos, "Antioch Review," 10 (March 1950), 85-98.
An excommunist traces Dos Passos' infatuation with communism and his subsequent disillusionment as reflected in his writings. Opposing capitalism as the cause of industrialization and war, Dos Passos, following the Sacco-Vanzetti case, accepted the Marxist conception of the class struggle. Alienated by communist tactics, he came to fear power and, along with it, government.

H219 .... The Liberals Who Haven't Learned: Why the Soviet Illusion Still Lingers, "Commentary," 11 (April 1951), 319-29.
Comment on the solicitude of liberals like the editors of the "Nation" for the USSR and its supporters. The communists benefited from the disintegration of the early depression years. Then came the antifascist united front, following which the USSR was our wartime ally. Pro-Soviet liberals pitilessly analyze U.S. shortcomings, while explaining away Russia's faults.

H220 .... Lincoln Steffens: He Covered the Future—the Prototype of a Fellow Traveler, "Commentary," 13 (Feb. 1952), 147-55.
Steffens' autobiography provides a clue to the attraction of communism for Americans during the 1930's. This clue was an uncritical quest for certainty—generalizing on insufficient evidence, knowing what he would find before looking, and finding what he sought. This also explains the panacea mania of liberals a generation later.

H221 .... How Red Was the Red Decade? "Harper's Magazine," 207 (July 1953), 53-61.
A former communist disputes the picture of an intellectual red terror, said by Eugene Lyons, author of "The Red Decade," to have existed during the depression years. The communists did not dominate the intellectual professions, although they had influence beyond their numbers. Given the widespread hunger and desperation of the depression years, it is surprising that communism was not more successful.

H222 .... "Where We Came Out." New York: Viking, 1954. 250 pp.
An account of his experience and motivation by a writer and literary critic who had long served as a contributor to and editor of the "New Masses," and who left the Party after holding membership for four years when the Hitler-Stalin pact was signed. He analyzes his motives and those of other intellectuals who became involved with communism in the 1930's. He explains his present position as an anticommunist, but deplores professional anticommunism and the confusing of liberal reform with subversive conspiracy.

H223 .... "Part of the Truth." New York: Harcourt, Brace & World, 1965. 314 pp. Ind.
The autobiography of the writer and critic who, for a few years prior to the Hitler-Stalin pact, had been one of the leading literary figures in the Party. Hicks tells of his acceptance of the communist position early in the depression 1930's, his experiences on the staff of the "New Masses" and in the Party, and his decision to quit the Party when Hitler and Stalin signed their nonaggression pact.

H224 HIELD, Wayne. What Keeps Harry Bridges Going? "Labor and Nation," 8 (Jan.-March 1952), 38-40 ff.
An analysis of Harry Bridges' procommunist control of the International Longshoremen's and Warehousemen's Union, attributing his strength to his effectiveness as a leader, and to the fact that his faction became firmly entrenched before a working opposition could be formed.

H225 HIGH, Stanley. Communism Presses Its Pants, "Saturday Evening Post," 211 (July 9, 1938), 5-6 ff.
A report on the CPUSA during its united front period, describing its organization, policies, activities, and leadership. Party members contribute generously in time and money and subject themselves to rigorous discipline. The Party has substantial influence in the CIO, and controls many front organizations. Its basic policies are made in Moscow.

H226 .... Who Organized the Unemployed? "Saturday Evening Post," 211 (Dec. 10, 1938), 8-9 ff.
An account of the history, program, and leadership of the Workers Alliance, the union of the unemployed. The origin of the Alliance is traced from its communist beginning in 1930. Biographical data is provided on its top leaders, most of whom are communists. The Alliance, whose political front is the New Deal, entices the unemployed through its "practical" programs.

H227 .... Rehearsal for Revolution, "Reader's Digest," 38 (June 1941), 89-93.
An analysis of communist objectives and tactics in the Allis-Chalmers strike in Milwaukee, January to April 1941. Local 248, UAW-CIO, long the pride of the Communist Party, is denounced with its leaders for calling a political strike. Events leading to the strike, personalities, union tactics, and the bitter aftermath are described.

H228 .... We Are Already Invaded, "Reader's Digest," 39 (July 1941), 122-26.
The communists first seek to win key positions in key unions, and then to stage sporadic strikes such as those in the aircraft industry in southern California. The final stage is the general strike and armed insurrection in which the communists will seize power. This strategy has been worked out in detail by Moscow's architects of revolution.

H229 .... Our Communists Are So Sorry They Were Good Boys, "Saturday Evening Post," 218 (Dec. 1, 1945), 17 ff.
A description of the effect on the CPUSA of French communist Jacques Duclos' article condemning Earl Browder's policy for postwar American communism. Browder has been purged for advocating class peace and replaced with William Z. Foster, an old hand at exploiting unrest. The Communist Political Association has been liquidated, and the reconstituted Party has returned to its strategy of disruption.

H230 .... Methodism's Pink Fringe, "Reader's Digest," 56 (Feb. 1950), 134-38.
Leaders of the Methodist Federation for Social Action, which operates within America's largest and most powerful Protestant church, attack the foreign policy of the U.S. and defend the internal and foreign policy of the USSR. Some of its heads are active in communist front organizations and contribute to Party publications.

H231 HILDEBRAND, J. H. The Communist Party and the Academic Profession, "Pacific Spectator," 3 (Spring 1949), 166-69.
Defense of the dismissal of two acknowledged communist professors by the University of Washington. The Party in the U.S., as in Russia, is the agent of a tyranny over the mind of man. Unlike those who merely hold unorthodox views, members of the Party submit themselves to discipline. (For a contrary view see Henry Nash Smith, "Legislatures, Communists, and State Universities," in "Pacific Spectator," Summer 1949.)

H232 HILL, Herbert. Communist Party—Enemy of Negro Equality, "Crisis," 58 (June 1951), 365-71; (July), 421-24.
The assistant field secretary of the NAACP traces the shifts in the Party program for Negroes, pointing out that it has changed with every shift in Russian policy. He concludes that the Party here is an instrument of Soviet foreign policy, that it is an enemy in the Negro's fight for equality, and that it stands for more efficient segregation. (Reprinted in pamphlet form.)

H233 ..., and GREENBERG, Jack. "Citizens' Guide to Desegregation: A Story of Social and Legal Change in America." Boston: Beacon, 1955. 185 pp.
An analysis (in "The Negro and the Communist Party," pp. 31-37) by two NAACP officials of Party activities in the Negro community, 1928-47. They discuss the "Self Determination of the Black Belt" slogan, its withdrawal with the advent of the people's front, the soft-pedaling of Negro protest during the war period, and the revival of "self determination" after the Duclos letter. They also deal briefly with the Party's use of the Scottsboro case for propaganda purposes.

H234 HILL, Joe [pseud.]. Anti-Red or Anti-Union? That Boston Labor Probe, "Nation," 180 (Jan. 8, 1955), 32-33.
An account of public hearings held in Boston by a Massachusetts legislative commission to investigate communism. Unions thus far investigated are the UE; the Distributive, Processing, and Office Workers; and the Fur and Leather Workers. The investigations, which served the interests of employers or rival unions or both, have frightened and confused workers.

H235 HILL, Sidney. "Housing under Capitalism." New York: International Pamphlets, 1935. 38 pp.
A "third period" communist analysis of housing in America, asserting that New Deal efforts cannot touch the real problem. Only in the Soviet Union has a housing solution been found. The author lists conditions for a genuine solution to the housing problem.

H236 .... The Housing Question—1937, "Communist," 16 (June 1937), 555-68.
A review of the housing crisis in the U.S. and an appraisal of measures adopted by the government to alleviate poor conditions. The Wagner-Steagall bill to set up a permanent U.S. Housing Authority and build 300,000 dwelling units in four years is endorsed, despite serious deficiencies.

H237 HILL, Stephen. CIO-PAC—A Survey: Record Shows the Communists Have Not Captured PAC, "New Leader," 27 (Nov. 4, 1944), 7.
A denial of statements in the Scripps-Howard newspapers that the communists have won control of the CIO's Political Action Committee. Evidence to the contrary is cited from Detroit, Cleveland, Pittsburgh, and leading Catholic periodicals. Sidney Hillman's errors, as in working with the left wing of the American Labor Party, are not evidence of a communist conspiracy.

H238 HILL, T. Arnold. Communism, "Opportunity," 8 (Sept. 1930), 278.
An official of the Urban League comments on communist efforts to recruit Negroes by championing their cause. He believes that the problem of communism among Negroes can be eliminated if prevailing injustices are removed.

H239 HILL, Warren P. A Critique of Recent Ohio Anti-Subversion Legislation, "Ohio State Law Journal," 14 (Autumn 1953), 439-93.

A law professor at Ohio State analyzes three recently passed Ohio laws dealing with subversion. He summarizes past antisubversion legislation in Ohio, and describes the legislative history and provisions of laws dealing with sedition, exclusion of subversives from state employment, and dismissal from public office for refusal to answer inquiries on subversion.

H240 HILLENBRAND, M. J. The Communist, "Commonweal,' 25 (Feb. 26, 1937), 493-95.
A sympathetic explanation of the appeal of individual communists and communism to the young intellectual. Communists are often idealists who hate Christians less than Christians hate them. We should give communists credit for their good points, and change our methods of fighting communism.

H241 HILLIARD, Raymond M. We Threw the Commies Out, "Saturday Evening Post," 223 (June 30, 1951), 20-21 ff.
A former New York City Commissioner of Public Welfare tells of his battle with the communist-controlled United Public Workers of America. He broke up the conspiracy by firing the ring leaders, transferring the less important troublemakers, and allowing the Party's dupes to make a fresh start. Today the Department of Welfare is no longer a communist cell.

H242 HILLMAN, Sidney. The Liquidation of Leftism in the Amalgamated, "Advance," 13 (Oct. 28, 1927), 6.
An editorial by the president of the Amalgamated Clothing Workers, asserting that the union came through its internal struggles by allowing the communists freedom. The administration presented a better program than the communists did. Recommendations that are right will ultimately be approved by the members, who know of the unscrupulous methods of the communists.

H243 HILLQUIT, Morris. The Socialist Task and Outlook, New York "Call," May 21, 1919. p. 8.
A leading socialist calls for a split between the right and left wings of the Socialist Party, which is dissipating its energies in fruitless controversies. The form and direction assumed by the left wing spell disaster, because they are reactionary and nonsocialistic, an emotional reflex of the situation in Russia. Two small organizations, each homogeneous, would be better than one big party torn by dissension.

H244 .... New Problems for Radicals, "New Leader," 1 (March 1, 1924), 7; (March 8), 7; (March 22), 7; (March 29), 7.
A series of lectures on problems faced by radicals in the postwar years, including communist disservices to the cause of socialism. These include generalizing from the Russian experience, discarding the concept of gradual growth, deprecation of parliamentarism, reversion to conspiratorial methods, revival of the theory of the dictatorship of the proletariat, and assertion that the end justifies any means.

H245 HIMELSTEIN, Morgan Y. "Drama Was a Weapon: The Left-Wing Theatre in New York, 1929-1941." New Brunswick, N.J.: Rutgers University Press, 1963. 300 pp. Notes. Bibliog. Ind.
A study of the Party's effort to infiltrate and control the American stage during the depression of the 1930's. The author describes the Party's attempts to organize new theatre troupes and dominate old ones, to formulate a theory of drama, and to force playwrights to conform to its line; and he records the Party's failure to reach these goals. The left-wing theatre, at its peak from 1934

through 1937, declined after 1938 and was dead by 1941. The Party had little success with antiwar plays, and its line was seldom reflected in anti-Nazi dramas. Though the Party line was reflected more frequently in plays dealing with social, political, and economic problems in American society, most dramas failed to offer the communist solution.

H246 HIMES, Chester B. "Lonely Crusade." New York: Knopf, 1947. 398 pp.
A left-wing but anticommunist novel, this is the story of an able young Negro who becomes a union organizer on the West Coast during World War II. A major theme is the use of his color for political purposes, as union members cultivate him for racial reasons and the employers seek to use him against the communists.

H247 HIMSTEAD, Ralph E. Correspondence with a Chapter Officer, "American Association of University Professors Bulletin," 35 (Autumn 1949), 545-56.
Clarification by its general secretary of the AAUP position toward communism and employment of communists as teachers. AAUP supports freedom of opinion and association, but does not condone subversive activities, use of classes for propaganda, or lack of scholarly objectivity. Those guilty of such offenses should be dismissed for professional unfitness.

H248 HINCKLEY, William W. "American Youth Acts: The Story of the American Youth Congress." New York: National Council, American Youth Congress, n.d. [1936]. 15 pp.
A brief history of the American Youth Congress since its founding in 1934, a summary of its campaign for passage of the American Youth Act, and a call for the election of youth group delegates to its third convention.

H249 .... "Youth Seeks Peace, Freedom and Progress: Report to Third American Youth Congress, Cleveland, Ohio, July 3, 4, 5, 1936." New York: National Council, American Youth Congress, n.d. [1936]. 22 pp.
A report by the chairman of the American Youth Congress, criticizing the youth program of the New Deal as inadequate and calling for passage of the American Youth Act, declaring support of organized labor, supporting Angelo Herndon, attacking the Supreme Court, announcing a decision to send delegates to the Geneva meeting of the World Youth Congress, and insisting on effective peace action and opposing militarization.

H250 .... "Youth Speaks for Itself." New York: American Youth Congress, n.d. [1936]. 16 pp.
The executive secretary of the American Youth Congress urges passage of the American Youth Act, introduced in Congress on January 14, 1936, and criticizes the National Youth Administration for its general inadequacy, its lack of democracy, and its threat to wage standards.

H251 HINDMAN, Jo. Reds Play the Circuit Again, "American Mercury," 88 (March 1959), 37-44.
Three and a half months after the Supreme Court in its decision in the Watkins case gave the "all's clear" signal to communist subversion, committees had been set up on the East and West Coasts to abolish the House Un-American Activities Committee.

H252 HINKEL, John V. Keep the Embargo on Munitions for Spain, "America," 60 (Jan. 14, 1939), 340-42.
An assertion that the bulk of the pressure on President Roosevelt to lift the arms embargo on Loyalist Spain comes from communist sources. The Joint Committee to Lift the Embargo is composed of six major communist

united-front organizations. Communist control of one of the six groups, the Medical Bureau and North American Committee to Aid Spanish Democracy, is shown.

H253 HINKEL, John V. Popular Front Forces Unite to Lift Arms Embargo, "America," 60 (Jan. 21, 1939), 366-68.
An exposé of the communist control of five of the six major groups comprising the Joint Committee to Lift the Embargo (the arms embargo on Loyalist Spain). These groups are the American League for Peace and Democracy, Friends of the Abraham Lincoln Brigade, Confederated Spanish Societies, American Friends of Spanish Democracy, and Lawyers Committee on Spain.

H254 . . . . Genesis of Conference to Lift the Embargo, "America," 60 (Jan. 28, 1939), 390-91.
A report on the communist-controlled Conference to Lift the Spanish Embargo, held in Washington, D. C., January 9-14, 1939. Each of the six organizations that called the conference is itself communist-controlled. Instructions to delegates and reactions of congressmen are reported.

H255 HINSHAW, Carl, and ROOSEVELT, James (George V. Denny, Jr., moderator). How Can the American Citizen Best Insure the Defeat of Communism? "Town Meeting," 16 (Sept. 19, 1950). 16 pp.
Asserting that communism has increased its Washington influence since Russia was recognized, Hinshaw calls for the election of candidates who will not appease communism. Roosevelt asserts that the communists will be defeated by positive programs such as the Marshall Plan.

H256 HIRSCH, Carl. "Public Enemies in Public Office." New York: New Century, 1951. 24 pp.
A communist author sees gangsterism and corruption as necessary concomitants of the capitalist system. Truman's political career is built on this morass, and the stench of corruption is nowhere greater than on Capitol Hill. The world's biggest racket today is the Korean "police action," where American Big Business is making super-profits. The author calls for socialism, independent political action, and a new political alignment for peace in 1952.

H257 HISS, Alger. "In the Court of Public Opinion." New York: Knopf, 1957. 424 pp. App. Ind.
An account of his investigations and trials by the former high State Department official, written after his release from prison. Accused by Whittaker Chambers of having passed confidential State Department papers to him for transmission to the Russians, Hiss sued for libel, and in turn was indicted for perjury. The real issue in the case, however, was espionage. Maintaining his innocence, Hiss ascribes his indictment and conviction to the political climate of the period, the tension generated by the Korean War, an unfair prosecutor, and a biased judge.

H258 HITZ, William. Criminal Prosecution for Contempt of Congress, "Federal Bar Journal," 14 (April-June 1954), 139-70.
The Assistant U.S. Attorney for the District of Columbia discusses statutes and decisions dealing with contempt of Congress. Among the cases are those who were cited for contempt for refusal to testify about alleged Communist Party affiliations before congressional committees.

H259 HOAR, Roger Sherman. Out of Their Own Mouths, "American Legion Magazine," 26 (May 1939), 10-11 ff.
An assertion, based on quotations from its director, Roger N. Baldwin, that the American Civil Liberties Union seeks to advance communism, using the half-hearted defense of the rights of conservatives as camouflage. Loyal Americans are advised to steer clear of the ACLU.

H260 HOBBS, Malcolm. The Subversive Drugstore, "Nation," 168 (Nov. 26, 1949), 517-18.
A case study of a "fifth amendment communist," Russian-born Mrs. Rose Anderson, owner of a Washington pharmacy, reciting the troubles which followed her refusal to answer the questions of an investigating committee and the injustices she suffered.

H261 HOCHMAN, Julius. The Labor Movement and Communism at Opposite Poles, "Justice," 9 (May 20, 1927), 7.
A speech to the convention of the Capmakers' Union by a vice-president of the ILGWU, contrasting the objectives of the American labor movement with those of communism. Communist attempts to infiltrate the union have been and will be rebuffed.

H262 HODGEMAN, Ralph. The Literary Marketplace, "Masses & Mainstream," 2 (July 1949), 7-15.
A discussion of economic conditions in American publishing and the status of creative writing, by a New York publishing executive. He shows that, with a controversial book of limited appeal, the publisher makes a profitless gesture in behalf of literature. The fortunes of American writing must not be left to the mercy of the market.

H263 HODGES, Clem. Crisis in Publishing, "Masses & Mainstream," 4 (Nov. 1951), 1-7.
A denunciation of Little, Brown and Company for accepting the resignation of D. Angus Cameron, editor-in-chief and vice-president, who was attacked as a communist sympathizer. The issue is the denial of freedom of speech and publication, under the fear and censorship that choke the publishing field today.

H264 HOFFMAN, Clare E. "Communism's Iron Grip on the CIO." New Haven, Conn.: Constitutional Educational League, n.d. [1937]. 60 pp.
Extracts from a speech by the Michigan Congressman in the House of Representatives, June 1, 1937, asserting that the CIO is led by men denounced by Lewis in 1924 as communists. The purpose of the CIO is to control the workers of all industries, which will permit the communists to take over the industries. Amendment of the Wagner Act, to make unions as responsible as industry, is advocated.

H265 HOFFMAN, Frederick J.; ALLEN, Charles; and ULRICH, Carolyn F. "The Little Magazine: A History and a Bibliography." Princeton: Princeton University Press, 1946. 440 pp. Bibliog. List of ref. Ind.
Chapter 9, "Political Directions in the Literature of the Thirties" (pp. 148-69), reviews and characterizes the leftist political-literary magazines of the depression 1930's. Among the magazines discussed are the earlier "Masses" and "Liberator," "New Masses," "Modern Quarterly," "Anvil," "Left Review," and "Partisan Review."

H266 HOFFMAN, Frederick J. "The Modern Novel in America: 1900-1950." Chicago: Regnery, 1951. 216 pp.
In chapter 6, "Violence and Rhetoric in the 1930's," the author discusses the proletarian novels of this decade. He examines the formula authors had to follow, and discusses briefly most of the proletarian novelists. He gives special treatment, however, to three outstanding novelists of the left or near-left, John Dos Passos, James T. Farrell, and John Steinbeck, analyzing both their literary qualities and their ideological orientation.

H267 HOFFMAN, Julius J. Whom Are We Protecting? Some Thoughts on the Fifth Amendment, "American Bar Association Journal," 40 (July 1954), 582-85.
An exploration of problems arising out of the use of the Fifth Amendment by communists or fellow-travelers. While the right to refuse to give self-incriminating testimony is basic in our country, cooperation with the government is equally basic. The privilege is narrowly construed and must not be abused.

H268 HOFSTADTER, Samuel H. "The 5th Amendment and the Immunity Act of 1954." New York: Fund for the Republic, 1955. 45 pp.
A historical and legal analysis of both the Fifth Amendment and the Immunity Act of 1954 by a justice of the New York State Supreme Court. The author distinguishes between a legal presumption of guilt, which the use of the Fifth Amendment forbids, and an inference of guilt, in the context of other facts, which may be valid. He condemns the improper use of the privilege by witnesses, and contends that, historically, the privilege has been a limited one. He approves of the Immunity Act as a means of accommodating the rights of the individual with the rights of society.

H269 HOLDEN, Bill. The Reorganization of the Workers Party of America, "International Press Correspondence," 6 (Jan. 13, 1926), 36-37.
Written for a special issue of "International Press Correspondence," prior to the second organizational conference of the Communist International. The article describes attempts to dissolve the language sections of the Workers (Communist) Party of America and to reorganize the Party on the basis of shop nuclei. Despite resistance by the language sections, the reorganization is now in progress.

H270 HOLDEN, Joseph M. On the 1952 Steel Strike, "Political Affairs," 31 (Nov. 1952), 36-45.
Though the steel workers won some gains in the 1952 strike, all their demands were not met because right-wing and reformist labor leaders supported the war-making policies of the ruling class. Among the needs are independent political action and protection of the rights of Negro steel workers.

H271 HOLDERMAN, Carl. The Internal Security Act of 1950, "Labor and Nation," 6 (Fall 1950), 44-46.
The president of the New Jersey State Council, CIO, criticizes the Internal Security (McCarran) Act of 1950 as threatening civil liberties; not only will it be ineffectual in controlling communists, but it will probably help them by its own built-in excesses and abuses.

H272 HOLLY, John P. "What If They Are Red?" New York: United Rank and File Education Committee, n.d. [1948?]. 25 pp.
Advice to rank-and-file members of communist-dominated unions who seek to restore control to the members. The author asserts that members of communist-led unions are handicapped legally, secretly manipulated, and sold out in collective bargaining. He urges them to stay in the unions and wage a two-front war against the communists and the employers.

H273 HOLMES, John Haynes. "Communism, Fascism, and Democracy." New York: Community Church, 1936. 19 pp.
A sermon stating the necessity of cooperation between communism and democracy if fascism is to be defeated.

H274 .... "What Shall We Do with These Communists?" New York: Community Church, 1949. 20 pp.

A sermon explaining our reasons for disliking communists, yet asserting that there is no excuse for the prevailing hysteria. In our own interests we must protect the rights of communists, while resisting them wherever they appear. We must remove conditions of inequality, injustice, and social misery that nourish communism.

H275 HOLT, Robert T. Age as a Factor in the Recruitment of Communist Leadership, "American Political Science Review," 48 (June 1954), 486-99.
An analysis of Party leadership in Italy, France, and the U.S., investigating the relationship between Party leadership and age of association with radical activity. Leaders were found to have joined the Party at an early age, most of them under 22, and to have become functionaries soon afterward.

H276 HONIG, Nathaniel. "The Trade Union Unity League Today: Its Structure, Policy, Program and Growth." New York: Labor Unity Publishers, 1934. 24 pp.
The official TUUL handbook, telling of the organization's formation in 1929, and outlining its basic policy as that of class struggle on the economic front and support of the Communist Party on the political front. It presents the TUUL platform, pledging the organization to guide militant opposition groups within reformist unions and to develop, through strike struggles, a powerful revolutionary trade union movement.

H277 .... "The Trade Unions Since the N.R.A.: The A.F. of L., Company Unions, T.U.U.L. Unions, Independent Unions." New York: Labor Unity Publishers, 1934. 32 pp.
Praise of the Party-controlled Trade Union Unity League as the only meaningful trade-union federation, and denunciation of the AFL for "blackest treachery" toward the workers. The NRA is attacked, as are workers who fell for the "sucker-bait" of Section 7(a). (A good example of the Party's trade-union line during the "third period.")

H278 .... NRA Builds Company Unions, "Labor Unity," 9 (April 1934), 6-8.
A charge that the NRA encourages company unions, leading even AFL leaders to protest. Revolutionary unions are told to work within company unions, to try to convert them into real shop committees.

H279 HOOK, Sidney. Why I Am a Communist: Communism Without Dogmas, "Modern Monthly," 8 (April 1934), 143-65.
Though he is a communist in that he accepts Marxian principles, Hook is not one in the sense of accepting the present principles and tactics of the Third International. He considers the arguments against communism from the standpoint of efficiency, democracy, morality, art, and necessity, and rejects official communist dogmas on the inevitability of communism, dialectical materialism, dictatorship and democracy, and the collective man. (Part of a symposium on communism, reprinted as "The Meaning of Marx: A Symposium.")

H280 .... The Anatomy of the Popular Front, "Partisan Review," 6 (Spring 1939), 29-45.
Max Lerner's "It Is Later Than You Think" illustrates the thought process behind popular frontism, an alliance of all classes to defend democracy. Experience in Kerensky's Russia, Germany, France, Spain, and in the U.S. during the Roosevelt Administration shows that in any popular front the most conservative wing prevails. A popular front, an agreement on a common political program, is distinguished from a united front of different political organizations for limited joint action.

H281 HOOK, Sidney. Unreconstructed Fellow-Travelers, "Call," 6 (Jan. 13, 1940), 2.
Critique of former communists or fellow-travelers who, instead of engaging in fundamental criticism of Stalinism, simply criticize the latest turn in the line as represented by the Hitler-Stalin pact. Hook foresees a lamentable retreat to the ivory tower on the part of intellectuals who have shaken off Stalinism, and who might be able to act with greater responsibility now.

H282 .... Communism and the Intellectuals, "American Mercury," 68 (Feb. 1949), 133-44.
An examination of the route by which intellectuals have become disillusioned with the Soviet experiment. Originally brought to the support of Soviet communism by the ideals of western democracy, the intellectuals were disenchanted by unnecessary cruelty and cultural terror in the USSR. Though the intellectuals were not blameless, their disillusionment shows growing maturity.

H283 .... Should Communists Be Permitted to Teach? "New York Times Magazine," Feb. 27, 1949), 7 ff.
Following expulsion of Party members from the University of Washington faculty, Hook argues that academic freedom does not extend to members of a group that is not itself free to search for truth. Evidence that the CPUSA is not free can be found in its teachings, its conditions for membership, and the behavior of members. All cases should be left to the faculties.

H284 .... The Fellow-Traveler: A Study in Psychology, "New York Times Magazine," April 17, 1949, 9 ff.
An analysis of the motivations and beliefs of fellow-travelers, sincere persons who believe that the Soviet Union is a progressive social order and that the CPUSA is a legitimate part of the movement of liberal reform. They should not be hounded, but educated to see that communism is reaction, and that the alternative is a courageous liberalism.

H285 .... The Literature of Political Disillusionment, "American Association of University Professors Bulletin," 35 (Autumn 1949), 450-67.
While the Bolshevik Revolution, like the French, produced a large literature of affirmation, it also produced a literature of disillusionment: Orwell, Gide, Silone, Koestler, and others were its principal exponents in Europe; and Eastman, Dos Passos, Hicks, and Farrell were its most noteworthy figures in the U.S. Analyzing the major elements in their disenchantment, the author argues that the change in the Soviet system was partly responsible, but that these intellectuals bear a heavy personal responsibility for their own illusions. (Adaptation of a paper read to the National Council of Teachers of English, Nov. 27, 1948; portions were published under the title, "Communism and the Intellectual," in "American Mercury," Feb. 1949.)

H286 .... What Shall We Do About Communist Teachers? "Saturday Evening Post," 222 (Sept. 10, 1949), 33 ff.
A professor of philosophy at New York University proposes that membership in the Communist Party be prima-facie evidence of unfitness to teach. He argues that Party members, because of Party directives on classroom teaching practices, organizational and campus activities, and research access to secret work, are unfit to teach in public schools and colleges.

H287 .... Academic Integrity and Academic Freedom: How to Deal with the Fellow-Traveling Professor, "Commentary," 8 (Oct. 1949), 329-39.
An assertion that fellow-traveling professors influence student political thought more than card-carrying Party members do. The solution must come from within the academic community, not from administrators or legislators. Communist theory and practice should be required study in colleges until the threat to the democratic culture of the West disappears.

H288 .... Communists in the Colleges, "New Leader," 33 (May 6, 1950), 16-18.
Criticism of AAUP officials and committee members for viewing membership in the Communist Party the same as membership in any other Party, and for doubting that the Party here is subservient to international communism. Communist teachers are instructed by the Party to use their position to indoctrinate for the Party line. The issue is one of professional conduct, not of belief or heresy.

H289 .... Dangers in Cultural Vigilantism, "New York Times Magazine," Sept. 30, 1951, 8 ff.
An assertion that indiscriminate charges of communism have hurt U.S. prestige abroad and injured liberty by stifling legitimate criticism. The cult of cultural vigilantism has attacked progressive education, demanded loyalty oaths, sought to eliminate subversive literature from schools and libraries, and urged censorship of the arts. The author presents a program to counteract this mania.

H290 .... What Is Guilt by Association? Clarifying a Catchphrase, "American Mercury," 75 (Nov. 1952), 37-43.
An assertion that much of the confusion concerning "guilt by association" arises from confusing moral guilt with criminal guilt, and from failure to assess the degree or kind of association. Enumerating the factors to be considered, the author calls for an intelligent evaluation if we are to keep both civil liberties and security.

H291 .... Lattimore on the Moscow Trials, "New Leader," 35 (Nov. 10, 1952), 16-19.
An attack on Owen Lattimore for his defense of the Moscow trials in 1937, a piece of special pleading in favor of the Kremlin. Almost every line breathes Lattimore's total commitment to the Kremlin's position on the trials. Yet he now hypocritically bemoans the state of civil liberties in the U.S.

H292 .... "Heresy, Yes—Conspiracy, No." New York: John Day, 1953. 283 pp. Ind.
An effort to define the problem of communists in relation to civil liberties by distinguishing between unpopular ideas, which deserve protection, and subversive movements, which should be destroyed. Hook emphasizes the conspiratorial nature of the Communist Party, which should be prima-facie evidence for excluding members from positions of trust or sensitiveness such as teaching. He criticizes both the overvigilant anticommunist and the undervigilant liberal for failure to meet the issue constructively. (A pamphlet of the same title by Hook was published in 1952 by the American Committee for Cultural Freedom.)

H293 .... Does the Smith Act Threaten Our Liberties? "Commentary," 15 (Jan. 1953), 63-73.
A discussion of the Smith Act, including the right of revolution, the meaning of conspiracy, and the context of the "clear and present danger" formula. While the aim of the Smith Act is justified, the method chosen is inept. Not speech, but organization by a foreign power for revolutionary overthrow, should have been proscribed.

H294 .... Indoctrination and Academic Freedom, "New Leader," 36 (March 9, 1953), 2-4.

A discussion of whether members of the Communist Party should be permitted to teach. Some persons argue that communists, like others, should be judged by performance, and that Party instructions to take advantage of their position is evidence only of intent. The author agrees with the New School that membership in a group which asserts the right to dictate in matters of scientific opinion thereby disqualifies one as a teacher.

H295 HOOK, Sidney. Freedom in American Culture, "New Leader," 36 (April 6, 1953), Section 2, 14 pp.
A discussion of heresy, conspiracy, security risks, campus fear, blacklisting, civil liberties, McCarthyism, communist teachers, and loyalty oaths by a professor of philosophy at New York University. (An adaptation of a chapter in Hook's forthcoming book, "Heresy, Yes—Conspiracy, No.")

H296 .... The Fifth Amendment—A Moral Issue, "New York Times Magazine," Nov. 1, 1953, 9 ff.
A discussion of the Fifth Amendment, and the privilege against self-incrimination, in relationship to members of the Communist Party. While a teacher has the legal right to plead the Amendment, his assertion that to answer a question as to Party membership would incriminate him would permit an assumption that he is a Party member. Reasons for refusing to answer as to past Party membership are discussed.

H297 .... Ethics of Loyalty: Security and Freedom, "Confluence," 3 (June 1954), 155-71.
An assertion that a security program is necessary for the U.S., given the aims of the communist movement. Liberals, both here and abroad, are criticized for their indifference to such a program. The alarm felt by the American public about the extent of communist infiltration is justified. Ways of countering the threat are examined.

H298 .... The Problem of the Ex-Communist, "New York Times Magazine," July 11, 1954, 7 ff.
A call for an intelligent acceptance of the excommunist on the basis of his present character, credibility, and allegiance, with opposition to any uniform policy of either acceptance or rejection. Not all excommunists have had the same experiences, nor do their political views agree. We should listen to their suggestions, without making them our guides to the future.

H299 .... Should Our Schools Study Communism? "New York Times Magazine," August 29, 1954, 9 ff.
Teaching about communism is advocated on the ground that hatred and fear of communism cannot adequately combat it. It should be studied systematically, not as incidental to other themes, and taught by qualified persons. No converts are made when objective study of communist theory is accompanied by study of its practice in communist countries.

H300 .... Fallacies in Our Thinking about Security, "New York Times Magazine," January 30, 1955, 15 ff.
A discussion of the proper functioning of a security system, pointing out that not all government positions require investigation and that accusations may be unfounded. There should be a minimum of political passion, and a pragmatic rather than a legalistic point of view. True security can be found only in positive action, not in a holding operation.

H301 .... The AAUP and Academic Integrity, "New Leader," 39 (May 21, 1956), 19-21.

A critical evaluation of the committee report, adopted by the AAUP, on academic freedom and national security. Hook challenges the AAUP view that Communist Party membership should not be a criterion of incompetence. The AAUP, he asserts, suggests that a college is failing in its educational duty unless members of the Party teach on campus.

H302 .... "Common Sense and the Fifth Amendment." New York: Criterion Books, 1957. 160 pp. App.
An argument that use of the Fifth Amendment to avoid self-incrimination, while legal, should permit common sense inferences of guilt or unfitness. Attitudes toward invocation of the Fifth Amendment have been influenced by its use in questions concerning communist involvement, put by controversial congressional committees. Chapters deal with logic, psychology, ethics, politics, and the individual, all in relation to the Fifth Amendment. Appendices contain excerpts of testimony before the House Committee on Un-American Activities.

H303 .... Liberalism and the Law: Justice Frankfurter and Professor Chafee, "Commentary," 23 (Jan. 1957), 46-56.
An argument against the thesis, put forward by Zechariah Chafee in "The Blessings of Liberty," that, though communists are bad because they have "double-crossed the community," those who have renounced communism are worse because they have double-crossed one time more. Justice Felix Frankfurter's views are commended with respect to his stand on liberty.

H304 .... The Fifth Amendment: A Crucial Case, "New Leader," 40 (April 22, 1957), 18-20.
An analysis of the case of Dr. Harry Slochower, alleged member of a CP cell at Brooklyn College, who was discharged for invoking the Fifth Amendment with regard to past Party membership. The majority opinion of the U.S. Supreme Court, under which he was ordered reinstated, is criticized. He subsequently resigned rather than face a hearing.

H305 .... Justice Black's Illogic, "New Leader," 40 (Dec. 2, 1957), 17-20.
Criticism of Justice Black's opinion in the Koenigsberg case, which held that state bar examiners may not infer bad moral character from an applicant's refusal, on First Amendment grounds, to answer questions about communist affiliation. The examiners had evidence that the applicant was a member of the Communist Party. Black's opinion is called bad logic, and a blow to the enforcement of legal ethical standards.

H306 .... "Political Power and Personal Freedom: Critical Studies in Democracy, Communism, and Civil Rights." New York: Criterion, 1959. 462 pp. Ind.
A collection of essays written over the past decade, many of them previously published in magazines. Among the topics are the conflict between communist and democratic philosophies, the literature of political disillusionment, the psychology of the fellow-traveler, ideological espionage, the problem of the excommunist, security and freedom, and academic freedom.

H307 ... (comp. and ed.). "World Communism: Key Documentary Material." Princeton, N.J.: Van Nostrand, 1962. 255 pp.
Part 4, pp. 132-77, deals with "Communism in the United States." It includes excerpts from Party publications, government documents, and other sources on control of the CPUSA by the Soviet Union, the method of achieving a Soviet America, self-determination for the Black Belt, the student movement, loyalty and war, and related issues.

H308 HOOVER, J. Edgar. Red Fascism in the United States Today, "American Magazine," 143 (Feb. 1947), 24-25 ff.
A disclosure by the head of the FBI of the aims and methods of American communists as portrayed by their own acts and words. Their objective is the destruction of the American way of life. They would bring the same terror, oppression, and tyranny that fascism would. Loyal to Russia, they use trickery and deceit to gain their ends.

H309 .... How to Fight Communism, "Newsweek," 29 (June 9, 1947), 30-32.
The director of the FBI asserts that the best defense against communism is the American way of life, and that our surest weapon is truth. We cannot meet the communist menace unless there is widespread knowledge of its designs. Union members, minority groups, schools, and churches should be alert to communist propaganda.

H310 .... Don't Be Duped by the Communists! "Redbook Magazine," 91 (June 1948), 40-41 ff.
An assertion that deceit is the essence of communism. Communists hide behind fictitious names and innocent-looking fronts, which give them a foothold in progressive organizations or a name for propaganda purposes. A criminal conspiracy to rob America of its freedoms, communism's greatest appeal is to foreign-born and their offspring.

H311 .... Communism—Enemy of American Labor, "American Federationist," 58 (Sept. 1951), 32-34.
The head of the FBI praises the magnificent work of American labor unions in fighting the communist menace and educating Americans to the evil character of communism. The communists are regrouping and attacking again, utilizing the revived communist shop clubs and the Stockholm peace petitions.

H312 .... Breaking the Communist Spell, "American Mercury," 78 (March 1954), 57-61.
An effort by the director of the FBI to enlist the help of excommunists in wiping out the Soviet conspiracy that threatens the U.S. Many are caught in a moral struggle between sympathy with former associates and duty to their country. One who breaks with the Party and yet remains silent is still aiding the enemy. (Reprinted from "This Week Magazine.")

H313 .... Communism in the United States, "American Legion Magazine," 56 (March 1954), 14-15 ff.
Questions and answers on the influence and activities of the Communist Party in the U.S. The head of the FBI reports a decrease by two-thirds of Party membership since January 1947, though many Party fronts remain active. Communist plans include infiltration of unions and of the two major political parties and continuation of the "peace offensive." Suggestions are given on how to fight communism.

H314 .... God and Country or Communism? "American Legion Magazine," 63 (Nov. 1957), 14-15 ff.
The head of the FBI, pointing to the current revitalization of the Party here and its expanding propaganda, asserts the falsity of its alleged break with its past and the cutting of its ties with Moscow. He asserts that communism is unchanged, and that Khrushchev's line of peaceful coexistence is simply a maneuver. (Also printed in the "American Mercury," Dec. 1957.)

H315 .... "Masters of Deceit: The Story of Communism in America and How to Fight It." New York: Holt, 1958. 374 pp. Ind. Bibliog. App. Gloss.
An analysis of communism by the director of the Federal Bureau of Investigation, who asserts that communism is a false, materialistic way of life, and that international communism has, over the course of its history, become a hard, dedicated, international conspiracy, whose chief target today is America. Chapters are devoted to the development of communist ideas by Marx, Lenin, and Stalin, and to a brief history of the CP in the U.S., with emphasis on the Party's subservience to Moscow. Other chapters analyze Party propaganda, and its appeals to Americans; the internal organization and discipline of the Party; Party agitation, united front, and infiltration tactics; and the Party underground espionage and sabotage activities.

H316 .... The Deadly Menace of Pseudo Liberals, "American Mercury," 86 (Jan. 1958), 7-11.
Though Party membership has gone down in the last ten years, there is still a hard core of conspirators. The influence of subversion is unbelievable, and complacency and softness are on the upswing. Aiding this trend are organizations of pseudo liberals, which seek, not freedom to protest, but license.

H317 .... The Communist Attack on Judaism, "ADL Bulletin," 15 (April 1958), 1-2 ff.
A review of the communist propaganda line for Jews in a publication of the Anti-Defamation League of B'nai B'rith, a Jewish fraternal organization. Attacking this propaganda as composed of half-truths and deceptions, the author calls on vigilant members of Jewish organizations to continue to counteract infiltration efforts by communists.

H318 .... "A Study of Communism." New York: Holt, Rinehart and Winston, 1962. 212 pp. Ind.
A study of the world communist movement, focusing on its attractions, its origins, its seizure and consolidation of power, its efforts at world expansion, and its challenge to freedom. Chapter 11, "Communism's Target—the United States" (pp. 156-81), discusses recent developments in the CPUSA, its current status, its loyalty to Moscow, its potential for sabotage, and communist intelligence and espionage activities here. Chapter 12, "Meeting the Communist Challenge" (pp. 182-91), deals with the role of the citizen in combating communism, the problem of internal security, and the response of a free society to the communist challenge.

H319 HORDERN, William. "Christianity, Communism and History." New York: Abingdon Press, 1954. 174 pp. Ind.
A comparison and contrast of Christianity and communism. Comparing communism as a dissident form of economic and political organization with Christian sects as a dissident form of Christian organization, the author shows why, despite their similarities, communism has led to totalitarianism whereas the sects have led to modern democracy. Pointing to half-truths in the communist creed, he emphasizes Christianity's basic opposition to communism. Social justice, he asserts, is a necessary part of the Christian answer to communism, though not the whole answer.

H320 HOROWITZ, Harold W. Loyalty Tests for Employment in the Motion Picture Industry, "Stanford Law Review," 6 (May 1954), 438-72.
A description of the loyalty program in the motion picture industry under the influence of congressional investigations, private groups outside the industry such as the American Legion, and the industry's own efforts. The industry now employs an informal screening process for prospective employees, and contracts contain specific clauses making past Party membership ground for dismissal.

H321 HORSCH, John. "Communism: A Deadly Foe to the Christian Faith Assuming the Guise of Christianity." Chicago: Bible Institute Colportage Assoc., 1937. 28 pp.
A fundamentalist statement of opposition to communism, seeing as the Party's most vital characteristic its fierce antagonism to religion. Quoting communist literature from Marx through Browder, the author calls upon his readers to oppose this greatest menace to Christianity.

H322 HOUSEWRIGHT, Vernon A., and SUFFRIDGE, James A. Retail Clerks Make History, "American Federationist," 55 (Sept. 1948), 16-18.
The president and secretary-treasurer of the Retail Clerks International Association, AFL, describe their organization's anticommunist activities, climaxed by the NLRB victory over the communist-dominated Local 1250 of the CIO's Retail, Wholesale and Department Store Union in Oppenheim, Collins & Co., New York.

H323 HOWARD, Milton. The President's Economic War Plan, "Communist," 21 (June 1942), 435-39.
Roosevelt's economic war plan calls for high taxes on profits and large incomes, price control and rationing, and wages adjusted to the price level. The defeatists demand a wage freeze, which would force labor to make most of the war sacrifices. Lewis and other labor betrayers call Roosevelt's plan a wage freeze. Labor must support Roosevelt's plan wholeheartedly.

H324 .... The 1942 Elections—and After, "Communist," 21 (Dec. 1942), 1005-11.
Republicans, including some defeatists, won new seats in Congress. Their success was due to the misdirected popular reaction to Roosevelt's hesitation in opening a second front and centralizing the war economy. The Administration can again mobilize the people behind it by energetically pursuing these goals.

H325 .... The Incoming Seventy-Eighth Congress, "Communist," 22 (Jan. 1943), 51-57.
The defeatist bloc in Congress has been strengthened as a result of Republican election gains. Instead of considering its enemies on certain issues to be enemies on all issues, the win-the-war camp should welcome support on any specific issue of men who are usually defeatists. The workers must now allow the defeatists to succeed in splitting labor.

H326 .... Lincoln, Roosevelt and the Fifth Column, "Communist," 22 (Feb. 1943), 135-45.
Lincoln, like Roosevelt, had to cope with the defeatists who conspired against the Northern war effort. Lincoln triumphed over the Copperheads only after he rallied mass support by proclaiming the emancipation of slaves, and by following Sherman's tactics of annihilating the enemy on his own soil.

H327 .... From Potsdam to Paris—One Year of Foreign Policy, "Political Affairs," 25 (June 1946), 483-89.
The Anglo-Soviet-American coalition was formed only after Britain and the U.S. gave up their futile hope of cooperation with German imperialism. The Paris conference is in line with British and American policy since the war ended. U.S. and British capitalists want their governments to renege on promises to Russia and seek world domination.

H328 .... Partisan Review: Esthetics of the Cage, "Mainstream," 1 (Winter 1947), 46-57.
An associate editor of the "Daily Worker" severely criticizes the "Partisan Review," using as a take-off point the publication of "Partisan Reader," a ten-year anthology of "Partisan Review' writings. Despite its "independent Marxist" tone, the "Partisan Review" assaults the Marxist view of the class nature of society and retreats from every real problem.

H329 ...; McMICHAEL, Jack R.; SHEPPARD, Harry R.; and MILLER, A. L., Should Congress Outlaw the Communist Party? "American Forum of the Air," 9 (April 29, 1947), 1-15.
The case for outlawing the Communist Party is presented by Representatives Sheppard and Miller, who call the Party an agent of a foreign power and an advocate of overthrow of government by force and violence. Howard, associate editor of the "Daily Worker," denies both charges. McMichael, executive secretary of the Methodist Federation for Social Action, would fight communism by preventing depressions.

H330 .... The Holy War on Reason: What Whittaker Chambers Means to America, "Masses & Mainstream," 5 (July 1952), 1-14.
An associate editor of the "Daily Worker" draws a parallel between the writings of Chambers and the "big lie" literature of the Nazi regime. Chambers is attacked for fabricated politics, faked social realities, cynical theology, shabby sophistries, and career slyness. Both his theory of American life and his account of his communism are fiction.

H331 .... "McCarthyism and the Big Lie." New York: New Century, 1953. 16 pp.
An assertion by a communist author that McCarthyism is a political policy as well as a method of hunting subversives. McCarthy's real targets are said to be democracy and the country's advances in political and social policies under Roosevelt. McCarthy looks on war with Russia and China as inevitable and good, while proclaiming Spanish and German fascism our only reliable allies.

H332 .... Orwell or O'Casey, "Masses & Mainstream," 8 (Jan. 1955), 20-26.
Denunciation of George Orwell, whose "Animal Farm" and "1984" are said to be among the most depraved works in contemporary literature. Orwell's fascist tendencies and hatred of humanity are contrasted with the humanism of Sean O'Casey. The world's people, seeking to balk an atomic war, are allied with O'Casey, as against Orwell, who preaches universal death.

H333 .... New Realities for the Intellectuals, "Masses & Mainstream," 8 (Feb. 1955), 35-42.
The Matusow confession forces intellectuals to re-evaluate the current myths in our country: that the cold war was instigated by the Soviet Union, that Marxism and the political movements based on it are criminal conspiracies with antidemocratic aims, that the Soviet Union is imperialistic, and that America must defend the world against Soviet imperialism.

H334 HOWARD, Sidney. Bailing the Bolshevist, "Collier's," 65 (Jan. 10, 1920), 15 ff.
A caution against ruthless persecution of aliens for supposed Bolshevism. Indiscriminate accusation is false, and makes for violence and terror by police, special government agents, and vigilante groups. We must assimilate and Americanize the aliens instead of answering their cry for education with a policeman's billy.

H335 HOWE, B. A. Reds Take to Stage and Screen, "National Republic," 23 (Jan. 1936), 22-23 ff; (Feb.), 22-23 ff.
An account of the communists' growing stage and screen

efforts in the U.S., emphasizing class hatred, atheism, and revolt. Soviet and communist films are listed, with the theaters in which they have been shown. Communist efforts in the areas of music and dance are also described.

H336 HOWE, Irving, and WIDICK, B. J. "The UAW and Walter Reuther." New York: Random House, 1949. 309 pp. Notes. Ind.
An analysis of the UAW-CIO from an "independent radical" point of view. The authors describe the background and history of the union, the formation of an anticommunist caucus led by Walter Reuther, and the final victory of the anticommunists in the union in 1946-47. Factional dissension in the union is analyzed, as is the role of the small but well-disciplined communist group. The communists called obstructionist strikes during the Hitler-Stalin pact period, supported incentive pay in 1943, and pushed the proposed merger with the Farm Equipment Workers in 1947.

H337 HOWE, Irving. Intellectual Freedom and Stalinists: Shall CP Teachers Be Prohibited from Teaching? "New International," 15 (Dec. 1949), 231-36.
A critique of Sidney Hook's view that communists should not be allowed to teach because CP membership is prima facie evidence of lack of intellectual independence. Other questions are whether the Stalinist surrender of intellectual independence differs from the non-Stalinist, whether Stalinist teachers behave in fact the way the CP demands, and whether the consequences of expulsion are more severe than those of permitting them to continue to teach.

H338 . . ., and COSER, Lewis. "The American Communist Party: A Critical History (1919-1957)." Boston: Beacon, 1957. 593 pp. Notes. Ind.
A critical account of the Communist Party in the U.S. from its inception in 1919 to its virtual disintegration in 1957. The authors trace the history of the communist movement here through its underground days, the 1920's and early 1930's, the popular front era, the Nazi-Soviet pact period, World War II, and the cold war. The book describes the Wallace campaign, the expulsions of Party-dominated unions from the CIO, the Smith Act prosecutions, the Khrushchev revelations, and the disintegration of the Party into impotent, quarreling factions.

H339 . . . . "On the Nature of Communism and Relations with Communists." New York: League for Industrial Democracy, n.d. [1966]. 14 pp.
A paper written for a conference of Students for a Democratic Society, Christmas week 1965. The author, a democratic socialist, approves cooperation with communists for limited purposes, while opposing organizational cooperation on a programmatic or political basis. Refusal to admit totalitarians to membership does not compromise the democratic outlook of a student group.

H340 HUBER, Eugene. Marxian Strike, "Catholic World," 153 (July 1941), 417-25.
An assertion that the CIO, from its inception, was so impregnated with Marxism that its policies and strikes bore a revolutionary taint. Catholics, who oppose an egalitarian concept of society, the use of force, and destructive violence impairing individual property, are urged to take a stand against this strike tactic.

H341 HUBERMAN, Leo. "The Great Bus Strike." New York: Modern Age, 1941. 167 pp.
An account, by a Marxist writer long friendly to the Party, of the New York City bus strike of March 1941. The strike was conducted by the Transport Workers Union, whose leadership was then close to the Party, against the Fifth Avenue Coach Company and the New York City

Omnibus Corporation. The author discusses the issues, gives a diary of the strike, denounces Mayor La Guardia and the newspapers, and concludes that the strikers won because of their solidarity against the combined forces of employers, politicians, and the press.

H342 . . . . "Storm over Bridges." San Francisco: Harry Bridges Defense Committee, 1941. 89 pp.
A denunciation of the immigration authorities, the FBI, and the "stoolies" for their renewed effort to deport Bridges. The author, long close to the Party and its causes, recites Bridges' achievements for the longshoremen, deplores his "persecution," and asserts that his militant trade unionism is the only reason for the deportation effort. The deportation hearings are seen as a threat to all citizens and to constitutional liberties.

H343 . . . . "Citizenship for Harry Bridges, Production Soldier." San Francisco: Harry Bridges Victory Committee and Citizens Victory Committee for Harry Bridges, 1942. 23 pp.
An assertion that Bridges, through patriotism, imagination, and devotion, has speeded the war effort and helped bring victory to the U.S. In return the government is urged to dismiss all charges against him and clear away any obstacles to citizenship.

H344 . . . . The Daggett-Sweezy Case, "Monthly Review," 6 (Aug. 1954), 142-50.
An account of the conviction of Paul M. Sweezy, an editor of the "Monthly Review," for contempt of court in connection with an investigation of subversive activities in New Hampshire. Sweezy refused to answer questions relating to the Progressive Party or a lecture on socialism at the University of New Hampshire as not pertinent to the inquiry or an invasion of freedoms guaranteed by the First Amendment.

H345 HUDSON, G. F. A New Whitewash of Alger Hiss, "New Leader," 36 (July 27, 1953), 15-22.
A critical evaluation of Lord Jowitt's book, "The Strange Case of Alger Hiss," originally published in the British journal, "Twentieth Century." The author of the article, a fellow at Oxford, concludes that Lord Jowitt does not understand acts of treason committed for the sake of a revolutionary ideology, by men convinced they owe an allegiance higher than loyalty to their own country.

H346 . . . . The Dexter White Case, "Twentieth Century," 155 (Jan. 1954), 22-35.
A review by a historian in a British journal of the FBI documents made public in the Harry Dexter White controversy. Judging the threat of communist infiltration of the U.S. government to be serious, the author asserts that Truman, by attempting to suppress information, made the situation worse.

H347 HUDSON, Roy B. Rooting the Party on the Waterfront, "Communist," 14 (Dec. 1935), 1161-70.
A speech to the November plenum of the Party's Central Committee, criticizing communist underestimation of activity in the International Longshoremen's Association and the International Seamen's Union. While the Seventh World Congress of the Comintern emphasized a broad united front and formation of a farmer-labor party, communists must win the workers in decisive industries such as the marine, and make them a factor in the united front.

H348 . . . . The Fight of the Seamen for Militant Unionism, "Communist," 15 (March 1936), 220-29.
Criticism of the convention of the International Seamen's Union for withdrawing the Sailors Union from the Maritime Federation of the Pacific. This action is contrasted

with that of the convention of the United Mine Workers, upholding industrial unionism.

H349 HUDSON, Roy B. "Who Are the Reds?" New York: Workers Library, 1937. 20 pp.
A communist recruiting pamphlet, addressed to seamen and longshoremen, outlining the Party's program on unionism, the people's front, war, and socialism. Denying that communists seek to capture control of unions or follow a rule-or-ruin policy, Hudson emphasizes the need for a popular front to defeat reaction, fascism, and war.

H350 .... Lessons of the Maritime Strikes, "Communist," 16 (March 1937), 220-40.
The successful strike of the Pacific maritime unions (united through the Maritime Federation of the Pacific and supported by maritime unions of the East and Gulf) has made a national maritime federation possible. The strike's conduct is reviewed.

H351 .... New Developments in Organizing the Marine Industry, "Communist," 16 (Nov. 1937), 1016-22.
A discussion of AFL attempts to block CIO efforts to form a national maritime federation. CIO forces have nevertheless been strengthened, and the AFL splitters placed on the defensive.

H352 .... The Struggle for Trade Union Unity, "Communist," 17 (March 1938), 242-50.
A report to a plenary session of the Party's Central Committee and National Party Builders Congress, February 18-21, 1938, declaring a unified labor movement as a central CP goal. The organization drives and philosophy of the CIO are praised, and the reactionary, anti-unification position of the AFL condemned. Party members are urged to work within the framework of the unions to develop a strong united front.

H353 .... The Charter of Party Democracy, "Communist," 17 (Aug. 1938), 704-10.
A report to the Party's tenth national convention, May 31, 1938, recommending improvements in the Party's constitution. Amendments considered dealt with religious beliefs, citizenship, democratic control, greater personal responsibility, and vigilance against the class enemy and his agents.

H354 .... Defeat the Foes of Labor Unity! "Communist," 17 (Oct. 1938), 881-90.
Big Business is supplementing its attack on the New Deal with a drive to disrupt the trade unions as the backbone of the democratic front. The union-wrecking offensive is being carried on under anticommunist slogans. Trotskyites and Lovestoneites are being exposed as union wreckers. The Party is helping to unify the labor movement. (Based on a report to the political committee of the Party's national committee, Aug. 19, 1938.)

H355 .... The A.F. of L. Convention and Tasks for Achieving Unity, "Communist," 17 (Dec. 1938), 1094-1104.
The recent AFL convention dramatized the division between the camp of reaction and the camp of progress and democracy. It made evident the growing sentiment of the membership for militant policies, and strengthened the forces of labor unity and the democratic front. Opposition to the reactionary leadership is mounting.

H356 .... The Path of Labor's United Action, "Communist," 18 (Oct. 1939), 927-38.
An examination of the possibilities for a united stand by CIO and AFL unions on behalf of New Deal candidates in the 1940 elections. The role of communists as trade union leaders is analyzed. Though communist factions in the unions have been abolished, communists remain responsible to the Party for their union activities.

H357 .... For a Greater Vote and a Stronger Party! "Communist," 19 (Aug. 1940), 707-15.
A report to the Election Campaign and Party Building Commission at the Party's national convention, asserting that the Party has stood firm in spite of strong attacks on it. Although membership has declined, a higher percentage of members are paying dues. Members must make great efforts to educate people and use mass campaigns to recruit new members.

H358 .... "The C.I.O. Convention and National Unity." New York: Workers Library, 1941. 15 pp.
Writing on the eve of Pearl Harbor when the communists were already emotionally in the war, the author lauds the convention for calling for all aid to Great Britain, the Soviet Union, and China in order to defeat Hitler, but criticizes the convention for insufficient understanding of the Soviet Union's role in the fight against fascism.

H359 .... "Trends in the Labor Movement." New York: Workers Library, 1941. 23 pp.
A communist pamphlet during the Hitler-Stalin pact period, urging workers to resist Roosevelt's war program. The author classes labor in three groups: a reactionary, anti-Soviet segment supporting the war program; a group hesitant to break with Roosevelt; and an advanced wing, to which the communists belong, which struggles to keep out of the war.

H360 .... The Real Reasons for Trade Union Progress, "Communist," 20 (Jan. 1941), 51-63.
A review of AFL growth, to discredit an analysis of its development by George Meany in the November "American Federationist." The CIO has done more in its short history to organize and unite labor than the AFL leadership has accomplished in 60 years. (Also published in pamphlet form.)

H361 .... The Trend in Labor's Ranks, "Communist," 20 (May 1941), 410-19.
An appraisal of the labor movement's opposition to the "imperialist war program of Wall Street," written shortly before the Nazi attack on the Soviet Union. The influence of social democrats is largely responsible for weaknesses in labor's policy, including its inability to see the aid-to-Britain program as a war policy.

H362 .... Labor's Great Responsibilities and Possibilities, "Communist," 20 (Aug. 1941), 685-95.
A reexamination of work in the labor movement in light of the Nazi attack upon Russia. Problems in rallying labor to anti-Hitlerism and support of the Soviet Union are considered. Labor must be represented on various government boards in order to accelerate aid to the USSR and Britain. (Based on a report to a plenary meeting of the Party's national committee, June 28-29, 1941.)

H363 .... "Two Questions on Winning the War." New York: Workers Library, 1942. 15 pp.
The text of a letter to the "Christian Science Monitor" dealing with the relations of the U.S. to the USSR in the prosecution of the war and with the role of the American communists in the struggle. The author, a Party leader, asserts that victory and the future of America depend on cooperation with the Soviet Union, and that the Party here is dedicated to the single task of helping to win the war.

H364 .... Labor and the National War Effort, "Communist," 21 (May 1942), 310-23.

A report to a plenary meeting of the Party's national committee, April 4-5, 1942, appraising organized labor's participation in the war effort. Conversion to war industry and increased production are acclaimed, while the labor movement is criticized for not calling for the opening of a second front in Europe.

H365 HUDSON, Roy B. The C.I.O. Convention, "Communist," 21 (Dec. 1942), 985-99.
A review of the Boston convention of the CIO, which is praised for its subordination of all other issues to a speedy victory in the war. It is also commended for friendly relations with the Soviet trade unions and the absence of Red-baiting.

H366 .... "The Communists and the Trade Unions." New York: Workers Library, 1943. 23 pp.
Criticism of labor leaders who disrupt the war effort with attacks on communists. This issue is a false one; unity to win the war and strengthen labor is the true issue. Communists seek only the same rights as other trade unionists.

H367 .... Forge World Labor Unity! "Communist," 22 (May 1943), 403-10.
Allied solidarity would be greatly strengthened by an alliance of labor forces among the united nations. The AFL is against such a move, while the CIO and Railroad Brotherhoods favor greater unity.

H368 .... Crucial Problems before Labor Today, "Communist," 22 (July 1943), 613-23.
A report to a plenary meeting of the Party's national committee, June 11-13, outlining labor's responsibilities to support the government's wartime policies and guarantee the production necessary for the invasion of Europe. Defeatists and obstructionists in the labor movement, particularly in the AFL Executive Council, are attacked, and their attempts to abandon the no-strike pledge are deplored.

H369 .... The Auto Workers' Convention, "Communist," 22 (Nov. 1943), 1005-17.
A review of the UAW convention in Buffalo, October 1943, stressing its patriotic character as illustrated in its resolutions on labor's participation in the war effort. Unity of win-the-war forces requires an end to factionalism.

H370 .... "Post-War Jobs for Veterans, Negroes, Women." New York: Workers Library, 1944. 24 pp.
The author, vice-president of the Communist Political Association and labor editor of the "Daily Worker," urges organized labor to prepare for the special problems of reconversion by permitting veterans, Negroes, and women to retain the rights won during the war period.

H371 .... Teheran and the Wage Policy Issue, "Communist," 23 (Feb. 1944), 140-47.
Due to the failure of many wartime controls, wage levels have not been maintained. This must be corrected, not by strikes, but by a national wage policy. Labor must continue to support the war effort, even though victory is certain. The Teheran conference provisions will insure lasting peace and favorable conditions for labor.

H372 .... Two Conventions of Labor, "Political Affairs," 24 (Jan. 1945), 31-42.
A contrast of the reactionary AFL and progressive CIO conventions with respect to their stands on a third party, international labor unity, Negroes, Red-baiting, the no-strike pledge, etc. The CIO is praised for declaring

against a third party, thereby consolidating the pro-Roosevelt coalition, whereas the AFL is criticized for its anti-Soviet, anti-CIO, and anti-Negro position.

H373 .... Labor's Victory Wage Policies, "Political Affairs," 24 (April 1945), 311-17.
The CIO Executive Board is praised for rejecting the plan of Rieve and Reuther to rescind the no-strike pledge and scuttle the War Labor Board; and also for its wage policy. The relation of wages to prices is discussed, as is the transition to peacetime production. The general functioning of the War Labor Board must be improved. (Based on a report to the national committee of the CPA, March 12, 1945.)

H374 .... Labor's Fight for Jobs and Wages, "Political Affairs," 24 (Nov. 1945), 1003-6.
A presentation of the minimum conditions that labor should accept in the reconversion to a peacetime economy. Labor should defeat compulsory arbitration, protect the right to strike, oppose wage ceilings, and prevent price increases by the monopolies.

H375 .... The I.L.W.U. Convention—A Victory for All Labor, "Political Affairs," 28 (July 1949), 45-57.
A description of the program adopted by the recently concluded convention of the International Longshoremen's and Warehousemen's Union headed by Harry Bridges. The progressive decisions of the ILWU are contrasted with the reactionary policies adopted by the CIO at its 1948 Portland convention.

H376 HUFF, Henry P. The Seattle Municipal Elections, "Communist," 23 (May 1944), 450-56.
An examination of the Seattle city elections by the secretary of the Party's Northwest District to determine the causes of the defeat of "win-the-war" candidates. The Party, which played a constructive role in the campaign, must increase its strength in the unions and intensify its educational activities.

H377 HUGHES, Langston. "A New Song." New York: International Workers Order, 1933. 31 pp.
Poems, with a Communist Party orientation, on political and economic injustice and in praise of communist heroes.

H378 .... "Not without Laughter." New York: Knopf, 1933. 324 pp.
A vivid picture of Negro working class life in midwest America, by a Negro author and poet who was a leading figure in Party cultural and race-front organizations.

H379 HUIE, William Bradford. Kilgore: West Virginia Water Boy, "American Mercury," 75 (Oct. 1952), 47-53.
An assertion that Kilgore has been the Senator most subservient to communism, as evidenced by his support in 1942 of a centralized administration to control scientific research, his admiration for the American Labor Party, his efforts to prevent an investigation of communism in Hollywood in 1947, his employment of two known communists, and the continuous adulation he receives from the "Daily Worker."

H380 HUISWOUD, Otto E. The Negro and the Trade Unions, "Communist," 7 (Dec. 1928), 770-75.
A brief description of the role of Negroes in the labor movement since the Civil War. Discrimination by AFL unions against Negro workers is reviewed. The Party must emphasize the organization of Negro workers in trade unions on the basis of equality.

H381 .... World Aspects of the Negro Question, "Communist," 9 (Feb. 1930), 132-47.

An analysis of the Negro question by the first Negro communist leader in the U.S., who sees the issue as a class and as a race question. The situation of the Negro masses where they are the majority, as in the West Indies and Africa, is compared to their situation in the U.S., where they are a minority. The Party should organize Negroes into TUUL unions and into the American Negro Labor Congress for full equality.

H382 HULCY, D. A. Management Sees Red, "Education," 72 (April 1952), 531-36.
A review by the president of the Chamber of Commerce of the U.S. of the Chamber's record of opposition to communism, and its exposure of communist subversion and influence in U.S. government and unions. Socialism will lead to communism, since socialism, once in power, would perpetuate itself by force.

H383 HULLINGER, Edwin W. Radicalism in the U.S., "Scribner's Magazine," 76 (Oct. 1924), 433-41.
A former Russian correspondent for the United Press takes stock of six years of the radical movement in the U.S. He concludes that Bolshevism is not an immediate threat; that its appeal is intellectual rather than vocational; and that forceful suppression, which strengthens it, should be replaced by social reform.

H384 HULTZEN, Lee S. Communists on the University Faculty: A Theoretical Discussion, "Journal of Higher Education," 21 (Nov. 1950), 423-29 ff.
Suppression of communist teachers is unnecessary, since they are numerically insignificant and ineffective. Suppression is risky. Students must achieve the tough-mindedness that comes only from the competition of ideas. This is the only way in which universities can serve the cause of democracy.

H385 HUMBOLDT, Charles. To the Mad Hatters, "New Masses," 62 (March 11, 1947), 13-17.
A denunciation of Philip Rahv, William Phillips, and Diana Trilling, whose recently published anthologies of Tolstoy, Dostoyevsky, and D. H. Lawrence contain introductions with distorted concepts of life, literature, and politics.

H386 .... I: What's Wrong with Our Short Stories, and II: Shop Talk on Short Stories, "New Masses," 63 (May 20, 1947), 6-8 ff; (May 27), 16-18.
A call for a reaffirmation of the view of literature as an instrument of struggle, knowledge, and change. Our writers must show that the war was to save mankind from fascism, and that now progressive forces everywhere will triumph. Few of our writers are free from bourgeois disillusionment and despair; they do not display enough of a "positive" view.

H387 .... The Novel of Action, "Mainstream" I (Fall 1947), 389-407.
The literary editor of the "New Masses," asserting that the bourgeoisie has infected the novel with its own defeatism, calls for the novel of action. The writer who identifies with the working class and the progressive forces in society, by accepting the philosophy of dialectical materialism, can bring social realism to age in the novel of action.

H388 .... How True is Fiction? "Masses & Mainstream," 2 (Jan. 1949), 20-34.
"Truth" in fiction requires the portrayal of human potentiality as well as human existence. Characters must be related to their class position, or they will ring false. Through Marxism, the creative potential of the human being can be projected.

H389 .... Communists in Novels, "Masses & Mainstream," 2 (June 1949), 13-31; (July), 44-65.
A review of the portraits of communists presented in novels, asserting that the quality most essential to the portrayal of communists in fiction is maturity compounded of action and understanding. Proletarian novels of the 1930's are reviewed; though many communists appeared, few were portrayed convincingly. The two most persuasive communist figures are in "Call Home the Heart" and "A Stone Came Rolling."

H390 .... Second Thoughts on Politics and Culture, "Masses & Mainstream," 9 (May 1956), 8-15.
A reappraisal of socialist realism and of the whole left cultural movement in the wake of Khrushchev's revelations about Stalin. The left made itself too dependent on Soviet views, stifling principled criticism and censuring or neglecting many talented artists.

H391 HUMPHREY, Hubert H. Fighting Communism in Unions, "U.S. News and World Report," 31 (Dec. 28, 1951), 20-26.
An interview with the chairman of a Senate subcommittee which is to investigate communist influence in labor unions. Senator Humphrey answers questions on the nature and extent of communist infiltration, the noncommunist affidavit, and legislative ways of combatting the problem.

H392 .... Should the Government Control Communist Unions? "New Leader," 35 (June 2, 1952), 6-7.
Problems facing the Senate Subcommittee on Labor and Labor-Management Relations in its 1952 hearings on communist-dominated unions, as outlined by its chairman. The committee will deal with such questions as whether a communist-led union is a hazard to national security, whether new legislation is needed, and whether noncommunist unions would be harmed.

H393 HUNT, Henry T. "The Case of Thomas J. Mooney and Warren K. Billings: Abstract and Analysis of the Record before Gov. Young of California." New York: National Mooney-Billings Committee, 1929. 444 pp.
An abstract and analysis of the record of Mooney's trial, prepared at the request of the Committee for presentation to Governor Young in support of Mooney's application for pardon. It contains a statement and chronology of the case, reviews the main points of the trial, traces the circumstances which led to Mooney's life imprisonment sentence, and tells of his subsequent appeals for pardon.

H394 HUNT, R. N. Carew (ed.). "Books on Communism: A Bibliography." London: Ampersand, 1959. 333 pp. Ind.
A bibliography, with brief annotations, of books on communism that have been published in English since 1945. The first half of the volume is devoted to studies of communism in general and in the USSR. Works dealing with the U.S. appear on pp. 176-84, and U.S. government publications on pp. 296-306. (A second, enlarged edition, edited by Walter Kolarz, was published in 1964.)

H395 HUNTER, Robert M., and FUCHS, Ralph F. Communists in the Colleges: Two Views, "Antioch Review," 9 (June 1949), 199-209.
Two law professors argue the pros and cons of academic freedom and tenure in relation to Communist Party membership. Hunter argues that Party membership is prima facie evidence of unfitness to teach, whereas Fuchs upholds the AAUP position that it is not.

H396 HURSTON, Zora Neale. Why the Negro Won't Buy

Communism, "American Legion Magazine," 50 (June 1951), 14-15 ff.
An account of the Party's efforts to recruit Negroes, viewing them as a permanent lower class on which the Party could be built. The Kremlin has sought to use the treatment of Negroes in the U.S. to build up Soviet influence in Asia. Communist action in the Scottsboro case is seen as a horrible example of Party methods. American Negroes are repelled by the Party's views on sex and religion, and by its propaganda based on color.

H397 HUTCHINS, Grace. "Labor and Silk." New York: International Publishers, 1929. 192 pp. App. Bibliog. Ind.
A study of the American silk industry, written as part of the "Labor and Industry" series of the Labor Research Association. It describes the textile industry and the conditions under which the workers live, and analyzes the efforts of the unions to organize the industry. The study emphasizes the forces operating in American industry to maintain the capitalist system and thwart the development of militant unions.

H398 .... "Women and War." New York: Central Committee, Communist Party of the USA, 1932. 31 pp.
A fictitious conversation among women factory workers, in which the one who is a communist shows the others the true nature of the capitalists. Women workers are urged to organize against imperialist war under the leadership of the Party.

H399 .... "Women Who Work." New York: International Publishers, 1932. 31 pp.
Communist pamphlet describing oppressive conditions for women workers in the depression. Capitalism in this country aims to keep women, especially Negroes, subordinate, whereas women in the Soviet Union are covered by insurance, maternity benefits, and have full equality with men. In the U.S., the various women's organizations aim to bring the working women under bourgeois influence. Working women are urged to join the Party and the TUUL.

H400 .... "Youth in Industry." New York: International Publishers, 1932. 31 pp. Ref.
An analysis of the plight of youth under the capitalist system. The hardships it suffers include low wages, long hours, disenfranchisement, lack of proper education, undernourishment and disease, and opposition from officials of the old trade unions. Only in the Soviet Union does youth get a fair chance to live and work. Youth is urged to join left-wing unions and the Young Communist League.

H401 .... "Children Under Capitalism." New York: International Publishers, 1933. 23 pp.
Communist pamphlet expressing grievances on behalf of the children of the working class. The author tells instance after instance of capitalism's inhumanity to the children, and concludes that children of the workers will really come into a full and joyous life only when the capitalist system is overthrown.

H402 .... "Women Who Work." New York: International Publishers, 1934. 285 pp. Ref. notes. Ind.
One of the "Books on American Labor" series sponsored by the Labor Research Association. The author deals with the plight of women under capitalism, especially during depressions, and with their double burden at home and on the job. She discusses the jobs that women do, on farms, in factories and in other urban employment, their working conditions and wages. She emphasizes the problems confronting the old, the sick, and the unemployed, contrasting

this with the position of women in the Soviet Union. She stresses the part women have played in strikes, attacks the class collaboration policies of the AFL leadership, and urges support of the Trade Union Unity League.

H403 .... "What Every Working Woman Wants." New York: Workers Library, 1935. 16 pp.
A plea for medical information and help for working-class women. The workers' bill for unemployment insurance is explained.

H404 .... "The Truth About the Liberty League." New York: International Publishers, 1936. 30 pp.
An account of the formation of the American Liberty League and of its ties to the Du Pont Company, to other leading industrial enterprises, and to the Republican Party. Representing fascist tendencies, the League is said to oppose every measure helpful to workers or labor organizations.

H405 .... "Women Who Work." Rev. ed. New York: International Publishers for the Labor Research Association, 1952. 96 pp. Ind.
A revised and updated version of the author's 1932 pamphlet, reflecting the Party's program of the post-World War II period. The first part tells of the difficulties of working married women, especially in agriculture, and of low wages, unequal pay, and the double standard in seniority lists. The second part tells why women join progressive unions, and such organizations as the Communist Party, the National Negro Labor Council, the Progressive Party, and American Women for Peace, which protests U.S. intervention in Korea.

H406 HUTCHINSON, John. Trade Unionism and the Communists: American and International Experiences, pp. 164-87 in "The Realities of World Communism," ed. by William Petersen. Englewood Cliffs, N.J.: Prentice-Hall, 1963. 222 pp. Bibliog. note.
Following an outline of Lenin's views of trade unionism in relation to the Party and the struggle for power, the author discusses (pp. 169-79) the role of the communists in the American labor movement, beginning with the TUEL. Party efforts to infiltrate both the AFL and CIO are evaluated. Whereas communist strength in the AFL was due to racketeering elements in various unions, within the CIO enormous victories created a demand for specialized services that the communists were uniquely prepared to provide.

H407 HUTCHINSON, Paul. The J. B. Matthews Story, "Christian Century," 70 (July 29, 1953), 864-66.
A sketch of the career of J. B. Matthews, from his early missionary experiences and scholarly achievements to the time when he was a leading fellow-traveler and finally a hunter of communists for congressional committees. His charges of extensive support for communists among the Protestant clergy are denied.

H408 HYATT, William. The NMU: Paid in Full, "American Legion Magazine," 42 (March 1947), 10-11 ff.
Opposition to NMU efforts to get for merchant seamen the same benefits given veterans of the armed forces. The position of the NMU on foreign policy is traced, showing that it has consistently followed the Party line since its formation in 1936, and that it is internationally-minded, in Moscow's direction. Merchant seamen avoided the draft, while earning high civilian wartime wages.

H409 HYMAN, Harold M. "To Try Men's Souls: Loyalty Tests in American History." Berkeley and Los Angeles: University of California Press, 1959. 414 pp. Notes. Bibliog. Ind.

A review of loyalty tests through American history, from the colonial period until the late 1950's. Chapter 13, "Path to the Patriotic Present" (pp. 316-45), deals with loyalty tests following World War I and during and after World War II. The author concludes that loyalty tests have never provided security, which has emerged from within; until this is recognized, American unity and Americans' rights will suffer.

H410　HYMAN, Nancy, and SPARKS, Leonard. "Public Enemy No. 1: William Randolph Hearst." New York: District 2, CPUSA, 1935. 22 pp.

An attack on Hearst for supporting fascism, striking at unionism, seeking to perpetuate poverty, and promoting imperialist wars. A boycott of the Hearst press is urged.

H411　HYMAN, Stanley Edgar. The Marxist Criticism of Literature. "Antioch Review," 7 (Dec. 1947), 541-68.

An analysis of Marxist literary criticism tracing its pre-Marxian origins, its role in the thought of Marx, Engels, and Plekhanov, and its contemporary manifestations in Britain and America. In America it led to political distortion by V. F. Calverton, Granville Hicks, and Michael Gold. Others, notably F. O. Matthiessen, have combined sociological criteria with esthetic appreciation.

I

I1   "ILLINOIS LAW REVIEW," The McCarran Act—Detection or Defection, 46 (May-June 1951), 274-91.
Criticism of the Internal Security Act of 1950. Despite a decade of consideration, the law to control communist subversion embodies many doubtful constitutional and practical issues. It is improbable, if not impossible, that the measure will achieve congressional objectives.

I2   ILMA, Viola. "And Now Youth." New York: Ballou, 1934. 56 pp.
The founder of the American Youth Congress analyzes youth problems in the depression, urging youth to support Roosevelt's New Deal as an alternative to traditional capitalist democracy, communism, and fascism. She also urges youth to fight against war, though she opposes isolationism and favors collective action. Noting that Nazism, fascism, and communism gained their strength in Europe from youth, she calls for mobilization of American youth and opposition to totalitarianism. (The author withdrew from AYC when a coalition of communists and socialists won control.)

I3   . . . . "The Political Virgin (as fathomed by L. Edgar Prina)." New York: Duell, Sloan and Pearce, 1958. 180 pp.
The biography of the founder of the American Youth Congress. Chapter 5 is devoted to the AYC, presenting the author's version of the communist take-over. Chapter 6 deals with a campaign, initiated by the "New Masses," to brand the author a fascist. It also tells of the author's first marriage, to Harry Carlisle, a British communist and writer who served for a time as guest editor of the "New Masses"; they were divorced in 1940. Security difficulties, resulting from these early associations, are discussed in chapter 9.

I4   "INDIANA LAW JOURNAL," Effectiveness of State Anti-Subversive Legislation, 28 (Summer 1953), 492-520.
An analysis and critique of state antisubversion laws, most of them enacted after the Internal Security Act of 1950. While all the laws seek to prevent activities aimed at overthrowing government by force, they vary in their provisions, some of which are probably unconstitutional. Judicial review requires proof of the necessity of these statutes and the sanctions they impose.

I5   "INDUSTRIAL WORKER," Communists and the I.W.W., 9 (Feb. 5, 1927), 2.
An IWW publication compares IWW philosophy with that of the Soviet Union. Communist efforts to ruin the IWW by draining off its active members are resented.

I6   INMAN, Mary. "Woman-Power." Los Angeles: Committee to Organize the Advancement of Women, 1942. 88 pp.
The author, a writer for the "Daily People's World" (San Francisco communist paper), presents a Marxist-Leninist view of the housewife's role in a capitalist economy—that of an underpaid producer of goods. She asserts that the bringing up of women to be cooks, nurses, and housekeepers is as necessary to capitalist production as is the raising and educating of laborers. It is necessary, in her view, both to win women for labor's struggle and to emphasize the dignity of housework.

I7   INSTITUTE FOR AMERICAN STRATEGY. "Education and Freedom in a World of Conflict: Guidelines for Teaching about Communism." Chicago: Regnery, 1963. 340 pp. App.
Selections from presentations by education, business, government, science, and military leaders at a conference sponsored by the Institute. Included are programs for education about communism at the high school, college, and graduate levels, together with views from business, labor, government, and the armed forces.

I8   INTERCHURCH WORLD MOVEMENT, Commission of Inquiry. "Report on the Steel Strike of 1919." New York: Harcourt, Brace and Howe, 1920. 277 pp. App. Ind.
A report on an investigation into the social conditions that lay behind the great steel strike of 1919, emphasizing the 12-hour day, the low level of wages, and the commitment of the industry to a policy of no conference with union representatives. The investigators found the charge of a Bolshevist plot or of industrial radicalism in the conduct of the strike, based largely on the syndicalist views of William Z. Foster, the strike leader, to be without foundation. The policies and conduct of the strike leadership, they concluded, were those of the American labor movement, which they criticized for indifference, selfishness, and narrow habit. Steel company policies, they discovered, included discharge for unionism, the use of blacklists and labor spies, and the abrogation of civil liberties in many of the steel towns of western Pennsylvania.

I9   INTERNATIONAL ALLIANCE OF THEATRICAL STAGE EMPLOYES AND MOTION PICTURE MACHINE OPERATORS. "Report of the International President on the Hollywood, California Studio Situation." New York: IATSE, 1945. 12 pp.
President Richard Walsh analyzes the jurisdictional strike in progress for the past 16 weeks as caused by an unholy alliance between the Carpenters Union and the communist-dominated Conference of Studio Unions. He asserts that the full weight of the communist apparatus in the Los Angeles area has been behind the strikers.

I10   INTERNATIONAL BROTHERHOOD OF CHRISTIANS. "Communism: Your Problem and Mine." Waldorf, Md.: The Brotherhood, 1948. 46 pp.
Letters and other writings in opposition to communism by Isaac Cramer, who answers communist propaganda and charges that a conspiracy prevents use of press and radio for that purpose. A radio speech by J. Parnell Thomas, chairman of the House Committee on Un-American Activities, is included.

I11   INTERNATIONAL LABOR DEFENSE. "The International Labor Defense: Its Constitution and

Organization Resolution Adopted by the Fourth National Convention Held in Pittsburgh, Pa., Dec. 29-31, 1929." New York: ILD, n.d. [1930]. 16 pp.
Progress made by the ILD since the last convention is reviewed and shortcomings are noted in the area of organization. Recommendations to help the ILD become a militant mass organization are made.

I12 INTERNATIONAL LABOR DEFENSE. "Free the Imperial Valley Prisoners." Foreword by J. Louis Engdahl. New York: Workers Library, 1932. 45 pp.
An appeal to the U.S. Supreme Court by seven workers convicted under the California criminal syndicalism law, following a strike of agricultural workers led by the Trade Union Unity League. Reversal of the conviction is asked on the grounds that the workers' civil rights were abridged, the criminal syndicalist law is a class instrument, and the employers and authorities used violence and despotism against the strikers.

I13 . . . . "Under Arrest! Workers' Self-Defense in the Courts." New York: ILD, n.d. [1932?]. 31 pp.
"Third period" instructions to workers who are arrested, on what to do when confronted by the police and court class-enemies. Obstructionist tactics are advised, since it is the duty of workers to fight such attacks on the working class with all their might.

I14 . . . . "Mr. President: Free the Scottsboro Boys!" New York: ILD, 1934. 30 pp.
A reprint of the statement presented to President Roosevelt's secretary, telling of the injustice done to the Scottsboro boys, and requesting presidential intervention. Although the President has refused to take jurisdiction, he must be forced to intervene by the mass pressure of millions.

I15 . . . . "What Is the I.L.D.?" New York: ILD, 1934. 24 pp.
An explanation of the need for a labor defense organization. Citing many cases of legal injustice to workers, the ILD traces the history of working-class defense activities to and through its formation in 1925. Its program, membership, and activities are described.

I16 . . . . "Charles Krumbein, No. 2379, Political Prisoner." New York: ILD, 1935. 14 pp.
An appeal for support for a prominent Party and trade union leader, sentenced for passport violation and denied parole. Asserting that he is in reality a political prisoner, jailed because of his political beliefs, the ILD calls upon readers to demand his unconditional freedom.

I17 . . . . "Ernst Thaelmann: Fighter against War and Fascism." Introd. by Anna Damon. New York: ILD, 1935. 14 pp.
The story of the leading German communist, imprisoned by the Nazis, is presented as an example of the fascist terror against which the ILD is waging a world-wide fight. Emphasis is placed upon Thaelmann's devotion to the workers' cause, the part he played in the revolutionary upsurge following World War I, and his leadership in the communist movement.

I18 . . . . "It's Happening in Spain." New York: ILD, 1937. 31 pp.
An appeal for funds to supply medical aid to the defenders of democracy in Spain. Emphasis is placed on fascist savagery, on military aid to Franco from Hitler and Mussolini, on the courage of the Spanish people and their sacrifices for the antifascist cause, and on their need for medical assistance.

I19 . . . . "Victory: Decision of the United States Supreme Court in the Case of Angelo Herndon, April 1937." New York: ILD, n.d. [1937]. 30 pp.
The text of the majority decision of the U.S. Supreme Court, in which Angelo Herndon, convicted for attempting to incite insurrection in Georgia, was ordered discharged. (See p. 251, Digest of the Public Record of Communism in the United States.) The minority dissenting opinion is also included. Anna Damon writes an introduction.

I20 . . . . "I. L. D. National Conference, Washington, D.C.: Proceedings and Report." New York: ILD, n.d. [1939]. 47 pp.
Excerpts from and resumés of speeches made at panels on civil rights, Negro people's rights, prison conditions, aid to refugees from fascist oppression, fascist organizations in the U.S., and Puerto Rico. Congressman Vito Marcantonio delivered the keynote address, and Anna Damon, ILD national secretary, reported on activities since 1937.

I21 . . . . "Equal Justice and Democracy in the Service of Victory." New York: ILD, 1944. 32 pp.
A pamphlet in memory of Anna Damon, who had been ILD secretary until her death. A number of Party members and fellow travelers write on such subjects as achievements of the ILD, labor in the postwar world, minorities, and the church.

I22 INTERNATIONAL LADIES' GARMENT WORKERS' UNION. "The End of the Communist Adventure in the Garment Unions." [New York]: ILGWU, n.d. [1926 or 1927]. 11 pp.
An account of the disastrous six-month strike of 35,000 workers in the New York cloak industry in 1926, allegedly called by the communist-controlled Joint Board for political reasons. Finally the union's general executive board removed the communist officials and ended the strike. The communists are now trying to set up dual unions.

I23 . . ., Joint Board of Cloak, Skirt, Dress and Reefer Makers' Unions. "The Left Wing in the Garment Unions." New York: Joint Board, 1927. 23 pp.
A publication of the left-wing leaders within the ILGWU, justifying their role in the strike of 1926, and giving a history of their struggle against union right-wing forces. Denying waste of funds in the conduct of the strike, they assert that the locals they controlled were expelled in violation of the constitution. They call for proportional representation, direct elections, amalgamation, and an end to expulsions and corruption.

I24 "INTERNATIONAL LITERATURE," Where We Stand—A Symposium, 3, no. 3 (1934), 80-96.
Answers by a number of American and British writers to questions by the secretariat of the International Union of Revolutionary Writers on the occasion of the Soviet Writers' Congress. The questions related to the influence of the October revolution upon their work, their views of Soviet literature, and the problems that most interested them then. The Americans included Theodore Dreiser, Malcolm Cowley, Louis Adamic, Joseph Freeman, Isidor Schneider, Granville Hicks, and Corliss Lamont.

I25 INTERNATIONAL LONGSHOREMEN'S AND WAREHOUSEMEN'S UNION. "A Postwar Perspective for Jobs: A Statement on Postwar Planning and Security." San Francisco: ILWU, 1944. 6 unnumbered pp.
A statement by the ILWU before the Duclos letter changed the Party line, when labor-management cooperation was still in vogue. Rejecting the "defeatist philosophy" that peace must be a signal for industrial warfare, the ILWU

guarantees that there shall be no strikes or stoppages during the war and beyond.

I26 INTERNATIONAL LONGSHOREMEN'S AND WAREHOUSEMEN'S UNION. "Union Busting New Model: The Case against the Coast Guard Screening Program." San Francisco: ILWU, 1951. 21 pp.
A denunciation of the Coast Guard's screening program aimed at keeping subversives off the docks during the Korean War. The real purpose, according to the ILWU, is to break up the union. The ILWU will fight this program as it has fought past blacklists, to protect members' rights to the ideas, associations, and programs they prefer.

I27 . . . . "The Everlasting Bridges Case." San Francisco: ILWU, 1955. 14 pp.
A denunciation of the forthcoming fifth effort by the federal government to deport Harry Bridges. Reviewing the four preceding investigations, the pamphlet concludes that the purpose of this fifth trial of Bridges is to silence the ILWU.

I28 "INTERNATIONAL PRESS CORRESPONDENCE," Statements of the Minority of the C.P. and of the C.E.C. of the C.P. of the U.S.A. on the Cannon Case, 9 (Feb. 8, 1929), 114-15.
Foster, Bittelman, and other members of the Foster caucus acknowledge their error in continuing to associate with Cannon after learning of his Trotskyist activities. The Central Executive Committee of the Party, controlled by Lovestone, points to shortcomings in the minority statement, and calls upon the Foster caucus to dissolve.

I29 . . ., Seventh Congress of the C.P. of America, 10 (July 17, 1930), 602-3.
A resume of reports and discussion at the seventh convention of the CPUSA, June 21-25, 1930. The report of the Central Committee, a report on political and organizational work, and a report on expulsions (most of them for Lovestoneism) are summarized. The convention heard reports on Negro work, and rejected a demand to seat a group of Lovestoneite delegates.

I30 . . ., The Extraordinary Party Conference of the CPUSA, 13 (Oct. 20, 1933), 1029-30.
The Open Letter adopted by the Extraordinary Party Conference of the CPUSA in July 1933 is not having the intended effect of turning the CPUSA into a mass party. The CPUSA can accomplish this task neither by republishing articles nor by holding district and section conferences. The CPUSA's leading comrades must personally see that the directives are carried out.

I31 INTERNATIONAL PUBLISHERS. "What is Leninism?" New York: 1936. 124 pp.
Readings in the meaning of Leninism, its historical roots, its method and theoretical foundations, and its development by Stalin, taken from the writings of Marx, Engels, Lenin, and Stalin, and arranged by V. Bystryansky and M. Mishin.

I32 . . . . "The Constitution of the United States, with the Amendments; also the Declaration of Independence." Introd. by Earl Browder. New York: 1937. 63 pp.
Issued in the popular front period, when the Party was rediscovering American progressive tradition. In his introduction (pp. 5-27), after reviewing early constitutional issues, Browder stresses the people's front against reaction and fascism, and denies that the Party would seek to establish socialism forcibly against the will of the people.

I33 . . . . "The Woman Question: Selections from the Writings of Marx, Engels, Lenin, Stalin." New York: 1951. 96 pp. Bibliog.
The views of world communist leaders regarding women, the family, birth-control, and sex, presented in historical, sociological, and economic context.

I34 INTERNATIONAL UNION OF ELECTRICAL, RADIO AND MACHINE WORKERS, CIO. "Ten Years of Communist Control of U.E." Washington, D.C.: IUE-CIO, 1950. 19 pp.
Comparison of the UE position, issue by issue, with the Communist Party line from 1939 to 1949, showing them consistent and identical throughout. The IUE's conclusion is that the UE is completely communist-controlled.

I35 INTERNATIONAL WORKERS ORDER, National Executive Committee. "A New Workers' Stronghold: What Is the International Workers Order and Why Every Worker Should Join It." New York: IWO, 1930. 16 pp.
A statement of the program of the IWO, the fraternal society allied to the communist movement, issued shortly after its formation. The sick and death benefits are outlined, as is the Order's cultural program. The publication attacks the Workmen's Circle, the Independent Workmen's Circle, and the Socialist Party for having made peace with capitalism, and appeals for support of the Communist Party.

I36 . . . (National Pioneer Council). "Poems and Recitations for Workers' Children." New York: IWO, n.d. [1930].
A "third period" collection of poems and recitations to further "class education" of workers' children, arouse hatred for their oppressors, and speed the fight for a workers' world. The poems are grouped into sections on the fight against war and fascism, our leaders, organizing children, holidays, Scottsboro, and songs and cheers.

I37 . . . . "Youth Section." New York: IWO, 1932. 15 pp.
A statement of the objectives of the youth organization of the IWO, a Party-controlled fraternal benefit society. The USSR is hailed as the fighting front of the working class.

I38 . . . . "Five Years of International Workers Order: 1930-1935." New York: National Executive Committee, IWO, 1935. 123 pp.
An account of the history of the communist fraternal organization and of the benefits it provides. Its growth among various ethnic groups in this country is described.

I39 . . . . "The IWO and the Negro People: A Message and an Appeal." New York: IWO, 1943. 22 pp.
A description of the program and benefits of the communist fraternal order, with an appeal to Negroes to join.

I40 . . ., Jewish American Section. "Our People: The Jew in America." New York: Co-operative Book League, Jewish American Section, IWO, 1944. 287 pp.
A volume for the IWO War Service Convention, held in 1944, to tell the story of the service of the Jewish people to our nation in peace and war. Included are a historical sketch by Philip Foner of Jews in America, an account of the war service and activity of the present Jewish-American community, the history of the formation of the IWO from the "reactionary" Workmen's Circle, a communist analysis of Jewish problems, and a discussion of Jewish literature, Jewish holidays, and Yiddish writers.

I41 INTERNATIONAL WORKERS ORDER. Fifteenth Anniversary Almanac, 1930-1945. New York: City Central Committee, IWO, 1945. 56 unnumbered pp.
An anniversary almanac, reviewing the activities and achievements of the Party-related fraternal organization and of its various nationality group affiliates.

I42 "INTERRACIAL REVIEW," Youth on the Left, 13 (Jan. 1940), 15.
A report on the allegedly communist-dominated convention of the American Student Union, held December 1939. The organ of the Catholic Interracial Council calls on Catholic youth to lead a united youth movement that is Christian in spirit as well as in name.

I43 . . ., Those C.P. Blues, 19 (Aug. 1946), 115-16.
An editorial argument addressed to Catholics, Negroes and whites, urging them not to give up the fight against racial bigotry from fear that by taking a strong stand against prejudice they may be labeled communists or Party-liners.

I44 "IOWA LAW REVIEW," Constitutional Issues Raised by the Proposed Loyalty Oath for Lawyers, 36 (Spring 1951), 529-35.
A discussion of legal problems raised by approval by the House of Delegates of the American Bar Association of the proposal that all lawyers be required to take a noncommunist oath. Constitutional issues include the prohibition of ex post facto laws, freedom of speech, equal protection of the law, and the privilege against self-incrimination.

I45 IRWIN, Leonard B. Communist Party Members as Teachers, "Social Studies," 40 (May 1949), 223-25.
A summary of events and arguments concerning the dismissal of six professors at the University of Washington because of past or present affiliation with the Communist Party. Arguments of Professor John L. Childs, who upheld the authorities, and of Carey McWilliams, who opposed them, are summarized. The author sides with Professor Childs.

I46 IRWIN, Will. The Lively Communists, "American Legion Monthly," 1 (Dec. 1926), 22-25 ff.
An account of the formation, history, methods of operation, and strength of the American communists. Formed from the left wing of the Socialist Party in 1919, the communists were largely an immigrant group whose revolutionary propaganda was ineffective. In 1925 the communists regrouped, with the factory nucleus as a basis, and currently they are leading the textile strike in Passaic, New Jersey.

I47 . . . . "How Red Is America?" New York: J. H. Sears, 1927. 219 pp.
A survey of "Reds" in America, a term that the author uses to cover syndicalists, anarchists, communists, and socialists. Chapter 5, "The Lively Communists" (pp. 119-63), describes the beginnings of the communist movement here, the structure of the Party, its labor union activities, and its agitational and educational activities. Party strength is listed at 16,000, with sympathizers raising the total to about 75,000.

I48 . . . . The Red Ballyhoo, "Saturday Evening Post," 203 (Nov. 22, 1930), 3-5 ff.
A review of the Party, of Party activities from the super-romantic days of 1920-22 to the present, and of expulsions and splits over doctrinal points. The movement is disciplined and heroic, even though the object is absurd. Most members are foreign-born or the children of recent immigrants; they have repudiated God and rejected bourgeois morals. Their threat to America is minimized.

I49 . . . . Riotous Publicity, "Today," 5 (Jan. 11, 1936), 8-9 ff.
The communists are viewed as a civic nuisance rather than a public menace. They constantly stage riots and public disturbances for the sake of propaganda. Their activities in the streets often result in tremendous publicity, far beyond what they could do themselves to publicize their cause.

I50 ISAACS, William. "Contemporary Marxian Political Movements in the United States, 1917-1939." New York: New York University, 1942. 49 pp.
An abridgment of a Ph.D. dissertation dealing with the principles, strategy, and tactics of the Communist Party. Based on official documents covering the militant period (1928-35) and the united front period (1935-39), the study highlights the dramatic shift in communist policies resulting from the Seventh World Congress of the Communist International.

I51 IVERSEN, Robert W. "The Communists and the Schools." New York: Harcourt, Brace, 1959. 423 pp. Notes. Ind.
A study of communist efforts to infiltrate the schools, part of the Fund for the Republic's inquiry into communism in American life. Though relatively few students or teachers ever became communists, the Party enjoyed its greatest success among students in the late 1930's, the result of depression, the rise of fascism, war threats, and a mild, idealistic Party line. In 1935 the Party had won control of the New York local, the largest in the American Federation of Teachers, and was influential in the national organization; in 1941, however, the communist-controlled locals were expelled. The communists had little or no impact on educational philosophy, methods, curriculum, or textbooks.

I52 IZUKA, Ichiro. "The Truth about Communism in Hawaii." Honolulu: The author, 1947. 31 pp.
A former communist and high-ranking officer in the ILWU exposes the activities of the Party in Hawaii and within the Longshoremen's Union. He tells how he was attracted to the Party, the training he received, the communists he knew, the cells in existence, the Party's political activities, and his expulsion. He denounces the conspiratorial and dishonest tactics of the Party.

J

J1　JACK, Homer. "Is McCarthy a Concealed Communist?" New York: Community Church, 1953. 19 pp.

A sermon by a Unitarian minister, attacking McCarthyism as the technique of the big lie and the smear, the cause of fear in America and of damage to our reputation abroad. McCarthy must be opposed as the most dangerous enemy to America. Though no concealed communist, he has damaged American civil liberties and democracy more than any communist.

J2　JACKSON, Esther Cooper. "This is My Husband: Fighter for His People; Political Refugee." Brooklyn: National Committee to Defend Negro Leadership, 1953. 36 pp.

An appeal by the wife of James Jackson, communist leader being sought by the FBI for violation of the Smith Act. Declaring that all his life he has worked for peace and an end to Jim Crow, she demands an end to the "frame-up" trials of the communists and the "fascist-like" Smith and McCarran laws.

J3　JACKSON, James [pseud. for Lovett Fort-Whiteman]. The Negro in America, "Communist International," n.s. no. 8, n.d. [1924 or 1925], 50-52.

An assertion by a leading American Negro communist that Party work among American Negroes must be based on the social grievances of the race. The Party must manipulate racial revolutionary sentiment to the advantage of the class struggle.

J4　JACKSON, James E. Theoretical Aspects of the People's Struggle in the South, "Political Affairs," 29 (Aug. 1950), 66-82.

A report to the national committee of the CPUSA by the Party's southern regional secretary, analyzing incipient revolutionary tendencies in the South: the proletarian class struggle, the struggle of the Negro nation in the Black Belt for national liberation, the struggle to complete the agrarian revolution, and the struggle for peace.

J5　. . . . On the Struggle for Negro Freedom, "Political Affairs," 36 (March 1957), 31-42.

Resolution presented to the sixteenth national convention of the Party by the chairman of its subcommittee on Negro rights and Negro-white unity. Calling Negro freedom the crucial domestic issue of the day, the resolution hails national Negro unity in the struggle, regrets the Party's isolation from it, and outlines a program for Negro rights.

J6　. . . . The Challenge of Little Rock, "Political Affairs," 36 (Oct. 1957), 1-10.

The Party's secretary for southern affairs analyzes the reasons why the politicians and racists chose Little Rock, Arkansas, for a show of force against school desegregation and democratization in the South. They hoped to convince the federal government that the South was united in opposing desegregation, so that the school desegregation ruling would not be enforced.

J7　. . . . The South's New Challenge, "Political Affairs," 36 (Dec. 1957), 1-18.

Based on a report to the Party's national committee by its secretary for southern affairs, November 9, 1957, and endorsed unanimously. The report discusses the industrialization of the South, the organization of agriculture, the Negroes' revolt against second-class status, tactical problems, the political outlook, and the position of the Party. (Published in pamphlet form by New Century.)

J8　. . . . A Reply to Comrade Healey, "Political Affairs," 36 [37] (April 1958), 29-33.

An attack on Dorothy Healey for her article, "On the Status of the Party," in "Political Affairs," March 1958. Her views represent the line rejected by the majority of the Party's national committee in February. A Party of multiple ideologies, which she wants, would make it a debating society; the Party can be effective only on a foundation of Marxism-Leninism.

J9　. . . . Some Aspects of the Negro Question in the United States, "World Marxist Review," 2 (July 1959), 16-24.

Calling the Negro question in the U.S. a national question, Jackson analyzes changes in the class structure of the Negro people and social forces in the Negro movement. The Party must have a more accurate and scientific solution to the Negro question. (Based on a report by the Party's secretary for southern and Negro affairs, to the December 1958 meeting of the national committee.)

J10　JACKSON, Robert H. Justice Jackson on Communism in America, "New York Times Magazine," May 21, 1950, 12 ff. Also published as Communists in America, in "Harper's Magazine," 201 (Sept. 1950), 21-27.

Excerpts from Justice Jackson's opinion in the Douds case, upholding the constitutionality of the Taft-Hartley non-communist affidavit. He finds Congress justified in concluding that the Communist Party is a conspiratorial junta, with methods and aims incompatible with our constitutional system. Congress, however, may not require disclosure of beliefs.

J11　JACOBS, Dan N. "The Masks of Communism." Evanston, Ill.: Harper & Row, 1963. 240 pp. Bibliog. Gloss. Ind.

An account of the rise of communism in Russia and its spread to other areas of the world. Chapter 8 (pp. 151-77) on "Communist Tactics in the United States," deals with communist tactics in action, the early years of the communist movement here, its heyday in the 1930's and early 1940's, and its decline since World War II.

J12　JACOBS, Joseph M. Communist Conspiracy in Packingtown, "Butcher Workman," 38 (Oct. 1952), 4-6.

An attorney for the Amalgamated Meat Cutters and Butcher Workmen (AFL) reports on testimony before the House Un-American Activities Committee by a former communist, who asserts that the Armour local of the rival United Packinghouse Workers (CIO) was dominated by communists. A list of CP officers and members is given.

J13 JACOBS, Paul. Should Communists Be Allowed to Eat? "Reporter," 12 (March 24, 1955), 26-27.
Critical comment on a decision by the California State Supreme Court, holding that any employer can discharge an employee who is a communist from any position. Overruling an arbitrator's decision under a union-management contract that the employee should be reinstated, the court holds that an employer has the duty to preserve order in its plant and protect its employees against sabotage and violence.

J14 .... Communists in Unions, "Commonweal," 63 (Jan. 20, 1956), 395-97.
Criticism of the government for attempting to have the United Electrical Workers declared a communist-infiltrated organization under the Communist Control Act. Such an effort shows the inadequacy of the Act, plus misunderstanding of the labor movement and of the role of the Party within it. Government action is a poor way of solving the problem.

J15 .... Crisis inside Communism, "Commonweal," 64 (May 18, 1956), 174-76.
An analysis of the impact of the Khrushchev revelations on the CPUSA. More fundamental tenets of Party ideology are being questioned in this crisis than in any previous one. The leadership must either follow Khrushchev or leave the Party. Loyalty to the Party will minimize membership losses.

J16 .... Good Guys, Bad Guys, and Congressman Walter, "Reporter," 18 (May 15, 1958), 29-31.
A satirical account of the Hollywood blacklist against those who invoked the Fifth Amendment before congressional investigating committees. With the assistance of Chairman Francis E. Walter of the House Un-American Activities Committee, Columbia Pictures has hired Carl Foreman, despite Foreman's refusal to name those who had been Party members with him.

J17 JACOBSON, David. Religion and Democracy Answer Communism, "National Jewish Monthly" (B'nai B'rith), 67 (March 1953), 242-43 ff.
A rabbi exposes the basic fallacies of Marxian dogma, emphasizing the threat of communism to individual freedom. To meet communism's challenge we need to reassert our faith in democracy, avoid communists' tactics and methods, and place our faith in God.

J18 JAHODA, Marie, and COOK, Stuart W. Security Measures and Freedom of Thought: An Exploratory Study of the Impact of Loyalty and Security Programs, "Yale Law Journal," 61 (March 1952), 295-333.
A report on the impact of loyalty and security programs, based on interviews with 15 university faculty members and 70 federal employees of professional rank. The effects on the climate of thought among federal employees is explored. The interview schedule appears on pages 331-33.

J19 JAMES, Daniel. Battle of A.V.C., "Nation," 164 (June 14, 1947), 706-8.
The forthcoming convention of the American Veterans Committee in Milwaukee will witness a battle between procommunist and anticommunist forces. Last year the noncommunists succeeded in reelecting Gilbert A. Harrison as vice-chairman, despite communist infiltration of AVC since early 1946 and capture by the Party of the AVC organization in New York City.

J20 .... CIO Expulsion of Red Unions Promises New Day for Labor, "New Leader," 32 (Nov. 5, 1949), 1 ff.

The author hails as long needed the action against communist-controlled unions being taken by the CIO convention now in session. At least three will be expelled, with eight more to follow. Damage done the CIO by these unions is reviewed.

J21 .... The Liberalism of Suicide, "New Leader," 34 (Aug. 27, 1951), 14-17.
A critique of the fellow-traveling politics of the "Nation," which avoids the truth about the Soviet Union, the basic moral issue of our decade. The editor and correspondents of the "Nation," are accused of obsessive apologetics for Russia. They urge us to take our minds off Stalin, to form a new popular front, and to unite with the Kremlin against the real enemy, fascism.

J22 JAMESON, Thomas. Labor and Third Party Perspectives: A Discussion Article, "Political Affairs," 31 (Oct. 1952), 37-46.
Conditions are favorable for a third party with a real working class base lacking in the Progressive Party, though too many workers and trade union leaders would resist leftist leadership. Such a party under conservative union leadership would be a step forward because of its break with capitalist politics and parties. Communists should work within such a broad coalition third party.

J23 JAMIESON, Stuart. "Labor Unionism in American Agriculture." U.S. Department of Labor, Bureau of Labor Statistics, Bulletin No. 836. Washington, D.C.: U.S. Government Printing Office, 1945. 457 pp. App. Bibliog.
A report on the development of unionism in agriculture in the U.S., including discussions of the agrarian program of the Communist Party, communist infiltration of AFL agricultural unions, and CIO efforts in which communists played a major role.

J24 JANEWAY, Elizabeth. Why They Become Communists, "New York Times Magazine," June 14, 1953. 13 ff.
In contrast to religions and democratic faiths which place responsibility on the individual, communism relieves the individual of choice and responsibility. The existence of Russia and the belief that she will win the cold war attract the power-hungry. The CPUSA, in no position to seize power, seeks instead to weaken American policies through propaganda.

J25 JASON, Walter. A Turning Point for the CIO: What Was Done and Not Done at the Cleveland Convention, "New International," 15 (Dec. 1949), 227-30.
A Trotskyist review of the November 1949 convention of the CIO, when for the first time the CIO openly faced the problem of Stalinism. The author analyzes the Stalinist problem in the labor movement, the reasons behind the present rupture, and the convention's actions against the UE, criticizing the CIO bureaucracy almost as severely as he criticizes the Stalinists.

J26 JEFFERSON SCHOOL OF SOCIAL SCIENCE. "The Economic Crisis and the Cold War: Reports Presented to a Conference on 'Managed Economy,' the 'Cold War,' and the Developing Economic Crisis, Held at the Jefferson School of Social Science in New York, May 14-15, 1949." Ed. by James S. Allen and Doxey A. Wilkerson. Introd. essay by William Z. Foster. New York: New Century, 1949. 113 pp.
A collection of reports presented at a conference on the U.S. postwar economy under the guidance of the Party's educational institution in New York City. Reports deal with the world position of the U.S. and the economic crisis,

the developing crisis in the U.S., the "cold war" and foreign markets, the conditions of the people, farm crisis perspectives, and the military economy and the ruling oligarchy. Foster's introductory essay discusses Truman's "managed economy" and the war danger.

J27 JEFFRIES, David. The Stalinist Youth Movement Today, "Fourth International," 4 (Sept. 1943), 279-82.

An analysis of the Young Communist League by a former YCL member, now a Trotskyite. The bulk of the YCL's 20,000 members have been recruited by win-the-war slogans, and hence are unreliable. A small group of revolutionary elements seek to defend the Soviet Union and bring socialism to America. Some of these can be won by theoretical discussion.

J28 JENKS, M. [pseud.]. "The Communist Nucleus: What It Is, How It Works." New York: Workers Library, 1928. 61 pp.

A handbook on the structure and functions of the nucleus, the Party's basic organizational form. Instructions are given on the organization of a nucleus, systematizing its work, the order of business at its meetings, and Party discipline. Advice is also given on propaganda among women, Negroes, youth, non-Party masses, and rank-and-file socialists, and on the work of a Party fraction in non-Party organizations. (M. Jenks was the pseudonym of a Comintern representative named Marcus who was assigned for a time to the U.S.)

J29 JENNER, William E. Communism Is a Lie: A Lie Can Always Be Successfully Resisted, "Vital Speeches of the Day," 23 (Aug. 15, 1957), 662-65.

A member of the Senate Internal Security Subcommittee outlines the advances that communism has made in the U.S. over the years. Communism has made too much progress in the U.S., in Eastern Europe, and in China. All assertions that communism is good are lies.

J30 JENNINGS, David. For a People's Tax Program, "Communist," 16 (Dec. 1937), 1119-26.

An appeal for revision of our tax laws to conform to Roosevelt's criterion of "ability to pay." The many loopholes which allow the rich to avoid payment of taxes must be eliminated. Reforms such as discontinuance of sales taxes, increased profit taxes, increased taxes on high income, and elimination of tax-exempt securities are needed. Sufficient revenue would be generated by this program to provide for new social legislation.

J31 JENNINGS, Howard. Revisionism and American History, "Political Affairs," 25 (Aug. 1946), 742-62.

An attack on Earl Browder's interpretations of American history, which are considered to be the basis of his revisionist theories. The basic fallacy in Browder's thought is his failure to analyze the role of the class struggle in American history.

J32 JENSEN, Vernon H. "Lumber and Labor." New York: Farrar & Rinehart, 1945. 314 pp. Bibliog. note. Ind.

An account of unionism and industrial relations in the lumber industry. Chapter 12, "Internal Conflicts and Jurisdictional Disputes" (pp. 225-45), deals with factional controversies within the International Woodworkers of America. Communists supported the administration faction, which cooperated with Harry Bridges, whereas the opposition group, supporting the national CIO leadership, took a strong anticommunist stand.

J33 .... "Non-ferrous Metals Industry Unionism,

1932-1954: A Study of Leadership Controversy." Ithaca, N.Y.: Cornell University, 1954. 328 pp. Bibliog. Ind.

A study of the Mine, Mill and Smelter Workers, and of the steps by which left-wing leadership gained control of the union. Democratic forces in the union lost, the author finds, because at crucial moments anticommunist support was not forthcoming from the national CIO headquarters, since the CIO leaders were also involved in struggles for power.

J34 JEROME, V. J. Unmasking an American Revisionist of Marxism, "Communist," 12 (Jan. 1933), 50-82.

An examination of the writings of Sidney Hook on Marxism. Jerome denounces Hook as a pseudo-Marxist who, in the tradition of other revisionists, revises Marx in the direction of reformist, bourgeois philosophies—in this case, that of John Dewey's instrumentalism. True Marxism, however, is a revolutionary philosophy. (See portions of Hook's response and Browder's comment in Earl Browder, "The Revisionism of Sidney Hook," in "Communist." February and March, 1933.)

J35 .... The Socialist Party Convention—A Communist Estimate, "Communist," 13 (July 1934), 616-38.

Notwithstanding the emergence of a left wing in the Socialist Party, its convention in Detroit once more emphasizes the bankruptcy of social democracy. The policy of "left" reformism is a desperate effort to run with the radicalized masses in order to betray them. There is no left socialism outside the Communist Party.

J36 .... Marxism-Leninism for Society and Science: A Year of "Science and Society"—a Critique, "Communist," 16 (Dec. 1937), 1146-63; 17 (Jan. 1938), 75-91.

A review and criticism of the first year of "Science and Society," a journal designed to meet the interest of college-educated in Marxism. Too few articles deal with social science topics or with current events, and many lack a communist perspective. They discuss questions too dispassionately, failing to give a communist analysis and solution.

J37 .... Charting the Course of the Democratic Front, "Communist," 17 (April 1938), 339-50.

The communist decision to organize a people's front is not a betrayal of Party principles, but a change in tactics due to the rise of fascism. Experience gained by the masses in a people's front against fascism will show them the need to abolish capitalism. Marx always distinguished between democratic and tyrannical forms of capitalist societies.

J38 .... A Year of "Jewish Life." "Communist," 17 (Sept. 1938), 850-60.

A critical review of "Jewish Life," an English-language monthly published by the Jewish Buro of the New York State Committee of the Party. The magazine cannot lead the Jewish masses until it fully equips its readers with the ideological weapons of Marxism-Leninism in the sphere of the national question.

J39 .... Forerunners (to Commemorate the Seventy-Fifth Anniversary of the First International and the Twentieth Anniversary of the Communist Party of the United States of America), "Communist," 18 (Sept. 1939), 836-56.

An appraisal of Marxist influence in the U.S. from 1850 to 1876, reviewing the activities of the First International and its affiliates. Modern communists are seen as the ideological descendants of these early Marxists.

J40   JEROME, V. J. Then—and Now, "Communist,"
       18 (Nov. 1939), 1028-36.
The socialists betrayed the working class in World War I.
Instead of seeking their nation's victory, they should have
welcomed their nation's defeat, as did the Russian Bolsheviks, as providing the opportunity for a proletarian
revolution. The present war, like World War I, is a
struggle between rival capitalist imperialisms.

J41   .... "Intellectuals and the War." New York:
       Workers Library, 1940. 63 pp.
Support of the Nazi-Soviet pact as application of Marxist-
Leninist theory to new world forces, with an attack on
intellectuals such as Granville Hicks who renounced the
Party following the pact. Far from deserting the antifascist fight, the Soviet Union, by limiting the zone of conflict, has promoted peace. All defenders of culture must
support the USSR policy.

J42   .... "Social-Democracy and the War." New
       York: Workers Library, 1940. 17 pp.
A brief examination of the role of socialists in various
countries, followed by a bitter denunciation of the Socialist Party as the war party of imperialism in the ranks of
the working class. Written during the Hitler-Stalin pact
period.

J43   .... One Year Since June 22, "Communist," 21
       (June 1942), 408-21.
In the struggle against Germany the U.S. should collaborate closely with Russia, take the offensive by launching a
second front, and seek the utmost national unity and
popular participation in the war effort. The defeatists
should be prevented from sowing discord through attacks
on the communists.

J44   .... The Twenty-Fifth Anniversary of the Soviet
       Power, "Communist," 21 (Nov. 1942), 869-85.
Russians put up such a gallant fight because they are
organized in a communist society. Besides bringing great
economic growth and cultural improvements, communism
has given Russians the most complete form of democracy.
Soviet Russia has never tried to subjugate any foreign
land; instead it has offered aid against fascist aggression.

J45   .... "The Path Dimitroff Charted." New York:
       Workers Library, 1943. 23 pp.
Following the line laid down by Georgi Dimitroff, Communist International leader, at the Seventh World Congress
in 1935, a leader of the Party in the U.S. calls for the
destruction of fascism as a prerequisite for peace. He
urges a united front against fascism, vigorous prosecution of coalition warfare, and international labor unity for
victory. (Reprinted from "Communist," October 1943.)

J46   .... Some Problems of Centralized War Produc-
       tion, "Communist," 22 (Feb. 1943), 126-34.
Because today's overriding task is defeating fascism, communists do not now press for socialism. Instead they seek
centralized economic planning because it will make the
war economy more efficient. The Party opposes management's desire to enslave workers in order to send them
where most needed. It proposes that the allocation of
manpower be handled by committees of labor and management representatives.

J47   .... Marx and National Wars, "Communist," 22
       (March 1943), 211-21.
The Marxist attitude towards wars is determined by their
political character. Imperialist wars are unjust, while
wars in which the goal is independence are just. As in the
case of the Russian attack on Finland, people engaged in a
war of national defense can take the offensive against
actual and imminent invaders.

J48   .... Marxism, Prussianism and Mr. Wallace,
       "Communist," 22 (May 1943), 411-24.
The Berlin "peace" offensive has inspired much anti-
Soviet propaganda in the U.S. By playing on American
fears of Russia, Germany hopes for a separate peace with
Britain and the U.S. Vice-President Wallace has contributed to anti-Soviet propaganda by calling Marxian
philosophy a child of Prussianism. Nothing could be more
false.

J49   .... The Communist Vanguard, "Communist," 23
       (April 1944), 310-18; (June), 558-72.
A presentation of the rationale for changing the name of
the CP from party to association. The various changes in
the movement since the First International were responses
to the needs of the time in order for communists to perform their vanguard role. At this time the needed support
for Roosevelt and the importance of working within the
unions and other victory movements make the change
necessary.

J50   .... "The Treatment of Defeated Germany."
       New York: New Century, 1945. 107 pp.
An editor of "Political Affairs" attributes the rise of
fascism in Germany to a dictatorship of monopoly capitalists. He calls for reparations to victim countries and
punishment of Axis war criminals. Progress in democratic
reeducation will depend on effective collaboration of the
Anglo-Soviet-American coalition and on changes in the
German people, primarily the working class.

J51   .... Lenin's Method—Guide to the Grasp of
       Reality, "Political Affairs," 25 (Jan. 1946), 3-17.
A repudiation of Browder's interpretation of Lenin's teachings. Whereas Lenin compromised to reach communist
goals, Browder compromised the Party's revolutionary
and socialist goals to collaborate with capital. He dis-
counted capital's imperialist designs, and accepted capitalism and the two-party system.

J52   .... The Vatican's War on Peace, "Political
       Affairs," 25 (April 1946), 310-26.
The Vatican, by mobilizing the masses ideologically in
the service of reaction, is taking the place held by social
democracy after World War I. Recent appointments of
cardinals reveal a direct correlation with this political
task. In the U.S. a wedge must be driven between the
reactionary hierarchy and the masses in the church.

J53   .... "Culture in a Changing World: A Marxist
       Approach." New York: New Century, 1947. 94 pp.
A view of culture in the cold war period by the Party's
leading cultural spokesman, asserting that two groups in
the U.S., finance capitalists and those with Marxist understanding, are aware of the significance of culture in the
class struggle. The current reactionary ideology of
American culture finds political manifestations in the
Truman Doctrine, imperialism, and Trotskyism. However, there are counteracting forces working towards a
people's culture.

J54   .... "A World Christian Front?" and "The Anti-
       Social Ethics of Red-Baiters." New York: New
       Masses, 1947. 15 pp.
Reprint of an article in "New Masses," November 26,
1946, charging that the Vatican and finance capital are in
alliance, and criticizing proposed Protestant-Vatican collaboration in an anti-Russian campaign as a facade to
further fascist and imperialist interests. Also reproduced is a letter published in the New York "Herald
Tribune" of December 1, 1946, charging Clare Boothe
Luce with distorting Marxist writings and urging peace
between the U.S. and the USSR.

J55   JEROME, V. J. Restore American-Soviet Cooperation for Peace! (An Editorial Article), "Political Affairs," 26 (Nov. 1947), 963-71.
An assertion that the Soviet Union, during its 30-year existence, has never engaged in an act of aggression, whereas the Dulles scheme, the Truman Doctrine, and the Marshall Plan add up to aggression for world domination. The domestic counterpart of U.S. imperialist foreign policy is the current fascist offensive. American-Soviet cooperation for enduring peace should be restored.

J56   . . . . Lenin and Opportunism in the American Labor Movement, "Political Affairs," 28 (Jan. 1949), 1-15.
An appraisal of political action in American trade unions from the mid-1930's to 1949, in the light of Lenin's teachings on the interaction of unionism and politics. Jerome calls for opposition to the Truman Doctrine and the Marshall Plan, a broad united front against war and fascism, international solidarity of workers, cooperation with the USSR, and struggle against capitalist exploitation.

J57   . . . . "The Negro in Hollywood Films." New York: Masses & Mainstream, 1950. 64 pp.
Expansion of a lecture in New York, February 3, 1950. Denouncing Hollywood's portrayal of Negroes, the Party's foremost cultural spokesman traces the characterization of the Negro in films made in the U.S., viewing current Hollywood "Negro interest" films as a continuation of the Uncle Tom tradition in modern dress. He urges work with the Party for a true representation of the Negro people on the screen. (Part appeared in "Political Affairs," June 1950.)

J58   . . . . Roots of Hollywood's Racism, "Masses & Mainstream," 3 (Oct. 1950), 48-60.
A review of Hollywood's early treatment of the Negro, from the first portrayal of Negroes as clownish subhumans to the Uncle Tom stereotype of 1910-14 and the treatment as a beast in "The Birth of a Nation." The myth of white supremacy is perpetuated to hold back the Negro liberation movement and prevent a Negro-labor alliance. (A chapter from a forthcoming book on the Negro in Hollywood films.)

J59   . . . . "Grasp the Weapon of Culture!" New York: New Century, 1951. 24 pp. Reprinted from "Political Affairs," Feb. 1951.
The text of a report to the December 1950 national convention of the Party. A leading Party official in the cultural field, and editor of "Political Affairs," Jerome denounces all phases of capitalist culture in America, particularly the perversion of science to militarism and modern Malthusianism allied to genocide and racism. He calls for an organic relationship of cultural work to the Party's main tasks among the masses.

J60   . . . . "A Lantern for Jeremy." New York: Masses & Mainstream, 1952. 288 pp.
The story of a Polish boyhood at the beginning of the century, written by a leading intellectual of the CPUSA.

J61   "JEWISH FRONTIER," Jewish Veterans Fight Communism, 6 (Feb. 1939), 3-4.
An editorial criticizing the Jewish War Veterans for wearing badges with the legend, "Fight Communism." The editors of this Labor Zionist publication urge the veterans' group to fight fascism as well as communism.

J62   "JEWISH LIFE," Freedom in the U.S.A., 5 (June 1951), 12-24.
A series of reports, from the communist point of view, on the state of freedom in the United States. Included are

Marion Bachrach, "The Case with the Built-In Verdict," on the case against the Communist Party before the Subversive Activities Control Board; "Deportation, McCarran Style," by Abner Green of the American Committee for Protection of Foreign Born; "AJC-NAACP Report on Civil Rights," by William L. Patterson of the Civil Rights Congress; Louis Harap, "New Stage in Anti-Semitism"; and Ben Gold, "Letter to a Friend on Ellis Island" (Paul Yuditch, labor editor of the "Morning Freiheit," held for deportation).

J63   . . ., Legacy of the Rosenbergs, 7 (Aug. 1953), 15-29.
A collection of material on the Rosenberg case, including the last letters of Ethel and Julius Rosenberg; an editorial article on "Meaning of the Execution"; "The Case for Morton Sobell," by Jacob Stein; a letter from Ethel Rosenberg describing a government offer to spare their lives for "talking"; comments from the Jewish press; "The International Reaction," by Alice Citron; the dissenting opinions of Justices Douglas, Black, and Frankfurter; and the funeral speech of Emanuel H. Bloch.

J64   . . ., Remember the Rosenbergs! First Anniversary of Their Execution, June 19, 8 (June 1954), 10-21.
Poems and articles in memory of Ethel and Julius Rosenberg, including an editorial introduction, "A Year Has Passed"; "The Rosenberg Cantata," by Michael Gold; "Toward Freedom for Sobell," by Alice Citron; "Personal Story of a Campaign," by Ray Waterman; and "The Children," three sonnets by Louis Aragon.

J65   . . ., Living Memory of the Rosenbergs: 2nd Anniversary of the Execution, 9 (June 1955), 7-14.
Contents include poems by Sam Swing and Max Rosenfeld; "Giant Step to Vindication" (a discussion of John Wexley's book, "The Judgment of Julius and Ethel Rosenberg") by Louis Harap; "Sobell Campaign Story," by Joseph Brainin; and a passage from a letter by Morton Sobell to his wife.

J66   . . ., Editorial Board. Review and Reappraisal, 10 (June 1956), 3-7 ff.
The members of the Board discuss their failure to perceive and protest crimes against Jewish culture and leaders in the socialist countries. They overlooked the shutting down of Jewish cultural institutions in the Soviet Union and the disappearance of leading Soviet Yiddish writers, and did not detect antisemitism in the Prague trial or in the campaign against "cosmopolitanism." They now expect Jewish cultural activity to be resumed in the USSR.

J67   JEWISH PEOPLE'S COMMITTEE. "Coughlin vs. Social Justice." New York: The Committee, 1940. 31 pp.
An attack on Father Coughlin by a communist front organization, in the form of showing a non-Jewish youth how a Jew feels when hearing Father Coughlin or reading his magazine, "Social Justice." Discussing youth's problems of unemployment, frustration, and fear, the authors urge youth to extend democracy and to fight against both war and the Father Coughlins.

J68   . . ., "Jews in Action: Five Years of the Jewish Peoples' Committee." New York: The Committee, n.d. [1940?]. 15 pp.
A statement by a Jewish Party front, during the Hitler-Stalin pact period, denouncing leaders of American Jewry for supporting the British against Hitler. The primary task, the Committee asserts, is to fight anti-Semitism at home now.

J69   JEWISH WAR VETERANS OF THE UNITED STATES, New York State. "The Communist: How To Recognize and Fight Him." New York: Jewish War Veterans, 1952. 46 pp.
Proceedings of a forum on communism held March 6, 1952, attended by delegates of veterans' organizations and other civic groups. Speakers denounced communist control of unions in vital defense industry, communist disruption in Korea, and communist hypocrisy regarding Jews and Jewish rights.

J70   JOHANNESSEN, Edward. "The Hawaiian Labor Movement: A Brief History." Boston: Bruce Humphries, 1956. 181 pp. App. Bibliog. Ind.
An account of the development of the labor movement in Hawaii and of its strength in the mid-1950's. Emphasis is placed upon the power of the ILWU, its virtual capture through ILWU-PAC of the Democratic Party in 1946, and the close relations of many of its leaders to the Communist Party. Communists were also influential in several other CIO unions. A campaign against communists on the islands was launched in 1947, participated in by Army Intelligence, the Territorial government, AFL unions, former Party members, and U.S. Senate committees.

J71   JOHN REED CLUBS OF NEW YORK. Draft Manifesto of John Reed Clubs, "New Masses," 7 (June 1932), 3-4.
A manifesto to be submitted to the John Reed Clubs of the U.S. by the John Reed Clubs of New York. The manifesto states that the general crisis of capitalism is reflected in its decadent culture. All honest intellectuals are urged to break with bourgeois ideas and join in forging a new art as a weapon in the battle for a new world.

J72   JOHNS, Orrick. The John Reed Clubs Meet, "New Masses," Oct. 30, 1934. 25-26.
A report on the second national conference of the John Reed Clubs, which represented a high level of revolutionary consciousness. The purpose of the Clubs is to win writers and artists to the revolution. The conference agreed to call a National Writers' Congress of antifascist writers within eight months.

J73   .... "Time of Our Lives: The Story of My Father and Myself." New York: Stackpole, 1937. 353 pp.
The former director of the WPA Federal Writers' Project in New York City tells of his experiences in the Communist Party from 1932 to 1937 (pp. 319-53). In the Party he worked with the National Committee for the Defense of Political Prisoners and as one of the editors of the "New Masses" before becoming a supervisor on a WPA newspaper project. He left the Party, not because of any disagreement over policy, but because he found life in his unit increasingly dull, dry, and repetitious.

J74   JOHNSEN, Julia E. (comp.). "Should the Communist Party Be Outlawed?" (Reference Shelf, 20:7.) New York: Wilson, 1949. 313 pp. Bibliog.
A collection of articles and speeches organized under three heads: general discussion, the case for outlawing the Party, and the case against outlawing it. Among the authors in the general discussion are William O. Douglas, Alexander Meiklejohn, Eric Johnston, J. Edgar Hoover, Louis Francis Budenz, and Harry D. Gideonse. Those who favor outlawing the Party include Harold E. Stassen, Dorothy Thompson, William Henry Chamberlin, and Morris Ernst. Among those opposing outlawry are Henry Steele Commager, Thomas E. Dewey, William C. Bullitt, Harry F. Ward, and Roger Baldwin.

J75   JOHNSON, Arnold. The Fight against Defeatism in Ohio, "Communist," 22 (July 1943), 653-56.

A report to a plenary meeting of the Party's national committee, June 11, 1943, describing the "treasonable" mine and rubber strikes and their tie-up with other forces working against Roosevelt.

J76   .... How to Defeat Universal Military Training, "Political Affairs," 27 (Jan. 1948), 19-26.
The author lists the organizations that are supporting the universal military training bill and proposes that communists and progressives incorporate opposition to it as part of the Party's antiwar and antifascist program in the 1948 election campaign. Universal military training is part of a plot to militarize the U.S.

J77   .... The Politics of the Truman Administration, "Political Affairs," 28 (March 1949), 1-14.
The Truman Administration is dashing the hopes of the American people for an enduring peace, economic security, and democratic rights. Truman is continuing the war-breeding Marshall Plan and Truman Doctrine. Three-fourths of his record-breaking budget is devoted to past, cold, and future wars. An intensive struggle is called for to change the Administration's war program.

J78   .... The North Atlantic Pact for Aggression, "Political Affairs," 28 (May 1949), 16-28.
The North Atlantic pact, inspired by the American capitalists, resembles the old Axis anti-Comintern pact, reflects American domination of Western Europe, undermines the UN, and violates the U.S. Constitution. It will mean high taxes on the masses and big profits for the capitalists. A mass campaign must be waged against it and in favor of an American-Soviet peace pact.

J79   .... The Bill of Rights and the Twelve, "Political Affairs," 28 (July 1949), 10-21.
An outline of the struggle for the Bill of Rights from its adoption in 1791 to 1949. The current struggle for the defense of the Bill of Rights is equated with the defense of 12 leading communists indicted in New York under the Smith Act.

J80   .... The 1958 Elections, "Political Affairs," 37 (June 1958), 1-13.
A discussion of issues, parties, and candidates in the 1958 elections. The Party's main objectives are to influence the outcome in the interests of the people, to promote labor independence and a broad people's coalition policy, and to strengthen the influence of the Party. A "United Socialist Ticket" is rejected as self-defeating and as isolating the left.

J81   .... The 1958 Elections, "Political Affairs," 37 (Dec. 1958), 1-15.
On November 4 the people voted for a leftward, liberal change in foreign and domestic policies. Labor was the main organized force that brought about the sweeping changes. The voters showed that they wanted peace, not the Dulles policy of brinkmanship, threatening war with China. The formation of the Independent Socialist Party proved premature and sectarian, as we predicted.

J82   JOHNSON, Bruce, and LOMENICK, Jean. Oklahoma's Loyalty Oath, "Nation," 173 (August 11, 1951), 106-8.
A description of the Oklahoma loyalty oath, its reception by the public, and its effects by two editors of the Oklahoma A. and M. college newspaper. Nearly 100 persons have lost their jobs because of their refusal to sign loyalty oaths, and state prestige, especially among educators, has been diminished.

J83   JOHNSON, Claudius O. The Status of Freedom of

Expression under the Smith Act, "Western Political Quarterly," 11 (Sept. 1958), 469-80.
An examination of the impact of the Smith Act, which makes it unlawful to advocate the overthrow of any government in the U.S. by force or violence or to promote an organization for such a purpose. The Dennis and Yates decisions of the U.S. Supreme Court are reviewed.

J84   JOHNSON, Frank Woodruff [pseud. for Elizabeth Dilling.]. "The Octopus." Omaha, Neb.: The author, 1940. 256 pp. Ind.
An anti-Semitic tract, asserting that there is a Jewish conspiracy to rob Gentiles of the right to speak or write facts unpleasing to Jewry. The B'nai B'rith Anti-Defamation League is attacked as pro-Red and anti-Christian. The backbone of the communist and socialist movements in the U.S. is said to be Jewish. Zionism in Palestine is called Marxist-socialist in leadership, theory, and practice.

J85   JOHNSON, Gerald W. Why Communists Are Valuable, "Harper's Magazine," 200 (Jan. 1950), 93-96.
Although communism is of no value in itself, the reaction it has produced from 1917 on has had educational and moral value for the ordinary American. The communists have made us think about racial prejudice and labor union democracy.

J86   .... Baltimore Report: A House Divided, "Reporter," 3 (Dec. 12, 1950), 31-32.
Baltimore, once dedicated to both loyalty and liberty, now finds them incompatible. It supports Owen Lattimore, target of McCarthy's wrath, but has endorsed the Ober Law, which bars from public office all members of organizations branded subversive by the U.S. Attorney General.

J87   JOHNSON, Hewlett. "The Soviet Power." New York: Modern Age, 1940. 352 pp.
The American edition of a study by the procommunist Dean of Canterbury, attempting to explain in simple terms an experiment in a new order of society, in which cooperation and planning replace competitive chaos and disorder. He ends with an apology for the Nazi-Soviet pact and the Soviet war on Finland. (The book had considerable influence in the U.S., particularly among the clergy.)

J88   JOHNSON, Howard. Aspects of Negro History and the Struggle against White Chauvinism, "Political Affairs," 29 (Feb. 1950), 13-22.
A brief history of the Negro people in the U.S., emphasizing the role of slavery in the development of American capitalism and the growth of the myth of white supremacy. The Party, opposing both white chauvinism and Negro bourgeois nationalism, must use Negro History Week to strengthen the struggle for a broad Negro people's liberation front.

J89   JOHNSON, J. R. "Why Negroes Should Oppose the War." New York: Pioneer Publishers for the Socialist Workers Party and the Young People's Socialist League (4th International), n.d. [1940?]. 31 pp.
An SWP pamphlet urging Negroes not to support the war, and assailing Roosevelt, anti-Negro Southern Democrats, and the Stalinists as deceivers of the Negro people. The pamphlet presents the SWP program for Negroes, urging them to struggle against the capitalists of America and the world, and to join the Fourth International.

J90   JOHNSON, M. Negro Rebellion Is Still Aim of Reds, "American Mercury," 80 (Feb. 1955), 97-102.
An analysis of the communist program of "self-determination in the Black Belt," put forth in 1930. The Scottsboro case was used to advance the program; so also were the National Negro Commission of the Communist Party, the Sharecroppers' Union, and the National Negro Congress. The Party is still working to bring American Negroes under Moscow's control.

J91   JOHNSON, Melvin M. " 'Red, White and Blue' or 'Red, Pink and White?' " Camden, N.J.: New Jersey State Bar Association, 1925. 33 pp.
An address to the New Jersey State Bar Association, June 6, 1925. The author outlines the early history and doctrines of the Communist Party, based primarily on Senate hearings, and pleads for education to combat the communist menace.

J92   JOHNSON, Oakley. The John Reed Club Convention, "New Masses," 8 (July 1932), 14-15.
An account of the National Organizing Conference of the John Reed Clubs, held in Chicago, May 29-30, 1932. Emphasis was placed on the struggle on the cultural front against capitalism and social fascism and on the relationship of revolutionary writers and artists to middle class intellectuals.

J93   .... Final Analysis: Madison Square Garden and the United Front, "Monthly Review," 1 (June 1934), 12-16.
A defense of the communists for breaking up the memorial meeting organized by the Socialist Party, following the crushing of the socialist workers of Vienna by the fascist Dollfuss. The communists, allegedly incensed by the scheduling of Mayor La Guardia and Matthew Woll as speakers, gave way to spontaneous resentment, not planned disruption.

J94   .... "The Day Is Coming: Life and Work of Charles E. Ruthenberg, 1882-1927." New York: International Publishers, 1957. 192 pp. Notes. Selected Writings. Ind.
A biography of the early Party leader and hero. Most of the book is concerned with Ruthenberg's early years, relatively little of it being devoted to Party politics or Ruthenberg's role in it. The final chapters, however, deal with Ruthenberg's transition to communism, and cover the period from the Cleveland May Day parade of 1919 through the criminal syndicalism trials, ending in 1925. The final chapter discusses Ruthenberg's efforts to create a labor party during the 1924 presidential election. Factional controversies in the Workers Party, following the failure of the 1924 venture into politics, are mentioned briefly.

J95   .... Ruthenberg and the Party's Founding, "Political Affairs," 39 [38], (March 1959), 1-13.
An appraisal of Charles E. Ruthenberg's role in the emergence and early years of the communist movement in the U.S., disagreeing sharply with Theodore Draper's estimate in "The Roots of American Communism." Johnson also attacks Draper's view of the importance of Louis Fraina in that early period, the reliance on force and violence, and the attitude toward trade unions. (Draper's reply and Johnson's rejoinder appear in "Political Affairs," May 1959, pp. 58-65.)

J96   JOHNSON, Robert H. How the Commies Take Over a Union, "America," 89 (Aug. 1, 1953), 436-38.
A case history of an election in UE Local 1150, Chicago, engineered by the communists. Based on the testimony of an ex-communist, a former UE field representative, the article shows how the communists gained control.

J97 JOHNSON, Tom. "The Reds in Dixie: Who Are The Communists and What Do They Fight for in the South?" New York: Workers Library, 1935. 47 pp.
Communists are working people who want adequate relief for the unemployed, unemployment insurance, higher wages, and militant and democratic unions. The division between black and white in the South lowers wages. Full equality in every field of life is advocated, along with a united working class and a Soviet America.

J98 JOHNSTONE, J. W. Two-Score Victories for the Left Wing, "Labor Herald," 2 (Nov. 1923), 21-22.
A progress report on TUEL successes in its efforts to amalgamate unions, form a labor party, and achieve recognition of the USSR. Unions that have endorsed these proposals are listed. Militant rank-and-file unionists are working to regenerate the trade union movement.

J99 .... Reaction in the Needle Trades, "Labor Herald," 2 (Feb. 1924), 25-27.
The first real battle between the growing left wing and the bureaucratic officials is under way in the needle trades. There is a reign of terror in the Furriers, and czaristic rule in the ILGWU. In the ACW the administration is in the center between right and left. The Needle Trades Section of the TUEL will soon meet.

J100 .... Two Battles against Reaction, "Workers Monthly," 4 (Nov. 1924), 38-39.
A brief review of conventions of the United Brotherhood of Carpenters and Joiners (Indianapolis, September 22) and the International Association of Machinists (Detroit, September 5). Left-wing activities in both unions are reviewed.

J101 .... The Carpenters Face Their Leaders, "Workers Monthly," 4 (March 1925), 228-29 ff.
Reactionary trade union leaders are meeting the challenge of the militants, organized by the TUEL, with a policy of expulsions. Latest autocrat to adopt this policy is Willian L. Hutcheson of the Carpenters, who has expelled 23 members so far and who will continue to expel TUEL supporters—those who oppose his class collaboration policies or expose his corruption. He is determined to control or destroy the Carpenters.

J102 .... The Martyrdom of the Coal Miners, "Workers Monthly," 4 (June 1925), 344-48.
A review of John L. Lewis' disastrous leadership of the United Mine Workers, and of his efforts to destroy the most militant and progressive sections. His record includes stolen elections, betrayals, declining membership, corruption, and expulsions. A mass revolt of the rank and file against miserable conditions and betrayal by their officials is urged.

J103 .... The 4th World Congress of the Red International, "Labor Unity," 2 (July 1928), 22-25.
A report on the Fourth Congress of the Red International of Labor Unions, held in Moscow in March and April, 1928, by the chairman of the American delegation. Sharply criticized at the Congress for not building new unions, the Trade Union Educational League leadership, which has traditionally opposed dual unionism, will seek to organize new unions in unorganized industries while continuing to work as a left wing within the old unions.

J104 .... The Work of Our Party in the Pittsburgh District, "Communist," 13 (April 1934), 346-55.
An assertion that the Party has failed to establish a foothold among Pittsburgh district miners, who are far more militant than the reformist leaders of the United Mine Workers. Application of the concentration policy, to establish a Party unit, will give the miners the leadership they lack.

J105 .... The Railway Labor Act: A Barrier to Militant Unionism, "Communist," 16 (May 1937), 465-70.
A protest against adoption for other industries of legislation similar to the Railway Labor Act, which has held back railroad labor from aggressive struggle. Like the B & O plan, the Act is a product of the poisonous capitalist theory of class collaboration.

J106 JOHNSTONE, Jenny Elizabeth. "Women in Steel." New York: Workers Library, 1937. 30 pp.
A pamphlet addressed to the women-folk of steel workers, describing the Steel Workers Organizing Committee, telling of its organization efforts culminating in its great victory, and urging them to form a Women's Auxiliary.

J107 JOINT COMMITTEE TO AID THE HERNDON DEFENSE. "The Case of Angelo Herndon." New York: The Committee, 1935. 15 pp.
An organizer for the Unemployed Councils, Herndon was convicted for attempting to incite insurrection after leading 1,000 unemployed to the Atlanta, Ga., courthouse in 1932 to seek relief. Emphasizing the civil liberties aspect of the case, the pamphlet asks signatures to a petition to the governor to free Herndon and repeal the law.

J108 JONES, Claudia. "Jim-Crow in Uniform." New York: New Age, 1940. 23 pp.
A pamphlet during the Hitler-Stalin pact period designed to arouse antiwar sentiment among Negroes. The author, a Negro Party leader, asserts that this is a white man's war, and that Jim Crow in the armed forces is another proof that the promises of democracy and liberty are false.

J109 .... New Problems of the Negro Youth Movement, "Clarity," 1 (Summer 1940), 54-64.
An assertion, in the theoretical organ of the Young Communist League, that the war situation has produced a movement for unification of Negro youth organizations and caused a rise in militancy among Negro youth to fight for their needs. Establishment of a National Federation of Negro Youth will develop ideological unity for keeping America out of war.

J110 .... "Lift Every Voice for Victory!" New York: New Age, 1942. 15 pp.
Addressing Negro youth, a Negro leader of the Young Communist League asserts that everything depends upon defeating Hitler and singles out Joe Louis as a symbol of American patriotism. Attacking "noisy traitors" such as Norman Thomas and George Schuyler, she states that the best friends of Negroes are patriotic citizens who want to win the war.

J111 .... On the Right to Self-Determination for the Negro People in the Black Belt (A Discussion Article), "Political Affairs," 25 (Jan. 1946), 67-77.
A discussion article following the rejection by the Party's national convention in July, 1945, of Browder's revisionist position on the Negro question. The article asserts the national minority status of Negroes in the North, and their existence as an oppressed nation in the Black Belt of the South. The right of self-determination should be raised once more as a programmatic demand.

J112 .... For New Approaches to Our Work Among Women, "Political Affairs," 27 (Aug. 1948), 738-43.

A pre-convention discussion article elaborating on the Party's policies toward women, which the author feels are not adequately emphasized in the draft resolution for the Party's national convention to be held August 3-6, 1948.

J113   JONES, Claudia. "An End to the Neglect of the Problems of the Negro Woman!" New York: National Women's Commission, CPUSA, 1949. 19 pp. Reprinted from "Political Affairs," June 1949.
A polemic against the neglect of the militant and progressive role of the Negro women, not only by bourgeois society, but in the ranks of progressive and labor movements and in the Party as well. This neglect is viewed as an important reason for the low degree of participation of Negro women in progressive organizations and in the Party.

J114   .... "Women in the Struggle for Peace and Security." New York: National Women's Commission, CPUSA, 1950. 16 pp. Reprinted from "Political Affairs," March 1950.
A cold war effort to mobilize women's opposition to American foreign policy and the atomic bomb. Women are said to be one of the most exploited sections of the working class. The Party is urged to combat male supremacist ideas and also the view of bourgeois feminism, to strengthen the Party's Women's Commission, and to concentrate more on women's problems.

J115   .... The Struggle for Peace in the United States, "Political Affairs," 31 (Feb. 1952), 1-20.
Though President Truman boasts of the armed strength of U.S. imperialism, Wall Street is suffering setbacks in the UN assembly. Sentiment for peaceful settlement of national differences is growing among the American people. The Communist Party works to produce an antifascist, antimonopoly, people's peace coalition.

J116   .... "Ben Davis: Fighter for Freedom." Introd. by Eslanda Goode Robeson. Brooklyn, N.Y.: National Committee to Defend Negro Leadership, 1954. 48 pp.
Denunciation of the conviction of Davis, one of the 11 communists found guilty in the trial under the Smith Act. Excerpts from his life, trial, and prison experiences are given to show that he was really jailed for advocating interracial democracy and Marxism-Leninism, for opposing the Korean War and Jim Crow, and for supporting Negro freedom. Readers are asked to seek amnesty for Davis and his colleagues.

J117   JONES, E. Stanley. "Christ's Alternative to Communism." New York and Cincinnati: Abingdon Press, 1935. 302 pp.
A statement of the social gospel by one who once looked with favor on the Soviet experiment. Now finding the USSR wanting, he opposes to its materialistic communism the Christian alternative, the Kingdom of God on earth. However, he favors the Soviet substitute of the cooperative ideal for the competitive motive. Unless Christians provide something better than communism offers, he warns, we will succumb to it. He suggests ways in which Christianity can become a more dynamic force.

J118   JONES, Hays. "Seamen and Longshoremen under the Red Flag." New York: Workers Library, 1935. 47 pp.
A recruiting pamphlet directed to seamen and longshoremen, telling what the maritime industry would be like in a Soviet America. To get rid of the American plutocratic dictatorship disguised as democracy, maritime workers are urged to join the Party, which leads the struggle

against fascism, for militant policies, for industrial unions, and for a mass labor party.

J119   JONES, Howard Mumford (ed.). "Primer of Intellectual Freedom." Cambridge, Mass.: Harvard University Press, 1949. 191 pp.
A collection of significant pronouncements on intellectual freedom, including the civil rights of communists, academic freedom in American colleges, and loyalty. Among the statements are those by President James R. Killian, Jr., of MIT, Chancellor Robert M. Hutchins of the University of Chicago, Grenville Clark and President James B. Conant of Harvard University, Dean Wilbur J. Bender of Harvard College, Professor Henry Steele Commager of Columbia University, and Professor Zechariah Chafee, Jr., of the Harvard Law School. Three dissenting opinions by Justice Oliver Wendell Holmes, one of them in a case involving Benjamin Gitlow, are included.

J120   JONES, Howard Mumford. Do You Know the Nature of An Oath? "American Scholar," 20 (Autumn 1951), 457-67.
A discussion of the University of California loyalty oath in particular and of loyalty in general. The author asserts that loyalty oaths for teachers are indefensible either to ensure loyalty or to weed out the tiny fraction of disloyal teachers.

J121   .... How Much Academic Freedom? "Atlantic Monthly," 191 (June 1953), 36-40.
A discussion by a Harvard professor of English of the issue of academic freedom, in view of current charges that colleges have communists or fellow-travelers on their faculties. No danger to education through efforts to indoctrinate students has yet been shown, nor is it evident that Party members are unfit to teach because their minds are closed.

J122   JONES, Ken. The FBI Wants You, "Reader's Digest," 58 (Feb. 1951), 65-68.
An account of communist espionage methods in the U.S., by one who spent six weeks with FBI spy-fighters. Behind the Moscow-trained professional spies are said to be at least 500,000 persons prepared for treasonable activities. Citizens are urged to be alert and to report any information on subversive activity to the FBI.

J123   JONES, Kitty, and OLIVIER, Robert. "Progressive Education Is REDucation." Boston: Meador, 1956. 246 pp.
An attack on progressive education as a technique for developing school children into socialists. Most of chapter 5 is devoted to showing the link between progressive education and communism. Progressive educators are said to want to change our economic system and social order, while the Communist Party supports progressive education. The book contains an account of the trial of Olivier, said to have been dismissed from a Louisiana teaching post for fighting against progressive education.

J124   JONES, L. P. Voice of America Hearing, "Foreign Service Journal," 30 (May 1953), 23-24 ff.
A condensation of a Senate Permanent Investigating Subcommittee hearing on the Voice of America, involving a high school teacher who had participated in a VOA broadcast to Czechoslovakia, and who declined to answer questions as to past membership in the Communist Party.

J125   JONES, Martin [pseud.?]. Organizational Steps toward Bolshevization in the American Party, "International Press Correspondence," 9 (May 24, 1929), 532-33.
A review of organizational changes adopted at the sixth convention of the American Communist Party in order to

"bolshevize" it. The changes seek centralized control of the Party, and increased working class composition of the leadership. The Party's name was changed from Workers (Communist) Party to Communist Party.

J126   JOSEPHSON, Leon. American Political Prisoners, "Masses & Mainstream," 3 (July 1950), 56-61.
The list of political prisoners, jailed for their beliefs, is growing steadily though they have committed no crime involving an intent or overt act. They are cold war prisoners, prosecuted as part of our government's preparation for war. While the pretense of democracy can be maintained in stable periods, the ruling class strikes out blindly when it feels its rule shaken.

J127   JOSEPHSON, Matthew. For a Literary United Front, "New Masses," 15 (April 30, 1935), 22-23.
Reflecting a shift in the Party line in the literary field, the author calls for establishment, at a proposed congress of American writers, of a literary united front broad enough to embrace people of various persuasions. The radical press is criticized for its left-literary infantilism and sectarianism of the past two years.

J128   . . . . "Sidney Hillman: Statesman of American Labor." Garden City, N.Y.: Doubleday, 1952. 701 pp. Ref. notes. Ind.
A well-documented, sympathetic portrait of Sidney Hillman, president of the Amalgamated Clothing Workers. Chapter 11, pp. 268-81, deals with the efforts of the TUEL to organize a faction within the union. On the whole they were unsuccessful, though for a time in the mid-1920's they controlled one of the large locals in New York City and challenged the union administration in other areas. Hillman took a tolerant view of such efforts, defeating them by militant economic action and an expanding social program. Communist influence within the CIO is treated briefly.

J129   . . . . The Battle of the Books, "Nation," 174 (June 28, 1952), 619-24.
An account of efforts by professional bigots and super-patriots to remove volumes they label as subversive from libraries and to intimidate textbook authors and publishers. Attacks on Little, Brown and others for publishing works by alleged communists have frightened book publishers into conformity.

J130   JOUGHIN, Louis. The Current Questionings of

Teachers: Notes for a Social Pathology, "Social Problems," I (Oct. 1953), 61-65.
Questionings of teachers about Party membership and sympathy may substitute a dynamics of fear for a previous tradition of rationality. This would be evidence of a pathological response within the social body. Legislators think communist teachers dangerous because they may be preparing traitorous acts or damaging youth by lies or distortions.

J131   "JOURNAL OF HIGHER EDUCATION," Academic Freedom: A "Journal" Symposium, 20 (Oct. 1949), 346-54 ff.
The case against allowing communists academic freedom is presented by Harold W. Stoke, who argues that the prospect of damage from communist toleration is greater than from communist suppression. John K. Ryan holds that error has no rights. Though Constance Warren would not knowingly engage a communist to teach, she would not dismiss him on that ground alone, but would judge him on his merits, relying on the estimate of his peers. (For comments by Sidney Hook, Peter A. Carmichael, and Raymond B. Allen, see "Academic Freedom," in "Journal of Higher Education," 20 [Nov. 1949], 422-28 ff.)

J132   JOWITT, William Allen (Earl Jowitt). "The Strange Case of Alger Hiss." Garden City, N.Y.: Doubleday, 1953. 380 pp. App. Ind.
A review of the evidence and procedures of the second Hiss trial, by a former Lord Chancellor of England. While the author expresses no opinion as to whether or not Hiss was guilty, he expresses doubts and lists baffling questions raised by the case.

J133   JOY, Henry B. "Our Pro-Socialist Churches." Detroit: The author, 1936. 61 pp.
A pamphlet purporting to show, by means of editorials, articles, and comments, that the Federal Council of Churches is a communist-dominated organization. Patriotic clergy and laymen are urged to save the churches from this control.

J134   . . . . "Reference Material." Detroit: The author, 1936. 162 pp.
A collection of 43 letters, circulars, reprints, and other items to show the connections of the Federal Council of the Churches of Christ, the American Civil Liberties Union, and the National Religion and Labor Foundation with communist, socialist, and pacifist activities.

K

K1 KAHN, Albert E. "Treason in Congress: the Record of the House Un-American Activities Committee." Introd. by O. John Rogge. New York: Progressive Citizens of America, 1948. 32 pp.

An accusation that the House Un-American Activities Committee has spied upon American citizens, compiled blacklists of liberals, cooperated with native fascist and subversive groups, and carried on an offensive against our democratic institutions and constitutional rights. An appeal is made for abolition of the committee, as part of a broader fight to build the Progressive Party and help elect Henry Wallace to the presidency.

K2 .... "High Treason: The Plot against the People." New York: Lear Publishers, 1950. 372 pp. Bibliog. Ind.

A communist interpretation of American history since World War I. Starting with a view of the Palmer raids as a crusade to crush the labor movement, the author pictures the 1920's in terms of the despoiling of the country by a moneyed minority. The golden years of the New Deal and World War II, when the people triumphed, were followed by the postwar betrayal of the Soviet Union, the return of reaction, the "witch hunt" in Washington, and the suppression of our liberties. Now cold war power politics threaten an atomic global war. The question facing the American people is whether their land shall be democratic or fascist.

K3 .... "The People's Case: The Story of the IWO." New York: Hour Publishers, n.d. [1951?]. 20 pp.

An appeal for the defense of the IWO, under indictment and under threat of liquidation by the Superintendent of Insurance of the State of New York. The author, a leader of the Jewish affiliate of this Party-controlled fraternal order, contends that the proceedings are based on political, not fiscal, grounds. He sees the defense of the IWO as an issue of democracy.

K4 .... "Agents of Peace," New York: Hour Publishers, n.d. [1952?]. 16 pp.

An attack on the Justice Department for its indictment of Dr. W. E. B. Du Bois and his associates of the Peace Information Center for failure to register as foreign agents. The author, leader of the Jewish section of the International Workers Order, tells the history of the Peace Information Center, describes its activities, and writes of its "gallant" work in printing and distributing the Stockholm world peace petitions.

K5 .... "The Crime against Jean Field." Croton-on-Hudson, N.Y.: Hour Publishers for the Jean Field Committee, 1952. 20 pp.

An appeal for sympathy and funds for Jean Field, who, allegedly because of her opposition to American intervention in Korea, was forcibly separated from her two children.

K6 .... "Vengeance on the Young: The Story of the Smith Act Children." New York: Hour Publishers, 1952. 21 pp.

An account of FBI harassment of the families of the communists who were indicted and imprisoned under the Smith Act. (Part of a forthcoming book to be called "The Game of Death: War Preparations for American Children.")

K7 .... "The Game of Death: Effects of the Cold War on our Children." New York: Cameron and Kahn, 1953. 256 pp. Ind.

An indictment of our nation's cold war policies for its effect on our children, written by a leader of the Jewish affiliate of the Party-controlled fraternal body, the International Workers Order. The author attacks the emphasis on militarism and violence, the loyalty checks on parents, and the neglect of children's health needs. He argues that we can safeguard children's welfare and happiness only by ending the cold war.

K8 .... Comics, TV, and Your Child, "Masses & Mainstream," 6 (June 1953), 36-43.

A selection from Kahn's new book, "The Game of Death," which analyzes the impact of the cold war on the youth of this country.

K9 ... (ed.). "McCarthy on Trial." New York: Cameron and Kahn, 1954. 64 pp.

A report on the "trial" of Senator McCarthy on January 6, 1954, before a "court of public opinion" on charges of illegal acts and violations of the U.S. Constitution. The prosecutor, witnesses, and jury were well-known fellow-travelers or members of front organizations. McCarthyism is condemned as warmongering, and the Truman Administration attacked for unleashing the cold war and an orgy of anti-Soviet Red-baiting.

K10 KAHN, Arthur D. "The Road to War: Rearming West Germany." New York: American Peace Crusade, n.d. [1952]. 15 pp.

A publication of a leading "front" organization of the cold war period. The author opposes the signing of an agreement by the U.S., Britain, and France with West Germany as a military alliance against the Soviet Union and hence a threat to world peace. The U.S. is urged to negotiate a peaceful settlement of the German question with the USSR.

K11 KAHN, Gordon. "Hollywood on Trial: The Story of the 10 Who Were Indicted." Foreword by Thomas Mann. New York: Boni and Gaer, 1948. 229 pp.

An account of the appearances of Hollywood authors, directors, and producers before the House Un-American Activities Committee in 1947, and of the indictment of ten authors and directors for contempt of Congress for refusing to answer questions as to membership in the Communist Party and in the Screen Writers' Guild. Hollywood's effort to fight back through the Committee for the First Amendment is described, as is the capitulation of the motion picture companies and their adoption of a blacklist. The book was written in collaboration with the indicted ten. (Later convicted of the contempt charges, the ten were given prison sentences ranging from six months to a year; the author, though not among those indicted, was dismissed by Warner Brothers for communist sympathy.)

K12 KAHN, Robert I. "An Affirmative Answer to Communism." Houston, Texas: Temple Emanu El, n.d. [1953?]. 28 pp.
A series of four sermons by an American rabbi who, in addition to exposing the fallacies of communism, appeals for an affirmative answer to it. The vital factor, he argues, is to develop a crusading democracy, to pay attention to race relations as the show window of democracy, and to gear our foreign policy to the crusade by bringing food and freedom to the underprivileged peoples of the earth.

K13 KAIN, R. S. The Communist Movement in the United States, "Current History," 32 (Sept. 1930), 1079-84.
A review of the history of the communist movement in the U.S. since 1919, stressing the propensity to split into rival factions, the close dependence on the Communist International, the predominant influence of the foreign-born and aliens, and the destructive influence on other radical or progressive groups.

K14 KALVEN, Harry, Jr.; MING, William R. Jr.; and SHARP, Malcolm. "A Look at Civil Liberties." Chicago: University of Chicago Round Table, Oct. 19, 1952. 24 pp.
A radio discussion covering the House Un-American Activities Committee, loyalty oaths, Senator McCarthy, and the government loyalty program. The participants, members of the University's law faculty, all express concern over the state of our civil liberties.

K15 KALVEN, Harry Jr. The Case of J. Robert Oppenheimer before the Atomic Energy Commission, "Bulletin of the Atomic Scientists," 10 (Sept. 1954), 259-69.
A review of the legal and evidential questions raised by the Atomic Energy Commission's denial of clearance to Oppenheimer. The decision weakened the Gray Board's findings, left the criteria of the security system undefined, and committed a serious error in judgment in applying such stringent standards of security.

K16 KAMMAN, Morris. Where Dies Stole His Technique, "New Masses," 33 (Nov. 7, 1939), 12-15.
A communist view of the Palmer raids of 1919-20 as the source of Dies' technique of Red-baiting to attack progressivism and organized labor.

K17 KAMP, Joseph P. "The Hell of Herrin Rages Again: A Story of Lawlessness, Violence and Death under the Reign of John L. Lewis." New Haven, Conn.: Constitutional Educational League, 1937. 122 pp.
An extremist right-wing view, blaming the CIO, Lewis, and the communists for violence in labor struggles. The author describes the violence committed by the United Mine Workers in Herrin in 1922, comparing it with CIO violence in strikes in Youngstown, Chicago, and Detroit in 1937. Violence is said to have been instigated by the communists, working closely with Lewis.

K18 .... "Join the C.I.O. and Help Build a Soviet America." New Haven, Conn.: Constitutional Educational League, 1937. 61 pp.
By a comparison of quotations from communist and CIO sources, the author seeks to prove that the CIO is helping to pave the way for a Soviet America. He points out communists in CIO leadership positions, and attacks the Garland Fund as one of the financial sources of red propaganda within the CIO.

K19 .... "The Fifth Column in the South." New Haven, Conn.: Constitutional Educational League, 1940. 42 pp.
A charge that the South has been invaded by a fifth column, threatening economic ruin and destruction of Southern traditions, and seeking social chaos and overthrow of the government. Participating in this fifth column are the Communist Party, the American Civil Liberties Union, the National Religion and Labor Foundation, Commonwealth College, Highlander Folk School, CIO unions, the Southern Conference for Human Welfare, the National Negro Congress, and others.

K20 .... "The Fifth Column in Washington!: Un-Americans on the Government Payroll." New Haven, Conn.: Constitutional Educational League, 1940. 33 pp.
An attack on liberals and leftists on government payrolls in Washington, with the charge that they constitute a communist fifth column. A list of government employees who were members of the Washington branch of the American League Against War and Fascism is included.

K21 .... "The Fifth Column Stops Defense." New Haven, Conn.: Constitutional Educational League, 1941. 12 pp.
An argument that current strikes are part of a subversive plot aimed at defense by communists occupying key posts in CIO unions. War industry production, the author asserts, has been stopped or slowed up on orders from Berlin via Moscow. A list of communists or fellow-travelers in the CIO is appended.

K22 .... "The Fifth Column vs. the Dies Committee." New Haven, Conn.: Constitutional Educational League, 1941. 34 pp.
A plea for enlarged appropriations for the Dies Committee to enable it to investigate and expose subversive activities, a task for which the FBI is not suited. The author asserts that President Roosevelt and a lot of his friends are trying to kill the Committee. He lists individuals and organizations, most of them in the communist camp, who are engaged in this effort.

K23 .... "Native Nazi Purge Plot." New Haven, Conn.: Constitutional Educational League, 1942. 66 pp.
Communists, socialists, liberals, progressives, internationalists, and interventionists are lumped together as plotters seeking to revamp the U.S. government into a super-collectivist state. They are said to further Hitler's purpose by causing disunity and disruption.

K24 .... "Vote CIO... and Get a Soviet America." New York: Constitutional Educational League, 1944. 64 pp.
Presidential campaign literature from the far right. Sidney Hillman, Earl Browder, the CIO's Political Action Committee, and the Communist Party are seen behind Roosevelt's bid for a fourth term. Browder and Hillman are said to seek control over the Democratic Party in order to seize the government and establish a communist state.

K25 .... "Strikes and the Communists Behind Them." New Haven, Conn.: Constitutional Educational League, 1947. 64 pp.
A denunciation of the postwar strike wave by a right-wing author, who asserts that the strikes, under communist instigation, are serving as dress rehearsals for violent revolution. He lists the communist-led unions of the CIO, charging that Philip Murray is now their captive.

K26 KAMP, Joseph P. "Behind the Lace Curtains of the YWCA." New York: Constitutional Educational League, 1948. 64 pp.
A report, from an extreme right-wing source, of infiltration by communist and other left-wing elements into the YWCA. The author finds touches of communist propaganda in YWCA publications, and names subversive organizations with which the YWCA has had dealings. He concludes that YWCA prestige and facilities are used to further communist interests.

K27 .... "America Betrayed: The Tragic Consequences of Reds on the Government payroll!" New York: Constitutional Educational League, 1950. 62 pp.
A discussion, by a right-wing extremist, of the communist triumph in China, which is termed a disastrous defeat for the U.S. at the hands of Soviet Russia. Communist influence, in and out of the State Department, is held responsible. A list of alleged communists in the State Department is included.

K28 .... "It Isn't Safe to be an American." New York: Constitutional Educational League, 1950. 58 pp.
Communist infiltration of the government is held responsible for the author's conviction for contempt of Congress and the troubles of the League with congressional committees. In contrast, subversives are treated gently by congressional committees under comparable circumstances.

K29 .... "We Must Abolish the United States: The Hidden Facts behind the Crusade for World Government." New York: Constitutional Educational League, 1950. 195 pp. Ind.
A condemnation of the crusade for world government as pro-Red and treasonable. An appendix lists Americans who support world government, with alleged communist-front organizations to which they belong.

K30 .... "Meet the Man Who Plans to Rule America." New York: Headlines, 1958. 32 pp.
Charges by an extreme rightist that Walter Reuther got his start in the labor movement by collaborating with communists, that he is a Marxist who has been both socialist and procommunist, that he is surrounded by leftist aides, and that he plans to establish and rule a socialist, Soviet America.

K31 KAMPELMAN, Max M. "The Communist Party vs. the C.I.O.: A Study in Power Politics." New York: Praeger, 1957. 299 pp. Bibliog. Ind.
A study of the effort made by the Communist Party to control CIO unions. The author briefly reviews communist influence in the American labor movement, and describes communist penetration of the CIO, the power battle which took place from 1945 through 1950, the intraunion struggles over the question of communism, and the final expulsion of communist-dominated unions. Analyzing the methods whereby the Party union leadership had been able to control large numbers of noncommunist members, the author observes that the communist trade union goal is not the overthrow of capitalism, but support of Soviet strategy in foreign affairs.

K32 .... Communists in the C.I.O., pp. 343-75 in "The Strategy of Deception: A Study in World-Wide Communist Tactics," ed. by Jeane J. Kirkpatrick. New York: Farrar, Straus, 1963. 444 pp.
An account of the rise and decline of communist influence within the CIO. By boring within key unions of the CIO, a small minority of communists was able to gain control over a substantial portion of the labor movement, though the membership did not respond to communist appeals. Rigidity on behalf of the USSR made identification of communist trade union leaders possible.

K33 KANTOROVITCH, Haim. The Thomas-Browder Debate, "Socialist Call," 1 (Dec. 7, 1935), 9.
Analysis of the new popular front line of the communists, as presented by Browder in a debate with Norman Thomas in Nov. 1935. Communists are no more sincere towards socialists than before, as shown by catcalls at Thomas when he criticized Stalin and the Soviet Union. Communists and socialists are no closer to a permanent united front, although local, temporary, united fronts may be possible.

K34 .... Notes on the United Front Problem, "American Socialist Monthly," 5 (May 1936), 7-11.
Arguments pro and con within the Socialist Party on whether to join in a united front with the Communist Party. While the author does not think such an alliance is necessary or advisable at present, he outlines concessions both parties would have to make should such an arrangement prove necessary later.

K35 KAPLAN, Nat. Youth and Industry, "Communist," 7 (Aug. 1928), 496-99.
Demands of the Young Workers (Communist) League for youth in the 1928 presidential elections, including enfranchisement, industrial reforms, a new status in society, and worker education.

K36 KARSAVINA, Jean. "Tree by the Waters." New York: International Publishers, 1948. 189 pp.
A book by a communist author for older boys and girls, dealing with the class conflict between the owners of a New England factory and the townspeople who work for them.

K37 KARSH, Bernard, and GARMAN, Phillips L. The Impact of the Political Left. In "Labor and the New Deal," ed. by Milton Derber and Edwin Young. Madison: University of Wisconsin Press, 1957. 393 pp. Bibliog. Ind.
In chapter 3, pp. 77-119, Karsh and Garman analyze the impact of communists and left-wingers on the trade unions from the time of the great depression through the New Deal. Organizations of the unemployed gave communists opportunity to develop leadership skills, which they used in the new unions of the CIO. Unlike previous periods, communist unionists gained influence during the New Deal years through the concealment, rather than the advocacy, of communist doctrines.

KATTERFELD, Ludwig E. See CARR, James.

K38 KATZ, M. "The Assassination of Kirov: Proletarian Justice versus White-Guard Terror." New York: Workers Library, 1935. 24 pp.
An account of the murder of Kirov, secretary of the Party Committee in the Leningrad Region, and of the energetic countermeasures taken by the Soviet state. The assassin is linked to the former Zinoviev-Trotzky opposition, White Guard elements, and foreign governments. Trotzkyites and Musteites in the U.S. are attacked.

K39 KAUB, Verne Paul. "Collectivism Challenges Christianity." Winona Lake, Ind.: Light and Life Press, 1945. 249 pp.
An attack on liberal Christianity as a bedfellow of Marxism and a view that socialism, the British Labour Party, Christian socialism, and technocracy are all part of the communist-socialist conspiracy. This conspiracy can be

fought only by rejecting collectivism in favor of the liberty of individualism.

K40 KAUB, Verne Paul. "Communist-Socialist Propaganda in American Schools." Boston: Meador Publishing Co., 1953. 192 pp.
A condemnation of progressive education as a means of indoctrinating our youth with communist-socialist ideology, and an attack on the National Education Association for endorsing progressive education. Progressive education is said to be subversive, based on atheist philosophy.

K41 KAUFMAN, Irving R. Representation by Counsel: A Theoretical Right, "American Bar Association Journal," 40 (April 1954), 299-302.
An address by the judge who presided at the trial of the Rosenbergs. He reminds lawyers that the duty to defend unpopular clients may be forgotten in the intensity of feelings about communists. Lawyers should assure to their clients every defense that the law provides.

K42 KAUFMAN, Morris, and WENNIES, Andrew. The United Fronters in the Fur Union. "New Leader," 2 (Oct. 24, 1925), 6.
An attack by the general president and general secretary-treasurer of the furriers' union on its communist-controlled New York Joint Board for failing to support the furriers' strike in Montreal. The Joint Board leaders are charged with discrediting the strike, thereby committing treason against the strikers.

K43 KAY, Helen. "We Demand: The Story of Anyboy and Anygirl." New York: National Committee, Unemployed Councils, and Young Pioneers of America, n.d. [1934?], 14 unnumbered pp.
An account of child labor and unemployment in the U.S., written for children, contrasting children's hunger here with happiness in the USSR. Children are urged to demand unemployment insurance, the soldiers' bonus, and an end to child labor.

K44 KAZIN, Alfred. "On Native Grounds: An Interpretation of Modern American Prose Literature." New York: Reynal & Hitchcock, 1942. 541 pp. Ind.
A review and analysis of modern American literature from 1890 to 1940. Writers like Hemingway and Dos Passos, who felt the impact of depression, war, and other social issues, are discussed at length. The communist appeal to writers beginning in 1930 is treated on pp. 373-83, and Marxist literary criticism on pp. 407-25.

K45 KEARNEY, Vincent S. The Case of John Stewart Service, "America," 86 (Jan. 12, 1952), 394-95.
An analysis of the loyalty dismissal of John Stewart Service, with a review of all aspects of the Truman loyalty order and the resulting program. Due process of law is not applicable here, since it is not a right to hold a government job.

K46 KEARNS, Lawrence. Non-Communist Affidavits under the Taft-Hartley Act, "Georgetown Law Journal," 37 (March 1949), 297-318.
A review of the legislative history of the provision, compliance under it, NLRB decisions bearing on it, and the constitutional issue involved. The provision has proved much more workable and effective than many critics anticipated.

K47 KEENAN, Charles. The Mundt-Ferguson Anti-Communist Bill, "America," 83 (Aug. 12, 1950), 488-90.
Analysis and approval of the bill, with reservations, by the managing editor, who asserts that the measure does not impinge on civil liberties. If it is passed, he urges that it be administered with wisdom and restraint.

K48 .... Free Speech or Free Conspiracy? "America," 85 (June 23, 1951), 309-10.
A discussion of judicial opinion on the conviction of the 11 communists under the Smith Act. The author approves of the court majority's concern with civil liberties and of its recognition of the menace of communism.

K49 KELLER, James. The Rubber Front in Akron, "Communist," 16 (March 1937), 241-49.
An appraisal of union organization and policy in the rubber industry in Akron. Party members must facilitate the forward movement of the rubber unions, while building the Party in Akron and particularly in the rubber unions.

K50 .... The Akron Municipal Elections, "Communist," 17 (Jan. 1938), 40-45.
An appraisal of the Akron elections in the light of people's front objectives, with an account of the work of Labor's Nonpartisan League. Errors made by the progressive camp are reviewed, and the role of the Party analyzed. Lessons of the Akron elections are summarized.

K51 .... The Strategy of the Packinghouse Workers' Strike, "Political Affairs," 25 (April 1946), 371-79.
An account of the successful Chicago strike for a wage increase, appraising the roles of the AFL, the CIO, and the Party. The government awards must now be enforced, and the wage increase put into effect everywhere. The union has been strengthened organizationally and ideologically.

K52 KELLEY, Hubert. Our No. 1 Communist, "American Magazine," 121 (Feb. 1936), 29 ff.
A portrait of Earl Browder, tracing his family background and early experiences that made him a convert to communism. A sentimentalist and dreamer before he became a revolutionary, he was ready to accept communism when he finished a prison term for opposing the draft in World War I.

K53 KELLEY, James Bernard. Science and Security, "Commonweal," 60 (Aug. 27, 1954), 506-10.
A review of the complex problems of scientific security involved in the Oppenheimer case. A scientist denied security clearance is almost unemployable in his profession. While security clearance is a privilege, not a right, government action should not appear capricious. The concept of security changes with time, and revisions are always retroactive.

K54 KELLOR, Frances A. "The Inside of Bolshevism— Addressed to Credit Men." New York: New York Credit Men's Association, 1920. 12 pp.
A plea to fight Bolshevism with economic weapons by creating better conditions for American immigrants and offering economic aid to Europe.

K55 KELLY, Alfred H. (ed.). "Foundations of Freedom in the American Constitution." New York: Harper, 1958. 299 pp. App. Ind.
Six essays on constitutional liberty, originally published by the Carrie Chapman Catt Memorial Fund. In chapter 4, "Constitutional Liberty and the Communist Problem," Jack W. Peltason surveys the measures taken in the U.S. to curb seditious speech from 1798 to the present. Robert K. Carr in chapter 5, "Constitutional Liberty and Congressional Investigation," traces the history of congressional investigations, considers the Fifth Amendment as grounds for refusal to testify, and suggests procedural and judicial reforms. In the final chapter, "Constitutional Liberty and

Loyalty Programs," Alan F. Westin traces the measures taken by the government to protect itself from infiltration by subversive elements.

K56   KELLY, John E. Little Red Schoolboys, "America," 60 (Jan. 14, 1939), 344-45.
A critical impression of the annual convention of the American Student Union, which is termed a youth outpost of the Comintern in the U.S. Only the pro-Soviet side of world issues was presented. A militant, patriotic student organization to drive communism from the campus is called for.

K57   . . . . The Erstwhile Pinks Are Now Tiger Lillies, "America," 64 (March 29, 1941), 682-83.
Comment on anticommunist sentiments now expressed by former radicals and dupes, since Stalin has been repudiated. Before the communist schism they had built a strong position in government, labor, education, press, cinema, and literature. Now the "Protestant Digest" appeals for tolerance, honoring several who never displayed tolerance.

K58   KELLY, Raymond J. Let's Outlaw It, "American Legion Magazine," 28 (March 1940), 16-17 ff.
A call by the national commander of the Legion for barring the communists from the ballot, as 13 states have already done. Three congressional committees have concluded that the communists constitute a foreign conspiracy masked as a political party.

K59   KEMLER, Edgar. Soft Impeachment: The Loyalty-Security Probe, "Nation," 181 (Dec. 24, 1955), 55-57.
Criticism of the Hennings subcommittee probe of the loyalty-security system, despite some minor successes, for failing to come to grips with the problem. Reform of security abuses are needed in government employment and the military service, and may soon be needed for workers in defense industry.

K60   KEMPTON, Murray. Robert Oppenheimer and the Iron Circle, "Progressive," 18 (Sept. 1954), 14-17.
A review by a New York "Post" columnist of the Oppenheimer case, covering his relations with communists, his reactions to security regulations, and the question of his loyalty. Currently he is a committed anticommunist. The root cause of his troubles was the fear and hostility of men with whom he disagreed.

K61   . . . . "Part of Our Time: Some Ruins and Monuments of the Thirties." New York: Simon and Schuster, 1955. 334 pp.
A series of sketches of communists or leftist anticommunists who were active in the 1930's. Drawing upon interviews and published biographical data, the author, a newspaper columnist, uses a fictionalized technique to show how they became involved and how they reacted. Among the subjects are Alger Hiss and Whittaker Chambers, Gardner Jackson and Lee Pressman, Joe Curran of the NMU, left-wing writers of the 1930's, J. B. Matthews, left-wing writers in Hollywood, Mary Heaton Vorse, Elizabeth Bentley and Ann Moos Remington, the Reuther brothers, and the student movement.

K62   . . . . The Achievement of Harvey Matusow, "Progressive," 19 (April 1955), 7-10.
An unflattering account of the career of Matusow, who joined the Party in 1947, became an underground FBI informant in 1950, was expelled from the Party in 1951, and later became a professional witness against the communists. Early in 1955, while writing his memoirs for a left-wing publishing house, he announced that he had lied

in his testimony against communist defendants. All brands of anticommunism are degraded by his spectacle.

K63   KENDRICK, Alex H. The Party and the Trade Unions in the Post-War Period, "Political Affairs," 31 (Dec. 1952), 41-56.
Since 1946 the U.S. government, preparing for a third world war, has destroyed the class unity of the labor movement, to make it powerless to prevent a full-fledged fascist state. However, the widening gulf between union leaders and workers, and also intolerable conditions, are causing strikes. The Party will continue to act on problems within trade unions.

K64   . . ., and GOLDEN, Jerome. Lessons of the Struggle against Opportunism in District 65, "Political Affairs," 32 (June 1953), 26-37.
District 65 of the Distributive, Processing, and Office Workers was a militant union in its early years, closely associated with the left and communist forces. Now its leadership substitutes class-collaboration for class-struggle wage policies, denounces communism along with fascism, and demonstrates its loyalty to the imperialist warmakers. (A scheduled concluding section to this article never appeared.)

K65   KENNAN, George F. Where Do You Stand on Communism? "New York Times Magazine," May 27, 1951, 7 ff.
A discussion of the communist problem by a leading State Department official. While opposing outlawry of the Party as ineffective, he urges elimination of fellow travelers from responsible government service and the use of wisdom in dealing with them in education. We should view the problem in perspective, not emotionally.

K66   . . . . Hope in an Age of Anxiety, "New Republic," 128 (June 1, 1953), 14-16.
A convocation address delivered at Notre Dame University by the former U.S. Ambassador to Russia, who warns against the direction and methods chosen by some anticommunists as negative and out of keeping with our democratic traditions. (This address also appears in "Bulletin of the Atomic Scientists," October 1953, under the title, "Communism and Conformity.")

K67   KENNEDY, Jack. Trade Union Capitalism Undermines the Brotherhoods, "Workers Monthly," 5 (June 1926), 352-55 ff.
An assertion that the railroad brotherhoods have become tamed in subservience to capitalism. The left-wing program should include amalgamation of railroad unions, organization of the unskilled and semi-skilled, creation of an American labor party, and control of the railroads by workers and technicians.

K68   . . . . The Watson-Parker Act, "Workers Monthly," 5 (Aug. 1926), 452-55.
An attack on the newly passed railway labor law, said to have been passed to forestall union wage demands as a legalized effort to avoid worker militancy. The membership of the board of mediation, the arbitration feature, and the provision for a presidential special board are all severely criticized. Repeal of this antistrike law is urged.

K69   KENNEDY, John C. The Future of the Federated Farmer-Labor Party, "American Labor Monthly," 2 (Dec. 1923), 47-51.
Defense of the Federated Farmer-Labor Party and participation of the Workers Party in it, by an official of the Washington State Farmer-Labor Party. Though not supported by most labor and farm groups, the organization serves a useful purpose. Progressive workers and farm-

ers will turn to it as they become disillusioned with La Follette.

K70   KENNEDY, John S. Witness of Whittaker Chambers, "Catholic World," 175 (July 1952), 260-65.
Whittaker Chambers' "Witness" sets forth powerfully the central issue of our age—the choice between communism and Christianity. Chambers, brought up in a home without God, tells of the faith and vision that communism represented to him, and of his return to Christianity from bondage.

K71   KENNEDY, Walter B. The Schneiderman Case—Some Legal Aspects, "Fordham Law Review," 12 (Nov. 1943), 231-51.
A professor of law at Fordham criticizes the Supreme Court majority in the Schneiderman denaturalization case for requiring clear and unequivocal proof rather than the "reasonable man" test. It erred in supposing that a communist could be attached to the Constitution and in doubting the Party's intent to use violence.

K72   KENT, Rockwell. "This Is My Own." New York: Duell, Sloan and Pearce, 1940. 393 pp.
The autobiography of an artist who was active in such communist-front organizations as the American League for Peace and Democracy, the International Workers Order, and the International Labor Defense. Some of the controversies resulting from these affiliations are described in the volume.

K73   . . . . "It's Me, O Lord." New York: Dodd, Mead, 1955. 617 pp.
The autobiography of an artist connected with many communist front groups. Though most of the volume deals with his family life, art, and trips, he also writes at some length about his political activities, including his postwar efforts to "win the peace" through the American Labor Party, the Progressive Party, and the Stockholm Peace Conference. He describes the achievements of the International Workers Order, of which he was an officer, and his appearance in New York State proceedings to liquidate that organization. He tells briefly of his appearance before the McCarthy Committee.

K74   KERBY, Phil. The Legion Blacklist, "New Republic," 126 (June 16, 1952), 14-15.
Criticism of the Hollywood film industry for submitting without protest to a political blacklist conducted by the American Legion, in order to stop picketing of motion pictures around the country. Some 200 to 300 industry personalities are now required to undergo a loyalty screening process conducted by the studios.

K75   KERNAN, William C. Snake in Suburbia's Garden, "Catholic World," 180 (Oct. 1954), 16-23.
A leading member of the Scarsdale Citizens Committee, organized to purge the public schools there of communist influences, analyzes "The Lonesome Train," a cantata telling the story of Lincoln's funeral train, which was performed in a Scarsdale school. Written by Millard Lampell, with score by Earl Robinson (both with long records of affiliation with communist causes), the cantata introduces communist propaganda into the Lincoln story.

K76   KERSTEIN, Morris. "Work or War?" New York: Workers Alliance, 1940. 15 pp.
A pamphlet of the Hitler-Stalin pact period opposing the New Deal and criticizing the Roosevelt administration for having changed its policy as a result of the war in Europe. Roosevelt's 1940 budget is said to emphasize war rather than domestic needs. The unemployed are urged to join the Workers Alliance and to support the American standard

work and assistance bill, H.R. 8615, introduced by Representative Marcantonio.

K77   KERSTEN, Charles J., and SHARP, Malcolm. "The Mundt-Nixon Bill." Chicago: University of Chicago Round Table, June 6, 1948. 44 pp.
A radio discussion between Representative Kersten of Wisconsin and Professor Sharp of the Law School of the University of Chicago. Kersten defends the measure which, among other anticommunist provisions, requires members of the Party to register. Ridiculing the notion that the Party is a present danger here, Sharp denounces the "thought control" bill as a violation of our traditions. Pertinent Supreme Court decisions are reproduced in a supplement.

K78   KERSTEN, Charles J. (as told to Carey Longmire). We Are Protecting Spies in Defense Plants! "Reader's Digest," 62 (Jan. 1953), 27-31.
An assertion by a Republican congressman from Wisconsin that the electronics industry, vital to our defense, is wide open to Soviet spies through the communist-controlled United Electrical, Radio and Machine Workers. He urges the Attorney General to put the UE on the subversive list and eliminate its NLRB protection.

K79   KERWIN, Jerome G. Red Herring, "Commonweal," 22 (Oct. 18, 1935), 597-99.
A Catholic layman deplores the witch hunt being conducted by patrioteers such as Hearst and Dilling, who lump together communists, socialists, pacifists, New Dealers, and all liberals. Progressives and liberals, not communists, bear the brunt of this reactionary drive. Catholics must not lend strength to this hysterical campaign because they abhor the atheism of communism.

K80   KEYES, Scott. Round Two on the Pecham Bill, "Nation," 173 (Sept. 22, 1951), 234-36.
A description by a Pennsylvania State College faculty member of the furor caused by the Pecham bill, requiring a loyalty oath of state employees and candidates for public office.

K81   KEYHOE, Donald E. Are You on the Communist Slave List? "Redbook Magazine," 92 (Nov. 1948), 36-37 ff.
A description of the communists' Master Plan for remaking America, under which two-thirds of our production would be shipped to the USSR. The population would be divided into five groups: essential general workers, workers in nonessential jobs (to be reassigned), enemies of communism (to be executed or imprisoned), top creative and technical brains, and those too old or infirm to be productive (to be starved or liquidated).

K82   KING, Carol, and GINGER, Ann F. The McCarran Act and the Immigration Laws, "Lawyers Guild Review," 11 (Summer 1951), 128-41.
An analysis of the immigration provisions of the Subversive Activities Control Act of 1950 (McCarran Act) and of their administration. The Act deprives foreign-born of the right to bail, excludes large numbers of immigrants, permits deportation hearings on the charge of Party membership, requires noncitizens to register, and permits denaturalization on political grounds.

K83   KING, Donald L. The Legal Status of the Attorney General's List, "California Law Review," 44 (Oct. 1956), 748-61.
Since the decision in the Joint Anti-Fascist Refugee Committee case in 1951, there has been no court test of an administrative designation of an organization as subversive. The Attorney General's list poses serious

threats for the citizen; the list, as presently constituted and compiled, should be withdrawn.

K84   KING, Jerome; EMERSON, Ralph; RENAUD, Fred; and McRYN, Lawrence. "We Accuse (from the Record)." New York: The authors, 1940. 192 pp. App.
An account of the way in which communists have penetrated and won control of the National Maritime Union and other U.S. marine unions, written by NMU dissidents who were later expelled for their activities. They charge Joseph Curran, NMU president, and the Party with using the seamen and the NMU to further communist purposes. Accusing NMU officials and members of being tools of the Party and agents of the Soviet government, they say these men will stop at nothing to subvert the union to the interests of the Party.

K85   KING, Joseph. Thou Shalt Not Bear False Witness, "Jewish Life," 2 (Dec. 1947), 1 ff.
An attack on Rabbi Benjamin Schultz of Yonkers for a series published in the New York "World-Telegram," October 14-16, exposing communist support among Protestant ministers, rabbis, and prominent Catholics, a series that led to his condemnation by the New York Board of Rabbis. His series is called part of the anti-Jewish plotting inside and out of the Truman Administration.

K86   KINIERY, Paul. The Catholic Answer to Communism, "Catholic World," 144 (March 1937), 652-60.
An assertion that the Catholic Church must be concerned with the physical welfare of workers as well as with mankind's spiritual needs. Workers are attracted to communism by the belief that better economic conditions will result. Catholics are criticized for often taking a purely negative stand on communism.

K87   KINTNER, William R. "The Front is Everywhere: Militant Communism in Action." Norman, Okla.: University of Oklahoma Press, 1950. 274 pp. Bibliog. Ind.
An assertion that the communist movement has world-wide military aims and is a military organization seeking to revolutionize existing society. Chapter 14, "Implications," relates the analysis to the U.S., asserting that the American CP might become a serious military threat in the event of war. In addition to existing legislation such as the Smith and Voorhis Acts and the Foreign Agents Registration measure, we should pass legislation to deprive the communist movement of its cover of secrecy.

K88   KIRCHWEY, Freda. Communists and Democracy, "Nation," 149 (Oct. 14, 1939), 399-401.
Criticism of the American Labor Party for adopting Dies Committee methods in expelling communists, with a plea for sanity in such prosecutions. General detestation of communists and Bundists may lead to repression supported by disgusted liberals as well as by reactionaries.

K89   .... Keep Cool on Labor, "Nation," 152 (June 21, 1941), 713-14.
Analysis of communist strategy in fomenting strikes in west coast defense industry. The President was right, despite the danger in this course, to use troops to break the North American Aviation strike. The government should support responsible leaders in both labor organizations.

K90   .... Stalin's Choice, "Nation," 158 (January 22, 1944), 89-90.
The editor of the "Nation" analyzes, in the light of Soviet interests, Browder's proposal that the Communist Party become a "political association" to encourage national

unity and avert class conflict. While the Party's existence here is an obstacle to Russia's interests in America, the situation in Europe is quite different, though it will be difficult to apply different strategies.

K91   .... American Labor Pains, "Nation," 158 (April 8, 1944), 409-10.
A discussion of the right-left split over the communist issue in the American Labor Party in New York. Following the capture of the party organization by the left wing, the right wing withdrew. Intervention on the side of the left by the CIO Political Action Committee headed by Sidney Hillman was unfortunate, and hastened the split.

K92   .... The Communist Arrests, "Nation," 167 (July 31, 1948), 117-18.
The editor of the "Nation" agrees with the American Civil Liberties Union that the indictment of 12 communist leaders under the Smith Act is an unjustified political move, an integral part of the current struggle against Russia. The results will be almost wholly evil, except for the testing of the constitutionality of the Smith Act.

K93   .... Communism in the Schools, "Nation," 174 (March 15, 1952), 243-44.
A description of New York's Feinberg Law and criticism of the U.S. Supreme Court's decision upholding its constitutionality. The law provides for the dismissal of school employees who belong to a subversive organization, no overt act being necessary. Justice Douglas' dissent is quoted with approval.

K94   KIRK, Russell. "Academic Freedom: An Essay in Definition." Chicago: Regnery, 1955. 210 pp. Notes. Bibliog. Ind.
Viewing academic freedom historically, the author argues that it is not an absolute right, that men who have made themselves unworthy of that special freedom should be expelled. How communists on university faculties should be handled is a matter for university, not political, authorities. Communists should not knowingly be hired, but where one is established at a university the standards for his dismissal should be the same as for any other professor.

K95   KIRKLAND, Edward C. Do Antisubversive Efforts Threaten Academic Freedom? "Annals of the American Academy of Political and Social Science," 275 (May 1951), 132-39.
A discussion of academic freedom in the U.S. There is a difference of opinion within the academic community as to whether membership in the Party should be prima facie evidence of unfitness to teach. Legislative investigations and loyalty oath laws are discussed. The current anti-Red drive has imposed a reign of terror, unexampled in the history of American higher education.

K96   KIRKPATRICK, T. C. "Communism: How It Works and What You Can Do about It." New Wilmington, Pa.: Economic and Business Foundation, 1948. 18 pp.
An address by the managing editor of "Counterattack" at a conference sponsored by the Foundation. He outlines the Communist Party's organization and describes Party efforts to infiltrate education, the mass media, trade unions, religion, and government. Emphasizing the Party's subordination to Moscow, he calls it a conspiracy, not a political party, with every member a potential saboteur. Suggestions for fighting communism are made.

K97   ..., and McNamara, F. J. Communism—What You Can Do about It! "Elks Magazine," 30 (July 1951), 4-5 ff.

Advice on the subject of combatting communism from the publisher and editor of "Counterattack," who call for knowledge of the Communist Party and organization and action to defeat it. They urge formation of a nationwide network of community organizations which would expose Party fronts and individuals who support them, and initiate letter-writing campaigns to public officials to counteract Party drives. Other specific actions to take in the community are outlined.

K98   KLINGENDER, F. D. "Marxism and Modern Art." New York: International Publishers, 1945. 48 pp.
One of a series of booklets by British Marxists on the 60th anniversary of Marx's death. The essays support "social realism" in art, as opposed to philosophical idealism and mysticism. All allusions in this pamphlet are British; since it was written in the Party's "win-the-war" phase, communism as such is not mentioned.

K99   KNEPPER, Max. Should We Outlaw the Communist Party? "Forum," 107 (June 1947), 497-501.
An argument against outlawing the Party, on the ground that democracy is superior and that any attempt to seize power should be punished. The Party is objectionable, not as a constitutional political party, but as a conspiracy to carry out the mandate of a foreign government. American democracy need not resort to totalitarian devices.

K100   KNORIN, V. "Fascism, Social-Democracy and the Communists." New York: Workers Library, 1934. 48 pp.
A speech delivered at the Thirteenth Plenum of the Executive Committee of the Communist International in December 1933, before the adoption of the popular front line. Left social democracy is called the most dangerous foe of communism, as the bourgeoisie's last line of defense. Those who will not join the communists will be fought.

K101   KNOX, Owen A. "Oklahoma Story." Note by Carey McWilliams. Washington, D.C.: National Federation for Constitutional Liberties, n.d. [1940]. 15 pp.
An account by the chairman of the Federation of the conviction of Robert Wood, state secretary of the Communist Party in Oklahoma and operator of a bookstore there, under the state's criminal syndicalism law passed during World War I. Seventeen others, communists or readers of communist books, are awaiting trial.

K102   KNUDSEN, William Ross. Amalgamate the Metal Trades, "Labor Herald," 1 (May 1922), 6-7.
An assertion that craft unionism, with its loose alliances or federation, is an anachronism in American industrial life. Industrial unions, united in an All Industries Congress, are needed; all metal trades should be organized into a militant industrial union.

K103   KNUTSON, Alfred. The Agricultural Situation, "Workers Monthly," 5 (March 1926), 218-23.
An assertion that farm economic distress is producing left-wing tendencies among farmers, although most farm organizations are not class conscious. Farmers must organize to secure relief from the bad conditions they suffer under capitalism, and ally themselves with city workers in a labor party. Both groups must turn to the Workers Party for inspiration and guidance.

K104   KOENIGSBERG, Samuel M., and STAVIS, Morton. Test Oaths: Henry VIII to the American Bar Association, "Lawyers Guild Review," 11 (Summer 1951), 111-26.
An objection to test and loyalty oaths of all kinds. Tracing the history of test oaths, the authors assert that the

American Bar Association's proposal would breach tradition. The Association would require from each member of the bar a periodic affidavit as to membership in or support of the Party or any organization seeking overthrow of the government.

K105   KOERNER, J. D. The Melancholy Road to Kronstadt, "Pacific Spectator," 9 (Autumn 1955), 372-81.
An analysis of the impact of communism on intellectuals, making use of personal documents by ex-communists. Questions explored include why they joined, why they stayed, why they quit, and how they were treated on their return. Usually they quit because of some event that followed a period of growing disillusionment.

K106   KOESTLER, Arthur. Complex Issue of the Ex-Communist, "New York Times Magazine," Feb. 19, 1950, 10 ff.
An analysis of the complex roles of Hiss and Chambers, and a defense of Chambers' exposure of espionage. Liberals find the role of informer repugnant because they value loyalty, even to perverted totalitarianism. Whether the public is attracted to or repelled by Chambers, it cannot let bias interfere with judgment.

K107   KOGAN, Herman. The Sucker State Sees Red, "New Republic," 120 (April 11, 1949), 18-19.
A report on the decision of the Illinois legislature to investigate subversive activities at the University of Chicago and at Roosevelt College. The investigation resulted from student efforts to lobby against bills to outlaw the Party, require a noncommunist oath of teachers, and punish membership in front groups.

K108   KOHANSKI, Alexander S. Communist Propaganda for Jews: The New Line, "Contemporary Jewish Record," 3 (Sept.-Oct. 1940), 470-83.
Present efforts of the Party and front groups to recruit Jews are failing because of the Nazi-Soviet pact. The new Party line minimizes the danger of Nazism, emphasizes British imperialism in Palestine, and extols the benefits to Jews in the USSR. The communists have made almost no imprint on Jewish community life.

K109   KOHLBERG, Alfred. The State Department's Left Hand, "Plain Talk," 1 (May 1947), 12-17.
An assertion that a pro-Soviet bloc in the State Department, headed by John Carter Vincent, is largely responsible for our failure to apply in the Far East the Truman Doctrine of stemming communism. America's traditional China policy has been scrapped in favor of Soviet appeasement. A thoroughgoing investigation by the Senate is long overdue.

K110   .... So Runs the World: More Light on the Spy Prodigies, "Plain Talk," 3 (March 1949), 32-34.
A commentary on the Soviet spy system in Japan and its connection with American communists and the personnel of the Institute of Pacific Relations, with bitter comments on American newspapers which give the story little attention and on elements in the government that seek to hush it up.

K111   .... Brainwashing, American Style, "American Legion Magazine," 56 (Jan. 1954), 14-15 ff.
An assertion that brainwashing is the most important communist weapon, as illustrated by the hullabaloo about book burning, the use of the words "guilt by association," and the term "McCarthyism." Examples in the field of foreign affairs include the UN, the destruction of arms after World War II, and the influence of the Institute of Pacific Relations on our foreign policy.

K112 KOLARZ, Walter. "Books on Communism: A Bibliography." 2d ed. New York: Oxford, 1964. 568 pp. Ind.
An enlarged edition of a bibliography originally edited by R. N. Carew Hunt that appeared in 1959, covering the period 1945-57. Coverage is now extended into 1963. The first half of the volume deals with studies of communism in general and in the USSR. Works dealing with the U.S. are on pages 282-96, and U.S. government publications are on pages 486-514.

K113 KONECKY, Eugene M. "Monopoly Steals FM from the People." New York: Provisional Committee for Democracy in Radio, 1946. 48 pp. Bibliog.
The author, managing editor of the International Workers Order's monthly publication, describes the monopoly control of FM radio, and asserts that the monopoly stranglehold on FM and on radio generally can be broken only by an organized mass struggle.

K114 KONVITZ, Milton R. "Civil Rights in Immigration." Ithaca, N.Y.: Cornell University Press, 1953. 216 pp. App. Ind.
A critical analysis of American immigration, deportation, naturalization, and denaturalization laws and their administration. The author deals with a number of aspects of the law (the McCarran-Walters Act) drafted to deal with the communist problem, discussing this (p. 65 ff) in the section on "Exclusion of Subversives." He also discusses (pp. 114-22) the attempts to deport Harry Bridges, as well as the denial of naturalization to communists under the McCarran Act.

K115 .... Justice and the Communist Teacher: A Reply to Sidney Hook, "New Leader," 36 (April 20, 1953), 16-19.
Taking issue with Sidney Hook, a Cornell University professor of law questions whether a person should be declared unfit to teach because he is a communist, without examination of all aspects of each case. Although some communists may thus escape punishment, it is essential to preserve academic justice as a guarantee of academic freedom.

K116 .... "Fundamental Liberties of a Free People: Religion, Speech, Press, Assembly." Ithaca: Cornell University Press, 1957. 420 pp. App. Notes. Table of cases. Ind.
Chapters 22-28 are primarily concerned with aspects of communist activity or government efforts to contain the communist movement. The noncommunist affidavit is discussed on pp. 209-23, loyalty oaths in chapter 24, and the clear and present danger doctrine in chapters 25-28. The trial of the top communist leaders for conspiracy under the Smith Act (the Dennis case) is treated in chapter 27. As a result of the communist convictions, little remains of the clear and present danger doctrine.

K117 .... "Bill of Rights Reader: Leading Constitutional Cases." 2d rev. ed. Ithaca, N.Y.: Cornell University Press, 1960. 849 pp. App.
An expanded edition of a work first issued in 1954, presenting cases dealing with civil and political rights guaranteed by the Constitution. The book contains a section on "Freedom of Speech and Press: The Clear and Present Danger Doctrine" (pp. 249-308), which includes the Dennis case, and one on "Freedom of Speech and Press: Problems of Loyalty and Security" (pp. 309-512). There is also a treatment (pp. 646-92) of self-incrimination, the privilege of immunity. (In 1963 the author published "First Amendment Freedoms: Selected Cases on Freedom of Religion, Speech, Press, Assembly," based on this work.)

K118 .... "First Amendment Freedoms: Selected Cases on Freedom of Religion, Speech, Press, Assembly." Ithaca: Cornell University Press, 1963. 933 pp.
A collection of constitutional cases, including a section on "Freedom of Speech and Press: The Clear and Present Danger Doctrine" (pp. 333-506), and one on "Freedom of Speech and Press: Problems of Loyalty and Security" (pp. 507-773). Included in the former section, among others, are the Dennis case and the registration of the Party under the Subversive Activities Control Act. The latter section includes cases involving loyalty regulations for trade union officers, loyalty or security regulations for government employees, the Attorney General's list of subversive organizations, limits on powers of legislative committees, and aliens and loyalty. (The volume is based in part on the author's earlier "Bill of Rights Reader: Leading Constitutional Cases.")

K119 KORETZ, H. Left Needle Workers Union Prepares for Struggles, "Labor Unity," 3 (Feb. 1929), 16-18.
An account of the formation at a recent convention of the Needle Trades Workers Industrial Union, based on an amalgamation of organizations of cloakmakers, dressmakers, and furriers under left-wing leadership. A constitution based on the shop delegate system and the class struggle was adopted, and preparations made for the coming strike in the New York City dress industry.

K120 KORNFEDER, Joseph Z. "Brainwashing and Senator McCarthy." Foreword by Archibald B. Roosevelt. New York: The Alliance, 1954. 18 pp.
A former prominent communist, a member of the Secretariat of the Communist International, describes the communists' propaganda attacks on Senator McCarthy. Communist influence in the press, and other agencies of opinion, is used to brainwash the public and engage in psychological warfare against McCarthy.

.... See also ZACK, Joseph.

K121 KOSA, John, and NUNN, Clyde Z. Race, Deprivation and Attitudes toward Communism, "Phylon" (Atlanta University), 25 (Winter 1964), 337-46.
Although deprived groups might be thought more receptive to communism, questionnaires administered to white and Negro college students showed the whites more tolerant to communism, and within each racial group those of the upper class were most tolerant and those of the lower class least. Some personality characteristics are associated with attitudes toward communism.

K122 KOVESS, Louis. The Socialist Party in the Election Campaign, "Communist," 9 (Oct. 1930), 914-22.
An attack on the Socialist Party for misleading workers by its radical phrases and for stepping between workers and the only leader of their class, the Communist Party. The Socialist Party, organizer of the small capitalists, furthers the cause of the imperialists. Its final goal is capitalism.

K123 KRAMER, Dale. The American Communists, "Harper's Magazine," 180 (May 1940), 587-97.
An analysis of the role of communists in America, written during the period of the Hitler-Stalin pact. Changes in the Party line since formation of the communist movement are reviewed. The communists, who gained real influence in the U.S. during the popular front period, have lost it as a result of the Hitler-Stalin pact.

K124 KRAUS, Henry. "The Many & the Few: A Chronicle of the Dynamic Auto Workers." Introd. by

George F. Addes and R. J. Thomas. Los Angeles: Plantin Press, 1947. 293 pp.
An account of the unionization of General Motors by the United Automobile Workers, in which the activities of procommunists are given great prominence, and anti-Stalinists are given little credit. The stories of the organizing drive in Flint, Mich., and of the great sit-down strike that followed in January, 1937, are told in detail and in dramatic form. The author was present as publicity man for the UAW. While he professes to tell a story of the rank and file, without heroes, greatest credit is given to vice-president Wyndham Mortimer for the organizing drive, while organizer Robert Travis is the hero of the sit-down strike.

K125　KRAUS, Henry. West Coast Report: Lessons from Longshoremen, "Masses & Mainstream," 2 (June 1949), 42-52.
A sympathetic account of the ILWU convention at which the main issue was autonomy—the right of CIO affiliates to oppose the Marshall Plan and endorse Henry Wallace. Condemning CIO pressure against officers of state and city CIO councils, the convention urged affiliation with the WFTU and denounced the Marshall Plan and the Atlantic Pact.

K126　.... "Here is Your Union! The Story of U.E. 430." Local 430, United Electrical, Radio and Machine Workers of America, n.d. [1952?]. 71 pp.
A popularly written story of Local 430 of the United Electrical, Radio and Machine Workers. The author asserts that the communist issue is used by employers and the rival International Union of Electrical Workers to attack the local and its collective bargaining gains, and tells of the failure of attempts by the "Red-baiting" IUE to raid Local 430.

K127　KRAVIF, Hy. "Tel and Tel: The Telephone and Telegraph Workers." New York: International Pamphlets, 1935. 31 pp.
Monopolistic control by American Telephone & Telegraph Co., Western Union, and other corporate giants is blamed in this "third period" pamphlet for unemployment and intolerable conditions among communications workers. The companies are attacked for high salaries and high profits, while workers suffer from wage slashes and speed-ups. Workers are urged to defeat company unions and form genuine ones.

K128　KRCHMAREK, A. The Ohio Smith Act Trial, "Political Affairs," 35 (June 1956), 58-65.
The partial victory in the Ohio trial, in which five of the 11 defendants were acquitted, was an important break-through in the pattern of automatic guilty verdicts. The hysteria surrounding earlier Smith Act trials was not in evidence. Ohio's and Cleveland's liberal traditions played an important part, as did the changing political climate and the work of defense counsel.

KREBS, Richard. See VALTIN, Jan.

K129　KRISTOL, Irving. Civil Liberties, 1952—A Study in Confusion, "Commentary," 13 (March 1952), 228-36.
Liberals and McCarthyites alike are blamed for existing confusion over the proper balance between fighting communism and preserving civil liberties. A liberal who defends the civil liberties of communists must recognize that an organized subversive movement such as communism threatens civil society and its liberties.

K130　KRUGMAN, Herbert E. The Appeal of Communism to American Middle Class Intellectuals and Trade Unionists, "Public Opinion Quarterly," 16 (Fall 1952), 331-55.
A preliminary report on the Appeals of Communism project, directed by Gabriel A. Almond at Princeton. Intensive interviews with 50 former members of the Party in the U.S. shed light on the varied attractions of communism, the needs which Party membership satisfied, and the effects of Party membership on the individual. The Party develops hostility and conformance in its members, and often brings about changes in the personality of its members, particularly the intellectual bourgeois.

K131　.... The Role of Hostility in the Appeal of Communism in the United States, "Psychiatry," 16 (Aug. 1953), 253-61.
An examination of psychoanalytic case reports of 35 present or former members of the CPUSA. For 18 of them the two main functions of communism were to permit expression of either hostility or submission without feelings of guilt. (Part of the Appeals of Communism project at Princeton under the direction of Gabriel A. Almond.)

K132　KRUMBEIN, Charles. Lessons of the New York Elections, "Communist," 17 (Jan. 1938), 29-39.
An appraisal of the election results, by the New York State secretary of the Party. In New York City the communist-backed American Labor Party enabled La Guardia to remain mayor, though Tammany elected most of its Assembly candidates. The communist vote increased, while the socialist vote declined. People's front parties that were broadly based were successful in other cities in New York State.

K133　KRUSE, William F. Workers Conquest of the Films, "Workers Monthly," 4 (Sept. 1925), 502-3 ff.
American communists have been less successful than the Russians in using the film as an instrument of propaganda and enlightenment because of difficulties of censorship and financing. With the support of the labor movement, however, American communists will be able to use the film as an effective weapon in the class struggle.

K134　KRUTCH, Joseph Wood. Communism and the Old Pagan, "Harper's Magazine," 165 (Oct. 1932), 544-51.
The author compares adoption of communism by some of his acquaintances to the pagan conversion to Christianity in Roman and Greek days. He looks with scepticism on the wisdom of the process or its ultimate effect on the world.

K135　.... Literature and Propaganda, "English Journal," 22 (Dec. 1933), 793-802.
An expression of dissent from the communist view that the value of a work of art depends upon the effectiveness with which it teaches and promotes the class struggle. The Marxian approach to literature is called a passing fashion. The real business of literature is the communication of an aesthetic experience.

K136　.... "Was Europe a Success?" New York: Farrar and Rinehart, 1934. 88 pp.
Literary essays dealing with various aspects of Marxism and communism. The author, who resisted communism's appeal when many of his fellow-writers, under the impact of the depression, were succumbing to it, denies the inevitability of the proletarian revolution, and lists the accomplishments of European culture. Rejecting the rosy predictions of both capitalists and communists, he asserts that literature means more in times of stress than it will in a communist utopia, and argues that communists, in

their call for class war, are as jingoist as any imperialist. A good presentation of the liberal opposition to the Marxist view.

K137 KUHN, Irene Corbally. Why You Buy Books That Sell Communism. "American Legion Magazine," 50 (Jan. 1951), 18-19 ff.
An assertion that the Party promotes the sale of pro-communist books and hurts anticommunist ones by its influence with publishing houses, book reviewers, book clubs, and retail book outlets. The assignment of reviews by the New York "Times" and New York "Herald Tribune," and the staff and author choices of Little, Brown and Co., are cited as examples.

K138 .... He Lobbies against Communism, "American Legion Magazine," 53 (July 1952), 14-15 ff.
A laudatory account of the activities of Alfred Kohlberg, American importer, who for years has fought the communists and their sympathizers who have fouled up our China policy. Discovering that American diplomats in China, and also the Institute of Pacific Relations, were discrediting our Chinese ally, he organized the American China Policy Committee and helped finance anticommunist publications.

K139 .... Who Are the Censors? "American Legion Magazine," 57 (July 1954), 14-15 ff.
An assertion that right-wing authors, not those of the left, are subjected to effective censorship by being ignored by book reviewers, whereas leading left-wing authors are virtually assured of favorable reviews. High school and public libraries may present only the leftists' side of controversial issues. Procommunist authors are assured of large audiences by book clubs, such as that run by the communist-dominated union, the UE.

K140 KUNITZ, Joshua. Max Eastman's Hot Unnecessary Tears, "New Masses," 9 (Sept. 1933), 12-15.
Criticism and ridicule of Max Eastman's lament over the alleged humiliation of art and letters in the USSR. Eastman is repelled by the revolutionary tinge of Soviet literature, and ignorant of the upsurge in the demand for the arts from the Soviet people. His escapist, art-for-art's sake esthetic is typical of the tired, petty-bourgeois radical.

K141 .... In Defense of a Term, "New Masses Literary Section," 28 (July 12, 1938), 145-47.
A reply to a suggestion that the term "people's literature" be substituted for "proletarian literature." The term "proletarian" not only describes the class, but indicates an ideology and recognizes the primacy of the proletariat in bringing about social change. To abolish the term after it has been finally accepted, even by the capitalist press, is a liquidationist proposal.

K142 KUSHNER, Sam. Some Problems in Illinois, "Political Affairs," 35 (July 1956), 54-60.
A mistitled article that criticizes sharply Eugene Dennis' report to the Party's national committee on the trade union movement. The author condemns the sectarian policy followed by the Party in the unions, that has resulted in its isolation. The major problem now is to become a more integral part of the working class.

K143 KUTNIK. The Revolutionary Trade Union Movement in the U.S.A. in the Conditions of the "New Deal" of Trustified Capital, "Communist International," 11 (Sept. 20, 1934), 598-606.
A review of the growth of labor organization and militancy in the U.S. Although the revolutionary unions played a big role in strike struggles, they did not consolidate their growing influence, despite membership gains in some industries. The AFL has made substantial gains, and the TUUL may become isolated. Tendencies to liquidate the TUUL unions must be combatted.

K144 KWAIT, John. Architecture under Capitalism, "New Masses," 8 (Dec. 1932), 10-13.
Criticism of Structural Study Associates, a group of architects and technicians interested in architecture as an instrument of social reform rather than revolution. They thereby commit themselves to the complete support of the status quo.

L

L1   "LABOR AGE," The Challenge to Progressives: An Editorial Statement, 18 (Feb. 1929), 3-7.

A manifesto of the Muste group, proposing, among other objectives, organization of the unskilled and semiskilled, organizing appeals to workers instead of employers, opposition to the National Civic Federation, union membership without regard to politics or race, the right of union oppositions to exist, recognition of Russia, the goal of a social order controlled by workers, a labor party, and a broad workers' education movement. (For the communist reaction, see Trade Union Educational League, National Committee, "A Manifesto of Reaction," and Earl Browder, "Reinforcements for a Discredited Bureaucracy," both in "Labor Unity," March 1929.)

L2   . . ., Communist Strike-Breaking and Union-Wrecking, 20 (Sept. 1931), 1-2.

An editorial attack on recent communist strikebreaking activities in Illinois minefields and Allentown, Pa., silk factories. The hollowness and sham of the communists' talk of united front is thus exposed. They will have nothing to do with strikes or unions not under their control.

L3   "LABOR HERALD," First National Conference of the Trade Union Educational League, 1 (Sept. 1922), 3-32.

A verbatim report of the proceedings of the first national conference of the TUEL. Reports of the national committee and the resolutions committee are included, along with programs in the building trades, the railroad industry, the metal trades, and the needle trades.

L4   "LABOR LEADER" (Association of Catholic Trade Unionists), Guild Members Oust Communist Leaders in Nation Wide Referendum, 4 (Oct. 17, 1941), 1 ff.

The membership of the American Newspaper Guild has voted its communist leadership out of national office by a substantial majority. Only one member of the old administration, whom the anticommunist group did not oppose, was elected to the new board.

L5   . . ., Reds Took Biggest Setback at CIO's Boston Convention, 10 (Oct. 31, 1947), 1.

Procommunist forces suffered their severest setback in CIO history at the convention held October 13-17 in Boston. They floundered on the Taft-Hartley resolution and failed to prevent a convincing stand on foreign policy. Efforts to identify the U.S. government with warmongering and imperialism failed.

L6   . . ., CIO, 33 to 11, Hits Wallace, Backs Marshall, 11 (Jan. 31, 1948), 1 ff.

The CIO Executive Board defeated the invitation to join Henry Wallace's third party by a vote of 33 to 11. Though this places a moral obligation on CIO unions, according to President Philip Murray, the spokesman for the Stalinists, Harry Bridges, made it clear that they would support Wallace vigorously. The Board also endorsed the Marshall Plan.

L7   . . ., 70,000 Members in 13 UE Locals Swing to Anti-CP's, 12 (Jan. 17, 1949), 1 ff.

As the result of recent elections 13 UE locals with 70,000 members moved into the union's anticommunist wing, doubling its strength. The communist-controlled union has 420,000 members in key industries. President Albert Fitzgerald, an ally of the communists, shows signs of breaking with them.

L8   . . ., UE Left-Wing Wins Again; May Bolt CIO, 12 (Sept. 30, 1949), 1.

Delegates to the UE convention set the stage for leaving the CIO by voting to withhold per capita tax unless CIO unions stopped all raiding activities at its expense. Though all left-wing officers were reelected, opposition candidates got 40 per cent of the vote.

L9   . . ., Three Commie Unions in N.Y. Merge into One, 13 (Sept. 19, 1950), 1.

A new union, to be known as the Distributive, Office and Processing Workers, will be formed on October 6 as a merger of the unaffiliated Distributive Workers Union and the remains of the United Office and Professional Workers and the Food and Tobacco Workers. The latter two, both dying, were recently expelled by the CIO for devotion to CP policies. The communist-controlled Distributive Workers Union is dominant in the department store and warehouse field in New York City.

L10   . . ., Commies Fight Over Affiliation with CIO, 15 (Feb. 14, 1952), 1 ff.

The General Council of District 65 of the Distributive, Processing and Office Workers, one of the most powerful communist-dominated unions in the U.S., is split over reaffiliation with the CIO. The district will reaffiliate only if it can continue to follow present policies, which parallel the Party line. Some officers have proposed that talks cease until approved by leaders of other communist-led unions.

L11   . . ., Osman Reaffirms Non-Red Oath, Will Return to CIO, 16 (April 14, 1953), 1.

The return to the CIO of 60,000 members of the Distributive, Processing and Office Workers of America is imminent, following negotiations that began in 1951 between CIO leaders and Arthur Osman, president of the DPOWA. The procommunist position taken in previous years by the DPOWA has disappeared, and now its leaders are denounced in Party publications.

L12   LABOR RESEARCH ASSOCIATION. Social Insurance and the T.U.U.L., "Labor Unity," 3 (Nov. 16, 1929), 6-7; (Dec. 14), 6.

The first article deals with the need for old age pensions, presenting the program of the Trade Union Unity League. Halfway measures, including the AFL proposal for state old age pensions, must be fought. The second article analyzes the unemployment problem and the inadequacy of social welfare schemes put forth by state and national legislatures.

L13   LABOR RESEARCH ASSOCIATION. "Labor Fact
      Book." 12 vols. New York: International Pub-
      lishers, 1931-55. Publ. biennially.
A communist source book presenting information about a
wide variety of economic, social, and political matters.
Although each volume includes additional facts, the series
tends to be repetitive; each volume, however, interprets
the facts consistent with the then current Party line.
Volume 6, "Labor and the War," is the only one with a
separate title. Subjects covered, among others, are
workers' organizations, economic trends, labor and social
conditions, trade unions in the U.S. and the world, farmers and farm workers, political developments and legislation. Special features include Negroes, civil rights,
postwar goals and problems, and the war economy.

L14   .... Aspects of the Depression of the Special
      Type in the U.S.A., "Communist," 14 (Feb. 1935),
      185-91.
A report, based on the period from March 1933 to October
1934, showing that the upswing from the lowest point of
the depression has been accomplished at the expense of
the working class.

L15   .... "Arsenal of Facts." New York: Inter-
      national Publishers, 1938. 126 pp. Ind.
Pocket handbook with data useful to Party workers. Topics
covered include population, government and policies, industry and commerce, agriculture, labor conditions,
labor legislation, the labor movement, social conditions,
civil rights, Spain, the Soviet Union, and wars and war
costs.

L16   .... "Railways in Crisis: A Program for Re-
      employment, Rehabilitation and Government
      Ownership." New York: International Publishers,
      1939. 48 pp.
An analysis of the crisis of the railroad industry as caused
by monopoly, overcapitalization, and banker control.
Public ownership is advocated, to operate the roads in the
public interest, with employment stabilized at the level
needed to provide efficient transportation.

L17   .... "Youth Arsenal of Facts." New York:
      International Publishers, 1939. 126 pp.
A handbook of statistics on unemployment and social problems of interest to youth, stressing the current Party line.

L18   .... "Labor against War: Statements and Reso-
      lutions by Labor Groups Opposed to American
      Involvement in the European War." New York:
      Labor Research Association, 1940. 20 pp.
Excerpts from antiwar resolutions of 60 labor groups,
including the CIO and AFL. Issued by the Communist
Party's research arm during the Hitler-Stalin pact period.

L19   .... "Wages and Profits in Wartime." New
      York: International Publishers, 1941. 32 pp.
A popularly written communist pamphlet, designed to show
that war is very profitable for the owners of industry,
while workers earn less than necessary for minimum
living standards for a family of four. Wages must rise
and bills to restrict labor must be opposed, and a world
built that is free of war and war profiteers.

L20   .... "The History of the Shorter Workday." New
      York: International Publishers, 1942. 64 pp.
An account of the history of the shorter work day movement in the U.S. from the first strike for this purpose in
1791 until the present time. Despite the need for greater
war production, the basic 40-hour work week, with time
and a half for overtime, is still maintained.

L21   .... "Monopoly in the United States: Facts
      Revealed by the T.N.E.C. Investigation." New
      York: International Publishers, 1942. 48 pp.
An indictment of American monopoly based largely on
hearings and reports of the Temporary National Economic
Committee, created by Congress in 1938 to study concentration of economic power. The people's forces, the
authors conclude, can expose the defeatist plans of Big
Business, while still seeking national unity to win the war.

L22   .... "Southern Labor in Wartime." New York:
      International Publishers, 1942. 30 pp.
A communist wartime pamphlet applauding the current
industrial expansion in the South and the contribution of
Southerners, white and Negro, to the war effort. Higher
wages are held necessary there, however, for increased
production now and for future economic development.
This will be achieved only as labor unions develop in the
South.

L23   .... Economic Review of 1946, "Political Af-
      fairs," 26 (Jan. 1947), 80-88.
A report stressing the maladjustments of the American
economy in 1946 and covering employment, industrial
production, wholesale prices, profits, workers' income,
consumer markets, and sale of gross national product.
An economic recession within the current year is predicted.

L24   .... Current Economic Trends, "Political Af-
      fairs," 26 (April 1947), 368-75.
A report on corporation profits, income trends, purchasing power, retail trade, unemployment, and private capital
formation in 1946, showing the imminence of a serious
depression.

L25   .... "Trends in American Capitalism: Profits
      and Living Standards." New York: International
      Publishers, 1948. 192 pp. Ind.
A Marxist interpretation of American economic trends,
including the rate of surplus value and profit, the conditions of the working class, and the future development
of the so-called free enterprise system. The authors
predict that capitalism will result either in another
depression or another world war, with catastrophe for the
American people in either event.

L26   .... Economic Review of 1947, "Political Af-
      fairs," 27 (Feb. 1948), 174-80.
A review of stock market trends, corporate profits, exports, industrial and farm output, consumption, etc.,
during 1947. The boom is based on war-created shortages, plus an accumulation of liquid capital. Some small
businesses lack credit, bankruptcies are rising, the
demand for goods is being satisfied, and a crisis lies
ahead.

L27   .... "Monopoly Today." New York: Interna-
      tional Publishers, 1950. 128 pp. Ind.
A collection of data showing the extent of monopoly in
industry and communications in the U.S. The volume up-
dates Anna Rochester's "Rulers of America," first published in 1936. It concludes that, unless the power of
Wall Street monopolies is effectively curbed, American
imperialism will bring fascism and war.

L28   .... "Billionaire Corporations: Their Growth
      and Power." New York: International Publishers,
      1954. 64 pp. Ref. notes.
A study of the power and influence of the 66 top monopolies
in the U.S., emphasizing their interrelationships, their
control over education and opinion, their domination over
government, and their vast profits. Also stressed are

their antilabor and Jim Crow policies. The corporations are alleged to be driving toward fascism, spearheaded by McCarthyism, to destroy the people's movement against war.

L29   LABOR RESEARCH ASSOCIATION. "Apologists for Monopoly." New York: International Publishers, 1955. 62 pp. Ref. notes.
A refutation by this communist research organization of arguments of prominent economists who assert either that monopoly is no problem here or that it is necessary to our economic development. These "economic fairy tales," the LRA asserts, serve to curtail antitrust activity and strengthen monopoly capitalism's drive to militarize the economy.

L30   .... "The Burden of Taxes." New York: International Publishers, 1956. 48 pp.
A report on taxes in the U.S. by a communist research group, pointing out how the tax structure discriminates against lower income families. Emphasis is placed on loopholes in the tax laws, the burden of the cold war budget, the profiteering and waste of taxpayers' money, and the aid given to monopoly through tax relief.

L31   .... "U.S. and the Philippines." New York: International Publishers, 1958. 64 pp. Ref. notes.
A communist view of U.S. relations with the Philippines, attacking the influence of American Big Business and the landlord-capitalist alliance represented by conservative Filipino political groups. The Huks are praised as valiant fighters for national independence and social justice.

L32   "LABOR UNITY," Program of Action for the Unemployed, 4 (April 5, 1930), 5 ff.
The program adopted at the National Preliminary Unemployed Conference, held in New York City, March 29-30. Sections of the program deal with the fight against unemployment, the demands of the unemployed, organization of the unemployed, and a program of action.

L33   LABOR YOUTH LEAGUE. "Our Generation Will Not Be Silent." New York: The League, 1953. 24 pp.
Statement of the Labor Youth League, in answer to Justice Department charges that it is a communist front organization under the McCarran Internal Security Act. The statement denies that the League is a front organization; asserts that it serves the needs of youth, not of the Party; and denies that it is controlled by the Party, though it admits that communists are members.

L34   .... "Constitution of the Labor Youth League: Adopted by Second National Convention, Feb. 22, 1954." New York: The League, n.d. [1954]. 15 pp.
The constitution of the Labor Youth League shows it to be an affiliate of the Communist Party. The preamble proclaims it a Marxist organization seeking to promote identification of youth with the working class, opposing Big Business, and striving for friendship between the U.S. and the USSR.

L35   .... "We Accuse McCarthyism." New York: The League, 1954. 48 pp.
The first motion made by the League at hearings before the Subversive Activities Control Board, in hearings initiated by Attorney General Brownell under the Internal Security Act of 1950 (the McCarran Act). The motion is an indictment of McCarthyism as the growing menace of fascism in the U.S. (The Labor Youth League, organized in 1949, operated as the youth section of the CPUSA.)

L36   LaFARGE, John. "Communism and the Catholic Answer." New York: America Press, 1936. 32 pp.
A reaffirmation of the stand of the Catholic Church against communism, condemning the communist solution to social problems as injurious to true social reform. The Catholic answer to communism is social morality plus spiritual values. Advice is given to Catholics on how to dispute with and compete with communists, on the street and in organizations.

L37   LA FOLLETTE, Robert M., Jr. Turn the Light on Communism, "Collier's," 119 (Feb. 8, 1947), 22 ff.
The former senator from Wisconsin discusses communist infiltration in industry and government, telling how he had to fight communist influences on the staff of his own Senate Civil Liberties Committee. He calls on liberals to dissociate themselves from communists and fellow-travelers, and to help keep the spotlight of publicity on their activities.

L38   LAHNE, Herbert J. "The Cotton Mill Worker." New York: Farrar and Rinehart, 1944. 303 pp. Bibliog. note. App. Ind.
A history of working conditions and labor organization in the cotton textile industry, with an account (pp. 217-19) of the 1929 Gastonia, N.C., strike led by the National Textile Workers Union of the Trade Union Unity League. There are other scattered references (pp. 212-14, 233-34, etc.) to communist influence in the industry and the activities of the NTWU.

L39   LAIDLER, Harry W. Present Status of Socialism in America, "Socialist Review," 8 (Dec. 1919), 33-37; (Jan. 1920), 106-14.
A history of events in the American socialist movement leading up to the creation of the left wing, a summary of the split in that group in 1919, and an analysis of the 1919 conventions in Chicago of the Socialist Party, the Communist Party, and the Communist Labor Party. Issues dividing the three groups are analyzed.

L40   LAING, Alexander. Three Ways of Swearing, "New Republic," 129 (Dec. 28, 1953), 9-12.
A Dartmouth College official explains his opposition to the New Hampshire law requiring teachers at state-financed schools to swear that they will not advocate the overthrow of government by force or violence. There are three ways of swearing—political, the simple oath of allegiance; religious, the oath of conscience; and disciplinary, the oath to refrain under penalty, from specified acts of faith or advocacy.

L41   LAMB, Edward. "No Lamb for Slaughter: An Autobiography." New York: Harcourt, Brace & World, 1963. 248 pp. Ind.
The autobiography of a liberal lawyer and business man, who had represented unions during the depression years and helped organize the National Lawyers Guild. Chapter 10, "McCarthyism in Flower" (pp. 123-36), tells of charges during the McCarthy period that Lamb had been a communist, and of his troubles in getting approval from the Federal Communications Commission of applications relating to his television interests. The FCC hearings, which ended in a victory for Lamb, are described in chapters 11-13 (pp. 137-90).

L42   .... " 'Trial by Battle': The Case History of a Washington Witch-Hunt." Santa Barbara, Calif.: Center for the Study of Democratic Institutions, 1964. 24 pp. App.
An account by a liberal attorney and business man of his four-year effort, at a cost of $900,000, to clear his name

of communist charges in order to renew radio and television broadcasting licenses. Named as a communist by former Party members, who were on the government's payroll as professional "consultants," Lamb was able to show that the witnesses gave perjured testimony that had been manufactured by attorneys on the Federal Communications Commission staff.

L43 LAMONT, Corliss. "You Might Like Socialism: A Way of Life for Modern Man." New York: Modern Age, 1939. 308 pp. Ind.
A popular effort by an upper class supporter of communist causes to win recruits to socialism from the middle and upper classes. The book contains chapters on the failures of capitalism, the virtues of planning, and the experiences of the Soviet Union. Other chapters are devoted to the problem of war, democracy and civil liberties, socialist philosophy, and the prospects for socialism in various areas of the world. (Chapter 1 appeared in the "New Masses," August 29, 1939, as "Why Members of the Upper Class Go Left.")

L44 . . . . "America and Russia." New York: National Council of American-Soviet Friendship, 1943. 15 pp.
A discussion, on the tenth anniversary of American-Soviet relations, of the bonds between the two countries. Parallel interests in the Pacific and democracy in the new Russia are emphasized, and cooperation in solving postwar problems is urged.

L45 . . . . "Are We Being Talked into War?" New York: Basic Pamphlets, 1952. 29 pp.
The author, long close to the Party, attacks the "sabre-rattling" minority of the American press for creating war hysteria, aimed at the Soviet Union. Included are quotations from books and magazines, some of them statements by present or former government officials, calling for war with the USSR. The author suggests that public opinion put an end to efforts to talk us into war.

L46 . . . . "Back to the Bill of Rights." New York: The author, n.d. [1952]. 16 pp.
Reprint of a paper read December 28, 1950, at a meeting of the American Political Science Association, together with an article published in the "Daily Compass," March 11, 1951. In the former, Lamont argues for full legal rights under democratic government for communist or fascist parties, distinguishing between opinions and overt acts. He criticizes HUAC, loyalty purges and oaths, the Smith Act, and the McCarran bill.

L47 . . . . Challenge to McCarthy, "Nation," 177 (Dec. 12, 1953), 510-13.
An account of the author's appearance before the Senate Internal Security Subcommittee, at which he denied the committee's right to question him on personal matters. He challenged its jurisdiction because it violated the First Amendment, because it invaded the powers of the judiciary, and because he is not a federal employee. (Also published in pamphlet form.)

L48 . . . . "The Congressional Inquisition." New York: Basic Pamphlets, 1954. 35 pp.
An analysis of the misuse of power by congressional committees in investigating subversive activities. Such committees, of which McCarthy's is the most flagrant example, flout the Constitution and trample on the rights of witnesses. The author advises witnesses to plead the First Amendment in refusing to answer questions, thus laying the basis for a legal test in a contempt case.

L49 . . . . "The Assault on Academic Freedom." New York: Basic Pamphlets, 1955. 39 pp. Reprinted as chapter 10 in Corliss Lamont, "Freedom Is as Freedom Does." New York: Horizon Press, 1956.
A history of the postwar controversy over academic freedom, emphasizing the issue of communist teachers. The author criticizes the view that members of the Communist Party should not be hired as teachers because they lack the necessary independence of thought and judgment. He argues that when communist teachers find themselves in substantial disagreement with Party beliefs they resign, showing that Party members do not inevitably lose intellectual freedom.

L50 . . . . "Freedom Is as Freedom Does: Civil Liberties Today." Introd. by H. H. Wilson. New York: Horizon Press, 1956. 322 pp.
A view of the "debased" state of civil liberties in the U.S., written by a lecturer in philosophy at Columbia University who has been a long-time supporter of communist causes. He discusses congressional investigations of subversive activities, antisubversive legislation, the loyalty-security program, the FBI, state activities in the field of subversion, the attack on nonconformity and on unpopular opinions, the assault on academic freedom, and the decline of the American Civil Liberties Union (from whose board he resigned in 1953 over the communist issue). He notes, however, a recent improvement in the state of civil liberties in the U.S.

L51 . . . . Conform—or Lose Your Job, "Monthly Review," 7 (Feb. 1956), 401-7.
An account of civil liberty crises in which political dissenters have been dismissed from their jobs and blacklisted. Illustrations are given from government, television and radio, movies, book publishing, professions, and business. The result is to silence all minority voices.

L52 LAMPMAN, Robert J. Red Probes and Academic Freedom, "Progressive," 13 (March 1949), 20-22.
An account of the controversy over CP membership at the University of Washington, culminating in the dismissal of three faculty members by the Board of Regents and the placing of three others on probation. The sole issue was whether communists were fit to teach. The Faculty Tenure Committee was divided on the issue, and the AAUP is now investigating the case.

L53 LANDAUER, Carl. How to Fight Communism, "Pacific Spectator," 4 (Autumn 1950), 498-506.
A call for stressing the positive issue of democracy in current struggles against the evils of communism. We can increase the stream of defectors from the communist movement by complementing our military program and our social reforms with emphasis on true freedom, especially civil liberties.

L54 LANDY, A. The Right of Revolution—An American Revolutionary Tradition, "Communist," 8 (July 1929), 360-68.
Revolutionary action is called a historic right of the American people in struggles against oppression. The development of this right in the practice of the bourgeoisie and the Southern slavocracy is traced.

L55 . . . . Cultural Compulsives or Calverton's New Caricature of Marxism, "Communist," 10 (Oct. 1931), 851-64; (Nov.), 941-59.
An indictment of V. F. Calverton, who, in a recent issue of "Modern Quarterly," called himself a communist. Yet Calverton is alien to the theory of revolutionary Marxism. He does not call upon the victims of capitalism to join or support the Party. He is guilty of revisionism and subjectivity.

L56 LANDY, A. Our Next Tasks in Party Education, "Communist," 17 (Sept. 1938), 842-49.
A plan for revitalizing and expanding the Party's educational program to include the mass of Party membership. Attention is paid to the channels of Party education, educating the new members, and use of new techniques.

L57 .... The Foreign Agent Fraud and the Battle for Democracy, "Communist," 19 (Feb. 1940), 122-32.
An effort to disprove the charges that the teachings of Marxism-Leninism are of foreign origin and hence un-American, and that Marxism-Leninism is opposed to democracy. Such charges are called an effort to discredit anyone who opposes U.S. involvement in the imperialist war.

L58 .... Two Questions on the Status of Women under Capitalism, "Communist," 20 (Sept. 1941), 818-33.
A theoretical analysis of the status of the housewife under capitalism, to show that her position is wretched because her husband is exploited. The questions relate to the usefulness of women's work in the home, and whether they get paid for this work.

L59 .... The National Groups in the National Front, "Communist," 20 (Oct. 1941), 917-36.
A discussion of the significance of Hitler's aggression for national groups in the U.S., and of the importance of winning their support for the defeat of Nazi Germany. The national groups can unite in a national front for the liberation of their countries of origin from Nazi enslavement. Obstacles in the way of unity must be overcome.

L60 .... "Marxism and the Woman Question." New York: Workers Library, 1943. 64 pp.
Criticism of Mary Inman's "Woman Power" for its incorrect application of Marxist-Leninist theory on woman's role in a capitalist economy. The housewife is seen as an unremunerated producer of goods who can be released from her exploited state only by helping on the assembly line to defeat Hitler.

L61 .... A Year of American Slav Unity, "Communist," 22 (June 1943), 552-61.
A description of the activities of the American Slav Congress, organized April 25-26, 1942, which represents nearly all the organized Slavs in the country. New objectives for the Congress' further development are outlined, and issues dividing the main Slav groups here—the Yugoslavs, the Czechoslovaks, and the Poles—are discussed.

L62 .... Comintern Aftermath, "New Masses," 47 (June 8, 1943), 11-12.
The Communist International has been dissolved to defeat the Hitlerite bloc sooner and assure friendship between the anti-Hitlerite nations after the war. It is not an obituary, but a weapon of war opening new paths to the future. Those who call for dissolution of the Communist Party are either Hitler's friends, fighting against national unity, or enemies of Hitler who misread the meaning of the Comintern dissolution.

L63 .... June 22 in the United States, "Communist," 22 (Aug. 1943), 742-52.
The significance of the anniversary of the Nazi attack on the Soviet Union is viewed in the light of the new temper and pattern of American-Soviet relations and revised public opinion regarding Russia.

L64 .... Three Years of the Soviet National-Liberation War, "Communist," 23 (June 1944), 507-20.
A review of Russia's conduct of the war and foreign policy to illustrate her efforts to liberate enslaved peoples. The Polish government-in-exile is criticized for non-cooperation with the Soviet Union.

L65 .... The Great Invasion, "Communist," 23 (Aug. 1944), 675-80.
The Normandy invasion, which spells Hitler's doom, has brought full coalition warfare in the spirit of Teheran. This military coalition would be undermined if Roosevelt is defeated by Dewey and the defeatists, who want to negotiate a separate peace with Hitler.

L66 .... A Lesson in Democracy: On the Occasion of the 25th Anniversary of the Communist Movement of the United States, "Communist," 23 (Sept. 1944), 798-805.
A rebuttal of views expressed in Walter Lippmann's "U.S. War Aims" that the Soviet Union is a totalitarian dictatorship, and that peace can be maintained only if the USSR agrees to the suppression of communist movements in Europe and America.

L67 .... The Twenty-Seventh Anniversary of the October Revolution, "Communist," 23 (Nov. 1944), 979-87.
Close ties between the U.S. and the USSR brought about by the war are hailed, and the anti-Soviet campaign of the Republicans is attacked. The Republicans seek to break up the Anglo-Soviet-American coalition, destroy national unity by attacking communists, and sabotage the budding United Nations organization by appealing to small nations' fears of being dominated.

L68 .... Internationalism and the American Working Class, "Political Affairs," 24 (May 1945), 407-14.
The importance of an international perspective on the part of American labor in face of the Anglo-Soviet-American alliance and the Teheran and Yalta decisions. The participation of American workers in the International Trade Union Conference is acclaimed.

L69 .... "Marxism and the Democratic Tradition." New York: International Publishers, 1946. 220 pp. Ref. notes. Ind.
A communist view of the relationship between democracy and communism, arguing that both democracy and communism are the offspring of an ascendant working class seeking political power and economic emancipation. Although communism and capitalism are opposite social systems, this does not make capitalism synonomous with democracy; the claim that democracy and communism are mutually exclusive rests on a distortion of both. The author traces the development of modern democracy from the British revolution of 1648 to the rise of Marxism.

L70 LANG, Daniel. Reporter at Large: The Days of Suspicion, "New Yorker," 25 (May 21, 1949), 37-54.
A sympathetic account of William W. Remington's background, thoughts, and activities from July 1948, when he was accused of being a communist by Elizabeth Bentley, to February 1949, when he was cleared and vindicated by the Loyalty Review Board.

L71 LANG, Frederick J. "Maritime: A Historical Sketch and a Workers' Program." New York: Pioneer Publishers, 1943. 171 pp.
A survey of the maritime industry from the point of view of the Socialist Workers Party. The Trotskyist author attacks the Stalinists for their role on the waterfront, and for their policy zigzags from the "third period" to their support of the capitalist war. He calls for a fight against the Stalinist bureaucracy, and a militant policy based on Marxist analysis.

L72　LANG, P. "Peace versus War: The Communist Position." New York: Workers Library, 1936. 31 pp.
A call, during the popular front period, for international proletarian unity to safeguard peace against fascist warmongers. The situation in Germany, Italy, Japan, France, Spain, and China is reviewed, and a world front of workers, peasants, and all friends of peace is urged against German fascists and Japanese militarists, the chief instigators of war.

L73　LANGBAUM, Robert. Cold War Troubles at Home, "American Scholar," 24 (Summer 1955), 265-79.
Criticism of both the right's exaggeration of the danger of communist infiltration and the liberal's exaggeration of McCarthy's power. In both cases we project a fear out of proportion to reality. We should have confidence in our laws, our minds, and our democratic traditions.

L74　LANGFORD, Howard David. "Education and the Social Conflict." Foreword by Alfred L. Hall-Quest. New York: Macmillan, 1936. 210 pp. Bibliog. Ind.
An exposition of Marxist philosophy on the functions of education in modern society. While some functions of education, such as transmitting information about the world and developing the individual, are compatible with capitalism, one—the organizing of exploited workers to control the means of satisfying material and cultural needs—is not. The author concentrates upon this latter problem, the relationship of education to social conflict or class struggle. He outlines the changes which must occur, in the mass media as well as in the schools, if education is to fulfill this function.

L75　LANNON, Al. "The Maritime Workers and the Imperialist War." New York: Waterfront Section, Communist Party, n.d. [1940]. 23 pp.
A defense of the Nazi-Soviet pact in a report to the Waterfront Section of the CP. The war in Europe is called an imperialist one, for which guilt is shared equally by the ruling classes of all belligerent countries. Party members are urged to support the USSR, build the Party, and keep America out of war.

L76　. . . . The West Coast Maritime Strike: Showdown for Labor, "Political Affairs,' 27 (Nov. 1948), 962-68.
Description of the background of a strike of five "progressive" maritime unions, in progress when the article was written. The strike is viewed as a focal point in the struggle of all unions against the Taft-Hartley Act.

L77　LAPHAM, Roger. Radical Unions Control American Shipping, "Sphere," 17 (June 1936), 13-15.
An address by the president of the American-Hawaiian Steamship Company to a meeting of the U.S. Chamber of Commerce, stressing the complete control that left-wing maritime leaders have obtained over Pacific Coast labor and outlining the methods used to achieve this. Their goals are to supplant all AFL unions in shipping and then to control all transport, including trucks and railroads.

L78　LAPIN, Adam. The Student Strike, "International Press Correspondence," 16 (May 30, 1936), 678-79.
A report on the third student antiwar strike, April 22, 1936, organized by the American Student Union. The strike compared favorably with those of previous years. School administrations and the government have opposed the student antiwar movement. The success of the strike was due in large measure to the united front of communist and socialist youth groups.

L79　. . . . "The Un-American Dies Committee." New York: Workers Library, 1939. 31 pp.
An attack by a Party publicist on the House Special Committee on Un-American Activities headed by Representative Dies. Though Dies had pretended a concern with Nazi activities in the U.S., his interests are in smearing the CIO, progressive and New Deal candidates, and the Communist Party. The author calls for abolition of the committee.

L80　. . . . Lessons from the 76th Congress, "National Issues: A Survey of Politics and Legislation," 1 (Sept. 1939), 8-10.
An attack upon the Tory coalition in Congress for scuttling the President's recovery program and refusing to repeal the arms embargo. The reactionaries used Redbaiting in the drive against WPA and the arts projects. The people must unite in preparation for the next session.

L81　. . . . "Your Stake in the Elections." New York: Workers Library, 1944. 35 pp.
Support for reelection of President Roosevelt because of his win-the-war record and his foreign and domestic program for the postwar period, written shortly after the transformation of the Communist Party into the Communist Political Association. Republican leaders are attacked for rejecting the Teheran conference, for a short-sighted foreign policy, for sabotaging the home front, and for double-talk on full employment.

L82　. . . . Trends in the Two Major Parties, "Communist," 23 (May 1944), 397-409.
The defeatists, who control the Republican Party, are opposed to war with Germany and to collaboration with Russia. Consequently, the Communist Party, the CIO, and progressive elements in the AFL support the Democratic Party and the nomination of Roosevelt as Democratic presidential candidate.

L83　. . . . The Republican Convention, "Communist," 23 (Aug. 1944), 696-704.
A review of the Republican convention, where the defeatists, who are suspicious of Russia and criticize the Teheran agreements, nominated Dewey. Nonpartisan support of Roosevelt is urged from all Americans who want the war to be won quickly.

L84　. . . . Republican Campaign Strategy, "Communist," 23 (Oct. 1944), 880-92.
The campaign strategy of Dewey, the Republican candidate, is to cast discredit on Roosevelt, attack United Nations cooperation, oppose government aid in industrial reconversion, and break up the progressive pro-Roosevelt coalition by attacks on the CIO and the communists.

L85　. . . . The Elections and the New Congress, "Communist," 23 (Dec. 1944), 1067-72.
The congressional elections gave popular support to the Administration's policies, with many of the isolationists defeated by pro-Administration candidates. As a result, there should be greater support for the Administration's policies in the 79th Congress.

L86　. . . . The President Alerts the Nation, "Political Affairs," 24 (Feb. 1945), 108-14.
The President's State of the Union message is praised for demanding a strengthening of the Anglo-Soviet-American coalition, at a time when reactionaries are agitating for a negotiated peace and casting suspicion on the Soviet Union. Roosevelt's message also calls for full employment, public works, and adequate social security.

L87　. . . . Strengthening National Unity under the

Truman Administration, "Political Affairs," 24 (June 1945), 511-17.

Reactionary pressure on Truman to abandon Roosevelt's domestic and foreign policy is increasing. The labor movement and all progressive organizations must now exert influence on Truman to carry out Roosevelt's policies. Greater labor unity and labor-management cooperation are imperative.

L88   LAPIN, Adam. Truman and the Republicans, "Political Affairs," 24 (Oct. 1945), 876-81.

A criticism of Truman's effort to conciliate the Republicans, who oppose his foreign policy and his reconversion program. They want the U.S. to cease cooperating with Russia and to limit unemployment benefits. Progressives must exert pressure on Truman to stand firm against Republican demands.

L89   .... The 79th Congress: An Estimate to Date, "Political Affairs," 25 (Jan. 1946), 78-88.

The reactionary 79th Congress created a committee on un-American activities, provided inadequate unemployment and veterans' benefits, emasculated the full employment bill, gave big corporations tax benefits, and opposed the Soviet Union. The reactionaries were well organized while the progressives, under the illusion that Truman was carrying out Roosevelt's policies, were not.

L90   .... "The Third Party: Challenge to the One Party System." San Francisco: Daily People's World, n.d. [1947]. 31 pp.

A pamphlet in anticipation of the 1948 presidential campaign, picturing the Henry Wallace candidacy as a spontaneous, grass roots movement based on workers, dirt farmers, Negroes, white collar workers, professionals, veterans, and small businessmen. Support of Wallace and the third party is called the only answer to Wall Street's domination of both major parties.

L91   .... "The Nation's Biggest Racket." New York: New Century, 1952. 15 pp.

Elaborating articles that appeared in "People's World," a communist publicist holds both Republicans and Democrats to blame for corruption in government, and for prolonging a senseless war in Korea to keep profits from falling. Readers are urged to support the Progressive Party peace candidates, Vincent Hallinan and Carlotta Bass.

L92   .... "Coexistence or No Existence: Which Way For America?" New York: New Century, 1955. 15 pp.

An assertion that the alternative to peaceful coexistence, now that the USSR has the atomic bomb also, is atomic war. The author claims that peaceful coexistence has been Soviet policy since 1917, and that the U.S. started the cold war. United pressure of trade unions, Negroes, farmers, and church groups can win recognition of red China, oppose German rearmament, and outlaw atomic bombs.

L93   LAPIN, Eva. "Mothers in Overalls." New York: Workers Library, 1943. 30 pp.

A call, during the Party's win-the-war phase, for women to get into overalls and production lines to aid the war effort. Employers and government are urged to take special measures, such as short-hour shifts for part-time workers and nursery care for children, to enable mothers to hold war jobs with a minimum of family dislocation.

L94   LARE, Mona. Brides of Marx, "American Mercury," 44 (May 1938), 11-19.

A characterization of the typical "lady comrade" as the antithesis of the heroine of proletarian literature, sexless, immoral, and prone to use insulting language. They come in two categories, she says, the Intellectual and the Guttersnipe. They serve only as call girls and mischief makers, as mere hangers-on of Earl Browder's circus.

L95   LARSEN, Emanuel S. The State Department Espionage Case, "Plain Talk," 1 (Oct. 1946), 27-39.

An account of the State Department espionage case that led to the arrest of six persons, including the author, in June 1945. The case, involving procommunist government specialists on China, was precipitated by the discovery of secret government documents in the files of "Amerasia" magazine. The author protests his innocence, though he pleaded nolo contendere and was fined $500.

L96   LARSON, Elmer. "Party Vigilance Against Enemy Infiltration." New York: New Century, 1953. 23 pp. Reprinted from "Political Affairs," Oct. 1952.

An attack on the FBI, which has infiltrated Party ranks with its informers, and used stool pigeons to do its dirty work. The need for constant Party vigilance against enemy penetration is stressed.

L97   LASCH, Robert. To Prevent Communism, "Forum," 106 (Nov. 1946), 417-18.

A columnist for the Chicago "Sun" belittles the internal threat of communism, or the possibility that the Soviet Union would try to extend its revolution other than through the consent of the people. Maintenance of a high standard of living is the best weapon against communism.

L98   .... Two Degrees Left of Hoover, "Reporter," 1 (Aug. 30, 1949), 8-9.

A brief sketch of poverty and politics in the 1930's to illustrate the causes and the insignificant proportions of the swing to communism at the time when its appeal was greatest.

L99   LASH, Joseph P. "The Campus Strikes against War." New York: Student League for Industrial Democracy, n.d. [1934]. 11 pp.

Background and story of the April 13, 1934, student strike against war, organized jointly by the socialist-controlled Student League for Industrial Democracy and the communist-controlled National Student League. The strike is viewed as having shattered the indifference of the American student, who is urged to join the SLID.

L100   .... "The Campus Strikes against War." Foreword by John Cripps. New York: Student League for Industrial Democracy, 1935. 47 pp.

An account of the 1935 student strike against war, with a brief description of antiwar sentiment and of today's student antiwar movement. The strike, substantially larger than the one in 1934, was directed by a National Student Strike Committee which included representatives from a number of student and youth groups. A rule of unanimity of decisions prevented domination by communists.

L101   ..., and WECHSLER, James A. "War Our Heritage." Introd. by Bruce Bliven. New York: International Publishers, 1936. 159 pp. Bibliog.

An antiwar book by leaders of the American Student Union. The authors assert that we are on the verge of another war, for which the capitalist countries are feverishly preparing. They oppose the ROTC, and endorse the Oxford Pledge (soon to be renounced by the authors and the ASU). The history of the student antiwar movement is traced. The final chapter presents a program around which the student antiwar movement must rally. (Lash, who came into the ASU from the socialist-controlled Student League for Industrial Democracy, cooperated with the communists and front groups until the Nazi-Soviet pact was signed. Wechsler, who was briefly a member of the Young Communist League, became the bitterly anti-communist editor of the "New York Post.")

L102 LASH, Joseph P. "The Campus: A Fortress of Democracy." New York: American Student Union, n.d. [1937]. 47 pp.
Report to the third annual convention of the American Student Union by its national secretary. The most controversial issue was the Oxford Pledge against participation in war. Agreeing with the communists' position, Lash supported collective security. (The socialists, from whose Student League for Industrial Democracy Lash had come into the ASU, still supported the Oxford Pledge.) The report also dealt with student economic security, education, relationship to the labor movement, and organizational issues.

L103 .... The Campus Debates War and Peace, "New Masses," 26 (Jan. 25, 1938), 6-7.
A review of the change in line of the American Student Union on peace, adopted at its third annual convention. The new policy supports the collective security line of the communists, adopted over the opposition of socialists, pacifists, and Trotskyists.

L104 .... Weekend at the Waldorf, "New Republic," 120 (April 18, 1949), 10-14.
A report of the simultaneous meetings held in New York of the Conference of Scientific and Cultural Workers for World Peace (at the Waldorf-Astoria) and Americans for Intellectual Freedom (at Freedom House). The former was well-controlled by communists, whereas the latter was forcefully anti-Soviet and anticommunist.

L105 LASKI, Harold J. Liberty on the American Campus: I. A Bill of Particulars; II. Conditional Freedom, "Nation," 169 (Aug. 13, 1949), 149-51; (Aug. 20), 181-82.
An analysis, by a leading English political scientist who is also a socialist, of the limitations on freedom of college and university faculty members here, resulting from the fear and dislike of communism. It is not easy, for example, to be sympathetic to Soviet Russia, to support Henry Wallace with vigor, or to recommend controversial books by left writers. Teachers not on tenure must be especially careful.

L106 LASKY, A. V. How Dead is Communism? "Commonweal," 32 (June 21, 1940), 187-90.
Despite the Nazi-Soviet pact and Soviet invasions of Poland and Finland, the Party has retained the bulk of its members and fellow travelers. Its new line, based on Soviet interests, stresses keeping the U.S. out of the European war. The Party, now building new fronts to support its new policies, finds John L. Lewis its biggest aid.

L107 .... Innocents at Home, "Common Sense," 10 (July 1941), 195-98.
A description of leading fascist and communist front organizations in the U.S. The latter include the American Peace Mobilization, the American Youth Congress, the National Federation for Constitutional Liberties, the Friends of the Chinese People, the Council for Pan-American Democracy, and the League of American Writers. "Friday" and "In Fact" are called communist front magazines.

L108 LASKY, Victor. Red Wedge in Hawaii, "Plain Talk," 2 (May 1948), 34-41.
An account of the rise of the International Longshoremen's and Warehousemen's Union in Hawaii, describing communist infiltration during and since the war and the procommunist leanings of Harry Bridges and of Jack Hall, ILWU local organizer. The author emphasizes the resulting danger to the islands' defense in event of war.

L109 .... Who Runs Wallace? "Plain Talk," 2 (June 1948), 1-13.
An account of the Wallace movement, asserting that it was conceived and is staffed and controlled from top to bottom by the Communist Party. The Party insists that its union leaders support Wallace even if it means splitting the CIO. All key positions at Wallace's national headquarters are held by communists or fellow-travelers.

L110 .... Americans against Communism, "American Legion Magazine," 48 (May 1950), 14-15 ff.
An account of a conference to fight communism, sponsored by the Legion, and attended by 66 organizations representing a hundred million people. Emphasis is placed on voting, the school system, radio, and films in the continuation work of the conference.

L111 .... The Case of the Hollywood One, "New Leader," 34 (Aug. 6, 1951), 14-15.
An account of the Party's attempt to discredit Edward Dmytryk, a member of the "Hollywood ten" who recanted, and how this failed. The communist blast against Dmytryk was printed in a two-page advertisement in the "Hollywood Reporter." A rejoinder by the Motion Picture Industry Council demolished the attack and encouraged others who might seek to escape communism.

L112 .... The Case of Howard Fast, "New Leader," 34 (Nov. 5, 1951), 14-15.
Fast is alleged to be one of the few communist intellectuals who really believes the Party line. His connections with Party activities and Party fronts are outlined. He served a short prison term for refusing to answer questions of the House Committee on Un-American Activities, thereby becoming a communist martyr.

L113 ..., and PHILBRICK, Herbert (Gunnar Back, moderator). Should the Communist Party Be Outlawed? "Town Meeting," 18 (Nov. 18, 1952). 16 pp.
Lasky advocates outlawing the Party as a conspiracy controlled by Moscow and a front for spies and traitors. Existing laws are inadequate to put the Party out of business. Philbrick opposes outlawry as a violation of civil liberties which would give us a false sense of security, since the communists would reorganize under another name.

L114 .... How to Understand Communism, "American Legion Magazine," 55 (Aug. 1953), 22 ff.
An assertion that Americans are thwarting a conspiracy of authors, publishers, and reviewers to keep them ignorant of the communist menace. Anticommunist authors and publications are listed, and suggestions given for the fight against communism.

L115 .... Benjamin Schultz: The Rabbi the Reds Hate Most, "American Mercury," 81 (Nov. 1955), 82-85.
A laudatory biographical sketch of the executive director of the American Jewish League against Communism and the coordinator of the Joint Committee Against Communism in New York, who is constantly exposing communist efforts to ensnare Jews.

L116 LASSWELL, Harold D., and BLUMENSTOCK, Dorothy. "World Revolutionary Propaganda:

A Chicago Study." New York: Knopf, 1939. 393
pp. App. Ind.

A comprehensive case study of communist propaganda in
Chicago during the great depression. The authors studied
the channels of propaganda, such as demonstrations,
publications, and organizations; the technique of propaganda, including slogans, symbols, and demonstrations;
the volume of propaganda; and its influence. Included in
their study are a bonus march, demonstrations, and riots,
along with schools, the theater, and social activities. The
authors conclude that, despite many favorable circumstances, the effectiveness of communist propaganda was
blocked by a number of factors, particularly by American
nationalism and individualism.

L117   LASSWELL, James. "Shovels and Guns: The CCC
in Action." New York: International Publishers,
1935. 23 pp.

An attack on the New Deal's Civilian Conservation Corps,
during the Party's ultramilitant "third period," as a
means of cutting wage rates and militarizing civilians.
The fight against the CCC is called an essential part of
the struggle against war and fascism.

L118   LATHAM, Earl. "The Communist Controversy in
Washington: From the New Deal to McCarthy.'
Cambridge, Mass.: Harvard University Press,
1966. 446 pp. App. Ind.

A comprehensive review of the communist issue in the
nation's capitol over a period of two decades, with material
drawn largely from hearings of Congressional investigating committees. The author traces the beginnings of
Soviet espionage in America, the first communist groups
of federal employees, the investigation of the NLRB, the
Hiss and "Amerasia" cases, the inquest on China, and
the politics of hysteria in the McCarthy period. He
accepts the main features of the accounts of Elizabeth
Bentley and Whittaker Chambers about espionage activity.
(One of the series on "Communism in American Life"
sponsored by the Fund for the Republic.)

L119   LATTIMORE, Owen. "Ordeal by Slander."
Boston: Little, Brown, 1950. 236 pp.

An account of the author's ordeal after being accused by
Senator McCarthy of being the top Russian espionage
agent in this country. Starting from the time he heard of
McCarthy's accusations while in Afghanistan, the author
tells in detail of events prior to and including his appearance before the Tydings Subcommittee, which was appointed
to investigate the McCarthy charges of communism in the
State Department. Lattimore declares that he is not and
never was a communist, nor has he ever supported communism. He condemns irresponsible witch-hunting as a
danger to American democracy.

L120   . . . . Lattimore Strikes Back, "New Republic,"
122 (April 17, 1950), 17-21.

Excerpts from the statement by Lattimore at a Senate
committee hearing, denying McCarthy's charges that he
was a communist, and in turn attacking McCarthy for
ignorant bigotry and for misusing his power as a Senator.
Denying that his views had influenced U.S. Far Eastern
policy, he asserts that, had he had more influence, the
communists would not now control China.

L121   LAVERY, Emmet. Communism and the Federal
Theatre, "Commonweal," 28 (Oct. 7, 1938), 610-12.

The program director of the Federal Theatre lists its
accomplishments and defends it from the charge of dis-
seminating communist propaganda. Job applicants are not
judged on political opinion, though an occasional communist supervisor may be guilty of such discrimination.
Critics should study the Federal Theatre before making
blanket condemnations.

L122   LAVINE, Harold. "Fifth Column in America."
New York: Doubleday, Doran, 1940. 240 pp.

A popularly written account of fifth-column organizations
in the U.S., with most attention to fascist groups but with
one chapter on the Communist Party. The Party reached
its greatest strength and influence during the four years
of the popular front, which collapsed with the Nazi-Soviet
pact. This in turn was followed by the Soviet invasion of
Poland and then of Finland. There is a brief discussion
of internal Party life.

L123   . . . . 21 G. I.'s Who Chose Tyranny, "Commentary," 18 (July 1954), 41-46.

A sociological analysis of the 21 American prisoners of
war in Korea who chose communism. A large number
were regular army men who came from broken homes
and from lives of social, psychological, and financial
poverty, and who had entered the service young. They
chose communism, which offered a home not unlike the
Army, rather than return to a dismal civilian life.

L124   "LAW AND LABOR," Criminal Syndicalism: The
Court's Charge in the Trial of William Z. Foster,
5 (May 1923), 134-35.

An analysis of the judge's charge to the jury in Foster's
trial under the Michigan criminal syndicalism statute for
engaging in Communist Party activities at Bridgman,
Michigan. The charge is unusually clear in setting forth
the conditions necessary for conviction.

L125   . . ., American Civil Liberties Union and Communist Activity, 13 (Feb. 1931), 23-24.

A reprint of the criticism of the ACLU made by the Fish
Committee of the House of Representatives. This committee, appointed by Congress to survey American communism, accused the ACLU of acting as a shield for the
communists.

L126   . . ., Recommendations of the Special Committee
of the House of Representatives on Communist
Activities in the United States, 13 (Feb. 1931),
25-28.

A reprint of the report of the House committee, which was
chaired by Hamilton Fish, Jr., and dealt with the history
of communism, the number of communists, and affiliated
organizations. Among its recommendations were deportation of alien communists, prohibition of interstate transportation of communist literature, and a declaration that
the Party was illegal.

L127   LAWRENCE, Bill, and BEGUN, Isidore. The New
York City Elections and the Struggle Against Hitlerism, "Communist," 20 (Dec. 1941), 1055-71.

In New York City, Mayor La Guardia won both the primary
and the election over opponents who resorted to Red-baiting. The Communist Party, which supported La Guardia,
played a key role, emphasizing winning the war as the
chief election issue. The results showed the New York
people to be anti-Hitler.

L128   LAWRENCE, David. Treason's Biggest Victory,
"U.S. News and World Report," 42 (June 28,
1957), 152 ff.

A condemnation of the Supreme Court's rulings concerning communism in the U.S. The Court has now in essence
taken away the investigatory power of Congress and has
made subversion and treason easy. Now the FBI will not
even get a "tip" over the phone.

L129   LAWRENCE, Lars. "Morning, Noon, and Night."
New York: Putnam, 1954. 340 pp.

A story of blacklisted miners, mostly Mexican-Americans,
in a mining town in the Southwest, who demonstrate against

being evicted from their homes. A riot results, after which the miners and left-wingers organize for their defense, while their adversaries seek to terrorize them. (First volume of a trilogy, "The Seed.")

L130 LAWRENCE, Lars. "Out of the Dust." New York: Putnam, 1956. 311 pp.
A story of Mexican-American miners, a sequel to "Morning, Noon, and Night." Left-wingers defend a jailed comrade, while bourgeois elements seek to use a riot to suppress labor and the left. The burial of a murdered miner turns into a communist demonstration. (Second part of a trilogy, "The Seed.")

L131 LAWSON, Elizabeth. "The Spy at Your Counter." New York: Workers Library, n.d. [193-?]. 31 pp.
An exposé of the activities of the Willmark Service System, Inc., of New York City, the largest agency spying on employees in the service industries. The author tells how spies are recruited and how workers in department stores, hotels, and other industries are informed on and blacklisted.

L132 .... "The Jobless Negro." New York: Workers Library (for National Committee, Unemployed Councils), 1933. 16 pp.
A plea for Negro-white unity and militancy, under the leadership of the Unemployed Councils, to break down racial discrimination and increase relief funds. The pamphlet attacks discriminatory unemployment and low pay among Negro workers, and praises the hunger marches of 1931 and 1932.

L133 .... "Scottsboro's Martyr, J. Louis Engdahl." New York: International Labor Defense, n.d. [1933?]. 7 pp.
A pamphlet commemorating the death in Russia of Engdahl, veteran U.S. communist leader. As national chairman of the Party-controlled International Labor Defense, Engdahl had toured 16 countries with Ada Wright, mother of two of the Scottsboro boys.

L134 .... "20 Years on the Chain Gang: Angelo Herndon Must Go Free!" New York: International Labor Defense, 1935. 14 pp.
An account of the life of Angelo Herndon, telling how he was imprisoned and found guilty of violating an antiquated Georgia law, how he was tortured, and how, at the last minute, let out on bail. The author calls for a mass campaign to free him.

L135 .... The Supreme Court, Citadel of Slavery, "Communist," 16 (April 1937), 322-33.
A review of the Supreme Court's decisions on slavery prior to the Civil War. The Court consistently upheld the property rights of slaveholders, making it unlawful to aid runaway slaves and holding in the Dred Scott case that slaves brought into states where slavery was prohibited did not become free.

L136 .... "Thaddeus Stevens." New York: International Publishers, 1942. 31 pp. Ref. notes.
A laudatory account of the career of the militant abolitionist, a leader in the fight to abolish slavery, to emancipate and arm the Negroes during the Civil War, and to secure the suffrage for the Negro people in the post-Civil War years.

L137 .... "Lincoln's Third Party." New York: International Publishers, 1948. 48 pp. Ref. notes.
An account of the formation and swift triumph of an early opposition party, the Republican, which in its youth represented a coalition of revolutionary forces against the slavocracy. For a brief period, on the slavery issue, the interests of workers and farmers coincided with those of manufacturing capitalists. (Written in the year of Henry Wallace's campaign, the pamphlet seeks to show that third parties are an integral part of American history.)

L138 .... "The Reign of Witches: The Struggle Against the Alien and Sedition Laws." Preface by William Patterson. New York: Civil Rights Congress, 1952. 64 pp. Bibliog.
A communist interpretation of the Alien and Sedition Acts of the eighteenth century as almost exactly paralleling the Smith Act cases today. The author gives the background of the original acts, their specific provisions, the "reign of terror" which these laws ushered in, the opposition of the people, and their final repeal and nullification. Contemporary parallels are shown at many points.

L139 ... (comp.). "The People's Almanac." New York: New Century, 1955. 64 pp.
A communist compilation of important dates and events in the history of the struggles of the people of the U.S. Emphasis is placed on labor and Negro struggles and Party history.

L140 LAWSON, John Howard. "A Southern Welcome (In Georgia and Alabama)." New York: National Committee for the Defense of Political Prisoners, 1934. 15 pp.
A report on a trip to Georgia and Alabama of a delegation sponsored by the national committee, with the ACLU, the ILD, and the Herndon Defense Committee, to visit Angelo Herndon, then in jail in Georgia. The delegation went to investigate the treatment of the Scottsboro boys, and to check on the state of civil and constitutional rights in both states. Both states are held in the process of Hitlerization, with free speech and constitutional rights endangered.

L141 .... Inner Conflict and Proletarian Art: A Reply to Michael Gold, "New Masses," 11 (April 17, 1934), 29-30.
Lawson takes issue with Mike Gold's attack on him ("A Bourgeois Hamlet of Our Time," in "New Masses," April 10, 1934). Gold disregards the historical background of Lawson's writings, and fails to recognize his inner conflict. Gold's attitude toward revolutionary themes is sentimental and mock-heroic.

L142 .... The Crisis in the Theater, "New Masses," 21 (Dec. 15, 1936), 35-36.
Tracing the history of the progressive movement in drama, the author suggests that the popular front line has tended to very un-Marxist generalizations. Today, we have new political needs and pressures, which should broaden the drama of the left, not dilute or conceal social content.

L143 .... Art Is a Weapon, "New Masses," 48 (March 19, 1946), 18-20.
Denunciation of the views of Albert Maltz on the social function of the writer ("What Shall We Ask of Writers?" in the "New Masses," February 12, 1946). By rejecting the slogan, "art is a weapon," Maltz denies political realities and rejects the artist's responsibility. He asks writers not to identify with the class struggle.

L144 .... Parrington and the Search for Tradition, "Mainstream," 1 (Winter 1947), 23-43.
A reevaluation of Parrington's "Main Currents in American Thought." Parrington accepted economic determinism with regard to the motivations of the privileged class, and saw the state as an instrument of class domination.

He failed to understand fully the role of the working class, however, and so was pessimistic of democracy's future.

L145   LAWSON, John Howard. Camera and Microphone, "Masses & Mainstream," 1 (May 1948), 36-47.
An analysis of the potentiality and misuse of these two instruments of the film art. The mobility of the camera, together with film strip cutting and arrangement (montage), determine film structure. The close-up provides the emotional insight that binds the action together. The microphone relates music and dialogue. Motion picture art, however, is limited by commercial production and monopoly control.

L146   . . . . "The Hidden Heritage: A Rediscovery of the Ideas and Forces that Link the Thought of Our Time with the Culture of the Past." New York: Citadel, 1950. 572 pp. Ref. Ind.
An interpretation of America's cultural history, by a leader of communist activities in Hollywood, completed just before he served a prison term for contempt of Congress. Sections of the work, which covers the period from 1075 to 1628, deal with the decline of Catholic power, the challenge of humanism, the colonial pattern, the European background of English colonization, and the English colonies. The author, who sees cultural history as a struggle between oppressors and oppressed, finds the roots of culture in the life of the people, their struggle for subsistence, and their battle against exploitation.

L147   . . . . Hollywood: Illusion and Reality, "Masses & Mainstream," 5 (July 1952), 21-33.
An assertion that the ideology of Hollywood films is based on the aims of American imperialism—propaganda for war and conquest, for white supremacy, and for colonial oppression. The films, with all other forms of art and communication, are class weapons, serving a specific purpose in the cultural superstructure of capitalism.

L148   . . . . Celluloid Revolution, "Masses & Mainstream," 5 (Aug. 1952), 28-38.
An attack on Hollywood's film about the revolutionary peasant movement in Mexico, "Viva Zapata!" The film, which teaches a lesson in the futility of people's movements, ignores the national uprising against U.S. imperial power. Elia Kazan, the director, groveled before the House Committee on Un-American Activities, before which he appeared as an informer.

L149   . . . . Can Anything Be Done About Hollywood? "Masses & Mainstream," 5 (Nov. 1952), 37-46.
An assertion that Hollywood mocks our democratic heritage, supporting fascism and war. Movies present workers only in subordinate or comic roles, ignore or stereotype Negroes, and degrade women. Films should be viewed with alertness and an awareness of their class bias. Audience organization is needed to tell Hollywood what the people want.

L150   . . . . "Film In the Battle of Ideas." New York: Masses & Mainstream, 1953. 126 pp.
A Marxist interpretation of Hollywood's film industry, by one who has consistently followed the communist cultural line. Films are called an important part of the superstructure of capitalist class culture, used by the ruling class to achieve conformity to its program. Hollywood movies distort history and reality, on the thesis that man is by nature depraved and aggressive. The author advocates a mass campaign against the propaganda art of Hollywood, along with a struggle for an independent motion picture art, free of Wall Street control.

L151   . . . . McCarthyism and Culture, "Masses & Mainstream," 6 (May 1953), 19-27.

As a reaction sets in against McCarthyism, a powerful coalition to defend culture and the Bill of Rights may be formed. The witch hunt, the burning of books, and the drive to put education in a totalitarian straightjacket have brought many allies to the anti-McCarthy side.

L152   . . . . The Tragedy of Eugene O'Neill, "Masses & Mainstream," 7 (March 1954), 7-18.
A review of O'Neill's work, pointing out where it ceased to be class conscious and concerned with social themes. The sickness in his work shows the disease of bourgeois literature in this century. When O'Neill the man died, O'Neill the artist had been dead for 20 years; society had damaged his art and paralyzed his creative will.

L153   "LAWYERS GUILD REVIEW," Extracts from Briefs to the United States Court of Appeals in National Lawyers Guild v. Herbert Brownell, Jr., 14 (Spring 1954), 11-38.
Extracts from briefs submitted to the Court of Appeals by the Guild's attorneys and by the Department of Justice in a case growing out of Attorney General Brownell's decision placing the Guild on his list of subversive organizations. The Guild appealed from a District Court decision denying its motion for a preliminary injunction.

L154   . . ., Special Issue Reporting Speeches at Guild Conference on Loyalty-Security and the Law, 15 (Winter 1955-56).
The proceedings of a conference, October 15, 1955, sponsored by the Constitutional Rights and Liberties Committee of the National Lawyers Guild. The leading speakers and their topics included Henry Mayer on the impact of the loyalty-security program on private employment, David I. Shapiro on government employment, Blanch L. Freedman on immigration and deportation, Harry I. Rand on naturalization and denaturalization, and Stanley Faulkner on the armed forces. (All of the above are abstracted separately.)

L155   LEAGUE OF AMERICAN WRITERS. "Writers Take Sides." New York: The League, 1938. 82 pp. App. Bibliog.
Replies of 418 writers (of over 1,000 queried) as to whether they favored Franco and fascism, or the legal government and the people of Republican Spain. Only one answer favored Franco. The appendix summarizes the aims of the Spanish Loyalists and those of the Franco leaders.

L156   . . . . "We Hold These Truths..." New York: The League, 1939. 128 pp. Bibliog.
Statements by 54 American writers, educators, clergymen, and others against anti-Semitism. The 54 persons quoted in this communist front publication include Party leaders like Earl Browder; writers such as Granville Hicks, who belonged to the Party; sympathizers for a time, such as Theodore Dreiser; liberals like John Haynes Holmes; and conservatives such as Thomas A. Dewey.

L157   LEAGUE OF PROFESSIONAL GROUPS FOR FOSTER AND FORD. "Culture and the Crisis: An Open Letter to the Writers, Artists and Other Professional Workers of America." New York: Workers Library, 1932. 32 pp.
An appeal by 52 intellectuals to fellow intellectuals and professionals to vote communist on November 8. Neither the Democrats nor the Republicans can alleviate the country's economic disaster, and the Socialist Party is one of mere reform. The country needs a basic social and economic reorganization; only the Communist Party stands for socialism of deeds.

L158 LEAGUE OF STRUGGLE FOR NEGRO RIGHTS. "Equality, Land and Freedom: A Program for Negro Liberation." New York: The League, 1933. 43 pp.

A publication of a Party front organization, calling for confiscation of large land holdings in the South, their distribution among small farmers and share croppers, and self-determination for the Negro people in the Black Belt. Negro leaders who propose reform and class collaboration are denounced, and assistance urged for Negroes elsewhere who are fighting imperialist oppressors.

L159 LEAGUE OF WOMEN VOTERS OF THE UNITED STATES. "Liberty and Security: Our Federal Loyalty-Security Programs: Origins, Operations, and Improvements Which Have Been Proposed." Washington, D.C.: The League, no. 239 (1956). 26 pp. Bibliog.

A review of Federal loyalty-security programs, their origin and evolution, their structure and stages, related operations such as the Attorney General's list, criticisms of the programs, proposals for improvement, and arguments for and against changes. Citizens are urged to think through the knotty issues, to help us achieve the best possible loyalty-security program.

L160 LEE, Brad. Communism on the Air, "National Republic," 42 (April 1955), 21-22.

A report on the fight behind the scenes between communists and anticommunists in the radio and television entertainment field. Because of communist control of the Radio Writers Guild, the anticommunists formed Aware, Incorporated, to disclose the facts about the communist invasion of the entertainment world.

L161 LEE, Hugh. Menace to Labor: The Cause of American Labor is Suffering from the Penetration of Communists into its Unions, "Current History & Forum," 52 (Jan. 10, 1941), 20-22 ff.

A discussion of communist infiltration of American trade unions, following dissolution of the Party's dual unions. Communist tactics, including attacks on old-line union leaders, planning in caucuses, and publication of shop papers, are outlined.

L162 LEE, Jack. The Save-the-Union Conference, "Labor Unity," 2 (May 1928), 3-6 ff.

An account of the National Save the Miners Union Conference of April 1-2, in which over 1,100 delegates from UMW locals and unorganized areas voted to take the union away from the Lewis machine and to extend and win the year-old strike. Relief and solidarity are needed to win despite Lewis, the operators, and injunctions.

L163 LEE, Kendrick. Loyalty in Government, "Editorial Research Reports," 2 (Sept. 11, 1946), 613-26.

An analysis of the problem of the loyalty of government employees, in the light of rising tension between the U.S. and the USSR and the disclosure of Soviet espionage operations in Canada. Particular attention is paid to the operation of wartime loyalty tests for civil servants and to proposals for better protection against disloyalty.

L164 .... Investigations of Un-Americanism, "Editorial Research Reports," 1 (Feb. 5, 1947), 89-106.

A discussion of investigations of subversive activities, criticisms of the House Committee on Un-American Activities, and its promises of reform. Earlier House and Senate investigations of communist propaganda and activity in the U.S. are reviewed, as are the loose procedure at Dies Committee hearings and the domination of the committee by the chairman.

L165 LEFEBVRE, R. R. Talks with Communists about Their Views on Religion, "America," 66 (Jan. 3, 1942), 343-44.

A discussion of the communist attitude towards religion during the united front period. Despite an appearance of religious tolerance, there has been no basic change in communism's relentless opposition to religion.

L166 LEFKOWITZ, Abraham. Communists Wreck the Teachers Union, "New Leader," 18 (Sept. 7, 1935), 1-2.

A report by the Union's legislative representative that Stalinist and Lovestoneite groups have invaded the Teachers' Union and used it as a battleground for their own quarrels. A committee headed by John Dewey, which investigated the situation in 1933, found it deplorable.

L167 LEHMAN, Lloyd. The Oakland General Strike, "Political Affairs," 26 (Feb. 1947), 173-81.

An account of a two and one-half day strike in seven cities of Alameda County, California, which began on December 3, 1946, when the police force was used to run merchandise through picket lines before two Oakland department stores. The general strike, marked by labor unity and militancy, ended in a major political victory.

L168 LEITER, Robert D. The Fur Workers Union, "Industrial and Labor Relations Review," 3 (Jan. 1950), 163-86.

An analysis of the union's development since the turn of the century, tracing the rise of communist influence and the completion of communist control by 1937. Though there is a strong noncommunist opposition, it is unlikely to win control so long as the administration continues its remarkable advances in wages, hours, and working conditions.

L169 LEITES, Nathan C., and POOL, I. De Sola. "Communist Propaganda in Reaction to Frustration." Washington: Library of Congress, 1942. 54 pp.

An analysis of the communist reaction to election and strike defeats, based upon communist writings in the U.S. and Europe, 1919-41.

L170 LENIN, Nicolai. "Should Communists Participate in Reactionary Unions?" New York: Workers Party, n.d. 14 pp.

A translation of a statement by Lenin calling on communists to enter and capture reactionary unions. He warns against men like Gompers who will seek to destroy their influence.

L171 ..., and TROTZKY, Leon. "The Proletarian Revolution in Russia." Ed. with Introd., notes, and supplementary chapters by Louis C. Fraina. New York: Communist Press, 1918. 453 pp.

The first collection of writings by Lenin and Trotzky published in this country. The volume was important in the crystallization of the left-wing of the Socialist Party here from which the communist movement emerged. Fraina, then editor of the left-wing socialist journal, "Revolutionary Age," saw the Russian revolution as a vindication of the position of the left wing.

L172 .... "The Soviets at Work." New York: Rand School of Social Science, 1918. 48 pp.

This pamphlet, dealing with the accomplishments of the Soviets and their remaining tasks, is important because of its influence upon left-wing socialists in the U.S. Published in at least five editions here, it was also in the volume of Lenin's and Trotzky's writings called "The Proletarian Revolution in Russia," edited by Louis C. Fraina, as well as in "Lenin's Selected Works."

L173 LENIN, V. I. A Letter to American Workers, "Liberator," 1 (Jan. 1919), 8-11. Also published in "Revolutionary Age," Dec. 28, 1918; Lenin's "Collected Works," 23:192-204; "Workers Monthly," Feb. 1926; and "Revolutionary Radicalism," 1:657-68.
Lenin's first letter to American workingmen, dated August 20, 1918. Defending the Bolsheviks against the charge that they brought devastation to Russia, Lenin argues that the Russian revolution is invincible, and that labor everywhere is breaking with its betrayers and preparing for the proletarian revolution. (This and a second letter, written five months later, were widely circulated among the Socialist Party's left wing, and were influential in converting it to Bolshevism.)

L174 .... "A New Letter to the Workers of Europe and America." Brooklyn: Socialist Publication Society, 1919. 13 pp. Also published in "Revolutionary Radicalism," and in "Communist," Jan. 1928.
Lenin asserts that, in the five months since his earlier letter, the proletarian revolution has matured. As in the previous letter, he bitterly attacks moderate socialism. He concludes that the forces of capitalism, though strong, have been unable to contain Soviet power, nor will they be able to crush the world proletarian revolution.

L175 .... " 'Left Wing' Communism: An Infantile Disorder." Detroit: Marxian Educational Society, 1921. 116 pp. Rev. ed. New York: International Publishers, 1934. Ch. 7 published as "Should Communists Participate in Reactionary Unions?" New York: Workers Party, n.d., 14 pp.
The textbook on Leninist tactics for European and American communists. Written in 1920, it was an attack on "infantile leftism," which makes a rigid principle out of illegal activity and rejection of compromises. Lenin calls for a flexible combination of legal and illegal work, understanding when each can be useful. Trade unions, despite reactionary leadership, are the only means by which the communist vanguard can ally itself to and educate the masses. Participation in parliamentary activity is the best way to dispel the bourgeois democratic prejudices of workers and peasants. Communists must be prepared to practice trickery, use illegal methods, conceal the truth.

L176 .... Capitalism and Agriculture in America, "Communist," 8 (June 1929), 313-18; (July), 395-401; (Aug.), 473-77. (A further installment, announced for the following issue, failed to appear.)
First publication in the U.S. of a work written by Lenin in 1913, dealing with general characteristics of U.S. agriculture, the industrial North, the formerly slave-owning agricultural section, the size of farms, and the capitalist character of agriculture. In relative terms the number of independent farmers is falling, while the number of hired laborers is increasing, showing the growth of capitalism in agriculture.

L177 LENS, Sidney. "Left, Right and Center: Conflicting Forces in American Labor." Hinsdale, Ill.: Regnery, 1949. 445 pp. Ind.
A survey of American labor history which attempts to explain the triumph of business unionism over labor radicalism. The author, an anti-Stalinist, examines the issue of Stalinism in unions, discussing the Trade Union Educational League and the motives, tactics, and leadership of American Stalinism. He shows how Stalinist labor activity is tied to Soviet policy, and contends that "Red-baiting" aids the Stalinist cause.

L178 .... "The Counterfeit Revolution." Boston: Beacon, 1952. 272 pp. Ind.
An inquiry into the rise and spread of Stalinism, and into its attractions for idealists, despite its dictatorship. Moscow's postwar appeal is held due to the failures of the West, to its confusion and unwillingness to change. America's foreign policy, obsessed with communism, allies itself with reactionary elements. The communist movement outside Russia, though completely in the service of a foreign government, wears a false mask of idealism. The author proposes that we destroy world poverty and under-industrialization, see that the fruits of industrialization are distributed equitably, and seek to widen the schisms within world Stalinism.

L179 .... Decade of the Ex-Reds, "Nation," 189 (Sept. 5, 1959), 105-8.
While the CPUSA is now down to about 4,000 members, the ex-communists, along with ex-Trotskyists and ex-socialists, are enjoying prosperity, with influential positions in the literary and diplomatic worlds, relief organizations, trade unions, and other organizations. For most of them, their most violent recent act has been to vote for Adlai Stevenson or argue at a PTA meeting.

L180 .... "The Mine Mill Conspiracy Case." Introd. by Norman Thomas. Denver: Mine-Mill Defense Committee, n.d. [1960]. 18 unnumbered pp.
Criticism of the government for its prosecution of past or present leaders of the Mine, Mill and Smelter Workers Union for "conspiracy to defraud the government" by falsely signing the noncommunist affidavits required by the Taft-Hartley Act. The government's behavior indicates a vendetta rather than an impartial application of justice.

L181 LERNER, James. "Twenty Years After, 1914-1934." New York: Youth Section, American League Against War and Fascism, n.d. [1934]. 18 pp.
The national chairman of the Youth Section finds the cause of World War I in the clash over colonies and markets. He denounces the current rush to war, pointing to fascist trends in the U.S. and the conditions of life for young people. Hailing USSR peace proposals, he calls for a fight against war, and election of delegates to the Second U.S. Congress Against War and Fascism.

L182 .... "Youth Demands Peace." New York: National Youth Committee, American League Against War and Fascism, 1936. 23 pp.
An analysis of war as caused by colonies, investment, trade, and profits, with an attack upon the U.S. for aiding aggressors through trade and for preparing for aggressive war in defense of big business abroad. Young people are urged to join the antiwar movement, to support neutrality legislation and student strikes against war, to stop shipments of war material, and to oppose military training in schools.

L183 LERNER, Max. After the Comintern, "New Republic," 108 (June 7, 1943), 753-55.
Stalin dissolved the Comintern as a wartime measure, and is unlikely to revive it after the war because of Russian national interests. Without its Russian support the Communist Party here, which never had real American roots, is through. The communists here may dissolve and join in the formation of a needed new national political grouping.

L184 ..., and MAGIL, A. B. Can Communists and Non-Communists Unite? "New Masses," 48 (July 13, 1943), 3-11.
An exchange of letters between a prominent liberal and an associate editor of the "New Masses" on the effect of the dissolution of the Communist International. Magil appeals

L214 LEWIS, Clyde A.; KIRSTEN, Charles J.; JAVITS, Jacob K.; and GIDEONSE, Harry D. (George V. Denny, Jr., moderator). Should the Communist Party Be Outlawed Now? "Town Meeting," 15 (Nov. 8, 1949), 24 pp.
Kirsten and Lewis favor outlawing of the Party as a criminal conspiracy whose objective is to destroy the government by violence and terror. Gideonse asserts that the Party is now in decline as a result of exposure, which would be made more difficult by outlawry. Opposing such outlawry as unconstitutional, Javits argues that present laws against conspiracy are adequate to deal with the communist meance.

L215 LEWIS, Flora. "Red Pawn: The Story of Noel Field." Garden City, N.Y.: Doubleday, 1965. 283 pp. Bibliog. Ind.
An account of the case of the former State Department official, a friend of Alger Hiss, who had been recruited into espionage work for the Soviets in 1935, and whose disappearance behind the Iron Curtain in 1949 was followed by the similar disappearances of his wife, his brother, and his foster daughter, when each in turn went to look for him. Finally released from prison, Field and his wife chose to remain in Hungary.

L216 LEWIS, Fulton, III. A Guide to Red Reading, "American Mercury," 88 (June 1959), 48-53.
Noting that school libraries throughout the U.S. contain many publications by members of the CP or front groups, the author argues that such books should contain a biographical sketch of the author's communist activities.

L217 LEWIS, H. "The Truth About Profits, Prices, Wages." Cleveland: Communist Party of Ohio, 1947. 16 pp.
An assertion that our economic system is controlled by a handful of gigantic corporations, which keep down wages by peddling phony economic theories and by dividing workers through Red-baiting. The workers must fight, not only for a higher share of the national income, but for the abolition of the profit system, as in the USSR.

L218 LEWIS, Theophilus. Negroes and Communism, "Interracial Review," 12 (Sept. 1939), 142-43.
A prediction that the Hitler-Stalin pact will open the eyes of some of the handful of Negroes who have accepted communism, for it is now apparent that little confidence can be placed in communist sincerity.

L219 .... Communism and Race Equality, "Interracial Review," 19 (July 1946), 108-9.
Negroes ask why the U.S. can't make racial discrimination illegal, as the Soviet Union has done. Lewis answers that as a democracy the U.S. cannot enforce equality as a dictatorship can. There is no guarantee that present Soviet policies will continue, whereas equality based on changes in people's minds cannot be reversed by government.

L220 .... Illusion of Negro Pinks, "Interracial Review," 20 (Sept. 1947), 142-43.
An assertion that fellow-travelers, in pointing out the inequities of capitalism, ignore the fact that the profit system, despite its many faults, provides more security than the closed economy they advocate.

L221 .... Sticks and Stones, "Interracial Review," 22 (Sept. 1949), 139-40.
A view of the anti-Robeson riots in Westchester County, N.Y., as a propaganda triumph for the communists, who were delighted when the citizens of Westchester foolishly "blew their collective top."

L222 .... Sowers of Tares, "Interracial Review," 23 (Aug. 1950), 125-26.
Instances of racism in the U.S. aid the communists to convince the darker peoples of the world that Americans are champions of white supremacy, determined to hold Asians and Africans in economic slavery. The Korean conflict increases the importance of this issue.

L223 LEWIS, Thurber. The Lenin School in Chicago, "Workers Monthly," 4 (May 1925), 320-21.
A description of a two weeks' course for revolutionary leaders at the Intensive Training School of District Eight of the Workers (Communist) Party, Chicago. The curriculum included Marxian economics, Leninism, history of the international labor movement and of the communist movement, the role of the Party and of its members and officers, and public speaking.

L224 .... A Solid Line of Proletarian Defense, "Workers Monthly," 4 (Aug. 1925), 460-61 ff.
A report on the conference in June 1925 which established the International Labor Defense as a united nonsectarian workers' defense organization to supply legal aid to all workers attacked for activity in the class struggle. James P. Cannon was elected chairman.

L225 LEWIS, Walter K. Profile of IWO: Communist Front, "New Leader," 30 (July 5, 1947), 4.
A detailed account of the International Workers Order, a fraternal benefit organization subservient to the Party. This is reflected in the interlocking leadership of IWO and CPUSA, and in IWO's faithful following of the Party line.

L226 .... A Front By Any Other Name—, "New Leader," 34 (March 26, 1951), 6-7.
Despite elaborate window dressing to conceal its communist domination, the Young People's General Assembly for Peace is part of the CP-dominated American Peace Crusade (itself the successor to the CP-dominated Peace Information Center). The Assembly repudiates the UN forces in Korea and supports the seating of Red China at the UN. It has already infiltrated several college student councils.

L227 .... Cominform Drive on Youth, "New Leader," 34 (July 9, 1951), 6-8.
An account of the recruiting through various fronts of American young people to attend the Third World Festival of Youth and Students for Peace, to be held in East Berlin in August. This is an effort to draw the young people of the world to communism.

L228 .... U.S. Reds Keep Heads Above Water (Gulp!), "New Leader," 38 (May 30, 1955), 19-20.
Quotations from the Party's monthly organ, "Party Voice," revealing communist efforts to infiltrate democratic organizations in fields like civil rights, housing, schools, etc. Though defensive measures against the CP have been effective, greater alertness is needed.

L229 .... U.S. Communists Convene, "New Leader," 40 (Feb. 25, 1957), 10-11.
A report on the recent convention of the CPUSA, which settled no major policy disputes. Neither Foster, head of the "Stalinist" faction, nor Gates, head of the anti-Stalinist group, is likely to win the struggle for power. Though Party membership has fallen to 10,000 or lower, the Party is still a threat to democratic and liberal organizations.

L230 "LIBERATOR," Reorganization of the Workers Party: Resolution of the Communist International, 7 (Oct. 1924), 26-27.

A resolution adopted at the Fifth Congress of the Communist International, requiring the world's communist parties to be organized on the basis of factory nuclei. This will distinguish the revolutionary parties from the reformist social-democratic parties based on electoral districts, and change the social composition of the Party so that the majority consists of proletarians.

L231 LIEBLING, A. J. Wayward Press: Spotlight on the Jury, "New Yorker," 25 (July 23, 1949), 60-68.
Criticism of the press' treatment of the jury in the first Hiss trial, particularly of the publicity given the jurors and their views of the trial, the comments of the judge on the "hung" jury, and comments on the trial by various congressmen. This treatment lessens the chance of a fair trial next time.

L232 "LIFE," Close-up of a Ghost, 35 (Nov. 23, 1953), 29-35.
A biographical sketch of Harry Dexter White, accused of being a member of a communist espionage ring in Washington, D.C. The economist, who rose to be assistant secretary of the Treasury, is said to have had a basic inferiority complex and to have gotten a feeling of importance from dealing with communist spy rings.

L233 . . ., U.S. Ponders a Scientist's Past, 36 (April 26, 1954), 35-39.
Text and pictures on the background of J. Robert Oppenheimer, who directed the laboratory at Los Alamos that perfected the atom bomb, and who was later barred from access to secret documents. His friendship with communists during the 1930's is reviewed, as is his early opposition to developing the hydrogen bomb.

L234 . . ., The Supreme Court and Liberty, 43 (July 1, 1957), 30.
An editorial assertion that the Supreme Court is naïve in its dealings with cases concerning communism. If the CPUSA is weak at present, it is due to the activities of the executive and congressional branches of government, while the Supreme Court has not yet shown cause for confidence and respect.

L235 LIGHTENBERG, John. Policy with Respect to Communist Teachers and the Fifth Amendment, "American Teacher," 38 (Feb. 1954), 4-7.
A statement by the attorney for the American Federation of Teachers, AFL, that the union will defend teachers dismissed solely for pleading the Fifth Amendment. While it will not defend a communist, it will defend a person accused of being one until guilt is established to its satisfaction.

L236 LIGHTFOOT, Claude. "An American Looks at Russia: Can We Live Together in Peace?" New York: New Century, 1951. 23 pp.
The text of a speech by the state secretary of the Communist Party in Illinois, on the occasion of the 33rd anniversary of the Russian Revolution. He reviews capitalism's record of wars, economic crises, and oppression of colonial peoples, contrasting it with Soviet progress and the USSR's peace policy. He calls for peaceful coexistence between the U.S. and the USSR.

L237 . . . . "'Not Guilty!' The Case of Claude Lightfoot." New York: New Century, 1955. 15 pp.
The author, an Illinois Party leader appealing a conviction under the Smith Act, asserts that his conviction, if upheld, will permit any type of accusation on the "guilt-by-association" principle. He denies being a foreign agent, and believes that the new climate of public opinion, as evidenced in the 1954 Congressional elections, will permit peace, democracy, and progress.

L238 . . . . The Struggle to End the Cold War at Home, "Political Affairs," 34 (Sept. 1955), 28-47.
A report to a Party national conference, August 2, 1955. Despite efforts to create a police state at home, a pro-democratic upsurge is maturing. Cases involving the Bill of Rights that will soon reach the U.S. Supreme Court include the McCarran Act, the Communist Control Act of 1954, the Lightfoot and Scales cases under the Smith Act, and the case of Pennsylvania vs. Steve Nelson. (Also published in pamphlet form.)

L239 . . . . "The Challenge of the '56 Elections: Report to the National Committee of the Communist Party, U.S.A." New York: New Century, 1956. 24 pp.
The full text of Lightfoot's report to the meeting of the Party's national committee, April 28-May 1, 1956, calling for stronger mass movements, legislative-electoral coalitions in 40 to 50 congressional districts, independent political action by labor, and an independent role for the Party.

L240 . . . . The Impending Elections, "Political Affairs," 35 (Oct. 1956), 5-14.
While the communists do not endorse any party or candidate in this campaign, they seek to help labor and allied forces to achieve their aims, as a step towards a people's coalition government. The problem of enforcing the Supreme Court decisions on civil rights, together with the fight for peace, will prove the key to victory in the 1956 election.

L241 LIGHTFOOT DEFENSE COMMITTEE. "The Case of Claude Lightfoot." Chicago: The Committee, n.d. [1955?]. 16 pp.
A popular presentation of the case of Lightfoot, Party leader in Illinois, who was being tried under the membership clause of the Smith Act. Other Smith Act trials, the pamphlet asserts, show little chance for a fair and impartial trial; if he is convicted, the Department of Justice will use the Smith Act to force any person or organization to do its bidding or face prosecution.

L242 LILIENTHAL, David E. Mystery in Oppenheimer Case: Trail of Inquiry That Vanished at the White House, "U.S. News and World Report," 37 (July 9, 1954), 89-95.
More testimony on the Oppenheimer case before the Personnel Security Board of the AEC. Lilienthal, chairman of the AEC in 1947, testifies that information of a derogatory nature about Oppenheimer was brought to the attention of the White House. There is no record of what happened there, and Oppenheimer's security clearance was continued.

L243 LIND, Robert L. The Crisis in Literature, "Sewanee Review," 47 (Jan.-March 1939), 35-62; (April-June), 184-203; (July-Sept.), 345-64; (Oct.-Dec.), 524-51.
Criticism of literature of the past 30 years for failure to exhibit new and deep currents of thought. Propaganda in its relationship to literature is explored, and discussion of this subject at the 1935 American Writers Congress is reviewed. Art cannot be separated from society and its problems, as proletarian literature and criticism show. Writers are finding in communist philosophy a modern world view that orients literature to its place in culture.

L244 LINVILLE, Henry R. How Communists Injure Teachers' Unions, "Social Frontier," 5 (March 1939), 173-76.
A discussion of communist influence within the New York City Teachers Union (Local 5 of the American Federation of Teachers) and the national union, written by the former

head of the local and leader of the rival Teachers Guild. Stalinist control of Local 5 is described, as is its affiliation with the Party-sponsored American League for Peace and Democracy. (For a denial of Linville's charges see Charles J. Hendley, "Unionism in the Educational Field," in "Social Frontier," May 1939.)

L245   LIPPAY, Z. "Behind the Scenes of the 'Disarmament' Conference." New York: Workers Library, n.d. [1932?]. 59 pp.
A communist view of the Geneva conference to limit armaments as a cover for efforts to transform the world economic crisis and the blockade against the USSR into active intervention and a new world war. Workers in capitalist countries are urged to struggle against their bourgeois war lords and defend the Soviet Union.

L246   LIPSET, S. M. Opinion Formation in a Crisis Situation, "Public Opinion Quarterly," 17 (Spring 1953), 20-46.
A report on a survey of student opinion taken at the height of the loyalty-oath controversy at the University of California. Though students were opposed to the oath, they were divided on the issue of employing communists at the university. Group affiliations and background characteristics were important factors in the formation of these opinions.

L247   LISSAMAN, Doris. The Taft-Hartley Non-communist Affidavit Provision, "Labor Law Journal," 5 (Oct. 1954), 697-707.
An evaluation of section 9 (h), the noncommunist-affidavit provision, of the Taft-Hartley Act, covering congressional sentiment and problems of compliance. Problems posed by the Communist Control Act of 1954 are discussed, as is the question of constitutionality. Proposals for changes in the provision are considered.

L248   "LITERARY DIGEST," Labor's Own View of the Red "Borers," 79 (Oct. 13, 1923), 17-18.
Editorial opinion from the labor press, in reply to a "Digest" questionnaire on kinds and methods of communist infiltration into labor unions. While the volume of red propaganda is large, the communist campaign has made little progress and is unlikely to make more.

L249   . . ., The Plot to Make Our Blacks Red, 87 (Nov. 21, 1925), 13-14.
A compilation of newspaper reports on the American Negro Labor Congress. Speakers included William Z. Foster, William Montgomery Brown, and Lovett Fort-Whiteman, a Negro newspaper correspondent who visited Russia in 1924. These attempts to sovietize the Negro will fail.

L250   LITTLE, John. "Wake Up and Live." New York: New York State Committee, Young Communist League, 1937. 47 pp.
A report of the New York State executive secretary to the state convention of the Young Communist League, held in Brooklyn, November 26-28, 1937. Written during the Spanish Civil War, emphasis is placed on building a people's front to quarantine the fascist aggressors. YCL branches are urged to train for leadership and to support the American Youth Congress, the American Labor Party, the Workers Alliance, the American Student Union, and the National Negro Congress. The Trotskyists are attacked bitterly.

L251   . . . . "Life for America's Sons and Daughters." New York: New York State Young Communist League, 1939. 47 pp.
This keynote speech at the second convention of the New York State Young Communist League, February 1939, presents the Communist Party's program for youth.

L252   "LIVING AGE," A Letter to John Dos Passos, 343 (Oct. 1932), 178-79.
A reproduction from a Soviet literary publication of a letter of praise to Dos Passos from two Soviet writers, who hail him as a trail blazer for the proletarian revolution of the future. Though Dos Passos is criticized for ideological errors, he is helping to build socialism and to expose and fight capitalist tactics.

L253   "LIVING CHURCH," Fr. Spofford and the Communists, 99 (Sept. 21, 1938), 253-55.
Editorial criticism of Rev. William B. Spofford, vice-chairman of the American League Against War and Fascism and executive secretary of the Church League for Industrial Democracy, for his replies to questions on communism, the American League, and the CLID. Spofford is called blind to the fact that communism, like fascism, denies Christianity and menaces the church. (The questions and answers appear on page 261 ff.)

L254   LLOYD, Jessie. "Gastonia: A Graphic Chapter in Southern Organization." New York: Committee on Progressive Labor Action, 1930. 31 pp.
The story of the communist-led textile strike in Gastonia, N.C., written from a leftist but noncommunist point of view. Attention is paid to working conditions in the mills, the history of the strike, the murder of the chief of police, the arrests of union members, and the public reaction. The main issue was unionism, not communism.

L255   LLOYD, R. Grann. Loyalty Oaths and Communistic Influences in Negro Colleges and Universities, "School and Society," 75 (Jan. 5, 1952), 8-9.
A survey of loyalty oaths and communist influences in Negro colleges and universities, compiled from questionnaires sent to college presidents. Since few, if any, communists are on the staffs, a loyalty oath or pledge of allegiance is unnecessary and derogatory.

L256   LLOYD, Roger Bradshaigh. "Revolutionary Religion: Christianity, Fascism, and Communism." New York and London: Harper, 1938. 190 pp.
The author, an Englishman, sees both communism and fascism as totalitarian, although of the two communism is by far the more creative force. Both can be combated only by the revolutionary spirit of Christianity. Rejecting the atheism and dialectic materialism of communism, the author asserts that only Christianity can produce the authentic revolution.

L257   LOGAN, Malcolm. These Terrible Reds, "Scribner's Magazine," 87 (June 1930), 649-55.
A review of the communist movement in the U.S. by a New York newspaperman who traces its history, estimates its strength, describes its leadership, and outlines its policy in the trade union and other fields. It has expanded its activities as a result of the unemployment that followed the stock market crash. The author suggests abolishing the conditions that make people listen to the Party's desperate counsels.

L258   LOGAN, Mark, and DOUGLAS, Sam. The Anatomy of McCarthyism, "Political Affairs," 32 (June 1953), 10-25.
McCarthyism is attacked as the technique of the Big Lie and the spearhead of fascism. Its biggest lie, that communism is a conspiracy plotting force and violence, endangers the civil rights of the entire nation. Eisenhower does not rebuke McCarthyism, because it draws the fire away from the sinister and oppressive acts of his administration.

L259   LOGAN, Rayford W. (ed.). "What the Negro

Wants." Chapel Hill: University of North Carolina Press, 1944. 352 pp.

The views of 14 leading American Negroes, among them Doxey A. Wilkerson, then a member of the national committee of the Communist Political Association. His contribution (pp. 193-216) stresses the Negro's stake in a military victory over the Axis and the gains Negroes are making in the war economy and in the armed services. He calls for unity among Negroes and with their allies among progressive whites and in organized labor. W. E. B. Du Bois (pp. 31-70) calls for full economic, political, and social equality, with no discrimination based on race or color. While giving his favorable impressions of a trip to the USSR, he views the program of the Party here as suicidal. (Du Bois joined the Party in 1961, two years before his death, after having supported communist causes for many years.)

L260   LOKOS, Lionel. "Who Promoted Peress?" New York: Bookmailer, 1961. 219 pp. Notes. Ind.
An account of the case of Major Irving Peress of the dental corps, written by a staunch supporter of Senator McCarthy, who tried to find out how an officer could be promoted and honorably discharged after invoking the Fifth Amendment on questions relating to communism. The Army's loyalty-security program is criticized severely.

L261   LOMASK, Milton. Feature X: Estimate of the Attitude of Many Catholics toward Communism, "America," 84 (March 3, 1951), 642-44.
A critical appraisal of the typical Catholic's anticommunist attitude. While Catholics have a sense of mission about their anticommunism, few understand it; their approach is lazy and anti-intellectual. Much of the anticommunist crusade has been negative; Catholics must have something positive to give as well.

L262   LONG, Anna. Women Workers after the War, "Political Affairs," 24 (March 1945), 258-67.
A discussion of postwar prospects for women workers, who are urged to consolidate their wartime gains, particularly through active participation in the labor movement. National progress is not possible without the progress of women workers.

L263   LONG, Hamilton A. "America's Tragedy Today." New York: Post Printing, 1950. 65 pp.
A military man's account of how the communists, with direct aid from the White House, infiltrated the U.S. defense establishment during World War II. He charges that the Party successfully kept communist radio operators on commercial ships, had armed forces' records on communists destroyed, sabotaged the armed forces' countersubversive system, and obtained commissions for members of its conspiracy, all with White House aid. The Truman Administration's high command, he asserts, is now a captive of the communist conspiracy.

L264   LONIGAN, Edna. N.K.V.D. in the U.S. (condensed from "Human Events"), "Catholic Digest," 13 (Dec. 1948), 1-7.
An assertion that the NKVD infiltrated the U.S. government beginning in 1933, and that its "plants" and dupes formulated the policies of Dumbarton Oaks, the United Nations, etc.

L265   . . . . Anatomy of the PAC, "Freeman," 1 (Nov. 27, 1950), 137-40.
An assertion that the Democratic Party is ruled by an outgrowth of the CIO's Political Action Committee, whose program has a remarkable resemblance to Browder's program for the Communist Party. The communists are asserted to have set up Wallace as the "left" in 1948 in

order to make Truman, whom they also supported, look like the "center."

L266   LORD, Daniel A. "What Catholicity and Communism Have in Common." St. Louis: Queen's Work, 1936. 32 pp.
Catholicity and communism are the two revolutions of our time, asserts the author. They are alike in demanding justice, but Catholicity preserves the human spirit, God, and freedom, whereas communism does not.

L267   LORE, Karl. Build the American Workers Party, "Labor Action," 1 (Dec. 20, 1933), 1-2.
An account of the transformation of the Conference for Progressive Labor Action, led by A. J. Muste, into the American Workers Party. An accompanying extract of the report of its national executive committee analyzes the various left-wing groups on the American scene. The communists are said to have alienated themselves by sectarian and disruptive activities.

L268   LORE, Ludwig. The United Front Gains Ground, "Nation," 139 (Dec. 19, 1934), 714-16.
An account of united front activities of socialists and communists, especially in France. Here the Norman Thomas-Dan Hoan wing of the Socialist Party now favors cooperation with the Communist Party. The American Workers Party, led by A. J. Muste, and the Communist League of America (Trotskyists) have merged into the Workers' Party of the U.S.

L269   LORING, Edward. Communists Set to Use Entire CIO Apparatus Again to Defy FDR, Cripple Defense Factories, "New Leader," 24 (June 14, 1941), 1 ff.
A report on the Party-led strike against the North American Aviation Company at Inglewood, California, with a prediction that communist-controlled unions will call even bigger defense strikes soon. The communists have their own organized faction within the CIO, whose leaders, with their union and Party-front affiliations, are listed.

L270   . . . . Attention! Phil Murray . . . Here is Why CIO Needs House-Cleaning! "New Leader," 24 (June 21, 1941), 1 ff.
A list of communists and communist-controlled unions in the CIO, with a call for President Philip Murray to cleanse the CIO of totalitarian leaders. Procommunists on the CIO national staff are listed, along with Party-controlled industrial union councils, national unions, and sections of national unions. Communists holding office in official CIO bodies are named.

L271   LORING, Norman R. Teachers Should Have Freedom of Thought: A Sermon, "Christian Register," 117 [116] (Jan. 7, 1937), 3-4.
A protest against teachers' oath laws, in effect in 22 states and the District of Columbia. The most atrocious of these laws, passed by Congress for the District of Columbia, forbids teachers to mention the philosophy of communism in the school or to discuss it anywhere else. The only way to defeat an idea such as communism is with a better idea—democracy.

L272   LORWIN, Lewis L. "Labor and Internationalism." New York: Macmillan, 1929. 682 pp. App. Bibliog. Ind.
A detailed treatment of international labor organizations, both political and economic. The origin of the Third International is traced, and its activities in its first decade, along with those of its satellites, are described. Attention is paid (ch. 21, pp. 517-58) to communist political organization, communist trade unionism, and auxiliaries among farmers, women, and youth, and in the field of relief.

(Revised and updated as "The International Labor Movement: History, Policies, Outlook," published in 1953.)

L273 LORWIN, Lewis L., with the assistance of Jean Atherton Flexner. "The American Federation of Labor: History, Policies, and Prospects." Washington, D.C.: Brookings, 1933. 573 pp. App. Bibliog. Ind.
A history of the AFL, with a brief treatment (see especially pp. 259-63) of the conflict between the Federation and the communists. From 1925 to 1927 the communists, organized in the Trade Union Educational League, sought to "bore from within" the AFL, and from 1929 on they organized rival unions affiliated with the Trade Union Unity League, with most success in clothing, textiles, and coal mining. Communist weaknesses in the trade union field are analyzed.

L274 .... "The International Labor Movement: History, Policies, Outlook." New York: Harper, 1953. 366 pp. Bibliog. Ind. Rev. Ed. of an earlier work, "Labor and Internationalism."
A comprehensive treatment of the international labor movement, including both economic and political aspects. The Second and Third Internationals are both covered, as are the International Federation of Trade Unions, the Red International of Labor Unions, the World Federation of Trade Unions, and the International Confederation of Free Trade Unions. Activities of the AFL and the CIO in the international labor field are reported. While emphasis is upon international organization of the communists and of noncommunist labor groups, the impact on the American scene is made clear.

.... See also LEVINE, Louis.

L275 LOSOVSKY, A. [pseud. for S. A. Dridzo]. "The International Council of Trade and Industrial Unions." New York: Union Publishing Association, 1920. 64 pp. App.
An account of the formation in Moscow, in July 1920, of an international organization of revolutionary trade unions, later known as the Red International of Labor Unions. Representatives from leftist trade unions in a number of countries, including America, participated. The new body, an affiliate of the Third, or Communist, International, will oppose the reactionary Amsterdam International Federation of Trade Unions.

L276 .... "Question of Organization." Moscow: Press Bureau, International Congress of Red Trade and Industrial Unions, 1921. 15 pp.
A discussion of the role of American trade unions by a Soviet expert on trade unions, who asserts that radical union groups, avoiding dual unionism, must enter the reactionary trade unions in order to conquer them. In the U.S. the AFL, the independent unions, and the IWW should be consolidated. If then the organization accepts the principle of revolutionary class struggle and submits to international proletarian discipline, it can affiliate with the communist trade union federation, the Red International of Labor Unions.

L277 .... "Lenin and the Trade Union Movement." Foreword by William Z. Foster. Chicago: Trade Union Educational League, n.d. [1924]. 36 pp.
Losovsky, secretary of the Red International of Labor Unions, reviews Lenin's ideas on trade unions, showing that he valued them as schools for the revolutionary education of workers. Foster, citing Lenin's ideas as justification for the TUEL's "boring from within" policy, asserts that the past four years have shown the soundness of the anti-dual-unionism policy.

L278 .... "Lenin: The Great Strategist of the Class War." Trans. and Introd. by Alexander Bittelman. Chicago: Trade Union Educational League, n.d. [1924]. 44 pp.
An effort by one of Lenin's co-workers in the USSR to present the essence of Lenin's thought in simple terms. In the Introduction, Bittelman, one of the early communist leaders here, asserts that American workers should consult Lenin on every doubtful point.

L279 .... "The World's Trade Union Movement." Introd. by Earl R. Browder. Chicago: Trade Union Educational League, 1924. 125 pp.
A translation of a series of lectures by the general secretary of the Red International of Labor Unions in Moscow in 1923, dealing with the world trade union movement before and after the war, the class collaborationist policies of the Amsterdam International, and the policies and tactics of the Red International (the Profintern). Browder's introduction describes the labor situation in the U.S. and the work of the TUEL, the American section of the RILU.

L280 .... On the Eve of the Third Congress of the Profintern, "Labor Herald," 3 (Aug. 1924), 179-84.
An analysis by the general secretary of the Red International of Labor Unions of the role of the revolutionary left wing in the trade unions of the world. He reaffirms Lenin's position of 1920 that the revolutionary wing must remain in reactionary trade unions in order eventually to oust the reactionary leadership.

L281 .... Struggle for Unity in the World Labor Movement, "Workers Monthly," 4 (Dec. 1924), 59-63.
The general secretary of the Red International of Labor Unions, while defending as necessary the splitting of socialist parties to form communist parties, demands the formation of a united trade union movement and a struggle within it for a revolutionary program and tactics. The RILU was created after the Amsterdam International declared war on the Russian Revolution and the Communist International.

L282 LOSSIEFF, V. Industrial Workers of the World, "Communist International," 3 nos. 16-17 [1921], 111-16.
A favorable review of the organization, history, structure, and tactics of the IWW, and of its relations with the socialist and communist parties. The question of affiliation with the Communist International is reviewed and arguments on both sides presented. The IWW is holding a referendum on the issue.

L283 LOUF-BOGEN, T. New Trends of Agriculture and the Crisis in the U.S., "Communist," 9 (June 1930), 538-57.
This analysis of proposed agricultural legislation argues that none of these plans, which fail to come to grips with problems of production, can solve the U.S. agricultural crisis.

L284 LOUGHRAN, John M. Layman to Layman, "Commonweal," 29 (Oct. 28, 1938), 13-15.
An enumeration of methods by which Catholics can counteract communist influence in organizations for social betterment. Catholics should join such organizations to make communist manipulation impossible; existing Catholic groups should develop programs of social action; and new nonsectarian groups should be formed to advance democracy, social justice, and peace.

L285 LOVE, Stephen S. An Analysis of the Sobell Case, "Jewish Life," 8 (Jan. 1954), 22-25.
An analysis of the evidence at the trial of Morton Sobell

by a professor of law at Western Reserve University, who calls the 30-year sentence a blight on the reputation of American justice and the product of hysteria. No documentary evidence of espionage was presented, and prejudice was aroused by the introduction of the element of communism.

L286   LOVE, Stephen S. The Sobell Case, "Nation," 182 (June 23, 1956), 526-28.
A professor of law at Northwestern University analyzes the case of Morton Sobell, now serving a 30-year sentence at Alcatraz, and concludes that he was convicted, not on a basis of reliable testimony, but as a result of hysteria generated by the label "communist."

L287   LOVENSTEIN, Meno. "American Opinion of Soviet Russia." Introd. by Broadus Mitchell. Washington, D.C.: American Council on Public Affairs, 1941. 210 pp. Ref.
A study of American attitudes toward the USSR, as disclosed in publications during three periods: war and its aftermath (1917-21), American expansion and Russia's New Economic Policy (1921-29), and the depression in the U.S. and the first five-year plan in Russia (1929-33). For each period the coverage includes labor organs, business and financial magazines, trade periodicals, economic magazines, learned journals, general magazines, books, newspapers, and government documents.

L288   LOVESTONE, Jay. "Blood and Steel: An Exposure of the 12-Hour Day in the Steel Industry." New York: Workers Party, n.d. [1922?]. 31 pp.
A call for the abolition of the 12-hour workday in steel. The author describes the oppressive working conditions, the starvation wages, and the rigors of the 12-hour day in the industry. Blaming the "brutal dictatorship" of the employing class for the 12-hour day, he calls for the building of a powerful steel union to reduce working hours.

L289   . . . . "The Government, Strikebreaker: A Study of the Role of Government in the Recent Industrial Crisis." New York: Workers Party, 1923. 364 pp. Ind.
A communist study of government intervention in the 1921-22 strike wave. The author pictures government labor policy as condoning the use of every weapon of repression against strikes. He tells how strikes of textile workers, miners, and railroad workers were defeated by the government's use of antilabor courts, the injunction, and the army, aided by employers' associations and the press. He calls for unity among workers and the organization of a labor party to win control of the government.

L290   . . . . "What's What—About Coolidge?" Chicago: Workers Party, n.d. [1923]. 16 pp.
A characterization of President Coolidge as the hero of Big Business, a dyed-in-the-wool reactionary and Red-baiter who breaks strikes, uses strong-arm tactics against labor, and serves as a machine man of the big bankers.

L291   . . . . "American Imperialism." Chicago: Workers Party, n.d. [1924]. 32 pp.
An analysis of American imperialism and a presentation of the anti-imperialist program of the Workers Party. Our foreign entanglements, Lovestone asserts, will soon draw American armies overseas to defend the foreign investments of our employing class. The AFL has permitted the interests of the labor aristocracy to be tied to imperialism. The Party urges a united front of workers and farmers in an anti-imperialist program.

L292   . . . . "The Labor Lieutenants of American Imperialism." New York: Daily Worker Publishing Co., n.d. [1924]. 14 pp. Also published in "Communist International, Jan. 30, 1927.
A denunciation of American trade union bureaucrats for serving as tools of capitalist interests and agents of American imperialism, and for paying themselves fabulous salaries. Thanks to them, the American labor movement is more backward politically than that of any other big capitalist country.

L293   . . . . "The La Follette Illusion: As Revealed in an Analysis of the Political Role of Robert M. La Follette." Chicago: Workers Party, 1924. 48 pp.
A communist denunciation of La Follette as more capitalist than progressive. By advocating trust busting, La Follette seeks a return to competitive capitalism, not social ownership and control by the working class. His political machine is called as corrupt as those dominated by big capitalist interests; workers' conditions in Wisconsin are shameful, and the La Follette government there aids antilabor activities.

L294   . . . . American Imperialism—America Today, "Communist International," n.s., no. 14, n.d. [1925], 3-12.
An analysis of the historical, economic, and political developments that have made America the dominant imperialist power in world affairs. The existence of a "labor aristocracy" in the U.S. is the result of imperialist bribery. Effective leadership in the class struggle can be provided only by a powerful, highly centralized, mass Communist Party.

L295   . . . . The New America: The American Empire, "Workers Monthly," 4 (July 1925), 391-94.
A review of American imperialism, which is backed by Wall Street and our growing military and naval force. The class struggle has thus become internationalized, affording a new basis for arousing the workers. Since the labor aristocracy defends the bourgeoisie, only a mass Communist Party can unify the ranks, provide leadership, and finally overthrow the American empire.

L296   . . . . More Communist Strongholds, "Workers Monthly," 4 (Oct. 1925), 540-42.
A discussion of bolshevization of the Party, as demanded by the Communist International. This cannot be achieved with 18 separate language federations. The Party must be reorganized into shop nuclei on the basis of employment and, where this is not possible, into street nuclei. The shop nuclei will give the Party leadership in shop struggles and guarantee its vanguard position.

L297   . . . . Class Divisions in the United States, "Workers Monthly," 5 (Nov. 1925), 18-20.
A comparison of the results of the 1910 and 1920 census, showing gigantic strides in industrialization and urbanization. The total number of wage earners is growing, while the agricultural proletariat, wage earners in domestic and personal service, and employers and the self-employed are decreasing in numbers. A big working class has developed, with a sharp trend toward proletarianization. (Also published in "Communist International," new series, no. 11 [1925].)

L298   . . . . Towards a World Bolshevik Party, "Workers Monthly," 5 (Dec. 1925), 73-80.
A discussion of problems within the communist movement, centering on a right-wing German group and its relations to the Communist International. Upholding the Comintern's criticism of the German group, Lovestone (expelled several years later for right-wing deviations) finds

lessons for the Party here in dangers of pessimism, a failure to use a proper approach to the masses, and attempted independence from the Comintern.

L299 LOVESTONE, Jay. The Great Negro Migration, "Workers Monthly," 5 (Feb. 1926), 179-84.
The reasons for, and character of, the mass migration of Negroes from South to North after World War I. Released from oppression on southern plantations, the Negro has become more race conscious while becoming an urban proletarian. His problems are inseparable from those of white unskilled workers. Communists must approach the Negro question on the basis of class, not race.

L300 .... Imperialism and the American Working Class, "Workers Monthly," 5 (March 1926), 203-5.
An abstract of a speech at a recent plenum of the Party's Central Executive Committee. Lovestone distinguishes between the effects of American imperialism on the AFL labor aristocracy and on the lower strata of the American working class. The working class is robbed of a major source of leadership, while its "revolutionization" must await a clash between European and American imperialism.

L301 .... Forces and Currents in the Present Political Situation, "Workers Monthly," 5 (April 1926), 249-55.
A discussion of factors impeding the rise of a labor party in the U.S. Among these factors are American imperialism, the corruption of the labor aristocracy, an increase in class-collaboration schemes, the oppression of the unskilled masses, and capture of the labor-party movement by La Follette. Favoring a labor party are a powerful centralized government and the development of a homogeneous working class.

L302 .... "The Coolidge Program: Capitalist Democracy and Prosperity Exposed." New York: Workers Library, 1927. 16 pp.
An attack by a leading American communist on a speech by President Coolidge, which is described as stating the program of American imperialism. Lovestone challenges the accomplishments of private initiative, conceding them for the capitalist class but not for the workers; he points to workers' low income, the concentration of wealth, and agricultural depression.

L303 .... America Facing Europe, "Communist," 6 (March 1927), 7-16.
An analysis of the state of American imperialism that disagrees with the views of Trotsky, who exaggerates the weakness of European capitalism and overestimates the strength of American imperialism. Trotsky assumes that American imperialists are the sole obstacle to revolution, whereas European capitalist nations increasingly resist New York. Trotsky's view that socialism in the USSR depends on a European or American revolution is false.

L304 .... Toward Another Wave of Revolutionary Struggles, "Communist," 6 (April 1927), 72-75; (May), 138-49.
A report on the prospects for communism from the perspective of the Seventh Plenum of the Executive Committee of the Communist International. Among the topics treated are the character of capitalist stabilization, the development of socialism in the Soviet Union, the decline of the British Empire, the growth of revolutionary China, the Trotsky opposition in the Russian Party, and problems of the Party in America.

L305 .... Perspectives for Our Party, "Communist," 6 (June 1927), 200-6; (July-Aug.), 287-94.

An evaluation of the economic and political situation in the U.S. American capitalism is still on the upward grade, despite weaknesses, and America today is the dominant imperialist power. Though chances for a mass labor party in 1928 are slim, U.S. class divisions are being sharpened. The Party's main tasks are to intensify its work in the trade unions and to mobilize the masses against the war danger.

L306 .... The Organizational Growth of the Workers (Communist) Party of America, "International Press Correspondence," 7 (June 30, 1927), 788-89.
A report on the membership of the Workers (Communist) Party of America from October 1925, when the reorganization from language bureaus to shop and street nuclei was made, until May 1927. The decline in new memberships and in dues payments following reorganization is now being overcome. Party membership is at the highest point since September 1925, the month before reorganization.

L307 .... Some Trade Union Problems, "Communist," 6 (Nov. 1927), 423-34.
In a speech at the fifth national convention of the Party, Lovestone analyzes the labor movement's failure to grow during a period of prosperity and reviews the work of the Trade Union Educational League. He appeals to Party members to keep factional considerations out of trade union work.

L308 .... "America Prepares the Next War." New York: Workers Library, 1928. 20 pp.
The head of the communist movement in the U.S., following the death of Ruthenberg, adapts the new line, as laid down at the Sixth World Congress of the Communist International, to American conditions. Lovestone asserts that the U.S. is entering the "third period" of capitalist development, in which it is preparing for war. (Less than a year later Lovestone was expelled from the Party.)

L309 .... "1928: The Presidential Election and the Workers." New York: Workers Library, 1928. 46 pp.
An analysis of existing parties and leading issues, first from a capitalist and then from the workers' point of view, by the Party's executive secretary (who was expelled the following year). Asserting that a labor party is best adapted to American conditions, Lovestone urges workers to form such a party, or at least a united labor ticket, for the 1928 election.

L310 .... The Present Economic Situation, "Communist," 7 (Feb. 1928), 75-89.
Lovestone reviews the year's economic developments. Although the general trend of American capitalism in 1928 is still upward, the peak of prosperity of the present cycle has passed, and the economy is being undermined by basic contradictions. These contradictions make for an aggressive policy in American imperialism.

L311 .... Ruthenberg as Fighter and Leader, "Communist," 7 (March 1928), 145-53.
A laudatory review of Ruthenberg's place in the communist movement by a factional associate who succeeded to Ruthenberg's position of leadership after his death. Lovestone praises Ruthenberg's fighting spirit, his organizing ability, his opposition to imperialist war, his understanding of Leninism, and his role as founder of the Party in the U.S. (Written as an introduction to a volume of Ruthenberg's speeches and writings, this article was also published in pamphlet form as "Ruthenberg, Communist Fighter and Leader.")

L312 .... Practical Phases of the Labor Party Campaign, "Communist," 7 (April 1928), 205-18.

While promoting a labor party, the communists' main task is to build the Workers Party into a mass party. Communists must maintain organizational independence and freedom of criticism and must recruit the best labor-party members into the Workers Party. Whenever possible, the Workers Party should nominate its own candidates. In Minnesota, communists should vote against objectionable Farmer-Labor candidates such as Shipstead.

L313 LOVESTONE, Jay. The Present Situation in the Labor Movement, "Communist," 7 (May 1928), 265-78.
Changes in the composition of the American working class and unfavorable developments in the labor movement have precipitated the current crisis in the trade unions. The reverses suffered by the United Mine Workers are due primarily to the treacherous policies of the Lewis clique. Nevertheless, a number of forces are undermining class collaboration.

L314 .... Some Immediate Party Problems, "Communist," 7 (July 1928), 421-33.
Excerpts of Lovestone's remarks to the meeting of the Central Committee of the Party on May 30, 1928. Although he finds America confronted by an economic crisis, Lovestone sees the national economy as still on the ascent and radicalization as less widespread than in 1922-23. While continuing work in the old unions, the Party's emphasis is shifting to the organization of the unorganized.

L315 .... How the American Communists are Conducting Their Election Campaign, "Communist International," 5 (Aug. 15, 1928), 412-16.
The Party, which will be on the ballot in at least 30 states, is conducting its most intensive parliamentary campaign, using its campaign to get on the ballot to spread its propaganda and bring its program before the masses. Its program emphasizes the class struggle—the unity of native-born, foreign, and Negro workers against the common enemy, trustified capital.

L316 .... Report on the War Question, "International Press Correspondence," 8 (Sept. 1, 1928), 1021-25.
Lovestone's report to the Sixth World Congress of the Communist International, analyzing the state of American capitalism and imperialism, outlining U.S. preparations for war, and summarizing the Party's antiwar and anti-imperialist campaigns. The aggressiveness of American imperialism is the result of its resources, which are enumerated.

L317 .... America's Fight for World Hegemony and the War Danger, "Communist," 7 (Oct. 1928), 605-21.
A "third period" analysis of American imperialism, its policies and areas of conflict. The reactionary trade union bureaucracy is part of the U.S. imperialist apparatus. The Party, which has made a good beginning in practical antiwar work, will combat imperialism and turn the next imperialist war into a civil war.

L318 .... The Sixth World Congress of the Communist International, "Communist," 7 (Nov. 1928), 659-75.
Lovestone's speech at the Party's membership meeting in New York City on October 2, describing the program adopted by the Sixth World Congress and the analysis of the world situation on which it was based. Emphasis will be on the "united front from below," to win social-democratic workers away from their leaders. The main danger is from the right, not from the ultra-left, both within the communist parties and the labor movement.

L319 .... The 1928 Elections, "Communist," 7 (Dec. 1928), 736-55.
A review of candidates and issues in the 1928 campaign. The Hoover victory represents the merger of Big Business and government. The Democratic Party, by no means dead, will continue to compete with the Republican Party as a representative of capitalism. The "progressives" lost ground, as did the Socialist Party, while the communists will clearly increase their vote substantially.

L320 .... "Pages from Party History." New York: Workers Library, 1929. 36 pp. Appeared also, in slightly different text, in "Daily Worker," Feb. 1, 6, 7, 8, and 11, 1929.
A factional document, criticizing the Foster group within the Party for its incorrect policies, recently criticized by the Communist International as right-wing and opportunistic. Denying the opposition's charge that his policies have led the Party to the right, Lovestone links the Foster caucus to deviationists expelled from the Party. (Although the Lovestone group elected a majority of the delegates to the Party convention held soon after this was published, Lovestone was expelled from the Party in June 1929.)

L321 .... Some Issues in the Party Discussion, "Communist," 8 (Jan.-Feb. 1929), 59-80.
Sections of a report made by Lovestone for the Political Committee of the Party to the Central Committee meeting in December 1928, dealing with issues between the Central Executive Committee majority and the Foster-Bittelman opposition. The issues concern the trend of American imperialism, the economic situation, industrialization of the South, and the question of radicalization and the perspective for struggle.

L322 .... The Crisis in the Communist International, "Revolutionary Age," 1 (Dec. 1, 1929), 10-11.
An assertion by the leader of the Communist Party (Majority Group) that a world-wide crisis exists in the communist movement, manifesting itself in a revision of Leninist strategy and tactics, a depletion of leading forces, a destruction of Party democracy, and a huge loss of membership. The leading role of the CPSU has become one of mechanical domination, with servility and unprincipledness the requisites for Comintern leadership.

L323 .... "The American Labor Movement: Its Past, Present and Future." New York: Workers Age, 1932. 22 pp.
The case for working within the existing unions as against the dual union policy of the official Party. The author, former Party head and now leader of the Communist Party (Majority Group), or Lovestoneites, analyzes the characteristics of American unions to show why the CP's union-splitting tactic violates traditional revolutionary policy.

L324 ..., and HILLQUIT, Morris. Where Was the Radical Vote? "Common Sense," 1 (Dec. 5, 1932), 23.
The light socialist and communist vote in the 1932 election is explained. Lovestone, who supported the communist ticket though he was out of the Party, asserts that Foster did not receive more votes because American workers were not yet far enough advanced and because the Communist Party followed wrong tactics.

L325 .... "What Next for American Labor?" New York: Communist Party of the U.S.A. (Opposition), 1934. 24 pp. Reprinted from "Modern Monthly," May 1934.
An attack on the Party's dual union position by a former Party leader now heading an opposition communist group. Presenting his group's program for labor in the NRA period, Lovestone argues that the Party's dual unionism

plays into the hands of conservative union officials. He advocates working within conservative unions to transform them into militant organizations.

L326 LOVESTONE, Jay. New Policies or Old Fallacies? Analyzing the Recent Party Statements, "Workers Age," 3 (Oct. 1, 1934), 4-5.
An analysis of conditions in Europe that are forcing a change in the line of the Communist International on the question of united fronts and the theory of "social fascism," followed by criticism of the CPUSA for its weak moves in that direction. The CP's trade union policies are criticized.

L327 .... "Soviet Foreign Policy and the World Revolution." New York: Workers Age Publishing Association, 1935. 31 pp.
An analysis and defense of Soviet foreign policy by a former leader of the American Party expelled as a right deviationist. While defending the USSR from criticism by Trotsky and others that it has abandoned world revolution, Lovestone attacks the Stalin hero cult as a curse in the Communist International. Praising the socialist construction achieved in the USSR and its foreign policy, he nevertheless denounces the sectarian and opportunist policies of the Comintern in capitalist and colonial countries.

L328 .... "The People's Front Illusion: From 'Social Fascism' to the 'People's Front.'" New York: Workers Age, 1937. 86 pp.
Criticism of the Party's people's front line by a former Party leader who in this period led an opposition communist group that was outside the Party. Asserting that the people's front is a policy of class collaboration and an abandonment of Marxist principles, Lovestone traces its background and its application in various countries. He charges that it is a distortion of the united front tactic in the direction of class collaboration and advocates dropping it in favor of revolutionary opposition to fascism.

L329 .... Stalinism and the Present World Situation, "Workers Age," 9 (April 27, 1940), 1 ff.
A discussion of the role of Stalinism in American economic and political life following the Hitler-Stalin pact. Unlike democratic parties, the CP is little more than an agency of the Hitler-Stalin bloc; Party aims coincide with American conditions only when the dictates of Russian foreign policy coincide with American aims.

L330 .... Can Communist Parties Be Independent of Moscow? "American Federationist," 63 (Aug. 1956), 6-11.
An assertion by a former communist leader that the June 24, 1956, Party declaration of independence from Moscow is only a maneuver. The political process through which the Party has gone since 1929 leaves no possibility of independent action. Changes in the international communist movement, while important, are not in the direction of democratization.

.... See also NELSON, Roger B., and ELL, Jay.

L331 LOVETT, Robert Morss. The Trial of the Communists, "Nation," 111 (Aug. 14, 1920), 185-86.
An account of the background, trial, and conviction of John Reed, William Bross Lloyd, and 18 other founders of the Communist Labor Party under a treason statute in Illinois. No evidence of overt acts to overthrow the government by violence was introduced; defendants were convicted because of their opinions.

L332 .... The Farmer-Labor Fiasco at Chicago, "New Republic," 35 (July 18, 1923), 198-200.
A review of the July 1923 conference called by the Farmer-Labor Party, and a critique of communist strategy there. The conference was taken over by the Workers Party, and a communist-controlled Federated Farmer-Labor Party emerged. Lovett doubts that the FFLP can overcome the suspicion aroused in the labor movement by communist bad faith maneuvering in Chicago.

L333 .... Farmer-Labor-Communist Party, "New Republic," 39 (July 2, 1924), 153-54.
A report on the "Farmer-Labor-Communist Party" convention held in St. Paul, Minnesota, June 17, 1924. After many groups had withdrawn because of the inclusion of communists, the convention nominated two nonentities. The author believes that a working agreement is possible between communists and progressive groups.

L334 .... Witch-Hunting in Massachusetts, "New Republic," 93 (Dec. 1, 1937), 96-97.
A denunciation of the organization and methods employed by the Massachusetts legislature's Committee on Communism and Other Subversive Activities and Propaganda. Questions asked at its hearings were irrelevant and insolent, and more concerned with communist subversion than with fascist tendencies.

L335 .... "All Our Years." New York: Viking, 1948. 373 pp. Ind.
The autobiography of a university professor often characterized as a fellow-traveler. Lovett stresses the need for a united front of socialists and communists in common causes (pp. 259-67) and tells of his work in the American League Against War and Fascism and its successor organization, denying that these were controlled by the communists. The sudden death of other fronts in which he participated made him suspicious of organizations dependent on a foreign power. While disapproving of communists, he asserts that free speech must be preserved.

L336 LOW, Nat. "The Negro in Sports." San Francisco: Daily People's World, n.d. [1948?]. 28 pp.
Pointing to the exceptional record of Negroes in sports, the author asserts that removing Jim Crow from baseball was a job begun by the Communist Party in New York. Asking readers to help, he asserts that the "Daily People's World" (actually the West Coast version of the "Daily Worker") carries on a consistent fight against Jim Crow in West Coast baseball.

L337 LOWE, Victor. A Resurgence of Vicious Intellectualism, "Journal of Philosophy," 48 (July 5, 1951), 435-47.
Opposition to arguments that all members of the Communist Party should be barred from the academic profession. To decide a professor's fitness to teach, one must look at the professor, not be content with an argument from the nature of communism. A hearing should not stop with a determination of Party membership, but should include all relevant evidence. (For criticism by Arthur O. Lovejoy and Sidney Hook, and a rejoinder by Lowe, see "Journal of Philosophy," February 14, 1952, pp. 85-121.)

L338 LOWENTHAL, Max. "The Federal Bureau of Investigation." New York: Sloane, 1950. 559 pp. Notes. Ind.
An exposé of the FBI, focusing on its methods, its antilabor bias, its tendency to investigate opinions and beliefs, and its anticommunist orientation (including all other types of radical thought). FBI activities directed against the IWW and against communists are outlined. The fear is

voiced that the collection in police files of rumors and suspicions represents danger to freedom of thought and speech in the U.S.

L339   LOWRIE, Donald A. America's Middle Way, "Christian Century," 66 (Oct. 26, 1949), 1262-64.
Marxist analysis has never really been applicable to American civilization, because one of the tenets of Americanism is that spiritual values are predominant. We can have a middle way between communism and capitalism by perfecting our social system, giving an effective reply to communism.

L340   LOWRY, Charles Wesley. "Communism and Christ." 3d ed. New York: Morehouse-Gorham, 1953. 177 pp. Bibliog.
A view of communism as a new universal salvation religion based on dialectical materialism as its ultimate dogma. The author looks upon communism's denial of love as antichrist, to be resisted by all possible means. Describing the needs being met by secular religions, he contrasts them with the Christian revolution, with the concept of love as its keystone. He asserts that Christianity remains central to modern democracy and the American way of life.

L341   LOWRY, W. McNeil. Hit and Run—How It Works, "Progressive," 14 (June 1950), 7-11.
A report by a Washington news correspondent on Senator McCarthy's charges that many CP members were employed in the State Department. The report covers the shifting nature of McCarthy's charges, his changes in the number of persons involved, the sources of his information, and his failure to make specific charges where he might be subject to suit for libel.

L342   .... The Price of Security, "Progressive," 15 (July 1951), 13-16.
A discussion by a Washington correspondent of the problem of balancing security with the rights of government employees. Statements by Paul Porter, Senator Paul H. Douglas, Professor William Yandell Elliott of Harvard, Congressman Christian A. Herter, Attorney General J. Howard McGrath, Senator Hubert H. Humphrey, Michael V. DiSalle, and Senator Estes Kefauver are included.

L343   LUCCOCK, Halford E. "American Mirror: Social, Ethical and Religious Aspects of American Literature, 1930-1940." New York: Macmillan, 1940. 300 pp. Ind.
An examination of the literature of the 1930's, viewed as a mirror reflecting current turmoil and conflict, written by a member of the Yale University Divinity School. The author analyzes many of the left-wing novels of the period, along with social drama and social poetry, tracing the influence of Marxism as one of the literary trends of the decade. Among the features of the times were depression, impoverishment, labor struggles, and skepticism about accepted codes and traditions.

L344   LUCE, Clare Boothe; CHAMBERLIN, William Henry; FOSTER, William Z.; and WARD, Harry F. Are Communism and Democracy Mutually Antagonistic? "American Forum of the Air," 8 (May 21, 1946), 1-15.
Representative Luce and Chamberlin assert, and Foster and Ward deny, the antagonism of communism and democracy. Foster views the communist movement as a major bulwark of world democracy. Both Foster and Ward point to American monopoly and imperialism as threats to democracy in the U.S. and throughout the world.

L345   LUCE, Clare Boothe. Doctrine of Communism (condensed from the Brooklyn "Tablet"), "Catholic Digest," 11 (Feb. 1947), 40-43.
A simplified explanation of Marxism and its objectives, as revealed by Russian and American communist leaders.

L346   .... "The Twilight of God." Chicago: Regnery, 1949. 39 pp.
A discussion of the godlessness of communism and of the indifference of Americans to the need to fight it with the Christian spirit. It is because of widespread irrationality and disbelief that communism has reached its present power. Only Christianity and God can prove stronger than the dynamic false faith of communism.

L347   LUCE, Phillip Abbott. "The New Left." New York: McKay, 1966. 214 pp. Ind.
An account of the various groups in the New Left and their programs, by a former member of the Progressive Labor Movement, who asserts that the Old Left has taken the New Left under its wing, subsidized much of it, and molded many young people into active communists. The role of the CPUSA in forming and controlling various youth front groups in recent years is described. The communist New Left condemns the U.S. and demands civil liberties here, while remaining silent on the question of freedom in the socialist states.

L348   LUMER, Hyman. "War Economy and Crisis." New York: International Publishers, 1954. 256 pp. Ref. notes. Ind.
A communist assertion that large-scale military spending in peacetime has become a permanent part of the economy in order to avoid depression and turn the U.S. into a permanent armed camp. The decline in real wages in time of war is contrasted with rising profits and the increased concentration of production and ownership. The only alternative to war and depression, which go hand in hand, are peace and a peacetime economy, for which a broad program is presented. A people's coalition for peace and democracy, directed against the monopolist instigators of war and McCarthyism, is advocated.

L349   .... "The Professional Informer." New York: New Century, 1955. 23 pp.
An exposé of the professional informer used by the Department of Justice to "finger" people accused of communist affiliation, written by a member of the Party's national executive committee. Asserting that informers lie for the sake of money, the author denounces their "communist conspiracy" falsehood and attacks the informer system as a threat to constitutional liberties.

L350   .... "The Promise of Automation and How to Realize It." New York: New Century, 1956. 23 pp.
A communist analysis of automation as leading to technological unemployment, the downgrading of skilled labor, the layoff and the speedup, and a new economic crisis. Though labor must demand a program to alleviate and prevent these conditions, the only real solution is socialism, as in the Soviet Union.

L351   .... The Problem of Inflation, "Political Affairs," 37 (Jan. 1958), 29-39.
Consumer prices are rising, with no apparent excess of demand to force them up. Inflation means growing hardship to workers, farmers, and small businessmen. It should be fought by higher wages, shorter hours, a curb on monopoly price-fixing, lower taxes, and a reduction in military expenditures.

L352   .... On Party Youth Work, "Political Affairs," 38 (June 1959), 1-13.

320

Based on a report presented to the Party's national committee April 26, 1959, and adopted unanimously. The report regrets the dissolution of the Labor Youth League, considers the status of the youth movement, and discusses the need for a socialist youth organization today. The organization should be broad in its appeal, friendly to the Party, and positive in its approach to socialist countries.

L353 LUMER, Hyman. The Economic Recovery in the U.S., "Political Affairs," 38 (July 1959), 1-12.
The recovery of the economy from its recent slump is less glowing than has been painted. A high rate of joblessness persists, foreign trade has declined, and jobs have been exported through American investments in western Europe. A fight for jobs remains important, along with a struggle against increased arms production and a campaign for trade with the socialist world.

L354 . . . . Forty Years of the Communist Party, "Political Affairs," 38 (Sept. 1959), 1-8.
An appraisal of 40 years of Party history, emphasizing the Party's vanguard role, which requires it to master Marxist theory while merging itself with the masses. The Party has been plagued by the right-opportunist evil of revisionism, and also by dogmatism and sectarianism. The key task today is to overcome isolation and rebuild the Party's mass ties.

L355 . . . . "Is Full Employment Possible?" New York: New Century, 1962. 128 pp. Tables. Charts. Ref. notes.
A presentation of the Marxist viewpoint on unemployment, with attention to current joblessness, depressed areas, the effect of automation, and foreign competition and the export of jobs. While permanent full employment is possible only under socialism, unemployment can be reduced by ending the cold war, disarming, and curbing the power of the trusts.

L356 . . . . "Poverty: Its Roots and Its Future." New York: International Publishers, 1965. 127 pp. Bibliog.
A discussion of the definition and extent of poverty in the U.S., the reasons for it, its nature and roots, the poverty of the Negro, depressed areas, and the Administration's antipoverty program. Proposals for dealing with the problems are presented.

L357 LUMPKIN, Grace. "To Make My Bread." New York: Macaulay, 1932. 384 pp.
A novel concerned with the movement of mountain people to the mills, culminating in events like those that occurred in Gastonia. After the heroine is shot during the strike, an indigenous leader urges the workers to join with others to fight for what rightfully belongs to them.

L358 . . . . "A Sign for Cain." New York: Furman, 1935. 376 pp.
A novel of Negro-white relations in the South, emphasizing economic exploitation, segregation, and lynchings. (The author later asserted to a Senate committee that the book contained Party propaganda because of threats by Party book reviewers to destroy her literary career if she followed any other course.)

L359 LUMPKIN, Katharine DuPre, and DOUGLAS, Dorothy Wolff. "Child Workers in America." New York: International Publishers, 1937. 321 pp. App. Ref. Bibliog. Ind.
A study of the extent of child labor in America, in industry, on the streets, in homes, and in agriculture. Child labor is in demand because it increases profits, whereas the supply is due to family poverty. The movement for control of child labor, and the opposition to control, are examined. Child labor can be curbed by direct federal legislation, by measures to relieve family poverty, and by improvements in the school system.

L360 LUMPKIN, Katharine DuPre. "The South in Progress." New York: International Publishers, 1940. 256 pp. Notes. Ind.
A procommunist discussion of problems of the South, including the type of economy, sharecropping, wages, poverty, the condition of Negroes, and hostility to labor organization. The South can forge ahead only under a progressive New Deal program.

L361 LUNDBERG, Ferdinand. Heywood Broun, Fellow-Traveller No. 1 Now Kremlin's Literary Hatchet Man, "New Leader," 22 (March 11, 1939), 5 ff.
An attack on Heywood Broun for following the Communist Party line in his syndicated column without having the courage to tell where he stands openly. The liberals he attacks are those who have come into head-on opposition with the Party. For years Broun has agreed with every twist in the Party line, attacked its enemies, and praised its friends.

L362 . . . . Communist Party Beaten Back on All Fronts, "New Leader," 22 (Sept. 2, 1939), 3.
An assertion that, following the signing of the Soviet-Nazi alliance, the Communist Party is rapidly losing strength here. Liberal individuals and magazines are turning anti-communist, communist fronts are dwindling, and it is a question whether the Party will continue to exist. Browder and his colleagues in the Party leadership are destroyed.

L363 . . . . PM-Crypticism-versus-Crypticism, "New Leader," 25 (June 13, 1942), 4; (June 20), 5 ff; (June 27), 4; (July 4), 4 ff.
A charge that the New York City newspaper "PM," under the editorship of Ralph Ingersoll, follows the Communist Party line, defending the USSR and all groups in the Party's orbit while posing as a progressive paper. The only exception was a strong anti-Axis and prowar position from the fall of 1940, when Marshall Field acquired full financial control, to June 22, 1941. Ingersoll's shift on John L. Lewis, in line with the Party's shift, is one of many examples cited. "PM" portrays Party supporters as lovers of freedom, while opposing any vigilance against the Party as Red-baiting.

L364 LUSCOMB, Florence. An Open Letter to a Member of the ADA, "Monthly Review," 4 (Feb. 1953), 359-63.
The Progressive Party candidate for governor of Massachusetts in 1952 declines to join Americans for Democratic Action because it has made anticommunism a basic plank. Denying that the communists would attempt violence against the government, she asserts that anticommunism, along with other evil results, has gone a long way toward destroying our civil liberties. (Reprinted in pamphlet form with an article by Arthur K. Davis under the title "Red Baiting and Civil Liberties.")

L365 LYND, Albert. Case History, "Commonweal," 25 (Dec. 11, 1936), 181-82.
The case history of a communist sympathizer, an intelligent young woman indignant at injustice, who was attracted to communism because it offered the most thoroughgoing opposition to present society. The pseudo education of young people of good will in secular colleges makes them susceptible to the communist appeal.

L366 . . . . "Quackery in the Public Schools." Boston: Little, Brown, 1953. 282 pp.

An attack on progressive education by a member of the Sharon, Massachusetts, school board, who charges that the progressive educators who control our school system lack the right or competence to suggest goals for society or educational institutions. The author traces John Dewey's influence on progressive education, stating that Dewey's philosophy, though prosocialist, is incompatible with Marxism; many of Dewey's disciples, however, are sympathetic to the USSR.

L367 LYONS, Eugene. Czardom or Democracy? "New Masses," 3 (June 1927), 5-9 ff.
An account of the struggle between right-wing union leaders and the left wing as represented in the Trade Union Educational League. Most attention is focused on the ILGWU, with brief attention to the furriers and others. The right-wing union heads, in their struggle against the rank and file, are supported by the AFL bureaucrats.

L368 . . . . Communist False Fronts, "Scribner's Magazine," 99 (Jan. 1936), 18-23.
An analysis of the Third International's 1935 policy switch to a united front, because of the fascist threat to the Soviet Union. In the U.S. the communist offer of friendship has been rejected by organized labor and the socialists, who long ago lost faith in any communist fair play. The present offer of a united front may be an honest tactic.

L369 . . . . War-Mongering on the Left, "American Mercury," 45 (Nov. 1938), 290-97.
The CPUSA now advocates instant American entry into war to defend the imperialist and colonial interests of Britain, France, and the U.S., provided they fight on the same side as the Soviet Union. This attitude is contrasted with the antiwar position of radicals and liberals in 1914-18.

L370 . . . . It Was Smart to Be Red, "Saturday Evening Post," 212 (Dec. 9, 1939), 25 ff.
A description of the influence of communism in literary and artistic circles before the Nazi-Soviet pact. Until then, there was almost an intellectual Red Terror in the New York area and in Hollywood. Many refused to speak up against Stalinist control because of the character assassination that would follow.

L371 . . . . Mrs. Roosevelt's Youth Congress, "American Mercury," 49 (April 1940), 481-84.
Criticism of Eleanor Roosevelt for lending prestige to the Youth Citizenship Institute of the American Youth Congress, held in Washington, D.C., in February 1940. Mrs. Roosevelt's support made it easier for the communists, in control of the conference, to jam through their views and suppress dissenting opinion.

L372 . . . . President Roosevelt and the Communists, "American Mercury," 50 (June 1940), 234-36.
The sudden end of the love affair between the communists and Roosevelt was the result of the Hitler-Stalin pact. The beginning, just as sudden, was due to Stalin's united front policy. Meanwhile Party members are entrenched in New Deal agencies.

L373 . . . . Strange Case of "PM," "American Mercury," 50 (Aug. 1940), 484-88.
An analysis of the newspaper "PM," which had appeared on the newsstands just ten days before. Lyons comments on the extensive colonization of the staff by communists and fellow-travelers. He traces the genesis of this "uptown edition of the 'Daily Worker,'" identifying procommunists on the staff and accusing the paper of slanting the news.

L374 . . . . "The Red Decade: The Stalinist Penetration of America." New York: Bobbs-Merrill, 1941. 423 pp. Ind.
A critical review of Communist Party activities during the 1930's, covering the sectarian "third period" that ended in 1935, the popular front period of 1935-39, and the Nazi-Soviet pact period of 1939-40. Pointing out that the only constant during this decade of Party-line flip-flops was the defense of the Soviet Union, Lyons elaborates on Party activities in peace, youth, Negro, cultural, labor, and other areas. He discusses the attitude of fellow-travelers toward the Moscow trials and the role of the communists in the Spanish Civil War.

L375 . . . . When Liberalism Went Totalitarian. Pp. 116-34 in "Whose Revolution?" ed. by Irving DeWitt Talmadge. New York: Howell, Soskin, 1941. 296 pp.
A review of liberal opinion in the 1930's, asserting that it blinded itself to the denial of freedom and civil rights in the USSR, condemning as reactionary any criticism of the Kremlin. The Hitler-Stalin pact of August 1939, which touched off World War II, brought many of the misguided liberals to their senses.

L376 . . . . End of the Comintern? "American Mercury," 57 (Aug. 1943), 205-7.
The editor of the "American Mercury" warns that dissolution of the Communist International means nothing if its duties have been transferred to other agencies.

L377 . . . . The Communist Influence in the American Labor Movement, "Commercial and Financial Chronicle," 163 (June 6, 1946), 3053 ff.
An analysis, for business readers, of the current fight between communist and anticommunist forces in the labor movement. Communist leaders already control CIO unions in industries vital to national defense. The communist unions, having zigzagged with the Party line, are now back on a class war basis.

L378 . . . . The Facts Behind "In Fact": Red Mouthpiece, "Plain Talk," 1 (March 1947), 3-13.
An assertion that the newsletter "In Fact" is a Party-line publication; that its editor, George Seldes, is an active fellow-traveler; and that he has concealed these facts from his subscribers, palming off the changing communist propaganda as his own independent views.

L379 . . . . The Myth of Jewish Communism, "Pageant," 3 (April 1947), 20-25.
An assertion that a large number of Jews have been in the forefront of the battle against communism. Although a number of Jews are rank-and-file Party members, there are very few Jewish Party leaders. The myth that communism is a Jewish movement has been fostered both by the Nazis and by reactionary elements in Russia.

L380 . . . . Wallace and the Communists, "American Mercury," 65 (Aug. 1947), 133-40.
Wallace is viewed as the great appeaser, the advocate of peace at any price, who constantly distorts Soviet reality, refusing to face up to its slave labor, its police government, its reign of terror in occupied countries. The communists, because of the Truman Doctrine, seek a third party to siphon off enough Democratic votes to guarantee a Republican victory.

L381 . . . . Who's Hysterical? "American Legion Magazine," 48 (March 1950), 20 ff.
Though the communist and the phony-liberal press assert that we are in the grip of red hysteria, with witch hunts of radicals and with civil liberties repressed, the truth is

that government agencies are infiltrated with Soviet spies, that the House Committee on Un-American Activities is abused and misrepresented, and that accused communists and fellow-travelers have attorneys and defense funds available.

L382 LYONS, Eugene. Lattimore: Dreyfus or Hiss? "New Leader," 33 (Sept. 2, 1950), 16-19.
An evaluation of Owen Lattimore's political views, centered on his book, "Ordeal by Slander." Lyons criticizes reviewers who took the book at face value. He analyzes Lattimore's consistently procommunist record, listing his connections with communist activists and fronts. Lattimore failed to sue when his accusers were not immune.

L383 .... The Men the Commies Hate Most, "American Legion Magazine," 49 (Oct. 1950), 14-15 ff.
A laudatory account of the work of the House Committee on Un-American Activities in investigating communist activities and exposing communists in U.S. employment. Congress' right to investigate is called the essence of democratic government. The Committee, investigating the powerful and secret communist group, has suffered from a hostile administration while it contended with fanatics and expert liars.

L384 .... Our New Privileged Class, "American Legion Magazine," 51 (Sept. 1951), 11-13 ff.
Cases of procommunists and anticommunists who have lost their jobs because of their convictions or attitudes are contrasted to show that public opinion is always aroused on behalf of the former but seldom of the latter. Illustrations are drawn from Hollywood, the ministry, academic life, government service, and journalism. The reason is the existence of Party-line defense groups such as the Civil Rights Congress to help publicize the case of the procommunist.

L385 .... What to Do with the Ex-Communist, "New Leader," 34 (Dec. 3, 1951), 16-18.
A plea for sympathetic, though cautious, reception of the ex-communist. Both fellow-travelers and old Red-baiters are too vindictive toward converts from Stalinism where compassion and understanding are called for. We should try to understand their natural distaste for denouncing former friends and comrades by name.

L386 .... Hysteria and the "Times": A Case Study in Journalism, "American Mercury," 80 (April 1955), 65-70.
A denunciation of the New York "Times" for asserting that the U.S. is in the throes of an ugly and dangerous hysteria. This nonsense, started by communists, has been taken up by liberals all over the country, and particularly by the "Times." A better case could be made for complacency than for panic.

L387 .... How Red the Decade? "American Mercury," 81 (Nov. 1955), 93-98.
An attack on "anti-anticommunists" who seek, belatedly, to soft-pedal the "redness" of the 1930's. The author discusses in particular an attack by Granville Hicks ("Harper's Magazine," July 1953) on Lyons' book "The Red Decade." This attack was aimed, not at the book's facts, but at its evaluation. Lyons suggests that Hicks' evaluation, not his own, is distorted.

L388 .... This Mean-Spirited Decade, "New Leader," 39 (Jan. 30, 1956), 18-19.
Replying to an attack on informers by Edward Shils, the author defends ex-communists who have given personal testimony about the Kremlin-directed conspiracy to destroy this country, and criticizes Shils' blanket denunciation of them.

L389 .... An Open Letter to Howard Fast, "New Leader," 39 (July 9, 1956), 6-8.
A letter reviewing Fast's column in the "Daily Worker" of June 12, which describes Fast's shock on reading Khrushchev's revelations about Stalin's regime. Though praising Fast's courage, Lyons asserts that his column is filled with routine communist self-deception. He urges Fast to break out of the world of communist alibis and rejoin the world of free men.

L390 .... Why the Reds are Gaining in America, "American Legion Magazine," 67 (Oct. 1959), 18-19 ff.
An assertion that American communism, despite its loss of membership, is growing stronger and more dynamic. Our vigilance against the communist menace is collapsing, the result of apathy. Meanwhile communist prestige is growing, accompanying Soviet military power and technological achievement. The current tactic of the communists here is a revived united front.

M

M1   MacDONALD, Andrew. How to Whip the Commies, "American Federationist," 54 (Oct. 1947), 16-17 ff.
The general chairman of the Radio Officers Union sketches his union's long fight against the communists, who took over the union of marine radio officers during the depression; the communists then purged their opponents. The Radio Officers Union, chartered by the AFL, has defeated the communists by getting better contracts. (Also published in "American Flint," November 1947.)

M2   MACDONALD, Dwight. "Henry Wallace: The Man and the Myth." New York: Vanguard, 1948. 187 pp. App. Postscript. Ref.
A critical view of Wallace, expanding on two articles that originally appeared in "Politics" in March-April and May-June 1947. The author argues that the real Wallace is a split personality, combining principle and opportunism, and contradicting himself incessantly. Wallace's pro-Russian views, beginning during World War II, seek to fill the political vacuum left by Roosevelt's wartime abandonment of the New Deal. Wallace has increasingly isolated himself from the once friendly liberal and labor movements, which are anti-Stalinist.

M3   . . . . The Wallace Campaign: An Autopsy, "Politics," 5 (Summer 1948), 178-88.
An analysis of the 1948 Progressive Party campaign, documenting Stalinist control of the convention and the campaign. The original purpose was to defeat the Marshall Plan; when this failed, the campaign supported the Soviet Union on other foreign policy issues.

M4   . . . . The Waldorf Conference, "Politics," 6 (Winter 1949), special insert, 32A-32D.
A critique of the Cultural and Scientific Conference for World Peace, held in New York City, March 26 and 27, 1949. The author, who was a delegate, concludes that the Conference was a front operation of the CP. The anticommunist left exposed the Conference as a front, through organization of an ad hoc group, Americans for Intellectual Freedom.

M5   MacDOUGAL, Donald. Unmasking the New Deal in the Cotton Patch, "Communist," 14 (May 1935), 459-69.
Discussion of the economic slavery of the Southern sharecropper and tenant and denunciation of the Bankhead bill intended to change tenants, sharecroppers, and laborers into small owners. The communist alternative, the farmers' emergency relief bill, is praised.

M6   MacGILLIVRAY, Arthur. Communist Influence in the New Poetry, "America," 60 (Feb. 18, 1939), 475-76.
The communists view literature as an important field of propaganda. Their poetry is the expression of disgruntled and exploited America, easily duped by the promise that so-called freedom under capitalism can be changed into a glorious freedom under communism, with material benefits.

M7   MacIVER, Robert M. "Academic Freedom in Our Time." New York: Columbia University Press, 1955. 320 pp. App. Bibliog. Ind.
A discussion of academic freedom in the U.S., including the rights and responsibilities of the educator and the place of the university in the social order. In chapter 11, devoted to the problem of communism, the author concludes that one who accepts the Party's principles without reservation is not fit to teach, though other factors must be considered before all communists are barred from teaching or any communist teachers dismissed. Any purge has perils, including an effect on students. The author outlines the principles that should be followed in dealing with communism on the campus.

M8   MACKAY, John A. "A Letter to Presbyterians Concerning the Present Situation in Our Country and in the World." Philadelphia: Office of the Presbyterian General Assembly, 1953, 7 pp.
The chairman of the Presbyterian General Council condemns our obsession with the threat of communism, blames it for an atmosphere of disquiet and an assault upon basic human rights, and warns against hatred of communism becoming hatred of individuals or whole nations. He calls for negotiation, reason, and support of the UN.

M9   MacLEISH, Archibald. Liberalism and the Anti-Fascist Front, "Survey Graphic," 28 (May 1939), 321-23.
A proposal by a leading poet that liberals adopt a prodemocratic policy in the current international situation, rather than the negative antifascist policy of the Communist Party. Liberals are urged to put irresponsible self-righteousness aside and to support action toward dynamic democracy.

M10   MADISON, Charles A. "American Labor Leaders: Personalities and Forces in the Labor Movement." New York: Harper, 1950. 474 pp. Bibliog. Ind.
A collection of biographies of prominent labor leaders, including Gompers, Green, Hutcheson, Mitchell, Lewis, Dubinsky, Whitney, Haywood, Murray, Hillman, Reuther, and Bridges. The expulsion of the communist-controlled unions from the CIO is treated in the chapter on Murray (pp. 326-33). The conflict within the ILGWU between right and left wings is discussed (pp. 215-21), as is the government's effort to deport Bridges as an alleged communist (pp. 414-21). While praising Bridges highly, the author criticizes the ILGWU leadership for an almost pathological dread of communists (p. 231) and attacks Reuther for "spleen" and "peevishness" in his attacks on leftist leaders at the 1948 CIO convention and for his relentless war on communists within the UAW (p. 402).

M11   MAGIL, A. B. The "Marxism" of V. F. Calverton, "Communist," 8 (May 1929), 282-85.
A criticism of Calverton's article "Revolt among American Intellectuals," which appeared in the April "New Masses," as an example of petty-bourgeois rather than Marxist thinking, because of its complete disregard of the class character of literature. Calverton is said to have a

shallow, pseudorevolutionary approach to literature and society.

M12 MAGIL, A. B., and NORTH, Joseph. "Steve Katovis: Life and Death of a Worker." New York: International Publishers, 1930. 31 pp.
An idealized biography of a Greek immigrant, an active member of the Communist Party, who was shot on a picket line of the Food Workers' Industrial Union. A member of the Building Maintenance Workers' Union of the TUUL, Katovis was also active in other Party-oriented organizations, and was planning to go to the USSR when he was killed.

M13 MAGIL, A. B. Toward Social-Fascism—The "Rejuvenation" of the Socialist Party, "Communist," 9 (April 1930), 309-20; (May), 462-68.
An application to the Socialist Party of the theory of social fascism. Its manifestations are found in the ILGWU, where finance capital and the police have been used to turn it into a company union. The Socialist Party has been rejuvenated by the capitalist class, as is shown by Norman Thomas' increased vote for mayor of New York in November 1929.

M14 .... Pity and Terror, "New Masses," 8 (Dec. 1932), 16-19.
A rejoinder to Philip Rahv's "The Literary Class War," in "New Masses," August 1932. While Rahv's theory of the psychology of consumption has some Marxist basis, his attitude toward literary fellow-travelers is more "leftist" than that adopted by the League of Revolutionary Writers at Kharkov. It reflects a lack of faith in the proletarian literary movement.

M15 .... "The Truth about Father Coughlin." New York: Workers Library, 1935. 47 pp.
A "third period" view of Father Coughlin and his National Union for Social Justice as fascist—cooperating with industrialists, attacking Jews, and working with the New Deal, itself a step toward fascism. Workers are urged, instead of following him, to seek to build a new society under the leadership of the Communist Party.

M16 .... "The People's Message to Congress." New York: Workers Library, 1938. 31 pp.
A picture of America during the depression, stressing the plight of labor, the unemployed, farmers, and the Negro people. A legislative program dealing with wages, WPA, farm relief, housing, social security, the trusts, taxation, and peace is advocated.

M17 ..., and STEVENS, Henry. "The Peril of Fascism: The Crisis of American Democracy." New York: International Publishers, 1938. 319 pp. Ref. notes. Ind.
An assertion that America is in a crisis, with a serious threat of fascism. Fascist forces here include economic royalists, reactionary Republicans, southern Bourbon Democrats, the American Liberty League, the Coughlin movement, the Ku Klux Klan, the Black Legion, professional patriots, and Trotskyites—all of them in the service of Big Business. Fascism, a product of capitalist decay, is a terrorist dictatorship of the most predatory sections of the capitalist class, with mass support from the impoverished middle classes and demoralized workers. The authors call for a single democratic front of all who are for progress and against fascism and war.

M18 .... Communism and Democracy: The Tenth Convention of the Communist Party, "New Masses," 27 (June 14, 1938), 14-17.
A report on the Party convention recently held in New York City. Its central emphasis was unity—of the labor movement, and of the entire American people, to defeat Big Business reaction. The Party has grown from 40,000 to 75,000 in two years; most convention delegates were American-born and industrial workers. The convention was more democratic than that of any other American political party.

M19 .... "The Real Father Coughlin." New York: Workers Library, 1939. 31 pp.
Father Coughlin is pictured as the chief mouthpiece of un-American, anti-Christian incitements against Jews; behind Coughlin are said to stand overlords of finance and industry, counterparts of the German industrialists who placed Hitler in power. Readers are urged to unite with the Communist Party against Coughlinism and the fascist danger it represents.

M20 .... "America Needs Earl Browder." New York: Workers Library, 1941. 15 pp.
A plea for the release of Earl Browder from federal prison, where he was sent for what this communist calls a "passport technicality."

M21 .... "Battle for America." New York: International Publishers, 1943. 48 pp. Ref. notes.
A reinterpretation of American history by a communist publicist, written during the Party's win-the-war phase. All who oppose a second front and an all-out production effort are condemned as monopolistic appeasers, outside the tradition of the American Revolution.

M22 .... "PM" and the Communists, "New Masses," 51 (April 11, 1944), 15-17.
A denunciation of the newspaper "PM" for a series of articles by Harold Lavine on the abolition of the Comintern. Issue is taken with the contents of the article, with Lavine's manner of quoting and writing, and with editor Max Lerner's use of Dies' ideology and methods against the Party.

M23 .... Where do the Liberals Go From Here? "New Masses," 54 (Jan. 23, 1945), 9-12.
A communist call, in the period of the Communist Political Association, for continued Big Three cooperation in the Teheran spirit and for maximum unity behind Roosevelt. The leading question regarding national unity is whether Big Business groups will follow their more progressive leaders in support of full employment and international prosperity.

M24 .... Roosevelt—Architect of American-Soviet Friendship, "Political Affairs," 24 (June 1945), 501-10.
A review of American-Soviet relations, which have become steadily closer since Roosevelt gave diplomatic recognition to Russia. The American delegation at the San Francisco conference is criticized for repudiating Roosevelt's policies in its stand on the Polish question.

M25 .... Speaking of Socialism, "New Masses," 57 (Oct. 2, 1945), 30-31.
An assertion that unemployment in the free-enterprise system contrasts unfavorably with the full employment possible under socialism.

M26 .... "Socialism: What's in It for You." New York: New Century, 1946. 64 pp.
A communist analysis of the contradictions in the capitalist system, and of the superiority of the USSR to the U.S. with regard to unemployment, education, etc. Criticisms of socialism with respect to incentives, freedom, religion, and democracy are answered. Formation of an antifascist and antimonopoly people's party is advocated; at the same

time the Communist Party must be built to achieve socialism.

M27 MAGIL, A. B. Reveille for Progressives, "New Masses," 62 (Jan. 14, 1947), 3-6.
An account of the formation of the Progressive Citizens of America by a merger of earlier groups. The new organization severely criticized the Democratic Party, serving notice that a new party may be necessary. Problems that stand in the way of forming an effective people's political coalition are discussed.

M28 .... Progressive Unity or Division? "New Masses," 62 (Jan. 28, 1947), 6-9.
Communist criticism of the newly formed Americans for Democratic Action for excluding communists and communist sympathizers, equating them with fascists. Communists believe in a superior brand of democracy and freedom, the socialist brand. A united progressivism would mean a political coalition out of which a new people's party could come.

M29 .... Schwellenbach Meant You, "New Masses," 62 (March 25, 1947), 3-6.
An assertion by a prominent communist that the proposal by Secretary of Labor Schwellenbach that the Communist Party be outlawed is the domestic part of a program for an American Century and an American Reich. Unionism will be outlawed next, and then all democracy will be stamped out. This reactionary course is dictated by monopolists who use violence against their workers and finance native fascists. The Party opposes forcible overthrow of government.

M30 .... Little Man, Big Lie, "New Masses," 63 (April 15, 1947), 6-9.
A reply to an anticommunist article by ex-Senator Robert M. La Follette, Jr. (See "Turn the Light on Communism," in "Collier's," February 8, 1947.) La Follette is accused of Red-baiting, distortions, and fabrications, and charged with betraying the liberal tradition and his father's name.

M31 .... Class Forces in Israel's Fight for Independence, "Political Affairs," 28 (March 1949), 72-86.
Communist criticism of Israel's independence struggle as under bourgeois leadership, utilizing reactionary social democracy to obtain mass support. American imperialism has supplanted Britain as the foremost enemy of Israel and of all Middle East people.

M32 .... "Israel in Crisis." New York: International Publishers, 1950. 224 pp. Ref. notes. Gloss. Ind.
A report on Israel by a veteran communist newspaper correspondent following a six-month stay there. He deals, among other topics, with Israeli political parties, the role of the labor movement and religion in the country's political life, and the relationship of Israel to world Jewry. His main theme is the threat of imperialism to Israel's independence, and the struggle of anti-imperialist forces against Anglo-American efforts to dominate the new nation's economy and politics.

M33 .... Wall Street, Zionism and Anti-Semitism, "Masses & Mainstream," 6 (March 1953), 12-27.
This attack on those who charge the USSR with anti-Semitism asserts that the recent Prague trials and the arrest of the Moscow doctors exposed agents of Zionist espionage. Communism opposes Zionism but abhors anti-Semitism. The author presents the case against Zionism and its espionage activities in the USSR.

M34 .... Government by Frameup, "Masses & Mainstream," 6 (Dec. 1953), 2-12.
An exposé of the frame-up charges against Harry Dexter White, a government economist accused of being a Soviet spy. Attorney General Brownell's charge that Truman knowingly promoted a spy shows that the drive toward fascism now seeks to destroy all opposition. There are signs of a counteroffensive, in which the role of the labor movement will be decisive.

M35 .... On the Struggle for Peace in the United States, "Political Affairs," 34 (Jan. 1955), 4-16.
Eisenhower supports imperialist expansionism and a war for world domination. The McCarthyite-Knowland, profascist, prowar Republican wing is seeking party control. The Democratic Party, the alternative party of Wall Street, supports the Eisenhower policy. Labor and the people must advance the independent fight for peace.

M36 .... "Crisis in the Middle East: Which Way Israel?" New York: New Century, 1956. 23 pp.
A communist view of problems of the Middle East in the cold war period. Attacking American and British oil trusts for seeking to make Israel part of Wall Street's economic empire, the author applauds the rise of Arab nationalist feeling and the strengthening of Arab relationships with the USSR. Israel is urged to negotiate on the Arab refugee problem and to become neutral in the East-West conflict.

M37 MAGNUS, Edward. "Professionals in a Soviet America." New York: Workers Library, 1935. 38 pp.
A picture of Utopia for professionals in a Soviet America, with a cultural and professional upsurge, public welfare and housing, and justice in the courts for all. Allaying any professional fears about leadership of the working class in a proletarian dictatorship, the author urges professionals to work through the Communist Party and specific professional organizations.

M38 MAGNUSON, Warren G., and MUNDT, Karl E. (George V. Denny, Jr., moderator). Are We Fighting Communism Wisely? "Town Meeting," 16 (June 6, 1950). 16 pp.
Senator Mundt of South Dakota charges the Administration with a patchwork program of inaction and timidity, both at home and abroad, with regard to the communist threat, and urges weeding communists out of the government. Defending the Administration, Senator Magnuson of Washington calls its program to reduce insecurity the best way to eliminate the breeding places of communism. He opposes substituting a witch hunt for a constructive program.

M39 MAHAN, Lawrence. "Who Are the Foreign Agents?" New York: Communist Party, USA, 1948. 15 pp.
A reprint of a radio broadcast, May 17, 1948, by the secretary of the Party in New Jersey, attacking the view in the Mundt bill, currently before Congress, that communists are foreign agents. The real foreign agents here are appeasers and financiers of Hirohito and Hitler, agents of Chiang Kai-shek, and European fascists and reactionaries.

M40 "MAINSTREAM," Painters and the Left, 10 (Aug. 1957), 1-7.
A group of progressive painters in California protest the replacement of aesthetic by political judgments, specifically condemning "Realism in Art," by Sidney Finkelstein, as an example of this type of criticism. In his study, they say, Finkelstein looks for work that will fit his conception of realism, seeing representative art as good and abstractions as bad.

M41 MALENKOF, G. M. "On the Threshold of Communism: Report to the XIXth Congress of the CPSU." New York: New Century, 1952. 94 pp. Appears also, in part, in "Political Affairs," Oct. 1952, pp. 6-17.
The main report to the Nineteenth Party Congress of the Communist Party of the Soviet Union, in which the secretary of the CPSU lays down a new line in international affairs, calling for peaceful coexistence of the USSR with capitalist states and emphasizing the building of united fronts and an antiwar coalition rather than the overthrow of capitalism. (The American Party, like all others accepting Moscow's discipline, had no choice but to adopt this line immediately.)

M42 MALLERY, David. "Teaching About Communism: A Definition of the Problem and a Description of Some Practices." Boston: National Association of Independent Schools, 1962. 72 pp.
There is now pressure to teach about communism in the schools. Communist societies should be studied in historical perspective. Students, suspicious of an adult "line," can be challenged to engage in free, independent exploration.

M43 MALLORY, Jim. Class War in Alabama, "Labor Unity," 9 (June 1934), 11-15.
An account of a wave of strikes in Alabama for the right to organize and for wages equal to those in the North and West. The AFL misleaders are supported by the bosses against left-wing influence, and sheriffs, troops, and company thugs are used against strikers. Workers are seeing the treachery of AFL officials and learning the need for rank-and-file control, Negro equality, and militant struggle.

M44 MALONE, Ross L. The Communist Resolutions: What the House of Delegates Really Did, "American Bar Association Journal," 45 (April 1959), 343-47.
An explanation by the president of the American Bar Association of the meaning of five resolutions offered by the Association's Committee on Communist Tactics, Strategy and Objectives, and approved by the House of Delegates in February. The resolutions dealt with the communist threat to internal security, the position of the Supreme Court as the final guardian of our liberties, and improvements in the procedure of congressional committees. (The resolutions, with accompanying discussion, appear on pages 406-10.)

M45 MALTZ, Albert. "The Underground Stream." Boston: Little, Brown, 1940. 348 pp.
A procommunist novel concerned with the life of a Party member and the basis of his faith. The action is a struggle between a hard-working but impulsive communist organizer in a Detroit automobile factory and the company personnel director, who belongs to a fascist group.

M46 . . . . What Shall We Ask of Writers? "New Masses," 58 (Feb. 12, 1946), 19-22.
An assertion that left-wing artistic activity has suffered from a too shallow approach to art. The "art-is-a-weapon" slogan has been vulgarized so that creative works have been judged primarily by their formal ideology, without appreciation of artistic content. The results have been bad art, plus the failure of much left-wing talent to mature. (Publication of these views led to a barrage of criticism by followers of the Party line.)

M47 . . . . Moving Forward, "New Masses," 49 (April 9, 1946), 8-10 ff.
An abject retraction of and apology for the views expressed in "What Shall We Ask of Writers?" "New Masses," February 12, 1946), following vigorous criticism by such leading literary Party-liners as Joseph North, Howard Fast, Alvah Bessie, and John Howard Lawson. Agreeing with his critics, Maltz now asserts that his earlier views were distorted, nondialectical, and revisionist.

M48 . . . . "The Citizen Writer." New York: International Publishers, 1950. 48 pp.
Speeches and articles on a writer's relationship to humanity and to his conscience. Two items emphasize the writer's role as the conscience of the people, and most of the remainder protest thought control by the House Committee on Un-American Activities, its questioning of the author's political beliefs, its invasion of the right of citizens, and its conspiracy against civil liberties.

M49 MALTZ, Margaret. Screen for Conquest, "Masses & Mainstream," 3 (Oct. 1950), 72-76.
A speech by the wife of Albert Maltz, protesting the jailing of her husband and the others of the Hollywood Ten who defied the Thomas committee and were sent to jail for contempt. She sees the blacklist of the Ten as an attempt to intimidate all intellectuals, to prevent them from using their gifts as organizers for peace.

M50 MANCHESTER, William. The Case of Luella Mundel, "Harper's Magazine," 204 (May 1952), 54-61.
The case of an art teacher at Fairmont State College, Fairmont, West Virginia, who was dismissed on vague charges of communism and atheism, the result of asking critical questions at an American Legion "Americanism seminar" addressed by several ex-communists. Her damage suit for slander against the board member who made the charges is described.

M51 MANDEL, William. "Man Bites Dog: Report of an Unusual Hearing before the McCarran Committee." New York: "National Guardian," 1952. 22 pp.
An active communist's account of his appearance before the McCarran investigating committee. Portions of the hearing transcript are presented, interspersed with explanations and elaborations of the author's views. The author defends the peaceful intentions of the USSR, supports the Moscow trials, and denies the existence of slave-labor camps in Russia.

M52 . . . . "Mandel vs. McCarthy." New York: "National Guardian," 1953, 23 pp.
Part of the record of Mandel's appearance before the McCarthy committee in March 1953. Mandel's exchanges with Senator McCarthy, Roy Cohn, and Senator Dirksen are interspersed with explanatory notes, commentary, and editorial comment. The author, an active communist, states that the Korean War is unjust, that the Attorney General's list violates the Constitution, and that the execution of the Rosenbergs in peacetime is unjustified.

M53 MANDELBAUM, Seymour J. "The Social Setting of Intolerance: The Know-Nothings, The Red Scare, and McCarthyism." Chicago: Scott, Foresman, 1964. 176 pp.
A volume in the Scott, Foresman series on "Problems in American History," organizing source materials around a facet of the nation's past. Each section contains an introduction by the author, followed by a collection of source materials. Pages 96-110 deal with the Palmer Raids of 1919-20 and an evaluation of the red scare of that period. The unit on McCarthyism (pp. 117-76) covers the demand for loyalty, McCarthy's charges, the problem of testifying, and an evaluation of McCarthyism.

M54 MANGOLD, William P. Forming a People's Front, "New Republic," 85 (Jan. 22, 1936), 310-11.

An enthusiastic report on the Third Congress of the American League Against War and Fascism, held in Cleveland on January 3, 1936. The wide appeal of the League is stressed, while the suspicion of some that the League was merely an instrument of the Communist Party is declared groundless.

M55 MANGOLD, William P. The Communist Convention, "New Republic," 87 (July 15, 1936), 292.
An enthusiastic report on the recently held ninth convention (the first public convention) of the CPUSA. Emphasis is placed on the youth, native birth, and proletarian origin of the bulk of the delegates, and on the stressing of the American revolutionary tradition.

M56 MANION, Clarence. We Fight Communism in the Wrong Places, "American Mercury," 85 (Dec. 1957), 58-62.
It is unlikely that the communists will ever attack the U.S. with bombs. They hope to take over the U.S. by weakening legislation against themselves, by undercutting the FBI and loyalty tests, and by promoting the idea that they are just another political party.

M57 MANLEY, Joseph. Anthracite, "Workers Monthly," 4 (Feb. 1925), 177-78.
A description of conditions in the anthracite coal fields, with support for the "outlaw" strike of the miners. The anthracite monopoly is attacked, as is the class-collaboration policy of the district and international union officers. Immediate demands, along with nationalization of the industry, are proposed.

M58 MANLY, Chesly. "The Twenty-Year Revolution: from Roosevelt to Eisenhower." Chicago: Regnery, 1954. 272 pp. Ind.
An attack upon both Democratic and Republican administrations of the past 20 years from a right-wing source, who asserts that communists and socialists have infiltrated the government, labor unions, schools, churches, radio and television, movies, and publishing. The primary menace to the U.S. is held to be, not the Soviet military threat, but internal subversion through control of foreign policy and related armaments programs. Big government, high taxing and spending programs, and inflation are associated with the leftist conspiracy.

M59 MANN, Charles P. Mr. I. F. Stone and the Negro Question, "Political Affairs," 31 (March 1952), 22-33.
A critical examination of "Who Will Free the Negroes?" by I. F. Stone, in the February 17, 1952, issue of the New York "Compass." Stone is commended for recognizing the Negroes' national character, but criticized for failing to locate the nation geographically, for offering no strategy to bring freedom, and for expressing defeatist attitudes.

M60 .... "Stalin's Thought Illuminates Problems of Negro Freedom Struggle." New York: National Education Dept., Communist Party, U.S.A., 1953. 47 pp. Mimeo. App.
A discussion outline on the Negro question for Party clubs and classes, with many quotations from Lenin and Stalin. Negroes in the U.S. are held to be a nation, entitled to self-determination. The class nature of Negro objectives is stressed, as is the point that only socialism can solve Negro problems. White chauvinism within the Party is attacked.

M61 ..., and BROWN, Wilbur H. "The South Today, and Labor's Tasks, "Political Affairs," 32 (Oct. 1953), 31-49.
An account of economic problems in the South, both in industry and agriculture, with an appeal for the organization of workers and farmers and for the elimination of the North-South wage differential. (A chapter from a planned larger work, "The Economic and Political Situation in the South Today.")

M62 MANN, Robert. "From Korean Truce to World Peace." New York: New York State Communist Party, n.d. [1953]. 16 pp.
A communist assertion that the Korean truce raises the question of why the world powers do not negotiate an end to the cold war. The pamphlet argues for peaceful coexistence, opposing the view of capitalists and militarists that war is inevitable. McCarthyism and Red-baiting are viewed as obstacles to world peace.

M63 MANN, W. Howard. Security and the Constitution, "Current History," 29 (Oct. 1955), 236-46.
A law professor at Indiana University examines the problem of internal security in the light of the Constitution and our legal traditions. He reviews the early sedition cases, the Espionage Act of 1917, the noncommunist oath under the Taft-Hartley Act, and the Smith Act of 1940. Cases arising under these laws are discussed. (This is an article in a special issue on security in a free society.)

M64 MANZON, Maximo C. "The Strange Case of the Filipinos in the United States." New York: American Committee for Protection of Foreign Born, 1938. 23 pp.
This publication by a communist-front organization depicts the sad plight of Filipinos in this country, who cannot become citizens and are treated as aliens, yet lack the national status of other foreign nationals and consequently suffer discrimination and injustice. The amendment of naturalization laws is urged to make all Filipinos eligible for American citizenship if they desire it.

M65 MARCANTONIO, Vito. "Labor's Martyrs: Haymarket, 1887, Sacco and Vanzetti, 1927." Introd. by William Z. Foster. New York: Workers Library, 1937. 15 pp.
The president of the International Labor Defense retells the story of these martyrs, calling upon all American progressives to honor their memories by helping to fight reaction and bigotry and by protecting the victims of the present and future.

M66 .... "We Accuse: The Story of Tom Mooney." New York: International Labor Defense, 1938. 31 pp.
A demand for the release of Mooney and Billings, telling the story of their imprisonment, the frame-up that took place, and the injustice that resulted. Freedom for Mooney, according to the Republican congressman who chaired the Party-controlled ILD, would be a staggering blow to reaction.

M67 .... "The Registration of Aliens." Introd. by Carey McWilliams. New York: American Committee for Protection of Foreign Born, 1940. 13 pp.
A protest against the Alien Registration Act of 1940 because it is the result of war hysteria leading to the destruction of free institutions and a step toward war. The law is attacked as malicious discrimination against the foreign born.

M68 .... "Congressman Vito Marcantonio Speaks Out Against This War." New York: American Peace Mobilization, n.d. [1941]. 7 pp.
A reprint from the "Congressional Record" of Marcantonio's speech opposing the lend-lease bill as an effort to launch a war for imperialism, both British and American.

He sees only a difference in degree between the tyranny of Hitler and the imperialism of Britain. (His argument is consistent with the Party's line during the Hitler-Stalin pact period.)

M69   MARCANTONIO, Vito. "Marcantonio Answers F.D.R.!" New York: American Peace Mobilization, 1941. 8 pp.
A radio speech during the period of the Hitler-Stalin pact, delivered by the congressman from New York who also served as president of the Party-sponsored International Labor Defense. Marcantonio accuses President Roosevelt of employing fear and deception to further his war scheme.

M70   . . . . "Should America Go To War?" New York: American People's Mobilization, n.d. [1941]. 15 pp.
A speech by Representative Marcantonio in the House, arguing that the invasion of the Soviet Union by Hitler in June 1941 has transformed an imperialist war into a war of national defense. Marcantonio argues that the defeat of the Soviet Union would place Hitler near Alaska and guarantee the defeat of the U.S., and that the interests of the U.S. and the USSR are interdependent.

M71   . . . . Trust the People! "Masses & Mainstream," 3 (Oct. 1950), 10-18.
Remarks of Congressman Vito Marcantonio (American Labor Party, New York), opposing antisedition bills. A parallel is seen between these bills and laws of fascist Germany and Italy. The work of the Civil Rights Congress is praised.

M72   . . . . "The Other Evil: The Truth about the 1952 Elections." New York: American Labor Party, 1952. 22 pp.
Adapted from a speech at an American Labor Party rally in October 1952 supporting Progressive Party candidates Vincent Hallinan for President and Charlotta Bass for Vice-President. Marcantonio criticizes both the Republican and Democratic parties for seeking to continue the Korean War and fearing peace; this leads them to similar positions on civil rights, Taft-Hartley, and McCarthyism.

M73   . . . . "I Vote My Conscience: Debates, Speeches and Writings of Vito Marcantonio, 1935-1950." Ed. by Annette T. Rubinstein and associates. New York: Vito Marcantonio Memorial, 1956. 494 pp. Ind.
Selections from the speeches and writings of the lawyer from East Harlem who represented his district in Congress from 1935 to 1950, except for one term. First a liberal Republican and then a leader of the American Labor Party, Marcantonio was connected with various Party fronts, serving as president of the International Labor Defense. Pages 441-82 reproduce parts of his arguments in court, addresses to the juries, or briefs in defense of W. E. B. DuBois of the Peace Information Center, William L. Patterson of the Civil Rights Congress, Ben Gold of the International Fur and Leather Workers Union, and the CPUSA.

M74   MARCHE, Henri. Communist Tactics—Phony and Real, "Reporter," 3 (Oct. 10, 1950), 31-33.
A Frenchman asserts that Western communist parties are window dressing to divert our attention from the real Soviet hidden agents. Repressive action against the communist parties would serve the Kremlin by equating everything not Soviet with fascism.

M75   MARDER, Murrey. The Fort Monmouth Story, "Bulletin of the Atomic Scientists," 10 (Jan. 1954), 21-25.
A report on the investigation by Senator McCarthy's subcommittee into alleged espionage at Fort Monmouth. Sample charges are reproduced, showing instances of guilt by association. Charges of espionage have been unproved, and many persons have been harmed by irresponsible accusations. (Condensed from a series of articles in the Washington "Post.")

M76   MARIN, C. S. The Campaign for the Federal Arts Bill, "Communist," 17 (June 1938), 562-70.
A discussion of the proposed federal arts legislation and a review of successful WPA arts projects. The Party will campaign for government support for cultural projects.

M77   MARINE WORKERS INDUSTRIAL UNION. "The Point Gorda Strike." New York: MWIU, n.d. 23 pp.
An account of the strike of the crew of a freighter against intolerable conditions, led by the Ship Committee and based on the day-to-day work of the Ship Delegate. The strike is called the first organized struggle on American ships in seven years. Lessons of the strike are outlined for use in other marine struggles. (The Marine Workers Industrial Union was an affiliate of the communist-led Trade Union Unity League.)

M78   . . . . "Centralized Shipping Bureau: Workers' Control of Hiring." New York: MWIU, 1934. 32 pp.
The case for workers' control of the hiring of marine workers, presented by an affiliate of the Party-controlled Trade Union Unity League. Workers' control of hiring, for which the union is leading a united-front fight, will smash the blacklist and racketeering. Experiences in the port of Baltimore are told about in detail.

MARINI, F. See BROWN, Fred.

M79   MARION, George. "The 'Free Press': Portrait of a Monopoly." New York: New Century, 1946. 48 pp.
An exposé of the American press, asserting that the industry is monopolistic and that only multimillionaires can enter the field. The press is seen as belonging to the state apparatus, and newsmen stationed abroad as forming part of a network of capitalist contacts and intelligence agents. The monopolistic Associated Press is contrasted with the democratic and truly free press of the Soviet Union.

M80   . . . . "Bases and Empire: A Chart of American Expansion." New York: Fairplay Publishers, 1948. 199 pp.
An American Marxist's view of world affairs today, refuting the view that Russia is responsible for the cold war. The U.S. is charged with forcibly spreading its military power over the globe and with provoking civil wars and world unrest by aggressive expansion. Attacking the Truman Doctrine and the Marshall Plan, the author calls for a return to the spirit of Roosevelt's policies and to the settlement with Russia reached at Teheran and Yalta.

M81   . . . . "The Communist Trial: An American Crossroads." New York: Fairplay Publishers, 1949. 192 pp.
A denunciation of the manner in which "class justice" was meted out to the 11 communists on trial under the Smith Act. The author attacks the "gross prejudice" of Judge Medina and denounces the stool pigeons who testified against the defendants. He asserts that justice is denied Negroes and workers, that the Smith Act was passed by trickery, and that the trial was a farce.

M82   . . . . Memo for Medina, "Masses & Mainstream," 2 (Dec. 1949), 3-10.

A review of judicial decisions regarding bail in the case of the 11 communist defendants tried under the Smith Act in New York City. The prosecution, in effect, sought without success a pretrial ban on communist activity as a condition of granting bail.

M83   MARION, George. Author Meets Critic, "Masses & Mainstream," 4 (July 1951), 11-18.
An analysis of the book-publishing monopoly, charging that it is the cleverest and most complete censorship known to the world. The channels of publication are closed to those holding unorthodox views. We must rely upon our own resources, not look to the Big Business press, for aid in a battle against Big Business.

M84   .... "Stop the Press!" Introd. by Howard Fast. New York: Fairplay Publishers, 1953. 224 pp.
A denunciation of the U.S. press as corrupt, dangerous, and monopolistic, with the New York "Times" and "Daily News" cited as examples. As a result of his criticism, the author's publishing house has been investigated for communist sympathy.

M85   .... For Millionaires Only: Price of the "Free Press," "Masses & Mainstream," 6 (June 1953), 26-31.
A report on fantastically expensive newspapers in America, such as the New York "Times" and the New York "Daily News." These tremendous capitalistic institutions, because of their fabulous cost of operation, reduce freedom of the press to a mockery.

M86   MARITIME FEDERATION OF THE PACIFIC, District Council No. 2. "The Yanks Are Not Coming." San Francisco: The Council, n.d. [1939 or 1940]. 16 pp.
Opposition to American entry into the European war, by a labor organization controlled by communists during the Party's isolationist phase, between the Nazi-Soviet pact and Hitler's invasion of the USSR. The war is viewed as an imperialist one between England and France and Germany for a redivision of the world.

M87   MARKMANN, Charles Lam. "The Noblest Cry: A History of the American Civil Liberties Union." New York: St. Martin's Press, 1965. 464 pp. Bibliog. App. Ind.
A sympathetic history of the ACLU, reviewing its long record of defending the civil rights of communists as well as of others, its opposition to loyalty oaths and the methods of some governmental investigating committees, and its work for victims of the loyalty-security programs. While approving the ACLU's barring of communists, as adherents of totalitarianism, from its offices or staff, the author deplores the Union's distinction between a communist as a member of a political party and as an agent of a foreign conspiracy.

M88   MARKOFF, A. The Training of New Cadres and Our School System, "Communist," 11 (Aug. 1932), 731-39.
A report on district, regional, and central full-time training schools conducted by the Party, with attention to selection of students, curriculum, methods of instruction, study groups, excursions, reading material, organization of the student body, and assignments to work after graduation.

M89   .... Lenin on Agitation and Propaganda, and the Tasks of the Communist Party, "Communist," 13 (Jan. 1934), 107-12.
A recommendation that communists follow Lenin's principle that agitation and propaganda not be artificially separated. Communists' speeches should contain lucid statements of communist doctrine, not meaningless slogans.

M90   MARKS, John. The Problems of the American Revolutionary Youth Movement: Ninth Plenum of the Young Communist International, "Communist," 12 (April 1933), 392-400.
At the Ninth Plenum of the Young Communist International, the American YCL was criticized for not taking advantage of widespread discontent among American youth. The YCL must work with other youth organizations and recruit large numbers of youth, without requiring too much discipline and Party activity. The Party can then try to convert them to communism.

M91   MARLEN, George [pseud. for George Spiro). "The Road: A Romance of the Proletarian Revolution." New York: Red Star Press, 1932. 623 pp.
A novel in which the hero is converted first to socialism and then to communism, as he recognizes the significance of the class struggle. Communist ideology is presented, and proletarian revolts around the world are described. (The author subsequently became the leader of a Trotskyist splinter group.)

M92   .... "Earl Browder, Communist or Tool of Wall Street—Stalin, Trotsky or Lenin." New York: The author, 1937. 493 pp.
A onetime member of each of the following groups—CPUSA, Communist League of America (Trotskyites), and Revolutionary Workers League—condemns them all, either for adherence to or misunderstanding of the Stalinist line. (Marlen finally organized his own group, the Lenin Circle, dedicated to the overthrow of Stalinism and the establishment of a Fourth International.)

M93   MARNIN, Irvin. The UE Faces the Split, "Fourth International," 10 (Nov. 1949), 298-303.
A Trotskyist analysis of the United Electrical Workers, written after the UE convention of 1949 but before the CIO convention at which the UE was expelled. The union has been victimized by two rival bureaucracies, Stalinist and anti-Stalinist, which serve the world's two major power blocs, not the union's rank and file.

M94   "MARQUETTE LAW REVIEW," Problems of the Fifth Amendment in Modern Times, 39 (Winter 1955-56), 179-217.
In a symposium on problems of the Fifth Amendment, the Rev. John R. Connery discusses "The Right to Silence," Dean Erwin N. Griswold of the Harvard University Law School writes on "The Fifth Amendment Today," and C. Dickerman Williams deals with "The Fifth Amendment in Non-Criminal Proceedings." (The Griswold and Williams articles are abstracted separately.)

M95   MARSHALL, James. The Defense of Public Education from Subversion, "Columbia Law Review," 51 (May 1951), 587-604.
An examination of academic freedom and its limits, the nature of subversion in education, the loyalty of teachers, loyalty oaths, administrative proceedings to remove teachers, and the use of school buildings by communists and front groups. While supporting uncensored teaching and academic freedom, the author would except teachers who pervert truth, teach hatred, or favor forceful overthrow of government.

M96   MARSHALL, James A. [pseud. for Max Bedacht]. The Socialist Party and Revolution, "Communist" (Organ of the Communist Party of America, affiliated with the Communist International), 1 (Nov. 1921), 7-8 ff.

An answer to socialist assertions that the immediate demands advocated by the Communist Party do not differ from those the Socialist Party has always urged. The difference between the two is that the communists use immediate demands to promote the class struggle, the socialists to avert it.

M97   MARSHALL, James A. [pseud. for Max Bedacht]. That Centrist, "Communist" (organ of the Communist Party of America), 1 (July 1922), 3-5.
An assertion that the term "centrist," as applied by extreme leftists, is meaningless. The true centrists are those who oppose centralization and discipline in the Party and who place organization above action. The major issue before the Party is extreme leftism, not centrism.

M98   MARSHALL, Margaret, and McCARTHY, Mary. Our Critics, Right or Wrong. IV: The Proletarians, "Nation," 141 (Dec. 4, 1935), 653-55.
An analysis of the problems faced by the Marxist critic as reflected in book reviews in the "New Masses," by the book-review editor of "The Nation" and a reviewer of "The Nation." The "New Masses" reviewer must berate the bourgeois, accommodate himself to every shift of the Party line, cater to both intellectual and working class audiences, and court young writers of talent for the revolutionary movement.

M99   MARTEL, Harry. Anti-Trust Laws and the Attack on Labor, "Communist," 19 (Jan. 1940), 58-66.
A protest against the invocation of the Sherman Act against trade unions by Attorney General Frank Murphy and Assistant Attorney General Thurman Arnold. A warning letter from Arnold to the Central Labor Union in Indianapolis is cited as an example of this perversion of the antitrust laws, which is part of the attempt to set up a war economy.

M100   . . ., and SISKIND, George. Psychoanalysis: Ideological Instrument of Imperialism, "Political Affairs," 29 (Dec. 1950), 61-74.
A Marxist analysis of Freudianism and its variants, ideological instruments at the disposal of the ruling class. The subjectivity of bourgeois psychology, according to the Marxist, leads to distortions of objective reality.

M101   MARTIN, Everett Dean, and BROWDER, Earl. Are We Going Communist? A Debate, "Forum and Century," 96 (Nov. 1936), 202-8.
Martin asserts that Americans do not want communism, that the dilemma of a choice between fascism and communism is a false one, that American workers are neither class-conscious nor revolutionary. Browder defines the present problem as the defense of democracy against reaction, fascism, and war, though the struggle of Americans for the things they want will finally lead them to socialism.

M102   MARTIN, Harold H. The Communist Party, U.S.A., "Saturday Evening Post," 235 (May 19, 1962), 17-23.
With its membership down to about 10,000, and spurned by intellectuals as well as by the masses, the Party is at its lowest ebb in 20 years. The author, a contributing editor of the "Saturday Evening Post," argues nevertheless that the Party can still be dangerous, because of its influence in unions in sensitive industries and because of the threats of espionage, sabotage, and subversion in Latin America. The country must be careful, however, lest in repressing the Party it will also cripple our basic liberties.

M103   MARTIN, Jack. "On Relief in Illinois." Chicago: Chicago Pen and Hammer, n.d. [1934?]. 30 unnumbered pp. App.

An account of the inadequate relief payments in Illinois during the depression, of the social-work system, and of the struggles of the Unemployment Council. Passage of the workers' unemployment insurance bill is urged.

M104   . . . . "Taxation Without Representation." Chicago: National Research League, [1935?]. 32 pp.
An assertion that a government tax program is written to benefit the class it represents, as the class nature of the federal budget shows. A people's taxation program can be achieved only by a rank-and-file farmer-labor party, based on the masses and built on an anticapitalist class struggle foundation.

M105   . . . . Legislative Problems in Illinois, "Communist," 18 (Aug. 1939), 712-20.
The Party's legislative secretary in Illinois reports on the successes of progressive forces in the 61st Illinois General Assembly. Emphasis is placed on the budget and taxes and on the need for sustained struggle by progressive forces. Legislative tasks facing the democratic front are outlined.

M106   . . .(ed.). "Voters Fact Book: A Handbook for the 1944 Elections. Facts..Issues..Candidates." Chicago: Illinois State Committee, Communist Party, 1944. 72 pp.
A call for unity of the American people to win the war, and for support of New Deal candidates in the 1944 national, state, and local elections. Voting records of candidates are evaluated, and information of use to canvassers and poll watchers is presented.

M107   MARTIN, Lawrence. "Faceless Informers and Our Schools." Denver: Denver "Post," 1954. 28 pp.
A study of charges of subversive connections against public school teachers, and of the evaluation and use of such charges. Assembling cases from across the country, the author charges that due process and constitutional rights of teachers have been violated by smear tactics and police state methods. In many communities, he asserts, guilt is presumed until innocence is proved.

M108   MARVIN, Cloyd H. Colleges and Communism, "Association of American Colleges Bulletin," 39 (Oct. 1953), 377-83.
An address to the graduating class of 1953 by the president of George Washington University, who contrasts the objectives and spirit of communism and democracy. Since a communist lacks a free mind, he cannot teach in college, though students must have opportunities to learn about communism.

M109   MARVIN, Fred R. "Are These Your Friends?" Denver: The author, 1922. 30 pp.
An exposé of radical organizations seeking to overthrow the government, outlining their goals and methods. The CPUSA, the IWW, and the left-wing socialists are grouped together. The Farmer-Labor Party and the Nonpartisan League are put in another group, as slightly less radical.

M110   . . . . "Ye Shall Know the Truth." New York: The author, 1926. 93 pp.
A survey of pacifist, liberal, and radical groups and activities in the mid-1920's, identifying the pacifist movement with socialism and communism, and pointing to the interlocking directorates of pacifist, civil-libertarian, liberal, and radical groups, all of them viewed as subversive. The American Civil Liberties Union and the American Fund for Public Service (the Garland Fund) receive special attention. The communists are charged with promoting pacifism so that they will be able to overthrow the government by force.

M111 MARVIN, Fred R. "Our Government and Its Enemies." New York: American Coalition of Patriotic Societies, 1932. 244 pp.
A series of 15 lectures delivered in 1929-31 designed to expose the economic, social, and political fallacies of socialism. "Socialism" is viewed as synonymous with communism, Bolshevism, liberalism, and pacifism; as responsible for unrest, class hatred, and the revolutionary spirit; and as an attack on church and home. Though communists propose mass or direct action involving violence, whereas socialists advocate legislative or parliamentary action, both seek to abolish private property and to overthrow our form of government.

M112 .... "Fool's Gold: An Exposé of Un-American Activities and Political Action in the United States since 1860." New York: Madison & Marshall, 1936. 184 pp. App. Ind.
A broad attack on the American left by a conservative, who criticizes communists and other elements on the left indiscriminately. Material on socialists, the Nonpartisan League, and third parties of the 1920's is included, along with a brief review of the communist movement. The New Deal is equated with socialism, and charges are made that it will destroy individual initiative, thrift, private industry, independent agriculture, freedom, constitutional government, and morale.

M113 MARX, Herbert, Jr. (comp.). "American Labor Unions: Organization, Aims and Power." New York: Wilson, 1950. 240 pp.
A "Reference Shelf" compilation on labor unions, representing both labor and management viewpoints. The section on "Division in Labor's Ranks" reprints in part three articles on communist influence in the CIO: Sam Stavisky, "Can the C.I.O. Get Rid of the Commies?"; Donald Robinson, "How Our Seamen Bounced the Commies"; and Robert Bendiner, "Surgery in the C.I.O."

M114 MARZANI, Carl. "We Can Be Friends." Foreword by W. E. B. DuBois. New York: Topical Books, 1952. 38 pp. App. Ind.
An analysis of the cold war and a plea for friendship with the USSR by a former U.S. civil servant, who was convicted of perjury for denying former membership in the Communist Party. Marzani holds America responsible for the cold war, asserting that Roosevelt's policy of peace and friendship was perverted into the Truman doctrine of arms and fear. Denying that Soviet leaders intend to spread communism by war, he looks upon the USSR, Red China, and the eastern European countries as forces for peace.

M115 MASON, Chick. "Sources of Our Dilemma: A Rejection of the 'Right Opportunist-Left Sectarian' Explanation by Our Leadership." n.p.: n.publ., 1956. 28 pp. Mimeo.
A pro-Browder view of the crisis within the Party precipitated by the Duclos letter of 1945, which permitted the isolationist, left sectarian wing headed by Foster to take over the leadership. This reversed the policy followed since 1933, when the Party had emerged from isolation. It now stands at the brink of bankruptcy, isolated from the people, and its leaders isolated from its members.

M116 MASON, Leonard J. "We Want to Live." New York: Young Communist League, n.d. [1938]. 31 pp. Bibliog.
A presentation of the YCL position on the issues of war, peace, neutrality, the Oxford Pledge, ROTC, etc. Urging economic as well as military sanctions against aggressors, the author calls upon the peace forces to unite. The Oxford Pledge, opposing any war the U.S. government may conduct, is supported, because of the present character of that government. While ROTC should be abolished, those who are ready to fight against fascism and war are urged to take advantage of the training.

M117 MASSACHUSETTS COUNCIL FOR CONSTITUTIONAL RIGHTS. "We Hold These Truths." Boston: The Council, 1953. 38 pp. Bibliog.
A critical commentary on threats to our constitutional rights posed by anticommunist measures such as loyalty oaths and legislative investigating committees. The Council membership includes Massachusetts and New England units of the American Friends Service Committee, the Civil Liberties Union, and the NAACP.

M118 MASSE, Benjamin L. Is the C.I.O. Ready to Resolve to Rid Itself of the Reds? "America." 66 (Nov. 15, 1941), 152-53.
A comment on the split within the CIO into left-wing and right-wing groups. An open fight against communism at the 1941 convention will split the CIO into two warring parties; as long as communists and their fellow-travelers are free to conspire, the CIO will lack the confidence of the public.

M119 .... Dies Committee Reports on the CIO, "America," 71 (April 8, 1944), 11-12.
An analysis of and disagreement with the Dies Committee's report on the CIO's Political Action Committee. The Dies Committee's charge that PAC is dominated by communists is false. PAC activities to date have been educational, contributions are voluntary, and five of the six-man PAC board are active anticommunists.

M120 .... Communism and the CIO-PAC, "America," 72 (Nov. 18, 1944), 124-25.
An elaboration and defense of statements by the author in the April 8, 1944, issue of "America," that communists do not control the CIO and its Political Action Committee. The CIO, however, gives a semblance of truth to the charge of communist domination by giving occasional support to Party causes.

M121 .... Communists Turn Left Again, "America," 73 (June 9, 1945), 189-90.
Speculation about the effect of the letter by French communist leader Jacques Duclos criticizing Earl Browder and the policies of the CPUSA. The reaction of the CPUSA shows that it is still subservient to Moscow. The communists in the CIO may be forced into an open break with Philip Murray.

M122 .... CIO at Atlantic City, "America," 76 (Nov. 16, 1946), 177-79.
A comparison of the coming convention of the CIO with its 1940 convention. The big issue is American foreign policy; a showdown fight is in the offing as a result of the boldness of communist efforts to subvert CIO unions. The question is whether Philip Murray can and will carry it off.

M123 .... Mr. Wallace and the CIO, "America," 78 (Jan. 3, 1948), 376-78.
Far from being an impractical dreamer, Henry Wallace is one of our most resourceful political operators. He tried to force the Democratic high command to make a place for him and his ideas by accepting left support. But the CIO repudiated him, and the Democratic leaders knew they could ignore him.

M124 .... Reds on the Run in the CIO, "America," 79 (July 24, 1948), 365-67.
The industrial-relations editor of a Catholic magazine describes the decline of communist influence in the CIO, citing the loss of key staff positions in the CIO national

office and the CIO's diminishing influence in the NMU, the TWU, and the CIO Council in New York City.

M125 MASSE, Benjamin L. The Issue in the West Coast Strike, "America," 79 (Sept. 25, 1948), 563-65.
Behind the strike of the West Coast longshoremen and other unions is the issue of communist control of the ILWU. The shipping interests insist that we stop temporizing with this fifth column directed from abroad.

M126 .... Stalinist Strength in the CIO, "America," 80 (Jan. 8, 1949), 373-74.
A survey of anticommunist victories in the CIO from 1946 to November 1949, when the CIO's Portland convention took a firm stand against communism. Included are the de-Stalinization of the industrial councils by John Brophy and the dismissal of de Caux and Pressman. It is hoped that Philip Murray will soon bring the struggle to a successful finish.

M127 .... Communism at Cleveland, "America," 82 (Oct. 22, 1949), 66-68.
A review of communist activities in the American labor movement, prior to the CIO Cleveland convention at which a showdown on this issue is expected. The issue is whether the CIO can ignore the challenge to its authority, to patriotism, and to democratic principles from the CP-led unions.

M128 .... Is Congress Framing UE? "America," 84 (Nov. 11, 1950), 159-61.
An open letter to Clifford T. McAvoy, Secretary of the UE Defense Committee, condemning as misleading the Committee's pamphlet "Stop the Frameups Against Our Union." Answering the pamphlet, the author applauds the House Committee on Un-American Activities for exposing Matles and Emspak as procommunist leaders of the UE.

M129 .... Public Policy toward Communist Unions, "America," 89 (April 25, 1953), 104-6.
A sketch of the main proposals advanced to a subcommittee of the Senate Committee on Labor and Public Welfare by leaders of labor and management regarding methods of combating communists in unions. The subcommittee's policy recommendations, based on these proposals, follow.

M130 .... Civil War in U.S. Communism, "America," 97 (Sept. 21, 1957), 637.
A report on current disagreements and disaffections within U.S. communist ranks, focusing on the resignation of Joseph Clark after 28 years in the Party because of its failure to establish its independence of Moscow. Hard-core Stalinists are gaining strength and may seize control of the Party.

M131 "MASSES & MAINSTREAM," American Message: A Reply to an Open Letter of Soviet Writers, 1 (May 1948), 3-6.
A May Day message signed by 32 communist and fellow-traveling writers and artists in response to a letter from Soviet writers. The signers concur with the Soviet concern about American warmongers, assert that honest artists are resisting the Un-American Activities Committee, and stand in international solidarity with the Soviet writers for peace and democracy.

M132 ..., Political Prisoners, 3 (July 1950), 1-96.
The bulk of this issue is devoted to articles by "political prisoners," communists jailed or about to be jailed for their "un-American activities." Among the contributors are John Howard Lawson, Howard Fast, Dalton Trumbo, Albert Maltz, Ring Lardner, Jr., Carl Marzani, and Leon Josephson. Also included (pp. 46-51) is a portion of a

letter from Eugene Dennis, refusing to appear before the House Committee on Un-American Activities. (The Fast, Josephson, and Dennis items are abstracted separately.)

M133 MASSING, Hede. "This Deception." Introd. by Morris L. Ernst. New York: Duell, Sloan and Pearce, 1951. 335 pp.
The experiences of a woman, Austrian by birth, who served Soviet espionage both in Europe and in America, until her break with communism in 1937. The wife, first of Gerhart Eisler, a leading German communist who was a Comintern representative to the American party in the early 1930's, and then of Paul W. Massing, German Party sympathizer, she throws light on the attractions of the movement in the 1920's and 1930's. Though she had experienced doubts while in Moscow in 1930-31, she did not break with communism until many of her German friends were liquidated in the Moscow purges. During her active period as a Soviet agent here she became a close friend of Noel Field, a State Department official who later disappeared behind the Iron Curtain. A witness at the second Hiss trial, she was the only one other than Chambers whose testimony connected Hiss with Soviet espionage.

M134 MATHER, Kirtley F. Scientists in the Doghouse, "Nation," 174 (June 28, 1952), 638-41.
A Harvard professor of geology discusses the plight of scientists in these times of irrational fear. Scientists, vulnerable because of their international outlook and their habits of independent thought and expression, are punished by withdrawal of federal subsidies and refusal to grant passports.

M135 MATLES, James J. "UE—The Members Run This Union! An Answer to the 'Saturday Evening Post.' " New York: UE, 1947. 40 pp.
Answering a "Saturday Evening Post" article by Joseph and Stewart Alsop charging Party control of the UE, its director of organization asserts that the rank and file got rid of James Carey, former president, because he was a tool of an outside group, the Association of Catholic Trade Unionists. A number of quotations praise the UE and its present leaders.

M136 MATTHEWS, J. B. "Odyssey of a Fellow Traveler." New York: Mount Vernon Publishers, 1938. 286 pp. Ind. of organizations.
The experience of a leading fellow-traveler before he became a political and economic conservative. Matthews tells of his youth, and of his successive embracing of religious fundamentalism, the social gospel, political reform, pacifism, socialism, and communism. In the period of 1932 to 1935 he participated in more than 20 front organizations, including the American League Against War and Fascism, of which he was national chairman. In a chapter on "Communists at Work," Matthews discusses Marxian ethics, the communists' attitude on civil liberties, their exploitation of discontent, their activities in trade unions, and their smearing technique.

M137 .... "The 'United Front' Exposed." New York: League for Constitutional Government, 1938. 30 pp.
The statement of a former "fellow-traveler" before the congressional committee (the Dies committee) investigating un-American activities. A former member of numerous communist front organizations and first national chairman of the American League Against War and Fascism, Matthews analyzes communist infiltration and united front tactics in the light of his experience.

M138 .... The Commies Go After the Kids, "American Legion Magazine," 47 (Dec. 1949), 14-15 ff.
In their efforts to reach children the communists use

songs, summer camps, comic strips, dramatic groups, and other devices. Among their front groups are the Labor Youth League, the chief auxiliary now for young people; Stage for Action, emphasizing the living-newspaper type of drama; and People's Songs, the International Workers Order, and the Young People's Record Club. Secret Party members seek to influence school policy and school textbooks.

M139 MATTHEWS, J. B. Did the Movies Really Clean House? "American Legion Magazine," 51 (Dec. 1951), 12-13 ff.
Despite exposures by congressional investigations of communist influence in Hollywood, the motion-picture industry has not really cleaned house. The communists, with their various fronts, achieved a shocking degree of penetration into the film industry. Only a few persons named as communists have so far lost their jobs.

M140 .... Communists in the White House, "American Mercury," 76 (Feb. 1953), 8-16.
An account of the relationship between the leadership of the American Youth Congress and Franklin D. and Eleanor Roosevelt. Matthews asserts that William Hinckley and Abbott Simon are Communist Party members, whose relationship with the Roosevelts included overnight visits at the White House.

M141 .... Communism and the Colleges, "American Mercury," 76 (May 1953), 111-44.
An account of communist infiltration in higher education, listing the better known of 3,500 professors claimed to be active supporters of the Party line. The author argues that progressive education, by relaxing old disciplines and loyalties, enables communists to undermine the loyalty of American students. The job of investigation cannot be left to university administrations, since none has investigated communists on its faculty until after legislative investigation.

M142 ..., and FLYNN, John T. Communists and the New Deal, "American Mercury," Part 1, by J. B. Matthews, 76 (June 1953), 33-40; Part 2, by John T. Flynn, 77 (July 1953), 57-62; Part 3, by J. B. Matthews, 77 (Aug. 1953), 17-25.
Matthews asserts in Part 1 that large numbers of Communist Party members were given government jobs during the New Deal, that Browder and other top Party leaders were welcome at the White House, and that Cabinet officers supported communist enterprises. Flynn asserts that the Morganthau plan for dismantling and punishing Germany was framed by Harry Dexter White, who followed the communist line, on instructions from Stalin. Part 3 deals with the case of Dr. William A. Wirt, who was sneered at and ridiculed for trying to expose communists in government in 1934.

M143 .... Reds and Our Churches, "American Mercury," 77 (July 1953), 3-13.
An assertion by a McCarthy committee investigator that the Protestant clergy form the largest single group supporting the communist apparatus in the U.S. today. He cites in particular the People's Institute for Applied Religion, the "Protestant" magazine, and the Methodist Federation for Social Action. Partial blame is placed on the social-gospel teachings of theological seminaries. (Controversy resulting from this article led to the discharge of the author from the committee staff.)

M144 .... Red Infiltration of Theological Seminaries, "American Mercury," 77 (Nov. 1953), 31-36.
An assertion, based in part on the seminary affiliation of "peace-petition" signers, that over 30 percent of the 177

Protestant theological seminaries in the U.S. have been infiltrated by the communist-front apparatus. The Party's grip in the religious field is strong, since these men teach tomorrow's ministers of religion.

M145 ...; OXNAM, G. Bromley; and NIEBUHR, Reinhold. Communism and the Protestant Clergy, "Look," 17 (Nov. 17, 1953), 33-37.
A symposium resulting from Matthews' charge that Protestant clergy form the largest single group supporting the communist apparatus in the U.S. today. In support of his charge Matthews asserts that most influential front organizations have been headed by Protestant clergymen and cites the contents of several religious publications. Bishop Oxnam challenges Matthews' trustworthiness, judiciousness, sincerity, and accuracy. Niebuhr asserts that the number of fellow-travelers in the churches is small, though some denominations may be blamed for undue toleration of them.

M146 .... America is Losing the War against Communism, "American Mercury," 78 (Jan. 1954), 3-10.
An assertion that the U.S. is rapidly losing the war against communism on both the domestic and international fronts, due to the work of American and UN anti-anti-communists. The communist use of front organizations, preferably headed by a clergyman, is described.

M147 .... The Years of Betrayal, "American Mercury," 78 (Feb. 1954), 34-45.
A bitter denunciation, not only of Presidents Roosevelt and Truman, but also of Eisenhower, for "covering up" the extent of communist infiltration into the government apparatus.

M148 .... World Communist Apparatus for Scientists, "American Mercury," 78 (March 1954), 17-28.
An exposé of the World Federation of Scientific Workers, formed in July 1946. The author tells the history of communist associations of the World Federation, its officers, and prominent members. Its affiliate, the American Association of Scientific Workers, is an integral part of the world communist espionage and propaganda apparatus for scientists.

M149 .... An Anti-Communist's Guide to Action. "American Mercury," 78 (May 1954), 21-28.
Advice on how to fight communism, including both "do's" and "don'ts." Readers are urged to promote anticommunist books, to support McCarthy and anticommunist legislation, to join an anticommunist organization, and to guard against communist infiltration. Anticommunist books and speakers are listed.

M150 .... Hutchins To Investigate Communism? "American Mercury," 80 (June 1955), 71-81.
A critical view of the forthcoming study of communist influence in American life sponsored by the Fund for the Republic. Matthews predicts that Robert M. Hutchins, Clinton Rossiter, and their staff will "whitewash" communism with a pile of "miseducational" material. Only Daniel Bell is considered competent.

M151 .... What and How of Communist Fronts, "American Mercury," 81 (Aug. 1955), 19-30.
An analysis of communist front operations, asserting that before 1935 the communists functioned openly in united fronts with noncommunists, whereas since that time the Party hides behind a facade to ensnare innocents. Congressional committees must investigate the Party's periphery as well as its core. The author shows how the Party ensnares dupes in a typical united front maneuver.

for unity of labor and all progressives, including the communists. Lerner calls upon the communists to focus on America instead of Russia, seek a fuller democracy, transform their intellectual tone, and play fair on a moral level.

L185 LESLIE, Alexander. Has the Communist Party a Future? "Monthly Review," 8 (July-August 1956), 106-11.
A discussion of the factors that suggest that the future of American socialism does not lie with the CP, which has been compromised politically, legally, and morally. Faced with the severest challenge of its history, the Party can again accept uncritically the newest Soviet version of history, make a clean break with the past, or compromise between these courses of action.

L186 LESLIE, John. Merrill's Marauders in Wall Street, "Plain Talk," 1 (Dec. 1946), 11-13.
An exposé of the United Office and Professional Workers of the CIO, now conducting a drive in New York City's financial district, as communist-dominated. Procommunist associations of Merrill and other leaders are cited. UOPWA secretaries have sent confidential information to Party sources.

L187 . . . . Book Club for Innocents, "Plain Talk," 1 (May 1947), 27-31.
An exposé of the Book Find Club as staffed with Party members and consistently following the Party Line. "Book Find News," heavily political, adheres closely to the current Party line. The club, formerly frank about the Party affiliations of its writers, now tries to conceal this.

L188 . . . . Lee Pressman as Portent: Profile of a Party-Line Unionist, "New Leader," 31 (April 10, 1948), 3.
Pressman's resignation as general counsel of the CIO is evidence of the steady decline of communist forces there. A political portrait of Pressman, stressing his Party allegiance since 1930, his participation in front activities, his legal contributions to Party causes, and his current enthusiasm for Henry A. Wallace.

L189 LE SUEUR, Meridel. The Fetish of Being Outside, "New Masses," 16 [14] (Feb. 26, 1935), 22-23.
A reply to an article by Horace Gregory (One Writer's Position in the "New Masses," February 12, 1935), who asserted that he could not join the Party although his sympathies were with it. Gregory's stand shows a middle-class malady common to all nourished on bourgeois soil. Objectivity is impossible; the writer must completely discard the old and completely embrace the new.

L190 . . . . "Salute to Spring." New York: International Publishers, 1940. 191 pp.
A volume of short stories by a communist writer, concerned largely with the struggles of the American proletariat.

L191 LETWIN, Alita. New Stirrings on the Campus, "Political Affairs," 34 (Oct. 1955), 54-63.
A report to the National Board of the Labor Youth League by its national student secretary. The cold war intensified the drive to cut off free inquiry and action on the campuses. Students resisted, in at least two struggles linking up the issues of academic freedom and peace and showing a new mood of boldness and militancy.

L192 LETWIN, Leon. Communist Registration Under the McCarran Act and Self-Incrimination, "Wisconsin Law Review," July 1951, 704-17.
Since the Supreme Court has held that admission of com-

munist membership is incriminating under the Smith Act, the registration provisions, which also connote criminality, are unconstitutional as self-incriminating. Individuals are not sufficiently protected by the immunity provision of the Act.

L193 LEVENSON, David. Left-wing Labor and the Taft-Hartley Law, "Labor Law Journal," 1 (Nov. 1950), 1079-94.
An appraisal of section 9(h), the noncommunist oath provision of the Taft-Hartley Act, reviewing the initial boycott and later compliance by labor. The provision has accomplished little, since CIO expulsion of its left-wing affiliates was based on more fundamental issues. Proposed alternatives to 9(h) are also criticized. Benefits that elimination of left-wing union leadership would produce are listed.

L194 LEVENSTEIN, Aaron. "Labor Today and Tomorrow." New York: Knopf, 1946. 253 pp. Ind.
An analysis of labor-management-government relations in the U.S. from 1938 through World War II. In a chapter, "Men Who Came to Dinner—The Left Wing," the author analyzes the shift in the communist labor policy from its anti-imperialist-war stand of the Hitler-Stalin pact period to its class-collaborationist, win-the-war policies after June 1941. He discusses the internecine fight within the CIO, showing how, once Jacques Duclos established the "hard line" after the war, the CIO was able to eliminate communists from influence.

L195 . . . . Troubles in the C.I.O., "American Mercury," 62 (June 1946), 706-12.
The director of the Labor Division of the Research Institute of America predicts an imminent fight between the pro- and anticommunist unions in the CIO, with Philip Murray still undecided on how to meet the challenge on the left. The AFL and John L. Lewis are looking forward to the controversy, with which Murray must deal.

L196 . . . . Travesty of the Hollywood Investigation, Hollywood Probe and Civil Liberties, "Socialist Call," 14 (Nov. 7, 1947), 6; (Nov. 14), 2.
A discussion of the investigative power of Congress, in the light of the probe of communism in Hollywood. Levenstein notes that misuse of the power threatens not only individual liberty, but also the congressional power of investigation into matters of public concern. He attacks liberals who defend civil liberties in the U.S. while remaining silent about their absence in Eastern Europe.

L197 . . . . What the Wallace Candidacy Means, "Socialist Call," 15 (Jan. 9, 1948), 8.
The Wallace candidacy in 1948 is called a triumph for communism and a setback for democratic socialist forces interested in a labor-based third party. By using Wallace's name, the CP will be able to attract many more votes than under its own name.

L198 LEVI, Maxine. "The Communists and the Liberation of Europe." New York: New Century, 1945. 63 pp.
A communist view of armed conflicts in various countries of Europe and of the part played in them by communists and by fascist and other reactionary interests. Among the countries reviewed are Yugoslavia, Greece, France, Italy, and Spain, with brief notes on others. Anticommunism is attacked as a cloak for fascism and reaction.

L199 LEVIN, E. The Veterans and the United Front, "Communist," 12 (July 1933), 684-95.
The economy bill cutting veterans' benefits was an attempt to solve the economic crisis by lowering living standards

of the masses. The bourgeoisie fears unity of the veterans with other sections of the masses. Despite the efforts of reactionary groups of veterans, a militant movement among rank-and-file veterans is on the upswing.

L200 LEVIN, Emanuel. The Veterans in the Struggle Against Fascism and Imperialist War, "Communist," 13 (Aug. 1934), 820-30.
A call to American veterans to join the international veterans' movement against war, and announcing that the Seventh International Congress of the International des Anciens Combattants will be held in Brussels, July 1934.

L201 LEVINE, Isaac Don. The Inside Story of Our Soviet Underground, "Plain Talk," 2 (Sept. 1948), 9-12; 3 (Oct. 1948), 18-22; (Nov.), 21-25; (Dec.), 19-22.
The author describes his contacts with Whittaker Chambers, whose story Levine helped take to federal officials; and with Walter Krivitsky, former high official of the Soviet secret service. Operations of the Soviet espionage network in this country and in Britain are revealed. The mystery surrounding the entry into this country of Russian-born Mrs. Earl Browder is examined.

L202 .... Sequel to Chambers' Story, "Plain Talk," 3 (Jan. 1949), 1-4.
The dates when, between 1940 and 1947, and the conditions under which the author contacted ten prominent Americans to acquaint them with Chambers' story, in an effort to convince them of the presence of treason in the capitol. The American people should be grateful for Chambers' revelations.

L203 .... The Plot to Kill the Reuther Brothers, "Plain Talk," 4 (Jan. 1950), 1-6.
After their defeat in the UAW-CIO, the communists are said to have originated a plot to kill the Reuther brothers. An alliance between the communists and gangster elements is said to be functioning. Both see Reuther as a major obstacle, the former for political reasons, and the latter because of his opposition to the numbers racket.

L204 LEVINE, Jack. Hoover and the Red Scare, "Nation," 195 (Oct. 20, 1962), 232-35.
An appraisal of FBI efforts to combat communism by a former FBI special agent, who asserts that J. Edgar Hoover exaggerates the present danger of domestic communism to maintain support for his agency. The shrunken Party is infiltrated from top to bottom with FBI informants, one for every 5.7 members. The Soviets must now rely on their own nationals for recruiting agents and establishing espionage networks.

L205 LEVINSON, Edward. The Dictatorship of the Hysterical, "New Leader," 2 (Dec. 19, 1925), 6.
An attack upon the communists for their demonstrations and "cheap dramatics" during the first eight days of the ILGWU convention. Isadore Nagler's speech defending the report of the Credentials Committee from communist attack is quoted at length.

L206 .... Communists in Control, "American Federationist," 34 (Jan. 1927), 87-92.
The assistant editor of the "New Leader" reports on communist leadership in a six-month strike of the ILGWU in New York City, analyzing the industry and giving the strike background. The communists have brought the union the most severe defeat in its history. The workers are turning to the International Union to free it from communist control.

L207 .... Who Are the Betrayers of Unity? Startling Revelations of Duplicity, "New Leader," 16 (Aug. 19, 1933), 6-7 ff.

Reasons for socialist withdrawal from the projected U.S. Congress Against War, the first united front effort with communists on a national scale. Instances of communist duplicity are cited, including attacks on the Socialist Party in the communist press despite assurances to the contrary, and publication of correspondence between SP units that could only have been acquired through a stool pigeon or a thief.

L208 .... "Labor on the March." New York: Harper, 1938. 325 pp. Bibliog. Ind.
A study of labor during the depression years, and of the formation and development of the CIO. There are a few references to communists in the CIO. The author asserts that, although they present problems in several unions, they are not an important factor in the U.S. labor movement, certainly not so far as the CIO is concerned.

L209 .... The CIO in Crisis, "Nation," 147 (July 2, 1938), 11-14.
An assertion that communists have caused serious difficulty in two CIO unions, the United Automobile Workers and the National Maritime Union, by seeking to silence all who disapprove of their views and tactics. Communists, who hope to drive Trotskyists, Lovestonites, and other dissenters from the labor movement, call anyone who opposes the Communist Party a Trotskyite.

L210 LEVINSON, Joseph. With American Communists Underground, "Justice," 9 (Feb. 25, 1927), 5 ff; (March 4), 5 ff; (March 11), 5 ff; (March 18), 5 ff; (March 25), 5 ff; (April 1), 5 ff; (April 8), 5 ff.
A series of articles, written by a former Party member, describing its inner life and activities. The first three articles deal with communist activities in the ladies' garment industry—with the cloakmakers' strike organized by the communists, with their intrigues in union elections, and with the activities of the Joint Action Committee in 1925. The remaining articles expose communist political methods and elections, corruption in Russian relief and trading agencies here, control of the Party by the emissary of the Moscow International, and promotion within the communist movement here of thieves and grafters.

L211 LEVNER, Bill. "Is it True What They Say about Cohen?" New York: American Jewish Labor Council, 1948. 32 unnumbered pp.
Cartoons and text published by a Jewish group allied to the communist movement, pointing out that most American Jews are wage workers, and that bosses are bosses regardless of religion. Calling for the outlawry of anti-Semitic and race hate literature, the author asserts that anti-Semitism serves Big Business.

L212 LEWIS, Alfred Baker. "Liberalism and Sovietism." New York: New Leader Association, 1946. 32 pp.
An assertion by a moderate socialist that communists and fellow-travelers are a wing of Russia's foreign office. He traces changes in the Party line to support each new need of the USSR. Liberals must insist that communists stop masquerading as liberals, and they must work for progressive measures without cooperating with communists.

L213 .... The Problem of Communist Infiltration, "Crisis," 61 (Dec. 1954), 585-88 ff.
A member of the NAACP board of directors discusses communist efforts to infiltrate and control the NAACP, warning that "cooperation" is a standard Party technique to create innocents' clubs or transmission belts under communist control. Communists, whatever the stated purpose of an organization, always put the interests of Russia first.

M152 MATTHEWS, J. B. Relief for America's Reds, "American Legion Magazine," 63 (Oct. 1957), 14-15 ff.
A critical review of four U.S. Supreme Court decisions involving rights of communists, issued June 17, 1957. The Court reversed the conviction of California Party leaders under the Smith Act, ruled that questions on communist associations by a New Hampshire legislative inquiry and the House Un-American Activities Committee did not have to be answered, and limited the power of the Secretary of State to discharge subordinates as security risks.

M153 .... The Communist Party, U.S.A.: How It Functions, "Social Education," 22 (April 1958), 173-77.
A brief account of the operations of the Party, emphasizing its control from Moscow, both in its underground organization and in its use of front groups. The Party's influence has always been greater than its membership size would suggest.

M154 .... Christ and Communism, "American Mercury," 88 (May 1959), 116-23.
The communists have had considerable success in gaining the backing of editors of religious periodicals, individual clergymen, and Christian denominations. A Gallup poll showed 12 per cent of the U.S. clergy unwilling to say that it was impossible to be a good Christian and a member of the Communist Party.

M155 MATTHIESSEN, F. O. "Theodore Dreiser." New York: Sloane, 1951. 267 pp.
A biography and critical review of Dreiser and his work by a literary critic sympathetic to communism. A chapter on "Dreiser's Politics" (pp. 213-35) explains his political development from 1927, when he visited Soviet Russia, until shortly before he died, when he requested membership in the Party.

M156 MATUSOW, Harvey M. (as told to Howard Rushmore). Reds in Khaki, "American Legion Magazine," 53 (Oct. 1952), 14-15 ff.
The experiences of an American soldier in World War II who was introduced to communist thought and activities by fellow soldiers and who joined the communist youth organization after demobilization. After three years, realizing his mistake, he became an informer for the FBI until the communists expelled him as a government agent.

M157 .... "False Witness." New York: Cameron & Kahn, 1955. 255 pp. Ind.
The autobiography of a man who, after having testified for the government in a number of cases involving communists, retracted his statements, asserting that he had lied. The author describes his testimony before House, Senate, and state committees and in court cases under the Smith and Taft-Hartley acts, and his other anticommunist activities, all of which he says he engaged in for self-glorification and publicity.

M158 MAURER, Herrymon. Lessons of the Anna M. Rosenberg Hearings, "Commentary," 11 (May 1951), 415-27.
An account of the Senate Armed Services Committee hearings into the loyalty of Anna M. Rosenberg and her fitness to be assistant secretary of defense. Mrs. Rosenberg was charged with possessing communist sympathies and with having been affiliated with communist-controlled organizations. The charges were found to be based on mistaken identities or the faulty memories of amateur anticommunists. The author praises the procedures followed by the committee.

M159 MAX, Alan. "May Day, 1938: For Democracy, Jobs, Security, Peace!" New York: Workers Library, 1938. 15 pp.
An assertion that May Day, 1938, because of the formation of the CIO and the victory of the New Deal, will see the American people better able than before to fight for security, jobs, and adequate relief. Party membership, now said to be 75,000, must be enlarged to cement the democratic front and lead America to socialism.

M160 .... "What Do You Read?" New York: Workers Library, 1941. 15 pp.
An indictment of the "advertiser-controlled" press and an appeal for support of the "Daily Worker," the only paper courageously supporting the workers. To the capitalist newspapers, freedom of the press means freedom to distort news, propagandize for the vested interests, and smear the labor and peace movements.

M161 MAXWELL, James A. Cincinnati's Phantom Reds, "Reporter," 3 (Sept. 26, 1950), 28-31.
The story of the effort of a Cincinnati newspaper, the "Enquirer," to exploit congressional immunity to publish an exposé of alleged communists. The technique was to publish a sensational lead story without names, have the reporter give the names in testimony to a congressional committee, and then publish the resulting story free from danger of a libel suit.

M162 MAY, George S. Communism in the Methodist Church, "New Leader," 34 (Aug. 20, 1951), 10-12.
An assertion that the Methodist Federation for Social Action is controlled by fellow-travelers Harry Ward and Jack McMichael, and that Willard Uphaus of its executive committee has a similar background. Though Methodist leaders have so far refused to face these facts, there is increasing opposition to McMichael, and the coming convention of the MFSA may attempt to unseat him.

M163 .... Communism Confuses the Methodist Church, "New Leader," 35 (Aug. 11, 1952), 9-10.
A report on the conflict within the Methodist Church over fellow-traveler control of the Methodist Federation for Social Action. Defeating conservatives who wanted to drop the social gospel, the moderates succeeded in establishing an official Board of Social and Economic Relations.

M164 MAYER, Henry. Labor's Responsibility to the National Security—and Its Due. Pgs. 473-521 in "Proceedings of New York University Seventh Annual Conference on Labor." Albany and New York: Bender, 1954.
A denunciation of the loss of freedom in the name of national security, citing the Oppenheimer and Fort Monmouth cases and the denial of due process in the discharge of defense workers on suspicion of disloyalty. The author reviews legislative proposals, opposed by the CIO, to curb communism and subversion, and summarizes private-employer loyalty measures.

M165 .... How the Loyalty-Security Program Affects Private Employment, "Lawyers Guild Review," 15 (Winter 1955-56), 119-30.
An assertion that the loyalty-security program menaces the livelihood of millions in private employment because it lacks even the few safeguards in the security provisions affecting federal employees. It can serve as a mask for antiunion activities, endanger trade unionism and collective bargaining, and influence arbitrators and the NLRB to uphold discharges.

M166 MAYER, Herbert Carleton. "New Footprints of the Trojan Horse: The Communist Program to

Conquer the World." Introd. by Lucius D. Clay. New York: Farrar, Straus and Young, 1952. 99 pp. A primer of communism, discussing its aims, its enslavement of the Russian and eastern European peoples, its plans for imperialist conquest, its methods of infiltration and subversion, and methods by which Americans can defend themselves. The author urges loyal Americans to be active in organizations to prevent communist infiltration, and to promote the American ideal.

M167 MAYER, James Andrew. Commies and the Constitution, "American Mercury," 78 (March 1954), 133-36.
A discussion of the Subversive Activities Control Board's decision ordering the CP to identify and label all its mailed material or broadcasts, to list its officers and members with the Attorney General, and to file annual financial statements with him. The legal basis for the SACB decision under the Internal Security Act is outlined.

M168 MAYER, Milton S. Chicago—City of Unrest: Even There Communism Has Made No Headway, "Forum and Century," 89 (Jan. 1933), 46-51.
Although Chicago has a high unemployment rate, a heterogeneous population, and an empty city treasury, the communists are making little progress. They have tried hard with unpaid school teachers, depositors of closed banks, Negroes, veterans, and relief recipients, all with little success.

M169 . . . . Mrs. Dilling; Lady of "The Red Network," "American Mercury," 47 (July 1939), 293-99.
A character portrait of the author of "The Red Network," whose lies and half-truths have spread steadily, branding almost every distinguished public person in the U.S. as subversive. Her writings show the traits of fascism: militarism, racism, and hysterical hatred for liberalism and intellectualism.

M170 . . . . Is Soviet Race Equality Worth the Price? "Negro Digest," 7 (Nov. 1948), 29-31.
A University of Chicago faculty member points out that in America Negroes are legally free but lack equality, whereas in Russia they would be legally equal with whites but would lack freedom. Though their bitterness about America's inequality is understandable, their hopeful view of the Soviet Union is not.

M171 MAYER-OAKES, S. R. Communism and Christianity, "Christian Register," 117 [116] (Feb. 25, 1937), 123-25.
A discussion of the meaning of Christianity and communism. Common sharing of goods was practiced in early Christianity, until crushed by church officialdom. The use of force, which may have been necessary in Russia, is our chief criticism of the dictatorship. Christianity necessarily includes economic democracy, which is the ultimate aim of communism.

M172 MAYLOTT, Marcia V., and CRYSTAL, Daniel. The Schneiderman Case—Two Views, "George Washington Law Review," 12 (Feb. 1944), 215-37.
Contrasting views on the 1943 decision of the U.S. Supreme Court, refusing to denaturalize William Schneiderman on the ground that he was a communist when naturalized. Miss Maylott criticizes the decision for creating doubt as to principles considered well established. Crystal welcomes the decision as preserving the right to hold unpopular beliefs.

M173 McALLISTER, Joseph B. Communism and the Negro, "Commonweal," 26 (July 9, 1937), 277-78.
A recital of communists' interest in American Negroes,

and of efforts to win them to communism. This influence should be challenged by the Catholic Church, which does not draw the color line, though many Catholics do. Catholics must actualize in their lives, and in their contacts with Negroes, the teachings of their church.

M174 McCARRAN, Patrick, and others. Can We Curb Subversives Without Losing Our Freedom? "Northwestern University Reviewing Stand," 15 (Dec. 10, 1950), 3-11.
A panel radio discussion on the need for legislation against subversive conspiracies. Senator McCarran and news-commentator Robert F. Hurleigh agree on the need for such legislation, whereas Professor Paul van Ripper calls for more positive laws, and Professor Nathaniel Nathanson urges the protection of freedom of speech.

M175 McCARRAN, Patrick. The Supreme Court and the Loyalty Program: The Effect of Refugee Committee v. McGrath, "American Bar Association Journal, 37 (June 1951), 434-37 ff.
The Nevada senator asserts that the Supreme Court's decision in Joint Anti-Fascist Refugee Committee v. McGrath has been misinterpreted as holding the loyalty program invalid. The Court merely held that the Committee must be given a hearing before being listed as subversive. It did not negate the executive order authorizing the Attorney General to make such a list.

M176 . . . . The Internal Security Act of 1950, "University of Pittsburgh Law Review," 12 (Summer 1951), 481-513.
A detailed analysis and defense of the statute bearing the author's name as a necessary measure to combat communism. The background of the law is given, and its provisions on registration and prohibitions, on reinforcement of espionage laws, and on immigration and naturalization are discussed. The communist problem is attacked in the statute without violating or ignoring the Constitution.

M177 . . . . The Value of the Ex-Communist, "American Mercury," 73 (Nov. 1951), 3-10.
An assertion that the former communist makes a vital contribution to the enlightenment of our people and the security of our nation. By our inimical attitudes toward him, we have prevented more from coming forth with information.

M178 McCARTHY, Joseph R.; HAYES, Edward Arthur; ARNALL, Ellis; and CHERNE, Leo (George V. Denny, Jr., moderator). Should the Communist Party Be Outlawed in the United States? "Town Meeting," 12 (April 3, 1947). 23 pp.
Hayes proposes outlawing of the Party as the servant of a foreign power, to rob it of its false appearance of respectability and make its functioning more difficult. While agreeing, McCarthy would go farther, requiring registration, publicizing of fronts, deportation of aliens, and barring communists from the use of government boards. Cherne proposes to expose communists rather than outlaw them, and enlarge rather than curtail democracy. Asserting that sufficient laws are now available against illegal communist activities, Arnall urges us to find a cure for the communist disease, not pass a law against it.

M179 McCARTHY, Joseph. "McCarthyism: The Fight for America." New York: Devin-Adair, 1952. 101 pp. Ind.
A rebuttal by the Senator of his assailants, a defense of his efforts to expose communists in government, and criticism of the press for misquoting and misrepresenting him. He discusses the Tydings hearings, the number of communists in the State Department, and his charges that Dean

Acheson, Philip Jessup, Owen Lattimore, and George C. Marshall aid the communist cause. He calls for the elimination of communist infiltrators from our schools and colleges.

M180 McCARTHY, Mary. My Confession: One Writer's Encounter with Communism, "Reporter," 9 (Dec. 22, 1953), 28-34; 10 (Jan. 5, 1954), 27-31.
The author tells how she moved in Stalinist literary circles in the mid-1930's and then, by accident, gave support to Trotsky's right to a trial and to asylum. This episode, combined with the obvious frame-ups of the Moscow trials, turned her into an anticommunist. Most of those who became anticommunists in 1936-37 have remained liberals.

M181 McCOLLOCH, Claude. The Strange Case of Alger Hiss: A Reply to Lord Jowitt, "American Bar Association Journal," 40 (March 1954), 199-202 ff.
The reaction of an American federal district judge to Earl Jowitt's book on the Hiss case, criticizing the book for omitting salient facts and for underemphasizing others in questioning the validity of the jury's verdict. The criticism of American courtroom procedures is seen as unfounded.

M182 McCONNELL, Dorothy. "Women, War and Fascism." New York: American League Against War and Fascism, 1935. 18 pp.
A protest against the use of women as cheap labor in factories and offices, in the U.S. as well as in the fascist states. Munitions plants employ women at dangerous tasks, with long hours and low wages. Discriminatory laws against women should be defeated and women's wages made equal with men's for equal work.

M183 McCORMACK, John W. Communism—Its Method, "National Republic," 24 (June 1936), 1-3 ff.
A discussion of communist techniques by a congressman from Massachusetts, who proposes legislation making it a crime to advocate overthrow of government by force and violence, and the strengthening of deportation laws for alien communists.

M184 McCORMICK, Robert R. "The Rising Red Tide in America." Chicago: Tribune Co., 1934. 12 pp.
A radio speech by the editor and publisher of the Chicago "Tribune," coupling Roosevelt's recognition of the USSR with industrial strife and communist-inspired riots in the U.S. Attacking the NRA as tyranny, McCormick calls for the rescue of the U.S. before it is too late.

M185 McCUISTION, William C. How Our Reds Are Made, "National Republic," 27 (April 1940), 3-4 ff; 28 (May), 22-23 ff; (June), 22-23 ff.
A former Party member, a leader in its Marine Workers Industrial Union, describes the process of education and training through which a communist progresses, and the discipline to which he is subjected. Those who are most susceptible to the communist appeal are the overexploited, the unemployed, the failures, the lazy discontented, and the intellectuals. Illegal activities in which communists engage are described.

M186 McDEVITT, Harry S. "Communism and American Youth." New York: America Press, 1936. 24 pp.
Two addresses by a Catholic, one dealing with the perversion of youth by communists, the other with communism in American education. Too many educators, under the guise of liberalism and academic freedom, are furthering atheism and un-Americanism.

M187 McDONALD, David J., and LYNCH, Edward A.

"Coal and Unionism: A History of the American Coal Miners' Unions." Silver Spring, Md.: Cornelius Printing Co., 1939. 227 pp. Bibliog.
A history of coal unionism from 1890 to 1940, told from the point of view of the United Mine Workers' administration. Brief attention is paid to developments involving communism, including the leftist miners' movement in Nova Scotia, the amendment to the UMW constitution barring Party members from the union, the "Save the Union" movement, and the Party-sponsored National Miners Union.

M188 McDONALD, Duncan. Let's Make the Issue Clear-Cut, "Liberator," 7 (Aug. 1924), 17.
Following the decision of the Conference for Progressive Political Action to support La Follette, the author, who was nominated for President by the National Farmer Labor Party, withdrew his candidacy. This action makes the issue more clear-cut; the lefts will now rally to the communists, and the middle class to La Follette.

McDONALD, Grace Lois. See GRAHAM, Margaret.

M189 McFARLAND, Dalton E. Left-Wing Domination of Labor Unions: A Case Study of Local Union Leadership, "ILR Research" (New York State School of Industrial and Labor Relations), 1 (June 1955), 2-3.
The problem of leadership in a local of the United Electrical Workers, whose communist-oriented president is continuously re-elected. His support rests upon his ability as a union leader, not upon his political activities. Perhaps the best way to eliminate left-wing leaders is not by attacking their character and political opinions, but by outperforming them.

M190 McFEE, William. Seagoing Soviets, "Saturday Evening Post," 213 (Sept. 21, 1940), 27 ff.
An account of communist activities in the merchant marine. The National Maritime Union, organized following the outlaw strike of 1936, is led by Joseph Curran, who is a stooge for Roy Hudson, the Party's labor director. The NMU follows the Party line in every particular. The Party control of the seamen is paralleled by its control of radio communications.

M191 McGINNIS, H. C. Must the Constitution Protect Those Who Would Destroy It? "America," 64 (Dec. 7, 1940), 230-31.
A call for legislation to outlaw the Communist Party. Despite its guise of independence, the Party is directed by foreign agencies. The Constitution does not require continued toleration of such un-American groups.

M192 . . . . Communist Shop Papers Incite Strikes and Sabotage, "America," 65 (June 21, 1941), 287-88; Communists Do the Planning, Innocents Do the Striking, (June 28), 315-16.
An exposé of the purposes of communist shop papers, taken from the CPUSA's "Shop Paper Manual." Editors of shop papers are shown how to interest workers in shop news while injecting subtle doses of red propaganda, gradually leading workers into the red fold.

M193 McGOVERN, W. M., and others. Should We Pass Laws to Curb Communism? "Northwestern University Reviewing Stand," 12 (April 10, 1949), 3-11.
A panel radio discussion. Professor McGovern of Northwestern favors freedom of speech for those willing to give it to others, not for those seeking to impose a totalitarian state by force. Nathaniel Nathanson of Northwestern asserts that we have enough laws against the evils of communism. Arthur Schlesinger, Jr., of Harvard favors

the use of the clear-and-present-danger test with regard to communists.

M194 McGOWAN, R. A. "Bolshevism in Russia and America." New York: Paulist Press, 1920. 45 pp.
Criticism of Bolshevism in a Catholic publication for belief in the seizure of power and the use of terrorism and civil war. Bolshevik Russia is attacked for disregard of property rights, subjection of religion, and offense against moral law. The rise of the communist movement here is reviewed. Revolutionary unrest may develop here unless economic wrongs are righted.

M195 McGUIRE, James. Deposing a Faker, "Workers Monthly," 4 (Sept. 1925), 508 ff.
An attack on the Johnston administration in the International Association of Machinists as determined to hold power regardless of the sentiment of the rank and file. Militant left-wing elements, under communist leadership, are in revolt against Johnston's class collaboration leadership.

M196 McHENRY, Beth, and MYERS, Frederick N. "Home is the Sailor: The Story of an American Seaman." New York: International Publishers, 1948. 250 pp.
A portrayal of the communist man, in the form of fictionalized biographies of worker radicals in the American merchant marine. Struggles to found the National Maritime Union are described.

M197 McINTIRE, Carl. "Russia's Most Effective Fifth Column in America." Collingswood, N.J.: Christian Beacon Press, 1948. 36 pp.
A reprint of a series of radio addresses by a leader of the fundamentalist American Council of Christian Churches, attacking the Federal Council of the Churches of Christ in America for seeking to destroy the free enterprise system, infiltrating communist ideas into Sunday-school literature, substituting Karl Marx for Jesus Christ, driving for world socialism through the World Council of Churches, and opposing the House Committee on Un-American Activities.

M198 . . . . "Servants of Apostasy." Collingswood, N.J.: Christian Beacon Press, 1955. 414 pp. App. Notes. Ind.
An attack on the World Council of Churches by a leader of the International Council of Christian Churches, a fundamentalist Protestant group opposed to "modernism" and liberalism in religion and to the ecumenical movement. The author centers his attack on the World Council's Second Assembly in Evanston in August 1954, on the grounds that communist clergy were received there and that the program served the communist cause. Chapters 6-8 deal with the communist clergy that attended and with the communist-controlled churches in eastern Europe.

M199 McKAY, Claude. "A Long Way from Home." New York: Lee Furman, 1937. 354 pp.
The autobiography of a West Indian Negro poet who lived in the U.S. during the early 1920's, a close friend of Max Eastman and for a time assistant editor of "Liberator." Though he considered himself a Marxist and was received enthusiastically in the USSR, he never joined the Party. He rejects the Party's proposal of a separate Negro state or economy within the U.S.

M200 . . . . "Harlem: Black Metropolis." New York: Dutton, 1940. 262 pp.
An analysis of Harlem, with attention to its religious, criminal, economic, political, and social aspects, by a Negro poet who attended the 1922 Comintern Congress in Russia but who later repudiated left-wing ties. In this book he criticizes the communists' campaigns against Negro nationalist or socialist leaders, their array of popular front organizations to lure the Negro, their sabotage of the cooperative movement in Harlem, their double-talk on Ethiopia, their undercover activity in the National Negro Congress, their control of the Harlem branch of the Workers Alliance, and their influence on the Negro intelligentsia through the Harlem Writers Guild and the Harlem Artists' Guild.

M201 McKAY, Kenneth Campbell. "The Progressive Movement of 1924." New York: Columbia University Press, 1947. 298 pp. Ind. Bibliog.
A doctoral dissertation on the La Follette campaign of 1924, with an analysis of the role of the communists. The Workers Party sought to gain control of the Farmer-Labor political machinery, nearly ruining the chances for independent political action in 1924. Though in this effort the communists demonstrated their talent for manipulation, parliamentary maneuver, and organizational discipline, their support was repudiated by La Follette, and the Conference for Progressive Political Action remained aloof from them.

M202 McKEE, Oliver, Jr. The Communist Power, "Commonweal," 13 (Feb. 4, 1931), 375-77.
A review and summary of the Fish Committee's report on communist activities in the U.S. Though Fish played to the galleries during the hearings, the report on the whole is good and thorough, showing the communist threat to the U.S. to be real, even if exaggerated.

M203 McKENNEY, Ruth. Meet the Communists, "New Masses," 27 (May 24, 1938), 3-6.
A popularly written account of the Communist Party and its membership, explaining that a Party of only 75,000 can accomplish miracles because of the devotion of its members. Democratic centralism is explained and stress placed on the Party's activity, discipline, and unity.

M204 . . . . What Every Red-Baiter Should Know, "New Masses," 27 (May 31, 1938), 6-9.
A popularly written description of the Communist Party at work, showing how the entire membership can be activated to implement a policy, such as collective security, once its convention has decided on the policy. The Party structure is described, along with its commissions and departments, and its publications, bookshops, and schools.

M205 . . . . "Industrial Valley." New York: Harcourt, Brace, 1939. 379 pp.
A story based on events in Akron, Ohio, 1932-36, which culminated in the establishment of the United Rubber Workers. The procommunist author gives much of the organizing credit to the communists.

M206 . . . . "Browder and Ford: For Peace, Jobs and Socialism." New York: Workers Library, n.d. [1940]. 15 pp.
An election pamphlet during the period of the Hitler-Stalin pact, denouncing the European war as an imperialist struggle for markets, having nothing to do with democracy. Proposing government jobs at union pay for every unemployed worker, the author asserts that socialism, the scientific way of organizing society, means work, freedom, and plenty for all.

M207 . . . . The Communists Nominate Peace, "New Masses," 35 (June 11, 1940), 5-7.
A day-to-day diary of the eleventh national convention of the CPUSA—impressions of the delegates, their hard work, and the nomination of Browder and Ford as presidential and vice-presidential candidates. Emphasis was placed on keeping America out of the war.

M208 McKENNEY, Ruth. "Jake Home." New York: Harcourt, Brace, 1943. 503 pp.
A procommunist presentation, in fiction form, of the communist personality and faith. The novel tells the story of Jake Home, whose career takes him from a white-collar railroad job into organizing activity for the Trade Union Educational League. Jake is last seen as "Big Red," happily leading a May Day parade in New York.

M209 McKEON, John. The Rosenbergs: Roots of Treason, "Commonweal," 57 (Jan. 9, 1953), 347-49.
A condemnation both of the liberals who tacitly approved of communism during the popular front days, and of the anti-Semitism in America which drove the Rosenbergs to affiliation with the Communist Party. These are the roots from which the Rosenberg tragedy grew.

M210 McKINNEY, Ernest Rice. Self-Annihilation for the Black Belt, "Labor Action," 2 (May 1, 1934), 4 ff.
The Communist Party's call for self-determination in the Black Belt is attacked in an American Workers Party publication as Jim Crowism. The slogan is viewed by Negroes as a foreign importation unconnected with realities of life in the U.S.

M211 McKINNON, Harold R. Are We Really against Communism? Reflections upon American Political Philosophy, "American Bar Association Journal," 36 (Jan. 1950), 5-8.
Our changed attitude toward the USSR and toward communists in the U.S. since the war is traced to the rise of Soviet military power. Our recognition of the evil of communism should not blind us to the injustices suffered by workers and racial minorities here as elsewhere.

M212 McLAUGHLIN, Wilmer L., and MENDOZA, John F. Privilege against Self-Incrimination in Federal Courts: Problem of Communist Affiliation, "Notre Dame Lawyer," 26 (Fall 1950), 68-81.
A defense of the privilege against self-incrimination as related to questions concerning Communist Party membership, and an explanation of the legal rationale behind the privilege. Some of the leading cases are reviewed. Though the general welfare and justice may at times be hampered, the purpose of the courts and legal system is to protect individual rights.

M213 McNICHOLAS, John T. "Communism: Its Evils and Its Causes." No publication information, 1937. 28 pp.
The Archbishop of Cincinnati attacks communism for its hatred of religion, its materialism, and its tyranny. Its causes are found in atheism, liberalism, capitalism, poverty, public education, radical unionism, legislative immorality, and effective propaganda.

M214 McPARTLAND, John. Portrait of an American Communist, "Life," 24 (Jan. 5, 1948), 74-78.
A fictional presentation of the activities of "Kelly," a prototype of the American communist, from his entrance into the Party in 1935 until 1947. The narrative traces the changes in line and describes the various causes supported by the Party during this 13-year period. (Reprinted in a pamphlet, "Life and Look Show Us Communism.")

M215 McRYN, Lawrence. Joe Curran's Maritime Union Is Comintern Agency on U.S. Waterfront, "New Leader," 23 (May 4, 1940), 4; C.P. Agents in Maritime Union Raided $165,000 Strike Fund, (May 11), 5-6; Comintern Ran School for Sabotage in Beacon, N.Y.; Trained Sailors to Cripple Merchant Marine, (May 18), 4.
An ousted anticommunist leader of the National Maritime Union tells how communist operatives on the waterfront captured the seamen's unions; how they perpetuated their control of the NMU, ousted opponents, and plundered the strike fund; and how they help maintain a courier service for Moscow and train their members in sabotage.

M216 McTERNAN, John T. Schware, Konigsberg and Independence of the Bar: The Return to Reason, "Lawyers Guild Review," 17 (Summer 1957), 48-53.
Comment on and approval of recent Supreme Court decisions on exclusion of applicants from the bar. Schware had been excluded from the New Mexico bar primarily because of admitted past membership in the Party, whereas Konigsberg was denied admission in California primarily because of his refusal to answer questions on political associations or opinions. In both cases the applicants were upheld.

M217 McWILLIAMS, Carey. "Factories in the Field: The Story of Migratory Farm Labor in California." Boston: Little, Brown, 1939. 334 pp. Bibliog.
Chapter 13, "The Great Strikes" (pp. 211-29), describes the strikes of agricultural workers in California between 1931 and 1935 under the leadership of the Cannery and Agricultural Workers' Industrial Union of the TUUL. Led by communists, this union was met by legal and illegal violence; its leaders were convicted under the state Criminal Syndicalism Act.

M218 .... "Race Discrimination—and the Law." New York: National Federation for Constitutional Liberties, 1945. 24 pp.
A reprint, by a Party-sponsored organization in the civil-rights field, of an argument for the elimination of social discrimination by means of legislation. The author asserts that although race prejudice cannot be eliminated by legislation, it tends to disappear with the abolition of discrimination. Segregation, in his view, can only further solidify Jim Crow in our legal system.

M219 .... Liberty in America: The Test of a Teacher, "Nation," 168 (March 5, 1949), 270-73.
A critical view of the action of the Board of Regents of the University of Washington for dismissing three faculty members for present membership in the CPUSA and placing three others on probation for past membership. The action is held to be clearly unwarranted in at least five of the six cases, and a gross violation of academic freedom. Punishment for beliefs may follow next. (For a defense of the decision see John L. Childs, "Liberty in America: Communists and the Right to Teach," in "The Nation," February 26, 1949.)

M220 .... "Witch Hunt: The Revival of Heresy." Boston: Little, Brown, 1950. 361 pp. Ind.
An examination of postwar anticommunism as a current manifestation of historic witch-hunting, caused by economic and political insecurity rather than by actual danger. The three sections of the volume deal with the question of loyalty and the cause of the current loyalty obsession, the University of Washington academic freedom case, and the nature and origin of heresy. The case of the Hollywood Ten and the University of California loyalty oath are discussed. The author believes that the more we yield to anticommunist hysteria, the more we minimize the differences between democracy and communism and apply the methods of the police state.

M221 .... The Registration of Heretics, "Nation," 171 (Dec. 9, 1950), 526-28.
An account of the requirement in Los Angeles County that

all "subversives" register. Condemning the ambiguity and blanket coverage of the requirement, the author asserts that registration in effect confesses violation of the Criminal Syndicalist Act. The next step, he suggests, will be selective internment in an effort to suppress the socialist heresy.

M222 McWILLIAMS, Carey. The Case of David Hawkins, "Nation," 172 (March 10, 1951), 228-29.
The case of a University of Colorado professor facing trial by a faculty committee on charges growing out of his admission, before the House Committee on Un-American Activities, of past membership in the Communist Party. Among the consequences at the university are loyalty oaths and an investigation by two former FBI agents.

M223 .... No Reds in Mill Valley, "Nation," 173 (July 7, 1951), 12-13.
An account of an effort by a California weekly newspaper to cleanse its small community of communists. Public opinion was so critical that the crusade was abandoned.

M224 ...; ZOLL, Allen; and BUNDY, McGeorge. "Can We Afford Academic Freedom?" Boston: Beacon, 1952. 34 pp.
In this "Harvard Law School Forum," moderated by Robert Brauchner, McWilliams favors academic freedom, opposing loyalty oaths as warning signs of the loss of civil liberties. Zoll, favoring freedom for research but not in teaching, argues that loyalty oaths are useful even though communists will lie. Bundy believes that teachers should have freedom to teach their own subject matter, but not to branch out into other areas.

M225 .... The Witch Hunt and Civil Rights, "Nation," 174 (June 28, 1952), 651-53.
An assertion that the federal loyalty program, with its fears and persecutions, has had an injurious effect upon civil rights here. Loyalty board members examine racial attitudes, because of communist belief in racial equality, and liberals shy away from civil rights cases in which left-wing elements are active. Human freedom is called indivisible.

M226 .... The Oppenheimer Case, "Nation," 178 (May 1, 1954), 373-79.
An article supporting J. Robert Oppenheimer and viewing the charges against him as part of an attack on all atomic scientists. This case, which exposes the contradictions in our security-loyalty program, arose primarily because Oppenheimer opposed the H-bomb. The FBI originated the case and kept it alive; this shows the dangers of entrusting political intelligence to a national police force.

M227 MEAD, George Whitefield. "The Great Menace: Americanism or Bolshevism?" New York: Dodd, Mead, 1920. 155 pp. App.
An attempt to awaken Americans to the menace of revolutionary radicalism, which seeks to overthrow the present social order and all its institutions, including the Church, confiscate all property, and level all classes. The author does not distinguish among socialism, syndicalism, and Bolshevism, using the terms as synonymous and condemning, as part of the same movement, radical demonstrations, strike violence, and IWW sabotage.

M228 MEANY, George. America, Russia and Peace, "American Federationist," 52 (Dec. 1945), 6-7 ff.
A catalogue of undemocratic communist methods and a protest against the tyranny in eastern Europe. The AFL president condemns those in the AFL who support the Soviet Union's aggressiveness, shows how they have used the labor movement as a front for their activities, and

calls upon our government to take a strong stand for freedom and against dictatorial control.

M229 .... "The Last Five Years: How the American Federation of Labor Fights Communism around the World." AFL, n.d. [1951]. 19 pp.
The then secretary-treasurer of the AFL reviews his organization's opposition to communism since the start of communist efforts to penetrate the labor movement and describes the work of its Free Trade Union Committee which carries on this fight on the world scene. Progress has been made in keeping European labor free from Moscow's control. (An address to the Catholic Labor Alliance in Chicago, March 31, 1951.)

M230 .... The A.F. of L. and the Fight for Freedom, "American Federationist," 58 (April 1951), 6-9 ff.
A discussion of the role of the AFL in combating communism in the international labor field. Through the Free Trade Union Committee and the Labor League for Human Rights, the AFL has helped turn the tide against the communists. As a result, trade union morale is improving in western Europe, and communists in trade unions have suffered severe setbacks.

M231 MEDINA, Harold R. The Crime of Conspiracy: Charge to the Jury, "Vital Speeches of the Day," 16 (Nov. 1, 1949), 34-46. Also published in "Current History," Nov. 1949.
The text of the charge to the jury by Federal Judge Harold R. Medina in the case of the 11 communist leaders charged with violating the Smith Act. The charge contains the indictment, a summary of contentions of prosecution and defense, instructions to the jury on credibility of witnesses and evidence, and an interpretation of Smith Act provisions.

M232 .... "A Look at America." Detroit: Chrysler Corporation, 1955. 28 pp.
A speech to the Economic Club of Detroit by the judge in the 1949 Smith Act trial of the 11 communist leaders, stressing the communists' efforts to intimidate or badger him. After the trial, however, the people of America showed their appreciation.

M233 MEGEL, Carl J. AFT Action on Communism, "American Teacher," 37 (April 1953), 2 ff.
A review of AFT actions on communism by the president of the American Federation of Teachers. Between 1931 and 1941, the issue was widely discussed and three locals were expelled; in 1941 the constitution was amended to bar communists from membership; and in 1952 a convention resolution stated the AFT's refusal to defend communist teachers.

M234 MEHLINGER, Howard D. (ed.). "Communism in Theory and Practice: A Book of Readings for High School Students." San Francisco: Chandler, 1964. 274 pp.
A collection of readings on communism in theory, Soviet economics and politics, and the international communist movement. Chapter 7, pp. 198-221, on communism in the U.S., deals with Comintern orders to American communists, rules for underground Party work, reasons for joining and leaving the Party, measures to control communism, and the Party line.

M235 MEIKLEJOHN, Alexander. Should Communists Be Allowed to Teach? "New York Times Magazine," March 27, 1949, 10 ff.
An answer to an article by Sidney Hook in the "New York Times Magazine," February 27, 1949, which asserts that Party members are not searchers after truth and hence are not entitled to academic freedom. Meiklejohn argues

that they should be allowed to teach, because a strong democracy must have free exchange of ideas, including those which seem repugnant to our society.

M236 MEIKLEJOHN, Alexander. What Does the First Amendment Mean? "University of Chicago Law Review," 20 (Spring 1953), 461-79.
An analysis of the "freedom of speech" amendment in the light of Justice Frankfurter's concurring opinion in Dennis vs. United States, which upheld the validity of the Smith Act. Frankfurter's reasoning is called a false and harmful construction of the First Amendment. The right to advocate revolution may not be abridged without violating political freedoms.

M237 MELBY, Ernest O., and PUNER, Morton (eds.). "Freedom and Public Education." New York: Praeger, 1953. 314 pp.
A selection of readings dealing with problems facing American public education, including federal aid, the teaching of religion, and academic freedom. The selections in general defend the public schools against attacks that they are subversive, communist, or collectivist.

M238 MELBY, Ernest O. Academic Fear and the Defense of Freedom, "New Leader," 36 (June 15, 1953), 13-14.
The dean of the School of Education of New York University argues that the biggest current problem regarding academic freedom is the removal of fear and hysteria. He would employ no communists, fascists, or others whose dedication to freedom is questionable; defend all teachers devoted to freedom, regardless of their views; and carefully investigate persons charged with subversion or indoctrination, basing dismissal on overt acts.

M239 MELDON, John. Swinging to the Offensive Against the N.R.A. in the Steel Mills, "Communist," 12 (Oct. 1933), 982-88.
A call for a strong Steel and Metal Workers Industrial Union to counter the AFL, which is supported by the steel trust and the government. The NRA, the AFL, and the Roosevelt government must be ruthlessly exposed.

M240 MELISH DEFENSE COMMITTEE. "The Melish Case: Challenge to the Church." Brooklyn: The Committee, n.d. [1949]. 64 pp.
A detailed statement of the case, including the long ministry of John Howard Melish at the Church of the Holy Trinity in Brooklyn, the appointment of his son as assistant minister in 1939, the younger Melish's chairmanship of the National Council of American-Soviet Friendship, the efforts of the vestrymen to depose them, and the appeal to the courts. The Committee views the case as a political heresy trial.

M241 MELISH, William H. Status of the Church, "New Masses," 53 (Nov. 14, 1944), 16-18.
The associate rector of the Church of the Holy Trinity in Brooklyn affirms that a satisfactory and probably permanent accommodation has taken place between organized religion and the government in the Soviet Union. He protests against the use of religious objections in anti-Soviet propaganda.

M242 .... "Religion Today in the U.S.S.R." New York: National Council of American-Soviet Friendship, 1945. 46 pp.
A denial by a Protestant minister that the Soviets spearhead a godless communism. He asserts that the Russian Orthodox Church supported the fight against the Nazis, that religious institutions survive and expand in Russia unhampered by the state, and that the Soviet constitution guarantees freedom of worship, although the state insists on freedom of antireligious propaganda.

M243 .... "Strength for Struggle: Christian Social Witness in the Crucible of Our Times." New York: Bromwell Press, 1953. 248 pp.
A book of sermons by a Protestant minister whose communist sympathies resulted in a court case against his father, the former rector, for refusing to fire him. Many of the sermons reflect his secular faith, commenting on the suppression of civil liberties in America, the need for coexistence with Russia, America's obsession with the inevitability of a third world war, etc. Addenda following some of the sermons contain material on the Melish case.

M244 MELTZER, Bernard D. Required Records, the McCarran Act, and the Privilege Against Self-Incrimination, "University of Chicago Law Review," 18 (Summer 1951), 687-728.
A discussion by a University of Chicago professor of law of the registration and record-keeping requirements imposed on communist organizations by the Internal Security Act of 1950 (the McCarran Act). Legal precedents support the access to records in the interests of effective administration, while barriers against unjustified invasions of privacy are available.

M245 ..., and KALVEN, Harry, Jr. Invoking the Fifth Amendment—Some Legal and Practical Considerations: A Discussion, "Bulletin of the Atomic Scientists," 9 (June 1953), 176-86 ff.
Differing interpretations of the Fifth Amendment by two University of Chicago Law School professors. Meltzer argues that its protection should be limited to self-incrimination. Kalven defends its use on other grounds, as the only way to fight improper and extralegal congressional investigations and invasions of privacy.

M246 MELTZER, Milton. Young America Has a Program, "New Masses," 32 (July 18, 1939), 12-14.
A report on the Fifth American Youth Congress. Charges of communist control, and efforts to split the Congress, were made by anticommunists, from Tories to Trotskyists. YCL members, while protesting that communism was not dictatorship, agreed to condemn all dictatorships, communist and fascist.

M247 MENCKEN, H. L. What Is Going On in the World, "American Mercury," 26 (May 1932), 1-7.
The editor of the "American Mercury" ridicules communist writers who intervened in a Kentucky strike. Free assembly and speech should not be invoked in the name of communism, since they are not permitted where communism prevails. Communism will not succeed here, because it challenges private property and Christianity.

M248 .... Illuminators of the Abyss, "Saturday Review of Literature," 11 (Oct. 6, 1934), 155-56.
A derisive commentary on the Marxist-inspired proletarian literature movement. Most of the writers are failures, and the critics are even more plainly inferiorities. The literature produced is amateurish and preposterous, and the movement, like other quackeries, will soon disappear.

M249 MEREDITH, Burgess. Confessions of a Fellow-Traveler, "Common Sense," 8 (Oct. 1939), 3-6.
A former president of the Actors' Equity Association tells of the troubles caused the organization by a small group of communists and fellow-travelers. At their suggestion he hired an able lawyer, who turned out to be an ardent Party member. Burgess tells of David Dubinsky's advice to dissociate himself from the communists and provide a militant democratic leadership.

M250 MERETO, Joseph J. "The Red Conspiracy." New York: National Historical Society, 1920. 398 pp. Ind. App.
An account of the socialist and communist movements abroad and in the U.S., stressing the development of American communism out of the socialist left wing, the revolutionary nature of the IWW, the red terror of the Bolsheviks in Russia, and the threat of the red conspiracy here to established government, religion, the family, and the race. The peril of socialism to workingmen is emphasized, as are socialist organizing methods and the use of deception. The author proposes a campaign of argument and education against socialism.

M251 MERIT, Donald. "The Labor Youth League Fights Back." New York: National Student Council, the League, n.d. 8 pp.
The chairman of the New York Student Division of the Labor Youth League replies to Attorney General Brownell's petition to have the League and 11 other organizations declared communist fronts. He attacks the McCarran Act, points to the danger to academic freedom, and denies that the League is controlled by the Party.

M252 MEYER, Frank. Philosophers of Capitalism in Decay, "Communist," 20 (April 1941), 368-76.
The philosophy of capitalism in decay is the philosophy of idealism and pragmatism. Both are escapist philosophies that attempt to refute Marxism by denying that objective truth exists.

M253 MEYER, Frank S. Principles and Heresies: The Meaning of McCarthyism, "National Review," 5 (June 14, 1958), 565-66.
A defense of McCarthy and a denunciation of liberals and intellectuals who persecuted him. The similarities between liberalism and communism were dramatized by McCarthy; it was this perception, rather than McCarthy's methods, that made liberal leadership attack him.

M254 .... "The Moulding of Communists: The Training of the Communist Cadre." New York: Harcourt, Brace, 1961. 214 pp. Notes. Ind.
A description of the theory and practice of communist training, written by a former communist activist. The philosophic system of Marxism-Leninism is described briefly, and major attention is given to the techniques of recruitment and of training, with emphasis on the functions, curriculum, and pressures of Party schools. The objective of the communist man is conquest of the world for communism with any weapons and by any means. The agency to achieve victory in this struggle is the Party, whose assigned tasks must be carried out without question or reservation. Faced with such a Party and such men, compromise and peaceful coexistence are impossible, the alternatives being victory or defeat.

M255 MEYER, Hershel D. "Must We Perish? The Logic of 20th Century Barbarism." New York: New Century, 1949. 171 pp. Ref. notes.
An assertion that war with the USSR, now urged upon us, would lead to disaster because the USSR also possesses the atom bomb. Recent history shows that monopoly capitalism and the needs of exploiting ruling classes lead to war. Only Marxism-Leninism shows the relationship between technology and poverty, between monopolistic industry and the drive to war. The USSR is offering peace and friendship, and America must choose between suicide and survival. American communists pave the way for an America free of profit, prospering in a peaceful world.

M256 .... "The Last Illusion: America's Plan for World Domination." New York: Anvil-Atlas Press, 1954. 447 pp. Bibliog. Distributed by New Century.
An assertion that America's ruling class seeks to bring about World War III and achieve world domination. Americans can combat these forces by supporting the world peace movement. Among topics dealt with are American foreign policy, the history of its development, colonialism, the Korean War, the development of U.S.-style fascism, the dynamics of the Soviet peace policy, the Pentagon design for World War III, and the alternative of coexistence.

M257 .... "The Krushchev Report and the Crisis in the American Left." Brooklyn: Independence Publishers, 1956. 111 pp.
An examination of the state of the CPUSA in the wake of the revelations of Stalin's excesses. Weaknesses in the Party here are traced to poor leadership, the surrounding social climate, and unsatisfactory class composition. Nevertheless the Party has made important contributions here; its dissolution would be a severe blow to progressive America, whereas a revitalized Party could enrich American life.

M258 .... "History and Conscience: The Case of Howard Fast." New York: Anvil-Atlas, 1958. 63 pp.
A procommunist appraisal of Howard Fast's career and of his "The Naked God," which expressed his disillusionment with communism and the Party. His spirit was broken by the fears and tensions of the cold war. Far from being a martyr to the Party and its cause, Fast had gained recognition, a world-wide audience, and wealth through Party support of his writings. "The Naked God" is remarkable for the poverty of its ideas. The charge of Soviet anti-Semitism is refuted.

M259 MEYER, J. Stalinism and Negro History, "Fourth International," 10 (Nov. 1949), 309-14; (Dec.), 337-41.
A Trotskyist analysis of Herbert Aptheker's writings on Negro history. Aptheker is charged with distorting Negro history in order to serve the needs of the Stalinists, who seek to manipulate American Negroes in the interests of Soviet policy.

M260 MICHAELS, C. H. The Deviationist Macaroon, "New Yorker," 26 (Sept. 2, 1950), 50-56.
An account of the infiltration of the Young Communist League into a campus dramatic group in the mid-1930's, of the repulse of Trotskyite efforts to work with the group, and of criticism by the Party organizer of one of the plays as ideologically incorrect.

M261 MICHELSON [pseud. for H. Valetski]. A Political Letter to the Party, from the Special Representative Sent to America by the C.I., "Communist" (organ of the Communist Party of America), 1, n.d. [Dec. 1922?].
A letter written by the Comintern representative to the CPA on the eve of his leaving the U.S. He urges the Party to publish propaganda, establish a research bureau, improve finances, help create a broad labor party, and "Americanize" the work of the foreign language federations.

M262 "MILITANT," On the Eve of the Party Convention, 2 (Feb. 1, 1929), 3.
An analysis of the situation in the Workers (Communist) Party following the 1928 expulsions of Cannon and his supporters and prior to the Party convention. Lovestone and Foster factions are engaged in a power struggle, while both denounce Trotskyism. The only hope for help

from Moscow for the genuinely proletarian elements is the overthrow by the Trotskyist Opposition of the present leadership of the CPSU.

M263 "MILITANT," The Party Is "United" Again! Latest "Open Address" of the E.C.C.I., 2 (June 1, 1929), 3.
An analysis of the address of the Executive Committee of the Communist International calling for the expulsion of the Lovestoneite leadership of the CPUSA. This action is linked to the struggle between the Stalin centrists in the Communist Party of the Soviet Union and the Bucharin-Rykov right wing. The Lovestone-Pepper regime in the CPUSA had been closely allied with Bucharin.

M264 ..., The T.U.U.L. Conference, 2 (Oct. 1, 1929), 2.
While recognizing the achievements of the Cleveland conference of the Trade Union Educational (now Unity) League, this Trotskyist publication emphasizes the shortcomings and blunders of the conference. Among these are gross exaggeration of its strength, mechanical control by the Party, no serious review of past activities, a program that guarantees expulsion of left-wingers from AFL unions, lack of faith in the masses, and ultraleftism.

M265 ..., Marine Workers' Rank and File Revolts against the Stalinist Union Bureaucracy! 3 (Nov. 1, 1930), 4-5.
A document, signed by a group of members (most of them Party members) of the Marine Workers Industrial Union, protesting the present leadership of the union, its incompetence, irresponsibility, and bankrupt policies. The group calls for union democracy, the election of new leadership, organizational responsibility, and an end to sectarianism and to adventurism in the handling of strikes. The "Militant" adds that the situation in the Marine Union is typical of the unions under Stalinist control.

M266 ..., Stalinist-Lovestone Unity Negotiations, 5 (May 7, 1932), 1 ff.
A reprint of two letters, one apparently written by a member of the CP and the other by a Lovestoneite, dealing with unity negotiations. Though no difference in principle exists, there is a question as to Lovestone's attitude toward the Brandler group in Germany. Old-time Fosterites are said to lack enthusiasm for unity and to be fearful of competition for office. If unity is achieved, the CPUSA will make a turn to the right.

M267 ..., The Intellectuals Revolt against Stalinist Hooliganism, 7 (March 10, 1934), 4.
A report in a Trotskyist paper of a meeting, sponsored by the Socialist Party to protest Austrian fascism, which was disrupted by the CPUSA. Subsequently 25 intellectuals who had been friendly to the Party signed an open letter to it and to the "New Masses," protesting the Party's action. The "Militant" urges them to recognize the need for a new revolutionary party in the U.S.

M268 MILLARD, Betty. "Women against Myth." New York: International Publishers, 1948. 23 pp.
A communist view of women's efforts to achieve equality in the U.S., contrasted with the full participation open to women in the USSR. Women here are urged to support efforts of the Congress of American Women for price and rent control, protective legislation, equal pay, and arresting the drive of the monopolists toward reaction and war.

M269 .... "Women on Guard: How the Women of the World Fight for Peace." New York: New Century, 1952. 31 pp.
A member of the secretariat of the Women's International Democratic Federation describes her travels through Europe and Asia, meeting "progressive" women, all of whom seek the end of our "madness for war." She describes the part American women have played and can play in "Women for Peace" activities.

M270 MILLER, Bert. Giant Power, "Communist," 7 (Aug. 1928), 473-80.
The power and public utilities industry exemplifies the intimate connection between Big Business and government. A list of individual Americans who link up power and politics is followed by a brief description of power developments in the Soviet Union, where the workers reap the profit.

M271 MILLER, Charles J. Devastating Exposure of the Workers' Party Machinations among Textile Mill Workers, "Industrial Solidarity," Dec. 19, 1928, 3; Dec. 26, 2.
A critical review in an IWW paper of Workers (Communist) Party activities in textile strikes, beginning with the Lawrence strike of 1919, charging the communists with leaving behind a trail of defeats and with seeking to make capital for their party at the expense of the working class. One of their specialities was collecting funds, but the accounts were very badly kept.

M272 MILLER, Charles R. "Christendom's Crusade against the Communist Peril." Los Angeles: Wetzel Publishing Co., 1949. 79 pp. Ind.
Arguing that the Kremlin has in fact declared war upon us through its aim of world conquest, the author calls for a Christian crusade of aggressive propaganda against communism. He proposes preparation of a brochure for permanent world peace, presenting the universal elements of Christian teachings that would appeal to reasonable people everywhere and help mankind achieve peace and happiness.

M273 MILLER, Kelly. Should Black Turn Red? "Opportunity," 11 (Nov. 1933), 328-32 ff.
Although the communists have shown sincerity in the Scottsboro case, a Negro leader warns Negroes against sedition and treason, urging them instead to trust in the American Constitution. The plight of Negroes would be the same if communism came to the U.S., in view of bigotry among the white proletariat.

M274 MILLER, Loren. One Way Out—Communism, "Opportunity," 12 (July 1934), 214-17.
An appeal to Negroes to consider communism; with the depression showing the last crack in the edifice of capitalism, Negroes should seriously consider "black self-determination" and other communist ideas. (See also the article by Kelly Miller in the November 1933 issue for the other side of the argument.)

M275 MILLER, Marion. "I Was a Spy." Indianapolis and New York: Bobbs Merrill, 1960. 224 pp.
The experiences of a woman who joined the Party as an undercover agent for the FBI, and whose husband had already served the FBI in that capacity. A Los Angeles resident during five years of Party membership, her career as an undercover agent ended when she testified publicly for the government in a case against the communists in 1955. She describes her experiences in the Party, the suspicions she aroused, and the abuse to which she was subjected when her mission became known.

M276 MILLER, Martin. Devaluation—Colonization Instrument of U.S. Capital, "Political Affairs," 29 (Jan. 1950), 78-96.
American capitalists forced devaluation of the British pound and other European currencies, making it easier for them to buy the properties and gain control of the European

economies. The workers in both Europe and America bore the cost of depreciation; in Europe there is pressure for wage cuts, whereas here workers and farmers suffer from the depression caused by reduced exports.

M277 MILLER, Merle. The Second Hiss Trial, "New Republic," 122 (Feb. 6, 1950), 11-14.
An account, sympathetic to Hiss and painting a derogatory picture of Whittaker Chambers, of the second Hiss perjury trial. While Hiss may have been guilty of perjury, he did what he felt was right, and what seemed right in the popular front 1930's.

M278 .... "The Judges and the Judged." Foreword by Robert E. Sherwood. Garden City, N.Y.: Doubleday, 1952. 220 pp.
A report of an investigation sponsored by the American Civil Liberties Union into blacklisting in the radio and television industries. Though the author was concerned with blacklisting from any source, including communists, the report deals primarily with the organized blacklist, initiated by "Counterattack" and "Red Channels," to keep communists and left-wingers off radio and television. The ACLU view is that employment in radio and television should be based on competence alone, so long as acts and associations are lawful.

M279 ...; RIESEL, Victor; and FORSTER, Arnold (Marquis Childs, moderator). Who Are the Troublemakers in our Democracy? "Town Meeting," 18 (May 27, 1952). 15 pp.
Forster asserts that the troublemakers are those who inflame racial and religious prejudices; Miller feels it is those who, in their anxiety to fight the communists, are willing to set aside the traditional American freedoms; and Riesel believes that communism is the troublemaker, not only here but across the world.

M280 .... Trouble on Madison Avenue, N.Y., "Nation," 174 (June 28, 1952), 631-36.
A discussion of the damaging effects of "Red Channels," "Counterattack," and their hysterical proponents on careers in radio, television, and motion pictures. The radio and television industry has not hired those named in "Red Channels" as having once belonged to a purported subversive organization. Neither "Red Channels" nor the industry checked on the truth of the allegations.

M281 MILLER, Moses. "A Jew Looks at the War." New York: Jewish People's Committee, n.d. [1940?]. 31 pp.
The Party line for Jews during the Nazi-Stalin pact period. The author alleges that refugees in French concentration camps fare no better than those in German camps and that leaders of the Polish government-in-exile have anti-Semitic backgrounds. A victory for either side, he asserts, would be equally disastrous.

M282 .... "A Message to American Jewry." New York: Jewish People's Committee, 1941. 63 pp.
A report, during the Nazi-Soviet pact period, picturing the tragic fate of Jews under the Nazis and asserting that they have found security and safety only in the Soviet Union and the U.S. Whereas there is no anti-Semitism in the USSR, in America Jewish security is threatened. Jews should unite with other progressives to defend democracy and peace.

M283 .... "Crisis in Palestine." New York: New Century, 1946. 32 pp.
The communist position on Palestine in 1946. Denouncing both British and American imperialism in Palestine, the author urges the unity of Jewish and Arab leaders and a joint struggle for independence and freedom. He attacks Zionist propaganda and philosophy, Jewish terrorism in Palestine, and partition schemes.

M284 .... "Soviet 'Anti-Semitism': The Big Lie." New York: Jewish Life, n.d. [1948?]. 31 pp.
A communist condemnation of the charge spread by portions of the daily press and by Jewish and socialist organizations, that the USSR has embarked on an official campaign of anti-Semitism. This is called one of the dirtiest lies ever to come from minds distorted by hatred.

M285 .... Zionism and the State of Israel, "Jewish Life," 3 (May 1949), 6-10; (June), 15-19; (July), 21-24; (Aug.), 22-26; (Sept.), 23-26.
A review of the communist policy toward Zionism and Israel by a member of the editorial board of a Jewish communist publication. The Party supports the struggle of the masses of Israel for independence, while opposing Zionism as a bourgeois nationalist movement. Feudal society and the growth of commerce are reviewed to show the rise of the bourgeoisie and the oppression of national minorities.

M286 .... "Nazis Preferred: The Re-Nazification of Western Germany." New York: New Century, 1950. 31 pp.
An assertion that the U.S. is laying the groundwork for another war by its policy of coddling the Nazis, allowing them to regain power under the pretense of building a bulwark against communism. The author sees Big Business, which is supporting the financial interests of the old German cartels, behind this treasonable policy.

M287 MILLER, Richard I. "Teaching about Communism." New York: McGraw-Hill, 1966. 355 pp. Bibliog. Ind.
A book designed to help educators who are organizing programs for teaching about communist totalitarianism. Sections deal with reasons for studying communism in the schools, what to teach, basic concepts, criteria for selecting material, approaches to teaching about communism, teacher education, and school programs in elementary and high schools.

M288 MILLER, Robert. The White Collar Workers and the War, "Communist," 22 (Jan. 1943), 88-96.
A plea for more widespread organization of white collar and professional workers, and for unity of the middle class and the labor movement in the war effort. The economic problems and social characteristics of white collar workers are reviewed. White collar unions can at the same time strengthen the war effort and solve their collective bargaining problems.

M289 MILLER, Robert Moats. "American Protestantism and Social Issues, 1919-1939." Chapel Hill: University of North Carolina Press, 1958. 385 pp. Bibliog. Ind.
Relations between Protestantism and communism are among the social issues discussed. Chapters 3-5 (pp. 63-112) analyze the general appeal of communism in the 1930's, with particular attention to the Methodist Federation for Social Service, the Episcopal Church League for Industrial Democracy, various left-leaning church journals, and the National Religion and Labor Foundation. Chapter 13 (pp. 181-200) deals with church attitudes toward treatment of communists as a civil liberties issue from 1919 on.

M290 MILLET, Martha. Modern Poetry: For or Against? "Masses & Mainstream," 8 (March 1955), 35-44.

An assertion that there cannot be a single form of poetry for all time, and that no one form is more appropriate for people's poetry than another. Progressive organizations, instead of insisting on traditional forms, should open channels of communication so that poetry becomes a vital force for understanding action.

M291 MILLET, Martha (ed.). "The Rosenbergs: Poems of the United States." New York: Sierra Press, 1957. 72 unnumbered pp. Bibliog.
A collection of poems on the Rosenbergs, pleading their cause; the editor contributes a poem and an introduction. Among the poets included are W. E. B. DuBois, Aaron Kramer, A. B. Magil, Dora Teitelboim, Michael Gold, Alfred Kreymborg, George Abbe, Yuri Suhl, Eve Merriam, and Helen Sobell.

M292 MILLION, Elmer M. Political Crimes, II, "Missouri Law Review," 5 (June 1940), 293-323.
A review of federal and state cases since World War I involving communists, among others, charged with criminal syndicalism, criminal anarchy, and sedition. Among the cases analyzed are Whitney vs. California, People vs. Ruthenberg, DeJonge vs. Oregon, Gitlow vs. New York, and Herndon vs. State. (Part I of the article, in the April issue, dealt with cases prior to World War I.)

M293 MILLIS, Walter. Are Subversives Really Subversive? "Saturday Review of Literature," 38 (Sept. 3, 1955), 16 ff.
A denial that there is any reason for the extreme measures advocated by the Attorney General to guard internal security; communists just are not that subversive. Indefinable fears and unverifiable assumptions are the only bases for our pervasive internal-security inquisitorial system.

M294 . . . . "Communism and Civil Liberties." New York: Fund for the Republic, 1956. 16 pp.
A view of the new "soft" line announced by the CPUSA in September 1956, as being more dangerous than the subversive one of the past. The Party now seeks to appear as just another political party, substituting a united front policy for the old one of capture and rule or ruin, and raising again difficult civil liberties issues. Allegiance to the basic principles of the Constitution will keep communists from gaining support.

M295 . . . . "Individual Freedom and the Common Defense." New York: Fund for the Republic, 1957. 80 pp.
An examination of the problem of the common defense from the point of view of individual freedom. "The Control of Sedition" is considered on pages 31-61, and "Secrecy and Security" on pages 63-80. Legislative measures against communist subversion are examined, as is their fate in the courts. The basic issue is whether the courts, in curbing antisubversion measures, have weakened defenses required for national security. The entire secrecy system needs clearer definition and greater flexibility.

M296 MILLS, C. Wright. "The New Men of Power: America's Labor Leaders." New York: Harcourt, Brace, 1948. 323 pp. Notes. Ind.
In chapter 11, "Communists and Labor Leaders" (pp. 186-200), the author shows why most American labor leaders fight the communists. He tells how communists entered the CIO and where their strength is today. He criticizes the communists for changes of policy determined by Russia's needs, for maintaining power by defamation and intrigue, for dictatorial rule, and for delaying the formation of a labor party.

M297 MILNER, Lucille. "Education of an American Liberal: An Autobiography." Introd. by Alvin Johnson. New York: Horizon Press, 1954. 318 pp. Ind.
The autobiography of the first secretary of the American Civil Liberties Union, who was associated with that organization from its beginning in 1920 until 1945. Pages 261-69 deal with the "purge" resolution of February 1940, declaring supporters of totalitarian dictatorship in any country ineligible to serve on the ACLU governing committees or staff. This resolution brought the resignation of Dr. Harry F. Ward, who was chairman both of the ACLU and of the American League for Peace and Democracy. It was followed by the trial and removal (pp. 270-94) of Elizabeth Gurley Flynn, the one CP member on the ACLU board.

M298 MIMS, Sam. Technique of the "Artful Dodger," "American Mercury," 78 (May 1954), 57-62.
A report on the insolence and disrespect exhibited by hostile witnesses before the Senate Internal Security and the House Un-American Activities committees. Their techniques include ridicule, offensive language, hysterical outbursts, and vilification of persons in authority. Use of the Fifth Amendment in other than criminal cases is condemned by the author.

M299 MINDEL, J. The Socialist Party and Its "Principles," "Workers Monthly," 5 (Nov. 1926), 601-4.
A characterization of the Socialist Party as demoralized organizationally and ideologically. No longer a Marxian party believing in the class struggle, it advocates a gentlemanly revolution through the ballot. It has no position on the League of Nations; it attacks the Soviet Union; it hates the proletariat and fears the big bourgeoisie.

M300 MINGULIN, I. The Struggle for the Bolshevization of the Communist Party of the United States, "International Press Correspondence," 9 (June 14, 1929), 605-8.
A comment on the decision of the Executive Committee of the Communist International on the factional quarrel in the CPUSA. Not only was Lovestone more responsible than the Foster-Bittelman faction for rightist errors, but he refused to accept Comintern decisions unreservedly, even threatening to split the Party. His views are criticized.

M301 MINGULIN, S. The Crisis in the United States and the Problems of the Communist Party, "Communist," 9 (June 1930), 500-18.
The Party is leading American workers in strikes and street struggles and is recruiting thousands of workers, many of them Negroes. Mass struggle is based on the growth of unemployment, with strikes interwoven with revolutionary demonstrations. The Party must build up the TUUL, organizationally and politically; it must improve its work among Negroes and make the "Daily Worker" a mass organ.

M302 MINOR, Robert. I Change My Mind a Little, "Liberator," 3 (Oct. 1920), 5-11.
An explanation of the author's transformation from an anarchist critic of Soviet Russia to a disciplined American communist. At first disenchanted with the Russian state bureaucracy, Minor gradually realized, after rereading the Marxist classics, that only through central authority and discipline could the revolution be brought to a successful conclusion.

M303 . . . . "Stedman's Red Raid." Cleveland: Toiler Publishing Association, 1921. 19 pp.
An attack on Seymour Stedman, prominent socialist attorney, growing out of a lawsuit over ownership of a commu-

nist clubhouse and educational center in Detroit. Stedman allegedly sought to prove that the communists advocated destruction of the U.S. government by direct or mass action, at a time when such beliefs were thought punishable by prison for citizens and deportation for aliens.

M304 MINOR, Robert. How I Became a Rebel, "Labor Herald," 1 (June 1922), 25-26.
Autobiographical details about one of the most famous communist cartoonists. He joined the Socialist Party in 1908, drifted out of it about 1912, and became interested in anarchism, particularly during his art studies in Paris. A rebel in the service of the communist revolution is the only kind that is important.

M305 . . . . We Want a Labor Party, "Liberator," 5 (Nov.-Dec. 1922), 13-17.
A call for the formation of a class political alliance between workers and dirt farmers. A labor party is desirable, historically inevitable, and the only way out of the present stagnation. A labor party, far from conflicting with communist principles, is a first step toward class consciousness. Labor will adopt a communist program if it is proved correct.

M306 . . . . The Black Ten Millions, "Liberator," 7 (Feb. 1924), 7-9; (March), 15-17.
An early communist examination of the Negro question, reviewing slave revolts, experiences after emancipation, the migration to northern industrial cities, the Marcus Garvey movement, and the shift of the Republican Party to white supremacy. The position of the Communist International on the Negro question is presented.

M307 . . . . The Handkerchief on Garvey's Head, "Liberator," 7 (Oct. 1924), 17-25.
A communist attack on Marcus Garvey, organizer of the Universal Negro Improvement Association to colonize American Negroes in Africa, comparing him with the "handkerchief-heads" or plantation house slaves who betrayed the insurrections of the field slaves. The author terms colonization a swindle, and calls upon Negroes to enter the class struggle as equals.

M308 . . . . Let Your Superintendent Be Your Labor Leader, "Workers Monthly, 4 (April 1925), 245-47 ff.
A denunciation of wage cuts, increased work loads, and feudal class relationships in the New England textile industry. A national organizing job led by the Workers (Communist) Party and the TUEL is called for, involving amalgamation of all existing unions and organization of the unorganized, to resist wage cuts and save unionism in the industry. Formation of a dual union is opposed.

M309 . . . . The First Negro Workers' Congress, "Workers Monthly," 5 (Dec. 1925), 68-73.
An account of the American Negro Labor Congress which met in Chicago in October. Though only a few thousand organized Negro workers were represented, many Negro federal locals failed to send delegates because of William Green's threats to revoke their charters. The organizational plan of the Congress is to form local councils in all centers of Negro population, with interracial labor committees in every locality.

M310 . . . . Death or a Program! "Workers Monthly," 5 (April 1926), 270-73 ff.
A protest against the impending split and destruction of the Universal Negro Improvement Association (the Garvey movement). Garvey is attacked for selling out the black workers for the illusory goal of a back-to-Africa movement. The organization is doomed unless the working class Negroes in it take a militant left-wing stand.

M311 . . . . After Garvey—What? "Workers Monthly," 5 (June 1926), 362-65.
The Universal Negro Improvement Association under the leadership of Marcus Garvey, whose program in effect calls for mass deportations of Negroes to Africa, is breaking up. Its fragments contain some of the best rank-and-file material to be found. The mass unrest of the Negro population will merge with the advanced section of the labor movement.

M312 . . . . The Party on the Trade Union Front in the United States, "Communist International," 4 (Feb. 28, 1927), 39-42.
The tendency in the American labor movement is toward class collaboration; every struggle opens up a gulf between the rank and file and the bureaucrats, providing an opportunity for the Trade Union Educational League. The Party enters struggles and offers leadership, as in the Passaic textile strike and the New York garment strikes.

M313 . . . . The Murder of Sacco and Vanzetti, "Communist," 6 (Sept.-Oct. 1927), 338-46.
Although Sacco and Vanzetti were anarchists, the demonstrations became in name and in fact "Bolshevistic." The executions resulted from the need of the American bourgeoisie to defy the working class of the U.S. and the rest of the world. The ups and downs in the seven years of the case responded to changes in class struggles at home and abroad.

M314 . . . . The Negro and His Judases, "Communist," 10 (July 1931), 632-39.
A denunciation of Negro petty-bourgeois elements who seek to divert Negro discontent into a bourgeois nationalist form, supporting the capitalist system and U.S. imperialism. The National Urban League, the NAACP, and the more prosperous Negro churches are examples.

M315 . . . . The EPIC Mass Movement in California, "Communist," 13 (Dec. 1934), 1214-33.
Upton Sinclair is called a capitalist tool, because of his program to have the unemployed use foreclosed farms and factories, exchanging products through barter. Though this would have freed the capitalists from taxation for relief, they opposed Sinclair for governor through fear that he would arouse workers into a readiness to accept communist leadership. (Based on a report to the Political Bureau of the Party's Central Committee; the remainder of the article failed to appear.)

M316 . . . . May Day under the Guns, "Communist," 14 (May 1935), 387-410.
An assertion that the decadent state of world capitalism is rapidly leading to World War II. Economic recovery, based on increased productivity and profits, is not benefiting the working masses and is actually a preparation for war, which will eventually bring about the end of capitalism.

M317 . . . . Somebody is Distressed—but Not Karl Marx, "Communist," 14 (Sept. 1935), 830-50.
A review of Earl Browder's "Communism in the United States," with an explanation of the change in Party tactics following the Seventh World Congress. The article bridges the gap between Browder's book (written before the Congress) and the new policy of working within U.S. unions to establish a labor party base. Quotations from Marx and Lenin answer the charge that the new united front line departs from Marxism-Leninism.

M318 . . . . "The Struggle against War and the Peace Policy of the Soviet Union." New York: Workers Library, 1936. 47 pp.

A report to the 1936 convention of the Party, in the early days of the popular front, asserting that the issue throughout the world is one of democracy against fascism. Not only the USSR, but every neighbor of Germany, is threatened with Nazi aggression. Praising the peace policy of the USSR, Minor calls for a world front of workers, farmers, and all friends of peace against the instigators of war.

M319 MINOR, Robert. Left Trends in the Socialist Party, "Communist," 15 (Feb. 1936), 147-64; (March), 253-69.
A critique of the draft program of the Socialist Party's left wing in the light of united front objectives. Though the socialist left-wingers claim to be the defenders of orthodox Marxism, Marxism calls, not for weasel words, but for unity of the working class in action.

M320 . . . . Lenin—His Meaning for Us Today, "Communist," 18 (Jan. 1939), 25-34; (Feb.), 114-27.
Lenin was a great cosmopolitan leader who was a keen observer of events in many countries, including the U.S. He saw that not all wars are imperialist wars. Today, when only the fascist states are the aggressors, peaceful capitalists, socialists, and the weak states should band together. Isolationism or appeasement will aid the fascist conquests of the weak states.

M321 . . . . The Second Imperialist War, "Communist," 18 (May 1939), 409-34.
Chamberlain's appeasement policy led to the fascist conquest of Czechoslovakia and Spain. American reactionaries are aiding the fascist states by fighting for American neutrality. The progressives must force the American government to collaborate with other democracies. Once united, the democracies would be much more powerful than the fascist states.

M322 . . . . Data on the Development of American Agriculture in the Twentieth Century, "Communist," 18 (Sept. 1939), 887-96.
An analysis of American agriculture, emphasizing the ruination of small farmers, the recent decline in the number of farm wage laborers, and the concentration of capital in agriculture. The deterioration and creeping ruin of the past half-century show that capitalism offers no solution to agrarian problems.

M323 . . . . "Free Earl Browder!" New York: Workers Library, 1941. 15 pp.
An assertion that Browder was jailed for speaking out against World War II as an imperialist war. The most convenient excuse on which Browder could be jailed—passport violations—was used, although the alleged violations occurred five years prior to the indictment.

M324 . . . . "One War: To Defeat Hitler." New York: Workers Library, 1941. 62 pp.
The communist position in the period between the Nazi invasion of the USSR and the Pearl Harbor assault. In a speech to the national council of the Young Communist League in July 1941, and in an article in September, Minor calls for U.S. entry into the war as necessary to defend America and liberate the world from the Nazis. A statement by Lenin on the Marxist view of war is included.

M325 . . . . Munich and Anti-Munich: September, 1938, to September, 1941, "Communist," 20 (Sept. 1941), 776-92.
A review of events from September 1938 to September 1941, justifying the changing Russian position. The war ceased to be an imperialist war when Russia was attacked. For the U.S. the war has become one of national existence,

since a Russian defeat would leave the U.S. to face a more powerful foe alone. U.S. entry into the war is urged.

M326 . . . . As We Fight, "Communist," 20 (Dec. 1941), 1045-50.
A summary speech by the Party's acting secretary at the close of its national committee meeting, December 7, 1941. Communists expected the Japanese attack on Pearl Harbor, knowing that Hitler would call on his Japanese ally when his Russian campaign ran into difficulties. The Party seeks close collaboration between Russia and the U.S., and the utmost war effort from the whole American population.

M327 . . . . "Our Ally: The Soviet Union." New York: Workers Library, 1942. 15 pp.
The text of a speech by the acting secretary of the Party, defending the Soviet Union as the most important ally of the U.S. in the war. He denounces as fascist those who question the fighting capacity of the Red Army, point to the Nazi-Soviet pact, call the Soviet government dictatorial, or deplore the Moscow trials. He calls for compulsory universal military training.

M328 . . . . "The Year of Great Decision, 1942." New York: Workers Library, 1942. 47 pp.
The text of a report to the national committee of the Party in April 1942, appraising the military situation. Minor stresses the importance of worker mobilization and a favorable outcome of the 1942 elections to the opening of a second front, which he considers vital.

M329 . . . . The Nation and the War, "Communist," 21 (Jan. 1942), 38-56.
Excerpts from the main report of the Political Committee to the Party's national committee, December 6-7, 1941, asserting that the German attack on Russia has transformed the war into one in which American national existence is at stake. The U.S. should enter the war, setting up other fronts to take the pressure off Russia. America must mobilize behind an all-out production drive, with strikes limited.

M330 . . . . A Biddle's-Eye View of the War and the Communist Party, "Communist," 21 (July 1942), 507-21.
U.S. Attorney General Biddle follows the Trotskyist conception of Marxists as terrorists when he accuses the Communist Party of seeking violent overthrow of the American government. Communists, like Lincoln, believe that only a mass popular revolt can legitimately overthrow the government by force. The present war is one of national freedom, not imperialism.

M331 . . . . "Invitation to Join the Communist Party." New York: Workers Library, 1943. 16 pp.
An appeal for membership from the assistant general secretary of the Party, who presents it as the party of the workers and the defender of democracy. The Party, he states, represents the spirit of international labor solidarity and of solidarity with the USSR. Proposals for socialism are not put forward now, in the interests of national unity and winning the war.

M332 . . . . What Are We Fighting For? "Communist," 22 (May 1943), 434-42.
Criticism of postwar plans in a symposium organized by the St. Louis "Post Dispatch." Although it is hoped that the war will free colonial peoples and continue the United Nations alliance, emphasis must remain on preventing foreign conquests rather than formulating plans for a postwar world. Otherwise Americans may not be the ones doing the planning after the war.

M333 MINOR, Robert. The Schneiderman Decision, "Communist," 22 (Aug. 1943), 688-97; (Sept.), 836-51.
A discussion of the U.S. Supreme Court's decision refusing to cancel the citizenship of William Schneiderman, state secretary of the Party in California. The main issue was whether or not the Party disbelieves in organized government and advocates overthrow of government by force. The decision protects the citizenship of naturalized Americans and reaffirms the American right of political thought, speech, and association.

M334 .... "The Heritage of the Communist Political Association." New York: Workers Library, 1944. 63 pp.
A sketch of the communist movement in America, of its theoretical views, its tactics, and its objectives, written by a veteran Party leader. The pamphlet is based upon a report made by the author at the founding convention of the Communist Political Association, May 20-23, 1944, following dissolution of the Communist Party. Following Browder in projecting the wartime unity into the postwar period, the report foresees prolonged world peace, full employment, rising living standards, and social gains after the war, with democratic rights safeguarded through the two-party system. (A shorter version appeared in "Communist," September 1944.)

M335 .... Not in Spite of but Because: An Answer to the Question whether the United Nations Coalition Can Endure in Spite of the Difference of Social Structure between the Capitalist and Socialist States, "Communist," 23 (Feb. 1944), 122-30.
The United Nations coalition is strengthened by the inclusion of the Soviet Union with its different social structure. The inclusion of the Soviet Union insures that the coalition will not be defeated or controlled by reactionaries. The Soviet Union, which can never commit aggression, also brings stability to the coalition.

M336 .... "Lynching and Frame-up in Tennessee." New York: New Century, 1946. 95 pp.
Condemnation of the police brutality and official incitement to riot which caused violence in Columbia, Tennessee, and resulted in the indictment of 30 Negroes for causing the riot. A mass movement of white and Negro people is called for to demand the conviction of the officials guilty of the attempted lynching.

M337 .... "Tell the People How Ben Davis Was Elected." New York: New Century, 1946. 24 pp.
A recruiting pamphlet directed principally to Negroes, asserting that Davis was elected to the New York City Council on the Communist and American Labor Party tickets by an alliance of Negroes with the most powerful sections of New York labor. White and Negro workers alike are urged to join the Communist Party, which fights for Negro rights.

.... See also BALLISTER, J.

M338 MINOT, Peter. The Wayward "New Yorker," "Plain Talk," 4 (Oct. 1949), 5-11.
Criticism of the magazine "The New Yorker" for deriding all mention of communist subversion in the U.S. and for belittling anticommunists who take a dim view of Stalin and his American followers. A. J. Liebling and his feature, "The Wayward Press," are censured for a mistaken sense of humor which, in effect, defends the communist underground.

M339 MINOW, Newton. Some Legal Aspects of the Hiss Case, "Journal of Criminal Law and Criminology," 40 (Sept.-Oct. 1949), 344-53.
A review of the first Hiss trial, analyzing the probable effects of developments there on the forthcoming second trial. Emphasis is placed on the effect of the two-witness rule on espionage evidence, and on the impact on the second jury of the disclosure of the balloting by the first jury.

M340 MINSKY, Louis. The United Front, "Commonweal," 25 (Feb. 19, 1937), 457-58.
A non-Catholic cautions churches and synagogues against joining with secular bodies for social action. In any such united front the secularists, who concentrate on economic solutions while ignoring ethical and religious aspects, would be in control. Churches, cooperating with each other, should take the leadership in social action.

M341 MINTON, Bruce [pseud. for Richard Bransten). Trial by Vigilantes: Criminal Syndicalist Cases in California, "New Masses," 14 (Feb. 19, 1935), 9-10.
An account of the trial of 18 militant union members under the California criminal syndicalism laws. Fascism is a growing reality in California, where owners were scared by the general strike. The decision, besides determining the status of the Communist Party, will directly affect all progressive forces.

M342 .... The Battle of Sacramento, "New Republic," 82 (Feb. 20, 1935), 37-39.
An account of the arrest and current trial of 17 agricultural union organizers, also members of the Communist Party, under the state's Criminal Syndicalism Act. In the wake of the terror following the general strike, California is closer to fascism than any other state.

M343 ..., and STUART, John. "Men Who Lead Labor." New York: Modern Age, 1937. 270 pp. Bibliog. Ind.
Biographical sketches of seven American labor leaders by two procommunist authors. William Green is attacked for class cooperation, William Hutcheson for reaction and corruption, and Edward McGrady for betraying workers at every chance. John L. Lewis, though a Red-baiter in the past, is now supported by the working class. Heywood Broun is praised for understanding the threat of fascism, A. Philip Randolph for supporting a working class political party to fight discrimination, and Harry Bridges for providing militant, class-conscious leadership. A final chapter on the newly formed CIO unions looks to creation of a national farmer-labor party, an American people's front.

M344 ..., and STUART, John. The Story of John L. Lewis, "New Masses," 22 (March 23, 1937), 3-6; (March 30), 13-16; (April 6), 17-19.
A laudatory series of three articles on John L. Lewis and the CIO, covering his biography, his astounding capacity for growth and development, and his newly found future. (Much the same as appears in the chapter in "Men Who Lead Labor.")

M345 ..., and STUART, John. William Green of Coshocton, O., "New Masses," 23 (May 18, 1937), 3-5; (May 25), 16-18; (June 1), 15-16.
Three articles on Gompers' successor as president of the AFL, dealing with his background in the UMW and in Ohio state politics, his selection as AFL president as a compromise candidate, his opposition to militancy, his toleration of racketeering, and his bitter fight against Lewis and the CIO.

M346 ..., and STUART, John. "The Fat Years and the Lean." New York: Modern Age, 1940. 454 pp. Notes. Bibliog. Ind.

An account of economic and political trends in the U.S. in the period between the two world wars, written from a communist point of view. Emphasis is placed on the moribund capitalism after 1919, the people's struggles against monopoly and hunger, and the drive toward socialism. Written during the period of the Nazi-Soviet pact, the book views the war in Europe as imperialist, praising the USSR as the exponent of peace. There are numerous sympathetic references to the Party, along with attacks on Red-baiting.

M347 MINTON, Bruce [pseud. for Richard Bransten]. The Plot against the Youth, "New Masses," 38 (Dec. 31, 1940), 9-10.
An assertion that the New Deal, since its break with the American Youth Congress (following the signing of the Hitler-Stalin pact), has sought to block AYC by reviving the International Student Service. ISS is urging AYC affiliates to join ISS instead, and is popularizing work camps that may lead to compulsory camps established by the government.

M348 .... Production for Victory, "Communist," 21 (March 1942), 171-78.
Criticism of the U.S. business community for its "business-as-usual" attitude and its skepticism regarding Roosevelt's war production goals while labor makes every effort to work with management to achieve maximum production.

M349 MITCHELL, Broadus. How to Traduce Teachers, "Nation," 175 (Dec. 27, 1952), 603-5.
A Rutgers economics professor reviews the recent dismissal of teachers suspected of communist connections from New York City schools and municipal colleges. He asserts that current persecutions have brought about an observable change in the candid conduct of classes.

M350 MITCHELL, John Bruce. Reds in New York's Slums, "Forum," 61 (April 1919), 442-55.
A sensational account of the spreading of Bolshevik propaganda in the slums of New York City's Lower East Side. Eighty per cent of the audiences at Bolshevik meetings are said to be Russian Jews, many of the others being writers and artists who are failures. Leaders include Russians smuggled into America, IWW's, and criminal types from Italy and Spain.

M351 MITCHELL, Jonathan. The Left Revives, "New Republic," 81 (Jan. 23, 1935), 300-1.
An account of how the communists worked successfully with other groups at the Unemployment Insurance Conference held in Washington, January 5-7, 1935, to support the Lundeen bill.

M352 MITCHELL, Louise. "Food Prices and Rationing." New York: Workers Library, 1943. 15 pp.
Support for price control and rationing by a "Daily Worker" staff member, who condemns efforts by congressional reactionaries to sabotage the program. She calls for rationing to prevent injustice and assure adequate production of consumer goods for military and civilian needs.

M353 .... "America's Housing Crisis." New York: New Century, 1946. 31 pp.
A "Daily Worker" staff member describes the hopelessness of finding a place to live in America in 1946, blaming manipulation by builders, speculators, and reactionary real estate groups. She calls for a crash program to build housing, and renewal of the Rent Control Act to protect existing housing.

M354 .... "Hold That Rent Ceiling." New York: New Century, 1947. 15 pp.
A call for support of rent control against the "wreckers" of the 80th, Republican-dominated, Congress. Labor, veterans, and women's organizations are urged to unite with communists and tenant groups to prevent the rent gouge.

M355 .... "How to Fight High Prices." New York: New Century, 1947. 15 pp.
An assertion that corporations, after having piled up profits during the war, are trying, through man-made scarcities, to force prices up even higher. A call for the return of price controls, and for the formation of a broad third party.

M356 MITCHELL, William. Personnel Security in the Atomic Energy Program, "Science," 125 (June 28, 1957), 1279-83.
A description of the personnel security program of the U.S. Atomic Energy Commission by its general counsel. The objectives are to assure that acts of sabotage will not occur and restricted data not disclosed to unauthorized sources. The author describes the investigative process, standards of evaluation, and review and appeal procedures.

M357 MITTELMAN, Edward B. Basis for American Federation of Labor Opposition to Amalgamation and Politics at Portland, "Journal of Political Economy," 32 (Feb. 1924), 86-100.
The Portland convention unseated William F. Dunne of Butte, Montana, spokesman for the Trade Union Educational League, for vilifying delegates; thereafter not one delegate supported amalgamation. The convention, in a confusing situation, overwhelmingly defeated a resolution for a labor party. Some groups, like the Workers Party, draw inspiration from Russia, whereas others want to copy the Labor Party of Britain.

M358 "MODERN MONTHLY," A Symposium on Communism, 8 (April 1934), 133-65.
Bertrand Russell, John Dewey, and Morris R. Cohen tell why they are not communists, and Sidney Hook tells why he is one, in the sense of accepting Marxian principles. The Dewey, Cohen, and Hook articles are abstracted separately. (Reprinted as "The Meaning of Marx: A Symposium.")

M359 "MODERN QUARTERLY," Democracy versus Dictatorship, 5, no. 4 [1931?], 397-406.
A discussion of economic and sociological factors behind democracy and dictatorship. The structure of modern society, with its disorganized production and division of classes, makes dictatorship, of either the communist or the fascist type, inevitable as the next step. Communism, the first sane solution to both the economic and the psychological problem, will rejuvenate our American Revolution.

M360 ..., Whither the American Writer (A Questionnaire), 6 (Summer 1932), 11-19.
Answers by a number of leading literary figures to questions about the collapse of capitalism, the writer's position in the social crisis, the relationship between a writer's work and the radical political party, whether becoming a communist deepens an artist's work, the path of American literature in the next decade, and the possibility of a proletarian literature in America.

M361 MONRONEY, A. S. Mike, and others. "The Strengthening of American Political Institutions." Ithaca, N.Y.: Cornell University Press, 1949. 134 pp.

Lectures at Cornell's symposium on "America's Freedom and Responsibility in the Contemporary Crisis." Thurman Arnold, in "The Case against the Federal Loyalty Program" (pp. 53-74), asserts that our real peril is not communism but the committees or loyalty boards which are instilling lack of confidence in the stability of American institutions. Arthur E. Sutherland, in "Additional Thoughts on the Federal Loyalty Program" (pp. 74-78), calls for a balance between individual immunity from undue harassment and undue license to the public enemy.

M362   MONTES, Luis. "Bananas: The Fruit Empire of Wall Street." New York: International Publishers, 1933. 23 pp.
A denunciation of conditions in the Central American "banana kingdoms" of the United Fruit Company, which oppresses the workers, controls governments with the aid of the military, and operates an imperialist empire. Only by solidarity of workers in the U.S. and Latin America through the Anti-Imperialist League will the workers be able to overthrow this imperialism.

M363   MONTGOMERY, J. L. "Socialism and Bolshevism: A Primer." New York: National Security League, 1919. 8 pp.
Questions and answers relating to socialism, Bolshevism, and the Soviet government, emphasizing the distinction between evolutionary and revolutionary socialists, the opposition of revolutionary socialists to U.S. participation in World War I, and denials of freedom in Russia.

M364   "MONTHLY LABOR REVIEW," Eleventh Convention of the CIO, 69 (Dec. 1949), 640-45.
A report on the recent CIO convention, which was preoccupied with the communist issue. The convention expelled the United Electrical and the Farm Equipment Workers, with ten other unions to be tried later by special committees. The history of the problem in the CIO is reviewed, and excerpts from speeches are reprinted.

M365   "MONTHLY REVIEW," Civil War in the CIO, 1 (June 1949), 33-35.
Analysis of the split in the CIO in a Marxist publication. The CIO right-wing majority supports the Truman Doctrine, the Marshall Plan, and the Atlantic Pact, and opposes the World Federation of Trade Unions. The national CIO demand that all unions follow CIO policy or be expelled violates the autonomous rights of the left-wing minority.

M366   . . ., Cooperation on the Left, 1 (March 1950), 334-44.
A discussion of the problem of cooperation by the American left, which is defined as including all classes and strata that are, actually or potentially, hostile to monopoly capitalism. This includes the communists, who are declared not to be agents of a foreign power, but who are blamed for often making cooperation with other groups difficult, if not impossible. While Red-baiting is deplored, the communists are held to be subject to criticism, just as is any other group.

M367   MOON, Henry Lee. "Balance of Power: The Negro Vote." Garden City, N.Y.: Doubleday, 1949. 256 pp.
A history of Negro suffrage and the franchise. Chapter 7, "Greener Pastures?" (pp. 119-31), discusses the Negro and the Communist Party. The author asserts that the Party has had an influence on Negro life and intellectuals, though it has failed to gain many Negroes for Party membership. He traces the shifting Party line with regard to Negro rights from the 1920's on, showing the complete subordination to Soviet interests.

M368   MOORE, Barrington, Jr. The Communist Party of the U.S.A.: An Analysis of a Social Movement. "American Political Science Review," 39 (Feb. 1945), 31-41.
An analysis of the Party at a time when it had abandoned its revolutionary policies. The Party is described as a propaganda agent for the Soviet Union, not a genuine American political party. Communist influence in the CIO and among ethnic minorities and intellectuals is outlined.

M369   MOORE, Harry Thornton. The Lady Patriot's Book, "New Republic," 85 (Jan. 8, 1936), 243-45.
A biographical sketch of Mrs. Elizabeth Dilling and a summary of her virulently anticommunist book, "The Red Network." The outstanding characteristic of the book is its inaccuracy. (A list of inaccuracies in the volume follows, on pp. 245-46.)

M370   MOORE, Herbert G. Marxism in the Pulpit, "National Republic," 39 (Sept. 1951), 7-8 ff; (Oct.), 13-14 ff; (Nov.), 17-18 ff; (Dec.), 17-18 ff; (Jan. 1952), 17-18 ff; (Feb.), 21-22 ff.
An exposé of communist penetration of churches in America. Three groups of clergy aid the communist cause: a small group of avowed communists and fellow-travelers, a larger number who preach the "social gospel," and innocents who allow free use of their names by front organizations. Attention is drawn to theological seminaries, the new Presbyterian curriculum, the Methodist Federation for Social Action, the Church League for Industrial Democracy, and the People's Institute of Applied Religion.

M371   MOORE, John [pseud. for John J. Ballam]. Report of the International Delegate to the Conference of the C.P. of A., "Communist" (organ of the United Toilers), 1 (June 1922), 6-8.
A report on a factional dispute before the Executive Committee of the Communist International in Moscow over the creation of a legal political party in the U.S. The CI ordered the two groups to unite. "Moore," leader of the Communist Party of America-Bolshevik Opposition, which opposed the legal party, comments that the CI cares nothing for majorities, insists that its policies be carried out, and considers splitting the greatest crime.

M372   MORAIS, Herbert M. "The Struggle for American Freedom: The First Two Hundred Years." New York: International Publishers, 1944. 320 pp. Ref. notes. Bibliog. Ind.
A procommunist interpretation of American history from 1607 to 1801, emphasizing the battles for democracy, social struggles and the role of the various classes, and connections between struggles for freedom here and in Europe.

M373   . . ., and CAHN, William. "Gene Debs: The Story of a Fighting American." New York: International Publishers, 1948. 128 pp. Bibliog.
A communist interpretation of the life of Debs, published during the struggle to expel communist-dominated unions from the CIO. Debs is characterized as a man who hated injustice and human exploitation. Emphasis is given to his endorsement of the Soviet Revolution, his support of labor unity, and his rejection of Red-baiting.

M374   MOREELL, Ben. "To Communism. . .Via Majority Vote." N.p.: 1952. 34 pp.
The chairman of the board of the Jones and Laughlin Steel Corporation asserts that we have adopted many of the measures proposed by Marx and Engels in their "Communist Manifesto." He points to government ownership of land, income and inheritance taxation, state control of credit and communication, government planning, etc., as "communistic ideas."

M375 MORGAN, Dwight C. "The Foreign Born in the United States." New York: American Committee for Protection of Foreign Born, 1936. 82 pp. Ind.
An analysis of the hardships and unfair treatment of the foreign born in this country, and of the advantage taken of them by exploiting employers. Reactionary elements, seeking to establish a fascist regime, attack noncitizens and the foreign born. Protection of them by the American Committee for Protection of Foreign Born therefore protects the rights of the native born.

M376 MORGAN, John A., Jr. The Supreme Court and the Non-Communist Affidavit, "Labor Law Journal," 10 (Jan. 1959), 28-44.
An analysis of Supreme Court cases involving the constitutionality of the noncommunist affidavit provision of the Taft-Hartley Act. Cases have dealt with the validity of the provision, who must file, and the effects of failure to file or of filing false affidavits. The provision as it presently stands is of little value and should be repealed.

M377 MORGENTHAU, Hans J. Government Administration and Security, "Current History," 29 (Oct. 1955), 210-16.
A University of Chicago professor of political science asserts that U.S. security policy has been highly unsuccessful, with problems both in the executive order and in its administration. Security regulations must deal with three problems: the kind of government operations that need protection, the groups from whom protection is needed, and the means that should be employed.

M378 "MORNING FREIHEIT," M. J. Olgin, Leader and Teacher. New York: Workers Library, 1939. 31 pp.
A communist pamphlet commemorating the death of M. J. Olgin, early leader of the Party, champion of Jewish rights, and editor of the "Morning Freiheit," the Yiddish communist daily.

M379 MORRIS, George. "The Black Legion Rides." New York: Workers Library, 1936. 47 pp.
A communist pamphlet exposing the fascistic Black Legion of Michigan, the northern equivalent of the Ku Klux Klan. The author blames a Liberty League-Hearst-Republican coalition for the Legion's formation, and urges support of a farmer-labor party to defeat this reactionary group and prevent further loss of liberties.

M380 .... The Elections in the USA, "World News and Views," 18 (Nov. 26, 1938), 1287-88.
New Deal losses in the 1938 elections are minimized, and Republican gains are held due to a sham progressivism that reflects dissatisfaction with New Deal slowness. The splitting role of the Socialist Party is contrasted with that of the Communist Party, which supported the American Labor Party for all candidates but one.

M381 .... Problems of War Manpower, "Communist," 22 (Nov. 1943), 1041-50.
Labor is urged to take an active role in the solution of war manpower problems. By demanding greater labor participation in planning, the leveling of wages in the same locality, and more efficient labor utilization, labor can correct the failures of the War Manpower Commission and prevent the passage of reactionary national service legislation.

M382 .... As We Face Reconversion, "Communist," 23 (Nov. 1944), 1027-38.
An appraisal of proposals for postwar reconversion. The communists support Philip Murray's program as contained in the Kilgore-Murray reconversion bill that was defeated in Congress, and urge increased activity by labor to strengthen its influence in reconversion.

M383 .... "Reconversion: 60,000,000 Jobs or 15,000,000 Jobless." New York: New Century, 1945. 39 pp.
The labor editor of the "Daily Worker" views with alarm cutbacks, unemployment, and rising living costs as reconversion starts. Labor's support of the program for a "New America," as proposed by Roosevelt and Wallace, will end the hardships and open up a new frontier of economic expression. (An example of the postwar labor-capitalist cooperation advocated by the Party until publication of the Duclos letter in June 1945.)

M384 .... "The Trotskyite Fifth Column in the Labor Movement." New York: New Century, 1945. 31 pp. App.
Denunciation of the Trotskyists for opposing the war, the Soviet Union, and labor's no-strike pledge, and for vilifying President Roosevelt and the Big Three war leaders. Fifth columnists guilty of collaboration with fascism, the Trotskyists should be driven out of the labor movement. Their call for labor support in their Minneapolis case is a mockery of democracy. (First published in "Communist," August 1944.)

M385 .... A.F. of L.-C.I.O.: What Kind of Unity? "Political Affairs," 24 (Feb. 1945), 158-68.
A discussion of the problem of AFL-CIO unity, following William Green's rejection of Philip Murray's proposal of collaboration on vital legislative issues, on the ground that organic unity is needed. Green's action is called a pretext for rejecting joint action. Since organic unity is improbable for some time, collaboration on vital issues is an urgent necessity.

M386 .... Reconversion—the Labor Aspect, "Political Affairs," 24 (Aug. 1945), 692-703.
An appraisal of reconversion to date as unfavorable to labor. A strong plea is made for progressive and labor backing of the Full Employment Bill, increased Social Security, wage readjustments upward, and other measures to benefit labor.

M387 .... Labor Achieves World Federation, "Political Affairs," 24 (Nov. 1945), 1007-17.
A report on the World Federation of Trade Unions, established at Paris on September 25, 1945. The participation of the CIO is called significant for American labor, and the AFL is criticized for its refusal to join.

M388 .... "How Wall Street Picks Your Pocket." New York: New Century, 1946. 15 pp.
The labor editor of the "Daily Worker" asserts that the cost of living rises under monopoly control while wages remain the same. Though immediate demands, such as those for a minimum real wage, price control, and increased wages, are important, only socialism, to be won under Party leadership, will solve the contradictions of capitalism.

M389 .... The New Stage in the Wage Struggle, "Political Affairs," 25 (Jan. 1946), 18-30.
Ascribing the current strike movement to low postwar wage levels, the author urges increased agitation for a 30 per cent increase. He also calls for labor unity, the defeat of pending antilabor bills, and coordination to finance the coming gigantic wage strikes.

M390 .... The A.F. of L. after 65 Years, "Political Affairs," 25 (Dec. 1946), 1073-83.
Never in its history has the AFL's controlling clique

collaborated with monopoly capital so openly as at its recent convention. The convention slandered the Soviet Union and declared war against the World Federation of Trade Unions. It conditioned wage increases upon speed-up of production and employers' "ability to pay," and carried the Red-baiting campaign to hysterical heights.

M391 MORRIS, George. "The Red-Baiting Racket and How it Works." New York: New Century, 1947. 39 pp.

An analysis by the labor editor of the "Daily Worker" of the use of Red-baiting against progressives. Asserting that there is real money in Red-baiting, with the U.S. Chamber of Commerce the major directing center for "pump-priming," he urges unity in labor's ranks and cooperation between unions and their allies as the most effective answer.

M392 .... Spotlight on the A.C.T.U., "Political Affairs," 26 (March 1947), 252-63.

An attack on the labor policies of the Association of Catholic Trade Unionists, as described in the Rev. William J. Smith's "Spotlight on Labor Unions." Smith would liquidate the class struggle in favor of labor-management partnership. His blueprint for a new order comes from Mussolini's and Franco's fascism and from right-wing social democracy.

M393 .... "How to Make Your Vote Count: The Communist Position on the Issues and Candidates in the 1948 Elections." New York: New Century, 1948. 23 pp.

Support for the Progressive Party as the main heir of the Roosevelt tradition is urged. While the Communist Party supports the Wallace movement, this does not make the Progressive Party communist, since the CP program goes far beyond. Answering objections to voting Progressive, the author appeals to liberals and labor to give their united support to Wallace.

M394 .... The Menace of Social-Democracy and Our Fight Against Opportunism, "Political Affairs," 27 (Aug. 1948), 756-62.

A pre-convention discussion of the danger of social-democratic or reformist tendencies creeping into the Party and supplanting revolutionary policies. Although social democracy has no mass support, many trade union leaders are social democratic in outlook.

M395 .... "Where is the CIO Going?" New York: New Century, 1949. 32 pp.

Recalling when left progressives were welcome in CIO organizing drives, a Party spokesman deplores the change since Murray and his associates gave support to the Truman Doctrine and the Marshall Plan. He denounces also the social democrats and the Association of Catholic Trade Unionists for siding with Murray in splitting the labor movement. The left wing, however, will continue to fight for free, vigorous, and united CIO unionism.

M396 .... The Vatican's Labor Philosophy, "Political Affairs," 28 (April 1949), 18-34.

A critical analysis of the labor influence of the Catholic Church. The papal encyclical "Rerum Novarum," of 1891, sought to stem socialism and trade unionism, and "Quadregesimo Anno," of 1931, supported clerical company unionism. The Association of Catholic Trade Unionists fosters class collaborationism and strikebreaking.

M397 .... "The C.I.O. Today." New York: New Century, 1950. 31 pp.

An attack by the labor editor of the "Daily Worker" on the 1949 CIO convention as a hysterical Red-baiting show.

The attack on left-progressives inside labor is part of reaction's attack on the labor movement as a whole. Reaction's influence in labor's ranks is expressed most viciously and aggressively by social democracy and the ACTU.

M398 .... "Inside Hotel Local 6!" New York: "The Worker," n.d. [1950?]. 23 pp.

A denunciation of the establishment of a trusteeship over Hotel Local 6 of New York City on the eve of elections at which the progressives would once more have won control. The author traces the perfidy of Jay Rubin, renegade left-winger, and the conspiracy of his clique with the reactionary heads of the International Union, directed against the rank and file.

M399 .... The Vatican Conspiracy in the American Trade-Union Movement, "Political Affairs," 29 (June 1950), 46-57.

An analysis of "Quadragesimo Anno," a papal encyclical on labor and the social order issued in 1931, to show that the Vatican favors reaction and opposes progressive unionism. An attack on the Association of Catholic Trade Unionists follows. The Vatican has formed alliances with every fascist power, and the ACTU proposes company unionism and class collaboration.

M400 .... "The Smith ... McCarran ... Taft-Hartley Conspiracy to Strangle Labor." New York: New Century, 1951. 24 pp.

An assertion by the labor editor of the "Daily Worker" that the Smith Act, the McCarran "police state measure," and the antilabor Taft-Hartley Act constitute part of a conspiracy against the labor movement. He urges protests to the President and the Attorney General against these measures, and restoration of the Bill of Rights.

M401 .... What the C.I.O. and the A.F. of L. Conventions Show, "Political Affairs," 30 (Jan. 1951), 69-79.

At both conventions there was only one theme: anticommunism and the war on the Soviet Union. Both conventions strikingly showed the gap between bureaucratic and conservative leaders and the 14,000,000 members. The left-progressive forces are in a state of confusion, with many of the left leaders living in the past.

M402 .... The Strike of the Steel Workers, "Political Affairs," 31 (June 1952), 38-50.

The background, demands, and conduct of the steel strike, still in progress when this was written. Steel workers are restless with the policy of clinging to the coattails of the Truman Administration, and are not willing to sacrifice for the Korean War program. Employers want new legislation to take the country further on the road to fascism.

M403 .... "Labor and Anti-Semitism." New York: New Century, 1953. 23 pp.

A pamphlet by the labor editor of the "Daily Worker," dismissing as ridiculous and deliberate slander the charge that the Soviet government follows an anti-Semitic policy. He attacks business spokesmen among American Jews, the American Jewish Committee, the Jewish Labor Committee, and the ILGWU for conniving with the State Department to promote imperialism and war and cover up racism.

M404 .... "Labor Unity: What AFL-CIO Merger Means for Workers." New York: New Century, 1955. 15 pp.

A welcome to the merger from a communist spokesman, who points out to Party followers in the ranks of the merged organization a chance to influence the kind of unity that will result. An opportunity now exists, he says, to arouse the rank and file to achieve a broader and progressively inclined coalition of forces.

M405 MORRIS, George. The AFL-CIO Merger, "Political Affairs," 34 (March 1955), 30-40.
The "Daily Worker" labor editor views the merger as a response to the growing economic and political threat to labor. The AFL leaders have not yet abandoned their reactionary outlook, and the CIO leaders will have to fight for racial equality, antiracketeering, and labor political action. AFL and CIO leaders have merged their anticommunism, endorsing the Administration's war-provoking line.

M406 .... "What I Saw in the Soviet Union Today." New York: New Century, 1959. 64 pp.
A report by the labor editor of the weekly "Worker" on an extensive trip through the USSR to see how workers and farmers live and to examine the role of the trade union. He reports on the collective agreement, the workings of the union, the economy, living standards, education and child labor, school reform, youth problems, and housing. Comparisons with conditions in the U.S. are made.

M407 MORRIS, Richard. "What's Happening in Korea?" New York: New Century, n.d. [1950?]. 23 pp.
A communist view of the Korean War. Though the State Department defends the action in Korea as necessary to stop Russian aggression, not one Russian is fighting there. The peace forces, having prevented use by Truman of atomic bombs in Korea, must demand admission of Red China to the UN, withdrawal of U.S. troops from Korea, and outlawing of the atom bomb.

M408 MORRIS, Richard B. "Fair Trial: Fourteen Who Stood Accused, from Anne Hutchinson to Alger Hiss." New York: Knopf, 1952. 494 pp.
Popularly written summaries of 14 American trials spread over more than 300 years. Pages 426-78 deal with the Hiss trial. The author is not primarily concerned with Hiss' innocence or guilt, but in showing that he was not properly convicted according to the law and evidence. Though both prosecution and defense employed questionable tactics, the author finds the prosecution most at fault. He implies that he has more faith in the Hiss than in the Chambers version of the case.

M409 MORRIS, Robert. Counsel for the Minority: A Report on the Tydings Investigation, "Freeman," 1 (Oct. 30, 1950), 78-81.
The counsel for the Republican minority of the Tydings subcommittee condemns the Democratic majority for its whitewash treatment of Owen Lattimore and the Institute of Pacific Relations. The majority, he charges, sabotaged the investigation of communist influence in the State Department and in the formulation of our Far East policy.

M410 .... Should Congress Investigate? I: The Case for the Senate Subcommittee on Internal Security, "Saturday Review of Literature," 38 (Feb. 19, 1955), 9-10 ff.
The former counsel for the Senate Internal Security Subcommittee defends legislative investigating committees for seeking to smash the power of the communist underground by exposure. He defends the practice of protecting the truly repentant defector from communism from public exposure, while calling upon the unrepentant to testify publicly. (A reply by Ernest Angell was published in the February 26, 1955, issue of "Saturday Review.")

M411 .... Is It Blacklisting? "America," 95 (July 21, 1956), 380-82.
A commentary on John Cogley's "Report on Blacklisting,"

criticizing it for equating the exposure of communists by private citizens with blacklisting, for glossing over the blacklisting of anticommunists by procommunists, and for indiscriminately labeling anticommunist forces as "extreme right-wing."

M412 .... Time Is Running Out! "American Mercury," 85 (Nov. 1957), 134-38.
The chief counsel for the Senate Internal Security Subcommittee criticizes the Supreme Court for its procommunist decisions. Our failure to take advantage of the Hungarian Revolution in 1956 and our hamstringing of anticommunist measures in the U.S. have cleared the way for Khrushchev's prediction that our grandchildren will live under communism to become a reality.

M413 .... "No Wonder We Are Losing." New York: Bookmailer, 1958. 238 pp. App. Ind.
An account of the author's role in the conflict between American democracy and communism. After assisting in a legislative investigation of communist activity in the New York City schools, Morris served in Naval Intelligence in communist counterintelligence work and then in the investigation of McCarthy's charges of disloyalty in the State Department. Later he was counsel to the Senate subcommittee that investigated the Institute of Pacific Relations, education, and the United Nations secretariat, followed by investigations of subversion in government and Soviet activity in the U.S. His volume was written in an effort to help awaken the U.S. to the proximity of the communist peril.

M414 MORROW, Felix. Red Unions and the A. F. of L., "Nation," 133 (Dec. 30, 1931), 722-24.
A comparison of communist trade union leadership, as shown in the Trade Union Unity League, with that of the AFL. The TUUL is criticized for its tactics—for the "united front from below" policy in strikes, for its inflexible demands, and for its unwillingness to make partial settlements. The TUUL has made its greatest gains in the sick industries.

M415 .... "The Bonus March." New York: International Publishers, 1932. 31 pp.
A communist account of the march on Washington, D.C., by World War I veterans in 1932. The author views this "mass action," especially the part taken by the Workers Ex-Servicemen's League, with satisfaction. He tells of the efforts by the government to smash the Bonus Army, of the struggle of rank-and-file veterans for all veterans' rights, and of their growing revolt against the reactionary veterans' organizations.

M416 .... "The Civil War in Spain: Towards Socialism or Fascism?" New York: Pioneer Publishers, 1936. 64 pp.
A Trotskyist view of the Spanish Civil War, indicting Stalinist participation in the popular front and charging that emphasis on an antifascist coalition prevents a socialist revolution. The Stalinist action is antiproletarian, a betrayal of the principles of the Russian Revolution to the bourgeoisie, and a sacrifice of the Spanish revolution to maintain the French-Soviet alliance.

M417 .... Malcolm Cowley: Portrait of a Stalinist Intellectual, Saga of the Literary Cop Who Patrols the "New Republic" Beat for Stalin, "New Militant," 2 (April 18, 1936), 2-3.
Denunciation of Malcolm Cowley following his critical article on Trotsky in the "New Republic," April 8. Seeking to escape a world of revolution he could not understand, Cowley embraced the Communist Party, still ignorant and unwilling to learn or think. He writes like a "literary

cop" patrolling the Stalinist line, not an intellectually honest critic.

M418 MORROW, Felix. "Revolution and Counter Revolution in Spain." New York: Pioneer Publishers, 1938. 202 pp. Ind.
A Trotskyist version of the Spanish Civil War, charging that Stalinist participation in a popular front with bourgeois forces led inevitably to the Franco victory, and asserting that independent, revolutionary, working class action would have defeated Franco.

M419 MORSE, Wayne L. Academic Freedom vs. Communistic Indoctrination. "Vital Speeches of the Day," 15 (April 15, 1949), 400-3.
An address to the graduating class of the FBI National Academy. Senator Morse asserts that communists in our educational system seek to indoctrinate in the name of academic freedom. However, we must not use police state methods in our counterattack. A line must be drawn between freedom and license.

M420 MORTON, J. K. The A.F. of L. Convention, "Communist," 22 (Dec. 1943), 1156-65.
A review of the 63d AFL convention, describing the resolutions adopted and the differences between its reactionary and progressive wings. The two groups are moving toward inevitable conflict over the Federation's position on the "win-the-war" leadership and policies of Roosevelt in the 1944 elections.

M421 .... The May Meeting of the A.F. of L. Executive Council, "Communist," 23 (June 1944), 533-40.
A review of the meeting, emphasizing the conflict between the provictory, Roosevelt majority headed by Daniel Tobin and the defeatist, Hooverite minority clique led by Woll and Hutcheson.

M422 MORTON, Joseph. "Depression: Hard Facts vs. Soft Soap." San Francisco: Pacific Publishing Foundation, n.d. [1954?]. 31 pp.
A Party view of the 1954 recession, asserting that armament production cannot cure an economic recession. A genuine antidepression program is needed, based on the people's peacetime needs. While such a program cannot prevent the profit system's economic cycle, it can make the decline less catastrophic.

M423 .... "McCarthy: The Man and the Ism." San Francisco: Pacific Publishing Foundation, n.d. [1954?]. 31 pp.
An unflattering biographical sketch by a procommunist author, bringing in McCarthy's questionable war record, his actions as a judge, his financial dealings, and his connection with Nazis, anti-Semites, and native fascist groups. Elements which contributed to the rise of McCarthyism include the cold war, the repressive hysteria at home, the use of the Big Lie against the communists, and the unpopular Korean War. The McCarthyite objective is fascism.

M424 .... "How the Cradle of Liberty Was Robbed." New York: New Century, 1955. 15 pp.
A denunciation of the Communist Control Law of 1954 as a grave blow to liberty. The author condemns its provisions, asserting that any political party could be outlawed and any person arrested under it. He urges readers to demand individually and through their unions and other organizations that it be repealed.

M425 MOTHER BLOOR CELEBRATION COMMITTEE. "Mother Bloor 75th Anniversary Souvenir Book." Staten Island, N.Y.: The Committee, 1937. 36 pp.

A book of tributes to Ella Reeve Bloor, an activist in the socialist and then in the communist movement, on her 75 birthday. Articles tell of her early years, her activities in strikes, and her work for political prisoners, women, farmers, and peace.

M426 MOWRER, Paul Scott. "Red Russia's Menace: How the Communist Dictators of Moscow Have Constructed a Militant Monster for Armed Aggression and Are Plotting World Conquest." Chicago: Chicago Daily News Co., 1925. 40 pp.
A discussion of Russian foreign and domestic policy, with emphasis on manipulation of the Communist International by the Russians to promote revolution. Greater effort, proportionately, is expended here than in Europe because of America's political "backwardness" and her decisive world position. The Workers Party here seizes every opportunity to create a disturbance.

M427 MUHLEN, Norbert. What Fellow-Travelers Read: The Book Find Club Finds Books With a Slant, "New Leader," 32 (Oct. 15, 1949), 5.
An assertion that the Book Find Club, while pretending to be nonpolitical, is in reality a Party front. Books by procommunist or fellow-traveling authors such as Owen Lattimore, Bartley C. Crum, Leo Huberman, Carey McWilliams, Stefan Heym, and Howard Fast are sandwiched between neutral selections. However, no books are chosen that oppose the Soviet viewpoint.

M428 .... The Hysteria of the Hisslings, "New Leader," 33 (May 13, 1950), 16-18.
An analysis of neurotic former fellow-travelers who defend Alger Hiss and express hatred for Whittaker Chambers. They hate the man who has made a clean breast of his guilt, which was their guilt, and they rationalize their implicit immorality by screaming "hysteria."

M429 .... The Phantom of McCarthyism, "New Leader," 34 (May 21, 1951), 16-18.
While deploring McCarthy's exaggerations of communist infiltration, the author attacks noncommunist liberals who see a greater threat in McCarthyism than in communism. This phantom danger is made to seem greater than the real threat of communism; those who assert this are contributing to the pro-Soviet cause.

M430 .... A Night with Fellow Travelers, "New Leader," 39 (Dec. 3, 1956), 11-12.
An account of the 1956 annual meeting of the National Council of American-Soviet Friendship. It was like a wake, following as it did the Hungarian revolt, with scarcely a word of praise for the Soviet Union. Criticism of the USSR was tolerated if one advocated peaceful coexistence, expressed fear of atomic warfare, and opposed American foreign policy.

M431 MUNDT, Karl E. The Mundt-Nixon Bill, "Vital Speeches of the Day," 14 (July 1, 1948), 555-60.
A speech in Chicago, on June 4, 1948, asserting that the CP is a conspiracy, not a political party as we understand one. The Mundt-Nixon bill would compel the CP, because of its intrigues and underground methods, to register with the Department of Justice, listing its members, sources of funds, and expenditures.

M432 ..., and HUMPHREY, Hubert H. (Theodore Granik, moderator). How Can We Best Combat Communism? "American Forum of the Air," 13 (Aug. 19, 1950), 1-12.
Senator Mundt proposes adoption of the Mundt-Ferguson-Nixon bill requiring communists to register and identify their propaganda and curtailing their privileges of getting

federal jobs or passports for travel abroad. Senator Humphrey supports the Administration measure for vigorous enforcement of existing laws and revision of some of them.

M433 MUNDT, Karl E., and CELLER, Emanuel (Theodore Granik, moderator). Do We Have Adequate Domestic Security? "American Forum of the Air," 14 (Jan. 28, 1951), 1-12.
Denying that we have adequate security, Senator Mundt applauds the establishment of the Senate Committee on Un-American Activities and the appointment of the commission headed by Admiral Nimitz to check on domestic security. Representative Celler, while agreeing on the danger of communist subversion, deplores hysteria and criticizes as unconstitutional some of the provisions of the Internal Security Act.

M434 MUNDT, Karl E. What Is a Communist? "National Republic," 39 (Dec. 1951), 3-4 ff.
A U.S. Senator from South Dakota gives 20 tests by which the pattern of action of communists may be recognized. Among these are opposition to the FBI, the House Committee on Un-American Activities, communist-control measures, and the loyalty program. Others include demand for more public housing, advocacy of complete control by the state, scorn of religion, and allegiance to Russia.

M435 MUNSON, Lyle H. (ed.). "For the Skeptic: Selected Readings on Communist Activity in the United States of America." New York: Bookmailer, 1959. 194 pp. Ind.
Readings on communist activity in the U.S., consisting of quotations from hearings of investigating committees. Selections deal primarily with Soviet espionage activities in the U.S. that utilize the services of government employees who were communists or fellow-travelers.

M436 MURPHY, Agnes. "An Evil Tree: The Story of Communism." Milwaukee: Bruce, 1961. 116 pp. Bibliog. Ind.
A Catholic view of communist theory and practice, written by a professor of history and philosophy at the University of San Diego, College for Women. The roots of communism are held to be atheism, dialectical materialism, naturalism, and the class struggle, whereas the trunk of the tree is the dictatorship of the proletariat, and the flowering is the classless society. The lives and work of communist leaders are reviewed, and special attention is paid to communism's appeal to youth, in the U.S. as elsewhere.

M437 MURRAY, Charles T. Questions of Wage Policy, "Political Affairs," 33 (Jan. 1954), 15-19.
An extract from the report on trade-union work to the Party's recent national conference. The first steps toward unity in wage negotiations, such as existed in 1946 and 1947, are being taken. Formulas such as escalator and productivity increases make workers more dependent on employers. Social democrats support incentives and piece rates, which increase exploitation.

M438 MURRAY, Milton, and BROWDER, Earl (George V. Denny, Jr., moderator). Are American Communists a Threat to Labor Unions? "Town Meeting," 12 (Oct. 24, 1946). 24 pp.
President Murray of the American Newspaper Guild, attacking the communists' rule-or-ruin program, asserts that there is no area of common agreement or interest between American workers and communists. Calling for labor solidarity embracing all workers, including communists, Browder denies that communists seek to control unions and calls for U.S.-USSR cooperation for peace.

M439 MURRAY, Philip. American Labor and the Threat of Communism, "Annals of the American Academy of Political and Social Science," 274 (March 1951), 125-30.
The president of the CIO outlines the causes of communist influence in the American trade union movement, the techniques by which it was established, and the lessons to be learned. Communists won control during the depression over a number of unions by conspiratorial organizational efforts, thus providing working bases for new members and organizers. Communism can best be combated by the intelligence of our citizenry, rather than by legislation or loyalty oaths.

M440 MURRAY, Robert K. "Red Scare: A Study in National Hysteria, 1919-20." Minneapolis: University of Minnesota Press, 1955. 337 pp. Bibliog. Notes. Ind.
A study of the fear of Bolshevism following World War I. The author deals with the history of individual communists and communist parties, the nationwide steel strike under the direction of William Z. Foster, and the January 1920 arrests by the Department of Justice and the subsequent deportations. He sees similarities between the anti-radicalism of 1919-20 and the present situation, and concludes that, as in 1919, there is the danger of exaggerating domestic communist activity and its influence.

M441 MURRAY, Sam. Is Communism Revolutionary? "Industrial Solidarity," 7 (July 20, 1927), 2.
A denial in an IWW publication that communism is revolutionary. "Revolution" means an economic overturn, whereas the communists emphasize political means. Marx's Manifesto stressed political action too strongly, and today the communists help keep the useless AFL alive.

M442 MURRAY, Sean. "Ireland's Fight for Freedom and the Irish in the U.S.A." New York: Workers Library for the Irish Workers' Club, 1934. 16 pp.
A call to Irish workers to join the Irish Workers' Club, which supports the struggle of the Irish people for national and social independence while fighting against imperialist war and deportations and supporting the campaign for unemployment relief and social insurance. Hailing the revolutionary traditions of the Irish in the U.S., the author calls for a united movement against the Yankee-Irish political bosses.

M443 MURRAY, William H. "The Negro's Place in the Call of Race." Tishomingo, Okla.: The author, 1948. 107 pp. App. Ind.
An extreme anti-Negro and anti-Semitic tract by a former governor of Oklahoma, who holds communism responsible for opposition to segregation, and who finds that American Jews are at least 95 per cent communist.

M444 MUSMANNO, Michael A. "Across the Street from the Courthouse." Philadelphia: Dorrance, 1954. 411 pp. Ref. Ind.
A Pennsylvania judge tells of communist cases, including the Smith Act conviction of Steve Nelson and other Pittsburgh communists. Espionage activities of communists in this country are reviewed. The author of legislation enacted in Pennsylvania in 1951 declaring the Party illegal, Musmanno calls for the passage of similar legislation by the federal government. Attention is also paid to communist influence in the motion-picture industry and the communist view of religion.

M445 MUSTE, A. J. The Opposition's "Why": How Dissenters Get That Way, "Labor Age," 16 (Jan. 1927), 15-17.
An analysis of the way in which left-wingers should operate

in the labor movement. Communists are criticized for insisting that they alone are fit for union leadership, for injecting extraneous issues, for seeking to make the labor movement the Party's puppet, and for undermining morale through unethical practices in factional fights.

M446 MUSTE, A. J. Militant Progressivism? "Modern Quarterly," 4 (May-Aug. 1928), 332-41.
A call for militant progressivism that will replace capitalism with a cooperative commonwealth while avoiding the pitfalls of doctrinaire communism. Though the communist analysis of the American scene is right, the tactics of the communists are wrong. Progressives, while much closer to the position of the communists, will not join either the Workers Party or the TUEL.

M447 .... "Still More about Brookwood College: A Reply to the Statement Issued by President William Green of the American Federation of Labor on Jan. 26, 1929." New York: Brookwood College, 1929. 12 pp.
A reply by the chairman of the faculty of Brookwood Labor College to a statement by William Green, urging AFL unions to withdraw support from Brookwood. Denying the charge that Brookwood is communist, Muste rebukes the AFL leadership for overlooking the organizing help the college has given the AFL and for ignoring testimonials of graduates.

M448 .... Socialism and Progressive Trade Unionism, "New Leader," 8 (April 6, 1929), 4.
The head of Brookwood Labor College denies the AFL charge that his institution is under communist influence, asserting that communist papers have attacked the school severely. Dual union sentiment, expressed by some at Brookwood, is connected, not with the communists, but with the lack of organizing zeal in the AFL.

M449 .... The Communists and the Unions, "Labor Age," 20 (June 1931), 5-8.
An assertion, in a debate with William Z. Foster, that the CP and the Trade Union Unity League are in collapse, without influence in any important union. Party tactics are called artificial and childish. The TUUL is playing into the hands of counterrevolutionaries by bureaucracy and contempt of the rank and file.

M450 ..., and others. An Open Letter to American Intellectuals, "Modern Monthly," 8 (March 1934), 87-92.
An open letter signed by Muste, Louis F. Budenz, Sidney Hook, James Rorty, V. F. Calverton, James Burnham, and 12 others, attacking the communists for sectarianism, disruption, and hooliganism, as evidenced by their breaking up the socialist-trade-unionist Madison Square Garden protest meeting against fascism in Austria. Asserting that the Socialist Party and Communist Party are equally hopeless, the letter calls for building the American Workers Party.

M451 .... Tactics of the United Front, "Labor Action," 2 (May 1, 1934), 1 ff.
The leader of the American Workers Party criticizes both the CPUSA and the Socialist Party for their united-front policies. The communists' "united-front-from-below" line is called asinine, and their vilification and double-crossing are denounced. The labor movement needs honesty, decency, and solidarity.

M452 .... "Which Party for the American Worker." New York: Pioneer Press for the Workers Party of the United States, 1935. 31 pp.
The program of the Workers Party of the U.S., formed by a merger of the American Workers Party (an outgrowth of the CPLA) and the Communist League of America (Trotskyites). One section deals with the Communist Party and the Communist International, explaining why they are no longer revolutionary. New revolutionary parties and a new International are needed in capitalist countries.

M453 .... The Convention and Democratic Socialism, "Liberation," 2 (March 1957), 7-10.
An evaluation of the recent Communist Party convention by a noncommunist observer, who cautiously approves the trend toward inner-Party democracy and genuine cooperation with others. The future of democratic socialism in the U.S. needs further discussion with all interested groups.

M454 .... A Letter to Mr. Hoover, "Fellowship," 23 (June 1957), 14-19.
An open letter to J. Edgar Hoover, challenging the charge by the FBI director that Muste had long fronted for the communists. This statement, says Muste, was contrary to the record of the past 20 years. (The controversy followed Muste's efforts to get impartial observers at the recent convention of the CPUSA.)

M455 MYERS, Alonzo F., and KERSTEN, Charles J. (Orville Hitchcock, moderator). Are Teachers Free to Teach? "Town Meeting," 16 (Aug. 1, 1950), 16 pp.
Dr. Myers, chairman of the Department of Higher Education at New York University, attacks intimidation of teachers by pressure groups, state legislative committees, and special loyalty oaths. He would dismiss teachers for what they do or fail to do, not for what they think. Advocating loyalty oaths along with other procedures to eliminate communist teachers, former Representative Kersten asserts that communists are instructed to inject Party principles into their teaching.

M456 MYERS, Frederick N. NMU: Storm Warning, "New Masses," 62 (March 18, 1947), 7-9.
A procommunist sketch of the problems and policies of the National Maritime Union, attacking President Joseph Curran for switching sides, for Red-baiting, and for quitting the Committee for Maritime Unity. In the plot against the NMU are the shipowners, the government, the AFL leadership, the Trotskyites, the ACTU, and renegade communists.

M457 MYERSCOUGH, Tom. "The Name is Lewis—John L.: Czar of the UMWA, Servant of the Big Coal Interests." Pittsburgh: The author, 1933. 39 pp.
A denunciation of Lewis by the president of the communist-controlled National Miners Union, who asserts that Lewis rose to power through machinations of the U.S. Steel Corporation, connivance with corrupt AFL leaders, and betrayal of the rank and file. Miners should form opposition groups in the UMW to smash Lewis, while building a union to fight for them.

N

N1 NAFT, Stephen. 100 Questions for the Comrades, "New Leader," 22 (July 22, 1939), 4; (July 29), 4 ff.; (Aug. 5), 4; (Aug. 12), 4 ff.; (Aug. 19), 4.
A series of questions addressed to Communist Party members and sympathizers, dealing with lack of civil rights in the USSR, inequalities of income there, Soviet trade relations with fascist countries, Soviet control of the CPUSA, CPUSA membership and funds, Party abuses in trade unions, totalitarianism and justice in the USSR, etc. (Reprinted in pamphlet form.)

N2 . . . . Questions for Communists: Answer Please! "New Leader," 31 (March 13, 1948), 6-7; (March 20), 4.
Another series of embarrassing questions for communists, on labor, living standards, social security, education, and "classlessness" in the USSR; democracy, freedom, and justice in communist countries; refugees and displaced persons; consistency; the "iron curtain"; cooperation; the "imperialist war"; and communists as agents of a foreign power. (Reprinted in pamphlet form.)

N3 NASONOV, N. Reformism in the U.S.A. Presidential Elections, "Communist International," 6 (Jan. 1, 1929), 86-90.
Though Hoover's victory in the U.S. is the victory of Big Business, Smith is also bound closely to finance capital. Yet the leftward trend of the workers is shown by the growth of the reformist attitude during the election. The La Follette campaign showed the strength of reformism in 1924, and in 1928 Smith represented reformism. Fear of communism is increasing in the U.S.

N4 NATHANSON, Nathaniel L. The Communist Trial and the Clear-and-Present Danger Test, "Harvard Law Review," 63 (May 1950), 1167-75.
A professor of law at Northwestern University criticizes Judge Medina's charge to the jury in the Dennis case. He finds it inconsistent with the clear-and-present danger test, insofar as it instructed the jurors to deal only with the intent of the defendants to overthrow the government.

N5 "NATION," Why Foster is Dangerous, 115 (Sept. 6, 1922), 222.
An editorial assertion that Foster is feared, not because of his views on Russia or because he favors violence, which apparently he does not, but because he may be able to reform the American trade union movement and direct it more effectively.

N6 . . ., Martin Dies and His Committee on Un-Americanism: A Special Supplement, 155 (Oct. 3, 1942), part 2.
A 20-page supplement reviewing the policy and personnel of the committee, in the belief that its unfounded accusations of communism against liberals in government constitute a menace to democratic processes. Among the contributors are Freda Kirchwey, Wilson Whitman, Richard H. Rovere, Kenneth G. Crawford, Will Chasan, Charles Van Devander, and James Wechsler.

N7 . . . . Reuther's Victory, 165 (July 26, 1947), 87-88.
Editorial comment on Reuther's success in defeating a proposed merger of the UAW with the communist-controlled Farm Equipment Workers. The campaign of the Reuther group, based on constitutionality and organizational soundness, is a model for unions troubled with communist infiltration tactics.

N8 . . ., How Free is Free? 174 (June 28, 1952).
A special issue devoted to the impact of the post-1945 "witch hunt" on American civil liberties, with special attention to occupations or categories under direct attack. These include government employees, scientists, authors and publishers, lawyers and ministers, students and teachers, the radio and television industries, the labor movement, the motion picture industry, aliens, and minority groups. (A number of these articles are abstracted separately.)

N9 . . ., Courage in Action: I: Philadelphia Theatre, 183 (Sept. 22, 1956), 233-37.
An account, told entirely through extracts from Philadelphia newspaper stories, of efforts by veterans' organizations to keep Gale Sondergaard from appearing in a local city-owned playhouse on the ground that she was a communist. She had earlier invoked the Fifth Amendment before the House Committee. Despite threats of picketing, she played her role as scheduled, and again invoked the amendment when questioned by the Committee.

N10 NATIONAL CATHOLIC WELFARE CONFERENCE, Department of Social Action. "Why Catholics Condemn Communism." Washington: The Conference, 1936. 42 pp.
A collection of official pronouncements by Pope Pius XI.

N11 . . ., Department of Social Action. "Communism in the United States." Washington: The Conference, 1937. 35 pp.
An appraisal of the Communist Party and its policies, tracing the history of the Party, its organization and membership distribution, organizations under Party control, activities in various areas, and methods of propaganda. A program of action to combat communism is presented.

N12 NATIONAL CIVIC FEDERATION, Committee on Subversive Activities. "Shall the United States Government Recognize the Soviet Regime? Discussion at Conference, Sept. 20, 1928." New York: The Federation, 1928. 25 pp.
Views of Ellis Searles, editor of the "United Mine Workers' Journal"; Whiting Williams, industrial consultant; L. I. Estrin, trust company official; and Matthew Woll, AFL vice-president and head of the National Civic Federation. All opposed recognition of the USSR, primarily because of Soviet revolutionary efforts here through the American communist movement.

N13 NATIONAL COMMITTEE FOR ACTION. "Farmers' Call to Action, Program Adopted by the Farmers' Second National Conference, Chicago, November 15-18, 1933." Washington, D.C.: The Committee, 1933. 15 pp.

A call to action to farmers to join with city workers in united action against impoverishment and exploitation. The pamphlet asserts that Roosevelt administers the farm policy of Wall Street, and calls for immediate relief through mass action, protests and demonstrations, united campaigns to refuse to pay debts, farmers' strikes, and joint struggles with city workers.

N14   NATIONAL COMMITTEE FOR REPEAL OF THE McCARRAN ACT. "What You Need to Know about the McCarran Act." Chicago: The Committee, n.d. [1964]. 94 pp.

The text of the Subversive Activities Control Act of 1950 (the McCarran Act), President Truman's veto message, and the majority and minority opinions of the U.S. Supreme Court, upholding, by a five-to-four vote, the constitutionality of the Subversive Activities Control Board's order requiring the Communist Party to register. The Committee argues that to force the registration of those with unpopular ideas is to destroy the democratic spirit and to attack traditional American views of a free society.

N15   NATIONAL COMMITTEE FOR THE DEFENSE OF POLITICAL PRISONERS. "Harlan Miners Speak: Report on Terrorism in the Kentucky Coal Fields." New York: Harcourt, Brace, 1932. 348 pp.

An account of a trip to the Harlan coal district in Kentucky of a committee organized by Theodore Dreiser from among the membership of the National Committee for the Defense of Political Prisoners. The committee sought to investigate the denial of constitutional and civil rights to miners affiliated with the National Miners Union. Chapters, written by various members of the committee, deal with class war in Kentucky, organization by the National Miners Union there, lawlessness and violence in the area, and living conditions. Testimony by miners, the sheriff, and the prosecuting attorney is reproduced.

N16   NATIONAL COMMITTEE TO SECURE JUSTICE FOR MORTON SOBELL IN THE ROSENBERG CASE. "The Scientist in Alcatraz: Questions and Answers on the Case of Morton Sobell." New York: The Committee, n.d. 11 unnumbered pp.

Questions and answers on the Sobell case, asserting that no evidence linked him to the atomic bomb project, that he was convicted of "conspiracy" without evidence that he committed a crime, that his 30-year sentence was of unprecedented severity, and that the Attorney General's office made a deal for false testimony.

N17   NATIONAL COMMITTEE TO SECURE JUSTICE IN THE ROSENBERG CASE. "New Evidence in the Rosenberg Case." New York: The Committee, n.d. [1953]. 15 pp.

A claim that two new accidentally discovered documents, reproduced here, cast doubt on the testimony of the Greenglasses. Readers are urged to write and wire the President to grant clemency to the Rosenbergs so that the full facts in the case may come to light.

N18   NATIONAL COMMITTEE TO WIN AMNESTY FOR THE SMITH ACT PRISONERS. "Can Americans Tolerate Prison for Ideas?" New York: The Committee, 1954. 24 pp.

An assertion that the communist defendants were convicted under the Smith Act for their ideas, not for any disloyal act, in an atmosphere of hysteria and intimidation. Readers are urged to petition the President to free the victims of "McCarthyism and its dictatorship of fear."

N19   NATIONAL COUNCIL FOR AMERICAN EDUCATION. Red-ucators series.

A series of pamphlets exposing the affiliations with communist fronts of faculty members at universities and colleges, including Chicago, Harvard, Yale, California, Stanford, Columbia, California Institute of Technology, Dartmouth, and leading women's colleges. A publication on the communist peace offensive is also in the series.

N20   . . . . "Communist and Communist Front Organizations in America: Compiled from Official Government Publications." New York: The Council, 1949. 23 pp.

Advice on recognizing communist fronts, with a listing of such organizations as determined by the Attorney General, the House Committee on Un-American Activities, and legislative committees of California, Massachusetts, New York, Pennsylvania, and Wisconsin.

N21   NATIONAL COUNCIL OF AMERICAN-SOVIET FRIENDSHIP. "Labor's Stake in American-Soviet Friendship." New York: The Council, n.d. [1944?]. 47 pp.

Excerpts from programs sponsored by the Council in commemoration of the tenth anniversary of diplomatic relations between the U.S. and the Soviet Union. Participating labor leaders include William Green, Philip Murray, William L. McFetridge, Joseph Curran, Michael Quill, and R. J. Thomas.

N22   . . . . "U.S.A.—U.S.S.R.: Allies for Peace." New York: The Council, 1946. 39 pp.

Text of addresses at the American-Soviet Friendship Rally, Madison Square Garden, November 14, 1945, by the Very Reverend Hewlett Johnson, Dean of Canterbury; Under-Secretary of State Dean Acheson; Hon. Nikolai V. Novikov; Hon. Joseph E. Davies; Paul Robeson; Corliss Lamont; Dr. John Howard Melish; Albert J. Fitzgerald; and Rev. Stephen H. Fritchman. Emphasis of the speeches is on the need for continued cooperation, in the postwar period, between the Soviet Union and the U.S.

N23   . . . . "A Statement on American Foreign Policy." Preface by William Howard Melish. New York: The Council, 1947. 11 pp.

An analysis by a Party front organization of tensions between the U.S. and the Soviet Union, with a program for relaxing them. Cooperation between the two countries requires abandonment of the thesis that the USSR is expanding, acceptance of it as a great power, and cooperation with it for economic development of Europe and Asia.

N24   . . . . "How to End the Cold War and Build the Peace." New York: The Council, 1948. 56 pp.

Contains official, semi-official, and unofficial documents at the time of the 1948 Berlin crisis, chosen and edited to place the blame on the U.S. for ending negotiations. The Council urges a rapprochement between the U.S. and the USSR.

N25   NATIONAL COUNCIL OF THE ARTS, SCIENCES AND PROFESSIONS. "We Can Have Homes: The Progressive Party Housing Program." n.p. [New York?]: n.publ., n.d. [1948]. 8 pp.

Progressive Party campaign literature arguing that Big Business wants a housing shortage, and that the Administration, representing militarists and monopolies, is not interested in people's welfare. A vote for the Progressive Party is called a vote for a decent government and good homes in decent communities.

N26   NATIONAL COUNCIL OF THE CHURCHES OF CHRIST IN THE U.S.A., Committee on World

Literacy and Christian Literature. "A Christian's Handbook on Communism." 3d ed. New York: The Committee, 1962. 86 pp.

The third edition, revised and enlarged, of a booklet that first appeared in 1952. Communism attracts support because it gives oppressed people a program of change, a well-organized plan of action, a hope that men can control their own destiny. Communism is a religion without God, a religion of men and machines. Communist practice in the USSR, in the Eastern European satellites, and in China is described, with attention to politics, the secret police, industrialization, agriculture, living standards, education, the family, and religion.

N27 NATIONAL FEDERATION FOR CONSTITUTIONAL LIBERTIES. "Investigating Committees and Civil Rights." Washington: The Federation, 1941. 23 pp.

A statement of the scope and methods of operation of congressional investigating committees, prepared by a communist front group. Among topics discussed are subpoenas, powers of investigative committee agents, the rules regarding documents, and punishment for contempt. The Dies Committee on Un-American Activities, and its counterparts in New York and California, are bitterly attacked.

N28 . . . . "Witch Hunt, 1941, Hits Government Workers." Washington, D.C.: The Federation, n.d. [1941?]. 24 pp.

A protest, by a Party front organization, against an early security check undertaken by the Roosevelt Administration, and the subsequent dismissal of government employees because of procommunist activity or sympathy. Two such cases are reviewed, and an appeal for help made.

N29 . . . . "Investigate Martin Dies!" New York and Washington, D.C.: The Federation, 1942. 51 pp. App. Ind.

A statement submitted to the Department of Justice, August 6, 1942, calling for a Grand Jury investigation of Rep. Martin Dies' relationship to the pro-Axis network in the U.S. An appendix documents the friendly relations between the Special Committee on Un-American Activities, headed by Dies, and pro-Axis propagandists indicted for conspiracy. The Federation urges discontinuation of the committee as a threat to national unity and a danger to the war effort.

N30 . . . . "600 Prominent Americans Ask President to Rescind Biddle Decision." New York and Washington, D.C.: The Federation, 1942. 32 pp.

The text of an open letter to the President, with 600 signatures, protesting the order of Attorney General Francis Biddle for the deportation of Harry Bridges, over the contrary recommendation of the Board of Immigration Appeals of the Department of Justice. The Federation attacks Biddle's order as a civil liberties violation, an antilabor move, and an action to disrupt the war effort.

N31 NATIONAL INDUSTRIAL CONFERENCE BOARD. "Industrial Security: 1. Combatting Subversion and Sabotage." Studies in Business Policy, no. 60. New York: NICB, 1952. 88 pp.

A discussion, toward the close of the Korean War period, of the threat to American industry and its vital defense production posed by communists and communist sympathizers. Management must learn what is a security risk, how to avoid hiring one, how to get rid of one already hired or make him ineffective, and how to prevent enemy agents and subversives from gaining access to the plant. The practices of a number of leading companies are described.

N32 NATIONAL LAWYERS GUILD, National Committee on Constitutional Liberties. The Constitutional Right to Advocate Political, Social and Economic Change—An Essential of American Democracy: An Analysis of Proposed Federal Legislation and Executive Order 9835, "Lawyers Guild Review," 7 (March-April 1947), 57-79.

Condemnation of the President's Loyalty Order as part of the effort to drive communists from U.S. political, social, and economic life. The discussion refers to the sedition laws, the "clear and present danger" doctrine, and the lack of proof that the Party's advocacy of overthrow of government was so imminent as to require abridgement of freedoms.

N33 NATIONAL LAWYERS GUILD. "Brief on the Unconstitutionality of the Mundt-Nixon Bill (H.R. 5852)." Washington, D.C.: The Guild, n.d. [1948]. 27 pp.

Prepared by the Committee on Constitutional Rights and Liberties under the chairmanship of O. John Rogge, the brief argues that the provisions of the proposed Subversive Activities Control Act, 1948 (H.R. 5852) are contrary to the Constitution and violate basic principles of constitutional law, and that they follow the historical pattern of repressive laws and are contrary to the human rights provisions of international law enunciated by the American government.

N34 . . ., Special Committee. Report on Certain Alleged Practices of the F.B.I., "Lawyers Guild Review," 10 (Winter 1950), 185-201.

An exposé of illegal practices by the FBI (principally wiretapping) as revealed in the Coplon case. The existence of dossiers on the "disloyal" facilitates fascism. Because FBI investigations violate our laws and threaten our democracy, the Committee recommends an investigation and restriction of the FBI from these practices.

N35 . . . . "An Appeal to Reason." New York: The Guild, n.d. [1953]. 19 pp.

Objection to the Attorney General's proposed placing of the Guild on his subversive list. The pamphlet denies that Guild leaders have subversive beliefs or affiliations, and asserts that the similarity of some Guild views with those of the Party, and the Guild's role in defending communists, in no way prove the Guild subversive. The Attorney General's action is challenged as usurpation of power and denial of due process.

N36 . . ., New York City Chapter. "Analysis of the Report of the New York State Bar Association for Implementing the American Bar Association's Proposal Relative to Loyalty among Lawyers." New York: The Guild, 1954. 46 pp.

A report reviewing and opposing proposals of the New York State Bar Association to suspend lawyers who invoke the Fifth Amendment or who remain members of organizations listed as subversive by the Board of Regents, and to investigate periodically under the Moreland Act attorneys whose loyalty is in doubt.

N37 NATIONAL MARITIME UNION. "Labor Spies in the NMU." New York: NMU, n.d. [1946?]. 63 pp.

A procommunist account of a battle for control of the NMU from 1937 to 1939, in which labor spies, Red-baiting, ballot fraud, and terror were allegedly used by the opposition group to win temporary control. Used as tools by the ship owners, the opposition group was finally exposed and expelled.

N38 . . . . "This is the NMU: A Picture History of the National Maritime Union of America, CIO." New York: n.d. [1955]. 145 pp.

An account of working conditions in shipping, of the formation and history of the NMU, and of its present administration. Pages 76-83 deal with the struggle between communists and anticommunists following World War II, ending in the defeat of the Party and the enactment of a constitutional amendment barring communists from the union.

N39 NATIONAL NEGRO CONGRESS. "Address and Resolutions." n.p.[Washington, D.C.?]. The Congress, 1936. 19 pp.
Speech of A. Philip Randolph, president of the congress, and resolutions dealing with Ethiopia, an antilynching bill, enforcement of the constitution, Hearst, and other subjects, adopted in Chicago, February 14-16, 1936. Randolph, denying connections of congress officers with communists, urged support for a farmer-labor party and a united front against fascism. (Randolph refused to run again in 1940 because of Party control.)

N40 .... "Official Proceedings, Second National Negro Congress, October 15, 16, 17, 1937." Washington, D.C.: National Negro Congress, 1937. 96 unnumbered pp.
A reproduction of speeches and resolutions of the 1937 meeting of this front group. Along with a number of noncommunists, the congress was addressed by such leading communists as James W. Ford, Clarence Hathaway, and Henry Winston, and such persons friendly to the Party as Max Yergan and Harry Ward. Resolutions were adopted on trade unionism, war and fascism, unemployment, civil liberties, and other subjects.

N41 ..., Los Angeles Council. "Jim Crow in National Defense." Los Angeles: The Congress, Los Angeles Council, 1940. 28 pp.
A denunciation of discrimination against Negroes in defense industries, with specific examples. The program of the National Negro Congress is presented as the weapon of unity for Negroes and whites to use in their common fight to end discrimination.

N42 .... "Negro Workers after the War." New York: The Congress, 1945. 23 pp.
An account of the advantages to employers and the nation when Negroes are hired in industry, with Sperry Gyroscope as the outstanding example. The congress proposes adjustments of seniority, veterans' rights, and job security to keep Negroes at work and to correct past injustices.

N43 .... "A Petition to the United Nations on Behalf of 13 Million Oppressed Negro Citizens of the United States of America." New York: The Congress, 1946. 15 pp. Notes.
An appeal to the UN by an organization frequently cited as a communist front to mobilize world influence on behalf of Negro rights in the U.S., and the elimination of discrimination and other abuses based on race and color. Evidence of the oppression of the Negro, prepared by Herbert Aptheker, deals with population, occupations, family income, housing, health, education, other public services, civil liberties, and peonage and violence.

N44 NATIONAL NEGRO LABOR COUNCIL. "Let Freedom Ride the Rails." Detroit: The Council, n.d. [1954?]. 24 pp.
An indictment of the railroad industry, the railroad brotherhoods, the government, and the courts for discriminating against Negroes in railroad employment. The council proposes a program of action for the right of equal employment, and full compliance with an outstanding presidential order to end discriminatory hiring.

N45 NATIONAL NON-PARTISAN COMMITTEE TO DEFEND THE RIGHTS OF THE 12 COMMUNIST LEADERS. "The Big Plot." New York: The Committee, [1950?]. 10 pp.
An attack upon the Smith Act convictions of communist leaders as a plan to impose a police state upon America. Readers are urged to insist upon repeal of the Smith Act.

N46 .... "Due Process in a Political Trial—the Record v. the Press." New York: The Committee, 1950. 64 pp.
A condemnation of Judge Medina's conduct of the trial for attempting to silence and immobilize defense counsel, for improper characterizations of defense counsel in the presence of the jury, for badgering defendants and defense witnesses, for deprecation of defendants' evidence, and for attributing to the defense ulterior and improper motives in the presence of the jury.

N47 NATIONAL POPULAR GOVERNMENT LEAGUE. "Report upon the Illegal Practices of the United States Department of Justice." Washington, D.C.: The League, 1920. 67 pp.
A report by a committee of leading lawyers and law professors, including Zechariah Chafee, Jr., Felix Frankfurter, Roscoe Pound, and Frank P. Walsh, of illegal actions by the office of the Attorney General in his campaign to suppress radical activities. Wholesale arrests have been made without warrant, men and women held incommunicado, homes entered without search warrant and property seized or destroyed, workers accused of radicalism maltreated, and agents introduced into radical organizations to inform or incite.

N48 "NATIONAL REPUBLIC," The Enemy within Our Gates.
A regular feature of this monthly magazine, devoted to exposing communist and also fascist activities in the U.S.

N49 NATIONAL STUDENT LEAGUE. "Building a Militant Student Movement: Program and Constitution of the National Student League." New York: NSL, n.d. [1935]. 23 pp.
The history, program, policies, and constitution of the NSL, the Party-sponsored student organization. Among the activities listed since its formation in 1931-32 were the student delegation to Kentucky, campaigns against retrenchment in education and increased tuition fees, antiwar demonstrations, and proposals for amalgamation with the socialist-led Student League for Industrial Democracy. Instructions for forming an NSL chapter are included. (An earlier version of this pamphlet was published in 1934.)

N50 .... "Students Fight War." New York: 1935. 31 pp.
An antiwar pamphlet by the Party-controlled student organization, criticizing U.S. higher education for its support of war and the ROTC. The NSL position is distinguished from that of the socialist-oriented Student League for Industrial Democracy. A brief history of student antiwar activity, with a description of the formation of NSL, is included.

N51 NATIONAL UNEMPLOYMENT COUNCIL OF THE U.S.A. "Constitution and Regulations." Foreword by Herbert Benjamin. New York: Workers Library, 1934. 22 pp.
The constitution of the National Unemployment Council, adopted at the National Convention Against Unemployment, February 3-5, 1934. Provision is made for state and local subdivisions, a national convention and national executive board, and united fronts with unions and other local groups.

N52   NATIONAL WALLACE FOR PRESIDENT COM-
MITTEE. "Facts to Fight with for Wallace and
the New Party." n.p. [New York?]: The Committee, 1948. 70 pp.
A campaign booklet attacking the Democratic and Republican Parties as indistinguishable. It presents the Progressive Party program; enumerates Wallace's and Taylor's records on labor, farmers, Negroes, and peace;
answers questions as to the reasons for, and organization
of, the Progressive Party; and meets the major criticisms
leveled at Wallace and the Progressive Party.

N53   NEARING, Scott, and FREEMAN, Joseph. "Dollar
Diplomacy: A Study in American Imperialism."
New York: Huebsch, 1925. 353 pp. App. Bibliog.
Ind.
A procommunist account, based largely on official government papers, of American economic and diplomatic policy
in undeveloped countries, emphasizing their oppression and
exploitation by American capital. The growth of U.S.
imperialism, based on economic penetration, spheres of
influence, armed intervention, conquest, and purchase, is
traced.

N54   NEARING, Scott. "World Labor Unity." New
York: Social Science Publishers, 1926. 31 pp.
World labor has broken into three camps: the Red International of Labor Unions, the International Federation of
Trade Unions (Amsterdam International), and the Pan-
American Federation of Labor. Tracing the causes of this
division, which include the Russian Revolution, the author
calls for uniting the scattered trade union forces of the
world into one federation.

N55   .... The Political Outlook for the Workers (Communist) Party, "Communist," 7 (Dec. 1928), 756-
59.
A discussion article, arguing that the Party's failure to
attract the masses in the 1928 campaign shows that it
cannot soon become a political mass force. The American
masses are not prepared ideologically for a communist
program, and the ruling class here is too powerful. Possibilities for a real farmer-labor party exist, however, and
the Workers (Communist) Party should play a role in leading it. (This article differs substantially from the Party's
position, which is presented by Jay Lovestone in "The
1928 Elections" in the same issue.)

N56   .... "Free Born: An Unpublishable Novel."
New York: Urquhart Press, 1932. 237 pp.
A novel that shows the Negro as oppressed in the North as
well as in the South. The Negro hero becomes a communist after witnessing a lynching in Georgia and a race riot
in Chicago, and after being jailed in Pennsylvania for
participating in a strike of coal miners.

N57   ...; THOMAS, Norman; and LESCOHIER, Don D.
"Which Offers More for the Future? Communism,
Socialism, Capitalism." Introd. by S. D. Schwartz.
Chicago: Popular Interest Series, 1932. 60 pp.
Nearing deals with the transition from capitalism to communism, the construction of a communist society, and its
administration. He asserts that no major social transition
has ever been accomplished except by direct action, that
communist society will be a world society, and that its
administration will be a functional one, not a class administration as with us. Presenting the case for socialism,
Thomas doubts that dictatorship is always necessary or
that it will wither away easily. Lescohier, speaking for
capitalism, attacks communism's crushing of the individual
and its destruction of freedom.

N58   .... The Communist Way Out, "Christian Century," 49 (Oct. 12, 1932), 1234-36.

Advocacy of the communist way out of the depression, with
an assertion that fascism is the only alternative. The
basic principles are social ownership of the means of production, production for use, social use of income, and a
unit economic plan. Economic planning in the USSR is
described.

N59   .... "An ABC of Communism." Ridgewood,
New Jersey: The author, n.d. [1934]. 28 pp.
Bibliog.
A portrayal of capitalism as a robbers' world, contrasted
with the workers' world of communism. The author
describes the proletarian revolutionary movement, the
seizure of power by workers, the organization of the
means of production under communism, communist institutions and ideas, and socialist construction in the USSR.
(Republished by the World Events Committee in 1948 as
"From Capitalism to Communism.")

N60   NEEDLE TRADES WORKERS INDUSTRIAL UNION.
"A Challenge to the A.F. of L. and Socialist
Union Bureaucrats." New York: NTWIU, n.d.
[1930?]. 15 pp.
An attack on the leadership of the noncommunist unions
in the needle trades by the needle trades affiliate of the
Trade Union Unity League. The NTWIU accuses the noncommunist leaders of a bloody pogrom of the furriers,
of hooliganism, of class collaboration, and of calling
strikes to defend the bosses from the revolt of the workers.

N61   NEFF, Walter S. The I.Q. Myth, "Masses & Mainstream," 1 (May 1948), 66-72.
The director of the Party-sponsored Abraham Lincoln
School in Chicago, formerly a professor of psychology at
Brooklyn College, discusses the relationship between I.Q.
scores and race, concluding that environmental factors
such as education and information account for substantial
differences in scores.

N62   "NEGRO DIGEST," Round Table: Have Communists Quit Fighting for Negro Rights? 3 (Dec.
1944), 57-70.
Three prominent Negro communists, William L. Patterson,
Benjamin A. Davis, Jr., and James W. Ford, deny that the
Communist Political Association has compromised on
Negro rights, arguing that all must concentrate now on the
war against fascism. George S. Schuyler and Horace R.
Cayton assert that communist support for the Negro is
verbal, not organizational, and that the Negro struggle has
been subordinated to the USSR's quest for world power.
(The articles by the communists were published in pamphlet form by New Century in 1945 as "Communists in
the Struggle for Negro Rights.")

N63   NEIKIND, Claire. U.S. Communists—1950: Their
Members and Influence Seem on the Wane, "Reporter," 2 (Jan. 6, 1950), 7-10.
The Party is steadily slipping in numbers and influence.
It has been rooted out of the CIO, its cultural influence has
collapsed, and it is far weaker than in the past among
youth and national groups. Only among Negroes has it
made slight headway, and only three of its front groups
retain any vitality. The quality of Party leadership is
steadily deteriorating.

N64   .... Joe Curran: Seaman in Deep Water, "Reporter," 2 (March 28, 1950), 27-31.
An account of the victory of the anticommunists over the
communists in the National Maritime Union. Two years
after the power of the communists was broken, Curran
and his faction are using the red scare to quell opposition.
This is a study in the self-destruction of a union.

N65 NEIKIND, Claire. U.S. Communism: Its Underground Plans and Its Secret Business Empire, "Reporter," 4 (Jan. 23, 1951), 5-9.

An account of the capitalist enterprises operated by the CPUSA. Robert William Weiner is the financial genius who set up this secret financial empire and who controls the expenditure of funds for Party activities. He has assured the Party of a full treasury.

N66 NELLES, Walter. "Seeing Red: Civil Liberty and Law in the Period Following the War." New York: American Civil Liberties Union, 1920. 12 pp.

The author, counsel for the ACLU, points out the denial of civil liberty implicit in much of the legislation enacted immediately after World War I to control subversives, i.e., the Espionage Act, the peacetime Sedition Bills, and actions which arose therefrom.

N67 NELSON, Louis. C. P. Covers Own Bankrupt Labor Policy by Attack on ILG for Discrimination, "Call," 9 (Oct. 22, 1943), 1 ff.

An ILGWU official replies to "Daily Worker" charges of discrimination against Negroes. Though all garment unions are affected by industry stratification by skill and socio-economic groups, the Fur Workers and the Amalgamated Clothing Workers, friendly to the CP, are not attacked. The attack covers the Party's abandonment of the struggle for Negro rights.

N68 NELSON, Roger B. [pseud. for Jay Lovestone]. Have We Retreated? "Communist" (Organ of the Communist Party of America, affiliated with the Communist International), 1 (Oct. 1921), 11-15.

An effort to show that it would not be a retreat for the Communist Party to take up workers' immediate demands. This would be accompanied by propaganda to show the limitations of such demands; opportunists and centrists do not make these limitations clear. A struggle of the masses for immediate needs will convince them of the impossibility of satisfaction under capitalism.

N69 NELSON, Steve. "The Volunteers: A Personal Narrative of the Fight against Fascism in Spain." New York: Masses & Mainstream, 1953. 192 pp.

A series of vignettes and short stories about the experiences in the Spanish Civil War of an American volunteer, a leading member of the Party. A prologue describes the beating of Nelson and his comrades by Chicago policemen during a 1930 demonstration of unemployed. Stories tell of the trip to France, arrangements in Paris, the journey across the Pyrenees, the welcome given the volunteers, the training camp, and the front.

N70 . . . . "The 13th Juror: The Inside Story of My Trial." New York: Masses & Mainstream, 1955. 252 pp.

An appeal by a communist convicted of sedition to the 13th juror, "bigotry, prejudice, and fear," against which he has fought all his life. The first half of the book describes Blawnox Workhouse, the prison in Pennsylvania where he served his sentence. The second half tells the story of his trial before Judge Montgomery in Pittsburgh for violation of the Smith Act, with Nelson acting as his own lawyer. The final chapter is an abridged version of his closing address to the jury.

N71 . . . . Foster and Steel, "Political Affairs," 35 (March 1956), 33-40.

A eulogistic account of Foster's role in organizing the steel workers. The strike that he led in 1919 laid the groundwork for the organizing success in the 1930's. The present-day Red-baiting policies of the steel union officials must be abandoned if labor is to march forward.

N72 NEMO [pseud.]. "From the First World War to the Second." New York: Workers Library, 1934. 75 pp.

A "third period" communist view of World War I and of the years that followed. Written after Hitler's rise to power but before the people's front tactic had been developed, the danger of war is laid to capitalism's drive for profits. Bitter attacks are made on the "social-patriotic treachery" of the socialists. Workers of all countries are urged to defend the Soviet Union and Soviet China, and to abolish fascist terror and imperialist danger of war.

N73 NEMZER, Louis. The Soviet Friendship Societies, "Public Opinion Quarterly," 13 (Summer 1949), 265-84.

A description of the basic features of the worldwide Soviet friendship societies, which reach an audience normally unreceptive to communist propaganda. The societies appeal for support of Soviet policy in the language of peace, humanism, and cultural understanding. A brief history is given of the American organizations of this type from 1927 to 1947.

N74 NEUBERGER, Richard. Bad-Man Bridges, "Forum," 101 (April 1939), 195-99.

An appraisal of Harry Bridges, balanced between sympathy and disapproval. Although he is intemperate, he is honest and he has won advantages for the workers where softer leaders have failed. Investigations have failed to prove him a communist, though he follows the Party line faithfully. His fate rests with the Supreme Court.

N75 . . . . Lewis and the Third Term, "Nation," 149 (Nov. 25, 1939), 571-73.

A discussion of the fight over communism in the CIO and its effect on labor issues on the West Coast. Communists and their allies have lost influence as a result of the Nazi-Soviet pact. Lewis, seeking to shake off communists and their supporters, is boycotting the Far Western Progressive Conference headed by Howard Costigan of the Washington Commonwealth Federation.

N76 . . . . The Tyranny of Guilt by Association, "Progressive," 19 (Sept. 1955), 12-14. Reprinted as a pamphlet by the Sidney Hillman Foundation.

A U.S. senator from Oregon condemns the concept of guilt by association, as illustrated by Senator McCarthy's attack on Milton Eisenhower for corresponding with security risks, and by the Army's "undesirable" discharge of a soldier whose father allegedly was a communist. Our Constitution should not be destroyed because communists shield themselves behind it.

N77 NEUMANN, Heinz. Marx and Engels on the Role of the Communists in America, "Workers Monthly," 5 (Nov. 1925), 32-36; (Dec.), 86-90.

A collection of Marx's and Engels' writings, many of them in letters to socialists in the U.S., on American labor and political problems. Topics dealt with include the forms of the American movement, its historical peculiarities, the formation of an independent working class party, the role of a Marxist nucleus within it, the modern development of America, and the international role of the American labor movement. (Also published in pamphlet form under the title, "Marx and Engels on Revolution in America." Chicago: Daily Worker Publishing Co., n.d. [1926?]. 43 pp.)

N78 NEVINS, Allan. What Is a Communist? How Can You Spot Him? "New York Times Magazine," May 2, 1948, 9 ff.

In dealing with the Communist Party we are concerned,

not with a movement, but with a militant minority, alien in allegiance. Though security measures of some sort are necessary, they should be limited to fields immediately associated with national security, and enforced with careful regard to the Bill of Rights.

N79 "NEW INTERNATIONAL," The Liquidation of the Communist Party, 10 (Jan. 1944), 7-10.
A Trotskyist analysis of Earl Browder's speech calling for liquidation of the CPUSA. Like every other CP action, this reflects the Kremlin's foreign policy needs. If the CPUSA is dissolved, communists can more easily work inside the labor movement and gag criticism of Stalin; similarly, Stalinists can penetrate the Democratic Party to defend Soviet foreign policy.

N80 . . ., The Upheaval in the Communist Party, 11 (Aug. 1945), 131-37.
Analysis, in a Workers Party of the U.S. publication, of the expulsion of Browder from the Communist Political Association. The similarities between the confessions of the CPA leadership and the confessions at the 1936 Moscow trials are emphasized, as are the criticisms of Browder by Jacques Duclos and William Z. Foster. None of the disagreements is over principle, the key to the fight being Browder's misinterpretation of the Teheran agreements.

N81 "NEW LEADER," Threatened Split at St. Paul Forces Communists to Give Up Plan to Form Labor Party; Conference Is Total Failure, 1 (June 21, 1924), 1 ff.
An account of a national conference held to form a labor party, in which the communists, coming as delegates from many paper organizations, largely captured themselves. Most labor groups boycotted the convention because of the danger of communist control. William Mahoney, leader of the Farmer-Labor Party of Minnesota, had threatened to bolt unless his plan for organization was adopted.

N82 . . ., Labor Organizes to Drive Communism from the Unions; N.Y. Cloakmakers in Revolt, 3 (Dec. 11, 1926), 1 ff.
Announcement of the formation of the Committee for the Preservation of the Trade Unions, with the purpose of eliminating communist disruption from the labor movement of New York City and vicinity. Pointing to disastrous strikes led by communists in the New York City cloak and fur industries, the committee issued a call for a union conference on December 21 to organize war to the finish against the communists.

N83 . . ., 300,000 Workers Organize to End Communist Disruption in Unions, 3 (Dec. 25, 1926), 1-2.
Report of a meeting called by the Committee for the Preservation of the Trade Unions to eliminate disruptive communist elements from the unions. Four hundred representatives of 150 unions in 17 trades in the New York area were reported in attendance, representing more than 300,000 workers. Full support was pledged from city and state federations of the AFL. (The committee's program is given on page 3.)

N84 . . ., The Meeting at the Garden, 17 (Feb. 24, 1934), 1 ff.
A report on communist efforts to break up a rally at Madison Square Garden, organized by the Socialist Party and friendly trade union and fraternal organizations in support of the heroic Austrian socialists. Deliberate communist provocation turned the demonstration of solidarity into a riot.

N85 . . ., Party Crisis Grows Acute As Socialists Strive

to Save the Organization from Disruption, 18 (June 15, 1935), 3-4.
Internal struggle within the Socialist Party, culminating in strife between the right-wing New York State organization and the leftist National Executive Committee, is declared the result of communist intrigue. The Revolutionary Policy Committee group within the SP, allied to the militants, is labeled communist, and militants told to line up either with the SP or with the Communist wreckers.

N86 . . ., Dubinsky Scores Communist-Left Alliance to Wreck Labor Unions, 19 (April 25, 1936), 5.
Resumé of a speech by the president of the International Ladies' Garment Workers' Union, charging that the united front between "militant" socialists and communists is attempting to dictate policy to labor unions. Dubinsky reviews the treacherous role played by the communists in the labor movement.

N87 . . ., The ALP and the Elections: An Editorial, 23 (Aug. 31, 1940), 5.
Answering criticism by Louis Waldman, the "New Leader" reaffirms the position of the Social Democratic Federation to remain in the American Labor Party so long as the trade unions that are fighting the communists there continue to do so with good prospects of success.

N88 . . ., Will the Comintern Turn to the Left Again? 28 (May 26, 1945), 7-8.
A review of the attack by Jacques Duclos, French communist leader, upon the ideas of Earl Browder, who serves as a convenient whipping boy because he went further to the right than any other communist leader in applying the collaborationist line between capitalist democracies and the USSR. Excerpts from the Duclos article are reprinted.

N89 . . ., The Motion Picture Studio Strike, 29 (June 29, 1946), 9-12.
A report on the Hollywood strike of the year before, showing how a disciplined and unscrupulous communist minority can spread its influence. A jurisdictional fight between two factions of the labor movement was exploited by the communists for partisan political purposes. Their objective was power over the organizations of men who influence opinion through the movies.

N90 . . ., The CIO—Purge or Housecleaning? 32 (Nov. 19, 1949), 1.
An editorial disputing the contention that the recent expulsion of communist-dominated unions by the CIO is a tendency toward conformity. The editorial asserts that communists can never be good trade unionists, and that the CIO has expressed in action its opposition to totalitarianism.

N91 . . ., The "Nation" Censors a Letter of Criticism, 34 (March 19, 1951), 16-18.
A letter by Clement Greenberg, long-time art critic for the "Nation," criticizing the pro-Soviet position of its foreign editor, J. Alvarez del Vayo. The letter, refused publication in the "Nation," was sent to the "New Leader." The author gives examples of many instances of special and specious pleading on behalf of the USSR by the foreign editor of the "Nation."

N92 "NEW MASSES," Are Artists People? 2 (Jan. 1927), 5-9.
Questions to a number of writers, artists, and critics, and their answers, dealing with decadence of American culture, the effects of the machine age, group action by artists, and attitudes to the revolutionary labor movement. Among those queried were Edmund Wilson, Upton Sinclair, Van

Wyck Brooks, Heywood Broun, Joseph W. Krutch, and Waldo Frank.

N93   "NEW MASSES," "How I Came to Communism: A Symposium," 8 (Sept. 1932), 6-10.
Statements by Waldo Frank, Clifton B. Fadiman, Granville Hicks, Sherwood Anderson, and Michael Gold in answer to requests by the "New Masses" for 1,500-word accounts of how they arrived at Marxism and evolved the revolutionary point of view in their works.

N94   . . ., Resolution on the Work of "New Masses" for 1931, 8 (Sept. 1932), 20-21.
A resolution sent to the "New Masses" editorial board by the International Union of Revolutionary Writers. While the magazine, on the whole, followed a correct course, the board is criticized for giving too little attention to the struggle against fascism and social fascists, the achievements of the Soviet Union, the dangers of war, the imperialistic grip of the U.S. on Latin America, and the content of the revolutionary proletariat's struggle.

N95   . . ., The Case of Mr. Harrison, 8 (Feb. 1933), 24-25.
An exchange of letters and statements between Charles Yale Harrison and the editors of the "New Masses." Resigning as a contributing editor, Harrison calls the magazine a servile mouthpiece of the Stalin apparatus, a charge that the editors deny.

N96   . . ., Unintelligent Fanaticism, 10 (March 27, 1934), 6-8.
Responding to John Dos Passos' criticism that communist behavior at the Madison Square Garden meeting represented unintelligent fanaticism, the editors attack literary intellectuals like Dos Passos and Upton Sinclair who vacillate between the upper bourgeoisie and the proletariat, between fascism and revolution, often ending up as Trotskyites.

N97   . . ., Author's Field Day: A Symposium on Marxist Criticism, 12 (July 3, 1934), 27-32.
Replies by a number of authors whose books had been reviewed in the "New Masses" to questions as to whether they found the criticism helped, and what they expected from Marxist criticism. Among the replies printed are those from Erskine Caldwell, Robert Cantwell, Jack Conroy, James T. Farrell, Josephine Herbst, John Howard Lawson, and Henry Hart.

N98   . . ., Art Young: His Life and His Times, 50 (Feb. 1, 1944).
An entire issue dedicated to Young, shortly after his death. Young, who had been a founder of and cartoonist for the old "Masses," had continued a member of the "New Masses" editorial board until his death. Some of his cartoons and excerpts from his speeches are in the issue, along with articles stressing his partisanship in the class struggle and his support of the war.

N99   . . ., The Readers Ask, 50 (Feb. 8, 1944), 7-8.
Answers by the editors to questions on Browder's recent report and the actions of the Party's national committee. While rejecting class collaboration, the editors support a coalition that includes the big bourgeoisie, in the spirit of Teheran. Members of the Party have been consulted, and they agree that a peaceful transition to socialism is possible.

N100   . . ., NM Evaluates Its Course, 55 (June 26, 1945), 17-19.
An editorial analysis of the magazine's stand in the light of the new situation created by the Duclos letter to the

Communist Political Association, ending the Browder era. Acknowledging that they had supported Browder's line projecting friendship between capitalism and communism into the postwar period, the editors now renounce Browderism.

N101   . . ., Washington-London Axis? 58 (March 19, 1946), 3-7.
An attack by the editors on Churchill's Fulton, Missouri, "iron curtain" speech as a call for a crusade against communism, following Hitler's plan. Churchill seeks a Washington-London axis to replace the Berlin-Tokyo axis. Churchill and Byrnes are worried about Iran and Manchuria, because these are bases from which to attack the USSR.

N102   . . ., The Minton-McKenney Flight, 60 (Sept. 24, 1946), 5-8.
Denunciation of Bruce Minton and Ruth McKenney, just expelled from the Party. They are accused of "puerile leftism" for disagreeing with the Party's effort to cooperate with progressive forces in labor and the Democratic Party, a policy they attacked as "Browderism."

N103   . . ., Think Hard, Think Fast; You May Be Next! 62 (Feb. 25, 1947), 3-7.
An editorial viewing the House Committee on Un-American Activities' treatment of Gerhart Eisler as the beginning of a fascist regime of terror in the U.S. Demanding the dissolution of the committee, the editors assert that there is no evidence that Eisler is a Comintern agent and secret chief of American communists.

N104   . . ., Freedom Train: A Special Issue, 65 (Sept. 1947).
On the occasion of the tour of the Freedom Train, carrying the Declaration of Independence, the Bill of Rights, and the Constitution among its documents, the "New Masses" directs attention to the Taft-Hartley Act, the President's "loyalty" order, and programs to deprive Negroes and other minorities of civil rights. Among the contributors are Richard O. Boyer, Howard Fast, Herbert Aptheker, A. B. Magil, Lloyd L. Brown, S. Finkelstein, and Alvah Bessie.

N105   "NEW REPUBLIC," Class War in North Carolina, 60 (Sept. 25, 1929), 134-38.
An editorial outlining the communists' class struggle philosophy, on the basis of which they are seeking to build revolutionary ideology among Gastonia, N.C., textile strikers. If they are to be proved wrong, progressives must achieve social justice without social warfare.

N106   . . ., A People's Front for America, 85 (Jan. 8, 1936), 240-42.
An editorial commenting on the chances for a united front of the left should the group led by Norman Thomas win control of the Socialist Party. Despite past bad mistakes by both socialists and communists, the only test now for united front action is whether one is for fascism or against it.

N107   . . ., The Atom and the Union, 119 (Nov. 8, 1948), 6-7.
Editorial discussion of the Atomic Energy Commission's order to the General Electric Company to break its contract with the communist-dominated U.E. in two atomic energy plants. While generally in agreement, the editors urge a clear statement of the standards and limits of government action, lest we move toward a Labor Front.

N108   . . ., Communism and Conspiracy, 123 (Aug. 14, 1950), 14-16.

An analysis of the U.S. Circuit Court's confirmation of the conviction of the 11 Communist Party leaders under the Smith Act. Portions of Judge Learned Hand's opinion are reproduced. The editors disapprove of the decision, a result of cold war pressures.

N109   "NEW REPUBLIC," Personal Freedom in Wartime, 123 (Sept. 4, 1950), 5-7.
Opposing any kind of sedition legislation, the editors summarize the provisions and discuss the implications of the McCarran-Mundt-Ferguson-Nixon bill. Such bills would violate freedom of speech and due process, drive communists underground, degrade us in the eyes of the UN, and damage noncommunist liberal activity.

N110   . . ., Democracy Is a Weapon, 123 (Oct. 9, 1950), 20-21.
An editorial outlining and supporting President Truman's reasons for vetoing the Communist Control Act, which was passed over his veto. He condemned the measure as a danger to our institutions, because it undermines our security, is useless against communists, would punish loyal Americans as supporters of front organizations, and saps our democracy.

N111   . . ., What the Court Has Destroyed, 124 (June 18, 1951), 5-6.
Editorial regretting the Supreme Court's decisions upholding the constitutionality of the Smith Act and loyalty oaths for state and local government employees. Though the immediate impact of the former falls only on a small band of conspirators, the latter affects 3,000,000 public servants. A deterioration of the American spirit of freedom is feared as a result.

N112   . . ., Conformity versus Freedom, 128 (March 9, 1953), 5-6.
The editors deplore the corroding of individual liberty in America under the guise of fighting communism. The result is the emergence of a neo-fascism and an enforced conformity that is equated with patriotism, while liberals and independent thinkers are labeled communist sympathizers. Loyalty inquisitions and attacks on public schools are evidence of the trend.

N113   . . ., Communists in the Churches, 128 (April 20, 1953), 5-6.
A condemnation of ministers who, as revealed by Herbert Philbrick's testimony, are Communist Party members selected by the Party for theological training to do the Party's work in the churches. These persons are not immune from investigation by Congress, provided its inquiry is not governed by malice, irresponsibility, or political gain. Action to remove communist infiltrators should be taken by the churches.

N114   . . ., The Crime and Punishment of Julius and Ethel Rosenberg, 128 (June 29, 1953), 6.
While believing that Julius Rosenberg had participated in a communist espionage network, the editors doubt that death was the appropriate punishment. Acting within his statutory power, Justice Douglas stayed the execution on an important legal point. It was improper for the full court to override the stay, to clear the way for execution the same day.

N115   . . ., The Case of Robert Oppenheimer, 130 (April 26, 1954), 8-15.
A review of events in the Oppenheimer case, including the charges against him, his reply, and his record on the "H bomb." The editors conclude that, if the President's Loyalty Order disqualifies Oppenheimer, then not he, but the Order, is at fault; and that scientists will correctly interpret the attack on him as one on the right and duty of scientists to hold and to express their doubts.

N116   . . ., Outlawing the Communists, 131 (Aug. 30, 1954), 7-8.
Although the editors agree that the Communist Party is the agency of a hostile foreign power, to be combatted by Americans, they denounce the Communist Control Act of 1954 as contrary to accepted legal principles, as unnecessary, and as dangerous to the innocent. Democratic senators who supported the measure are criticized.

N117   . . ., The Court on the Right to a Passport, 138 (June 30, 1958), 5-6.
Though the Supreme Court has called a halt to the right of the Secretary of State to deny passports to communists or suspected communists, it has done so without directly invoking the Constitution. Whereas Congress had delegated its power over such matters to the Executive, it must now make its wishes explicit and direct.

N118   NEW THEATRE LEAGUE. "Censored!" New York: National Committee against Censorship of the Theatre Arts, 1935. 29 pp.
A protest against censorship of the theatre by an organization cited as a communist front. Mark Marvin, national secretary of the League, gives the background of political censorship in the past, and tells of the formation of the National Committee to Combat Censorship of the Theatre Arts. Richard Pack describes efforts to repress such plays as "Waiting for Lefty," "Till the Day I Die," and "They Shall Not Die."

N119   NEW YORK STATE LEGISLATURE, Joint Committee Investigating Seditious Activities. "Revolutionary Radicalism: Its History, Purpose and Tactics." 4 vols. Albany: Lyon, 1920. 4450 pp. Ind.
The "Lusk Report," the first two volumes of which deal with "Revolutionary and Subversive Movements Abroad and at Home" and the final two volumes with "Constructive Movements and Measures in America." Among the American movements included are the Socialist Party, with particular reference to its left wing; the Communist Party and the Communist Labor Party; the Socialist Labor Party; the anarchists; and the IWW and other revolutionary industrial unions. Radical documents and editorials are reproduced, together with a large amount of miscellaneous material. Attention is paid to the spread of socialism in educated circles through pacifist, religious, and collegiate societies.

N120   NEW YORK TEACHERS UNION, Local 555, United Public Workers of America. "Academic Freedom in a Time of Crisis." New York: The Union, 1948. 31 pp.
An assertion that fear increasingly pervades campus and classroom, the result of President Truman's loyalty order, the Attorney General's subversive list, and the activities of HUAC. Academic freedom may be destroyed, as part of the drive to silence all opposition to official policies. Books are banned, teachers punished for "unbecoming conduct," courses dropped, and students sheltered from ideas.

N121   NEW YORK WORLD-TELEGRAM. "The Facts." New York: n.d. [1948]. 24 pp.
A reprint of articles by Frederick Woltman for the "World-Telegram" and the Scripps-Howard newspapers on the December 1947 meeting of the Methodist Federation for Social Action, which he charged with following the Party line, defending the USSR, and denouncing U.S. foreign policy. Editorials in the "World-Telegram" are

also reproduced, along with charges against the Woltman reports in a letter by Clyde R. Miller and a factual rebuttal to each of Miller's points.

N122 "NEWBERRY LIBRARY BULLETIN." Communism and the American Writer: A Report of the Tenth Newberry Library Conference on American Studies, 5 (Aug. 1959), 84-116.
A report on the discussion by a group of scholars of a paper by Daniel Aaron on "Communism and the American Writer." Aaron divided the "left" period in American literature into four segments: the "joyous season" of 1912-19, the disenchantment of 1919-28, the migration to communism of 1929-35, and the schisms and defections of the Browder period, 1935-45. The sharpest criticism related to Aaron's definitions.

N123 NEWHOUSE, Edward. "You Can't Sleep Here." New York: Macaulay, 1934. 252 pp.
A novel about a declassed reporter who agitates for unemployment insurance and is converted to communism. A strike is made to appear, not as just a battle in the class war, but as the class war itself.

N124 .... "This Is Your Day." New York: Furman, 1937. 313 pp.
A novel about a Communist Party organizer who works with upstate New York farmers. His career is contrasted with that of his brother-in-law who, while interested in the Party, is a career university teacher.

N125 .... Hollywood on Strike, "New Masses," 23 May 18, 1937), 6-7.
An account of the strike of sound technicians in the new Federated Motion Picture Crafts against the ten major studios. The rival AFL unions, particularly the IATSE, are denounced, and the equivocal stand of the Screen Actors' Guild is chided.

N126 NEWMAN, Edwin S. (ed.). "The Freedom Reader." 2d ed. Dobbs Ferry, N.Y.: Oceana Publications, 1963. 222 pp. Table of cases. Bibliog. Ind.
A collection of materials on civil rights and civil liberties in America, including excerpts from Supreme Court decisions and commentary of eminent persons. Among the topics dealt with are loyalty, registration of communist organizations, legislative investigations and the Fifth Amendment, and academic freedom. (Revision of a work that first appeared in 1955.)

N127 NEWMAN, Edwin S. "Civil Liberty and Civil Rights." Dobbs Ferry, N.Y.: Oceana Publications, 1964. 90 pp. App. Ind.
A revised edition of a work originally published in 1949 as "The Law of Civil Rights and Civil Liberties." Part 2 of chapter I, "Protection of National Security" (pp. 14-34), includes discussion of the Smith Act of 1940, state sedition laws, disclosure requirements for subversives, alien subversion, loyalty-security programs, loyalty oaths, and legislative investigations.

N128 NEWMAN, Henry. Myth and Realities of U.S. China Policy, "Political Affairs." 28 (Aug. 1949), 77-91.
A review of U.S. relations with China since 1785, attacking the imperialist drive of the American economic royalists and hailing the victory of the Chinese communists. The author calls for recognition of the new people's government in China, trade with long-term credit, financial and technical aid, and solidarity with the Chinese people and their organizations.

N129 "NEWSWEEK," What Communists Are Up To, 29 (June 2, 1947), 22-29.
A survey of communist efforts in various areas of American life, including front group activities, infiltration in the CIO and AFL, minority groups, the churches, publishing, stage and screen fellow-travelers, and radio. Leaders in the fight to expose communist infiltration are listed.

N130 NIEBUHR, H. Richard. The Irreligion of Communist and Capitalist, "Christian Century." 47 (Oct. 29, 1930), 1306-7.
Both capitalism and communism seek to break up old religious attitudes without assisting in formulating new ones: they are both essentially secular, seeing the spiritual forces of the church as irrelevant. As such both creeds bind the church; the ties are best broken so that faith may return.

N131 NIEBUHR, Reinhold. The Religion of Communism, "Atlantic Monthly." 147 (April 1931), 462-70.
An assertion by a religious thinker that communism, while ostensibly a scientific and irreligious social philosophy, is really a new religion. In Russia the Party is a monastic order within the church, employing rigorous discipline and periodically purging itself of heretics. Not until Soviet Russia fulfills its dream of industrialization will it realize how many problems remain unsolved.

N132 .... Our Romantic Radicals, "Christian Century." 52 (April 10, 1935), 474-76.
An assertion that American radicalism, because of its irresponsible romanticism, can offer no effective alternative to our dying capitalist system. The author criticizes the Socialist Party, A. J. Muste, the Workers Party, and the Communist Party.

N133 .... Communism and the Clergy, "Christian Century." 70 (Aug. 19, 1953), 936-37.
While applauding Bishop G. Bromley Oxnam's vigorous defense before the House Committee on Un-American Activities, a leading liberal Protestant theologian regrets Oxnam's statement that no Christian could possibly be a communist sympathizer. Though the number is small, there are a few Stalinists and fellow-travelers in the churches. Clerical Stalinism, Niebuhr asserts, could not have developed except for the Marxist dogmatism in liberal Protestantism.

N134 .... The Cause and Cure of the American Psychosis, "American Scholar." 25 (Winter 1955-1956), 11-20.
An attempt to explain why the U.S. reacted to the postwar communist threat with so much hysteria. Suggested explanations are our inexperience for international leadership, and our disillusionment in the face of twentieth century terrors. This conflict of moods was obscured until it reached catastrophic proportions. Our best chance for survival lies in modesty and patience.

N135 NIKOLORIC, L. A. Our Lawless Loyalty Program, "Progressive." 12 (Oct. 1948), 5-8.
An assertion by a Washington attorney, whose firm has handled many of the major loyalty cases, that the federal government's loyalty program is a failure. Vagueness of charges makes it difficult to prepare a defense. The author outlines safeguards essential to preserve dignity and decency in the public service. The present program lowers efficiency and morale, and shakes faith in our domestic institutions.

N136 .... AVC—Innocent No More, "Progressive." 13 (May 1949), 11-13.
The story of the infiltration by communists of the American Veterans Committee and of their defeat by noncommunist progressives after a bitter fight. The AVC's third

convention directed that communists be cleaned out. Meanwhile membership has dwindled and the treasury has been drained as a result of the long battle.

N137 NIKOLORIC, L. A. The Government Loyalty Program, "American Scholar," 19 (Summer 1950), 285-98.
Criticism of the Truman loyalty program as violating the tenets of freedom and liberty because of its failure to provide safeguards of fair procedure. The loyalty program is said to have been a failure so far as security is concerned.

N138 NIN, Andreas. "Struggle of the Trade Unions against Fascism." Introd. by Earl Browder. Chicago: Trade Union Educational League, 1923. 40 pp.
Nin describes the struggle of the trade unions of Europe against fascism. In his introduction, Browder asserts that actual and potential fascist groups, such as the Ku Klux Klan and the American Legion, exist in the U.S. Browder finds here the open shop movements typical of fascism; he finds the characteristic violence of fascism—its anti-communism, antiunionism, anti-Semitism and anti-Negroism.

N139 NIXON, Richard M. "Six Crises." Garden City, N.Y.: Doubleday, 1962. 460 pp.
An account of six crises in the life of Nixon, the first being the Hiss case (pp. 1-71), which brought Nixon popular fame and contributed to his election to the U.S. Senate and then to his selection as Eisenhower's running mate. Nixon tells the story of the Hiss case as he experienced it—as an acute personal crisis, and as a case study of the continuing crisis caused by aggressive international communism.

N140 NOBLE, Elizabeth. "Billions for Bullets." New York: American League Against War and Fascism, 1937. 23 pp.
An attack on the Administration's peacetime military budget, as well as on the ROTC, the CCC, and the use of the military against workers. Asserting that the trend is toward fascism, the author calls upon the American people to demand that military appropriations be used for relief purposes.

N141 NOLAN, William A. Communism and the Negro; Are Negroes Communistically Inclined? "Interracial Review," 22 (Oct. 1949), 153-56.
A partial explanation of the Party's failure to recruit any sizable number of Negroes is its insistent repetition of "self-determination in the Black Belt." The slogan is a weird importation from eastern Europe.

N142 .... What Makes Communists Tick? "America," 82 (Oct. 8, 1949), 9-12.
A list of reasons why persons become Party members or sympathizers, taken from accounts of those who broke away or from interviews. Reasons are classified under six heads: more or less honest reasons; motives based on excessive self-interest; motives related to personal disintegration; motives related to sex; motives occasionally effective among the well-to-do such as a sense of guilt or boredom; and motives related to religion.

N143 .... "Communism versus the Negro." Chicago: Regnery, 1951. 276 pp. Bibliog. Ind.
A detailed analysis of the Party's approach to Negroes in America. After describing the Comintern and the Soviet Union, the author, who is with the Institute of Social Order at St. Louis University, reviews chronologically the communist propaganda among Negroes here, from the formative period, through the "Self-Determination of the Black Belt" era, to 1951. He concludes that Party propaganda among Negroes has been a failure, and that it will not succeed as long as conditions continue to improve here and the Party continues to put Russia first.

N144 .... The Totalitarian "Liberal," "Social Order," 2 (March 1952), 99-104.
An assertion that some American "liberals," duped by Marxist propaganda, are a grave threat to American democracy. They have accepted the views that the CPUSA is only a political party, that conservatives can be attacked in the most irresponsible language, and that no one can incur guilt by association with communists.

N145 NOLL, John F. "The Decline of Nations: Its Causes and Cure." Huntington, Ind.: Our Sunday Visitor Press, 1940. 424 pp.
A Catholic view of the evils of communism, pointing to the Catholic Church as the most bitter foe of socialism and communism. Chapter 4 (pp. 84-209), dealing with communism in the U.S., lists communist control of labor unions, federal government sympathy toward radicals, support for communist ideology from liberal writers and teachers, communist control of peace and youth organizations, and Protestant clergymen's cooperation with communism as among the reasons for the rise of communist influence here.

N146 NOMAD, Max [pseud.]. "Rebels and Renegades." New York: Macmillan, 1932. 430 pp. Bibliog. Ind.
One chapter (pp. 338-91) in this series of portraits of outstanding revolutionaries is devoted to William Z. Foster, whose career is traced, from his early days in the Socialist Party and then the IWW, to his conversion to a "boring from within" trade union policy. Attention is paid to his leadership of the great steel strike of 1919, his conversion to communism, his role in factional conflicts within the Party, and the Party's adoption of a dual union policy in 1928.

N147 .... "Political Heretics from Plato to Mao Tsetung." Ann Arbor: University of Michigan Press, 1963. 367 pp. Notes. Ind.
Pages 294-316 deal with American communists, covering the early years, William Z. Foster and his factional rivals, the ultra-revolutionary "third period" of 1928-35, the succeeding popular front of 1935-39, the Moscow-Berlin pact interlude, the war period, and postwar developments.

N148 NORMAN, Loren. Communists Force Line Down Throat of Jobless Union, "Socialist Call," 3 (July 10, 1937), 8.
A socialist account of the 1937 convention of the Workers Alliance of America, one year following the merger of socialist and communist-controlled unemployed groups. The communists imposed upon the convention their full line—democracy versus fascism, collective security, support for "good" capitalist politicians, and support for major Party fronts.

N149 NORMAN, William. The Struggle for National Unity in New Jersey, "Communist," 22 (Oct. 1943), 944-52.
The nomination of Vincent J. Murphy, mayor of Newark and AFL official, as Democratic candidate for governor will aid the pro-Roosevelt, "win-the-war" forces. The election is significant in view of the crucial stage in the war and the coming presidential elections.

N150 .... Lessons of the New Jersey Elections, "Communist," 22 (Dec. 1943), 1138-46.

The Democratic defeat in the New Jersey elections is attributed to weak organization among the "win-the-war" forces. The defeat showed that the people were confused on the real issues; that unity, once achieved, must be strengthened; that a win-the-war coalition must be based on action; and that the issue of the war cannot be side-tracked.

N151 NORRIS, Mary. The Economic Outlook, "Political Affairs," 33 (Feb. 1954), 30-47.
The general economic decline since the spring of 1953 increases the war danger, though monopoly capital alternatively considers a "controlled recession" to reduce wages and living standards. Changes in the economy since 1929 include the arms economy, "automatic stabilizers," growth of state monopoly capitalism, changes in foreign trade and investment, and a more highly organized working class.

N152 . . . . The Economic Situation: Proposals for Action, "Political Affairs," 33 (March 1954), 16-31.
An evaluation of the current economic policy of monopoly capital and of the economic programs to combat depression being developed by the labor movement. The only major difference between the Republican and Democratic leadership is on the farm program. The Party must engage in the economic struggles of workers and farmers, put forward its own antidepression economic program, and clarify its economic thinking.

N153 . . . . Is the Economic Cycle under Control? "Political Affairs," 34 (June 1955), 24-40.
Despite three depression threats in the past ten years, full-scale economic decline has been prevented through government intervention. Postwar economic trends show profound underlying instability, distortion of the cycle by war production and inflation, and intensification of the basic contradictions. A major change in the Eisenhower policies is necessary if war or economic crisis is to be avoided.

N154 NORTH AMERICAN COMMITTEE TO AID SPANISH DEMOCRACY. "Catholics Speak for Spain." New York, 1937. 31 pp. App.
A collection of statements by Spanish Catholic lay and church leaders supporting the Loyalist cause, and asserting that prominent Catholics have sided with the people against fascism. The appendix contains similar statements by Catholics in other countries.

N155 NORTH, Joseph. Earl Browder: A Profile, "New Masses," 15 (April 30, 1935), 13-15.
A biographical sketch of the Party's general secretary, tracing his family background, his early activities in the Socialist Party, his imprisonment for opposing the draft in World War I, and his Party activities since his release. His experiences with the Trade Union Educational League, the Red International of Labor Unions, the Communist International, and the Pan Pacific Trade Union Secretariat are described.

N156 . . . . Herndon Is Free, "New Masses," 23 (May 11, 1937), 13-14.
An account of the freeing of communist organizer Angelo Herndon, who had been sentenced to 18 to 20 years on a Georgia chain gang for "insurrection." The article tells how he discovered communism, and how he never lost faith. His freedom came on a five-to-four decision by the Supreme Court.

N157 . . . . "Why Spain Can Win." New York: Workers Library, 1939. 15 pp.

A popularly written pamphlet in support of Republican Spain by the editor of the "New Masses," who for 14 months was special correspondent of the "Daily Worker" in Spain. He calls for lifting the American embargo against Spain and aiding Spain in order to prevent a world war.

N158 . . . . The People, Yes, "New Masses," 35 (June 18, 1940), 7-8.
A description of the personnel and program of the Communist Party, as evident at its national convention. It is the party of the working class, seeking power for the common people. Its demands are to keep America out of the imperialist war, provide jobs and an American living standard, and protect and extend civil liberties.

N159 . . . . "The Case of Earl Browder: Why He Should Be Freed." New York: Citizens' Committee to Free Earl Browder, 1942. 15 pp.
A resumé of the Browder passport case, asserting that Browder was jailed in 1941 for technical irregularities on a passport application filed years earlier. Charging that the severity of the sentence was due to Browder's political opinions, the author asks for signatures on petitions to President Roosevelt to free Browder.

N160 . . . . "Washington and Lincoln: The American Tradition." New York: Workers Library, 1942. 15 pp.
Written during the Party's "patriotic" phase, this pamphlet seeks to ally the communists with the tradition of Washington and Lincoln, as well as Frederick Douglass. Earl Browder is viewed as their modern counterpart. His release from prison is called for, along with national unity and fullest collaboration with our allies to win the war.

N161 . . . . "Labor Faces '44's Challenge." New York: Workers Library, 1944. 15 pp.
A wartime communist pamphlet appealing for solidarity of all patriots on the national as well as the international front, and urging President Roosevelt to seek reelection in November. The author attacks enemies of victory who seek a negotiated peace on the eve of the second front, and their lieutenants within the camp of labor such as Dubinsky, Lewis, and Woll.

N162 . . . . From a Convention Notebook, "New Masses," 51 (June 6, 1944), 3-8.
The editor of the "New Masses" reports on the Communist Party convention held in May 1944 at which the CPUSA was dissolved and replaced oy the Communist Political Association. Browder's economic and political proposals for the country are reviewed, and the unity of the convention is emphasized.

N163 . . . . "What Are We Doing in China?" New York: New Century, 1945. 23 pp.
A communist call for the immediate removal of our troops from China; for the halting of all shipments of material to the Kuomintang, which uses them for civil war against the communists; and for the resolution of the question of China by Big Three and Big Five unity.

N164 . . . . What the Communists Did, "New Masses," 56 (Aug. 14, 1945), 3-6 ff.
A report on the convention in New York City, July 26-28, 1945, that reconstituted the Communist Party. The delegates corrected the Marxist revisionism of the past year and a half, and rooted out harmful bureaucratic practices and opportunistic approaches. Browder is blamed for all the mistakes of the recent period.

N165 NORTH, Joseph. No Retreat for the Writer, "New Masses," 48 (Feb. 26, 1946), 8-10.
An attack on Albert Maltz' position on communism and writers ("What Shall We Ask of Writers?" in the "New Masses," Feb. 12, 1946) by the "New Masses" editor. Maltz is condemned for anti-Marxism, for ignoring the achievements of left-wing writers, and for not understanding that a writer cannot be divided into two parts, citizen and artist.

N166 ..., and MAGIL, A. B. The Struggle for the Urban Middle Class, "Political Affairs," 26 (June 1947), 520-30.
Although the middle class cannot lead the struggle between Big Business and labor, it can be decisive as an ally of either. The working class must gain middle class allegiance by helping it solve its problems. The "New Masses" can play an outstanding role in reaching the city middle class.

N167 .... Torquemada in Technicolor, "New Masses," 65 (Nov. 4, 1947), 3-6; "Crossfire," (Nov. 11), 7-9.
A report on the House Un-American Activities Committee's hearings on communism in Hollywood. The first article criticizes Hollywood producers for their spineless behavior, while the second applauds Alvah Bessie and the Hollywood Committee for the First Amendment for their defiance of HUAC. The hearing is viewed as a forerunner of fascism.

N168 .... How to Stop the Fire, "New Masses," 65 (Nov. 18, 1947), 6-9.
An appeal to all Americans to unite to overcome the near hysteria fostered by J. Parnell Thomas and other "Un-Americans," written shortly after the House Committee on Un-American Activities investigated the movie industry.

N169 .... "Verdict against Freedom: Your Stake in the Communist Trial." New York: New Century, 1949. 23 pp.
A denunciation of the verdict of guilty in the trial of the communist leaders at Foley Square. This was a twentieth century heresy trial, the author asserts, in which men, for the first time in our history, were convicted for their ideas. Americans are urged to protest against this verdict.

N170 .... Justice, Inc., "Masses & Mainstream," 2 (April 1949), 7-19.
Communist commentary on the trial of the 11 communist leaders under the Smith Act in New York City in 1949. Emphasis is placed on the bias of the judge, the presence of police outside and stool pigeons within the courtroom, and the challenge by the defendants to the method of selecting the jury.

N171 .... Bill Foster, An American Epic, "Masses & Mainstream," 4 (March 1951), 9-20.
A eulogistic biography of Foster, telling of his career as class-conscious worker, labor leader, strike organizer, and leading communist. He is the foremost theoretician of Marxism-Leninism in the U.S., as well as the greatest strategist and tactician that our working class has produced.

N172 .... A Man of Dangerous Thoughts, "Jewish Life," 6 (Dec. 1951), 10-12.
The story of Alexander Bittelman, who faces imprisonment and deportation. He is charged with conspiracy to advocate forcible overthrow of the U.S. government, his "overt acts" consisting of two articles written for "Political Affairs."

N173 .... "Behind the Florida Bombings." New York: New Century, 1952. 23 pp.

A report by a "Daily Worker" staff member of the bomb killing of Harry T. Moore, Florida NAACP leader, and his wife, and the bombing and defacing of Miami synagogues. The Moore murder is held related to the government's foreign and domestic policy, controlled by bankers and industrialists, and the death can be avenged only by marching for Negro equality, freedom, and peace.

N174 .... Fighting Bob Minor: Artist and People's Leader, "Masses & Mainstream," 6 (Jan. 1953), 15-28.
A eulogy of Robert Minor, Texas-born artist and writer who became a communist in 1920 and remained a leading Party figure until his death. A great cartoonist and a great reporter, he was also orator, organizer, and editor. He was active in the Mooney-Billings and Scottsboro cases, in the International Labor Defense, and in Negro work.

N175 .... "William Z. Foster: An Appreciation." New York: International Publishers, 1955. 48 pp.
An account of Foster's life and of his leadership in the American communist movement, written for his 75th birthday. His early experiences in the Socialist Party and the IWW are sketched, as is his leadership in the packing-house strike of 1917, the steel strike of 1919, the TUEL, and the TUUL. Emphasis is placed upon his writings, on trade union and political themes.

N176 .... "Robert Minor, Artist and Crusader: An Informal Biography." New York: International Publishers, 1956. 284 pp.
A biography of a Party leader, a journalist and former cartoonist, who for a number of years edited the "Daily Worker." North emphasizes Minor's role in various communist causes: Sacco-Vanzetti, the Scottsboro case, the New York hunger riots of 1930, Spain, the fight for a second front in World War II, and the post-World War II trials of communist leaders. A "Party man," heart and soul, from the moment he joined, Minor was in effect killed by his devotion to the movement. (An excerpt appeared in "Masses & Mainstream," Nov. 1954, under the title, "Young Artist from Texas.")

N177 .... "No Men Are Strangers." New York: International Publishers, 1958. 255 pp.
The autobiography of a newspaper man who became a publicity man for the International Labor Defense and later a leading communist reporter and editor. He reports on demonstrations of unemployed during the depression, strikes and picket lines, the Scottsboro case, his work on the editorial staff of the "New Masses" and the Sunday edition of the "Daily Worker," the civil war in Spain, his trip to Cuba, and his impressions of Europe as World War II ended.

N178 .... "Cuba: Hope of a Hemisphere." New York: International Publishers, 1961. 95 pp.
An enthusiastic account of Castro's revolution in Cuba, by a communist journalist who made two trips there, and who views it as the highest level that the democratic, anti-imperialist revolution has reached in America. The Cuban communists are among Castro's most loyal backers. The U.S. must stop using armed force and economic reprisals against Cuba.

N179 "NORTHWESTERN UNIVERSITY LAW REVIEW," Control of Communist Unions: Comment, 50 (July-Aug. 1955), 364-409).
An analysis of legislative efforts to control communist labor unions following World War II. Section 9(h) of the Taft-Hartley Act (the noncommunist affidavit provision), the Subversive Activities Control Act of 1950, and the

Communist Control Act of 1954 are the major statutes discussed.

N180 "NORTHWESTERN UNIVERSITY LAW REVIEW." Communism and the First Amendment: The Membership Clause of the Smith Act, 52 (Sept.-Oct. 1957), 527-42.
An analysis of the membership clause of the Smith Act, providing a criminal penalty for membership in or affiliation with a group advocating overthrow of government in the U.S. by force or violence. The "affiliation" clause seems too vague for constitutional enforcement. With regard to membership, our security against hard-core communists can be protected by legislation more compatible with civil rights.

N181 NORTON, John K., and BALDWIN, Roger (Theodore Granik, moderator). Should Members of the Communist Party Be Employed as Teachers? "American Forum of the Air," 12 (July 18, 1949). 12 pp.
Dr. Norton, professor of education at Teachers College, Columbia University, asserts that Party members have given up the right to think and have joined an international conspiracy to abolish the free way of life. Roger Baldwin of the ACLU, while supporting discharge of communist teachers who try to indoctrinate their students, declares that mere Party membership should not be a disqualification in all subjects.

N182 NORTON, John K. Communists as Teachers, "American School Board Journal," 119 (Aug. 1949), 49.
An argument by a professor of educational administration at Teachers College that communists should not be allowed to teach, because the special role of communist teachers is to destroy the loyalty of children and youth and indoctrinate them with communist ideology. (Abstract of a paper read before the Boston convention of the National Education Association, July 6, 1949.)

N183 .... Should Members of the Communist Party Be Employed as Teachers? "Teachers College Record," 51 (Oct. 1949), 1-6.
An assertion by a professor of education at Teachers College, Columbia University, that communism is more than a political party; it is a conspiracy that would take over by force and regulate every phase of a citizen's life. It looks upon the school and education as choice means of achieving its evil ends. (An address at Teachers College, July 19, 1949.)

N184 .... Keeping American Education Free, "Educational Forum," 14 (March 1950), 277-87.
A defense, in an address to the Maryland State Teachers' Association of a report of the Educational Policies Commission of the National Education Association, calling for teaching about communism while asserting that Party membership makes one unfit to be a teacher. State laws on subversion in the schools, such as that sponsored by Ober in Maryland, are ill advised.

N185 NOSKIN, Bernard. Leadership and the Communists, "American Labor Monthly," 2 (Feb. 1924), 48-51.
Criticism of the communists for seeking to impose policies on the working class, instead of seeking to educate rank-and-file workers. As a result the Workers Party has concluded, incorrectly, that there is mass sentiment for a labor party, and the Trade Union Educational League advocates dual unionism.

N186 .... The Communist Party's New Turn, "Jewish Frontier," 12 (Dec. 1945), 18-21.

The new CP line, abandoning the popular front and the identity of interest of the three principal allied powers for the old phrases about monopoly capitalism and imperialism, is due to the changed power situation of the USSR, now that Nazi Germany has been defeated. The American Negro, as a representative of the oppressed colonial peoples, has become a valuable pawn in the Soviet struggle against Britain and the U.S.

N187 NOSONOV. Prospects of Unemployment in the U.S.A., "Communist International," 8 (March 1, 1931), 156-62.
An effort to expose the propaganda of optimism about unemployment in America. The proposals of the bourgeoisie and reformist socialist groups must be exposed as efforts to spread unemployment, not solve it. The struggle for public work, unemployment relief, etc., must be at the expense of the capitalists. The main organizational form must be the unemployment committee, made up of both the employed and the unemployed.

N188 NOSOVITSKY, Jacob. How Soviet Spies Worked Way into U.S. Secret Service, New York "American," Oct. 4, 1925. (Other articles in the series appeared on Oct. 11, 18, and 25; Nov. 1, 8, 15, and 22; and Dec. 13.)
A series of nine articles by a former Bolshevik who was a spy for the Justice Department and Scotland Yard, and also a courier between top Russian agents in charge of communist activities in England and the U.S.

N189 .... How They Tried to Paint the La Follette Movement Red, "Labor Age," 17 (Jan. 1928), 3-5; (Feb.), 15-17; (March), 11-14; (April), 18-21.
A former "undercover man" tells how he had been hired to link La Follette with the communists when La Follette ran for President in 1924. Nosovitsky worked at the assignment, concentrating on the La Follette state chairman in Louisiana, until double-crossed by the man who had hired him. (Earlier Nosovitsky had been active in the Russian federation of the communist movement in the U.S., while serving as a Department of Justice agent within the Party.)

N190 NOSSITER, Bernard. The Butler Bill: Iron Maiden for Labor, "Nation," 179 (Sept. 4, 1954), 192-93.
A description of and attack on Senator Butler's proposal, passed by Congress, authorizing the Subversive Activities Control Board to declare a union "communist-infiltrated" on the basis of vague and tenuous criteria. Such unions would then be deprived of all NLRB services. While the new measure will be used first against such unions as UE and Mine, Mill, it could also destroy the orthodox unions.

N191 NOVACK, George. American Intellectuals and the Crisis, "New International," 3 (Feb. 1936), 23-27; (April), 44-47; (June), 83-86.
An analysis of the appeals of Stalinism to American intellectuals and of the possibilities for providing an anti-Stalinist radical alternative for them. Disillusioned with the New Deal's failure to shift class power, many intellectuals have come under Stalinist influence, unaware of Stalin's betrayal of the world revolution. Communist Party leaders put these intellectuals to good use within the network of paper organizations that surround the Party.

N192 NOVICK, Paul. "Palestine—the Communist Position: The Colonial Question." New York: Jewish Buro, Central Committee, CPUSA, 1936. 27 pp.
An attack on the Jewish Zionist bourgeoisie and the Jewish Zionist "socialists," both of whom are alleged to support

British imperialism. The communists support the oppressed Arab people and the Jewish workers who join them in opposing Zionism and British imperialism.

N193 NOVICK, Paul. "Zionism Today." New York: Jewish Buro, Central Committee, CPUSA, 1936. 58 pp.

Analyzing the proceedings of the 19th Zionist World Congress held in Lucerne, Switzerland, August 20-27, 1935, the author denounces its stand for unlimited Jewish immigration, and deplores seeking the aid of British imperialists. Zionism is not a solution, he asserts, but a hindrance to united struggle.

N194 .... Palestine—Land of Anti-Imperialist Struggle, "Communist," 15 (June 1936), 508-22.

A communist view of Zionism as an organic part of British imperialism in the Near East. Zionists, leading only a small minority among Jews in the world, seek to build a state using imperialist force and racial aggression. Palestine communists advocate unity of Arab and Jewish toilers for national and social liberation.

N195 .... A Solution for Palestine, "Communist," 17 (Sept. 1938), 785-96.

An assertion that British imperialism and fascism have set Arabs and Jews against each other in Palestine, and that the new scheme of British imperialism to partition Palestine is tricky and impossible. The communists and all progressive elements in Palestine are seeking an understanding between Jews and Arabs, to guarantee the national rights of the Jewish minority and give Palestine self-rule.

N196 .... "Solution for Palestine: The Chamberlain White Paper." New York: National Council of Jewish Communists, 1939. 32 pp.

The communist line on Palestine in 1939, by the editor of the Yiddish communist paper in New York. British rule in Palestine is denounced, and Zionist leaders attacked for urging unlimited immigration. The author proposes abolition of the Balfour Declaration, full democratic rights for all in Palestine, preservation of the existing numerical ratio between Jews and Arabs, and protection of peasant and tenant farmers against dispossession.

N197 .... Zionism and the Imperialist War, "Communist," 19 (May 1940), 463-79.

The communist line on Zionism during the period of the Hitler-Stalin pact, attacking Zionism for seeking to drag the Jewish people and America into the imperialist war. British policy in Palestine is critically reviewed, and Zionism criticized as an instrument of imperialism and reaction. The Jewish people have nothing to gain from the imperialist war.

N198 .... Thomas' "Socialists" Aid Fascism, "Communist," 23 (Aug. 1944), 705-12.

The Socialist Party's election platform, which calls for a negotiated peace with Germany to prevent Russia from becoming too powerful in Europe, helps Hitler. Similarly, the socialists' attacks on the trade unions' no-strike pledge and on Roosevelt aid Hitler by undermining the war effort and national unity.

N199 ..., and BUDISH, J. M. "Jews in the Soviet Union: Citizens and Builders." New York: New Century, 1948. 47 pp.

Two separate articles on the life and work of Jews in the USSR. In "The New Jew in the Soviet Union," Paul Novick, editor of the "Morning Freiheit," points to the Soviet Union as the only country in Europe where millions of Jews have survived, anti-Semitism has been eradicated, and Jewish cultural activity is at its peak. J. M. Budish, in "A Jewish State Rises in Birobidjan," describes the richness of the area and the realities of Jewish self-government and Jewish culture. He rejoices, with the Soviet delegation to the UN, over the establishment of a Jewish state in Palestine.

N200 NYGARD, Emil. "America's First Red Mayor in Action: Address of Emil Nygard, Communist Mayor of Crosby, Minn., in Webster Hall, New York City, Oct. 19, 1933." New York: Workers Library, 1933. 15 pp.

Speech by the communist mayor of Crosby, Minnesota, during the election campaign of Robert Minor, Party candidate for mayor of New York City. Nygard tells of his leadership of political and economic struggles of the workers in Crosby for relief and higher wages. He attacks the Farmer-Laborites of Minnesota as dominated by the social fascists of the Socialist Party.

O

O1   OAK, Liston M. The Communists and the Coming War, "Modern Monthly," 10 (Dec. 1937), 8-11.
On the basis of his experiences as a newspaperman in Spain, the author concludes that the Communist International has lost all claim to working class support and exists merely as a tool of Russian policy in other countries.

O2   OAKES, Clarence Perry (ed.). "Education and Freedom in a World of Conflict: Guidelines for Teaching about Communism." Chicago: Regnery, 1963. 340 pp. App.
A selection from papers presented at a conference sponsored by the Institute for American Strategy. Selections deal, among other topics, with programs for education about communism at the high school, college, and graduate school level; and with the views of various government officials on aspects of education and communism.

O3   OBER, Frank B. Communism vs. the Constitution: The Power to Protect Our Free Institutions, "American Bar Association Journal," 34 (Aug. 1948), 645-48 ff.
The text of an address to the Maryland State Bar Association by the chairman of the Maryland Commission on Subversive Activities. He reviews the communist danger, citing efforts of Congress to deal with seditious activities and Supreme Court Rulings that have often defeated congressional intent. He urges that the Communist Party be outlawed.

O4   .... Communism and the Court: An Examination of Recent Developments, "American Bar Association Journal," 44 (Jan. 1958), 35-38 ff.
A Maryland attorney, reviewing Supreme Court decisions affecting communists, finds that the present Court has extended the Bill of Rights so that it presents great obstacles to the Executive, Congress, and the States in the fight against communism. He calls for greater emphasis on internal security, to thwart the communist conspiracy.

O5   O'BRIAN, John Lord. Loyalty Tests and Guilt by Association, "Harvard Law Review," 61 (April 1948), 592-611.
A protest against use of "guilt by association" to determine loyalty, and against creation of dossiers on thousands of Americans under the federal loyalty program. The hysteria and fear of the present are compared with the 1920's. (Based on an address to the New York State Bar Association.)

O6   .... New Encroachments on Individual Freedom, "Harvard Law Review," 66 (Nov. 1952), 1-27.
A review of tendencies, in statutes and in executive and administrative rulings, affecting our traditional freedoms, from World War I to the present. Attention is paid to the Espionage Acts of 1917 and 1918, the "Red Raids" of 1919-20, the Smith Act of 1940, loyalty orders, treatment of aliens, the Internal Security Act of 1950, and Supreme Court decisions involving loyalty.

O7   .... "National Security and Individual Freedom." Cambridge, Mass.: Harvard University Press, 1955. 84 pp.
The Godkin lectures at Harvard in April 1955. Reviewing the government's measures to combat communism and subversion, the author denounces abuses in the program as a departure from constitutional procedures. He calls for drastic revision of the security programs by men versed in our history of freedom and constitutionalism.

O8   O'BRIEN, John A. Fighting for Social Justice, "Commonweal," 26 (May 28, 1937), 117-19; (June 4), 148-50; (June 11), 179-80.
An outline of communism's challenge to religion, with a program of remedial social action. Though the Church regards communism as the greatest menace to Christianity and to all religious faith today, it likewise opposes fascism. The real defense against communism is the removal of the injustices in our economic and social order. Too often the Church has been silent on the grossly unfair distribution of income, and its silence has alienated the poor.

O9   .... "The Struggle for Social Justice: Removing the Breeding Ground of Communism." New York: Paulist Press, 1938. 31 pp.
Analysis of the roots and dangers of communism by the Catholic chaplain at the University of Illinois. Opposed both to communism and fascism, the Catholic Church views communism as the greater menace. The author urges Catholics to stop communism, not through denunciation, but through good works, by removing the abuses against which communism protests.

O10   .... Communism and Christianity, "Vital Speeches of the Day," 14 (Jan. 1, 1948), 174-76.
A speech delivered at the Harvard Law School Forum, November 14, 1947. The author sketches the historical background of modern communism, explains the four essential points of Marxian communism (materialism, dialectic, overemphasis on economic factors, and class struggle), and emphasizes the incompatibility of Christianity and communism.

O11   O'BRIEN, Thomas L. "The Plot to Sovietize Hawaii." Hilo, Hawaii: Hawaii News Printshop, 1948. 79 pp. App.
An exposé of the ILWU as seeking the political conquest and economic overthrow of Hawaii in order to sovietize it. The author describes the 1946 sugar strike fomented by the ILWU, the revolt within the union in 1947, and the union's defeat in the 1948 election. Though the people then kept the ILWU leaders from control of the legislature, the fight to loosen the union's stronghold on the island's life continues.

O12   O'BRIEN, Tim. All Out for May Day, "Commonweal," 32 (May 17, 1940), 77-79.
An account of the 1940 May Day parade in New York City, during the Hitler-Stalin pact period, analyzing the speakers, slogans, and participants. The parade was anti-New

Deal, and there was, by almost complete silence, a defense of the Hitler program. There was almost no union representation.

O13   OCKO, Edna. The Revolutionary Dance Movement, "New Masses," 11 (June 12, 1934), 27-28.
A description of current revolutionary dancers and dance leagues, affiliated with the Workers Dance League. The League seeks to build performing troupes to reach the masses and to activize their audiences into sympathy and cooperation with the working class movement.

O14   O'CONNOR, Harvey. "How Mellon Got Rich." New York: International Pamphlets, 1933. 23 pp.
A communist version of Andrew Mellon's life and fortunes; he stands as the supreme expression of predatory, acquisitive capitalism, which the workers must fight to exterminate.

O15   O'CONOR, J. F. The Fifth Amendment: Should a Good Friend Be Abused? "American Bar Association Journal," 41 (April 1955), 307-10 ff.
Exploration of the problem of suspected communists who invoke the privilege against self-incrimination. While pleading the Fifth Amendment protects a suspect from criminal action, he is asserting that telling the truth would incriminate him. He is therefore unworthy of a position of trust which a communist should not hold.

O16   ODALE, Walter B., and BACON, M. R. "Does America Want Communism?" Portland, Ore.: Citizens' Educational Service, 1934. 45 pp.
An anticommunist polemic, endorsed by the director of the Immigration Service at Portland, examining methods used by the Party in its attempt to overthrow the U.S. government by force. Using quotes from Party sources, the authors explore the historical background of communism, its labor tactics, propaganda methods, influence on youth, and front groups.

O17   ODALE, Walter B. "Americanism or Communism?" Portland, Ore.: The author, 1935. 49 pp.
An anticommunist exposition of the structure, aims, and tactics of American communism, including in this category many noncommunist elements of the left. Sections on youth, labor doctrine, and organizations are included. Fascism is called an "imaginary monster."

O18   OEHLER, Hugo. The Communists in the South: A Review and Criticism, "Militant," 3 (July 12, 1930), 7; (July 26), 7; (Aug. 15), 7; (Sept. 1), 7.
An analysis, by a leading member of the Trotskyist group, of the shortcomings of the 1929-30 drive by the TUUL in the textile industry of the South. Despite some success, in the face of violence from police and hired gunmen, he finds weaknesses in inadequate support, poor leadership, organizational mistakes, and blunders resulting from "third period" tactics, under which all outside the Party are viewed as fascists or social fascists.

O19   O'FLAHERTY, T. J. The I.L.D. and Its Mission, "Workers Monthly," 5 (March 1926), 206-8 ff.
A description of the founding, the tasks, and the achievements of the International Labor Defense, which defends class war prisoners in the U.S. and abroad. Its current task is to free all class war prisoners in American jails, and wipe out anti-free-speech and antisyndicalism laws. It also looks after the material needs of dependents of such prisoners.

O20   . . . . For the Candidates of the Workingclass, "Labor Unity," 2 (Nov. 1928), 1-3 ff.
A call for workers to support Foster and Gitlow, the presidential and vice-presidential candidates of the Workers (Communist) Party. The Republican, Democratic, and Socialist parties are all denounced as supporters of the capitalist system and enemies of the workers. A special appeal is made to the unemployed and to Negroes.

O21   O'GARA, James. What Price Anti-Sedition? "Commonweal," 50 (July 8, 1949), 312-15.
An analysis of Illinois' proposed antisedition laws, introduced by State Senator Broyles. From the legal point of view, the bills seem poorly worded and are probably unconstitutional, and the attendant investigations are felt to be politically motivated. Legislation against subversive activity, if needed, must be framed cautiously.

O22   . . . . McCarthy—the Case against Him, "Commonweal," 57 (Oct. 31, 1952), 91-95.
McCarthy's methods are said to do more harm than good. Most cases of subversives that McCarthy claims to have exposed had been disposed of earlier, and the rest were borderline cases. McCarthy's isolationist voting record shows him to be shortsightedly anticommunist; he is opposed by anticommunist publications and legislators.

O23   . . . . Communism in the Thirties, "Commonweal," 62 (July 29, 1955), 424-27.
A discussion of the appeal of communism during the depression years and of the types of persons who joined, suggested by Murray Kempton's "Part of Our Times: Some Monuments and Ruins of the Thirties." Many joined for the sake of action, or because they were prompted by idealism and moved by compassion. The alternative seemed the ineffective capitalism of Herbert Hoover.

O24   OGDEN, August Raymond. "The Dies Committee." Washington, D.C.: Catholic University Press, 1944. 295 pp. Bibliog.
A study of the work of the Dies Committee from its creation in 1938 through 1944. The study reviews the committee's investigations, and its relations with Congress, the executive branch of government, and the public. An introductory chapter summarizes legislative investigations of communism before 1938. While the committee has not wholly failed, the author recommends that it be discontinued and that a joint Senate-House standing committee, with competent investigators, be created for a continual investigation of subversive affairs. He also recommends procedural rules to protect the rights of citizens.

O25   O'HIGGINS, Harvey. The Nervous American, "American Mercury," 16 (March 1929), 257-63.
America's fear of communism is traced to subconscious fear and secret insecurity. Whereas the governing class in England is secure, in the U.S. wealth and political power are rarely inherited. Less self-confident, our business leaders are more fearful of revolts threatening their privileges.

O26   "OHIO SOCIALIST," Official Proceedings of the Communist Labor Party Convention, Sept. 17, 1919, 2-3.
These proceedings contain minutes of the left wing caucus, held August 29, the evening before convening of the emergency convention of the SP; minutes of the numerous left wing caucuses of August 30, on the strategy to be used in the right-wing controlled convention; the call by the ousted left wing delegates to a rump convention; minutes of the emergency convention called by the left wing delegates (the group which eventually constituted itself the Communist Labor Party of America). (The platform and program adopted at the Communist Labor Party convention appear on page 4 and are reprinted in "Revolutionary Radicalism," 1:809-17; excerpts appear in "American Labor Yearbook," 1919-1920, pages 414-19.)

O27 "OHIO SOCIALIST," The Question of Unity between the Communist Labor Party and the Communist Party, Sept. 17, 1919, 1 ff.
The texts of all the official documents that passed between the two communist conventions at Chicago. Each group sought a basis for seating delegates that would insure its control. (The "Ohio Socialist" supported the Communist Labor Party; the Communist Party, which was dominated by the Russian Language Federation, charged that not all of the CLP were revolutionary socialists.)

O28 OLGIN, Moissaye J. The Fur Workers' Strike, "New Masses," 1 (Aug. 1926), 15-17.
A left-wing report on the 1926 furriers' strike in New York City, describing the earlier union bureaucracy, the deterioration of working conditions, and a triumphant rank-and-file rebellion. Success was due to confidence between workers and strike leaders, a democratic strike apparatus, and leaders guided by the ideology of the class struggle.

O29 .... Politics and the Fly Hunt: Finance Capital and the 1928 Elections, "Communist," 7 (Sept. 1928), 538-47.
Finance capital has eliminated actual political struggle in the U.S. and made democratic forms useless. The election campaign, as conducted by the capitalist parties, amuses and distracts the masses by an elaborately staged fly hunt. The 1928 campaign, as compared with 1924, is more openly manipulated by finance capital. Only the Workers (Communist) Party expresses the fundamental interests of the masses.

O30 .... The Socialist Party Offers Itself, "Communist," 7 (Oct. 1928), 595-604.
Denunciation of the Socialist Party platform in 1928 as a denial of all Marxian and working class precepts. The socialists favor the capitalist state, support imperialism, make water power their main issue, make much of "public ownership of natural resources," and spread innumerable falsehoods. The Workers (Communist) Party is the leader of the working class, and the Socialist Party is one of the enemies of that class.

O31 .... The Socialists Have a Real Value, "Communist," 9 (Oct. 1930), 923-31.
Socialists have real value to capitalism—their democratic phrases provide an outlet for the masses' distrust of the existing order. The Socialist Party, shedding its class outlook and proletarian orientation, has openly become the savior of the capitalist economy and capitalist state.

O32 .... "Capitalism Defends Itself through the Socialist Labor Party." New York: Workers Library, 1932. 38 pp.
An explanation of the Socialist Labor Party's attack on Foster, denouncing the SLP as unwittingly procapital in its advocacy of the ballot, its fight for industrial unions, and its criticism of the CP.

O33 .... "Life and Teachings of Friedrich Engels." New York: Workers Library, n.d. [1932]. 39 pp.
An account of the life and thought of the co-founder with Marx of the theory of class struggle and socialist revolution, and the builder of the first revolutionary working class organizations. Among the topics discussed are dialectical materialism, historical materialism, the class struggle, the dictatorship of the proletariat, and internationalism.

O34 .... "The Socialist Party: Last Bulwark of Capitalism." New York: Workers Library, n.d. [1932]. 30 pp.
Denunciation of the Socialist Party as indistinguishable from the capitalist parties. Economic struggles, freedom, the Negro, private property, the ballot, war, imperialism, and the Soviet Union are among the issues analyzed. The SP is called social-fascist; only the CPUSA advances a clear-cut revolutionary program.

O35 .... "Trotskyism: Counter-Revolution in Disguise." New York: Workers Library, 1935. 160 pp.
An unflattering account of Trotsky's career, asserting that he fought Bolshevism as a Menshevik until late in the summer of 1917, and has been fighting it again ever since 1923. He is said to represent the interests of the petty bourgeoisie. The basis of all his ideas and policies is the denial that socialism is possible in one country. He has falsified the history of Bolshevism. The danger of Trotskyism is that its deception is not easily detected because it is covered with revolutionary phrases. One chapter (pp. 126-44) deals with the Trotskyites in the U.S., where their aim is to discredit revolutionary theory and practice.

O36 .... "Why Communism? Plain Talks on Vital Problems." 2d rev. ed. New York: Workers Library, 1935. 72 pp.
Revision of a pamphlet that first appeared in 1933, describing the beliefs and objectives of communists while they still openly advocated the revolutionary overthrow of capitalism and the dictatorship of the proletariat. Though Hitler was already triumphant in Germany, the communists had not quite yet adopted the people's front tactic, still viewing Roosevelt's New Deal as incipient fascism. Olgin, editor of the Jewish communist daily, "Freiheit," calls for turning imperialist war into civil war, overthrowing the capitalist state, and establishing the dictatorship of the proletariat.

O37 .... "That Man Browder, Communist Candidate for President." New York: Workers Library, 1936. 23 pp.
A biography of Browder, communist candidate for president in 1936. His early career in the Socialist Party and in the Syndicalist League of North America is traced, as is his imprisonment during World War I for opposition to the war. His activities in the Comintern, both in Moscow and in China in 1927, are told. The pamphlet concludes with a discussion of the 1936 platform.

O38 OLIN, John M. "Review of the Mooney Case; Its Relation to the Conduct in This Country of Anarchists, I.W.W. and Bolsheviki." Madison, Wis.: The author, 1920. 104 pp.
A detailed analysis of the evidence in the case, with approval of the conviction. Opposition is declared due to the International Workers Defense League and other radical groups.

O39 OLNEY, Warren, III. The Use of Former Communists as Witnesses: The Propriety of Practice in Federal Trials, "Vital Speeches of the Day," 20 (Aug. 15, 1954), 646-50.
An Assistant U.S. Attorney General defends the propriety of using and paying ex-communists and planted informants as expert witnesses concerning the aims of the Communist Party and the identification of members. He asserts that their assistance has been invaluable, and that the services of the ex-communists show a change of heart and a desire to serve their country.

O40 OLSON, Sidney. The Movie Hearings, "Life," 23 (Nov. 24, 1947), 137-48.
A report on the House Un-American Activities Committee's Hollywood hearings in Washington. Adverse witnesses included Dalton Trumbo, John Howard Lawson,

Albert Maltz, and Samuel Ornitz. Emmet Lavery, head of the Screen Writers Guild, and refugee screen writer Berthold Brecht convinced the committee that they were not communists.

O41 ONEAL, James (aff.), and MINOR, Robert (neg.). "Debate. Resolved: That the Terms of the Third International Are Unacceptable to the Revolutionary Socialists of the World." New York: Academy Press, 1921. 32 pp.
Oneal criticizes the Communist International's terms as Bakuninist, not Marxist, as imposing conspiratorial techniques and programs on other countries despite great variety in historical development and present conditions. Defending the Comintern, Minor argues that the 21 conditions permit both lawful and unlawful methods, depending on national conditions, and that the Comintern correctly rejects American socialists, who refuse to choose between "democracy" that shoots workers and working class revolution.

O42 ONEAL, James. Communist Hoax, "American Mercury," 1 (Jan. 1924), 79-84.
A history of the communist movement from 1919 to 1924, asserting that the communists now number less than 20,000, about half of the number in 1919. Oneal describes the numerous sects in existence, the shifts in line, and the hostile relations between the IWW and communism. The Trade Union Educational League, under communist influence, is distrusted by most of organized labor.

O43 .... The Record of the Communist Party, "New Leader," 1 (Sept. 27, 1924), 9.
A pre-election article on the Communist Party record, pointing to contradictions in policy on election activity, labor parties, united fronts with like-minded political groups, La Follette, etc. The CP record since 1919 has ranged from support of civil war, armed insurrection, and boycotting of elections to support of La Follette, opposition to him, and final denunciation of him as an "enemy."

O44 .... The Latest Wrinkles in American Communism: Convention Completes a Two-Year Cycle of Internal Controversies and Splitting, "New Leader," 2 (Oct. 3, 1925), 6.
An article originally written for the Baltimore "Sun," following the August 1925 national convention of the Workers Party. Factions in the WP are surveyed and the major issues reviewed, including the Party's labor party policy, the meaning of "bolshevization," and the status of language federations. The WP has been plagued with factional caucuses.

O45 .... Eclipse of American Communism, "Current History," 23 (Nov. 1925), 208-12.
The editor of the socialist "New Leader" traces the history of the Workers Party from 1921 to 1925. On Moscow's orders the communists supported the farmer-labor party in 1924; the WP then viewed this united front policy as a mistake, only to have the Communist International reverse this decision. The Party, which is contracting, must be subsidized from abroad.

O46 .... Militancy's Record of Wreckage: How a Progressive Labor Movement Has Been Thwarted, "New Leader," 3 (May 22, 1926), 3.
An attack upon communists' "militancy" in the trade unions, which in practice consists of falsehoods, intrigue, and character assassination of all who oppose them. The anarchists in the 1870's and 1880's, and later the Socialist Labor Party and then the IWW, followed similar tactics, with disastrous results. Tolerance of varying views is urged.

O47 .... "American Communism: A Critical Analysis of Its Origins, Development and Programs." New York: Rand Book Store, 1927. 256 pp. App. Ind.
A critical account of the first eight years of the communist movement in the U.S. by a veteran socialist, who describes the development of the early communist parties out of the left wing of the socialist movement, their splits and mergers in the underground phase of communism, the emergence of the legal Workers Party, and the political and trade union ventures in which it engaged in the mid-1920's. The 1919 program of the left wing Socialists and the 21 conditions for membership in the Communist International are reproduced as appendices.

O48 .... "A History of the Amalgamated Ladies' Garment Cutters' Union Local 10, Affiliated with the International Ladies' Garment Workers' Union." New York: Local 10, 1927. 450 pp. App. Ind.
Three chapters in the volume deal with the fight between communists and the right-wing faction for control of the local in the mid-1920's. Chapter 14, pp. 297-332, outlines the formation, policies, and activities of the communist nucleus within the local. Chapter 15, pp. 333-56, deals with the special convention of 1925, called as a result of the left-right struggle within the ILGWU. Chapter 16, pp. 357-89, describes the communist-led strike in the New York City industry in 1926.

O49 .... Whence This Communism? "New Leader," 3 [4] (Jan. 1-May 28, 1927).
A series of 19 articles on facets of communism, in Europe and in the U.S. Most of the material deals with predecessor movements, including the Socialist Party "impossibilists," the IWW, the Socialist Labor Party, etc. Some of the material appears in the author's book, "American Communism."

O50 .... Where Is That Half-Million? The Communists' Unsavory Part in the Sacco-Vanzetti Case, "New Leader," 4 (Sept. 10, 1927), 4 ff.
An assertion by a leading socialist that the communists injected discord and intrigue into the movement for Sacco and Vanzetti, distorting the motives of all others working to save them. Nearly all the money that the communists raised, ostensibly for Sacco and Vanzetti, went into their own coffers.

O51 .... About This United Front Offer, "New Leader," 15 (April 1, 1933), 3 ff.
A warning to socialists not to participate in united front activities with the communists until so advised by the Second International. Communist invitations have been frequent in various countries since Hitler's rise to power. United front efforts here are reviewed. The communists' goal in such activities is to strengthen their own organization.

O52 .... "Socialism versus Bolshevism." New York: Rand School Press, 1935. 27 pp.
A contrast of socialist aims and methods with those of communists, written by a leading right-wing American socialist. He accuses Lenin and the Bolsheviks in Russia of utopianism, of abandoning Marxist views, of contradictions and futility, of inviting capitalist exploitation, of collaborating with the Nazis, and of justifying low cunning and rule-or-ruin policies.

O53 ...., and WERNER, G. A. "American Communism: A Critical Analysis of Its Origins, Development and Programs." New York: Dutton, 1947. 416 pp. App. Ind.

A revision of a work originally published in 1927, to cover two additional decades of communist history in the U.S. Additional chapters deal with the rise of Trotskyism in America, communist youth activities, the dissolution of the Comintern, the communists during World War II, and postwar trends. New appendices include instructions to communist factions from the ECCI, the constitution of the Third International, and parts of its program.

O054   O'NEIL, James F. How You Can Fight Communism, "American Legion Magazine," 45 (Aug. 1948), 16-17 ff.
The national commander of the Legion gives advice on spotting and fighting the communists, who seek to disguise themselves as "progressives." Each Legion post should have a trained specialist on subversive activities, oppose appearances of pro-Soviet apologists, and expose communist fronts. The House Un-American Activities Committee should be supported.

O055   O'NEILL, Richard. "Vote for John L. Lewis and Communism: A Tale of Three Cities." New Haven: Constitutional Educational League, 1937. 30 pp.
The author sees the hand of communism in the recent primary victory of Pat O'Brien in Detroit, in an American Labor Party endorsement of La Guardia in New York City, and in Earl Browder's support of Judge Patterson for mayor of Akron. If voters support these CIO and communist endorsed candidates in 1940, he warns they may later vote for John L. Lewis to be president of a Soviet America.

O056   OPITZ, Edmund A. Presbyterians and a Letter, "Freeman," 5 (Sept. 1954), 91-93.
An attack on the "Letter to Presbyterians" written by President John Mackey of Princeton Theological Seminary, and endorsed by the Presbyterian General Assembly. Although Mackey is aware of the menace of communism, he condemned the methods of congressional investigating committees, slandered ex-communists, and attacked one of the great churches to which they have turned.

O057   OPPENHEIMER, J. Robert. A Letter from the Chief of Los Alamos, "New Republic," 120 (June 6, 1949), 8-9.
A letter from Oppenheimer to Senator Brien McMahon, chairman of the Joint Committee on Atomic Energy, opposing the proposal that fellowships of the National Research Council be screened for potential subversives. No access to restricted data is granted to fellows. Secret investigations inevitably bring preoccupation with conformity and fear of ruin.

O058   "OPPORTUNITY," Communism and the Negro Tenant Farmer, 9 (Aug. 1931), 234-35.
A discussion of the clash at Camp Hill, Ala., where racial violence flared up following organizational efforts of the communist-controlled Negro Share Croppers Union. Blame for the violence is placed on the sheriff and deputies, who broke up the meeting and denied participants the right of peaceful assembly.

O059   OSSINSKY, N. Agrarian Relations in America, "Workers Monthly," 5 (July 1926), 416-18; (Aug.), 72-74.
Condensed version of a report by a former Soviet Commissar of Agriculture, following a trip through the U.S. He presents data to show that U.S. farm-tenancy has increased and that it is becoming more difficult for farmers to rise from tenants to owners.

O060   OVERSTREET, Harry and Bonaro. "What We Must Know about Communism." New York: Norton, 1958. 348 pp. Bibliog. Notes. Ind.
An analysis of communism as a world force led by the USSR, which has practiced totalitarianism at home and piecemeal conquest abroad. The CPUSA, like all other such parties, has always served the interests of the Soviet Union, using the united front tactic to extend its influence. Particular target groups in the U.S. have been the workers, any underprivileged minority, the armed forces, young people, and intellectuals. The CPUSA teaches its members to flout the law, to destroy the respect of the masses for it, and yet to demand every legal safeguard for themselves.

O061   OXNAM, G. Bromley. "I Protest." New York: Harper, 1954. 186 pp.
A protest by a Methodist bishop against the use of improper procedures by congressional investigating committees. Describing his experiences before the House Un-American Activities Committee, in which his association with allegedly procommunist organizations was attacked, the author criticizes committees that intimidate rather than investigate, that employ incompetent staff members, and that use unverified information as a device to discredit.

O062   OZANNE, Robert Willard. "The Effects of Communist Leadership on American Trade Unions." Unpubl. doctoral dissertation, University of Wisconsin Library, 1954. 329 pp. Bibliog.
An examination of communist leadership of American trade unions, with attention to communist techniques of control at the local and national union levels. A case study of a communist-led local, Local 248 of the United Automobile Workers at Allis-Chalmers, is included. The author concludes that communist leadership maintains itself through regular use of machine politics, that communist unions are generally militant in collective bargaining and grievance handling, that the economic interests of the members are sacrificed to advance Soviet foreign policy, and that this conflict results in lack of union democracy.

P

P1 PACIENZA, Francis A., Jr. Communism, Inferences, and the Privilege against Self-Incrimination, "Catholic University of America Law Review," 4 (Jan. 1954), 51-61.
An assertion that the protection afforded by the Fifth Amendment bar against self-incrimination is applicable in criminal but not in civil proceedings. A failure in the latter to explain incriminating circumstances permits the jury to draw an adverse inference. Public employees who claim the privilege in congressional investigations, which are not criminal proceedings, may therefore be discharged.

P2 PACKER, Herbert L. A Tale of Two Typewriters, "Stanford Law Review," 10 (May 1958), 409-40.
An examination of the evidence relating to Hiss' charge that he was the victim of forgery by typewriter. Though the Hiss defense has raised doubts about the case, these doubts, if proved well-founded, would exonerate Hiss in only the most technical sense. Besides the unresolved issue of the two typewriters, there are many loose ends that should still be pursued.

P3 .... "Ex-Communist Witnesses: Four Studies in Fact Finding." Stanford, Calif.: Stanford University Press, 1962. 279 pp. App. Notes. Ind.
A study of the testimony of four former communists—Whittaker Chambers, Elizabeth Bentley, Louis Budenz, and John Lautner—with attention to the shortcomings of the processes used to elicit and test the evidence. While evidence supports the main outlines of their stories, problems are raised by the urge for self-vindication, the pecuniary motive, and the pursuit of publicity. The advantages and disadvantages of congressional investigations, court trials, and administrative inquiries are examined, and alternatives in the British tradition considered.

P4 PACKMAN, Martin. Security Risks in Government, "Editorial Research Reports," 1 (Feb. 3, 1954), 81-100.
An analysis of the evolution of the federal loyalty-security program during and after World War II. A comparison is made of security standards and the operation of the security program in the Eisenhower and Truman Administrations, and our system is compared with that of the British. Disagreement exists as to how to protect the national interest without undue interference with the rights of citizens.

P5 PADMORE, George. "The Life and Struggles of Negro Toilers." London: R.I.L.U. Magazine, 1931. 126 pp.
The international role of Negro workers as seen by the Red International of Labor Unions. (Written in conjunction with the first International Conference of Negro Workers called by the RILU in July 1930; the author was a Negro born in the British West Indies and educated in the U.S.) While primary emphasis is given to Negroes in colonial and semicolonial countries, the "intolerable" conditions of the American Negro are also given consideration (pp. 46-55, 109-10). Negro workers in the U.S. are said to be coming into closer alliance with class-conscious white workers under leadership of the Party and the Trade Union Unity League.

P6 .... An Open Letter to Earl Browder, "Crisis," 42 (Oct. 1935), 302 ff.
An open letter by a former Party member, who had been secretary of the Party-controlled Negro Trade Union Committee, complaining of the campaign of lies and slander against him in Party organs. (In a reply, in the December issue of "Crisis," Browder asserts that Padmore was removed because he accepted the Japanese imperialist view that Negroes will be liberated through a race war of darker races against the whites.)

P7 PAGE, [Dorothy] Myra. "Southern Cotton Mills and Labor." Introd. by Bill Dunne. New York: Workers Library, 1929. 96 pp.
A communist view of conditions in Southern textile mills and of the history and prospect of unionism. The author describes oppression in the Southern mill town, the exploitation of the mill hands, and the repeated failure of unionism until 1928, when the Party-led National Textile Workers Union entered the Southern field. She contrasts the heroic activity of the NTWU with the "sell-out" tactics of the United Textile Workers.

P8 .... Inter-racial Relations among Southern Workers, "Communist," 9 (Feb. 1930), 154-65.
An analysis of the origin and development of antagonisms between poor whites and Negroes in the South. Party history has shown that these workers can be drawn into joint struggle and into militant organizations for common objectives.

P9 .... "Gathering Storm: A Story of the Black Belt." New York: International Publishers, 1932. 374 pp.
A presentation, in fiction form, of the Gastonia strike, emphasizing the need for Negro-white unity on an equal basis in a communist front. All the characters, except for several who are belatedly converted, are well grounded in communist ideology.

P10 .... "Moscow Yankee." New York: Putnam, 1935. 292 pp.
A novel dealing with an average American worker who leaves a production line at Ford's for the production line of the Red Star truck plant in Moscow. Falling in love with Russia, he settles down in the Soviet Union to assist in building a workers' society.

P11 PAGE, John. "Drouth." Philadelphia: Farmers National Committee for Action, n.d. [1935]. 31 pp.
Criticism of the New Deal farm program for creating another million surplus farmers, leading the nation to the doorstep of famine while talking of surpluses, and increasing the debt burden of farmers. Scrapping of the AAA and passage of the Farmers Emergency Relief Bill is urged.

P12 PAGE, Kirby (ed.). "A New Economic Order." New York: Harcourt, Brace, 1930. 387 pp.

A symposium on capitalism, fascism, and communism. Anna Rochester presents "A Favorable Interpretation of Communism" (chapter 5, pp. 67-88), emphasizing the class struggle, the history and goals of the Communist International, and the achievements of the Soviet Union. In chapter 6, "A Critical Examination of Communism" (pp. 89-102), Jerome Davis points out that the Soviet Union does not permit freedom of religion, that it relies on mass violence, denies the worth of the individual, and considers anyone who opposes the Party in action to be a traitor.

P13   PAGE, Kirby. Socialism versus Communism, "World Tomorrow," 15 (Sept. 14, 1932), 258-60.
A discussion, from a pacifist-socialist point of view, of the different approaches of the Socialist and Communist Parties to American politics and social problems. The author prefers the peaceful persuasion of the socialists to the revolutionary emphasis of the communists, whose method of reaching the classless society is through class war.

P14   . . . . "Individualism and Socialism: An Ethical Survey of Economic and Political Forces." New York: Farrar & Rinehart, 1933. 367 pp. App. Notes and ref. Ind.
The editor of "World Tomorrow" devotes chapter 6 (pp. 200-35) to "A Socialist Critique of Communist Strategy." He discusses the communist theory of social change, and contrasts the decisive factors in the Russian Revolution with those on the American scene. Opposing a united front with the communists because of their desire to disrupt socialist organizations, he rejects the communist strategy of violent class war as pragmatically indefensible and morally unjustified.

P15   . . . . Class War and Religion, "World Tomorrow," 16 (March 8, 1933), 225-28.
An examination of the concept of class war, primarily from the ethical-religious point of view. The communist hope of seizing power by means of a disciplined minority would result in a long dictatorship, using terror to liquidate counterrevolutionaries. The social consequences of prolonged civil war in a highly industrialized nation would be devastating.

P16   . . . . Can Socialists and Communists Unite? "World Tomorrow," 16 (May 1933), 395-96.
The communists attack the socialists as bankrupt and insincere, at the same time proposing a united front on the basis of a violent seizure of power as advocated by the CP. Socialists could join such a united front only by abandoning the principles that have set them apart from the communists.

P17   . . . . What Is behind the United Front? "World Tomorrow," 16 (Oct. 26, 1933), 587-88.
The success of the U.S. Congress Against War, organized by the communists, calls for an examination of the united front tactic. The communists still seek to destroy socialist and pacifist movements that oppose violent revolution and civil war. So long as this hostility remains, there is no foundation for united action.

P18   . . . . Can Communism Capture America? "Christian Century," 52 (Oct. 9, 1935), 1275-77.
The success of communism here appears very doubtful, though we are in the sixth year of depression. Analyzing the factors unfavorable to communism, the author asserts that the attempt to establish a just society through resort to violence is wholly unjustified.

P19   PALMER, Edward E. (ed.). "The Communist Problem in America: A Book of Readings." New York: Crowell, 1951. 496 pp. Ind. App.

A compilation of 42 selections under four heads: (1) "The Strategy and Tactics of World Communism," providing an understanding of communist ideology; (2) "The Communist Party in America," giving insight into the history of the CPUSA, its major goals, and its connection with the Kremlin; (3) "Toward an Informal Solution," dealing with the impact of communism on American education, civil liberties, politics, labor unions, and civil service; and (4) "Toward a Formal Solution," a presentation of the legal methods of combating communism.

P20   PALMER, Frederick. How Strong Are the Reds? "American Legion Monthly," 20 (Feb. 1936), 8-9 ff.
Stressing the connections of the communists in the U.S. to the Communist International, the author reports Browder's speech to the Seventh Congress of the Comintern, held in Moscow, and Foster's reception there. The teachings of Lenin are contrasted with the traditions of America. Recent communist gains here are reported.

P21   . . . . The Reds, the Army, the Navy, "American Legion Monthly," 20 (March 1936), 10-11 ff.
An account of communist propaganda leaflets addressed to American servicemen, picturing their officers as scabs and agents of imperialism, and preaching mutiny and sedition. Similar agitation is conducted in the CCC camps, protesting regimentation and militarism. The author contrasts the liberty to dissent here with repression in the USSR.

P22   . . . . The Reds Look to Youth, "American Legion Monthly," 20 (April 1936), 12-13 ff.
An account of communist appeals to young people, of the Young Pioneers (the communist substitute for Boy Scouts), and of the Young Communist League plans to infiltrate other youth organizations. On the basis of attendance at a joint socialist-communist mass meeting, the author sees little difference between the two movements. He emphasizes the youth and native birth of those who attended.

P23   . . . . Peace, the Reds and the Rest of Us, "American Legion Monthly," 20 (May 1936), 12-13 ff.
An account of red pacifist propaganda in the U.S., particularly that conducted by the League Against War and Fascism and the student antiwar movement. American Legion members are pictured by such groups as glorifiers and racketeers of war. Communists are not against war and militarism as such; they favor revolutionary wars while opposing military training.

P24   PANUCH, J. Anthony. The Inside Story of the Marzani Case, "Plain Talk," 2 (Oct. 1947), 27-38.
A former Deputy Assistant Secretary of State tells how Carl A. Marzani, who went from the wartime Office of Strategic Services to a highly confidential bureau of the State Department, was found to be a former member of the CPUSA under the name of Tony Whales. He was dismissed and convicted of fraud, for concealing his communist connections.

P25   PANUNZIO, Constantine M. "The Deportation Cases of 1919 - 1920." New York: Commission on the Church and Social Service, Federal Council of the Churches of Christ in America, 1921. 104 pp. App.
A report based on 200 deportation cases, which concludes that only a small number of those involved were dangerous radicals, and that the present law needed serious modification. Among the aspects discussed are deportation laws, the arrests and trials of aliens, the treatment of those arrested, the organizational affiliations of the arrested, and the effect on the aliens' families.

P26 PARKER, Alex (pseud.). "Organizing the Party for Victory over Reaction." New York: New Century, 1953. 48 pp.
A report to a national conference of the Party in 1953. Party emphasis in the coming period must be on mass work, rejecting defeatist acceptance of illegal status. Proposals for creating a united front Marxist party must be combatted. The author criticizes the Party for a serious decline in recruitment, "mechanical" work in bourgeois-led organizations, and an alarming loss in circulation of the Marxist press.

P27 PARSONS, Talcott. McCarthyism and American Social Tension: A Sociologist's View, "Yale Review," 44 (Dec. 1954), 226-45.
The transition from laissez-faire capitalism and isolationism to increasing government intervention and internationalism have produced strains in the American social structure. McCarthyism is a highly emotional overreaction to the difficulties communism creates for us. Communism has become a symbol for many "evils" associated with our new situation.

P28 PARSONS, Wilfrid. Popular Front and Catholicism, "Commonweal," 25 (Feb. 19, 1937), 464-66.
Catholics are cautioned against seeing the present crisis as an alternative between democracy (of which communism pretends to be a part) and fascism. Communism is a greater evil than fascism because it is an article for export, it is a "religion" as well as a state system, and it has produced fascism as a reaction. Catholics are urged to take a third position, the defense of democracy and peace.

P29 "PARTISAN REVIEW & ANVIL," What Is Americanism? A Symposium on Marxism and the American Tradition, 3 (April 1936), 3-16.
A symposium on the concept of Americanism and its relationship to the cultured tradition of western Europe, the native revolutionary heritage of the U.S., and Marxism, with particular reference to the growth of revolutionary literature. Participants are Theodore Dreiser, Newton Arvin, Josephine Herbst, Robert Herrick, Matthew Josephson, Kenneth Burke, Waldo Frank, William Troy, William Carlos Williams, and Joseph Freeman.

P30 "PARTY ORGANIZER," Mine Strike Issue, 4 (Aug. 1931), 1-29.
Notes by various authors on the coal miners' strike in Pennsylvania, Ohio, and West Virginia, under the leadership of the National Miners Union and the Party. Items deal with preparations for the strike, building the union and the Party, relief activities of the unemployed, unity of Negro and white workers, ex-servicemen, picket lines, and leadership.

P31 . . ., Special Plenum Issue, 5 (May-June 1932), 1-33.
A series of short items by various authors dealing with the Fourteenth Plenum of the Central Committee of the CPUSA. Among the topics are work in factories, the election campaign, sectarianism, work among Negroes, strike preparations, work in reformist unions, the struggle against provocateurs and spies, literature distribution, and training of cadres.

P32 . . ., Special Shop Issue, 6 (Feb. 1933), 1-96.
The entire issue is devoted to problems in building organization and winning leadership in the shops. Short articles deal with particular industries, such as steel, metals, railroads, printing, longshoremen, and autos; with special problems of dealing with Negro or women workers; or with general issues such as the united front, or work with-in reformist unions or in shops controlled by the revolutionary union.

P33 . . ., Special Issue: Extraordinary Party Conference, 6 (Aug.-Sept. 1933), 1-96.
Excerpts from speeches at a July 1933 Party conference at which an open letter to the membership was adopted, demanding mobilization of all resources for a turn towards mass work. Reports criticize Party work in the basic industries and among other groups, discuss building of opposition groups in AFL unions and work in Party-oriented mass organizations, and deal with united front action and with strengthening political understanding.

P34 . . ., Excerpts from Speeches Made at the Seventeenth C.C. Plenum Held Recently, 6 (Nov. 1933), 1-32.
Excerpts from speeches at the Seventeenth Plenum of the Central Committee, CPUSA, in the fall of 1933, reviewing Party work since the Extraordinary Party Conference in July. Speakers criticize the Party's lack of progress among steel, mining, and marine workers, and in the South; and also among women, youth, and the unemployed. White chauvinism must be rooted out, and leadership and communication improved.

P35 . . ., Eighth Convention Issue, 7 (May-June 1934), 1-64.
Excerpts from speeches and reports at the Party's eighth national convention, April 2-8, 1934. Emphasis was upon meeting the threat of fascism and imperialist war, overthrowing capitalist dictatorship, and setting up a Soviet government. Topics included organizational status and tasks of the Party; work among steel, metal, marine, mining, textile, stockyard, and needle workers; use of the united front to win over socialist workers; organization of farm women; and the League of Struggle for Negro Rights.

P36 . . ., Special Issue: Central Committee Plenum, 8 (March 1935), 1-48.
Excerpts from reports and discussion at the Central Committee plenum on organization and agitation-propaganda problems. Among the topics are organization in steel and among city transport workers, penetrating Negro organizations, women's work, mass agitation, schools, literature, and shop papers.

P37 . . ., May Meeting of Central Committee, 8 (July 1935), 1-48.
Excerpts from reports and discussion at the meeting of the Party's Central Committee, May 25-27, 1935. The excerpts deal with the work of shop nuclei, the united front movement, the building of a mass labor party, and Party training and methods of agitation.

P38 . . ., Special Pre-Convention Discussion Issue, 9 (March 1936), 1-48.
Discussion of Party work, in preparation for the coming Party convention, following the Seventh World Congress of the Communist International. Articles deal with work in Party branches, in industrial and shop units, and in trade unions and on WPA projects. Other topics include work among women, the use of shop papers and leaflets, and taking part in city and state politics.

P39 . . ., Special Issue on Party Building, 10 (Aug. 1937), 1-48.
Excerpts from speeches and reports at the plenary meeting of the Party's Central Committee, June 17-20, 1937. Topics include problems in building the Party among workers in particular industries or in various parts of the country, along with experiences in strike struggles, among Negro women, and with national groups.

P40 "PARTY ORGANIZER," Special Education Issue, 11 (Feb. 1938), 1-40.
The entire issue is devoted to various phases of the Party's educational work—key educational problems, agitation for collective security, ways to keep new members, shop and neighborhood papers, self-education, and building an educational organization.

P41 . . ., National Party Builders' Congress Issue, 11 (April 1938), 1-48.
The entire issue is devoted to excerpts from reports submitted at the National Party Builders' Congress held in New York City, February 18-21, 1938. Pages 24-25 list pointers on recruiting condensed from these reports.

P42 . . ., 10th National Convention Discussion Issue, 11 (May 1938), 1-32.
The entire issue is devoted to discussion articles in preparation for the Party's tenth national convention, May 26-31, 1938. Topics covered include Party education, organizational problems, work among the masses, experience with Catholics, building the democratic front among national groups, work in Akron, and youth in the democratic front.

P43 . . ., Tenth National Convention Issue, 11 (July 1938), 1-32.
The entire issue is devoted to excerpts from reports and speeches at the Party's tenth national convention, May 26-31, 1938. Topics include building the Party, the struggle against wage cuts, election activities, vigilance against Trotskyist and Lovestoneite groups, and shop unit reports.

P44 PASCHELL, William, and ROSE, Theodore. Anti-Communist Provisions in Union Constitutions, "Monthly Labor Review," 77 (Oct. 1954), 1097-1100.
A BLS report on formal anticommunist provisions in 59 of 100 national union constitutions studied. The trend toward adoption of such provisions began after 1935. The article discusses specific versus general provisions, the extent of coverage of these provisions, the severity of restrictions or discipline, and types of trial procedure.

P45 PATCH, Buel W. Anti-Radical Agitation, "Editorial Research Reports," 1 (March 28, 1935), 221-40.
A review of antiradical agitation in the U.S. before and since World War I, with attention to the 1919-20 communist scares, the deportation of alien radicals, state laws on criminal syndicalism and sedition, and the revival of anti-red agitation in the depression.

P46 . . . . Communism in America, "Editorial Research Reports," 2 (Nov. 13, 1946), 779-98.
An analysis of communist influence in the U.S. in the immediate postwar period, when wartime collaboration with the Soviet Union had given way to the cold war. Particular attention is paid to communist infiltration of unions, particularly of the CIO, and also to Party strength, methods, and subservience to Moscow. Problems of loyalty and civil liberties, in the light of the communist challenge, are also discussed.

P47 . . . . Loyalty and Security, "Editorial Research Reports," 1 (April 4, 1950), 231-54.
A review of loyalty probes and the national security, precipitated by Senator McCarthy's charges of communist infiltration of the State Department. The development of the federal loyalty program is traced, and three years of the current loyalty program evaluated. Loyalty policies of the British government are outlined briefly.

P48 PATES, Gordon. California—the Oath Epidemic, "Reporter," 3 (Dec. 26, 1950), 29-31.
A survey of the multiplicity of loyalty oaths instituted in California between 1945 and 1950. Activities of the Tenney Committee are reviewed. Oaths for University of California faculty, civilian defense oaths, and oaths for state officials proliferate the point of absurdity.

P49 PATTERSON, Haywood, and CONRAD, Earl. "Scottsboro Boy." Garden City, N.Y.: Doubleday, 1950. 309 pp. App.
The story of Patterson, one of the defendants in the Scottsboro case, written by Conrad as though Patterson were speaking. Tried and convicted four times in Alabama on the rape charge, Patterson was sentenced to death the first three times and to 75 years in prison the fourth time. After serving 12 years of this term he escaped and went North. Some references are made to the roles played by the International Labor Defense and the Scottsboro Defense Committee.

P50 PATTERSON, Samuel C. "A New Approach to Negro Work." New York: International Workers Order, 1943. 24 pp.
A report to the general executive board of the IWO, proposing establishment of a Negro section. Denying that this is a Jim Crow measure, the report urges this action as recognition of the peculiar history and traditions of the Negro community. Far from isolating Negro work, the result would be the building of a mass base among Negroes.

P51 . . . . "The Program and Plans for the Establishment of the Frederick Douglass Fraternal and Benevolent Society of the International Workers Order." New York: IWO, 1943. 23 pp.
Report of the subcommittee on Negro Work of the IWO, proposing establishment of Negro branches. Asserting that the IWO has based itself on national groups, the report calls for an organization within the Order under Negro leadership to guide Negro work. The important position and necessary functions of fraternal societies in the Negro community are emphasized.

P52 PATTERSON, William L. The I.L.D. Faces the Future, "Communist," 13 (July 1934), 718-27.
A review of the problems and policies of the ILD on its ninth anniversary. Though other civil liberties groups such as the ACLU exist, they obscure the class essence of civil liberties. The task of the ILD is to expose the class character of democracy and justice, and stimulate the class consciousness of the masses. The ILD, guided by the Party, must struggle against social-fascist agents of the ruling class.

P53 . . . . "Sikeston—Hitlerite Crime against America." St. Louis: Communist Party of Missouri, 1942. 23 pp.
A speech by the national vice-president of the International Labor Defense, protesting the lynching of Cleo Wright at Sikeston, Missouri. Lynchers are called Hitler's fifth column in America. The second-rate citizenship of Negroes must be ended.

P54 . . . . We Charge Genocide! "Political Affairs," 30 (Dec. 1951), 42-52.
An address by the national executive secretary of the Civil Rights Congress on the occasion of the publication of its book, "We Charge Genocide—The Crime of Government against the Negro People." Attacking the Ku Klux Klan, segregation, lynching, and poll taxes, Patterson charges that the South is becoming a vast torture chamber for Negroes and calls upon the UN for action.

P55 PATTON, James M. The Pennsylvania Loyalty Act, "University of Pittsburgh Law Review," 14 (Fall 1952), 90-102.

An examination of the constitutionality of the state law requiring loyalty oaths for state employees. Among objections considered are that they are bills of attainder or ex post facto laws, that they conflict with the exclusive oath of office required by the constitution, and that they infringe upon free speech, religion, and belief. Despite procedural unfairness, the statute is probably constitutional.

P56   PAVLOVA, V. "Party Organizer," "Communist International," 8 (Oct. 15, 1931), 580-82.
Criticism of the American Party's internal organ, "Party Organizer." While individual suggestions are valuable, they are not linked up with each other or with the main political tasks confronting the Party. The magazine must be changed into an organ that helps the Party consolidate its work.

P57   PEALE, Norman V., and GAINFORT, John. Five Ways You Can Help Your Church Fight Communism, "Woman's Home Companion," 71 (Oct. 1954), 42 ff.
An assertion that communists are trying to infiltrate American churches, with suggestions for starting a counteroffensive by praying about the problem, by learning to answer the communists, by being active in organizations that make the community a better place in which to live, by making one's own church tolerant of other races and faiths, and by having faith in the superior values of religion.

P58   PEARSON, Norman Holmes. The Nazi-Soviet Pact and the End of a Dream. Pp. 327-48 in "America in Crisis: Fourteen Crucial Episodes in American History," ed. by Daniel Aaron. New York: Knopf, 1952. 363 pp. Bibliog.
An effort to explain the belief of American writers and intellectuals in the communist experiment during the 1930's. Attention is paid to the spiritual as well as the economic crisis of the depression decade, and to the menace of fascism. The Nazi-Soviet pact was the final disenchantment to those whose faith had survived disillusioning episodes like the Moscow trials.

P59   PEASE, Frank. "Technicians and Revolution: An Exposé of Communist Tactics for Overthrowing the State." Coral Gables, Florida: The author, 1939. 34 pp.
A pamphlet from the extreme right, by an author who sees the communists' bid for power in a CIO drive to organize technicians in industry. He advocates outlawing communism, industrial preparedness, and shipping or shooting communists.

P60   PEGLER, Westbrook. What Strange Bedfellows! "American Legion Magazine," 26 (April 1939), 10-11 ff.
An assertion that communism and nazi-fascism are both varieties of Bolshevism, with inconsequential differences. Nazi-fascism is the response to communist aggression. Union meetings are controlled by cliques of disciplined communists, seeking to bring about strikes in order to create public disorder and bankruptcies.

P61   PELTASON, Jack. "Constitutional Liberty and Seditious Activity: Individual Liberty and Governmental Security." New York: Carrie Chapman Catt Memorial Fund, 1954. 57 pp. Bibliog.
One of the Freedom Agenda pamphlets, by a professor of political science at the University of Illinois, tracing the problem of liberty versus security through our history. Included are the Sedition Act of 1798, laws against syndicalists and anarchists, the Espionage Act of 1917, the Gitlow case, the Taft-Hartley oath and the Douds case, the Smith Act and cases under it, the Internal Security Act of 1950, the Communist Control Act of 1954, and state anti-subversive legislation. Alternatives for public policy are presented.

P62   PENDRELL, Nan and Ernest. "How the Rich Live and Whom to Tax." New York: Workers Library, 1939. 31 pp.
A picture of the idle rich, Tommy Manville, Brenda Frazier, the Rockefellers, and the Mellons, as dodging taxes while the poor must pay. The authors demand that we tax the trusts, and set up a tax program to aid the masses of the people.

P63   PEPPER, Claude. "An American Policy for Peace: A Program for Big Three Unity and American-Soviet Friendship." New York: National Council of American-Soviet Friendship, n.d. [1946]. 16 pp.
Abridgement of a speech delivered in the U.S. Senate in March 1946 urging reestablishment of Big Three unity, upon which the UN was founded. Negotiations among the Big Three are proposed to deal with the problems of Germany and Japan, atomic power, economic development, and other issues.

P64   PEPPER, John [pseud. for Josef Pogany]. "For a Labor Party: Recent Revolutionary Changes in American Politics." New York: Workers Party of America, 2d ed. 1923. 68 pp.
The second edition of a publication that went through three editions, each representing a substantial change in policy. The first, issued in 1922 under the authorship of the Workers Party of America (see separate entry), came before the December 1922 meeting of the Conference for Progressive Labor Action which refused admission to the communists. The second edition, following the CPLA meeting, analyzes that meeting and the 1922 elections. It appeared just prior to the July 1923 conference called by the Farmer-Labor Party headed by John Fitzpatrick. (The third edition, also authored by John Pepper, appeared in August 1923, after that conference, at which the Federated Farmer Labor Party was formed under Workers Party leadership. Formation of the FFLP is defended, and communist domination is denied. "John Pepper" was one of several pseudonyms used by Josef Pogany, an early Comintern representative in the U.S.)

P65   . . . . "Underground Radicalism: An Open Letter to Eugene V. Debs and to All Honest Workers within the Socialist Party." New York: Workers Party of America, n.d. [1923?]. 48 pp.
An attack upon the Socialist Party for opportunism and treachery, combined with an appeal for a united front for concrete actions. The author, a Comintern representative to the Party here, holds the right-wing socialist leaders, not the left wing, responsible for the split in 1919. Opposed both to "underground radicalism" and to "above-ground opportunism," he asserts that the right-wing socialist leaders will expose themselves by daily betrayals.

P66   . . . . Gompers Refuses to Recognize the U.S. Government, "Labor Herald," 2 (June 1923), 20-22.
An answer to assertions by Gompers and others that the movements for union amalgamation and a labor party are led by agitators and Reds. The conditions for these movements are created by capitalism, not by the TUEL. Denouncing the nonpartisan activities of the AFL, the author calls for a labor party to fight the bosses and the government.

P67   . . . . Declaration of Independence of the American Working Class, "International Press Correspondence," 3 (July 12, 1923), 511-12.

An analysis of factors that make formation of a revolutionary mass party in America possible. Emerging class conflicts will break the old, two-party framework; the current third party movement reflects these conflicts, without being representative of any single class. Only a party of the working class can represent the laboring masses of factories and farms alike.

P68   PEPPER, John [pseud. for Josef Pogany]. The First Mass Party of American Workers and Farmers, "International Press Correspondence," 3 (July 26, 1923), 552-54.
A report on the formation of the Federated Farmer-Labor Party in Chicago in July 1923. Criticisms by socialists, Gompers, and John Fitzpatrick of the Chicago Federation of Labor are answered. Denying that the Workers Party dominates the new party, Pepper asserts that it has a membership of 600,000. The next tasks of the FFLP are outlined.

P69   .... The Workers Party and the Federated Farmer-Labor Party, "Liberator," 6 (Aug. 1923), 10-14.
A report on the Chicago conference of July 1923, at which the Federated Farmer-Labor Party was formed, and on its relationship to the Workers Party. While the new party is not communist, it is fundamentally revolutionary. Pepper gives the WP point of view on the factional struggles with John Fitzpatrick of the Chicago Federation of Labor over convention organization, organization of the new party, and policy issues.

P70   .... The Slogan of the Workers' and Farmers' Government, "International Press Correspondence," 3 (Aug. 16, 1923), 602-4.
A discussion of the Comintern decision to broaden its slogan of a workers' government to that of a workers' and farmers' government. American communists were the first to apply the new slogan. The U.S. situation and the lessons of European revolutions show that farmers are necessary for a successful proletarian revolution, though the initiative and leadership must remain with the industrial working class.

P71   .... A Revolt of Farmers and Workers in the United States, "International Press Correspondence," 3 (Aug. 23, 1923), 616-18.
An analysis of the election of the Minnesota Farmer-Labor Party's gubernatorial candidate, Magnus Johnson. The real victors were not the exploited workers and farmers, but the confused politicians of the lower middle class and well-to-do farmers. Only a class party such as the Federated Farmer-Labor Party can represent the workers and farmers.

P72   .... The Workers Party at a Turning Point, "International Press Correspondence," 3 (Sept. 27, 1923), 698-99.
From September 1919 to August 1922, the American communist movement was preoccupied with internal problems. From then until July 1923 it fought for standing in the labor movement, using the united front tactic to influence the masses. It is now entering a third stage, in which it must lead the masses under its influence into the political struggle.

P73   .... Shall We Assume Leadership? "Liberator," 6 (Oct. 1923), 9-11.
A defense of the Workers Party's labor party policy, in particular its formation of the Federated Farmer-Labor Party. Though its formation has alienated some progressive labor leaders, it offers the Workers Party the opportunity to reach larger trade union audiences. The

fact that the Workers Party is the only group favoring immediate creation of a labor party should not keep it from assuming leadership.

P74   .... From a People's Upheaval to a Class Movement, "International Press Correspondence," 3 (Oct. 27, 1923), 770-72.
The Minnesota Farmer-Labor Party is contrasted with the Minnesota Farmer-Labor Federation, which expresses the discontent of the workers and exploited farmers with the Farmer-Labor Party machine. The new organization urges organization of the Farmer-Labor Party on the basis of economic rather than geographical units, to insure control by the advanced workers and farmers.

P75   .... "The General Strike and the General Betrayal." Chicago: Daily Worker Publishing Company, 1926. 100 pp.
An account of the nine-day general strike in England by a former Comintern representative to the Party here, who emphasizes the necessity for uncompromising revolutionary mass action on the political and economic fronts.

P76   .... Why a Labor Party? "Workers Monthly," 5 (Jan. 1926), 99-102.
Arguments for a labor party by a former Comintern representative to the Party here, currently a leader of the Ruthenberg faction. Pepper asserts that a labor party corresponds to the stage in class consciousness of the left wing, and that such a party, based on the trade unions, is feasible here. He answers the arguments of those, both members of the Party and others, against the labor party slogan.

P77   .... "American Negro Problems." New York: Workers Library, 1928. 16 pp.
An early Party advocacy of the right of self-determination of the Black Belt, written by a former Comintern representative to the Party here. The Black Belt in the South is said to be virtually a colony within U.S. borders. The Party must battle the Negro bourgeoisie, develop Negro cadres, and organize American Negroes as champions of Negroes everywhere against imperialism. (Reprinted from "Communist," Oct. 1928.)

P78   .... "Why Every Miner Should Be a Communist." New York: Workers Library, n.d. [1928]. 16 pp.
Recruiting literature addressed to striking coal miners. Praising the heroism of the strikers engaged in a struggle against the capitalist class, the author denounces the Lewis machine in the UMW, supports the Save-the-Union movement, and urges miners to join the Party.

P79   .... America and the Tactics of the Communist International, "Communist," 7 (April 1928), 219-27.
Though the Comintern has initiated a sharp left turn in Europe, this does not mean that the labor party policy should be abandoned here. American capitalism, contrary to European, is still on the upgrade; the American working class is in a relatively privileged position; no marked leftward tendency exists here yet. The labor party slogan will remain a propaganda slogan this year, but may become a slogan of action soon.

P80   .... Certain Basic Questions of Our Perspective, "Communist," 7 (May 1928), 297-306.
Examination of the relationship between Party work in the reactionary trade unions and the formation of new unions under sponsorship of the Trade Union Educational League. Because of the strength of the established unions, these two phases of Party work must go together. Criticism of

the Party's trade union work by Losovsky, leader of the Red International of Labor Unions, is considered.

P81   PEPPER, John [pseud. for Josef Pogany]. A Program of Action for America, "Communist," 7 (June 1928), 327-39.
A program of action sums up the tactical tasks of the Party at a given time, whereas a program is permanent. A program of action needs general slogans or demands, to link up transitional and partial demands into a system. Past programs and platforms of the Party suffered from lack of immediate demands. The program of action for 1928 must avoid mistakes of previous platforms.

P82   PERLMAN, Mark. "Labor Union Theories in America: Background and Development. White Plains, N.Y.: Row, Peterson, 1958. 313 pp. Bibliog. Ref. Ind.
An analysis of theories on American unionism, with a section (pp. 87-95) on William Z. Foster. The author sketches Foster's union activities, with special attention to the TUEL-TUUL period. He summarizes Foster's theory of unionism as based on subordination of union tactics to the strategy of revolutionary leaders. Emphasis is placed on the capture of labor unions by disciplined minority groups.

P83   PERLMUTTER, Nathan. Evangelist Demagogue, 1952 Model: Both Sides of the Coin, "Commentary," 14 (Oct. 1952), 334-38.
A portrait of Kenneth Goff, former minor functionary of the Communist Party and now an evangelist of reaction and anti-Semitism. Similarities in the appeals of communism and fascism are pointed out.

P84   PERLO, Victor. "American Imperialism." New York: International Publishers, 1951. 256 pp. Ref. notes. Ind.
A critical view of American Imperialism, a historical stage of capitalism in which the small group that owns and controls America exports capital, participates in international cartels, and seeks territorial expansion for the U.S. The rise of American imperialism, with its strategy of world domination and its system of military bases and alliances, is traced. War is viewed as the escape from economic crisis, providing a certain market for goods and work for the unemployed. A great peace mobilization is called for, to prevent world war, support the struggle of colonial peoples for national liberation, and permit the peaceful coexistence of capitalism and socialism.

P85   .... Trends in the Economic Status of the Negro People, "Science and Society," 16 (Spring 1952), 115-50. Reprinted in pamphlet form.
A procommunist economist presents evidence to prove that Negroes have suffered serious economic and social losses since World War II. The fundamental cause of this deterioration is the cold war, showing that improvement in conditions of Negroes is associated with the struggle for peace.

P86   .... "Israel and Dollar Diplomacy." New York: New Century, 1953. 48 pp.
An assertion that Zionist leadership seeks to make Israel an economic, political, and social dependency of the U.S., with a resulting decline in Israeli living standards and a campaign of vilification against the Soviet Union. Israel, however, can prosper without reliance on foreign capitalists. Peace is a necessity, to divert the swollen military budget to constructive channels.

P87   .... "The Negro in Southern Agriculture." New York: International Publishers, 1953. 128 pp. Ref. notes. Ind.

An economic analysis of the position of the Negro in the South. The author examines the plight of the Negro farmer and sharecropper, his living standards, the class structure, and the organization of Southern agriculture. The solution to the South's problem lies in land reform, government protection of farm tenants and laborers, elimination of discrimination, and world peace.

P88   .... (In collaboration with Labor Research Association). "The Income Revolution." New York: International Publishers, 1954. 64 pp. Ref. notes.
A critique of Simon Kuznets' book, "Shares of Upper Income Groups in Income and Savings," by a procommunist author who denies that an equitable and widespread redistribution of income is taking place in the U.S. This can occur only if trade unions and progressives unite to curb monopolies and fight against war and McCarthyism.

P89   .... "The Empire of High Finance." New York: International Publishers, 1957. 351 pp. App. Ref. notes. Ind.
A study of American monopoly capitalism from a communist point of view, asserting that eight prime centers of power control most of the major companies and most of the profits. The government and the main political parties have become increasingly merged in this corporate power structure, while Washington has become the alter ego of Wall Street, with a common board of directors. Attention is focused on finance capital—on the relations between finance and industry, the main financial empires, and the relations between government and Big Business.

P90   .... State-Monopoly Processes in the U.S. Economy, "World Marxist Review: Problems of Peace and Socialism," 2 (June 1959), 46-51.
A discussion, in an international communist journal, of the development of state-monopoly capitalism in the U.S., forms of state regulation in industry and agriculture, the war economy and Big Business, the export of capital, the capitalist economic cycle, and the working class and reforms.

P91   .... "USA and USSR: The Economic Race." New York: International Publishers, 1960. 127 pp. Ref. notes.
A comparison by an American communist economist of economic progress in capitalist America and communist Russia. Starting from a backward position but growing more rapidly, Soviet production in many key areas will reach or surpass that of the U.S. by 1965. Efforts of American writers to explain away the Soviet gains are reviewed. America can remain with the leaders, achieving a growth rate equal to that of the USSR, by changing its social system from capitalism to socialism.

P92   .... "Militarism and Industry: Arms Profiteering in the Missile Age." Preface by J. D. Bernal. New York: International Publishers, 1963. 208 pp. App. Ref. notes. Ind.
A study of American armament profits by a communist economist, who finds that Big Business benefits from a militarized economy through higher-than-average rates of profit, as well as through foreign investment and related overseas business. For Big Business as a whole, foreign and military business will provide over half its profits in the near future. Militarism is responsible for many U.S. economic problems. The business groups most heavily involved in munitions and related industries take the most consistently promilitarist position.

P93   PERRY, Frederick A. "Radical Organizations and Subversive Movements in America." Detroit: Coalition Committee for the State of Michigan, 1922. 18 pp.

An address praising the work of the Lusk Committee in New York State, and attacking the communists, along with all other radicals and the AFL, as subversive. The results of their teachings will be immorality, labor unrest, and the undermining of home, church, and the Ten Commandments.

P94   PERRY, Pettis. Destroy The Virus of White Chauvinism, "Political Affairs," 28 (June 1949), 1-13.
White chauvinism is an inseparable part of the propaganda barrage of chauvinist nationalism used by American finance capital in its drive to war and fascization. Communists must raise the level of understanding of the masses on the question of Negro rights, not accommodate to their backwardness.

P95   . . . . Next Stage in the Struggle for Negro Rights, "Political Affairs," 28 (Oct. 1949), 33-46.
A report to the national committee, CPUSA, September 1949, enumerating "bestial" attacks on the Negro people. Emphasis is placed on the danger of Negro reformism, the struggle against white chauvinism, and the need for a united front of the Negro masses.

P96   . . . . Lessons of the Civil Rights Mobilization, "Political Affairs," 29 (March 1950), 58-67.
A report on the Civil Rights Mobilization initiated by the NAACP and held in Washington, D.C., January 15-17, 1950, emphasizing the Red-baiting and disruptive tactics of the reformist unions and Trotskyite representatives. Weaknesses of the left-progressive forces are analyzed.

P97   . . . . Press Forward the Struggle against White Chauvinism, "Political Affairs," 29 (May 1950), 138-49.
A sub-report to the plenum of the national committee, CPUSA, March 23-25, 1950, asserting that anti-Negro terror is increasing. Though the Party's struggle against white chauvinism has advanced, major weaknesses still exist. All communists must agitate for passage of legislation for FEPC and jobs, and against police brutality.

P98   . . . . Further Strengthening of the Fight against White Chauvinism, "Political Affairs," 29 (Dec. 1950), 50-60.
A report to the plenary session of the national committee, CPUSA, September 19-20, 1950. The author reports on the Trade Union Conference for Negro Rights in Chicago on June 10-11, warns against chauvinism among white members and bourgeois nationalism among Negro members, and discusses the Party's fight for jobs and rights for Negroes.

P99   . . . . "This, too, Is Lynch Law." New York: Self Defense Committee of the 17 Smith Act Victims, n.d. [1951?]. 7 pp.
An assertion that the Smith Act defendants were being tried under lynch law conditions because the jury selected for the case was all white and included no manual workers.

P100   . . . . "Negro Representation — A Step toward Negro Freedom." New York: New Century, 1952. 24 pp. Reprinted from "Political Affairs," Dec. 1951.
A call for unrestricted Negro suffrage and representation, and for the smashing of Jim Crow in our political life. While Marxists should seek to lead the movement, they should support Negro candidates who are registered Republicans or Democrats as well as those who run on the Progressive, ALP, or communist tickets.

P101   . . . . "Pettis Perry Speaks to the Court." New York: New Century, 1952. 16 pp.

Opening statement to the court and jury at the Smith Act trial. Perry gives his background, tells how he became involved with the International Labor Defense, how he joined the Party in 1932, and how he and the Party have sought since to improve the lot of the working class and the Negro people by legal means. The issue today is to prevent World War III and fascism.

P102   . . . . "White Chauvinism and the Struggle for Peace." New York: New Century, 1952. 22 pp. Reprint of Certain Prime Aspects of the Negro Question, in "Political Affairs," Oct. 1951.
Condemnation, by a Negro Party leader, of the growth of white chauvinism in Party ranks. This tendency, allied to right opportunism, stimulates bourgeois nationalism on the part of Negro comrades. White chauvinism must be defeated to achieve a peace movement based on unity of white and Negro workers.

P103   . . . . Puerto Rico and the Fight for Its Independence, "Political Affairs," 31 (June 1952), 30-37; (July), 24-34.
The economy of Puerto Rico, an American colony, is controlled by a few sugar trusts. It is characterized by mass unemployment, poor living conditions, starvation wages, and poor educational facilities. The Party supports Puerto Rico's independence, while opposing discrimination against Puerto Ricans in the U.S. mainland.

P104   . . . . Perspectives in the 1952 Elections, "Political Affairs," 31 (Sept. 1952), 6-20.
A report to the national election conference of the CPUSA, September 6, 1952. Both major parties are the parties of Wall Street, standing for war and the destruction of civil and democratic rights. The largest possible vote must be obtained for the Progressive Party; where it is not on the ballot, coalitions must be built around specific candidates, while not neglecting the CP's own candidates.

P105   . . . . "The Communist Party: Vanguard Fighter for Peace, Democracy, Security, Socialism. New York: New Century, 1953. 64 pp.
Summation speech to the jury at the second Smith Act trial, asserting that the Party represents the interests of the working class, the Negro people, and all who suffer at the hands of the monopolists. Perry denies that the defendants are conspirators, since dictatorship of the proletariat means majority rule. The Party leads the struggle for peace, Negro equality, a people's front, and people's democracy. (A portion of the pamphlet was published independently under the title, "The Party of Negro and White.")

P106   . . . . "The Party of Negro and White." Introd. by Herbert Aptheker. New York: New Century, 1953. 15 pp.
Part of Perry's summation speech to the jury at his trial under the Smith Act, January 13, 1953. Negro enslavement must end, and Negroes in the Black Belt of the South allowed to exercise their right to self-determination. Communists seek to unite the Negro people and the labor movement around the struggle for Negro rights.

P107   . . . . The Defense of the Party Is the Defense of the Bill of Rights, "Political Affairs," 32 (Sept. 1953), 29-42.
Attacks on democracy, initiated by Truman, have been intensified by the Eisenhower Administration. These include the Subversive Activities Board's decision against the Party, indictments of Party leaders under the Smith Act, and the murder of the Rosenbergs. The people can be aroused for the repeal of the Smith and McCarran Acts, and for an amnesty for the Party leaders.

P108 PERRY, Pettis. The Third Annual Convention of the National Negro Labor Council, "Political Affairs," 33 (Feb. 1954), 1-8.
The convention dealt with a number of basic questions facing Negro workers, and also with such issues as McCarthyism, peace, and the fight against colonial oppression. The Council should be supported because of its influence on the labor movement and its work in bringing together Negro and white workers.

P109 .... The November Elections and the Struggle for Jobs, Peace, Equal Rights, and Democracy, "Political Affairs," 33 (Sept. 1954), 13-46.
The main report to the national election conference held August 7-8, 1954. Emphasis is placed on the fight for peace, the need to elect an anti-McCarthy congress, the danger of depression, the struggle for Negro rights and representation, and the growing independent political action of labor and its allies. The role of the advanced electoral bodies in the November elections must be strengthened. (Issued by New Century in pamphlet form.)

P110 PETERS, Clarence A. (comp.). "American Capitalism vs. Russian Communism." (The Reference Shelf, 18: 7) New York: Wilson, 1946. 305 pp. Bibliog.
A collection of writings on Russia, the Soviet way of life, the American way of life, criticism of the Soviet system, and criticism of the American system. Among the critics of the American system are Paul M. Sweezy, Sam Adams Darcy, and Anna Rochester, who write, respectively, on capitalist development, the evils of American capitalism, and the nature of capitalism.

P111 PETERS, J. [pseud. for Alexander Goldberger]. Organizational Problems in the Light of the Open Letter, "Communist," 12 (Sept. 1933), 948-54.
The main emphasis of the Open Letter to the Party membership was on the Party's failure to become the revolutionary mass party despite favorable circumstances for recruitment. Shop nuclei in the basic industries are the main device through which membership will be increased.

P112 .... Problems of Party Growth, "Communist," 13 (Oct. 1934), 1005-14.
Fewer than one-third of those joining the Party in 1930-34 have remained in it. Fluctuation can be reduced by better functioning of unit leadership. The Party must raise the ideological level of unit membership, and bring itself before the masses by distributing the "Daily Worker," issuing Party leaflets to peripheral organizations, and similar methods.

P113 .... "The Communist Party: A Manual on Organization." New York: Workers Library, 1935. 127 pp. Ind.
The definitive Party handbook, written by a Comintern representative in the U.S. Sections deal with fundamentals of the Party program, the basic principles of Party organization, the structure and functions of Party organization, Party membership and cadres, and rules and methods for disciplinary cases. The nature of democratic centralism is explained, as are Party discussion and self-criticism. Attention is also paid to Party structure, the work of Party officials, Party fractions in mass organizations, recruiting, dues, and discipline.

P114 .... "Secrets of the Communist Party Exposed!" Columbus, Ohio: State Publishing Co., 1947. 63 pp.
A reprint of Peters' "Manual on Organization," with a vigorously anticommunist preface.

P115 PETERSEN, Arnold. "W. Z. Foster—Renegade or Spy?" New York: New York Labor News Co., 1932. 31 pp. App. Rev. ed., 1945.
A personal and political attack on Foster by a Socialist Labor Party leader, who reviews Foster's early apprenticeship in social-democratic reform, his change to anarcho-syndicalism, his support of World War I, and his subsequent career in the communist movement, where he has successfully negotiated all the switch-backs in the Party line.

P116 .... "Burlesque Bolshevism: American Communism as an Auxiliary of Capitalism." New York: New York Labor News Co., 1934. 63 pp.
Four essays reprinted from the "Weekly People," organ of the Socialist Labor Party. The first underscores the burlesque, naive, and imbecile nature of the communist movement in America; the second exposes its lying, Jesuitical character; the third is concerned with its sinister, slum-proletarian aspect; and the fourth deals with the freakishness of its "arty" and literary fringes. The communist movement is termed a reform party, seeking its ends by noise, hooliganism, and physical violence.

P117 .... "Communist Jesuitism." Introd. by Eric Hass. New York: New York Labor News Co., 1939. 110 pp. App.
A Socialist Labor Party indictment of the communists' people's front line as a Russian-dictated betrayal of the working class and socialism. The communists are called stooges of capitalism who, having repudiated the class struggle, now defend bourgeois democracy, the New Deal, and Roosevelt's imperialism. They are charlatans and imposters, with opportunism their only principle.

P118 .... "Stalinist Corruption of Marxism: A Study in Machiavellian Duplicity." New York: New York Labor News Co., 1940. 124 pp.
A Socialist Labor Party condemnation of the betrayal of socialism in the USSR and the slavish idolatry of Stalin. The communists are called the modern disciples of Machiavelli. Reversals of the Party line here, as shown in successive statements by Browder, are reviewed and ridiculed.

P119 PETTIS, Ashley. Two Worlds of Music, "New Masses," 8 (Feb. 1933), 12-14.
A comparison of the sad state of opera, radio, musical education, and musical composition in the U.S. with their flourishing condition in the USSR. The American government's lack of interest in serious music is reflected in the pseudo-music of Tin Pan Alley.

P120 PFEFFER, Leo. "Church, State and Freedom." Boston: Beacon, 1953. 675 pp. Bibliog. Table of legal cases. Ind.
An extensive treatment of the separation of the church and state in the U.S. Some cases concern state intervention in church affairs where the churchmen are procommunist. One is the Russian Church Schism (pp. 248-51), in which the U.S. Supreme Court upheld the right of the Metropolitan appointed by the Russian Orthodox Church in Moscow to church property in the U.S., over the claim of the noncommunist Russian Church in America. Another case discussed is the Melish controversy (pp. 251-56), between the procommunist Melishes (father and son) and their supporters on the one side, and anticommunist vestrymen and the bishop on the other.

P121 .... "The Liberties of an American: The Supreme Court Speaks." Boston: Beacon, 1956. 309 pp. Ind.
An account of the leading decisions of the U.S. Supreme Court interpreting and applying the Bill of Rights. Of

particular interest are chapter 3, "Liberty of Speech and Silence," and chapter 4, "Liberty of Petition, Assembly, and Association." The author believes that liberty for all is indivisible, and that the Supreme Court has in large measure fulfilled its responsibilities as guardian of the Bill of Rights.

P122　PHELPS, Wallace, and RAHV, Philip. Problems and Perspectives in Revolutionary Literature, "Partisan Review," 1 (June-July 1934), 3-10.

An editorial review of the growth of revolutionary literature in America in the past year, with comments on conflicting currents in this literature. On the leftist extreme writings are steeped in the Party's political program, resulting in sloganized writing; at the right-wing extreme the work resembles that of liberal, bourgois writers. "Partisan Review," will stress creative experimentation and critical perception.

P123　PHILBRICK, Herbert A. "I Led Three Lives: Citizen, Communist, Counterspy." New York: McGraw-Hill, 1952. 323 pp.

A description of communist activities in eastern Massachusetts, written by a participant. Philbrick, a Boston advertising man, joined the Young Communist League and Communist Party as an informant for the FBI, observing and reporting on communist activities for nine years. A leading prosecution witness at the trial of the 11 communist leaders, he has also testified before the House Committee on Un-American Activities. Philbrick asserts that the Party secretly preached revolution while denying its adherence to this objective in its publications. He feels that the real danger from communism is not from its overt activities or leaders, but from "invisible" communists and their innocent aides.

P124　.... The Communists Are After Your Church! "Christian Herald," 76 (April 1953), 18-20 ff.

A citizen who served for nine years as a volunteer counterspy for the FBI in the CPUSA asserts that the communist threat to the church is greater now than for 20 years. The Reds have planted secret communists in pulpits and infiltrated seminaries. In Boston there was an underground Party cell composed of ministers. Ways in which the Party uses religious leaders are described.

P125　PHILLIPS, George. "What Price Philippine Independence?" New York: New Century, 1946. 32 pp.

A communist view of American imperialism's stake in the Philippines. While giving the Philippines independence, we make the new republic our puppet, under our economic control for years to come, and crush the Hukbalahap, the backbone of the independence movement.

P126　.... American Imperialism and the Colonial World, "Political Affairs," 26 (July 1947), 596-611.

All colonial and semi-colonial countries, led by those in Asia, are struggling for independence and democratic rights. The imperialist countries are responding either with violence or with grudging constitutional reform. The U.S., the dominant imperialist power, aims at world domination. It is directly responsible for the Chinese civil war and the war against the Filipino peasantry.

P127　PHILLIPS, Lyle G. The Reds in Hawaii, "American Mercury," 83 (Dec. 1956), 149-54.

A review of Party control of labor unions, particularly the ILWU, in Hawaii. The CP, through unions under its control, sought unsuccessfully to take over the Hawaiian Democratic Party in 1948. However, it continues to play an influential role in Hawaii, with greater success than anywhere else in the U.S.

P128　PHILLIPS, William. The Esthetic of the Founding Fathers, "Partisan Review," 4 (March 1938), 11-21.

Contrary to assertions by Stalinist literary critics, Marxist general theories do not contain specific esthetic principles. Up to 1935 the communists viewed art as a weapon and sought to build a proletarian literature, but neither Marx nor Engels ever implied that art was only a class weapon. Literary analysis consistent with a materialist version of society is compatible with Marxist philosophy.

P129　PIATNITSKY, O. Conference of the Sections of the Comintern on Organization, "Communist International," n.s., no. 11, n.d. [1925], 22-34.

Report on a conference on organization held by the Communist International, dealing with reorganization of national parties on the basis of factory nuclei. Pages 31-34 describe the chaotic situation in the Workers Party of America, especially the dependence of its Central Committee on the good will of 17 separate language organizations to carry out its decisions.

P130　.... "World Communists in Action." New York: Workers Library, n.d. [193-?]. 64 pp.

This self-critical Comintern publication contains a brief appraisal of the CPUSA and other Communist Parties, with extensive treatment of communism in France and Germany. It attributes the decline in Communist Party membership to poor organization.

P131　.... "The Immediate Tasks of the International Trade Union Movement." New York: Workers Library, n.d. [1930?]. 40 pp.

An analysis of the weakness both of independent communist trade unions and of communist fractions in conservative unions, written on the eve of the Fifth Congress of the Red International of Labor Unions. Both "left" and "right" errors of the various national sections are enumerated. (Though the U.S. is not specifically mentioned, the analysis is important for the Party's trade union policy here.)

P132　.... "The Twenty-one Conditions of Admission into the Communist International." New York: Workers Library, 1934. 32 pp. App.

An elaboration of the basic conditions for admission adopted by the Comintern in 1920. Attention is given to the expulsion of petty bourgeois elements, the split with reformism, the exposure of social patriotism, and the establishment of democratic centralism in Party structure. The 21 conditions are listed in the appendix.

P133　PICKARD, Walt. "Burlington Dynamite Plot." New York: International Labor Defense, n.d. [1934?]. 23 pp.

A popularly written pamphlet about union struggles in a North Carolina mill town. The author, president of a local of the United Textile Workers, tells how six mill hands were framed for a dynamiting they knew nothing about, and sentenced to prison. Only the ILD came to their defense.

P134　PILAT, Oliver R. "The Atom Spies." New York: Putnam, 1952. 312 pp.

A dramatic account of wartime atomic espionage by U.S. communists under directions from the Soviet Union. The author tells the complex story of the atomic espionage rings in the U.S., Canada, and England, documented from government reports and trial evidence and testimony. Communist espionage rings, in his view, are among the most successful of all time. He emphasizes the relationship between political heresy and subversive conspiracy, between open Party membership, underground Party work, and Soviet espionage.

P135 PILAT, Oliver R. The Truth about the Atom
Spies, "New Leader," 36 (Jan. 12, 1953), 6-8.
A review of the propaganda aspects of the Rosenberg
case, by a New York "Post" reporter. He concludes that,
while keeping the Rosenbergs available until they confess
and thus meeting communist propaganda, may be grounds
for clemency, the general fairness of the sentence has not
been challenged, even by the American Civil Liberties
Union.

P136 PIRINSKY, George. "Slavic Americans in the Fight
for Victory and Peace." New York: American
Slav Congress, 1946. 61 pp.
An account of the American Slav Congress (a Party front
working among Americans of Slavic birth or descent) and
of its activities in the war. The author, executive secretary of the Congress, protests abandonment of Roosevelt's
policies for an "atomic policy" of threats and coercion.

P137 .... "The Struggle for Peace and Democracy in
USA." New York: American Slav Congress, 1947.
20 pp.
The report of the executive secretary of the American
Slav Congress to the national committee meeting in
February 1947 deploring the postwar drift from the policies
of Roosevelt, and pledging the organization to fight for
restoration of Big Three cooperation and social advancement at home.

P138 PITKIN, Robert B. The Movies and the American
Legion, "American Legion Magazine," 54 (May
1953), 14-15 ff.
An account of communist penetration of the motion picture
industry from 1934 to 1947, of exposures by the House
Un-American Activities Committee and resistance by AFL
film unions, and of efforts by the companies, with American
Legion cooperation, to clean house. Since 1947, the policy
of major film companies has been to get rid of all identified and unrepentant communists, and of all who would not
testify frankly before congressional committees.

P139 .... The Legion's 40 Years against Communism,
"American Legion Magazine," 67 (Dec. 1959), 22-
23 ff.
An account of the Legion's fight, still continuing after 40
years, against the international communist conspiracy, a
subversive and destructive influence in America. While
opposing intellectual fads inspired by communists, the
Legion has supported the FBI and congressional and state
investigating bodies.

P140 PITTMAN, John. A Perspective for Forging
Negro-White Unity, "Communist," 23 (Jan. 1944),
86-91; (Feb.), 174-81.
Wartime conditions have brought an unprecedented growth
of unity between Negroes and other Americans, following
outrages in Los Angeles and elsewhere incited by Axis
agents. Nevertheless new outrages are being planned by
the American fifth column. Crushing of the fifth column
and full integration of Negroes and other minorities in the
war effort are advocated.

P141 .... The Negro People Spark the Fight for Peace,
"Political Affairs," 25 (Aug. 1946), 724-33.
A petition from the National Negro Congress to the Economic and Social Council of the UN "for the elimination of
political, economic and social discrimination against
Negroes in the United States of America" signals a
dramatic struggle for Negro rights.

P142 .... War on Korea: Point IV in Action, "Political Affairs," 29 (Aug. 1950), 40-50.
American capitalism has a surplus of capital to use in a

Point Four program to gain economic domination of the
backward countries. Wall Street now opposes Point Four
because it prefers the approach used in Korea—subjugation
by force. The communist answer to Point Four is working
class internationalism.

P143 PITTMAN, Martin. This Proletarian Stuff, "North
American Review," 234 (Dec. 1932), 519-23.
A humorous report, ostensibly written by a coal miner,
on the lack of interest among proletarians like himself in
the product of the "literary left."

P144 PITTS, Rebecca. Women and Communism, "New
Masses," 14 (Feb. 19, 1935), 14-18.
An assertion that the root of woman's dilemma is social,
not biological. The subjection of women was necessary to
early capitalism; later women were set free to become a
reserve labor-army in the interests of employers. Within
class society women can expect only a return to slavery.
Only communism offers woman the right to be an independent productive worker, along with the right to a freer
sex happiness.

P145 PITZELE, Merlyn S. Can American Labor Defeat
the Communists? "Atlantic Monthly," 179 (March
1947), 27-32.
An analysis, by the labor editor of "Business Week," of
the extent of communist control of the labor movement,
the means of achieving it, and ways to defeat the communists. Today the Party controls more than a dozen
national unions, because communists have posed as militant unionists and have worked hard, and because everything new or forceful in the labor movement has been
indiscriminately labeled "red."

P146 PLATT, Leon. The Struggle for the Comintern in
America, "Communist," 8 (Sept. 1929), 502-11.
The Party must continue its uncompromising struggle
against Lovestone and all other manifestations of the right
danger. Lovestone's struggle and slanders against the
Comintern undermine its prestige and weaken our struggle
against imperialist war. Lovestone and his group will
further degenerate into social democracy and go over to
the camp of capitalism.

P147 .... The Roosevelt Program of Industrial Recovery, "Communist International," 10 (Oct. 15,
1933), 687-97.
An analysis of Roosevelt's industrial recovery program,
including discussion of the NIRA, the economic situation of
the U.S., the meaning of the Roosevelt program for the
working class, the gains of the American bourgeoisie from
the NIRA, the strike wave, and the attitude toward American and international socialism. The capitalist economy
is not recovering from its crisis.

P148 PLATT, Myles M. Red Hearing in the Motor City,
"America," 87 (July 5, 1952), 348-51.
Praise for the conduct of the hearing held by the House
Committee on Un-American Activities in Detroit, February 26 to March 1, 1952. The history and background of
the committee are described. While the hearings did not
uncover any sizable conspiracy, they were a far cry from
"a fanatical lynching," as the communists asserted.

P149 PLAVNER, Murray. "Is the Youth Congress a
Communist Front? Here Are the Facts." New
York: The author, 1939. 93 pp.
An assertion that the American Youth Congress contains
Party members and fellow-travelers among its leaders.
Though the author supports AYC, he argues that it should
pass resolutions against communism as well as against
Nazism and fascism. He documents Party activities in

AYC by quoting from resolutions, by noting AYC leaders who are communists, and by relating Party activities in AYC to directives on united front work of the Young Communist International and the CPUSA.

P150 PLOTT, L. The Youth and the Labor Movement, "Workers Monthly," 6 [5] (Jan. 1927), 698-700; 5 (Feb. 1927), 737-40.

An analysis of the importance of the working youth in production, including a discussion of the decline of the apprenticeship system and reasons for leaving school. Young workers are largely unskilled, underpaid, and non-union. The church is one of the means used by the bourgeoisie to keep workers in subjection. The Young Workers' (Communist) League can approach young workers on vital problems through the shop nucleus.

POGANY, Josef. See PEPPER, John.

P151 POLING, Daniel A. Clergymen Are Citizens, Too! "Saturday Evening Post," 226 (April 24, 1954), 26-27 ff.

The editor of the "Christian Herald" asserts that the Protestant ministry has not been as alert as other groups in uncovering the communist menace in their midst. Protestant clergy wrongly invoke the doctrine of the separation of church and state in protesting congressional investigation of communism in the churches.

P152 "POLITICAL AFFAIRS," Speeches in Discussion on the Draft Resolution of the National Board at the Plenary Meeting of the National Committee, C.P.A., June 18-20, 1945, 24 (July 1945), 591-639.

Speeches by Gilbert Green, Morris Childs, Roy Hudson, Elizabeth Gurley Flynn, Doxey A. Wilkerson, Samuel Donchin, Carl Winter, and V. J. Jerome in support of the resolution which culminated in the dissolution of the Communist Political Association and the reconstitution of the Communist Party. They admit their responsibility in concurring with Browder's revisionist line of accepting the leadership of capital and failing to base Party activities on the principle of democratic centralism.

P153 . . ., Statement of the Secretariat of the Communist Political Association on the Charter of the United Nations, 24 (Aug. 1945), 688-91.

A pledge of the Communist Political Association to support the ratification of the United Nations Charter, which it considers a democratic and antifascist pact that binds the Big Three to work together to preserve peace.

P154 . . ., The Imperialist Threat to Peace: An Editorial, 25 (April 1946), 294-304.

An analysis of alleged imperialist motives of the U.S. and Britain, and of the role of "peace" forces in defeating the imperialist powers. The propeace forces include the USSR, the working class everywhere, the new people's democracies, the colonial masses, and communist parties. The peace forces here must oppose the Administration's armament program and fight against monopoly.

P155 . . ., Special Plenum Issue: Meeting of National Committee, C.P.U.S.A., July 16-18, 1946. 25 (Sept. 1946), 770-854.

Included in the special issue are William Z. Foster's opening remarks, Eugene Dennis' report for the National Board entitled "Defeat the Imperialist Drive Toward Fascism and War," John Williamson's report on "Improve and Build Our Communist Press," Morris Childs' report on "The Daily Worker—Problems and Prospects," and Max Weiss' report on "The Struggle on the Ideological Front." (The Dennis, Williamson, Childs, and Weiss reports are abstracted separately.)

P156 . . ., America's First Postwar Elections: An Editorial, 25 (Dec. 1946), 1059-72.

The congressional elections placed Congress even more firmly in the grip of Big Business. Communists are for a third party because the Democratic Party cannot be transformed into a people's party. A third party may or may not mean a separate presidential ticket; a coalition with the Democrats is possible.

P157 . . ., Lenin on the Struggle for Genuine Political Consciousness: A Basic Lesson for American Labor Today: An Editorial, 26 (Jan. 1947), 3-7.

Commemorating the twenty-third anniversary of the death of Lenin, the editorial calls on American labor to follow his teachings by abandoning the leadership of the AFL and supporting the formation of an independent, antimonopoly party of labor, farmers, the Negro people, and progressives.

P158 . . ., The December 3-5 Plenary Meeting of the National Committee, C.P.U.S.A., 26 (Jan. 1947), 8-79.

Leading speeches and reports to the national committee, including Eugene Dennis' "Concluding Remarks on the Plenum Discussion," John Williamson's report on "The Situation in the Trade Unions," Robert Thompson's "Conclusions from the New York Elections," Arthur Bary on "The Denver Elections," William Z. Foster on Negro self-determination, Benjamin J. Davis, Jr. on Negro rights, and Henry Winston's report, "Toward a Party of 100,000." (The Dennis, Williamson, Thompson, Bary, and Winston reports are abstracted separately.)

P159 . . ., The June 27-30 Plenary Meeting, National Committee, C.P.U.S.A., 26 (Aug. 1947), 675-738.

Leading reports and speeches to the national committee meeting. Included are William Z. Foster's report on "American Imperialism and the War Danger," Eugene Dennis' "Concluding Remarks on the Plenum Discussion," John Williamson's report on "The Taft-Hartley Law and Labor's Tasks," John Gates' report on "The 80th Congress and Perspectives for 1948," and Henry Winston's report on Party organization problems entitled, "Not Against but With the Stream." (The Foster, Dennis, Gates, and Winston items are abstracted separately.)

P160 . . ., "Secure These Rights": From the Eugene Dennis Brief in the U.S. Appellate Court, 26 (Dec. 1947), 1066-76.

Excerpts from Dennis' brief to the U.S. Court of Appeals, growing out of his contempt citation by the House Committee on Un-American Activities. The brief argues that personal beliefs of citizens are protected from inquiry by the First Amendment, and that the committee is illegal because one of its members, John Rankin of Mississippi, was illegally elected in that Negroes were excluded from the franchise.

P161 . . ., Outlook for 1948 and the Third Party, 27 (Jan. 1948), 3-10.

Editorial asking support for Henry Wallace and the Progressive Party in the 1948 elections. It asserts that the Democratic and Republican Parties are alike since Truman came into power and embarked on a reactionary domestic policy and an imperialistic foreign policy.

P162 . . ., American Labor Faces May Day: An Editorial, 27 (May 1948), 389-99.

Less than three years after V-J Day, the American working people again confront the danger of war and fascism. Because U.S. trade union leadership denies the class struggle and promotes imperialist chauvinism, the key task of the Party is to develop class consciousness and promote working class internationalism. The new people's party led by Wallace rallies all who fight for peace and against fascism.

P163 "POLITICAL AFFAIRS," Pre-Convention Discussion, 27 (July 1948), 586-614.
Discussion of the draft resolution for the Party's national convention to be held August 3-6, 1948. Included are articles on the peace program, labor issues, the new people's party in relation to Negroes, and China.

P164 . . ., 14th National Convention of the Communist Party, U.S.A., 27 (Sept. 1948), 773-947.
A special convention issue, including William Z. Foster's keynote address, "The 1948 Elections and the Struggle for Peace"; Eugene Dennis' main political report, "The Fascist Danger and How to Combat It"; Foster's "Concluding Remarks at the Convention"; Henry Winston's organizational report, "For a Fighting Party Rooted among the Industrial Workers"; John Williamson's report, "Only Militant, United Action Can Defeat the Drive against the Unions!"; Benjamin J. Davis' report, "The Negro People's Liberation Movement"; John Gates on "The South—The Nation's Problem"; Robert Thompson's report, "The Party's Responsibility for Work among the Youth"; Betty Gannett's "Win the Youth for Peace, Democracy and Socialism!"; and the "1948 Election Platform of the Communist Party." (Each of the above is listed separately.)

P165 . . ., From the Briefs on the Unconstitutionality of the Smith Act, 27 (Nov. 1948), 1013-32.
Excerpts from briefs submitted by defense attorneys for the 12 members of the Party's national committee who were indicted under the Smith Act. The briefs argue that Congress is without power to enact legislation such as the advocacy sections of the Smith Act; that the First Amendment forbids interference with speech, press, assembly, or religion; and that the advocacy sections of the Smith Act as applied to these indictments are unconstitutional.

P166 . . ., The Defense Prosecutes, 28 (Feb. 1949), 5-19.
An excerpt from the brief asking the U.S. Supreme Court to void the indictments of the 12 communist leaders. The brief argues that the grand jury that returned the indictments was selected unlawfully.

P167 . . ., World Labor Unity for Peace and Democracy, 28 (May 1949), 3-15.
An editorial outlining the special responsibilities of American workers on May Day 1949: resistance to the Taft-Hartley law and to the North Atlantic pact, and support of the World Federation of Trade Unions.

P168 . . ., The Struggle against White Chauvinism, 28 (June 1949).
The entire issue is devoted to a discussion of the American Negro's economic, social, and political status, and the Party's past and present role in bettering this.

P169 . . ., From the Court Testimony of the Communist Leaders, 28 (Sept. 1949), 25-48.
Selections from the opening address to the jury by Eugene Dennis at the trial of the 11 communists in New York under the Smith Act, followed by excerpts from the testimony of John Gates, Gilbert Green, Benjamin J. Davis, and Robert Thompson.

P170 . . ., 15th National Convention, Communist Party, U.S.A.: Organize the Peace Front of the People, 30 (Feb. 1951).
The entire issue is devoted to reports and speeches to the Party convention held December 28-31, 1950. Included

are William Z. Foster's message on "American Capitalist Hegemony, the National Emergency, and 'Isolationism,'" Henry Winston's "Gear the Party for Its Great Tasks," John Williamson's "The Main Direction of the Party's Trade-Union Work," and V. J. Jerome's "Let Us Grasp the Weapon of Culture." (All of the above are listed separately.) Other reports and speeches are by Gus Hall, Carl Winter, John Gates, Robert Thompson, Jim Jackson, Elizabeth Gurley Flynn, Pettis Perry, Claudia Jones, Irving Potash, Carl Ross, Betty Gannett, Robert Minor, Israel Amter, and Cesar Andreu.

P171 . . ., Notes on Recent Developments in the South, 31 (May 1952), 41-51.
Reports on Louisiana, Alabama, and Texas state that Truman's war policy has brought some new industries to the South, increasing Wall Street's domination without providing many jobs, especially for Negroes. The reactionaries dominating the state governments are enforcing policies and laws that discriminate against Negroes, Mexicans, and Puerto Ricans.

P172 . . ., The Real Issues in the 1952 Elections, 31 (Aug. 1952), 1-12.
An editorial article asserting that the real issues of our day are peace or war, democracy or fascism. The bourgeoisie prevents any real debate on foreign policy. The monopoly-class essence of the two-party system must be exposed through struggle, and an antimonopoly, antifascist, and antiwar people's party crystallized.

P173 . . ., National Election Conference of the Communist Party, 33 (Sept. 1954).
A special issue devoted to reports and documents pertaining to the Party's National Election Conference, held in New York City, August 7-8, 1954. Contents include the national committee's statement on the Communist Control Act, "Answer the Attack on the Communist Party and the Labor Movement!"; Foster's message to the conference; the main report by Pettis Perry, "The November Elections and the Struggle for Jobs, Peace, Equal Rights, and Democracy"; Betty Gannett's report on the discussion of the draft program; and Leon Wofsy's speech on youth unity. (The National Committee's statement and Perry's report are listed separately.)

P174 . . ., William Z. Foster 75th Anniversary Issue, 35 (March 1956).
An issue commemorating Foster's 75th birthday, devoted largely to eulogistic articles on various phases of his career. (The article by Steve Nelson, "Foster and Steel," is separately abstracted, as is one by Foster entitled, "Has World Capitalism Become Stabilized?")

P175 . . ., On Social Democracy in the U.S., 36 (Jan. 1957), 5-18.
A report of a Party subcommittee, stressing the need for a new approach to social democrats, who in the U.S. comprise three currents—bourgeois reformism, labor reformism, and social reformism. We can find common ground with them in the fight for peace, democracy, and other immediate issues. We look upon them as workers' organizations, including the elected leaders, and we deal with them fraternally.

P176 . . ., The Communist Party National Convention, 36 (March 1957), 1-42.
The first 42 pages of this issue contain material on the Party's sixteenth national convention, including Eugene Dennis' keynote address, Fred M. Fine's report "On the Draft Constitution," the resolution presented by James E. Jackson entitled "On the Struggle for Negro Freedom," and reports by William Schneiderman, Max Weiss, and

Nemmy Sparks. (The Jackson resolution is listed separately.)

P177 POLLAK, Katherine H. "Our Labor Movement Today." [Katonah, N.Y.]: Brookwood Labor College, 1932. 112 pp. Ind.
A simply written account of the contemporary labor movement, including the AFL, the progressives, the Socialist Party, and the communists. Chapter 5 on the communists (pp. 91-102) deals with the Gastonia strike, the communist structure, communist beliefs, activities in the U.S., attacks on all other groups, splits among the communists, and criticism by progressives.

P178 POLONSKY, Abraham. "A Season of Fear." New York: Cameron Associates, 1956. 224 pp.
A novel about the climate of loyalty oath informers and the effect on the integrity of a typical American. An engineer who signs a routine loyalty oath, and whose mind becomes corroded with fear, is linked in friendship with an informer.

P179 PONTIFICAL ACADEMY OF ST. THOMAS AT ROME. "The Philosophy of Communism." Introd. by Charles Boyer. New York: Fordham University Press, 1952. 308 pp.
Papers on the philosophy of communism read at meetings in Rome, April 19-24, 1949. Topics included the antithetical theologies of Marxism and Christianity, the social function of property, communism as an economic system, communism and democracy, communist ideology and the problem of truth, political atheism, labor in the USSR, human value and Marxism, dilemmas in communist ideology, Marxism and penal law, ethics of communism, science in Soviet culture, and human freedom under communism. Participants agreed that, had there been any attempt to satisfy the legitimate aspirations of the working classes, there would be no communism today.

P180 L. P. [Liston Pope]. Democratic Strategy toward the Communists, "Christianity and Crisis," 8 (March 15, 1948), 25-26.
An assertion that the communists have damaged liberal movements here, especially the trade unions, though they are being exposed and removed from leadership. The author's program includes loyalty tests for government employees, abolition of the House Committee on Un-American Activities, legality of the Party but prosecution whenever communists break the law, ignoring them where possible, and becoming more active champions of democracy ourselves.

P181 PORTER, Harry W. How High School Seniors Feel about Communism, Fascism, and Democracy, "Social Education," 5 (Feb. 1941), 110-14.
Results of a test given to 83 high school seniors to determine their attitudes toward communism, fascism, and democracy. Though most expressed favorable attitudes toward democracy, they also revealed an appalling ignorance of its real meaning. None of the students was favorable toward communism, and only nine were neutral; all who had a thorough understanding were opposed to it.

P182 PORTER, Paul. Factions and Unity in the C.I.O., "American Scholar," 8 (April 1939), 131-43.
A prediction that centralized power in the CIO, one of its basic differences from the AFL, can and will soon be used by Lewis, Murray, and Hillman to purge the Stalinists who have entrenched themselves in more than a dozen CIO unions.

P183 POST, Louis F. "The Deportations Delirium of Nineteen-Twenty. Chicago: Kerr, 1923. 338 pp. App. Ind.

A critical account of the anti-red crusade of 1919-20, which resulted in the deportation of hundreds of aliens under the Immigration Act of 1919. The author, Assistant Secretary of Labor during the period, was threatened with impeachment for cancelling warrants for the arrest of alien "Reds." He describes the widespread raids organized by the Department of Justice and the deportations of aliens that followed, holding the Department largely responsible for stimulating the delirium. Aliens were deported for harmless expression of harmless opinion, and legislation was proposed to punish citizens also who proposed peaceful change in government.

P184 POTAMKIN, Harry A. "The Eyes of the Movie." New York: International Publishers, 1934. 31 pp.
An assertion that the movie industry magnates use their medium in behalf of their class, to debase the Negro and the Jew, to glorify war and the nation, and to engage in anti-Soviet propaganda. The Film and Photo Leagues, John Reed Clubs, and workers' cultural organizations must expose the bourgeois film.

POTASH, Irving. See EDWARDS, H.

P185 PRAGO, Albert. Notes on Keynes' Concepts of Saving and Investment, "Political Affairs," 27 (April 1948), 367-75.
A Marxist analysis of certain of Keynes' economic theories to show that they do not remove the contradictions and injustices of capitalism. Keynes would free capitalism of its contradictions by manipulating the currency, especially the rate of interest. He does not consider the role of monopoly.

P186 PREIS, Art. "Stalinists on the Waterfront: A Documented Record of Betrayal." New York: Pioneer Publishers, 1947. 31 pp.
A Trotskyist attack on Stalinists in the National Maritime Union as corrupt bureaucrats and disrupters of maritime unity. Stalinist treachery and betrayal, long charged by the Trotskyists, was finally exposed by a leadership rift.

P187 PRENDERGAST, William. State Legislatures and Communism: The Current Scene, "American Political Science Review," 44 (Sept. 1950), 556-74.
A review of antisubversive measures adopted by state legislatures in 1949, including legislation to strengthen attachment to American ideals, to prevent unemployed communists from receiving benefits, to keep educational scholarships from communists, to rid school systems of communist teachers, and to keep communists off the public payroll. In no state was any need for the legislation demonstrated.

P188 .... Do State Antisubversive Efforts Threaten Civil Rights? "Annals of the American Academy of Political and Social Science," 275 (May 1951), 124-31.
A review of state legislation to combat subversion, concluding that these efforts contain threats to civil liberty in their ambiguity with regard to speech and in the power to exclude from public employment. Civil liberty has not been seriously damaged, however, except in a few western states after World War I. Improved procedures are badly needed.

P189 PRESSMAN, Gabriel. They Howl for Justice, "American Legion Magazine," 47 (Sept. 1949), 16-17 ff.
Contrasts between two trials held this year—that of Cardinal Mindszenty in Budapest, Hungary, and that of Eugene Dennis and 11 other American communist leaders in New York City. A reporter who covered both trials

390

contrasts the scenes, with attention to the behavior of judges and attorneys, the rights afforded the defendants, ability of the outside press to attend, the number of armed police, and the right of sympathizers to picket.

P190   PRESTON, John Hyde. "The Liberals: A Novel." New York: John Day, 1938. 386 pp.
A problem novel by a procommunist, attempting to state the case of the liberals versus the revolutionaries. Set in Connecticut, the story is pro-CIO, in line with the popular front line of the communists in 1938.

P191   PRESTON, John W. Recent Developments in the Negro People's Movement, "Political Affairs," 31 (Feb. 1952), 32-42.
A report on developments since the Party's fifteenth national convention in December 1950. Increased assaults upon the Negro people by big capital have been countered by a rise in national consciousness, a corresponding struggle against Negro reformists, and a rise in progressive, anti-imperialist Negro leadership.

P192   PRINGLE, Jack [pseud.]. The Situation in U.S.A., "Communist International," 9 (Oct. 15, 1932), 668-72.
A speech at the Twelfth Plenum of the ECCI, reviewing Party activities and growth in the U.S. and analyzing the Party's weaknesses. The major problems are to get rid of sectarianism, establish the Party in the workshops and trade unions, and develop daily work among the factory masses.

P193   PRITCHETT, C. Herman. "Civil Liberties and the Vinson Court." Chicago: University of Chicago Press, 1954. 297 pp. Notes. Table of cases. Ind.
A critical study of the way in which the U.S. Supreme Court, over the years 1946-53, faced the problem of subversion. The author analyzes judicial interpretations or views of the Smith Act, the noncommunist affidavits of the Taft-Hartley law, the McCarran Act, the McCarran-Walter Act, the Hiss and Rosenberg trials, legislative investigating committees, and loyalty oaths for public employees.

P194   .... The Supreme Court and Our Civil Liberties, "Nation," 179 (Oct. 9, 1954), 302-5.
Criticism of the Supreme Court by a political science professor for failing to defend basic civil liberties with regard to legislative and executive programs aimed at subversion. Particularly criticized is the Court's acceptance, in the Dennis case, of the constitutionality of the Smith Act as a device for jailing Party leaders. Also discussed are loyalty oaths and the power of congressional committees.

P195   .... "The Political Offender and the Warren Court." Boston: Boston University Press, 1958. 74 pp.
The Bacon Lectures on the U.S. Constitution. The author believes that the Warren Court has performed its function creditably as a protector of personal and civil liberties. He considers three types of cases involving political offenders: 1) criminal punishment under statutes of proscribed political activities; 2) forced exposure of activities or associates by congressional committees; and 3) punishment of political offenders by administrative officials.

P196   PRITT, D. N. "The State Department and the Cold War: A Commentary on Its Publication, Nazi-Soviet Relations, 1939-1941." New York: International Publishers, 1948. 96 pp.
Criticism by a British lawyer and labor member of Parliament of a U.S. State Department publication containing captured German documents on the Hitler-Stalin pact.

Pritt charges that the selection of documents is biased, and that the publication seeks to turn public opinion against the Soviet Union, thereby justifying military expenditures and the Marshall Plan.

P197   .... "The Search for Peace." Introd. by Jessica Smith. New York: International Publishers, 1952. 63 pp.
The communist answer to Western "charges" against the Soviet Union on the Hitler-Stalin pact, use of the veto power in the UN, atomic power, Russian "imperialism," Russian armament and attitudes toward war, lack of freedom, and slave labor in the Soviet Union.

P198   .... "The Rosenberg Case." New York: National Committee to Secure Justice in the Rosenberg Case, n.d. [1953?]. 15 pp.
An analysis by a British lawyer, asserting that the case against the Rosenbergs rests on the uncorroborated evidence of three persons, all of them unreliable. The behavior of the trial judge is criticized. The duty of securing a review rests on world public opinion.

P199   .... "The Case of Morton Sobell." New York: National Committee to Secure Justice for Morton Sobell in the Rosenberg Case, n.d. [1954?]. 31 pp.
A review of Sobell's case by a procommunist Briton, who concludes that evidence to support the verdict was lacking and that a fair trial was denied by linking Sobell with the Rosenbergs. Letters urging review of the case are requested.

P200   "PROGRESSIVE," McCarthy: A Documented Record, 18 (April 1954), 1-94. Ind.
The entire issue is devoted to a rebuttal of McCarthy's charges and a review of his public record. The issue analyzes the original charges of communists in the State Department made by McCarthy; and reviews the activities of McCarthy and his committee, highlighting his character assassination tactics. The magazine concludes that McCarthy has not exposed the extent of communist infiltration of our government, and that in addition he has destroyed the very weapon, truth, on which we depend to combat communism.

P201   PROGRESSIVE BUILDING TRADES WORKERS. "What's Wrong in the Carpenters Union?" Chicago: PBTW, 1925. 54 pp.
An account by a Trade Union Educational League affiliate of corruption in the Carpenters Union under the Hutcheson administration. The union leadership is charged with graft, machine tactics, vote stealing, the expulsion of militants, and threats against political opponents. The TUEL group asks for a united front, with the right to propagandize for its program.

P202   PROGRESSIVE CITIZENS OF AMERICA, The Arts, Sciences, and Professions Council. "Conference on the Subject of Thought Control in the United States: Papers and Proceedings. Beverly Hills, Calif: The Council, 1947. 432 pp. Ind.
Proceedings of a Party-dominated conference held in Los Angeles, Calif., June 9-13, 1947. Publication is in six sections: (1) opening session: legal aspects of thought control; (2) the press and radio; (3) literature, music, the arts and architecture; (4) health and medicine, science and education; (5) the film, the actor; and (6) closing session. The reports agree that there is an alarming trend to control the cultural life of the American people in accordance with reactionary conceptions of our national interest. Many resolutions are included, together with a letter to the President, calling on him to halt this dangerous trend.

P203 PROGRESSIVE PARTY. "Peace, Freedom and Abundance: The Platform of the Progressive Party Adopted July 23-25, 1948." New York: The Party, 1948. 19 pp.

Platform of the Progressive Party, denouncing the Republican and Democratic Parties as putting forth the same program. Planks are grouped under the heads of peace, freedom, and abundance. Among specific planks are those calling for negotiations with the Soviet Union, opposition to anti-Soviet hysteria, repudiation of the Truman Doctrine and the Marshall Plan, outlawing of atomic bombs, abolition of the House Un-American Activities Committee, and abolition of the federal loyalty program.

P204 PROKOPEC, Jos. Negroes as an Oppressed National Minority, "Communist," 9 (March 1930), 239-45.

An attempt to clarify the Communist International resolution on the American Negro question. Negroes in the Black Belt are like any other national minority or colonial people. Without self-determination, the struggle for equality is meaningless. A national revolutionary movement of the Negro peasantry and bourgeoisie will hasten the proletarian revolution.

P205 "PROPAGANDA ANALYSIS," Communist Propaganda, U.S.A., 1939 Model, 2 (March 1, 1939), 1-8.

Communist propaganda and communist activity in labor and so-called liberal organizations are widespread, although the Party has very few members and very little money. It is able to disseminate this propaganda successfully through discipline, fanatical devotion, and industry. The specific propaganda depends on the momentary policy and program of the Party.

P206 PROVISIONAL COMMITTEE TO FREE STEVE NELSON. "Steve Nelson: A Tribute by 14 Famous Authors." New York: The Committee, n.d. [1952]. 32 pp.

A tribute to the Pittsburgh communist who was currently being tried under the Smith Act. There are poems written to his heroism, reminiscences of his fighting in the Spanish Civil War, condemnation of Judge Musmanno and Matthew Cvetic, and appeals to him to remain steadfast. Among the contributors are Howard Fast, I. F. Stone, Luis C. Aragon, John Howard Lawson, Alvah Bessie, Albert E. Kahn, William L. Patterson, and Albert Maltz.

P207 PUBLIC AFFAIRS COMMITTEE. "Loyalty in a Democracy: A Roundtable Report." New York: PAC, 1952. 32 pp.

A discussion of the federal loyalty program, the House Committee on Un-American Activities, state loyalty oaths, and private loyalty investigations. The group, chaired by Professor Robert E. Cushman of Cornell, concludes that present loyalty measures constitute a threat to basic American freedoms.

P208 PUNDEFF, Marin. "Recent Publications on Communism: A Bibliography of Non-Periodical Literature, 1957-1962. Research Institute on Communist Strategy and Propaganda, School of International Relations, University of Southern California, 1962. 66 pp. Mimeo.

A compilation of recent books and pamphlets published in English on communism. While the bibliography is primarily concerned with communism abroad, some items pertaining to the U.S. are included.

P209 PURCELL, Obed. The Supreme Court and Civil Liberties, "Communist," 16 (April 1937), 313-21.

An examination of the Supreme Court's record, emphasizing its denials of civil liberties. The Court uses the Fifth, Tenth, and Fourteenth Amendments to protect property rights over human rights. The Court's record in minimum wage, espionage, criminal syndicalist, and Negro rights cases is reviewed, and Roosevelt's plan for reorganization endorsed.

P210 PURCELL, Theodore V. "The Worker Speaks His Mind on Company and Union." Cambridge, Mass.: Harvard University Press, 1953. 344 pp. Bibliog. Ind.

Primarily concerned with the relationship of workers in a Swift & Company meatpacking plant in Chicago to the company, to fellow-workers, and to the union, the book also deals (especially pp. 64-72) with communist influences in Local 28 and in District 1 of the United Packinghouse Workers of America.

P211 PURO, H. The Tasks of Our Party in Agrarian Work, "Communist," 10 (Feb. 1931), 147-52.

An elaboration of the November plenum line on agrarian work. The Party's plan of work in this field calls for ideological clarification, a practical program of action, preparation and distribution of literature, development of local demands, organization of the Agricultural Workers Union, and special efforts among Negroes in the South.

P212 .... The Class Struggle in the American Countryside, "Communist," 12 (June 1933), 547-58.

The Party and militant farmers' organizations are leading mass struggles against foreclosures and for immediate relief. Solidarity between farmers and city workers has grown. We must give a revolutionary orientation to farmer militancy, and build the Party in farm communities.

P213 .... The Tasks of Our Party in the Work among the Farmers, "Communist," 12 (Sept. 1933), 875-87.

Objectives and techniques in the Party's farm program, as outlined in a speech to the Extraordinary Conference of the Party, July 7-10, 1933. While the Party's main orientation must be toward the basic industries, the rural toiling masses are an indispensable ally of the industrial proletariat, and political gains must be made among them.

P214 .... The Farmers Are Getting Ready for Revolutionary Struggles, "Communist," 13 (June 1934), 569-80.

Farmers have shown their militancy by strikes and other struggles, many of which the Party has led along class struggle lines. We are making progress among Negro sharecroppers in the South and agricultural wage workers on the West Coast. We must combat social-fascist influence in the farmers' movement, and show the revolutionary way out of the crisis.

Q

Q1 QUIN, Mike [pseud. for Paul William Ryan]. "The C.S. Case against Labor." San Francisco(?): International Labor Defense, n.d. [1935]. 31 pp.
An account of a 1935 trial of 18 communists and members of the Cannery and Agricultural Workers' Industrial Union under the California criminal syndicalist law. In the background were successful agricultural strikes, the growing power of the Unemployed Council, and agricultural worker support of the San Francisco maritime strike of 1934. Only one defendant, a former communist now a Trotskyite, broke solidarity during the trial. Seven defendants were found guilty of conspiracy to violate the criminal syndicalist act.

Q2 . . . . "Ashcan the M-Plan." San Francisco: The Yanks Are Not Coming Committee, 1940. 24 pp.
A communist antiwar pamphlet of the Hitler-Stalin pact period. The M-Plan, called the iron heel of Wall Street and Big Business, is to go into effect if America declares war, replacing American democracy with an industrial-military dictatorship.

Q3 . . . . "The Yanks Are Not Coming." San Francisco: Yanks Are Not Coming Committee, District Council No. 2, Maritime Federation of the Pacific, n.d. [1940]. 16 pp.
An antiwar pamphlet, written during the Nazi-Soviet pact period, asserting that this is a war to impose fascism at home and further imperialist ambitions abroad. The Roosevelt Administration is uniting with Big Business in preparing for war. The peoples of all the fighting countries are equally victims. We should solve our own problems at home.

Q4 . . . . "The Enemy Within." San Francisco: People's World, 1941. 32 pp.
A short story by a communist writer, dramatizing fascist tendencies of Big Business.

Q5 . . . . Postscript by Harry Bridges. "The Big Strike." Olema, Calif.: Olema Publishing Co., 1949. 259 pp. App.
An account, from a communist point of view, of the West Coast maritime strike of 1934 and the San Francisco general strike that followed. Attention is paid to municipal corruption in San Francisco, the life and work of seamen and longshoremen, incompetence of conservative union officers, efforts by the Industrial Association to open the port of San Francisco, violent police action against pickets, the general strike called by the San Francisco Labor Council, anticommunist raids, the arbitration award, and the establishment of union power on the waterfront.

Q6 QUITMAN, Gertrude, and ALLEN, William H. "Dictator Isms and Our Democracy: Nazism . . . Fascism . . . Communism 'Made in America' Brands." New York: Institute for Public Service, 1940. 55 pp.
Emphasizing the similarities of fascism and communism, the authors describe the disappearance under either type of dictatorship of civil liberties, free politics, free education, free labor, and free business. Pointing to a dangerous tendency in this country to trade freedom for the glamor and showmanship of a dictator, they call for vigilance in our government units, in our political parties, in business and labor, in our civic agencies, in education, in our homes, and in our hearts and minds.

R

R1   RABINOWITCH, Eugene. What Is a Security Risk? "Bulletin of the Atomic Scientists," 10 (June 1954), 241 ff.

The editor of the "Bulletin" asserts that the decision of the Personnel Security Board in the Oppenheimer case is absurd on its face and dangerous in its implications. The security regulations need revision if so great a scientist is excluded from working for our country.

R2   RABINOWITZ, Victor. Slow Down for the Witch-Hunt, "American Socialist," 3 (July 1956), 12-14.

A discussion of the case of Steve Nelson, Communist Party official in Pennsylvania. Convicted under a state sedition law, with little evidence of his activities presented, Nelson was sentenced to 20 years. His conviction was overturned by the U.S. Supreme Court, which held state sedition laws unenforceable because the federal government, by passing the Smith Act in 1940, had occupied the field.

R3   RADIN, Max. The Loyalty Oath at the University of California, "American Scholar," 19 (Summer 1950), 275-84.

A discussion of the loyalty oath controversy by an emeritus professor of law at the University. The faculty opposed a noncommunist, loyalty oath, although a majority accepted a "compromise" which attached a noncommunist statement to the employment contract. A great many will refuse to sign this statement.

R4   RAHV, Philip. The Literary Class War, "New Masses," 8 (Aug. 1932), 7-10.

An assertion that bourgeois literature is at a stage of decline and imminent collapse, whereas proletarian literature is militant and creative. Bourgeois literature reflects the vacuum of bourgeois psychology, based on consumption. Unless writers make the Marxist world view their own, they will desert to the bourgeoisie. (See criticism by A. B. Magil, "Pity and Terror," in the "New Masses," Dec. 1932.)

R5   . . . . Two Years of Progress—From Waldo Frank to Donald Ogden Stewart, "Partisan Review," 4 (Feb. 1938), 22-30.

A comparison of the writers' congresses that met in 1935 and 1937. Whereas the first was revolutionary and anti-capitalist as well as against war and fascism, the second was merely antifascist, since in the meantime the communists had adopted the popular front slogan. Frank, first president of the League of American Writers, was dropped for questioning the Moscow trials, and replaced by the more pliant Stewart.

R6   . . . . Proletarian Literature: A Political Autopsy, "Southern Review," 4 (Winter 1939), 616-28.

The rise and fall of proletarian literature can be understood only in its relationship to the Communist Party. In the early 1930's the Party attracted many writers, who shifted leftward as a result of the depression. A novel or play was certified as "revolutionary" only when its political ideas corresponded to those of the Party. After 1935, when the Party line shifted right, the proletarian literary movement was dissolved.

R7   RAILROAD BROTHERHOODS UNITY MOVEMENT. "Revolt in the Railroad Unions." Chicago: RBUM, n.d. [1935]. 36 pp.

A critical account of wage cuts, disappearing jobs, and accidents on the railroads. Conservative craft unions are charged with sell outs, cooperation with management to speed up production, discrimination against Negroes, and raiding sister unions. The unity movement seeks one union in the industry, along with protection of jobs and wages.

R8   RAMSEY, David, and CALMER, Alan. The Marxism of V. F. Calverton, "New Masses," 8 (Jan. 1933), 9-27.

A long, detailed, and acid attack on V. F. Calverton, editor of the "Modern Quarterly," debunking his reputation as a Marxist. He is charged, not only with never having understood the fundamental principles of Marxism, but with being a concealed fascist, a Lovestoneite, a renegade, and a plagiarist. In attitude and ethics, he reflects a decadent capitalist civilization. (For Calverton's response, see his "An Open Letter to the 'New Masses,'" in "Modern Monthly," March 1933.)

R9   RAMSEY, David. The A.A.A.—And After, "Communist," 15 (Feb. 1936), 130-38.

An analysis of the nullification by the Supreme Court of the Agricultural Adjustment Act. Following the nullification of the NRA, the decision foreshadows the same fate for other New Deal legislation. Communists must rally farmers against any cuts in benefits, and show city workers that any benefits from the nullification will not aid them, but line capitalist pockets.

R10   . . . . Platforms and Issues in 1936, "Communist," 15 (July 1936), 600-17.

Republican candidate Landon is controlled by Wall Street, the Liberty League, and the Hearst Press. The Republican program would overthrow the limited gains of the New Deal and set up a finance capital-fascist dictatorship. While not as dangerous, Roosevelt still retreats under capitalist pressure, and socialist candidate Norman Thomas is also unsatisfactory.

R11   . . . . Roosevelt and the Democratic Platform, "Communist," 15 (Aug. 1936), 707-20.

Strong criticism of Republican policy and tactics, with qualified praise for the Democratic platform. Labor and other progressive pressures have forced Roosevelt to take a stand against Wall Street and achieve the best platform of either major party to date. Without actually endorsing Roosevelt, the CP regards the defeat of Landon as a necessity.

R12   RAND, Ayn. Screen Guide for Americans, "Plain Talk," 2 (Nov. 1947), 37-42.

An analysis of totalitarian propaganda, written for motion picture producers at the request of the Motion Picture

Alliance for the Preservation of American Ideals. The author points out that the communists seek to destroy every form of independence, and to undermine faith in American political institutions. She equates the free enterprise system with Americanism.

R13 RAND, Harry I. Loyalty-Security and the Foreign-Born Citizen: Naturalization and Denaturalization Statutes, "Lawyers Guild Review," 15 (Winter 1955-56), 139-44.
While the foreign-born citizen, like the native-born, suffers the full impact of our loyalty-security programs, his lot is ever more burdensome because of restrictions on naturalization and, once citizenship has been achieved, threats of denaturalization. Our new laws deny naturalized citizens the liberties guaranteed all by the Constitution.

R14 RAND SCHOOL OF SOCIAL SCIENCE, Labor Research Department. "American Labor Year Book." Vols. 1-13. New York: The School, 1916-1932.
Source books on labor issues from a radical but (except for the early years) noncommunist point of view, with many of the sections written by experts in specific fields. Although the categories vary, the volumes generally contain sections on the industrial and social conditions of the country, trade union organization, the AFL and specific unions, labor disputes, labor politics, labor legislation, court decisions affecting labor, civil rights, international relations of labor, and labor abroad. Information is included on strikes and lockouts in which the communists played a part, left-wing unions, political prisoner cases, Communist Party platforms and internal frictions, and the RILU and its international affiliates.

R15 RANDOLPH, A. Philip. Why I Would Not Stand for Re-election for President of the National Negro Congress, "Black Worker" (Brotherhood of Sleeping Car Porters), 6 (May 1940), 1 ff.
The president of the Brotherhood of Sleeping Car Porters attacks the Communist Party for its control of the National Negro Congress, which he asserts is kept alive by the CIO and the communists rather than by Negroes. (Also published in "American Federationist," July 1940, pp. 24-25.)

R16 .... Two-Edged Sword against Communism, "Interracial Review," 20 (Dec. 1947), 182-84.
A Negro union leader emphasizes the necessity of fighting against communist encroachments on American life, and at the same time strengthening the democratic system.

R17 .... The Menace of Communism, "American Federationist," 56 (March 1949), 19-20.
The president of the Brotherhood of Sleeping Car Porters enumerates the ways in which communism threatens democratic organizations. Their antidemocratic program, their subservience to the Soviet Union, and their dishonest tactics make them a menace to democratic organizations.

R18 RAPHAEL, A. [pseud. for Alexander Bittelman]. The Task of the Hour, "Communist" (Organ of the Communist Party of America, affiliated with the Communist International), 1 (Oct. 1921), 3-6.
A call for the creation of a legal political party to coexist with the underground Communist Party, in order to end its isolation from the working masses. In any revolutionary situation, the underground party, not the legal one, will take leadership. That is what the Communist International meant by requiring its parties to combine legal with illegal work.

R19 RAPORT, Morris. The Washington State Elections, "Communist," 16 (Feb. 1937), 173-79.
Although the communists were denied affiliation with the Commonwealth Federation, they supported its successful attempts to get progressive candidates nominated in the Democratic primaries in the state of Washington. Now the communists must try to convert the Federation into an independent party.

R20 .... The Commonwealth Federation Moves On, "Communist," 16 (April 1937), 366-72.
With many of its candidates now in the Washington state legislature, the Federation has proposed bills that will enlarge civil rights, improve social security, end the sales tax, and aid education. Some of its bills were passed, though it did little to organize public pressure to override the governor's veto. The Federation has increasingly come to appreciate and accept aid from the Communist Party.

R21 .... The Democratic Front and the Northwest Elections, "Communist," 18 (Jan. 1939), 66-75.
The secretary of the Party in the Northwest District analyzes election results in Oregon and Washington, evaluating the roles played by the Commonwealth Federation, the AFL and CIO, and the Communist Party.

R22 .... The Communist Party in the State of Washington and the 1940 Elections, "Communist," 18 (Aug. 1939), 730-39.
A description of the struggle between reactionary and progressive forces in the Washington legislature. Red-baiting and the Party's role in defeating Red-baiting resolutions are discussed. Progressive forces are looking forward to the 1940 elections by developing the organizations which contributed to New Deal victories.

R23 RASCOE, Burton. You Should Know about This Book, "American Legion Magazine," 50 (May 1951), 28 ff.
Although 96 per cent of "Good Reading" is meritorious, the remainder recommends communist propaganda and omits anticommunist works. Among the sections criticized are those on politics, China, philosophy, and economics.

R24 .... "Goodwin Watson: His Record." New Rochelle [?]: American Legion, Department of New York, Westchester Co. Committee, Americanism Commission, n.d. [1953]. 40 pp.
The record of Dr. Watson's connections with the communist conspiracy in America as shown by his sponsorship or participation in organizations and other activities controlled by Soviet agents. Eighty-two instances of his championship of communist objectives are listed.

R25 RASKIN, A. H. Report on the Communist Party (U.S.A.), "New York Times Magazine," March 30, 1947, 12-13 ff.
A report on how the Party is organized, what its members believe, and how they spread their doctrine. Five charges frequently made against the Party are listed, with comments on each by Eugene Dennis, general secretary of the Party. The opposing point of view is presented by AFL vice-president Matthew Woll.

R26 .... Taft-Hartley and Labor's Perspective, "Commentary," 4 (Nov. 1947), 435-40.
An analysis of the political views of the American labor movement, with a discussion of the role that communists are playing in it. The communists, opposing the Truman Doctrine and the Marshall Plan, are pursuing an anti-CIO foreign policy. While Murray has shown resistance to the

communists, Lewis may resume cordial relations with them.

R27 RASKIN, A. H. Presenting the Phenomenon Called Quill, "New York Times Magazine," March 5, 1950, 11 ff.
A portrait of Michael J. Quill, president of the Transport Workers Union of the CIO, for 14 years a champion of communist causes and now a leading labor opponent of the communists. He uses all the tricks he learned from the communists to destroy their influence in the union. After breaking with the communists in 1948, he cleaned them out from the TWU leadership and staff in nine months.

R28 RAUH, Joseph L., Jr. Informers, G-Men, and Free Men, "Progressive," 14 (May 1950), 9-11.
An assertion by a prominent Washington attorney, counsel in civil liberties cases, that many FBI informers are irresponsible and unreliable. The FBI places particular reliance on ex-communists and ex-undercover agents in the Party. The growing system of informing is producing a timid and insecure civil service.

R29 . . . , and BURNHAM, James (James F. Murray, Jr., moderator). Is the Fear of Communism Endangering Our Freedom? "Town Meeting," 20 (Oct. 12, 1954), 1-8.
Rauh asserts that our biggest threat is Soviet aggression from without, and that we endanger our own liberties by becoming obsessed with the fear of communist infiltration. Charging the communists with originating the idea that the fear of communists endangers our freedom, Burnham calls for the rejection of communism to preserve our liberties.

R30 RAUSHENBUSH, Winifred. Paul Robeson: Messiah of Color, "Freeman," 1 (Nov. 13, 1950), 111-14.
A biographical sketch of Robeson, emphasizing incidents in his life which indicate and explain his communist sympathies, and culminating in an account of the Peekskill riots. Robeson's communist assignment, as spokesman for the colored people of the U.S., is to help topple the white race from power in the coming world struggle.

R31 RAWICK, George P. From Faith to Dogma: The Development of the Communist Party Line, 1928-1939, "South Atlantic Quarterly," 53 (April 1954), 193-202.
A tracing of the Party line from the softness before 1928 through the hard "third period" to the soft popular front and the even softer democratic front of the late 1930's. With the Hitler-Stalin pact the Party showed again that it was merely a sounding board for Soviet needs.

R32 RAYMOND, Anan. Prairie Fire: A Footnote to Contemporary History, "American Bar Association Journal," 38 (Nov. 1952), 911-14 ff.
An account of the 1934 trial of "Mother" Bloor in Sherman County, Nebraska, on charges of unlawful assembly and incitement to riot. The author discusses the historical background, the publicity obtained by the Party, and the defendant's ambivalent attitude toward the U.S. and the USSR.

R33 RAYMOND, Harry. "The Milk Steal." New York: Workers Library for the New York State Committee of the Communist Party, 1936. 15 pp.
An election pamphlet accusing the Borden and Sheffield milk trusts of starving children, driving farmers from the land, robbing workers of their wages, and fleecing the consumer. The capitalist parties will never act against the milk trusts; only the Communist Party will give relief.

R34 . . . . "Dixie Comes to New York: Story of the Freeport GI Slayings." New York: Daily Worker, 1946. 14 pp.
An account by a staff writer of the "Daily Worker" of the shooting of two Negroes by a policeman at Freeport, Long Island, which the city officials and the courts were attempting to "whitewash."

R35 . . . . "The Ingrams Shall Not Die: Story of Georgia's New Terror." New York: Daily Worker, 1948. 14 pp.
The story of Mrs. Rose Ingram and her two boys, sentenced to die for the killing of a neighboring sharecropper in Americus, Ga. The author, a "Daily Worker" reporter, calls for mass protests, funds for defense, and communications to the governor of Georgia and President Truman demanding the freedom of the Ingrams.

R36 RAYMOND, Phil. The Briggs Auto Strike Victory, "Labor Unity," 8 (March 1933), 21-24.
A report, in the organ of the Trade Union Unity League, of the successful strike of the Briggs workers in Detroit against a wage cut, under the leadership of the Auto Workers' Union. AFL misleaders first ignored the strike, then sought to disrupt the local of the Auto Workers' Union.

R37 REARDON, B. E., and HOPE, R. S. The Government Loyalty Program Cases, "George Washington Law Review," 20 (Jan. 1952), 294-313.
A discussion of the legal position of persons and organizations adversely affected by the loyalty program. U.S. Supreme Court rulings in "Bailey v. Richardson" and "Joint Anti-Fascist Refugee Committee v. McGrath" are analyzed. One was a case of a federal employee dismissed on security grounds, the other of an organization designated by the Attorney General as subversive.

R38 RECORD, Jane Cassels. The Red-Tagging of Negro Protest, "American Scholar," 26 (Summer 1957), 325-33.
The idea that desegregation and communism are linked has gained currency among white Southerners, who can find no other explanation for southern Negro protest. The author refutes this view.

R39 RECORD, Wilson. "The Negro and the Communist Party." Chapel Hill: University of North Carolina Press, 1951. 340 pp. Ind.
A comprehensive, documented account of communist activities among Negroes, tracing the twists and turns in the Party line toward Negroes to the changing needs of the Soviet Union. In some periods self-determination of the Black Belt is the goal; in others it is complete integration in American society. Sometimes Negro protest and betterment organizations are denounced as reactionary, sometimes their cooperation is sought, sometimes they are attacked for protesting too vigorously. Though the Party has little Negro membership or support to show for its efforts, it has helped to dramatize the Negro's plight.

R40 . . . . The Negro and the Communists, "New Leader," 34 (April 23, 1951), 15-18.
A survey of the Communist Party's 30-year record of attempting to capitalize on and channel Negro discontent. The Party has failed because the Kremlin does not understand Negro problems, because Negroes have found sincere allies elsewhere, because Negroes have developed protest organizations of their own, and because Negroes appreciate the potential of the Constitution and Bill of Rights.

R41 . . . . The Development of the Communist Position

on the Negro Question in the United States, "Phylon Quarterly," 19 (Fall 1958), 306-26.
An examination of the ideological origins of the communist position on the American Negro, showing how the positions of Marx, Engels, Lenin, and Stalin were modified in response to changing definitions of the world situation. Interpretations and analyses by early leaders such as Jay Lovestone and John Pepper, and by later writers such as James S. Allen and Harry Haywood, are described.

R42   RECORD, Wilson. "Race and Radicalism: The NAACP and the Communist Party in Conflict." Ithaca: Cornell University Press, 1964. 237 pp. Ind.
An account of the relations between the NAACP and the CPUSA, a part of the study of the impact of communism on American life and institutions sponsored by the Fund for the Republic. American Negroes have been among the prime objects of communist efforts. The author presents an overview of relations between the two organizations from 1919 to 1962, emphasizing the disparity of goals and methods, and focusing on their interaction in specific periods marked by shifts in the Party's program for Negroes as well as in its general line. The Party has found it difficult to recruit Negroes when it spoke in revolutionary language, and its ranks have split many times over the dilemma of reform or revolution. The NAACP has swum with the mainstream of American life during the past 20 years, whereas the CP has not.

R43   RED LABOR INTERNATIONAL [RED INTERNATIONAL OF LABOR UNIONS]. "Resolutions and Decisions of the First International Congress." Introd. by A. Losovsky. Chicago: "Voice of Labor" for American Labor Union Educational Society, 1921. 96 pp.
The framework of organization of the RILU. The Congress adopted a revolutionary position, called for the dictatorship of the proletariat, favored closest cooperation with the Communist International, and attacked the Amsterdam International. Tactics approved included direct action, workers' control, and formation of shop committees. Conditions for affiliation were agreed upon. (The IWW delegates withdrew after the Congress decided against dual unions in favor of "boring from within" AFL unions.)

R44   RED INTERNATIONAL OF LABOR UNIONS. "Resolutions and Decisions, Second World Congress of the Red International of Labor Unions, Held in Moscow, November, 1922." Chicago: Trade Union Educational League, n.d. [1923]. 46 pp.
Resolutions of the Congress held in Moscow in November 1922 denouncing the evils of capitalism and the class collaboration policy of the unions of the Amsterdam International. In the U.S., the Trade Union Educational League is urged to cooperate with independent revolutionary unions (the IWW) and seek to stay within the AFL, while seeking to organize workers who are outside it.

R45   .... "Third World Congress: Resolutions and Decisions." Chicago: Trade Union Educational League, 1924. 78 pp.
Resolutions of the Congress that met in Moscow in July 1924 reaffirming the necessity of struggling against the reformist unions. With regard to the U.S., the Congress prescribed TUEL structure, its stand on specific issues, and its relations to the Workers Party. At all times the TUEL must emphasize the revolutionary aims of the left wing.

R46   .... Report of the Fourth Congress of the RILU, May, 1928." London: National Minority Movement, 1928. 200 pp.

The RILU Congress that changed the communist trade union line. In America (pp. 135-42), the decision was to replace the previous "boring from within" policy with organization of left-wing unions by the Trade Union Educational League, concentrating in the metal, transport, mining, food, textile, and needle industries.

R47   .... The Red International Program, "Labor Unity," 2 (May 1928), 25-26; (July), 25-26; (Aug.), 27-28; (Sept.), 27-29; (Oct.), 26-27.
The main thesis adopted by the Fourth World Congress of the Red International of Labor Unions, that met in Moscow from March 17 to April 3. Topics covered include the capitalist offensive, the leftward movement of the masses, capitalist rationalization, trade unions in the workers' state, the Amsterdam International, RILU work in reformist unions, the united front, and a program of action.

R48   ..., International Trade Union Committee of Negro Workers. A Trade Union Program of Action for Negro Workers, "Communist," 9 (Jan. 1930), 42-47.
The program of this committee of the Red International of Labor Unions, among other planks, calls for equal pay for equal work and civil rights, and opposes class collaboration, racial barriers in trade unions, and church and bourgeois influence. (The program was developed for Negroes of the world, particularly in colonial areas, not especially for those in the U.S.)

R49   ..., Central Council, Sixth Session. Lessons and Perspectives of the Economic Struggles, "Labor Unity," 4 (Feb. 8, 1930), 2; (Feb. 15), 7; (March 8), 3; (March 15), 11.
Theses of the Sixth Session of the RILU Central Council, following the 1929 economic crash. As a result the U.S. ruling class is carrying out its war program against the USSR, class contradictions are being sharpened, and the crisis in the reformist trade unions is growing. Tasks of the RILU in both advanced and underdeveloped countries, where the revolutionary unions are legal and where they are illegal, are outlined.

R50   ..., Tasks of the Trade Union Unity League of the USA, "Labor Unity," 4 (Feb. 8, 1930), 1 ff.
Approving the establishment of a new revolutionary trade union center, the RILU lists the most favorable fields of struggle for the TUUL. The depression has killed the bourgeois-Lovestone theories of "American exceptionalism." AFL and socialist groups, which are part of the strikebreaking apparatus, must be fought mercilessly. The TUUL has been weak with regard to the question of self-determination in its Negro work.

R51   .... "Resolutions of the Fifth World Congress, Held in Moscow, August, 1930. London: Minority Movement, 1931. 173 pp.
Resolutions of the RILU Congress held at the depth of the depression, hailing the militancy of the working class. A section on Negro workers (pp. 156-65) emphasizes their exploited condition in the U.S., condemns as social-fascist the Garvey movement and the NAACP, and calls for intensified recruiting of Negro workers by the revolutionary unions.

R52   ..., Executive Bureau. Immediate Tasks of TUUL, Revolutionary Unions: Resolution of Executive Buro of Red Int'l. of Labor Unions Shows Way to Real Struggles, "Labor Unity," 5 (May 23, 1931), 6-8.
Resolution of the RILU dealing with the work of the TUUL, appraising its successes and its failures, and noting that

the situation in the U.S. is favorable for revolutionary work. Mistakes in TUUL strike activity are pointed out, and immediate tasks are outlined. The TUUL must stimulate and lead strike movements, build the revolutionary unions, and intensify work among Negroes.

R53   RED INTERNATIONAL OF LABOR UNIONS, The Tasks of the T.U.U.L., "Labor Unity," 7 (June 1932), 5-9.
The text of the resolution on revolutionary trade union work in the U.S. adopted by the eighth session of the Central Council of the RILU, of which the TUUL was the American section, at its December 1931 meeting in Moscow. Among other directives, the TUUL was told to prepare systematically for strikes, learn to work among the masses, organize the unemployed, form strong groups within the reformist unions, and reorganize the TUUL unions on a factory basis.

R54   REDFIELD, A. "The Ruling Clawss." Introd. by Robert Forsyth [pseud. for Kyle Crichton]. New York: "Daily Worker," 1935. 183 pp.
A collection of satirical cartoons from the "Daily Worker."

R55   REDLICH, Norman. Spies in Government. I: The Bentley Story, "Nation," 178 (Jan. 30, 1954), 85-88; II: The Jenner Report, (Feb. 6), 109-11.
The author discredits most of the story of Elizabeth Bentley, which was the basis for the report of the Senate Subcommittee on Internal Security (the Jenner report). The Bentley testimony dealt with alleged espionage groups in Washington that collected secret documents for transmission to Russia.

R56   REECE, B. Carroll. Communist Base in Hawaii, "National Republic," 44 (Jan. 1957), 3-4 ff.
A review of inquiries by Senate committees into communist influence in Hawaii. Using the ILWU, which they controlled, as a base, the communists first assisted, then took over, the Democratic Party in Hawaii.

R57   .... Tax Exempt Subversion, "American Mercury," 85 (July 1957), 56-64.
A review of evidence from congressional hearings to support the author's assertion that tax-exempt foundations have become a principal source of communist infiltration and subversion in the U.S. Criticism is directed at the Rockefeller and Carnegie Foundations and the Fund for the Republic, as well as at the Garland Fund of earlier years.

R58   .... Hawaii—Red Citadel, "National Republic," 45 (Aug. 1957), 1-2 ff.
A review of communist infiltration in Hawaii, as disclosed by the Senate Subcommittee on Internal Security. The ILWU, directed by Harry Bridges, is the chief vehicle of Party penetration. The communist problem in Hawaii is often one of the division of jurisdiction between territorial and Washington authorities.

R59   .... Private War on Communism, "National Republic," 46 (Sept. 1958), 1-2 ff. Reprinted in "American Mercury," March 1959.
A call to Americans to be aware of the communists' blueprint for power, and to realize that merely being against communism is not enough. They are urged to understand the subject, to be effective citizens and opinion-makers, to expose communists, to support their church, to examine their schools, and to preach Americanism.

R60   REED, John. "Ten Days That Shook the World." New York: Boni and Liveright, 1919. 371 pp. Notes. App.
A sympathetic, carefully documented narrative of the Bolshevik Revolution of 1917. Reed, who subsequently became a leader of one of the early communist parties, became convinced that the uncompromising policy of the Bolsheviki was the best path to socialism. His eyewitness account of the Bolshevik Revolution enhanced Reed's influence in the emerging American communist movement, and had an impact on American opinion of the Soviet regime.

R61   .... The World Congress of the Communist International "Communist" (organ of the United Communist Party), 1, no. 10 n.d. [1920], 1-3.
A report on the Second World Congress of the Communist International by the UCP representative, pointing out that each party is the national section of the world party, bound by decisions of the Executive Committee of the Communist International. Comintern decisions on conditions for unity in the American communist movement and on the labor union question are discussed.

R62   .... Daughter of the Revolution, and Other Stories. Introd. by Floyd Dell. New York: Vanguard, 1927. 164 pp.
Stories and sketches by an early communist hero about New York, Pancho Villa's army in Mexico, and Russia during the Revolution.

R63   REEVE, Karl [Carl]. The New Imperialist Offensive against the Philippines, "Communist," 8 (April 1929), 190-203.
The appointment of Henry L. Stimson as secretary of state in the Hoover cabinet shows U.S. intent to intensify exploitation in its colonies. Stimson's record as governor-general of the Philippines is attacked. His appointment illustrates the alliance of the Philippine landlords and bourgeoisie with American imperialism.

R64   .... Lessons of the Great National Textile Strike, "Communist," 13 (Nov. 1934), 1106-24.
The national textile strike confirms the Party's view that the economic struggles of the workers are becoming more militant and political in character. However, the strike was sold out by the AFL leaders, who opposed spreading the strike, undertook a Red-baiting campaign, and advocated an industrial truce on the basis of the report of a Roosevelt-appointed mediation board which granted none of the workers' demands.

R65   .... Lovestoneism—Twin of Fascist-Trotskyism, "Communist," 17 (Aug. 1938), 732-42.
Lovestoneites are defeatists who think American capitalism is too strong to be overthrown. When influential in trade unions, they settle for poor bargains. They are allied with Trotskyites in attacking Russia and the people's front, in advocating neutrality for the U.S., in working for the defeat of progressive candidates. They use revolutionary phrases to promote fascist goals.

R66   .... The Elections in Pennsylvania, "Communist," 17 (Oct. 1938), 927-36.
The Party's educational director for eastern Pennsylvania reviews policies and personalities in the Republican and Democratic parties in his state, explaining the reasons for and aims of an independent communist campaign.

R67   .... Benjamin Franklin—Champion of Democracy, "Communist," 18 (July 1939), 594-605.
A discussion of Franklin's role in the extension of American democracy, part of the communists' effort in this period to align themselves with American traditions. Franklin's analysis of exchange value is compared with that of Karl Marx.

R68 REHWINKEL, Alfred M. "Communism and the Church." St. Louis: Concordia Publishing House, 1948. 143 pp. Bibliog.
A brief survey of American communism and a program for church anticommunism. The author, professor at Concordia Theological Seminary, St. Louis, and a pastor of the Missouri Synod of the Lutheran Church, analyzes the early history of communism in Marx's day, tells of its present spread in Europe, Asia, and the U.S., and summarizes its economic and social principles and its basic antireligious tenets. The menace of communism, the sworn enemy of the Church, can be countered by information, direction by the pastors, and the godliness of individual Christian lives.

R69 REINEMER, Vic. How Our Commies Defame America Abroad, "Saturday Evening Post," 222 (Feb. 11, 1950), 30 ff.
An account of the World Youth and Student Festival held in Budapest, Hungary, in 1949. The American delegation was controlled by communists and procommunists who presented a distorted picture of the U.S. by emphasizing slums, prejudice against Negroes, war preparations, monopolists, and imperialists.

R70 REINER, Margrit. The Fictional American Woman, "Masses & Mainstream," 5 (June 1952), 1-10.
Bourgeois writers reflect and perpetuate male supremacist attitudes, showing fictional women as passive, emotional, erotic, and childlike, while all references to the heroines of history are obliterated. Some progressive and socially conscious writers also perpetuate this double standard, though others stress the nobility of women.

R71 REINHARDT, Guenther. "Crime without Punishment: The Secret Soviet Terror against America." New York: Hermitage House, 1952. 322 pp. Ind.
An exposé of the operations of the Soviet secret services and police in the U.S., Latin American countries, and Europe, by one who worked with the FBI for seven years, and with the U.S. Counter Intelligence Corps in Europe. Among the activities in the U.S. that are discussed are the disappearance and alleged murder of Juliet Stuart Poyntz (chapter 1, pp. 19-37), the murder of Carlo Tresca (chapter 4, pp. 71-83), and the communist-instigated riots in connection with demonstrations of the unemployed in New York City in 1930 (pp. 251-61).

R72 REISS, Marvin. The Struggle for Peace, "Political Affairs," 28 (April 1949), 5-17.
The American government, controlled by capitalists who scheme for world domination, is forming an alliance with the western European countries which it dominates through the Marshall Plan. This alliance, directed against Russia, undermines the UN. The reactionaries fear that the communists will mobilize opposition to the Atlantic alliance among the mass of Americans who want peace with Russia.

R73 REISSIG, Herman F. Time to Speak Up! "Christian Century," 68 (Dec. 26, 1951), 1510-12.
A defense of those who supported causes such as Loyalist Spain in which the communists were active, or who, like the communists, criticized Chiang Kai-shek. Since the Nazi-Soviet pact, Americans who join hands with communists are either procommunist or blind to their real character and purposes. In the 1930's, however, more people should have been interested in objectives of united front organizations.

R74 RELIGIOUS FREEDOM COMMITTEE. "A Conspiracy to Destroy Religion." New York: The Committee, 1953. 20 pp.
Ridiculing assertions made to the House Committee on Un-American Activities about a conspiracy to destroy religion in the U.S., the pamphlet attacks the House Committee for enlarging this alleged conspiracy into one to overthrow the government and spy for the USSR. The House Committee is criticized for entering the field of religion, in which Congress has no jurisdiction under the Constitution.

R75 REMES, Carol. The Heart of Huckleberry Finn, "Masses & Mainstream," 8 (Nov. 1955), 8-16.
The birth of Samuel L. Clemens (Mark Twain) 120 years ago is the occasion for reevaluation of his finest work, "The Adventures of Huckleberry Finn." Clemens grew up in a Missouri town where slaves were among his friends. Throughout his life he had a deep personal concern over the sufferings of Negroes in bondage in America.

R76 "REPORTER," The Case of Alger Hiss, 1 (Aug. 30, 1949), 4-7.
An account of the first Hiss trial, emphasizing the exploitation of emotion and drama, and the repudiation of the New Deal implicit in the public response. The ghosts of the New Deal, not the defendant, are on trial before the public.

R77 REPPY, Alison. "Civil Rights in the United States." New York: Central Book Co., 1951. 298 pp. Ind.
A study of civil liberty cases in the U.S. in 1948-50. Chapter 5, "Communism and the Constitution" (pp. 31-67), deals with the investigatory powers of Congress, the important decisions in this area, and Congress' use of the contempt power. The author discusses the President's loyalty order, the Attorney General's listing of organizations, bills of attainder, the noncommunist affidavit under the Taft-Hartley Act, and the trial of communist leaders under the Smith Act.

R78 REPUBLICAN PARTY, National Committee. "Red Herring and Whitewash: The Record of Communism in the Government." Washington: Research Division, Republican National Committee, 1950. 50 pp.
A charge that the Democrats have been soft toward communists and fellow-travelers over many years, have obstructed attempts to expose the communist menace in government, have been indifferent to communist penetration, and have instituted an inadequate loyalty program. The cases of Alger Hiss, "Amerasia," and communists in the State Department are cited, and those responsible are condemned.

R79 RESEARCH INSTITUTE OF AMERICA. "The Communist in Labor Relations Today." [New York?]: The Institute, 1946. 18 pp. Multilithed.
A pamphlet addressed to employers, emphasizing the importance of the Party in the U.S. labor movement. The pamphlet explains the political strike called by communist-dominated unions, tells how communists control unions, gives tests for spotting a communist union, suggests employer policy in negotiations with such unions, and lists the communist-dominated unions in the AFL and the CIO.

R80 REUBEN, William A. "To Secure Justice in the Rosenberg Case." New York: National Committee to Secure Justice in the Rosenberg Case, n.d. [1951]. 32 pp.
An abridged version of articles in the "National Guardian" in August 1951 asserting that the Rosenbergs were victims of a political frameup. The author describes the background of the Rosenbergs, the unlawful behavior of the FBI, the manufacture of evidence against the Rosen-

bergs, the prejudicing of the jury, the inhumanity of the death penalty, and the heroism of the defendants.

R81   REUBEN, William A. Truth about the Rosenbergs' Case, "Jewish Life," 6 (Nov. 1951), 4-7.
A review of the testimony against the Rosenbergs, concluding that the government's case was flimsy and suspicious. All three witnesses who testified against the Rosenbergs had strong material motives for doing so. No documentary evidence was introduced. The mysterious "Julius" referred to may have been Klaus Emil Julius Fuchs, not Rosenberg.

R82   . . . . What Was the Rosenbergs' Crime? "Jewish Life," 6 (Dec. 1951), 21-23.
An argument that the Rosenbergs were condemned to die, not for espionage, but because of alleged radicalism. The Administration is said to be using the "Reichstag fire" device of the Nazis to connect radicalism with espionage.

R83   . . . . "The Atom Spy Hoax." New York: Action Books, 1954. 504 pp. Ind.
A denial that there is any direct connection between radical ideas and Soviet espionage. The author denies that there were any atom bomb secrets that could be stolen, that the Soviet Union was dependent on spies to produce its atomic bomb, or that communists are primarily loyal to Russia and are actual or potential spies. He asserts that all defendants in the Rosenberg case were railroaded, and that the testimony of Bentley, Budenz, Chambers, and others shows no real evidence of a communist conspiracy.

R84   . . . . "The Honorable Mr. Nixon and the Alger Hiss Case." New York: Action Books, 1956. 142 pp. App.
An analysis of the role played by Richard Nixon in getting Alger Hiss convicted. The author asserts that Nixon had ulterior purposes in mind and that, now that all the evidence is in, it is clear that the Hiss case constitutes a great deception of the American people.

R85   REUTHER, Walter P. How to Beat the Communists, "Collier's," 121 (Feb. 28, 1948), 11 ff. Reprinted in Henry M. Christman (ed.), "Walter P. Reuther: Selected Papers." New York: Macmillan, 1961. Pp. 22-35.
Drawing upon his experience in combatting the communists in the United Automobile Workers, the UAW president asserts that communism cannot win, in the union or in the nation, if the people know the issues and are offered democratic leadership and a positive program. We can defeat communism by making democracy work and by fighting against injustice. Obstacles are the united front psychology and a fear of character assassination by communists.

R86   . . . . The People with Captive Mentalities, More to Be Pitied Than Despised, "Ammunition" (United Automobile Workers—CIO), 7 (Nov. 1949), 46-47.
The text of Reuther's speech at the 1949 CIO convention, demanding the ouster of the communists from the CIO.

R87   REUTTER, E. Edmund. "The School Administrator and Subversive Activities." New York: Teachers College, Columbia University, 1951. 136 pp. Bibliog. Ind.
A study of methods prescribed in state and local laws, including the loyalty oath, which bind teachers to uphold the U.S. form of government. The author is not concerned with the necessity or desirability of various restraints on alleged subversive activities, but rather with their administration. He deals with the problem as it relates to personnel in public elementary and secondary schools,

although he includes experiences from the field of higher education.

R88   "REVOLUTIONARY AGE," The Bolshevik Call for an International Communist Congress, 2 (March 1, 1919), 1.
This Russian call sets up a working program for the Communist International, including revolutionary overthrow of the bourgeoisie, seizure of government power, and dictatorship of the proletariat. Groups invited from the U.S. were the Socialist Labor Party, the IWW, the Workers International Industrial Union, and the left wing of the Socialist Party.

R89   . . ., The National Left Wing Conference, 2 (July 5, 1919), 4-5.
An account of the national conference of the left wing of the Socialist Party, held in New York, June 21-24, 1919. The main dispute was between those hoping to take control of the emergency SP convention on September 1, 1919, and those favoring immediate formation of a communist party. The former won. (This struggle was the major factor in the creation of two communist parties in Chicago in Sept. 1919.)

R90   . . ., The Left Wing Unites, 2 (Aug. 1919), 3.
A report on the decision of the National Council of the left wing in the Socialist Party to form a communist party rather than make a last effort to take over the Socialist Party. This represents a reversal of the Council's earlier position. The realignment of forces resulting in this change is described.

R91   "REVOLUTIONARY AGE" [organ of the Communist Party, (Majority Group)]. "The Achievements" of the C.C. Plenum, 1 (Nov. 1, 1929), 17.
A Lovestoneite denunciation of the first plenum of the Central Committee of the Party held since December 1928. The faction led by William Z. Foster is accused of revisionism, Trotskyism, and following policies that have resulted in membership losses, collapse of mass work, and demoralization.

R92   . . ., An Appeal to All Party Members and Revolutionary Workers, 1 (Nov. 1, 1929), 1-2.
The newly formed CPUSA—Majority Group (Lovestoneite) gives its version of the internal war in the Party since 1923, holding William Z. Foster responsible. The relationship of events in the American party to factional struggles in the Communist International is described. Consolidation of all communist forces is urged.

R93   . . ., The Truth about the Corridor Congress, 1 (Dec. 1, 1929), 12; (Dec. 15), 13.
A description of an unofficial "corridor congress" during the Sixth World Congress of the Communist International, which undermined the prestige of Bukharin. Delegates of the Foster faction of the CPUSA participated in this caucus. Though the Sixth World Congress endorsed the Lovestoneite leadership of the CPUSA, Stalin promised Foster that the decision would be reversed. Subsequently the Lovestoneites were expelled.

R94   . . ., Unite the Communist Party! Appeal to the Seventh Convention and to the Party Membership, 1 (July 1, 1930), 1-2 ff.
An appeal by the Lovestoneite organization for reinstatement into the CPUSA. Despite the most favorable "objective" conditions for growth, the CPUSA has been reduced to impotence because present CPUSA and Comintern policies are non-Leninist. The Lovestoneites were expelled for disagreeing with these policies.

R95   . . ., "The Party Has Been Unified": The Seventh

National Convention of the Party, 1 (Aug. 1, 1930), 14.

A Lovestoneite review of the seventh national convention of the CPUSA, held in July 1930. The "unity" of which Browder boasts is the unity of a graveyard. Vital questions such as membership inactivity and losses, and the failures of the TUUL unions, were not discussed at the convention, which acted as a rubber stamp.

R96   REVOLUTIONARY AGE, Communists and the Trade Unions, 1 (Oct. 1, 1930), 8; (Nov. 22), 8-9.
A resolution adopted by a national conference of the Communist Party (Majority Group), criticizing the Communist Party's trade union policy and the TUUL. The CP's splitting of the labor movement has destroyed the organized left wing and left workers under reformist influence. Trade union unity must be reestablished.

R97   REVUSKY, Abraham. Understanding or Capitulation? The Jewish Communists and Their New Attitude towards Zionism, "Jewish Frontier," 6 (Aug. 1939), 5-9.
Although Jewish communism has been hostile toward Zionism since its inception, the united front has produced a more sympathetic view. Nevertheless, the communists are inconsistent and evasive. A number of questions are addressed to two communists, Moissaye Olgin and Paul Novick.

R98   REYNARD, Dick. Lee Pressman Lies, "New Leader," 33 (Sept. 9, 1950), 6-8.
An assertion that Pressman, formerly legal counsel to the CIO, deliberately lied when questioned by a congressional committee about communist connections during that period. He collaborated with Party leaders in making CIO decisions and was closely involved with front groups. Pressman may have lied to regain respectability or to get back into the CIO's good graces.

R99   REYNOLDS, Bruce. "The Communist Shakes His Fist." New York: George Sully, 1931. 460 pp.
An account of communist activities in the U.S., including a comparison of conditions in the U.S. with those in the USSR to show that communism is a menace and that communists seek, in an effort planned and financed by Moscow, to overthrow the government of the U.S. by violence and bloodshed.

R100   REYNOLDS, Quentin. "Courtroom: The Story of Samuel S. Leibowitz." New York: Farrar, Straus, 1950. 419 pp.
Chapter 10, "Two Southern Ladies" (pp. 248-87) and chapter 11 "...And Nine Southern Boys" (pp. 288-314) tell the story of criminal lawyer (now judge) Samuel Leibowitz's part in the Scottsboro case as attorney for the defendants. The use of the case by communists for their own propaganda purposes is discussed.

R101   RICE, Charles Owen. Debating the Outstretched Hand, "Commonweal," 29 (Jan. 20, 1939), 351-53.
A Catholic priest describes preparation for and participation in a debate with Clarence Hathaway (substituting for Earl Browder) on whether a Catholic could accept communism. The author asserts that there is no prospect of cooperation between Catholics and communists, now or ever.

R102   .... Philip Murray and the Reds, "Catholic Digest," 11 (May 1947), 97-101. Condensed from "Our Sunday Visitor."
The history of communism in the CIO, with praise for Murray's actions in a difficult situation. Murray has changed the rules governing state and city industrial union councils, and obtained the passage of an anticommunist resolution at the last CIO convention. Catholics and others of good will should aid him.

R103   .... "How to De-Control Your Union of Communists." Pittsburgh: n.publ., n.d. [1948?]. 11 pp.
Advice by a priest, a leader of the Association of Catholic Trade Unionists in Pittsburgh, on winning control of a communist-dominated local union. He tells how to start a caucus, how to plan meeting strategy, what issues to fight for, and which arguments to use.

R104   RICH, J. C. How the Garment Unions Licked the Communists, "Saturday Evening Post," 220 (Aug. 9, 1947), 23 ff.
An account by the editor of the "Hat Worker" of communist tactics in the needle trades unions. Dynamic leaders like Dubinsky in the ILGWU, Hillman and Potofsky in the Amalgamated Clothing Workers, and Zaritsky in the Hatters, using democratic procedures, have defeated the communists by organizing the majority against a disciplined and crafty minority.

R105   .... 60 Years of the "Jewish Daily Forward." "New Leader," 40 (June 3, 1957), sect. 2, 38 pp.
An account of the history of this Jewish socialist publication, written by a member of its editorial staff who also edits the "Hat Worker." He tells of its long and bitter struggle during the 1920's and 1930's against communist influence in the Jewish community.

R106   RICHARDS, David H. "Milk for Millions." New York: New York State Committee, Communist Party, n.d., [1930?]. 45 pp.
An exposé of the methods used by the Milk Trust—Borden and Sheffield—to swindle farmers, charge exhorbitant prices, and make huge profits. The author advocates a program to unite the farmers with the progressive movement led by the American Labor Party.

R107   .... "Your Taxes: An Explanation and a Program." New York: New York State Committee, Communist Party, n.d. [1939]. 31 pp.
An analysis of the Big Business position on taxes, arguing that Big Business wants to cut only its own taxes, not those that oppress the people. The author discusses various taxes, and presents a "people's tax program" as proposed by the Communist Party for New York City, New York State, and the country.

R108   RICHARDSON, Elliot L. Freedom of Expression and the Function of Courts, "Harvard Law Review," 65 (Nov. 1951), 1-54.
An examination of the constitutionality of restraints on speech, with a review of relevant cases from the Gitlow case to the trial of the communist leaders under the Smith Act. The author indicates which issues in free speech cases are wholly committed to the courts, especially the U.S. Supreme Court, and which belong primarily to the legislatures and to the states.

R109   RICHARDSON, Seth W. The Federal Employee Loyalty Program, "Columbia Law Review," 51 (May 1951), 546-63.
An examination of the loyalty program for federal employees established by President Truman on March 21, 1947, with attention to the procedural framework, the program in operation, and the objectives. The author concludes that cries of thought control and interference with personal rights are unjustified. The executive order is reproduced in full.

R110   RICHMAN, A. B. The Economics of American

Agriculture, "Communist," 7 (June 1928), 355-63; 8 (Jan.-Feb. 1929), 88-94.
A picture of agriculture, the weakest part of American capitalism, with attention to size of farms, production, indebtedness, bankruptcies, taxation, living conditions, and mechanization. The agrarian population is being expropriated and reduced from ownership to tenancy or day labor.

R111 RICHMOND, Al. "Native Daughter: The Story of Anita Whitney." San Francisco: Anita Whitney 75th Anniversary Committee, 1942. 199 pp.
A sympathetic biography of the daughter of an American "first family" and her evolution from social work and the women's suffrage movement to socialism and then to communism. There is a dramatic account of her 1920 trial and conviction in California for criminal syndicalism, her imprisonment, and her pardon in 1927. Her later activities with the International Labor Defense and other communist causes are outlined.

R112 RIDEOUT, Walter B. "The Radical Novel in the United States, 1900-1954: Some Interrelations of Literature and Society." Cambridge, Mass.: Harvard University Press, 1956. 339 pp. Bibliog. Ind.
A comprehensive examination of the radical novel in the U.S., including the fiction influenced by socialism in the earlier years of the century and the writing in the 1930's influenced by communism. All the important proletarian novels of the 1930's are analyzed, with attention to the characteristics of this body of literature, specific categories and classifications, defects and possible virtues, and the direct or indirect influence of the Party on the authors.

R113 RIESEL, Victor. Communist Grip on Our Defense, "American Mercury," 52 (Feb. 1941), 202-10.
A warning that communists, having invaded trade unions in defense and related industries, can slow up and confuse our defense plans. The strike against Vultee is a case in point. The author lists unions dominated by communists, points out the strategic position of most of them for defense purposes, and calls upon labor to clean house.

R114 .... Carey Ouster Gives Communists Added Power, Widens Split in CIO, "New Leader," 24 (Sept. 6, 1941), 1 ff.
Since 1939 James Carey has been fighting the communists within the United Electrical, Radio and Machine Workers. Now they have defeated him as union president, because he refused to abandon the fight. The Party, following the Nazi invasion of Russia, is putting pressure on other CIO leaders (Curran, Quill, Bridges) to switch from isolationism to support of the British and Soviet war effort.

R115 .... Ten Men Who Could Paralyze America for Thirty Days, "Cosmopolitan," 132 (April 1952), 38-39 ff.
A popular exposé of the ten leaders of communist-controlled unions in defense industries that could paralyze American production at word from Moscow. Unions controlled by them include the ILWU, the Mine, Mill and Smelter Workers, the United Electrical Workers, the American Communications Association, the Marine Cooks, and the Fur and Leather Workers.

R116 .... They Blacklist Themselves, "American Mercury," 76 (May 1953), 43-53.
An attack on those liberals, especially in the entertainment industry, who refused to dissociate themselves from proved pro-Soviet front groups and who now cry out against blacklisting. The author argues that they have in fact blacklisted themselves.

R117 .... Revolution in the Sun! "American Legion Magazine," 61 (Oct. 1956), 14-15 ff.
An assertion by a leading columnist that Harry Bridges and his communist associates in the ILWU have fastened a death grip on the Hawaiian Islands, which are vital to U.S. military activities. A wide variety of union services, combined with hard-hitting propaganda, have built a close-knit political machine under leftist control.

R118 RING, Harry. The Struggle in the Communist Party, "International Socialist Review," 19 (Spring 1958), 52-55.
A Trotskyist account of the crisis within the Communist Party since the Khrushchev revelations about Stalin. The alternatives are an ideologically independent party sympathetic to the Soviet Union, or an isolated sect functioning as an instrument of Kremlin foreign policy. The group headed by Foster seeks the latter solution; efforts to compromise with Fosterite leaders cripple the struggle for independence and democracy. Meanwhile Party membership dwindles at an accelerated pace.

R119 RIORDAN, Arthur. Murray Serves Notice: I Am Not Going to Permit CP Infiltration, "CIO News," 11 (Nov. 29, 1948), 3 ff.
An account of Philip Murray's speech at the CIO convention, denouncing the philosophy and splitting methods of communists and fellow-travelers. In a move aimed at communist leadership, the executive board was authorized to investigate evidence of incompetence.

R120 .... The Left-Right Battle within CIO—Why It Heads toward Convention Showdown, "CIO News," 12 (Oct. 10, 1949), 6-7 ff.
A review of events in the CIO which have led to the coming showdown between communist and anticommunist forces. Key issues were Henry Wallace's candidacy on the Progressive Party ticket in 1948 and the Marshall Plan. Matters of CIO policy and issues within the maritime, auto, transport, mine-mill, and electrical workers' unions are reviewed.

R121 .... CIO Convention Cracks Down on Left Wing, "CIO News," 12 (Nov. 7, 1949), 3 ff.
An account of the Cleveland convention of the CIO which expelled the United Electrical Workers and the Farm Equipment Workers unions as communist-dominated. Ten other unions and their leaders are to face trial boards. The resolutions, speeches, and final votes are reported.

R122 RIVINGTON, Ann. "No Gold Stars for Us—Our Boys Stay Home!" New York: Workers Library, 1940. 30 pp.
A communist pamphlet issued during the Hitler-Stalin pact period, denouncing the war as an imperialist one and calling for jobs for sons instead of gold stars for mothers. Women are reminded that World War I was also imperialist, and that it was followed by reaction and depression. Organization of the Women's Council for Peace is urged.

R123 .... "Women—Vote for Life!" New York: Workers Library, 1940. 15 pp.
An antiwar pamphlet during the period of the Hitler-Stalin pact, denouncing the peacetime draft as a plot of Big Business and the two major parties to overthrow democracy and get the U.S. into the war despite the desires of the people.

R124 ROBERTS, Benjamin C. Arbitration and Security Risk Disputes, "Arbitration Journal," 10 n.s., no. 1 [n.d.], 13-30.
A review of arbitration cases concerning known or suspected communists who had been discharged, laid off, or

transferred. Some discharges have been sustained on the grounds of adverse publicity, failure by the employee to make a denial or secure a retraction, or employee unrest and disruption. The necessity for company self-preservation has been a paramount consideration. Still undecided is whether mere Party membership, without the showing of injury, is grounds for discharge.

R125 ROBERTS, Joseph. The Connecticut Story, "Political Affairs," 26 (April 1947), 336-45.
An account of the secession movement in the Mine, Mill and Smelter Workers in Connecticut and the expulsion of 27 members of the Bridgeport General Electric local of the UE as communists or fellow-travelers. Those responsible include the monopolies, the ACTU, the Republican Party, James Carey's Committee for Democratic Action, and the CIO shipyard workers. The labor tactics proposed by right and left opportunists in the Party must be rejected.

R126 .... Twenty-five years of the "Daily Worker," "Political Affairs," 28 (April 1949), 72-79.
A tribute to the communist press and a report on the recent circulation drive of the "Daily Worker" and the "Worker." The importance of the press in the work of the Party is emphasized.

R127 ROBESON, Paul. "For Freedom and Peace," New York: Council on African Affairs, 1949. 14 pp.
Robeson's address at a Welcome Home Rally, June 19, 1949, attacking those who challenged his patriotism for asserting that Negroes would never join in a war against the Soviet Union. He recites his record against segregation and oppression, and voices his support of Wallace and the Progressive Party; and he denounces the Marshall Plan and the Atlantic Pact.

R128 .... "Forge Negro-Labor Unity for Peace and Jobs." New York and Chicago: Harlem Trade Union Council and South Side Chicago Negro Labor Council, 1950. 15 pp.
The text of an address to the National Labor Conference for Negro Rights, June 10, 1950, denouncing President Truman and the U.S. government for enslaving Negroes and others at home, and colonial people abroad with the Marshall Plan and the Point Four program. Our government's drive toward war and destruction can be stopped if we take the Stockholm pledge, as in the Soviet Union and China.

R129 .... "The Negro People and the Soviet Union." New York: New Century, 1950. 15 pp.
The text of a speech made to the National Council of American-Soviet Friendship in November 1949. The Soviet Union, because of its heroic stand for race equality and abolition of discrimination, is the hope of the Negro people in the U.S.

R130 .... The Negro Artist Looks Ahead, "Masses & Mainstream," 5 (Jan. 1952), 7-14.
Addressing the Conference for Equal Rights for Negroes in the Arts, Sciences and Professions, Robeson protests the exclusion of Negroes from publishing houses and theatres, from radio and television (except as occasional guests), and from significant roles in Hollywood. He demands recognition of Negroes' rights to all kinds of jobs, including technical ones, in the arts.

R131 .... "Here I Stand." New York: Othello Associates, 1958. 128 pp. App.
An autobiography of the noted Negro singer and actor who was active in Party front organizations. Robeson tells of the attraction of the Soviet Union because colored people walked secure and free as equals (p. 44); of his appearance before the House Committee on Un-American Activities because of his remarks to the 1949 World Peace Conference (pp. 49-50); and of the denial of his passport by the State Department (pp. 71-74).

R132 ROBINS, Eva. Marxist-Leninist Education of Our Membership in the Light of the May Plenum of the C.C., "Communist," 14 (Sept. 1935), 851-65.
Communists must fully understand Marxist-Leninist theory if they are to indoctrinate others successfully. Marxist-Leninist theory is not too difficult for the uneducated industrial worker to grasp. The work of agitation and propaganda should not be left to the untrained.

R133 ROBINSON, Donald B. "Spotlight on a Union: The Story of the United Hatters, Cap and Millinery Workers International Union." New York: Dial Press, 1948. 320 pp. Ind. Bibliog.
A popularly written history of the United Hatters, Cap and Millinery Workers International Union. The story of the left-right fight in the Cap Makers Union in the 1920's is told in chapter 10, "The Union Sees Red" (pp. 175-97), which deals with communist efforts to win control of the union.

R134 .... How Our Seamen Bounced the Commies, "Saturday Evening Post," 221 (Dec. 25, 1948), 14-15 ff.
A discussion of communist influence in the National Maritime Union, CIO, 1945-47; of President Joseph Curran's adoption of a strong anticommunist position; and of the union's gradual throwing off of communist control, beginning with its 1947 convention.

R135 .... Ideological Experts, Not Policemen—to Wage War on Communism, "Labor and Nation," 5 (Sept.-Oct. 1949), 25-28.
A summary of the current anticommunist campaign in the U.S., concluding that the biggest result has been to establish precedents for undemocratic, intolerant actions. Communists can be beaten by ideas better than by clubs, as the American labor movement has shown.

R136 ROBINSON, Edward G. How the Reds Made a Sucker Out of Me, "American Legion Magazine," 53 (Oct. 1952), 11 ff.
The well-known actor admits that he was duped by the communists into contributing to Party-controlled organizations sponsoring worthy causes. He took advice on joining organizations from "liberals" later disclosed to be Party members. He will now scrutinize the background of the executive secretary of any organization, and be careful about personal secretaries and sources of counsel for political activity.

R137 ROBINSON, Harry. The Struggle for Puerto Rican Independence, "Communist," 15 (July 1936), 629-42.
Responding to U.S. capitalist exploitation, the Puerto Ricans are making a strong bid for independence. The Tydings bill in Congress provides for an independence vote and, if this wins, a gradual transition to independent status. The CP must fight for immediate and complete independence.

R138 ROBINSON, James A. "Anti-Sedition Legislation and Loyalty Investigations in Oklahoma." Norman, Okla.: Bureau of Government Research, University of Oklahoma, 1956. 61 pp.
A review and analysis of the state's record on the problem of loyalty and security, starting with treatment of draft dodgers and the IWW in World War I. An account is given of the state's criminal syndicalism law of 1919 (under

which a number of communists were tried in 1940), of the legislative investigations of subversive activities in 1941 and 1949, and of the loyalty oath controversy in the 1950's.

R139 ROCHESTER, Anna. "Labor and Coal." New York: International Publishers, 1931. 255 pp.
One of a series prepared by the Party-affiliated Labor Research Association, the book analyzes the coal mining industry, the conditions under which the miners work and live, and the unsuccessful efforts to unionize them. The United Mine Workers are seen as a reactionary union whose control is being broken by the National Miners Union, a militant organization based on the class struggle.

R140 .... "Profits and Wages." New York: International Publishers, 1932. 31 pp.
Contrasting capitalist incomes with workers' wages, the author asserts that the economic crisis is widening the gap between the classes. Though workers lacked minimum living standards even during prosperity, the mass unemployment and wage cuts of the depression have pressed down their standards. Calling for strikes against wage cuts and for the overthrow of capitalism, the author urges organization in the TUUL and the CP.

R141 .... "Wall Street." New York: International Pamphlets, 1932. 15 pp.
An assertion that Wall Street power is in the hands of a few interlocking banks and corporations that control the economic life of the country. The author asserts that these economic rulers control government, plan another war, and stack the cards against the working class. The CP is the only political party threatening Wall Street's power.

R142 .... "Your Dollar under Roosevelt." New York: Workers Library, 1933. 23 pp.
A prediction that inflation will occur under Roosevelt's New Deal, which is only for the capitalists. The answer to Roosevelt's inflation, according to this "third period" pamphlet, is for workers to engage in mass struggles for higher wages and for federal unemployment insurance at the expense of capitalists.

R143 .... The Banking Crisis in the United States, "Communist," 12 (April 1933), 337-51.
An examination of the American financial situation, based on Marx's analysis of the credit system. The banking crisis in the U.S. reflects the deepening general crisis of capitalism, which will lead inevitably either to war or to revolution.

R144 ..., and TOOHEY, Pat. "In a Soviet America: The Miners' Road to Freedom." New York: Workers Library, 1935. 47 pp.
A recruiting pamphlet addressed to coal miners, describing the miseries of workers now and picturing their brighter lot under a Soviet form of government. The authors outline the organization of the coal industry and the management of work in a Soviet America, and also life outside the mine, at home and club. The revolutionary overthrow of capitalism is held necessary, and the unity of all existing miners' unions into one fighting, class-struggle union is advocated.

R145 .... "Rulers of America: A Study of Finance Capital. New York: International Publishers, 1936. 367 pp. App. Ind.
An exposé of the Morgans, Mellons, Rockefellers, and Du Ponts, sponsored by the Labor Research Association. The author shows how finance capitalists maintain control over the American economy, and what this means to the working class. She anticipates a revolutionary crisis in the future when capitalism will be overthrown by the working class and its allies from all other groups which have suffered from finance capital rule.

R146 .... Finance Capital and Fascist Trends in the United States, "Communist," 15 (June 1936), 523-36.
A review and denunciation of Big Business organizations of the right such as the American Liberty League, which are considered fascist enemies of the working class. They have successfully opposed all New Deal measures that had some hope of really helping the workers. The united front must oppose this conspiracy.

R147 .... "Why Farmers Are Poor: The Agricultural Crisis in the United States." New York: International Publishers, 1940. 317 pp. App. Ref. notes. Ind.
A Labor Research Association book holding capitalism responsible for the poverty of the farmers and the farming economy. Tracing the development of capitalism within agriculture, the author emphasizes the hardships of the farm tenants, the plight of small and middle-income farmers burdened with debt, and the efforts of the trusts to crush the farmers. She urges wage workers and working farmers to unite in a fight for socialism.

R148 .... The Farm Problem and the Working Class, "Communist," 14 [19] (June 1940), 565-74.
A discussion of farm problems in the light of the general crisis of capitalism, stressing the importance of workers and farmers joining forces and asserting that all farmers except the very largest, who are tied in with the financial world, are vitally interested in weakening the power of finance capital.

R149 .... "Farmers and the War." New York: Workers Library, 1943. 30 pp.
A plea to American farmers for all-out production to feed our Soviet and British allies as a patriotic duty. The author shows why higher farm production is needed, and how it can be achieved through Roosevelt's farm policies.

R150 .... "The Populist Movement in the U.S." New York: International Publishers, 1943. 128 pp. Ref. notes.
A sympathetic analysis of the Populist movement by a leading communist writer, who discusses the rise of the movement, the forces from which it developed, and the reasons why it failed to achieve the desired economic and political freedom. She views Populism as an expression of the struggle of farmers and other small producers to protect themselves from monopoly and finance capital. Populism contributed much to the struggle for political democracy, but it could not cope with the economic problems of monopoly capitalism; only the outlook provided by socialism can do that.

R151 .... "Capitalism and Progress." New York: International Publishers, 1945. 111 pp. Bibliog. ref. Ind. Rev. ed. as "The Nature of Capitalism."
A communist study of American economic development and of the operation of the capitalist economic system, written at the close of World War II when the Party hoped that enlightened capitalism and communism could cooperate for peace and progress. The author concludes that American capitalism, despite negative aspects and depressions, has played a progressive role, and that it faces a long period of useful existence here.

R152 .... "The Nature of Capitalism." New York: International Publishers, 1946. 96 pp. Ind. Ref. notes. Rev. of "Capitalism and Progress."

A Marxist cold war view of capitalism, with discussion, among other topics, of surplus value, cyclical crises, monopoly, imperialism, and fascism. With the end of the war, the working class and those desiring broad political and economic democracy are opposed by the forces of capitalist property and monopoly. The Soviet Union shows what can be achieved when human rights are fully realized.

R153   ROCKMAN, Joseph. Tasks in Broadening the Fight for Peace, "Political Affairs," 31 (June 1952), 15-29.
Though American imperialism has accelerated the tempo of war preparations, the world peace camp has been decisively strengthened; and American imperialism has suffered several major defeats. A united front for peace must be built, with sectarianism eliminated. The Negro masses must be more actively involved in the fight for peace. (Expanded in pamphlet form as "Broaden the Fight for Peace and Democracy.")

R154   RODMAN, Selden. Youth Meets in Washington, "Nation," 138 (Jan. 17, 1934), 70-71.
Report on the National Conference of Students in Politics held in Washington, D.C. in December 1933. The conference was dominated by the socialist-led League for Industrial Democracy and the communist-led National Student League. The NSL rejected a proposed political program because of its failure to support the American League Against War and Fascism.

R155   ROE, Wellington. "Juggernaut: American Labor in Action." Philadelphia: Lippincott, 1948. 375 pp. Ind.
A story of dictatorship in the labor movement, critical of both the right-wing and of left-wing leaders like Harry Bridges of the Pacific Coast longshoremen. There is a discussion of the relationship between John L. Lewis and the communists in the CIO, and briefer treatment of their relations with Philip Murray and the struggle within the ILGWU.

R156   ROEMER, William F. Loyalty Oath and Freedom to Teach, "Notre Dame Lawyer," 28 (Spring 1953), 364-72.
A defense of the loyalty oath, with an outline of the California cases. The common good is prior in moral and legal value to academic freedom, not the other way round. Teachers should help society rid itself of its enemies within.

R157   ROGERS, C. E. Red Propaganda: An Informative Study of Communist Party Organization and Methods, "Kansas Magazine," 1933. 69-75.
The Party views itself as the militant vanguard of the proletariat army, employing agitation for mass mobilization on issues and propaganda for political education. The Party organization, from the smallest nucleus to the International, is highly integrated. The individual communist, directed by the Party, carries on person-to-person agitation and propaganda.

R158   ROGERS, Edward. "A Christian Commentary on Communism." New York: Praeger, 1952. 238 pp.
A commentary on Marx and his theories, on Lenin's interpretation of Marxism, and on the Soviet experiment. Viewing the questions posed by communism as essentially religious, the author advocates application of Christian social doctrine to the problems which communism proposes to solve.

R159   ROGGE, O. John. "Our Vanishing Civil Liberties." New York: Gaer Associates, 1949. 189 pp.
A pessimistic view of civil liberties in the U.S. by a former

assistant attorney general of the U.S. who later participated in a communist-led peace movement. He condemns the House Un-American Activities Committee, defends the innocence of Harry Dexter White and Harold Christoffel, and denounces Truman's loyalty program and the indictment of Party leaders under the Smith Act. The communist scare, in his view, is a hoax masking the threat of a police state and a third world war.

R160   .... Report on Civil Liberties, "Lawyers Guild Review," 9 (Winter 1949), 13-17.
A report on civil liberties to the convention of the National Lawyers Guild, criticizing "police state" measures that have taken us near fascism. Among these measures are Truman's Loyalty Order, activities of federal and state un-American activities committees, and the indictment of the 12 communist leaders.

R161   ROGIN, Lawrence. The Case for Labor, "Education," 72 (April 1952), 537-41.
Although American labor has proved its fidelity to American institutions and its abhorrence of communism, some who are opposed to unionism equate the two. Communists today control only an infinitesimal portion of the labor movement. More democracy is the cure for communism.

R162   ROGOFF, Harry. 25 Years of American Communism, "New Leader," 27 (Nov. 18, 1944), 6.
An assertion that the communists are the only American "left" group that has no heroic leaders, has caused nothing but trouble, and has betrayed social progress in America. Unlike the other groups, which changed only their tactics, the communists change their basic ideas. Their history is full of shameful acts, disruptions, and scandals.

R163   ROLAND, Joseph. The Economic Basis of Current U.S. Imperialist Policy, "Political Affairs," 26 (Feb. 1947), 144-51.
An application of Lenin's theory of the "superabundance of capital" in monopoly development to the economic policies of the U.S. Contradictions of American imperialist policy are considered. The main economic question is how to turn government economic intervention from its present reactionary course, which is tending toward fascism.

R164   .... The Question of the National Debt, "Political Affairs," 27 (March 1948), 266-78.
An analysis of the process of creating and maintaining the U.S. national debt, viewed by the communists as a means of fleecing the people and enriching financial speculators. A Marxist program for controlling the national debt is presented. The debt should be sharply reduced and a progressive tax program adopted.

R165   ROLFE, Edwin. "The Lincoln Battalion: The Story of the Americans Who Fought in Spain in the International Brigades." New York: Random House, 1939. 321 pp. Ind.
The story of the 2,800 Americans, most of them young communists, who fought in the International Brigades during the Civil War in Spain. In the front lines from February 1937 to September 1938 the Americans, like the other international volunteers, made a remarkable military record in the struggle of the Spanish Loyalists against fascism.

R166   ROLLINS, William. "The Shadow Before." New York: McBride, 1934. 389 pp.
The story of a strike, placing the Gastonia struggle in a northern setting. The author portrays the life of a Communist Party member, and shows antagonism toward both Christianity and patriotism.

R167 ROMER, Samuel. Disruption in CIO, "New Leader," 30 (Sept. 6, 1947), 4.
An account of factional conflict within the Mine, Mill and Smelter Workers Union, and Party control of it. Reid Robinson, Party-liner president, had been replaced by Maurice Travis, Party commissar in the union. Following a CIO investigation, John Clark, nominated by Travis, was chosen president, while Travis became secretary-treasurer and Robinson a vice-president.

R168 ROMERSTEIN, Herbert. "Communism and Your Child." New York: Bookmailer, 1962. 123 pp. App. Ind.
An account of communist efforts to use young people in their drive for world conquest, written by a former Party member who joined at the age of fifteen and left the movement two years later. Topics dealt with include the communist plan for conquering the world, the campaign against HUAC, student riots, and Party efforts to recruit children. Communist youth activities in which the author participated and the international communist youth movement are also discussed.

R169 ROOSEVELT, Eleanor. "This I Remember." New York: Harper, 1949. 387 pp. App. Ind.
In chapter 12, "The American Youth Congress" (pp. 199-205), Mrs. Roosevelt tells of her association with AYC and its leaders when they strongly supported the New Deal, as well as during the Hitler-Stalin pact period, when hostility developed. She tells of her growing awareness of communist domination, and her final conclusion that the leaders could not be trusted.

R170 ROOSEVELT, Franklin D. "The Public Papers and Addresses of Franklin D. Roosevelt." 1940 Volume: "War—and Aid to Democracies." Comp. by Samuel I. Rosenman. New York: MacMillan, 1941. 741 pp. Ind.
The President's address to delegates of the American Youth Congress to the Youth Citizenship Institute, February 10, 1940, appears on pages 85-94. The President defended the New Deal's seven-year record, criticized a resolution passed by the New York City Council of AYC opposing aid to Finland as an effort to force America into the imperialistic war, and attacked the Soviet Union for invading Finland, for being a dictatorship, and for allying itself with Nazi Germany.

R171 ROOT, E. Merrill. Our Academic Hucksters, "American Legion Magazine," 53 (Dec. 1952), 18-19 ff.
A college professor of English asserts that at least 3,000 American professors have engaged in communist front activities, that they are promoting dogmatic collectivism under the slogan of liberalism. Those who believe in collectivism now have good business jobs and foundation support available to them. The leading newspapers and magazines give favorable attention to those who subscribe to the cultural left.

R172 .... "Collectivism on the Campus: The Battle for the Mind in American Colleges." New York: Devin-Adair, 1955. 403 pp. App. Ind.
An assertion that the colleges and universities of America are dominated by collectivists, including communists, who subtly influence social science textbooks and who bring strong pressures on noncollectivist teachers to teach the philosophy of the total state. Sections deal with communist professors and students, fellow-travelers and dupes, and liberals. Instances are given of the alleged contemporary academic purge of conservatives, and of the pressures for conformity brought on the few individualist students by the forces of collectivist liberalism.

R173 ROOT, Jonathan. "The Betrayers: The Rosenberg Case—A Reappraisal of an American Crisis." New York: Coward-McCann, 1963. 305 pp. Ind.
A review and interpretation of the Rosenberg case, accepting the guilt of the Rosenbergs as evidenced by their own behavior. Products of a slum, they were communists who wanted to reform society by revolution. The prosecutor is criticized for his pre-trial publicity and his courtroom innuendo and oratory, while Judge Kaufman's conduct of the trial is praised. The committee organized to defend the Rosenbergs is criticized for seeking to intimidate the judiciary by mob action and for seeking to vilify American justice rather than to save the Rosenbergs.

R174 RORTY, James. Mobilizing the Innocents: Communism behind the Scene, "Forum and Century," 99 (Jan. 1938), 43-47.
An exposure of communist methods of operation through innocent clubs or front organizations. Their most successful creation, the American League Against War and Fascism, is really a holding company of innocent clubs. The farce of the Congress of American Writers, another Stalinist innocent creation, is also exposed.

R175 ..., and RAUSHENBUSH, Winifred. The Lessons of the Peekskill Riots: What Happened and Why, "Commentary," 10 (Oct. 1950), 309-23.
A report on the two Peekskill riots of 1949, involving local veterans groups and Paul Robeson concerts sponsored by the Civil Rights Congress. The anti-Jewish and anti-Negro, along with the anticommunist, aspects of the riots are examined. The authors criticize the communists for their provocative behavior, the veterans group for violence, the police for inadequacy, and the ACLU for naively accepting the communists' view of the riots.

R176 .... The Anti-Communism of Senator McCarthy: It Slays More Friends Than Foes, "Commentary," 16 (Aug. 1953), 122-29.
An evaluation of Senator McCarthy's record on communism. While a relatively small number of his accusations proved correct, either he does not know enough to distinguish a communist from a socialist, an ADA liberal from a subversive, or he doesn't care. Now his time appears to be running out.

R177 ..., and DECTER, Moshe. "McCarthy and the Communists." Boston: Beacon, 1954. 163 pp. App. Ind.
An analysis of McCarthy's role in the fight against communist infiltration of the U.S. government, with particular examination of his investigations of the State Department's International Information Administration and the Army's Signal Center at Fort Monmouth, N.J. The authors find that McCarthy has ignored criteria of an effective fight against the communist threat, using tactics and strategy destructive of the ends sought by anticommunists. They present a constructive program of anticommunism, with suggestions on loyalty and security in government service, the operation of congressional committees, immigration policy, and the role of private organizations.

R178 .... Thirty Days That Shook Norwalk, "Commentary," 17 (April 1954), 330-36.
An account of the controversy over communists in Norwalk, Conn., started by an assertion made during a membership drive of the Veterans of Foreign Wars that the names of some local residents had been reported to the FBI. Norwalk is called an enlightened community in which this stupid snafu, largely due to newspaper publicity, helped only the communists and their camouflaged followers.

R179 .... What Price McCarthy Now, "Commentary," 19 (Jan. 1955), 30-35.

A review of a McCarthyite meeting in Madison Square Garden on November 29, 1954, three days before his Senate censure. A party movement for McCarthy is unlikely, though the For America organization, already in existence, embodies his principles. McCarthy, who has lost his support in the Republican Party, is on his way to political oblivion.

R180 RORTY, James. Storm over the Investigating Committees: The Charges against them and the Record, "Commentary," 19 (Feb. 1955), 128-36.
A favorable analysis of the role of the congressional investigating committee. While noncommunist liberals argue for corrections in procedure, the communists assert that Congress has no right to investigate totalitarian subversion.

R181 .... The Dossier of Wolf Ladejinsky: The Fair Rewards of Distinguished Civil Service, "Commentary," 19 (April 1955), 326-34.
The case of Wolf Ladejinsky, who was not reappointed agricultural attaché in Tokyo because of lack of security clearance, based on employment with Amtorg Trading Corporation 23 years earlier and a visit to Russia to see members of his family. The fact that his land reform program had impeded communism in the Far East was overlooked.

R182 ROSEBURY, A. Disruption in the Name of Revolution, "Labor Age," 14 (March 1925), 20-22.
Criticism of communist tactics in the labor movement. The author does not oppose on principle the tactic of boring from within, but he does oppose the communists' use of it as an antidemocratic effort to either control an organization or destroy it. The "education" of the Trade Union Educational League is in reality a systematic campaign of slander and libel.

R183 ROSENBERG, Bernard. The Communist Party Convention, "Dissent," 4 (Spring 1957), 152-56.
A report from an observer of the recent convention of the Party. The convention was the "death rattle of an impotent party." An interminable factional fight, primarily over semantics, will not reduce the Party's isolation. John Gates, supposedly leading a split, proved the biggest Party patriot, and was silent on the Hungarian revolt.

R184 ROSENBERG, Ethel G., and Julius. "Death House Letters." New York: Jero Publishing Co., 1953. 168 pp.
A volume of selected letters written by the convicted atomic spies to each other and to their attorney, Emanuel Block, while in prison. The volume includes the chronology of the case, excerpts from the Rosenbergs' petition for clemency, and statements from people who believed the Rosenbergs innocent or felt their sentence was too severe.

R185 ROSENBERG, Harold. The Communist: His Mentality and His Morals, "Commentary," 8 (July 1949), 1-9.
A portrait of the communist personality, drawing on two recent biographies of Lenin. The chief trait of the communist is his knowingness; he is an intellectual, belonging to an elite of the knowing, who seeks to control the activities of others and whose primary law is combat. His ability to reverse judgments and feelings is not cynicism.

R186 .... Couch Liberalism and the Guilty Past, "Dissent," 2 (Autumn 1955), 317-28.
A critique of efforts, such as those by Leslie Fiedler in "An End to Innocence," to heap the sins of Stalinist fellow-travelers onto the heads of the naive but non-Stalinist liberals of the 1930's. Whatever its weakness in under-

standing communist power and techniques, liberalism was not responsible for communist vileness.

R187 ROSS, Allan. "Reconversion: Security or Crisis." New York: Communist Political Association of New York State, 1944. 32 pp.
A discussion of economic problems facing workers in the late war period. Millions face unemployment as war contracts are terminated, permitting fifth columnists to attack the entire war effort. Reactionaries block passage of the Kilgore bill, which would protect workers in the reconversion period. The author calls for a square deal to ex-servicemen, improvement of living standards, and protection to women and Negro workers. Emphasis is placed on problems facing New York City.

R188 ROSS, Carl. Problems of Reconstructing the Young Communist League, "Communist," 16 (July 1937), 661-67.
At the eighth convention of the YCL, it was proposed that the YCL be reconstructed into a mass organization to attract noncommunist youths through broad educational, social, and athletic programs. In addition to their other skills, communists in the YCL must be soundly trained Marxists. The YCL must assist trade unions and recruit young industrial workers.

R189 .... After the Youth Congress, "Communist," 16 (Oct. 1937), 954-61.
The Fourth American Youth Congress, to which many youth organizations are now affiliated, seeks to become an ever broader youth movement that will fight for peace and progressive education. The Young People's Socialist League has refused to join the Congress.

R190 .... "Let's Pull Together for Jobs, Security, Democracy and Peace." New York: Workers Library for National Council of Young Communist League, 1938. 16 pp.
A pamphlet by the national executive secretary of the YCL attacking the "Copperheads" and Tories of today, urging passage of the American Youth Act, and calling for peace and a democratic front to defeat reaction.

R191 .... The World Youth Congress, "Communist," 17 (Oct. 1938), 950-56.
A report by the national executive secretary of the Young Communist League on the Second World Youth Congress, stressing American contributions and the Congress' influence upon the U.S. movement. The Congress supported collective security, though a minority opposed sanctions against aggressors. Socialists tried to break up a democratic coalition against fascism by urging opposition to colonial powers.

R192 .... America's Youth in the Struggle for Social and National Security, "Communist," 18 (April 1939), 317-23.
After the progressives won control of the American Youth Congress, the AYC dramatized youth problems, winning widespread support among the youth. The New Deal Administration responded to AYC demands by establishing the CCC and the NYA. Now that the reactionaries are trying to regain control of youth, AYC must strengthen youth unity by rallying youth support for the entire New Deal.

R193 .... America's Youth in the Struggle against the Imperialist War, "Clarity," 1 (April-May 1940), 8-21.
A review, in the theoretical organ of the Young Communist League, of attitudes toward the war on the part of various youth organizations, criticizing pacifist groups for their

failure to oppose the war as imperialist. Young communists must help to build anti-imperialist unity of working, farm, and student youth.

R194 ROSS, Carl. The Town Meeting of Youth, "Clarity," 2 (Spring 1941), 17-30.
A report on the Town Meeting of Youth, organized by the American Youth Congress, which mobilized 5,500 young people to challenge Roosevelt's imperialist policy. The top boards of bourgeois youth organizations are trying to break youth's growing antiwar sentiment.

R195 .... Let Freedom Ring for Earl Browder, "Communist," 21 (March 1942), 163-70.
A plea for the release of Earl Browder, based on a report to an enlarged meeting of the National Council of the YCL, January 31, 1942.

R196 .... Universal Military Training, "Political Affairs," 24 (Jan. 1945), 60-68.
Universal military training is necessary if the U.S. is to play its part in maintaining peace. It would become an instrument of war only if the U.S. followed the imperialistic policy desired by the reactionaries. Universal military training is the most effective and democratic way to meet our international commitments and assure our national security.

R197 .... The National Labor Conference for Peace, "Political Affairs," 28 (Nov. 1949), 40-47.
The program, policies, and representative character of the National Labor Conference for Peace, held in Chicago, October 1-2, 1949. The conference expressed the growing peace sentiment in the ranks of labor, despite the prowar line of the dominant labor leadership. The broad general program must be translated into concrete programs for given shops and industries.

.... See also J. D.

R198 ROSS, David Allan. The Professional Communist, "American Mercury," 37 (April 1936), 425-32.
A portrait of the typical small man in communist ranks, the legman or "heeler" who does the dirty work. Usually the son of hard-working immigrant parents, he believes that America owes him a living. Unwilling to work and living on relief, he embraced communism, the refuge of the frustrated, in the hope of becoming one of the Ins instead of one of the Outs.

R199 ROSS, Irwin. The Student Union and the Future: The Communists Win One Round, "New Republic," 102 (Jan. 8, 1940), 48-49.
The convention of the American Student Union was the first of a popular front organization since the Hitler-Stalin pact. While the communists controlled the majority vote, they temporized in order to maintain the united front. The anticommunist forces coalesced into a National Liberal Caucus that will seek a referendum on the Finnish question.

R200 .... Youth Goes to Washington, "New Republic," 102 (Feb. 26, 1940), 275-76.
A report on the American Youth Congress' Citizenship Institute held in Washington during the Hitler-Stalin pact period. Presenting evidence that the Youth Congress is communist-dominated, the author argues that it nevertheless manages to articulate the real problems of youth—jobs, peace, and civil liberties.

R201 .... Why Communists Stay That Way, "New Republic," 102 (March 25, 1940), 403-4.
Many American communists continued in the Party after the Hitler-Stalin pact because of the type of organization the Party is, the type of theory it accepts, and the psychological security it affords loyal members.

R202 .... It's Tough to Be a Communist, "Harper's Magazine," 192 (June 1946), 528-36.
Earl Browder's difficulties and his eventual expulsion from the Party illustrate the hazards faced by all communists in trying to follow the zigzags of the official line. The future is uncertain for the occasional reflective comrade, who might pine for the bourgeois luxury of private convictions.

R203 .... Harold Medina—Judge Extraordinary, "Reader's Digest," 56 (Feb. 1950), 85-90.
A biographical sketch of Judge Medina and a laudatory review of his conduct of the Dennis trial, an ordeal lasting nine months. The communists tried to goad him into an intemperate remark or judicial error, to prove the unfairness of "capitalist justice" or to get a mistrial or a reversal on appeal; yet he remained urbane and painstaking in judicial scruple.

R204 .... "The Communists: Friends or Foes of Civil Liberties?" New York: American Jewish Committee, 1951. 26 pp.
A denial that communists are champions of civil liberties, since they deny to others the rights that they demand for themselves. Applauding the enforcement of the Smith Act against their enemies, they protest vehemently its application to themselves. They betray the rights of Negroes or Jews whenever it suits the interests of the Kremlin.

R205 ROSS, Lillian. Onward and Upward with the Arts: Come In, Lassie! "New Yorker," 23 (Feb. 21, 1948), 32-36 ff.
An account of the reactions of Hollywood personalities to the investigation of the movie industry by the House Committee on Un-American Activities. The communist scare is viewed by the author as fictitious, and the blacklisting of the ten Hollywood writers cited for contempt is itself contemptible.

R206 ROSS, M. "A History of Soviet Foreign Policy." New York: Workers Library, 1940. 80 pp.
A survey of Soviet foreign policy, with detailed attention to the Hitler-Stalin pact and events since then in Poland, Finland, the Baltic countries, etc. The pact is defended as a move by the USSR to achieve universal peace and safeguard its own security in the face of efforts by the Anglo-French bloc to provoke war between Germany and the Soviet Union.

R207 ROSS, Malcolm H. "Machine Age in the Hills." New York: Macmillan, 1933. 248 pp.
An examination of technological unemployment in coal mining areas, with attention to efforts by the National Miners Union to organize Harlan County. The author decries the use of class hatred on either side, and asserts that the investigating group led by Dreiser purposely increased antagonism in both camps. The Quakers, who followed, brought industry and some stability out of chaos.

R208 ROSS, Mike. Expelling Progressive Carpenters, "Labor Unity," 2 (Nov. 1928), 8-10.
An account of the expulsion of left-wing leaders at the recent convention of the Carpenters, including Morris Rosen, who had opposed Hutcheson for the national presidency in 1924, and who attacked Hutcheson for irresponsibility, treachery, and despotism, and accused him of protecting corruption and strikebreaking. Progressive delegates are criticized for failure to run for office or introduce resolutions.

R209 N. R. [N. Ross]. A Note on the Development of Post War Capitalism in the U.S., "Communist," 8 (Sept. 1929), 512-27.
Statistical data on the development of American capitalism since the end of World War I. The author concludes that American capitalism is following an orthodox Marxian line of development, in which its internal contradictions parallel its external, imperialist contradictions. (The article justifies the line of the Comintern and opposes the Lovestone theory of American exceptionalism, although Lovestone's views are not explicitly mentioned.)

R210 ROSS, Nat. The N.R.A. in the South, "Communist," 12 (Dec. 1933), 1179-88.
The South is being victimized by Roosevelt's NRA program. NRA codes will legalize the lower standards of Southern workers as compared with the rest of the country. The program is supported by the Southern ruling class and their Democratic and Ku Klux Klan agents.

R211 .... Some Problems of the Class Struggle in the South, "Communist," 14 (Jan. 1935), 61-75.
A discussion article in preparation for the Seventh Congress of the Comintern. The main tasks of the Party are to develop the united front between Negro and white workers and an aggressive rank-and-file trade union movement inside the AFL. The united front between the Sharecroppers Union and the Southern Tenant Farmers' Union must be broadened, and the CP must build its influence in Southern industrial centers.

R212 .... The Next Steps in Alabama and the Lower South, "Communist," 14 (Oct. 1935), 968-76.
An analysis of industrial conditions and trade union organization in Alabama, pointing up the need for a concerted united front movement. White Southern workers must be convinced that Jim Crow and white supremacy constitute a class attack on their economic interests as well as on those of Negroes.

R213 .... The Election Campaign in Minnesota, "Communist," 17 (Oct. 1938), 937-44.
A denunciation of Harold Stassen's campaign as Big Business masked by liberalism. The communists support the Farmer-Labor-New Deal alliance in Minnesota.

R214 .... What the South Faces Today, "Political Affairs," 25 (March 1946), 254-65.
Big Business has carried out an "economic blitz" against Negro and white workers in the South, along with a reactionary political offensive. Negroes and whites are urged to join forces to sponsor a program, which is outlined, for the South's recovery. The Southern Negro Youth Congress and the National Negro Congress must be built.

R215 .... What's Happening in the South, "Political Affairs," 26 (July 1947), 612-23.
Reaction is using the South to test fascism in the U.S., with the Negro people as the victims and the lynch drive as the pacesetter. Red-baiting and Negro-baiting are used against labor organizations. An economic and political program for the South is outlined. The Party must show the white masses that they cannot improve their own lot until they join the fight for Negro rights.

R216 .... The Dixiecrat Fascist Menace, "Political Affairs," 28 (July 1949), 33-44.
The Dixiecrats are fascists, secretly backed by the Wall Street capitalists. Their objectives are to continue to oppress the Negroes and to prevent union organization in the South. In return for their support of the North Atlantic pact, Truman has left them in powerful congressional positions and does nothing to make civil rights effective.

R217 .... An Imperialist Agent's Three Years in Moscow, "Political Affairs," 29 (March 1950), 86-96.
A review article on Walter Bedell Smith's "My Three Years in Moscow," characterizing it as a book of slanders and distortions. The foreign policy, economy, and culture of the Soviet Union are defended.

R218 ROSS, Norman, and SAVAGE, Murray. The Rochester General Strike, "Political Affairs," 25 (July 1946), 614-24.
An examination of the May 28 Rochester general strike which followed the dismissal of 498 city workers for joining an AFL union. The dismissal was the first step in the big corporations' plan to destroy trade unions in Rochester. However, the AFL and CIO cooperated in a general strike that forced the city manager to reinstate the workers and permit union activity.

R219 ROSS, Norman. The Struggle for the Negro-Labor Alliance, "Political Affairs," 28 (June 1949), 79-87.
Emphasizing the community of interest between the Negro liberation movement and a militant, progressive labor movement, the author asserts that such an alliance existed in the early stages of the CIO but has since been dissolved. CIO leaders now seek to deflect the struggles of the Negro people into safe channels. Militant, class conscious Negro leadership is needed.

R220 ROSSITER, Clinton. "Marxism: The View from America." New York: Harcourt, Brace, 1960. 338 pp. App. Notes. Ind.
A critical analysis of Marxist teachings by a leading political scientist, seeking to confront Marxism with the American tradition. The author analyzes the Marxist idea, Marxist man, classes and institutions in the Marxist view of society, the Marxist interpretation of the state, and the Marxist temper. He finds irreconcilable conflicts between Marxism and Americanism. Indicting Marxism for its many political errors, the author sees little to choose between Marx and Stalin, between the old and the new Marxist theories of the state. Yet he holds that there are Marxist insights that we can use in moderation without surrendering any of the values of American democracy.

R221 ROSTEN, Leo C. "Hollywood: The Movie Colony, the Movie Makers." New York: Harcourt, Brace, 1941. 436 pp. App. Ref. notes. Ind.
Pages 140-58 deal with the communist issue in Hollywood—the organization of communist fronts such as the Hollywood Anti-Nazi League and the Motion Picture Democratic Committee, the attacks on Hollywood by Dies and others for harboring communists, and the charge that Hollywood films contained communist propaganda. The movie colony will not accept the discipline and deprivations of a fanatical cause.

R222 ROSTOW, Eugene V. Needed: A Rational Security Program, "Harper's Magazine," 215 (July 1957), 33-40.
A critical review of ten years of loyalty-security programs, by the dean of the Yale Law School, who finds that these programs deny basic values of our law. While the strength of the USSR makes the communist threat to U.S. internal security real, the communist fifth column here is weak and ineffective. A new screening system for employees in government and defense industries is proposed to better protect the public interest and innocent persons.

R223 ROVERE, Richard H. The Student Convention: What the ASU Wants, "New Masses," 30 (Jan. 10, 1939), 11.

A report on the fourth convention of the American Student Union, at which support for the New Deal reached its height. In the sphere of foreign policy, collective security was endorsed over token opposition by socialists. Whereas in the past ROTC was opposed, now ASU voted for democratization and an end of compulsion.

R224 ROVERE, Richard H. On Joining the Socialist Party, "Socialist Call," 6 (Jan. 27, 1940), 4.
A former associate editor of the "New Masses," who resigned from the Communist Party following the Hitler-Stalin pact, joins the Socialist Party and gives his reasons. He explains the communist's ability to justify to himself and others such events as the Moscow trials, Stalinist policy in Spain, and the Hitler-Stalin pact.

R225 .... Factions on the Far Left, "New Republic," 102 (April 8, 1940), 468-70.
A survey of parties and factions on the left, including the Socialist Party, the Communist Party, Trotskyite splinters, the Lovestone group, and the Social Democratic Federation. Though the left is pulverized, the noncommunist left will not work with the communists on anything because the communist line is uncertain, dependent on the mood in the Kremlin.

R226 .... The American Left: 1. The Decline of the Communist Party. "Common Sense," 9 (Nov. 1940), 9-11.
An account of the decline of the Party in numbers and influence since the signing of the Hitler-Stalin pact. The communists built a powerful movement since 1935, largely as a result of popular front policies. Now Jews and middle class members are leaving in large numbers, trade union leaders are breaking alliances, and front organizations are collapsing or losing support.

R227 .... How Free Is the "Nation"? "New Leader," 35 (July 14, 1952), 12-14.
A condemnation of the special issue on civil rights in the "Nation," which encourages acceptance of Moscow's view of the U.S. as a disintegrating democracy in which the hooligan element has achieved power. The major purpose of the issue is not to assess freedom in the U.S., but to weaken U.S. resistance to Soviet aggression.

R228 .... The Kept Witnesses, "Harper's Magazine," 210 (May 1955), 25-34.
An exposé of the "professional witnesses" used by the Department of Justice in cases against communists. Rovere counts at least 83, all of whom are former members of the Party and receive fairly high wages for appearing as witnesses. This practice of subsidizing testimony violates the spirit of our law and jurisprudence.

R229 .... "Senator Joe McCarthy." New York: Harcourt, Brace, 1959. 280 pp. Ind.
An unflattering picture of McCarthy as a seditious demagogue, showing how he used the communist issue as a vehicle to power. His attacks on the State Department for harboring communists, his investigations of communist influence in various areas of American life, and his clash with the Army are reviewed, and the factors that contributed to his rise and fall are analyzed.

R230 ROY, Ralph Lord. "Apostles of Discord: A Study of Organized Bigotry and Disruption on the Fringes of Protestantism. Boston: Beacon, 1953. 437 pp. Bibliog. notes. Ind.
Two chapters deal with the problem of communism and its influence in the Protestant churches. Chapter 11, "The Hammer and Sickle behind the Cross" (pp. 251-84), tells how the Party uses a small but active group of Protestant ministers to further its cause. Chapter 13, (pp. 308-36), deals with "The Struggle within Methodism." The author concludes that church parroting of the Party line has strengthened groups opposed to any social reform.

R231 .... "Communism and the Churches." New York: Harcourt, Brace, 1960. 495 pp. Bibliog. essay. Notes. Ind.
A study of Communist Party attempts to infiltrate American churches, of the methods employed, and of the degree of success. Changing attitudes of the Party over the years are surveyed, from its view of religion as an opiate, to its efforts at cooperation or infiltration. Particular attention is paid to the creation of "front" groups to appeal to religious leaders, among others, in the 1930's, and to the communist peace campaign during the era of the cold war. The author concludes that the Party never attempted a full-scale campaign to infiltrate the churches, that only a small number of clergymen ever joined the Party, and that communist influence within American churches was near the zero mark by 1960.

R232 RUDAS, L. The Meaning of Sidney Hook, "Communist," 14 (April 1935), 326-49.
An attack on Hook's interpretation of Marxism by a Soviet professor, who denies that Hook is a Marxist and charges that Hook aims to create confusion. Hook falsely alleges that one can be outside the Communist Party and still be a communist or remain a dialectical materialist.

R233 RUSHMORE, Howard. Rebirth of an American, "American Magazine," 129 (April 1940), 16-17 ff.
A tenth-generation American tells why—because of poverty, cynical politics, and accounts of social progress in the USSR—he joined the Communist Party. He rose in Party ranks to become managing editor of the "Sunday Worker." After six years in the Party he left, disillusioned by the maneuverings of Party members for power and the dishonesty of communist reporting.

R234 .... Life on the "Daily Worker," "American Mercury," 50 (June 1940), 215-21.
An account, by a reporter on the "Daily Worker" from 1937 until December 1939, of his disillusionment. News was fitted into the Party line of the moment or ignored, and editors, chosen for their political loyalty to the right faction, rewrote stories as they pleased without regard to facts.

R235 .... Robert Morris, "American Mercury," 76 (March-April 1953), 78-85.
The career of a Republican lawyer in investigating and exposing communists, as staff member for a New York legislative committee in 1940, as naval intelligence officer during World War II, and as counsel for U.S. Senate committees in 1950 and 1951. His Senate work dealt with McCarthy's charges of communists in the State Department and with the Institute of Pacific Relations.

R236 .... Mr. Anti-Communist, "American Mercury," 76 (May 1953), 79-86.
Praise for the methods and achievements of J. B. Matthews in his work with the Dies Committee, the Broyles Committee of the Illinois legislature, and McCarthy. His life history, including his four and one-half years as a fellow-traveler, is related, and his communist "vilifiers" are condemned.

R237 .... Pekin Farm Boy, "American Mercury," 77 (July 1953), 77-82.
A laudatory portrait of Illinois Representative Harold H. Velde, Chairman of the House Un-American Activities Committee, which condemns the campaign of the "anti-anti-Communists" against him.

R238 RUSHMORE, Howard. The Class Struggle in Suburbia, "American Mercury," 77 (Nov. 1953), 43-46.
An account of the controversy in Scarsdale, N.Y., over the presence of books by procommunist authors in public school libraries, and the use of school facilities by leftist speakers. The fight against communist influence is led by the Scarsdale Citizens' Committee, which has won some minor victories.

R239 RUSSELL, Charles Edward. "Bolshevism and the United States." Indianapolis: Bobbs-Merrill, 1919. 341 pp.
An account of the seizure of power in Russia by the Bolsheviks, and of the new forms of government and society introduced by them. Attention is paid to rights and liberties, the peasantry, government efficiency, labor and transportation, and the old and new autocracies. Chapter 12 (pp. 296-326), devoted to the rise and progress of American Bolshevism, lists socialists, pacifists, labor sympathizers, liberal intellectuals, anarchists, and the IWW as potential Bolsheviks here. To combat Bolshevism, Russell proposes fairer distribution of the product of industry and fairer recognition of labor in government.

R240 RUSSELL, William F. Divided We Fall, "Pattern Makers' Journal," 46 (March-April 1939), 1-7.
The dean of Columbia Teachers College, Columbia University, asserts that America, like France, is in danger of becoming split between fascism and communism; he advances a program to combat the drift toward extremes in America.

R241 .... How to Tell a Communist and How to Beat Him, "Atlantic Monthly," 163 (May 1939), 603-8.
An address by the dean of Teachers College, Columbia University, to a convention of the New York Department of the American Legion, pointing out that communism flourishes under conditions of widespread misery, suppressed civil rights, and general ignorance. Removal of these conditions is the best way to beat communism.

R242 .... The American vs. European Policies Regarding Communism and Education, "Teachers College Record," 54 (Jan. 1953), 175-83.
Europe views communism as merely a political movement which does not threaten liberty and which has little appeal for the masses. The American view, which the author supports, is the contrary. However, he proposes citizenship education rather than loyalty oaths and textbook inquiries to deal with the problem.

R243 .... Communism and Education, "Vital Speeches of the Day," 19 (Jan. 1, 1953), 185-89.
An address by the president of Teachers College, Columbia University, contrasting the reaction of American and European schools and teachers to the threat of communism. The firm stand in the U.S. against communism in education is viewed with alarm in Europe. The Europeans run grave dangers by underestimating the communist threat.

R244 RUSSO, Michael. The Textile Crisis in New England, "Political Affairs," 31 (Aug. 1952), 42-52.
A discussion of the factors contributing to the increasing unemployment in the New England textile mills—the cut in military expenditures, the movement of industry to the South, and the ineffectual policies of the Textile Workers Union of America.

R245 RUTHENBERG, C. E. Statement of the Executive Secretary to the Majority Group of the Executive Council, "Communist" (organ of the Communist Party of America), 2 (May 1, 1920), 5-8.
The executive secretary of the CPA discusses his dispute with the majority of the Central Executive Committee. The Chicago district organization censured the CEC and threatened to secede; Ruthenberg, though in sympathy with the Chicago group, convinced them to submit their grievances to the CPA convention. The CEC, however, attempted to replace the Chicago district organizer. The motivation can only be an effort by the CEC majority to oust its opponents prior to the convention.

R246 ..., and FERGUSON, Isaac E. "A Communist Trial." New York: National Defense Committee, 1921. 80 pp.
Excerpts from Ruthenberg's testimony and Ferguson's closing address to the jury in their trials under the Criminal Anarchy Law of New York. The defendants asserted that the existing industrial system should be abolished, and that prison sentences would not change their views. They argued that they were not guilty of criminal anarchy as defined by New York law, and that they did not write the Manifesto of the left wing as charged.

R247 .... "Why Every Worker Should Be a Communist and Join the Workers Party." [Chicago?]: Workers Party, n.d. [1923]. 7 pp.
A recruiting pamphlet by the executive secretary of the Workers Party, attacking capitalism for not supplying workers' needs. The Party calls for industrial unionism and a farmer-labor party to transform capitalism into a communist society.

R248 .... The Skirmish in Cleveland, "Liberator," 5 (Jan. 1923), 9-11.
A communist analysis of the Conference for Progressive Political Action, held in Cleveland, December 1922. A right-wing group made up of railroad brotherhoods, farm organizations, and the Socialist Party opposed a labor party. Workers Party delegates, favoring a labor party, were not seated. The conference opposed a labor party, though formation of state labor parties is permitted.

R249 .... Communism in the Open Again, "Liberator," 6 (Feb. 1923), 12-14.
A report on the second convention of the Workers Party of America, held in New York City, December 1922. No longer is there spontaneous enthusiasm for a proletarian revolution; the workers must learn its need through their own experience. The Party works for a labor party, and penetrates existing unions to amalgamate them into industrial unions.

R250 .... The Workers Party of America, "International Press Correspondence," 3 (Feb. 20, 1923), 144-45.
A report on the second convention of the Workers Party of America, summarizing the delegate makeup of the convention, the report of the Central Executive Committee, and the debate on such major policy questions as the labor party, trade union policy, and protection of foreign born workers. The absence of all factionalism is reported.

R251 .... American Democracy on Trial, "International Press Correspondence," 3 (April 12, 1923), 270.
A secret convention of the underground Communist Party, held at Bridgman, Mich., was raided, and 32 leaders now face trial under the Michigan Criminal Syndicalism Law. Communists will use the trial to fight for their right to work in the open in the U.S. The Workers Party is now the Communist Party in everything but name.

R252 .... "The Farmer-Labor United Front." Chicago: Workers Party, 1924. 29 pp.

The limits of the Workers Party united-front policy in politics. In Minnesota Party candidates must announce themselves as communists, even if this endangers the united front. In Michigan communists must oppose a Republican candidate, even though this splits the united front. Where there is a third party, as in the case of La Follette on the national scene, with farmer and industrial worker support, the Workers Party will endorse him.

R253 RUTHENBERG, C. E. The Revolutionary Party, "Liberator," 7 (Feb. 1924), 12-13.
An outline of the program of the Workers Party, which educates the workers through daily struggles, not abstract discussions. Party policies include support for a labor party, protection of foreign born, amalgamation of trade unions, and opposition to discrimination against Negroes.

R254 .... Third Party or Farmer-Labor Party? "Liberator," 7 (March 1924), 10-11.
The Workers Party supports the St. Paul convention of the Farmer-Labor Party to be held May 30, and opposes the Conference for Progressive Political Action, to meet in Cleveland on July 4. The CPPA has fallen into the hands of reactionary farm and labor leaders and middle class elements. Only the Federated Farmer Labor Party expresses the demands of the exploited.

R255 ...; ONEAL, James; and REYNOLDS, V. L. Is America Ripe for a Labor Party? "Modern Quarterly," 2 (Summer 1924), 33-51.
Viewpoints on working class politics, on the eve of the 1924 election, of the Workers' Party, the Socialist Party, and the Socialist Labor Party. Ruthenberg argues that economic conditions, for the first time, favor emergence of a class-oriented labor party. Oneal, while criticizing communist tactics, hopes for the emergence of a permanent labor party from the Conference for Progressive Political Action. Reynolds argues that a bona-fide labor party, the Socialist Labor Party, already exists in the U.S.

R256 .... Workers and Farmers on the Mark, "Liberator," 7 (July 1924), 16-21.
A report on the Farmer-Labor Party convention, held in St. Paul on June 17, 1924. The convention adopted communist proposals to oppose La Follette and to organize on a long-range basis. A National Organization and Campaign Committee was empowered to negotiate with any other group favoring a national farmer-labor party.

R257 .... The Communist Campaign for Class Action, "Liberator," 7 (Aug. 1924), 16.
A defense of the Workers Party's decision to withdraw support from National Farmer-Labor Party candidates and run candidates in its own name. Blame for the failure of a mass farmer-labor movement is placed on Senator La Follette and the Socialist Party. The Workers Party will use creation of a mass farmer-labor party as one of the central slogans of its election campaign.

R258 .... Progressive, But Not Labor, "Workers Monthly," 4 (Nov. 1924), 21-23 ff.
An assertion that the La Follette-Wheeler Progressive movement is opposed to formation of a labor party, and that its class appeals, organization, leadership, and program show it to be merely an appendage to a petty-bourgeois organization. Nevertheless the revolt of many workers against the two old capitalist parties is progress. The task of the Workers Party is now to hasten the disillusionment of the workers with La Folletism.

R259 .... Is the Movement towards Class Political Action Dead? "Workers Monthly," 4 (Dec. 1924), 77-79.

Criticism of the Foster group's proposed abandonment of the farmer-labor party slogan in order to build the Workers Party. The Pepper-Ruthenberg policy has been to use the united front tactic as the best method of building a mass WP, by bringing the most radical workers under WP leadership. Foster would repudiate the united front on the political field.

R260 .... "The Workers (Communist) Party: What It Stands for, Why Workers Should Join. Chicago: Workers (Communist) Party, n.d. [1925?]. 14 pp.
The program of the Workers (Communist) Party, outlined by its general secretary. The program covers the class struggle, trusts in industry, farmers and capitalists, government and the workers' struggles, the breakdown of capitalism, socialized industry, labor union militancy, organizing the unorganized, a labor party, Negro workers and imperialism, and the program of the Communist International.

R261 .... From the Third through the Fourth Convention of the Workers (Communist) Party, "Workers Monthly," 4 (Oct. 1925), 531-38.
A summary of the development of American communism by the Party's executive secretary, written following intense struggle between the Foster and Ruthenberg factions. Stages in the Party's history are reviewed, as is the factional conflict and the intervention of the Communist International in support of the Ruthenberg group. Methods of bolshevizing the Party are outlined. (Republished in pamphlet form.)

R262 .... Capitalism Mobilizes against the Social Revolution, "Workers Monthly," 5 (Nov. 1925), 5-9.
Though the Dawes Plan and the Locarno treaty may have brought capitalism a breathing space, they have not overcome the forces which are preparing for the destruction of capitalism. The task of the Workers (Communist) Party in the U.S. is to put pressure on the main center of capitalist power, thereby weakening capitalism's offensive against the Soviet Union.

R263 .... The Program of American Capitalism, "Workers Monthly," 5 (Feb. 1926), 151-53.
A communist view of President Coolidge's report to Congress on the state of the union as in reality the program of the capitalist class. The program calls for partial stabilization of European capitalism, strengthening of American capitalism, entry into the League of Nations, increase in the American military establishment, attacks on foreign-born workers and the right to strike, and unbearable conditions for farmers.

R264 .... The Session of Enlarged Executive Committee of the Communist International, "Workers Monthly," 5 (June 1926), 339-42 ff.
A report by the general secretary of the Workers (Communist) Party on the meeting of the enlarged ECCI, held February 17 to March 15, 1926, at which one of the topics was the American question. Capitalism is viewed as still on the upgrade in the U.S., with American imperialism looting the entire world. The labor movement here is moving to the right, with conditions favorable to communist growth.

R265 .... The Tasks of the Party in the Light of the Comintern, "Workers Monthly," 5 (July 1926), 401-5.
Summary of the report of the Political Committee to the Party's Central Committee, May 1926. The report deals with the inner Party situation, the economic situation in the U.S., the political situation, and the work of the Party.

(This report follows the meeting of the ECCI, which laid down the line for the American Party.)

R266 RUTHENBERG, C. E. Seven Years of the Communist Party of America, "Workers Monthly," 5 (Sept. 1926), 483-85.
A brief sketch of the founding and early organizational histories of rival American communist parties. The unified party's goals remain what they were in 1919—the overthrow of capitalism and the establishment of a proletarian dictatorship. No longer sectarian, the Party now participates in workers' struggles, urging more aggressive action, and teaching the necessity of the proletarian revolution.

R267 .... What Is the Election About? "Workers Monthly," 5 (Nov. 1926), 579-81.
No major issues separate the Democratic and Republican parties in the 1926 election. While the parties represent conflicting economic interests, neither represents workers. Only the Workers (Communist) Party has a program for the working class; it calls for united labor tickets, labor parties, or farmer-labor parties.

R268 .... "Speeches and Writings of Charles E. Ruthenberg." Introd. by Jay Lovestone. New York: International Publishers, 1928. 96 pp.
A collection of 35 excerpts from the writings and speeches of the former head of the Workers (Communist) Party, covering the period from 1910 until his death in 1927. The excerpts, some from Ruthenberg's statements at various trials, relate to capitalist chaos, socialism, capturing power, imperialism, war and revolution, class justice, and the class struggle. Included in these also are Ruthenberg's opinions on the development of communism in the U.S., revolution versus reformism, the role and aims of the Party, and the labor party. Lovestone's introduction is a laudatory review of Ruthenberg's radical development and activities. (The introduction also appeared as "Ruthenberg as Fighter and Leader" in "Communist," March 1928, and as a pamphlet entitled "Ruthenberg, Communist Fighter and Leader.")

.... See also DAMON and DAMON, David.

R269 RYAN, Eleanor. Toward a National Negro Congress, "New Masses," 15 (June 4, 1935), 14-15.
A report on a conference protesting injustices to Negroes in such New Deal programs as the NRA and land redistribution under the Agricultural Adjustment Act. The Party, and most delegates, called for a National Negro Congress to work out a program on which all mass Negro organizations could cooperate.

RYAN, Paul William. See Quin, Mike.

R270 RYAN, T. W. War and the Militarization of the American Marine Transport Industry, "Communist," 9 (Nov.-Dec. 1930), 1006-15.
Military aspects of the U.S. shipbuilding and marine program make it important to root the Marine Workers Industrial Union in the industry. In the coming war the marine workers and the revolutionary proletariat, under Party leadership, will turn the imperialist war into a civil war.

R271 RYAN, Tim. The National Recruiting Campaign of the CPUSA, "International Press Correspondence," 17 (Dec. 24, 1937), 1391-92.
A report on a recent recruiting drive which brought in 10,000 new members, raising membership of the Communist Party to 60,000. Data on national origins, geographical location, union membership, and industrial composition are presented. Methods contributing to the success of the drive are discussed.

R272 RYAN, William G. Medical Bureau for Spain Reeks with Respectability, "America," 61 (July 29, 1939), 364-65.
The Medical Bureau and North American Committee to Aid Spanish Democracy are treated as a case study of the luring of innocents into communist front organizations.

R273 .... Art Rhymed with Marx while Scribes Salaamed to Moscow, "America," 63 (May 18, 1940), 150-51.
Criticism of the proletarian novel as crude propaganda, with a single basic plot, in which the underprivileged hero develops social consciousness, then mouths communist slogans and sings the glories of the Soviet Union. The Hitler-Stalin pact will unmask communists and fellow-travelers.

R274 .... The Communist Column Remains a Constant Threat, "America," 63 (July 13, 1940), 371-72.
An appraisal of the techniques and objectives of the communist fifth column in the U.S. by a former member of it, who contrasts its subtlety and intelligence with the crudeness and stupidity of the Nazi fifth column here. Newspapers and radio commentators are criticized for failing to identify communist front activities as such.

R275 RYAN, William J. How the Left Wing of the Shoe Workers Won a Strike at Haverhill, "Labor Unity," 2 (April 1928), 16-20.
An account of a successful strike in January by 5,000 shoe workers in Haverhill, under the leadership of a secret rank-and-file committee, that forced the Haverhill Shoe Manufacturers Association to rescind a wage cut. Rejecting the advice of the top union officers to accept a compromise, the strikers won their demands in full.

R276 RYHLICK, Frank. "Congress and You." New York: Workers Library, 1943. 64 pp.
Indictment of Congress for failure to support President Roosevelt's war policy. Unity is urged behind a program including a second front in Europe in 1943, total economic mobilization, strengthening the United Nations concept, support of Roosevelt's rationing and economic stabilization program, and abolition of the poll tax and of discrimination against Negroes. Readers are urged to help block defeatists and isolationists in Congress.

S

S1 "ST. JOHN'S LAW REVIEW," Communism and the Constitution—Internal Security Act of 1950, 25 (May 1951), 397-416.
An examination of McCarran Act provisions and of constitutional questions raised by them. Among the provisions considered are those relating to sedition, registration of communist action and front organizations, registration of individuals belonging to communist action organizations, consequences of registration, immigration, and naturalization.

S2 SALISBURY, Harrison E. Writers in the Shadow of Communism, "New York Times Magazine," June 9, 1957, 10 ff.
Reprint of correspondence between Howard Fast and Soviet writer Boris Polevoi, following Fast's resignation from the CPUSA. Salisbury contributes an introductory analysis. The Russian author rebukes Fast for aiding the reactionaries by resigning as he did. Fast answers by asking about anti-Semitism and the orgy of murder under Stalin, just revealed by Khrushchev.

S3 SALOFF-ASTAKHOFF, N. I. "Real Russia from 1905 to 1932 and Communism in America." New York: The author, 1932. 125 pp.
The bulk of the book criticizes Russian communism. The last three chapters warn of increasing communist membership in the U.S. and urge all "true Americans" to unite in the fight against communism.

S4 SALTER, Paul, and LIBROME, Jack. Dewey, Russell and Cohen: Why They Are Anti-Communist, "New Masses," 12 (July 17, 1934), 24-27; (July 24), 22-23.
Comment on a discussion between Sidney Hook, advocating communism, and philosophers John Dewey, Bertrand Russell, and Morris R. Cohen, who disagree with him. Russell is characterized as a philosophical opportunist, Dewey as suffering from his petty bourgeois background, and Cohen as the most reactionary of the three.

S5 SALTZMAN, R. "A Crime against Jewish Unity: The Jewish Labor Committee Owes the Jewish Public an Explanation." New York: Cooperative Book League, Jewish-American Section, International Workers Order, 1942. 23 pp.
An attack on the Jewish Labor Committee, N. Chanin of the Workmen's Circle, and Hillel Rogoff of the "Jewish Daily Forward" for their criticism of Russian War Relief. Despite them, U.S. Jews will continue to answer the call, to aid the battle against the Hitlerite enemy.

S6 SALUTSKY, J. B. [J. B. S. Hardman]. Wanted: A Genuine Labor Party in the U.S., "American Labor Monthly," 1 (May 1923), 8-16.
An assertion that no mass labor party will be formed at the conference called by the Farmer-Labor Party for July 1923. Those in favor are a few trade union progressives, the TUEL, the Workers Party and, half-heartedly, the socialists. Absence of the bulk of the trade union movement will turn leadership over to the radicals. More educational work in the trade unions is needed.

S7 . . . . Chicago—A Study in Collapse: How the Federated Farmer Labor Party Came to Be, "American Labor Monthly," 1 (July 1923), 4-15.
The editorial feature, "The World We Live In," is used by one of the editors for a critical analysis of the Chicago conference of July 3-5 that launched the Federated Farmer Labor Party. The conference, though called by others, was captured by the Workers Party. Few, if any, large unions or farmers' organizations participated; the new party is reminded that a labor party can be formed only by the masses of organized labor. (Salutsky was expelled from the Workers Party shortly after this article was written.)

S8 . . . . The W. P. Expelled Me a Little: A Personal Statement on a Non-Personal Matter, "American Labor Monthly," 1 (Sept. 1923), 85-96.
An account by one of the editors of the "Monthly" of the charges filed against him in the Workers' Party of America in February and March 1923, his trials, the negotiations that followed, and his expulsion late in July. Salutsky, a member of the Party's first Central Executive Committee, was charged with failing to defend the Party's position at the Cleveland Conference for Progressive Labor Action, and with editing a magazine (the "American Labor Monthly") that was not under Party control.

S9 SALZMAN, Max. Some Notes on the Socialist Party, "Communist," 8 (Aug. 1929), 438-44.
An effort, based on quotations from the "New Leader," to show that the Socialist Party denies the existence of a class struggle in the U.S., consists mainly of non-proletarian elements and labor aristocrats, helps American imperialists prepare for war, endorses the murder of German workers, and supports the use of police terror against the workers.

S10 . . . . Building the United Front in Ford-Controlled Dearborn, "Communist," 12 (Aug. 1933), 793-99.
To obtain adequate relief in Dearborn, the communists organized a committee, staged hunger marches, and sent delegations to the state government. They attracted the support of enough other organizations to be able to launch a united front political movement, with a communist candidate for mayor.

S11 SAMSON, Leon. Freud and Marx, "New Masses," 3 (March 1928), 15-16.
It is an error to lump Freudianism with Marxism as "materialist" or "determinist." Whereas psychoanalysts assume that man's fundamental passions are wrong and his institutions right, the Marxist assumes that man's instincts are sound but that bourgeois institutions have corrupted him.

S12 SAMUELS, Gertrude. American Traitors: A Study in Motives, "New York Times Magazine," May 22, 1949, 17 ff.
A study of the various types of seditionists, traitors, and espionage agents, both fascist and communist, in recent American history. Whittaker Chambers and Elizabeth

Bentley are discussed as ideological traitors, the report of the Royal Commission of Canada on the motives of the communist spy is explained, and disloyalty is analyzed in psychiatric terms.

S13 SANCTON, Thomas. Hiss and Chambers; A Tangled Web, "Nation," 167 (Dec. 18, 1948), 691-92.
A Washington reporter's comment on and interpretation of the Chambers-Hiss controversy after the disclosure of the "pumpkin" papers, which provided evidence of Soviet espionage in Washington in the 1930's. Chambers is shown up as a troubled, unfathomable character.

S14 SAPOSS, David J. What Lies Back of Foster, "Nation," 116 (Jan. 17, 1923), 69-70.
A discussion of radical union tactics by a labor historian. Whereas in an earlier period radicals, when ignored by conservative union leaders, withdrew to form dual unions, they have learned that this merely isolated them. William Z. Foster's Trade Union Educational League and his "boring from within" campaign seek to bring radical ideas to workers in their established unions.

S15 .... "Left Wing Unionism: A Study of Radical Policies and Tactics." New York: International Publishers, 1926. 192 pp. Ind.
A study of the two ways used by radicals to influence the labor movement, "boring from within" and formation of dual unions. Whereas the objective of socialist boring from within was to obtain endorsement of their principles, the communist objective was control of the union machinery. The author describes various types of dual unions, shows that they occur throughout the world, and analyzes the factors that produce them. Radical dual unionism, as exemplified by the IWW, eventually becomes evangelical and propagandistic. (A rare example of noncommunist writing published by International Publishers.)

S16 .... "How Communists Operate in Labor Unions." Washington, D.C.: Bureau of National Affairs, 1954. 12 pp.
A description of means used by communists to control labor unions, directed to a lay audience. The author describes the techniques communists use, their methods of broadening their influence, the pressures they exert on officials, and the means they employ to discourage or defeat opposition.

S17 .... "Communism in American Unions." New York: McGraw-Hill, 1959. 279 pp. Ind.
A discussion of communist penetration of American unions from the mid-1930's on, of their tactics, and of the role of union leaders, members, employers, and government in combating communist domination. In the AFL the communists had their greatest success in the movie industry, and were also influential in the Hotel and Restaurant Workers. They were far more successful in the CIO, where they dominated many of the newly formed unions and held important staff positions in CIO headquarters. Eventually the CIO expelled the communist-dominated unions, creating rival unions that raided them successfully. Following passage of the Communist Control Act, denying NLRB facilities to communist-controlled unions, the latter have sought entry into noncommunist unions.

S18 .... "Communism in American Politics." Washington, D.C.: Public Affairs Press, 1960. 259 pp. Ref. Ind.
A review of the political efforts of the American communist movement, from its emergence in 1919 to its re-examination following the Khrushchev report on Stalinist excesses. After sketching the united front maneuvers of the early 1920's, the author describes communist efforts to infiltrate parties in the states of Washington, California, and Minnesota. Detailed accounts are given of the capture of the American Labor Party of New York and its subsequent decline, and of the communists' creation and control of the Progressive Party in 1948 led by Henry A. Wallace. Though the Party was greatly weakened in the aftermath of the Khrushchev disclosures, it continues as part of an international conspiratorial movement controlled by a foreign power.

S19 "SATURDAY REVIEW," Was Alger Hiss Framed? A Debate, 41 (May 31, 1958), 14-17 ff.
Fred Rodell, professor of law at Yale, asserts that Alger Hiss was framed with the help of the U.S. government, his conviction based largely on phoney, fabricated evidence. Victor Lasky, co-author of "Seeds of Treason," charges that Fred J. Cook's "The Unfinished Case of Alger Hiss" is a work of special pleading, tricky selection, and suppression of evidence. Walter Millis describes the climate of the Hiss trials.

S20 SAXTON, Alexander P. "The Great Midland." New York: Appleton-Century-Crofts, 1948. 352 pp.
A novel, laid in a railroad yard in Chicago, portraying the daily lives of communists. (The communists in this book are more lifelike than the crude sketches in the proletarian novels of the 1930's.)

S21 SAYERS, Michael, and KAHN, Albert E. "Sabotage: The Secret War against America." New York: Harper, 1942. 266 pp. Ind.
A procommunist account of Axis sabotage in the U.S. during World War II. The authors deal with psychological as well as physical sabotage—with supporters of the America First Committee, native fascists, and other groups tending to undermine our wartime morale.

S22 .... "The Great Conspiracy: The Secret War against Soviet Russia." Boston: Little, Brown, 1946. 433 pp. Bibliog. notes. Ind.
A communist view that a conspiracy linked intervention in Siberia in the 1920's, espionage activity in the Soviet Union by western countries, the establishment of the "cordon sanitaire," the Trotskyite "fifth column," Nazi designs on the Soviet Union, and American anti-Soviet organizations. Chapter 23 (pp. 342-78) is devoted to "American Anti-Comintern," consisting of various right-wing, isolationist, anti-Soviet, and profascist groups that flourished in the U.S. in the 1930's and early 1940's. The authors, who take the Stalinist treason trials and purges at face value, conclude that illusions about the Soviet Union were not shattered until she proved her strength during World War II.

S23 SCANLAN, Alfred Long. The Communist-Dominated Union Problem, "Notre Dame Lawyer," 28 (Summer 1953), 458-96.
An appraisal of communist union influence and suggestions for combating it. Communist leadership, despite CIO expulsions, is still entrenched in some important unions. The existing legislative authority meant to deal with this problem is found deficient. Various proposals to strengthen legislative sanctions are analyzed.

S24 SCHAAR, John H. "Loyalty in America." Berkeley and Los Angeles: University of California Press, 1957. 217 pp. Notes. Ind.
A study of the nature and meaning of loyalty in American democracy. Chapter 5 (pp. 130-74) deals with the background and operations of the federal loyalty program, including the exclusion of communists from federal employment. The author concludes that the real problem of

disloyalty in the U.S. is posed, not by the weak band of the actively disloyal, but by the large numbers without loyalty.

S25 SCHACHNER, E. A. Revolutionary Literature in the U.S. Today, "Windsor Quarterly," 2 (Spring 1934), 27-64.
A comprehensive analysis of revolutionary writing—criticism, drama, poetry, and fiction—by a leading Party literary functionary. The author, a leading member of the John Reed Club in New York, has also been on the "Daily Worker" staff. While praising some of the Marxist literary critics, Marxist poetry, the Theatre Collective, and the Theatre Union, he finds revolutionary literature at its weakest in fiction. The greatest progress in the creation of revolutionary literature will come in the theatre and in poetry, the two art forms closest to the hearts of oppressed classes.

S26 SCHAFFER, Louis. "Stalin's Fifth Column on Broadway: A Cue to Theatre People." New York: Rand School Press, 1940. 31 pp.
The socialist producer of "Pins and Needles" charges the Theatre Arts Committee with being Stalin's fifth column in the theatre. He tells of the vilification he suffered for organizing theatre benefits for Finnish relief during the Russian-Finnish war when the Theatre Arts Committee, following the Party line, opposed such activity.

S27 SCHAPPES, Morris U. "Letters from the Tombs." Ed. by Louis Lerman. Foreword by Richard Wright. New York: Schappes Defense Committee, 1941. 119 pp.
A collection of letters written during the 34 days that the author was imprisoned in the Tombs of New York, following his conviction for perjury before the Rapp-Coudert Committee, before being released pending appeal. His address to the court on July 11, 1941, is included. Richard Wright likens the letters to those of Debs, and Sacco and Vanzetti.

S28 .... Communist Identity, "New Masses," 48 (July 27, 1943), 14-16.
An assertion that communists cannot reveal their identity, as proposed by liberal critics, without inviting discharge and sometimes blacklisting. Legislation to prevent discrimination on political grounds by government and by private employers is called for, along with abolition of government committees investigating communism.

S29 .... "The Daily Worker: Heir to the Great Tradition." New York: Daily Worker, 1944. 31 pp.
An historical account of "freedom-loving" labor and socialist journalism. The "Pilot" (National Maritime Union), the "UE News," and the "Daily Worker" are called outstanding examples of excellence.

S30 .... Culture and Anti-Semitism, "New Masses," 65 (Nov. 4, 1947), 10-12.
Anti-Semitism is viewed as a potent weapon in the arsenal of reaction; today the ruling class, which has converted the U.S. into an imperialist power, threatens to extinguish Jewish rights. Jewish American cultural workers should look to their history for inspirational themes amidst the Jewish working class.

S31 .... "Problems of Jewish Culture." New York: School of Jewish Studies, 1950. 13 pp.
An analysis of two approaches to Jewish culture in America: the bourgeois-nationalist and the working-class internationalist. The former views the Jew in isolation, seeing a single world Jewish nation centered in Israel. The latter approach, the correct one, is based on the class conscious Jewish worker and seeks to unite Jew and non-Jew against anti-Semitism.

S32 SCHATZ, Phil. Some Lessons of the United-Front Victory in the Ford Elections, "Political Affairs," 29 (July 1950), 79-86.
The March and April elections in Ford Local 600, United Auto Workers-CIO, in which every notorious Red-baiter was defeated, are viewed as a communist victory and as confirmation of the correctness of the Party's united front policy.

S33 SCHEIBER, Harry N. "The Wilson Administration and Civil Liberties, 1917-1921." Ithaca: Cornell University Press, 1960. 69 pp. App. Bibliog. note. Ind.
A study of civil liberties during and after World War I, with attention to security measures, censorship, Justice Department activities, and the red scare. Wilson, harshly critical in his public addresses of groups accused of disloyalty, left the fate of civil liberties to subordinate officials, the judiciary, and the public. The appendix lists criminal prosecutions under the Espionage Act.

S34 SCHERER, Gordon H. I Was the Target, "American Legion Magazine," 56 (April 1954), 20-21 ff.
A member of the House Committee on Un-American Activities complains of the abuse and intimidation suffered by members of the Committee at the hands of communists and their fellow-travelers. Those called before the Committee enjoy wider protection than in a courtroom. Expert propaganda against the Committee has given the country a distorted picture of its work.

S35 .... Are Americans Aware? Subversion, Not Arms, the Chief Red Weapon, "Vital Speeches of the Day," 24 (Aug. 1, 1958), 633-36.
Because of the indifference, cynicism, and withdrawal of the American people, the communists have had great success in subversive activities. Even congressional staffs are not immune. The Supreme Court and people like Cyrus Eaton are held largely responsible.

S36 .... Communists in Your Own Back Yard, "National Republic," 46 (April 1959), 1-2 ff.
A review of testimony before the House Committee on Un-American Activities in 1957 concerning communist activities in and around Baltimore, Maryland.

S37 SCHLAMM, William S. Apropos Apostasy, "Freeman," 1 (March 26, 1951), 400-2.
A discussion of the position of the excommunist, disliked by some conservatives because he was once a communist, but hated by some "liberals" because he is now a renegade. The excommunist's information might help the "liberal" to understand.

S38 SCHLESINGER, Arthur M., Jr. The U.S. Communist Party, "Life," 21 (July 29, 1946), 84-96.
A brief history of the Communist Party and an appraisal of its status in 1946. Among the topics dealt with are Party discipline, turnover, appeal, and exploitation of the race issue. Party-dominated labor unions and front organizations are discussed, along with the nature and mechanics of Moscow control. Shifts in Party tactics, the expulsion of Browder, and postwar policies are also covered.

S39 .... What Is Loyalty? A Difficult Question! "New York Times Magazine," Nov. 2, 1947, 7 ff.
While it is not disloyal to criticize capitalism, individuals such as communists and fellow-travelers, whose loyalties go elsewhere, do not belong in agencies important to security. The Truman Administration has compromised on civil liberties to head off more extreme congressional action. Civil libertarians, the press, the American left,

and American conservatives should propose security measures with proper safeguards.

S40   SCHLESINGER, Arthur M., Jr. "The Vital Center: The Politics of Freedom." Boston: Houghton Mifflin, 1949. 247 pp. Ind.
In chapter 6, "The Communist Challenge to America," the author discusses the relationship of the CPUSA to the world communist movement, and its apparatus, techniques, and danger (which he believes overrated) to the U.S. In chapter 7, "The Restoration of Radical Nerve," he argues that the American left, no longer intoxicated with Russian communism, is developing new confidence in its own insights and values. Chapter 9, "The Techniques of Freedom," deals with methods of combating communism without undue sacrifice of individual freedom.

S41   .... The Right to Loathsome Ideas, "Saturday Review of Literature," 32 (May 14, 1949), 17-18 ff.
A review of the University of Washington academic freedom cases. Despite the fair conduct of the proceedings, there was a miscarriage of justice, since there was no "clear and present danger." Only an emergency justifies repression, and no one even pretended that the communist teachers constituted an emergency.

S42   .... The Life of the Party: What It Means to Be a Communist, "Saturday Review of Literature," 32 (July 16, 1949), 6-7 ff.
An analysis of the communist movement in the U.S., telling of reasons for joining, discipline enforced, Party activities, and front organizations. The Browder expulsion illustrates the way in which the Party overdoes the shifts required by Moscow. The Party forces its writers to conform to its political line. Despite its espionage efforts, it is not dangerous to U.S. security now.

S43   .... "What about Communism?" New York: Public Affairs Committee, 1950. 32 pp.
A popularly-written account of communist history, philosophy, and organization, with attention to the rise of Marxism, Lenin and the Russian Revolution, stages in communist policy, and the role of the Party in the U.S. Among questions discussed are whether communists advocate force, whether they are agents of a foreign power, and whether the Party should be outlawed.

S44   .... Whittaker Chambers & His "Witness," "Saturday Review," 35 (May 24, 1952), 8-10 ff.
An essay review of Chambers' autobiography, "Witness." No evidence is presented that the Soviet spies within the U.S. government ever influenced domestic or foreign policy decisions. The book, despite Chambers' dogmas in politics and philosophy, is an invaluable account of the communist conspiracy in the U.S. (Reprinted in Schlesinger's "The Politics of Hope." Boston: Houghton Mifflin, 1962.)

S45   .... The Oppenheimer Case, "Atlantic Monthly," 194 (Oct. 1954), 29-36.
An analysis of the 992-page Atomic Energy Commission report on the security hearing of J. Robert Oppenheimer. Schlesinger concludes that the denial of clearance for Oppenheimer was an injustice to the man and a disservice to the real security of our nation. (Reprinted in the author's "The Politics of Hope.")

S46   .... "The Age of Roosevelt: Vol. 3, The Politics of Upheaval." Boston: Houghton Mifflin, 1960. 749 pp. Notes. Ind.
In chapter 11, "Radicalism: European Plan" (pp. 162-80), Schlesinger discusses the native American radicals' dislike of communism and the widening communist influence among the lower ranks of the intelligentsia. Chapter 12,

"Growth of a Conspiracy" (pp. 181-207), outlines the communist commitment to revolution as opposed to the evolutionary approach of the New Deal, the growth of communist front organizations, and the development of espionage activities. Pages 563-70 discuss the people's front tactic, the Party's response to the rising threat of Hitlerism.

S47   SCHLOSSBERG, Joseph. Factional Divisions in the American Labor Movement, "Advance," 12 (April 29, 1927), 10-13.
An attack on TUEL factionalism in the Amalgamated Clothing Workers as unlike past factionalism, which reflected real conditions and vital principles. The TUEL attack on the Amalgamated for class collaboration is without meaning, as its call for the shop delegate system is camouflage. However, the Amalgamated opposes repressive measures.

S48   SCHMALHAUSEN, Samuel D. These Tragic Comedians, "Modern Quarterly," 4 (Nov. 1927-Feb. 1928), 195-229.
A sarcastic survey of the state of American liberalism, socialism, and communism, with leading figures of each group found wanting in character, tactics, or devotion. Among the communists thus treated are Floyd Dell, Scott Nearing, Max Eastman, William Foster, Rose Pastor Stokes, Mossaye Olgin, Mike Gold, and Trachtenberg.

S49   SCHMIDT, Karl M. "Henry A. Wallace: Quixotic Crusade, 1948." Syracuse: Syracuse University Press, 1960. 362 pp. App. Bibliog. Ind.
A study of Wallace's Progressive Party and of his 1948 presidential campaign, covering the background of the movement, the leaders, the organization that was built, the campaign itself, and the disintegration of the movement. The charge of communist domination, persistently made, was one of the party's greatest disadvantages. In chapter 11, "Communist Bogey" (pp. 252-79), the author concludes that the movement was influenced but not dominated by the communists, who were more influential in the organizational sphere than in policy.

S50   SCHNEIDER, David M. "The Workers' (Communist) Party and American Trade Unions." Baltimore: Johns Hopkins Press, 1928. 117 pp. App. Ind.
An account of the activities of the Trade Union Educational League in the early 1920's in six trade unions: the Machinists, the Carpenters, the United Mine Workers, the Amalgamated Clothing Workers, the Furriers, and the ILGWU. The author appraises the policies and tactics of the Workers Party, outlines the "class struggle" program of the communists, and attributes their lack of success to their leaders' ignorance of American conditions.

S51   SCHNEIDER, Isidor. "From the Kingdom of Necessity." New York: Putnam, 1935. 450 pp.
An autobiographical novel by an editor of the "New Masses," telling the story of a boy who comes to America with his parents at the age of six. The years covered in the story bridge the first two to three decades of the twentieth century, during which the boy grows into manhood and learns to understand the proletarian revolution.

S52   .... Poetry: Red-baiting Victim, "New Masses," 50 (Jan. 18, 1944), 24-26.
The young "social poets" of the depression have been so victimized by Red-baiting that only the "New Masses" and a few other small magazines are open to them. Perhaps with the development of a mature trade union press, social poetry will find a base of operation and influence.

S53 SCHNEIDER, Isidor. Probing Writers' Problems, "New Masses," 57 (Oct. 23, 1945), 22-25.
A summary of three meetings on problems of writers held by the staff and friends of "New Masses." Since no formulated Marxist criticism exists, progressive writers should be guided by their own experiences, though these should be aligned with those of the labor movement. No writer need worry about being politically correct, if his work is faithful to reality.

S54 .... "The Judas Time." New York: Dial, 1946. 361 pp.
A satirical novel by an editor of the "New Masses" about a communist who breaks with the Party, becomes a Trotskyite, and goes to Russia on an espionage mission for Trotsky. Though the chief character is portrayed as repulsive, Party members appear weak and inept in comparison.

S55 .... Background to Error, "New Masses," 58 (Feb. 12, 1946), 23-25.
A review of the development of the successes and the problems of left-wing criticism since 1932, criticizing the left culture for its emergency-mindedness during the reactionary counteroffensive beginning in 1936. A program to help develop a left culture, including more publications and longer range objectives in writing, is advocated.

S56 .... Monopoly in Book Publishing, "New Masses," 58 (March 5, 1946), 23-24.
The book publishing business is being "stabilized" by the book clubs, which provide mass distribution and permit invasion of the field by monopoly capital. The result is the draining of thought from books, with a threat to cultural standards and freedom of book publication. The progressive Book Find Club and the chain of progressive book stores provide a contrary influence.

S57 .... Writers after Two Wars, "Masses & Mainstream," 1 (Nov. 1948), 31-40.
A contrast of the progressive current in literature after World War I with the present period. Progressive writers in the 1920's were concerned with literary values, glorified the avant guarde, and hailed the new socialist state in Russia. Today they do not challenge anti-Soviet propaganda. The monopolistic book industry strangles the remaining progressive voices.

S58 SCHNEIDERMAN, William. "The Pacific Coast Maritime Strike." San Francisco: Western Worker Publishers, 1937. 31 pp.
The story of the 1936 strike, by a California Party leader, denouncing the attempts by Red-baiters and Trotskyite disrupters to sabotage the Party's work in support of the maritime workers. (This material originally appeared in the "Western Worker.")

S59 .... The Pacific Coast Maritime Strike, "Communist," 16 (April 1937), 342-57.
A review and evaluation of the strike, led by the Maritime Federation of the Pacific, which ended in victory after 99 days with new and decisive gains. The victory was made possible by the success of the progressives in the district elections in the ILA last year; strong support from the labor movement and the middle classes contributed to it.

S60 .... The Election Struggle in California, "Communist," 17 (Oct. 1938), 919-26.
The state secretary of the Party in California describes struggles for political unity among progressive forces in advance of the 1938 congressional elections. The Democratic primaries resulted in a victory for progress.

S61 .... The California Elections, "Communist," 21 (Aug. 1942), 602-9.
A discussion of prospects for the California primaries, to be held August 25, 1942. The communists will support Roosevelt on a "win-the-war" program. California's incumbent congressmen are criticized as labor-baiters and Administration obstructionists.

S62 .... California and the Coming Elections, "Communist," 22 (July 1943), 648-52.
A report to the plenary meeting of the Party's national committee, June 11, 1943, describing political developments in California in advance of the 1944 presidential elections.

S63 .... The San Francisco Elections, "Communist," 22 (Dec. 1943), 1133-37.
Factional splits among Democrats and labor groups resulted in a Democratic defeat in San Francisco. The Communist Party's role in support of "win-the-war" forces is reviewed.

S64 .... The Defense of the Party, "Political Affairs," 28 (Oct. 1949), 19-25.
Excerpts from a report to the Party's national committee, September 16-18, 1949, asserting that the communists are being tried at Foley Square for advocating their political faith. A mass campaign must be organized to protect civil liberties from further attack. The Party must train its cadres, be vigilant against the infiltration of enemy agents, beware of opportunist deviations, and organize united fronts against the reactionaries.

S65 SCHNEIR, Walter and Miriam. "Invitation to an Inquest." Garden City, N.Y.: Doubleday, 1965. 467 pp. Sources. Ind.
A comprehensive review of the cases of Ethel and Julius Rosenberg and Morton Sobell, by authors who believe that they were convicted on perjured testimony prompted by the FBI. The trial is called the result of the cold war atmosphere, plus the belief that Soviet scientists were incapable of discovering the secret of the atomic bomb for themselves. No evidence, other than the doubtful testimony of government witnesses and a fellow-defendant, linked the Rosenbergs with espionage, though their communist connections were well known.

S66 SCHNERING, Farrell. Mr. Duper Communist Flatters Mrs. Wealthy White: A Revelation of the Process by a Former Duper, "America," 60 (Jan. 21, 1939), 364-66.
An account of how the communists recruit wealthy, influential "innocents" to head their united front groups. The Party retains control, spreads its influence, and receives a large share of the money. Innocents who become troublesome, especially about accounting for the funds, are quickly dropped.

S67 .... Innocents and Travelers Hold Conferences for Reform: Clever Preludes to the Revolution Are Being Staged, "America," 61 (May 13, 1939), 100-1.
A discussion of communist techniques in staging united front activities, written by one who had helped to promote them. The people's front tactic was devised by the Comintern to disguise its power drive. Communists can be detected by their noisy antifascism, while praising "Soviet democracy."

S68 .... Communists Burrow Way into Key Positions in C.I.O., "America," 61 (Aug. 12, 1939), 416-17.
A description of communist influence in the CIO in Wisconsin by a former communist organizer and editor, who asserts that a Party member, Emil Costello, played a

leading role in forming the state CIO council, which the Party has since controlled.

S69 SCHNERING, Farrell. The Wisconsin C.I.O. and the In-Borers, "America," 61 (Aug. 26, 1939), 463-65.
An exposure of undemocratic practices in communist-controlled CIO councils in Wisconsin, and of communist influence behind Local 248 of the UAW (Allis-Chalmers) and its president, Harold Christoffel. Back in power following a suspension, Christoffel called an unnecessary strike, accompanied by violence, which gained nothing.

S70 .... Why I Suspect the Youth Congress, "America," 63 (May 25, 1940), 176-77.
A former communist youth leader describes the control exercised by the communist-dominated American Student Union over the American Youth Congress, a "transmission belt" for the Kremlin. The craftiness of secret Party fractions is described, and the support given AYC by persons in high positions is deplored.

S71 SCHRENK, William J., Jr. Constitutional Law—The President's Loyalty Order—Standards, Procedure and Constitutional Aspects, "Michigan Law Review," 46 (May 1948), 942-52.
Comment on the standards, procedure, and constitutional aspects of President Truman's executive order on loyalty. Although the Supreme Court may not pass on the order, serious questions are raised by vagueness and procedural lacks. "Guilt by association" and denial of confrontation or cross examination violate our system of legal safeguards.

S72 SCHUBART, Henry. The Housing Crisis, "Political Affairs," 25 (March 1946), 240-53.
A discussion of the current housing shortage, with proposals for legislation. Housing, a major economic and political question, should be a vital issue in Party campaigns. Labor must support the Wagner-Ellender-Taft bill, the Wyatt program, continuation of rent control, organization of tenant unions, and labor participation in all city planning and housing boards.

S73 SCHULBERG, Budd. Collision with the Party Line, "Saturday Review of Literature," 35 (Aug. 30, 1952), 6-8 ff.
The story of Schulberg's childhood and youth, his early trip to Russia, his subsequent affiliation with the Party as student and young writer, and his ending of communist ties on the issue of the social responsibility of a writer. The aims and techniques of communist literary and artistic circles in the Soviet Union and in the U.S. are reviewed.

S74 SCHULTZ, Benjamin. Commies Invade the Churches: I. Red Fronts Find Dupes in Protestant Pulpits; II. Red Crocodile Tears Ensnare Some Rabbis; III. Reds Use Prominent Catholics as Bait to Lure Masses, "New York World Telegram," Oct. 14, 15, 16, 1947. Reprinted by the American Jewish Committee in pamphlet form.
An assertion by the rabbi of a Westchester congregation that, despite official opposition to communism in all three faiths, pro-Soviet apologists or dupes exist among prominent church leaders.

S75 SCHUYLER, George S. The Separate State Hokum, "Crisis," 42 (May 1935), 135 ff.
A bitter attack both on the 49th state proposal of "black fascists" and on the Negro republic in the Black Belt advocated by the communists. Of the two proposals, the latter is the more fantastic, though Congress would never

adopt either. Should such action be possible, the revolution would be here and a separate state would be unnecessary. (Part of a symposium on "Which Way Out for the Negro?")

S76 .... Negroes Reject Communism, "American Mercury," 47 (June 1939), 176-81.
An assertion that the American Negro remains cold to communism because he is cynical, doubting that prejudice will disappear with the revolution. The author traces Party efforts among Negroes, arguing that results have been negligible because the Negro is militant only when there is hope of success.

S77 .... The Negro and Communism, "Interracial Review," 19 (April 1946), 54-55.
An assertion that communists have been relatively unsuccessful in recruiting Negroes because Negroes resent outside interference in their organizations, because communists introduce too many programs in which Negroes have no interests, and because Negroes suspect that the communists are trying to use them.

S78 .... Reds Outwit NAACP in Drive to Capture Negro Leadership, "New Leader," 29 (Aug. 10, 1946), 5.
An assertion by a leading Negro editor that the communist drive to capture leadership of American Negroes is in full swing and is succeeding. In many places the communists have infiltrated the NAACP, which may become a hollow shell, if not a communist front. Meanwhile the communists are winning the support of Negro professionals.

S79 .... Stalin's Blueprint for a Soviet Negro Belt in the U.S.A., "Plain Talk," 1 (June 1947), 3-9.
A critical analysis of the Party's plan for self-determination of Negroes in the Black Belt. The Party is ready to sacrifice Negro lives to promote Stalinist power here. Using injustices toward Negroes for propaganda purposes, the Party has won some Negro intellectuals but not the average Negro.

S80 SCHWARTZ, Murray L., and PAUL, James C. N. Foreign Communist Propaganda in the Mails: A Report on Some Problems of Federal Censorship, "University of Pennsylvania Law Review," 107 (March 1959), 621-66.
An examination of the federal government's program for withholding from American addresses "foreign communist propaganda" mailed from abroad. Attention is paid to the character of the addressee, the source of the mailing, and the character of the material. Legal bases for the operation are considered, and legislative alternatives are weighed against the constitutional guaranty of free expression.

S81 SCHWARZ, Fred. "You Can Trust the Communists (....to do exactly as they say!) Englewood Cliffs, N.J.: Prentice-Hall, 1960. 187 pp. Ind.
An account of the communist movement, based on the premise that the communists intend to carry out their objectives, using the organization they have described and following the moral code they have announced. The author describes the recruiting and molding of communists, the communist organization, communist fronts, techniques for seizing and consolidating power, the recruitment of allies, brainwashing, and the Marxian dialectic. He outlines a program for survival, discussing motivation, knowledge, and organization.

S82 SCHWEITZER, Leonard J. Communist Influence in the A.L.P., "America," 79 (Sept. 18, 1948), 533-35.

419

A study of American Labor Party membership in New York City, concluding that most members are Party-liners, and that a small minority are confused idealists.

S83   SCOTT, Adrian. Hollywood Liberals' Dilemma, "Masses & Mainstream," 8 (Oct. 1955), 15-28. Reprinted from "Hollywood Review."
The dilemma of Dore Schary of Metro-Goldwin-Mayer and others is to reconcile their words against book burning with their actions, which reject the works of known writers because of advanced political ideas. Since the 1947 hearings of the Un-American Activities Committee on Hollywood, blacklisting has continued, to the detriment of the victims and the public.

S84   SCOTT, Louise. Some Problems of Party Work in the Countryside, "Communist," 14 (May 1935), 429-43.
A description of communist organization among farmers, deploring the lack of effective guidance to rural units by section and district organizers, and the tendency of comrades in the countryside to regard themselves solely as organizers of the United Farmers' League, a Party front group.

S85   SCOTTSBORO DEFENSE COMMITTEE. "Scottsboro: The Shame of America." New York: The Committee, 1936. 30 pp.
A restatement of the Scottsboro case, in which nine Negro boys were accused of raping two white girls on a freight train in Alabama. After eight were convicted and sentenced to death, the International Labor Defense, a legal agency allied to the communist movement, entered the case. The Defense Committee, now in full charge of the case, also includes noncommunist Negro, civil liberties, and church groups.

S86   SCRATCH, Walter L. "God vs. Communism." Hollywood: House-Warven, 1952. 137 pp.
A discussion of the ideological conflict between communism and Christianity, with historical analysis to prove the irreconcilability of individual freedom with communism's atheistic materialism. The author describes the Hollywood Marxists whom he met at communist meetings; frustrated, many of them are more to be pitied than censored.

S87   "SEAMEN'S JOURNAL," Strategists or Disrupters? 50 (Dec. 1, 1936), 329-30 ff.
An attack by the general counsel of the International Seamen's Union upon Joseph Curran and communists in the Strike Strategy Committee on the Atlantic Coast. Red groups are seeking to force a general strike of seamen in violation of agreements. The ISU will not take orders from any political body, communist or otherwise.

S88   SEARS, Lawrence. Security and Liberty, "American Scholar," 20 (Spring 1951), 137-49.
An evaluation of our security-loyalty program concluding that, in our concern with security, we are using methods which not only threaten our liberty but fail to provide for the national security we seek.

S89   SEAVER, Edwin. Literature at the Crossroads, "New Masses," 7 (April 1932), 12-13.
The American writer of integrity is at a literary crossroad. He does not understand the relationship between his social function and his art, and accuses the revolutionary writer of talking politics, not art. The revolutionary writer is one who carries out the obligations agreed to by the International Union of Revolutionary Writers.

S90   .... American Writers and Kentucky, "New Masses," 7 (June 1932), 9-10.
Theodore Dreiser's decision to visit the striking miners of Harlan, Ky., and Sherwood Anderson's defense of Dreiser, show a revolution in the thinking of our established writers. This is the first step away from the ivory-tower literature of the 1920's, and a phase on the road to class consciousness.

S91   .... Sterile Writers and Proletarian Religions, "New Masses," 8 (May 1933), 22-24.
The author attacks the current vogue of literary editors of asserting that "our younger writers, grown sterile, had gone in for proletarian religions." A revolutionary orientation is not a sign of sterility, but the refutation of the sterility and bankruptcy of the 1920's.

S92   .... Another Writer's Position, "New Masses," 14 (Feb. 19, 1935), 21-22.
A rebuttal to Horace Gregory's rejection of Party membership despite sympathy with its views (One Writer's Position, "New Masses," Feb. 12, 1935). It is impossible to separate political from artistic activity; to claim "objectivity" is to cling to individualism. If a writer sees communism as a solution, he must function through the Party as a member or dependable ally.

S93   .... Socialist Realism, "New Masses," 17 (Oct. 22, 1935), 23-24.
An analysis of socialist realism as presented by the 1934 Congress of Soviet Writers, as well as by the book, "Problems of Soviet Literature." Socialist realism demands the ability to generalize, to seek out the main phenomenon. It does away with the split between realism and romanticism.

S94   SECURITY MINDED, Federal Employee Security Procedures, "Foreign Service Journal," 31 (Sept. 1954), 20-23 ff.
A review and evaluation of the federal government's employee security procedures, criticizing their slowness, the lack of minimum standards of proof, the failure to give the accused employee full information, and the time and money spent before a hearing is held. Need exists for more complete information, standards of proof and judgment, and objectivity.

S95   SEEGER, Peter. People's Songs and Singers, "New Masses," 60 (July 16, 1946), 7-9.
A favorable account of People's Songs, which publishes union and topical songs, and which issues monthly bulletins listing new recordings, songbooks, and critical articles. Its objective is a singing labor movement, using music as a weapon.

S96   SEGAL, Benjamin D., and KORNBLUH, Joyce L. The Insecurities of Our Security Program, "Progressive," 21 (Aug. 1957), 15-17.
Criticism of the industrial personnel security program, intended to safeguard classified information in the hands of private companies with Defense Department contracts. The program employs loose criteria, follows disturbing procedures, denies basic constitutional freedoms, injures workers accused of being security risks, and permits misuse by employers.

S97   SEGAL, Edith. "Give Us Your Hand! Poems and Songs for Ethel and Julius Rosenberg in the Death House at Sing Sing." New York: People's Artists. 1953. 24 pp.
A booklet of poems and songs on behalf of the Rosenbergs, representing the conviction that they are the innocent victims of terror, and that they have not received a fair trial.

S98 SEIDMAN, Joel. Communism in the American Labor Movement, "American Teacher," 25 (May 1941), 21-23.
A review of communist activities in trade unions, including the formation of the TUEL, its reorganization into the TUUL in 1929, the shift back to the AFL in 1933, the switch to the newly formed CIO in 1935, and the developing communist influence in that body. Though communist influence has been weakened since the Nazi-Soviet pact, the Party still controls many unions. (Part of a symposium on communism, fascism, and democracy.)

S99 . . . . "The Needle Trades." New York: Farrar & Rinehart, 1942. 356 pp. Bibliog. App. Ind.
Chapter 9, "Civil War in the Needle Trades" (pp. 153-85), describes the left-right strife in the needle trades unions in the 1920's. Unions dealt with include the ILGWU, the Amalgamated Clothing Workers, the Cap and Millinery Workers, and the Fur Workers. The communists were most successful in the Fur Workers, where they won complete control, and in the New York Joint Board of the ILGWU, where they led a disastrous strike in 1926.

S100 . . . . Labor Policy of the Communist Party during World War II, "Industrial and Labor Relations Review," 4 (Oct. 1950), 55-69.
A review of the labor policy of the Party from the popular front period of the 1930's to the postwar, cold war period, showing that the explanation for the Party's policy changes is to be found in the needs of the USSR. The Party line is traced through the popular front coalition against fascism, the supermilitancy of the Nazi-Soviet pact period, the superpatriotism of the war period, and the militancy of the postwar era.

S101 . . . . "American Labor from Defense to Reconversion." Chicago: University of Chicago Press, 1953. 307 pp. Notes. Ind.
A survey of labor in America during World War II, showing the changes in the attitudes and activities of the communists in the labor movement from 1939 to 1947. After opposing war efforts during the Nazi-Soviet pact period, the Party became vehemently interventionist with the attack on Russia. It supported the war effort and opposed all strikes, changing to a "hard" line with publication of the Duclos letter in June 1945.

S102 SEILER, Conrad. Orange Groves and Jails: The California Red Flag Law Finds Its First Victims, "New Republic," 61 (Nov. 27, 1929), 15-16.
An account of the arrest and conviction, in the first application of California's law against displaying the red flag, of women who helped operate a children's summer camp sponsored by the Young Workers' League and the International Labor Defense.

S103 . . . . Cantaloupes and Communists, "Nation," 131 (Sept. 3, 1930), 243-44.
An account of the conviction of nine leaders of the Agricultural Workers Industrial League of the Trade Union Unity League for criminal syndicalism, June 16, 1930. The author describes labor conditions in the Imperial Valley in California where the union was formed, the militant action of the union, and the mob action that resulted in arrests and subsequent conviction.

S104 . . . . The Redmongers Go West, "New Republic," 64 (Nov. 12, 1930), 346-48.
An account of the Fish Committee hearings on communism in Los Angeles, October 8-9, 1930. The witnesses, most of them obtained through the Better America Federation, testified to communist activity in the high schools, and Bolshevik propaganda in films. A representative of the ACLU received a brief and unfriendly hearing.

S105 SELDES, George. "Witch Hunt: The Technique and Profits of Redbaiting." New York: Modern Age, 1940. 300 pp. Ind.
A study of the use of the term "Red" as a smear-word directed, not against members of the Communist Party, but against liberals or trade unionists to divert attention from real issues. Sample Red-baiters include Ralph M. Easley, George E. Sokolsky, J. B. Matthews, Father Coughlin, Elizabeth Dilling, Harry A. Jung, and Merwin K. Hart. The author concludes that Red-baiting is itself a big business, that it is a political weapon, that it is conducted chiefly for profit, that the biggest Red-baiters in America are leading businessmen seeking to preserve their wealth, and that Red-baiting is one of the important forces in present-day America.

S106 . . . . "The People Don't Know: The American Press and the Cold War." New York: Gaer Associates, 1949. 342 pp. App. Ind.
An indictment of the U.S. press for its reporting of news from Europe after World War II, by a reporter and editor who had been associated with Party fronts. The American press is said to suppress or distort news from eastern Europe. Seldes found on a European tour that the Marshall Plan had increased fears of war, that the Eastern bloc has enjoyed great success, and that the charge of religious persecution in Eastern nations is false.

S107 SELIGMAN, Daniel. Communists Organize the Women, "New Leader," 29 (June 29, 1946), 5.
Behind a facade of respectable names, plus Party-liners, the communists have organized the Congress of American Women, an affiliate of the Women's International Democratic Federation. The activities of the leaders of the organization and the parent body show that they follow the world communist line.

S108 . . . . U.E.—The Biggest Communist Union, "American Mercury," 69 (July 1949), 35-45.
A discussion of the United Electrical Workers, the largest communist-dominated union in the U.S., written by an assistant editor of "American Mercury." He analyzes UE structure, its leadership, its past history, and present anticommunist efforts within the union. He sees encouraging signs of a break with the communists.

S109 . . . . How Elastic Is a Communist? Dilemma in New York, "Fortune," 55 (Feb. 1957), 101 ff.
An evaluation of the state of American communism during the de-Stalinization period. Though the present turn in line, like all past turns, was triggered by the turn in line of the Communist Party of the Soviet Union, this time the CPUSA led western communist parties in an impassioned attack on the CPSU. The CPUSA is expected to return to the control of pro-Stalinists William Z. Foster and Eugene Dennis.

S110 SELIGMAN, Edwin R. A.; BROCKWAY, Fenner; and NEARING, Scott. "Resolved: That Capitalism Offers More to the Workers of the World Than Socialism or Communism." New York: Rand Book Store, 1930. 64 pp. Also pub. by the Political Science Pocket Library.
A debate held in New York City, February 2, 1930, under the auspices of the League for Public Discussion. Professor Seligman emphasizes the production of wealth and growth of freedom under capitalism. Brockway, a British socialist, criticizes the inequitable distribution of wealth and limitations on freedom under capitalism. Nearing, for the communists, asserts that the choice is between a dying capitalist imperialism and a planned world economy under working class control.

S111 SELLIN, Thorsten (ed.). Internal Security and Civil Rights, "Annals of the American Academy of Political and Social Science," 300 (July 1955).
Papers delivered at the annual meeting of the Academy in April 1955. Included are papers on "Subversives in Government," by Francis Biddle; "Controlling Subversive Groups," by Ernest van den Haag; "The Dismissal of Fifth Amendment Professors," by Harold Taylor; "The Operation of Personnel Security Programs," by Ralph S. Brown, Jr.; and "Due Process in Security Dismissals," by Eleanor Bontecou. (All these items are separately abstracted.)

S112 SELSAM, Howard. "Socialism and Ethics." New York: International Publishers, 1943. 223 pp.
An analysis of the ethical basis of Marxist philosophy, asserting that Marxism, by pointing to moral issues and identifying itself with the needs of progressive humanity, takes a position of the highest morality. The author emphasizes Marx's belief in the justice of the proletarian cause, and surveys changes in moral ideals in human history to illustrate Marx's assertion that right cannot be higher than the economic structure and the cultural development of society determined by it.

S113 . . . (ed.). "Handbook of Philosophy." New York: International Publishers, 1949. 128 pp.
A Marxist philosophical dictionary, a translation and adaptation of a work, "Short Philosophic Dictionary," by M. Rosenthal and P. Yudin, that was first published in the Soviet Union in 1939. The handbook was planned to enable the reader without technical training to guide himself through the classic works of Marxist-Leninist philosophy.

S114 . . . . Shall Communists Teach in Our Colleges? "New Foundations for Peace, A Democratic Education and a Socialist Future," 6 (June 1953), 4-7.
A defense of the right of communists to teach. There can be no academic freedom unless it includes freedom for communists, who believe in freedom of thought and speech no matter where it leads. It is not the intellectual honesty of Marxists that is in question, but their conclusions concerning peace, democracy, and socialism.

S115 . . . . "Philosophy in Revolution." New York: International Publishers, 1957. 160 pp. Ind.
A discussion of the dynamics of social conflict by a leading Party theoretician and educator, who asserts that those who embrace Marxist views or accept Marxist leadership in the struggle for national liberation, progress, and socialism transform themselves ideologically, reaching a new understanding of man and his world. The author discusses Marxist historical materialism, attacking other philosophic schools as reactionary, demagogic, or destructive.

S116 . . . . "What Is Philosophy? A Marxist Introduction. 3d rev. ed., New York: International Publishers, 1962. 190 pp. Bibliog. Ind.
An introduction to dialectical materialism by a Marxist educator, who analyzes the nature and problems of philosophy as a social-historical enterprise. Discussing the conflict between philosophic systems of materialism and idealism, the author develops the Marxist conception of history, showing that its theory of the world serves as a basis for progressive social action. (The first edition of this work appeared in 1938.)

S117 . . ., and MARTEL, Harry (eds.). "Reader in Marxist Philosophy: From the Writings of Marx, Engels, and Lenin." New York: International Publishers, 1963. 384 pp. App. Sources. Bibliog. ind.

Selections from the writings of Marx, Engels, and Lenin, organized into sections on what Marxism is, materialism versus idealism, dialectics and the dialectical method, the theory of knowledge and the philosophy of science, the materialist interpretation of history, religion, and ethics.

S118 SELZNICK, Philip. "The Organizational Weapon: A Study of Bolshevik Strategy and Tactics." New York: McGraw-Hill, 1952. 350 pp. Ind.
A sociological analysis of Leninist organizational strategy and tactics. While many groups use organizational weapons, their aims are limited; in Leninism, however, organization becomes an adjunct to ideology as a means of gaining power. The Leninist party is in part a military organization, involving development of cadres who sever all other ties to become professional revolutionaries. United fronts and front organizations are devices by which the party hopes to gain access to diffuse populations, to transform them into mobilizable sources of power. Methods of dealing with communist penetration are discussed.

S119 "SENIOR SCHOLASTIC," Outlaw the Reds? 65 (Sept. 15, 1954), 9-11.
A pro and con discussion, in a publication for high school senior classrooms, of the wisdom of outlawing the Party in the U.S. Six reasons for and six against the outlawing of the Party are given, with supporting arguments. No conclusion is reached.

S120 SENTNER, William. The Missouri Valley Authority, "Political Affairs," 24 (May 1945), 453-60.
A plea for the establishment of a Missouri Valley Authority, to coordinate irrigation, flood control, and power generation. The proposal, supported by most farmers and workers, is opposed by utility companies, Big Business, and big farmers.

S121 SHACHTMAN, Max. "1871: The Paris Commune." Chicago: Daily Worker Publishing Co., n.d. [192-?]. 64 pp.
Account of the rise and fall of the Paris Commune, called the first great attempt to establish working class rule through the dictatorship of the proletariat. The weaknesses of the Commune are analyzed, their main source found to be the absence of a determined and conscious revolutionary party.

S122 . . . . A Communist Milestone: The Fourth Convention of the Workers Party of America, "Workers Monthly," 4 (Aug. 1925), 451-52.
An anticipation of problems of the Party convention to be held in August 1925, ranging from fighting imperialism to reorganizing on the basis of shop nuclei. Though there is a united front against the Workers Party, ranging from the reactionary parties of capitalism through trade bureaucrats and socialists, the WP leads the way to working-class revolution.

S123 . . . . "Sacco and Vanzetti, Labor's Martyrs." New York: International Labor Defense, 1927. 80 pp.
An assertion that Sacco and Vanzetti were victims of capitalist class justice, and that future labor defense cases must be fought, not merely in the courtroom, but in the streets with the weapons of class struggle. A living labor defense movement, such as the International Labor Defense, is the only vindication of the martyrs. (Shachtman was expelled from the Party the following year for helping organize a Trotskyist group.)

S124 . . . . Limitations of American Imperialism, "Communist," 6 (March 1927), 25-31.
A discussion of weaknesses of American imperialism in

the Orient and in Europe. Though American imperialism may achieve temporary success in China, it will fail, thanks to the Chinese revolution. In Europe, America faces strong industrial nations that compete for world markets; the collapse of Europe, resulting from this competition, will shake the structure of American imperialism. (A concluding section of this article failed to appear.)

S125   SHACHTMAN, Max. "Lenin, Liebknecht, Luxemburg." Introd. by Robert Minor. Chicago: Young Workers (Communist) League, n.d. [1929?]. 32 pp.
An account of the lives and work of Lenin and two of his disciples, communist martyrs Karl Liebknecht and Rosa Luxemburg.

S126   .... Lovestone's Appeal to Party, "Militant," 2 (Aug. 15, 1929), 7.
Analysis of the CPUSA leadership on the occasion of Lovestone's appeal to the Communist International for reinstatement. The dispute in the CPUSA is an unprincipled power struggle, in which both groups have equal claim to leadership. The crisis in the CPUSA will not be solved by the Stalinists. What is required is a principled return to the line of Lenin and the reinstatement of the Trotskyite opposition.

S127   .... "Ten Years: History and Principles of the Left Opposition." New York: Pioneer Publishers, 1933. 79 pp.
A history of the Trotskyist left opposition inside the Communist Party of the Soviet Union and the Comintern from 1923 to 1933. The Bolshevik party has gone through a period of social and political reaction that will lead to counterrevolution. In the Comintern, there is a similar crisis, stemming from opposition of Trotskyists to the theory of socialism in one country. The left opposition, which for many years sought to act as a faction of the official party, now seeks to build new Communist Parties and a new Communist International dedicated to the concept of permanent revolution.

S128   .... A Stupendous Bureaucracy, "New International," 1 (Aug. 1934), 78-80.
The CPUSA is called the most bureaucratized Stalinist party outside the Soviet Union. Of 3,000 Party members in New York City, about 1,000 depend upon the good will of Party leaders for the posts they occupy in nearly 100 organizations staffed exclusively by Party members.

S129   .... Stalinists in a Panic as Organization of New Party in U.S. Approaches, "Militant," 7 (Oct. 20, 1934), 4.
A review of CPUSA abuse of the Trotskyists, on the occasion of their impending merger with the American Workers Party led by A. J. Muste. The abuse conceals from the CPUSA membership the disgraceful situation inside the Party, which is seriously threatened by emergence of a new revolutionary center.

S130   .... The Problem of the Labor Party, "New International," 2 (March 1935), 33-37.
A review, in a Trotskyist journal, of the changing attitudes of the official communist movement in the U.S. toward a labor party. The first organized legal communist party, the Workers Party, tried to organize such a party in 1922. Browder's current advocacy of a labor party is a resurrection of Pepperism, even cruder and more opportunistic.

S131   .... People's Front—New Panacea of Stalinism, "New Militant," 2 (Jan. 11, 1936), 2.
A Trotskyist critique of the "popular front" line adopted at the Seventh World Congress of the Communist Inter-

national, and of its American application. Stalin's foreign policy has abandoned the international working class for alliances with bourgeois states. Soviet diplomacy therefore becomes a tool for preserving the bourgeoisie in those states with which Stalin makes alliances.

S132   .... The Stalinist Convention, "New International," 4 (July 1938), 202-5.
A Trotskyist reaction to the tenth convention of the CPUSA, at which the Party sought to show independence from Moscow and replaced the People's Front with the Democratic Front. The convention docilely accepted this reformist line because of the political inexperience and self-deception of the delegates, who were recruited from the middle class, and hand picked from Party functionaries. Ideological terrorism was used.

S133   .... Stalinists Start a New Union Busting Drive, "Labor Action," 6 (June 1, 1942), 1 ff.
Trotskyist commentary on the communists' drive to purge the unions of "Trotskyists," by which they mean anyone who will not accept their current line of all-out production for the war effort and opening of a second front. Both issues show their concern to protect the Stalinist regime.

S134   .... After the Dissolution of the Comintern: New Stalinist Plans to Undermine Labor, "Labor Action," 7 (July 19, 1943), 3; (July 26), 3.
A Trotskyist analysis of the situation resulting from Stalin's dissolution of the Comintern. This was a mere gesture to the Allies, since the Comintern had been buried by the Russian bureaucracy years before. It does not follow that Stalin intends to destroy the Stalinist parties, his principal means for operating inside the labor movement of capitalist countries.

S135   .... A Left Wing of the Labor Movement? Two Concepts of the Nature and Role of Stalinism, "New International," 15 (Sept. 1949), 204-10.
A discussion, from a Trotskyist point of view, of Stalinism and its reactionary role. The Stalinist movement does not resemble left-wing tendencies in any of its important characteristics. Labor's reformist bureaucracy, however, continues to play into Stalinist hands. The first task of militants is to remove Stalinism from the working class movement.

S136   .... Twenty-five Years of American Trotskyism: Part 1, The Origins of American Trotskyism, "New International," 20 (Jan-Feb., 1954), 11-25.
An account of the history of American Trotskyism, emphasizing developments since the expulsion of the Trotskyists from the CP in 1928. The factional struggle within the CP prior to the expulsion is treated, however, as are the formative influences on James P. Cannon, early Trotskyist leader, and the pattern of Stalinist gangsterism as experienced by the Trotskyists.

S137   .... American Communism: A Re-Examination of the Past, "New International," 23 (Fall 1957), 207-45.
An account of the development of the American communist movement, along with a review of Theodore Draper's "The Roots of American Communism." Shachtman deals with the emergence of the movement out of the socialist left wing, its factional quarrels, its control by the Comintern, its splits and expulsions, and the changes in its opinions over the years. He concludes that the American socialist movement must be reconstructed as a united, democratic movement, not in the image of the Communist Party, but based on American social conditions. (For a reply by Draper and Shachtman's rebuttal, see the "New International," Winter 1958, pp. 49-58.)

S138   SHAFER, Paul W. Communist Expansion in the United States, "National Republic," 40 (March 1953), 1-2.
An account by a Michigan congressman of communist activities in Philadelphia, the city said to harbor the most dangerous communist underground in the U.S. Communist control of a local of the United Electrical Workers is described.

S139   SHAFFER, Helen B. Red Teachers and Educational Freedom, "Editorial Research Reports," 1 (Feb. 11, 1953), 101-19.
An account of communist infiltration of school systems, of action to combat subversion in schools, and of the effect of red hunts on freedom of teaching. The McCarran Internal Security subcommittee had reported evidence of a communist conspiracy to indoctrinate youth by infiltrating the school system. Educators are seeking to safeguard academic freedom.

S140   . . . . Security Risks and the Public Safety, "Editorial Research Reports," 1 (Feb. 23, 1955), 137-56.
Procedural changes in the federal employee security program, to protect the rights of employees, are soon to be proposed. The security program has been the subject of controversy, particularly over the barring of J. Robert Oppenheimer from access to classified data, the dismissal of John Paton Davies from the Foreign Service, and the ousting of Wolf Ladejinsky as agricultural attaché in Tokyo.

S141   SHAIR, David I. How Effective Is the Non-Communist Affidavit? "Labor Law Journal," 1 (Sept. 1950), 935-44.
An analysis of Section 9 (h) of the Taft-Hartley law after three years of operation. The author gives its legislative history, a historical background for this type of affidavit, and a brief summary of communism in American unions. He concludes that the affidavit is hastening the elimination of communists from union posts.

S142   SHANNON, David A. "The Decline of American Communism: A History of the Communist Party of the United States since 1945. New York: Harcourt, Brace, 1959. 425 pp. Bibliog. essay. Notes. Ind.
A history of the Party from its left turn in the closing months of World War II to the period of disillusionment and decay following the Khrushchev disclosure of Stalinist excesses and the crushing of the Hungarian revolt. The Party's role in the Henry Wallace-Progressive Party campaign of 1948 is outlined. The Party declined from its 1947 peak because of postwar prosperity, the impact of the cold war, anticommunist legislation and prosecutions, and the development of left-of-center groups into strong centers of anticommunism. The Party reacted to anticommunist attacks with hysterical repression. However feeble, it will continue to exist until the Soviet regime finds it no longer useful.

S143   SHANNON, William V. Hollywood Returns to the Stand, "New Republic," 124 (June 25, 1951), 21-22.
The Washington correspondent for the New York "Post" reports on the second portion of the investigation of communism in the movie industry by the House Committee on Un-American Activities. Asserting that the hearings serve no purpose, the author views the witnesses as lonely men who prostitute and degrade themselves.

S144   SHAPIRO, David I. Government Employment and the Loyalty-Security Program, "Lawyers Guild Review," 15 (Winter 1955-56), 131-34.
A review of cases that have reached the courts under the Truman loyalty-security program. Most attention has been centered on procedural fairness, though the question of coverage is also important. The author argues that procedural fairness is lacking, and that there is no justification for application to nonsensitive employment.

S145   SHAPIRO, Meyer. Architecture and the Architect, "New Masses," 19 (April 7, 1936), 30-31.
A discussion of the problems facing architecture before and during the depression. Building is at an impasse despite immense technical resources, an army of unemployed architects, and miserably housed masses. Only a socialist state can guarantee the large scale planning and the high living standards of the masses essential to building.

S146   SHAPLEN, Robert. Scarsdale's Battle of the Books: How One Community Dealt with "Subversive Literature," "Commentary," 10 (Dec. 1950), 530-40.
An account of the two-year (1948-50) struggle in Scarsdale, New York, between the "Committee of Ten," which sought to purge school libraries of books by communists, and the Board of Education. The Board, backed by the majority of citizens, refused to ban the books.

S147   SHARP, Malcolm. "Was Justice Done? The Rosenberg-Sobell Case." Introd. by Harold C. Urey. New York: Monthly Review Press, 1956. 216 pp. App.
Defense of the Rosenbergs and Morton Sobell by a professor at the University of Chicago Law School, who expresses grave doubt as to the justice of the convictions. He reviews the case presented against the three, shows where doubt has arisen as to the reliability of Greenglass' testimony, points out weaknesses in the case as a whole, and reviews efforts to get a new trial on new evidence. He concludes that the Rosenbergs, who are superior persons, have become scapegoats for hidden guilts and hatreds.

S148   SHAULL, M. Richard. "Encounter with Revolution." New York: Association Press, 1955. 145 pp.
An argument by a missionary with long experience in South America that communism appeals to people in underdeveloped countries, who are passing through a profound social revolution, because it offers an explanation and solution, a strong movement, and a total philosophy. The U.S., he asserts, must recognize the limitations of military power alone in a revolutionary world, and show an interest in the social and economic problems confronting other peoples. Christians must be active in the struggle against injustice, particularly in the treatment of Negroes here, as they must be free from obsession with material things and concerned with the material well-being of others.

S149   SHAW, Irwin. "The Troubled Air." New York: Random House, 1951. 418 pp.
The story of the director of a radio show who tries to protect his actors against charges of communism made by a rabid anticommunist magazine. The director loses his job in the process, only to find out that one of the actors he defended is a fanatical communist.

S150   SHAW, J. G. [pseud.]. Will the Communists Get Our Girls in College? "Liberty," 12 (Sept. 7, 1935), 12-15.
The plaint of a father whose daughter, a student at a leading state university, had joined the Communist Party, lost her religion, and forgotten her career. Similar cases of other college girls are recited. The blame is put upon the

socialist Student League for Industrial Democracy as well as upon the communist National Student League. (For his daughter's reply see Nancy Bedford-Jones, My Father is a Liar, "New Masses," Sept. 3, 1935.)

S151 SHAW, Marvin. The Reawakening of the American Student Movement, "Political Affairs," 26 (Feb. 1947), 132-43.
A report on the Chicago Conference of Students held December 28-30, 1946. The conference is praised for bringing different groups of students together to discuss national and educational problems. Catholics are criticized for acting as a bloc at the conference. The conference set up a national organization to speak for U.S. students on matters of common interest.

S152 .... Student America Convenes! "Political Affairs," 26 (Oct. 1947), 872-86.
An account of the founding convention of the National Student Association and of the program adopted. The NSA is criticized for its weak position on segregation in education. The Catholic student bloc is criticized for its reactionary role, as are the leaders of Students for Democratic Action for their pathological fear of communism. Left and progressive students, though few in number, made important contributions.

S153 SHAW, Ralph. Initiating Labor Party Tickets: Experiences in the Recent Elections in Southern Illinois Mining Towns, "Communist," 14 (June 1935), 548-57.
Experiences in Illinois mining communities are reviewed to show the possibilities of building a broad labor party. Weaknesses included sluggishness in starting the campaign, too few Party members in the local unions, and capitulation to Red-baiting.

S154 SHEEN, Fulton J. "The Tactics of Communism," New York: Paulist Press, n.d. [1936?]. 24 pp.
A description of communist tactics presented in questions and answers, with most of the answers in the form of brief quotations from communist sources, both American and foreign. Questions deal with revolution and violence, private property, the ties between the Communist Party of the U.S. and the international communist movement, and the Party's united front tactics against war and fascism.

S155 .... "Communism and Religion." New York: Paulist Press, n.d. [1937?]. 22 pp.
An assertion that communism is antithetical to religion, despite the fact that western communists, in this popular front period, profess to respect religious beliefs and despite the provisions of the new Soviet constitution. Communism, the author asserts, has two faces—persecution for religion in Russia, where it is established; and kindly and even religious appearance in countries it hopes to sovietize, in order to avoid antagonizing at the beginning.

S156 .... When Stalin Kissed Hitler the Communists Blushed Red, "America," 62 (Oct. 21, 1939), 32-33.
A review of pronouncements from Party sources prior to the Hitler-Stalin pact. Though the union of communists and Nazis surprised many, including leaders of communist front groups, it was no great surprise to Catholics.

S157 .... Moscow Makes Confusion for Reds and for Nations, "America," 62 (Oct. 28, 1939), 60-61.
A report on the reaction to the Hitler-Stalin pact of communist leaders in France and in the U.S. The "New Masses" has run a column of questions and answers relating to the new line. The Party here will not have a new line until Moscow gives it to them.

S158 .... "Freedom under God." Milwaukee: Bruce, 1940. 265 pp. Notes.
An appraisal by a Catholic clergyman of the meaning of liberty. Chapter 5 (pp. 55-92) deals with "Communism, Capitalism, and Liberty," with a critical evaluation of communism on pages 71-92. Communism is charged with speaking only of the use of property and forgetting its rights, and with taking over all the bad features of capitalism while ignoring its better ones.

S159 .... "Communism Answers Questions of a Communist." Helena, Montana: Americanism Committee, American Legion, Department of Montana, 1946. 15 pp.
A reprint of a series of articles originally printed in the Catholic press in January 1937 in response to questions posed by Louis F. Budenz in the "Daily Worker" in December 1936. The author quotes communist sources to show that communism is for the downtrodden only when it seeks converts, that it is wrong in its methods, and that a united front with communists would be camouflage and deceit.

S160 .... "Communism and the Conscience of the West." Indianapolis and New York: Bobbs-Merrill, 1948. 247 pp. Notes.
A popularly written analysis of the communist philosophy and its basic defects, and of the failings of the Christian world for having given birth to the materialist philosophy from which Soviet philosophy developed. The author tells how communism can be combatted, and enumerates the differences between the Church's social concern and the Russian attitude. The basic struggle today is over whether man shall exist for the state, or the state for man; whether freedom is of the spirit, or a concession of a materialized society. Communism has dehumanized man by making him a social animal for whom an economic machine is the total meaning of existence.

S161 SHEIL, Bernard J. McCarthy vs. Morality, "UAW-CIO Ammunition," 12 (April 1954), 14-17.
In an address to a UAW education conference in Chicago, April 9, 1954, a Catholic bishop discusses the form that anticommunism should take in a freedom-loving country such as ours. He singles out McCarthy as a proponent of an immoral and ineffective type of anticommunism.

S162 .... The Immorality of McCarthyism, "Progressive," 18 (May 1954), 10-12.
Adapted from a speech by Bishop Sheil to the 1954 education conference of the United Automobile Workers. Bishop Sheil urges us to meet the challenge of communism by improving social and economic conditions and breaking down the barriers that separate people. By this test, as well as because of his lies and deceit, Senator McCarthy is found wanting.

S163 SHELTON, Willard. Inside the C.I.O., "New Republic," 116 (March 24, 1947), 38-39.
A discussion of the leadership and the arguments of both the anti- and the procommunist factions within the CIO. The war over communism is sure to continue, and the leftists, recently on the defensive, are trying to organize a counteroffensive. Philip Murray is still walking a tightrope.

S164 .... Amerasia Case, "Nation," 170 (June 17, 1950), 590-92; (June 24), 613-15.
A review of the charges, the background, the evidence, and the sentences in the "Amerasia" case, in which classified government documents were found in the magazine's files. Asserting that the uproar that followed represents McCarthyism, the author suggests the need for legislation to

protect classified materials. There is no evidence of a procommunist State Department bloc which "sold out" Chiang Kai-shek.

S165   SHELTON, Willard. C o m m u n i s t s in Unions, "Nation," 174 (Feb. 23, 1952), 170-71.
A discussion of the problem facing Senator Humphrey's subcommittee in finding just and effective means to control communist-led unions. A democracy may properly see whether security is jeopardized by communist leadership of key unions. Among the suggestions are denial of bargaining rights to communist-led unions in defense industries, or in all industries.

S166   . . . . Paul Crouch, Informer, "New Republic," 131 (July 19, 1954), 7-9.
Crouch is called the best paid of the career informers on communist activities. His contradictory statements under oath have raised questions as to his reliability. Frequently he puts himself in "imaginary" positions in his testimony.

S167   SHERMAN, B. The Eighth Convention of the Communist Party of the U.S.A. and Some Conclusions, "Communist International," 11 (June 20, 1934), 390-94.
The Party convention showed substantial growth and strengthened Party leadership. Rejecting "left" tendencies, it focused the main attention on building a mass opposition in the reformist unions while building the revolutionary unions. Great improvement in the political development of Negro cadres was evident.

S168   SHERMAN, Charles Bezalel. "The Communists in Palestine: The Mufti's Moscow Allies." New York: League for Labor Palestine, 1939. 29 pp.
An exposé of communist policy toward Palestine and Zionism, based on declarations in the American and international communist press. Attention is drawn to Soviet opposition to a Jewish homeland in Palestine and to its efforts to foment anti-Jewish and anti-Zionist outbursts among the Arabs.

S169   SHERMAN, Ray W. "How to Win an Argument with a Communist. New York: Dutton, 1950. 251 pp. App. Bibliog.
An account of communism, both utopian and Marxist, in America, with a point-by-point refutation of the Communist Manifesto. The experience of the leading utopian colonies in America, including Brook Farm, the Shakers, the Oneida community, and the Amana Society, is presented, along with brief comments on communism in the USSR. Questions to be asked communists are listed. The text of the Communist Manifesto is given in an appendix.

S170   SHIELDS, Art. "The Killing of William Milton." Introd. by Simon W. Gerson. New York: Daily Worker, 1948. 15 pp.
The story of the killing of Milton by police in Brooklyn, N. Y. Milton, a Negro and a communist, had scuffled with a neighborhood bartender who disliked serving Negroes and was killed by police as he fled home.

S171   . . . . Pittsburgh: Peace on Trial, "Masses & Mainstream," 4 (April 1951), 17-30.
A report on the trial of three communists—Steve Nelson, Andy Onda, and James Dolsen—under a Pennsylvania sedition law passed in 1919, and unused for almost 20 years. The suit is really aimed at peace, militant unionism, and resistance to fascism. Unflattering pictures are painted of Judge Musmanno and prosecution witness Matt Cvetic.

S172   . . . . "Unemployment: The Wolf at the Door." New York: New Century, 1958. 22 pp.

A simply written pamphlet by a "Daily Worker" reporter, who reviews the march of Coxey's army on Washington in 1894, the Unemployed Councils and hunger marches of the 1930's, and the winning of unemployment insurance. A program to combat the current recession is outlined.

S173   SHILS, Edward A. "The Torment of Secrecy: The Background and Consequences of American Security Policies." Glencoe, Illinois: Free Press, 1956. 238 pp.
A discussion of postwar America, the insecurity caused by the atomic bomb and the danger of subversion, and the exaggeration and distortion of the legitimate concern with security. The author traces the sources of the obsession with security and its effects on our society. The laws aimed at the communist movement contribute little to security, and policies to ensure personnel security hurt many innocent persons. The committee investigations and perjury cases have had little impact on espionage or security. (An excerpt was published in the "New Leader," Jan. 9, 1956.)

S174   SHUB, Boris. American League, CP's Innocent Front No. 1, "New Leader," 21 (Dec. 31, 1938), 2 ff.
A comparison of the policies of the American League for Peace and Democracy, and of its predecessor, the American League Against War and Fascism, with the Communist Party line. Emphasis is placed on the relationship between these and the foreign policy needs of the Soviet Union. (The first of two articles on the American League.)

S175   . . . . How Communism Inc. Controls the League for Peace and Democracy, "New Leader," 22 (Jan. 7, 1939), 3 ff.
The Party is a holding company which controls the American League for Peace and Democracy through such subsidiaries as the IWO, the ILD, the National Committee for Defense of Political Prisoners, the American Writers Congress, and the Youth Congress. These Party-controlled affiliates are overrepresented in the League's congress, national committee, and executive board. (The second of two articles on the League.)

S176   SHUB, David. Socialism, Communism and Trade Unionism, "New Leader," 18 (Oct. 5, 1935), 10.
The big issue before workers is said to be democratic socialism or communism, which seeks a new order through revolution, dictatorship, and mass terror. Stooping to any tactics in the belief that the end justifies the means, communists seek to capture unions to place them under Party control. Unions must drive communists from leadership, or be wrecked by them.

S177   . . . . Why Socialists Are against a United Front with the Communists, "New Leader" (Magazine Section), 18 (Nov. 23, 1935), 9-12.
A review of the change in line on the united front adopted at the Seventh World Congress of the Communist International, and defense of the rejection by the Second International of the Comintern proposal for united front activity. The Comintern reflects the foreign policy interests of the Soviet Union. In the U.S., the Communist Party is encouraging dissension inside the Socialist Party.

S178   SHUBIN, P. The Bourgeoisie of the U.S.A. Put Their Stake on War, "Communist International," 10 (Aug. 15, 1933), 545-51.
A communist view of the depression crisis in the U.S., asserting that the American bourgeoisie sees war as the only solution, with the National Industrial Recovery Act a means of preparing for war. American imperialism, in preparing for war, hopes to enlarge the foreign as well as the domestic market.

S179 SHULL, Leo. Exit Theatre? "New Masses," 65 (Dec. 23, 1947), 6-8.
A view of the New York theater as controlled by a monopoly. Showing how other countries manage the theater, the author concludes that only a subsidy will solve American theater problems.

S180 SHULTZ, Lillie. Spies or Sappers? "Nation," 175 (Dec. 20, 1952), 576-79.
A critical review of the loyalty purge of United Nations employees, under which employees who refuse to answer questions relating to espionage or Communist Party membership in the U.S. are to be dismissed, along with those believed by the UN Secretary General to be engaged in subversive activities here. These provisions are alleged to violate the UN charter, the authority of the secretary general, and U.S. concepts of jurisprudence.

S181 SHUSTER, George N. Communism or the Catholic Church, "Forum," 86 (Oct. 1931), 207-12.
Catholic and communist cures for our present social disorders are contrasted. Today's only source of reconstructive energy is the Catholic Church, which could put corrective measures into effect immediately, preventing communism from influencing the dispossessed.

S182 SIBLEY, Mulford Q.; HARTMANN, George W.; and SMITH, Tucker P. The Roots of McCarthyism: A Symposium, "Socialist Call," 22 (Sept. 1954), 14-18.
Sibley traces the sources of McCarthyism to neo-isolationism, fear of communism, and the fear-insecurity-power complex. Hartmann finds the primary cause in hostile rejection of anyone who is not a 100 per cent anticommunist. Smith emphasizes the evasion of reality in current American political choices.

S183 SIGMAN, Morris. The Communist Plague in Our Union, "New Leader," 2 (July 4, 1925), 4.
Declaring that the communists have declared war upon the ILGWU, the president of the union asserts that no member or follower of the Workers Party should be allowed to hold office, paid or unpaid, in the union.

S184 SILBER, Irwin (ed.). "Lift Every Voice! The Second People's Songbook." Foreword by Paul Robeson. New York: People's Artists, 1953. 96 pp.
A collection of songs of the common people—union songs, love songs, play songs, songs of struggle for democracy and freedom, all of them contributing to the struggle for peace.

S185 SILLEN, Samuel. The Response to "Native Son," "New Masses," 35 (April 23, 1940), 25-27.
The first of two articles on Richard Wright's "Native Son," concentrating on an analysis of press and literary reaction to the book. Though there is agreement that Wright is one of the leading American novelists, opinion is divided as to whether the novel is communist or anticommunist.

S186 .... The Meaning of Bigger Thomas, "New Masses," 35 (April 30, 1940), 26-28.
The second of two articles on Richard Wright's "Native Son." Critics who have seen the novel as anticommunist have misinterpreted it. Though the communist characters in the book are not "mature" at the beginning, Wright's portrayal of them is generally positive.

S187 ... (ed.). "Walt Whitman: Poet of American Democracy." New York: International Publishers, 1944. 175 pp.
Selections from the poetry and prose of Walt Whitman, arranged and edited so as to present him as a living force in the war against fascist barbarism and in the peace which America and its allies seek. (Whitman was one of the prominent American figures whom the communists adopted as forerunners of democracy, as they interpret it.)

S188 ... (ed.). "William Cullen Bryant." New York: International Publishers, 1945. 94 pp.
Selections from the poetry and prose of William Cullen Bryant, who is seen as one who carried forward the revolutionary tradition, bringing it to bear on the fight against slavery. (One of the efforts by the communists in this period to identify with leading American historical and cultural figures, of whose tradition they now claim to be the bearers.)

S189 .... Writers and the American Century, "Masses & Mainstream," 2 (Feb. 1949), 44-52.
A review of modern literature, emphasizing the fight of our best writers against entrenched privilege and smugness. John Chamberlain is criticized for his complaint about the mistreatment of the businessman in American literature. No serious writer sympathetic to democracy has ever glorified capitalist relations in America.

S190 .... Behind the Ivy Curtain, "Masses & Mainstream," 2 (March 1949), 7-17.
A defense of the right of communists to teach at American colleges and universities, with criticism of the University of Washington for dismissing three Party members and of the other institutions for dropping supporters of Henry Wallace. Increasingly, colleges and universities are instruments of Big Business, controlled by wealthy and conservative trustees.

S191 .... "Cold War in the Classroom." New York: Masses & Mainstream, 1950. 24 pp.
An assertion by the editor of "Masses & Mainstream" that the cold war spells ruin for the American school system, from kindergarten to college. He attacks snooping into textbooks, dismissal of leftist teachers, control of college boards of trustees by Big Business, and militarization of colleges. A program to save the schools is presented.

S192 .... Mrs. Stowe's Best Seller: 100th Anniversary of an American Classic, "Masses & Mainstream," 5 (March 1952), 20-29.
An account of the writing of "Uncle Tom's Cabin," the problems in getting it published, its reception and influence. Defects include the characterization of Uncle Tom, the idealization of some slaveholders, and generalizations about Negroes bordering on racism. Its achievement was the powerful indictment of chattel slavery.

S193 .... Charles W. Chesnutt: A Pioneer Negro Novelist, "Masses & Mainstream," 6 (Feb. 1953), 8-14.
The forgotten career of this able Negro novelist, who lived from 1858 to 1932, illustrates the Jim Crow pattern of publishing in this country, and white supremacist literary tastes. Chesnutt's themes—injustice in Southern towns, problems of "passing," interracial marriages—were not popular with publishers or the general public.

S194 .... Van Wyck Brooks and the Literary Crisis, "Masses & Mainstream," 6 (Oct. 1953), 20-27.
A critical review of Brooks' book, "The Writer in America." While sharing Brooks' dismay at the state of American letters, Sillen criticizes Brooks for unwittingly supporting the social forces responsible for the cultural

crisis. Brooks does not understand the effects of the system of war and oppression; moreover, he denounces communist writers and traditions.

S195   SILLEN, Samuel. "Women against Slavery." New York: Masses & Mainstream, 1955. 102 pp. Bibliog.
Sketches of 16 women abolitionists who fought for the Negro, the Bill of Rights, and freedom. Now as then, according to this communist author, minorities are being officially persecuted for advanced social views.

S196   . . . . Notes on Dreiser, "Masses & Mainstream," 8 (Dec. 1955), 12-19.
Notes on Theodore Dreiser's life and work, written on the tenth anniversary of his death. Dreiser is compared to Balzac, who influenced him greatly, and contrasted with Henry James, whom Balzac also influenced. Dreiser, long a storm center of American criticism, joined the Communist Party in the last year of his life.

S197   SILVER, A., and AMTER, I. "Proletarian Dictatorship or Industrial Unionism?" New York: N. Y. Labor News Company, 1927. 40 pp.
A debate between A. Silver of the Socialist Labor Party and I. Amter of the Workers (Communist) Party over whether industrial democracy is to be achieved through proletarian dictatorship, as advocated by the communists, or through industrial unionism, as proposed by the SLP.

S198   SILVER, Henry. Knowledge of Communist Activities as Self-Incrimination, "Lawyers Guild Review," 10 (Summer 1950), 71-74.
A historical survey of the Fifth Amendment privilege and of recent cases involving it. The privilege against self-incrimination applies not only to a witness' own participation in communist activities, but also to his knowledge of such activities by others.

S199   SILVERMAN, Harriet. "J. Louis Engdahl: Revolutionary Working Class Leader." New York: Workers Library, 1935. 31 pp.
A memorial pamphlet to the national secretary of the International Labor Defense, who died in Moscow while on a European tour on behalf of the Scottsboro defendants. A member of the left wing of the Socialist Party which evolved into the communist movement, Engdahl served the latter as editor and official of the ILD until his death.

S200   . . . . The Health Status of American Workers, "Communist," 17 (Feb. 1938), 177-87.
Attention is called to a health crisis in the U.S., and compulsory national insurance is proposed as the first step in alleviating deplorable health standards.

S201   SILVERSTEIN, Louis. The Lefts Right About Face: Communism in Slogan and Practice in the Garment Workers' International, "New Leader," 3 (March 20, 1926), 3.
An assertion that the communists, now in control of the dress division of the New York Joint Board of the ILGWU, follow the same policies as their right-wing predecessors, although at the recent union convention they had sponsored a militant resolution opposing class collaboration, arbitration, and limitations on the strike.

S202   SIMMONS, George E. The Communist Conspiracy Case: Views of 72 Daily Newspapers, "Journalism Quarterly," 27 (March 1950), 3-11.
An analysis of editorial comment on the trial of the communist leaders, revealing division of opinion on the meaning of "clear and present danger." The author discusses editorial stands for and against the constitutionality of the

Smith Act and the extensive news coverage of the trial, concluding that the press acquitted itself well in its reporting and editorial task.

S203   SIMON, Hal. The Rank-and-File Strike of the New York Longshoremen, "Political Affairs," 24 (Dec. 1945), 1088-96.
The New York strike of AFL longshoremen shows the growing militancy in the labor movement against monopolistic profiteering. The activities of communists among the striking longshoremen are described.

S204   . . . . Some Lessons of the Recent Strike Struggles, "Political Affairs," 25 (June 1946), 493-501.
The recent strike struggles were worthwhile because of the wage increases won, as well as for other reasons, even though lack of unity prevented winning of the full demands. The war aims of the imperialists and their union supporters can be combated only by a fight for trade union unity. Major goals for the trade union movement are outlined.

S205   . . . . The Struggle for Jobs and for Negro Rights in the Trade Unions, "Political Affairs," 29 (Feb. 1950), 33-48.
A report by the trade union secretary of the CP in New York State to a trade union conference, October 7-8, 1949. White chauvinism today is used to divide and disrupt the struggle for peace and democracy. By driving the Negro worker out of industry, by pitting white and Negro workers against each other, the top CIO and AFL leaders serve the interests of American imperialism.

S206   . . . . The Labor Merger, "Political Affairs," 35 (Jan. 1956), 51-65.
A report to the Party's national conference, December 3-5, 1955, viewing the AFL-CIO merger as a step forward, praising the merger convention's actions on civil rights and organizing the unorganized, but criticizing its support of the Administration's imperialist foreign policy. Tasks of progressive forces within the merged organization are outlined.

S207   . . . . Some Concepts of Our Trade-Union Work, "Political Affairs," 36 (Feb. 1957), 49-57.
The Party's biggest problem is to overcome its isolation from the labor movement. Left sectarian errors of the past, which have estranged the communists from millions of workers, are reviewed. The Party should contribute to the broadest unity of the workers in daily struggle, while infusing consciousness and welding a firm antimonopoly coalition.

S208   SIMON, Harold. The Current Communist Party Line, "New Leader," 26 (July 17, 1943), 5 ff.
An assertion that the Communist Party, despite the "dissolution" of the Comintern, is continuing its hypocrisy and internationally coordinated disruptiveness. It is attacking the labor and socialist movement, continuing its old union splitting policy in new forms, and opposing the formation of a national labor or farmer-labor party.

S209   SIMONS, William. "Hands Off Cuba!" New York: Workers Library, 1933. 16 pp.
A protest against the American warships in Cuban waters, which are preparing to land marines in order to protect Wall Street property. American rule in Cuba has meant reaction, terror, heavy taxation, and corruption. The Cuban people have the right to throw off the American yoke.

S210   SINCLAIR, Upton. Communist "C r i m i n a l s" in California, "Nation," 129 (Nov. 20, 1929), 582-84.

An account of the conviction, under California's "red flag law," of Yetta Stromberg and four other Russian working women, who conducted a children's summer camp at which communist doctrines were taught. (The convictions were later reversed by the U.S. Supreme Court.)

S211 SINCLAIR, Upton. "The Way Out: What Lies Ahead for America." Los Angeles: The author, 1933. 64 pp.
A pamphlet by an independent radical consisting of letters "addressed to a young capitalist," telling what is wrong with the American economy. Although he does not advocate the "complete communism" that has taken place in Russia, Sinclair asserts that there is much that we can learn from the Russians. Communists consider him a social-fascist; nevertheless both know that the time is not far distant when government will take over industry, and socialism will be here.

S212 SINGER, Herman. The Modern Quarterly: 1923-1940, "Modern Quarterly," 11 (Autumn 1940), 13-19.
An analysis of the magazine and of the personality and intellect of V. F. Calverton, its editor and publisher. The main concern of the "Modern Quarterly" was with Marxist influence on the social sciences, literature, and literary criticism. The magazine presented a balanced, critical view of the USSR, and consistently criticized the activities of the Communist Party.

S213 SINGER, Kurt. "Communist Agents in America: A Who's Who of American Communists." New York: News Backgrounds, 1947. 20 pp.
One of a series of news reports on world affairs, this pamphlet provides a listing of leading communists and front organizations.

S214 . . . . Red Watch in Our Harbors, "Plain Talk," 1 (July 1947), 20-24.
A review of communist control over our waterfronts, primarily through the American Communications Association, the Marine Cooks and Stewards, and the International Longshoremen's and Warehousemen's Union. There is danger of espionage and sabotage so long as communists control American harbors and ships.

S215 . . . . "The World's 30 Greatest Women Spies." New York: Funk, 1951. 318 pp.
A popularly written account of the conspiratorial activities of 30 women spies and counterespionage agents, including Elizabeth Bentley, Ruth Fischer and Judith Coplon. Through them the stories of Harry Gold, the Rosenbergs, and David Greenglass are told as well (pp. 70-128).

S216 . . . . "Repentant Communists—Maybe." New York: Overnight Duplication Service, n.d. [1952?]. 10 pp.
A lecture delivered in San Francisco, December 3, 1952, warning Americans against trusting excommunists. While they should be forgiven, they should be put where they belong in public life—at the bottom and not on the top.

S217 . . . . "The Men in the Trojan Horse." Boston: Beacon, 1953. 258 pp. Ind.
A discussion of spies, traitors, and espionage agents, by a counterespionage agent, with emphasis on communist spies and with an analysis of the psychology of intelligence forces. There is a chapter on Gerhart Eisler (pp. 163-73), and one on the Noel Field mystery (pp. 224-42). The author urges caution in trusting the excommunist until he has proved his new idealism for democracy over a long period of time.

S218 SISK, John P. On Hearing Mr. Budenz, "Commonweal," 50 (July 22, 1949), 360-63.
The author is depressed by the black-and-white view of a very complex issue presented by Budenz, whose formula for detecting communists is not necessarily infallible. Many now confuse freedom with security, both of which are threatened by the communists.

S219 SISKIND, Beatrice. Despotism and Deportation, "Political Affairs," 28 (Dec. 1949), 60-73.
An analysis of attacks on the foreign born in American history, with particular attention to arrests of communists in 1949 under the Alien Registration Act of 1940. Chauvinism and racism have traditionally accompanied attacks on the foreign born in the U.S. Top leaders of the CIO and AFL have cooperated with the Department of Justice drive to deport progressive trade unionists.

S220 SISKIND, George. The Wall Street-Washington Peace Panic, "Political Affairs," 27 (Nov. 1948), 951-61.
The Wall Street overlords fear that a peaceful agreement with the Soviet Union will ruin business, that the economy will collapse without war expenditures. American capitalism narrowly averted disaster when the State Department rejected Soviet proposals to destroy atomic stockpiles and reduce armaments. Soviet leaders stand for peaceful coexistence, while asserting that capitalism and imperialism breed war.

S221 . . . . Leninism—Guide to Unity for Peace, Democracy, Socialism, "Political Affairs," 29 (Jan. 1950), 4-13.
The U.S. has reached the decaying stage in the Leninist analysis of capitalism, with its productive capacity so overreaching the available markets that it must turn to imperialist adventures. The main thrust of its aggression is against Russia, which responds with an offer of a peace pact. The masses can be united to put pressure on the government to accept the offer.

S222 . . ., and MARTEL, Harry. Psychoanalysis: Ideological Instrument of Imperialism (An Article for Discussion), "Political Affairs," 29 (Dec. 1950), 61-74.
A communist analysis of Freudianism and its variants, which constitute an ideological instrument at the disposal of the monopolist ruling class. The subjectivity of this bourgeois psychology leads to distortions of objective reality. Psychoanalysis helps to conceal imperialism's brutality, as it provides justification for fascism and war. Bourgeois psychology, like every other aspect of bourgeois science, has been affected by the general crisis of capitalism.

S223 SKOUSEN, W. Cleon. "The Naked Communist." Salt Lake City: Ensign Publishing Company, 1958. 343 pp. Bibliog. Ind.
An effort to compress the main facts about communism in a single volume and to present the communist in his native elements, stripped of propaganda and pretense. Chapter 7, pp. 131-54, on "Communism in the United States," deals with violence attributed to the communists, their labor union drive, communist growth, and communist espionage. Attention is paid to the revelations of espionage by Whittaker Chambers and Elizabeth Bentley.

S224 SLESINGER, Zalmen. "Education and the Class Struggle: A Critical Examination of the Liberal Educator's Program for Social Reconstruction." New York: Covici-Friede, 1937. 312 pp. Bibliog.
A Marxist evaluation of the educational philosophy of a group of liberal educators, including George S. Counts,

William H. Kilpatrick, and the Progressive Education Association, advocates of social reconstruction through democratic means. The Marxist position held by Slesinger is that economic and social relations are class structured, and that fundamental reconstruction can take place only if revolutionary means are used.

S225 SMALL, Sasha. "Scottsboro: Act Three." New York: International Labor Defense, 1934. 15 pp.
A communist version of the third part of the Scottsboro trial, at which Heywood Patterson and Clarence Norris were again convicted of murder. Although the verdicts were adverse, the ILD has not abandoned the fight.

S226 .... "Hell in Georgia: What Angelo Herndon Faces!" New York: International Labor Defense, 1935. 14 pp.
The horrors of a Georgia chain gang are described. This is the fate awaiting Angelo Herndon unless the widest possible defense is mobilized for him. Readers are urged to join the ILD for a united front defense.

S227 .... "Ten Years of Labor Defense." New York: International Labor Defense, 1935. 31 pp.
A history of the ILD and of the legal battles it has fought for the working class since its formation in 1925. The ILD has never forgotten labor's heroes, such as Mooney and Billings, Sacco and Vanzetti, J. B. McNamara, and hundreds of others.

S228 .... "Women in Action." New York: Workers Library, 1935. 16 pp.
A review of women's participation in recent strike struggles in the U.S., stressing the heroic deeds of communist women here and in other countries. The Communist Party is the only party fighting for equal rights for women and the everyday needs of women of every nationality and color.

S229 .... Ten Years of the I.L.D., "New Masses," 16 (July 23, 1935), 13-14.
A review of American labor defense efforts on the tenth anniversary of the International Labor Defense. The author tells of American labor victims before this time; describes the formation in 1920 of the National Defense Committee which, with the Labor Defense Councils, became the ILD in 1925; and reviews the program carried on since then.

S230 .... "20,000 Unknown Soldiers." New York: International Labor Defense, 1936. 14 pp.
A denunciation of political persecution in this country, and an appeal for financial and moral support of the ILD. Case histories are cited of working class families that lack food and support because their heads are in prison for loyalty to their beliefs.

S231 .... "Heroines." New York: Workers Library, n.d. [1937]. 48 pp.
A collection of biographies of heroic women who have spoken for peace, freedom, and democracy. Among the sketches are those of Clara Zetkin, Krupskaya, La Pasionara, Mother Jones, Mother Bloor, and Elizabeth Gurley Flynn.

S232 .... "You've Got a Right Defending Democracy." New York: International Labor Defense, 1938. 31 pp.
A call for readers to join with the ILD to fight for the civil and democratic rights of the American people. The pamphlet tells what the ILD is doing to defend civil rights.

S233 .... "Civil Liberties in the U.S.A.; A Short History of the Origin and Defense of the Bill of Rights." New York: Workers Library, n.d. [1940?]. 63 pp.
Americans who have loved liberty, according to this communist author, have been hounded by the Dies Committees of their day from 1620 to the present. Though the civil liberties of the American people are today threatened with disaster, for every blow at the Bill of Rights an answering blow for democracy is struck by the progressive forces.

S234 SMERKIN, George, and LARKS, Sol. "From Young Socialists to Young Communists." New York: Youth Publishers, 1934. 30 pp.
Former members of the Young People's Socialist League in Chicago tell why they left the YPSL for the Young Communist League. Depression taught them that the only way to achieve workers' demands was through militant action, in which the SP would not engage. The authors also favored participation in united front activities with communists, which the socialists opposed.

S235 SMITH, Al. Our Union in the Printing Trades, "Labor Herald," 1 (Aug. 1922), 3-6.
The International Typographical Union, the only large union able to maintain itself in the open shop struggle in the printing industry, has come out again for the principle of industrial unity. Smaller unions must see that amalgamation or annihilation faces them.

S236 SMITH, Asbury. What Can the Negro Expect from Communism? "Opportunity," 11 (July 1933), 211-12.
A Negro minister asserts that communists, to attract Negroes, used the Scottsboro case, together with support for racial equality and economic betterment. Nevertheless the communist label would increase the oppression of Negroes. Communist language and tactics have blocked desirable legislation.

S237 SMITH, Bernard. "Forces in American Criticism: A Study in the History of American Literary Thought." New York: Harcourt, Brace, 1939. 401 pp. Ind.
A study of American literary criticism from the Colonial period to the late 1930's, with attention to the rise of Marxist criticism. Marxist literary thought is defined, and attention given to the pioneering of Floyd Dell of the "Masses." There is also discussion of later Marxist critics, such as V. F. Calverton, Joseph Freeman, and Michael Gold, and of the role of the "New Masses." Changes in Marxist criticism during the 1930's are outlined, and its contributions evaluated.

S238 SMITH, Beverly. How Will Our Law against Traitors Work? "Saturday Evening Post," 223 (Jan. 13, 1951), 22-23 ff.
A popular explanation of the McCarran Internal Security Act of 1950 by the Washington editor of the "Post." Mere exposure has failed to control communist conspiratorial methods, and legislative proposals to outlaw the CP would probably be unconstitutional. The McCarran Act seeks to strike at the communist conspiracy without violating the Constitution.

S239 SMITH, Bradford. The Making of a "Communist," "American Scholar," 22 (Summer 1953), 337-45.
A conservative writer tells how he found himself under suspicion of being a communist. He tells how the rumors about him started and of their effect upon him, concluding that irresponsible Red-baiting is communism's strongest ally.

S240 SMITH, C. The Problem of Cadres in the Party, "Communist," 11 (Feb. 1932), 110-23.

The current line of the CPUSA, calling for leadership of workers' mass struggles, emphasizes the lack of well-trained cadres as one of the greatest internal shortcomings. Greater efforts must be made to recruit into the Party from its periphery in the trade unions, among Negroes, and among the unemployed; those recruited must be given political education.

S241 SMITH, Chard Powers. Static on the Red Network: The Menace of Reaction in America, "Scribner's Magazine," 99 (May 1936), 257-65.
A denunciation of inaccuracies and exaggerations in Elizabeth Dilling's "The Red Network." Instead of limiting herself to radicals involved in an insurrectionary plot, she included loyal and pacific liberals, encouraging repression which threatens American liberty far more than communism. Opinions of ten of those liberals on the use of violence are included.

S242 SMITH, Edwin S. "Organized Labor in the Soviet Union." New York: National Council of American-Soviet Friendship, 1943. 41 pp.
A call by the executive director of the Council for close collaboration among the trade unions of the U.S., Britain, and the Soviet Union. He discusses the membership and functions of the Soviet trade unions, their collective bargaining procedures, wages and working conditions, and labor's contributions to the war effort.

S243 SMITH, Ellington. The Electrical Workers Meet, "New Republic," 121 (Sept. 19, 1949), 14-15.
An outline of the battle for control between the communist and noncommunist factions of the UE during 1948-49. Though American workers are overwhelmingly anticommunist, the UE rank and file has not yet found right-wing challengers for leadership to support.

S244 SMITH, Henry Nash. Legislatures, Communists, and State Universities, "Pacific Spectator," 3 (Summer 1949), 329-37.
Criticism of the dismissal of two professors by the University of Washington for admitted membership in the Party. A university requires freedom of discussion, including political discussion; it is more in danger from a legislative investigating committee than from a few communists on the faculty. (For a contrary view see J. H. Hildebrand, The Communist Party and the Academic Profession, "Pacific Spectator," Spring 1949.)

S245 SMITH, Jessica. "Jungle Law or Human Reason? The North Atlantic Pact and What It Means to You." New York: Soviet Russia Today Publications, 1949. 48 pp.
An attack on the North Atlantic pact prior to its ratification by the Senate. Denying that there is any threat from the USSR, the author asserts that the aims of the pact are consideration of aggressive war against the Soviet Union, an effort to put down the communists within the signatory countries, and keeping of war hysteria at a pitch to justify military expenditures.

S246 .... "Negotiations: The Way to Peace." New York: New World Review, 1954. 65 pp.
The editor of the "New World Review" discusses the Berlin four-power foreign ministers conference, asserting that Soviet proposals there have had biased treatment in the American press. The Soviet position is presented on the three items on the agenda: (1) a five-power conference, including Red China, to discuss Korea and Indo-China; (2) Germany and European security; and (3) an Austrian treaty.

S247 .... How the McCarran Act Threatens You, "New World Review," 22 (Jan. 1954), 36-41.

A demand for the repeal of the McCarran Act, the Subversive Control Act of 1950, which is called part of the effort to establish fascism here and unleash a new world war. After communists are outlawed, you are next.

S248 .... "The American People Want Peace: A Survey of Public Opinion." New York: Soviet Russia Today Publications, 1955. 47 pp.
An assertion that the American people changed U.S. foreign policy, as reflected in the Geneva summit conference, and an effort to contribute to that pressure by telling what other Americans interested in peace have been doing and saying. The contributions made by labor, religious, peace, Negro, student, and youth groups are presented, whether or not the groups are communist controlled.

S249 .... "Hungary in Travail." New York: New Century, 1956. 23 pp. Reprinted from "New World Review," Dec. 1956.
A communist interpretation of the events in Hungary. Unlike the people in the Soviet Union, the Hungarian people had not been prepared for the de-Stalinization campaign initiated by the twentieth Congress of the CPSU. While the Hungarians had legitimate grievances, fascist elements took advantage of these. Soviet military intervention is criticized as having inflamed the Hungarians, but defended as legitimate under the Warsaw Pact.

S250 SMITH, Lucy. "No Middle Ground." Philadelphia: Writer's Division, Philadelphia Council of the Arts, Sciences and Professions, 1952. 30 pp.
Free verse by a Negro poet who pleads for peace and understanding, published by a Party front organization.

S251 SMITH, Rembert Gilman. "Moscow over Methodism." St. Louis and Chicago: John S. Swift Co., 1936. 280 pp. Planographed.
A right-wing condemnation of socialist and communist influence within the Methodist church. The author attacks the Methodist Federation for Social Service, denouncing liberal church leaders such as G. Bromley Oxnam, Francis J. McConnell, and James Myers. Asserting that socialism and communism are the greatest enemies of real Methodism, he urges Methodists to join his Methodist League against Communism, Fascism and Unpatriotic Patriotism. (A revised edition under the same title was published in 1950.)

S252 .... "Communism versus Civilization." Tulsa, Okla.: The author, 1938. 11 pp.
An assertion that communism seeks to destroy civilization as we know it, through the destruction of private property, the family, religion, morality, and existing governments.

S253 SMITH, Vern. "The Frame-up System." New York: International Pamphlets, 1930. 31 pp.
An exposé of the "frame-up" used by employers when it is inexpedient to use violence. The author cites outstanding cases of frame-ups in American history, and asserts that only through mass protests and widespread publicity, led by the TUUL, the ILD, and the Party, can the workers fight against frame-ups.

S254 .... The Roosevelt Program of Attack upon the Working Class! "Communist International," 10 (Sept. 15, 1933), 596-603.
A communist publicist (formerly editor of an IWW paper) calls the Roosevelt legislative program an effort to capture foreign markets by reducing workers' living standards, a scheme to set farmers against workers and the employed against the unemployed, and a plan to further concentrate industry in the hands of finance capitalists.

S255 SMITH, Vern. Beginnings of Revolutionary Political Action in the U.S.A., "Communist," 12 (Oct. 1933), 1039-54.
A brief historical survey of the working class political movements leading to a Bolshevik left wing in 1919. At first labor supported movements like Populism and Single Tax; later it supported revisionist Marxist parties, like De Leon's Socialist Labor Party and Debs' Socialist Party.

S256 . . . . Farmer-Labour Party Developments, "International Press Correspondence," 16 (May 16, 1936), 626-27.
A review of developments in the farmer-labor party movement. Unfavorable factors include opposition by AFL and CIO, Dubinsky's endorsement of Roosevelt, and opposition by the socialists. Among favorable factors are united front support in 30 states, endorsement by the Workers Alliance and many state labor federations, and the more militant position of the Minnesota Farmer-Labor Party.

S257 . . . . Trotsky Will Not Win American Labour, "International Press Correspondence," 17 (Feb. 27, 1937), 250-51.
An attack on Trotsky and American Trotskyists, timed with Trotsky's arrival in the western hemisphere. The American Committee for the Defense of Trotsky has had no impact on American workers. Trotskyist splitting and defeatist tactics in the Socialist Party and in recent strikes are outlined.

S258 SMITH, William J. "American or Communist? You Can't Be Both." Brooklyn: International Catholic Truth Society, 1938. 31 pp.
Pointing out that the CPUSA is part of an international conspiracy against all nations, with the specific mission of overthrowing democratic government here, the author proposes that communism be declared criminal, while freedom of speech and press are preserved. Questions for study club review are included.

S259 . . . . "Spotlight on Labor Unions." New York: Duell, Sloan & Pearce, 1946. 150 pp. Ind.
An essay on the role of labor in the U.S. by a priest who is "sympathetic to legitimate trade unions, but who views the communist infiltration of the CIO with alarm and sees the Political Action Committee as a cloak for communist propaganda." Communist philosophy in labor unions makes progress, however, only if its leaders conceal its true nature.

S260 . . . . Attention Van Bittner of CIO, "Plain Talk," 1 (Dec. 1946), 21-22.
A charge that Van Bittner of the CIO hides the seriousness of the communist menace in the CIO. Though the CIO understandably plays down the communist issue in its drive to organize in the South, the result is that many potential friends of the CIO fail to support it. A list of Stalinists in the CIO is attached.

S261 SOCIAL DEMOCRAT. Thomas-Browder Debate, "New Leader," 18 (Nov. 30, 1935), 4.
A right-wing socialist review of the Madison Square Garden debate between Norman Thomas and Earl Browder. Thomas is criticized for endorsing the united front policy in principle and for believing in the sincerity of the new CP line.

S262 "SOCIALIST CALL," The American Forum: An Editorial, 25 (June 1957), 3-5.
Comment on creation of "The American Forum—For Socialist Education" in May by communists, Trotskyists, fellow-travelers, and independent radicals, following the new line toward socialists enunciated by Khrushchev.

Rejecting an invitation to join, the "Call" invites those concerned with democracy and socialism to join the Socialist Party—Social Democratic Federation.

S263 SOCIALIST LABOR PARTY. "Manifesto of the Socialist Labor Party to the Working Class of America: Changing Tides around the Rock of Gibraltar." New York: National Executive Committee, SLP, 1920. 41 pp.
An attack on rival radical groups, including the Socialist Party, the communist sects, and the anarcho-syndicalist IWW. The communists are ridiculed for ranting and phrase-mongering, for failing to understand the functions of a labor political movement or the meaning of mass action. Anarcho-syndicalists are viewed as a cancerous growth.

S264 . . . . "The Russian Soviets and the American Socialist Labor Party." New York: National Executive Committee, SLP, 1921. 29 pp. App.
A statement supporting the Russian Soviet Republic, together with an open letter to Chairman Lee S. Overman of the Senate Judiciary Committee. The SLP asserts that it is the real exponent of American Bolshevism, that its proposal for reconstruction of society on industrial lines closely resembles the Soviet program.

S265 . . . . "The Socialist Labor Party and the Third International." New York: SLP, 1926. 64 pp. App.
An assertion that the activities of the Third International, far from helping the revolutionary socialist movement of the world, have created confusion and alienated millions. The history of the communist movement in the U.S. has been ludicrous and shameful. The revolutionary socialist movement in each country must be shaped in accordance with the country's economic, political, and historic conditions.

S266 . . . . "Who Are the Falsifiers?" New York: New York Labor News Co., 1926. 28 pp.
A compilation of articles from the Socialist Labor Party newspaper "Weekly People," showing how the communists doctored up Marxist classics for their own semianarchist purposes.

S267 . . . . "The World War and Soviet Russia." New York: New York Labor News Company, 1941. 16 pp.
Denying that the war is being fought to protect liberties or Christian civilization, the SLP finds it due to a clash of rival capitalists for world markets. While castigating the Stalinist bureaucracy for its betrayal of socialism and, because of the Hitler-Stalin pact, holding it responsible for the war, the SLP condemns Hitler's treacherous attack on the USSR.

S268 . . . . "Workers of the World, Unite! Declaration on the Dissolution of the Communist International." New York: New York Labor News Company, 1943. 31 pp.
The dissolution of the Third International is viewed as a surrender to world capitalism and an admission that Stalinism does not represent Marxism. The Third International is charged with having disrupted world labor, disgraced Marxism, and distorted its principles in the service of the Stalinist bureaucracy. The Party here under Browder is attacked for its servility to Russia and its wartime support of capitalism.

S269 SOCIALIST PARTY OF AMERICA, Left Wing Section, Local Greater New York. "Manifesto and Program." New York: The Section, 1919. 14 pp. Also reprinted in "Revolutionary Age," Feb. 8 and

March 23, 1919, and in New York State, Joint Committee for the Investigation of Seditious Activities, "Revolutionary Radicalism," 1: 706-16.

A call to the Socialist Party to support the Bolshevik Revolution in Russia and the Spartacus group in Germany, to embrace revolutionary industrial unionism, to engage in mass political action instead of limited parliamentary action, and to hold a national emergency convention immediately. (The left wing was in the process of splitting away from the Socialist Party to form the communist movement.)

S270   SOCIALIST PARTY OF AMERICA, National Left Wing Council. Left Wing Manifesto: Issued on the Authority of the Conference by the National Council of the Left Wing, "Revolutionary Age," 2 (July 5, 1919), 6-8 ff.

The so-called "June Manifesto" adopted by the National Left Wing Conference of the Socialist Party in June 1919. Reformist socialism is condemned; revolutionary socialism aims, not to "capture" the bourgeois parliamentary state, but to overthrow it. Of all the radical groups, only the Communist International offers a revolutionary socialist program.

S271   SOCIALIST PARTY, U.S.A., National Executive Committee. About Socialist-Communist Unity, "Socialist Call," 2 (Feb. 20, 1937), 6.

A Socialist Party statement on joint action and united front with the Communist Party. On some subjects, such as a labor party, there may be insufficient agreement on principles to provide the basis for united action. On other subjects, such as war, the parties are so far apart that united action is impossible.

S272   SOCIALIST WORKERS PARTY. "Teachers and the War." New York: Pioneer Publishers, n.d. [1940]. 23 pp.

A Trotskyite pamphlet calling upon teachers to join the antiwar program of the SWP. War means salary cuts, lower educational standards, and the death of academic freedom and democracy. The Communist Party is ridiculed for its swing from support of Roosevelt's war program to support of the Moscow-Berlin axis.

S273   SOKOLSKY, George E. "Labor's Fight for Power." Garden City, N.Y.: Doubleday, Doran, 1934. 275 pp.

An argument in the first part of the book that AFL and communist unions, while apparently different, would have the same effect, since even conservative union leaders would increase labor's share of profits until none remained for capital. The second part of the book, discussing the New Deal, argues that the NIRA introduces communist measures in a capitalist structure.

S274   SOLL, George. Civil Liberties and Security, "Survey," 86 (Dec. 1950), 541-44.

An ACLU attorney analyzes the issues of academic freedom for communists, loyalty oaths for government employees, laws requiring registration by the Communist Party or its members, and labeling of propaganda. Both contribution to internal security and impact on individual freedom must be considered.

S275   SOLOMON, Charles. You Can't Compromise with Communism, "American Federationist," 57 (Jan. 1950), 24-25 ff.

An assertion that communism represents a fundamental break with the morality and way of life of the democratic world, that communists see democracy as the chief barrier to their triumph, and that their exclusive loyalty is to Soviet Russia. As a result, compromise in democratic terms is impossible with them.

S276   SOLOW, Herbert. Minutiae of Left Wing Literary History, "Partisan Review," 4 (March 1938), 59-62.

A review of contributors to the "New Masses" over the years, noting whether they now stand in or out of favor with the Party. The more a person contributed to the publication, the greater have been his chances of falling from grace. Extensive quotes show that present enemies were once exuberantly praised, and present friends vehemently denounced.

S277   . . . . Missing a Year! Where Is Julia Poyntz? "New Leader," 21 (July 2, 1938), 3 ff.

A review of events surrounding the disappearance of Juliet Stuart Poyntz. The evidence indicates that Miss Poyntz, a communist who recently became critical of the Stalin regime, has been abducted by Stalin's agents in the U.S.

S278   . . . . Passport Ring on Trial Here Linked to Soviet's GPU, "New Leader," 22 (April 15, 1939), 1 ff.

First of a series of articles on the trial of three American communists for passport fraud. Other GPU activities in the U.S. are reviewed. (Other articles in this series by Solow are: "Moves to Cover C.P. Mark N.Y. Passport Trial," April 29, 1 ff; "USSR Spies Here Guilty; Moscow Show Trial Near," May 6, 1 ff; and "U.S. Attorney Links Convicted Spies to USSR," May 13, 1 ff.)

S279   . . . . Stalin's American Passport Mill, "American Mercury," 47 (July 1939), 302-9.

A description of the persons and processes involved in the Soviet false passport organization, working in collaboration with the American communists. Adolph Arnold Rubens, the most notorious forger in this racket, was recently caught and imprisoned. A reservoir of Kremlin spies has resulted from the racket.

S280   . . . . Stalin's Great American Hoax: The League for Peace and Democracy, "American Mercury," 48 (Dec. 1939), 394-402.

A history of the League, which was set up by the Kremlin and which has always been directed by the Party. Though it has a respectable facade, the important executive posts are reserved for Party members or fellow-travelers. The League, now facing a crisis because of the Hitler-Stalin pact, always follows the Moscow line.

S281   . . . . The Techniques of Communism, "American Teacher," 25 (May 1941), 26-28.

A discussion of the totalitarian nature of Stalinist technique, which uses OGPU agents to liquidate Stalin's enemies outside as well as within the USSR. Milder techniques are to deprive opponents of their means of livelihood or to conduct whispering campaigns against them. (Part of a symposium on communism, fascism, and democracy.)

S282   SOLTIN, J. "The Struggle against Anti-Semitism: A Program of Action for American Jewry." New York: Jewish Buro of the National Committee, CPUSA, 1938. 62 pp.

A popular front document urging unity of all progressive forces against fascism and reaction. The author calls for a struggle against discrimination and anti-Semitic propaganda, and urges popularization of the role of Jews as champions of progressive ideas and liberalization of our immigration laws to admit Jewish refugees.

S283   SOMERVILLE, John. "The Communist Trials and the American Tradition." New York: Cameron, 1956. 256 pp.

An account by a defense witness of the trials of the second-string communists in Pennsylvania and Ohio. He asserts that Marx, Engels, Lenin and Stalin advocated revolution only if and when it expressed the will of the majority, and that communists teach the possibility of violent revolution against an oppressive government only. He denies that communists teach the necessity of overthrowing the U.S. government by violence.

S284 SOMERVILLE, John. Law, Logic and Revolution: The Smith Act Decisions, "Western Political Quarterly," 14 (Dec. 1961), 839-49.
An examination of the relationship of the Smith Act cases, and of the Act itself, to the tradition of American democracy. Criticizing the Supreme Court's distinction between the Dennis and the Yates cases, the author points out that the evidence in both was the body of Marxist-Leninist teachings. He predicts that the Smith Act will eventually be held unconstitutional.

S285 SONDERGAARD, Gale, and MALTZ, Albert. "On the Eve of Prison." Hollywood: Arts, Sciences and Professions Council, n.d. [1950?]. 14 pp.
Speeches at two rallies, called to protest the jailing of the Hollywood Ten. The authors denounce the bigots who send the men to prison, but note with satisfaction the many who are present to protest injustice.

S286 SOSKIN, William. Rhapsodies in Red, "Forum," 88 (Dec. 1932), 349-53.
An account of the frustrated writers who turn to communism, or its literary face, proletarianism, as an escape. Some of the books and conversions along the leftward path are cited. The author hopes that writers will realize that communist formulas are bound to hamper an artist's free growth.

S287 SOULE, George. William Z. Foster: A Henry Ford of the Labor Movement, "New Republic," 72 (Oct. 5, 1932), 196-99.
A sympathetic portrait of the workingman-intellectual who is a leading communist here. Despite his ten years of work, no revolutionary movement has developed because the situation is not as revolutionary as the communists imagine. Foster could command an army, but he cannot improvise one.

S288 SOULE, Isobel Walker. "The Vigilantes Hide behind the Flag." Introd. by Vito Marcantonio. New York: International Labor Defense, 1937. 31 pp.
An account of vigilante and antilabor activities in the U.S., including the "Mohawk Valley Formula," the Silver Shirts, and the Black Legion. Vigilantism is viewed as the American pattern for Hitlerism. The threat of vigilante action in strikes is seen as a threat to democratic rights.

S289 SOUTHWORTH, Gertrude Van Duyn, and SOUTHWORTH, John Van Duyn. "What about Communism? A Report to the American People." Syracuse, N.Y.: Iroquois Publishing Co., 1948, 36 pp.
Prepared for use in elementary schools, this pamphlet looks at communism through the eyes of a housewife, a farmer, a clergyman, a businessman, a member of a labor union, a newspaper editor, a teacher, and a former member of the Communist Party. Each considers what his lot would be in the USSR, and tells why American democracy is preferable.

S290 SPARGO, John. "The Psychology of Bolshevism." New York: Harper, 1919. 150 pp.
A former leader of the right wing of the Socialist Party seeks to explain the appeal of Bolshevism, despite its illiberal and undemocratic character, to educated people. He finds that Bolshevism is the madness of men goaded to despair by a sense of injustice. Some are embittered by a hatred of capitalism and its injustices, some are disillusioned by the postwar world or disturbed by the savage repression during the war, some are obsessed by a fixed idea, and some are adventurers. To prevent the rise of Bolshevism, we should eliminate the wrongs of the past.

S291 SPARKES, Boyden. Seeing Red, "Saturday Evening Post," 205 (Sept. 10, 1932), 14-15 ff.
Communist marches and demonstrations are stage-managed, often held on silly pretexts, and directed by minds steeped in social revolutions. Police are deliberately provoked by communists, who pretend to be injured to make good propaganda pictures. The deportation of revolutionary aliens is advocated.

S292 SPARKS, Leonard. "How to Win Jobs!" New York: Communist Party, USA, 1934. 23 pp.
A "third period" pamphlet, viewing the lack of good housing and jobs as part of the capitalist conspiracy. While the Party prepares to fight for the overthrow of capitalism, immediate demands for housing and jobs must be forced upon the capitalists and their government.

S293 SPARKS, Nemmy. "The Struggle of the Marine Workers." New York: International Publishers, 1930. 63 pp.
A review of the intolerable conditions among marine workers, the result of concentration of ownership and exploitation. Calling the old marine unions one of the curses of the industry, the author presents the program of the Marine Workers Industrial Union of the TUUL, the only agency through which the workers can solve their problems.

S294 .... The Northwest General Lumber Strike, "Communist," 14 (Sept. 1935), 811-29.
An account of the formation of the Party-controlled National Lumber Workers Union in 1933, its development, and its role in the 1935 general lumber strike. The NLWU comrades are criticized for a sectarian approach toward the creation of a united union of lumber workers affiliated with the AFL.

S295 .... The Hand of God—and the Lack of Flood Control, "Communist," 15 (May 1936), 434-47.
The Pittsburgh flood is reviewed to point out inadequacies in flood control and relief measures. The National Guard was sent in to enforce class rule. Neither flood relief nor control can be expected from the capitalist class unless mass pressure is mobilized.

S296 ..., and BLAIR, F. B. Exit Mayor Hoan: Lessons of the Socialist Party Defeat in Milwaukee, "Communist," 19 (Sept. 1940), 842-55.
Socialist Mayor Hoan has lost power in Milwaukee. In his many years in office, he was primarily concerned with clean government. He served the interests of the capitalists, suppressed radical meetings, failed to provide adequate relief and public housing, and did not help union organization or promote AFL-CIO unity.

S297 .... The Two-Party System, "Communist," 23 (May 1944), 415-24.
American political life has been characterized by the two-party system; no third party has ever succeeded. Consequently, labor and the communists have abandoned attempts to form a third party in favor of support of and participation in the Democratic Party.

S298 .... Marxism and Science, "Political Affairs," 27 (Dec. 1948), 1114-28.
A lecture delivered by the Los Angeles County chairman of the Party in the spring of 1948, in commemoration of

the centennial of Marxism. Scientific advances have outstripped the capitalist system, and only through the acceptance of dialectic materialism and socialism can scientific discoveries be used for the full development of man. At present a backward social organization retards this development.

S299 SPARKS, Nemmy. Towards a United Party of Socialism: Discussion Article, "Political Affairs," 35 (July 1956), 49-53.
Criticism of Party policy of viewing itself as the only constructive bearer of socialist thinking in the U.S. The author suggests that exploratory discussions between communist- and socialist-minded groups be undertaken as a step toward a united mass party of socialism.

S300 SPECTOR, Frank. "Story of the Imperial Valley." New York: International Labor Defense, n.d. [1930]. 29 pp.
A pamphlet by a California Party leader describing wretched labor conditions in the Imperial Valley, where nine strikers were convicted under the California criminal syndicalism law in 1930. An appeal for support of the ILD, which is campaigning for repeal of criminal syndicalism laws.

S301 SPELLMAN, Francis Cardinal. Communism Is Un-American, "American Magazine," 142 (July 1946), 26-28 ff.
A cardinal of the Roman Catholic Church raises his voice against communism as the enemy of Americanism, and as an "ism" based on bloodshed, barbarism, suppression, and slavery. Picturing the suffering of those under communism, he asserts that America is infected with its germs.

S302 SPENCER, Harold. "In Danger: The Right to Speak for Peace." Philadelphia: Committee to Defend the Pittsburgh Six, 1952. 16 pp.
An appeal for support for the communists on trial in Pittsburgh on charges of violating the Smith Act. The background of Steve Nelson, main defendant is given; the actions of Judge Musmanno and Matt Cvetic, main government witness, are denounced; and the threat of fascist, police-state thought control is raised.

S303 SPERO, Sterling D., and HARRIS, Abram L. "The Black Worker: The Negro and the Labor Movement." New York: Columbia University Press, 1931. 509 pp. Ind.
An early study of Negroes as a working class minority, with a chapter, "Socialism and Communism" (pp. 414-29), on communist policy toward Negroes. The authors analyze communist trade union emphasis and tactics, the efforts of the communists to "bore from within" Negro organizations such as the Garvey movement and the American Negro Labor Congress, and the slogan of self-determination for Negroes.

SPIRO, George. See MARLEN, George.

S304 SPITZ, David. Why Communists Are Not of the Left, "Antioch Review," 9 (Dec. 1949), 495-508.
An assertion that communists today, in spirit, thought, and action, are alien to the left. They are totalitarians, not democrats; conformists, not radicals; harbingers of a new slavery and a new privileged class, not fighters for freedom. Fidelity to the Kremlin is the key.

S305 SPITZ, George N. DPOWA: Red Toehold in NY Labor, "New Leader," 34 (Oct. 29, 1951), 6-8.
The history and politics of the Distributive, Processing and Office Workers of America (independent), one of the last communist strongholds in the American labor movement. Mainstay of the union is District 65, which has contracts with a number of New York City department stores. The careers of the two top leaders, Party-liners Arthur Osman and David Livingston, are traced.

S306 .... The Struggle for Control in the DPOWA, "New Leader," 35 (March 3, 1952), 8-9.
An analysis of the leadership conflict within the Distributive, Processing and Office Workers of America between overt communists and those who seek reaffiliation with the CIO. The author describes the revolt of the former procommunist leaders, Arthur Osman and David Livingston, concluding that they merit the support of organized labor, but should be watched.

S307 .... DPOWA Goes Anti-Communist, "New Leader," 35 (June 9, 1952), 10-11.
A review of the bitter struggle between the Osman-Livingston leadership of District 65 of the Distributive, Processing and Office Workers of America, who sought to break away from communist control, and the Stalinists in and out of the union, prior to their recent Atlantic City convention. The delegates overwhelmingly endorsed the leadership's new anticommunist stand.

S308 SPIVACK, Robert G. Growth of an American Youth Movement, 1905-1941, "American Scholar," 10 (Summer 1941), 352-61.
A review of the youth movement, including the pre-World War I Intercollegiate Socialist Society, the "New Student" magazine of the 1920's, the Student League for Industrial Democracy and the National Student League, the united front American Student Union formed in 1935, and the American Youth Congress. The communists defected from the FDR camp following the Hitler-Stalin pact.

S309 SPIVAK, John L. "On the Chain Gang." New York: International Publishers, 1932. 15 pp.
An exposé of the horrors of the chain gangs in Georgia, as witnessed by the author, a New York newspaper reporter.

S310 .... "Georgia Nigger." London: Wishart, 1933. 241 pp.
An account, in fictional form, of Negro life in the South, centering on the experiences of a sharecropper on a cotton plantation, his attempt to escape from peonage, his conviction for this, and his life in a prison camp. The book makes the points that former white trash are now in power, that the "free" Negroes are treated worse than slaves, and that prison camps, bad as they are, are better than some plantations. Illustrations showing prisoners at work, the cages in which they sleep, and methods of punishing them are appended, as are reproductions of prison documents.

S311 .... "Anti-Semitism Exposed! Plotting America's Pogroms." New York: New Masses, 1934. 95 pp.
A reprint of a series of articles in the "New Masses," October 2 to December 4, 1934, exposing organized anti-Semitism in the U.S. The author asserts that certain Americans, some of them in high government positions, are acting as Nazi agents, circulating anti-Semitic propaganda; and that reactionary nationalist organizations (such as the American Jewish Committee and the American Jewish Congress) have been abetting anti-Semitism, not opposing it. He urges Jews to ally themselves with the working class to oppose fascism and overthrow exploitation.

S312 .... "America Faces the Barricades." New York: Covici, Friede, 1935. 287 pp.

A series of anecdotes dramatizing conditions of workers in the 1930's. Spivak criticizes the NRA as ineffectual, and stresses the great strikes in Toledo, Minneapolis, and San Francisco as prophetic of a long and bloody road of future labor struggles, leading to the mounting of barricades. While American workers merely want to get food, not to overthrow the government, national revolt will be inevitable when government can grant no more concessions to the hungry. Some group will then seize control, and the Communist Party is the only one which knows what it wants.

S313 SPIVAK, John L. "Pattern for American Fascism." New York: New Century, 1947. 72 pp.
A communist exposé of America's drive toward fascism. The author sees the postwar drive against communism as an antilabor move by Big Business, paralleling the tactics of Hitler in his rise to power. The Chamber of Commerce of the U.S. spearheads this drive, aided by a new organization called American Action, the House Committee on Un-American Activities, and the President's loyalty order. The anti-red propaganda drive has led to the Taft Hartley law weakening unions, an important step on the road to fascism.

S314 .... "The Save the Country Racket." New York: New Century, 1948. 63 pp.
An exposé of American Action, Inc., a "patriotic" organization formed by Merwin K. Hart and financed by anti-union industrialists. This organization has been sending money into congressional districts to oppose progressive congressmen.

S315 SPOFFORD, William B. Talking It Over, "Witness," 22 (Sept. 22, 1938), 4-6.
The managing editor devotes his weekly comments under this title to questions submitted by Clifford P. Morehouse, editor of the "Living Church," and to Spofford's replies. Denying that he is a communist, Spofford states his willingness to cooperate with communists in areas of agreement, as in the struggle against war and fascism. He denies that the American League for Peace and Democracy is dominated by the communists. (Further comment by Spofford on this subject appears in "Talking It Over" in "Witness" for Sept. 29.)

S316 SPOLANSKY, Jacob. "The Communist Trail in America." New York: Macmillan, 1951. 227 pp.
The story of a special agent of the Department of Justice, who for 30 years specialized in uncovering subversive activities. He tells of his work in the deportation cases of 1919 and 1920, of early U.S. communist meetings, of the Bridgeman, Mich., arrests, and of particular communists he knew. He gives a history of the CP, analyzes its program and objectives, and discusses the defendants at the Foley Square trials.

S317 .... Red Threat to American Industry, "American Mercury," 76 (May 1953), 32-40.
A description of communist plans for sabotage and espionage in American industry, with an appeal for more concern by American executives with industrial security. Communists are penetrating American industry, our strongest line of defense. Communist sabotage instructions are quoted and the Party's plan for underground organization is described.

S318 SPRAD [pseud.]. "A Dangerous Woman": Stella Petrosky, Held for Deportation. New York: American Committee for Protection of Foreign Born, 1935. 24 pp.
The case of Stella Petrosky, miner's wife and alien, who faces deportation to Poland because she was active in the

Unemployed Councils and helped striking miners. Her fearless example will build a united front of native and foreign born to gain better conditions for all.

S319 SPROUL, Robert G. Why Communists Should Not Teach, "American Affairs," 12 (Jan. 1950), 44-46.
Part of an address by the president of the University of California to the American Bankers Association, defending the policy of the Regents of the University that Communist Party membership is incompatible with the objectives of teaching and the search for truth. A college professor must be free to accept the duties as well as the privileges of academic freedom.

S320 STACHEL, Jack. Our Factory Nuclei, "Party Organizer," 2 (May-June 1928), 5-10.
A report, by area and industry, on shop nuclei throughout the country, made to the organization conference held May 28, 1928. Not more than 10 per cent of Party membership is now organized in shop nuclei. There are now about 100 real shop nuclei with approximately 1,500 members, whereas in May 1927 there were 158 nuclei with 1,524 members. Shop papers are also discussed.

S321 .... Organization Report to the Sixth Convention of the Communist Party of the U.S.A., "Communist," 8 (April 1929), 179-89; (May), 234-49.
The report deals with the size and social composition of Party membership, factory nuclei, shop committees, factory papers, Party committees and fractions, Party campaigns, distribution of literature, work among Negroes and young workers, and the draft constitution.

S322 .... Coming Struggles and Lessons in Strike Strategy, "Communist," 10 (March 1931), 204-13.
Recent strike struggles have shown that the workers will strike in protest against cuts in their living standards during periods of economic crisis. The Trade Union Unity League must not be content to assume leadership once a strike begins; it must be an active force in organizing and preparing these struggles.

S323 .... Some Lessons of the Lawrence Strike, "Communist," 10 (May 1931), 433-43.
An analysis of the Lawrence, Mass., textile strike, under the leadership of the National Textile Workers Union of the Trade Union Unity League. Starting as a protest in one department against speed-up, the strike spread to include 10,000 workers. The strike, a partial victory, was well prepared, though some serious mistakes were made.

S324 .... The Preparation of Struggles, "Labor Unity," 7 (April 1932), 3-5.
A Party trade union specialist describes the meeting of the Central Council of the Red International of Labor Unions, held in Moscow in December, and applies its decisions to the work of the TUUL. The TUUL was criticized by the Council for poor preparation of strikes, for failure to learn other forms of struggle than the mass strike (as the short protest strike and the slow-down), for failure to organize on a factory basis, and for neglecting to work among the unemployed.

S325 .... Lessons of Two Recent Strikes, "Communist," 11 (June 1932), 527-42.
An examination of the two leading strikes conducted by the Party in 1932, the miners' strike in Kentucky and the dress strike in New York, in the light of the Resolution of the ECCI (see Communist International, Lessons of the Strike Struggles in the U.S.A.: Resolution of the E.C.C.I. in "Communist," May 1932). The strikes showed many of the same weaknesses pointed out by the ECCI, and proved the correctness of the ECCI analysis.

S326 STACHEL, Jack. Struggle for Elementary Needs—The Main Link in Winning the Masses, "Communist," 12 (Jan. 1933), 18-32.
With the end of capitalist stabilization, the economic struggles of the proletariat are assuming a revolutionary character. The Party and the revolutionary unions must intensify their work, without separating Party work from trade union work. The CP must develop more contact with the masses through the "united front from below" tactic.

S327 .... The Strikes in the Auto Industry, "Labor Unity," 8 (March 1933), 3-7.
An account by a Party union specialist of the strikes against Briggs and Hudson under leadership of the Auto Workers Union. The growth of the strike movement in heavy industry is noted, as is the fact that some concessions were gained in every strike. The union is urged to emphasize work among Negroes in the industry, and to develop a united front of all workers against AFL attempts to divide their ranks by organizing an industrial union.

S328 .... The Fight for the United Front in the USA, "International Press Correspondence," 13 (May 19, 1933), 484-85.
A review of Communist Party efforts to get units of the AFL, the Socialist Party, and the Conference for Progressive Labor Action to join in "united front from below" activities. The CPLA has been more willing than the AFL or SP to enter into joint action on specific programs. Greater united front results could be achieved if the CPUSA's organizations would be more active.

S329 .... Some Lessons of Recent Strike Struggles, "Communist," 12 (Aug. 1933), 784-92.
Excerpts from a report to a Party conference, evaluating the Party's strike policy and calling for concrete radicalization in specific industries and factories. The report urges greater united front support of strike situations, and more effective factory organization.

S330 .... Recent Developments in the Trade Union Movement, "Communist," 12 (Dec. 1933), 1155-68.
The number of strikes is rising despite government terror and treachery of AFL bureaucrats. The Party should exploit the increasing trade union membership, particularly in the AFL federal unions organized in basic industries on an industrial basis. TUUL unions should not be liquidated, however.

S331 .... Lessons of the Economic Struggles, and the Work in the Trade Unions, "Communist," 13 (March 1934), 272-301.
Survey of the Party's trade union work, submitted as a basis for discussion of a new Resolution. Trade union organization has increased in spite of the NRA, not because of it. However, membership of the Red trade unions has declined while AFL, independent, and company unions have grown. The Party must intensify trade union work, and prevent liquidation of the TUUL unions.

S332 .... The Independent Unions and Fight for Unity in the Trade Unions, "Labor Unity," 9 (June 1934), 26-30.
A discussion, by the acting secretary of the Trade Union Unity League, of the rise of independent unions in the mining, automobile, shoe, and other industries, and a proposal that the TUUL unite with them to form an Independent Federation of Labor, on the basis of an elementary class struggle program. The new federation would seek to unite with AFL workers for common struggle against capitalists and AFL bureaucrats.

S333 .... Some Problems in Our Trade Union Work, "Communist," 13 (June 1934), 524-35.
Because of recent AFL growth, the Party's trade union emphasis must be on developing opposition within AFL unions, especially in the basic industries, while also working in independent unions and building the TUUL unions wherever possible. The objective remains the same, to gain influence among the masses.

S334 .... The Great Textile Strike and Its Betrayal, "Labor Unity," 9 (Oct. 1934), 3-7.
The textile strike of 1934 was the greatest single strike in U.S. history, and also the greatest betrayal by AFL bureaucrats. The heads of the United Textile Workers were powerless to prevent the strike, which brought red scares and unprecedented terror against the workers. The bosses and the government are ready to crush every struggle of the workers with force.

S335 .... Our Trade Union Policy, "Communist," 13 (Nov. 1934), 1087-1105.
A report to the Political Bureau of the CPUSA Central Committee, outlining the extent to which tactics must be modified to reach the masses of workers in AFL unions. Since the TUUL was not successful in organizing, it is now necessary to work within AFL unions even where the mass of the workers are unorganized, as, for example, in steel.

S336 .... The Fight of the Steel Workers for Their Union, "Communist," 14 (June 1935), 483-99.
A discussion of the expulsion of a number of lodges from the Amalgamated Association of Iron, Steel and Tin Workers by Mike Tighe, the union's leader. Communists got the expelled locals to set up an Emergency Committee to carry on the fight for unity; failing this, they will seek AFL recognition as the Amalgamated Association.

S337 .... Organizational Problems of the Party, "Communist," 14 (July 1935), 625-40.
An abridged report to a meeting of the Party's Central Committee, giving membership in basic industries. The report shows an increase in membership, with a slight improvement in membership composition. The report also discusses the work of street and shop nuclei and of trade union fractions, and the need for greater cadre development.

S338 .... A New Page for American Labor: An Evaluation of the Fifty-fifth Convention of the American Federation of Labor, "Communist," 14 (Nov. 1935), 1015-33.
A detailed report on the convention, stressing the division of delegates into reactionary and progressive camps on the question of industrial unions and on most other issues. Communist delegates and sympathizers aided the Lewis forces in every way insofar as they made a genuine fight for industrial unionism and other progressive measures.

S339 .... Problems Before the 56th Annual Convention of the A.F. of L., "Communist," 15 (Nov. 1936), 1046-55.
The efforts of reactionary AFL officials to oust the CIO will be resisted by the progressive elements. The progressives will present a program advocating labor unity, the organization of Negro and other unorganized workers, the formation of a labor party, antifascism, and international labor affiliation.

S340 .... The 56th Convention of the A.F. of L., "Communist," 16 (Jan. 1937), 50-62.
Criticism of the Tampa convention for its reactionary policies in general, and specifically for endorsing the Executive Council's suspension of the CIO unions. This conflicts with the united labor front sought by the communists. Unity of the suspended CIO unions is advocated.

S341 STACHEL, Jack. Build the Party for Peace, Democracy and Socialism, "Communist," 17 (March 1938), 220-41.
A report to the plenary session of the Party's Central Committee and National Party Builders Congress, February 18-21, 1938, tabulating the results of the recruiting campaign begun in June, and discussing the education and training of the new members.

S342 .... Lessons of the Strike Struggles, "Political Affairs," 25 (March 1946), 195-208.
The AFL does not speak for labor in the current wage disputes, and the Truman Administration more and more bends to the will of the big trusts. The CIO is leading the fight of all labor. The lesson of the present wage and strike struggles is that labor and progressives must organize politically as an independent force.

S343 .... Highlights of the Recent Labor Developments, "Political Affairs," 25 (July 1946), 579-87.
The Truman Administration's threat of force against railroad strikers reveals its complete break with Roosevelt's domestic policies, following its break with his foreign policy. Yet the recent victories of the maritime workers, organized in the Committee for Maritime Unity, shows that monopoly capital's offensive can be beaten back.

S344 .... The Third Party Movement in the 1948 Elections, "Political Affairs," 26 (Sept. 1947), 780-93.
Not since the La Follette campaign of 1924 has there been so much support for a third party as today. Today's third party movement and the Wallace-for-president movement are closely linked. The social democrats serve reaction by seeking to label the third party movement as communist. The Truman Administration has abandoned Roosevelt's foreign and domestic policies.

S345 STALIN, Joseph. "Interviews with Foreign Workers' Delegations." New York: International Publishers, 1928. 63 pp.
Among the interviews is one with the first American labor delegation to the USSR, September 9, 1927. The delegates asked questions relating to Marxist theory and Soviet practices and problems, and in return Stalin asked questions on the weakness of trade union organization in the U.S., the absence of state insurance, the lack of a mass workers' party, and the reactionary policies of U.S. labor leaders.

S346 .... "Stalin's Speeches on the American Communist Party." New York: Central Committee, Communist Party, U.S.A., n.d. [1931]. 39 pp.
Three speeches by Stalin on the Communist Party, U.S.A., one delivered in the American Commission of the presidium of the ECCI on May 6, 1929, and the other two on May 14, 1929, in the presidium of the ECCI during discussion of the American question. Dealing with the factional struggle between the Fosterites and the Lovestoneites in the CPUSA, Stalin criticized both groups for opportunism and for exaggerating the specific features of American capitalism. (Shortly thereafter Lovestone and his followers were expelled from the Party.)

S347 .... "Marxism and the National and Colonial Question." New York: International Publishers, n.d. [1936]. 304 pp. App. Notes. Ind.
A collection of articles and speeches by Stalin on the issue of national minority groups, asserting the right of self-determination and proposing regional autonomy. (While Stalin was primarily concerned with minority peoples in Russia, his ideas, including his definition of a nation, were applied by American communists to the problem of Negroes in the U.S.)

S348 .... "Marxism and the National Question." Moscow: Foreign Languages Publishing House, 1945. 80 pp. Also pub. in other editions in English.
Stalin's classic work on nationalism, originally published in 1913, with the definition whose application by the Party established the Negroes in the U.S. as an oppressed nation with the right of self-determination. "A nation is a historically constituted, stable community of people, formed on the basis of a common language, territory, economic life, and psychological make-up manifested in a common culture. ... A nation has the right to arrange its life on autonomous lines. It even has the right to secede."

S349 STANDARD, William L. "Merchant Seamen: A Short History of Their Struggles." New York: International Publishers, n.d. [1948?]. 224 pp. Ind.
A procommunist interpretation of the history of merchant seamen in the U.S., with particular attention to the Marine Workers Industrial Union of the 1930's, the West Coast strike of 1934, and the formation of the National Maritime Union. The communist line on the various unions and their activities is followed throughout. The account ends with the dissolution of the Committee on Maritime Unity (when Curran turned anticommunist), and a call for unity.

S350 "STANFORD LAW REVIEW," Control of Communist Activities, 1 (Nov. 1948), 85-107.
A survey of existing and proposed anticommunist legislation. Most existing legislation requires specific identification of the group or individual seeking overthrow of the government, which is often very difficult to determine. To overcome these shortcomings, legislation has been proposed that would regulate the Communist Party by name or by characteristics.

S351 STANLEY, Herbert Wilton. Red Pacifism, "American Mercury," 38 (Aug. 1936), 394-406.
An account of Party activities in the pacifist movement in the U.S. The Party entered the peace field to support the foreign policy of the USSR, and to open up another channel for recruiting. Its chief organization for innocents in this field is the American League Against War and Fascism. Noncommunist peace organizations are also described.

S352 STANLEY, Louis. Ghost of Trotskyism Turns Up in America But Is Promptly Squelched, "New Leader," 7 (Dec. 1, 1928), 3.
A socialist view of the expulsion from the Workers (Communist) Party of James P. Cannon, Martin Abern, and Max Shachtman for organizing a Trotskyist faction. Most of the points at issue concern the Stalin-Trotsky dispute in the CPSU, as well as Comintern policy.

S353 .... Communists Form New Union Unity League at Cleveland Session, "New Leader," 9 (Sept. 7, 1929), 3.
News article on the transformation of the Trade Union Educational League into the Trade Union Unity League, and on the change in tactics that accompanied it. Communists now hope to capture the union movement by operating outside the previous union structure, rather than by "boring from within."

S354 .... Communist Dual Unionism, "Labor Age," 18 (Oct. 1929), 9-12.
A report on the Cleveland convention that transformed the Trade Union Educational League into the Trade Union Unity League, in response to the Communist Party's shift to dual unionist tactics. The delegates were largely Party members. The author attacks the TUUL for submitting to Party dictatorship.

S355 STANTON, N. [pseud.?]. The Extraordinary Conference of the CP of the USA, "Communist International," 10 (Oct. 1, 1933), 652-57.
A self-critical report on the Party's failure to compete with reformist groups and the Roosevelt Administration for the allegiance of American workers. Party work inside nonrevolutionary unions is taking on increasing importance. The Party's concentration policy, the "Daily Worker," recruiting, and membership composition are also criticized.

S356 STAPLES, Elizabeth. Langston Hughes: Malevolent Force, "American Mercury," 88 (Jan. 1959), 46-50.
An assertion that Hughes' record was from the first procommunist, and that it remains so. His record of affiliation with Party fronts is reviewed. Protestant churches are criticized for recommending his writings for study by church groups.

S357 STARK, Louis. Tares in the Wheat, "Survey Graphic," 30 (Nov. 1941), 584-87 ff.
A leading labor reporter reviews the history of communist penetration of the labor movement, describing the TUEL, the TUUL, and communist entrance into and influence in the CIO. Communist leadership swings with the foreign policy of the USSR. During the Hitler-Stalin pact period communists promoted defense strikes; with Hitler's attack on Russia, they urge U.S. intervention in the war. They subordinate union to Party objectives.

S358 STARK, Robert. The Economic Crisis, "Communist," 17 (May 1938), 429-44.
A statistically documented analysis of the 1938 crisis. By attacking government spending, social legislation, WPA, and wage-hour legislation, finance capitalists narrowed the base of purchasing power and increased the severity of the crisis. A working class solution of the crisis is presented.

S359 STARNES, Joe. They're on the Run, "American Legion Magazine," 28 (April 1940), 16-17 ff.
An account by an Alabama congressman of the work of the Dies Committee in exposing fascist and communist activities. The Communist Party, the largest subversive group at work here, has sought to win control of labor unions, to infiltrate schools and colleges, and to create united-front organizations. A legislative program to combat fascism and communism is presented.

S360 STAROBIN, Joseph. "The Life and Death of an American Hero: The Story of Dave Doran. New York: New Age, 1938. 45 pp.
The story of a young communist who organized for the Young Communist League in the South and participated in relief struggles and strikes in other parts of the country. A political commissar in the International Brigades fighting with the Loyalist army in Spain, he was killed in action there.

S361 . . . . "It's Up to You." New York: New Age, 1939. 23 pp.
A popularly-written recruiting pamphlet for the Young Communist League during the popular front period. Young people are urged to defend the principles of the New Deal, to be on the side of democracy as against profascist reaction. Red-baiting is attacked as a technique to confuse the issue.

S362 . . . . Fifth American Youth Congress, "World News and Views," 19 (July 29, 1939), 830.
A report on the Fifth American Youth Congress, July 1939, emphasizing the tactics of Red-baiters. The Young Communists, in order to preserve harmony, did not openly oppose a resolution opposing all forms of dictatorship, fascist and communist, and guaranteeing rights of all groups abiding by the democratic procedure of the Congress.

S363 . . . . The Youth vs. Roosevelt, "New Masses," 34 (Feb. 20, 1940), 5-6.
A report on the American Youth Congress' Citizenship Institute, held in Washington, D.C., February 1940, during the Hitler-Stalin pact period. The President was blamed for whittling away at the New Deal and the Neutrality Act. In a speech to the delegates, Roosevelt sharply criticized the Soviet Union for the attack on Finland.

S364 . . . . "The Great Offensive," "Communist," 22 (Jan. 1943), 73-82.
Max Werner's book, "The Great Offensive," gives an accurate account of Russian military successes in the war. Although Werner recognizes the necessity of close Allied collaboration and a second front, he does not recognize that Soviet foreign policy has always been correct. He also fails to see that the source of the Russian power of resistance is the superiority of its communist form of society.

S365 . . . . A Great Summer of Coalition Warfare, "Communist," 23 (Oct. 1944), 867-79.
The Anglo-Soviet-American coalition has won great successes on the second front. It has unified democratic forces in the liberated countries, where communists are now included in the governments. In the U.S., Republican efforts to prevent the extension of the coalition into the postwar world must be defeated.

S366 . . . . "The San Francisco World Security Conference." New York: New Century, 1945. 25 pp.
The foreign editor of the "Daily Worker" discusses the problems of forming a world organization that will confront representatives of 40-odd nations in San Francisco. The proposed plan for the United Nations worked out at Dumbarton Oaks will link the socialist and capitalist worlds and check aggression before it starts.

S367 . . . . From Teheran to Crimea, "Political Affairs," 24 (March 1945), 210-19.
During the period between the Teheran and Yalta conferences, the Anglo-Soviet-American coalition has won great military victories, and helped to bring democratic groups to power in the liberated and defeated countries. Only in Belgium, Italy, and Greece has progress toward democratic rule been arrested.

S368 . . . . The Truman Doctrine, "Political Affairs," 26 (May 1947), 403-14.
The Truman Doctrine is one of unabashed imperialism, flowing from the "get tough" program of the biggest monopoly capitalists. Its purposes are to prevent the stabilization of the new Europe and to encourage fascist, antidemocratic conspiracies throughout Europe. The arguments advanced for the Doctrine, which has an inherently warlike character, are false.

S369 . . . . "Should Americans Back the Marshall Plan? New York: New Century, 1948. 23 pp.
The foreign editor of the "Daily Worker" asserts that the Marshall Plan seeks to organize Western Europe against Russia and Eastern Europe. It would cost the U.S. heavily, in money, civil liberties, taxes, and inflation. He proposes instead cooperation with the USSR and allocation of American aid to an international organization under the UN.

S370 STAROBIN, Joseph. A Communication, "Nation," 183 (Aug. 25, 1956), inside front cover, ff.
A letter to the editor from a former member of the CPUSA, for 12 years foreign editor of the "Daily Worker," calling for a democratic socialist movement willing to absorb former and present communists. The writer criticizes liberal journals for not discussing the Party objectively, and for not including Marxist views.

S371 .... A Communication, "Political Affairs," 36 (Jan. 1957), 60-65.
A former leading member of the Party denies that he opposed the Party's fight against the war danger or that he supported American imperialism. Though he does not advocate liquidation of the Party, he doubts that a regeneration of it is possible. The left may have to go through a period of rethinking; the forms of organization which emerge will be far different from those assumed by the Party in the past.

S372 STARR, Isidore. Recent Supreme Court Decisions: Communism and Loyalty, "Social Education, 15 (Nov. 1951), 327-30.
A summary of Supreme Court decisions during the 1950 term concerning communism and loyalty. Majority and minority opinions in the most important case (Dennis vs. U.S., involving constitutionality of the Smith Act) are discussed, as are rulings on self-incrimination.

S373 STARR, Mark. Trebled Membership Seen Result of Ouster of Stalinite Officials from Teachers Union, "New Leader," 23 (Sept. 7, 1940), 5-6.
The convention of the American Federation of Teachers has re-elected George S. Counts as president; the author expects the union to boom as a result of this anticommunist victory. New York Local 5, a communist center, was criticized by AFL President William Green at the convention.

S374 STASSEN, Harold E., and DEWEY, Thomas E. Should the Communist Party in the United States Be Outlawed? "Vital Speeches of the Day," 14 (June 1, 1948), 482-89.
Transcript of a radio debate between the former governor of Minnesota and the governor of New York in the course of their campaign for Oregon support for the Republican presidential nomination. Stassen calls for outlawing the CP, urging passage of the Mundt-Nixon bill. Denying that this bill would outlaw the Party, Dewey asserts that efforts at outlawry would merely force the communists into new front organizations.

S375 STAVISKY, Sam. Can the C.I.O. Get Rid of the Commies? "Collier's," 124 (Oct. 29, 1949), 18-19 ff.
A labor reporter for the Washington "Post" predicts that the CIO will rid itself of the communists, though the fight will be a long and desperate one. Philip Murray, once hesitant and conciliatory, is now tired of vilification and Party maneuverings. Drastic action against the communists is planned for the coming CIO convention.

S376 STEADMAN, R. W. A Critique of Proletarian Literature, "North American Review," 247 (Spring 1939), 142-52.
An analysis of American proletarian literature from 1928 to date, covering some 50 novels, short stories, several hundred poems, and a dozen plays. Langston Hughes is the one important proletarian poet; of the plays, "Waiting for Lefty" is by far the best. The weakest element in proletarian literature is the novel, which requires emotional honesty as well as accuracy.

S377 STEEL, Johannes. "Will the Marshall Plan Renazify Germany?" Introd. by Rockwell Kent. New York: People's Forum, n.d. [1948]. 30 pp.
An attack on the Marshall Plan by a radio news commentator who was close to the Party line. He argues that the basis of the Marshall Plan is the future of Germany; under the Plan other European countries are to become economic satellites of Germany, which could be turned into an industrial base of aggression against the USSR.

S378 STEELE, James [pseud. for Robert L. Cruden]. "Conveyor." New York: International Publishers, 1935. 22 pp.
A novel exposing working conditions in the Ford River Rouge plant, in which the proletarian hero slowly awakens to the injustice of capitalism. After he is evicted from a company-owned house and beaten by labor spies, he decides to help the communists, who have been organizing an auto workers' union.

S379 STEELE, Walter S. Communistic Cultural Front, "National Republic," 22 (May 1934), 17-18 ff; (June), 21-22; (July-Aug.), 23-24 ff.
An assertion that the communists have set up a widespread net in the U.S. to catch intellectuals, artists, musicians, writers, and youth. Cultural organizations created by the Party since 1931 include the Workers Cultural Federation, the Workers Theatre League, the Film and Photo League, the Workers Music League, the Young Workers Dance League, and various writers' organizations. Communistic ideas are becoming well rooted among the working masses through films, theaters, books, newspapers, music, singing, and dancing.

S380 .... Solid South Battles Reds, "National Republic," 22 (Nov. 1934), 25 ff.
The once peaceful southern states are becoming a battle front between Americanism and communism, with the Reds facing well organized opposition of patriots. Textile owners are the chief targets of the Reds, who seek to incite racial and labor strife in the South.

S381 .... Red, Black, White in Dixieland, "National Republic," 24 (March 1937), 17-18 ff.
An account of communist agitation among Negroes in the South, stressing equality, distribution of land, and the right of self-determination for the Negro people in the Black Belt. Communist propaganda here is contrasted with actual conditions in the Soviet Union.

S382 .... Reds Plan for America: Force and Violence—A Soviet America, "National Republic," 27 (Nov. 1939), 4-5 ff.
Assertions, supported by quotations from American and Russian communist sources, that communism does not expect to gain power here through the ballot, that its political activity is a smokescreen for its plan to seize power illegally, and that it is not an American movement because its policies and activities are controlled by the Communist International.

S383 .... Communism in Schools, "National Republic," 29 (May 1941), 21-24 ff.
The Coudert Committee of the New York State legislature has discovered a red network in most colleges and public schools in the state. Professors and their textbooks seeking to destroy our system of government, individual enterprise, and security should be cleaned out. The charters of three locals of the American Federation of Teachers will soon be revoked because of communist control.

S384 .... Turning Searchlight on Reds, "National Republic."

A column with this heading was a regular feature of this monthly publication for some years, beginning in the late 1940's.

S385 STEFFENS, Lincoln. "The Autobiography of Lincoln Steffens." New York: Harcourt, Brace, 1931. 884 pp. Ind.
The autobiography of a well-known American muckraker and reformer who became, after the Soviet revolution, a leading fellow-traveler. Disillusioned with reform, Steffens concluded that only revolution could change the system. The autobiography presents his favorable views of the Soviet regime, including his oft-quoted remark after a visit, "I have been over into the future, and it works."

S386 STEIN, Bruno. Loyalty and Security Cases in Arbitration, "Industrial and Labor Relations Review," 17 (Oct. 1963), 96-113.
A review of arbitration awards, published between 1945 and 1961, dealing with loyalty cases. Three types of cases are analyzed: (1) discharges for alleged communist or "fellow-traveling" activity; (2) discharges stemming from refusals to testify before congressional or state legislative committees as to present or past communist associations or activities; and (3) discharges or layoffs of security risks in defense employment under the government's security program.

S387 STEIN, Rose. Lewis and the Communists, "Nation," 153 (Aug. 16, 1941), 140-42.
Discussion of the dilemma of communists in the CIO, whose survival depends on their loyalty to Lewis; but Lewis' antiwar, anti-Roosevelt stand conflicts with Party support of American defense measures and aid to Britain. The author predicts that Party-liners in the CIO will support Lewis, in which case the Party will turn on them.

S388 STEIN, Sid. As the C.I.O. Convention Nears, "Political Affairs," 28 (Aug. 1949), 35-49.
Workers' conditions have deteriorated since the 1948 election. Labor will remain on the defensive so long as it supports the "cold war" of the Marshall Plan and North Atlantic Pact. Progressive unionists in the CIO are fighting for a militant trade union policy and for the right of each international union to adopt its own policies. The frame-up of the 12 communist leaders is a threat to the existence of trade unions.

S389 . . . . The C.I.O. Convention and the Struggle for Labor Unity, "Political Affairs," 28 (Dec. 1949), 35-45.
A report on the 1949 CIO convention in Cleveland, the central theme of which was Red-baiting and anticommunism. Instead of a program to unite trade unions against the employers, Murray and Reuther split the CIO in the interests of Wall Street's war policies. Despite the expulsion of the UE-FE, the fight for labor unity continues.

S390 STEINBECK, John. "In Dubious Battle." New York: Viking, 1936. 343 pp.
A fictional account of the violent course and tragic end of a communist-organized struggle of apple pickers in California, written by a leading author who was once close to the Party line.

S391 STEINBERG, Julien. Communist Merry-Go-Round in the UE, "New Leader," 29 (Nov. 16, 1946), 5 ff.
An account of changes in views of the United Electrical, Radio and Machine Workers on national and international issues as the Communist Party line changes. The communist affiliations of leading UE officials are presented. A rank-and-file opposition group is being formed.

S392 . . . . The CIO Starts to Clean House, "New Leader," 30 (Feb. 15, 1947), 4 ff; (March 1), 5 ff. Part one, "Purge from Below," describes the growing revolt of the rank and file and of some leaders, previously friendly to the CP, against the communists in the CIO. Part two, "Purge from Above," tells of the strengthening of anticommunist sentiment in the national office, resulting in strong stands at the 1946 convention against communist efforts to interfere in CIO affairs and to exploit state and city CIO councils.

S393 . . . . The Meaning of the Proposed UAW Merger, "New Leader," 30 (July 12, 1947), 4.
An analysis of the proposed merger of the UAW and the Farm Equipment Workers. The communist-sponsored proposal would provide the margin of votes to defeat Reuther as UAW president. Its approval would lead to internal civil war, whereas its defeat would signal an anticommunist drive throughout the CIO.

S394 . . . . The Coming Communist Rout in the CIO, "New Leader," 31 (Jan. 3, 1948), 5 ff; (Jan. 17), 5 ff.
The tide has turned against the communists in the CIO. In a number of CIO state councils the Party has been decisively defeated. The communists have suffered severe defeats within the National Maritime Union and the UAW, at the hands of Joseph Curran and Walter Reuther, respectively. Within the UE an opposition group is making its influence felt.

S395 . . . . The CP and the NMU Treasury, "New Leader," 31 (Jan. 24, 1948), 5 ff.
An exposé of the effect of Stalinist control on the finances of the National Maritime Union. Expenditures were based on the political needs of the Party, as well as on the needs of the union. The payroll was loaded with communists, and huge sums were spent on all types of Party-line causes.

S396 . . . (ed.). "Verdict of Three Decades: From the Literature of Individual Revolt against Soviet Communism, 1917-1950." New York: Duell, Sloan and Pearce, 1950. 634 pp. Ind.
A collection of articles from anticommunist literature, most of it pertaining to developments in the USSR. Two selections, Granville Hicks on "Communism and the American Intellectuals" (pp. 388-401) and Louis Budenz on "Communist Confessions" (pp. 594-603), deal specifically with communism in the U.S. Other American authors in the volume include Alexander Berkman, Emma Goldman, Max Eastman, Eugene Lyons, William Henry Chamberlin, Louis Fischer, Solomon M. Schwarz, Bertram D. Wolfe, David J. Dallin, and Sidney Hook.

S397 STEINBERG, Max. Achievements and Tasks of the New York District, "Communist," 14 (May 1935), 444-58.
An organizational report submitted to the New York Party District Conference, February 23-24, 1935, analyzing the communist campaign in that city and presenting a statistical report on recruitment, shop nuclei, dues payments, shop papers, etc. Despite weaknesses, decisive gains have been made in the past year.

S398 . . . . Problems of Party Growth in the New York District, "Communist," 15 (July 1936), 643-75.
A survey of Party life and activity in the New York District from March 1934, to June 1936, as reported to the district convention, June 14, 1936.

S399 . . . . The Party Building Drive in New York State, "Communist," 16 (Dec. 1937), 1135-45.
A review of the Party building drive over the period of

intensive election campaigning in September and October. Weaknesses in Party work are analyzed.

S400 STEINBERG, Max. Rooting the Party among the Masses in New York, "Communist," 17 (Sept. 1938), 829-41.
A survey of membership gains in New York State by the Party's organization secretary, who asserts that the increase has not been sufficiently large in certain industries and districts. Election district groups, participating in neighborhood problems, will aid recruiting.

S401 . . . . Under a "Socialist" Mantle, "Communist," 22 (May 1943), 469-80.
Formation of the American Labor Conference on International Affairs headed by AFL president William Green is a sinister intrigue aimed at disrupting unity of the labor movement. This evaluation is based on the anti-Soviet bias of the Conference's leaders and supporters.

S402 STERLING, Philip. The Songs of War, "New Masses," 7 (Dec. 1931), 18-21.
An assertion that Tin Pan Alley played a vital part in mobilizing mass sentiment for war and is ready to do so again. Examples are given of the songs published from 1915 on.

S403 STERN, Madeleine. Propaganda or Art, "Sewanee Review," 45 (July-Sept. 1937), 306-27; (Oct.-Dec.), 453-68; 46 (Jan.-March 1938), 45-69.
A discussion of the literary reaction to Nazi persecution, Marxism in recent European fiction, and the problem of art versus propaganda with reference to American proletarian literature. In all three instances the most effective propagandists are those who employ traditional literary devices. The plots and artistic techniques of the leading proletarian novels are reviewed.

S404 STETIN, Sol. Stalinist Disruption in the N.J. CIO, "New Leader," 29 (Dec. 21, 1946), 5.
The speech of the regional director of the Textile Workers Union at the convention of the New Jersey State Industrial Union Council, urging the CIO to rid itself of the communist disease. He denounces communist efforts to dominate the labor movement, which the Party would use to support the Soviet line.

S405 STEUBEN, John. Recent Developments in the Steel Industry and Our Tasks, "Communist," 13 (Dec. 1934), 1234-40.
An outline of the Party's practical tasks in the light of the Central Committee's recent decision to throw its entire weight into the AFL organization drive in the steel industry, though most steel workers are neither in the AFL nor in the TUUL union.

S406 . . . . "Labor in Wartime." New York: International Publishers, 1940. 159 pp. App. Ind.
An analysis of labor's experiences in wartime by a Party labor expert, written during the period of the Hitler-Stalin pact. Examining the 1914-18 period, Steuben concludes that workers' economic conditions did not improve during or after the war, that protective legislation was weakened, and that labor did not gain a greater degree of recognition. He emphasizes the parallels between the last war and the present situation.

S407 . . . . "Strike Strategy." New York: Gaer Associates, 1950. 320 pp. App. Bibliog. Ind.
A manual on strike strategy as advocated by the Communist Party at this time, with numerous quotations from William Z. Foster and other communist sources. The author, who was associated with communist-controlled

unions, compares strike strategy with military strategy, and gives directions on how to carry on strike warfare.

S408 STEVENS, Andrew. "New Opportunities in the Fight for Peace and Democracy." New York: New Century, 1953. 94 pp.
Report delivered at a Party national conference in the summer of 1953. The report contains sections on the struggle for peace, democratic liberties, perspectives on the economic situation, a program of political action in the 1954 congressional elections, and a discussion of the Party's organizational problems. The Progressive Party is abandoned in favor of independent political action within the framework of the Democratic Party. Liquidationist tendencies within the Party, and the problem of Party security under pressure of government prosecution, are discussed. (Excerpts from the report appear in "Political Affairs," Sept. and Oct. 1953.)

S409 . . . . The Fight against White Chauvinism, "Political Affairs," 34 (May 1955), 43-65.
The influence of white chauvinism among the masses has decreased, especially in the labor movement. The struggle against white chauvinism must continue within the Party. The main danger is left sectarianism and isolation with regard to the Party's work among the Negro masses; but in our work with the white masses the main danger is right opportunism, under white chauvinist pressures.

S410 STEVENS, Bennett. "The Church and the Workers." New York: International Publishers, 1932. 31 pp.
A "third period" view of all churches as capitalist propaganda agencies, which have always used their influence and resources to maintain reactionary rulers in power, and supported imperialism and war. In return, the state perpetuates agencies like the church. Only by organizing a militant workers' antireligious movement can the workers be freed from the churches' oppression.

S411 STEVENS, Dan. Policy and Tactics of the New York Teamsters' Strike, "Political Affairs," 25 (Dec. 1946), 1104-11.
An account of the background, issues, tactics, and results of a 58-day teamsters' strike. Red-baiting was successfully repudiated, and the rank and file played a decisive part in the strike. AFL members must struggle for a correct wage policy, repudiating the Executive Council's surrender to Big Business.

S412 Stevenson, Adlai E. On Liberty, "New Republic," 126 (Feb. 18, 1952), 9-11.
Part of the message of June 26, 1951, by the governor of Illinois, vetoing the antisubversive Broyles bill, asserting that the bill endangered the liberties we seek to protect.

S413 STEWART, Donald O. (ed.). "Fighting Words." New York: Harcourt Brace, 1940. 168 pp.
A report of the Third Writers Congress, held before September 1939, although the report was written during the period of the Nazi-Soviet pact. The report is a folksy, running commentary on the Congress. Sections deal with folklore, writing craft problems (including a brief mention of proletarian literature), the novel, the Negro in fiction, radio, movies, the writer as a trade unionist, and the writer in politics (dealing with the need for writers to enter the political fight against fascism). Section titles are used to contrast the aims of writers with war aims, and the volume ends on an antiwar, anti-imperialist note.

S414 STEWART, George R. "Year of the Oath: The Fight for Academic Freedom at the University of

California. New York: Doubleday, 1950. 156 pp.
App.
One of the dissenting professors in the loyalty oath controversy at the University of California recounts the year's
struggle between the Regents and the small group of
professors who stood firm in their contention that the oath
was a denial of academic freedom.

S415 STEWART, Maxwell S. (ed.). "Loyalty in a Democracy: A Roundtable Report." New York: Public
Affairs Committee, 1952. 32 pp.
A report of a roundtable held by the Public Affairs Committee on May 26, 1951, on national security and individual
freedoms. The report condemns efforts to guard national
security by means of the federal loyalty program, congressional investigating committees, and loyalty oaths.
Participants suggest that strengthening of our democratic
institutions will aid national security.

S416 STILLER, Allen. Communism Changes C o l o r.
"Modern Monthly," 9 (June 1936), 22-26.
Comment on the Party's sharp change of line on the labor
party issue. While Party publications were still opposing
a farmer-labor party, Earl Browder, just returned from
Moscow, championed a labor party. Since essential conditions have not changed and there has been no admission
of past errors, the sincerity of Party leaders in the matter
of tactics may be questioned.

S417 STODDARD, William Leavitt. An Open Letter to
the Communist Party, "Outlook," 135 (Feb. 14,
1923), 313.
Criticism of communists, who speak nonsense because
they do not understand America, as "futile and childish."
Communists are called upon to prove the worthiness of
their cause, if they can, by abandoning secrecy and openly
advocating their program.

S418 STOKE, Harold W.; RYAN, John K.; WARREN,
Constance; HOOK, Sidney; CARMICHAEL, Peter
A.; and ALLEN, Raymond B. Academic Freedom
Symposium, "Journal of Higher Education," 20
(Oct. 1949), 346-54 ff; (Nov.), 422-28 ff.
Varying points of view on the current status of academic
freedom, and on problems of academic freedom raised by
membership in the CUPSA. The authors disagree on
whether Party membership is evidence of unfitness to
teach, and on the policies that should be followed with
respect to communist teachers.

S419 STOKES, Dillard, Catspaws for the Communists,
and SCHLESINGER, Arthur M., Jr., Dangerous
Nonsense, "Progressive," 17 (Sept. 1953), 6-10.
A debate on liberals, communists, and McCarthy. Stokes
accuses liberals of ignoring the issue of communists in
government by calling, not for a fair investigation, but for
no investigation at all. Schlesinger argues that men such
as Dies, McCarthy, Jenner, and Velde will not investigate
fairly, because their anticommunism is not genuine, but a
means for political aggrandizement.

S420 STOKES, Dillard. How Insure Security in Government Service: Past Failures and Present Remedies, "Commentary," 17 (Jan. 1954), 25-36.
The present Eisenhower security program balances national safety with the rights of individuals. The government's emphasis should be on security, not loyalty; government, like private employers, must decide on an employee's
ability to do his job. The excesses of congressional committees must be regretted, but the committees were faced
with aggressive noncooperation and abuse from liberals.

S421 STOKES, Jeremiah. "C o m m u n i s m on Trial:

Photographic Evidence Compiled for a World
Court and Jury. Salt Lake City: Federated Libraries, n.d. [1939]. 160 pp. Mimeo.
A compilation of material on communism, most of it taken
from official Party sources, by an active supporter of
criminal syndicalism statutes. Selections deal with the
communist program, communist organization, espionage
and sabotage, strikes, revolutionary tactics, the people's
front, appeals to youth and women, religion, and other
topics.

S422 .... "Master Key Reference on Communism."
Salt Lake City: Federated Libraries, 1940. 150 pp.
A collection of quotations and documents compiled by the
author in his successful fight against repeal of Utah's
criminal syndicalism law. Along with material issued by
the Party in this country, the author has included some
from international communism and others from anticommunist sources. Quotations deal with doctrines,
tactics, and practices of the Party and of international
communism. The author argues that communism is in
power in Mexico and Chile, that it was the cause of
dictatorship in Germany and Italy and of civil war in
Spain, and that only communists oppose criminal syndicalism legislation in the U.S.

S423 .... "Americans' Castle of Freedom: Under
Bolshevik Fire on Our Home Front." Salt Lake
City: Federated Libraries, 1944. 78 pp.
An assertion, while we were allied with Russia during
World War II, that international communism seeks to
destroy the U.S. government by revolution. The dissolu-
tion of the Communist International is viewed as a hoax.
Communists in the U.S., as in other capitalist countries,
plan armed insurrection. The communist-supporting New
Deal should be defeated, and the Communist Party and all
other subversive groups should be outlawed.

S424 STOKLITSKY, Alexander. On the Party Horizon,
"Communist" (organ of the Communist Party of
America, National Organization Committee), 1
(July 19, 1919), 3.
Reasons why the Communist Party of America, National
Organization Committee, opposes efforts to take over the
Socialist Party as a prior step to organization of the
Communist Party of America. Some argue that such an
effort, exposing SP members to the injustice of the SP
National Executive Committee, will turn them to the left
wing. Stoklitsky asserts that supporters of the Third
International will not "run after the masses" in this
fashion.

S425 STOLBERG, Benjamin. The Mouse That Frightens
Hughes, "Hearst's International," 45 (March 1924),
18-19 ff.
An appraisal of the weakness of the communist movement
in the U.S. by a labor journalist who emphasizes the
mistaken trade union and political tactics of the Workers'
Party. He ridicules the exaggerated fears of communism
professed by such men as Secretary of State Charles
Evans Hughes and President Samuel Gompers of the AFL.

S426 .... Revolutionary Radicalism in A m e r i c a n
Labor, pp. 182-94 in "Linking Science and Industry," ed. by Henry C. Metcalf. Baltimore:
Williams & Wilkins, 1925. 206 pp.
A brief survey of the background, spirit, and works of
communism in the U.S. from its inception until early 1924.
Leaders of the communist movement are sketched, and
their efforts in both political and trade union areas are
described. The communists are hampering the natural
progressive forces in American labor.

S427 STOLBERG, Benjamin. The Peter Pans of Communism: A Study of Bolshevism in America, 1919-1925, "Century Magazine," 110 (June 1925), 219-27.
An assertion that the leadership of the Communist Party is attempting to build in the U.S. a professional revolutionary organization such as Lenin developed out of necessity in Russia, with the result that American labor is being treated to a burlesque show. America lacks the first prerequisite of a communist revolution—a radical trade union movement.

S428 .... The Collapse of the Needle Trades, "Nation," 124 (May 4, 1927), 496-99; (May 11), 524-25; (May 18), 554-56.
Three articles on the progressive needle trades unions, emphasizing the left-right struggle within them. The articles deal, respectively, with the ILGWU, the Amalgamated Clothing Workers, and the Furriers. Out of the present chaos the author sees a growth of cynicism among the workers and a swing to the far right in the unions.

S429 .... "The Story of the C.I.O." New York: Viking, 1938. 294 pp. Ind.
The history of the CIO by an anti-Stalinist, based on a series of articles in the Scripps-Howard newspapers early in 1938. The author appraises the influence of Party-liners on CIO industrial unions, asserting that these have been hurt by Stalinist disruption. The automobile, maritime, and white collar unions are among those examined in detail. While opposing the exclusion of workers for political beliefs, Stolberg urges the CIO to rid itself of Stalinist officials, staff members, and organizers.

S430 .... Communism in American Labor. Pp. 21-25 in "Report of the Ninth Annual New York Herald Tribune Forum on Current Problems." New York: New York Herald Tribune, 1939. 256 pp.
From 1928 to 1934 the communists here had their own unions, largely paper organizations. In January 1935 they liquidated the Trade Union Unity League and infiltrated the AFL. When the CIO was founded in November 1935 they got control of the CIO national headquarters and a number of the new CIO national unions. Now the progressive opposition to the CIO is on the offensive and growing in strength.

S431 .... Communist Wreckers in American Labor, "Saturday Evening Post," 212 (Sept. 2, 1939), 5-7 ff.
An analysis of the role played by communists and fellow-travelers in the formation and development of the CIO. Reasons are advanced as to why Lewis cooperates with the communists, love of power being the most important. The author outlines the techniques by which communists obtain and maintain control. Except for the American Federation of Teachers, the AFL is fairly free of communists. (Jerome Davis of the AFT, called a communist in this article, sued the "Saturday Evening Post" for libel.)

S432 .... Muddled Millions: Capitalist Angels of Left-Wing Propaganda, "Saturday Evening Post," 213 (Feb. 15, 1941), 9-10 ff.
Disclosure of the financial backers of radical propaganda in the U.S. A comprehensive listing of left-wing publishers and periodicals is given, including their origins, affiliations, subsidies, and editorial policies. The work of the Garland Fund is described in detail and individuals are named, along with the "Nation," the "New Republic," and "PM."

S433 .... Inside Labor "American Mercury," 53 (Aug. 1941), 174-83.
An analysis of communist influence in the labor movement. During the Nazi-Soviet pact period the communists conducted political strikes in defense industries. Now that Russia and Germany are at war, communists will oppose even the most legitimate strike. We should not tolerate a totalitarian group taking orders from a foreign dictatorship.

S434 .... "Tailor's Progress: The Story of a Famous Union and the Men Who Made It." New York: Doubleday, Doran, 1944. 360 pp. Ind.
A history of the International Ladies' Garment Workers' Union with an analysis of ideological conflicts within the union. Chapter 7 (pp. 108-55) deals with the civil war in the union in the 1920's between the communist and anti-communist factions. In the Trade Union Educational League period the communists won control of leading New York City locals of the ILGWU and led a long and disastrous strike in 1926. In the subsequent Trade Union Unity League period of dual unionism the communists organized the Needle Trades Workers Industrial Union, which was dissolved in 1935.

S435 STONE, I. F. Biddle and the Facts, "Nation," 154 (June 13, 1942), 674-77; (June 20), 702-3.
A critical examination of Attorney General Biddle's decision in the Harry Bridges deportation case in the light of the three preceding decisions, showing weaknesses in interpretation of both law and facts. Testimony as to whether Bridges is or was a Party member was very tenuous, and the Party's present policies do not bring it within the force or violence provisions of the immigration laws.

S436 .... The Army and the Reds, "Nation," 160 (March 3, 1945), 238-39.
A review and evaluation of the congressional controversy over the Army order lifting bars against communists. (Under the earlier rules, the Army had barred communists from commissions and certain confidential posts.)

S437 .... Problems of the Progressive Party, "Monthly Review," 1 (April 1950), 379-89.
Criticism of Henry Wallace for turning against the communists in the Progressive Party. Though the communists lack able leadership, follow a Party line, and are primarily concerned with the USSR, they have been the dominant influence in the Progressive Party because Wallace has failed to provide real leadership. Wallace is also criticized for his advocacy of "progressive capitalism" rather than socialism.

S438 STONE, Martha. The Youth, "Political Affairs," 35 (Jan. 1956), 36-50.
A review of problems and developments affecting American youth, including youth movements, civil liberties, the coming elections, juvenile delinquency, jobs, and economic views. The youth issue is one around which nonyouth groups, particularly labor, must be mobilized. Labor Youth League members should continue to be involved in mass work. (Based on a report to the Party's national conference, Dec. 3-5, 1955.)

S439 STONE, Sherman. Story of the California Fifteen, "Jewish Life," 6 (Feb. 1952), 17-19.
An account of the 15 California Smith Act defendants, finally released on reasonable bail after four and one-half months of popular struggle against their detention. The basic issue in the case is the right of advocacy.

S440 STORK, A. Mr. Calverton and His Friends: Some

Notes on Literary Trotskyism in America, "International Literature," 3 (July 1934), 97-124.
An attack, translated from the Russian, on V. F. Calverton, who through his "Modern Monthly" has become the official corrupter of the left intelligentsia, serving up counterrevolutionary rubbish under the flag of Marxism. Max Eastman, Leon Trotsky, and Edmund Wilson are included in this group of blundering falsifiers.

S441 STORM, Henry. The Crisis on the Campus, "New Masses," 7 (June 1932), 12-14.
An analysis of the impact of the depression on the political attitudes of American students. Economic need and the intellectual bankruptcy of college professors help to radicalize students. The National Student League is the most politically advanced student organization of recent years. Student struggles from which the NSL emerged are summarized.

S442 STORMER, John A. "None Dare Call It Treason." Florissant, Missouri: Liberty Bell Press, 1964. 254 pp. Ref. Ind. Rec. reading.
A review of communist successes from a right-wing source, who believes that communists and "liberal internationalists" have controlled the presidential nominations in both parties for the past 30 years. He finds part of the explanation in progressive education, "social gospel" religion, collectivist influence in mass communications and in psychiatry, communist influence in the CIO, support of subversive activity by tax-exempt foundations, and infiltration of government by collectivist thinkers. He calls upon conservatives to get into politics, to rid the government of those who have aided the communists.

S443 STOUFFER, Samuel. "Communism, Conformity, and Civil Liberties: A Cross Section of the Nation Speaks Its Mind." New York: Doubleday, 1955. 278 pp. App.
A report by a leading sociologist on the opinions of the American people on communism and civil rights, based on interviews with a national sample and with a separate sample of community leaders. The author concludes that community leaders champion civil liberties more than do the people as a whole, and that the country is not suffering from fear or an anxiety neurosis about the internal communist threat.

S444 STOUT, Jonathan. Will Communists Infiltrate the Democratic Party? "New Leader," 27 (May 27, 1944), 1 ff.
A suggestion that the Democrats face the same problem of communist infiltration suffered by the American Labor Party. When the latter was captured by the communists, its anticommunist members formed the Liberal Party, barring communists and fascists from membership.

S445 STRACK, Celeste. The American Students Unite, "New Masses," 18 (Jan. 14, 1936), 19-21.
A report on the founding convention of the American Student Union, through merger of the communist-controlled National Student League with the socialist-controlled Student League for Industrial Democracy. The major issue was the peace program; the communists won acceptance of the Oxford Peace Pledge, despite efforts of the socialists to make the pledge more concrete.

S446 .... The Student Movement in the United States, "Communist," 16 (Feb. 1937), 142-52.
A discussion of the amalgamation of the communist-led National Student League and the socialist-led Student League for Industrial Democracy to form the American Student Union. The Trotskyists, who are active in the Young Peoples Socialist League and in the ASU, are denounced as counterrevolutionaries who are opposed to the ASU's popular front views.

S447 .... The Economic Theory of J. M. Keynes, "Political Affairs," 25 (July 1946), 625-39.
A Marxist evaluation of Keynesian economic theory. The variables on which Keynes erects his theoretical structure are inadequate, he lacks an objective theory of value, and his analysis of the growth of chronic unemployment is poor.

S448 .... The Keynesian Palace Revolution, "Political Affairs," 27 (May 1948), 448-59.
A Marxist critique of Lawrence B. Klein's book, "The Keynesian Revolution," evaluating the economic theories of John Maynard Keynes. (Part of the Party's campaign against Keynesian influence in the Wallace campaign, to guard against its spread in the Party.)

S449 STRAIGHT, Michael. The Right Way to Beat Communism, "New Republic," 122 (May 1, 1950), 10-13.
There are two methods of combatting communism, the archconservative stressing of power associated with James Burnham, and the liberal point of view as represented by Paul Hoffman and George Marshall. Only the latter can bring about communism's defeat.

S450 STRAUSS, Harold. Realism in the Proletarian Novel, "Yale Review," 28 (Dec. 1938), 360-74.
Though the literary purpose of the proletarian novelists was sound, their techniques were misguided. They were trapped and defeated by their addiction to photographic realism, and they failed to achieve the social objectivity demanded of a good revolutionary novel.

S451 STRAUSS, Lewis L. "Men and Decisions." Garden City, N.Y.: Doubleday, 1962. 468 pp. App. Ind.
Chapter 14 (pp. 267-95) deals with the case of Dr. J. Robert Oppenheimer, consultant to the Atomic Energy Commission, and the suspension of his security clearance for access to confidential materials. Hearings and reports on the case are reviewed. Strauss, who had voted to clear Oppenheimer in 1947, found him untrustworthy in 1954 because of additional information that had become available.

S452 STREATOR, George. The Black Man Turns Away from the Communist Appeal: 13,000,000 Negro Americans Wait for Saner Leader, "America," 61 (Oct. 7, 1939), 608-9.
Though the communists were the first to fight against injustices to Negroes, their preoccupation with Russia and their unpredictable shifts in the Party line have decreased their influence. While the problems of the Negro still demand solution, the Party cannot provide leadership. Saner leaders must give aid.

S453 .... Politics of Self-Determination, "Commonweal," 42 (Aug. 17, 1945), 425-27.
Commenting on the dropping by Benjamin Davis, Jr. (Negro City Councilman from Harlem), of the self-determination line, the author traces the historical background of the self-determination thesis and chides Davis for Marxist "immaturity." The self-determination line is the communists' way of making Negroes the expendable shock troops of the revolution.

S454 STRINGFELLOW, G. E. Fraternalism Fights Communism, "American Mercury," 83 (July 1956), 109-14.
An official of the Shrine organization asserts that the 700 fraternal organizations of America stand as a bulwark

against communist infiltration. Firm in their faith in God, Freemasonry and other fraternal groups are loyal to this country and defenders of our liberties.

S455 STRIPLING, Robert E. "The Red Plot against America." Ed. by Bob Considine. Drexel Hill, Pa.: Bell, 1949. 282 pp.
An account of communist subversion in America as disclosed by investigations of the House Committee on Un-American Activities, 1938-48, written by the Committee's chief investigator. Included are the cases of Gerhart and Hanns Eisler, communist activities in Hollywood, atom bomb espionage, the disclosures of Elizabeth Bentley, and the Hiss-Chambers case. The Committee's pamphlet, "500 Things You Should Know about Communism," is reprinted. The author denies that the Committee ignored fascism to concentrate on communism, or that it ever smeared the reputations of good citizens.

S456 STRONG, Anna Louise. "I Change Worlds: The Remaking of an American." New York: Henry Holt, 1935. 422 pp.
An autobiography of a communist who lived most of her adult life (since 1921) in Soviet Russia. She tells of her introduction to socialism and her work with the Socialist Party, of her experiences in the IWW general strike in Seattle in 1919, and of her pilgrimage to Russia as a writer. She writes of revolution in Mexico and China, as well, but most of the book tells of the glories of the new society in the USSR.

S457 STRONG, Earl D. "The Amalgamated Clothing Workers of America." Grinnell, Iowa: Herald-Register Publishing Co., 1940. 306 pp. Bibliog. Ind.
A summary of the 1924-27 struggle within the union between the right and left wings appears on pages 185-99. The left-wing group was led by members of the Workers Party and by the Trade Union Educational League.

S458 STRONG, Edward E. On the 40th Anniversary of the N.A.A.C.P., "Political Affairs," 29 (Feb. 1950), 23-32.
The background and past achievements of the NAACP, which more than ever before represents broad sections of the Negro people. While there is a left, anti-imperialist trend in the Association, the leadership remains with the Negro petty bourgeois. Progressives must form a united front within the rank and file, to expose the reformist role of the leaders and insure adoption of a genuine anti-imperialist policy.

S459 .... The Till Case and the Negro Liberation Movement, "Political Affairs," 34 (Dec. 1955), 35-51.
The murder in Mississippi of Emmett Louis Till reveals the continued existence here of an oppressed people. The major Negro organizations are achieving greater unity along all-class lines. The Negro liberation movement, in which great Negro Marxists have participated, urgently needs the science of Marxism-Leninism.

S460 .... Developments in the Negro-Labor Alliance, "Political Affairs," 35 (Feb. 1956), 35-52.
The AFL-CIO convention's position on Negroes was a major defeat for the racist policy of Gomperism, though much remains to be done on the racial issue within the Federation. A Negro caucus movement, which is not dual unionism, has developed to bring about more resolute action.

S461 STUART, John. The Aim of Soviet Policy, "New Masses," 59 (April 16, 1946), 10-13.

A defense of Soviet foreign policy after Winston Churchill delivered his Fulton, Mo., "iron curtain" speech. The author denies that the USSR seeks imperialist domination or that the Red Army is a weapon of aggressive expansion. Since Russia is a workers' state, its national interests will never collide with those of the working masses anywhere.

S462 .... Schlesinger: Rankin Historian, Luce Liberal, "New Masses," 60 (Aug. 13, 1946), 7-10; (Aug. 20), 16-19.
The magazine's managing editor replies to Arthur M. Schlesinger, Jr.'s attack on communism and the Communist Party in the July 29, 1946, issue of "Life." Schlesinger is charged with falsehood in asserting that there is a communist conspiracy and that the Party is subservient to Soviet foreign policy.

S463 .... Empire: Why They Can't Win, "New Masses," 62 (March 25, 1947), 6-9.
An outline of the Party's opposition to President Truman's proposal to send financial and military aid to Greece and Turkey, totalitarian police states that are favored because they are anti-Soviet and will act as servile U.S. colonies. Truman has accepted Churchill's belief that war with the USSR is inevitable.

S464 .... The Living John Reed, "Masses & Mainstream," 3 (Nov. 1950), 13-25.
An account of Reed's career, abridged from the introduction to a volume of his writings to be issued by International Publishers. Emphasis is placed upon his Harvard years, his strike experiences, his reporting of the Mexican revolt, his refusal to support World War I, and his experiences in Russia during the Bolshevik seizure of power.

S465 ..., and BRANSTEN, Richard (eds.). "The Education of John Reed." New York: International Publishers, 1955. 224 pp.
Selections from the writings of John Reed, including journalistic work, poetry, and excerpts from "Ten Days That Shook the World," all showing Reed's revolutionary spirit. A short biography is included. "Ten Days That Shook the World," Reed's famous description of the Russian October Revolution, is described as a masterpiece, despite Reed's failure to appreciate Stalin's great role in the revolution.

S466 SULLIVAN, Edward Dean. "This Labor Union Racket." New York: Hillman-Curl, 1936. 311 pp.
A view that racketeers, with communist participation, have usurped power in the American labor movement, with AFL leaders sitting by. John L. Lewis, though no radical, is supported by them in his fight for industrial organization. The author quotes Stalin, Foster, and the "New Masses" to show that communists, intent on violent revolution, foment strikes for the sake of chaos and disruption, supply agitators and organizers to working class struggles, and train revolutionary leaders in their schools.

S467 SULLIVAN, George Edward. "Wolves in Sheep's Clothing." Washington, D.C.: Sodality Union, 1937. 93 pp.
A Catholic view, in question-and-answer form, of the evils of communism, which is termed a monstrous formula for human enslavement. Jewish influence in the Soviet regime is emphasized, as is Jewish participation in communist activities in the U.S. Communist influence in American educational institutions is portrayed. The communists, who prepare for violent revolution, are waging an undeclared war against civilization.

S468 SULLIVAN, Kevin. Two Party Lines, "America," 69 (July 17, 1943), 409-10.

A comparison between Catholic and proletarian literature, ascribing the failure of both as art to an emphasis on theories and institutions rather than on things and men. Qualities in art are not measured by creeds or ideologies, but by degree of success in interpretation of human life in forms of beauty.

S469 SUMMERS, Robert E. (comp.). "Federal Information Controls in Peacetime." (Reference Shelf, 20:6.) New York: Wilson, 1949. 301 pp. Bibliog.
A collection of readings on problems of secrecy, loyalty, and federal controls. Sections deal, among other topics, with the extent of communist infiltration, the federal loyalty program, loyalty vs. civil rights, and loyalty checks and justice.

S470 . . ., (ed.). "Freedom and loyalty in our Colleges." (Reference Shelf, 26:2.) Wilson, 1954. 214 pp. Bibliog.
Excerpts from various articles on academic freedom and loyalty. Sections are included on communism and national security, indictments against the schools, federal investigation of education, the states and subversion, the loyalty oath battle, the Fifth Amendment controversy, and academic freedom. Among the authors are J. B. Matthews, William F. Buckley, Jr., Wayne Morse, the American Association of University Professors, the Jenner Committee, Alan Barth, Walter Gellhorn, A. Powell Davies, Benjamin F. Wright, Alexander Meiklejohn, Sidney Hook, Norman Thomas, and Thomas C. Hennings.

S471 SUTHERLAND, Arthur E. Freedom and Internal Security, "Harvard Law Review," 64 (Jan. 1951), 383-416.
Recognizing the grave threat of Soviet imperialism to the U.S. and the world, the author analyzes the Internal Security Act of 1950 and forecasts its probable results. He doubts whether the new statute, and, in particular, its registration provision, will produce the desired disclosure.

S472 SVOBODNY, Bogdan. "The Soviet of Deer Island, Boston Harbor: January-February, 1920." Boston: American Civil Liberties Union, Boston Branch, n.d. [1920]. 39 pp.
A pamphlet by one of the alien communists arrested for deportation during the Palmer raids of 1920. The author tells of their imprisonment at Deer Island, the conditions they found, and their formation of a "soviet" which organized work and leisure time activities.

S473 SWABECK, Arne. The Building Trades Problem, "Labor Herald," 1 (June 1922), 3-5.
The building trades unions, in a bitter struggle against the employers' open shop assault, are weakened by division and disunity. They must amalgamate or face annihilation. Amalgamation will lay a foundation for workers' control and ultimately for a workers' republic.

S474 . . . . The R.I.L.U. World Congress, "Labor Herald," 2 (March 1923), 22-24.
A report on the RILU Congress, analyzing the world scene and the role played by RILU unions and their affiliates since the last Congress. The TUEL in America is commended, and independent unions are told to campaign for reentry into the AFL as organized groups.

S475 . . . . The Makers and Masters of Steel, "Workers Monthly," 4 (Aug. 1925), 455-59.
A description of the steel industry and of life and working conditions in the steel towns, where the steel trust dominates municipalities. Attention is paid to profits and investments, labor struggles of the past, the black-list, and the low level of wages.

S476 . . . . Organizing to Fight the Steel Trust, "Workers Monthly," 4 (Sept. 1925), 512-15.
A review of labor history in the steel industry, emphasizing the power of the Amalgamated Association of Iron, Steel and Tin Workers in the 1880's and 1890's and its decline with the rise of the big steel corporations. It is now a feeble organization under reactionary leadership, though a progressive opposition has recently developed within it. Communists in the mills are preparing plans for organization.

S477 . . . . The Presidential Elections of 1928, "Communist," 7 (Sept. 1928), 548-54.
A discussion of candidates and parties in the 1928 elections. With the identity of interest of the two major parties, the repudiation of the class struggle by the Socialist Party, and the absence of a labor party movement, the Workers Party is the only one representing the interests of the workers.

S478 . . . . The National Miners Union: A New Conception of Unionism, "Communist," 7 (Oct. 1928), 622-27.
A description of the formation of the National Miners Union in Pittsburgh; it is the fruit of a militant working class movement in which communists have played a large part.

S479 . . . . The New Industrial Unions: The Mass Organizations of the Workers or Narrow Party Sects? "Militant," 3 (Feb. 1, 1930), 8.
A leading member of the Trotskyist opposition group criticizes the serious failures of the new unions. He finds the reasons in the Party's wrong conception of the role of revolutionary unions, which makes their organizing efforts caricatures; in the mechanical control exercised by the Party; and in the splitting policy which isolates leftists from the masses, strengthening the control of the AFL bureaucrats.

S480 . . . . "Unemployment and the American Working Class." New York: Pioneer Publishers for the Communist League of America (Opposition), n.d. [1932?]. 23 pp.
A pamphlet by the Shachtman opposition to the Communist Party, condemning the Party's "opportunistic" role with regard to the unemployed. Mere demands for a shorter workday, unemployment relief, etc., are not enough; demonstrations have become smaller and organizations have declined because the Party has not followed a united front policy.

S481 . . . . The Decay of the Stalinist Party, "New International," 1 (July 1934), 20-22.
Of all parties in the Communist International, the CPUSA is the most poorly equipped to analyze the current American economic life. It ignores deep-going changes in class relations, sees fascism in both the Hoover and Roosevelt regimes, writes off the AFL as moribund, and adopts a perspective in 1934 similar to that adopted in 1930.

S482 . . . . American Trade Union Problems: II, "New International," 2 (March 1935), 64-66.
In the second of two articles analyzing the labor movement from a Trotskyist viewpoint, the author discusses the transition from the Trade Union Educational League to the Trade Union Unity League. The movement completed a cycle back to its original form, but sapped of its revolutionary and progressive qualities.

S483 SWACKHAMER, John W. The Impact of Communist Domination Charges on the Rank and File. Pp. 100-2 in "Proceedings of the Twenty-Eighth Annual

Conference of the Western Economic Association."
Western Economic Association, 1954.
A case study of the International Union of Mine, Mill and Smelter Workers in Montana and the Coeur d'Alene area of Idaho, to assess the impact on the rank and file of charges that the union was dominated by communists. The rank and file were found to judge leaders by their efficiency on economic matters rather than by their political activities.

S484 SWEARINGEN, Rodger. "The World of Communism: Answers to the 100 Questions Most Often Asked by American High School Students." Boston: Houghton Mifflin, 1962. 278 pp. App. Bibliog. Ind.
A text, with answers to 100 commonly asked questions, for the study of communism in high school. While most of the book deals with Marxist-Leninist theory, the world communist movement, and communism in the USSR and in China, chapter 8 (pp. 197-210) deals with communism in the U.S. Subjects dealt with include the origin and background of the communist movement here, the nature of the Party and its front organizations, and the extent of its threat to the U.S.

S485 SWEENEY, Charles P. Picuro: A Post-Mortem Red, "New Republic," 30 (April 5, 1922), 163-64.
"What really happened" in a bomb explosion in New York City, March 13, 1922. No evidence existed that Peter Picuro, the maker of the bomb, was a radical of any kind, certainly not the "Red Menace" the newspapers alleged him to be.

S486 SWIFT, John [pseud. for Gilbert Green]. The Parasitism of the U.S. War Economy, "Political Affairs," 31 (March 1952), 51-64.
Truman's arms program can at best bring a temporary boom; it cannot increase consumption because taxes reduce consumer spending. A tapering off of arms expenditures at this time will cause recession because consumer demand and world markets are lacking. The capitalists will pressure government to continue arming; the communists instead propose vast public works and social welfare programs.

S487 .... Some Problems of Work in Right-Led Unions, "Political Affairs," 31 (April 1952), 30-41; (May), 30-40.
Communists are cautioned against assuming that reactionary policies of right-led unions reflect workers' desires. Occasional progressive measures by conservative union leaders are viewed as skillful use of camouflage to hide their true motives. Actions of the ILWU and the Mine, Mill and Smelter Union illustrate the role of left-led unions in the struggle for unity of action of all workers.

S488 .... Reuther's Seizure of the Ford Local, "Political Affairs," 31 (July 1952), 7-23.
A discussion of weaknesses in the work of progressive and communist members of Local 600 of the United Automobile Workers, which allowed Walter Reuther to take over the union's leadership against the wishes of a majority of the workers. The progressive coalition can win if it works together; Ford workers have learned to resist Red-baiting as an effort to destroy their unity.

S489 .... The Ford Local Union Election, "Political Affairs," 31 (Nov. 1952), 18-35.
An analysis of the September 1952 election within Local 600 of the UAW-CIO, in which four top officers who were removed by Reuther in March were reinstated. This shows that it is possible to establish progressive-led coalitions within right-led unions despite all attempts of reactionary officials to destroy them.

S490 .... The Struggle for a Mass Policy, "Political Affairs," 32 (Feb. 1953), 16-34.
A leading Party weakness is its isolation from the masses, especially organized labor. The 1948 election proved our estimate of a mass breakaway from the two old parties as premature. Our problem in the labor movement is to maintain our identity with the mass and also our distinctiveness. Sectarianism warps the thinking of sections of the Party.

S491 .... The Left and the Struggle for Labor Unity, "Political Affairs," 32 (July 1953), 33-42; The Left-Led Unions and Labor Unity (Aug), 37-50.
In America, as in every capitalist country, labor has two wings which cannot be reconciled, the left and the right-wing reformists. Nevertheless labor unity must be achieved, based on an economic and political program of united action and recognition of the right of conflicting tendencies to exist. The left-led unions should play an important role in the struggle for labor unity, emphasizing Negro rights, the struggle for peace, and international labor solidarity.

S492 .... Some Thoughts on Independent Political Action: A Discussion of the National Guardian's Call for a Third Party, "Political Affairs," 34 (April 1955), 4-18.
Comment on the call by John T. McManus of the "National Guardian" for a new national party of peace, jobs, rights, and socialism for the 1956 election. The author regrets that only an abortive effort could be made now. Progressive forces must not cut themselves off from organized labor, whose backing is needed for a broad coalition party.

S493 SWING, Raymond Gram. Patriotism Dons the Black Shirt, "Nation," 140 (April 10, 1935), 409-11.
Under the guise of patriotism a campaign against civil liberties is under way, which would take the Communist Party off the ballot, require loyalty oaths from teachers, and imprison anyone advocating overthrow of the government by force. Laws to curb economic and political unorthodoxy are the foundation for fascism.

S494 SYKES, Jay G. The Investigated, "Progressive," 19 (April 1955), 25-29.
A report by a Seattle attorney of an investigation by the House Un-American Activities Committee into communist activities in the Northwest. Unions whose members were named stampeded to endorse the Committee. Others were discharged from their jobs. Two citations for contempt of Congress are pending.

S495 .... Post-McCarthy Delusions of Liberty, "Monthly Review," 7 (Feb. 1956), 394-400.
A denial that domestic liberty has been revitalized in the post-McCarthy period. Although excesses are less frequent, the institutional pattern of the inquisition is now established. Attention is focused on Seattle, and on persons there who have lost their jobs or union memberships as a result of identification as communists or pleading the Fifth Amendment.

S496 SYMES, Lillian. Blunder on the Left, "Harper's Magazine," 168 (Dec. 1933), 90-101.
An analysis of the relative unpopularity of communists and other radical groups during the depression. Increases in radical strength came from the American intelligentsia, not its laboring masses. Marxist theory underestimated the virility and capacity for action of the middle classes. Communists and other radical groups have made many tactical and organizational blunders.

S497 SYMES, Lillian. Our Liberal Weeklies. "Modern Monthly," 10 (Oct. 1936), 7-10.
An analysis of the political line of the "New Republic" and the "Nation." Frankly liberal prior to 1932, both reflected the leftward migration of American intellectuals of that year. Since then the "New Republic" has been a polite echo of the Party line. Though the "Nation" has been less consistent, it is now supporting the popular front advocated by the Party.

S498 .... Communism Twenty Years After, "Harper's Magazine," 177 (June 1938), 85-94.
A discussion of the Communist Party's methods of infiltrating liberal organizations during the period of the united front. The widespread view that the CPUSA is a revolutionary organization is mistaken. In spite of its current, seeming pro-Americanism, the Party is a foreign legion of the Soviet Union.

S499 .... "Communism: World Revolution to Red Imperialism." Chicago: Socialist Party, n.d. [1940]. 42 pp.
A socialist critique of the Hitler-Stalin pact, arguing that the Bolshevik revolution degenerated first into Stalinism, an oppressive nationalist caricature of a socialist society, and now into a new Russian imperialism. The author asserts that Stalin used negotiations with England and France as a smoke-screen for negotiations with Hitler, as well as a club to extract the most favorable terms. Since communists are agents of an antiworking-class regime, labor unions should keep them from positions of control.

S500 .... The Joke about the Dissolution of the Communist International, "Call," 9 (June 4, 1943), 3.
A socialist writer asserts that the "dissolution" of the Communist International, hailed by liberals and conservatives alike as a momentous event, will result in no change in the status of the world's communist parties as tools of the Russian foreign office. If the CP changes its name, it will be to increase its electoral effectiveness.

S501 .... Bedfellows Make Strange Politics, "Call," 10 (Jan. 28, 1944), 3.
A socialist discussion of the victory of the Communist Party—Sidney Hillman alliance in the two-year old factional struggle inside New York's American Labor Party. Hillman's role has been to tie the labor movement to the Democratic chariot. Dubinsky of the ILGWU, who has no taste for cooperating with the CP, has threatened to pull out.

S502 SYRKIN, Marie. "The Communists and the Arab Problem." New York: United Socialist Zionist Party, n.d. [1936]. 14 pp.
The author, associate editor of "Jewish Frontier," denounces the communists for instigating the Arab peasantry against the Jewish population. She tells of communist disruption, attacking the communist Yiddish paper "Freiheit" for falsifying news from Palestine. Asserting that Zionism is not incompatible with Arab interests, she calls for an end to the alliance of Palestine communists with Arab terrorists and fascists.

T

T1   TAFT, Philip. Some Problems of the New Union-ism in the United States, "American Economic Review," 29 (June 1939), 313-24.

One of the problems discussed is the tendency of many unions to recruit organizers, such as communists, who primarily seek an agitation center for a political program. While top CIO leadership has no sympathy for the communists, this is not true of all its international unions.

T2   . . . . Strife in the Maritime Industry, "Political Science Quarterly," 54 (June 1939), 216-36.

An analysis of union growth and strife in the industry, emphasizing the importance of communism in the International Longshoremen's and Warehousemen's Union on the Pacific coast and in the National Maritime Union on the Atlantic.

T3   . . . . Attempts to Radicalize the Labor Movement, "Industrial and Labor Relations Review," 1 (July 1948), 580-92.

A review of communist efforts to infiltrate and control the labor movement. Whereas before World War I Marxists sought merely to dominate the labor movement intellectually, the communists seek to subordinate all unions to the Party. The author describes the activities of the TUEL and the TUUL, and the influence of the communists in many of the newer CIO unions.

T4   . . . . Communism in American Trade Unions. "Proceedings of the Sixth Annual Meeting, Industrial Relations Research Association, December 28-30, 1953," pp. 14-25.

A review of communist policy in the American labor movement, including TUEL efforts in the AFL reformist unions, the dual unionism of the TUUL, and communist penetration of the newly formed unions of the CIO. Management was partly to blame for having prevented earlier organization, whereas early CIO leaders were opportunistic and lacked knowledge of communist methods.

T5   . . . . "The Structure and Government of Labor Unions." Cambridge, Mass.: Harvard University Press, 1954. 312 pp. Ind.

Chapter 1, "Radicalism in American Labor," traces left-wing influence in American trade unionism, with a history of communist activity in unions from 1917 until the expulsion of the communist-dominated unions from the CIO. Chapter 5, "The Unlicensed Seafaring Unions," deals with a group of unions which have been the scene of unusually bitter struggles over the communist issue. Chapter 6, on the auto and steel workers' unions, explores the differences between the two unions, including the presence of disputes over political questions in the UAW and their absence in the Steelworkers.

T6   . . . . Independent Unions and the Merger, "Industrial and Labor Relations Review," 9 (April 1956), 433-46.

Pages 438-40 deal with the experiences of the left-wing unions since their expulsion from the CIO, with particular attention to the Mine, Mill and Smelter Workers, the ILWU,

and the United Electrical Workers. Most of the left-wing unions have suffered severely since their expulsion.

T7   TAFT, Robert A.; NIXON, Richard M.; ARNOLD, Thurman W.; and McGILL, Ralph E. (George V. Denny, Jr., moderator). How Should Democracy Deal with Groups Which Aim to Destroy Democracy? "Town Meeting," 14 (May 18, 1948), 23 pp.

Arnold and McGill oppose the Mundt-Nixon bill on communism as a symptom of panic and lack of confidence in American democracy. While opposing the outlawing of communism unless it advocates seizure of government by violence, Taft supports exposure of communists, dismissal from government service, and refusal of NLRB services. Nixon defends his measure as striking at the subversive activities of communism and as exposing its foreign domination by requiring it to register.

T8   TAFT, Robert A. Address on Communism, "U.S. News & World Report," 33 (Oct. 31, 1952), 84-88.

A campaign address by Senator Taft for General Eisenhower, pointing out errors by the Democratic Administration which enabled communists to make gains in government and labor and to subvert our foreign policy. Taft asserts that a demonstrated softness to communism, both domestically and in foreign affairs, permitted communist infiltration of government.

T9   TAGGARD, Genevieve (ed.). May Days: An Anthology of Verse from Masses-Liberator. New York: Boni & Liveright, 1925. 306 pp. Ind.

An anthology of "revolutionary" poetry published in the old "Masses" and the "Liberator" by various poets, many of whom became closely associated with the Communist Party. Included are contributions by Claude McKay, Carl Sandburg, Joseph Freeman, Floyd Dell, John Reed, Max Eastman, and many others.

T10   . . . . Romanticism and Communism, "New Masses," 12 (Sept. 25, 1934), 18-20.

An assertion that the faith of communism cannot be reconciled with the romantic ideology of Shelley, Whitman, and Swinburne. The Romantic is more at home with anarchism or utopian schemes, from which he turns defeatist. The good artist knows that he needs society, that he works best with right authority.

T11   TALMADGE, Irving DeWitt (ed.). "Whose Revolution? A Study of the Future Course of Liberalism in the United States." New York: Howell, Soskin, 1941. 296 pp.

A re-evaluation of liberalism and democracy in a changing world, including a discussion of totalitarian influences on liberal thought. Granville Hicks, in his chapter, "Communism and the American Intellectuals" (pp. 78-115), explains the attraction of communism in the 1930's, using his experience as an example. In "When Liberalism Went Totalitarian" (pp. 116-34), Eugene Lyons writes of the same period. Roger N. Baldwin, in "Liberalism and the United Front" (pp. 166-84), supports the united front against fascism and war, despite the Party's attempts to dominate such fronts to its own advantage. (These three items are abstracted separately.)

T12   TANK, Herb. "Communists on the Waterfront." New York: New Century, 1946. 112 pp.
An organizational pamphlet directed at seamen, combining an interpretation of communist theory as related to seamen and their problems with a presentation of the current Party line. Episodes of waterfront labor history are told. Asserting that the imperialists are trying to build a reactionary anti-Soviet bloc, the author calls on seamen to join the Communist Party.

T13   . . . . "Inside Job — The Story of Trotskyite Intrigue in the Labor Movement." New York: New Century, 1947. 64 pp.
A communist attack on Trotskyite activities, with emphasis on their ballot stealing, racketeering, "stooling" for the bosses, gangsterism, etc. Since honest, militant workers may support a Trotskyite program without being aware of the fascist content of Trotskyism, the author exposes their splitting tactics and disruption.

T14   TAYLOR, Alexander. Browder, "New Masses," 20 (Aug. 11, 1936), 38-39.
A laudatory account of Browder's career, as part of a symposium on presidential candidates in 1936. Successively a member of the Socialist Party and the Syndicalist League of North America, Browder was in jail for opposition to the draft when the communist movement was founded. Joining it upon his release, he has been a leader since in Party and union work.

T15   TAYLOR, Frank J. Behind the San Francisco Strike, "Nation's Business," 23 (March 1935), 25-27 ff.
An account of the San Francisco waterfront and general strikes of 1934, asserting that they represented a war between the present social order and those who seek to wreck it. The waterfront strike was planned months in advance and engineered from communist headquarters in New York. The CP directed the boring from within by which radical groups seized control of local unions.

T16   TAYLOR, Glen H.; SHEPPARD, Harry R.; KEEFE, Frank B.; and HAYS, Arthur Garfield. Should We Outlaw the Communist Party? "American Forum of the Air," 9 (Dec. 16, 1947), 1-11.
Representatives Keefe and Sheppard advocate outlawing the Communist Party as a criminal conspiracy to overthrow our constitutional system of government. Denying that the communists are strong here, Senator Taylor and Mr. Hays fear that liberals will be suppressed once the communists are outlawed. Taylor supports laws against treasonable acts, not names of parties.

T17   TAYLOR, Harold; ALLEN, Raymond B.; BALDWIN, Roger; and SMITH, T. V. (George V. Denny, Jr., moderator). Should Communists Be Allowed to Teach in Our Colleges? "Town Meeting," 14 (March 1, 1949), 22 pp.
Defending the communists' right to teach, Taylor and Baldwin hold the test to be one of professional competence. Allen argues that communists should be barred from college faculty posts because they are not free men, and Smith denies the right of communists to teach in schools whose means they subvert.

T18   TAYLOR, Harold. A Vote for Academic Freedom, "Reporter," 1 (Aug. 30, 1949), 29-30.
Examining the arguments of those who would bar communists from academic life, a prominent educator asserts that we are in little danger from internal communism, and that we should not endanger intellectual quality, since we have more to fear from the harmlessness of the academic mind than from the vigor of occasional radicals.

T19   . . . . "On Education and Freedom." New York: Abelard-Schuman, 1954. 320 pp. Ind.
An examination of the ability of American colleges to remain free of political, intellectual, or economic dictation, by the president of Sarah Lawrence College. A final chapter on "Communism and American Colleges" is included. Minimizing the dangers of free education, Taylor calls for exposure to new ideas and freedom from political pressure to substitute indoctrination for education. He also evaluates legislative attacks on academic freedom, discusses the rights of the scholar, and opposes a "double standard" of judgment for communist and noncommunist teachers.

T20   . . . . The Dismissal of Fifth Amendment Professors, "Annals of the American Academy of Political and Social Science," 300 (July 1955), 79-86.
A discussion of the problem of college teachers who invoke the Fifth Amendment before a congressional committee in regard to affiliation or association with the Communist Party. Retention on the faculty should be determined by the individual's worth as a scholar and teacher and by his integrity as a member of the academic community.

T21   TAYLOR, Harry. Toward a People's Theatre, "Mainstream," 1 (Spring 1947), 239-49.
A former dramatic critic of the "New Masses" calls for the building of a people's theatre in America. He tells the history of the people's theatre movement from the 1920's until the war. Though reaction is rife, factors favorable to a people's theatre include a large trade union membership, the Progressive Citizens of America, and the American Labor Party.

T22   . . . . The Dilemma of Tennessee Williams, "Masses & Mainstream," 1 (April 1948), 51-55.
An analysis of four plays by Tennessee Williams, whose great failing as a writer is his inability to escape a tragic boyhood in which those whom he hated or feared always won. In his plays, similarly, evil always triumphs. Since great drama arises out of genuine conflict, Williams must recognize that the forces of good have both will and power to change our environment.

T23   . . . . Theatre for the People, "Masses & Mainstream," 2 (March 1949), 61-70.
A reexamination of the "epic theatre," a form of theatre which has proved itself to be on the side of the people. The Living Newspaper project of the Federal Theatre of the 1930's is called its characteristic American form. Today it can be produced again in little theatre groups.

T24   TAYLOR, Henry J.; GIDEONSE, Harry; CHAMBERLIN, William Henry; and BALDWIN, Roger (George V. Denny, Jr., moderator). Is Communism a Threat to the American Way of Life? "Town Meeting," 10 (Jan. 11, 1945), 24 pp.
Taylor and Chamberlin view communism as a threat; Taylor emphasizes its threat as a system of collectivism, while Chamberlin views the American communists as the organized fifth column of a foreign power. Gideonse looks upon American Stalinists more as an irritating group of conspirators than a serious threat. Denying that the communists are a menace by virtue of size or methods, Baldwin sees them as a threat only if Americans fail to make democracy work.

T25 TAYLOR, Paul S., and KERR, Clark. Uprisings on the Farms, "Survey Graphic," 24 (Jan. 1935), 19-22 ff.
An examination of underlying conditions and immediate causes of farm-labor disturbances in the West and Southwest. While communists and communist farm organizations have been active in this area, employers resort to the "red scare" to quell the uprisings.

T26 TAYLOR, Telford. "Grand Inquest: The Story of Congressional Investigations." New York: Simon and Schuster, 1955. 358 pp. App. Notes. Ind.
An analysis of the investigating power of Congress, paying particular attention to issues of loyalty and subversion. The congressional loyalty investigation has been captured by a group of extreme right-wing members of Congress, concerned with exposure and punishment outside the law rather than with obtaining information. The methods and objectives of committees headed by Senators McCarthy and McCarran and by Representatives Dies and Thomas, among others, are reviewed. The Communist Control Act of 1954, which outlaws the Party, is traced to fears and pressures generated by the loyalty investigations.

T27 TEACHERS UNION OF THE CITY OF NEW YORK, Local 5. "Statement of Local 5 on Proposed Revocation of its Charter." New York: The Union, 1941. 43 pp.
A statement in response to an action of the Executive Council of the American Federation of Teachers, January 2, 1941, calling on Local 5 to show cause why its charter should not be revoked. Local 5 asserts that the AFT wants to expel it for communist domination, though this does not appear in the official list of charges. The council action evades the AFT constitutional provision barring discrimination against members for political activities. Local 5 denies that it is dominated by communists.

T28 TELLER, Judd L. "Scapegoat of Revolution." New York: Scribner, 1954. 352 pp.
A refutation of the "Jewish Bolshevik" claim. Not only have the Jews not been instigators of revolution, but they have been the scapegoats of all revolutions. The author draws upon history to demonstrate this, stressing the anti-Semitic strain in the socialist tradition after World War I, and the anti-Semitic policy of the Soviet Union from its founding. In parts of chapter 18 (pp. 319-30), he tells of the resistance of American Jews to the Communist Party, asserting that the extremely radical element among American Jewish youth has always been small.

T29 TENAYUCA, Emma, and BROOKS, Homer. The Mexican Question in the Southwest, "Communist," 18 (March 1939), 257-68.
The state chairman and secretary of the Party in Texas survey the social status of the Mexican people in the southwestern U.S. They cite the work of the League of United Latin American Citizens in the movement for Mexican rights in this area, and describe its tie-up with the democratic front in the U.S.

T30 TENNEY, Jack B. "Red Fascism: Boring from Within, by the Subversive Forces of Communism. Los Angeles: Federal Printing Co., 1947. 727 pp.
A compilation of material on communists and communist subversive activities by the chairman of the California legislature's Joint Fact-Finding Committee on Un-American Activities. The reports of Tenney's legislative committee constitute the basis, with extracts of other U.S. and Canadian reports included. The findings, interwoven with Tenney's interpretation and editorial comment, deal with the philosophy of the Party; its history abroad and in the U.S.; and its structure, strategy, activities, and techniques of penetration into labor unions and other organizations. Known Marxists are named, and a list of front organizations presented.

T31 .... "The Tenney Committee... The American Record." Tujunga, Calif.: Standard Publications, 1952. 100 pp. Ind.
The former chairman of the California Legislative Committee on Un-American Activities answers his critic, Professor Edward L. Barrett, Jr., who had written a book, "The Tenney Committee." After telling of his involvement with the communists in Local 47, Musicians Union, and of his awakening to the communist menace, Tenney attacks Barrett for smears, biased assumptions, and outright falsehoods. He relates the legislative history of his committee to show its popular mandate and points to the Korean War as vindication of his views.

T32 THOMAS, Norman. Timely Topics: The United Front Situation, "New Leader," 17 (Dec. 8, 1934), 8.
Discussion of the decision by the national executive committee of the Socialist Party to end united front negotiations with the Communist Party. Such negotiations are a waste of time in view of the disruptive tactics of the communists. Thomas reviews differences of opinion regarding the communists among SP leaders.

T33 ..., and BROWDER, Earl. "Debate: Which Road for American Workers, Socialist or Communist?" New York: Socialist Call, 1936. 46 pp.
The stenographic record of the debate between the national leader of the Socialist Party and the general secretary of the Communist Party, held in Madison Square Garden, November 27, 1935. Thomas criticized the communists for their emphasis on dictatorship and the inevitability of violence, for the lack of civil liberties in Russia, and for disrupting labor's ranks here. Browder called for a people's united front against the dangers of war and fascism, praised the peace policies of the USSR, and advocated the dictatorship of the proletariat as opposed to the reformism of socialists.

T34 .... How Should America Deal with Communism? "Socialist Call," 17 (May 12, 1950), 4.
Thomas' statement to the House Un-American Activities Committee, opposing the Mundt-Ferguson-Nixon bill for registration of communist organizations and their members. Although the Communist Party is undemocratic and conspiratorial, it should not be outlawed; this measure would be a blow to democracy, and would prove ineffective to its intended goal.

T35 .... Civil Rights—But Not Conspiracy, "New York Times Magazine," January 7, 1951, 11 ff.
A discussion of the problem of preserving civil liberties while protecting the nation from communist subversion. The communist conspiracy presents a real menace. A socialist leader calls for a common sense balance of rights and interests, not such measures as the Smith and McCarran Acts and loyalty tests.

T36 .... "The Test of Freedom." New York: Norton, 1954. 211 pp. Ind.
A statement by the socialist leader on the menace of communism, with an appraisal of the state of civil liberties in the U.S. since World War II. Thomas gives his view of congressional investigations, loyalty and security tests, the Smith and McCarran Acts, and the impact of McCarthyism on American life. Although he recognizes the conspiratorial nature of communism and the communists' abuse of freedom, he opposes outlawing the Party. He would permit communists in the arts and professions,

though not as teachers. (One chapter appeared in the "Progressive," Feb. 1954, under the title, "Liberals and Communists.")

T37 THOMAS, Norman. The Communist Record Repudiated, "Socialist Call," 24 (June 1956), 10-13.
The socialist leader rejects united action with the communists, proposed in Eugene Dennis' report to the national committee of the Communist Party. Noting that the Russian communist leaders who now denounce Stalin participated in many of his outrages, Thomas doubts that any basic change in communist views has taken place.

T38 THOMPSON, Craig. Here's Where Our Young Commies Are Trained, "Saturday Evening Post," 221 (March 12, 1949), 38-39 ff.
A report on the Party's Jefferson School of Social Science in New York City, covering its trustees, faculty, student body, and teaching, based on notes of a researcher who attended classes. Most students are discontented youths, no more than half of them Party members, some from comfortable, middle-income homes.

T39 .... America's Millionaire Communist, "Saturday Evening Post," 223 (Sept. 9, 1950), 29 ff.
A report on the career and Party ties of Frederick Vanderbilt Field. As an officer of the Institute of Pacific Relations he helped influence U.S. policy in favor of the Chinese communists. He was the guiding spirit of "Amerasia," whose editor was involved in an espionage case, and a contributor to and fund raiser for many Party fronts.

T40 .... The Communists' Dearest Friend, "Saturday Evening Post," 223 (Feb. 17, 1951), 30 ff.
A biographical sketch of Carol King and a review of her career as the leading defense lawyer for American communists, and activist in the International Labor Defense, the International Juridical Association, and the National Lawyers Guild.

T41 .... The Sinister Doings at the U.N., "Saturday Evening Post," 224 (Nov. 17, 1951), 155-57.
An assertion that the communists are seeking to sabotage the secretary-generalship of Trygve Lie and gain control of the UN Secretariat. A number of staff members, some of them Americans, have been discharged by Lie for disruption and disloyalty. The Staff Association of the Secretariat was dominated by the Party.

T42 .... Moscow's Mouthpiece in New York, "Saturday Evening Post," 226 (Sept. 12, 1953), 19-21 ff.
Information on the function, finances, and some of the personnel of the "Daily Worker" during its money-losing, 29-year career. An eight-page tabloid, it is least of all things a newspaper. It is an amalgam of libel and gibberish, with legitimate news class-angled or Party-angled beyond recognition. It hates all except the Party line and Party-liners.

T43 THOMPSON, Dorothy. "The Truth about Communism." Washington, D.C.: Public Affairs Press, 1948. 17 pp.
A brief appraisal of communist aims, quoting from official communist documents. The author shows that American communists are subject to foreign discipline; that the Party is pledged to illegal methods, secrecy, and armed rebellion; and that communists hold war, international and civil, inevitable until the entire world is organized into a union of socialist soviet republics.

T44 .... To Protect Civil Liberties, "Ladies' Home Journal," 65 (Jan. 1948), 11-12.
A defense, as necessary to preserve our civil liberties, of the right of government to investigate all activities dangerous to constitutional order. Communists are organized, not like a normal political party, but like an army or semisecret religious order, with many members engaged in extralegal activities.

T45 .... How I Was Duped by a Communist, "Saturday Evening Post," 221 (April 16, 1949), 19 ff.
A distinguished journalist tells how, out of pity, she employed a European refugee for four years as part-time research assistant, despite warnings that he had communist connections. Now he is in the Russian zone of Germany as professor of sociology and propagandist for the Soviet forces.

T46 THOMPSON, Leo. The Second American Youth Congress, "International Press Correspondence," 15 (Aug. 31, 1935), 1083-84.
A report on the second American Youth Congress, held in Detroit, in July 1935. A united front between the Young People's Socialist League and the Young Communist League welded the AYC into an effective agency to struggle against war and fascism and for the rights of American youth. The greatest weakness of the AYC is its failure to penetrate the trade unions and working class youth.

T47 THOMPSON, Louise, and PATTERSON, Samuel C. "The IWO and the Negro People: A Message and an Appeal." New York: IWO, 1943. 22 pp.
An appeal to Negroes to join the IWO. The authors present the IWO program for Negroes, listing its benefits and policies, stressing its nondiscrimination policy, and asserting that IWO represents the most progressive force in America fraternalism.

T48 THOMPSON, Robert. Enemies of Teheran, "Communist," 23 (May 1944), 425-30.
The defeatists are trying to sabotage the decisions of the Teheran Conference by urging the U.S. to negotiate a separate peace with the fascists. They oppose the opening of a second front and try to destroy American confidence in United Nations cooperation by slandering the Soviet Union.

T49 .... Nearing Conclusive Victory in Europe, "Political Affairs," 24 (May 1945), 392-96.
With victory over Germany at hand, we must prevent any future revival of Nazism. This means that Germany must long be occupied, and the Nazis brought to trial. We must also help reconstruct the liberated countries and insure their government by democratic regimes.

T50 .... "The Path of a Renegade: Why Earl Browder Was Expelled from the Party." New York: New Century, 1946. 23 pp.
A report to the national committee of the Party, asking approval of the expulsion of Earl Browder by the national board. Thompson sees three stages in the struggle against Browderism: first, Browder promoted illusions with regard to the alleged "progressive" role of American capitalism; then opposition to Browder took on new scope, thanks to the Duclos article; and finally Browder, by an active struggle against Party policy, has made his ideology that of a class enemy.

T51 .... Party Policy in the Veterans' Field, "Political Affairs," 25 (Jan. 1946), 42-49.
Veterans, a nonhomogeneous group, cannot play an independent role, but will be allies of one or the other class forces. A labor-veteran alliance can be achieved if labor fights for veterans' demands and extends its influence in veterans' organizations. Fascist-oriented veterans groups must be exposed. The Party must recruit the most militant and advanced veterans into its ranks.

T52　THOMPSON, Robert. Conclusions from the N.Y. Elections, "Political Affairs," 26 (Jan. 1947), 37-46.

Though New York State contributed to the Republican election victory, labor-progressive forces made limited advances; while fighting the Dewey program, they differentiated themselves from the Truman Administration and the Democratic Party. The results substantiate our Party's policy of working to establish a new people's party nationally. The ALP should become the mass independent people's party in New York.

T53　.... Basic Aspects of the Negro People's Struggle, "Political Affairs," 26 (Feb. 1947), 159-72.

A report to a meeting of club, section, and county leaders of the CP of New York City, January 13, 1947. Topics dealt with include the present activity and struggles of the Negro people's movement, the Party's position on self-determination, and the Party's tasks in the struggle for Negro equality.

T54　..., and LYONS, Eugene. What Do the Communists Really Want? "Commercial & Financial Chronicle," 166 (Sept. 4, 1947), 15-16.

Reproduction of statements in a CBS radio program, August 28, 1947. Thompson, state chairman of the Party in New York, defends the patriotism of the Party, and asserts that it seeks lower living costs, Taft-Hartley repeal, and world peace. Lyons accuses the communists, blindly allied to the Moscow power machine, of aiming to destroy our free economy and democratic government by violence.

T55　.... The Party's Responsibility for Work among the Youth, "Political Affairs," 27 (Sept. 1948), 910-15.

Excerpts from a report on its youth panel to the Party's fourteenth national convention, August 2-6, 1948, stressing the importance of winning youth's support of the Progressive Party, the possible formation of an independent non-Party youth organization, and the need for communists to play a greater role in American Youth for Democracy.

T56　.... Strengthen the Struggle against White Chauvinism, "Political Affairs," 28 (June 1949), 14-27.

An analysis of white chauvinism, with specific instances of its appearance in the Party in New York and of the necessary expulsions that followed. The Party is not yet militantly hostile to all forms of white chauvinism; this is connected with insufficient attention to ideological problems. Reluctance to struggle against white chauvinism is a vicious form of opportunism.

T57　.... Truman's Perspective and America's Reality, "Political Affairs," 29 (Feb. 1950), 1-12.

Truman's messages to Congress in January 1950 holding out the prospect of a four-fold increase in national production in 50 years, represent a pipe dream, that can only be based on Wall Street's insane dream of a third world war to destroy the USSR and the people's democracies. Truman's social welfare proposals are not inconsistent with fascist reaction and war preparations.

T58　.... Two Paths for American Labor (On the Occasion of the 67th Anniversary of the Death of Karl Marx), "Political Affairs," 29 (March 1950), 7-17.

The alternatives for American labor are endorsement of the "profascist" leadership of the CIO and AFL, or acceptance of working class internationalism with resumption of ties between the trade unions of the country and the World Federation of Trade Unions.

T59　.... "Patriotism against McCarthyism." New York: New York State Communist Party, n.d. [1954]. 16 pp.

The full text of a speech made by the Chairman of the Communist Party of New York State before being sentenced for contempt for failing to surrender in the original Smith Act case. Part of the speech was undelivered, stopped by the judge when Thompson sought to describe McCarthyism as the real danger to America.

T60　.... On the 12-Party Declaration, "Political Affairs," 37 (Feb. 1958), 26-35.

The views of one of the seven members of the Party's national executive committee who opposed the majority statement on the declaration issued by 12 communist parties in Moscow in November. (See CPUSA, National Executive Committee, Statement on the Declaration of 12 Communist Parties, "Political Affairs," Jan. 1958.) The members of the majority are said to seek respectability, which they find by criticizing the Soviet Union; their formula will make the Party isolated and impotent.

T61　.... On the Work and Consolidation of the Party, "Political Affairs," 37 (Aug. 1958), 37-52.

A report to a meeting of the Party's national committee, June 28-29, 1958, stressing labor activity, the Party's role among youth, the Negro people's movement, and political action. The need to build Party morale and rout revisionism is emphasized along with the importance of ending factionalism and halting Party-wrecking.

T62　THOMPSON, William O., and others. "N.R.A. from Within." New York: International Pamphlets, 1934. 23 pp.

Part I contains, with other material, Thompson's letter of resignation from the National Recovery Review Board, stating that NIRA is an instrument for increasing the power of monopoly capital. In Part II, Earl Browder contends that the New Deal leads to trustification, prepares for a new war, and displays tendencies to fascism.

T63　THOMSON, George. "Marxism and Poetry." New York: International Publishers, 1946. 71 pp. Ref. notes.

An analysis of poetry from the Marxian point of view, by an Englishman who asserts that under capitalism the bourgeoisie has ceased to be a progressive class, and poetry has lost touch with the underlying forces of social change. In Russia, however, a cultural renaissance has taken place. When the class struggle has been overcome, the English will recover their sense of poetry, with the rest of their heritage.

T64　THOREZ, Maurice. Culture and Peace, "Masses & Mainstream," 3 (June 1950), 43-47.

Excerpts from the report of the general secretary of the French Communist Party to its Twelfth Congress in April, arguing that the decadence of American culture is reflected everywhere, and is in line with Marshall Plan warmongering.

T65　THORMAN, Donald J. Anti-Communist Record of the Catholic Press, "America," 92 (Feb. 5, 1955), 473-75.

An account of a study by the author of the effectiveness of the Catholic press in fighting communism. He explains the methods of his research, sampling techniques, and sources consulted. He concludes that, while the Catholic press has done a good job on the dangers of communism, it has been inadequate in presenting positive social doctrine.

T66　THORNHILL, Thomas J. (compiler). "The Plight

of the Nation." Vol. 4. Dallas: Wilkinson Printing Co., 1948. 192 pp. (Only volume published.)
A collection of materials designed to show that communism is the cause of the present world chaos and an imminent threat to this nation. Much of the material is drawn from "Reader's Digest," "Plain Talk," "Newsweek," Southern newspapers, and reports of the Dies Committee. Lists of communist front organizations and leading fellow-travelers are included, and attention is focused on communist activities in the labor and peace movements.

T67 THORNING, Joseph F. "Communism in the U.S.A." New York: America Press, n.d. [1937]. 32 pp. Bibliog.
A Catholic view of the communist movement in the U.S., with attention to its progress among the native-born and Negroes, efforts to undermine conservative unions, work among the unemployed and youth, and the united front tactic. The communists hope to call a nationwide strike, to be transformed into a civil war.

T68 THORP, Willard. American Writers on the Left. In Donald Drew Egbert and Stow Persons (eds.), "Socialism and American Life," vol. 1, ch. 13, pp. 599-620. Princeton, N.J.: Princeton University Press, 1952.
After a brief sketch of leftist literature before 1920, the author discusses the problems faced by leftist writers between 1920 and 1940: hewing to the correct political line, following the correct literary fashion, and selecting and treating material in an approved manner. He uses the literary careers of Max Eastman, Joseph Freeman, Philip Rahv, and Isidor Schneider as examples. He also discusses writers' congresses, with emphasis on Party control.

T69 THORPE, Merle. New Labels on Old Bottles, "Nation's Business," 23 (July 1935), 25-26 ff.
An assertion that the communist platform is being incorporated in the American system of government. Marx's program included the centralization of credit, means of communication, and transport in the hands of the state; the combination of agriculture with manufacturing; the liability of all to labor; a graduated income tax; and the abolition of property in land.

T70 TICHENOR, George H. Why It Is Difficult for a Communist to Be a Cooperator, "New Leader," 27 (Aug. 19, 1944), 6.
An assertion by an official in the cooperative movement that communists cannot be cooperators because they will neither abide by democratic decisions, nor work for the common good rather than for a partisan clique. Several attempts by communists to capture coops are described.

T71 TIGNER, H. S. Communism and Christianity, "Christian Century," 63 (Nov. 20, 1946), 1405-7.
Anyone who believes that communism is an idealistic political movement, seeking moral goals in kinship with Christianity, totally misunderstands its character. Communism, which seeks unlimited power, is utterly opposed to Christianity. It is brutal and inhuman, seeking a human omnipotence that defies the sovereignty of God.

T72 .... Academic Freedom and the Communist Teacher, "Christian Century," 66 (Sept. 28, 1949), 1136-37.
An assertion that communists cannot properly teach in the schools of a democracy, since they cannot meet the standards of fair play, integrity, and lawful procedures. Communism is a technique of winning power, and communist teachers are disciplined servants of a ruthless political conspiracy. "Truth" is prepared for the communist by the Party rulers.

T73 TIMASHEFF, Nicholas S. The Schneiderman Case—Its Political Aspects, "Fordham Law Review," 12 (Nov. 1943), 209-30.
A sociologist dissents from the opinion of U.S. Supreme Court Justice Murphy in "Schneiderman vs. U.S." that it is possible for a Communist Party member to be attached to the principles of the U.S. Constitution. The communist creed, which is endorsed by the Party as a section of the Communist International, is explicitly revolutionary.

T74 TIMON [pseud.]. The Troubled Mandarins, "Masses & Mainstream," 9 (Aug. 1956), 35-47.
Using Simone de Beauvoir's "The Mandarins" as his text, the author poses questions that have troubled communists since the revelations about Stalinist excesses. He appeals for intellectual freedom; the artist in particular has a duty to stimulate thought and to experiment, not to give absolute allegiance to the state or a political party.

T75 TIPPETT, Tom. War in Gastonia, "Labor Age," 18 (July 1929), 15-16.
A review of the Gastonia, N.C., textile strike, in which 14 union men have been charged with murdering the chief of police. Although the National Textile Workers Union was started by the Party and most organizers are Party members, the union operated only as a militant, class-conscious one.

T76 .... "When Southern Labor Stirs." New York: Cape and Smith, 1931. 348 pp. Ind.
A description of several Southern textile strikes in 1929, all with violence and severe anti-union measures by employers. The methods of the communist-affiliated National Textile Workers Union, which led the strike in Gastonia, N.C., are compared with those of the AFL United Textile Workers, which led the other major strikes. Although communism was a handicap to the Gastonia strikers, the author suggests that the AFL could learn from the communists how to conduct a more militant fight.

T77 TODES, Charlotte. "Labor and Lumber." New York: International Publishers, 1931. 208 pp. Ref. notes. App. Ind.
One of a series of volumes on different industries prepared by the Labor Research Association. The author analyzes the lumber industry, the working and health conditions of the workers, the organizational efforts of unions, and their future in an industry suffering from overdevelopment, chaotic production, and fierce competition. She sees hope for the workers in an industrial union in lumber affiliated with the Trade Union Unity League, to gain increased wages and improved working conditions, and help bring about the end of capitalism.

T78 .... "Injunction Menace." New York: International Pamphlets, 1932. 15 pp.
The history of the injunction, emphasizing its continued use against militant unionists by employers and their AFL "handmaidens" despite an anti-injunction law. To fight the injunction menace, a broad united front of workers must build strong TUUL unions and expose the class function of the courts.

T79 .... "William H. Sylvis and the National Labor Union." New York: International Publishers, 1942. 128 pp. Ref. notes. App. Ind.
A communist eulogy to Sylvis, post-Civil War labor leader, who took a militant stand against those who had usurped the people's rights. Although he did not fully understand the dynamics of the new class situation, he was

a great pioneer leader, outspoken on the issues of international class solidarity and the rights of women and Negroes.

T80   TOM MOONEY MOLDERS DEFENSE COMMITTEE. "Labor Leaders Betray Tom Mooney." San Francisco: The Committee, 1931. 50 pp.
An indictment of AFL leaders for allegedly sabotaging the demands of the rank and file for Mooney's unconditional pardon. Asserting that the betrayal of Mooney and Billings is but part of the AFL leadership's betrayal of American workers, the Committee, which is headed by veteran communist Robert Minor, urges the AFL rank and file to wrest control from the present leaders and expose the Mooney frame-up.

T81   TOMPKINS, W. F. The Communist Control Act: The Communists and Organized Labor, "Vital Speeches," 21 (Aug. 1, 1955), 1396-98.
An assistant attorney general, in charge of internal security, reviews communist efforts to control the trade union movement. The noncommunist affidavit of the Taft-Hartley Act has proved impotent. The Communist Control Act of 1954 provides means by which rank-and-file members of communist-dominated unions can clean house of communist dictators.

T82   TOOHEY, Pat; NEARING, Scott; SHIELDS, Art; and DUNN, Robert W. "The Fight of the Young Coal Miners." Springfield, Ill.: Coal Miner, n.d. [1926?]. 14 pp.
A plea to young miners to support the opposition slate to John L. Lewis, led by John Brophy, within the United Mine Workers. (Later many of this "Save-the-Union" group, including Toohey, helped form the National Miners Union of the Trade Union Unity League.)

T83   TOOHEY, Pat. The Miners Surge Forward, "Labor Unity," 2 (March 1928), 4-5 ff.
The communist secretary of the National Save-the-Union Committee, which heads the fight of the left wing in the United Mine Workers against the Lewis machine, tells of the mass meetings being held throughout the union, building up sentiment for ousting Lewis and winning the strike. Sentiment is growing for a national left-wing conference, he asserts.

T84   .... The Anthracite: A Record of A.F. of L. Betrayal, "Labor Unity," 3 (Feb. 1929), 9-12 ff.
An account of anthracite conditions by the secretary of the National Miners Union, who attacks the employers for maintaining a monopoly, making stupendous profits, union-busting, and wage-cutting. He reviews the long and bitter struggles of the anthracite miners, attacks the United Mine Workers for company unionism and corruption, and promises militant leadership by the NMU.

T85   .... Greater Attention to the Problems of the Negro Masses! "Communist," 19 (March 1940), 278-88.
A speech to the Party's national committee, February 19, 1940, stressing the need to combine the struggle for equal rights and national liberation of Negroes with creation of a broad antiwar and anti-imperialist people's front. A deep-seated antiwar feeling, to which national expression must be given, exists among Negroes. Issues around which anti-imperialist unity of Negroes may be rallied are outlined.

T86   .... Some Reconversion Problems in the Automotive Industry, "Communist," 23 (June 1944), 541-57.
A study of problems involved in reconverting the automotive

industry to peacetime production. The joint participation of management, labor, and government in the solution of these problems is urged.

T87   TOOLE, H. M. "Communist Action vs. Catholic Action." New York: American Press, 1936. 16 pp.
A Catholic view of the Party line, Party organization and propaganda, the "Daily Worker," and the League of Militant Atheists, by which the Party promotes an antireligious program of action. The Party's propaganda can be fought by Catholic efforts to promote social justice.

T88   TORMEY, Jim. Some New Approaches to Party Organization and Concentration Work, "Political Affairs," 27 (June 1948), 551-60.
A report, based on examination of the Party's organizational structure in New York City over a period of several months, recommending that the Party concentrate its efforts in six specific areas where Negroes, Jews, or particular national groups predominate.

T89   TOWN CLUB, Education and School Budget Committee. "Report on Allegations of Communist Infiltration in the Scarsdale Schools," 1953. 27 pp.
A review of the long controversy over alleged communist influence in the Scarsdale school system, as evidenced by appearance of books by communists on reading lists and in the school library, and participation of communist speakers in a program of lectures for teachers. The controversy over the books centered on the use of historical novels written by Howard Fast. The committee concludes that there is no evidence to support the charges.

T90   TRACHTENBERG, Alexander. "The Heritage of Gene Debs." New York: International Publishers, 1930. 31 pp.
A communist account of Debs' career, emphasizing Debs' advocacy of revolutionary industrial unionism, his hatred of class collaboration, his disagreements with reformist elements within the Socialist Party, his opposition to all wars except that of the social revolution, and his sympathetic response to the Russian Revolution. Debs is criticized, however, for opposing the formation of the Third International, and for remaining with the socialists after the revolutionary elements split off to form the communist movement.

T91   .... "The History of May Day." New York: International Pamphlets, 1930. 31 pp.
A communist view of May Day as a day of struggle for the immediate political demands of workers, bound up with the struggle for the shorter workday. Hailing the revolutionary history of the American labor movement, the author asserts that the Communist International now carries on the traditions of May Day. He attacks AFL leaders who, though they initiated this day, now advocate and practice class collaboration.

T92   TRADE UNION COMMITTEE TO DEFEND LOUIS WEINSTOCK. "The Smith Act—A Threat to Labor: Louis Weinstock, Working Painter, Frame-up Victim." New York: The Committee, 1951. 30 pp.
An appeal for support for Weinstock, indicted for alleged Smith Act violations. Quotations praise the defendant, a Party leader in the Painters Union, and emphasize the dangers of persecuting persons for their beliefs. Denying that he is a Party functionary, Weinstock asserts that the indictment seeks to suppress unpopular ideas and weaken the labor movement.

T93   TRADE UNION COMMITTEE TO FREE IRVING POTASH. "Free Irving Potash." New York: The Committee, n.d. [1952?]. 25 pp.

An appeal to trade unionists and democratic-minded Americans to preserve the Bill of Rights by seeking to free Potash, leader of the Fur and Leather Workers Union and one of the 11 communist leaders imprisoned under the Smith Act. His union activities are reviewed, and messages of support from within this country and abroad are reproduced.

T94   TRADE UNION EDUCATIONAL LEAGUE. The Principles and Program of the Trade Union Educational League, "Labor Herald," 1 (March 1922), 3-7.
The American labor movement is conservative and backward because progressives have left it to form dual unions. The TUEL, an organization of progressive and revolutionary elements, operates within trade unions with a program against class collaboration, in support of industrial unionism, and in favor of affiliation with the Red Trade Union International.

T95   ..., National Committee. A Political Party for Labor, "Labor Herald," 1 (Dec. 1922), 3-6.
Endorsement of the struggle for a labor party, and condemnation of the political policy of Gompers and the AFL. Sentiment in labor ranks for immediate formation of a labor party is growing. It must be a class political party, permitting existing working class parties to retain their identity through a federated structure.

T96   .... Second General Conference Issue, "Labor Herald," 2 (Oct. 1923). 35 pp.
The proceedings of the September 1-2, 1923, session of the TUEL. Included are the report of the national committee, reports of the national industrial sections, reports from the various districts on progress of TUEL work, and a list of resolutions adopted by the convention.

T97   .... The Program of the T.U.E.L., "Labor Herald," 3 (July 1924), 151-54.
A draft of the TUEL program prepared for the Third World Congress of the Red International of Labor Unions, which is to meet in Moscow July 5. The program includes formation of a labor party, amalgamation of unions, exposure of bureaucracy, recognition of Soviet Russia, affiliation of all unions with the RILU, formation of shop committees, and workers' control of industry.

T98   ..., Needle Trades Section. "Needle Trades Left Wing Program." New York: The Section, 1926. 93 pp.
Program adopted at the third conference of the Needle Trades Section, held September 12-14, 1925, including economic demands, amalgamation of all needle trades' unions, decentralization of the union into shop committees, and formation of an all-inclusive labor party based upon the unions and all workers' political and fraternal organizations.

T99   .... "Program of the TUEL, Adopted by the 3rd National Conference, New York, December 3-4, 1927." New York: TUEL, 1927. 14 pp.
A restatement of the TUEL program, including militant trade unionism, a fight against class collaboration, the building of unions, formation of a labor party, organization of the left wing, and international labor unity. Workers are urged to form opposition groups, take control of their unions, and throw misleaders out of office.

T100   .... Statement of the Trade Union Educational League on the American Federation of Labor Convention, "Labor Unity," 2 (Nov. 1928), 6-7 ff.
Asserting that the American labor movement is in the greatest crisis of its history, as a result of mechanization,

collaboration with employers, narrow craft unionism, and corruption, the TUEL calls for workers to organize factions under its leadership within mass unions and separate TUEL unions in unorganized industries, break barriers of race and nationality, and fight for their own class political party.

T101   ..., National Committee, A Manifesto of Reaction: Expose the Fake Progressives of the "Labor Age" Muste Group! "Labor Unity," 3 (March 1929), 14-15.
An attack upon the manifesto, A Challenge to Progressives, in the February "Labor Age." Though the manifesto is directed against the right-wing AFL bureaucracy, it is really an effort to revive the illusions of workers and hinder the building of the TUEL new unions. Members of the group, led by A. J. Muste and Norman Thomas, are said to have intervened in recent strikes to aid discredited labor bureaucrats.

T102   TRADE UNION UNITY LEAGUE. "Problems of Strike Strategy: Decisions of the International Conference on Strike Strategy Held in Strassburg, Germany, January, 1929." Foreword by A. Lozovsky. Pref. to American ed. by Bill Dunne. New York: Workers Library for Trade Union Unity League, 1929. 49 pp.
Resolutions and decisions of the International Conference on Strike Strategy called by the Executive Bureau of the Red International of Labor Unions, with which the TUUL is affiliated. Revolutionary strike strategy is designed to win victory for the working class both in everyday "bread-and-butter" struggles and in the political struggles into which serious economic conflicts quickly develop.

T103   .... "The Trade Union Unity League: Its Program, Structure, Methods and History." New York: The League, n.d. [1930?]. 29 pp.
The history and program of the TUUL, labor center of the Communist Party, successor to the Trade Union Educational League, and American Section of the Red International of Labor Unions. Whereas the TUEL sought only to organize revolutionary minorities within the AFL, the TUUL in addition will organize the unorganized into industrial unions outside the AFL, which is attacked as fascist and an instrument of capitalists to exploit the workers. A program based on class struggle is presented, opposing imperialist war and pledged to defense of the Soviet Union.

T104   .... Trade Union Unity League's Program of Work — Adopted Feb. 17, "Labor Unity," 4 (Feb. 1930), 2-3 ff.
The program adopted by the TUUL's National Executive Board, endorsing the resolutions of the RILU General Council's sixth session. The TUUL must intensify the fight against the AFL and SP, win the leadership of the masses of workers, and organize and lead the unemployed. It must organize the unorganized, and work among Negroes and youth.

T105   ..., National Executive Board. For Unification of the Trade Union Movement, "Labor Unity," 9 (Oct. 1934), 27-30.
A letter addressed to the delegates to the AFL convention, as well as to all AFL locals and the entire membership, proposing unification of the trade union movement. Arguing that TUUL policies have been proved correct and that AFL leaders have followed wrong policies, the letter suggests united action to defeat the bosses' attack. Unification will be possible if the AFL will open its unions to all workers, readmit expelled members, and guarantee full rank-and-file democracy.

T106 TRAGER, Frank N. Bogus Friends of Freedom, "North American Review," 248 (Winter 1939-40), 366-73.
Criticism of magazines and writers that employ double-bookkeeping, attacking fascist repression while remaining silent as to the betrayal of freedom in the USSR. Among those attacked are the "Nation," the "New Republic," Max Lerner, and Vincent Sheean. The values of a free society are indivisible.

T107 .... Frederick L. Schuman: A Case History, "Partisan Review," 7 (March-April 1940), 143-51.
A resumé of the political career of a professor of government at Williams College, who ceased being a Stalininst fellow-traveler after almost a decade, because of the Red Army's invasion of Finland. In 1935, during an investigation of radicalism at the University of Chicago, he repudiated his 1932 support of Foster and Ford. In 1937, however, he supported the Stalinist line on the Moscow trials.

T108 TRILLING, Diana. A Memorandum on the Hiss Case, "Partisan Review," 17 (May-June 1950), 484-500.
An analysis of motives and hidden preferences that may explain why both sides, but particularly the defenders of Hiss, could see only the evidence that supported their convictions. The passions of loyalty roused on Hiss' side represent a case of "There but for the grace of God go I." The entire episode may make liberals aware that political ideas are also political acts.

T109 .... A Communist and His Ideals, "Partisan Review," 18 (July-Aug. 1951), 432-40.
An explanation of how deprecation of self and country has led many middle-class American idealists toward communism. Seeking the international brotherhood of man, the idealist may see the Soviet Union as the embodiment of internationalism, and thereby move from refusal of concern for his own country to total concern for one other country.

T110 .... The Oppenheimer Case: A Reading of the Testimony, "Partisan Review," 21 (Nov.-Dec. 1954), 604-35.
An analysis of Oppenheimer's hearing before the Gray Board, concluding that the very strict standards by which he was judged were standards by which virtually anyone might fail. Before Oppenheimer understood the true nature of the Soviet Union, it was a grave risk to trust him; but he never told the secrets then. It is inept to take away clearance after he learned the error of his way.

T111 .... McCarthy, the Liberals and a New Communist—non-Communist Forum, "New Leader," 40 (May 27, 1957), 12-14.
Criticism of the American Forum, newly organized to promote discussion among persons, including communists, who are related to socialist and labor traditions. Pointing to the slaughter of Hungarian freedom fighters, the author asserts that freedom of culture here still has much to fear from communist totalitarianism.

T112 TRILLING, Lionel. "The Middle of the Journey." New York: Viking, 1947. 310 pp.
A novel of ideas, laid in a Connecticut farming district in the late 1930's. The central figure, an intellectual fellow-traveler, reexamines the ideological and cultural foundations of his life. Rejecting the communist movement and the intellectual atmosphere surrounding it, he seeks a new philosophy more adequate to his needs.

T113 TRIMBLE, Peter. Thought Control on the Waterfront, "Nation," 173 (July 14, 1951), 27-29.

A labor reporter discusses the loyalty screening program as administered by the Coast Guard on the West Coast waterfront. The rights of individuals are not sufficiently protected; security must be reconciled with freedom.

T114 TRUMAN, Harry S. The Internal Security Act: Veto Message, "Vital Speeches of the Day," 17 (Oct. 15, 1950), 2-6.
President Truman's veto message analyzes shortcomings, inconsistencies, or illegalities of various sections of this legislation. He concludes that expediency cannot justify enactment of a bill which would so greatly weaken our liberties and give aid and comfort to our enemies.

T115 TRUMBO, Dalton. "Johnny Got His Gun." Philadelphia: Lippincott, 1939. 309 pp.
A communist antiwar novel, written during the Hitler-Stalin pact period. A "basket case" veteran of World War I asks to be exhibited to people everywhere as a protest against war.

T116 .... "Harry Bridges: A Discussion of the Latest Effort to Deport: Civil Liberties and the Rights of American Labor." Los Angeles: League of American Writers, 1941. 28 pp.
The case against the proposed deportation of Bridges, published by a front organization. The author builds a legal case against the deportation by quotations from authorities from Alexander Hamilton to Justice Brandeis. Bridges' background is said to be exemplary, and his union democratic and hard-hitting.

T117 .... "The Time of the Toad: A Study of Inquisition in America." Hollywood, Calif.: Hollywood Ten, 1949. 38 pp.
An account of the investigation by the House Committee on Un-American Activities of communist infiltration into the Hollywood motion picture industry, written by one of the ten persons indicted for refusing to answer questions as to political beliefs. The title is taken from a remark by Emile Zola.

T118 .... "The Devil in the Book." Los Angeles: California Emergency Defense Committee, 1956. 42 pp.
An analysis of the Smith Act trial in California by one of the Hollywood figures indicted for refusing to answer questions on political beliefs before the Un-American Activities Committee. He describes the courageous defendants, the "vindictive" judge, the informers who testified in the case, the verdict, the denial of appeals, and the present status of the case. He calls for repeal of the Smith Act as a travesty of law.

T119 TRUMBULL, Walter. "Life in the U.S. Army." New York: Young Communist League, n.d. [1931?]. 47 pp.
A contrast of the rights and treatment of enlisted men with the privileges of officers, written by a soldier who was court-martialed for inciting fellow soldiers to refuse to participate in exploiting natives in Hawaii. Asserting that enlisted men are victims of class exploitation and that the army is a tool of imperialism, he contrasts the working class army of the USSR with the capitalist army of the U.S.

T120 TSIRUL, S. "The Practice of Bolshevik Self-Criticism: How the American Communist Party Carries Out Self-Criticism and Controls Fulfillment of Decisions." New York: Central Committee, CPUSA, 1932. 32 pp. Reprinted from "Communist International," Aug. 15, 1932.
Sharp criticism of the American Party for failure to take

positive action on the basis of its resolutions. The author cites bureaucratic leadership, steretyped campaigning, and lack of political interest as causes of instability of Party membership in the U.S. Improvement is called for in the work of the Party cells, in membership recruitment, and in leadership practices.

T121 TUNNEY, Gene. American Youth Congress: Nature Will Take Its Course, "America," 63 (July 27, 1940), 424-26.
An assertion that the American Youth Congress, despite its good start, degenerated under communist leadership into a collection of cry-babies, stooges, parasites, and seditionists.

T122 TWOHY, James F. The Feinberg Law, "St. John's Law Review," 24 (April 1950), 197-220.
A discussion and defense of the New York statute barring communists from teaching in the public schools. World War II gave the Stalinists opportunities, particularly in education. The Feinberg law was passed to curb this influence. Defending its constitutionality, the author asserts that teachers may not teach doctrines whose fulfillment would eliminate all our freedoms.

T123 TYLER, Gus. "The United Front." New York: Rand School Press, 1933. 19 pp.
A socialist appraisal of the communists' united front tactic. The Bolsheviks split every Socialist Party in Europe and America after taking power in Russia, then promoted abortive revolutions in Italy and Germany. Now they call for united fronts, not to unite, but with the objective of destroying all noncommunist working class organizations.

T124 . . . . "Youth Fights War!" Chicago: Young People's Socialist League, n.d. [1936?]. 23 pp.
A socialist criticism of the communist line on war, asserting that the original communist slogan of turning imperialist into class war has been replaced by the collective security line. Having lost faith in the power of the international working class, the Comintern has turned to capitalist nations for alliances. YPSL believes that the best Soviet ally is the international working class.

T125 . . . . A Party of Labor Must Break from the Friends of Labor, "Socialist Call," 3 (Sept. 11, 1937), 8.
American labor must choose between a popular front, advocated by the Communist Party, and an American labor party, advocated by the Socialist Party. Contrary to communist claims, the people's front is not a step toward a labor party, since it tries to amalgamate classes, and thereby disarm labor when class struggle is most needed.

T126 . . . . ADA Fights Reds—and Reactionaries, "New Leader," 34 (March 5, 1951), 6-7.
An analysis of the fourth annual convention of Americans for Democratic Action. The author asserts that this convention reflected the two-front battle being fought by ADA: the fight against communism as a military menace, and against conservatism as a threat to living standards and civil liberties.

T127 . . . . The New Line of the Communist Party, "New Republic," 128 (Jan. 26, 1953), 13-15.
A review of the new line of the CPUSA, embodied in the national committee's draft resolution of December 1952. The two main directives are to liquidate the Progressive Party, and to infiltrate both left and right noncommunist organizations. This new infiltration tactic, designed to end the communists' isolation of recent years, will affect conservative as well as liberal and left groups.

T128 . . . . The Communists' New Line, "New Republic," 130 (March 22, 1954), 13-14.
An analysis of the CPUSA draft program of March 7, 1954. The Party has embarked on a new popular front policy aimed at disrupting our alliance with European powers, whereas in the 1930's it sought to cement such an alliance. The CPUSA will seek to use McCarthyism to discredit Eisenhower "internationalism" and isolate America from the noncommunist world.

T129 "Typographers Journal" (International Typographical Union), Beware of Borers from Within, 85 (July 1934), 8-10.
A warning to union members that communists are beginning to organize within the union. A document issued by the "Unemployed Association" within the union is cited as evidence.

U

U1   UHLER, John Earle. Russia's Advance in the United States, "Catholic World," 166 (Oct. 1947), 11-18.
A recital of communist penetration in American life, a penetration made possible by our many minorities, heavy taxes, the dole, lawlessness, labor union abuses, immorality, divorces, lack of discipline, and political conditions. Communist success throughout the world makes it essential that we resuscitate American democracy.

U2   ULMAN, Ruth, (ed.). "University Debaters' Annual: 1948-1949." New York: Wilson, 1949. 347 pp. Bibliog. Ind.
Chapter 5 (pp. 151-85) reproduces a debate between New York University and Barnard College on the topic, Resolved: That the Communist Party should be outlawed. Arguments by both sides are first summarized in outline form, then presented in full text.

U3   . . . . "University Debaters' Annual: 1949-1950." New York: Wilson, 1950. 355 pp. Ind.
Chapter 8 (pp. 280-306) reports a mock television trial participated in by debating teams from the University of Pittsburgh and Western Reserve University on the subject, Resolved: That communists should be prohibited from teaching in American colleges and universities. A bibliography on the subject is included.

U4   . . . . "University Debaters' Annual, 1950-1951." New York: Wilson, 1951. 256 pp. Ind.
Chapter 4 (pp. 85-121) reproduces a debate between the Agricultural and Mechanical College of Texas and Baylor University on the subject, Resolved: That the Communist Party should be outlawed in the United States. Chapter 5, (pp. 122-54) reports a debate on the subject, Resolved: That loyalty oaths in colleges should be outlawed, between Temple University and the University of Pennsylvania. Bibliographies on both subjects are included.

U5   UNEMPLOYED COUNCILS OF U.S., National Committee. "The National Hunger March in Pictures." New York: The Councils, 1931. 15 unnumbered pp.
Pictures of the National Hunger March on Washington in December 1931, in which 1,670 delegates from all over the country participated. A brief text describes the march, which was under Party leadership, and calls for unemployment insurance and immediate relief.

U6   . . . . "Poverty 'Midst Riches. Why? We Demand Unemployment Insurance." New York: Unemployed Councils, n.d. [1932?]. 46 pp.
The indictment of mass starvation and the program for unemployment relief and insurance as presented to Congress by the National Hunger March on December 7, 1931.

U7   . . . . "Why We March." New York: Workers Library, 1932. 16 pp.
The reasons and aims of the National Hunger March, for immediate unemployment relief and unemployment insurance at the expense of government and employers.

U8   . . . . "Make the Democrats Keep Their Promises." New York: Workers Library, 1933. 23 pp.
An attack on the Democrats for having done virtually nothing since the election to help the millions of unemployed and for ignoring the needs of exploited Negroes and desperate farmers. The Unemployed Councils which, under Party leadership, are becoming fighting organs of the workers, will force the government to keep its pledges.

U9   UNITED COMMUNIST PARTY OF AMERICA, Program and Constitution of the United Communist Party of America." The Party, 1921. 32 pp.
The program and constitution of the United Communist Party, formed by the merger of the Communist Labor Party and the Communist Party of America. Sections of the program deal with parliamentary democracy, "socialist" reform parties, mass action, penetration of military units, imperialism and war, colonial problems, unemployment, Negroes, agriculture, and labor unions and shop committees. Workers can achieve freedom only through revolution and workers' dictatorship.

U10   UNITED ELECTRICAL, RADIO AND MACHINE WORKERS OF AMERICA, District Council No. 7. "The Story of 'Police,'" Cleveland: District Council No. 7, UE, n.d. [1942?]. 14 pp.
An attack on a publication called "Police," which "plays up the communist bogy" and slanders militant CIO leaders. Its editor, John P. Moran, engages in Red-baiting to undermine the war effort and slander the democratic UE.

U11   UNITED ELECTRICAL, RADIO AND MACHINE WORKERS OF AMERICA. "It's Your Union They're After." New York: UE, 1948. 30 pp.
An attack on the Hartley Committee of the House of Representatives for accusing the UE of communist infiltration and for performing anti-union dirty work. Testimony of UE officers is quoted, with a resolution of its 1948 convention denouncing the committee and proclaiming the right of UE members to hold whatever political opinions they choose.

U12   . . . . "UE vs. Company Unionism." New York: UE, 1948. 23 pp.
Justification to UE members of the union's withholding of per capita payments to the CIO, which it attacks for Red-baiting and for sanctioning raids. The UE denies as slanderous the charge that it is communist controlled.

U13   . . . . "Stop the Frame-ups against Our Union." New York: UE, 1949. 14 pp.
A denunciation of the Un-American Activities Committee for its persecution and harassment of the union and its leaders on the charge of communist infiltration and control.

U14   . . . . "Red-Baiting: Road to Lower Wages, Fewer Jobs and Company Unionism." New York: UE, 1950. 23 pp.
An assertion that the UE is attacked as red because of its record of devotion to the American people in war and peace. The enemies of the union are denounced.

U15 "UNITED MINE WORKERS JOURNAL," Communists Are Again Making an Attempt to Gain Control of the United Mine Workers of America, 37 (Nov. 1, 1926), 3-5 ff.
Reprint and discussion of a letter said to indicate a close link between the "rebels" in the union (headed by John Brophy), Jay Lovestone of the Communist Party, and the TUEL. The scheme of the communists to take over the miners' union is discussed in speeches by President Lewis and Vice-President Wilson of the UMW.

U16 . . ., Communists Have Made Desperate Attempts to Seize Control of United Mine Workers of America, 41 (Nov. 1, 1930), 8-10 ff.
Statement by Ellis Searles, editor of the "Journal," before the House committee investigating communism, headed by Hamilton Fish. Searles tells of communist attempts to seize control of the UMW, and of the communist-inspired Save-the-Union Committee and National Miners Union. Only congressional regulation of the coal industry can prevent the spread of communism.

U17 . . ., Progressive Miners Union Backed by Communists, Pete Allard Discloses to State's Attorney, 44 (May 1, 1933), 3-5 ff.
Reprint of an affidavit by a brother of Gerry Allard, a leader of the Progressive Miners of America, which was fighting the United Mine Workers in Illinois. The affidavit asserts that Allard and all the other leaders are part of the left-wing communist group known as Trotskyists. Added is a reprint of a 1929 letter from Gerry Allard denouncing the Trotskyists and asking for readmission to the CPUSA.

U18 UNITED MINE WORKERS OF AMERICA. "Attempt by Communists to Seize the American Labor Movement." Indianapolis: UMW, 1923. 63 pp.
Reprint of a series of six articles prepared by the UMW on the communist attempt to seize control of the organized labor movement in America and use it as the base for overthrow of the government. Emphasis is placed on control of the communist conspiracy from Moscow, and on its efforts to win control of labor organization in the coal fields. (Reprinted as Senate Document No. 14, 68th Congress, 1st Session. The articles originally appeared in "United Mine Workers Journal," Sept. 15-Dec. 1, 1923.)

U19 . . . . Miners Reject and Repudiate Moscow, "American Federationist," 30 (Feb. 1923), 139-41.
A report unanimously adopted by the international executive board of the United Mine Workers, ordering its District 26 to disaffiliate from the Red International of Labor Unions or be suspended from the UMW. The RILU was found to be a dual union, in opposition to the policies and laws of the UMW.

U20 "UNITED STATES NEWS," Friction inside the CIO Affecting Defense Work, 10 (June 27, 1941), 18-19.
An assertion that national leaders of the CIO will not purge the communists, as had been expected. Though right-wing CIO leaders seek a showdown, the left wing controls the CIO. The government sides with Sidney Hillman of the ACW. Philip Murray is the man in the middle.

U21 . . . . CIO Split with Communists? Trend against Party Pressure, 21 (Aug. 30, 1946), 18-19.
The split between the factions over strike and political policies may come to a showdown at any time. Communists are demanding militant strike action, whereas Murray wants to honor existing contracts and softpedal strikes. Communists favor a third party, but Murray prefers working within the two old parties.

U22 . . ., Communist Tactics in Unions, 21 (Oct. 25, 1946), 44-46.
A description of communist tactics in unions, showing how disciplined efforts have led to their control of many local CIO unions, and how they use their control to solidify and exploit their position. Though resentment against them is high, efforts to purge them in several unions have been unsuccessful.

U23 . . ., Story of Capture of a Union: Allis Chalmers Charge That Communists Forcibly Run Plant Local, 22 (Feb. 21, 1947), 30-32.
The story of the 10-month Allis Chalmers strike led by a communist-controlled local of the United Automobile Workers, as told by a company vice-president to the Senate Labor Committee.

U24 . . ., Rein on Communists in Unions, 22 (June 20, 1947), 22-23.
The noncommunist affidavit of the new labor law will have widespread effects in the CIO. Known communists will have to leave the Party or resign from union office, though communist-dominated unions may choose to boycott the NLRB. Policing will be a major administrative job for the NLRB and the FBI.

U25 "U.S. NEWS & WORLD REPORT," Communist-Control Plans: Spy Hunt as Preparation for New Laws, 25 (Sept. 10, 1948), 18-19.
Investigations have shown that communist groups operated in Washington and elsewhere in the U.S. during and before the war, and that some Party sympathizers obtained important government posts. Legislation has been proposed to require Party members to register, deny federal jobs to communists, restrict issuance of passports, tighten espionage laws, etc.

U26 . . ., Shift in Communist Strategy: Concentration of Effort on Key Industries, 25 (Oct. 8, 1948), 40-42.
The new policy of the communists is to concentrate in basic industries, so that they can engage in strikes and sabotage should we get in a war with Russia. Employers can expect more communist use of nationality groups, more plant cells, more pressure on right-wing leaders, and more internal union strife.

U27 . . ., Communist Hunt Is Spreading: Who's Being Investigated by Whom, and Why, 26 (June 24, 1949), 22-23.
A summary of investigations and spy trials currently in progress. Congressional committees are investigating communists in defense industries and seeking to bolster anticommunist laws. Court cases include those of 10 Hollywood writers, Alger Hiss, Judith Coplon, and 11 Party leaders. Federal workers are being investigated for loyalty, and states are active in legislation and investigations.

U28 . . ., How Russia Got U.S. Secrets: 10,000 Spies in Key Places, 28 (Feb. 17, 1950), 11-13.
The Soviet spy network in the U.S. includes thousands, many of them American citizens. While atomic secrets are the chief objective, information about guided missiles, rockets, and big bombers is sought. Spy networks are built into government, labor unions, key industries, and research organizations. Party members and fellow-travelers are potential spies.

U29 . . ., F.B.I. Director Hoover Tells How Communists Work in the U.S., 28 (June 23, 1950), 11-13.
J. Edgar Hoover comments on operations of American communists in answer to questions of a Senate committee.

461

The FBI director discusses the use of European immigrants and aliens in Party work, the role of front organizations, and the secrecy of communist activities. Their underground apparatus will make detection of their activities more difficult in the future.

U30 "U.S. NEWS & WORLD REPORT," How Communists Operate: An Interview with J. Edgar Hoover, 29 (Aug. 11, 1950), 30-33.
An interview with the FBI chief on communist tactics and how to combat them. He explains the Party's cell organization, the meaning of Party membership, the difficulties in proving illegal acts, and the use of publicity in exposing communists. He asks the public to be alert, and to report information promptly to the FBI.

U31 . . ., Communists in the New Deal? At Least One Cell Is Brought to Light, 29 (Sept. 15, 1950), 22-23.
Lee Pressman's testimony before a congressional committee confirms suspicion that a small group of communists in key positions in the New Deal sought to stir up trouble. Pressman reveals that members of a communist cell were employed in the Department of Agriculture, the WPA, the FSA, and the NLRB.

U32 . . ., Inside Story of a Native American Who Turned Spy, 29 (Nov. 24, 1950), 15-17.
The case history of Alfred Dean Slack, who first sold industrial information to Soviet agents, and finally transferred the formula of a new explosive to Harry Gold, the lead contact in a Russian spy apparatus. He was apprehended in 1950 and sentenced to 15 years in prison.

U33 . . ., Interviews with Sen. Benton of Connecticut and Sen. McCarthy of Wisconsin: The McCarthy Issue Pro and Con, 31 (Sept. 7, 1951), 24-41.
Senator Benton, who has introduced a resolution to expel McCarthy, charges him with making irresponsible accusations and with degrading the standards of the Senate. He asserts that McCarthy has made it more difficult to get communists out of government. Senator McCarthy calls his work necessary because the executive branch is not prosecuting communists in government. He criticizes the Tydings Committee and the record of Loyalty Boards.

U34 . . ., Communist Threat inside U.S.: Interview with Sen. McCarran, 31 (Nov. 16, 1951), 24-30.
Senator McCarran describes communist infiltration into government, educational institutions, and organizations. He tells how the Internal Security Committee evaluates information on communists, and discusses the charges against the Institute of Pacific Relations.

U35 . . ., Catching the Disloyal: Interview with Hiram Bingham, 31 (Nov. 23, 1951), 22-27.
The chairman of the Loyalty Review Board describes previous loyalty programs and tells how his board evaluates the decisions of the 100 or more lower loyalty boards. The board's jurisdiction does not extend to security, which is much broader; its job is to find out whether there is reasonable doubt as to loyalty.

U36 . . ., Interview with Senator Humphrey, 31 (Dec. 28, 1951), 20-26.
Senator Hubert H. Humphrey, head of a Senate subcommittee investigating communist influence in labor unions, asserts that communist-dominated unions get their orders from the Party, which is directed by the Soviet Politburo. One remedy would be to deprive communist-dominated unions of bargaining rights.

U37 . . ., How Communists Rule a Union, 32 (March 28, 1952), 28-33.

A former officer of Local 600 of the UAW at the Ford Motor Company plant near Detroit tells how a small number of communists dominated a local union of 60,000 members by means of a caucus and stacking of meetings.

U38 . . ., "Fewer Communists in U.S.," 32 (April 11, 1952), 35.
A report on the Communist Party based on FBI findings asserts that, while the Party has lost numerical strength, it remains a threat to American security, particularly through infiltration of defense industries.

U39 . . ., Communists in Government, 33 (July 11, 1952), 53-74.
The text of a report and recommendations by the Senate Judiciary Committee on responsibility for the communist conquest of China. The report asserts that a group associated with the Institute of Pacific Relations sought between 1941 and 1945 to change U.S. policy so as to accommodate communist ends. Owen Lattimore is called a conscious instrument of the Soviet conspiracy.

U40 . . ., What's McCarthyism: Pros and Cons of Bitter Controversy, 33 (Sept. 26, 1952), 16-19.
An account of the controversy over McCarthyism, a major issue in the 1952 presidential campaign. Its beginning came with McCarthy's 1950 speech charging that communists in the State Department were helping to shape U.S. foreign policy. "McCarthyism" is presented, as explained by the senator and as described by its opponents.

U41 . . ., Interview with Robert Morris: The Story of Communism in U.N., 33 (Dec. 5, 1952), 18-19.
The special counsel of the Senate Internal Security Committee asserts that high-ranking Americans at the UN hold procommunist views. FBI files against many of these people have been ignored. The UN should clean house of these people who are undermining the confidence of Americans in the UN.

U42 . . ., What Grand Jury Found in U.N., 33 (Dec. 12, 1952), 88-92.
The text of the grand jury's report on disloyalty of certain U.S. citizens at the UN. The jury found evidence of infiltration into the UN of a large group of disloyal U.S. citizens, many of them associated with the communist movement. Their presence at the UN menaces our national security.

U43 . . ., Interview with Nathaniel Weyl: I Was in a Communist Unit with Hiss, 34 (Jan. 9, 1953), 22-40.
An interview with an excommunist, a former government economist, who asserts that he was in the same Party unit with Alger Hiss in 1933. The Party then appeared to many in a humanitarian guise, as the left wing of the progressives. It was common knowledge that Lee Pressman took communist orders. Weyl advises other excommunists to go straight to the FBI.

U44 . . ., Bishop Oxnam—Committee Hearing, 35 (Aug. 7, 1953), 40-48 ff.
The text of the ten-hour hearing of Bishop G. Bromley Oxnam of the Methodist Church before the House Committee on Un-American Activities. Bishop Oxnam, former head of the Federal Council of Churches of Christ in America, appeared at his own request to answer his critics in Congress and to protest the Committee's practice of releasing unverified information associating him with communist fronts. Asserting his active opposition to communism, he declares that we cannot beat the communist menace by bearing false witness against fellow Americans.

U45 "U.S. NEWS & WORLD REPORT," The Great Conspiracy: Communism inside U.S., 35 (Aug. 28, 1953), 11-19.
The report of the Senate Internal Security Subcommittee on the operation within the U.S. government of a group of highly placed procommunists who advised Cabinet members and influenced government policy. The records of 12 members of the conspiracy are examined in detail. The full text of the Committee's report and recommendations is presented.

U46 . . ., Interview with Herbert Brownell, Jr.: Communists in the U.S. a Greater Menace Now, 35 (Sept. 4, 1953), 40-44 ff.
Transcript of an interview with the Attorney General on questions of communist infiltration, the FBI, investigating committees, and related issues. Brownell explains the Attorney General's list and tells of improvements in security rules and of pending investigations by the Department of Justice.

U47 . . ., Mr. Nixon Attacks Communist Conspirators, 35 (Sept. 11, 1953), 28-31.
Excerpts from a speech by Vice-President Nixon to the American Legion national convention, asserting that congressional committees have exposed the communist conspiracy where courts have no jurisdiction. All members of the communist conspiracy will be immediately removed from federal employment.

U48 . . ., "I Refuse to Answer"—and U.N. Pays Him Off with $40,000, 35 (Oct. 16, 1953), 27-30 ff.
Excerpts from hearings by the Internal Security Subcommittee of the Senate Committee on the Judiciary, looking into the communist activities of U.S. citizens employed by the United Nations. The UN is awarding up to $40,000 to Americans, discharged as security risks, who refused to answer Subcommittee questions as to communist connections.

U49 . . ., Communism: Religious Faith or Police Problem? 35 (Nov. 13, 1953), 116-18.
The text of a letter from the General Council of the Presbyterian Church in the U.S.A. to its 8,000 congregations, warning that some of the methods used against communists raise moral problems, threaten freedom of thought, and could lead to fascism. (A statement by Dr. Carl McIntire of the International Council of Christian Churches, attacking the letter's basic philosophy and assumptions, is appended.)

U50 . . ., All about the White Case, 35 (Nov. 20, 1953), 110-26.
The entire official record, with explanatory material, on Harry Dexter White, accused of spying for the Soviet Union while serving as a top official in the U.S. Treasury Department. Included are statements by high government officials, government correspondence, and statements by White's accusers and by White himself.

U51 . . ., Did Communist Ring Circle White House? 35 (Nov. 20, 1953), 17-20.
A congressional committee has disclosed that at least two spy rings encircled the White House in the late 1930's and 1940's: one set up by Harry Ware, including Alger Hiss; and the other by Nathan Silvermaster, including Harry Dexter White. Both Roosevelt and Truman, though informed of the poor security record of these and other alleged spies, took no action.

U52 . . ., The Spy Story as Told By: Truman, Brownell, FBI's Hoover, 35 (Nov. 27, 1953), 104-23.
Current developments in the case of Treasury Department official Harry Dexter White, accused of espionage for the Soviet Union. Former President Truman's radio-TV address, testimony of Attorney General Brownell and FBI Director J. Edgar Hoover before a Senate subcommittee, and President Eisenhower's comments at a press conference are reproduced.

U53 . . ., McCarthyism Pro and Con, 35 (Dec. 4, 1953), 104-9.
The texts of two speeches on November 24, one by Adlai Stevenson to the Georgia legislature, and the other by Senator McCarthy over television and radio networks. Stevenson accused Eisenhower's lieutenants of "McCarthyism" in attacks on the Truman Administration for disloyalty. McCarthy, charging communist infiltration of our government, asserted that Truman had promoted a Soviet spy.

U54 . . ., What It Takes to Catch a Spy, 35 (Dec. 4, 1953), 26-27.
Though the FBI knew of communist spy rings in Washington, it could not jail them because of the inadequacy of our laws to deal with the communist conspiracy. Inhibiting factors include the stringency of required proof, the ban against use of wiretapped information, and the statute of limitations.

U55 . . ., Strange Case of John P. Davies, 35 (Dec. 11, 1953), 26-32 ff.
The case of John P. Davies, State Department career diplomat, many times investigated for loyalty and now under study as a security risk. Formerly part of the State Department group guiding U.S. policy on China, he allegedly helped block aid to the Chinese Nationalists and recommended communist sympathizers as advisors on China.

U56 . . ., Gouzenko Talks, 36 (Jan. 1, 1954), 34-45.
An interview with the former Soviet intelligence agent who, in breaking away, touched off the spy inquiry in Canada, gave evidence leading to the conviction of the British atomic spy, Allan Nunn May, and opened up many leads into the Soviet espionage apparatus in the U.S.

U57 . . ., Senator McCarthy Reports—Reds at Work on Secret Files . . . Defense Plants . . . Libraries . . . Ships, 36 (Jan. 29, 1954), 110-15.
The text of portions of the annual report of Senator McCarthy's Subcommittee on Investigations, asserting that State Department files are in deplorable state from the security standpoint, that U.S. Information Centers abroad carry procommunist books, and that communists are infiltrating the armed forces and defense industry.

U58 . . ., Loyalty of the Clergy—O.K., 36 (Feb. 19, 1954), 126-27.
The text of the section on religion in the 1953 annual report of the House Committee on Un-American Activities. Religious institutions as such are cleared of involvement in the communist conspiracy, though some individuals, including Jack McMichael, are found to have consistently followed the Party line.

U59 . . ., Story of How Reds in U.S. Army Get Honorable Discharge, 36 (March 12, 1954), 72-87.
The text of the McCarthy-Army hearings in the case of Major Irving Peress of the Army Dental Corps, honorably discharged after refusing to testify whether he was a communist. (The investigation led to a controversy involving General Ralph W. Zwicker, Army Secretary Stevens, and President Eisenhower.)

U60 . . ., Security Risks in the Armed Forces—The Pentagon's Own Story, 36 (March 26, 1954), 116-20.

Testimony before the Senate Armed Services Committee about communists in the armed forces. Secretary of Defense C. E. Wilson tells of the armed forces' security precautions, and representatives of the Navy, Army, and Air Force deny that communists are "coddled."

U61   "U.S. NEWS & WORLD REPORT," The Strange Case of Dr. Oppenheimer, 36 (April 23, 1954), 20-24 ff.
An analysis of the security charges against J. Robert Oppenheimer, and of his ideas, associations, activities, and opposition to the H-bomb. The AEC charges and Oppenheimer's reply are published in full.

U62   . . ., Findings in the Case of Dr. Oppenheimer, 36 (June 11, 1954), 82-101.
The text of the majority report and minority dissent of the Personnel Security Board in the case involving J. Robert Oppenheimer. The majority, though finding him loyal, ruled him unsafe for top security secrets because of past associations with communists and susceptibility to influence. Oppenheimer's appeal is also reproduced.

U63   . . ., Testimony That Decided the Oppenheimer Case, 36 (June 25, 1954), 79-106.
Excerpts of testimony before the Personnel Security Board by William L. Borden, former executive director of the Congressional Joint Committee on Atomic Energy, who believed that Oppenheimer was probably a Soviet agent; and by Dr. Edward Teller, who asserted that Oppenheimer's disapproval of the H-bomb delayed its development.

U64   . . ., General Groves Sizes Up Scientists, 37 (July 2, 1954), 79-84.
An excerpt from testimony before the Personnel Security Board in the case of J. Robert Oppenheimer. General Leslie R. Groves, director of the original A-Bomb project, asserts that the opposition of scientists to the "compartment" system for atomic information made it possible for Russia to steal the A-bomb details. This does not imply espionage effort by Oppenheimer, however.

U65   . . ., Final AEC Decision—Why Dr. Oppenheimer Is Called a Security Risk, 37 (July 9, 1954), 71-81.
The text of the AEC's four-to-one decision against Oppenheimer, upholding the AEC Personnel Security Board and denying the scientist access to restricted information. This is because of character defects; his opposition to the H-bomb is not a factor. The majority decision, supplementary statements, and dissenting opinion are reproduced.

U66   . . ., Interview with Martin Dies: They Tried to Get Me, Too, 37 (Aug. 20, 1954), 56-71.
The first chairman of the House Un-American Activities Committee (1938-45) tells of efforts by the Roosevelt Administration to discredit him and minimize communist influence in government and in the CIO. He describes Mrs. Roosevelt's coddling of communists in the American Youth Congress, communist efforts to unseat him, and communist methods and infiltration tactics.

U67   . . ., Jolt for Communists in Unions; New Plan Takes Rights from Infiltrated Groups, 37 (Aug. 27, 1954), 72-74.
An analysis of the proposed communist control bill of 1954 to outlaw the Communist Party and give the Eisenhower Administration power to curb the activities of the red unions.

U68   . . ., Red Tactics in Upsetting Committee Investigations, 37 (Aug. 27, 1954), 100-7.
Testimony before a Senate subcommittee by Bella V. Dodd,

telling of the strength of the Party in segments of American public opinion and its infiltration of congressional committee staffs. She shows how the Party uses smears, works against investigating committees, infiltrates newspapers, colors the news, and works with the underground.

U69   . . ., No Place for Communists to Hide? 37 (Sept. 3, 1954), 42-43.
An analysis of new anticommunist measures passed by Congress, which will make it harder for communists to operate here and impose greater penalties if they are caught conspiring against the U.S. The Party is outlawed, communists are required to register with federal authorities, and they can be jailed if they refuse to talk.

U70   . . ., End of an Era in China Policy: Men Who Served U.S. during Red Rise Now Out of Power, 37 (Nov. 19, 1954), 56-60.
Case histories of men who advised the U.S. on its China policy while the communists were getting a grip on that country. They include John Paton Davies, Jr., John Stewart Service, John Carter Vincent, Oliver E. Chubb, Lauchlin Currie, and Owen Lattimore.

U71   . . ., New Debate on the Oppenheimer Case, 37 (Dec. 24, 1954), 86-103.
Excerpts from an article in "Harper's" by Joseph and Stewart Alsop, attacking the Atomic Energy Commission for its handling of the Oppenheimer case. Roger Robb, former counsel to the AEC Personnel Security Board, replies in detail. A statement by the Alsops, rebutting an AEC attack on their article, is included.

U72   . . ., Communists in Government—The Issue Comes Up Again, 38 (Jan. 28, 1955), 102-5.
Two statements printed in full, each with corroborating evidence. One, by Senator Olin D. Johnston of South Carolina, asserts that, of the 205 Communist Party members alleged by Senator McCarthy to be in the State Department, not one has been proved a communist. Senator McCarthy sharply disagrees, pointing out that 32 resigned while under investigation.

U73   . . ., What Reds Are Up to in Unions, 38 (March 4, 1955), 107-10.
Communists, their strength in U.S. unions waning, now are telling left-wing groups to infiltrate the AFL-CIO. The Party line seems to be to find a way to join some AFL union at any cost, in order, it is believed, to obtain some protection from the 1954 Communist Control Law.

U74   . . ., Former AEC Counsel Explains Why Oppenheimer Was Ousted, 38 (April 1, 1955), 92-95.
The text of an address by Roger Robb at Amherst College, explaining that "security risk" is broader than disloyalty, since it includes character and associations as well. Robb reviews the evidence against Oppenheimer, showing why an adverse verdict was reached.

U75   . . ., Interview with Herbert Brownell, Jr.: Shall Doors Be Opened to Spies and Subversives? 38 (April 29, 1955), 54-66.
Attorney General Brownell defends the government's practice of using confidential sources to detect spies and fight the communist conspiracy. He denounces the attack on the government informant system as part of the communist strategy, and asserts that wiretapping evidence should be legal and that the Attorney General's list serves an important and useful function.

U76   . . ., The Case of John Peters: Test of Security Program, 38 (May 13, 1955), 55-59.
The case of Professor John P. Peters of Yale, dismissed

as part-time consultant to the U.S. Surgeon General under the security program. His record of communist associations is given. The Supreme Court will decide in this case whether the government can be forced to reveal its informers when discharging an employee on security grounds.

U77 "U.S. NEWS & WORLD REPORT," Onetime Spy Tells His Story: How U.S. Press Was Infiltrated by Communists, 39 (July 8, 1955), 70-80.
Excerpts from the testimony of Winston Burdett before the Senate Internal Security Subcommittee, telling how he joined the Party in 1937 while a reporter on the Brooklyn "Eagle," how he was used as a spy by the Soviets in Finland and Turkey, and how he broke with communism.

U78 . . ., Senators Question Newsman, 39 (July 8, 1955), 92-95.
Extracts from the testimony of Charles Grutzner, New York "Times" reporter, before the Senate Internal Security Subcommittee. Grutzner had been a member of the Party from 1937 to 1940. Questions put to him concerned the infiltration of the press by the CP, and the propriety of two news stories he filed from the Korean War zone.

U79 . . ., Case of Paul Robeson: Why Some Americans Can't Get Passports, 39 (Aug. 26, 1955), 79-81.
Extracts from a court hearing on Robeson's motion for an injunction to compel the State Department to issue him a passport, on the ground that political considerations are invalid grounds for denial. The motion was denied, the court ruling that the Secretary of State had not abused his discretion or acted arbitrarily.

U80 . . ., Communists on Broadway—Walter Committee Studies Reds in the Theater, 39 (Aug. 26, 1955), 75-78.
Extracts from hearings on communism in the New York area, held by the Walter Subcommittee of the House Committee on Un-American Activities, August 17, 1955. George Hall, an actor, admitted former Party affiliation and threw some light on communists in the theater and in Actors Equity.

U81 . . ., Risks in Government: Security Cases Bring New Charge of Politics, 39 (Oct. 7, 1955), 122-29.
Extracts from the testimony before a Senate Subcommittee by Philip Young, chairman of the Civil Service Commission, on security dismissals. He denies that the Commission has engaged in a "numbers racket" as to security firings designed to discredit the previous administration.

U82 . . ., A Handbook for Americans: How to Detect the Activities of the Communists in U.S., 40 (Jan. 6, 1956), 94-109.
Excerpts from a report of the Senate Internal Security Subcommittee, explaining the motives and methods of American communists. The article describes how communists exert influence in voluntary organizations and the armed forces, how recruiting takes place, what leads a person to join and stay in the Party, and the "benefits" the Party offers. The underground and front activity of the Party, and how it can be detected, is also discussed.

U83 . . ., Committee of Congress Says: U.S. Can't Let Up Now in Fighting Communism, 40 (Feb. 3, 1956), 124-25.
The text of a statement by the House Committee on Un-American Activities, January 17, 1956. It describes the success of the hearings held by the Committee in 1955, and makes recommendations to strengthen the government's hand in dealing with the Soviet conspiracy.

U84 . . ., A New Study of the U.S. Security System: New York Lawyers Say Keep the Program, Correct Its Weaknesses, 41 (July 13, 1956), 118-23.
The report of a study of the federal loyalty-security program by a committee of the Association of the Bar of the City of New York. This study analyzes the problem of communism in government, summarizes loyalty and security programs, and evaluates the present security program. It concludes that the security system should be continued, but that its weaknesses should be corrected.

U85 . . ., Newest Plan to Bar Risks from Government, 41 (Aug. 3, 1956), 104-6.
Excerpts from a statement by Senator Olin D. Johnston of South Carolina, chairman of a Senate Subcommittee that recently reported on the subject. He asserts that legislation is needed, since executive department orders and judicial interpretation have conflicted with public will and congressional intent. Disloyal persons should be barred from the federal service, with safeguards to protect the innocent.

U86 . . ., Here's Latest Official Report on Red Activities in U.S., 42 (March 15, 1957), 144-53.
After another year of investigating communist activities, the Senate Subcommittee on Internal Security finds that Soviet agents are using diplomatic passports; that the press, radio, and strategic labor unions have been infiltrated; and that British diplomatic spies Burgess and Maclean, working in behalf of the USSR, have been linked to Americans. Legislation to combat these problems is proposed.

U87 . . ., In the Court's Own Words . . .: The New Line on Communists, Investigations, Power of Congress, 42 (June 28, 1957), 35-36 ff.
Excerpts from the Supreme Court's decision in Watkins vs. U.S. and several other cases, along with editorial comments. The majority decisions handed down will greatly affect the investigatory powers of Congress, academic freedom in political expression, the rights of federal employees with respect to security investigations, and the prosecution of communist leaders.

U88 . . ., The Plan That Started New Fight over Loyalty Problem, 43 (July 5, 1957), 86-89.
Recommendations of a congressional commission on government security. Among its proposals are those for a Central Security Office in the executive branch, a statutory basis for the Attorney General's list, and a security program for the legislative and judicial branches.

U89 . . ., The Supreme Court and the Communist Threat, 43 (July 5, 1957), 46-48.
An analysis of the decisions since 1955 in which the U.S. Supreme Court has limited or denied executive or legislative powers to deal with subversion. Included are decisions on loyalty, sedition, dismissals, citizenship, sensitive jobs, deportation, admission to the bar, and the Smith Act.

U90 . . ., What Two Critics Say about Court's Ruling on Reds, 43 (Aug. 9, 1957), 112-15.
Two critical reports on the decisions of the Supreme Court concerning communism in the U.S., one by Attorney General Louis C. Wyman of New Hampshire, and the other by Senator William E. Jenner of Indiana. Wyman asserts that the Constitution is being tortured out of all historical proportion, while Jenner declares that the decisions have weakened national security.

U91 . . ., Supreme Court Rulings Criticized by Bar Association Committee, 43 (Aug. 16, 1957), 135-39.

Excerpts from a report by the American Bar Association's Committee on Communist Tactics, Strategy and Objectives, dealing with recent Supreme Court rulings on U.S. communists. New legislation is proposed to overcome the Court's rulings with which the Committee disagrees. A proper balance between liberty and authority is needed.

U92　"U.S. NEWS & WORLD REPORT," Communism and Supreme Court—A Growing Debate: Pro and Con by Senator Eastland and Senator Morse, 45 (July 18, 1958), 81-82.
Excerpts from a speech by Senator James O. Eastland of Mississippi, with rebuttal by Senator Wayne Morse of Oregon. While Eastland, reviewing the record of the Supreme Court, concludes that some justices consistently favor the Reds, Morse believes that the Court is preserving the basic rights of Americans.

U93　. . ., Passports for U.S. Reds—Both Sides of Growing Debate, 45 (Dec. 5, 1958), 103-6.
Since the decision by the Supreme Court in June concerning passports for communists, hundreds of known communists and fellow-travelers have traveled abroad. Both sides of the issue are presented: Roderic L. O'Connor of the State Department calls for tighter congressional regulations, whereas a committee of the New York City Bar Association urges fewer restrictions on passports.

U94　. . ., Now Lawyers Speak Out about Supreme Court, 46 (March 17, 1959), 48-49.
Disturbed by Supreme Court rulings on U.S. communists, the American Bar Association recommends legislation to overcome their effect on U.S. security. The Association would restore state authority to enforce sedition laws, make it a crime to advocate violent overthrow of the U.S. government, and authorize dismissal of security risks from nonsensitive as well as sensitive positions.

U95　UNITED WORKERS PARTY OF AMERICA. "Bolshevism or Communism?" Chicago: United Workers Party of America, 1934. 15 pp.
Criticism of both Stalinism and Leninism-Trotskyism, by a Marxist group which rejects the whole Bolshevist policy, beginning with Lenin, as a corruption of Marxism. Calling for an overthrow of the present state of capitalism in Russia, the UWP calls for power in the hands of the soviets, not the state or party.

U96　"UNIVERSITY OF ILLINOIS LAW REVIEW," The McCarran Act—Detection or Defection, 46 (May-June 1951), 274-91.
A criticism of the communist registration provisions of the Internal Security Act of 1950, and also of its provision making it a crime to conspire to do any act that would "substantially contribute" to establishing a totalitarian dictatorship in the U.S.

U97　"UNIVERSITY OF PENNSYLVANIA LAW REVIEW," State Control of Political Thought, 84 (Jan. 1936), 390-99.
A criticism of existing state statutes directed against sedition, criminal syndicalism, criminal anarchy, and loyalty oaths which impede the free dissemination of ideas. An assertion that the expression of ideas, even of dangerous political ideas, is essential to democracy.

U98　. . ., Restraints on American Communist Activities, 96 (Feb. 1948), 381-401.
A critique of ways of restricting communist activities, including criminal sanctions (such as deportation or denaturalization), electoral sanctions, loyalty probes of federal employees, congressional investigations, and expulsion of Party members from labor unions. Most of these devices endanger civil liberties, which need to be safeguarded.

U99　UPHAUS, Willard. "Commitment." New York: McGraw-Hill, 1963. 266 pp. App.
An autobiographical account of the life and work of a leader in religious and peace organizations, who served a year in jail for refusing to turn over a list of guests at the World Fellowship Center in New Hampshire to the state attorney general. Uphaus had served for 17 years as executive secretary of the Religion and Labor Foundation, before being forced to resign for attending the communist-inspired World Peace Congress in 1950 and speaking behind the Iron Curtain. His conviction for contempt was sustained by the U.S. Supreme Court in 1959 over the dissenting opinion of four justices. The majority and dissenting opinions are reproduced in an appendix.

U100　UTLEY, Freda. "The China Story." Chicago: Regnery, 1951. 274 pp. Ind.
Criticism of U.S. China policy, emphasizing mistakes made during the Roosevelt and Truman Administrations. The author asserts that our policy hastened communism's expansion in the Far East. She charges that pro-Soviet forces influenced some of our diplomats dealing with Chinese affairs, and that communist subversion as well as errors in judgment contributed to our failure to save China from communism. The case of Owen Lattimore is discussed in detail. (An excerpt, "Case of Owen Lattimore," appeared in "American Mercury," Sept. 1951.)

U101　. . . . The Strange Case of the I.P.R., "American Legion Magazine," 52 (March 1952), 16-17 ff.
An account of the investigation of the Institute of Pacific Relations by the Senate Internal Security Committee, which found evidence that the Institute helped communist agents get key government jobs and that its writers and research workers supported the Party line. Nevertheless the advice and services of the Institute were sought by the State Department and other government agencies. Communists connected with the Institute are identified.

U102　. . . . The Book Burners Burned, "American Mercury," 77 (Dec. 1953), 35-37.
Testimony to the preponderance of procommunist literature in our overseas libraries, with criticism of the State Department's response to the McCarthy exposures: instead of adding anticommunist works, the Department eliminated all "controversial" books—meaning those by authors with any political or moral convictions.

U103　. . . . The Triumph of Owen Lattimore, "American Mercury," 80 (June 1955), 21-26.
Though Owen Lattimore has been exposed, our support of the Chinese Nationalists is equivocal. The support of the Chinese communists by Lattimore, John Davies, John Service, and other State Department officials of the Lattimore school may determine our policy in time. The Republican Administration today is just as responsible for this as the Truman Administration.

V

V1 VAIL, Sol. "This Is Treason!" Forewords by Joseph Curran and Samuel Dickstein. New York: Jewish-American Section, International Workers Order, 1943. 28 pp.
An attack on anti-Semitism in the U.S. as treasonable, as a propaganda spearhead of Hitlerism. The Nazi formula is to discredit the Jews, identify them with the main objectives under attack, and follow with physical assault. National unity is necessary for victory.

V2 VALE, Rena M. Stalin over California, "American Mercury," 49 (April 1940), 412-20.
An account of communist infiltration of the California state government in 1938. Democratic Governor Olson and Lieutenant Governor Patterson, whose views paralleled the Kremlin line, opened the patronage machinery to the comrades. The Moscow-Hitler pact ended this opportunity.

V3 [VALETSKI, H.]. A View of Our Party Condition: Extract from Report of the Representative of the C.I. to the Presidium of the C.I., "Communist" (organ of the Communist Party of America), 1 (Aug.-Sept. 1922), 10-14.
An analysis by the Comintern representative for the Comintern Presidium of the second annual convention of the CPA, held at Bridgeman, Mich., in August 1922. The report reveals that the Comintern representative, Valetski, forced the factions to maintain unity, and drafted many of the resolutions.

. . . . See also MICHELSON

V4 VALTIN, Jan [Richard Krebs]. Communist Agent, "American Mercury," 48 (Nov. 1939), 264-71.
A former agent of the Communist International describes the training he underwent and the duties, including industrial espionage in the U.S., to which he and his fellow agents were assigned. A number of leading American communists have undergone such training. The nominal head of the Party here must take orders from agents assigned to the U.S.

V5 . . . . ABC of Sabotage, "American Mercury," 52 (April 1941), 417-25.
A dramatization of the menace of Stalin's agents in America, by presentation of a document which a Comintern agent in the U.S. might receive. It lays down the line ("This war is not our war") and gives instructions on committees to be formed, tactics to be followed, and sabotage methods to be employed and where.

V6 . . . . Moscow's Academy of Treason, "American Mercury," 53 (July 1941), 39-43.
The author of "Out of the Night" tells how espionage is taught to communist leaders from all over the world at Lenin University, Moscow. He lists Americans who have attended, the curriculum followed, and the implications of this training course. Graduates are future officers of civil war armies and political police machines.

V7 VAN DEN HAAG, Ernest. The Communist Teacher Can't Be Free, "New Leader," 36 (May 25, 1953), 12-14.
A college lecturer in the social sciences, agreeing with Sidney Hook of New York University and disagreeing with Milton R. Konvitz of Cornell, asserts that Communist Party membership makes a professor unfit to hold a teaching position. Unlike a court, which must prove guilt, a university need only establish unfitness to teach.

V8 . . . . Controlling Subversive Groups, "Annals of the American Academy of Political and Social Science," 300 (July 1955), 62-71.
An argument that subversive organizations, including communist ones, should be prohibited; that we should distinguish between the study of dialectics and membership in a group organized to abolish democracy; that the government should not tolerate subversive employees; and that membership in the party should be sufficient grounds for the dismissal of professors.

V9 VARNEY, Harold Lord. Left Wing or IWW—The Way to Unity, "Revolutionary Age," 1 (April 19, 1919), 8.
A representative of the IWW, while greeting the Bolshevik Revolution, points out that the left wing of the Socialist Party speaks a European language that American labor does not understand. He urges unity around the IWW program of industrial unionism.

V10 . . . . Are the Capitalists Asleep? "American Mercury," 37 (March 1936), 266-72.
An assertion that the Reds are rapidly gaining influence in American life, especially in literature, the arts, and teaching. Capitalists, who have generally been indifferent to criticism from the left, should launch a slashing counter-offensive.

V11 . . . . Civil Liberties Union: Liberalism à la Moscow, "American Mercury," 39 (Dec. 1936), 385-99.
An assertion that the American Civil Liberties Union aids the communist cause, and that its director, Roger N. Baldwin, is bound "in the communist straight jacket." The author concludes that the ACLU mobilizes unsuspecting liberal idealism to the service of the Kremlin.

V12 . . . . Red Road to War, "American Mercury," 41 (May 1937), 6-18.
Warning Americans against the new communist united front tactics, the author points to the growing power of the Red Army and to the danger of a collapse of western Europe before Stalinism. He proposes an attitude of unyielding anti-Sovietism.

V13 . . . . Radicals in Our Churches, "American Mercury," 43 (Jan. 1938), 51-67.
An account of socialist and communist penetration into American Protestantism, centering attention on the Church League for Industrial Democracy within the Protestant Episcopal Church, the Methodist Federation for Social Service, the interdenominational United Christian Council for Democracy, and leftist tendencies within the Federal

Council of Churches. The beginnings of a countermovement are described.

V14 VARNEY, Harold Lord. Sovietizing Our Merchant Marine, "American Mercury," 44 (May 1938), 31-43.
An assertion that service and discipline on American ships have deteriorated because of communist influence in CIO maritime unions. The author traces the history of communist infiltration in the ILWU and the NMU. With these unions in control, the outlook for continued private ownership of America's shipping industry is almost hopeless.

V15 .... The Left Kidnaps American Youth, "American Mercury," 44 (Aug. 1938), 391-402.
A summary of the growth and activities of communist-dominated youth groups, on the eve of the World Youth Congress meeting. Cooperation between communists and socialists enabled them to take over the American Youth Congress and create the American Student Union, both now controlled by the communists. The radical minority, with leadership and solidarity, appears to speak in the name of all American youth.

V16 .... They're All Anti-Communists Now, "American Mercury," 76 (March-April 1953), 104-12.
An attack on the sincerity of eleventh-hour anticommunists by an old hand, who enumerates some of the tricks and dodges of bogus anticommunists. Though a sincere anticommunist may exhibit some of these attitudes out of stupidity, anyone who exhibits them all is masquerading as an anticommunist. James Wechsler and Joseph P. Lash are attacked.

V17 .... The Truth about Joe McCarthy, "American Mercury," 77 (Sept. 1953), 3-11.
A vigorous defense of McCarthy, arguing that his only real offense is his amazing effectiveness as a battler against communism. McCarthy has exposed, not only the card-carrying Stalinists, but also the men behind them.

V18 .... What Has Joe McCarthy Accomplished? "American Mercury," 78 (May 1954), 3-14.
A laudatory account of McCarthy's career of attacking communists in government service. Cited are his lists of serious security risks in the State Department, and his investigations of the Voice of America, the General Printing Office, and the Army Signal Corps. McCarthy's side is taken in his clash with Secretary of the Army Stevens and General Zwicker.

V19 .... The Risk in Hawaiian Statehood, "Freeman," 4 (May 3, 1954), 557-59.
A valid reason for opposing statehood for Hawaii is the influence of communism on the islands, primarily the power of the ILWU and the United Public Workers, both communist controlled. Many Americans would prefer to defer statehood until American-minded leadership replaces that of Harry Bridges and Jack Hall among Hawaii's plantation and dock workers.

V20 .... The Egg-Head Clutch on the Foundations, "American Mercury," 78 (June 1954), 31-37.
Through aid given by the Carnegie, Rockefeller, and Ford Foundations, the Institute of Pacific Relations was able to carry on its procommunist propaganda. Persons known to be procommunist received sizable grants, Alger Hiss was given respectability, and the Fund for the Republic entered the civil liberties field to protect leftists.

V21 .... Why the Rich Become Reds, "American Mercury," 85 (Oct. 1957), 111-17.
Many millionaires become socialists or communists.

Seeking a path to idealism and finding fault with the world as it is, such millionaires as Frederick Vanderbilt Field and Corliss Lamont have crossed the "ideological line." Most who have done so soon become disillusioned.

V22 VELDE, Harold H., and MALIN, Patrick Murphy (Erwin Canham, moderator). Are We Losing Our Civil Liberties in Our Search for Security? "Town Meeting," 18 (Feb. 19, 1952), 14 pp.
Mr. Malin, national director of ACLU, charges that the House Committee on Un-American Activities has cut into our civil liberties needlessly in the quest for security. Congressman Velde, a member of the Committee, argues that we are justified in using every legal protection against the communist threat, which would leave us with no rights at all.

V23 VELIE, Lester. Red Pipe Line into Our Defense Plants, "Saturday Evening Post," 225 (Oct. 18, 1952), 19-21 ff.
A survey of the Communist Party's tactics, influence, and personalities in the United Electrical, Radio and Machine Workers Union, with special emphasis on Local 301 at General Electric's Schenectady plant. Pro-CP leaders use work stoppages to plague company production, while bargaining hard to keep worker loyalties. Such locals represent a loophole in our national security.

V24 .... Red Pipeline into Our Uranium Sources, "Reader's Digest," 66 (June 1955), 81-86.
The International Union of Mine, Mill and Smelter Workers, the dominant union in the nonferrous metals industry, has been branded as Red-led by the CIO, by Senate probers, and by some of its own leaders. This union has control of the men who work our uranium sources.

V25 VERITAS [pseud.]. "Pro-war Communism!" Brooklyn: Advance Publishers, 1937. 48 pp.
Protest by a former member of the Party's executive committee against its current war talk. Now writing as a socialist, he refuses to acknowledge the USSR as world leader of socialism, and criticizes the Party's reversal of its earlier opposition to wars and international tribunals.

V26 VETERANS OF THE ABRAHAM LINCOLN BRIGADE. "Volunteer for Liberty: A Complete Collection of the Publications of the International Brigades during the Spanish War Years of 1937-38." New York: Veterans of the Abraham Lincoln Brigade, 1949. 535 pp.
A memorial volume, reproducing the weekly paper published by the Abraham Lincoln Battalion from May 24, 1937, to November 7, 1938. (The Lincoln Battalion was composed of American volunteers who fought for the Spanish Loyalists.)

V27 VIERECK, Peter. Sermons of Self-Destruction, "Saturday Review of Literature," 34 (Aug. 18, 1951), 6-7 ff.
An inquiry into why the fellow-traveling, pro-Soviet bias continues to be influential today. The author considers the domestic roots of neutralist and fellow-traveling sentiments abroad, the motivation of non-Party "communist dupes" in the U.S., and leading English and American journals that show a softness toward the Soviet Union. Policies of the "Nation" are reviewed.

V28 .... "Shame and Glory of the Intellectuals: Babbitt Jr. vs. the Rediscovery of Values." Boston: Beacon, 1953. 320 pp. Ind.
An attack on liberal intellectuals for their failure to fight Stalinist totalitarianism with the vigor with which they

opposed Nazism. These liberals used their influence, the author asserts, to blind the country to the magnitude of Soviet inhumanity.

V29   VILLARD, Oswald Garrison. "Fighting Years: Memoirs of a Liberal Editor." New York: Harcourt, Brace, 1939. 543 pp. Ind.
The memoirs of the editor and publisher of the "Nation" from 1918 to 1933. A pacifist during World War I, Villard's magazine was attacked as "red" and Bolshevik. The "Nation" under Villard criticized the Palmer raids and the attacks on the civil liberties of liberals and radicals during the "red scare" following World War I. Never sympathetic to communism, Villard deplored the weakening of civil liberties that accompanied the anti-communist campaign.

V30   "VIRGINIA LAW REVIEW," The Legal Status of the Communist Party, 34 (May 1948), 450-56.
A review of state efforts to keep the Communist Party off the ballot or to make it difficult for it to qualify, and also of anticommunist legislation pending before Congress. The constitutional problems involved are examined. Although legislation banning the Party from the ballot seems unwise and unnecessary, government should protect itself from foreign agents.

V31   .... The Status of Communists under Federal Law, 34 (May 1948), 439-50.
An examination of federal restrictive techniques against communism, and of constitutional restrictions on congressional actions. Congressional investigations, anti-subversive legislation, and employee loyalty probes are considered. A distinction is drawn between unorthodox political views and dangers to national security.

V32   VON KUEHNELT-LIDDIHN, Erich. Do Jews Tend toward Communism? "Catholic World," 164 (Nov. 1946), 107-13.
A denial of the popular Gentile thesis that Jews tend toward communism. An orthodox Jew could never be a communist; if agnostic or atheistic Jews sometimes embrace communism, it is for sociological reasons, not because of Jewishness. Many Jews occupy leading positions in parties which oppose or compete with communism.

V33   VÖÖBUS, Arthur. "Communism's Challenge to Christianity." Maywood, Ill.: Chicago Lutheran Theological Seminary, 1950. 98 pp.
An account of Soviet terror in Estonia by an Estonian refugee who is professor of theology at Chicago Lutheran Theological Seminary. Asserting that communism is unique in its systematic development of brutality, he decries the failure of most Protestant theologians to criticize communist propaganda. The church must free itself of illusions about communism and fight for human values that are endangered by aggressive communism implemented by military power.

V34   VOROS, Sandor. "American Commissar." Philadelphia and New York: Chilton Co., 1961. 477 pp.
An account of the personal and Party experiences of a Hungarian immigrant who became an American citizen and a Party member, who edited Hungarian Party papers in the United States and Canada, and who served in Spain with the International Brigade. He quit the Party shortly afterward, disillusioned by despotic practices in the Soviet Union and in the Party everywhere, as well as by major policies of the Soviet Union culminating in the Nazi-Soviet pact.

V35   VORSE, Mary Heaton. "Passaic." Chicago: International Labor Defense, n.d. [1926]. 23 pp.
An account of the current Passaic textile strike, under the leadership of Albert Weisbord, a communist. Low wages and police brutality are emphasized, as is the indictment of Weisbord on charges of inciting hostility against the government.

V36   .... "The Passaic Textile Strike, 1926-27." Passaic, N.J.: General Relief Committee of Textile Strikers, 1927. 126 pp.
An account of the 13-month strike of 16,000 Passaic textile workers, which ended in partial victory. Led in its early phases by Albert Weisbord, a communist, the strike was later turned over to the AFL. Starvation wages, police brutality, strikebreaking by a Citizens' Committee, and worker solidarity are emphasized.

V37   .... Gastonia, "Harper's Magazine," 159 (Nov. 1929), 700-10.
A sympathetic account of the 1929 textile strike in Gastonia, N.C., led by the communist-controlled National Textile Workers' Union. Mob and police violence against strikers, Northerners, and real or suspected communists is described, as is the murder trial of union leaders that followed the killing of the local chief of police.

V38   .... "Strike!" New York: Liveright, 1930. 376 pp.
A novel of mill workers in North Carolina manufacturing towns, based on the Gastonia and Marion strikes. A young communist, idol of the mill workers, sacrifices himself in their cause.

V39   .... "Labor's New Millions." New York: Modern Age, 1938. 312 pp. Bibliog. Ind.
An account of the resurgence of the labor movement by a procommunist author, who enthusiastically supports the CIO and bitterly denounces the AFL. She praises the organization of steel and auto workers, Harry Bridges and the West Coast longshoremen, the National Maritime Union, the UE, the transport workers, and the packing-house workers; and she vigorously criticizes Red-baiting attacks on CIO unions and leaders. She endorses Labor's Nonpartisan League, the American Labor Party, and the Commonwealth Federation in the state of Washington.

W

W1 WAGNER, J. Addington. No Compromise with Communism, "American Mercury," 84 (Feb. 1957), 67-68.
An individual cannot be a loyal American and a communist at the same time, for the communists share neither truth, logic, nor morality with the rest of mankind. There can be no compromise with communism without sacrificing Americanism.

W2 WAHLKE, John C. (ed.). "Loyalty in a Democratic State." Boston: Heath, 1952. 111 pp. Bibliog.
Readings selected by the Department of American Studies, Amherst College, dealing with the meaning of loyalty in a democracy and with legislative and administrative measures to safeguard the nation. Excerpts center on four measures: the conviction of 11 communist leaders under the Smith Act, the federal employee loyalty program, the Internal Security Act of 1950, and the exclusion of communists from college teaching.

W3 WAKEFIELD, Lowell. "Hitler's Spy Plot in the U.S.A." New York: Workers Library, 1939. 31 pp.
Written shortly before the Hitler-Stalin pact, the pamphlet describes German espionage in this country and the trial and conviction of a group of Nazi spies in the fall of 1938. Praising the trial as a service to democracy, the author attacks Trotskyites as apologists for the spy ring and agents of Hitler.

W4 WALDMAN, Louis. The Real Issue before the Party, "New Leader," 19 (March 28, 1936), 1 ff.
Discussion of the primary fight in New York between the "regular" Socialist Party candidates and the opposition slate filed by the SP left wing under the leadership of Norman Thomas. Waldman argues that the fundamental question is democracy versus communism. Major issues separating the two factions include united fronts with communists, allowing splinter communist groups within the SP, and advocacy of revolutionary methods.

W5 . . . . "Labor Lawyer." New York: Dutton, 1944. 394 pp. Ind.
Waldman, socialist leader and labor lawyer, tells the story of 30 years in the American labor movement. His book deals in part with the birth and growth of the Communist Party and its offshoots. Bitterly anticommunist, Waldman withdrew with others from the Socialist Party to form the Social Democratic Federation when the SP favored a united front with the communists. Among other topics the book deals with communist activities in the CIO and in the American Labor Party, and with the case of Fred Beal, communist union organizer in Gastonia, N.C.

W6 WALDMAN, Seymour. "Guns Are Ready." New York: American League Against War and Fascism, 1935. 19 pp.
An assertion that the Roosevelt Administration is preparing tirelessly for M-Day, by the largest war appropriations in our peacetime history, unprecedented peacetime military maneuvers, military men in key NRA posts, and war propaganda more open and widespread than ever before.

W7 WALKER, Charles R. Relief and Revolution, "Forum," 88 (Aug. 1932), 73-78; (Sept.), 152-57.
Part I describes the state of unemployment and relief in 1932, and the government's shift to federal aid to ease the crisis. Part II analyzes the "charity" philosophy of relief and the opposition to it by the Unemployed Councils. Although communists organize and usually lead the Unemployed Councils, the Councils are structured democratically and the majority rules.

W8 WALKER, Richard. American People Can Halt the War! "Political Affairs," 31 (June 1952), 1-14.
Wall Street's imperialist aggression against the Korean people, now entering its third year, can be halted by the people if peace sentiment is mobilized. Tasks in the drive to win a cease-fire are outlined.

W9 WALKER, Richard L. Lattimore and the IPR, "New Leader," 35 (March 31, 1952), sect. 2, 15 pp.
A detailed review of the evidence disclosed by the McCarran Committee's investigation of Owen Lattimore and the influence of the Institute of Pacific Relations on U.S. Far Eastern policies. The author, a Far Eastern expert on the Yale faculty, concludes that the IPR was successfully infiltrated by the communists, who were able to influence the thinking of scholars and the behavior of government officials. (Objections by the secretary general of the IPR and Walker's reply appear in the issue of April 21, 1952, pp. 10-12; Lattimore's protest and Walker's reply are in the issue of June 2, 1952, pp. 16-19.)

W10 WALLACE, George. Deterioration of Labor Conditions during the Last Decade, "Communist," 18 (March 1939), 245-56.
A review of labor conditions between 1928 and 1938, showing a continuous lowering of workers' living standards.

W11 WALLACE, Henry. "Stand Up and Be Counted! Why I Choose to Run." New York: New Republic," 1947. 14 pp.
Wallace's final article as editor of the "New Republic," announcing his candidacy on a third party ticket. His program will seek one world through cooperation with the Soviet Union, emphasis on the UN, and opposition to the bipartisanship of the Democrats and Republicans. He asserts that those who oppose his policies because the communists favor them are using Hitler's weapons.

W12 . . . . A Bad Case of Fever, "New Republic," 116 (April 14, 1947), 12-13.
The editor of the New Republic voices strong opposition to the federal loyalty program, which tends to punish people for their beliefs and not for their acts. The present drive against subversives is seen as only a witch hunt, since we have little to fear from communism if we make our democracy work.

W13 WALPIN, Bernard G. Cancellation of Citizenship Because of Communism, "Yale Law Journal," 51 (May 1942), 1215-23.
The lower court decision in the Schneiderman case, order-

ing denaturalization because of communist membership at time of naturalization, results in two classes of citizenship, since no natural citizen could be similarly punished for like activities. Criminal statutes, when a clear and present danger exists, should be the means of punishing advocacy of force and violence.

W14   WALSH, William Thomas. Is Communism Dangerous? "Commonweal," 21 (Feb. 8, 1935), 420-22.
An analysis of the attraction of communism, and of collectivism generally, to Americans of all social classes. A large and growing body of opinion is now almost neutral toward communism, which is a species of religion, not merely an economic and political theory. Catholics tend to belittle communism's appeal, and to make less progress than the communists among the neutral population.

W15   WALSTED, Julius. "An American Farmer Sees the Soviet Union." Philadelphia: Farmers' National Committee for Action, n.d. [1935?]. 30 pp.
A South Dakota farmer discusses his trip to Russia as a guest of the Friends of the Soviet Union. He describes the happiness of the people, the freedom of church worship, the voluntary nature of collective farming, and the tremendous drive for production and mechanization.

W16   WALTON, William. Kangaroo Court under Klieg Light, "New Republic," 17 (Nov. 3, 1947), 8-9.
An attack on the House Un-American Activities Committee, chaired by J. Parnell Thomas, now holding hearings on communism in Hollywood. The author criticizes the movie stars who gave Thomas ammunition for his witch-hunting. The Committee is flouting American traditions, invading the privacy of citizens, pillorying them without fair trial, and spreading fear and hatred.

W17   WALZER, Michael. The Travail of the U.S. Communists, "Dissent," 3 (Fall 1956), 406-10.
An expression of skepticism with regard to the newly discovered critical mind of the CPUSA following the Khrushchev revelations. With few exceptions, the Party will fall back into line when Moscow indicates that the era of criticism is over. One of the exceptions is Howard Fast, whose revulsion must lead him out of the Party.

W18   WANGERIN, O. H. The Railroad Amalgamation Movement, "Labor Herald," 2 (Sept. 1923), 3-5.
An optimistic report on the amalgamation movement in the railroad industry since April 1922. The movement is seen as firmly rooted in every union and every railroad center in the country.

W19   WARD, Courtney. "The A. F. of L. and One World of Labor." Cleveland: Brotherhood of Painters, Decorators and Paperhangers, District Council Six, 1945. 31 pp.
An appeal by a procommunist union observer at the World Trade Union Conference (precursor to the World Federation of Trade Unions) for AFL membership in the WFTU. AFL members are asked to urge their organization to support AFL participation and to bring pressure on President William Green for such action.

W20   WARD, Estolv E. "Harry Bridges on Trial: How Union Labor Won Its Biggest Case." New York: Modern Age, 1940. 240 pp.
A pro-Bridges account of the 1939 deportation hearings of the West Coast labor leader, decided in his favor on the ground that the evidence did not prove him to be a member of the Party. Bridges' role as leader of the 1934 longshore strike and champion of the people is reviewed.

W21   WARD, Harold. "National Defense—for Whom?"

New York: American League Against War and Fascism, 1935. 18 pp.
An assertion that national defense has nothing to do with ordinary people, but protects finance-capitalists against threats to their control of the country or to their share of the world's wealth and markets, profits, and dividends. Commercial relations between American companies and foreign firms and governments are exposed, as are profits by leading U.S. defense contractors in World War I.

W22   WARD, Harry F. "Which Way Religion?" New York: MacMillan, 1931. 221 pp.
A professor of Christian ethics at Union Theological Seminary pleads for greater emphasis on social values and for regard for the individual in a secular as well as a religious sense. In a brief discussion of religious aspects of communism (pp. 197-203), he sees hope in the renaissance in Russia, asserting that communism, stripped of its dogmatic glorification and use of force, constitutes a religion of humanity.

W23   . . . . "In Place of Profit: Social Incentives in the Soviet Union." New York and London: Scribner, 1933. 458 pp.
A favorable analysis of the Soviet social and economic system by a professor of Christian ethics at the Union Theological Seminary. He writes of the new forms of social approval and disapproval in the USSR, the new attitudes toward work, the nature of mass initiative, and the new types of control.

W24   . . . . "The Development of Fascism in the United States." New York: American League Against War and Fascism, 1935. 8 pp.
An attack on the New Deal as containing tendencies toward fascism. The granting of widespread power to the President, the subordination of the labor movement, and the curtailing of labor's right to strike are viewed as foreshadowing the totalitarian state.

W25   . . . . Christians and Communists, "Christian Century," 52 (Dec. 25, 1935), 1651-53.
A plea for a Christian united front with communists to oppose fascism. The author, president of the American League Against War and Fascism, argues that such a united front need not mean loss of the right to criticize and oppose communism.

W26   . . . . "Democracy and Social Change." New York: Modern Age, 1940. 293 pp.
An argument that democracy can no longer be maintained within the framework of the capitalist system, and that there is urgent need for an economic democracy. The author, prominent in Party front organizations, asserts that the communist goal is similar to the American democratic ideal, that the Soviet is the equivalent in Russia of the old New England town meeting, that communism cannot be totalitarian because it views the state as evil and seeks to abolish it, and that the communists here are committed to the democratic process. Other topics discussed include the fascist threat, the role of religion, civil liberties, and the danger of war.

W27   . . . . The Communist Party and the Ballot, "Bill of Rights Review," 1 (Summer 1941), 286-92.
A review of recent proposals, passed in a number of states, to bar the Communist Party from the ballot. Yet the communists do not advocate force and violence in social change, though they do prophesy it. Our traditional democratic rights must be kept open for all if they are to be available for any.

W28   WARD, Lynd, and HICKS, Granville. "One of Us:

The Story of John Reed." New York: Equinox Cooperative Press, 1935. 60 unnumbered pp.
The highlights of Reed's career, with 30 pages of narrative by Hicks, illustrated by as many lithographs by Ward. Attention is paid to Reed's Harvard days, his pageant for the striking Paterson silk workers in 1913, his connection with the "Masses," his service as a war correspondent during World War I, his experiences in Russia during the Bolshevik Revolution, his trial in this country for sedition for opposing the war, his activities in the early communist movement here, his election to the Executive Committee of the Communist International, and his death and hero's burial in Moscow.

W29   WARD, Theodore. Five Negro Novelists: Revolt and Retreat, "Mainstream," 1 (Winter 1947), 100-10.
Criticism of contemporary Negro writers of fiction for their literature of despair, a trend started by Richard Wright's "Native Son," and carried on today by William Attaway, Carl Ruthaven Offord, Chester B. Himes, Ann Petry, and Frank Yerby. These authors, all portraying bleakness and defeat, are false to Negro needs and aspirations, failing to show that Negroes will ultimately embrace Marxism.

W30   WARE, Clarissa S. "The American Foreign-Born Workers." New York: Workers Party, n.d. [1924?]. 39 pp.
An analysis of the foreign-born in our country: who they are, where they came from, and the oppression and discrimination to which they are subjected. Since capitalist attacks on the foreign-born are a prelude to attacks on native American workers, all members of the working class must unite against the capitalist class.

W31   WARNER, David R. Criminal Syndicalism, "Nebraska Law Bulletin," 14 (May 1936), 365-84.
A summary of state laws on criminal syndicalism and of the principal cases under them, involving communists and members of the IWW. Pros and cons of this type of legislation are listed, and injustices and abuses are reviewed. Though the laws serve a useful purpose, they should be narrowly construed and applied.

W32   WARNER, John. Labor Unions and Security Risks, "Reporter,' 11 (July 6, 1954), 14-18.
The Industrial Personnel Security Clearance Program is condemned as a blacklist, and a threat to civil liberties. The shift from the Truman criteria of "loyalty" to that of "security"—a lot broader—endangers union members who have had contact with left-wing unions. The program may provide an excuse for anti-union action by employers.

W33   WARREN, Frank A., III. "Liberals and Communism: The Red Decade Revisited." Bloomington and London: Indiana University Press, 1966. 276 pp. Notes. Ind.
An effort to gauge the nature and extent of communist influence on liberal thought during the 1930's by an examination of liberal writings of the period, particularly in such periodicals as the "Nation," the "New Republic," and "Common Sense." The author seeks to recreate the atmosphere of the period—the economic crisis here, the attractions of the Soviet Union, the dangers of fascism and war, the rise and fall of the popular front, the collective security issue, and the Moscow trials. ("The Red Decade," published by Eugene Lyons in 1941, alleged that Stalinism had dominated American liberal thinking in the 1930's.)

W34   WARREN, Sidney. The Threat of Internal Communism, "Current History," 29 (Oct. 1955), 204-10.
Perspective, while essential, is difficult in view of emotion and exaggeration of the communist threat. Fluctuations in Party strength and influence are traced. Our traditions of freedom will withstand the threat, the appeal of communism being primarily to the emotionally immature. (An article in a special issue on security in a free society.)

W35   WARSHOW, Robert. The Legacy of the 30's: Middle Class Mass Culture and the Intellectuals' Problem, "Commentary," 4 (Dec. 1947), 538-45.
Using Lionel Trilling's novel, "The Middle of the Journey," as a point of departure, the author discusses the Stalinist impact on American intellectuals and their writings in the thirties. The question for intellectuals is how to regain the use of their experience in the world of mass culture.

W36   . . . . The Idealism of Julius and Ethel Rosenberg, "Commentary," 16 (Nov. 1953), 413-18.
A review article on the recently published death cell letters of Julius and Ethel Rosenberg. For all their sincerity, they are a complete fabrication, with "we are innocent" standing for "my resolve is unshaken; I will not confess." In their alienation from truth and experience, these letters express the communism of 1953.

W37   WARTH, Robert D. The Palmer Raids, "South Atlantic Quarterly," 48 (Jan. 1949), 1-23.
An account of the raids on anarchists and communists in 1919-20 under the direction of Attorney General A. Mitchell Palmer. A boatload of 249 alien deportees, including well-known anarchists, sailed on December 21, 1919, and nationwide raids on members of the Communist Party and the Communist Labor Party were staged on January 2, 1920. Palmer's methods were severely criticized by liberal groups.

W38   WASHINGTON (STATE) UNIVERSITY, Board of Regents. "Communism and Academic Freedom: The Record of the Tenure Cases at the University of Washington. Seattle: University of Washington Press, 1949. 125 pp. App.
Documents in the cases of six tenured members of the faculty who were charged with being present or former members of the Communist Party. Following recommendations by President Raymond B. Allen, three were dismissed by the Board of Regents and three retained on two-year probation, subject to filing affidavits that they were not then Party members. The report of the faculty Committee on Tenure and Academic Freedom and President Allen's analysis and recommendations to the Regents are printed in full.

W39   WASSERMAN, Jack. "The Challenge of Our Immigration Laws." Introd. by Abner Green. New York: American Committee for Protection of Foreign Born, n.d. [1945]. 31 pp. Notes.
The history of our immigration laws and a discussion of our present legislation, written by a member of the Board of Immigration Appeals of the Justice Department. Condemning their restrictive and discriminatory character, he urges amendments to remove race classifications and arbitrary standards. (A reprint of an article which first appeared in the "Journal of Legal and Political Sociology.")

W40   WATKINS, Gordon S. Present Status of Socialism in the U.S., "Atlantic Monthly," 124 (Dec. 1919), 821-30.
An analysis of the divided state of American socialism, written shortly after the split from which the communist movement emerged. The author sees three wings in American socialism—right (Socialist Party), center (Communist Labor Party,) and left (Communist Party). Asserting that the major issues are those dividing the SP from the CP, the author predicts that soon there will be only two major groups within American socialism.

W41 WATKINS, Gordon S. Revolutionary Communism in the United States, "American Political Science Review," 14 (Feb. 1920), 14-33.
A contemporary analysis of the initial period of the American communist movement, written by a University of Illinois professor. The article deals with the organization of the left wing within the Socialist Party early in 1919 and its split from the socialists late that summer to form the Communist Party and the Communist Labor Party. There is a critical review of the philosophy and program of American communism.

W42 WATT, John J. Launching the National Miners Union, "Labor Unity," 2 (Oct. 1928), 2-6.
The president of the National Miners Union, launched in September as an outgrowth of the Save-the-Union Committee, describes the organizing convention and the onslaughts upon the delegates by Lewis' organizers, aided by the police.

W43 WATTS, Rowland. "The Draftee and Internal Security." New York: Workers Defense League, n.d. [1955]. 251 pp. App.
A study of the Army's military personnel security program, through a detailed analysis of 49 case histories. The author discusses the criteria and procedures used, and criticizes a program that can give an "undesirable" or "general" discharge to draftees for allegedly disloyal activities prior to induction. Procedural protections, he points out, are inferior to those given civilian government employees. Included are cases of Communist Party membership, or attendance at meetings of groups on the Attorney General's list of subversive organizations.

W44 WAX, Melvin S. The Red Tide Reaches Vermont's White River Valley, "Reporter," 4 (Jan. 23, 1951), 13-14.
An account of vigilant anticommunism in Vermont inspired by Senator McCarthy and led by a Vermont matron, Mrs. Lucille Miller. Although the FBI knows of only 10 communists in Vermont, Mrs. Miller claims that there are 18 in a single area where the Hisses summered and Owen Lattimore and others owned farms.

W45 WEATHERWAX, Clara. "Marching! Marching!" New York: John Day, 1935. 256 pp.
A strike novel laid in Aberdeen, Washington, which ends with the strikers marching defiantly into the guns of the National Guard. The book attacks the New Deal and AFL officials, corrupt leaders of a capitalist labor front. (Winner of a "New Masses" contest for a novel on an American proletarian theme.)

W46 WEAVER, George B. Liberation—Red Bait for Negroes, "American Mercury," 87 (Nov. 1958), 32-39.
The explosiveness of race relations in the U.S. offers an almost unparalleled opportunity for the communists to exploit. The school desegregation issue is one that they have used. The communists have infiltrated the NAACP, even to top levels.

W47 WECHSLER, James. "Revolt on the Campus." Introd. by Robert Morss Lovett. New York: Covici Friede, 1935. 458 pp. Ind.
An account of student liberal, leftist, and pacifist activities, 1917-35, by a participant. The formation and activities of the National Student League, a communist-controlled student organization of the 1930's, are described, as are Hearst's 1934 college faculty "red scare" (pp. 222-35), the dropping of Granville Hicks from the Rensselaer Polytechnic Institute faculty in 1935 (pp. 236-42), and the 1935 investigation of communism at the University of Chicago (pp. 258-66). (The author, briefly a member of the Young Communist League while a student, shortly afterward became a staunch opponent of communism.)

W48 .... American Pacifism Seeks a Policy, "New Republic," 85 (Jan. 8, 1936), 249.
Favorable comment on the objectives of the American League Against War and Fascism, the third congress of which opened on January 3, 1936, in Cleveland. Differences of opinion with regard to neutrality on combined action against aggressors are outlined.

W49 .... The Student Union Begins, "New Republic," 85 (Jan. 15, 1936), 278-80.
Formation of the American Student Union was possible because most students do not harbor the hatreds of present liberal-radical groups. These differences are overshadowed by the threat of American fascism, opposition to which is the unifying force within ASU.

W50 .... Student Unity at Stake, "New Masses," 22 (Dec. 29, 1936), 17-19.
The American Student Union is threatened, prior to its second convention, with a struggle over its peace program, between communist and socialist delegates, particularly Trotskyist socialists. Criticizing them as sectarians, Wechsler opposes actions that will bewilder students, undermining ASU's organizational strength.

W51 .... Stalin and Union Square, "Nation," 149 (Sept. 30, 1939), 342-45.
A description of reactions on the left to the signing of the Nazi-Soviet pact. A number of intellectuals have left the Party and its related cultural organs, though Party ranks still appear firm. The Party here has been reduced to apologizing for Moscow's actions without understanding them. There are gropings toward a new alignment, based on American radical independence.

W52 .... Politics on the Campus, "Nation," 149 (Dec. 30, 1939), 732-33.
A report on the American Student Union, just prior to its 1939 convention. A cleavage between communists and noncommunists has developed since the Nazi-Soviet pact. Joseph Lash, ASU executive secretary, who has criticized the pact, opposes ousting the communists, though not at the price of whitewashing Russian foreign policy.

W53 .... Carey and the Communists, "Nation," 153 (Sept. 13, 1941), 224-25.
An assertion that James B. Carey was ousted from the presidency of the UE because he would not submit to the communist machine in the union. His defeat is a measure of the CIO's internal chaos. Carey's inability to build a counter-machine, together with rank-and-file bitterness over the Dies Committee's Red-baiting, contributed to his defeat.

W54 .... "Labor Baron: A Portrait of John L. Lewis." New York: Morrow, 1944. 278 pp. Bibliog. Ind.
An incisive portrait of John L. Lewis, his policies and programs, and his role in the new labor movement. Chapter 8 on Lewis and the Communists (pp. 122-51), tells of Lewis' early reliance upon the left wing for support in the CIO, and shows how the Nazi invasion of Russia caused a crisis in this relationship. Until the invasion both Lewis and the Party had been critical of Roosevelt and had opposed U.S. involvement in the war. When Lewis remained isolationist after the invasion, the communists attacked him bitterly, declaring him disqualified for CIO leadership.

W55 WECHSLER, James. How to Rid the Government of Communists, "Harper's Magazine," 195 (Nov. 1947), 438-43.
An analysis of the Truman loyalty program by a New York "Post" correspondent, who denies that Truman's loyalty program is a police state prelude to wholesale suppression of dissent. He suggests procedural changes to safeguard our security within our traditional democratic framework.

W56 .... The Philadelphia Pay-Off, "Progressive," 12 (Sept. 1948), 8-10.
An account of the Philadelphia convention that launched Henry Wallace's Progressive Party. Meeting under the cloud of charges of communist control, the convention made the cloud blacker than ever. Party leaders and fellow-travelers, occupying key positions in the convention, kept foreign policy decisions to the communist line and avoided the slightest criticism of the USSR.

W57 .... The Trial of Our Times, "Progressive," 13 (Feb. 1949), 10-12.
A discussion of the Hiss-Chambers case by a Washington correspondent, who covered the hearings of the House Committee on Un-American Activities. Many liberals who participated in popular front ventures in the 1930's are reluctant to admit that communists engaged in espionage. Reactionaries, in self-justification, are convinced Hiss is guilty.

W58 .... "The Age of Suspicion." New York: Random House, 1953. 333 pp. Ind.
A political biography of the editor of the New York "Post," written after he had been charged by Senator McCarthy with serving as a communist undercover agent to attack those trying to expose communists. A member of the Young Communist League from 1934 to 1937 and briefly on its executive committee, Wechsler was repelled by its ruthless orthodoxy, and then shaken by the Moscow trials. He found the communist movement an enemy of freedom of thought, justice, and tolerance, and the USSR a place of fear. For many years thereafter he was active in the struggle against communists. He was summoned before McCarthy's committee, ostensibly because his writings appeared in U.S. libraries overseas, after publishing a series of articles critical of McCarthy.

W59 WECTER, Dixon. Commissars of Loyalty, "Saturday Review of Literature," 33 (May 13, 1950), 8-10 ff.
A University of California history professor describes the loyalty oath controversy there. Even had there been serious danger of communist infiltration, a loyalty oath would have been ineffective in combatting it. A committee of alumni effected a compromise, substituting an anticommunist declaration and review of cases by a faculty committee.

W60 WEEDON, Ann. "Hearst: Counterfeit American." New York: American League Against War and Fascism, 1936. 23 pp.
A condemnation of Hearst and his newspapers for provoking war in order to sell papers, for attacking union labor and the working class, and for seeing good in fascism. A boycott of Hearst publications is urged.

W61 "WEEKLY PEOPLE," Who Are the Falsifiers? New York: New York Labor News Co., 1926. 28 pp.
A compilation of articles from the Socialist Labor Party newspaper, the "Weekly People," to show how the communists doctored the Marxist classics for their own purposes.

W62 WEINBERG, Jules. Priests, Workers, and Communists: What Happened in a New York Transit Workers Union, "Harper's Magazine," 197 (Nov. 1948), 49-56.
An analysis of the anticommunist battle in the Transport Workers Union, CIO, climaxed in March 1948 by Mike Quill's break with the communists and the end of CP domination of the union. The leaders of the anticommunist faction were two students in the Catholic Church's labor program.

W63 WEINBERG, S. "An American Worker in a Moscow Factory." Moscow-Leningrad: Co-operative Publishing Society of Foreign Workers in the USSR, 1933. 69 pp.
Written for the American worker, the pamphlet tells the story of an unemployed American worker who goes to Russia and finds a workers' utopia there. The author describes life in Leningrad and Moscow, the bustling industry, the excitement of getting on the job and organizing his brigade, and the watch factory that he "owns."

W64 WEINGAST, David E. "This Is Communism: The Communist Conspiracy in the United States and in the World." Foreword by Edward F. Kennelly. New York: Oxford Book Co., 1959. 178 pp.
A textbook designed for high school and junior college use, as well as for adult and trade union classes. Chapters with particular relevance to the movement in the U.S. include those dealing with front organizations, propaganda, and fellow-travelers. Strategy to oppose the communists is outlined.

W65 WEINMAN, S. "Hawaii: The Story of Imperialist Plunder." New York: International Pamphlets, 1934. 31 pp.
A communist pamphlet addressed to Hawaiian workers, denouncing American imperialists who paint a rosy picture of Hawaii in order to attract tourist trade. Instead drawing a picture of misery and exploitation on the islands, the author calls for the overthrow of foreign domination and the establishment of a workers' and peasants' republic.

W66 WEINSTEIN, Jacob J. Drift to the Left—or Why Jews Balk at Communism, "Jewish Frontier," 2 (Feb. 1935), 12-14.
While in agreement with many of the Party's social welfare concepts, the author asserts that Jews will not become communists in large numbers. Their middle class status fosters a gradualistic approach, a preference for nonviolent abolition of capitalism. They fear that a communist state would have no sympathy for Jewish group integrity.

W67 WEINSTONE, William. The C.P. of the U.S.A. and the Address of the Communist International, "International Press Correspondence," 9 (Aug. 9, 1929), 817-18.
A report of events in the CPUSA following the decision of the Communist International to end the factional struggle and oust Lovestone from Party leadership. Many of Lovestone's former associates refused to go along with his splitting tactics and his refusal to accept Comintern discipline. Lovestoneism was also rejected by a decisive majority of the Party.

W68 .... The Coming of an Economic Crisis in the United States, "International Press Correspondence," 9 (Dec. 6, 1929), 1448.
Writing shortly after the 1929 stock market crash, Weinstone asserts that the crisis is more serious than capitalists will admit, and that the bourgeoisie will attempt

to overcome it at the expense of the workers and by more feverish preparations for war. The crisis confirms the correctness of the CP line of bolshevizing the party and intensifying its struggle against social reformism.

W69 WEINSTONE, William. The Economic Crisis in the United States and the Tasks of the Communist Party, "Communist International," 6 (Feb. 15, 1930), 1225-33.
Though the crisis has not fully matured, its depth is visible. The army of unemployed is increasing, wages are being cut, and tremendous strike struggles are foreshadowed. The Party must develop from a small propaganda organization to a real leader of the masses. The Labor Party slogan must be dropped, the fighting spirit of the masses aroused, and demonstrations and strikes organized.

W70 . . . . The XI Plenum of the Executive Committee of the Comintern: Extracts from Report to 13th Plenum of the C.C., C.P.U.S.A., "Communist," 10 (Oct. 1931), 771-96.
The function of the CPUSA is to crystallize growing class consciousness and focus it on the revolutionary way out of the crisis. The CPUSA has mistakenly thought this could occur spontaneously. It must struggle against social fascists, Democrats, the AFL, and other misleaders of labor. It must sharpen its antiwar struggle, and work among the Negro masses.

W71 . . . . The United Front Tactics in the Lawrence Strike, "Communist," 11 (Jan. 1932), 9-16.
Criticism of the leadership of the National Textile Workers Union in the Lawrence, Mass., strike for not understanding and using correctly the united front tactic. AFL bosses got a considerable number of workers under their influence, thereby splitting the workers' forces, and the NTWU did not conduct a persistent struggle to bring the workers into the united front on the basis of the struggle itself.

W72 . . . . The Intensified Drive toward Imperialist War, "Communist," 12 (Sept. 1933), 922-38.
The world economic crisis and the rise of the USSR have forced the capitalist nations to arm for a new imperialist war. The Second International, renouncing internationalism, has become the main ally of the bourgeoisie against proletarian revolution. The Communist Party must lead the antiwar struggle and defend the Soviet Union.

W73 . . . . Experiences in United Independent Political Action—The Road to the Farmer-Labor Party, "Communist," 14 (Dec. 1935), 1142-60.
A speech to the November plenum of the Party's Central Committee, describing Party efforts in Toledo and Detroit to collaborate with socialists and promote a farmer-labor party.

W74 . . . . Advancing against Reaction in the Center of the Motor Industry, "Communist," 15 (Aug. 1936), 747-58.
A report to the Party's ninth convention describing union activity in the steel and automobile industries in the Detroit district, one of the Party's four major areas of concentration.

W75 . . . . "The Great Sit-Down Strike." New York: Workers Library, 1937. 45 pp.
An enthusiastic account of the successful 44-day sit-down strike in the automobile industry, written by the secretary of the Michigan District of the Party. He praises the militancy and solidarity of the strikers, the quality of their leadership, and the use of modern mass methods of fighting.

Describing the sit-down tactic, he tells why it is more effective than the walk-out. He pays tribute to the support given the strike by the communists and the "Daily Worker."

W76 . . . . The Great Auto Strike, "Communist," 16 (March 1937), 210-28.
A description of the sit-down strike fought against General Motors by the newly organized United Automobile Workers. The defeat of the reactionaries in the last election created more favorable conditions for winning the strike. Negotiation of an agreement on wages, hours, and working conditions still remains. The communists supported the strike loyally.

W77 . . . . "The Case against David Dubinsky." New York: New Century, 1946. 112 pp.
The educational director of the Party in New York State accuses Dubinsky and the social-democratic labor officials around him of betraying the progressive past of the ILGWU. Weinstone charges Dubinsky with spearheading the conspiracy to undermine the CIO, with splitting the American Labor Party, with building the splinter Liberal Party, and with supporting "strikebreaking" Truman. In addition, Dubinsky has deliberately misrepresented the Nazi-Soviet pact, and helped disrupt world trade unionism by opposing the World Federation of Trade Unions.

W78 . . . . The Tactics of the Party in the New York State Elections, "Political Affairs," 25 (Oct. 1946), 904-14.
The primary aim of the Party in the coming election is to defeat Dewey. To achieve this goal the Party must support Democratic candidates, while criticizing the Democratic Party's platform on foreign policy and preparing the formation of a third party. "Pseudo-left" ideas in the Party, rejecting in principle any alliance with bourgeois forces, are attacked as anti-Leninist.

W79 . . . . An Important Chapter in the Party's History of Industrial Concentration, "Political Affairs," 28 (Sept. 1949), 71-81.
A review and appraisal of the Extraordinary Party Conference held in July 1933, recalled on the Party's thirtieth anniversary. The 1933 conference began the turn to the shops and factories, gave the Party a firmer proletarian footing, and made possible its part in the labor upsurge of 1934-38. This emphasis on shops and factories is an integral part of the reconstituted Party's program.

W80 . . . . The Fight to Repeal the Legislative Blueprint for Fascism, "Political Affairs," 29 (Oct. 1950), 32-46.
An outline of the McCarran Act, with a discussion of its implications for the entire working class, as well as for the communists. Congress cynically trampled on the Constitution in passing this fascist measure. Though the communists are attacked first, the Act shows that the anticommunist drive will destroy all progressive organizations and gag all decent people.

W81 WEISBORD, Albert. "Passaic: The Story of a Struggle against Starvation Wages and for the Right to Organize." Chicago: Daily Worker Publishing Co., 1926. 64 pp.
The story of the Passaic textile strike by its leader, then active in the Party, who attests to the contribution of the Party and affiliated organizations to the militancy and education of the workers and to strike relief. He discusses police brutality, liberal support of the strike, and the reactionary role of the AFL officialdom. (Later Weisbord became a Trotskyist, and then the head of a Marxist splinter group.)

W82 WEISBORD, Albert. Lessons from Passaic, "Workers Monthly," 5 (Dec. 1926), 636-40.
An account of the ten-month-old Passaic strike by its communist leader, who calls it an important experience for the whole working class. Since the AFL has conditioned its entry on the removal of Weisbord and the other communist leaders, settlement of the strike is now up to the Federation.

W83 . . . . Some Aspects of the Situation in New Bedford, "Communist," 7 (July 1928), 442-50.
An analysis of the strike of 26,000 cotton textile workers of New Bedford, Mass., emphasizing the role of the American Federation of Textile Operatives, an independent union, and of the National Textile Mill Committee, the left-wing section of the textile workers.

W84 . . . . Three Strategies in the New Bedford Strike, "Communist," 7 (Aug. 1928), 481-85.
An outline of the strategies of employers, "labor bureaucrats," and left-wing leaders in the thirteenth week of the textile strike in New Bedford, Mass. The left-wing union is growing, and the strike is still on the upgrade.

W85 . . . . The Fall River Strike, "Labor Unity," 2 (Sept. 1928), 11-14.
An account of the strike of 3,000 Fall River textile workers, under left-wing leadership, against a wage cut, and of the attacks upon the strikers by the mill owners, police, judges, and AFL labor fakers.

W86 . . . . Passaic—New Bedford—North Carolina, "Communist," 8 (June 1929), 319-23.
Three textile strikes—Passaic in 1926-27, New Bedford in 1928, and North Carolina in 1929—mark important steps forward by the left wing in the task of organizing textile workers. The National Textile Workers Union, formed after the New Bedford strike, must prepare for greater tests yet to come.

W87 . . . . Trotsky on America, "Common Sense," 1 (June 8, 1933), 11-13.
A report by Weisbord, then a Trotskyite, on an interview with Trotsky, who viewed Europe as a satellite of the U.S. and who observed a developing conflict between the U.S. and the USSR. He found the Socialist Party here servile and the Communist Party immature. If a Labor Party is formed the communists should "bore from within" it to expose its limited role.

W88 . . . . "The Conquest of Power: Liberalism, Anarchism, Syndicalism, Socialism, Fascism and Communism." 2 vols. New York: Covici, Friede, 1937. 1208 pp. Ind.
An analysis of the history, philosophy, and characteristics of various social and political systems by the leader of the Passaic textile strike of 1926, the first successful mass action of American communists. Weisbord, who was briefly a Trotskyist after his expulsion from the Party, formed his own splinter group in 1931; he attacks the Party in this country as decayed and hopelessly reformist, its sudden turns of policy serving the interests of Russian nationalism and Soviet diplomacy. Declaring that the Third International has broken down, he urges establishment of a Fourth International to concentrate on the strategy of world revolution in the period of wars and revolutions into which the world has passed.

W89 WEISS, Abraham S. The Communist Party and Dual Unions, "Student Outlook," 3 (April 1935), 11-13.
An account of the Party's trade union policy, published in a student socialist magazine. After first advocating dual

unionism and supporting the IWW, the Party was forced by RILU policy to "bore from within" the reformist unions. In 1928, with the "third period," communists sought to destroy AFL affiliates and build TUUL unions. With the advent of the NRA, the TUUL is liquidating some unions while seeking to strengthen others.

W90 WEISS, Max. "In a Soviet America: Happy Days for American Youth." New York: Workers Library, 1935. 46 pp.
A Young Communist League pamphlet contrasting the hunger of American youth in the depression with the happiness possible in a workers' and farmers' America, under a government patterned after that of the Soviet Union. This can be achieved through a united struggle of workers and farmers, Negro and white, young and old, against capitalism.

W91 . . . . "In Flanders Field . . ." New York: Youth Publishers, 1935. 23 pp.
A popularly written antiwar pamphlet from the Young Communist League. World War I was a war for profits. Workers in all countries should follow the example of the Russian workers and farmers and overthrow their own capitalists.

W92 . . . . "Youth's Road to Peace and Security." New York: New Age, 1940. 46 pp.
A report to the plenum of the National Council of the Young Communist League, New York, December 21, 1940, during the Nazi-Soviet pact period. The report strongly opposes both the war in Europe and the draft, and criticizes Mrs. Roosevelt and former American Student Union head Joseph Lash for encouraging the draft.

W93 . . . . New Developments in the Youth Movement, "Clarity," 1 (Fall 1940), 19-35.
Youth opposition to America's involvement in the war is disturbing to the bourgeoisie and the warmongers. Tendencies in various youth groups, particularly with regard to the war issue, are reviewed. The need of youth for jobs and training must be emphasized.

W94 . . . . "Destroy Hitlerism." New York: New Age, 1941. 31 pp.
A communist plea, after Hitler's attack on the Soviet Union, for the destruction of Hitlerism. The president of the Young Communist League asserts that USSR involvement has transformed the war into a just one. U.S. defense demands the military defeat of Hitler's fascism and its satellites.

W95 . . . . For a National Anti-Fascist Youth Front! "Communist," 20 (Aug. 1941), 737-52.
The war has ceased to be an imperialist war, and youth has begun to see that Russian entry guarantees democratic, antifascist results from victory. The Party will build an antifascist youth front.

W96 . . . . Earl Browder—Champion of U.S.-Soviet Collaboration, "Communist," 20 (Nov. 1941), 977-87.
In their agitation for American-Soviet collaboration, Browder and the communists have been accused of subordinating American national interests to Russian foreign policy. There is no such conflict, since American-Soviet collaboration has always been in the national interests of the U.S.

W97 . . . . "Youth Serves the Nation." New York: New Age, 1942. 43 pp.
The president of the Young Communist League calls for world unity against the Axis and for national unity in the

war effort. Youth is being mobilized to serve the nation, in the armed forces, in production, and in civilian defense. Red-baiting is called Hitler's main weapon. (Based on a report to the National Committee of the YCL, Jan. 31, 1942.)

W98   WEISS, Max. The Twentieth Anniversary of the Young Communist League, "Clarity," 3 (Spring 1942), 7-15.
A review, in the League's theoretical organ, of YCL accomplishments in its 20-year history, emphasizing its consistent service to America, its carrying on of the American tradition, and its educational work in the spirit of socialism.

W99   .... The Nation and the Armed Forces, "Communist," 22 (Feb. 1943), 146-56.
The Party recommends development of a democratic fighting front that stresses political education of servicemen, allows soldiers to vote without poll tax, trains young officers from the ranks, and integrates Negroes fully into the armed services. Trade unions should build close ties with servicemen.

W100   .... Youth in the Fight for Victory, "Communist," 22 (April 1943), 316-31.
Communists want a mass army, solidarity between the army and labor, incentive wages, greater emphasis on job training, recruitment of young workers into trade unions, the vote for youths old enough for military service, and unity of youth in support of full war mobilization. To achieve Party goals respecting youth, the YCL must become a mass organization.

W101   .... Fifth-Column Diversion in Detroit, "Communist," 22 (Aug. 1943), 698-710.
The race riots in Detroit and other American cities did not arise from a deterioration of relations between Negroes and whites. They were instigated by Nazi fifth-columnists intent on disrupting the war effort.

W102   .... Toward a New Anti-Fascist Youth Organization, "Communist," 22 (Sept. 1943), 792-805.
A proposal to change the name of the Young Communist League and reorganize it into a broad youth organization with a program of mobilization behind the war effort, support of democratic ideals and institutions, alliance with the working class, support of Negro integration, and international fellowship. The new organization is to be independent of the Party. (Reprinted in pamphlet form.)

W103   .... Oust the Trotskyites from the Labor and Progressive Movement, "Political Affairs," 25 (Feb. 1946), 130-48.
The counter revolutionary Trotskyists falsely attack the Soviet Union for expansionism, support the imperialist aims of the U.S., and act in the interests of Big Business on the domestic front by creating factionalism. They have penetrated industrial centers such as Detroit because the Party has relaxed its struggle against them. The Party must arouse a spirit of hatred of Trotskyists.

W104   .... Toward Clarity on the Negro Question (A Discussion Article), "Political Affairs," 25 (May 1946), 457-78.
Sharp disagreement with Francis Franklin's view (in "The Status of the Negro People in the Black Belt," in the same issue of "Political Affairs") that the Negro people have exercised the right of self-determination in favor of amalgamation. This view, which stems from Browder's revisionism, is an argument for disintegration of the Negro nation. Self-government means separation, autonomy, or federation, but not amalgamation.

W105   .... The Struggle on the Ideological Front, "Political Affairs," 25 (Sept. 1946), 837-52.
A report delivered July 18 at the plenary meeting of the Party's national committee, calling for a political-ideological campaign within the Party for the mastery of Marxism-Leninism. Ideological understanding weakened under the influence of Browder's revisionism. We need a Marxist-Leninist analysis of U.S. imperialism and of the masses' economic struggles against the monopolies.

W106   .... "What Price Profits?" New York: New Century, 1947. 48 pp. Ref.
An analysis of wage-price economics by the secretary of the national education commission of the Party, who denies that higher wages cause higher prices. Labor's wage policy must be based upon the need for rising living standards, as well as its strength and the support from allies. Only the establishment of socialism will permanently solve the wage-price problem.

W107   .... The Nathan Report, "Political Affairs," 26 (Feb. 1947), 99-108.
A discussion of the implications to labor of a report on the 1945-46 industrial-economic situation, prepared at the request of the CIO. The Party's largely favorable opinion of the report is contrasted with the attacks made on it by the camp of monopoly. The report is limited by its unquestioning acceptance of the capitalist system.

W108   .... Henry Wallace's "Toward World Peace," "Political Affairs," 27 (May 1948), 400-11.
A review of Henry Wallace's "Toward World Peace," praising Wallace for stressing the fight for peace and American-Soviet friendship. It criticizes Wallace for viewing the Soviet Union as an expansionist power, and for believing that American capitalism can be made into a progressive capitalism.

W109   .... "The Meaning of the XXth Congress of the Communist Party of the Soviet Union." New York: New Century, 1956. 40 pp.
Report by the Party's educational director to the meeting of its national committee held April 28-May 1, 1956. The report analyzes the speeches and decisions of the Congress, held three years after Stalin's death, which demolished the "cult of the individual" and castigated Stalin for violations of socialist democracy and legality. The author advocates inner-party democracy as a guard against one-man leadership, and urges communists here to rediscover America.

W110   .... Geneva and '56, "Political Affairs," 35 (Jan. 1956), 1-18.
A report to the Party's national conference, December 3-5, 1955, viewing the Geneva conference between the U.S. and the USSR as a turn in favor of peace. Representatives of monopoly in both major parties favor continuation of the cold war and an armed truce. The peace camp wants to advance from armed truce to peaceful coexistence.

W111   WEISSMAN, Aaron. "The Best Years of Their Lives." New York: New Century, 1955. 15 pp.
A Labor Youth League leader denounces Eisenhower's proposal for a military reserve program as containing all the objectionable features of universal military training. The social consequences of a militarized young generation are emphasized, while the threat of Soviet aggression, used to justify it, is labeled a myth.

W112   WEISSMAN, David L. Sacher and Isserman in the Courts, "Lawyers Guild Review," 12 (Winter 1952), 39-47.
A discussion and criticism of the summary contempt pro-

ceedings against the lawyers for the communists in the Dennis case, instituted by Judge Medina and subsequently affirmed on appeal.

W113 WEISSMAN, David L. Harvey Matusow and the Role of the Prosecutors in United States v. Flynn, "Lawyers Guild Review," 15 (Fall 1955), 103-7.
A discussion of the problem of administering justice in times of popular passion. After testifying that he had heard some of the defendants in the Smith Act case and others assert that the Party sought to overthrow the government by force and violence, Harvey Matusow retracted this testimony. Government prosecutors were so eager to hear what they wanted that they cast all doubts aside.

W114 .... The Issue: Freedom; Place: The Court, "Nation," 181 (Nov. 26, 1955), 450-53.
Comments on the Party's case before the Supreme Court, challenging the order that it register under the Internal Security Act of 1950. Describing the registration provisions of the Act, the author summarizes the arguments of the government, the Party, and the civil libertarians. The American heritage of freedom is at stake.

W115 .... The Proceedings to Disbar Leo Sheiner: A Story of Judicial Maladministration, with a Portrait of Informer Joseph D. Mazzei, "Lawyers Guild Review," 16 (Winter 1956), 137-48.
The case of a Florida lawyer ordered disbarred because of pleading the Fifth Amendment regarding past activities in the Communist Party and the Southern Conference on Human Welfare. Though the chief witness against him has been proved unreliable, the disbarment order has not been vacated.

W116 WELBORN, Lewis [pseud.]. The Ordeal of Dr. Condon, "Harper's Magazine," 200 (Jan. 1950), 46-53.
A news correspondent attacks the practice of accusing public figures of communism without public hearing, as in the case of Dr. Edward N. Condon, accused of being "one of the weakest links in our atomic security" by J. Parnell Thomas of the House Un-American Activities Committee. The author presents the case Dr. Condon might have argued.

W117 WELCH, Robert [H. W., Jr.]. Why People Become Communists, "American Mercury," 86 (May 1958), 124-31.
People become communists because of idealism, loneliness, intellectual snobbishness, coercion, desire for power, or opportunism. Opportunists, the largest single group, believe that communism is "the wave of the future." Communists will continue to win the cold war until America realizes that communism has an appeal to and a membership among great numbers of people.

W118 .... "The Blue Book of the John Birch Society." N.p.: n.publ., 4th printing, 1961. 180 pp. Multilith.
Welch's view of the communist conspiracy in the U.S., that led him to form the John Birch Society in December 1958. He finds communism steadily advancing throughout the world, aided by members of the conspiracy highly placed in Washington. Among the leading political figures he names as part of the communist conspiracy or seeking similar objectives are Franklin D. Roosevelt, General George C. Marshall, Nelson Rockefeller, and Chief Justice Earl Warren. Once the communist conspiracy here is destroyed, the Society will seek its ultimate goals of less government, more responsibility, and a better world.

W119 .... "The Politician." Belmont, Mass.: Belmont Publishing Co., 1963. 448 pp. Bibliog. Notes. Ind. Planographed.
An account of the career of Dwight Eisenhower by the founder of the John Birch Society, who believes that Eisenhower, completely controlled by communist influences, put the diplomatic and economic power of this country to work on the side of Russia and the communists in connection with every problem and trouble spot in their empire. Eisenhower is called either a stooge, or a communist, assigned as a political front man.

W120 WELLMAN, Saul, and GANLEY, Nat. The Auto Workers Advance, "Political Affairs," 34 (Oct. 1955), 31-43.
Gains made by the auto workers, following the pattern-setting Ford settlement, fell far short of union demands. The Marxist left, making a wrong estimate of the situation, strained the administration coalition in Ford Local 600 by calling for a plant-wide "no" vote on the settlement. The left forces should have worked within the coalition, not disrupted it by an independent stand.

W121 WELLS, Harry K. "Pragmatism: Philosophy of Imperialism." Introd. by Howard Selsam. New York: International Publishers, 1954. 221 pp. Ref. Ind.
A communist view of pragmatism as the philosophy of capitalism in the era of imperialism. Its method is that required by the exploiting class; its theory is the direct opposite of Marxist materialism, the scientific world view and method of the proletariat and the Communist Party.

W122 WELSH, Edward K. What's What about the National Negro Congress, "Workers Age," 5 (March 21, 1936), 3 ff.
A Lovestoneite analysis of the National Negro Congress recently held in Chicago. Though charged with being communist-dominated, it is, thanks to the logic of the popular front, overrepresentative of bourgeois and church groups. The CP is criticized for failing to lead a fight on the labor party issue and for voting for resolutions pushed by petty bourgeois Negro groups.

W123 WEST, George P. California Sees Red, "Current History," 40 (Sept. 1934), 658-62.
A reporter for the San Francisco "News" describes the events leading up to the July 16 general strike, led largely by communists, and followed by a wave of reaction against every form of radicalism.

W124 .... Communists and Liberals, "New Republic," 108 (May 10, 1943), 631-33.
A discussion of the Harry Bridges deportation case, emphasizing the relations between liberals and communists. The author, presenting a flattering picture of Bridges, calls for frankness and understanding between liberals and communists. To this end the Party, while admitting its past policy of conspiracy and secrecy, should repudiate this policy for the future.

W125 WEST, James, and ROSS, Carl. Teheran and the Young Generation, "Communist," 23 (April 1944), 336-46.
A proposal that all youths, except the defeatists, join a mass youth organization, the American Youth for Democracy, that backs the Teheran Conference decisions. The communists have disbanded their Young Communist League in order that young communists can join with noncommunists to build the AYD.

W126 WEST, Jim. "Can Everybody Be Rich and Still Be Honest?" New York: CPUSA, 1951. 32 pp.

A recruiting pamphlet addressed to steel workers, asserting that the steel industry is making huge profits while the workers' standard of living sinks. Workers are urged to enter independent political action, with a new peoples' party representing the interests of all who suffer from the trusts.

W127 WEST, John. "War and the Workers." New York: Workers Party of the U.S., 1935. 47 pp.
The answer of the Workers Party of the U.S. (formed by a merger of the American Workers Party with the Communist League of America) to the Communist Party's united front tactic. The workers are urged to seize power as the only way to end imperialist wars, avoiding the Stalinist rapprochement with the capitalists.

W128 WEST, Rebecca. Review of "A Generation on Trial: USA vs. Alger Hiss," by Alistair Cooke, "University of Chicago Law Review," 18 (Spring 1951), 662-77.
Criticism of Cooke's account of the Hiss trial as inadequate and inaccurate. The author asserts that Cooke has failed to deal with the primary problem, the reliability of Whittaker Chambers' testimony regarding Hiss.

W129 .... Whittaker Chambers, "Atlantic Monthly," 189 (June 1952), 33-39.
A discussion of the personality of Whittaker Chambers as revealed in "Witness," and of the significance of the Hiss trial as compared to the Dreyfus and other trials with ideological significance. The author concludes that Chambers, with his "intuitive" judgments, does more to confuse than clarify the issues.

W130 .... As a Briton Looks at McCarthyism, "U. S. News & World Report," 34 (May 22, 1953), 60-81.
Reproduction of a series of four articles written for the London "Sunday Times," dealing with security and the civil service in the U.S., investigations by the House Un-American Activities Committee, communists and the schools, and Senator McCarthy. Emphasizing revelations by Elizabeth Bentley and Whittaker Chambers, the author denies that the U.S. is gripped by anticommunist hysteria or has banished free speech. She attacks Soviet espionage, sabotage, and infiltration of unions in other countries.

W131 WESTERMAN, George W. "Blocking Them at the Canal: Failure of the Red Attempt to Control Local Workers in the Vital Panama Canal Area." Panama City: Panama Tribune, 1952. 67 pp.
A reprint of a series of 32 articles by the associate editor of the paper that appeared between February 2, 1948, and May 23, 1952, exposing the communist leadership of the United Public Workers of America, a CIO union organizing in the Canal Zone. The author appeals to the local membership and leadership to repudiate these leaders for the good of their union and for the sake of proper consideration of their just grievances. (This series played a role in the expulsion of the UPWA from the CIO.)

W132 WESTIN, Alan F. Our Freedom—and the Rights of Communists: A Reply to Irving Kristol, "Commentary," 14 (July 1952), 33-40.
Criticism of Irving Kristol's stand ("Commentary," March 1952) on the civil rights of communists, asserting that Kristol has corroded the liberal stand on civil liberties. The civil liberties of communists should be defended to protect the rights of all, to avoid harmful effects on our society, and to preserve our moral leadership in the world.

W133 .... Do Silent Witnesses Defend Civil Liberties? The Course of "Profoundest Wisdom," "Commentary," 15 (June 1953), 537-46.

While most reluctant witnesses before congressional committees investigating subversion are communists or former communists, some of those invoking the Fifth Amendment may be liberals who are "conscientious objectors." The course of wisdom for the latter group is to answer all questions freely, not to claim the protection of the Fifth Amendment, or of the First.

W134 .... "The Constitution and Loyalty Programs: Public Employment and Governmental Security." New York: Carrie Chapman Catt Memorial Fund, 1954. 53 pp. Bibliog.
A "Freedom Agenda" pamphlet, discussing the background of the loyalty problem, the federal loyalty-security programs, the Supreme Court and the loyalty programs, the constitutional aspect of fidelity programs, the question as to their necessity, their proper concerns, the administrative procedure, and past and future fidelity programs. The task must be approached with sanity and justice.

W135 .... Winning the Fight against McCarthy: The Need to Struggle on Two Fronts, "Commentary," 18 (July 1954), 10-15.
An analysis of a communist booklet, "McCarthy on Trial," revealing that the communists plan to work in mass organizations, capitalizing on growing anti-McCarthy sentiment. We must keep communists and united fronters out of the organizations that fight McCarthy, to prevent perversion of the anti-McCarthy fight.

W136 .... Libertarian Precepts and Subversive Realities: Some Lessons Learned in the School of Experience, "Commentary," 19 (Jan. 1955), 1-9.
A discussion of problems of civil liberties and security raised by communist espionage and infiltration of government. The author considers government loyalty programs, and inferences to be drawn from the use of the Fifth Amendment or from one's associations. He criticizes the position taken on these issues by civil libertarians.

W137 .... The Supreme Court Decisions: The New Balance on Civil Liberties, "New Leader," 40 (Aug. 5, 1957), 5-8.
A review and discussion of U.S. Supreme Court decisions in May and June, 1957, affecting civil liberties. Among them were a prosecution for falsifying a Taft-Hartley noncommunist oath, contempt prosecutions arising from federal and state antisubversive investigations, convictions of communist leaders under the Smith Act, and a State Department discharge on loyalty grounds.

W138 WESTON, Hugh. Hunting Witches in the Church, "American Socialist," 1 (Dec. 1954), 9-12.
A Universalist minister in Massachusetts reviews the government-inspired attack on the clergy for radical activity, some of it in cooperation with the Communist Party or in peace or other organizations in which the Party also participated. Among the instances cited are loyalty oaths for churches, removal of tax exemption, contempt citations for clergymen, and church "heresy trials."

W139 .... The Vindictive Execution of Julius and Ethel Rosenberg, "American Socialist," 2 (June 1955), 22-24.
Two years earlier the Rosenbergs were executed, following conviction as members of a Soviet spy ring to steal the atomic bomb secret. The evidence against them was of the weakest kind, most of it uncorroborated testimony by a witness who wanted to save his own life. The judicial authorities involved were biased and ferocious, and an atmosphere of hysteria surrounded the entire case.

W140   WESTON, Thomas. Bridges on Angel Island Fig-
       ure-Heads for Stalinism, "America," 61 (Aug. 19,
       1939), 436-37.
Beyond question the Communist International, with which
the CPUSA is affiliated, teaches and advocates violent
overthrow of government. It is up to the government to
prove that Harry Bridges is a member of the Party, in
which case he will be deported.

W141   WEXLEY, John. "The Judgment of Julius and Ethel
       Rosenberg." New York: Cameron & Kahn, 1955.
       672 pp. App. Ind.
A view of the Rosenberg case as a gross miscarriage of
justice, and of the prosecution's evidence as full of
contraditions and improbabilities. The Rosenbergs are
seen as innocent victims of a frame-up and an unfair trial.
The volume contains a synopsis of the government's case
and a chronology of events. The events of January-
December 1950 preceding the trial are described, and the
trial of January-April 1951 is headed "The Empty Ritual."
Judge Kaufman's conduct of the trial is bitterly attacked.

W142   WEYBRIGHT, Victor. Communists and Civil Lib-
       erties, "Survey Graphic," 29 (May 1940), 290-93.
An examination of the controversy over the 1940 resolution of the national committee of the American Civil
Liberties Union barring defenders of totalitarian dictatorship anywhere from its governing committees or staff.
The ACLU supports civil liberties, not as a means to the
end of a good society, but as a good end in itself.

W143   WEYL, Nathaniel. "Treason: The Story of Dis-
       loyalty and Betrayal in American History." Wash-
       ington, D.C.: Public Affairs Press, 1950. 491 pp.
       Ind.
A study of the role of treason and sedition in the U.S. since
the beginning of the Republic, and of the measures taken to
guard national security. Chapters deal with the nature
and extent of pro-Soviet espionage in the U.S., the cases
of Alger Hiss and Judith Coplon, and the trial of the 11
Communist Party leaders under the Smith Act. Exploring
the hold of communism upon its agents, the author urges
us to combat communist ideas with debate rather than
with imprisonment.

W144   . . . . "The Battle against Disloyalty." New York:
       Crowell, 1951. 342 pp. Ref. notes. Ind.
A historical survey and analysis of 175 years of American
struggle against disloyalty, sedition, and espionage, with
particular attention to measures adopted from 1919 to
1950 to control the inroads of communism. The author
discusses stolen documents, atomic espionage, the merits
and drawbacks of the federal loyalty program, FBI investigations, congressional investigating committees, and
the Internal Security Act of 1950. He weighs the civil
rights of the individual against the duty of the state to
protect itself.

W145   . . . . The Art of Spy-Catching, "Reporter," 4
       (Jan. 23, 1951), 9-10.
A critique of the Internal Security Act of 1950 (the
McCarran Act), questioning its effectiveness. It cuts the
heart out of the 1940 Smith Act by denying that membership or office-holding in the Party is a violation of law.
The registration provision is thus almost useless, and
other provisions are unwise or of doubtful constitutionality.

W146   WHARTON, Don. American Red, "Today," 5 (Dec.
       21, 1935), 8 ff.
A biographical sketch of Earl Browder, tracing his rise to
leadership of the Party. Early a radical, Browder was
jailed for opposing the war, and he outmaneuvered Foster
to become Party secretary when Lovestone was expelled.

Though the Party has grown under his leadership, the
masses have turned elsewhere.

W147   WHEILDON, L. B. Control of Communism in the
       United States, "Editorial Research Reports," 1:
       1948 (Feb. 11), 91-106.
An examination of present laws and proposed measures to
control communism. Arguments for and against outlawing
the Party are reviewed, and existing federal and state
laws to control subversive activity are analyzed. Alternatives to outlawing the Party, such as exposure, registration, and tightening espionage laws, are presented.

W148   WHIFFIN, Peter. A Few Communists, "Common-
       weal," 24 (May 29, 1936), 22-24.
A Catholic priest describes his attendance, without the
clerical collar, at communist meetings, and his differences
with the speakers. Opposed to abuses in capitalism and
in organized religion, he favors reform, not revolution.

W149   WHITE, Charles. "Free Angelo Herndon." New
       York: Youth Publishers, 1934. 16 pp.
A call for the liberation of Herndon, sentenced to 20 years
on the Georgia chain gang for leading Negro and white
unemployed in the struggle for relief. At his trial for
"insurrection" Herndon placed the Southern white ruling
class on trial, denouncing capitalism. He has become the
symbol of growing black and white unity.

W150   . . . . Path of a Negro Artist, "Masses & Main-
       stream," 8 (April 1955), 33-44.
An autobiography of a procommunist artist, telling of the
prejudice he met, his struggles to become an artist, the
lessons he learned from Soviet and Chinese artists, and
his concerns for the future.

W151   WHITE, David McKelvy. "Franco Spain . . . Amer-
       ica's Enemy." New York: New Century, 1945.
       24 pp.
A call by the executive secretary of the Veterans of the
Abraham Lincoln Brigade, the organization of Americans
who fought for Loyalist Spain, to break American diplomatic and business relations with fascist Spain. Franco's
record as Hitler's ally is reviewed, and a plea made for a
free and democratic Spain.

W152   WHITE, H. V. Christianity and Communism,
       "Christian Century," 49 (Nov. 23, 1932), 1440-42.
An assertion that Christianity is faced with a new and
serious rival in communism, a materialistic and authoritarian creed with no inner strain between doctrine and
practical program. It offers the way of salvation with
enthusiasm and zeal. Christianity, standing valiantly for
its faith, must incorporate communism's good into its own
program.

W153   WHITE, Howard B. Materialists and the Sociology
       of American Literature, "Social Research," 7
       (May 1940), 184-200.
An attack on sociological analysis by such literary
"materialists" as Granville Hicks, Bernard Smith, and
V. F. Calverton, for attempting to coordinate the history of
American letters with economic life, and for frequently
assuming that in the study of letters there is no need for
aesthetic appreciation. The author criticizes the narrow-
ness of their approach and their political formalism.

W154   WHITE, Josh. I Was a Sucker for the Communists,
       "Negro Digest," 8 (Dec. 1950), 27-31.
Accused of fronting for communists, singer Josh White
tells how he was fooled and misled by left wingers. Not
until 1947 did he realize that some groups with which he
was affiliated were communist-inspired. While reaffirm-

ing his belief in America, White asserts that injustice here must be removed.

W155 WHITE, Nathan I. "Harry D. White—Loyal American." Waban, Mass.: Bessie (White) Bloom, 1956. 415 pp. App.
A defense of Harry Dexter White by his brother from charges of communist sympathy and participation in a Soviet espionage ring. White, an economist, had held a number of government posts, including that of Assistant Secretary of the Treasury. He was charged by Elizabeth Bentley, a self-confessed spy, with giving information to be relayed to her, and was named by Whittaker Chambers as a fellow-traveler and a source of information meant for Russia. A grand jury that heard all the testimony against White refused to indict him. The volume defends White's record as a loyal American and conscientious public servant.

W156 WHITE, Ray B. "The False Christ of Communism and the Social Gospel." Zarephath, N.J.: Pillar of Fire, 1946. 248 pp. Add.
Written as a reply to "The Soviet Power," by the Very Reverend Hewlett Johnson, Dean of Canterbury, this work by a fundamentalist leader is an attack on the liberal church as well as an indictment of communism and the Soviet Union. The author asserts that communist morals originated with the devil, that the "all-in-common" principle of communism embraces sex as well as economic matters, and that sex perversion and crime are the result of communist propaganda. The addendum holds the Federal Council of the Churches of Christ in America to be anti-Christian, guilty of false claims, false creeds, and false conclusions.

W157 WHITE, W. L. The Story of a Smear, "Freeman," 2 (Oct. 22, 1951), 51-53.
A description of the infiltration and manipulation of the Bonus Expeditionary Force's march on Washington in 1932, as revealed in the confessions of former communists. After their infiltration the communists fomented violence, which was exploited by the communist press.

W158 WHITE, Walter F. The Scottsboro Case: Race Hatred Run Riot, "New Leader," 12 (June 13, 1931), 4.
A discussion of the Scottsboro case by the head of the NAACP, who contrasts the painstaking legal methods of the NAACP with the campaign of propaganda waged by the communist-dominated International Labor Defense. Race hatred, combined with prejudice against communists, is likely to lead the Scottsboro boys to the electric chair.

W159 .... The Negro and the Communists, "Harper's Magazine," 164 (Dec. 1931), 62-72. Reprinted in "Crisis," 57 (Aug.-Sept. 1950), 502-6 ff.
An account of the Scottsboro case by the executive secretary of the NAACP, who tells of the events, the NAACP's initial role, the intrusion of the CP and the ILD, the Party's methods, the financial manipulations, and the disillusionment when it became evident that the Party wanted to make martyrs of the boys to spread propaganda among Negroes.

W160 .... "A Man Called White: The Autobiography of Walter White." New York: Viking, 1948. 382 pp. Ind.
The autobiography of the national secretary of the NAACP. The Scottsboro case and the part played by the Communist Party in it are described (pp. 125-33), as are the role of the communists and the Civil Rights Congress in the Columbia, Tennessee, disturbances in 1946 (pp. 308-21).

W161 .... Portrait of a Communist, "Progressive," 14 (Nov. 1950), 17. Reprinted in "Negro Digest," 9 (Feb. 1951), 84-85.
A sadly sympathetic portrait of Benjamin J. Davis, Jr., convicted communist. Raised in a wealthy and privileged Negro family in Atlanta, Georgia, Davis became a communist as a result of the Angelo Herndon case, in which he served as a defense attorney.

W162 .... The Strange Case of Paul Robeson, "Ebony," 6 (Feb. 1951), 78-84.
An analysis of the personality and motivations of a man of great talent who became the leading American Negro supporter of the USSR. Together with some ideological rejection of capitalism, Robeson grasped the Soviet way as the answer to racial slights and discrimination in the U.S. Most Negroes prefer to fight for freedom in a faulty democracy.

W163 WHITE, William C. The Good Communist: Is This What the Newly-Become Radicals Want? "Scribner's Magazine," 92 (Aug. 1932), 91-94.
America's younger intellectuals, turning in large numbers to communism as a result of the depression, do not realize that the communist movement distrusts them. The Soviet leaders want Party members who never waver from the Party line, who submit to Party discipline without question.

W164 WHITEHEAD, Don. "The F.B.I. Story: A Report to the People." New York: Random House, 1956. 368 pp. Ind.
A sympathetic history of the FBI, with attention to its role in combatting communism in the U.S. from 1919 until the present. The author outlines Communist Party history as seen through FBI activities; he discusses FBI surveillance over the Party, the loyalty screening program, and the FBI role in the Hiss and Coplon cases. He describes the FBI part in the trials of leading communists under the Smith Act, and in the exposure of the atomic espionage ring.

W165 WHITNEY, Richard M. "LaFollette, Socialism, Communism." New York: Beckwith Press, 1924. 64 pp.
Criticizing radical and liberal organizations indiscriminately, the author asserts that communism will be the ultimate result if socialist measures are adopted. He labels La Follette a socialist.

W166 .... "The Reds in America." New York: Beckwith Press, 1924. 287 pp. Ind. App.
A broad survey of communist activities (based primarily on documents seized in the Bridgman raid) by an officer of the American Defense Society, who advocates stringent anticommunist legislation. There are chapters on communist publications and organizations, and on communist programs directed at schools, industry, the arts, the government, and Negroes. The appendix contains a number of important communist documents.

W167 .... "Back to Barbarism." New York: American Defense Society, 1925. 25 pp.
A presentation, based on quotations from original sources, of the socialist-IWW-communist program for Negroes, concluding that such a program would result in barbarism.

W168 WHITTEN, Woodrow C. Trial of Charlotte Anita Whitney, "Pacific Historical Review," 15 (Sept. 1946), 286-94.
An account of the trial of Anita Whitney, charter member of the Communist Labor Party, who was convicted in 1920 under California's criminal syndicalism statute and sentenced to imprisonment for up to 14 years.

W169 WHITTY, R. H. T. Report from America, "Lawyers Guild Review," 9 (Spring 1949), 78-88.
A British lawyer's report on the 1949 convention of the National Lawyers Guild, the Dennis trial, and the trial of the "Trenton Six." The Guild's support of the defense in the Dennis case is held justifiable as a civil liberties issue. The author agrees with the Guild that Judge Medina may be prejudiced and views the Trenton Six as unjustly accused.

W170 WICKETS, Donald Furthman. What the Dies Committee Overlooked, "Liberty," 15 (Dec. 24, 1938), 13-14; (Dec. 31), 37-38; 16 (Jan. 7, 1939), 49-51; (Jan. 14), 45-47.
A series of articles on the communist movement in the U.S., dealing with control from Moscow, Party organization and functioning, antireligious propaganda, OGPU executions in the U.S., communist influence in our schools, and communist plans for the revolution. The Party expects to seize power by means of strikes and armed demonstrations, that will culminate in a general strike accompanied by armed insurrection.

W171 WICKS, H. M. The Democratic Party, "Workers Monthly," 5 (Jan. 1926), 123-29; (March), 223-27; (May), 323-28.
A communist interpretation of the history and class basis of the Democratic Party, which has served three distinct classes: chattel slave owners of the South prior to the Civil War, the middle class from 1896 to 1908-10, and the House of Morgan, or imperialism, since.

W172 .... Herbert Hoover, "Communist," 7 (Feb. 1928), 69-74.
A scathing review of the "imperialist" record of Herbert Hoover, Republican presidential candidate in 1928. His election would place in the White House an unscrupulous president adept at utilizing misery and devastation for imperialist purposes. The only effective weapon is a movement for class political action through a labor party.

W173 .... The Anti-Comintern Opposition in the American Party, "International Press Correspondence," 9 (Aug. 2, 1929), 801-2.
A review of Lovestone's resistance to Comintern decisions following the sixth convention of the CPUSA. Lovestone planned to resist the Comintern even after going to Moscow to appeal its decision that ousted him from Party leadership. After this plan was frustrated, Lovestone returned to the U.S. in violation of Comintern orders, for which he was expelled. Since then his efforts to win over Party members have failed.

W174 .... On the End of Capitalist Stabilization in the U.S.A., "Communist," 12 (Feb. 1933), 123-32.
Despite optimistic statements by capitalist leaders that the economic crisis was passing, the production trend in heavy industry is still downward. The social fascists try to help the capitalist class stop the growing movement of the masses. Although the economic situation is desperate, capitalism will not collapse, but must be crushed by the revolutionary proletariat.

W175 .... "Eclipse of October." Chicago: Challenge Publishers, 1957. 464 pp. Ind.
A history of the world communist movement, emphasizing the twists in the party line under Stalin and his successors, written by an early American participant. One of the founders of the Communist Party of America in 1919, Wicks from that time until 1936 held high office in the communist movement. Under Stalin, in his view, a Kremlin tyranny arose that turned to its own designs the various communist parties in other countries. Wicks shows the response of the Party leadership here to each turn of the line emanating from Moscow.

W176 WIDENER, Alice. The UN Has a Rule for It, "Freeman," 3 (Oct. 20, 1952), 47-50.
A discussion of the employment by the UN of American citizens who were associated with procommunist organizations. A large number of Americans on the UN staff, in the aftermath of a federal grand jury probe, are being removed as poor security risks. The UN has a rule barring employees associated with fascism, but not with communism. (First in a series of articles on communist influence in the UN.)

W177 .... Hiss Led the Way, "Freeman," 3 (Nov. 17, 1952), 127-30.
Alger Hiss, who was director of the State Department's Office of Special Political Affairs, is held responsible for the movement of American subversives from U.S. government agencies to employment with the UN. A number of these have refused, on grounds of self-incrimination, to testify as to present or past membership in the Communist Party. (One of a series of articles on communist influence in the UN.)

W178 WIGMORE, John H. Abrams v. U.S.—Freedom of Speech and Freedom of Thuggery in War-time and Peace-time, "Illinois Law Review," 14 (March 1920), 539-61.
A professor of law at Northwestern University asserts that the Bolshevik Revolution, having introduced a dictatorship of force and violence, seeks to promote civil disobedience everywhere. Abrams, propagandizing on its behalf, presented a clear and present danger, outside the protection of the "freedom of speech" amendment.

W179 WILCOX, Clair (ed.). "Civil Liberties under Attack. Philadelphia: University of Pennsylvania Press, 1951. 155 pp.
A series of lectures delivered at Swarthmore College on the subject of civil liberties. Henry Steele Commager deals with the danger of conformity and the need for nonconformist thinking. Zechariah Chafee, Jr., attacks investigations of radicalism as bound to bring thought control and denounces the House Un-American Activities Committee, the McCarran Act, and the Subversive Activities Control Board. Walter Gellhorn condemns the secrecy surrounding scientists' work under military or government jurisdiction, as well as the loyalty probes of scientists working in "sensitive" areas. Curtis Bok, in discussing censorship and the arts, touches on the subject of communism and the loyalty oath. James P. Baxter, III, while upholding academic freedom and condemning loyalty oaths for teachers, denies that there is a place for communists on a college or university faculty, since they put Party interests ahead of truth.

W180 WILCOX, Thomas. "The Anti-Bolshevik Bibliography." Los Angeles: The author, 1954. 76 pp. Mimeo.
A list of some 300 works critical of communism, each with a brief annotation. Though most of the publications deal with the USSR and lesser numbers on other communist states, a number of American items are included.

W181 WILKERSON, Doxey A. The Negro in the War, "New Masses," 49 (Dec. 14, 1943), 18-19.
The original doubts of the Negro people as to whether this war had meaning to them are now largely cleared away, except for defeatist, antiwar leaders such as A. Philip Randolph, who have no following. Much must still be done to remove racial bars, but with the defeat of fascism the Negroes will march forward.

W182 WILKERSON, Doxey A. Freedom—Through Victory in War and Peace. Pp. 193-216 in Rayford W. Logan, ed., "What the Negro Wants." Chapel Hill: University of North Carolina Press, 1944. 352 pp.
An assertion by a leading Negro communist, then a member of the national committee of the Communist Political Association, that Negroes want complete economic, political, and social equality. He urges unconditional Negro support of the war effort, along with unity between progressive white and Negro Americans for victory and a democratic peace. Demands for the correction of specific injustices must be raised as war measures to promote victory.

W183 .... "The Negro People and the Communists." New York: Workers Library, 1944. 23 pp.
A call to the Negro people, during the Communist Political Association period, to ally themselves with democratic friends: most clearly the communists, but also the CIO, enlightened sections of Big Business, small business groups, farmers, and all who are for a pro-Teheran coalition, dedicated to German defeat.

W184 .... The Negro and the Elections, "Communist," 23 (Sept. 1944), 819-29.
The Negro vote is cited as a decisive factor in the coming elections. Democratic policies are contrasted with those of Republicans to illustrate their greater concurrence with the interests of the Negro people.

W185 .... "Why Negroes Are Joining the Communist Party." New York: CPUSA, 1946. 15 pp.
An assertion that thousands of Negroes are joining the Party because its members are the most militant and effective leaders of struggles. The author tells of his reasons for joining the Party and urges Negroes to fight with the CIO, the WFTU, and the Party for a genuinely democratic America.

W186 .... The Negro and the American Nation (A Discussion Article), "Political Affairs," 25 (July 1946), 652-68.
The proposed revival by the Party of the slogan of "Self-Determination in the Black Belt" would be theoretically incorrect and tactically disastrous. The slogan is un-Marxian, militates against the unity of the whole Negro people, and aggravates divisions between the white and Negro masses of the South. A new theoretical approach to the Negro question is suggested. (For replies by James S. Allen see "Political Affairs" for Nov. and Dec. 1946. The latter article, "The Negro Question: The Negro People as a Nation: A Discussion Article," is abstracted.)

W187 .... Negro Culture: Heritage and Weapon, "Masses & Mainstream," 2 (Aug. 1949), 3-24.
An interpretation of Negro culture as related to Negro freedom struggles. Negro spirituals, jazz, poetry of freedom—all are examples. Two big problems are the struggle for literacy and the struggle for content. The great dangers are the need to conform to Negro stereotypes in order to have a job, and the tendency of some to escape into cosmopolitanism and formalism.

W188 .... Henry Luce's Revolutionaries, "Masses & Mainstream," 4 (Sept. 1951), 7-15.
An attack on the volume, "U.S.A.—The Permanent Revolution," by the editors of "Fortune." The volume's thesis is that U.S. imperialism has the moral obligation and power to dominate the world by starting another world war. Bourgeois economic and political theory thus shows its bankruptcy in the period of capitalist decay.

W189 .... Race, Nation and the Concept "Negro," "Political Affairs," 31 (Aug. 1952), 13-26.
The necessity of viewing the Negro problem in the U.S. as a national question does not mean that Marxists can reject the concept of race. A leading Negro communist denounces as false the "ultra-leftist" position he took on this subject the previous year.

W190 .... The Fight to Abolish Segregated Schools, "Political Affairs," 33 (July 1954), 29-43.
A review of the fight against segregation in education in the light of the recent Supreme Court decision. The fight to abolish segregated schools shows that educational inequalities are a major issue among the Negro people; that the Negro nation plays a key role in the struggle for Negro liberation; and that the Negro liberation movement has an all-class, national character, with Negro workers in the leading role.

W191 .... "The People versus Segregated Schools." New York: New Century, 1955. 15 pp.
A communist analysis of the Supreme Court decision outlawing segregation in public schools. While the decision is a major blow to Jim Crow oppression, Dixiecrats are already flouting it. Eisenhower may be seeking peace with the Dixiecrats. All peoples' organizations must unite in an all-out struggle to abolish segregated schools.

W192 .... The 46th Annual Convention of the NAACP, "Political Affairs," 34 (Aug. 1955), 1-18.
The NAACP, the vital center of the Negro people's movement today, reaffirmed the goal of an end to Negro second class citizenship by 1963. Repeated calls for independent political action were sounded. The NAACP is the key to building a Negro-labor alliance; its weaknesses flow from the reformist ideology of its middle class leadership.

W193 WILKINS, Roy. Stalin's Greatest Defeat, "American Magazine," 152 (Dec. 1951), 21 ff.
The Party's attempt to recruit millions of Negroes has been its greatest failure, according to the head of the NAACP. Communist efforts have been blocked by the Negro church and by Negroes' aspirations and loyalties. Negroes want to be fully integrated Americans, not part of a segregated Black Belt republic.

W194 WILLIAMS [pseud.]. The Veterans' Movement in the U.S.A., "Communist International," 9 (Sept. 1, 1932), 562-66.
An analysis of the veterans' movement, and particularly the bonus march on Washington, emphasizing its mass character and its objectively revolutionary character. The role and influence of the Workers' Ex-Servicemen's League, the Party front for veterans, are examined. The American government is attacked for brutally showing its class character in the assault on the marchers. (The author may have been Boris Mikhailov, a Comintern representative in the U.S. in 1929-30, who used this pseudonym.)

W195 WILLIAMS, Albert Rhys. "Soviet Russia." Chicago: Kerr, 1919. 60 pp.
An address in Chicago on February 19, 1919, presenting one of the first sympathetic, eye-witness accounts of the Russian Revolution. (Williams' contribution to the winning of American support for the new Russian regime was second only to that of John Reed.)

W196 WILLIAMS, C. Dickerman. Problems of the Fifth Amendment, "Fordham Law Review," 24 (Spring 1955), 19-52.
A review of problems raised by the privilege against self-incrimination, including the extent of the privilege, the

circumstances in which it may be invoked, the question as to whether it applies to congressional investigations, the inferences drawn from silence, and the propriety of action based upon its invocation. Its use by a former member of the CPUSA is discussed.

W197 WILLIAMS, C. Dickerman. The Law of the Land: Reflections on the Fifth Amendment, "National Review," 1 (Dec. 21, 1955), 15 ff.
A disagreement with Dean Erwin N. Griswold of Harvard Law School regarding the Fifth Amendment and its proper use. The author takes issue with Griswold's support of those who have invoked the Fifth Amendment in congressional hearings.

W198 . . . . The Fifth Amendment in Non-Criminal Proceedings, "Marquette Law Review," 39 (Winter 1955-56), 205-17.
A review of the historical rationale of the privilege, showing its inapplicability in noncriminal cases. The assertion of the privilege by a lawyer should be grounds for disbarment, because he has a social duty, a level of expected conduct, that requires nonsilence. Resort to the Fifth Amendment in congressional hearings is usually unwarranted.

W199 WILLIAMS, Claude. "Religion: Barrier or Bridge to a People's World? A Handbook for Progressive Leaders." Birmingham, Ala.: People's Institute for Applied Religion, 1946. 64 pp.
An attack on religious barriers to a people's world, which are found in Catholicism, reactionary Protestantism, upper class Jewish organizations, and fascist sponsored religious groupings. These groups are all antilabor, anti-Negro, anti-Semitic, and reactionary. True religion is based on knowledge of the class struggle and the nature of the world. The author calls for a people's interpretation of the Bible and democratic collectivism.

W200 WILLIAMS, David C. The Menace of McCarthy, "20th Century" (London), 154 (Aug. 1953), 86-94.
A discussion of the communist menace in the U.S. by the research director of Americans for Democratic Action. Senator McCarthy, who has discovered communism very late in the day, receives dishonorable support from responsible men in government, and cannot be stopped until the President so decides.

W201 WILLIAMS, George. "The First Congress of the Red Trade Union International at Moscow, 1921." Chicago: Industrial Workers of the World, n.d. [1922?]. 68 pp.
The IWW delegate to the First Congress of the Red Trade Union International asserts that the congress was dominated by the political group in the Communist International. He reports on the controversies between syndicalists and communists, and opposes the abandonment of revolutionary dual unions. A statement by the general executive board of the IWW, recommending that it not affiliate, is included.

W202 WILLIAMS, John Henry. "A Negro Looks at War." New York: Workers Library, 1940. 31 pp.
An assertion, during the Nazi-Soviet pact period, that the conflict in Europe is just an imperialist war, and that "the Black Yanks are not coming." Protesting Jim Crowism, the author describes war as part of capitalist oppression.

W203 WILLIAMSON, John. The Success of the Party Recruiting Job in the U.S.A., "International Press Correspondence," 10 (March 6, 1930), 213-14.
The efforts of the CPUSA to transform itself into a mass party as demanded by the Communist International reveal only partial success. It has achieved a correct perspective on the general crisis of capitalism and liquidated factionalism. But its membership campaign, its efforts to bring working class elements into positions of leadership, and its efforts to recruit Negroes show varying degrees of success.

W204 . . . . Some Burning Problems of Organization, "Communist," 9 (June 1930), 519-29.
On four occasions during the last year the workers responded to the Party's call in numbers far exceeding expectations. A goal of 25,000 Party members should be reached by January, and tens of thousands of demonstrators brought into class struggle organizations. Greater emphasis on recruitment through shop nuclei is called for.

W205 . . . . The Party Nucleus—A Factor in the Class Struggle, "Communist," 10 (May 1931), 424-32.
Party resolutions and directives are meaningless unless the Party nucleus, which must carry these into life, is properly equipped. The nuclei are not active in mass work, particularly in the larger cities, where they depend on the district office for everything. Directives for improving the situation are presented.

W206 . . . . "Program of Action." Cleveland: Communist Party State Election Campaign Committee, n.d. [1934]. 19 pp.
The keynote speech by the district organizer of the Party in Ohio to the State Ratification Conference, July 29, 1934. Attacking the Democratic Administration and its "Wall Street Twin," the Republican Party, he calls for a revolutionary workers' government to distribute surplus food and clothing and reorganize industry for socialist production.

W207 . . . . The Lessons of the Toledo Strike, "Communist," 13 (July 1934), 639-54.
An analysis of the Auto-Lite strike in Toledo, contrasting the united front against the workers—arbitration, sell-out, the red scare, armed force, injunctions, Roosevelt, Green, and the Musteites—with the communist policies—mass picketing, rejection of arbitration, and a general strike.

W208 . . . . Akron: A New Chapter in American Labor History, "Communist," 15 (May 1936), 411-26.
The Goodyear rubber workers' strike is seen as a partial victory for industrial unionism. The leadership of the United Rubber Workers, though progressive, has too much faith in Roosevelt. While CIO organizers should generally be supported, the industrial union structure should be given a class struggle content.

W209 . . . . Strengthening the Trade Union Backbone of the Farmer-Labor Party Movement in Ohio, "Communist," 15 (Aug. 1936), 784-93.
A report to the Party's ninth convention from the Cleveland district, one of the Party's four major areas of concentration. The report deals with progress in forming a farmer-labor party, problems in trade union work, and Party membership and personnel.

W210 . . . . Party Mobilization in Ohio, "Communist," 16 (March 1937), 250-57.
A review of union successes in Ohio and of legislative proposals by progressive trade union bodies. The Party and its members are playing an important role in strikes and other mass activities.

W211 . . . . The Rubber Workers Show the Way, "Communist," 16 (Dec. 1937), 1127-34.
The second convention of the United Rubber Workers, held September 12-20 at Akron, is hailed for its democracy and

unity. The program and resolutions of the convention are outlined.

W212 WILLIAMSON, John. The Ohio Relief Crisis, "Communist," 19 (Jan. 1940), 67-72.
An account of the plight of Ohio workers under the Republican Administration of Governor John W. Bricker. Labor organizations are urged to resist wage and relief cuts and fight against attacks on labor by state and city governments. These immediate goals should be connected with the central objective of keeping America out of the imperialist war.

W213 .... Shifting Political Alignments in Ohio, "Communist," 19 (April 1940), 336-43.
The economic situation in Ohio under a predominantly bourgeois administration is called deplorable. The work of the CP in forwarding a progressive movement there is reviewed.

W214 .... The People vs. the 77th Congress, "Communist," 20 (Feb. 1941), 120-31.
A Hitler-Stalin pact period attack on the war program of the 77th Congress as contrary to the wishes of the American people. It will lead to a lower worker standard of living and an abridgment of democratic rights. The communists hope to arouse the people to oppose the government's war policy.

W215 .... Strengthen the War Effort by Building the Party, "Communist," 21 (May 1942), 324-35.
To make the utmost contribution to the war effort, the Party must strengthen itself by recruiting more members, increasing circulation of its newspaper, participating in common war tasks like Civilian Defense, and improving its organization. The Party resists the call of the reactionaries that the Party be liquidated in the interests of national unity.

W216 .... Strengthening Communist Collaboration in National Unity, "Communist," 21 (Sept. 1942), 692-707.
In order to make even greater contributions to the war effort, the Party must be strengthened. It must engage in independent political activity to fulfill its leadership role. It also must lead mass organizations, expose the lies of the Red-baiters, and attract more recruits by increasing membership participation in branch activity.

W217 .... The Role and Problems of a People's Cadre of Win-the-War Leaders, "Communist," 21 (Oct. 1942), 826-34.
A proposal for the formation of "people's cadres"— individuals trained to rally workers in war activities around objectives held indispensable by the Party to a victorious people's war.

W218 .... Prepare the Party for a Nationwide Party Building and Press Campaign, "Communist," 22 (Jan. 1943), 30-37.
A speech at the Party's national conference, outlining the importance of strong, informed branch leadership and increased circulation of printed material. Requirements for party membership are liberalized and all members are encouraged to participate actively in civic and job-oriented activities.

W219 .... Lessons of the Party Building Campaign and the Next Tasks, "Communist," 22 (June 1943), 539-51.
The entire Party participated in a three-month recruiting campaign that brought in 15,000 new members. The Party's success was largely due to its good work in struggling for the war effort and workers' rights. Too few coal miners and women shop workers were recruited, however. Changes in Party branch meetings are suggested to better integrate the new members.

W220 .... Gearing Organizational Forms and Methods to the War Effort, "Communist," 22 (July 1943), 624-32.
A report to a plenary meeting of the Party's national committee, June 11-13, proposing that the Party become more like other American parties. The Party's industrial sections are to be abolished to encourage communists to work as trade unionists rather than as factions in the trade unions, and large community branches are to be organized. The democratic nature of the Party will be maintained.

W221 .... The Organizational and Educational Tasks of Our Party, "Communist," 22 (Oct. 1943), 922-33.
Decisions of the national committee's June meeting to improve the Party's functioning in the light of liquidation of the Comintern and the successful recruiting drive. Changes look to deeper inner-Party democracy, liquidation of industrial units and transfer of their members to community branches, indoctrination of new members, greater propaganda efforts, and further recruitment and registration of new members.

W222 .... Urgent Questions of Party Growth and Organization, "Communist," 23 (Jan. 1944), 63-71.
The Party's new recruiting campaign is to provide people to carry out the Party's tasks of strengthening the United Nations coalition and aiding the war effort. The community branches are to be the main organizational units in the recruiting drive.

W223 .... New Problems of Communist Organization, "Communist," 23 (Feb. 1944), 131-39.
The change in its name and organization does not alter the communists' task of using Marxist theory to lead and enlighten the workers. The new name of "association" rather than "party" enables the communists more easily to approach and influence the workers and the public.

W224 .... Perspectives on the Functioning of the Communist Political Association, "Communist," 23 (June 1944), 521-32.
The reorganization of the communist movement has helped the recruiting drive to almost reach its goal. The drive has brought large numbers of Negroes and industrial workers into the movement. The Communist Political Association is a nonpartisan association that enlightens people with Marxist theory and organizes them politically to work for communist objectives.

W225 .... The Role of the Club in the Communist Political Association, "Communist," 23 (July 1944), 608-13.
The task of the members of a club, the basic organizational unit of the Communist Political Association, is to work as individuals with noncommunists to achieve progressive goals. The club's function is to indoctrinate the members in Marxist theory in order that they can fulfill their task.

W226 .... Problems of Club Leadership and Democracy in the C.P.A., "Communist," 23 (Nov. 1944), 1018-26.
A discussion of the need for building the Communist Political Association, with suggestions of ways to accomplish this. Democratic practices within the organization must be extended.

W227 .... The CPA—Our Most Indispensable Weapon, "Political Affairs," 24 (Jan. 1945), 43-55.

485

While the Communist Political Association has increased its influence in mass organizations, it has become less cohesive, with looser relations between leaders and members. CPA members in mass organizations must no longer conceal their identity, and the organization must develop independent activities.

W228 WILLIAMSON, John. A Program for Developing Communist Cadres, "Political Affairs," 24 (April 1945), 358-67.
A program to train functionaries for the Communist Political Association. A systematic training program must be provided for leadership in the CPA, the trade unions, and national groups. Communist leaders must have perspective and principle, understand the use of flexible tactics, show political and personal courage, and be practical in achieving results.

W229 .... The Reconstitution of the Communist Party, "Political Affairs," 24 (Sept. 1945), 800-15.
A report to the special convention of the Communist Political Association, July 26-28, 1945, which reconstituted the Communist Party. The Party is to resume its vanguard role as leader of the working class. All members must be active in Party work, democratic centralism within the Party will be restored, and the shop clubs reestablished.

W230 .... New Organizational Problems of the Communist Party, "Political Affairs," 24 (Dec. 1945), 1109-27.
A report to a meeting of the Party's national committee, November 17, 1945, asserting that progress in revitalizing the membership since reconstitution of the Party has been uneven and insufficient. Party clubs must assume a more creative role in mass activities. The Party must free workers of bourgeois influences, train its cadres more adequately, and concentrate recruitment among industrial workers, returning veterans, and youths.

W231 .... For a Mass Marxist Party of the Working Class! "Political Affairs," 25 (March 1946), 224-39.
A report to the February 12-15 plenary meeting of the Party's national committee, describing Party activity in the present wage-strike movement and emphasizing the need to play a vanguard role, build a mass party, root the Party in vital industries and areas, and recruit Negroes, veterans, and youth.

W232 .... Improve and Build Our Communist Press— The Next Step in Party Building, "Political Affairs," 25 (Sept. 1946), 810-26.
A report delivered July 18, 1946, at the plenary meeting of the Party's national committee, discussing the successes and failures of the Party's recruiting efforts. It suggests that the "Daily Worker" be used to integrate the Party's new members and clubs. To better fulfill this role, the "Worker's" circulation must be increased.

W233 .... Problems and Tasks before Labor Today, "Political Affairs," 25 (Nov. 1946), 976-87.
Monopoly capital is engaged in a planned attack to lessen trade union effectiveness. Labor must win new wage increases without further price rises, organize the unorganized, establish AFL-CIO joint action, and defeat Red-baiting. Unity in the CIO must be established under Philip Murray's leadership.

W234 .... The Situation in the Trade Unions, "Political Affairs," 26 (Jan. 1947), 20-36.
John L. Lewis is criticized for calling off the coal miners' strike, and the need for united action by all labor is emphasized. Militancy of rank-and-file workers in the AFL, when given leadership, is applauded. The place of Negro workers in the AFL is assessed. (Based in part on a report to the December 3-5 meeting of the Party's national committee.)

W235 .... Organic Unity: Next Point on Labor's Agenda, "Political Affairs," 26 (April 1947), 295-301.
Today's urgent need is for joint action by the AFL and CIO to preserve the trade union movement, as urged by the CIO, while realizing that joint action is the path to organic unity, as proposed by the AFL. The beneficial effects of organic unity far outweigh possible dangers. A basis for organic unity is proposed.

W236 .... The Recent Wage Settlements and Labor's Course, "Political Affairs," 26 (June 1947), 483-92.
Recent wage increases in the electrical, steel, and auto industries have been won without strikes because of union strength, the mood of the workers, and bourgeoisie fears that strikes might be transformed into political struggles. Labor must now grapple with major policy questions such as labor unity, independent political action for 1948, and labor-farmer unity.

W237 .... The Trade Unions and the Negro Workers, "Political Affairs," 26 (Nov. 1947), 1007-17.
The unity of the labor movement and the Negro people's movement is jeopardized by inadequate union efforts to retain Negro wartime gains in industry, too little Negro union leadership, and too little union effort for equal rights in other areas. Discontent among Negro trade unionists can be exploited by employers and certain forces among the Negroes. (Based on a report to a Party conference on Negro problems, Sept. 19-20, 1947.)

W238 .... The A.F. of L. and C.I.O. Conventions, "Political Affairs," 26 (Dec. 1947), 1077-89.
While the conventions of the two labor federations showed some similar features, the CIO, despite its confusion on foreign policy, is clearly the most progressive sector of organized labor. Left and progressive forces must seek to unite their unions and to establish joint CIO-AFL action against the growing attacks of reaction.

W239 .... Trade Union Problems and the Third-Party Movement, "Political Affairs," 27 (March 1948), 224-37.
Despite reactionary trade union leadership, millions of unionists can be won to progressive political action in 1948. Left-progressive unions in the CIO are propeace, anti-Marshall Plan, and anti-Truman. Trade union unity can be advanced on the basis of the Wallace candidacy and the struggle against the Taft-Hartley Act. (A report to a meeting of the Party's national committee, February 3-5, 1948.)

W240 .... The Imperative Need for United Labor Action, "Political Affairs," 27 (June 1948), 514-28.
The big trusts, encouraged by the Taft-Hartley Act, have launched a new offensive against the entire labor movement. The unions must adopt a fighting policy of wage gains, and combine their struggles on the economic and political fronts regardless of political differences. The communists are ready to join with all others in a united struggle.

W241 .... Only Militant, United Action Can Defeat the Drive against the Unions! "Political Affairs," 27 (Sept. 1948), 857-79.
A report to the Party's fourteenth national convention,

asserting that American monopolists, bent on world domination, are in an unprecedented attack on the working class and trade unions. Workers need a fighting policy, union involvement in the Progressive Party, maximum unity of labor, and higher levels of class consciousness.

W242 WILLIAMSON, John. Two Conventions of Labor: The Situation in the Trade Union Movement, "Political Affairs," 28 (Jan. 1949), 23-44. (Reprinted in pamphlet form.)
An examination of the policies and decisions of the 1948 CIO and AFL conventions, both under right-wing leadership. For the first time the left-progressive groups at a CIO convention fought for its program on fundamental issues. The central task now is to win the rank and file to progressive policies, that will defend their economic and political interests.

W243 .... Lessons of Recent Strikes and United Labor Action, "Political Affairs," 29 (May 1950), 83-100.
A report to the plenum of the national committee, CPUSA, March 23-25, 1950, analyzing strikes in the auto, steel, and mining industries in 1949-50, with particular attention to the communist role in the mining strikes. Left forces in the trade unions must be united ideologically with maximum unity of action.

W244 .... For a United-Front Policy among the Jewish People—Sharpen the Struggle against Bourgeois Nationalism, "Political Affairs," 29 (July 1950), 55-70.
A critical analysis of the Party's work among Jewish people, with suggestions for improving the "Morning Freiheit" and "Jewish Life," and for increasing unity between the Negro and Jewish minorities. (A report on behalf of the national committee of the Party, May 3, 1950, to a conference of comrades working among the Jewish people.)

W245 .... Trade-Union Tasks in the Struggle for Peace, Jobs, and Negro Rights, "Political Affairs," 29 (Nov. 1950), 37-59.
The Party's goals in the trade unions are to fight for higher wages, opposing all proposed wage freezes; to support the Labor Conference for Peace; to achieve equal rights for Negroes in industry; and to emphasize work in basic industries and in conservative-led trade unions. (A report to the plenary session of the Party's national committee, September 19-20, 1950.)

W246 .... The Main Direction of the Party's Trade-Union Work, "Political Affairs," 30 (Feb. 1951), 54-73.
The labor director of the Party urges united front action on the shop and local union level to resist a wage freeze, longer hours, higher taxation, and denial of the right to strike. Criticizing progressive union leaders for defensive tactics, he calls for a return to militancy and organization of rank-and-file movements within reformist-led unions. (Part of a special issue of "Political Affairs" devoted to reports and speeches at the Party's fifteenth national convention.)

W247 .... An American Labor Leader without Peer, "Political Affairs," 30 (March 1951), 22-35.
A tribute to William Z. Foster, national chairman of the Party, on his 70th birthday. Emphasis is placed on Foster's work as trade union organizer and as communist leader and theoretician.

W248 ..., and STEIN, Sid. The Defense of Labor's Living Standards and the Fight for Peace, "Political Affairs," 30 (May 1951), 19-33.

A May Day declaration clarifying the CP position on labor by the heads of its trade union department. Among the goals are a negotiated peace in Korea, a "big five" peace pact, opposition to fascist reaction, defense of workers against a war economy and inflation, united labor action with Negroes and farmers, and international working class solidarity.

W249 WILLNER, S. Building the Revolutionary Trade Union Movement, "Communist," 10 (Dec. 1931), 995-1005.
The TUUL, in spite of weaknesses, is making serious efforts to penetrate the basic industries. It must build its organization on a factory basis. The Party must build the union factory branches, while winning the best workers for the Party and organizing them as a shop nucleus. The members of the Party shop nucleus then work within the union factory branch as a fraction.

W250 .... Some Lessons of the Last Miners' Strike, "Communist," 11 (Jan. 1932), 27-45.
A critical analysis of the role of the National Miners Union in the recent wave of strikes in the mining fields. Despite weaknesses, the NMU-led strikes prevented wage cuts, and the Party recruited many new members. The Party underestimated the miners' readiness to struggle, and a "worship for spontaneity" prevented the development of Party leadership at crucial times. (Also published in "Communist International," Feb. 1, 1932.)

W251 .... Organizational Problems in Our Unemployment Work, "Communist," 11 (March 1932), 215-29.
A discussion of the united front policy of the movement of the unemployed and part-time workers, and of the relationship between the revolutionary unions and the unemployed committees. The revolutionary movement of the unemployed is dangerously isolated from the working masses. Despite mass participation in hunger marches, the revolutionary trade unions have failed to recruit.

W252 WILLOUGHBY, Charles A. Espionage and the American Communist Party, "American Mercury," 88 (Jan. 1959), 117-23.
A retired major general, MacArthur's Chief of Intelligence in the Pacific (1941-51), links the CPUSA to Russian espionage agents through personal relations and the Institute of Pacific Relations.

W253 WILSON, Edmund. Foster and Fish, "New Republic," 65 (Dec. 24, 1930), 158-62.
An account, very favorable to William Z. Foster, of his appearance before the House Committee investigating communist activities, headed by Hamilton Fish. Members of the committee revealed almost complete ignorance of the Party and its methods of operation. Israel Amter of the Party and Roger Baldwin of the ACLU also testified.

W254 .... Communists and Cops, "New Republic," 65 (Feb. 11, 1931), 344-47.
An account of a communist "Hunger March," staged in New York City, January 20, 1931. The communists, many of them Jews and some Negroes, called for work or wages and presented a long list of demands at City Hall. Their demonstration was finally broken up by the police.

W255 .... Freight Car Case, "New Republic," 68 (Aug. 26, 1931), 38-43.
An account of the factual background and trial procedure of the Scottsboro case, presented in a manner sympathetic to the International Labor Defense. The author tells how the communists and the ILD entered the case, and how a split developed between the ILD and the NAACP.

W256 WILSON, Edmund. "The American Jitters: A Year of the Slump." New York: Scribner, 1932. 313 pp.
An account of events in 1932 by a prominent literary figure who was sympathetic to the communists at that time. Chapter 3 describes Foster and Amter before the Fish Committee, chapter 7 reports on a communist-led parade of unemployed to New York City Hall, and chapter 26 deals with the Lawrence, Mass., strike of 1932, in which communists played an important part. Chapter 23, "The Case of the Author," tells of his favorable view of Marxism, and of his emotional, but not organizational, attachment to the communists.

W257 .... Literary Class War, "New Republic," 70 (May 4, 1932), 319-23; (May 11), 347-49.
A discussion of Michael Gold's assault on Thornton Wilder's "bourgeois" writings. Wilson defends Wilder, asserting that a first-rate book by an agonizing bourgeois may have more human value and more revolutionary power than second-rate Marxists who attack it. In the second article, Wilson deals with the relationship between art and propaganda, arguing that propaganda may be great literature if the writer's ability is great enough.

W258 .... Detroit Paradoxes, "New Republic," 75 (July 12, 1933), 230-33.
A picture of Detroit as a rootless and planless community, left with nothing by the deflation of the motor industry boom. Diego Rivera, though expelled from the Communist Party of Mexico, painted murals of Detroit industries that alarmed and antagonized the clergy and the papers. The Reynolds family, 100 per cent American communists, have independence and influence.

W259 .... Art, the Proletariat and Marx, "New Republic," 76 (Aug. 23, 1933), 41-45.
An assertion that most Marxists and Marxist critics do not understand the Marxian stand on art. In Russia, Lenin and Trotsky intervened for bourgeois writers and artists in order to extend the benefits of literature to the masses. The chances of building a "proletarian" culture in a socialist America without the aid of bourgeois artists are even less than in Russia.

W260 .... Complaints: I. The Literary Left, "New Republic," 89 (Jan. 20, 1937), 345-48.
An assertion that the critical literature of the far left has been dominated by the quarrels of Russian factional politics. To introduce a "party line" in literature is alien to both the English and the American literary tradition; the resulting literature will neither save civilization nor preserve aesthetic standards. The writer must defend the highest standards of his craft, even in times of social crisis.

W261 .... Marxism and Literature, "Atlantic Monthly," 160 (Dec. 1937), 741-50.
A review of the writings of Marx, Lenin, and Trotsky on literature and revolution. Only since Stalin have the communists sought to use literature to manipulate the population. Those who seek to apply Marxist principles in literary criticism attempt to measure works of literature by tests with no validity in that field.

W262 .... "Classics and Commercials: A Literary Chronicle of the 40's." New York: Farrar, Straus, 1950. 534 pp. Ind.
A selection of essays originally written in the 1940's, including "Max Eastman in 1941" (pp. 57-69), analyzing Eastman's literary and political writings. Eastman's books on the Russian Revolution are called the most valuable commentaries in English on the subject.

W263 .... "The Shores of Light: A Literary Chronicle of the Twenties and Thirties." New York: Farrar, Straus and Young, 1952. 814 pp.
A collection of essays and reviews, all of which have appeared earlier. Included are a number of pieces on literature and the economic-social-political area in which the communists played a part, particularly "Dos Passos and The Social Revolution" (pp. 429-35), and "The Economic Interpretation of Wilder" (pp. 500-3).

W264 .... "The American Earthquake: A Documentary of the Twenties and Thirties." Garden City, N.Y.: Doubleday, 1958. 576 pp.
A collection of Wilson's nonliterary writings between 1923 and 1934. Several of the pieces included in the section on "The Earthquake: October 1930-October 1931," deal with aspects of the communist movement in the U.S. Among these are "Foster and Fish" (pp. 179-95), "Communists and Cops" (pp. 206-13), and "The Scottsboro Freight-Car Case" (pp. 334-47).

W265 WILSON, H. H. Crisis of Democracy, "Nation," 177 (Nov. 21, 1953), 417-20.
Criticism of Attorney General Herbert Brownell for asserting that the late Harry Dexter White was a Russian spy and for accusing former President Truman of knowingly tolerating spies and traitors in the government. Behind this effort of Republican officials to discredit the Democratic Party lies the power of the FBI as a shadow government.

W266 WILSON, J. R. A National Budget for Full Employment, "Political Affairs," 24 (April 1945), 348-57.
The President's budget message outlined a budget in accord with America's commitment to the International Monetary Fund and the Export-Import Bank. The budget also implements the Full Employment Act of 1945, by undertaking measures to boost consumer purchasing power and provide public works.

W267 WILSON, Lawrence. California's Red Trial, "Christian Century," 52 (March 13, 1935), 330-32.
The trial of 15 alleged communists for violation of California's criminal syndicalism act was accompanied by vigilantism on the part of the state and the people, and by factional bickering between the Stalinists and the Trotskyists among the defendants. The author criticizes the state of California for giving the communists a lot of free publicity.

W268 .... California Convicts Itself, "Christian Century," 52 (April 17, 1935), 506-8.
A criticism of the prosecution's methods in securing the conviction of eight alleged communists under California's criminal syndicalism law in Sacramento, April 1935. The central figure in the prosecution was a professional labor spy who joined the Party and functioned as an agent provocateur. The newspapers were unfair in their reporting on the trial.

W269 WILSON, Raymond J., Jr. "Communism: A Catholic Survey." Cincinnati: Catholic Students' Mission Crusade, 1949. 121 pp. Bibliog.
A source book with discussion club outlines, covering the meaning of communism, reasons for Catholic opposition, and a program of action for students. Chapters 7 and 8, on communist propaganda (pp. 71-92) deal with the Party here, its control by the USSR, the Party line, propaganda media used by the communists (newspapers, magazines, theater, movies, radio, publishing houses, and lecture bureaus), the united front tactic, front groups, and infiltration in labor unions.

W270 WILSON, Walter. Atlanta's C o m m u n i s t s, "Nation," 130 (June 25, 1930), 730-31.
An account of the indictment of six communist agitators in Atlanta as a result of their circulation of communist literature. The ancient insurrection law under which they are to be tried is discussed.

W271 .... "Forced Labor in the United States." New York: International Publishers for the Labor Research Association, 1933. 192 pp. Ind.
A discussion of the prevalence of convict labor, peonage, and chattel slavery in the U.S. and in its colonies and semi-colonies. Charging that wage labor under capitalism differs from forced labor not in content but only in form, the author asserts that the Soviet Union is the only free labor country in the world. Because of this the international capitalists, including those of the U.S., perpetrate the lie about forced labor in the USSR.

W272 .... Georgia Suppresses Insurrection, "Nation," 139 (Aug. 1, 1934), 127-28.
A discussion of the use of a Georgia insurrection statute as a criminal syndicalist law against communists and other labor organizers. The author calls for civil liberties action in defense of Angelo Herndon, convicted under the law, and the "Atlanta six" awaiting prosecution.

W273 .... "The American Legion and Civil Liberty." New York: American League Against War and Fascism, 1936. 32 pp.
An exposé of the "unfortunate" record of American Legion officials and posts in the area of civil liberties. Asserting that the Legion, in the main, has reflected the interests of Big Business, the author gives some typical cases of violations of civil rights. He calls for pressure by rank-and-file legionnaires on their officers.

W274 WINDMULLER, John P. "American Labor and the International Labor Movement, 1940 to 1953." Ithaca, N.Y.: New York State School of Industrial and Labor Relations, Cornell University, 1954. 243 pp.
An analysis of American labor's foreign affairs since 1940. The author deals with the origins of the WFTU, AFL policies and activities with regard to it, the problems of the CIO with the WFTU leading to the final break, and the formation and activities of the ICFTU. Attention is paid to the conflict within the CIO between the communist-dominated unions and the others with regard to the USSR and its trade unions.

W275 WINROD, Gerald B. "Communism and the Roosevelt Brain Trust." Wichita, Kansas: Defender Publishers, 1933. 26 pp.
An assertion that Roosevelt's New Deal, led by the Brain Trust, has plunged us into a socialistic experiment. Leaders of the Brain Trust, many of whom are Jewish, are described. Many of their plans resemble recent experiments in Russia; they are turning the country first "pink," then "red."

W276 .... "Communism in Prophecy, History and America." Wichita, Kansas: Defender Publishers, 1946. 86 pp.
An anticommunist, anti-Semitic, anti-New Deal tract viewing modern communism as stemming from Satanic forces of the remote past. The ideas for Franklin Roosevelt's New Deal are traced to a book, "Philip Dru: Administrator," published in 1912, which charted the course of the revolutionary movement in the U.S.

W277 WINSTON, Henry. "Life Begins with Freedom." New York: New Age, 1937. 37 pp.
An appeal by a leading Negro communist to Negroes to join the Young Communist League in order to help liberate the Negro people. The YCL is part of the people's front; it has no Jim Crow; and it provides facilities for recreation, along with opportunities to meet people and attend classes in socialism.

W278 .... "Character Building and Education in the Spirit of Socialism." New York: New Age, 1939. 31 pp.
A report to the ninth national convention of the Young Communist League in 1939, emphasizing the social and cultural as well as the political role of the YCL.

W279 .... The Young Communist League Prepares for Growth, "Communist," 18 (April 1939), 324-33.
The YCL has been carrying out the policy set forth at its eighth convention. Its branches have become broad social clubs which noncommunist youths can join. It should try to bring Negroes into its branches and build branches among college and farm youths. Its leaders must be good Marxists who will try to convert the youths to communism.

W280 .... Negro and White Unity against War, "Clarity," 1 (April-May 1940), 22-35.
Writing in the theoretical organ of the Young Communist League during the period of the Nazi-Soviet pact, a leading Negro communist asserts that the war in Europe is one between rival imperialist powers. He opposes U.S. aid to either side, defends the Soviet attack on Finland, and stresses Negro opposition to the war and the economic hardships suffered by Negroes during the drive toward war.

W281 .... "Old Jim Crow Has Got to Go!" New York: New Age, 1941. 15 pp.
The national administrative secretary of the Young Communist League, prior to the Nazi attack upon the USSR, asserts that the YCL program offers the only solution to Negro discrimination in industry and in the army, and urges opposition to the "imperialist" war.

W282 .... Organizational Problems of the Y.C.L., "Clarity," 2 (Spring 1941), 39-49.
A discussion in the theoretical organ of the Young Communist League of organizational problems that it faces. The League must give more attention to the problem of the individual, defend the economic needs of youth, concentrate in the basic industries, build youth unity, improve the League's ideological and political work, and recruit systematically.

W283 .... Party Tasks among the Negro People, "Political Affairs," 25 (April 1946), 349-61.
A report to the plenary meeting of the Party's national committee, February 12-15, 1946, praising Negro militancy and Negro-white solidarity in the current strike struggles. Trade union and Party tasks to aid Negroes are outlined. Progressive NAACP activities must be strengthened, and a fighting National Negro Congress built.

W284 .... Toward a Party of 100,000, "Political Affairs," 26 (Jan. 1947), 64-79.
The full text of a report on problems of Party organization and activities to the December 3-5 meeting of the national committee. Included in the discussion are the electoral showing, the Red-baiting attack, Party growth and membership goals, the policy of concentrating in key industries, shop and industrial clubs, the community club, the press, and the Party registration.

W285 .... "Not against But with the Stream," "Political Affairs," 26 (Aug. 1947), 730-38.

Excerpts from the organization report to a meeting of the Party's national committee, June 27-30, 1947, asserting that attacks on the Party show the desperation and weakness of the opponents. While maintaining its vanguard role, the Party is moving along with the mass of Americans in the fight against the trusts; within the unity of the masses, the Party is the most advanced sector.

W286 WINSTON, Henry. Some Aspects of Party Work, "Political Affairs," 27 (March 1948), 238-50.
A report to the February 3-5 meeting of the Party's national committee. The reactionary drives of Truman, the Republican and Democratic Parties, and others are strengthening the progressive, third party forces. In order to fulfill its vanguard role in the progressive movement, the Party must increase its recruiting and propaganda efforts.

W287 .... Against the Militarization of Our Youth, "Political Affairs," 27 (May 1948), 412-18.
A statement on behalf of the Communist Party, submitted on April 2, 1948, to the Senate Armed Services Committee. It declares the Party's opposition to universal military training and a peace-time draft.

W288 .... For a Fighting Party Rooted among the Industrial Workers! "Political Affairs," 27 (Sept. 1948), 834-56.
A report to the Party's fourteenth national convention, held August 2-6, 1948, on the Party's organizational and ideological tasks. The report reviews the Party's growth and organization, its work among Negroes and in the basic industries, its failure to increase its trade union membership, and the dangers it faces from left sectarianism and right opportunism. (Part of this report was republished in "Political Affairs," Aug. 1952, under the title, "The Meaning of Industrial Concentration.")

W289 .... Building the Party—Key to Building the United Front of Struggle, "Political Affairs," 29 (May 1950), 59-82.
A report to the plenum of the national committee, CPUSA, March 23-25, 1950, asserting that a united front struggle can defeat the fascist Mundt-Ferguson bill. Party registration figures are given, by states, industries, and race. The Party must emphasize building its clubs, especially in the shops and working-class communities; its policy of industrial concentration; and the training of new cadres.

W290 .... Strengthen the Party among the Basic Industrial Workers, "Political Affairs," 29 (Nov. 1950), 21-36.
A report to the plenary session of the national committee, CPUSA, September 19-20, 1950. Labor must be convinced that the McCarran Act and local anticommunist laws are directed against the entire working class. The Party must concentrate in the basic industries, winning the workers for united action on concrete issues in the shops.

W291 .... "What It Means to Be a Communist." New York: New Century, 1951. 15 pp.
A section of the report of the national organization secretary of the Party to its fifteenth national convention, dealing with the training of communist cadres. Among the topics discussed are the communist concepts of personal integrity, loyalty to and confidence in the working class, and relations between members and leaders.

W292 .... Gear the Party for Its Great Tasks, "Political Affairs," 30 (Feb. 1951), 21-53.
The fifteenth national convention is urged by the Party's organization secretary to carry out the program for concentration in the basic industries, to build the shop and community clubs, and to develop a cadre training program. Renegades and bureaucrats are attacked, and communists are defended from charges of conspiracy and of being foreign agents.

W293 WINTER, Carl. Background of the Auto Strike, "Political Affairs," 24 (Dec. 1945), 1069-78.
An analysis of factors involved in labor's demands in the Michigan auto industry. The auto workers' demand for a wage raise of 30 per cent is a fight to preserve take-home pay and maintain purchasing power. Curtailment of the work week necessitates a wage raise. Management is accused of a monopolistic postwar program.

W294 .... The Face of a Social-Democrat—Walter P. Reuther, "Political Affairs," 25 (May 1946), 407-22.
Reuther's campaign for the presidency of the United Automobile Workers was supported by all the agencies of capitalist propaganda. Through his election the social democrats have entered top CIO circles. Reuther represents the core of opportunism, makes "socialist" pretensions, seeks to save capitalism, fears the class struggle, shows concern for profits, fosters the speed-up, and curbs labor militancy.

W295 .... "19 Questions and Answers about Communist Party Suppressed by the Detroit News." Detroit: Michigan State Committee, CPUSA, 1947. 16 pp.
The complete text of answers by the Michigan state chairman of the Party to questions submitted by the Detroit "News," which the "News" has not published. Among the topics covered are the objectives of the Party, its relation to the Comintern, dictatorship, private property, war with the Soviet Union, and the Party's program for Michigan.

W296 WINTER, Frederick, and FULLER, Edmund. Jim Crow: Editor and Publisher, "New Masses," 63 (April 1, 1947), 9-12.
An analysis of racial attitudes as shown in magazines, comic books, and serious books. Included is a study by a Columbia University group of attitudes toward non-Nordic, non-Aryan peoples as shown in fiction in widely-read magazines, and a survey of the portrayal of Negroes in the "Reader's Digest." The authors conclude that racist mythology dominates our books and magazines.

W297 WINTERS, Paul. Case Study in Stalinism: Morris Muster and the UFW, "Call," 13 (July 29, 1946), 3.
A socialist publication, reviewing the communist take-over in the United Furniture Workers, largely blames the ousted president, Morris Muster, who first became an ally, and later a prisoner, of the communists. The way to fight the communists, as in the Upholsterers International Union, is to be more progressive, militant, and active than they are.

W298 WIRIN, A. L., and ROSENWEIN, Sam. The Smith Act Prosecutions, "Nation," 177 (Dec. 12, 1953), 485-90.
A summary of the status of the "second string" communist leaders convicted under the Smith Act. The authors, who have been defense attorneys in Smith Act cases, analyze the indictments and the pattern of the trials. The trials, in their view, confirm fears that enactment of the peacetime sedition law endangers the liberties of every American.

W299 ..., and .... "The Smith Act Score, "Nation," 180 (Feb. 26, 1955), 177-80.
Two attorneys active in civil liberties cases assert that all citizens have lost some of their rights under the Smith Act. They urge repeal of the act, the end of all prosecutions

under it, and pardon for those convicted. The repressive process has slackened as a result of growing protests.

W300 WIRT, Sherwood E. Can the Church Stand a Probe? "Christian Century," 70 (May 20, 1953), 604-5.
A clergyman discusses a proposal for a congressional investigation of the clergy. While the church can stand up under such a probe, the minister who calls for loyalty investigations in his clerical role is dealing with matters outside his purview as shepherd or prophet of God; the minister who does so as a citizen must be aware that charges of "communism" may conceal a theological attack on those of different biblical views.

W301 WISCONSIN CITIZENS' COMMITTEE ON McCARTHY's RECORD. "The McCarthy Record." Madison, Wis.: The Committee, 1952. 136 pp. Ind.
An unflattering review of McCarthy's record, concluding that he actually played into the hands of the communists. He failed to expose a single communist in the State Department and engaged in a smear campaign against the Administration. He produced confusion at home, unjustly discredited our representatives abroad, stirred up smears and hysteria, and threatened to paralyze American policy in a critical period.

W302 WISE, James Waterman. "Meet Henry Wallace." New York: Boni and Gaer, 1948. 91 pp.
A biography of Henry Wallace, written following the announcement of his candidacy for President on the Progressive Party ticket in 1948. The first five sections are biographical; the last two deal with creation of the new party and with its program. The author denies that Wallace is a communist or is under communist influence.

W303 WITTENBERG, Philip (ed.). "The Lamont Case: History of a Congressional Investigation." Introd. by Horace Kallen. New York: Horizon Press, 1957. 331 pp.
Documentary material in Corliss Lamont's contempt of Congress case for refusing to answer questions before the McCarthy committee on first amendment grounds. Cited by the Senate for contempt, Lamont was cleared by the U.S. District Court and the U.S. Court of Appeals. Lamont's attorney, who edits the volume, provides a running commentary, arguing that the American people are indebted to Lamont for his resistance to McCarthyism. In his introduction Kallen attributes Lamont's actions to libertarianism and sentiment for the weaker side, not to procommunist sympathy.

W304 WITTMER, Felix. Freedom's Case against Dean Acheson, "American Mercury," 74 (April 1952), 3-17.
An assertion that Acheson's record of disservice was evident both in his private law practice (in 1933 his firm represented the Soviet government) and as Secretary of State, when he supported such men as Philip Jessup, John Carter Vincent, and John Stewart Service, who precipitated our China debacle.

W305 .... Now Hear This! "American Legion Magazine," 54 (Feb. 1953), 18-19 ff.
An assertion that speakers for school and other programs are overwhelmingly procommunist or prosocialist, whereas conservatives are hard to get. The author, a former teacher who believes that freedom is possible only under free enterprise, urges formation of committees to watch speakers at school, church, and club meetings, and at public forums.

W306 .... "Conquest of the American Mind: Comments on Collectivism in Education." Boston: Meador, 1956. 352 pp.

A collection of articles and essays by a right-wing author who asserts that a pattern of collectivistic subversion has been established in American intellectual life, especially in literature and education. Most of the articles had previously appeared in "National Republic." Though the author is concerned with state control and state ownership rather than communism specifically, some of the chapters, such as "Communist Tactics in the Lecture Hall" (pp. 61-70), deal with the latter topic.

W307 WOFSY, Leon. Fighting for the Needs of the Young Workers, "Political Affairs," 28 (March 1949), 34-45.
In order to win young workers to the Young Communist League and the Young Progressives of America, the Party must fight for more than just the demands made for all workers. It must also fight for repeal of the draft, unemployment insurance for first-job seekers and laid-off young workers, a dollar minimum wage, public works and job-training programs, jobs for young Negroes, and equal pay for women. (Based on a report to the Party's national committee, Jan. 24, 1949.)

W308 .... Toward Unity of the Working Youth for Peace, Jobs and Democracy, "Political Affairs," 29 (May 1950), 155-67.
The Labor Youth League has been organized under communist leadership to strive for peace, oppose the Taft-Hartley Act, support strikers, and oppose discrimination against Negroes. It has been successful in some districts in getting jobs, relief, and unemployment insurance for unemployed youths. It is trying to recruit many more young workers.

W309 .... "Youth Fights for Its Future." New York: Labor Youth League, 1952. 40 pp.
The main report to the May 1952 national conference of the Labor Youth League by its national chairman, who asserts that youth has no future under capitalism, and that peace can be achieved only through the unity of youth. The LYL should participate in more united actions with groups not under progressive leadership. A big vote for Progressive Party candidates is urged.

W310 .... "Stop McCarthy Now!" New York: Labor Youth League, 1954. 30 pp.
The keynote report to the second national convention of the Labor Youth League, February 1954, by the national chairman, who sees McCarthyism as the main danger to American youth and to the LYL. McCarthyism can be defeated if youth unites against it and mobilizes to vote against it in the 1954 and 1956 elections.

W311 WOLF, Robert. What There Isn't and Why Not, "New Masses," 3 (Feb. 1928), 18-21.
While America has produced a good quantity of poetry in the last decade, it has not been proletarian or even revolutionary poetry. The writings of Joe Hill, Carl Sandburg, Mike Gold, Ralph Chaplin, Claude McKay, Langston Hughes, and others are analyzed.

W312 WOLFE, Bertram D. "How Class Collaboration Works." Chicago: Daily Worker Publishing Co., 1926. 32 pp.
An analysis of class collaboration by labor, under which a privileged section of labor shares in the exploitation of their fellow workers. This collaboration is encouraged by American industry, which gives part of its surplus profits to the labor aristocracy. The left wing of the labor movement, backed by every honest trade unionist, seeks to counteract this tendency to class collaboration.

W313 ...; LOVESTONE, Jay; and DUNNE, William F.

"Our Heritage from 1776: A Working Class View of the First American Revolution." New York: Workers School Library, n.d. [1926]. 23 pp.
A reprint of articles from the "Workers Monthly" and the "Daily Worker," as part of a communist campaign to present the American Revolution as a class revolution, and to show that the American working class has a native revolutionary tradition.

W314 WOLFE, Bertram D. Economics of Class Collaboration, "Workers Monthly," 5 (Jan. 1926), 117-20; (March), 228-31.
An analysis of techniques by which American industry "bribes" segments of the working class, cutting them off from the militant, class-conscious elements. Among the techniques used are permitting some workers to share in monopoly profits, paying high wages derived from surplus value extracted from others, rewarding strikebreakers, permitting direct exploitation by petty subcontractors, and making high payments in industries strategic to imperialism.

W315 . . . , and STACHEL, Jack. Lenin, the American Working class and Its Party, "Workers Monthly," 5 (Feb. 1926), 154-60.
An effort to show that Lenin's doctrines are valid for the U.S. Though objective conditions are ripe for the revolution Lenin predicted, much must be done to educate the backward American workers. The Party's fundamental task is to accelerate the class formation of the American working class. It must develop professional revolutionaries who give full time to the movement.

W316 . . . . Problems of Party Training, "Workers Monthly," 5 (June 1926), 374-77.
Practical problems of a program to educate rank-and-file communists to be leaders. Greater theoretical training of the Party's rank and file will bridge the gulf separating it from the leadership, while Party reorganization and training will transform the Party into one of leaders. Party training must be shifted from the central school to the shop nucleus.

W317 . . . . Whose Revolution Is It? "Workers Monthly," 5 (July 1926), 387-92.
On the 150th anniversary of the American Revolution the maturing American working class should begin to discover America and its revolutionary traditions. The task of mature communists must be to debunk the history of 1776, throw away its chauvinism and reaction, and use its revolutionary traditions, methods, and lessons.

W318 . . . . Towards Leninism, "Workers Monthly," 6 [5] (Jan. 1927), 675-80 ff.
An appraisal of the degree of progress toward Leninism made by the Party in the U.S. Advances have been made toward organization of a labor party, toward organizing a progressive bloc within the trade unions, and toward Party unification. Among the problems which have slowed the progress are the Party's lack of Americanization, its revisionist views, its Trotskyist view of farmers, and its illusions as to the stability of American capitalism.

W319 . . . . A Program for the Period of Prosperity, "Communist," 6 (July-Aug. 1927), 275-86.
A communist program for American labor in prosperity, calling for amalgamation of craft into industrial unions, organization of the unorganized, development of class consciousness and class struggles, and formation of a labor party to struggle for social legislation and against imperialism, war, and the political power of capital.

W320 . . . . Eastman Revises Marx—and Corrects Lenin, "Communist," 6 (Nov. 1927), 403-12.

An attack on Max Eastman's article, "Lenin Was an Engineer," in the November "New Masses." Wolfe disputes Eastman's interpretation of Marxism and his characterization of Leninism, including Lenin's view of professional revolutionaries. He accuses Eastman of snobbery and anti-working-class prejudice.

W321 . . . . "The Trotsky Opposition: Its Significance for American Workers." New York: Workers Library, 1928. 96 pp.
An attack on the opposition group led by Trotsky within the Communist Party of the Soviet Union, asserting that Trotsky and his followers have abandoned all the basic Leninist views on the question of the revolution. They attack the Party program, violate Party rules and Soviet law, and try to rally the non-Party population against the Party. Expulsion was long overdue. (Some of this material appeared in "Communist," Jan. and Feb. 1928.)

W322 . . . . Atheism and "Evolution," "Communist," 7 (March 1928), 160-68.
Criticism of "Evolution," a new magazine opposing laws that forbid the teaching of evolution. By refusing to take a stand in favor of atheism, the magazine is serving an antirevolutionary purpose. The fight against fundamentalism is really the fight for dialectical materialism and a scientific approach to the universe.

W323 . . . . Pacifism and War, "Communist," 7 (May 1928), 285-96.
The antiwar resolution adopted recently at the Havana meeting of the Pan-American Union is denounced as the product of American imperialism, which conceals its war preparations. Communists oppose imperialist "pacifism," as well as the "left pacifism" of social democrats. Opposed to imperialist wars, they support and lead revolutionary wars of the proletariat. (The concluding portion of the article, announced for the June issue, failed to appear.)

W324 . . . . The Right Danger in the Comintern, "Communist," 7 (Dec. 1928), 723-35.
American Trotskyism is a "right" danger in the present period, even though it was a "left" danger when it appeared in the Soviet Union and in Germany. Earlier the "left" danger lay in overestimating the strength of capitalism and calling for revolution in Europe as a prerequisite for socialism in the USSR. Now the "right" error lies in underestimating the danger of war and the degree of radicalization of the masses. (In Oct. 1928, the American Trotskyists, led by James P. Cannon, were expelled from the Party.)

W325 . . . . Results of Elections to Sixth American Party Congress, "International Press Correspondence," 9 (Feb. 15, 1929), 129-30.
A Lovestone supporter discusses the defeat of the opposition caucus led by Foster in elections to the coming convention of the Workers (Communist) Party. Reasons include the opposition's reservations about decisions of the Communist International, its refusal to drop the factional fight, the expulsion of the Cannon group for Trotskyism, and the defeat of Foster by Bittelman as the opposition's leader.

W326 . . . . Is the Sixth Congress Being Revised? "Revolutionary Age," 1 (Nov. 15, 1929), 3-4.
The Executive Committee of the Communist International has "revised" the decisions of the Sixth World Congress of the Communist International. Delegates of the Foster faction at the Sixth World Congress participated in a "corridor congress" that secretly opposed Congress decisions while publicly supporting them. Stalin's support gave Foster control of the CPUSA.

W327 WOLFE, Bertram D. "What is the Communist Opposition?" New York: Communist Party (Opposition), 1933. 52 pp. App.
A Lovestoneite outlines a Marxist program, neither Stalinist nor Trotskyite. The defeat of the German proletariat is the fruit of the "social-fascist" theory of the Communist International; and the dual union policy of the CP has split the trade union movement, in the U.S. as elsewhere.

W328 .... "Marx and America." New York: John Day, 1934. 32 pp.
A Lovestoneite reviews the writings of Marx and Engels on America, pointing out that their predictions have all been verified, though no Marxist party worthy of the name has yet developed. He suggests absorption of the writings of Marx and Engels and mastery of their method.

W329 .... In Memoriam: The Communist Party; Born 1919—Died 1937, "Workers Age," 6 (Sept. 29, 1937), 1 ff.
A sardonic critique by a Lovestoneite leader of the speech by Earl Browder to the 1937 convention of the Communist Party of Massachusetts. The "death" of the Party is ascribed to bourgeois democratic illusions and reformist hallucinations.

W330 .... The American War Party: Stalinists Follow Holy War Policy to Reaction, "Workers Age," 7 (Sept. 24, 1938), 2 ff.
A Lovestoneite assertion that all of Browder's domestic politics seek to involve the U.S. in war with any of the potential enemies of the USSR. American Stalinites may struggle against warmakers in Italy and Germany, but not against our own warmakers. The people's front seeks to weaken class lines in the event of war.

W331 .... "Strange Communists I Have Known." New York: Stein and Day, 1965. 222 pp.
Sketches of ten communists, five of whom the author knew personally and five of whom he knew only through historical research. Of the former group, three had been active in the communist movement in the U.S.: John Reed, the poet, reporter, and revolutionary leader, who was buried under the Kremlin wall; James Larkin, the Catholic Irish labor leader and nationalist who was a leader of the left wing of the Socialist Party here; and Samuel Putnam, translator, author, and lecturer, who followed the Party line for a decade.

W332 WOLFE, Ella G. Mexico and Nicaragua, "Workers Monthly," 5 (Feb. 1927), 723-25.
A blast at American imperialism in Mexico and Nicaragua. The objective of American intervention in Nicaragua, ostensibly to fight the influence of Mexican Bolshevism, is really Mexican oil. Our long-range objective is to swallow all of Central America, and then South America.

W333 .... Preparing for the Pan-American Conference, "Communist," 7 (Jan. 1928), 25-37.
An attack on the Pan-American Union, about to hold its sixth conference, as a weapon of American imperialism. Latin-American protest to American intervention in hemisphere affairs is growing. The communists must utilize the conference to expose the reactionary nature of the Pan-American Union to Latin-Americans.

W334 WOLFF, Milton. "Western Front Now!" New York: Veterans of the Abraham Lincoln Brigade, 1941. 14 pp.
The democracies of the world are urged, by an organization found to be Party dominated, to unite in an all-out attack on Hitler while the Soviet armies keep the bulk of his troops occupied in the East.

W335 WOLIVER, Irving. "Now We Are Six." [New York]: American Student Union, 1940. 25 pp.
A series of cartoons commemorating various events in ASU history: the defense of Spain, the attack on the student movement by President Robinson of CCNY, the Vassar College embargo on Japan and China, the protest against the Munich pact, the campaign for the Youth Act, etc.

W336 WOLL, Matthew. The Communists Dissolve, "American Photo Engraver," 36 (Feb. 1944), 107-9.
A leading AFL official attacks the recent dissolution of the Communist Party as "just another tactic." The Party, he asserts, was never one in the American sense, but always an international conspiracy.

W337 .... Warning to Hollywood, "American Photo Engraver," 38 (Sept. 1946), 895-97.
A call by an AFL leader for a "Legion of Political Decency" to drive the Reds out of Hollywood, which he says is the third largest communist center in the U.S.

W338 .... World Issues and the A.F. of L., "American Federationist," 55 (May 1948), 10-11 ff.
An outline of the AFL's program for fighting communism on an international scale, by a member of its Executive Council.

W339 .... The CIO Role in the WFTU, "New Leader," 31 (July 3, 1948), 8-9.
An account of the session of the Executive Board of the World Federation of Trade Unions in Rome, with criticism of James Carey of the CIO for failing to support the European Recovery Program. The conference is said to have constituted a great gain for the Kremlin. (Carey's reply appeared in the "New Leader" for July 24, 1948.)

W340 WOLTMAN, Frederick. Camouflaged Communist Press, "American Mercury," 57 (Nov. 1943), 578-87.
An examination of the lesser known communist papers in this country by a staff member of the New York "World-Telegram." Though these journals deny being communist, the truth can be found by a study of their swings each time Russia's foreign policy changes. "U.S. Week" and "Friday" have just died. Others that follow the Party line are "Science and Society," "The Protestant," and "In Fact," whose publisher, George Seldes, has long labored for communist causes.

W341 .... "The Shocking Story of the Amerasia Case." New York: Scripps-Howard Newspapers, 1950. 44 pp. App.
An exposé of the "Amerasia" affair by a newspaperman, who sees it as the key to America's postwar diplomatic debacle in Asia. He tells of the original arrests, the pro-communist orientation of the publication, its relationship to the pro-Soviet China group in the State Department, and the whitewashing of the case by the Justice Department and the Tydings Committee.

W342 ..., and LASKY, Victor. Mystery of the Amerasia Case, "American Mercury," 71 (Sept. 1950), 274-85.
A summary of the "Amerasia" case by two staff writers of the New York "World-Telegram and Sun." Although the FBI seized 1,700 confidential government documents in a raid on the "Amerasia" offices and arrested six people on espionage charges, those responsible were let off lightly. Despite a congressional investigation, the whole ugly story of "Amerasia" has yet to be told.

W343 .... Pravda, U.S.A., "Collier's," 126 (Oct. 21, 1950), 15-17 ff.

A reporter who specializes in exposing communist subversion shows how the "Daily Worker" takes its orders from Moscow and how editors must toe the Party line or be fired. The paper's policies, ownership, finances, circulation, and wage scale are treated, and its attitude toward minorities and its propagandist interpretation of music are discussed.

W344 WOOD, Charles G. "Reds and Lost Wages." New York: Harper, 1930. 280 pp.
A discussion of strikes in specific industries, such as textiles and shoes, in which the author had been involved as Commissioner of Conciliation for the Department of Labor. He asserts that communists lead workers to certain ruin through strikes that are expensive and certain to be lost, while they themselves collect money for which they never account. Communists cannot succeed with American workers because their program, based on unsound principles, is doomed to failure.

W345 WOOD, Charles W. Don't Fight with Sex: The Scientific Attitude for Proletarian Revolutionists, "New Masses," 2 (Feb. 1927), 7-9 ff.
An argument that the property or ownership attitude toward women is no longer workable, that love should be treated as a joyous human enterprise, not as a means of having and holding one woman or a flock of them. The revolutionist must try to find out what sex is, how it acts, and what can be done with it.

W346 WOOD, Junius B. Trained to Raise Hell in America, "Nation's Business," 35 (April 1947), 33-35 ff.
An account of the program of the International Lenin School in Moscow, from which 800 disloyal Americans, trained in communist philosophy and practical revolutionary activity, have graduated. A plan for seizing a city like Chicago, part of the training program, is described.

W347 WOOD, Mabel Travis. Teachers' Fifth Column, "Plain Talk," 1 (June 1947), 32-34.
An exposé of the procommunist teachers' union locals affiliated with the United Public Workers, CIO. The Teachers Union of New York, ousted from the American Federation of Teachers in 1941 for communist tactics, is the spearhead of the new organizing drive. Party line tactics of the leaders of the union are described.

W348 .... Our Stalinist Hotel Unions, "Plain Talk," 4 (April 1950), 17-20.
An assertion that communists and their stooges control Local 6 of the Hotel Employees, AFL, of New York City. Communist affiliations of the local's president and other officers are given. Although noncommunist himself, Hugo Ernst, president of the International, is said to have abetted the entrenchment of communists in the local.

W349 WOOD, Robert. "To Live and Die in Dixie." New York: Southern Workers Defense Committee, n.d. [1935?]. 31 pp.
An account of tyranny and oppression in the South, by the secretary of the Southern District of the International Labor Defense. Among the topics touched on are exploited city workers, wretched farm conditions, frame-up of Negroes, and the Georgia chain gang. Also discussed are illiteracy, violence against unions, police brutality, mob law, and vigilante terrorism.

W350 WOODBURY, Clarence. That Man Budenz, "American Legion Magazine," 49 (Nov. 1950), 18-19 ff.
An account of the career of Louis F. Budenz, managing editor of the "Daily Worker" for five years and a member of the Party's national committee for six, who is the government's most valuable witness against communism.

Now a professor at Fordham University, his information has helped in the cases of J. V. Peters, Alger Hiss, John Santo, Harold Christoffel, Judy Coplon, Harry Bridges, and the 11 leading communists tried for conspiracy.

W351 .... A Man Named Brewer, "American Legion Magazine," 61 (Dec. 1956), 14-15 ff.
An account of the fight, led by Roy M. Brewer, against the communists on the Hollywood labor front. A bitter jurisdictional fight between two rival unions was really an effort by the communists to win control of the motion picture industry. Brewer proved that he could be as rough as the communists were, defeating them on the picket line, in an NLRB election, and in the struggle to influence public opinion.

W352 WOODBURY, Sam. A Community Fights the Reds, "National Republic," 41 (Aug. 1953), 3-4 ff.
An account of the activities of the Shoshone County Anti-Communist Association in the lead-zinc mining district of northern Idaho. A counterattack against communist propaganda in that area followed a broadcast sponsored by a local of the Mine, Mill and Smelter Workers, praising Russia as a workers' paradise.

W353 WOODS, Steve. How to Capture an Island, "Plain Talk," 3 (July 1949), 1-8.
A report on the strike by Harry Bridges' ILWU which has paralyzed Hawaii. The ILWU, which has developed great power since 1943, has a top leadership of communists, who seek to capture this strategic island group. The community, hampered by inexperience, will need help soon.

W354 WORDEN, William L. U.C.L.A.'s Red Cell: Case History of College Communism, "Saturday Evening Post," 223 (Oct. 21, 1950), 42-43 ff.
A description of communist activities at UCLA and their impact on the college community and the reputation of the university. Factors favoring communist activity include commuting students, a public institution, an excitable school administration and local press, and discontented minorities.

W355 "WORKERS AGE," Exchange of Correspondence between the CPUSA and the CPO (Lovestoneites), on the Question of Unification, 4 (Jan. 19, 1935), 2-4.
The Lovestoneites sought unity when the CPUSA began to abandon the "third period" ultra-leftist line. The effort failed, both groups refusing to modify their political lines, and even disagreeing as to the conduct of negotiations.

W356 .... , Communist Party Draft Resolution Mile-Post of Opportunist Course, 5 (June 27, 1936), 1 ff.
Lovestoneite criticism of the draft resolution submitted by Earl Browder to the ninth convention of the CPUSA, one year following adoption of the popular front line by the Communist International. Most of the criticism is leveled at the resolution's positions on war and fascism, and the blurring of class lines in the popular front policy.

W357 "WORKERS COUNCIL," The Open Communist Party: The Task of the Hour, 1 (Oct. 15, 1921), 120-21.
A manifesto of the Workers Council of America, calling on the membership of the underground American communist movement to join in creating an open, above-ground communist organization. While the Palmer raids drove the Communist and the Communist Labor Parties underground, the idea of an American underground movement was part of the atmosphere of revolution and romanticism created by the Russian upheaval.

W358 "WORKERS COUNCIL," New Era Dawns for America's Working Class, 1 (Dec. 15, 1921), 152-53.
An article welcoming a convention call for creation of a legal arm of American communism, the Workers Party of America. The development of the Workers Council is reviewed. Its members split from the Socialist Party in 1921 because of its reformism, yet felt that the policies of the organized communist movement prevented building a mass movement.

W359 WORKERS CULTURAL FEDERATION. Art Is a Weapon! Program of the Workers Cultural Federation, "New Masses," 7 (Aug. 1931), 11-13.
A declaration that capitalist culture is decaying imperialist culture, in contrast to the cultural revolution in the USSR. In America the leftward ferment among the intellectuals may stimulate proletarian culture. With the creation of the Workers Cultural Federation of New York, we can expect a national federation, to be organized on the Kharkov Conference platform. (See Fred Ellis, and others, The Kharkov Conference of Revolutionary Writers, in the "New Masses," Feb. 1931.)

W360 WORKERS EX-SERVICEMEN'S LEAGUE. "Veterans—Close Ranks! Fight for the Bonus!" New York: Workers Library, 1932. 31 pp.
A communist plea for benefits to veterans, outlining the program of the League.

W361 WORKERS LIBRARY. "Where Do the Communists Stand: Communist Election Pamphlets." New York: Workers Library, 1932. 312 pp.
Fifteen pamphlets presenting the Communist Party's official stand in its militant period on Negroes, farmers, women, youth, prohibition, and socialism. Written by candidates William Z. Foster and James W. Ford, and by C. A. Hathaway, Israel Amter, and others.

W362 .... "The Menace of a New World War." New York: Workers Library, 1936. 47 pp.
A communist antiwar pamphlet, emphasizing the slaughter and suffering which workers endure while capitalists pile up profits. Workers are urged to follow the example of the USSR, and unite against war in a people's front led by the communists.

W363 .... "Songs of the People." New York: Workers Library, 1937. 64 pp.
Words and music of 43 "proletarian" songs.

W364 .... "The American Legion and the Communists Discuss Democracy: A Debate." New York: 1938. 79 pp. App.
Verbatim report of a debate between three Legionnaires and three Party members on the question: Resolved: That the American form of democracy is superior to communism. Speakers were Edward E. Fuchs, William Davis, and Richard Fuchs for the J. W. Person Post of the Legion, and Peter V. Cacchione, James W. Ford, and Israel Amter for the Party. The Legionnaires quoted Marxist sources on revolution and dictatorship, whereas the communists asserted that the Party's program was consistent with American traditions.

W365 .... "Songs for America." 1939. 64 pp.
A communist collection of songs and ballads appropriate to the popular front period. Included are marching songs, American ballads and folk songs, songs from other lands, and novelties and songs for socials.

W366 .... "Campaign Book: Presidential Elections, 1940." New York: Workers Library, 1940. 128 pp. Ind.

The election platform of the Communist Party in 1940, during the period of the Nazi-Soviet pact. The Party's views are presented on other political groups, peace, jobs, social security, civil rights, monopoly, farmers, Negroes, youth, women, and the USSR. The war in Europe is denounced as an imperialist one, and socialism is advocated as the economic foundation for democracy and peace.

W367 .... "The Hour for Action Has Struck." New York: Workers Library, 1942. 15 pp.
A communist pamphlet proclaiming May Day 1942 as a day for dedication to an all-out offensive against Hitler.

W368 "WORKERS MONTHLY," The Youth Conference in East Ohio, 5 (April 1926), 264-67.
Description of an Ohio youth conference sponsored by the Young Workers (Communist) League at which immediate demands for young workers were developed. Organizational problems of youth work are discussed in the light of the directives of the Young Communist International.

W369 ..., The Aswell Bill Shall Not Pass, 5 (Feb. 1927), 734-36.
Arguments against House Resolution 5583, introduced by Representative Aswell of Louisiana. The alien registration proposal is seen as a repressive measure aimed at the whole working class, with provisions that would turn American consulates into hirers of contract labor for strikebreaking purposes. (Article prepared by the Chicago Office of the Council for the Protection of the Foreign Born.)

W370 WORKERS MUSIC LEAGUE. "Red Song Book." New York: Workers Library, 1932. 32 pp.
A collection of 26 revolutionary and militant union songs, with words and music.

W371 .... "Workers Song Book." New York: The League, 1935. 48 pp.
Words and music for 48 songs of protest.

W372 WORKERS PARTY OF AMERICA. "Program and Constitution: Adopted at National Convention, New York, Dec. 24-26, 1921." New York: Workers Party, 1921. 31 pp.
The first program and constitution of the legal political party established by American communists following their underground ventures. Immediate demands were proposed, but for revolutionary purposes; and parliamentary action was sanctioned, but only to unmask fraudulent capitalist democracy. The Party remained centralized and disciplined, though no calls were made for armed insurrection and civil war.

W373 .... "For a Labor Party: Recent Revolutionary Changes in American Politics." New York, 1922. 48 pp.
Written just before the December 1922 meeting of the Conference for Progressive Political Action, the pamphlet urges formation of a labor party that will be based on the trade unions, and that will admit communists and adopt a class-conscious program. The failure of past labor parties in America was due to the lack of centralized government power and absence of a uniform working class. For the first time the conditions for a mass labor party exist. (Later editions of this pamphlet, substantially changed and separately abstracted, were published under the authorship of John Pepper.)

W374 .... "For a United Front of Labor." New York: Workers Party, 1922. 4 pp.
An outline of the communist program pending the revolution, urging unity, support of Russia, and a separate labor party.

W375 WORKERS PARTY OF AMERICA, Central Executive Committee. "Our Immediate Work: Program Adopted by the Central Executive Committee of the Workers Party of America." Chicago: Workers Party, n.d. [1924]. 21 pp.

A program of action for the Workers Party, including its policy in the 1924 elections, membership and "Daily Worker" campaigns, educational work, trade union and industrial work, and reorganization on the basis of shop nuclei.

W376 . . . . "The Second Year of the Workers Party of America: Report of the Central Executive Committee to the Third National Convention, Held in Chicago, Illinois, Dec. 30, 31, 1923, and Jan. 1, 2, 1924: Theses, Program, Resolutions." Introd. by C. E. Ruthenberg. Chicago: Literature Department, WP, 1924. 128 pp.

Included are the report of the Central Executive Committee, dealing with the united front, protection of foreign-born workers, labor party developments, propaganda, membership, and finances; theses on the economic and political situation and on labor party policy; a letter from the Communist International; and reports and resolutions on industrial work, the Communist International, American imperialism, recognition of the USSR, shop nuclei, class war prisoners, the Negro question, etc.

W377 . . . . The Situation in the United States: Theses on the Present Economic and Political Situation and on Labour Party Policy, Adopted by the C.E.C. of the Workers Party of America, "International Press Correspondence," 4 (May 1, 1924), 256-59.

These theses, written by John Pepper [Josef Pogany] and C. E. Ruthenberg, were adopted by the convention of the Workers Party, except for the portion on the relationship of the third party and the farmer-labor party, which was referred to the Communist International for decision. The theses see a sharpening economic conflict that will reflect itself in increased sentiment for a third party. Communists must distinguish between a third party and a class farmer-labor party.

W378 . . . . "Leninism or Trotskyism." Pref. by Alexander Bittelman. Chicago: Daily Worker Publishing Co., 1925. 75 pp.

Articles and speeches by Zinoviev, Stalin, and Kamenev attacking Trotskyism as an ideology irreconcilable with Leninism. Bittelman's preface reviews the fundamental disagreements between Lenin and Trotsky dating back to 1903. (Publication of this material in the U.S., several years before the expulsion of Trotsky and his followers, helped spread anti-Trotskyist views among members of the Party here.)

W379 . . ., Central Executive Committee, Results of the Discussion in the American Party, "International Press Correspondence," 5 (Feb. 26, 1925), 241-42.

Statement of the majority group in the Central Executive Committee, Workers Party of America, led by William Z. Foster, claiming overwhelming Party support for its policy of abandoning the united front farmer-labor political policy of the Ruthenberg group. The opportunist Ruthenberg group underestimates the need both for trade union work and for building the WP.

W380 WORKERS (COMMUNIST) PARTY OF AMERICA. "For a Communist Party of Action." New York: Cooperative Press, 1925. 27 pp.

A call for the Party to become more militant, with an assertion that nothing can be gained by the formation of a farmer-labor party as proposed by C. E. Ruthenberg and Jay Lovestone. Instead the Party should form "united fronts from below" on specific issues. (Though not so stated, this represented the program of the Foster-Cannon opposition group; publication was authorized by the Central Executive Committee of the Party.)

W381 . . . . "The Fourth National Convention of the Workers (Communist) Party of America." Chicago: Daily Worker Publishing Co., 1925. 166 pp.

The reports and resolutions submitted to the fourth national convention of the Workers (Communist) Party held in Chicago, August 21-30, 1925. Following a Comintern decision, the Foster group received minority representation on the Party's leading committees, while the Ruthenberg group retained majority control. Despite this decision, the convention was dominated by factional battles. The main issues dividing the two groups related to the farmer-labor party question. Other major problems included reorganization into shop and street nuclei, centralization, and liquidation of language federations as necessary to the bolshevization of the Party.

W382 . . . . "The Party Organization." Introd. by Jay Lovestone. Chicago: Daily Worker Publishing Co., n.d. [1925]. 48 pp. Ind.

Pages 10-25 reproduce a letter from the Communist International to the Central Executive Committee of the Workers (Communist) Party, calling for a restructuring of the Party organization on the basis of shop and street nuclei, which are to be combined in turn into city, district, and the national organization. The constitution and organizational charts of the Party are included.

W383 . . ., National Election Campaign Committee. "The Platform of the Class Struggle: National Platform of the Workers (Communist) Party." New York: Workers Library, 1928. 64 pp.

The election program of the Workers (Communist) Party in 1928, calling for class struggle to end capitalist rule and establish a workers' and farmers' government. Among the topics covered are unemployment, colonies and imperialist war, the defense of the Soviet Union, the government as strikebreaker, a labor party, social legislation, the plight of farmers, Negroes, foreign-born workers, education, and housing.

W384 . . ., Central Executive Committee, A Program on Unemployment, "Communist," 7 (June 1928), 374-77.

Policies adopted by the Central Executive Committee of the Workers (Communist) Party on questions of unemployment insurance, working hours, women's and child labor, public works, etc.

W385 . . ., Resolution on the Report of the Political Committee (May 1928, Plenum of the C.E.C. of the Workers Party), "Communist," 7 (July 1928), 413-20.

An analysis of the current political situation in the U.S. The task of the Workers Party is to gain a foothold among the masses by entering labor struggles and building a left-wing movement generally. The Party's stand on Negro work, the Socialist Party, and a labor party is also discussed.

W386 . . ., Central Executive Committee, Resolution on Trade Union Work, "Communist," 7 (July 1928), 388-98.

Resolution adopted at the May 1928 plenum to place the main emphasis in the Party's industrial work on the formation of new unions to organize the unemployed, while intensifying activities in the old unions. The resolution followed criticism of the Party's union work by Comrade Losovsky, leader of the Red International of Labor Unions.

W387 WORKERS (COMMUNIST) PARTY OF AMERICA. Central Executive Committee, Declaration of the C.E.C. of the C.P. of America on the Decision of the VI World Congress of the C.I. Regarding the Situation in and the Tasks of the Workers (Communist) Party of America, "International Press Correspondence," 8 (Nov. 2, 1928), 1444-46.
A statement of the CEC (then controlled by the Lovestone group) accepting and endorsing the demand of the Sixth World Congress of the Communist International that factionalism in the Workers (Communist) Party be ended. The CEC pledges to correct all the weaknesses pointed out by the CI.

W388 .... The Struggle against Trotskyism and the Right Danger: Declaration by the Central Committee of the Workers (Communist) Party of America, "International Press Correspondence," 8 (Dec. 13, 1928), 1684-86.
Declaration issued in connection with the ouster, on October 28, 1928, of James P. Cannon, Max Shachtman, and Martin Abern from the Party as Trotskyists. The Foster minority in the Party, with which Cannon was associated, is praised for exposing the Trotskyists, but criticized for not having done so earlier. Foster, now that he has broken with Cannon, is urged to drop his opposition to Lovestone.

W389 WORKERS PARTY OF THE U.S. "Declaration of Principles and Constitution of the Workers Party of the U.S." New York: Pioneer Publishers for the WP, n.d. [1934 or 1935]. 31 pp.
The principles and constitution of the WP, formed by merger of the American Workers Party and the Communist League of America, a Trotskyist group. The CPUSA, like other sections of the Communist International, has lost all semblance of Party democracy, the result of complete domination by the bureaucracy of the CPSU. Defense of the Soviet Union against capitalist attack is pledged.

W390 WORKERS, SOLDIERS AND SAILORS COUNCIL, Propaganda Committee. "Industrial Democracy." Toledo: The Council, 1919. 40 pp.
Articles from Louis C. Fraina's "Revolutionary Age," urging the spread of the revolutionary movement. An article by John Reed, advising industrial workers how to take power, is included.

W391 "WORLD NEWS AND VIEWS," Election Programme of the CPUSA, 20 (Sept. 21, 1940), 523-24.
The 1940 election program of the CPUSA attacks the Democratic Party for abandoning the New Deal in favor of defense expenditures, and for whipping up war hysteria to justify a peacetime military dictatorship. Other left-wing groups seek to subordinate the labor movement to the defense program; only the Communist Party fights against the war.

W392 ..., American Communists and the Communist International, 20 (Nov. 30, 1940), 691-92.
A report on the cancellation by the CPUSA of affiliation to the Communist International, in order to comply with the Voorhis Act and continue as a legal party in the U.S. The Party knows that such a step is not a surrender of the principles of internationalism or of its ability to propagandize the American working class for these principles.

W393 WORTIS, Rose. Trends in the A.F. of L., "Communist," 21 (Nov. 1942), 922-37.
A review of the Toronto convention of the AFL, pointing to new trends within it as a result of U.S. participation in the

war. The convention's support of many of Roosevelt's policies is approved, as is the development of united action with the CIO. Regret is voiced that the convention did not call for opening a second front.

W394 .... Labor Day 1943, "Communist," 22 (Sept. 1943), 775-88.
The tasks of American labor in 1943 are to promote maximum war production, achieve trade union unity, give political support to Roosevelt, and promote close international relations with foreign (especially Russian) trade union movements.

W395 .... International Labor Moving toward Unity, "Communist," 22 (Nov. 1943), 989-1001.
An examination of the possibilities for an international trade union alliance, with strong criticism of the AFL Executive Council's refusal to affiliate with the Anglo-Soviet Trade Union Committee.

W396 .... The I.L.G.W.U. at the Crossroads, "Communist," 23 (March 1944), 267-74.
The International Ladies' Garment Workers' Union is said to repudiate the decisions of Teheran in its Red-baiting, its refusal to join an international trade union body with the Soviet Union, and its general political stand.

W397 WRIGHT, Lloyd. A Leading Lawyer Explains Use and Abuse of 5th Amendment, "U.S. News & World Report," 39 (Nov. 25, 1955), 86-94.
The text of an address by the president of the American Bar Association, February 25, 1955. While the self-incrimination section of the Amendment should not be repealed, it should not be misused. A man can claim the privilege only if disclosure would put him in danger of criminal prosecution.

W398 WRIGHT, Richard. "Native Son." New York: Harper, 1940. 359 pp.
The story of a Negro slum youth who accidentally murders a rich, young, white woman, a communist sympathizer, and who tries unsuccessfully to cast suspicion upon a Party functionary who had been close to her. Caught and tried for murder, he is ably defended by a communist attorney, who tries in vain to save him. Ambiguous in its attitudes toward the communists, the book expresses the hopelessness, the fear and rage, the hatred and violence of Negro slum youth. (The author, a leading Negro writer, had been a member of the Party for two years in the mid-1930's.)

W399 .... I Tried to Be a Communist, "Atlantic Monthly," 174 (Aug. 1944), 61-70; (Sept.), 48-56.
A recital of how Wright, author of "Native Son," became interested in the John Reed Clubs and joined the Communist Party. Wright tells of his disillusioning experiences in the Clubs and the Party, and the character assassination he suffered from the Party after he left it. He describes his revulsion with all that the Party stands for.

W400 .... "The Outsider." New York: Harper, 1953. 405 pp.
An anticommunist book, a drama of ideas analyzing the communist use of power. The central figure, after being declared dead in an accident, takes on a new name, becomes involved with communists, and turns murderer. In the end he is killed by a member of the Party.

W401 WRIGHT, Thomas H. The American Communist Party, "American Teacher," 25 (May 1941), 23-25.
A discussion of Party objectives and agitation, emphasizing its current propaganda line against Britain and its peace-at-any-price agitation, both of which are undermin-

ing the fight against fascism. Control of Party policies by the USSR is emphasized, as is the rule-or-ruin policy of the Party in its struggle for power in trade unions. (Part of a symposium on communism, fascism, and democracy.)

W402 WRONG, Dennis H. Theories of McCarthyism—A Survey, "Dissent," 1 (Autumn 1954), 385-92.
Recent writings on McCarthyism reflect three views—that it is a peculiarly American phenomenon, that it is a fascist movement like those of Europe, and that it is an incident in the drift toward a garrison state. The author leans to the third view, adding that McCarthy has helped to brutalize American politics.

W403 WYNN, Daniel Webster. "The NAACP versus Negro Revolutionary Protest." New York: Exposition Press, 1955. 115 pp. Bibliog. Ind.
A comparison of the legal protest action of the NAACP with revolutionary protest action with regard to their effectiveness in securing civil rights for Negroes. Paul Robeson and W. E. B. Du Bois are viewed as Marxian socialist types and leaders of Negro revolutionary protest; the Council on African Affairs and the Peace Information Center, both dominated by communists, and the Party itself are examined with a view to their effectiveness. The author concludes that the legal protest methods of the NAACP are more effective. A short history of the Negro protest movement in America is presented as background.

W404 WYZANSKI, Charles E., Jr. The Communist Party and the Law, "Atlantic Monthly," 187 (May 1951), 27-30.
A U.S. District Court judge recommends reliance upon our federal criminal conspiracy statutes to prosecute the Communist Party. This approach, which condemns as unlawful such means as espionage and perjury, places communists under normal criminal rules and common law procedures and reaffirms our tolerance of non-conspiratorial radical groups.

X

X1   "X." Hollywood Meets Frankenstein, "Nation,"
       174 (June 28, 1952), 628-31.
A group of Hollywood writers deplores Hollywood's
appeasement of right-wing pressure groups after the
firing of the Hollywood Ten. American Legion picketing
has ended with the setting up of a clearance committee to
rule on all film industry employees charged with supporting subversive organizations.

Y

Y1 "YALE LAW JOURNAL," Deportation of Alien for Membership in the Communist Party, 48 (Nov. 1938), 111-17.
A discussion of the case of Joseph Strecker, ordered deported by the Department of Labor on the charge of past membership in the Communist Party. The Circuit Court of Appeals denied the Department's application, holding that mere membership was no basis for deportation. The criterion should be the actual policy of the Party, at the date of membership, as evidenced by official documents.

Y2 . . ., In re Harry Bridges, 52 (Dec. 1942), 108-29.
A discussion of legal aspects of the Bridges deportation proceedings, including earlier deportation efforts, the constitutionality of the statute invoked, and the administrative application of the statute. The "Journal" concludes that Bridges is not deportable, and that seldom has one been subjected here to so relentless a hunt.

Y3 . . ., Loyalty and Private Employment: The Right of Employers to Discharge Suspected Subversives, 62 (May 1953), 954-84.
Discussion of the few existing statutes and agreements that could restrain employers in dismissal of employees for disloyalty. The NLRB, until 1950 suspicious of such firings, now gives employers wide leeway. Private union contracts have done the same. An employee who is unjustly and publicly discharged has little recourse to protect his job and name under present laws.

Y4 . . ., The Communist Control Act of 1954, 64 (April 1955), 712-65.
A section-by-section analysis of constitutional problems raised by the Communist Control Act of 1954. In many respects the measure is obscure, ambiguous, and incongruous; much of it was proposed on the floor of Congress, without hearings and with little opportunity for analysis. It is questionable whether this is an effective or desirable way to combat communism.

Y5 YARMOLINSKY, Adam (ed.). "Case Studies in Personnel Security." Washington, D.C.: Bureau of National Affairs, 1955. 310 pp.
An account of 50 cases from a sample of 230 under federal security programs: 31 relate to the Truman-Eisenhower loyalty-security programs, 15 are from industrial security programs, two are from the armed forces, one deals with port security, and one involves a UN employee. These case studies show our procedures to be unsatisfactory and often grossly at fault. The charges are apt to be petty and security officers incompetent in this type of evaluation.

Y6 YATES, Oleta O'Connor. The Struggle against Deviations and Factionalism in San Francisco, "Political Affairs," 25 (Dec. 1946), 1092-1103.
A description of the right and left deviations apparent in California elections, strike struggles, and intra-Party issues. A number of persons have been expelled for participating in an anti-Party, left sectarian factional grouping. The Party has become more united, vigilant, and politically mature in the course of this struggle.

Y7 YELLEN, Samuel. "American Labor Struggles." New York: Harcourt, Brace, 1936. 398 pp. Notes. Ind.
An account of the leading U.S. labor struggles, including the Southern textile strikes of 1929 and the West Coast longshoremen's strike of 1934 (chapters 9 and 10, pp. 292-358). The communists played leading roles in both the Gastonia, N.C., textile strike and the 1934 longshore strike, which culminated in the general strike in San Francisco. In both cases the red issue was used against the strikers, though Southern textile manufacturers fought the conservative AFL textile union with equal determination. The longshore strike established the leadership of Harry Bridges, who was closely allied to the communists, on the San Francisco waterfront.

Y8 YERGAN, Max. "Democracy and the Negro People Today." Washington, D.C.: National Negro Congress, 1940. 15 pp.
An address by the president of the National Negro Congress (since cited by the Attorney General as subversive), opposing U.S. involvement in the current imperialist war, and stressing the interest of Negroes in jobs, the right to vote, the abolition of social ghettos, and the end of Jim-Crowism in the armed services.

Y9 . . ., and ROBESON, Paul. "The Negro and Justice: A Plea for Earl Browder." New York: Citizens' Committee to Free Earl Browder, 1941. 11 pp.
Speeches at a rally at Madison Square Garden, September 29, 1941, at which pleas for Earl Browder's release from prison were made. One of the themes was that Browder's release would aid the fight against fascism here.

Y10 YERXA, Fendall, and REID, Ogden R. "The Threat of Red Sabotage." Foreword by J. Edgar Hoover. New York: New York Herald Tribune, 1950. 36 pp.
Reprint of a series of ten newspaper articles, telling how vital plants are "fingered" for destruction by sabotage should war come. The authors find subversive communist tactics behind the Stockholm peace appeal, the disruption of our courts, appeals to get the GI's home from Korea, and labor union, church, and community organization infiltration. They demand that our vital plants be better protected and that sources of intelligence data be kept from communist hands.

Y11 YOUNG, Art. "On My Way: Being the Book of Art Young in Text and Picture." New York: Liveright, 1928. 303 pp.
Memoirs of the popular cartoonist who was long associated with the radical movement in the U.S. Critical of many aspects of the society of his day, Young was attracted to the socialists, the liberal reformers, the communists, the IWW, the Single Taxers, and the anarchists. He served on the art staff of the "Masses," and with other staff members was indicted and twice tried under the Espionage Act because of opposition to World War I, with the jury in both cases being unable to agree.

Y12 . . . . "Art Young: His Life and Times." Ed. by

John Nicholas Beffel. New York: Sheridan House,
1939. 467 pp. Ind.
The autobiography of the well-known radical cartoonist,
who was closely associated with the "Masses" and the
"Liberator," and who stood trial with Max Eastman,
Floyd Dell, and others under the Espionage Act of World
War I. In 1922 Young agreed to the merger of the
"Liberator" with the communists' "Workers Monthly,"
and with the birth of the "New Masses" in 1926 he
became a contributing editor. Nevertheless Young had
little sympathy for the communists; he supported Norman
Thomas for the presidency in 1936, and was only mildly
critical of Franklin Roosevelt.

Y13   YOUNG, Harris. 1952 and Labor's Political
       Course, "Political Affairs," 30 (Dec. 1951), 53-62.
Truman has not fulfilled any of his 1948 campaign pledges,
and his Korean war has shattered the myth that he is for
peace. Though widespread worker disappointment has led
to many strikes, the workers have not supported the peace
movement. They must be shown that capitalist warmongering brings low living standards. Trade union
leaders still endorse Truman, and even progressive-led
unions have not supported a third party dedicated to
peace.

Y14   YOUNG, Jack. "'The People Be Damned!' A
       Record of the 53rd Session of the State Legislature
       of California." San Francisco: "Daily People's
       World," 1939. 48 pp.
An assertion by the Sacramento correspondent of the
"Daily People's World," West Coast organ of the Party,
that the legislature killed nearly all the progressive
legislation backed by Governor Olson. Every major piece
of labor legislation was defeated, as were the measures
wanted by dirt farmers and the unemployed. Lobbyists
for Big Business were in control. Voting records are
shown.

Y15   YOUNG, Marguerite. The Little Poison Flower,
       "New Masses," 10 (Feb. 27, 1934), 12-14.
Father Coughlin is denounced as a demagogue who leads
an embryonic fascist movement of great influence, particularly regarding currency and monetary control. Fortunately not all of Catholic labor approves of him, though
the Catholic Church will not interfere with his activities.

Y16   YOUNG, Max. Sharpen the Fight for the Central
       Slogan of the World Communist Party—Soviet
       Power! "Communist," 14 (Jan. 1935), 45-60.
A discussion article in preparation for the Seventh World
Congress of the Comintern, analyzing the struggle for
Soviet power in America. Too much effort is expended in
the struggle for immediate demands, too little in linking
up immediate demands with the struggle against the
capitalist state.

Y17   YOUNG, William and Pauline. On Wage Stabiliza-
       tion, "Communist," 22 (May 1943), 443-51.
Critical comment on Gilbert Green's Some Problems of
Economic Stabilization (in "Communist," March 1943),
arguing that the cost of living index does not reflect
decline in quality or black market prices paid for shortages. Green rejoins that the Youngs' opposition to the
cost of living formula would end wage stabilization.

Y18   YOUNG COMMUNIST INTERNATIONAL. "Pro-
       gramme of the Young Communist International."
       New York: Young Communist League of America,
       n.d. [1929]. 83 pp.
The world youth program of the Young Communist International in the militant period preceding the rise of
fascism. The YCL tasks are to struggle energetically

against all bourgeois youth organizations, and to eliminate
social-democratic, syndicalist, and anarchist influences
over youth.

Y19   . . ., Executive Committee. "Resolution of the
       Executive Committee, Young Communist Inter-
       national, on the Report of the National Executive
       Committee, Young Communist League of the
       U.S.A." New York: Young Communist League,
       n.d. [1932]. 16 pp.
The resolution criticizes the League for opportunist
theories, for underestimating the war danger, and for
failure to lead daily struggles or expose social-fascists.
The YCL must bolshevise itself, lead young workers'
economic struggles, expose the U.S. imperialist war
policy, and struggle against white chauvinism.

Y20   YOUNG COMMUNIST LEAGUE OF THE U.S.A.
       "Program, Constitution, Theses and Resolutions
       Adopted by the First National Convention." New
       York: YCL, National Executive Committee, n.d.
       [1920?]. 31 pp.
The first program of the YCL, a copy of the Party's
program.

Y21   . . . . "Report of the Fifth National Convention of
       the Young Communist League of U.S.A." New
       York: YCL, n.d. [1929]. 49 pp.
Included are an introduction by John Harvey, national
secretary of the YCL; a thesis on the tasks of the YCL;
the speech of the representative of the Young Communist
International; and resolutions on the fight for young workers in industry and on building the League organization.

Y22   . . . . "Who Are the Young Communists?" New
       York: Workers Library, n.d. [1932?]. 23 pp.
An assertion that the YCL leads the fight for better conditions for young workers, the rightful owners of America,
who are deprived of their just due by capitalism.

Y23   . . . . "Fix Bayonets—Against Whom?" New York:
       YCL, 1933. 39 pp.
An assertion that the National Guard is run by the bosses
for use against workers; episodes of Guard use to break
strikes are related. The Guard is being trained for war
because the bosses are afraid of the Soviet Union. Guards-
men are urged to join the YCL.

Y24   . . . . "Towards a Mass Young Communist League:
       Resolutions Adopted by the July Plenum of the
       Young Communist League, U.S.A." New York:
       Youth Publishers, 1933. 16 pp.
The main resolution of the July 1933 plenum, criticizing
sectarianism and calling for struggles against American
imperialism and against incorrect tendencies within the
YCL. Shop and trade union work are called vital to the
League. Resolutions on work among children and on
building the "Young Worker" are included.

Y25   . . ., New York State. "An Election Message to
       All Young People of New York." New York: YCL,
       n.d. [1934?]. 15 pp.
An assertion that a vote for any other party than the Communist Party is a vote for the enemy. Youth's hope is in
a Soviet America.

Y26   . . . . "Let's Fight Together!" New York: Youth
       Publishers, n.d. [1934]. 11 pp.
The text of an appeal by the Young Communist International
to the Young Socialist International for coordinated action
to support the Spanish proletariat, with a similar appeal
by the YCL to the Young People's Socialist League here
for a united front to demonstrate before Spanish consulates
and raise funds for the revolutionary Spanish youth.

Y27　YOUNG COMMUNIST LEAGUE OF THE U.S.A. "A Program for American Youth." New York: Youth Publishers, 1934. 32 pp.

Manifesto and resolutions of the seventh national convention of the YCL, June 22-27, 1934. Despite progress, the YCL lags because of sectarianism and opportunism covered with radical phrases. The major task is to win the young workers in the decisive war industries.

Y28　. . . (Dist. 13), Educational Department. "Young Communists in Action: Handbook for Young Communists." Compiled by Lewis Miller: YCL (Dist. 13), n.d. [1936?].

(See Chamber of Commerce of the U.S., "Communist Propaganda among American Youth.")

Y29　. . ., New York State. "Youth Faces the Elections." New York: Workers Library, 1936. 14 pp.

Support is urged for the Communist Party, whose election platform includes passage of the American Youth Act and the child labor amendment, lowering of the voting age, and abolition of military training and the Civilian Conservation Corps.

Y30　. . ., New York State. "Extracts and Resolutions, Empire State Convention, November 26-28, 1937." 1937. 71 pp. Mimeo.

Panel reports and resolutions at the convention of the New York State unit of the YCL. Panel reports deal with branch work, Negro youth, education, the labor movement, students, girls, and high schools.

Y31　. . . . "We Take Our Stand." New York: YCL, 1937. 22 pp.

Principles and by-laws of the YCL, as adopted by its eighth national convention, May 2-5, 1937. Emphasis is placed on unity in a People's Front to block war and reaction, as well as on industrial unionism, collective security to preserve peace, the achievements of the Soviet Union, and Negro equality.

Y32　. . . . "Year Book." New York: YCL, 1937. 64 pp.

A magazine published on the fifteenth anniversary of the YCL, with names and pictures of branch members throughout the country.

Y33　. . . . "The Constitution of the Young Communist League." New York: New Age, 1939. 12 pp.

Constitution adopted at the ninth national convention, May 1939.

Y34　. . . . "Youth Meets the Challenge of 1940." New York: New Age, 1939. 46 pp.

A collection of three reports delivered to the National Council of the Young Communist League in 1938, urging support of the New Deal and organization of youth in the democratic front.

Y35　. . . . "Youth Fights for Peace, Jobs, Civil Rights." New York: New Age, 1940. 76 pp.

Reports delivered to the national council of the YCL, May 5-7, 1940. The main report, by Max Weiss, deals with economic and political developments. Other reports include those by Henry Winston on organization, John Gates on Negro rights, Bob Thompson on industrial youth, and Carl Ross on problems of the youth movement. The report of the election campaign commission is also included.

Y36　YOUNG WORKERS LEAGUE OF AMERICA. "Resolutions and Theses: 1923." Chicago: The League, 1923. 57 pp.

Resolutions and theses adopted at the second national convention of the League, held in Chicago, May 20-22, 1923. Discussion centered on reorganization of the League on the basis of job activity or shop nuclei, and a program for children's sections.

Y37　YOUTH PUBLISHERS. "Fighting Fascism in the Factories." New York: 1934. 32 pp.

A handbook of shop organization for communists, showing how the YCL of Germany fights in the factories to overthrow the fascist dictatorship.

Z

Z1 ZACK, J. A. [Joseph Kornfeder]. Against the Labor Party (Militant Reformism) in the U.S.A., "Communist," 8 (Dec. 1929), 682-86; 9 (Jan. 1930), 67-80.
The labor party tactic, which was overruled by the Comintern, was the mistaken idea of Comrade Pepper, who committed the Party to La Follettism. All forms of a labor party, including organization of one "from below" (militant reformism) must be rejected. The Party should become the strike party of the unorganized and the leader of all the exploited.

Z2 . . . . The United Front: Based on Recent Experience, "Labor Unity," 7 (Jan. 1932),25; (Feb.),26-27.
A discussion of united front tactics by the secretary of the Trade Union Unity League of Greater New York, who argues that the AFL is declining while the TUUL is growing, and that the masses should be organized outside the AFL, not into it. Explaining the tactic of the united front from below, he proposes that workers in AFL and TUUL unions should be united against the bosses, but in the direction of building up the new unions.

Z3 . . . . How to Apply the Open Letter, "Communist," 13 (Feb. 1934), 207-17.
Suggestions for revitalizing Party work in industry by an active unionist, who argues that building unions is the best mass approach to the building of the Party. The Party must cease to be a sectarian group, isolated from the masses. (For criticism of Zack's views see accompanying editorial comment and Gertrude Haessler, "How Not to Apply the Open Letter," in the "Communist," March 1934.)

Z4 . . . . The Line Is Correct—To Realize It Organizationally Is the Central Problem, "Communist," 13 (April 1934), 356-62.
A discussion article prior to the eighth convention of the CPUSA, asserting that, while the Party's program is correct, organizationally it has been unable to take advantage of the leftward swing of the masses to increase its membership and influence. The eighth convention therefore must concentrate on organizational questions, not program.

Z5 . . . . Conflict in Auto Workers Union, "New Leader," 29 (May 25, 1946), 9.
An account of the conflict within the UAW-CIO between Walter Reuther, newly elected president, and the faction led by George Addes, secretary-treasurer, which follows the Communist Party line.

Z6 . . . . Red Plan for Labor, "Freeman," 3 (Oct. 20, 1952), 57-59.
A former Comintern agent and graduate of the Lenin School shows how communists seek to transform unions into a political movement aiming at abolition of a free society. Describing the extent of communist influence in American labor, he asserts that recent losses have stemmed from moral disintegration inside the communist movement.

Z7 ZAM, Herbert. The Plenum of the Executive Committee of the Young Communist International, "Workers Monthly," 5 (June 1926), 343-46.
Zam, Secretary of the Young Workers (Communist) League of America and the first American on the presidium of the Young Communist International, summarizes the criticisms of Young Communist Leagues made at this plenum. The YCI calls for more effective efforts at mass work through capturing the leadership of the young masses in nonpolitical organizations.

Z8 . . . . Winning the Youth, "Communist," 6 (April 1927), 84-91.
The membership of the Communist Youth International has grown, primarily in the Soviet Union, though losses occurred elsewhere. In December 1926, there were 2,100,000 members, almost 2,000,000 of whom were in the Soviet Union. It now regards as enemies only those youth organizations, such as the Socialist Youth Leagues, the YMCA and YWCA, and Catholic youth organizations, that cannot serve the interests of the working class.

Z9 . . . . The Youth and the Elections, "Communist," 7 (April 1928), 242-46.
Youth is disfranchised and exploited in capitalist countries. The Young Workers (Communist) League demands the extension of the franchise to youth between 18 and 21, and advocates a program of social legislation. Youth is urged to help in the formation of a labor party.

Z10 . . . . The Youth Movement and the Sixth Anniversary of the Young Workers (Communist) League, "Communist," 7 (June 1928), 340-45.
A review of the development of the League, tracing its roots to the Young Peoples Socialist League, and a statement of its aim to win working youth for the class struggle. The League is finally on the road to becoming a mass organization, the leader of young workers in the fight against capitalism.

Z11 . . . . The New Turn Twists the New Line, "Revolutionary Age," 1 (June 15, 1930), 8-9; (July 1), 4.
A Lovestoneite examination of the proposed thesis for the coming (seventh) convention of the CPUSA. The thesis seeks scapegoats for the disastrous effects of the ultra-left line. The first article criticizes Earl Browder's analysis of the world situation; the second discusses current tactics of the Communist International.

Z12 . . . . After Two Years: Balance Sheet of the New Line, "Revolutionary Age," 2 (May 30, 1931), 3.
A Lovestoneite review of the state of the CPUSA on the second anniversary of the expulsion of the Lovestoneites. Covering membership statistics, trade union work, fraternal societies, and strike struggles, it concludes that the new ultra-left line has brought failure, weakness, and the loss of old support.

Z13 . . . . The New Turn Twists Back Again, "Workers Age," 1 (May 7, 1932), 1 ff; (May 14), 3 ff.
A Lovestoneite analysis of a resolution on "left social

fascists'' (left-wing splinter groups) published by the Central Committee of the Communist Party. Zam criticizes the suggestion that the revolution will be achieved if the communists defeat the social fascists.

Z14 ZAM, Herbert. Ninety Years after the Communist Manifesto. "Socialist Call," 4 (Feb. 26, 1938), 2; (March 5), 2.
The ideas of the Communist Manifesto are still sound today. The revisionist "twentieth century Americanism" line of the Communist Party, by removing the threat of revolution by the working class, seeks to persuade the middle class not to turn to fascism. Only the working class, following a class struggle policy, can defeat fascism; the communists, in wooing the middle class, have abandoned the class struggle, thereby hastening fascism.

Z15 . . . . After the Soviet Munich. "Socialist Review," 6 (Sept.-Oct. 1939), 6-8.
An attack on the communists for justifying the Stalin-Hitler pact, while continuing to condemn Munich. Stalin's motives are said to be German economic assistance. United fronts between communists and fascists in other countries are now to be expected, while communists will again fight other working class groups as the main enemy.

Z16 ZAUSNER, Philip. "Unvarnished: The Autobiography of a Union Leader." New York: Brotherhood Publishers, 1941. 381 pp.
The story of an Austrian immigrant who joined a New York local of the Brotherhood of Painters, Decorators and Paperhangers in 1912 and steadily rose to union leadership. In chapter 15, "Thunder on the Left" (pp. 183-98) and in succeeding chapters he tells the story of a long conflict with a communist faction for control of the local.

Z17 ZELMAN, Annette. "Teaching about Communism in American Public Schools." New York: Humanities Press for American Institute for Marxist Studies, 1965. 74 pp. App. Bibliog.
A review of the types of courses about communism taught in the public schools and the materials used, concluding that often the objective is to instill hatred, not understanding, of communism, and that the courses are a source of confusion rather than clarification. Much of the impetus for the programs has come from right-wing groups, and many of the programs, devoid of scholarship, seek merely to indoctrinate.

Z18 ZINOVIEV, G. September First Statement of the Executive Committee of the Communist International. "Communist" (organ of the Communist Party of America), 2 (March 1, 1920), 4. (Reprinted in New York State Legislature, Joint Legislative Committee Investigating Seditious Activities, "Revolutionary Radicalism," 1: 468-84.)
Letter from the president of the Executive Committee of the Communist International to revolutionary socialists in France, America, England, and Germany, opposing parliamentarism as a form of government, but favoring parliamentary activity to further communist work. Principal efforts are to be directed toward establishing the Party, capturing unions, and organizing soviets. Revolutionary socialists must unite.

Z19 ZITRON, Celia L. Teachers under Fire. "Masses & Mainstream," 5 (April 1952), 28-37.
One of eight teachers, dismissed from the New York City public school system in May 1950, on security grounds, defends the ability and devotion of eight other teachers dismissed in February 1951. These teachers were dismissed for antiwar utterances, though anti-Semitism and racial bias played a part.

Z20 ZOOBOCK, Louis. Employers Association[s] in the United States. "Workers Monthly," 4 (Feb. 1925), 182-84.
A description of employers' associations in the U.S., both belligerent ones such as the National Association of Manufacturers and the National Metal Trades Association, and negotiating ones such as in the foundry, building construction, and newspaper publishing industries. The methods used by the belligerent type to defeat unionism are described.

Z21 ZUCKER, Dora. "Young Communists at Work." New York: Youth Publishers, 1934. 31 pp.
A fictionalized version of the experiences of four unemployed young workers and an organizer for the Young Communist League, dealing with the economic crisis. Workers can end the crisis by joining revolutionary working class organizations such as the CP, the YCL, and the revolutionary unions, that will create a Soviet America.

Z22 ZUGSMITH, Leane. "A Time to Remember." Random House, 1936. 352 pp.
One of the leading proletarian novels of the mid-1930's, dealing with a strike of department store workers and the efforts of businessmen and public officials to defeat it. "Justice" under capitalism is viewed as a conspiracy of the owning against the working class.

Z23 ZUR MUHLEN, Herminia. "Fairy Tales for Workers Children." Chicago: Daily Worker Publishing Co., 1925. 66 pp. Translated from the German by Ida Dailes.
A book of working class stories to delight children and instill in their minds the spirit of revolt.

ZYSMAN, Dale. See HARDY, Jack (1935-37).

A

Abraham Lincoln Battalion, A8, V26

Abramovich, B436

academic freedom, A61, A62, A75, A142, B63, C75, C78, C98, C133, C154, C170, E54, F21, G110, H144, H205, H301, H306, H395, J119, J121, J131, K94, K95, L49, L50, L105, M7, M95, M220, M224, M238, M251, M419, N120, N126, S41, S274, S418, S470, T19, see also colleges, education, teachers

Acheson, Dean, W304

Actors' Equity Association, B131, M249

Actors Guild, F7

advertising, G120

Affiliated Schools for Workers, G245

Africa, F185

agrarian protest, 16, 17, 29, 55, 61

agriculture, B56, B416, C205, C219, C230, C300, C315, C571, D199, E68, G93, H78, H152, J26, K103, L13, L15, L176, L283, M5, M217, M322, P211, R9, R110, T25, see also farmers, United Farmers League

Alabama, M43

Aldridge, Ira, B190

Alien and Sedition Acts, L138

aliens, B763, C81, E64, G221, H334, M67, S219, W369, see also denaturalization, deportation, foreign born, immigrants, immigration laws, Walter-McCarran Act

Altgeld, John Peter, F38

Amalgamated Association of Iron, Steel, and Tin Workers, S336, S476

Amalgamated Clothing Workers, A14, F98, H242, J128, S47, S457, see also Hillman, Sidney; needle trades

amalgamation, B79, B424, B425, F241, F242, F247, F266, F271, F322, F494, G320, H52, K102, W18

"Amerasia," A135, C228, C623, E57, L95, L118, R78, S164, W341, W342

American Action, Inc., S314

American Association for the United Nations, F12

American Association of Scientific Workers, M148

American Association of University Professors, H247

American Bar Association, K104, M44, see also lawyers

American Civil Liberties Union, A94, A95, B728, D178, D292, H259, L50, L125, M87, M109, M297, V11, W142, see also civil liberties, civil rights

American Communications Association, H56

American Federation of Labor, 21, 53, 105, 124, 132, 133, A108, A112, B93, B441, B446, B690, C469, D294, D296, D301, D304, D309, D311, D319, E61, E66, E86, F175, F250, F264, F279, F292, F324, F336, F369, F395, F475, G3, G138, G194, G216, H109, H154, H277, H352, H355, H372, H406, K143, L273, L274, L292, L300, M229, M230, M239, M357, M390, M401, M414, M420, M421, P66, S17, S338, S339, S340, S342, S405, T80, T105, W234, W238, W242, W274, W338, W393, Z2, see also AFL-CIO merger; Gompers, Samuel; Green, William; labor unity; particular unions

AFL-CIO merger, C574, M404, M405, S206, S460, see also

American Federation of Labor, Congress of Industrial Organizations, labor unity

American Federation of Teachers, A145, B444, C652, H170, I51, M233, S373, S431, T27, see also colleges, education, schools, teachers, Teachers Union of New York

American Forum, S262, T111

American Fund for Public Service, M109, S432

American Jewish Committee, H43, H46, see also Jews

American Jewish League Against Communism, L115

American Labor Conference on International Affairs, S401

American Labor Party, A182, A194, B519, C14, C653, E79, K88, K91, N87, S18, S82, S444, S501, W5

American League Against War and Fascism, B209, C113, L335, M54, S174, S351, W48, see also American League for Peace and Democracy

American League for Peace and Democracy, C113, S174, S175, S280, S315, see also American League Against War and Fascism

American Legion, B15, B733, G48, G73, K74, P139, W273, see also veterans

American Liberty League, H404, R146

American Medical Association, F339, see also health

American Negro Labor Congress, L249, M309, see also Negroes

American Newspaper Guild, L4, see also Broun, Heywood; newspapers

American Peace Crusade, L226

American People's Mobilization, E12

American Railway Union, 84, see also Debs, Eugene V.

American Slav Congress, C713, L61, P136, P137, see also Slavs

American Student Union, E28, I42, K56, L102, L103, R199, R223, S445, S446, V15, W49, W50, W52, W335, see also National Student League, Student League for Industrial Democracy, students, youth

American Veterans Committee, G47, J19, N136, see also veterans

American Workers Party, L267

American Writers' Congress, C124, C665, C666, H93, L243, S413, see also writers

American Youth Act, A153, C190, C191, H248, H250, R190, see also youth

American Youth Congress, B314, C209, C619, D249, E12, F228, G244, G274, H248, I3, L371, M140, M246, M347, P149, R169, R170, R189, R192, R194, R200, S70, S362, T46, T121, U66, V15, see also youth

American Youth for Democracy, D167, W125, see also youth

Americanism, P29

Americans for Democratic Action, L364, M28, T126

Americans for Intellectual Freedom, L104

anarchism, 8, 41, 42, 52, 109, 123, 138, see also Goldman, Emma; Industrial Workers of the World; syndicalism

anarchists, 25, 56, 93, 109, 120, 121, N119, see also Haymarket Affair

anticommunism, B143, C121, C220, D177, K97, L198, L364, W44, see also federal legislation, loyalty-security program, state legislation

anticommunist oath, A84, B683, see also loyalty oaths, loyalty-security program, noncommunist affidavit

anticommunists, B733, F520, K66, V16

Anti-Defamation League, F14

anti-Semitism, A257, B43, C138, D76, D78, F102, F206, G4, J62, L156, M33, M209, S30, S282, S311, V1, see also Jews

antitrust laws, B694, M99

B

C

communism, appeal of, (continued), N93, N142, O23, R198, R201, R233, S38, S42, S73, S148, S234, S290, S467, T109, V21, W14, W117, W185, W399, see also Party membership, Party recruiting, Party strength

    causes of, D168, H274, M213, S484, see also communism, measures against

    criticism of, B162, C123, F163, G106, K12, M211, N1, N2, N145, W148, W156

    fear of, O25

    measures against, B742, C130, C241, C624, D186, K54, L53, L97, L110, L114, L178, L339, M38, M146, M149, M279, M432, O8, O9, O54, P180, R16, R59, R85, R135, R177, R240, R241, R242, S40, S160, S161, S162, S449, see also communism, causes of

    menace of, A80, A124, B146, B168, B191, B365, B366, B399, B590, C152, C210, C229, C272, C274, C624, C683, D40, D74, D166, F1, F21, F121, F122, F123, F167, H3, H309, K87, L73, M8, M58, M102, M202, M250, N134, P93, P123, R17, R99, S40, S252, S425, S443, S484, T24, T36, T66, T71, W34

    nature of, B30, B146, B165, B166, B310, B367, C134, C135, C705, F61, F64, F535, F550, F552, G92, H244, H339, M110, M434, M436, N58, N59, N183, O10, S158, S301, S304, S422, W1, W118, see also Bolshevism

    rejection of, B680, C132, C135, C224, C238, C689, F55, F56, F57, F170, F529, G53, G55, G172, H28, H210, H222, H285, K105, M234, M358, R224, R233, S73, S371, W399, see also ex-communists

    study of, H299, N184, O2

communist cases, B25, B198, B556, B642, C104, C180, C264, C268, C269, C394, F506, G133, H142, L238, L331, M73, M152, R77, R159, R246, S102, S171, S210, S278, S285, S316, U27, U87, U89, W178, W270, see also criminal anarchy, criminal syndicalism, federal legislation, particular statutes and cases, sedition, Smith Act, state legislation, U.S. Supreme Court

Communist Control Act of 1954, B68, B120, C136, C187, C569, E54, F506, G82, H4, J14, L247, M424, N110, N116, N179, P61, P173, S17, T26, T81, U67, Y4

communist countries, C584, F427, F450, J66, N2, N26, S106, see also Bolshevism

communist fronts, see front groups

communist ideology, B30, C94, C118, C207, C475, C688, H279, M374, P19, see also class struggle, dictatorship, Marxism, revisionism, revolution

Communist Information Bureau, C538, F426

Communist International, A170, B173, B178, B233, B343, B550, B650, C118, C253, C296, C298, C330, C331 C337, C339, C340, C347, C355, C357, C363, C371, C381, C387, C440, C463, D89, D202, D203, D205, D206, D248, D262, F370, F472, G5, G202, H53, H111, K13, L62, L183, L184, L210, L230, L272, L274, L298, L304, L318, L322, L326, L327, L376, M22, M261, M263, M371, O1, O41, O53, P12, P79, P129, P130, P132, R61, R88, R93, R264, S127, S134, S265, S268, S423, S500, W88, W140, W326, W392, Z18

Communist Labor Party, B317, C275, C297, C327, C330, C368, E1, E18, L39, N119, O26, O27, W40, W41

Communist League of America, M92

Communist League of Struggle, C372

Communist Manifesto, S169, Z14

Communist Party of America, C275, C280, C283, C284, C286, C287, C288, C289, C290, C292, C293, C294, C295, C297, C327, C330, C335, C336, L39, M97, N119, O27, R245, S424, V3, W40, W41

Communist Party (majority group), see Lovestone group

Communist Party (opposition), see Lovestone group

Communist Party, U.S.A., see various headings under "Party"

communist personality, L94, R185,

Communist Political Association, B615, C518, C519, C590, C591, C592, C593, C594, C595, C596, C597, C598, C627, D247, F407, F409, G43, G44, G195, G208, G285, H229, M334, N162, W224, W225, W226, W227, W228, W229, see also Browderism, revisionism

Communist Youth International, Z8

communists, cooperation with, B164, B288, H339, M366, S315

    registration of, A77, M221, N126, T7, U69, see also federal legislation, state legislation

company unions, C12, D281, D283, D290, F270, F275, G64, H278, see also labor unions

Condon, Edward N., W116

Conference for Progressive Labor Action, F300, F303, L1, L267, see also Muste, A. J.

Conference for Progressive Political Action, B214, C43, D295, F256, R248

Conference of Scientific and Cultural Workers for World Peace, L104

Congress, see U.S. Congress

Congress of American Women, S107

Congress of Industrial Organizations, A21, A67, A107, A274, B24, B36, B133, B135, B139, B141, B665, B690, B723, B724, C59, C61, C62, C66, C70, C99, C482, C604, C605, C606, C618, C636, C639, C640, C642, E49, E79, F120, F126, F132, F134, F232, F233, F316, F324, F326, F330, F369, F395, F396, F475, G3, G194, H51, H75, H76, H264, H340, H352, H360, H365, H372, H406, J20, J25, K17, K18, K21, K24, K25, K31, K32, K125, L5, L6, L10, L11, L195, L208, L269, L270, L274, L377, M10, M113, M118, M123, M124, M126, M127, M296, M343, M364, M365, M395, M397, M401, N75, N90, P59, P182, R86, R102, R119, R120, R121, R155, R219, S17, S23, S68, S69, S163, S259, S260, S339, S340, S342, S357, S375, S387, S388, S389, S392, S394, S404, S429, S430, S431, S442, U20, U21, V39, W5, W233, W238, W239, W242, W274, see also AFL-CIO merger; labor unity; Lewis, John L.; Murray, Philip; particular unions; Reuther, Walter

CIO—Political Action Committee, C137, G2, G228, H237, L265, M119, M120, M122, S259

congressional committees, B25, B356, B387, C109, L118, M75, M87, M157, M298, M409, M410, M435, N27, R180, U47, see also congressional investigations, contempt of Congress, particular committees, U.S. Congress

congressional investigations, A213, A216, B2, B195, B367, B642, C77, C133, C227, C647, D192, D195, D261, E25, E26, G79, G127, G128, J124, K55, L48, L50, L164, L196, M44, M161, M413, O61, S173, S415, S419, T26, T36, U98, V31, W144, see also congressional committees, contempt of Congress, loyalty-security program, particular committees, U.S. Congress, "witch hunt"

Consumers Union, F26

contempt of Congress, B86, H258, see also Congress, congressional committees, congressional investigations

convict labor, W271

Coolidge, Calvin, L290, L302

cooperatives, H29, H30, T70

Coplon case, C623, N34, W143, W164

Corey, Lewis, B227

Cornell University, G104

corporations, L28

corruption, B285, F279, G12, H256

Coudert Committee, S383

Coughlin, Father, B239, G85, J67, M15, M19, Y15

Cowley, Malcolm, M417

Coxey's army, 89

Crane-Gartz, Kate, C128

criminal anarchy, G133, M292, R246, see also communist cases, federal legislation, state legislation, U.S. Supreme Court

criminal syndicalism, 34, A87, C105, C206, C240, D17, D31, E71, F551, G83, G263, H105, I12, K101, L124, M217, M292, M341, M342, P45, Q1, R138, R251, S300, S422, W31, W168, W267, W268, see also communist cases, federal legislation, state legislation, U.S. Supreme Court

Crosby, Minnesota, N200

Crouch, Paul, S166

Crusade for Freedom, F10, F13

Cuba, D209, N178, S209

Cultural and Scientific Conference for World Peace, B61, C654, F46, M4

culture, A128, F420, G183, G240, G241, J53, J59, J71, L146, P170, P202, W359, see also art, dance, music, theater

Curran, Joseph, A218, B377, F227, K61, M456, N64, S87, see also maritime unions, National Maritime Union

Czechoslovakia, H47

D

"Daily Worker," C167, C367, C391, C539, D7, D9, D305, E63, H126, M160, P155, R126, R234, S29, T42, T87, W232, W343, see also Party press

Damon, Anna, I21

dance, O13, see also culture, entertainment, Workers Dance League

Darrow Report, C309

Davies, John P, U55

Davis, Benjamin J., Jr., J116, M337, W161

Davis, Horace B., A76

Debs, Eugene V., 23, 50, 51, 75, 88, 91, E13, F138, F154, M373, T90, see also American Railway Union, Socialist Party

defense industry, G302, K78, K89, N41, R113, R115, S165, U27, U57, V23, see also war economy, World War II

De Leon, Daniel, 51, 88, 100, 111, 119, see also Socialist Labor Party

Dell, Floyd, G180

democracy, B62, D99, D238, F440, K88, L69, L344, L348, M9, M112, O29, S289, W26, W364

democratic front, A195, B247, B248, B250, B522, B537, C237, D100, D101, F202, F204, F205, F338, F341, F346, F348, F350, H136, J37, R190, see also national front, people's front, united front

Democratic Party, B698, C407, S297, S444, W171

demonstrations, B436, G201, S291

denaturalization, B23, F497, K82, see also aliens, deportation, foreign born, immigrants, immigration laws, particular cases, Walter-McCarran Act

Dennis, Eugene, B10, E55, F154

Dennis case, B136, B137, B185, B358, B412, C249, C644, C712, D244, E35, G239, G306, H65, J83, K116, K117, K118, M236, N4, P160, R203, S372, W112, W169

deportation, B7, B27, B28, B122, C79, C105, C635, D246, D259, F497, G258, G259, H99, J62, K82, L154, M183, P25, P45, P183, S219, S316, S318, S435, S472, T116, W37, Y1, see also aliens, denaturalization, foreign born, immigrants, immigration laws, particular cases, Walter-McCarran Act

depression, A178, B241, B457, B757, C65, D255, F305, G11, G76, G185, L14, L98, L208, L348, M16, M346, M422, see also economic crisis, economic trends, hunger march, recession, relief, social security, Unemployed Councils, unemployment, unemployment insurance, Workers Alliance

Detroit, W74, W258

Dewey, Thomas E., G36, G99, G229, L84

dictatorship, C377, N57, Q6, T33, W295, W364, see also communist ideology, Marxism, revolution, violence

Dies, Martin, B596, G74, K16, N29

Dies Committee, A100, A122, B549, C496, C608, D291, G57, K22, L79, L164, M119, M137, N6, O24, S359, see also House Un-American Activities Committee

Dilling, Elizabeth, M169, M369

Dimitroff, C452

disarmament, A249, C197, L245, see also armed forces, peace

Distributive, Processing and Office Workers, K64, L9, L10, L11, S305, S306, S307

Distributive Workers Union, L9

Dmytryk, Edward, E75, L111

Doran, Dave, S360

Dos Passos, John, F29, H218, L252, W263

Douds case, C712, J10

Douglass, Frederick, F173, F179

Draper, Theodore, J95

Dreiser, Theodore, F41, F107, M155, S196

Drew, James LeRoy, C6

dual unionism, C602, F289, F290, H175, L323, L325, S15, see also labor unions

Dubinsky, David, D21, W77, see also International Ladies' Garment Workers' Union

DuBois, W. E. B., E50, K4

Duclos letter, B622, B623, M121, N88

Dumbarton Oaks conference, B179, B604

Dunne, William, M357

E

Eastman, Max, K140, S440, W262

economic crisis, A54, B261, B268, B272, B275, B278, B286, B448, B475, B477, B518, B631, B634, B754, C344, C446, C453, C629, D274, F298, F351, F450, L314, M316, R143, S358, W68, W69, W174, see also depression, economic trends, recession, unemployment

economic trends, A45, A52, A54, B391, B435, L13, L23, L24, L25, L26, L310, L314, L353, M346, M422, N151, N152, N153, R151, R265, see also depression, economic crisis, employment, recession

economics, B183, H171

education, A59, A61, A82, A227, B395, B396, B403, B485, B578, B709, C94, C257, C655, D34, D87, D220, E23, E24, E34, G73, G114, H33, H138, H155, H171, H202, H203, I7, I51, L74, education (continued), M186, M237, M287, R87, R243, S224, S467, S470, W306, Z17, see also academic freedom, American Federation of Teachers, colleges, progressive education, schools, teachers, textbooks, workers' education

Eisenhower, Dwight, C243, M147, W119

Eisler, Gerhart, A131, E38, E39, E40, G28, G29, G30, N103, S217, S455

Eisler, Hanns, S455

election platform, 1928: W383; 1933: C425; 1934: C439, C442; 1935: C451, C457; 1936: C464, C466; 1937: C473, C474; 1938: C483, C491, C492; 1940: C499, C501, W366, W391; 1948: C544; 1952: C561; 1954: C567; see also elections, particular parties, political action, political developments

elections, A200, C359, Z9; 1924: A172, A173, B433, B434, F261, R255, R256, R257; 1926: B97, B98, R267; 1928: B345, E70, F283, G139, G140, L309, L315, L319, N3, O20, O29, S477; 1931: C399; 1932: C351, C406, E72, L324; 1934: B354, C311; 1936: A190, B501, B506, B510, B512, C314, C472, D96, F198, R10, R11, R19, Y29; 1937: A191, K50, K132, O55; 1938: C236, D101, H135, M380, R21, R66, S60; 1939: A196, D278; 1940: B537, B551, B558, B569, D106, H356, R22; 1941: L127; 1942: A204, B50, C165, D196, D280, H324; 1943: D30, N149, N150, S63; 1944: B614, C326, D111, D113, D115, D116, F397, F398, G288, H376, L81, L82, L83, L85, M106, W184; 1945: C597, G231, G232, G289; 1946: B72, C123, G233, H25, P156, P158, T52; 1947: G290; 1948: B628, C546, D137, D143, F217, F447, G100, M393, P161, P164; 1950: F96; 1952: C564, M72, P104, P172; 1953: C144; 1954: B323, C243, P109, P173; 1956: B325, B327, H48, L239, L240; 1958: D164, D165, J80, J81; 1964: H21; see also election platform, particular parties, political action, political developments

electrical workers, see United Electrical, Radio and Machine Workers

employers' associations, Z20

employment, B77, B123, B257, B676, C523, G287, H370, H374, L23, S292, W266, see also economic trends, unemployment

Engdahl, J. Louis, L133, S199

Engels, Friedrich, N77, O33, S117, see also Marx, Karl; Marxism

England, F225, F238, P75

entertainment, F16, R116, see also dance, Federal Theatre, Hollywood, motion pictures, music, plays, radio-television, sports, theater

EPIC, M315

equal rights amendment, C660

espionage, A125, B170, B361, B417, B705, B729, B744, C76, C92, C130, C612, C711 D12, D175, E20, G150, G317, H140, H306, H318, J122, K78, K110, L95, L118, L201, L215, L264, L381, M75, M435, N188, P134, R55, R71, R83, S12, S46, S215, S217, S223, S317, S421, S455, U27, U51, U54, U56, U75, U77, U86, V4, V6, W3, W143, W144, W155, W252, W265, see also particular cases

Espionage Act, C104, M63, P61, S33

Ethiopia, C436, F191

European Recovery Program, see Marshall Plan

European War, A198, C2, C15, C85, C193, C497, C498, C502, C506, F351, F353, F354, F355, F357, F358, F361, F362, F364, F365, F366, F368, F372, F374, F375, J40, J89, L57, L75, M68, M69, M70, M86, M206, M281, M324, M325, M346, N197, Q2, Q3, R122, R123, R193, W92, W93, W94, W95, W202, W212, W214, W280, W281, W401, Y8, see also World War II

ex-communists, A253, A261, B25, C645, C692, D65, D183, D185, D265, E84, E85, F221, H281, H298, H303, H306, H312, K57, L179, L385, L388, M177, O39, P3, P6, R228, S37, S216, S217, U43, see also communism, rejection of; expulsions

existentialism, H41

expulsions, C51, C351, C352, C388, C524, C526, C529, C638, M262, M263, N80, N102, S8, S137, S352, T50, W388, Y6, see also ex-communists, Party discipline

F

factionalism, A19, B92, B105, B124, B144, B211, B213, B440, C46, C47, C48, C49, C53, C74, C213, C277, C278, C296, C298, C341, C344, C349, C350, C420, C579, C581, C627, D14, D15, D18, D252, F182, F259, F458, F480, F481, G53, G94, G148, G200, G298, H53, H74, H156, H188, H338, I28, K13, L320, L321, M115, M130, M262, M263, M266, M300, M371, N147, O44, R91, R92, R93, R118, R183, R245, R259, R261, S126, S136, S137, S346, T60, W325, W326, W379, W380, W381, W387, W388, Y6

factory nuclei, see shop organization

Fair Employment Practices Commission, H27, see also Negroes

Far East, C260, C262, C263, D175, F85, G15, see also particular countries

Farm Equipment Workers, C604, M364, S393

farmer-labor party, A171, A173, A192, B431, B434, B494, B497, B499, B504, B505, B661, C43, C191, C341, C462, D298, E68, F189, F194, F260, F473, G146, H115, H116, H117, L333, M188, P74, R247, R252, R254, R256, R257, R259, S256, W73, W209, W377, W379, W380, W381, see also labor party, particular parties, people's party, political action, political developments

Farmer-Labor Progressive Federation, D96

farmers, A37, A166, A223, A224, B51, B52, B55, B56, B57, B111, B117, B405, C217, C231, C232, C301, C357, C398, C408, C416, D3, D80, D196, D197, D198, H1, H79, H128, H133, H167, H168, J23, L272, M5, N13, O58, O59, P11, P70, P212, P213, P214, R147, R148, R149, S84, S103, T25, U8, see also agriculture, United Farmers League

Farrell, James, G186

fascism, A117, A118, A121, A184, A202, B236, B318, B543, B618, C305, C362, C419, C463, D232, F63, F64, F333, F335, F363, F406, F454, F456, G16, G203, G272, H91, H273, J45, P60

in U.S., B106, B381, B428, B655, C443, C461, D120, D142, D154, D203, D206, D207, F50, F135, F310, F371, F471, F477, G33, H45, L181, M17, M29, M101, M169, N138, S21, S313, W24

Fast, Howard, L112, L389, M258, S2, W17

Faulkner, William, G119

Federal Bureau of Investigation, B202, B340, B381, C623, C713, C714, J122, K6, L50, L96, L204, L338, M56, M156, M275, N34, W164, see also Bureau of Investigation; Hoover, J. Edgar

Federal Communications Commission, L41, L42

Federal Council of Churches, J133, J134, M197, see also Protestants

federal legislation, A7, A86, A96, A99, B312, C98, C105, E33, F69, F471, G107, H105, K87, M174, M183, M193, O3, P19, S23, S350, S359, U25, U69, V30, V31, W147, W404, see also anticommunism; communists, registration of; criminal anarchy; criminal syndicalism; particular statutes; Party, outlawing of; sedition; U.S. Supreme Court

Federal Theatre, B418, F128, F129, G39, L121, see also entertainment, theater

Federated Farmer-Labor Party, B661, F249, G217, K69, L332, P68, P69, P71, R254, S7

Feinberg law, B307, C127, C680, K93, T122

fellow-travelers, A226, H281, H284, H287, H306, L220, L374, M249, M428, R186, T66, V27, W64, see also Party, influence of; Party membership

fiction, B667, C17, D233, D234, E48, F35, F36, F38, F42, F44, F53, F113, G108, G121, G167, G168, G246, H32, H197, H216, H246, H378, H387, H388, H389, J60, K36, L129, L130, M45, M205, M208, P178, P190, Q4, S20, S51, S54, S149, S193, S310, S390, T112, T115, V38, W296, W398, W400, see also literature, Marxist literary criticism, proletarian literature, short stories, utopian novel, writers

Field, Frederick V., B290, T39

Field, Jean, K5

Field, Noel, D179, L215, S217

Fifth Amendment, B674, B766, C249, D260, E24, F131, F530, G314, G315, H182, H260, H267, H268, H296, H302, H304, K55, L235, M94, M245, M298, N126, O15, P1, S198, S470, S495, T20, W133, W136, W196, W197, W198, W397, see also Bill of Rights, civil liberties, self-incrimination

Filipinos, M64

Finkelstein, Sidney, M40

Finland, A197, B414

First Amendment, M236, see also Bill of Rights, civil liberties

First International, J39

Fish Committee, A92, F297, L126, M202, S104, W253, W256

Fitzpatrick, John, F252

five-day week, B442

flood control, H63, S295

Flynn, Elizabeth Gurley, B385

Food and Tobacco Workers, L9

Ford, Henry, A70

Ford, James W., D43, H120

Ford Local (UAW), S488, S489, W120

Ford Motor Co., A70, B337, C694

foreign born, B651, B653, F534, G158, G256, G257, G260, K13, M375, R13, S219, W30, see also aliens, denaturalization, deportation, immigrants, immigration laws, national groups, Walter-McCarran Act

foreign policy, A48, A57, A251, B15, B47, B259, B336, B360, B535, B540, B547, B555, B577, B580, B629, B741, C260, D42, D118, D121, D122, D147, D175, E16, E21, F51, F165, F427, F430, F438, H327, J114, K10, see also co-existence; cold war; collective security; imperialism; particular countries; peace; USSR, relations with; U.S. imperialism; war

foreign trade, B632, B756, F130

Fort Monmouth, B720, C92, F60, M75, M164

Foster, William Z., B573, B633, B639, B640, B646, D240, E81, F152, F219, G143, G153, H50, N5, N71, N146, N147, N171, N175, P82, P115, P174, S14, S287, W247, W253, W264

foundations, R57, S442, V20

Fraina, Louis C., C285, C379

frame-ups, S253

France, F238, L268

Frank, Waldo, G160, H82

Frankfurter, Felix, C682

Franklin, Benjamin, R67

fraternal organizations, B110, S454, see also International Workers Order

Fredrickson, Arvo, C510

Free Trade Union Committee, M229, M230

Freistadt, Hans, A132

Freud, E5, G159, S11

Frey, John P., F132

front groups, A85, A124, A125, A126, A139, A226, A273, B21, B58, B184, B363, B365, B366, B367, B368, B704, B705, C108, C118, C137, C271, C602, C671, C683, D190, D191, E12, F226, F510, G57, G173, H58, H61, H140, H225, K97, L107, L335, M136, M137, M146, M151, M153, N20, N73, N129, O16, R136, R174, R231, R272, S42, S46, S66, S81, S118, S213, S379, S484, T30, T66, U29, W64, W154, W269, see also Attorney General's list; particular organizations; Party, influence of

Fund for the Republic, M150

fur workers, A16, A271, D306, F98, F178, G137, K42, L168, O28, see also needle trades

furniture workers, see United Furniture Workers

G

Garland Fund, see American Fund for Public Service

Garvey, Marcus, see Universal Negro Improvement Association

Gates, John, C582

Gellert, Hugo, G193

General Electric Company, N107

Geneva Conference, C204, L245, W110

genocide, C184, P54

George, Henry, 1, 47, 88, 128, see also single tax

Georgia, C394, S309

Germany, B177, B254, B299, B524, C198, C199, C204, C419, C443, F238, F363, J50, L298, M286, T49, Y37, see also Hitler-Stalin pact

Gitlow case, J119

Goff, Kenneth, P83

Gold, Ben, B187, F557, F558

Gold, Mike, B339, G192, L141

Goldman, Emma, 35, 88, see also anarchism

Gompers, Samuel, 105, B424, H109, see also American Federation of Labor

"Good Reading," R23

government, A125, B68, B252, B709, B729, B744, C488, L289

government employees, B671, C60, C119, C122, C228, C683, K20, K28, L37, L118, L154, L342, M142, M147, M179, R78, S111, S419, T8, U25, U31, U33, U34, U43, U45, U46, U47, U72, V2, V8, see also United Public Workers

Great Britain, see England

Greece, A106

Green, Gilbert, D174

Green, William, M345, see also American Federation of Labor

Greenback-Labor party, 92

"guilt by association," C149, C258, C259, H290, N76

Gwinn Amendment, B397, H107, see also housing

H

Hague, Frank, C485

Hall, Gus, D 174

Harlan County, Kentucky, D256, N15

Harlem, B302, F193, F203, F207, M200, see also Negroes

Harlem Legislative Conference, F204, F205

Harrison, Charles Yale, N95

Hart, Merwin K., S314

Hartley Committee, U11

Harvard, A74, E25

Hat and Cap Workers Union, G262, see also needle trades

Hawaii, E76, G10, I52, J70, L108, O11, P127, R56, R58, R117, V19, W65, W353

Hawkins, David, M222

Haymarket Affair, 25, 136, F38, M65, see also anarchists

Haywood, William, 51, F138, see also Industrial Workers of the World

Healey, Dorothy, J8

health, F328, F339, F546, S200, see also American Medical Association

health insurance, B736

Hearst, William Randolph, A120, C87, D327, H410, W60

Herndon, Angelo, D16, J107, L134, L140, N156, S226, W149, W272

Herndon case, B188, H142, H191, H192, I19

Hicks, Granville, G161, L387, W47

Hill, Joe, F180

Hillman, Sidney, C637, J128, see also Amalgamated Clothing Workers

Hiss, Alger, A130, A239, C126, C158, C623, D176, D181, K61, K106, R78, W177, see also Hiss-Chambers case

Hiss-Chambers case, A214, B126, B138, B142, B206, B689, B759, C132, C620, C622, C626, C646, D172, F75, F77, H257, H345, J132, L118, L231, M133, M181, M277, M339, M408, M428, N139, P2, R76, R84, S13, S19, S455, T108, W57, W128, W143, W164, see also Hiss, Alger; Chambers, Whittaker

Hitler-Stalin pact, B175, B249, B308, B552, B574, J41, L218, L374, S156, S157, S499, V34, W51, Z15, see also Germany, Stalin, USSR

Hoan, Daniel, S296

Hollywood, B313, C67, C68, C221, D193, D194, E75, F3, F5, F6, F7, F9, F11, F107, G117, G118, I9, J16, K11, K61, L111, L147, L148, L149, L150, L196, N89, N125, N167, O40, R205, R221, S83, S86, S143, S455, T117, W16, W337, W351, X1, see also entertainment, motion picture industry, motion pictures

Hollywood Ten, M49, M220, S285

Hook, Sidney, B470, F21, J34, R232, S4

Hoover, Herbert, C410, G140, W172

Hoover, J. Edgar, B381, C623, L204, M454, see also Federal Bureau of Investigation

Hoover-Laval pact, B454

hotel employees, M398, W348

hours, L20, L288

House Un-American Activities Committee, A138, B10, B80, B84, B86, B196, B201, B378, B387, B689, B733, C76, C98, C177, C179, C221, C228, C609, C646, D72, D120, D128, D130, D134, D135, D136, D146, D151, D222, E85, F48, F74, F132, F402, G26, G27, G74, G78, G79, G131, H251, K1, K11, K14, L46, L164, L381, L383, M48, M128, M131, M132, M152, N103, N167, N168, O40, O61, P148, P203, P207, R159, R168, R205, R237, S34, S36, S143, S455, S494, U13, U44, U83, V22, W16, W130, W179, see also congressional investigations, Dies Committee, U.S. Congress

housing, B397, C467, G56, G307, H107, H235, H236, M353, N25, S72, S292, see also Gwinn Amendment, rent control

Hughes, Langston, E50, S356

humanism, C26

humor, D213, F223

Hungary, A245, C576, S249

hunger march, A177, B349, U5, U6, U7, W254, see also depression, Unemployment Councils, unemployment, Workers Alliance

hunger strike, B7, D246

Hutchins, Robert M., M150

hydrogen bomb, C201, D162, see also atom bomb, nuclear tests

I

Illinois, C164, C166, K107, M103, M105

immigrants, A12, E64, K114, see also aliens, denaturalization, deportation, foreign born, immigration laws, Walter-McCarran Act

immigration laws, B717, W39, see also aliens, denaturalization, deportation, foreign born, immigrants, Walter-McCarran Act

imperialism, A55, B235, B253, B259, B336, B350, B454, B566, C344, C409, C527, D55, D248, D268, E69, F184, F185, F195, F357, F502, G9, G10, G15, G22, G209, G211, G291, see also colonialism, foreign policy, particular countries, U.S. imperialism, war

"In Fact," L378

income distribution, P88, see also living standards, poverty, wages

India, A38

industrial injuries, B735

industrial security, S317, W32, Y5

industrial unionism, 82, 108, C469, F313, F319, R247, S197, S235, W319

Industrial Workers of the World, 13, 14, 22, 39, 56, 58, 70, 76, 79, 82, 83, 87, 97, 102, 108, 121, 122, 124, 126, 133, B411, B412, B663, C339, F175, F180, G5, G88, H154, I5, L282, M250, O49, V9, W201, see also anarchism; Haywood, William; syndicalism

inflation, B49, L351, R142, see also prices

informers, C645, L96, L349, L388

Ingersoll, Ralph, C235

Ingram case, R35

injunction, T78

Institute of Pacific Relations, B743, F165, K110, M409, U34, U39, U101, W9, W252

K

J

L

Minnesota Farmer-Labor Party, B355, C148, P71

Minor, Robert, N174, N176

Minton, Bruce, N102

Missouri Valley Authority, S120

"Modern Quarterly," S212

Moley, Raymond, D323

monopoly, 85, B259, B286, B390, B392, B714, C309, F400, F417, G292, G294, L21, L27, L28, L29, L344, P89, P90, see also big business, capitalism, milk trust

"Monthly Review," B281

Mooney-Billings case, H393, M66, O38, T80

Morganthau Plan, M142

Morris, Robert, R235

Mortimer, Wyndham, K124

Moscow Conference, B605, D112, see also World War II

Moscow trials, A105, B244, B308, B528, B540, D27, D28, D188, F321, H291, M133, M180, W33, see also USSR

Most, Johann, 93

motion picture industry, B196, C177, C252, H320, K74, M139, P138, P184, see also Hollywood

motion pictures, B747, D194, H335, J57, J58, K133, L145, M280, N129, R12, see also entertainment, Hollywood

Mundel, Luella, M50

Mundt bills, A83, B670, C91, C106, C107, C108, C225, C641, C646, D149, E58, F68, F155, G101, K47, K77, M39, M431, M432, N33, N109, T7, T34, W289

Munich, B535, G17

Murray, Philip, A274, B135, C605, R102, R119, see also Congress of Industrial Organizations

music, B189, C100, F104, F108, F110, F116, F514, P119, see also culture, entertainment

Muste, A. J., F300, F303, L1, M454, see also Conference for Progressive Labor Action

Muster, Morris, W297

N

Nagler, Isidore, H110, L205, see also International Ladies' Garment Workers' Union

Nathan Report, B266, W107

"Nation," H187, H207, J21, N91, R227, S497, V29

National Association for the Advancement of Colored People, B389, C679, D308, F533, L213, R42, S78, S458, W46, W192, W403, see also Negroes, Scottsboro case

National Committee for the Arts, Sciences and Professions, C654

National Council of American—Soviet Friendship, M430

National Council of Churches, A222, H59, H60, see also churches, Protestants, religion

national debt, R164

national defense, W21, see also armed forces, militarism

national front, C318, L59, see also democratic front, people's front, united front

national groups, A193, A198, A202, B647, B648, B649, C315, H15, L59, P42, S347, S348, see also foreign born

national income, see income distribution

National Industrial Recovery Act, A176, B234, B468, B469, B473, C309, C441, C450, D289, D318, D319, D322, G14, G265, H277, H278, M239, R210, T62, see also New Deal; Roosevelt Administration; Roosevelt, Franklin D.

National Labor Relations Board, D245, H69

National Lawyers Guild, E52, L153, see also lawyers

National Lumber Workers Union, S294, see also lumber workers

National Maritime Union, A218, B377, C701, H84, H85, H408, K84, L209, M190, M196, M215, M456, N37, N38, N64, P186, R134, S349, S395, T2, V14, W42, see also Curran, Joseph; maritime unions; maritime workers; merchant marine; seamen

National Miners Union, D256, F304, F511, F512, G13, G122, M187, N15, P30, S478, U16, W250, see also coal miners

National Negro Congress, B76, B77, D73, F196, F197, F200, G248, N39, N40, P141, R15, R269, W122, see also Negroes

National Negro Labor Council, P108, see also Negroes

National Religion and Labor Foundation, M289

National Research Council, O57

national security, see loyalty-security program

National Student Association, S152, see also students, youths

National Student League, D250, L99, N49, S441, S445, S446, W47, see also American Student Union, Student League for Industrial Democracy, students, youth

National Textile Workers Union, B309, L38, P7, W71, W86, see also textile strikers, textile workers

National Union for Social Justice, M15

national unity, B48, B583, B584, B587, B600, B603, B607, B608, B613, C165, C166, C593, D112, D113, D115, D116, D118, F119, F379, F387, H358, L87, M23, see also World War II

National Youth Administration, H250, see also youth

"Native Son," S185, S186

Navy, see armed forces

Nazi-Soviet pact, see Hitler-Stalin pact

needle trades, A15, B438, F269, F282, G134, G175, H54, H180, I23, J99, N60, R104, S99, S428, T98, see also Amalgamated Clothing Workers, fur workers, Hat and Cap Workers Union, International Ladies' Garment Workers' Union, millinery workers, Needle Trades Workers Industrial Union

Needle Trades Workers Industrial Union, B666, K119, S434, see also needle trades

Negroes,
Party's conservative period 1921 - summer 1928, A139, A165, C364, D302, D303, J3, L299, M306, M309, W167

revolutionary "third period," summer 1928 - summer 1935, A24, A26, A29, A31, A162, A163, A164, B329, B406, B407, B450, B464, B474, C301, C345, C348, C353, C397, C436, C678, C696, D211, F79, F183, F184, F187, F188, F190, F192, F514, G123, G222, G223, G242, H120, H141, H145, H146, H147, H148, H150, H151, H172, H238, H380, H381, L132, L158, M273, M314, N56, O58, P5, P204, R48, S61, S75, S236, S303, S310, U8

popular front period, summer 1935 - August 1939, A32, B188, B302, C99, C486, D44, D73, F189, F194, F195, F198, F199, F200, F201, F202, F204, F205, F320, F526, G124, M173, P6, S76, S347, S381, T67, W277

Hitler-Stalin pact period, August 1939 - June 1941, A70, A228, B74, B75, B76, C315, C500, D191, F208, J89, J108, J109, L218, M200, N41, S452, T85, W202, W280, W281, W398, Y5

World War II period, June 1941 - May 1945, A229, A230, B19, B20, B77, B609, B615, C690, D45, D46, F210, F211,

Negroes,
World War II period, June 1941 - May 1945 (continued),
F212, F213, F214, F215, F216, I39, J110, L259, N62,
N67, P50, P51, S348, T47, W181, W182, W183, W184

Stalinist "cold war" period, May 1945 - March 1953, A49,
A63, A231, A232, A236, B21, B78, B189, B296, B344,
B667, B668, B669, B745, C1, C184, C531, C536, C553,
C668, C679, D10, D48, D49, D50, D51, D52, D53, D54,
D55, D57, D58, D269, F218, F219, F421, F425, F431,
F527, G50, G169, H17, H90, H153, H169, H232, H396, J4,
J57, J58, J88, J113, L219, L220, L255, M59, M60, M170,
M259, M337, M367, M443, N42, N43, N104, N141, N143,
P54, P85, P87, P95, P100, P106, P141, P158, P164, P168,
P191, R34, R39, R40, R127, R128, R129, R130, R219,
S77, S78, S79, T53, W29, W185, W187, W189, W193, W237,
W245, W283, W296

post-Stalin period (after March 1953), A243, B388, B389,
B746, C587, D59, D61, D274, F110, F464, F467, F474,
G158, G295, H113, H114, H233, J5, J9, K121, L139, N44,
P108, P176, R38, R41, R42, S195, S459, S460, W46, W150,
W190, W403, see also American Negro Labor Congress,
civil rights, Fair Employment Practices Commission,
Harlem, Jim Crow, League of Struggle for Negro Rights,
lynching, National Association for the Advancement of
Colored People, National Negro Congress, National Negro
Labor Council, race, race relations, Scottsboro case,
self-determination, slavery, South, Universal Negro Im-
provement Association, white chauvinism

Nelson, Steve, F52, F125, P206, R2

neutrality, A35, B554, B555, B659, F354

New Deal, A176, A185, A252, B56, B57, B184, B224, B234, B354,
B469, B553, B683, C236, C397, C435, C443, C446, C687,
D103, D289, D317, D322, F181, F456, K2, K37, L117, M111,
M142, R269, S273, S423, T62, W24, W275, W276, see also
National Industrial Recovery Act; Roosevelt Administration;
Roosevelt, Franklin D.; social security; unemployment in-
surance; Works Progress Administration

New Left, L347

"New Masses," E43, F544, G190, N94, N95, N100, S276

"New Republic," S497

New York City School for Workers, G245

New York "Compass," H186

New York "Times," L386

"New Yorker," M338

newspapers, M79, M84, M85, M160, M161, see also American
Newspaper Guild, particular papers

Nicaragua, E69

Nixon, Richard, C646, R84

noncommunist affidavit, A1, A96, C247, D83, D241, E54, H391,
J10, K46, K116, L180, L193, L247, M63, M376, N179, P61,
R77, S141, U24, see also anticommunist oath, Taft-Hartley
Act

North American Committee to Aid Spanish Democracy, R272

North Atlantic Pact, C139, J78, P167, S245, S388

Norwalk, Conn., R178

novel, see fiction

nuclear tests, D162, see also atom bomb, hydrogen bomb

Nygard, Emil, N200

O

Oak Ridge, Tenn., G72

Ober Act, B14, F523, J86

O'Casey, Sean, H332

Ohio, W210, W212, W213

Ohio Un-American Activities Commission, B368

Oklahoma, J82, K101, R138

Olgin, M. J., M378

One Big Union, 108

O'Neill, Eugene, L152

Oppenheimer, J. Robert, A69, A258, B69, B664, B718, B719,
B721, C704, D169, F521, G317, K15, K53, K60, L233, L242,
M164, M226, N115, R1, S45, S451, T110, U61, U62, U63, U64,
U65, U71, U74

opportunism, B95, B439, B738, C373, C583, D328, E27, F94,
F432, F452, H129, L354, M394, see also Marxism, Party
program

Orwell, George, H332

outlawing of party, see Party, outlawing of

Oxford Pledge, M116, see also pacifism, peace

Oxnam, G. Bromley, B80, F74, U44

P

Pacific maritime strike, H350, S58, S59

pacifism, B218, M109, P23, W323, see also Oxford Pledge,
peace

Padmore, George, F187

Paine, Thomas, A34

painters, E29, M40, Z16

Palestine, B253, B256, B262, B263, B264, B265, B267, B270,
B503, B509, F414, M283, N192, N194, N195, N196, S168,
S502, see also Israel, Jews, Zionism

Palmer raids, 102, 126, B733, C623, D293, K2, K16, M53, M440,
N47, O6, P183, S472, V29, W37, see also Justice Department

Panama Canal, D171, see also Canal Zone

Pan-American Union, W333

Paris Commune, S121

parliamentarianism, C282, C283, L175, see also Marxism,
Party program, Party tactics

Parrington, L144

Parsons, Albert A., 19

"Partisan Review," H328

Party activities, B462, B465, B654, B680, C272, C313, C356,

Q

R

S

T

U

United Packinghouse Workers, B762, J12, P210

United Public Workers, C119, D171, H241, W131, W347, see also government employees

United Retail, Wholesale and Department Store Employees, B35, F90, see also retail clerks

United Rubber Workers, M205, W208, W211, see also rubber workers

U.S. Congress, B321, B326, E62, G26, G49, G237, H325, L80, L89, L126, see also congressional committees, congressional investigations, contempt of Congress, particular committees

U.S. Congress Against War, L207

U.S. Constitution, B516, C192, D270, I32

U.S. history, A247, H55, M21, M372, N160, see also Revolution of 1776

U.S. imperialism, A36, A47, A117, A119, A165, A240, C383, D23, D126, D127, F373, F400, F406, F422, F434, F443, F445, F451, F455, F456, F457, F463, F469, L147, L148, L291, L292, L294, L295, L300, L302, L316, L317, L344, M35, M80, M256, M276, M362, N53, P84, P126, P154, P155, P159, R63, R153, R163, R268, S124, S178, S221, W188, W332, W333, see also foreign policy, imperialism, war

U.S. Information Centers, U57

U.S. Supreme Court, A98, A116, A136, B185, B198, B234, B307, B382, B400, C73, C78, C182, C183, C185, C555, C560, C672, D16, D244, D326, F500, G16, G25, G238, G239, G325, H132, H160, H304, H305, I19, L128, L135, L192, L234, M44, M152, M172, M175, M333, M376, M412, N14, N111, N156, O3, O4, O6, P193, P194, P195, P209, R37, S372, T73, U87, U89, U90, U91, U92, W137, W190, W191, see also communist cases, criminal anarchy, criminal syndicalism, federal legislation, particular cases and statutes, sedition, state legislation

United Textile Workers, B32, see also textile strikes, textile workers

United World Federalists, F4, F6, F8, F12, F14

Universal Negro Improvement Association, F195, M307, M310, M311, see also Negroes

University of California, B116, C97, C154, F127, F493, H67, J120, L246, M220, R3, S414, W59, W354

University of Chicago, A206, B127, H194, K107, W47

University of Colorado, M222

University of Kansas City, A76

University of Washington, A62, A142, C256, H231, I45, L52, M219, M220, R21, S41, S244, W38

Uphaus, Willard, M162, U99

Upholsterers International Union, W297

uranium, V24

Urey, Harold C., D253

utopian novel, 1, 7, 45, 68, 98, see also fiction, literature

utopian socialism, see socialist communities

V

Vatican, J52, J54, M396, M399, see also Catholic Church, Catholics

Veblen, Thorstein, 1, 32, 33, 51, 88, 128

Velde, Harold H., R237

Vermont, W44

veterans, B409, B410, C66, C357, C534, D236, J61, L199, L200, M415, T51, W194, W360, see also American Legion, American Veterans Committee, bonus march, Workers' Ex-Servicemen's League

Vietnam, A251, H157

vigilantes, S288

Villa, Pancho, R62

violence, 2, A23, A248, C12, F440, F477, G175, K17, N173, P18, S43, S223, S485, T33, T54, W27, W178, see also dictatorship, revolution

Voice of America, J124

Voorhis bill, B557

Vorse, Mary Heaton, K61

W

wages, B258, B266, B594, B600, C357, C523, C550, C585, F418, G42, H371, H373, H374, L19, L23, L217, M388, M389, M437, P43, R140, W106, W212, W233, W236, W245, Y17, see also income distribution, living standards

Wall Street, C8, R141

Wallace, Henry A., A158, B78, B628, B701, C632, J48, L380, M2, M123, S437, W108, W302, see also Progressive Party, Wallace movement

Wallace movement, C170, D140, D141, F18, F438, F442, G49, G58, G100, H70, L6, L90, L109, L197, M3, N52, P162, P163, S18, S49, S344, W11, W239, see also Progressive Party; Wallace, Henry A.

Walter-McCarran Act, A103, G259, G260, G261, see also aliens, denaturalization, deportation, foreign born, immigrants, immigration laws

war, 12, A118, A121, B113, B218, B226, B235, B236, B293, B350, B393, B455, B693, B703, B737, B739, B755, C38, C344, C390, C393, C409, C463, D159, D214, D232, D248, D287, D288, F224, F333, F352, F411, F416, F429, F434, F436, F443, F455, F457, F469, F528, G276, H11, H165, H178, H398, J47, K76, L15, L18, L19, L43, L45, L101, L102, L181, L182, L200, L308, L316, L317, L348, L369, M35, M101, M255, M256, M316, M318, M320, M321, N50, N72, P162, Q2, R270, S178, S220, S272, T124, V25, W72, W91, W323, W324, W330, W362, see also armed forces, cold war, foreign policy, imperialism, militarism, particular wars, peace, U.S. imperialism

war economy, A52, B49, F384, G282, M381, S486, see also defense industry, World War II

War Labor Board, H373, see also World War II

war preparations, B280, B285, F462, W6, see also cold war

war production, B581, B588, B595, B600, C319, C511, D29, F401, J46, M348, see also World War II

Ward, Harry F., C273, M162

Washington (State), C648, H57, R19, R20, R22

Washington Commonwealth Federation, F169

Watson, Goodwin, R24

Weinstock, Louis, T92

Western Federation of Miners, 73, 108

White, Harry Dexter, B202, C623, H346, L232, M34, U50, U52, W155 white chauvinism, B406, B408, B464, C400, C549, F464, H147, H169, J88, P34, P94, P97, P98, P102, P168, S205, S409, T56, see also Negroes, race relations

white collar workers, D279, G226, M288, see also United Office and Professional Workers

Whitman, Walt, S187

Whitney, Anita, F142, R111, W168

Wilder, Thornton, G182, W263

Williams, Claude, B121

Williams, Tennessee, T22

Willmark Service System, L131

Wilson, Edmund, S440

Wilson Administration, S33

Winston, Henry, D174

"witch hunt," A213, C10, C254, D239, K79, see also congressional investigations, loyalty-security program

Woltman, Frederick, N121

women, A125, B318, C15, C315, C392, C491, C657, C659, C660, C661, F143, F144, F145, F147, F148, F150, F448, G223, H398, H399, H402, H403, H405, I6, I33, J112, J113, J114, L58, L60, L93, L94, L262, L272, M182, M268, M269, P144, R70, S107, S228, S231, W345

Workers Alliance, B154, B155, B156, B157, B159, H226, N148, see also depression, hunger march, relief, unemployed councils, unemployment

Workers Cultural Federation, W359

Workers Dance League, O13, see also dance

workers' education, B91, see also education

Workers Ex-Servicemen's League, W194, see also bonus march, veterans

Workers Party, A169, B92, B317, C291, C338, C341, C342, C344, C349, E3, E45, F259, G298, H269, P129, R249, R250, R253, R260, R261, S8, S50, S122, W372, W374, W375, W376, W377

Workers School, B546

workmen's compensation, B735

Works Progress Administration, B152, B311, M76, see also New Deal, relief, unemployment

World Congress Against War, A104

World Council of Churches, M198

World Federation of Scientific Workers, M148

World Federation of Trade Unions, C61, C63, D11, D219, F405, F475, L274, M387, P167, T58, W19, W274, W339, see also world labor movement, World Trade Union Conference

world government, B205, K29, see also United Nations

world labor movement, B128, B129, B697, H367, see also International Confederation of Free Trade Unions, International Federation of Trade Unions, World Federation of Trade Unions, World Trade Union Conference

World Trade Union Conference, E86, F404, W19, see also World Federation of Trade Unions, world labor movement

World War I, S406

World War II, A12, A39, A40, A201, B48, B49, B50, B538, B544, B545, B548, B559, B560, B561, B562, B563, B564, B567, B575, B576, B581, B583, B586, B591, B596, B696, C129, C326, C509, C519, D29, D45, D104, D105, D107, D110, D111, D257, F80, F118, F119, F139, F143, F144, F172, F210, F211, F216, F376, F377, F378, F379, F380, F382, F384, F386, F390, F393, F507, F508, G46, G252, G277, G278, G279, G281, G324, H1, H98, H323, H358, H359, H361, H362, H363, H364, H365, H366, H368, J43, J48, J110, K2, L13, L65, L263, M326, M327, M328, M329, M330, M332, N161, N198, O53, R149, R276, S100, S101, S267, S365, S367, W97, W99, W100, W181, W182, W215, W216, W217, W367, W394, see also defense

industry, European war, Moscow Conference, national unity, postwar policy, reconversion, second front, Teheran Conference, war economy, War Labor Board, war production

World Youth and Student Festival, R69

World Youth Congress, B145, R191

Wright, Richard, E50, S185, S186

writers, A2, A149, A254, B64, B193, B372, B570, B668, B751, C19, C30, C35, C125, C238, C245, C662, C667, D62, D92, D93, D94, D173, E7, E14, E47, E89, F28, F31, F33, F39, F55, F91, F105, F517, F518, G37, G105, G169, G178, G188, G191, G222, G310, H209, H212, H386, I24, J72, J127, K44, K61, L114, L141, L155, L370, M14, M46, M47, M48, M180, M360, N92, N122, N165, P58, R5, R70, S53, S57, S73, S89, S90, S91, S92, S93, S189, S194, S286, S413, T10, T68, T106, W29, W35, W257, W260, see also American Writers Congress, fiction, intellectuals, League of American Writers, literature, Marxist literary criticism, proletarian literature, short stories

Y

Yalta Conference, B615, B619

Yates case, J83

yellow dog contract, C222

Young, Art, N98

Young Communist International, Y18, Y19, Y26, Z7

Young Communist League, C103, C117, C193, D226, F555, G264, G266, G271, G272, G273, G274, H177, J27, L250, L251, M90, M116, M260, R188, S361, W98, W102, W125, W277, W278, W279, W281, W282, W307, Y19, Y20, Y21, Y22, Y23, Y24, Y25, Y26, Y27, Y28, Y29, Y30, Y31, Y32, Y33, Y34, Y35, Z7, Z21, see also Labor Youth League, Young Workers League, youth

Young People's General Assembly for Peace, L226

Young Pioneers, C40

Young Progressives of America, W307

Young Women's Christian Association, K26

Young Workers (Communist) League, H108, Y36, Z10, see also Labor Youth League, Young Communist League, youth

youth, A150, A151, A152, A153, A154, A155, A156, A185, A215, B19, B20, B21, B40, B41, B145, B314, B376, B745, C190, C447, C552, D22, D167, D191, D225, D226, E28, G8, G20, G109, G171, G173, G265, G267, G268, G269, G270, G271, G272, G273, G274, G276, H249, H400, I2, I37, J109, K35, L17, L227, L272, L347, L352, M138, M186, O16, O17, P22, P42, P150, P164, P173, R69, R168, R190, R191, R193, S308, S361, S421, S438, T55, T67, V15, W90, W100, W102, W368, Z9, see also American Student Union, American Youth Act, American Youth Congress, American Youth for Democracy, Labor Youth League, National Student Association, National Student League, National Youth Administration, Student League for Industrial Democracy, students, Young Communist League, Young Workers League

Z

Zionism, B503, C471, M33, M285, N193, N194, N197, R97, S168,
  see also Israel, Jews, Palestine